Revised Second Edition

Masterplots

1,801 Plot Stories and Critical Evaluations
of the World's Finest Literature

Revised Second Edition

Volume 10
Rid – Spo
5611 – 6240

Edited by
FRANK N. MAGILL

Story Editor, Revised Edition
DAYTON KOHLER

Consulting Editor, Revised Second Edition
LAURENCE W. MAZZENO

SALEM PRESS

Pasadena, California Englewood Cliffs, New Jersey

∞ The paper used in these volumes conforms to the American National Standard for Permanence of Paper for Printed Library Materials, Z39.48-1984.

Library of Congress Cataloging-in-Publication Data

Masterplots / edited by Frank N. Magill; consulting editor, Laurence W. Mazzeno. — Rev. 2nd ed.

p. cm.

Expanded and updated version of the 1976 rev. ed.

Includes bibliographical references and indexes.

1. Literature—Stories, plots, etc. 2. Literature—History and criticism. I. Magill, Frank Northen, 1907- . II. Mazzeno, Laurence W.

PN44.M33 1996

809—dc20 96-23382

ISBN 0-89356-084-7 (set) CIP

ISBN 0-89356-094-4 (volume 10)

Revised Second Edition

First Printing

PRINTED IN THE UNITED STATES OF AMERICA

LIST OF TITLES IN VOLUME 10

LIST OF TITLES IN VOLUME 10

Revised Second Edition

RIDERS IN THE CHARIOT

Type of work: Novel
Author: Patrick White (1912-1990)
Type of plot: Parable
Time of plot: After World War II
Locale: Sarsaparilla, an outlying suburb of Sydney, Australia
First published: 1961

Principal characters:

MRS. RUTH GODBOLD, a mother, wife, and washerwoman of good and simple heart
MORDECAI HIMMELFARB, a former professor of English and Jewish immigrant
MISS MARY HARE, an elderly spinster and the owner of Xanadu
ALF DUBBO, an aborigine painter
HARRY ROSETREE (born HAIM ROSENBAUM), a factory owner
MRS. JOLLEY, the gossiping, malicious widowed housekeeper at Xanadu
MRS. FLACK, her friend and a woman of genteel malevolence
BLUE, Mrs. Flack's illegitimate son

The Story:

The seventeen chapters of the novel are organized in seven unequal parts to describe the events in and near the Australian town of Sarsaparilla, which Patrick White has fixed on as his recurrent locale. The novel occupies itself with the last few weeks in the lives of three of the protagonists: Alf Dubbo, a consumptive and diseased aborigine painter; Miss Mary Hare, an aging spinster from a good family; and Mordecai Himmelfarb, an elderly Jewish immigrant or "New" Australian working in a factory.

Miss Hare and Himmelfarb died on Good Friday; Dubbo died later. At the end of the novel, Mrs. Ruth Godbold, the fourth protagonist and a local washerwoman, remained with her children and grandchildren to bury Himmelfarb and watch the destruction of Xanadu, Miss Hare's dilapidated mansion.

Parts 1 and 2 of the novel tell the past histories of Miss Hare and Himmelfarb; the fourth and fifth parts tell the stories of Mrs. Godbold and Alf Dubbo in less detail and at shorter length, a modification caused by the increasing pace of the plot in the later sections. The plot is launched in the first scene when Miss Hare's allowance from an English cousin, which had resumed after World War II, enabled her to hire a housekeeper for Xanadu. She hired Mrs. Jolley, a widow who had been rejected by her family as the probable murderess of her husband. Miss Hare soon learned to fear Mrs. Jolley's ordinariness and her spite. Three aspects of Miss Hare's past were central: She was the only, ugly, and unwanted daughter of English parents whose delusions of grandeur were reflected in the name of their house—Xanadu; she had been nursed back to life by Mrs. Godbold; she saw the "Chariot" and was therefore marked as a "rider," as she believes Mrs. Godbold is also. By the end of the first part, she also had met fleetingly the two other riders, Dubbo and Himmelfarb, and Mrs. Jolley had met her peer in gossip and evil, Mrs. Flack. Therefore, the plot, protagonists, and theme were all introduced by the end of the first part.

As Miss Hare, perhaps inexplicably, told her story to Mrs. Jolley in the first part, so Himmelfarb told his to Miss Hare when they met by chance in the overgrown grounds of

Xanadu. Himmelfarb's prewar career as a professor of English in Germany resulted in the loss of his Jewish faith, a betrayal compounded by the cowardice which resulted in his wife's being taken by the Nazis. Himmelfarb was sheltered for a time by old friends, but when they, too, were taken by the Nazis, he gave himself up as a Jew and tried ineffectually to help his people while on the train to the gas chambers. Although he failed, he was miraculously delivered from the extermination camp, and, half-blinded by the symbolic loss of his glasses, made his way to Israel, with aid given by many helping hands. Later, he rejected that haven and accepted emigration to Australia. There he worked in the factory of a Jew turned Gentile, Mr. Rosetree, bought a dilapidated shack, and became thoroughly orthodox.

Himmelfarb's story is possibly the most remarkable of the four past histories that make up the bulk of the book, although each is a triumph of White's imagination and narrative skill. His technical problem is to relate thematically the four characters by more than coincidental meetings in and around Sarsaparilla. As the plot advances through the parallel subhistories of the Rosetrees and of Mrs. Jolley and Mrs. Flack, the theme is gradually explicated and illustrated. All the protagonists are burnt by different aspects of love. Himmelfarb rejects it; Miss Hare's affection for her parents is stunted; Dubbo's encounters with love all turn to perversion and lust; only Mrs. Godbold, finally apostrophized as "the rock of love," can fully express and enjoy it, even for her most unattractive (and very Australian) husband, who loads her with six daughters and leaves her to rear them by taking in Sarsaparilla's washing.

By the end of part 5, the formal arrangement of the quartet of protagonists is taking shape in at least three aspects: sex, marital state, and native or "New" Australian. Miss Hare is unmarried and born in Australia; Dubbo represents the aborigines or older Australians; Mrs. Godbold and Himmelfarb are or have been married, and both are immigrants, although at different periods of Australian history. White seems to be using as universal a cast as possible, and postwar Australia gives him the opportunity to select representative human types in order to make his novel at once Australian and universal. The most important criteria to the theme is the experience of love, expressed in terms of marriage. The two most evil figures in the novel are both widows, and the more sinister is Mrs. Flack, whose son, Blue, is introduced as her nephew in the third part. This denial of a loving relationship is contrasted to Mrs. Godbold's nursing of Miss Hare, Himmelfarb, and Dubbo.

By the beginning of part 6, all the protagonists have met one another, and the "Chariot" link has been established between two pairs, the women and the men, when Himmelfarb finds Dubbo reading Ezekiel at the factory in preparation for a canvas of the "Riders in the Chariot" that he is trying to paint. He can do this after watching the death of Himmelfarb attended by Miss Hare and Mrs. Godbold on the Good Friday following his mock crucifixion by Blue at Rosetree's factory on Easter Thursday. Following Himmelfarb's death, Miss Hare wanders away and is presumed dead, Dubbo dies of a tubercular hemorrhage, and Rosetree commits suicide when he learns that Himmelfarb has had a Christian burial at the hands of Mrs. Godbold. Mrs. Jolley has nosed out Blue's true parentage, but Mrs. Flack knows that Mrs. Jolley's family has rejected her as Blue has been rejected; the two widows live together in a hell of their own making. Only Mrs. Godbold is left with her family to watch brick bungalows gradually spreading over the site of Xanadu. On a visit to the real-estate development, Mrs. Godbold achieves a perfect vision of the "riders in the chariot."

Critical Evaluation:

Patrick White, who received the Nobel Prize in Literature in 1973, has created through *Riders in the Chariot* a striking parable—complex in its design and structure, yet altogether lucid in its meaning. Most often in White's novels, a single character acts as a visionary, grappling with life's mysteries, finally to receive illumination, usually through death or madness. In this novel, however, the stories of four prospective illuminati unfold individually, then intertwine as they move toward their single destiny as riders in the chariot. Their destiny is to glimpse life's great mystery, whose central force is love.

In some ways an unlikely quartet to embark on such a mission, the four riders include the introverted offspring of decadent aristocracy, a Jewish refugee who has turned his back on religion, a tubercular Aboriginal painter who had been seduced by a priest, and the local washerwoman whose husband had deserted her and their six daughters. Nor is the setting one of grandeur. The action unfolds in Sarsaparilla, a dreary Australian suburb outside of Sydney. Superimposed on the stories of the four strange riders are those of other residents of White's imaginary suburb. Their drab surroundings are the symbols and teachings of world religion and Jungian philosophy. In spite of being what might appear an impossible task for any novelist to undertake, *Riders in the Chariot* succeeds immensely as a narrative.

Its success rests first of all on the storytelling itself, which never lags. In order to explore the present actions of the four riders, the narrator must rely on flashbacks, an unfashionable technique in contemporary writing. The most striking of these visits into the past is Mordecai Himmelfarb's story, beginning in his native Germany, where he taught at a university, then moving into the Nazi period, when Himmelfarb and his wife are taken to a concentration camp, and then finally progressing to Himmelfarb's miraculous escape, which brings him first to Israel, then to Australia. For each of the other characters, there is a similar unfolding of the past: Mary's miserable childhood, Dubbo's unhappy experience in a white Christian household, and Mrs. Godbold's bleak life, first as a servant, then as a deserted wife taking in washing to support her daughters. The quality that dominates all of these past experiences is the absence of love. It might be as extreme as what Himmelfarb faced in Hitler's Germany or as persistent as what Dubbo encounters as the member of a colonized race. It may be more subtle, such as the humiliation Mary suffered at the hands of her father, who disliked her because she was ugly and awkward. In Mrs. Goldbold's case, it might be a matter of love's turning into possessiveness.

Hate, which is a subtext of the novel, finally reveals itself completely through the book's most memorable scene, which is the mock crucifixion of Himmelfarb, which takes place at the bicycle factory on Maundy Thursday of Passion Week. Led by Blue, a simple-minded and cruel man, the workers conduct the grisly rite: "The Jew had been hoisted as high as he was likely to go on the mutilated tree. . . . a burlesque. . . . what they suspected might be blasphemy. . . . The Jew hung." The onlookers relish the bleeding Jew, especially his one hand that looks as though it has been pierced. They laugh and spit water at him; one throws an orange but misses her target; a purple-haired old woman offers to buy Blue a drink as a reward for his cleverness. This may well be the most unpleasant passage in modern literature. The four illuminati are integrated into this pivotal scene—Dubbo is a stunned witness; Mrs. Godbold is at home ironing sheets thinking of how the women had lovingly prepared such sheets to receive Christ's body after the crucifixion; Miss Hare is in her crumbling mansion watching "the marble shudder, the crack widen," which is suggestive of the quaking described in the original Crucifixion.

This scene has often been criticized as melodramatic, unlikely, or unmotivated. Regardless, it not only remains essential to the overall pattern of the novel but it also demonstrates White's rare technique of consistently implanting idea into action. First, the hatred is directed toward immigrants to Australia after World War II, especially Jewish ones. This becomes evident when some of the onlookers shout: "Go home to Germany!" Second, the painful events, which take place near the end of the novel, expand in meaning when considered as the climactic moment in the riders' movement toward the chariot and the truth within. To eliminate or to alter the crucifixion scene would be to unbalance the intricate structure of *Riders in the Chariot*, from a narrative and a thematic standpoint.

The antidote to hatred is love, to darkness is light, to death is life. As the complex story of the riders comes to an end, love and light and life triumph. Such a conclusion might appear contradictory because only Mrs. Godbold survives. Mary Hare disappears into the night after Himmelfarb's death in the burning house. Alf Dubbo dies in his room, where "The sharp pain poured in crimson tones." Most often in White's novels the visionary fails outwardly and can unravel life's mystery only in death or madness.

For a visionary to survive whole, as Mrs. Godbold does, is indeed a rare occurrence; but Mrs. Godbold lacks the complexity of Himmelfarb, the European Jew, of Mary Hare, the daughter of sophisticates, of Alf Dubbo, the gifted painter. That the washerwoman appears last, in a sense as the mediator for her more accomplished fellow riders, illustrates the move from complexity to lucidity, the leap from condemnation to celebration. In spite of the novel's record of cruelty, cultural desolation, ignorance, and malevolence in all its forms, the ending tempers the bleak picture. Mrs. Goldbold, trudging upward—if it is only up the hill toward the shed where she lives, has experienced a reconciling vision that redeems and heals: "She had her own vision of the Chariot. Even now, at the thought of it her very center was touched by the wings of love and charity."

"Critical Evaluation" by Robert L. Ross

Bibliography:

Bliss, Carolyn. "*Riders in the Chariot*." In *Patrick White's Fiction*. New York: St. Martin's Press, 1986. Argues that the four protagonists, the "riders in the chariot," represent qualities, if they were combined, that "would produce a complete human being or society." Concludes that they reach wholeness through their "acceptance of failure."

Chapman, Edgar L. "The Mandala Design of Patrick White's *Riders in the Chariot*." In *Critical Essays on Patrick White*, edited by Peter Wolfe. Boston: G. K. Hall, 1990. Examines the novel in the light of its mythological sources, including William Blake's visionary poetry, the biblical prophets, the apocalypse, the Jewish cabbalistic tradition, Jungian thought, and the mandala symbol. A complex but readable and illuminating essay.

Dutton, Geoffrey. "White's Triumphal Chariot." In *Critical Essays on Patrick White*, edited by Peter Wolfe. Boston: G. K. Hall, 1990. Admires all aspects of the work—its scope, vision, characterization, and language. An excellent general introduction to the novel.

Edgecombe, Rodney S. "*Riders in the Chariot*." In *Vision and Style in Patrick White: A Study of Four Novels*. Tuscaloosa: University of Alabama Press, 1989. Analyzes each of the chariot's riders in detail, showing their roles in the elaborate allegory and their relationships with one another. Combines this discussion with an examination of the work's complex structure.

Morley, Patricia. *The Mystery of Unity: Theme and Technique in the Novels of Patrick White*. Montreal: McGill-Queen's University Press, 1972. Remains an important and standard study. Places White's work in the mainstream of European writing and investigates how it employs the Western tradition along with archetypes that dominate Western literature. Helpful as a background for *Riders in the Chariot*.

RIDERS TO THE SEA

Type of work: Drama
Author: John Millington Synge (1871-1909)
Type of plot: Tragedy
Time of plot: Late nineteenth century
Locale: Island off the west coast of Ireland
First published: 1903; first performed, 1904

Principal characters:
MAURYA, an old woman
BARTLEY, her son
CATHLEEN, her daughter
NORA, her younger daughter

The Story:

Maurya, an old peasant woman, was worried about her son Michael. Her husband, her father-in-law, and her four other sons had drowned in earlier sea accidents, leaving her with two sons, Michael and Bartley, and two daughters, Cathleen and Nora. Now Michael was missing at sea. As Maurya slept, Cathleen worked at her spinning and made a cake for Bartley, the youngest brother, to take on a trip. Bartley was planning to go to the horse fair on the mainland. Nora came in the house with a bundle of clothes a priest had given her. The clothes, a shirt and a stocking, had been taken from the body of an unidentified young man found floating off the coast of Donegal to the north. Hearing their mother stir, Cathleen and Nora decided to hide the clothes. They planned to examine them later to see if they were Michael's before saying anything to Maurya.

Cathleen asked Nora if she had asked the priest to urge Bartley not to sail in the stormy weather. Nora said the priest told her to trust God not to leave Maurya without any sons. Cathleen climbed into the loft and hid the clothes. When she heard her mother getting up she pretended she was fetching turf for the kitchen fire. Maurya scolded her for wasting turf.

Maurya asked where Bartley was. Nora said he had gone to check on the boat schedule. Moments later, Bartley hurried into the room looking for a piece of rope to make a horse halter. His mother tried various arguments to stop Bartley from going to the horse fair. She told him he ought to leave the rope where it was because they might need it to lower Michael's coffin into his grave if he had drowned. When Bartley told her it was supposed to be a good fair Maurya replied that a thousand horses could not be worth as much as a son, but Bartley continued with his plans, knotting the rope into a horse halter and giving Cathleen last-minute instructions for looking after things during his absence. Bartley and Maurya left, and Nora hid Michael's clothes and decided not to mention anything until Bartley returned safely. When Maurya returned after seeing Bartley off she sat by the fire and began to moan and cry. Nora and Cathleen demanded to know what was wrong. She said she had seen Bartley riding the red horse with Michael in fine clothes and new shoes riding behind him on the gray pony. When she had tried to call her blessing, her voice choked in her throat.

Shocked by her mother's words, Cathleen gave in and told her Michael had drowned. Maurya continued to speak as if to herself, recounting her losses one by one, as other old women came into the house, crossed themselves, and knelt to pray. Cathleen handed Maurya the bit of Michael's clothing. Then Maurya knew it was true.

They heard a sound outside. It was the men carrying Bartley's wet body. The gray pony had knocked Bartley down in the surf and he had been swept out with the tide and drowned. Now Maurya realized the finality of loss. She would never see Michael again and Bartley, her last son, was also dead. She said there was nothing left to threaten her now. The men prepared to build a coffin for Bartley from the white boards Maurya had gotten for Michael's burial. Maurya sprinkled the last of the holy water on Michael's clothes in final benediction and asked for God's blessing. She said no one could live forever and mankind must be satisfied with a decent grave.

Critical Evaluation:

John Millington Synge is considered the greatest playwright of the Irish Literary Revival, a movement in Ireland associated with the poet William Butler Yeats and other Irish writers. This revival took place at the end of the nineteenth and the beginning of the twentieth centuries. Irish born, Synge studied at Trinity College in Dublin and received a scholarship to study music. He traveled to the Continent and lived in Paris, where he taught English and began writing poetry. In Paris, in 1896, Synge met Yeats, a leading writer and one of the founders of the Abbey Theatre in Dublin, a theater dedicated to performing Irish plays. Yeats advised Synge to return to Ireland and take as a model for his writing the people of the Aran Islands off the west coast of Ireland.

Synge followed Yeats's advice. From this experience came Synge's book, *The Aran Islands* (1907), a travel memoir recounting island folklore and daily events in the lives of the local people. From this same material Synge took inspiration and material for his plays. Writing of actual events, Synge used expressions and speech patterns of the old-fashioned local dialect to give a poetic, particularly Irish quality to his drama. The Aran Islands are the inspiration for *Riders to the Sea*. The details regarding the drownings are realistic; drownings were not uncommon there and all the adult men regularly went to sea. A young woman wonders if the drowned man is her missing brother. She puts together information about his clothing and an object found on him to confirm that the dead man must be her brother Mike.

Synge weaves this and other material into the tragic story of Maurya, her two daughters, and the lost men of the family. In doing so he takes the story beyond a local to a mythic level. *Riders to the Sea* begins with the image of the daughter Cathleen at her spinning wheel. Later, when Cathleen and Nora examine the clothing of the drowned man, trying to determine whether it is Michael's or not, Cathleen cuts the string that holds the bundle. Examining a stocking, Nora speaks of knitting, dropping and picking up stitches. These images of spinning, knitting, and cutting suggest the actions of the Fates, classical goddesses of destiny who determine the length of human life as they spin and cut the thread of life. Maurya's speech of resignation at the end of *Riders to the Sea* has been compared to the ending of a Greek tragedy, Sophocles' *Oedipus Tyrannus*, in which the chorus says that no mortal is happy until he has passed beyond life's pain. Her vision of the dead Michael riding the gray horse as an omen of doom has a biblical flavor. It would be a mistake, however, to read Synge's allusions too strictly. Some of these images may have been suggested by other sources. Synge does not force such parallels but rather uses them to add color and a mythic scale.

Synge also uses images of sacraments. Water, often a sign of baptism and life, here takes away life, but the people have no choice but to turn to it for their living. The bread of life, a cake which is baking on the turf fire, goes uneaten by Bartley as he leaves without his mother's blessing. When she tries to correct this oversight he is already beyond her help. Color images are also important. The few colors in the play stand out against a gray and stormy world. Nora speaks of "the green head" of land where the tide is turning and of the likelihood that Bartley will sail in spite of his mother's wishes. Later Cathleen refers to Bartley riding "over the green head" on his way to the boat. The rope that Bartley wants to use to tie the gray horse has been chewed on by the pig with the black feet. The boards the mother is saving for Michael's casket are white boards. The red mare and the gray pony are vivid images in the otherwise bleak landscape. Maurya cries out that when the black night falls she will not have a son left. When Nora tells of how Michael's body was found by two men rowing past the black cliffs to the north, the birds that fly over the sea where his body was found are described as "black hags." Maurya describes seeing the body of Patch, an older son, brought home dripping on a red sail. The women who come into the house to pray and mourn, like a tragic chorus, are wearing red petticoats, the color of the sail. Finally Maurya says that Bartley will have a "fine coffin out of the white boards." Green, black, red, gray, and white create a pattern of life, death, and resignation.

The humble cottage in which the play is set is like an island itself, small and vulnerable in comparison to the large, dangerous world outside. The beauty of Synge's one-act play, which takes approximately half an hour to perform, is in its language and in its simplicity. It presents the clear line of the tragedy itself, seen in its final hours. The players in this drama are not at fault. Instead, this is a tragedy of a fate that can not be avoided and in the face of which there is no alternative but stoicism and acceptance.

Barbara Drake

Bibliography:

Gerstenberger, Donna. *John Millington Synge*. New York: Twayne, 1964. Excellent basic reference book on Synge with one chapter devoted to *Riders to the Sea*. Points out that *Riders to the Sea* was the only one of Synge's plays that did not occasion angry outbursts from Irish audiences. Discusses imagery and symbolic use of color. Selected bibliography.

Grene, Nicholas. *Synge: A Critical Study of the Plays*. New York: Macmillan, 1975. Discusses Synge's Aran experience. Extensive discussion of *Riders to the Sea* and how it differs from Synge's other plays. Praises the economy of the play and delineates way in which props such as the spinning wheel, the bread, the bundle, the boards, and other objects are used for dramatic effect. Cautions against overemphasizing comparisons to classical tragedy and argues for authenticity and originality of the play.

Skelton, Robin. *J. M. Synge*. Cranbury, N.J.: Bucknell University Press, 1972. A summary of Synge's background and analysis of the plays, including *Riders to the Sea*. Chronology and bibliography.

____________. *The Writings of J. M. Synge*. Indianapolis: Bobbs-Merrill, 1971. Chapter on *Riders to the Sea* discusses folklore and mythology referred to in the play.

Thornton, Weldon. *J. M. Synge and the Western Mind*. Gerrards Cross, Buckinghamshire, England: Colin Smythe, 1979. Compares views of a wide variety of critics and scholars on Synge. Excellent introduction to what has been written about Synge's work.

THE RIGHT STUFF

Type of work: New journalism
Author: Tom Wolfe (1931-)
First published: 1979

The Right Stuff, Tom Wolfe's account of America's space program up to Project Mercury, evolved from his curiosity about the kind of men who were willing to sit on top of a thirty-six story container of explosives waiting for the fuse to be lit. His interest in these men—who they were, where they came from, and how they felt while perched atop twenty thousand pounds of liquid oxygen—fueled the research that resulted in this entertaining and enlightening look at America's astronauts. Wolfe explores the fraternity of fliers, the military lifestyle, the function of the press, and the nature of courage, providing the reader with an insightful journey into the heart of American culture. Although factual, the book allows itself liberties in the description of events and, for example, the re-creation of conversations or the thoughts that someone may have had.

Wolfe first discovers the "right stuff" among the close-knit group of military fighter and test pilots stationed at bleak air bases scattered throughout the United States in the late 1940's and early 1950's. He describes this "stuff" as "the ability to go up in a hurtling piece of machinery and . . . have the moxie, the reflexes, the experience, the coolness, to pull it back in the last yawning moment—and then go up again *the next day*, and the next day, and every next day . . . and . . . do so in a cause that means something to thousands, to a people, to a nation, to humanity, to God." This ability and willingness to "push the outside of the envelope" was the sole quality upon which the "True Brotherhood" of fliers judged themselves and each other. The "right stuff" determined, more surely than military rank, the fliers' status in the rigid hierarchy of flying.

Moving from one desolate outpost to another, these fliers aspired to Edwards Air Force Base, the mecca of flying, where pilots who had reached the pinnacle of their careers were assigned. In their quest to fly ever higher and faster in the most advanced American aeronautical technology available, the Edwards pilots risked their lives daily with the offhand calm that marked their breed, hoping to achieve what many considered impossible. The supreme impossible goal was reaching the speed of Mach 1, the sound barrier. The "most righteous of all the possessors of the right stuff," Chuck Yeager, while flying with two broken ribs, achieved the impossible, reaching Mach 1 on October 14, 1947. Yeager and his fellow pilots at Edwards, living what Wolfe termed the "Flying & Drinking and Drinking & Driving" lifestyle, continued achieving even greater speeds for the next decade, until a monumental shift in the direction of American space exploration occurred.

On October 4, 1957, ten years minus ten days after Yeager broke the sound barrier, the Soviet Union sent *Sputnik I* into orbit. Panic followed the Soviets' first foray into space. It appeared to the people of the United States and their government that the control of the heavens was at stake, and an effort to launch an American into space, to close the gap with the Soviets, began immediately. After lengthy consideration about how to select the first American in space (at one point the field was to be open to any young male college graduate with experience in dangerous pursuits—mountain climbers, deep sea divers, skydivers, and the like) President Eisenhower ordered that the first astronauts be chosen from the ranks of military test pilots.

These pilots were not overwhelmingly eager at first to volunteer for this new program, uncertain as to whether it would represent a step up in status, or a leap into obscurity. The position of "astronaut" was unprecedented, and the fliers had to reach a consensus on where an astronaut would fit in their hierarchy. Many fliers argued that astronauts would be no better than passive lab animals, with little or no opportunity to exhibit the right stuff. Motivated largely by the fear of being left behind, the pilots volunteered in large numbers for the assignment, despite their misgivings. Those who decided to volunteer for Project Mercury very soon discovered a whole new set of assumptions at work in the space program. The seven finalists would not be chosen for their prowess as pilots, but rather for mental and physical stamina and adaptability. The rules were understood only by the doctors and scientists, who subjected the fliers to exhaustive and often humiliating examinations and tests, which made it abundantly clear that the fliers were merely lab rats in the brave new world of space exploration.

When the seven men chosen—Alan Shepard, Virgil I. (Gus) Grissom, John H. Glenn, Jr., M. Scott Carpenter, Walter M. (Wally) Schirra, L. Gordon Cooper, and Donald K. (Deke) Slayton—were presented to the press and the American public, not only was no mention made of their experience and qualifications as fliers, no one was really interested. The press asked about their wives and children, their religious affiliation, and their feelings of patriotism, not their stellar records as fighter jocks and test pilots. Determined to take a fitting tone and express the proper sentiment in a matter of serious national concern, the press (or, as Wolfe calls them, the Victorian Gentleman or Genteel Beast) played a major role in the drama of the space race by portraying the astronauts as clean-cut, clean-living repositories of the highest moral virtues, whether or not the facts warranted such an interpretation. The press allowed no hint of the hard drinking, hard driving lifestyle of the astronauts to reach the American public, believing it their duty to provide their readers with the "proper and fitting" images of America's newest heroes.

The press made instant heroes of the astronauts' wives as well, whose faces, airbrushed almost beyond recognition, appeared on the cover of *Life* magazine, which bought exclusive rights to their stories. No mention was made of the fact that Betty Grissom spent only a handful of days a year with her husband or that Gordon Cooper and his wife had been separated before he was chosen as an astronaut, because these facts did not fit conveniently with the required wholesome image. As test pilots' wives, the fear they endured while their husbands flew dangerous missions was private. As astronauts' wives, their anxiety not only became a public spectacle (as their homes were invaded by hordes of reporters), but it paled in comparison to the agony they suffered facing the idiotic and largely unanswerable questions of the press after the splashdown.

As the astronauts proceeded with their training they found themselves pitted against the establishment of the National Aeronautics and Space Administration (NASA), which wanted to use them only as experimental subjects, while they wanted at least some control over the operation of their capsules. Their job description evolved through continuing compromises with NASA concerning how much control they would be allowed over their flights, with the end result being that the astronauts were to be something between passengers and pilots. The astronauts lobbied for and got several changes in the design of the capsule, including a window, a hatch they could "blow," or open by explosives from the inside, an override control on re-entry, and other operational functions.

Although the public was led to believe all of the Mercury flights were successful, and all seven of the astronauts heroes, the astronauts themselves judged each other by their own standards as test pilots, and some were found wanting. Gus Grissom, for example, apparently lost his cool while waiting, floating in the middle of an ocean, to be picked up and blew his capsule's hatch prematurely, sinking the capsule and losing all of the valuable information recorded inside. Among themselves, the other six pilots believed he panicked, or "screwed the pooch," exhibiting an alarming lack of the right stuff. Scott Carpenter, who considered his orbital flight a great success, was considered less than successful by the others because he immersed himself in the in-flight science experiments assigned by NASA, at the expense of operational efficiency. Gordon Cooper probably exhibited the most impressive demonstration of the right stuff by actually falling asleep atop the rocket before his liftoff.

The unprecedented hero-worship that the Mercury astronauts inspired surprised no one so much as the astronauts themselves. Until their first meeting with the press no one suspected the level of hysteria their existence would produce. They were great heroes before they donned a space suit or put a foot inside a capsule, worshipped for offering themselves up as sacrifices to the space race. Wolfe traces this phenomenon back to an ancient element of warfare, the single-combat warrior. Hero-worship of the single-combat warrior was common throughout the pre-Christian world and the Middle Ages. Single-combat warfare pits each army's fiercest and most talented warrior against the other in lieu of a full flight between the entire armies. Sometimes this one-on-one fight settled the affair, with no full-scale fight taking place, and sometimes the result of the single combat was taken as an omen of what was to come, as an indication of which side was God's chosen in the fight. These single-combat warriors were treated as national heroes before they went into battle, much as the astronauts were treated as heroes before they were launched into space. According to Wolfe, the astronauts were the Cold War's single-combat warriors, offering to sit on top of the rockets in order to keep the Soviets from domination of the heavens.

Wolfe's distinctive style and narrative voice permeate *The Right Stuff*, setting a tone of high energy, enthusiasm, and humor. His use of exclamation points, italics, alliteration, and repetitive terms gives an almost cartoonlike feel to the narrative. This tone effectively offsets the bland, wholesome image of the astronauts promulgated by the press and NASA officials. This book provides one of the first glimpses behind the official propaganda of the space program and offers a fascinating insight into the history, technology, and personalities of one of America's most remarkable and ambitious enterprises.

Mary Virginia Davis

Bibliography:

Stokes, Lisa. "Tom Wolfe's Narratives as Stories of Growth." *Journal of American Culture* 14, no. 3 (1991): 19-24. Focuses on Wolfe's distinctive narrative voice and the relationship he establishes between his characters and narrator.

Stull, James N. "The Cultural Gamesmanship of Tom Wolfe." *Journal of American Culture* 14, no. 3 (1991): 25-30. Discusses Wolfe's use of arcane subcultures in his work, and his exploration of status within these cultures, including the fraternity of pilots in *The Right Stuff*.

Wolfe, Tom. "Literary Techniques of the Last Quarter of the Twentieth Century." In *The Writer's Craft: Hopwood Lectures, 1965-81*, edited by Robert A. Martin. Ann Arbor: The University of Michigan Press, 1982. Discusses Wolfe's philosophy of writing and literature, which stresses the importance of reporting as a literary technique.

______________. "The *Rolling Stone* Interview: Tom Wolfe." In *Conversations with Tom Wolfe*, edited by Dorothy Scura. Jackson: University Press of Mississippi, 1990. Discusses the origins of *The Right Stuff*, revealing which astronauts agreed to be interviewed and how Wolfe came to discover the reality behind the hype. Other informative interviews about *The Right Stuff*.

RIGHT YOU ARE (IF YOU THINK SO)

Type of work: Drama
Author: Luigi Pirandello (1867-1936)
Type of plot: Parable
Time of plot: Early twentieth century
Locale: A small Italian town, the capital of a province
First performed: Così è (se vi pare), 1917; first published, 1918 (English translation, 1922)

Principal characters:

LAMBERTO LAUDISI, an observer of human nature
PONZA, secretary to the provincial councillor
SIGNORA FROLA, his mother-in-law
SIGNORA PONZA, his wife
COMMENDATORE AGAZZI, a provincial councillor
AMALIA, his wife
DINA, their daughter
THE PREFECT
CENTURI, a police commissioner

The Story:

There was much talk in the small capital of an Italian province about the peculiar family arrangements of old Signora Frola and her daughter, the wife of Ponza, a newly appointed secretary to Commendatore Agazzi, the provincial councillor. Why was Signora Frola living by herself in a fine apartment next door to the Agazzis and not with her daughter and her son-in-law? Why were Ponza and his wife living in fifth-floor tenement rooms on the edge of town? Why did Ponza visit the old lady every evening and sometimes during the day, but always by himself? Why did Signora Frola never visit her daughter, and why did her daughter, whom no one except Ponza ever saw, never visit her? Why would the old lady not even permit Signora Agazzi and her daughter to pay a social call?

While the enigma was being discussed by Agazzi, his family, and several visitors in the Agazzi parlor, Signora Frola came in to apologize for having refused to admit the Agazzis when they came calling and also to explain why she lived apart from her daughter. She did not want to interfere, she said, in the home life of her daughter and Ponza. She lived by herself, it was true, but she was not unhappy about it; she kept in contact with her daughter, although there were no face-to-face visits. Signora Frola had hardly left when Ponza—a fierce, nervous, sinister-looking man—came in to explain about his poor mother-in-law. The truth was she was mad. Her daughter had been dead for four years, and he had married again two years later. He had prevailed upon his second wife to humor the old woman by carrying on shouted conversations from a fifth-floor balcony and writing notes to be let down in a basket from the balcony to the old woman on the ground.

No sooner had Ponza gone than Signora Frola returned. Although the company at first denied it, she knew what Ponza had been telling them. The sad truth was, however, that he was the mad one. The real truth, which she wished she did not have to tell, was that when he married her young and innocent daughter he so frightened her with his passionate attentions that she had to be put into an institution for a while. When she finally returned, Ponza himself was in such a nervous state that he could not be convinced that she was his wife; she was prevailed upon to pretend that she was a second wife taking the place of the one he had lost.

Before long, a plot was hatched to have Signora Frola and Ponza confront each other in the presence of Agazzi and the others, in order that the truth might be uncovered. From the beginning of the gossipy, inquisitorial discussion, Lamberto Laudisi, the brother-in-law of Agazzi, had maintained that the private domestic lives of the Ponzas and Signora Frola were their own affair and should remain so. They were harming no one; they were not seeking anyone's aid; they should be left alone. Laudisi was overruled. Agazzi left and came back shortly to get some papers that he had purposely left in his study so that he might bring Ponza back with him to get them. As they came in, Ponza heard a piano in the next room playing a tune that had been a favorite of his wife, Lena. Signora Frola was playing; when she stopped, her voice could be heard through the doorway. She was discussing her daughter's cherished melody in such a way as to suggest that Lena was still alive. When she confronted Ponza a moment later in the study, he furiously insisted that Lena was dead, that he was now married to Julia, and that the piano that Lena used to play had been smashed to pieces long ago.

While he was frenziedly shouting at her, she occasionally glanced about at the others in the room as if to call attention to his piteous state and to her forbearance in humoring him. After bursting into tears, Ponza suddenly ordered her out of the room, and she soon left, sobbing. When she had gone, Ponza immediately grew calm again and explained the reason for his actions. The old woman, he said, was so convinced of his madness that he had to pretend to be mad. Now he must go and see her. Laudisi, who had earlier insisted that truth is a relative thing and that what is one person's truth is not necessarily another's, laughed at the confusion of the Agazzis and their visitors. Now, he mocked, they had the truth they had wanted.

Still the puzzle remained: Who was telling the truth and who was lying, either knowingly or unknowingly? Earlier, someone had suggested that documents, such as a marriage certificate for the second marriage or the letters that the second—or first—Signora Ponza wrote to the old woman, might be secured to prove who was right. One of those interested, Commissioner Centuri, arrived with some data that he had uncovered, which might yet clear up the puzzle; but the data turned out to be as inconclusive as the information already at hand.

A chance remark that Signora Ponza might as well be in another world, since no one had ever seen her, made Laudisi wonder whether there really was a Signora Ponza. It was then suggested that Ponza go and get his wife so that she might be seen by everybody, to prove that she existed, and that she be questioned by the prefect in the presence of everyone so that the truth might be generally known. Ponza left after he had been assured that his wife and his mother-in-law would not be compelled to face each other. In his absence, the old woman returned to say that, since she could not live her own life in peace, she would leave town and not come back. To pacify her, the prefect pretended to believe her version of the truth, although he had earlier said he believed Ponza's. When Ponza returned with a heavily veiled woman dressed as if she were in deep mourning, he was shocked and angry to see his mother-in-law, since he had been assured that she would not be there. Signora Ponza, to quiet the clamor, asked Ponza to take the old woman away. Ponza and his mother-in-law went out weeping and with their arms about each other's waists.

Now the truth would finally come out: Signora Ponza would tell the entire group the whole truth. For the final time, however, the decision was left to each of her hearers. She was, it seemed, the daughter of Signora Frola; she was also the second wife of Ponza; and, for herself, she was nobody. When the prefect insisted that she must be one or the other of the two women, she answered that she was the person she was believed to be. Hearing that reply, Laudisi, saying that everybody now knew the truth, burst out laughing.

Critical Evaluation:

Pirandello's *Right You Are (If You Think So)*, which has been given varied English titles, may be Pirandello's most extreme statement on one of his favorite themes: the relativity of truth. Laudisi, who mocks the townspeople's determination to pry out the secret of Signora Frola and the Ponzas, and who several times vainly tries to stop them, serves as the author's spokesman and the explicator of his theme. Despite the philosophic nature of the theme, the drama is an eminently actable one.

Pirandello sets up a situation in which the truth, as people are accustomed to verifying it, cannot be determined, because of the inability to establish a single truth for all. An earthquake has destroyed the village from which the Ponza-Frola family came, dispersed or killed most of its inhabitants, and destroyed the official birth and death records. The author further indicates that even if factual evidence such as documents were to be found, a single truth acceptable to all could not be found because the documents would be interpreted differently. This point, the theme of the play, is shown through the manner in which truth is perceived by various groups or characters within the play.

The first group consists of the townspeople (the Agazzi family and their friends). To them, truth is specific and concrete. It represents what one can see and feel, a decidedly empirical approach to reality. They assume reality appears the same to all. It never occurs to them that they cannot find the truth because reality may appear differently to different people at different times. Thus, they vacillate from belief in Ponza's version of the truth to belief in Signora Frola's version, depending upon who is telling the tale.

For Ponza and Frola, truth is the illusion they have created in order to permit themselves to live. They have suffered a misfortune (exactly what it is, is never made clear), but they have created a truth that permits them to overcome their individual sorrow and continue to live. Their truth is based on love and consideration for each other. For this reason, Signora Ponza can state at the end of the play that she is "the daughter of Signora Frola . . . and the second wife of Signor Ponza." When the townspeople insist that she must be one or the other, she replies that she is "whom you believe me to be."

For Laudisi, truth is relative. He points out that one can never really know the truth about others, because each person perceives reality according to his or her own point of view. People perceive themselves in one way, but others perceive them differently. Which view is correct? Laudisi would suggest that all views are correct. Although the townspeople insist on a single reality that is the same for all, the mocking laughter of Laudisi that closes each act of the play would seem to indicate that finding the truth is impossible.

Pirandello called this play a parable, presumably about how one must respect the truths of others. When one person attempts to force other people to face "reality," that is, his or her version of the truth, there is a danger of upsetting the delicate balance others have achieved in order to make their existence viable. Pirandello also suggests that one person's version of the truth is in no way more reliable or verifiable than anyone else's version.

Bibliography:

Büdel, Oscar. *Pirandello*. New York: Hillary House, 1966. Overview of the dramatist's achievements, organized thematically. Discusses *Right You Are (If You Think So)* as an example of Pirandello's extreme relativism and his use of humor to highlight the absurd plight of humanity.

Matthaei, Renate. *Luigi Pirandello*. Translated by Simon Young and Erika Young. New York: Frederick Ungar, 1973. Critical study of Pirandello's major plays. Examines *Right You Are*

(If You Think So) as a social satire; reviews its critical reception in Europe and the United States.

Oliver, Roger W. *Dreams of Passion: The Theater of Luigi Pirandello*. New York: New York University Press, 1979. Reads *Right You Are (If You Think So)* and other plays in light of the theory of the theater outlined in Pirandello's essay *On Humor* (1908).

Ragusa, Olga. *Luigi Pirandello: An Approach to His Theater*. Edinburgh, Scotland: Edinburgh University Press, 1980. Shows how Pirandello's works illuminate the dramatist's vision of humankind and humans' place in the world. Discusses *Right You Are (If You Think So)* as one of a group of plays published between 1916 and 1921 that share certain dramaturgic and thematic qualities.

Vittorini, Domenico. *The Drama of Luigi Pirandello*. 2d ed. New York: Russell & Russell, 1969. Examines Pirandello's works in light of the tradition of Italian theater. Claims the central idea of *Right You Are (If You Think So)* is that humankind is essentially subjective; only if people accept others' points of view as being equally as valid as their own can true social harmony be achieved.

THE RIME OF THE ANCIENT MARINER

Type of work: Poetry
Author: Samuel Taylor Coleridge (1772-1834)
Type of plot: Allegory
Time of plot: Late medieval period
Locale: High seas
First published: 1798

Principal characters:
THE ANCIENT MARINER
A HERMIT
A WEDDING GUEST

The Story:

Three young gallants on their way to a wedding were stopped by an old gray-headed sailor who detained one of them. The ancient Mariner held with his gaze a young man whose next of kin was being married in the church nearby and forced him to listen, against his will, to the old seaman's tale. The ancient Mariner told how his ship left the home port and sailed southward to the equator. In a storm the vessel was blown to polar regions of snow and ice. When an albatross flew out of the frozen silence, the crew hailed it as a good omen. The sailors made a pet of the albatross and regarded it as a fellow creature. One day the ancient Mariner killed the bird with his crossbow. The superstitious sailors believed bad luck would follow.

Fair winds blew the ship northward until it reached the equator, where it was suddenly becalmed and lay for days without moving. The thirsty seamen blamed the ancient Mariner and hung the dead albatross about his neck as a sign of his guilt.

In the distance a ship appeared, a skeleton ship which moved on the still sea where no wind blew. On its deck Death and Life-in-Death were casting dice for the crew and the ancient Mariner. As a result of the cast, Death won the two hundred crew members, who dropped dead one by one. As the soul of each dead sailor rushed by, the ancient Mariner was reminded of the sound of the rushing bolt of his crossbow when he shot the albatross. Life-in-Death won the ancient Mariner, who lived on to expiate his sins. Furthermore, the curse lived on in the eyes of the men who died accusing him. One night the ancient Mariner, observing the beauty of the water snakes around the ship, blessed these creatures in his heart. The spell was broken. The albatross fell from his neck into the sea.

At last the ancient Mariner was able to sleep. Rain fell to quench his thirst. The warped vessel began to move, and the bodies of the dead crew rose to resume their regular duties as the ship sailed quietly on, moved by a spirit toward the South Pole. The ancient Mariner fell into a trance. He awoke to behold his own country, the very port from which he had set sail. Then the angelic spirits left the dead bodies of the crew and appeared in their own forms of light. Meanwhile, the pilot on the beach had seen the lights, and he rowed out with his son and a holy Hermit to bring the ship in to harbor. Suddenly the ship sank, but the pilot pulled the ancient Mariner into his boat. Once ashore, the old man asked the Hermit to hear his confession and give him penance. The ancient Mariner told the Wedding Guest that at times since that moment, the agony of the seaman's guilt returned and he had to tell the story of his voyage to one who must be taught love and reverence for all things God has made and loved. The merry din of the wedding had ceased, and the Wedding Guest returned home a sadder and a wiser man.

Critical Evaluation:

Perhaps what is most strange about *The Rime of the Ancient Mariner* is not its uniqueness, which makes it seem strange, but its transparency. It is about what it says it is about. An epigraph, marginal glosses, and a moral at the end state the poem's ideas so clearly that one may try to second-guess them. A reader may also argue that the poem succeeds in its stated aim—to teach lessons of the spirits, of guilt, of expiation, and of love for all of God's creations—and that the poem's oddity is instrumental in this success. Without the novelty of the tale, the ancient and simple lessons would be easier to ignore.

The epigraph by Thomas Burnet states that "[*f*]*acile credo*" (I believe with ease, or I may easily believe) that there are many invisible beings in the universe. Burnet next points out that, while it is also easy to get bogged down in questions regarding such creatures, and therefore, implicitly, create an attitude of cynical skepticism, it is spiritually enriching to contemplate the invisible realm, and thereby to imagine a greater and better world. Such thought gives one better perspective on the trivial concerns of daily life. Such contemplation, Burnet concludes, is not intended to lead away from truth. This epigraph may be interpreted, in the context of the poem, to state the following ideas: First, there is a spiritual realm, and its mysteries are to be respected although not fully understood. The Mariner makes the mistake of showing contempt for the spiritual world by killing what seems to be one of its representatives. Second, spiritual mysteries are wonderful, miraculous, and terrible. They can be described, but they are best understood emotionally rather than through analysis. When the Mariner "blessed them unaware," (part four, line 285), his spiritual rebirth begins. Third, the marvels of the invisible can lead one to greater understanding. This is clear in the Mariner's case. Fourth, the marvels of the spiritual world are not intended to lead one away from truth. Perhaps to Burnet, truth meant doctrinal orthodoxy. To the Mariner, truth may mean, as Burnet says, avoiding extremes and telling day from night. In the Mariner's case, this means putting his hard-won knowledge to use in the world. He tells others what he has learned. Perhaps to Coleridge, truth was the practice of his art, the creation of *The Rime of the Ancient Mariner.*

The Rime of the Ancient Mariner was published in the famous volume *Lyrical Ballads* (1798), a collaboration between Coleridge and William Wordsworth. The volume contains two kinds of poetry. In one type, as Coleridge would later write in chapter 14 of his *Biographia Literaria* (1817):

> The incidents and agents were to be, in part at least, supernatural, and the excellence aimed at was to consist in the interesting of the affections by the dramatic truth of such emotions, as would naturally accompany such situations, supposing them real. . . . In this idea originated the plan of the *Lyrical Ballads*, in which it was agreed that my endeavors should be directed to persons and characters supernatural, or at least romantic; yet so as to transfer from our inward nature a human interest and a semblance of truth sufficient to procure for these shadows of imagination that willing suspension of disbelief which constitutes poetic faith. . . . With this view I wrote *The Ancient Mariner.*

Whether the faith be Christian, poetic, or pagan, *The Rime of the Ancient Mariner* is about, among other things, faith. For example, in part 1 of the poem, the albatross appears to guide, or seems to guide, the ship out of the ice. "As if it had been a Christian soul,/ We hailed it in God's name." A bird, after all, is not foreign to Christian symbolism. Coleridge hedges somewhat ("as if" and "supposing them real"), but this hedging is the test of faith. Readers may decide to take the poem literally, to accept it as a work of imagination that tells important spiritual truths, or to consider the poem simply a strange story of no consequence.

The quotation from Burnet (translated in most modern editions) should alert readers to the fact that Coleridge, who had once planned to be a clergyman, is concerned in this poem with demonstrating the inadequacy of materialism and rationalism as interpretations of reality. Materialism is the belief that only matter and motion exist (as opposed to spiritual reality of any kind). Rationalism is the belief that reason is capable of comprehending the totality of nature. Although Coleridge was inconsistent as a philosopher, he regularly opposed both of these suppositions.

In a letter of December 31, 1796, for example, he opposed materialism and regarded himself as "a mere apparition—a naked Spirit!—And that Life is I myself I!" In January, 1798, he described himself as a committed defender of religion, regarding scientific discoveries of any kind as being important primarily for their theological revelations. In later years also, Coleridge would emerge as a significant religious teacher who always believed in a spiritual reality beyond the material one. *The Rime of the Ancient Mariner*, defying both reason and materialism, is something of a sermon on the sanctity of life, which in all its forms is a manifestation of the divine. It may be said that the poem argues, with perhaps deceptive simplicity and candor, that the laws that govern living things are not physical but moral and come from God.

Close reading of the poem can reveal how its spiritual themes, often discussed in reference to text not belonging to the poem, are developed. The poem's frame (the Mariner telling his story to the Wedding Guest), for example, may be examined in terms of Christian symbolism, the psychology of the reader (whose responses to the Mariner may be much like the guest's), and the creation of the willing suspension of disbelief. The Mariner's story follows a clear pattern of guilt, penance, expiation, and confession, and this pattern may be examined in terms of the flow of the narration and the uses of the irregular stanzas and of the glosses. Finally, what may be the poem's most memorable element—its descriptions of natural and supernatural phenomena—may be examined in terms of sheer poetic technique. In any case, *The Rime of the Ancient Mariner*'s uniqueness is indisputable, and its spiritual themes may be considered to be no less authentic for being stated clearly.

"Critical Evaluation" by Dennis R. Dean

Bibliography:

Boulanger, James D., ed. *Twentieth Century Interpretations of "The Rime of the Ancient Mariner": A Collection of Critical Essays*. Englewood Cliffs, N.J.: Prentice-Hall, 1969. A useful collection of scholarly articles dealing with the poem, including an introduction that attempts to reconcile some of the differences of critical opinion.

Coleridge, Samuel Taylor. *The Annotated Ancient Mariner*. Edited by Martin Gardner. Illustrated by Gustave Doré. Cleveland: World Publishing, 1967. Includes the last and the first versions of the poem, together with interpretive comments of varying utility. Doré's illustrations (and those by other artists) remind readers how intensely visual the poem is.

House, Humphry. *Coleridge: The Clark Lectures, 1951-52*. London: Hart-Davis, 1953. This book of fewer than 170 pages maintains its reputation as a sound introduction to the poet and his works. A thirty-page chapter on *The Rime of the Ancient Mariner* is sensible and straightforward.

Lowes, John Livingston. *The Road to Xanadu: A Study in the Ways of the Imagination*. Rev. ed. Boston: Houghton Mifflin, 1931. In this classic work of literary scholarship, Lowes attempts to illuminate *The Rime of the Ancient Mariner* by a seemingly exhaustive examination of the poet's reading, which was wide. Captivating as the source hunt is, Lowes tells readers little about what the poem might actually mean.

Piper, H. W. *The Active Universe: Pantheism and the Concept of Imagination in the English Romantic Poets*. London: Athlone Press, 1962. Proposes the influence of various scientific and philosophical ideas upon Coleridge, with several chapters on the poet's intellectual development and one devoted entirely to *The Rime of the Ancient Mariner*.

THE RING AND THE BOOK

Type of work: Poetry
Author: Robert Browning (1812-1889)
Type of plot: Dramatic
Time of plot: Seventeenth century
Locale: Italy
First published: 1868-1869

Principal characters:
PIETRO COMPARINI, an aged Roman
VIOLANTE, Pietro's wife
POMPILIA, the Comparini's adopted daughter
GUIDO FRANCESCHINI, Pompilia's husband
GIUSEPPE CAPONSACCHI, a priest

The Story:

Count Guido Franceschini, descended from an ancient house of Aretine, had married Pompilia Comparini, a young and beautiful Roman woman. Unhappy with her husband, the young wife fled back to Rome in the company of a young priest, Giuseppe Caponsacchi. Guido and four accomplices followed her, and on Christmas night he found his wife at the home of her parents, Pietro and Violante. He murdered the seventy-year-old man and woman and fatally wounded seventeen-year-old Pompilia.

The aged parents were laid in the church where the people of Rome came to stare and to speculate. The Comparinis had been childless until somehow Violante had tricked Pietro into thinking that she had given birth to the child she had secretly bought. It was Violante's mischief that had led to evil, asserted the Roman people. She had spied Guido, of a noble family, and had persuaded him to take Pompilia for his wife. Then all three, parents and daughter, had moved to his estate in Arezzo and there learned of Guido's poverty. Leaving Pompilia behind, the Comparinis returned to Rome. Back in Rome, Violante confessed to Pietro that she had bought the child from a prostitute, and by disowning her parentage the aged couple denied Guido his dowry rights. Pompilia, meanwhile, had written a letter to the archbishop in Rome, telling him that since her parents' departure life in Arezzo had become unbearable. In Arezzo, Pompilia had begun a flirtation with Caponsacchi, the Roman gossipers related, and at last had run away with him.

As the guilty pair neared Rome, Guido overtook them and brought them to Rome and to the Pope. Pompilia and Caponsacchi declared themselves innocent and disavowed love letters that Guido claimed had passed between them. When the court treated the case as a slight marriage quarrel, Guido returned to Arezzo and the taunts of his townsmen. Soon afterward news reached him that Pompilia, who had returned to the Comparinis, had given birth to a son. Then Guido took four men, went to Rome, killed the parents, and left Pompilia dying. The Romans excitedly awaited the trial, for Caponsacchi would be one of the witnesses.

Another group of spectators in Rome took a different view of the murderer and his wife. Pompilia had been a blessing to her foster parents, no matter how she came to them. They had considered it a blessing when Guido married their daughter, only to reach horrible disillusionment when they went to Arezzo and saw his cruelty and poverty. She was Guido's victim, these gossips said.

The tribunal tried to determine the truth in the case. Pietro and Violante had been poor, struggling creatures. When the mother of Pompilia was with child, Violante had bargained with her for the baby and deceived her husband by pretending that it was she who was pregnant. Her act was judged criminal. When Guido came to Rome to find a wife to bear him sons, and a dowry to pay his debts, Pietro and Violante gave him their daughter so that she could rise in name and fortune. When they learned that Guido was penniless, they cried that they had been cheated. Meanwhile it was Pompilia who suffered between the rival factions of parents and husband. She was tricked by Guido to trace letters to Caponsacchi, which were offered at the trial. Guido's friends claimed that he could not have so mistreated his young wife, that she must have written the letters herself.

Guido told his own story. His family had once been wealthy and great, but in his lifetime they had known only poverty. His brothers were priests; he alone remained to carry on the Franceschini name. His brother Paul, a priest in Rome, had advised him that Pompilia would make a suitable wife. He was to give the woman his name and state in return for her dowry and her son. Pompilia had, he said, shirked her wifely duties from the first. One day she caught the eye of Caponsacchi at the opera. Afterward Caponsacchi's way to church led him past Guido's house and past Pompilia's window. Then one night Pompilia drugged Guido and all the servants and fled with her priest to the inn where Guido located them. He found some letters Caponsacchi had exchanged with her, letters that she claimed had been forged. He brought them to court to have his marriage annulled, but the court upheld the marriage and sent Caponsacchi away for a short confinement. Pompilia returned to Pietro and Violante and there she had a child that Guido believed Caponsacchi's. He had no other course, he said, but to go to Rome and cleanse his family name, and he threw himself upon the justice of the court.

Caponsacchi took the stand to describe his first sight of Pompilia at the opera. Not long after he received a letter, signed by Pompilia, confessing love and asking him to come to her window. Suspecting the letter to be a forgery, he answered it with a refusal. He received more letters. At last he became curious and went to stand outside Guido's house. Pompilia, seeing him, rebuked him for his unseemly letters to her, a married woman. They decided that they were victims of Guido's plot. Pompilia begged Caponsacchi to take her to her parents in Rome. His heart softening at her plight, he arranged for her to go away with him.

Pompilia, Caponsacchi said, had been victimized by her cruel husband. The testimony of the dying Pompilia upheld what Caponsacchi had said. At the time of her marriage she had been only thirteen years old. She had been brought to Arezzo, to an impoverished home where Guido's brother had tried to seduce her. For three years she lived in misery. Then she received letters from Caponsacchi. She tried to understand what was happening regarding the letters, knowing that somehow she was being tricked, but finally she sent for the priest because she had decided to seek help from the outside world.

The testimony of others followed, some in defense of Guido, others exposing his carefully laid plot to rid himself of Pompilia. Testimony of Pompilia's innocence was also presented. The Pope, condemning Guido for the crime, pronounced Pompilia innocent of guilt and told the court of the tremendous burden of justice that a Pope must carry on his shoulders. Guido and his four accomplices were sentenced to be hanged.

Humbled and fearful of death, Guido made one last plea for his life. Pride and self-love colored his statements as he confessed his crime but rationalized his motive. He was to be pitied; he wanted to live. He pleaded for mercy, which was not granted.

Critical Evaluation:

This poem reveals Browning's deep perceptive and poetic powers at their greatest heights.

Based upon a murder trial in the city of Florence in 1698, the poem attempts to probe the inner motivations of the people involved in an old, sordid tale of passion and crime. A series of dramatic characterizations and episodes carries the reader to the magnificent conclusion. Pompilia and Caponsacchi are among Browning's most notable creations. Too long to be one of the widely read poems of Browning, yet too masterful to be disregarded by any of his admirers, *The Ring and the Book* is written with tremendous power of language.

Compared to Shakespeare's greatest plays when it first appeared, *The Ring and the Book* put the final stamp of unqualified distinction on its author and confirmed his equality with Alfred, Lord Tennyson, the other giant of Victorian poetry. The Shakespearean comparison was a tribute to Robert Browning's poetic range and to his capacity to dig deep into experience in order to raise up forms and people larger than life. John Keats had thought Shakespeare divine because he could create both an Iago and an Imogen. Similarly, Browning was admired for the variety and complexity of his characters. In *Men and Women* (1855) he reveals his gift for penetrating character analysis in such brilliant dramatic monologues as "Fra Lippo Lippi" and "Andrea del Sarto." The joyous realism of Lippi, his relish for portraying things "just as they are," contrasts sharply with the self-delusion of del Sarto, who betrays his talent and reputation for the sake of a worthless wife.

What Browning accomplished with monologues (his characteristic poetic form) became the basis for a cosmic view of human evil in *The Ring and the Book*. For four years he worked on this ambitious project and published it at intervals in 1868-1869. It is a narrative poem consisting of many long monologues, each expressing a different view of the central action—Guido's murder of Pompilia and her parents. By reflecting each character in the thoughts of the other, Browning's monologues achieve dazzling effects in point of view and psychological revelation—despite the syntactical obscurity of much of the verse (Browning shares with the later Henry James a peculiar blend of impenetrable style with striking psychological insight). The monologue form enables the characters to speak their minds and speculate on the thoughts and feelings of the others with a depth denied the conventional drama. The effect is similar to what would happen if all the best soliloquies of a Shakespearean play were juxtaposed and still constituted a unified drama despite the absence of intervening dialogue and action. The analytical power of Browning's approach is reinforced by the variety of the characters. They are so divergent in temperament and nature it is difficult to imagine them together in a conventional drama: ruthless, sensual, and manic-depressive Guido; saintly but dangerously immature Pompilia; the venal and pathetic parents, petty in their thinking and vulnerable because of it; worldly but impressionable Caponsacchi, the priest; and finally, the humanist Pope, who must judge Guido and does so with a mixture of compassion and contempt that captures perfectly the realism and tough-minded spiritualism of the Renaissance Church.

The blend of people, values, and emotions that informs this poem is anticipated by the opening part, in which the poet explains the title of his work. The book of the title is the Yellow Book, the old record of the story and trial that Browning found in a Florence book stall. The ring is the result of mixing the raw gold of the Yellow Book with the alloy of his art. In other words, the ring is the crafted result of the artist's sympathetic imagination—a power that penetrates the mysteries of experience with greater revelation than any other human effort. Browning's ring is also a symbol of the poem's circular reflection. The ring is a house of mirrors in which the characters' several minds reflect on one another in the mind of the reader.

Browning's willingness to base a dramatic poem, full of what Matthew Arnold would have called "high seriousness," on a sordid story of crime and mayhem stems largely from his conviction that anything representative of life as it truly is, is worthy of serious study. For

Browning the only absolute evil is the rejection of life. Anything that affirms life is finally good, even if human vileness is part of it. To recognize the existence of evil is not to condone it; Browning simply believed that an objective consideration of the vast range of evil in the world—from petty indifference to sadistic murder—only revealed ultimate moralities in bolder terms.

Elizabeth Barrett, Browning's wife, took issue with his insistence on the relevance of the sordid and the ugly to a moral art. She wanted him to drop his *dramatis personae* and speak with his own voice. He insisted that his objective dramatizations, his dramatic monologues, were the best he had to give the world. He was right. Browning could put himself momentarily into someone else's psyche. Browning's ability to enter other people's minds enabled him to achieve states of perception beyond the mere self. What seemed an absence of identity, or even personal involvement on his part, became finally a means to a poetic understanding greater than that exemplified in the ardent subjectivity of his wife's poetry. Browning may have started off as an amoral dramatizer, but he ended as one of the major poet-teachers of his period.

It is the Pope, and his function in *The Ring and the Book*, that vindicates Browning's dramatic objectivity to his wife and all the other Victorians. The Pope is a spokesman for Browning's hard-won ethical vision; he represents a projection of Browning's own power to sermonize and idealize in the very act of demonstrating the venality and terrifying corruptibility of the human soul. Browning, finally, is not a tragic writer. There is too much of a sometimes naïve robustness in him. Human flaws do not define his fate. On the contrary, Browning saw in the very imperfection of life the seeds of God's power. Browning, like John Milton, sought to justify the ways of God. People must strive to know all they can, as does the Pope in his soul-searching effort to comprehend Guido's crime, but the Pope's limited understanding is God's design. In passing judgment on Guido, the Pope realizes that his own moral vision is being tested and shaped: "All to the very end is trial in life." For some this means anxiety and alienation. For Browning it merely marks off the arena of human experience.

"Critical Evaluation" by Peter A. Brier

Bibliography:

Altick, Richard D., and James F. Loucks II. *Browning's Roman Murder Story: A Reading of "The Ring and the Book."* Chicago: University of Chicago Press, 1968. An intensive study of the work's artistry as well as of its treatment of religious themes such as the infallibility of the Pope.

Browning, Robert. *The Complete Works of Robert Browning, with Variant Readings and Annotations.* Edited by Roma King, Jr. Athens: Ohio University Press, 1985. Professor King's variorum edition contains extensive and invaluable notes.

Hines, Susan C. "A Trial Reading of Robert Browning's *The Ring and the Book.*" *Studies in Browning and His Circle* 18 (1990): 28-33. Postulates that Browning's method of telling a legal story through several narrators places the reader in the position of juror. Through the experience of the poem, the reader realizes the difficulty of seeing the truth.

King, Roma, Jr. *The Focusing Artifice: The Poetry of Robert Browning.* Athens: Ohio University Press, 1968. Traces the development of Browning's art, focusing on the aesthetic devices Browning uses to examine morality and values.

Raymond, William O. *The Infinite Moment and Other Essays in Robert Browning.* Toronto: University of Toronto Press, 1950. Reviews criticism from the first half of the twentieth century.

Sullivan, Mary Rose. *Browning's Voices in "The Ring and the Book": A Study of Method and Meaning*. Toronto: University of Toronto Press, 1969. Examines how Browning uses narrative to create meaning.

Wasserman, George. "The Meaning of Browning's Ring Figure." *Modern Language Notes* 76 (1961): 420-426. Discusses Browning's use of the ring as a symbol for the poem.

RIP VAN WINKLE

Type of work: Short fiction
Author: Washington Irving (1783-1859)
Type of plot: Tall tale
Time of plot: Eighteenth century
Locale: New York state
First published: 1819

Principal characters:
RIP VAN WINKLE, a henpecked husband
DAME VAN WINKLE, his wife

The Story:

Along the reaches of the Hudson, not far from the Catskill Mountains, there was a small, Dutch town. The mountains overshadowed the town, and there were times when the good Dutch burghers could see a hood of clouds hanging over the crests of the hills. In that small town lived a man named Rip Van Winkle. He was beloved by all his neighbors, by children, and by animals, but his life at home was made miserable by his shrewish wife. Though he was willing to help anyone else at any odd job that might be necessary, he was incapable of keeping his own house or farm in repair. He was descended from an old and good Dutch family, but he had none of the fine Dutch traits of thrift and energy.

He spent a great deal of his time at the village inn, under the sign of King George III, until his wife chased him from there. During these times, he would take his gun and his dog, Wolf, and head for the hills. Wolf was as happy as Rip was to get away from home. When Dame Van Winkle berated the two of them, Rip raised his eyes silently to heaven, but Wolf tucked his tail between his legs and slunk out of the house.

One fine day in autumn, Rip and Wolf walked high into the Catskills after squirrels. As evening came on, he and his dog sat down to rest before starting home. When Rip started down the mountainside, he heard his name called. A short, square little man with a grizzled beard had called Rip to help carry a keg of liquor. The little man was dressed in antique Dutch clothes. Although he accepted Rip's help in carrying the keg, he carried on no conversation. As they ascended the mountain, Rip heard noises that sounded like claps of thunder. When they reached a sort of amphitheater near the top, Rip saw a band of little men, dressed and bearded like his companion, playing ninepins. One stout old gentleman, who seemed to be the leader, wore a laced doublet and a high-crowned hat with a feather.

The little men were no more companionable than the first one had been, and Rip felt somewhat depressed. Because they seemed to enjoy the liquor from the keg, Rip tasted it a few times while they were absorbed in their game. Then he fell into a deep sleep.

On waking, he looked in vain for the stout old gentleman and his companions. When he reached for his gun, he found it was rusted. His dog did not answer his call. He tried to find the amphitheater where the little men had played, but the way was blocked by a rushing stream.

The people he saw as he walked into town were all strangers to him. Since most of them, upon looking at him, stroked their chins, Rip unconsciously stroked his and found that his beard had grown a foot long. The town itself looked different. At first, Rip thought the liquor from the keg had addled his head, for he had a hard time finding his own house. When he did locate it at last, he found it in a state of decay. Even the sign over the inn had been changed to one carrying the name of General Washington. The men gathered under the sign talked gibberish to him, and they accused him of trying to stir up trouble by coming armed to an election. When he was finally able to inquire into the whereabouts of his old friends, he was told that men by those names had moved away or that they had been dead these twenty years.

Finally, an eager young woman pushed through the crowd to look at Rip. Her voice started a train of thought, and he asked who she was and who her father had been. When she claimed to be Rip Van Winkle's daughter Judith, Rip asked after her mother. When Judith told him that her mother had died after breaking a blood vessel in a fit of anger at a Yankee peddler, Rip identified himself as Judith's father.

Although another old woman claimed that she recognized him, the men at the inn only winked at his story until an old man, a descendant of the village historian, vouched for Rip's tale. He assured the men that he had it as a fact from his historian ancestor that Hendrick Hudson and his crew came to the mountains every twenty years to visit the scene of their exploits, and that the old historian had seen the crew in antique Dutch garb playing at ninepins just as Rip had related.

Rip spent the rest of his life happily telling his story at the inn until everyone knew it by heart. Ever afterward, when the inhabitants of the village heard thunder in the Catskills, they would say that Hendrick Hudson and his crew were playing ninepins, and many a henpecked husband would wish in vain for a draught of Rip Van Winkle's quieting brew.

Critical Evaluation:

As children, many readers have been told some version of "Rip Van Winkle" before they ever get around to reading Washington Irving's tale. Moreover, a number of theatrical adaptations have made the basic elements of the story familiar to many who have never read it. As a consequence of this, "Rip Van Winkle" comes across as a story without an author, a product of the folk imagination, and there is much in the genesis of the tale that reinforces this impression. In these circumstances, it is altogether too easy to overlook the art involved in Irving's telling of his tale, especially since it would be difficult to find anywhere in American literature a more compelling example of an art that conceals art.

The story first appeared in *The Sketch Book of Geoffrey Crayon, Gent.* (1819-1820). Much of the content of this book, the first by an American to enjoy a transatlantic reputation, focuses on subject matter derived from Irving's stay in England, to which he had sailed in 1815. It expresses an attitude toward England, announced as that of Geoffrey Crayon, Irving's persona, that is often critical and sometimes melancholy. In this context, the American qualities of "Rip Van Winkle," set in the time of the revolution that established the independent United States of America where previously there had been only British colonies, make themselves emphatically felt. Irving, however, places the tale in a second context as well. The story was found, we are told, among the papers of Diedrich Knickerbocker. Knickerbocker is, of course, one of Irving's earlier creations, the fictional author of Diedrich Knickerbocker's *A History of New York* (1809-1812), Irving's first masterpiece. How the papers of Diedrich Knickerbocker came into the possession of Geoffrey Crayon is never explained. Two personae, Geoffrey Crayon and Diedrich Knickerbocker, separate Irving, the actual author, from the work; the separation encourages in the reader an air of ironic detachment toward the story Irving tells. It may also constitute a sort of authorial self-effacement, a disappearance of the author behind his work. It is ironic that this success results in a diminished sense of the author's accomplishment.

The actual source of the story is a German folktale. It is Irving's genius, however, that resets this tale in America and in history. The twenty years that Rip sleeps are not merely an arbitrary period, suggesting simply a long time, as is common in folktales. They are rather the twenty years during which the American nation was born in revolution. Rip himself is also historically situated. At the beginning of the story, he is a loyal subject of England's King George III. As his name suggests, however, he is descended from the Dutch settlers who preceded the English in the area that became New York. Before that, the Dutch the area was inhabited by American Indians. They are present in the story only as figures in the tales Rip tells to frighten and amuse the children of the village. History has pushed them to the margins, to dwell with the witches and ghosts who otherwise populate Rip's yarns, yet they remain in memory and imagination.

Thus, Irving suggests a multiplicity of historical layers beyond the surface of his tale. Even the most fantastic element, the apparition of Hendrick Hudson and his crew playing at ninepins, recalls the importance of Dutch exploration in American history. The background to the dynamic of history is provided by the Catskills, emblematic on this occasion of the American landscape, the theater in which the acts of the historical drama are played out. The latest (and not the last) act of this drama is the age to which Rip awakens. His awakening leads swiftly to a crisis of identity. He no longer knows who he is.

In his confusion, as he begs someone to identify him to himself, Rip articulates a version of one of the central questions of classic American literature: What are these new beings called Americans? Do they represent a new beginning in human history? Or is the change from British colonists to American citizens as superficial as the coat of paint that transforms the George III inn into the George Washington inn? In fusing the materials of a German folktale with the stuff of American history, Irving encourages in his readers an ironic reflection on just such questions.

Part of the art of this story, then, rests in the mastery of touch that allows Irving to bring into play such complexities of time and place, while maintaining without rupture a surface of unruffled urbanity and humor. There is a mastery of narrative craft at work here as well. The story opens on a panorama of the geographical setting. The passages in the Catskills, including Rip's encounter with the little men, are developed in more tightly focused, scenic terms. Viewpoint becomes strictly limited as we move to Rip's discovery, through observing the reactions of others, of his long beard. This prepares us for the inspired confusion of election day in the village as perceived by a befuddled old man who thought he was coming home. "Rip Van Winkle" is a marvel in its author's manipulation of point of view.

"Critical Evaluation" by W. P. Kenney

Bibliography:

Bowden, Mary Weatherspoon. *Washington Irving*. Boston: Twayne, 1981. A general introduction to the work, including a chronology and an annotated bibliography. Bowden emphasizes the integrity of *The Sketch Book of Geoffrey Crayon, Gent.*, in which "Rip Van Winkle" first appeared, and suggests that Irving's greatest literary accomplishment was his style.

Hedges, William L. *Washington Irving: An American Study, 1802-1832*. Baltimore: The Johns Hopkins University Press, 1965. Although Hedges believes that Irving reached an intellectual dead end by 1825, he asserts that in his greatest works, including "Rip Van Winkle," Irving stands as an important forerunner in style to Nathaniel Hawthorne and Henry James and in narrative and thematic concerns to Edgar Allan Poe and Herman Melville.

Myers, Andrew B., ed. *A Century of Commentary on the Works of Washington Irving*. New York: Sleepy Hollow Restorations, 1976. A representative sampling of critical writing about Irving.

Roth, Martin. *Comedy and America: The Lost World of Washington Irving*. Port Washington, N.Y.: Kennikat Press, 1976. Argues that "Rip Van Winkle" is one of the few exceptions to a decline in Irving's work already underway by the writing of *The Sketch Book of Geoffrey Crayon, Gent.*

Rubin-Dorsky, Jeffrey. *Adrift in the Old World: The Psychological Pilgrimage of Washington Irving*. Chicago: University of Chicago Press, 1988. Emphasizes the "Americanness" of Irving, the way he was shaped by, and came to identify himself with, his country and its particular heritage. The tale Irving tells in "Rip Van Winkle" reenacts Americans' doubts about identity and their fantasies of escape.

THE RISE OF SILAS LAPHAM

Type of work: Novel
Author: William Dean Howells (1837-1920)
Type of plot: Domestic realism
Time of plot: Nineteenth century
Locale: New England
First published: 1885

Principal characters:
SILAS LAPHAM, a self-made manufacturer
MRS. LAPHAM, his wife
PENELOPE and
IRENE, his daughters
TOM COREY, the Laphams' friend
MR. ROGERS, Mr. Lapham's former partner

The Story:

Silas Lapham was being interviewed for a Boston paper. The journalist was secretly mocking Lapham's way of life, but Lapham was content with his success and paid little attention to his interviewer as he proudly exhibited a photograph of his two daughters and his wife. He told how he had been brought up in a large family and gone West with his brothers, how he had returned, bought a stage route, married the village schoolteacher, and finally hit upon the idea of making paint from a mineral his father had discovered on his farm. The story of his success was a story of determination and hard work. During the Civil War, his wife had kept the paint works going, and after the war, he had taken a man named Rogers as a partner for a short time.

After the interview, Lapham and his wife drove out to see the site of a house they were building in a more fashionable part of Boston. Although both looked with pride upon the place soon to be their residence, they pretended not to want the house at all. They merely suggested the new home would be a greater advantage for Penelope and Irene when their friends came to call. Neither Penelope nor Irene anticipated their coming change of living with great joy. They thought the present house was more convenient for the horsecars. Secretly, both realized that their parents were awkward in social life, and they themselves had not been brought up to feel comfortable in the presence of people whose families had been accustomed to wealth for generations.

One day, as Mr. and Mrs. Lapham were dismounting from their carriage, Lapham's former partner appeared unexpectedly. Rogers had provided money to help get the business started, but Lapham had eventually bought Rogers out. Lapham insisted that what he had done had merely been good business, but Mrs. Lapham maintained that she never felt quite right about what had happened to Rogers. Seeing him again took all the happiness out of her plans for the new house.

The next time the family ventured out to visit the partly completed house, Irene was surprised by the arrival of Tom Corey, a young man who had shown some interest in her. Immediately, Mr. Lapham began to dominate the occasion, and by his bragging he greatly embarrassed his daughters. That evening, young Corey talked to his father, Bromfield Corey, who did not agree with his son's easy acceptance of the Laphams but did not object when his son announced his intention of applying for a position in Lapham's firm.

Young Corey visited Lapham in his office in order to ask for a job. Lapham was so pleased that he invited Corey to go with him to Nantasket where Mrs. Lapham and the girls were expecting Lapham for the weekend. At the Nantasket cottage, the girls and their mother could not understand what had brought young Corey for the weekend visit. They had thought Lapham's bragging would have kept him away forever.

That evening, Lapham discussed Corey with his wife. Mrs. Lapham contended that Corey was interested not in the paint but in Irene. Her husband commented that unless the young man were interested in the paint he would never get a chance to be interested in Irene. When Lapham said he intended to give the young man a chance, Mrs. Lapham warned him that he was playing with a situation that was bound to bring trouble. Tom Corey's mother was concerned when she heard about her son's new employment. She admitted she would not object if he made a fortune from the paint business, but she did not want him to fall in love with either of the Lapham girls.

After Corey entered Lapham's employ, he was invited frequently to the Lapham home, for Irene was beginning to fall in love with him. Bromfield Corey grew more and more curious about the Laphams. He decided that he would encourage his wife to give a dinner for them in the autumn. The cost of the new house worried Mrs. Lapham, and she asked her husband to stop his lavish spending. She learned that he had given a substantial loan to Rogers, his former partner.

When Mrs. Corey returned from Bar Harbor, she debated a long time about giving a dinner party for the Laphams. In the first place, the Laphams were newcomers. On the other hand, she wanted to give public recognition of the new connection between her son and the Lapham family. She finally decided to give a formal dinner early in the season, before her more prominent friends returned to the city.

On the night of the dinner, the Laphams tried to appear at ease. Penelope had refused to attend, thus causing her mother considerable embarrassment. Lapham watched the other men carefully, feeling sure that he had not made too many social blunders. The next day, however, he was not so sure, for he had taken too much wine at dinner.

At the office, Lapham sought out Corey and mentioned with embarrassment his behavior of the night before. He offered Corey his liberty to seek another job, a position among gentlemen, but Corey refused to go, saying that Lapham's tipsy talk had been only an unfortunate accident. When they parted, Corey insisted that Lapham's conduct had been proper and entertaining. That night, feeling that he had actually patronized Lapham, Corey resolved to go to his employer and apologize. Lapham was out, but Penelope received Corey. At the end of a long talk, he stammeringly confessed his love for her. In great confusion, he left without waiting to speak to Lapham.

The next day, Mrs. Lapham informed her husband that Corey had been coming to see Penelope all the time. She could only imagine what the shock would do to Irene. They felt, however, that Penelope would never permit Corey to become her suitor, for Penelope was convinced that he belonged to Irene, who was informed of the situation by her mother that evening. Irene immediately carried to her sister's room every memento of Corey's attentions that she possessed. After a few days, Lapham took her to his boyhood village in Vermont. Corey called on the Laphams to present his explanation, saying that he had cared for Penelope all the time. Penelope refused to give him any satisfaction. She said she owed more to her sister's hurt feelings.

At the same time, Lapham's finances were troubling him greatly. People who owed him money were unable to pay, and his own creditors were pressing him. Lapham determined to take a trip West to inspect some mills held as security for his loan to Rogers. When he returned, he was even more concerned. Rogers had drawn him into a trap with his securities, for a railroad controlled the value of the property. Lapham decided it would be necessary to sell the new house unfinished. Learning of Lapham's difficulties, Corey offered to lend his employer thirty thousand dollars, but Lapham rejected the offer.

Lapham's affairs took a turn for the worse. An added blow was the destruction of the unfinished Back Bay house. Wandering through the house one night, he decided to test one of the chimneys and made a fire from blocks and shavings that the workmen had left scattered about. He thought the fire had burned out before he left. That night the house burned to the ground. The insurance policy had expired a week before.

Determined to raise money by selling everything he could, Lapham visited his competitors who were working on a new mineral paint. They were willing to merge with him if he could raise money to help develop their plant. While he was trying to secure a loan, he learned from Rogers that some English gentlemen were interested in buying the property that Rogers had put up as security and that Lapham had thought valueless. Lapham refused to sell the mills, however, because he believed a sale would be unethical as long as the railroad controlled their value.

He asked for time to think over the proposition. Shortly afterward, the railroad forced him to sell the mills at a ruinous figure. Lapham felt that his honesty, which had kept him from selling the property to the Englishmen, had been unjustly abused. Rogers claimed that Lapham had made it impossible for him to recover his losses. Lapham was now ruined, for he could not raise capital to merge with the rival paint firm.

Tom Corey was determined to marry Penelope in spite of her father's impending ruin. He did marry her after Lapham went into bankruptcy, and his family accepted her for their own sake as well as for his. Irene, who had returned from Vermont as soon as she heard of her father's troubles, was pleased with her sister's happiness. Lapham managed to save a part of his fortune, but more important to him was the belief that he had acted honestly in all his business dealings.

Critical Evaluation:

According to many critics, *The Rise of Silas Lapham* is the most important book William Dean Howells ever wrote. Howells, a prolific though never a brilliant writer, attempted to deal conscientiously with the everyday experiences of rather ordinary people. By presenting character and situation in a straightforward manner, he wrote novels characterized chiefly by their moral atmosphere and authentic domestic realism.

The reputation of Howells suffered much from the charge of many critics that his scope was too limited to satisfy the requirements of complexity demanded by the sophisticated twentieth century reader. It is argued that his insights into human being's social existence, for example, were based on tenets from a past age that no longer applied; the lack of intense passions and obsessions in the novels, as well as Howells' failure to explore in depth such areas as human sexuality and capacity for violence, are cited as evidence. Similarly, *The Rise of Silas Lapham*—the author's most popular work and in many ways his masterpiece—has been adversely judged by some on the grounds that its plot is too slender to support the weight of its own implications. To support such charges, however, is either to misunderstand the nature of Howells' moral vision of life, or to overlook its depth and breadth, universality, and applicability to all times and places.

Howells believed in people's interdependence with one another; he viewed each person's life as inextricably caught up with the lives of others, thus creating the web of interrelationships that forms societies. Such a belief meant that, for Howells, individual's personal moral lives and their lives as social beings were fused; there was no such thing as a purely individual moral act, whether good or evil, since each personal act had its inevitable consequences in the interpersonal or social realm. This in turn led to the morally pragmatic stance that the proper course of action can often be chosen on the basis of which course will result in "the most good for the greatest number" of people. This utilitarian viewpoint is reflected in such concepts as "the economy of pain" principle, propounded by Howells through the character of David Sewell in the scene from *The Rise of Silas Lapham* in which Silas and his wife seek the minister's advice concerning the love complication between their two daughters and Tom Corey. He tells them that in such a situation, for which no one is to blame, the best solution is the one that will cause suffering to the fewest number of people. In this case, therefore, Penelope would be wrong to sacrifice Tom to Irene, which would make all three persons suffer miserably; she should marry him herself, which would result in the great happiness of two people and the temporary hurt of only one.

Underlying this moral outlook were three basic assumptions: that all aspects of human life, including the social, are infused with moral purpose, thus making society an extremely precious commodity; that the preservation of society depends on human beings overcoming their destructive passions with reason; and that the function of art reveals the superiority of the civilized and reasoning side of human nature over the primitive and ignorant side. Howells' first assumption was shared by most people in his age, but it was his fervent espousal of the last proposition that placed him at the philosophical head of a group of writers whose aim it was to reveal the morality of life through the use of realism in their fiction. Yet Howells abhorred sermonizing and attacked the didactic element in writing whenever he encountered it.

This seeming paradox is cleared up, however, when one examines more closely Howells' theory of literature. What he objected to was not the presence of moral purpose in a work but rather any attempt by an author to force artificially his set of beliefs into a fictional structure without regard to the organic dictates of the work itself. When Howells was asked to summarize explicitly his theory of the moral purpose of literature, he began by identifying the three progressively worse stages of "immorality" often practiced in fiction. The first involves the obscuring of the reader's judgment through indulgence of his "gross appetite for the marvelous"; the second, the elevation of passion over principles; and the third (and most pernicious), the presentation of characters who commit serious sins but are left unpunished by the penalties that follow such sins in the real world. The true function of the writer, Howells argued, is first to reject any absolute standard of morality and then to portray lives of characters in honest and careful detail; as the characters meet each new situation in their everyday lives, and as they are faced with decisions over what is right and what is wrong, they will respond as people do in life. Sometimes they will act in morally responsible ways and will be rewarded, if not with worldly success, with inner peace; at other times, they will commit wrongs and will suffer the inevitable consequences. Thus, Howells believed, all the author need do is describe reality truthfully, and the morality of life will become apparent through the narrative as naturally as it does in life.

Howells carried out his theory to near perfection in *The Rise of Silas Lapham*. This novel tells the story of a man who has been led astray from the true values in life by the corrupting influence of wealth. The action centers around Silas Lapham's fall into financial ruin, which turns out to be his salvation and his rise (hence the title) back into a morally healthy state. The plot is organic, reflecting the theme of the novel and growing out of the main character's growth. The beginning and end are linked masterfully, while the midway point in the story—the dinner party given by the Coreys—serves to pull together the threads spun out until then, suspending them momentarily for the reader's contemplation, and then directing them toward their climax and natural conclusion. In his interview with Bartley Hubbard at the opening of the novel, Silas is seen in all the glory of his material success: He is proud of his rise from humble beginnings, of his newly acquired social position, and of the new house he is just starting to build. The house becomes a symbol of Silas' fortunes; destined to be a magnificent mansion, it rises quickly until its construction is slowed down because of lack of funds. In the end, it is burned to the ground. The destruction of the house represents Silas' rebirth, since his moral regeneration can only occur after he has been stripped of the false trappings of materialism. In his talk with David Sewell at the end, Silas' transformation is set in dramatic contrast to his initial appearance in the Bartley interview: He has grown humble and honest, and his bragging has been replaced by sincerity.

Lapham has been able to reach this new stage of awareness by progressing through a series of moral tests, culminating in the legal, but morally dishonest, deal urged on him by Milton Rogers and the Englishmen; when he refuses to participate, both his financial ruin and his personal salvation are secured. He has painfully but steadily moved from the easiest stages of redemption—acts of unselfishness and generosity on a personal, one-to-one basis—through a wider area of commitment to people in large groups, and has finally reached the highest, most difficult level of good action. This level involves an individual's commitment to the social body as a whole, to the welfare not of a personally known individual or group but of all human beings of a larger society.

Howells' efforts to uncover the underlying morality of all human action by focusing on the commonplace and familiar in his fiction reached a pinnacle in *The Rise of Silas Lapham*, but he was not fully conscious of the nature of his achievement until a year after the novel's publication. It was in that year, 1886, that he began reading the works of Leo Tolstoy. His exposure to the Russian novelist was like a religious experience; he wrote, "What I had instinctively known before, I now knew rationally." Following this illumination of his own motives and absorbing concerns as an artist, Howells was able to sum up the vision that had inspired not only *The Rise of Silas Lapham* but all of his other work: "Morality penetrates all things, it is the soul of all things."

"Critical Evaluation" by Nancy G. Ballard

Bibliography:

Carrington, George C. *The Immense Complex Drama: The World and Art of the Howells Novel*. Columbus: Ohio State University, 1966. A classic study that remains influential in the field. Analyzes *The Rise of Silas Lapham* in relation to Howells' other novels. Considers theme, subject, technique, and form.

Eby, Clare Virginia. "Compromise and Complicity in *The Rise of Silas Lapham*." *American Literary Realism 1870-1910* 24, no. 1 (Fall, 1991): 39-53. Analyzes the use of class, privilege, and the businessman in *The Rise of Silas Lapham*. Argues that in his depiction of the conflict between the Coreys and the Laphams, Howells advocates greater flexibility and compromise between class groups.

Pease, Donald E., ed. *New Essays on "The Rise of Silas Lapham."* New York: Cambridge University Press, 1991. A stimulating collection of essays on the novel. Includes topics ranging from Howells' treatment of the middle class and suffering under capitalism to a reexamination of realism and Howells' relationship with Samuel Clemens (Mark Twain).

Tanselle, G. Thomas. "The Architecture of *The Rise of Silas Lapham*." *American Literature* 37, no. 4 (January, 1966): 430-457. A structural analysis of the novel that notes two separate plots (the bankruptcy plot and the love plot) and diagrams their intersections and parallels to argue for the overall unity of the novel.

Vanderbilt, Kermit. *The Achievement of William Dean Howells: A Reinterpretation*. Princeton, N.J.: Princeton University Press, 1968. The chapter on *The Rise of Silas Lapham* examines revisions of the novel and personal letters to show Howells' concern with social eruption, class, and ethnicity in Boston during the Gilded Age.

THE RISING OF THE MOON

Type of work: Drama
Author: Lady Augusta Gregory (1852-1932)
Type of plot: Protest
Time of plot: Early twentieth century
Locale: Ireland
First published: 1905; first performed, 1907

Principal characters:
SERGEANT, an older police officer
POLICEMAN X, Sergeant's assistant
POLICEMAN B, Sergeant's assistant
A RAGGED MAN, a ballad singer

The Story:

On a moonlit night at an Irish wharf by the sea, three Irish policemen in the service of the occupying English government pasted up wanted posters for a clever escaped political criminal. Convinced that the escaped rebel might creep to the water's edge to be rescued by sea, they all hoped to capture him for the hundred-pound reward and perhaps even a promotion. The Sergeant sent his two younger assistants with the only lantern to post more flyers around town while, uneasily, he kept watch at the water's edge.

A man in rags tried to slip past the Sergeant, explaining that he merely wanted to sell some songs to incoming sailors. The Ragged Man identified himself as "Jimmy Walsh," a ballad singer. When the man headed toward the steps to the water, the Sergeant stopped him, insisting that "Jimmy" leave by way of town. Trying to interest the officer in his songs, the man sang a few ballads to the protesting Sergeant, who wanted only to keep the area clear so he could catch the fleeing prisoner if he appeared. He ordered the man to leave the area immediately.

The Ragged Man pretended to start toward town but stopped to comment on the face on the poster, saying that he knew the man well. Interested, the Sergeant's changed his mind about sending the Ragged Man away, and insisted that the stranger stay to furnish more information about the fugitive. The Ragged Man described a dark, dangerous, muscular man who was an expert with many weapons, then he hinted at previous murders of policemen on moonlit nights exactly like the present one.

Frightened, the Sergeant gladly accepted the Ragged Man's offer to stay with him on the wharf to help look for the escaped murderer. Sitting back-to-back on a barrel in order to have full view of the dock area, the two men smoked pipes together to calm the Sergeant's nerves. The Sergeant confessed that police work was difficult, especially for family men, because the officers spent long hours on dangerous missions. Accompanying the Sergeant's lament, the Ragged Man started to sing a traditional, sentimental song about lovers and the beautiful Irish countryside. Then he began a nationalistic ballad about a legendary, oppressed old Irishwoman named Granuaile. The Sergeant stopped him, protesting that it was inappropriate to sing about Irish oppression when political tempers were flaring between Ireland and England. His ragged companion replied that he was only singing the song to keep up his spirits on their dangerous and lonely watch.

Then the Ragged Man grabbed his chest as if the forbidden singing was necessary to calm his frightened heart, so the pitying Sergeant allowed him to continue his ballad. Again, the man sang about the fabled Irish martyr, Granuaile, but this time he inserted the wrong lyrics.

Immediately, the Sergeant corrected the man and sang the proper line, revealing his knowledge of a rebel song, even though he was supposed to be loyal to the English rulers.

The ballad-man slyly began to probe the Sergeant's memories of former days when, as a young man, the Sergeant lovingly sang several traditional Irish ballads, including "Granuaile." Confidentially, the Sergeant admitted that he had sung every patriotic ballad the Ragged Man named. The man suggested that the Sergeant and the fugitive perhaps shared the same youthful memories; in fact, the escaped prisoner might even have been among the Sergeant's close friends in their younger days. When the Sergeant admitted the possibility, the ballad-man described a hypothetical scene in which the Sergeant joined in with those former singing friends to free Ireland. Therefore, the Ragged Man, concluded, it might have been fated that the Sergeant would be the pursued instead of the pursuer.

Caught up in the hypothetical scenario, the Sergeant mused that if he had made different choices—not going into the police force, not marrying and having children—he and the fugitive could well have exchanged roles. The possibility became so real for him that he began to confuse his own identity with the escapee and imagined himself stealthily trying to escape, violently shooting or assaulting police officers. He was startled out of his reverie by a sound from the water; he suspected that the rescuers had at last arrived to carry away the fugitive.

The Ragged Man contended that the Sergeant in the past sympathized with the Irish nationalists and not with the law he currently represented. In fact, he suggested that the Sergeant still doubted the choice he made for the English law but against "the people." Boldly singing the rebel tune, "The Rising of the Moon," as a signal to the rescuers on the water and ripping off his hat and wig, "Jimmy," the "ballad-man," revealed that he was in fact the fugitive himself, with a hundred-pound reward on his head.

Startled and struggling with his heretofore suppressed sympathies for the rebels, the Sergeant threatened to arrest the escapee and collect the reward when his younger police companions approached. He protested that his own rebel sentiments were buried in the past. Slipping behind the barrel seat they had shared to hide from the nearing officers, the fugitive called on the Sergeant's love for Ireland to keep his presence secret. Quickly hiding the fugitive's wig and hat behind him, the Sergeant denied to his subordinates that he seen anyone. When the officers insisted that they stay to aid their superior on his dangerous watch, the Sergeant gruffly rebuked their noisy offers and sent them away with their lantern.

The escaped rebel gratefully retrieved his disguise, promising to return the favor when, "at the Rising of the Moon," roles would inevitably be reversed between oppressors and oppressed. Quickly, he slipped into the rescue boat. Left musing alone on the moonlit wharf, the Sergeant thought of the lost reward and wondered if he had been a great fool.

Critical Evaluation:

Lady Gregory's contribution to the Irish Literary Renaissance was twofold: co-founding the Abbey Theatre with William Butler Yeats and writing what became the Abbey's most popular plays, including *The Rising of the Moon*. Most of her drama featured Irish peasants and was not overtly political; she insisted that she was not promoting political rebellion with this play. Nevertheless, in 1907, when the play was first performed, many Irish knew the popular old ballad "The Rising of the Moon," in which the ascending moon is a signal for "rising," or rebellion. Lady Gregory's sympathies were with the people of Ireland. She was, however, adamantly against violence. She sympathized with Irish calls for independence from English rule, but she chose not to join the more strident Irish voices. Her chosen form of political statement was to highlight Irish language and customs. She was convinced that if the English saw the true Gaelic soul, they would sympathize with Irishmen's desire to rule themselves. In this play, the rebel's cleverness is depicted, not his crimes.

As in other Gregory plays, the dialogue evokes native Irish rhythms and lore. The Ragged Man and the Sergeant share Irish speech and knowledge of old sentimental and patriotic songs, a feature of nearly all Gregory plays. Granuaile, the bound and wailing old woman in the song the Ragged Man sings, is a symbol for suffering Ireland. The line the Ragged Man leaves out and which the Sergeant furnishes is the most agonizing of all: "Her gown she wore was stained with gore," a reference to Irish martyrs that would not be lost on Lady Gregory's audience. In fact, when reviewers suspected that the play was a patriotic statement, though Lady Gregory denied it, the Dublin police force withdrew their uniforms, which had previously been lent to the drama company as costumes.

In *The Rising of the Moon*, moonlight plays an important role. Giving the lantern to his deputies, the Sergeant is at a disadvantage in the dim moonlight. He cannot see clearly. Also, the dimness helps the Ragged Man enhance his frightening stories of the rebel's past violence to policemen. The moonlight inspires the Sergeant's reveries and weakens his sense of duty to the British authorities. At the end, when the Sergeant refuses the lantern, he is left alone in the moonlight puzzling over his identity—as an upholder of the law or as an Irish sympathizer.

The fugitive's cleverness precedes his entrance onstage, as the policemen recall that he is the head of the rebel organization, that he probably won sympathy and assistance from his jailers. This foreshadows the rest of the play. The Ragged Man cleverly wins sympathy from his would-be captor. He sets his trap for the Sergeant's heart once it is clear that the officer will not let him pass to the water. First, he sings "Johnny Hart," a romantic song about two lovers who are forbidden to marry. The sad song creates a melancholy mood and convinces the officer that the man is, indeed, a balladeer. Next, he intrigues the Sergeant into needing him by saying that he knows the escapee personally. Craftily, the man paints a deadly picture of the powerful fugitive to frighten the Sergeant into wanting company. Then he shows sympathy for the Sergeant's weariness and suggests they share a seat on the barrel. Back to back, the Sergeant cannot compare the man to the poster, but their bodies share space and a friendly pipe. The man pretends to be so frightened that he needs to sing a forbidden Irish political ballad, then tricks the Sergeant into revealing his knowledge of the patriotic song. He springs the trap with his assertion that the Sergeant himself harbored Irish sympathies years before and constructs a scenario of the Sergeant's being part of a rebel group had fate not intervened. Caught, the Sergeant admits the possibility. Startled by the arriving rescue boat, however, he snaps into his uniformed role and acts as protector of the law.

As his fellow officers approach with the lantern the Sergeant must choose between his admitted rebel sympathies and his official duty, which promises rewards. Refusing the lantern and sending the other men away to protect the escaping fugitive, the Sergeant is unsure that he has made the right choice after all. He loses money, promotion, recognition for himself and his family. The audience is left with admiration for the Ragged Man's successful strategy but sympathy for the officer who had two legitimate but conflicting loyalties. The brief play voices its author's political message: concern for the human dimensions of a complicated conflict.

Nancy A. Macky

Bibliography:

Adams, Hazard. *Lady Gregory*. Cranbury, N.J.: Bucknell University Press, 1973. A fine overview of Lady Gregory's career, with clear critical analysis of her plays.

Gregory, Lady Augusta. *Our Irish Theatre*. New York: Capricorn Books, 1965. A lively account of the Abbey Theatre, its plays and controversies, with discussion about Lady Gregory's writing strategies and problems.

Mikhail, E. H. *Lady Gregory: An Annotated Bibliography*. Troy, N.Y.: Whitston, 1982. A thorough listing of books, periodicals, dissertations, manuscripts, and reviews of all Gregory plays.

Saddlemyer, Ann. *In Defence of Lady Gregory, Playwright*. Dublin: Dolmen Press, 1966. An easily accessible discussion of themes and motifs of Lady Gregory's plays.

Saddlemyer, Ann, and Colin Smythe, eds. *Lady Gregory, Fifty Years After*. Gerrard's Cross, England: C. Smythe, 1987. Many excellent essays on aspects of Lady Gregory's career and writings, including drama.

THE RIVALS

Type of work: Drama
Author: Richard Brinsley Sheridan (1751-1816)
Type of plot: Comedy of manners
Time of plot: Eighteenth century
Locale: Bath
First performed: 1775; first published, 1775

Principal characters:
CAPTAIN JACK ABSOLUTE or ENSIGN BEVERLEY, a young officer
SIR ANTHONY ABSOLUTE, his father
FAULKLAND, Jack's friend
BOB ACRES, a country squire
SIR LUCIUS O'TRIGGER, a fiery Irishman
LYDIA LANGUISH, an heiress
MRS. MALAPROP, her aunt
JULIA MELVILLE, her cousin

The Story:

To beautiful and wealthy young Lydia Languish, who had been brought up on romantic novels, the only lover worth considering was one whose position in life was in complete contrast to her own. To this end she had fallen in love with a penniless young ensign named Beverley. To this same Beverley, her aunt, Mrs. Malaprop, raised serious objections. Her antipathy to young Mr. Beverley was partly aroused by letters that the ensign had written to Lydia, letters that made uncomplimentary references to her aunt's age and appearance. Mrs. Malaprop had some moments of extreme discomfiture, when she wondered whether she did resemble the she-dragon to which Beverley had compared her.

Mrs. Malaprop herself had fallen hopelessly in love with a quixotic Irishman named Sir Lucius O'Trigger, who presumably returned her affection. Sir Lucius, who had never seen Mrs. Malaprop, had been hoodwinked by a maidservant into believing that the romantic creature with whom he was exchanging love letters was Lydia.

The situation was further complicated by the fact that Beverley was in reality young Captain Jack Absolute, the son of Sir Anthony Absolute, and as wealthy and aristocratic as Lydia herself. Jack very early sensed that he would get nowhere if he wooed the romantic Lydia in his own person, and so he assumed a character more nearly resembling the heroes of the novels that Lydia enjoyed.

Nor did Jack's friend, Faulkland, fare any better in his own romantic pursuit of Lydia's cousin, Julia Melville. In fact, it might be thought that he fared worse, for unlike Jack, he was forever placing imaginary obstacles between himself and his beloved. Whenever they were separated, Faulkland imagined all kinds of horrible catastrophes that might have befallen her, and when he found that she was alive and well he tormented himself with the thought that she could not be in love and remain so happy. At last Jack Absolute lost patience with his friend's ridiculous behavior, and even Julia became a little tired of her lover's unfounded jealousy. This curious love tangle reached a crisis when Sir Anthony Absolute informed his son that he had selected the woman for him to marry, threatening, if he refused, to cut him off without a penny. Not having the faintest idea as to the identity of the woman his father had picked out for him, and conjuring up pictures of some homely heiress his father intended to force on him against his will, Jack rebelled. He declared that, whatever the consequences, he would have nothing to do with his father's choice.

Having been quite a connoisseur of pretty women in his youth, and being not exactly immune to their charms in his old age, Sir Anthony Absolute was not the man to saddle his son with an unattractive wife. He had made an agreement with Mrs. Malaprop for the bestowal of her niece's hand upon his son. Mrs. Malaprop, in turn, was only too glad to save Lydia from a foolish marriage to Beverley. When Jack refused to marry anyone not of his own choosing, Sir Anthony flew into a rage and insisted that the marriage take place regardless of what the lady might be like.

By chance, however, Jack discovered that the woman Sir Anthony had selected as his bride was Lydia Languish, the same one he had been wooing as Ensign Beverley. He immediately assured his father that he would be willing to marry anyone his father might choose. Sir Anthony, not used to such tractability on Jack's part, became suspicious and a little worried. Sir Anthony nevertheless made arrangements for his son to meet the bride-to-be, thus placing Jack in a neat dilemma. Jack realized that Lydia would have none of him as Sir Anthony Absolute's son. Finally the supposed Ensign Beverley pretended to Lydia that in order to gain access to her aunt's house, he would be forced to pose as Jack Absolute.

Lydia had another suitor in the person of Bob Acres, a wealthy country squire and a neighbor of Sir Anthony, who had ambitions to become a man about town. Before Sir Anthony proposed his son as a husband for her niece, Mrs. Malaprop had favored Bob Acres as a likely candidate for Lydia's hand. When Acres discovered he had a rival in Ensign Beverley, he was disheartened. Encouraged by his friend, Sir Lucius O'Trigger, he challenged Beverley to a duel. Never having seen young Beverley, he was forced to give the challenge to the ensign's friend, Jack Absolute, to deliver.

The great crisis in Jack's love affairs came when he was forced to face Lydia in the company of his father. With his true identity revealed, Lydia's dreams of a romantic elopement with a penniless ensign vanished. She dismissed Jack from her life forever. Chagrined by his abrupt dismissal, Jack accepted with positive gusto another challenge to a duel from Sir Lucius O'Trigger. Sir Lucius named the place as King's Mead Fields at six o'clock that very evening, when he had an appointment to act as a second to his friend, Acres, in a duel with a certain Ensign Beverley.

When Lydia learned that Jack had involved himself in a duel on her account, he became a different person in her eyes, and she hurried with her aunt to King's Mead Fields in an effort to halt the duel. Meanwhile Sir Lucius O'Trigger had alarmed Acres with his bloodthirsty stories of dueling, so that when Acres recognized his opponent as his old friend, Jack Absolute, he heaved a sigh of relief.

With the arrival of Lydia and Mrs. Malaprop, the whole situation was quickly explained. Sir Lucius, much to his chagrin, was forced to realize that the writer of tender love letters to whom he addressed his own impassioned correspondence was not Lydia but Mrs. Malaprop. Faulkland was content to accept Julia's love for the wholehearted thing it was. Lydia at last saw Ensign Beverley and Jack Absolute as the same person with whom she was in love. Bob Acres, happy because he would not be forced to fight a duel with anyone, ordered fiddles and entertainment for all in the fashionable parlors of Bath.

Critical Evaluation:

Together with that other masterpiece of late eighteenth century comedy, Oliver Goldsmith's

She Stoops to Conquer (1773), Richard Brinsley Sheridan's *The Rivals* represents a successful reclaiming of the essential spirit of English comedy. Too long subject to "the goddess of the woeful countenance—the sentimental muse" (as Sheridan addressed her in his prologue to *The Rivals*), English comedy had forgotten its boisterous heritage; a theater nurtured in the rich buffoonery of a Falstaff and the satirical malice of a Volpone had dissipated its energies in the moralizing and saccharine "genteel" comedies. Although reluctant, and perhaps incapable, of returning to the cynicism of Restoration comedy, Sheridan was anxious to rescue the healthy psychological realism traditional not only to English comedy but also, ever since Chaucer, to English literature generally. Sentiment was a French value. Sheridan's insistence on steering a middle course between sentiment and wit, between morality and reality, puts him at the center of the English literary tradition.

At the heart of all comedy is the ridicule of affectation. People may not all be fools, but all are, at times, foolish. Sheridan exploits the inevitable tendency in people to be foolish, regardless of their accomplishments in life. He does not resort to flat or stock characters, amusing only because they represent totally unrealistic or exaggerated foibles. His people are always human, and their foolishness often makes them more so.

Despite the stock character aspect of their names (Absolute, Languish, and Malaprop), these characters are all larger than the epithets. Captain Absolute may be absolute about refusing his father's choice in a wife, but he is forced into a profound relativity when he has to be two people at the same time. When Absolute is at last revealed as having masqueraded as Beverley, he is, in any case, no longer absolute. Lydia Languish is ridiculed for languishing over sentimental novels, but she overcomes her foolishness when she refuses, finally, to languish in wounded pride for being duped by her Beverley. Mrs. Malaprop's name was coined by Sheridan from the French *malapropos*, which means "not to the purpose." The word malapropism entered the language in honor of Sheridan's character, and her abuses of the English language are still hilarious.

Sheridan, however, does not reduce Mrs. Malaprop to the one affectation of commanding a vocabulary that she does not, in truth, command. Her speaking "not to the purpose" is only symptomatic of a much deeper affectation; she is not to the purpose. She favors the wrong suitor, Acres, for Lydia; Mrs. Malaprop presumes, incorrectly, that the letters Sir Lucius O'Trigger has been writing are intended for her when they are in fact directed to Lydia; and finally, at the end of the play, she blames her own willful and deluded misconceptions on the opposite sex. She is *malapropos* in more than diction; it is her human condition. Sheridan is careful not to pickle her in the brine of absolute ridicule. In her weakness lie the seeds of her vitality; by refusing to adhere "to the purpose" of her age and limited intellect, she achieves a touching transcendence that seems to turn the heart of Sir Anthony at play's end. There is hope for her.

Sheridan's fascination with human weakness led him to create a character that many critics feel is at odds with his avowed purpose in the play, which is essentially a broad attack on the sentimental in literature and life. The character in question is Faulkland. On the surface, it is clear that Faulkland's excessive concern with the pitch and nuance of his feelings for Julia, and hers for him, is so laden with anxiety that it is meant to be ridiculous. As such, Sheridan must have intended Faulkland's misplaced sentiment in life to complement Lydia Languish's misplaced sentiment in art. She models her love-in-life after the sentimental romances she has read, and Faulkland constantly measures his relationship with Julia against an unrealistic idea of bliss in an imperfect world. Lydia's sentimental values are wrecked by the empirical fact that the man she loves turns out not to be the penniless Ensign Beverley, but the rich and titled Captain

Absolute. What sentimental art had decreed acceptable—the poor but dashing suitor—turns out to be the thing reality withholds. The revenge of life on a superficial idea of art is absolute. In Faulkland's case, the comic exposure is not as brilliant. As one critic puts it, while Sheridan laughs at Faulkland, he also identifies with his tortured sensibility.

Faulkland's constant anxiety is too serious a thing to dismiss categorically with laughter. His doubt is of the kind that a true awareness of reality implies. He may seem ridiculous in questioning his Julia's right to be healthy and happy in his absence, but his anxiety over the authenticity, as well as sincerity, of her love is the fate of his kind of mind.

Almost as if Sheridan senses that Faulkland does not completely succeed as an attack on the sentimental, the playwright created another character in whom those anxieties are clearly absurd; namely, Acres. Acres's cowardice is finally ridiculous because it is dehumanizing; he is less a person for falling prey to O'Trigger's theatrical overdramatizing of dueling. Faulkland's anxiety, although uncalled for, is finally metaphysical; Acres' is completely venial and selfish.

Sheridan wrote this play at the age of twenty-three. It is a work of youthful genius and together with *The School for Scandal* (1777) easily confirms his reputation as the outstanding dramatist of the eighteenth century. In his work the wit of Restoration comedy and the best of sentimental comedy—its gift for feeling characterization—come to full fruition.

"Critical Evaluation" by Peter A. Brier

Bibliography:

Auburn, Mark. *Sheridan's Comedies: Their Contexts and Achievements*. Lincoln: University of Nebraska Press, 1977. Treats Sheridan's comedies as exemplary manifestations of the comic aesthetic. Discusses *The Rivals* as a practical play, designed to appeal to a specific audience, and attempting no innovations or departures from popular stage practice.

Mikhail, E. H. *Sheridan: Interviews and Recollections*. New York: St. Martin's Press, 1989. A biography composed of excerpts from the writings of those who knew Sheridan. Includes contemporary accounts of *The Rivals*, opinions on the play from Sheridan's friends, relatives, and other contemporaries. Shows the range of opinion that accompanied the initial run of the play; reveals the nature of Sheridan's audience.

Morwood, James. *The Life and Works of Richard Brinsley Sheridan*. Edinburgh: Scottish Academic Press, 1985. Reassesses Sheridan's political career and his management of Drury Lane for thirty-two years. Section on *The Rivals* comments on Sheridan's use of autobiographical allusions, his revisions of the play after opening night, and his debt to William Shakespeare. Discusses the two plots and their equation of moral judgment with common sense.

Sherwin, Oscar. *Uncorking Old Sherry: The Life and Times of Richard Brinsley Sheridan*. New York: Twayne, 1960. The chapter on *The Rivals* covers production history, the initial failure of the play, and Sheridan's revisions, which led to the play's later success. Includes a brief discussion of the play's effect on Sheridan's career as a playwright and theater manager.

Worth, Katharine. *Sheridan and Goldsmith*. New York: St. Martin's Press, 1992. Treats Sheridan and Goldsmith as two Irish dramatists whose work is firmly rooted in the eighteenth-century English theater. Discusses *The Rivals* in the context of the pantomime tradition.

ROAN STALLION

Type of work: Poetry
Author: Robinson Jeffers (1887-1962)
Type of plot: Symbolism
Time of plot: 1920's
Locale: Carmel Coast, California
First published: 1925

Principal characters:
CALIFORNIA, a farm wife
JOHNNY, her husband
CHRISTINE, their daughter

The Story:

California was the daughter of a Scottish father and a Spanish and Indian mother. From her mother she had inherited a dark beauty and a passionate nature. When she was still very young, she married a farmer named Johnny; by the time she was twenty-one, her features were already beginning to show the marks of hard work.

Johnny spent much of his time away from the farm drinking and gambling. One evening, he brought home a splendid roan stallion he had won. It was shortly before Christmas, and California, pleased with his good fortune, decided to go into town to buy some Christmas presents for their young daughter, Christine. Johnny delayed her departure in the morning so that it was quite late before she could hitch their old mare to the buggy and set out for Monterey. By nightfall, when she was ready to return home, a heavy rainstorm had started. The water was high when she reached the ford. Before trying to cross in the darkness, she lashed the presents around her body, hoping they would keep dry. The mare refused to cross the swollen stream and floundered back to shore. California soothed the mare and tried once more to guide her across the ford, but the animal was too frightened. Desperate, California prayed for light. Suddenly, the heavens lit up brilliantly and she saw in them the face of a child over whom hovered angels. The mare, startled by the light, scrambled back to shore. Sobbing, California climbed out of the buggy, fastened the presents securely to her back, and mounted the horse. By the light of the heavens she was able to guide the mare across the stream and reach home safely.

California thought she hated the roan stallion, but she could not forget the magnificent beast. When she told young Christine of the miraculous light at the ford and described the birth of Christ, she could hardly restrain herself from identifying the stallion with the deity. She knew that outside Johnny was mating the stallion with a neighbor's mare.

That evening, Johnny went down the valley to the home of a neighbor. After Christine was asleep, California stole out to the stable. She leaned against the fence, listening to the far-off cries of the coyotes and watching the moon rise over the hill. Once before she had seen God. If she were to ride to the top of the hill, perhaps she might do so again. She hurried down to the corral. The stallion heard her as she approached. She caressed his flanks, wishing that nature had not made it impossible for him to possess her. Then she sprang upon his back and reveled in the feel of his muscles as he galloped up the hillside. At the top they halted, and she tethered him lightly to a tree. Overwhelmed by his majesty and her desire, she threw herself at his feet.

The following night, California could not bear the thought of being with Johnny. He had brought home some wine and, half drunk, ordered her to drink some. Revolted at the thought of the night ahead, California stole to the door, opened it, and fled. Excited by the prospect of a chase, Johnny called to his dog to help him. When California heard them approaching, she crawled under the fence into the corral, the dog close behind her. The stallion plunged, frightened by the snarling, snapping dog. Johnny climbed into the corral, where the fierce stallion trampled him.

Christine had awakened from the noise. Frightened by the lonely house, she made her way to the corral. When she saw her injured father, she ran back to the house for the rifle. California took the gun and shot the dog. While she watched, the stallion struck again at Johnny, killing him. Then, prompted by a remnant of fidelity to the human race, she raised the rifle and shot the stallion. She felt as if she had killed God.

Critical Evaluation:

With the publication of *Roan Stallion, Tamar, and Other Poems* in 1925, Robinson Jeffers finally achieved recognition and financial reward. In a literary career that spanned forty-two years, from *Flagons and Apples* (1912) to *Hungerfield and Other Poems* (1954), the poet reached the height of his popularity in the early 1930's. Jeffers, the son of a minister, had been educated in the classics, and many of his poems draw upon biblical and classical sources. His treatment of these sources is, however, extremely unconventional. He did not avoid those topics of violence and sexual abnormality that sometimes shocked his reading public, yet the center of his vision is at once religious (though not in the ordinary sense) and philosophical. His poetry, marked by dramatic power, has been called both "romantic" and "naturalistic." Certainly nature figures prominently in his thinking and in his works.

The title poem, "Roan Stallion," the shortest of Jeffers' long poems, combines elements of myth, Christianity, and the poet's own philosophy to produce a work that many consider one of his best. The story of the poem draws on those Egyptian and Greek myths in which a mortal falls in love with a powerful beast. In "Roan Stallion," a woman falls in love with a magnificent horse whom she comes to identify with God. Unlike the situation in traditional myth, however, here the union of woman and horse/god does not produce gods or demigods but leads to a heightened psychological awareness on the part of the woman. "Roan Stallion" is to some extent the story of California's initiation and journey toward identity.

At the beginning of the poem, the woman California stands "at the turn of the road," symbolic of the journey she is about to undertake. Throughout, she is opposed to her degenerate husband Johnny. Johnny, as the diminutive form of his name implies, has never become an adult; brutish and domineering, he spends much of his time gambling and drinking. He has no appreciation of his wife other than as an object for sex; indeed, he once gambles her away to another man for two nights. Johnny also has no appreciation for the majesty of the stallion, whom he thinks of merely as a commodity for his use.

California, as her name implies, is "of the earth," and her name is also suggestive of the far West, a land of freedom and possibility. She is connected with the forces of nature, has a profound love for her daughter Christine, and is aware of a spiritual plane. It is this connectedness that places California so far above her husband Johnny. California's prayers when trying to ford the stream are answered with the vision of the Christ child and light; she also sees angels with "birds' heads, hawks' heads." Although this combination of Christian and pagan elements disconcerted some of Jeffers' readers when the poem first appeared, it is consistent with Jeffers' pantheistic theme that the universe is a single organism and that there is a holiness in nature that can transcend the human sphere.

Unlike her husband, California comes to view the stallion as a pure embodiment of the natural world—he is beautiful and free, the "exultant strength of the world." The stallion also represents a pure, unadulterated male force that is superior to the human male in this poem, a theme somewhat similar to the one developed by the English novelist, short-story writer, and poet D. H. Lawrence in his novel *St. Mawr*, which was published in the same year as "Roan Stallion."

"Roan Stallion" is an unrhymed narrative poem divided chronologically into three main sections. The first takes place on Christmas Eve and consists of California's journey to Monterey and back to bring presents to her daughter Christine. On this journey, California experiences the vision, is symbolically baptized in the swollen stream, identifies with the mare, Dora, and in a daydream envisions a dangerous water-stallion whose sexual force has the power to crush her.

The second episode begins in springtime, symbolic of fertility and rebirth, and involves California's ride with the stallion to the hilltop. Though California is first afraid of being thrown or trampled, she ends up lying under the stallion's hooves in an act of submission and worship. This section of the poem is complicated by the intrusion of two verses that amplify the narrative in much the same way a Greek chorus does. These verses reinforce Jeffers' philosophical creed. The first intrusion occurs near the beginning of the second episode, right after Johnny has left for the night, and begins with the line that came to be used to explain Jeffers' philosophy of "inhumanism": "Humanity is the mould to break away from . . . The Atom to be split." The second intrusion occurs at the end of the second episode, while California is lying under the stallion's hooves. Both mystical and surreal, this verse elaborates on myth, religion, and the nature of human consciousness. Lying at the foot of the godlike stallion, California becomes the human race itself wedded to pure nature. The hilltop is appropriately likened to calvary, since it is here that California completely dies to her old self and undergoes a transformation.

The third and final section of the poem occurs the following evening and includes the stallion's death at California's hands. Significantly, California's previous apathy for her husband has turned to hate, exemplifying her new awareness of herself and her environment. With the powerful ending, Jeffers implies that California is human and loyal to humanity. Because the stallion has killed a human being, however insignificant that human being may have been, the animal must die. This fact, Jeffers seems to imply, is both tragic and inevitable.

In an alternative interpretation, California could be seen to have been initiated through the stallion from innocence into a profound knowing. Though California once believed that the stallion might kill her, it is she who at the end wields the godlike power of death. Symbolically, the stallion's sacrifice and death in spring indicate a return to mother earth and the process of regeneration for California. Knowing love, knowing God, and knowing suffering and death, California now also knows what it is to be truly human.

"Critical Evaluation" by Candace E. Andrews

Bibliography:

Brophy, Robert J. *Robinson Jeffers: Myth, Ritual, and Symbol in His Narrative Poems.* Cleveland, Ohio: Case Western Reserve University, 1973. Uses a myth-ritual approach to *Roan Stallion*. Equates California with a marelike earth-goddess, Johnny with a doomed year-spirit beast, Christine with a solstice-child, the stallion with a Poseidon-like steed of God, and California's dream with a Christian-pagan conflation lighted by natural dynamism.

Coffin, Arthur B. *Robinson Jeffers: Poet of Inhumanism.* Madison: University of Wisconsin

Press, 1971. In the context of tracing Jeffers' ideological advance toward inhumanism, Coffin regards *Roan Stallion* as a work of primary importance. The heroine temporarily frees herself from accustomed social behavior by shedding human attributes, seeing God's eminence in a horse, and letting it kill her contemptible husband.

Everson, William. *The Excesses of God: Robinson Jeffers as a Religious Figure*. Stanford, Calif.: Stanford University Press, 1988. Contends that Jeffers, habitually combining paganism and mysticism, regards the religious aspect of sex as a primordial force, a supernatural wrath, and an analogy of divine life and that he dramatizes this belief in *Roan Stallion*.

Nolte, William H. *Rock and Hawk: Robinson Jeffers and the Romantic Agony*. Athens: University of Georgia Press, 1978. Interprets the figure of California in *Roan Stallion* as enacting an unwilled, unconscious, beautiful microcosmic recapitulation of one of the several dark, macrocosmic myths ruling humanity.

Squires, Radcliffe. *The Loyalties of Robinson Jeffers*. Ann Arbor: University of Michigan Press, 1956. Divides Jeffers' poetry into diffuse, sagalike works and classically unified shorter poems. In the first category, Jeffers explores the ramifications of sinning. In the second category, best exemplified by *Roan Stallion*, Jeffers espouses breaking free of life as the solution to problems occasioned by sin.

ROB ROY

Type of work: Novel
Author: Sir Walter Scott (1771-1832)
Type of plot: Historical
Time of plot: 1715
Locale: Northumberland and Glasgow
First published: 1817

Principal characters:

WILLIAM OSBALDISTONE, a man employed by the firm of Osbaldistone and Tresham
FRANK OSBALDISTONE, his son
SIR HILDEBRAND OSBALDISTONE, Frank's uncle
RASHLEIGH OSBALDISTONE, his son
SIR FREDERICK VERNON, a Jacobite
DIANA VERNON, his daughter
ROB ROY (MACGREGOR CAMPBELL), a Scottish outlaw

The Story:

Frank Osbaldistone was recalled from France, where his father had sent him to learn the family's mercantile business. Disappointed in his son's progress, the father angrily ordered the young man to Osbaldistone Hall, home of his uncle, Sir Hildebrand Osbaldistone, in northern England. His father gave him fifty guineas for expenses and instructions to learn who among Sir Hildebrand's sons would accept a position in the trading house of Osbaldistone and Tresham.

On the road, Frank fell in with a traveler named Morris, who was carrying a large sum of money in a portmanteau strapped to his saddle. That evening, they stopped at the Black Bear Inn, in the town of Darlington, where they were joined at dinner by a Scotsman named Mr. Campbell, who was really Rob Roy, the Scottish outlaw. The next morning, Campbell and Morris left together. At a secluded spot along the road, the men were halted and a highwayman robbed Morris of his saddlebag. Meanwhile, Frank rode toward Osbaldistone Hall. As he neared the rambling old mansion, he saw a fox hunt and met Diana Vernon, Sir Hildebrand's niece. Outspoken Diana told Frank that each of his cousins was a mixture in varying proportions of sot, gamekeeper, bully, horse jockey, and fool. Rashleigh, she said, was the most dangerous of the lot, for he maintained a private tyranny over everyone with whom he came in contact. It was Rashleigh, however, who was prevailed upon to accept Frank's vacant position.

Frank and his cousins disliked one another. One night, while drinking with the family, Frank became enraged at Rashleigh's speech and actions and struck him. Rashleigh never forgot the blow, although to all intents and purposes he and Frank declared themselves friends after their anger had cooled.

Shortly after Frank's arrival, he was accused of highway robbery. He went at once to Squire Inglewood's court to defend himself and to confront his accuser, who turned out to be Morris. Rob Roy, however, appeared at the squire's court of justice and forced Morris to confess that Frank had not robbed him.

When Rashleigh departed to go into business with Frank's father, Frank became Diana's tutor. Their association developed into deep affection on both sides, a mutual attraction marred only by the fact that Diana was by faith a Catholic and Frank a Presbyterian.

One day, Frank received a letter from his father's partner, Mr. Tresham. The letter informed him that his father, leaving Rashleigh in charge, had gone to the Continent on business, and that Rashleigh had gone to Scotland, where he was reportedly involved in a scheme to embezzle funds from Osbaldistone and Tresham.

Frank, accompanied by Andrew Fairservice, Sir Hildebrand's gardener, set off for Glasgow in an attempt to frustrate Rashleigh's plans. Arriving in the city on Sunday, they went to church. As Frank stood listening to the preacher, a voice behind him whispered that he was in danger and that he should not look back at his informant. The mysterious messenger asked Frank to meet him on the bridge at midnight. Frank kept the tryst and followed the man to the Tolbooth prison. There he found his father's chief clerk, Mr. Owen, who had been arrested and thrown into prison at the instigation of MacVittie and MacFin, Glasgow traders who did business with his father. Frank learned that Campbell was his mysterious informant and guide, and for the first time, he realized that Campbell and Rob Roy were one and the same.

Shortly thereafter, Frank saw Morris, MacVittie, and Rashleigh talking together. He followed them, and when Morris and MacVittie departed, leaving Rashleigh alone, Frank confronted his cousin and demanded an explanation of his behavior. As their argument grew more heated, swords were drawn, but the duel was broken up by Rob Roy, who cried shame at them because they were men of the same blood. Rob Roy considered both men his friends. Frank also learned that his father's funds were mixed up with a Jacobite uprising, in which Sir Hildebrand was one of the plotters. He suspected that Rashleigh had robbed Morris on information supplied by Rob Roy.

Frank and Andrew were arrested by an officer on their way to meet Rob Roy, and the officer who searched Frank discovered a note that Rob Roy had written to him. On the road, the company was attacked by Scotsmen under the direction of Helen, Rob Roy's wife, who captured or killed all the soldiers. Helen, a bloodthirsty woman, ordered that Morris, who had fallen into the hands of the Highlanders, be put to death. In the meantime, Rob Roy too had been captured, but he made his escape when one of his captors rode close to him and surreptitiously cut his bonds. Rob Roy thereupon threw himself from his horse into the river and swam to safety before his guards could overtake him.

With a Highland uprising threatening, Frank thought he had seen Diana for the last time; but he met her soon afterward riding through a wood in the company of her father, Sir Frederick Vernon, a political exile. She gave him a packet of papers that Rashleigh had been forced to give up; they were notes to the credit of Osbaldistone and Tresham. The fortune of Frank's father was safe.

In the Jacobite revolt of 1715, Rashleigh became a turncoat and joined the forces of King George. At the beginning of the revolt, Sir Hildebrand had made his will, listing the order in which his sons would fall heir to his lands. Because Rashleigh had betrayed the Stuart cause, he substituted Frank's name for that of Rashleigh in the will. Sir Hildebrand was captured by the royal forces and imprisoned at Newgate, where he died. His four sons died from various causes, and Frank inherited all the lands and properties belonging to Sir Hildebrand. When Frank went to Osbaldistone manor to take over, Rashleigh showed up with a warrant for Diana and her father; but he was killed in a fight with Rob Roy. Frank became the lord of Osbaldistone Hall. At first, Frank's father did not like the idea of having his son marry a Papist. In the end, however, he relented and Frank and Diana were married.

Critical Evaluation:

Rob Roy, which captures the raging cultural and religious debates of the early eighteenth century, is considered one of Sir Walter Scott's Waverley novels because it too employs the technique the author first used in his *Waverley* (1814), that of using historical fact within a novelistic setting. To read this novel profitably, it is important to get a sense of the history that frames its characters and events. *Rob Roy* is set in northern England and in Scotland at the time of "the fifteener." This was an attempted invasion in 1715 by the son of James II, whose Catholic family line was ousted in the so-called Glorious Revolution of 1688. His two daughters, Mary and Anne, were allowed to finish the Stuart legacy, which ended with the accession of King George I in 1714. James II's son was known as the Old Pretender, and by some Jacobites as James III. Those who supported the newly crowned King George were known as Royalists, and those who were for the Stuart family line were known as "Jacobites" because they were supporters of the Old Pretender, James III. That name was used because the names James and Jacob have the same linguistic root. It is important to keep these lineages and names in mind while reading *Rob Roy*.

After the Act of Union with Scotland in 1707, Scotland became a subordinate part of Great Britain, a position it was not happy to assume. The vast majority of people in the south of England solidly supported George I, but in the north, and especially among the Highland clans of Scotland, there was much support for the Stuart line and fervid anti-English sentiment. One reason for this is that both the Stuarts and the Highlanders were nominally Catholic, and they were able to establish lasting ties while the Stuarts were trying to remain in power during the Civil War. Memory of this loyalty was so strong that as late as 1745 the son of the Old Pretender tried one last invasion, again by way of Scotland, to place himself on the throne. It failed, but is shows the great cultural differences between Scotland and England. These cultural differences lie at the heart of *Rob Roy*.

Rob Roy, or Robert MacGregor, was a historical figure who became an outlaw as a result of political intrigue and shifts in cultural values. He was also a Jacobite. At times a cattle thief and always at the fringes of the law, he skirmished and raided his way along the Scotland-England border and was seen as a sort of Robin Hood. The relation between this historical character and the one in the novel is important, for it marks Scott's attempt to combine authentic or true history with fictive romance. Indeed, Rob Roy was already the stuff of legend, and Scott was able to make use of this popular fascination and combine it with the more realistic elements of law and culture. The result was one of the groundbreaking novels in literary history.

Scott's melding of the romance and historical genres is an important contribution to the history of the novel, as well as a fascinating element within *Rob Roy* itself. At the time Scott wrote *Rob Roy*, it was popularly assumed that the novel genre was dominated by women and what was considered feminine "romance" discourse. Scott began to change this not only by creating strong male and female characters but also by interfusing historical elements and those of chivalric romance. This combination of what most people considered opposing traditions began a new development in the history of the novel.

The figure of Rob Roy in Scott's novel is interesting not only because he is an outlaw but also because at many times his lawlessness is more legitimate than the laws wielded by the state. Rob Roy's ultimate contribution in the novel, killing Rashleigh after he tries to serve a warrant for Diana, aids in establishing Frank as the legitimate lord of Osbaldistone hall. Furthermore, his apparently irresponsible and lawless act creates a marriage that transcends the limits of the anti-Catholic and anti-Protestant cultures that threaten to destroy the union between Frank and Diana. Rob Roy's actions in the novel show the ambivalence of power as it is wielded by the government, and they show that the correct use of power and law cannot be fully claimed by the state alone. *Rob Roy* also shows that the normal conventions of society do not prove to be useful and valid at all times. Even Frank's father realizes this. When he allows the marriage to take place, the novel shows that it is possible to transcend the given prejudices of any culture.

The epistolatory structure of *Rob Roy* is on the surface rather traditional, following in a long line of novels that includes Samuel Richardson's *Clarissa* (1747-1748) and Madame de Staël's *Delphine* (1802). Mary Shelley's *Frankenstein* (1818), which was published the same year as *Rob Roy*, also has a similar format. Much has been made of the fragmentary style of these novels, but it must be kept in mind that these authors assumed they were telling the complete story and that nothing was left out or incomplete. However, a more verifiable antitraditional element in *Rob Roy* is its emphasis on things that many people considered real.

Rob Roy centers on legalistic elements such as wills, courts, and other things a trained lawyer such as Scott would have known about. In fact, Scott was interested in reforming many of the law practices at the time, and it has been argued that the legalistic elements in this novel are a part of this agenda. *Rob Roy* also centers on religious and ethnic issues that, just seventy-five years earlier, were considered too inflammatory to discuss openly. All these elements combine to create a novel that was quite revolutionary for its time and continued to demand attention in subsequent times. Its analysis of power, ethnicity, culture, and the proper use of law speaks powerfully to any century.

"Critical Evaluation" by James Aaron Stanger

Bibliography:

Anderson, James. *Sir Walter Scott and History*. Edinburgh: Edina, 1981. Presents Scott as an innovator in the historical novel who possessed the ability to delve into the embers of the Jacobite and Scottish/English conflicts of the eighteenth century.

Beiderwell, Bruce John. *Power and Punishment in Scott's Novels*. Athens: University of Georgia Press, 1992. Foucauldian approach that examines Scott's representations of the shifting structures of state power and punishment. Argues that Scott's *Rob Roy* represents the (mis)uses of power and his ambivalence about paradigms of punishment and state discipline.

Ferris, Ina. *The Achievement of Literary Authority: Gender, History, and the Waverley Novels*. Ithaca, N.Y.: Cornell University Press, 1991. Revisionist history that argues how the Waverley novels inscribe masculinist rhetoric and authority within the then female-dominated genre of the historical novel. Also discusses how the feminine voice remained in Scott's writings. Illuminates the role of gender in the novel and accounts for Diana as a strong character.

Murray, W. H. *Rob Roy MacGregor: His Life and Times*. Glasgow, Scotland: R. Drew Publishers, 1982. Excellent biography of the historical figure Robert MacGregor and his part in the confusing and constantly shifting loyalties and political currents that existed in Scotland of the early eighteenth century. Portrays MacGregor as a Scottish Robin Hood.

Sutherland, John. *The Life of Walter Scott: A Critical Biography*. Oxford, England: Basil Blackwell, 1995. Authoritative biography on Scott. Useful in gaining insights into how his life and identity as a Scotsman helped shape such heroes as Rob Roy.

ROBERT ELSMERE

Type of work: Novel
Author: Mary Augusta Ward (Mrs. Humphry Ward, 1851-1920)
Type of plot: Social realism
Time of plot: 1882-1886
Locale: Westmoreland, Oxford, Surrey, London
First published: 1888

Principal characters:
ROBERT ELSMERE, a clergyman
CATHERINE LEYBURN ELSMERE, his wife
ROSE LEYBURN, her sister
EDWARD LANGHAM, Robert's Oxford tutor
HENRY GREY, an Oxford don
SQUIRE WENDOVER, a landowner and scholar
HUGH FLAXMAN, Rose's suitor

The Story:

Catherine, Agnes, and Rose Leyburn, sisters living in a remote valley in Westmoreland, in England's Lake District, learned of the imminent arrival of Robert Elsmere, a young Anglican clergyman who was coming to visit his uncle and aunt before he assumed responsibility for a parish in southern England. Once he had met the Leyburns, Robert was quickly drawn to Catherine's seriousness and spirituality. Catherine resisted her own attraction to Robert, having promised her deceased father to remain in Westmoreland and devote herself to her mother and sisters and to preserving the centrality of religion in their lives. Rose, a talented violinist, was already trying to break away to study music, but Catherine thought music frivolous. Catherine was grateful when Robert persuaded her to treat Rose's interests more sympathetically, but she felt she had to break off her relationship with him. She told him that she could not desert her family and had resolved to continue her life in Westmoreland. Her resolve was shaken when her mother, learning of her interest in Robert from Robert's matchmaking aunt, assured Catherine that she would be pleased with the match. Catherine felt her life's purpose had been undermined. On a stormy evening, she attended the deathbed of a woman who had borne an illegitimate child. Robert followed her and persuaded her to marry him, promising that together they could live a life dedicated to God and helping others.

This promise seemed borne out as the Elsmeres enthusiastically embarked on their work with Robert's new parishioners at Murewell, in Surrey. At the end of their first year, though, Catherine was troubled by Rose's interest in the disillusioned Edward Langham, a man with no sympathy for religious belief. Langham and Rose hoped briefly that she might rouse him from the despair of his solitary, empty life, but Langham, believing himself unable to change, departed suddenly. Rose was embarrassed to have shown her interest in him.

A more serious crisis developed when Robert became friendly with Squire Wendover, the local large landowner and a scholar famous for his skeptical views of Christianity. Robert pursued his own study of history with the help of Wendover's library, and together they discussed nineteenth century German philosophy and historical research. Although Robert had hoped his faith would be strong enough to withstand modern scholarship, he had to conclude that it compellingly refuted traditional beliefs in miracles, the Resurrection, and the divinity of

Christ. He maintained a deep religious commitment to Jesus' life as an ethical model, but the loss of other orthodox beliefs was wrenchingly painful. Some other Anglican clergymen were able to doubt privately yet continue their lives of church service, but Robert knew this would be impossible for him. Not only did he have to end his ministry in Murewell, he was terrified that his changed faith would mean an irreparable breach with Catherine.

Robert went to Oxford to ask the advice of Mr. Grey, an Oxford don he had admired when he was a student, and someone whose religious beliefs were close to those Robert now held. The understanding Grey advised Robert immediately to seek Catherine's help. When he did so, Catherine almost broke down: Robert's loss of faith was incomprehensible to her. She told Robert that she would continue to love and support him, but the distance between them grew.

In London, Robert found a socially useful role in the slums of the East End. Here, he lectured and discussed his new beliefs with skeptical but interested artisans, with whom he founded a new church, the New Brotherhood of Christ. Because Catherine refused any contact with this work, the rift between them widened and their unhappiness in their life together intensified.

Meanwhile, musical study in Germany had developed Rose's artistry. Taken up by socially prominent friends of Squire Wendover, she attracted the interest of the aristocratic Hugh Flaxman. Flaxman became fascinated with Robert's East End projects and gave financial support to the New Brotherhood. During this time, Rose was also seeing Edward Langham, who was unable to stay away from her. Once again their relationship deepened and they declared their love, but the next morning, Langham wrote Rose that his nature made marriage impossible. Rose decided that her love for him had been an immature romantic illusion. Her sense of propriety made it difficult for her to accept a new lover, however, and when Hugh Flaxman, after waiting patiently, proposed to her, she asked him to wait six more months.

The Elsmeres' marriage regained its strength after advances from the amoral Madame de Netteville made Robert face his estrangement from Catherine and after Flaxman gave Catherine a moving account of Robert's experience with the New Brotherhood. Catherine was finally able to agree that Robert's beliefs, though she thought them wrong, were still fundamentally religious. Robert's health, never strong, had however broken under the strain of his work. Told that he would soon die from tuberculosis, he and Catherine went to Algiers in the hope that warm air would prolong his life. Rose and Flaxman joined them and were there when he died. After Rose and Flaxman married, Catherine continued to attend an Anglican church but also worked for the New Brotherhood, which thrived.

Critical Evaluation:

Mary Ward's *Robert Elsmere* was the most popular novel of its time in England and the United States. It was widely read and discussed and became the subject of innumerable sermons. Its author had interesting family connections, as she was the niece of the eminent Victorian essayist and poet Matthew Arnold and the granddaughter of Dr. Thomas Arnold, the famous headmaster of Rugby School. *Robert Elsmere* aroused more interest among readers, however, than Matthew Arnold's writing ever had. William Gladstone, Britain's former prime minister, called it "eminently an offspring of the time" and wrote a much-quoted critique of its treatment of orthodox Christianity. *Robert Elsmere*, Ward's second novel, launched her career as one of the most successful novelists of the late Victorian era. By the early twentieth century, though, she came to be seen as the epitome of everything a younger generation of writers wanted to reject in their Victorian heritage, particularly given her role as a leader in the battle against women's suffrage. After World War I, her work sank into obscurity.

Of her Victorian predecessors, Ward said she greatly preferred Charlotte Brontë to George

Eliot. There are several references to Brontë in *Robert Elsmere*, but in form, style, and themes the book is actually much closer to Eliot's novels. It resembles Eliot in its organization into seven books, in the central role that ideas play in the characters' lives, in its moral earnestness and preoccupation with problems of vocation, and in the detail with which it represents the changes taking place in nineteenth century society. Like many earlier Victorian novels, *Robert Elsmere* also owes a debt to Romantic poetry. The novel's first section includes lyrical descriptions of the Lake District landscape celebrated in William Wordsworth's poems, and Elsmere and Catherine Leyburn quote Wordsworth to each other.

The novel's central subjects are Elsmere's spiritual crisis and his marriage. Ward makes Elsmere a receptor of major developments in Victorian thought, including Charles Darwin's theory of evolution and German historical study and biblical "higher criticism"—the effort by nineteenth century scholars to establish the historical contexts in which the Bible was written. Ward dramatizes the moral and psychological bankruptcy many Victorians feared would be the consequence of this new thought by making its leading representative in the novel the arrogant Squire Wendover, whom she portrays as emotionally starved and isolated, living only for scholarship, deeply in need of the companionship he finds with Elsmere but also trying ruthlessly to coerce Elsmere into accepting his own skeptical beliefs. As a balance for Wendover, Ward gives Elsmere a more satisfying mentor, the Oxford don Henry Grey, who combines a skeptical rejection of Christian belief in miracles with a humanitarian commitment to social service. Grey, whom Ward based on the philosopher T. H. Green, is a model whose life inspires Elsmere in his final phase as the founder of a new workers' church, the New Brotherhood of Christ.

Ward dramatizes the emotional agony of Victorian religious doubt through her study of the Elsmeres' marriage as a complex relationship of two people who share many values and a strong mutual love but have come from very different social worlds. These differences are defined not by social class—they are both children of university-educated professional fathers—but by relationships to cultural change. Following his early upbringing by an open-minded mother who encouraged his curiosity in many directions, Robert was exposed to theological disputes and other modern trends during his student days at Oxford. This background is in contrast with Catherine's much narrower education, sheltered by a clergyman father who had moved his family back to his native Westmoreland because he was determined to protect his family from the influences of an increasingly secular world. Although Robert falls in love with Catherine partly because of her saint-like spiritual dedication, and though they share a reformist dedication to improving the lives of the poor, their differences in temperament and social experience threaten to destroy their marriage when Catherine refuses even to try to comprehend Robert's altered religious views.

Robert Elsmere's preoccupation with its era's pull toward the *fin de siècle* is also apparent in the novel's subplot centered on Catherine's sister Rose. Whereas the older sister identifies with their father's resistance to the modern, the musically gifted Rose is a rebellious free spirit. At the beginning of the novel, she seems destined to emerge from adolescence as a late nineteenth century New Woman who will challenge conventional expectations about female propriety and find a profession and a life in the cosmopolitan world of the arts. The possibilities of a musical career for Rose fade, though, as she becomes one more Victorian heroine moving through a courtship plot in which her most important action is choosing the right husband. The wrong husband, significantly, is the bored aesthete Edward Langham, whose cynicism makes him like Squire Wendover, an embodiment of the emptiness of excessive modernity. The right husband, Hugh Flaxman, who, though politically progressive, scornfully labels Langham an *enfant du siècle*, is older and wiser than Rose and the nephew to a duke. One of Ward's friends was the novelist Henry James, who wrote to her that he wished she had made Rose "serious, deeply so, in her own line, as Catherine, for instance, is serious in hers." A few years later, Ward followed his advice when she created the New Woman heroine of another popular novel, *Marcella* (1894).

Anne Howells

Bibliography:

Colby, Vineta. *The Singular Anomaly: Women Novelists of the Nineteenth Century.* New York: New York University Press, 1970. Colby, who sees Ward as a flawed novelist but a reliable documentarian of her times, discusses *Robert Elsmere* and the reasons for its popularity at some length.

Peterson, William S. *Victorian Heretic: Mrs. Humphry Ward's "Robert Elsmere."* Leicester: Leicester University Press, 1976. The only book-length treatment of the novel. Peterson situates *Robert Elsmere* in its biographical and literary-historical contexts and describes its publication history and treatment by reviewers.

Smith, Esther Marian Greenwell. *Mrs. Humphry Ward.* Boston: Twayne, 1980. Reviews changes in Ward's reputation as a novelist, summarizes comments by other late twentieth century critics, and argues for the continuing relevance of *Robert Elsmere*'s religious issues.

Sutherland, John. *Mrs. Humphry Ward: Eminent Victorian, Pre-eminent Edwardian.* New York: Oxford University Press, 1990. The best available biography of Ward, a sympathetic account of her life and a richly detailed analysis of the changing social contexts in which she wrote. Describes her struggles with the composition and revision of *Robert Elsmere*, which Sutherland does not think her best novel.

Wolff, Robert Lee. *Gains and Losses: Novels of Faith and Doubt in Victorian England.* New York: Garland, 1977. Introductory chapter of this study usefully summarizes religious developments in England since the Reformation. Chapter on Ward includes an extensive description of *Robert Elsmere*, which Wolff, a historian, calls "the climactic Victorian novel of religious doubt."

ROBIN HOOD'S ADVENTURES

Type of work: Fiction
Author: Unknown
Type of plot: Adventure
Time of plot: Thirteenth century
Locale: England
First published: c. 1490

Principal characters:
ROBIN HOOD, Earl of Huntingdon
LITTLE JOHN,
FRIAR TUCK,
WILL SCARLET,
A TINKER, and
A COOK, the members of the band of merry men
THE SHERIFF OF NOTTINGHAM
SIR RICHARD OF THE LEA, Robin Hood's friend

The Story:

Before he became an outlaw, Robin Hood was the rightful Earl of Huntingdon. The times were corrupt, however, and Robin's father had been dispossessed of his estates. Young Robin was driven into the forest. His method of protest was to organize a band of outlaws in Sherwood Forest and prey upon the rich to give to the poor.

His career as an outlaw began when he was on his way to a shooting match in Nottingham. Some of the king's foresters met him in Sherwood Forest and mocked his youth. One of the foresters wagered that Robin could not slay a deer, so Robin Hood killed one of the king's stags. The penalty for his deed was death. When the foresters gave chase, Robin was forced to hide in the forest. There he found other landless, hunted men and became their leader.

While seeking adventure one day, Robin Hood encountered a tall stranger at a bridge. Calling his merry men after the stranger had tumbled him into the stream, Robin and his companions soon overcame the stranger. Then a shooting match took place between the two. Robin Hood won the match, and the stranger good-naturedly acknowledged defeat and joined Robin's band. The outlaws called him Little John because he was so big.

The Sheriff of Nottingham was angered because Robin flouted his authority, and he issued a warrant for his arrest. This warrant was carried by a tinker into the forest. When the tinker met Robin Hood, however, the tinker failed to recognize the fugitive because Robin was disguised. Robin took the tinker to the Blue Boar Inn, got him drunk, and stole the warrant. Later, the tinker met Robin in the forest and fought with him. Robin Hood won the bout, and the tinker happily joined the other merry men in Robin's band.

The Sheriff of Nottingham grew more and more enraged by Robin's boldness. When the king rebuked him for not capturing the outlaw, the sheriff devised another plan. Knowing that Robin Hood prided himself on his skill in archery, the sheriff proclaimed a shooting match in Nottingham Tower. There he hoped to catch Robin Hood and his men. They outwitted him, however, for they went to the match in disguise. As a tattered stranger, Robin won the golden arrow given as a prize. After he returned to Sherwood Forest, he sent the sheriff a note of thanks for the prize. This act infuriated the officer even more.

Now the band of outlaws lay low in the forest for a time. At last, Robin Hood sent one of his men to learn the sheriff's next plan. When he was captured, the band set out to rescue him. As the man was being dragged forth to be hanged, Little John leaped into the cart and cut the prisoner's bonds. The other outlaws ran from their hiding places and overcame the sheriff's men.

Next, Robin Hood bought some meat and took it to Nottingham to sell to the poor at half price. Disguised as a butcher, he was thought by most people to be either a foolish peasant or a wealthy nobleman in disguise. When Robin Hood offered to sell him a herd of cattle at a ridiculously low price, the sheriff gleefully accepted the offer. Then Robin took the sheriff to Sherwood Forest, took his money, showed him the king's deer, and told him that there stood his herd.

As a lark, Little John went to the Fair at Nottingham Tower, where he treated all the people to food and drink. He was asked to enter the sheriff's service because of his great size. Little John decided such employment might be fun. He found life in the sheriff's household so pleasant that he stayed six months, but he gradually grew bored and became arrogant toward the steward. The steward called the cook to fight Little John. Both men ate such a huge meal before fighting that neither could win. Finally, they decided to stop because they did not really dislike each other. Then Little John persuaded the cook to join the band of merry men.

On another day, Robin Hood and his men went out to find Friar Tuck of Fountain Dale, supposedly a rich curate. Spying a strange monk singing and feasting beside a brook, Robin joined him. When Robin wished to go across the water, he persuaded the man to carry him on his back. On the return trip the monk, who was in reality Friar Tuck, dumped Robin into the water. After another great fight, with Robin the victor, the friar joyfully joined the outlaw band.

The queen had heard of Robin's prowess and was fascinated by stories told about him and his men; she invited him to come to London. In an attempt to outwit the king, she proposed an archery match at which she would put up three archers against his best three. If her team won, the king was to issue a pardon of forty days to certain prisoners. The king accepted the wager. The queen's archers were Robin Hood, Little John, and Will Scarlet, all in disguise. Naturally, the outlaws won, although Will Scarlet was bested in his match. When the king learned that the queen's archers were Robin Hood and two of his men, he was angry, and they escaped capture only with the queen's help. The others returned safely to Sherwood Forest, but Robin Hood met with many dangerous adventures on the way. During his journey, he encountered Sir Richard of the Lea, a knight whom he had once aided, and Sir Richard advised him to return to London and throw himself on the queen's mercy. She persuaded the king to give Robin Hood safe escort back to Sherwood Forest and so pay the wager of the shooting match.

Returning from the Crusades, King Richard the Lion-Hearted decided to seek out Robin Hood and his outlaw band. With six others, all disguised as friars, Richard encountered Robin and his men and bested them. Richard then revealed himself and pardoned Robin and his men. Robin he restored to his rightful honors as the Earl of Huntingdon.

On a visit to Sherwood Forest several years later, Robin Hood became so homesick for his old life that he gave up his title and returned to live with the outlaws. His action infuriated John, the new king, and the Sheriff of Nottingham. They sent their men to capture the outlaws. During the fighting, the sheriff was killed. Robin Hood, ill and much depressed by this bloodshed, went to Kirkley Abbey, where his cousin was prioress, to be bled. She was a treacherous woman and had him bled too long, so that he lay dying. At last Little John, having pulled down bolts and bars to get to Robin, reached his leader's bedside. As Robin Hood lay dying in Little John's arms, he asked for his bow and arrows and said that he wished to be buried wherever his arrow fell. Then Robin shot an arrow through the window of the priory. Little John marked its flight, and Robin was buried beneath the ancient oak, which was his last target. His merry men disbanded after his death, but the stories of their brave deeds and the prowess of Robin Hood live on.

Critical Evaluation:

Robin Hood's Adventures is one of the best-loved stories of all time. It has the elements that make for entertaining reading: romance, adventure, the stage of history, and lofty characters. As a work of prose fiction, however, it is quite unusual in one respect: comparatively few have actually read the book, whereas millions have heard about the story. Those who have not read the original have nevertheless come to know and love the characters of the Robin Hood legend through the countless versions of the story in prose, fireside tales, motion pictures, and more recently television.

The Robin Hood story goes back well into the Middle Ages. Legends developed about a "good" outlaw who protected and supported the poor while he stole from the rich. Early legends, however, did not center on one bandit. There appear to have been several similar heroes of this type who were eventually coalesced into the character of Robin Hood, Earl of Huntingdon, as he appears in this story. Whether or not the prototypes of Robin Hood were real, as some historians believe them to have been, is a moot point. It is the legend and not the reality of the story that has excited people for centuries.

Although the first recorded reference to Robin Hood occurred in the writings of the Scottish historian John of Fordun, who died in approximately 1384, the first known compilation of prose and poetry of the Robin Hood legend came in 1490 with the publication of the *Lytel Geste of Robin Hood*, by Wynkyn de Worde, a noted British printer. If there had been records for best-sellers in those days, certainly this tale would have been high on the list. It proved so popular that this version appeared again several decades later and has been reprinted and retold for centuries. It was used as a basis for works of later novelists such as Sir Walter Scott in *Ivanhoe* (1819) and more recently on film in motion picture and television adaptations.

Its popularity may also be measured by considering that playing Robin Hood is a fantasy game popular with children. To the English especially, Robin Hood is a great hero. He and King Arthur are the most revered characters in British legends, and their popularity continues to thrive throughout the world.

Although *Robin Hood's Adventures* may not be classed as one of the great works of world literature, it is so entertaining that it may be read with delight over and over again. Readers can forgive a lack of character analysis when they are able to feel as if they were riding through Sherwood Forest by Robin Hood's side, engaging in adventures that are noble in spirit and yet full of mischief.

The story line of the tale is quite simple: The underdog, Robin Hood, fights oppression and injustice in the form of the Sheriff of Nottingham and Prince John, to protect the poor and rally them around the good, but absent, King Richard I. Robin Hood represents an early attempt to personify noblesse oblige. He is a highborn man who helps the unfortunate. He does not condescend in his assistance, however, because he lives and works among the poor in Sherwood Forest. By contrast, Prince John is a powerful, oppressive leader. Persecuting Robin Hood, he inadvertently encourages Robin's followers. King Richard, Prince John's brother, represents the colorful "good king" who is away fighting in the Holy Land during the Third Crusade.

The narrative of Robin Hood makes for entertaining reading, but it is quite far removed from historical fact. As the legends grew about Robin Hood, the actual historical events surrounding the reigns of Richard and John became blurred. In reality, Richard was rarely seen in England after he became king. He preferred traveling and fighting in other countries. John was not a particularly bad leader, merely unlucky. He was called John Lackland because he had the unfortunate habit of losing English territories to the French. For this reason, he became very unpopular and has had a bad reputation down through the centuries. The possibility of real Robin Hood-type bandits existing in the period surrounding the signing of the Magna Carta may be admitted, but the legend has been expanded so much that historical accuracy is not an element of the Robin Hood story. The Robin Hood story is a folktale, the kind of literature that is re-created from generation to generation, responding to such basic human needs as justice and having fun. Reading *Robin Hood's Adventures*, however, one should bear in mind that the tale is not historically accurate.

History aside, the book's adventures can be appreciated by almost anyone. Its characterizations, however, are weak. They are too black-and-white to be true reflections of life. One should realize, however, that English literature in the fifteenth century had not developed the novel. Literature was largely based on characters and events already familiar to readers: types, mythology, history, legend. The artistic goal of faithfulness to the shadings and complexities of good and evil in real people did not exist then, and furthermore Robin Hood is a figure of legend, not reality. One should approach *Robin Hood's Adventures* as one would approach a film made with no greater, and no lesser, intent than entertainment.

"Critical Evaluation" by Patricia Ann King

Bibliography:

The Ballad of Robin Hood. Sung by Anthony Quayle. Lyre by Desmond Dupré. Caedmon TC 1177, 1963. The Robin Hood ballads were intended to be sung, not read. Many of them seem banal until they are heard in Quayle's and Dupré's excellent renditions.

Dobson, R. B., and John Taylor, comps. *Rymes of Robyn Hood: An Introduction to the English Outlaw*. Pittsburgh: University of Pittsburgh Press, 1976. Invaluable in studying Robin Hood. Collects the very best of the medieval and early modern versions of the Robin Hood story into one volume. Contains an excellent introduction describing the history and development of the legend.

Holt, J. C. *Robin Hood*. Rev. and enlarged ed. London: Thames and Hudson, 1989. This highly readable book discusses at length the various claims for the existence of an actual historical Robin Hood.

Keen, Maurice. *The Outlaws of Medieval Legend*. Rev. ed. London: Routledge & Kegan Paul, 1977. Gives the historical context for the medieval legend of Robin Hood by relating it to the stories of other outlaws. Examines the social causes of the rise of such legends.

Peacock, Thomas Love. *Maid Marian*. Edited by Richard Garnett. London: J. M. Dent, 1891. This is a humorous and largely neglected version of the Robin Hood legend.

ROBINSON CRUSOE

Type of work: Novel
Author: Daniel Defoe (1660-1731)
Type of plot: Adventure
Time of plot: 1651-1705
Locale: An island off the coast of South America and the Several Seas
First published: 1719

Principal characters:
ROBINSON CRUSOE, a castaway
FRIDAY, his faithful servant

The Story:

Robinson Crusoe was the son of a middle-class English family. Although his father desired that he go into business and live a quiet life, Robinson had such longing for the sea that he found it impossible to remain at home. He took his first voyage without his parents' knowledge. The ship was caught in a great storm, and Robinson was so violently ill and so greatly afraid that he vowed never to leave land again should he be so fortunate as to escape death.

When he landed safely, however, he found his old longing still unsatisfied, and he engaged as a trader, shipping first for the coast of Africa. The ship on which he sailed was captured by a Turkish pirate vessel, and he was carried as a prisoner into Sallee, a Moorish port. There he became a slave. His life was unbearable, and at the first opportunity he escaped in a small boat. He was rescued by a Portuguese freighter and carried safely to Brazil. There he bought a small plantation and began the life of a planter.

When another English planter suggested that they make a voyage to Africa for a cargo of slaves, Robinson once more gave in to his longing for the sea. This voyage was destined to bring him his greatest adventure of all, for the ship broke apart on a reef near an island off the coast of South America; of the crew and passengers, only Robinson was saved. The waves washed him ashore, and he took stock of his situation. The island seemed to be completely uninhabited, and there was no sign of wild beasts. In an attempt to make his castaway life as comfortable as possible, he constructed a raft and brought away food, ammunition, water, wine, clothing, tools, sailcloth, and lumber from the broken ship.

He set up a sailcloth tent on the side of a small hill and encircled his refuge with tall, sharp stakes; he entered his shelter by means of a ladder that he drew up after him. Into this area he brought all the goods he had salvaged, being particularly careful of the gunpowder. His next concern was his food supply. Finding that there was little that had not been ruined by rats or water, he ate sparingly during his first days on the island.

Among the things Robinson had brought from the ship were a quill and ink; before long, he began to keep a journal. When he considered the good and evil of his situation, he found that he had much for which to thank God. He began to make his shelter permanent. Behind his tent he found a small cave, which he enlarged and braced. With crude tools, he made a table and a chair, some shelves, and a rack for his guns. He spent many months on the work, all the time able to feed himself with wildfowl and other small game. He also found several springs that kept him supplied with water.

For the next twenty-four years, his life was spent in much the same way as his first days on the island had been. He explored the island and built what he was pleased to call his summer home on the other side. He was able to grow corn, barley, and rice. He carefully saved the new kernels each year until he had enough to plant a small field. With these grains, he learned to grind meal and bake coarse bread. He caught and tamed wild goats to supply his larder and parrots for companionship. He made better furniture and improved his cave, making it even safer from intruders, whom he still feared, although he had seen no sign of any living thing larger than small game, fowl, and goats. He had also brought three Bibles from the ship, and he had time to read them carefully. At a devotional period each morning and night, he never failed to thank God for delivering him from the sea.

In the middle of Robinson's twenty-fourth year on the island, an incident occurred that altered his way of living. About a year and a half previously, he had observed some savages who had apparently paddled over from another island. They had come in the night and gorged themselves on some other savages, obviously prisoners. Robinson had found the bones and the torn flesh the next morning and had since been terrified that the cannibals might return and find him. Finally, a band of savages did return. While they prepared for their gruesome feast, Robinson shot some of them and frightened the others away. Able to rescue one of the prisoners, he at last had human companionship. He named the man Friday after the day of his rescue, and Friday became his faithful servant and friend.

After a time, Robinson was able to teach Friday English. Friday told him that seventeen white men were prisoners on the island from which he had come. Although Friday reported that the men were well treated, Robinson had a great desire to go to them, thinking that together they might find some way to return to the civilized world. He and Friday built a canoe and prepared to sail to the other island, but before they were ready for their trip, another group of savages came to their island with more prisoners. Robinson discovered that one of the prisoners was a white man and managed to save him and another savage, whom Friday found to be his own father. There was great joy at the reunion of father and son. Robinson cared for the old man and the white man, who was a Spaniard, one of the seventeen of whom Friday had spoken. A hostile tribe had captured Friday's island, and now the white men were no longer safe.

Robinson dispatched the Spaniard and Friday's father to the neighboring island to try to rescue the white men. While waiting for their return, Robinson saw an English ship one day at anchor near shore. Soon he found the captain of the ship and two others, who had been set ashore by a mutinous crew. Robinson, Friday, and the three seamen were able to retake the ship, and Robinson was at last delivered from the island. He disliked leaving before the Spaniard and Friday's father returned, and he determined to go back to the island some day and see how they had fared. Five of the mutinous crew chose to remain rather than be returned to England to hang. Robinson and Friday sailed to England. Robinson returned to his homeland after an absence of thirty-five years, arriving there, a stranger and unknown, in June of 1687.

His adventures were not over. When he visited his old home, he found that his parents had died, as had all of his family but two sisters and the two children of one of his brothers. Having no reason to remain in England, he went to Lisbon to inquire about his plantation. There he learned that friends had saved the income of his estate for him and that he was now worth about five thousand pounds sterling. Satisfied with the accounting, Robinson and Friday returned to England, where Robinson married and had three children.

After his wife died, Robinson sailed again in 1695 as a private trader on a ship captained by his nephew and bound for the East Indies and China. The ship put in at his castaway island, where he found that the Spaniards and the English mutineers had taken native wives from an adjoining island; consequently, the population was greatly increased. Robinson was pleased with his little group and gave a feast for them. He also presented them with gifts from the ship.

After he had satisfied himself that the colony was well cared for, Robinson and Friday sailed away. On their way to Brazil, savages attacked the ship, and Friday was killed. From Brazil, Robinson went around the Cape of Good Hope and on to the coast of China. At one port, after the sailors had taken part in a massacre, Robinson lectured them so severely that the crew forced their captain, Robinson's nephew, to set him ashore in China, as they could no longer tolerate his preaching. There Robinson joined a caravan that took him into Siberia. At last, he reached England. Having spent the greater part of fifty-four years away from his homeland, he was glad to live out his life in peace and in preparation for that longer journey from which he would never return.

Critical Evaluation:

The Life and Strange Surprising Adventures of Robinson Crusoe of York, Mariner, Written by Himself, as Daniel Defoe entitled his novel, is read as eagerly today as when it was first published. An exotic novel of travel and adventure, *Robinson Crusoe* functions primarily as Defoe's defense of his bourgeois Protestantism. Crusoe's adventures—the shipwrecks, his life as a planter in South America, and his years of isolation on the island—provide an apt context for his polemic. A political dissenter and pamphleteer, Defoe saw as his enemies the Tory aristocrats whose royalism in government and religion blocked the aspirations of the middle class. Like Jonathan Swift in *Gulliver's Travels* (1726), Defoe in his novel also presented a religiously and politically corrupt England. Both authors were intent on bringing about a moral revolution and each used his hero as an exemplum. Gulliver, however, represents a moral failure, whereas Crusoe's adventures reveal his spiritual conversion, a return to the ethics and religion of his father. As one critic has said of *Robinson Crusoe*,

> We read it . . . in order to follow with meticulous interest and constant self-identification the hero's success in building up, step by step, out of whatever material came to hand, a physical and moral replica of the world he had left behind him. If *Robinson Crusoe* is an adventure story, it is also a moral tale, a commercial accounting and a Puritan fable.

Significantly, Crusoe's origins are in northern England, in York, where he was born in the early part of the seventeenth century and where his father had made a fortune in trade. He belongs to the solid middle class, that class that was gaining political power during the early eighteenth century, when Defoe published his book. Crusoe's father is an apologist for the mercantile, Puritan ethic, which he tries without success to instill in his son. As Crusoe says, "Mine was the middle state," which his father "had found by long experience was the best state in the world, the most suited to human happiness, not exposed to the miseries and hardships, the labour and sufferings of the mechanick part of mankind, and not embarrassed with the pride, luxury, ambition and envy of the upper part of mankind." Its virtues and blessings were those of "temperance, moderation, quietness, health [and] society."

His father's philosophy, which is designed to buy a man happiness and pleasure in both this life and the next, nevertheless fails to persuade the young Crusoe, who finds nothing but boredom in the comforts of the middle class. He longs to go to sea, to follow a way of life that represents the antithesis of his father's. He seeks the extremes of sensation and danger, preferring to live on the periphery rather than in the middle where all is secure. Crusoe's decision to become a sailor is an act of adolescent rebellion, yet it is also very much in the tradition of Puritan individualism. Not content with the wisdom of his class, the young man feels it is necessary to test himself, and to discover himself and his own ethic.

Even after the first stage in his adventures, which culminates in Crusoe's gaining a modest fortune in South America, he refuses to settle down. Intent on his own "inclination," as he says, he leaves his plantation and once again takes up the uncertain life of sea trade. It is at this point in the narrative that Crusoe is shipwrecked and abandoned on a tropical island without any hope of rescue.

Crusoe's first response to his isolation and the prospect of living the rest of his life alone is one of despair. He has, however, a strong survival instinct and courageously he sets about the task of staying alive and eventually of creating a humane, comfortable society. One of the first things he does is to mark time, to make a calendar. Despite all of his efforts to continue his own life and environment, he falls ill, and it is at this point that he realizes his complete vulnerability, his absolute aloneness in the universe. Stripped of all his illusions, limited by necessity to one small place, Crusoe is thrown back upon himself and confronted by an immense emptiness. He asks desperately: "What is this earth and sea of which I have seen so much? Whence is it produced? And what am I and all the other creatures, wild and tame, human and brutal? Whence are we?"

All of these questions predate Crusoe's religious conversion, the central and most significant event of the novel. His answer to the questions is that all creation comes from God and that the state of all creation, including his own, is an expression of the will of God. Upon this act of faith, he rebuilds not only his own life but also his own miniature society that reflects in its simplicity, moderation, and comfort the philosophy his father had taught. Furthermore, his faith brings him to an acceptance of his own life and station, an acceptance that he was never able to make before: "I acquiesced in the dispositions of Providence, which I began now to own and to believe ordered everything for the best." Later, after two years on the island, he says,

> It is now that I began sensibly to feel how much more happy this life I now led was, with all its miserable circumstances, than the wicked, cursed, abominable life I led all the past part of my days; and now I changed both my sorrows and my joys; my very desires altered, my affections changed their gusts, and my delights were perfectly new from what they were at my first coming.

Once he was able to answer the overwhelming question of the novel—"Whence are we?"—the rest of the narrative and Crusoe's adventures justify, to his aristocrat readers, his religious faith and the middle-class Puritan ethic. Apart from this justification, there also remains the glorification of the self-reliant and self-directing man. This was a man unfamiliar to Defoe's readers, a new man beginning to appear on the fringes of the power structure and about to demand his place in a society that was evolving toward a new political structure that became recognized as middle-class democracy.

"Critical Evaluation" by David L. Kubal

Bibliography:

Damrosch, Leopold, Jr. *God's Plot and Man's Stories*. Chicago: University of Chicago Press, 1985. Damrosch devotes a chapter to *Robinson Crusoe*, which he reads largely within the context of Puritan doctrine. The result is a first-rate and highly recommended discussion of the work.

Defoe, Daniel. *Robinson Crusoe*. Edited by Michael Shinagel. New York: W. W. Norton, 1994. The perfect beginner's guide to Defoe's great novel. In addition to an authoritative text of *Robinson Crusoe*, Shinagel provides selections from twentieth century criticism, a bibliography, and a set of very useful contextual materials.

McKeon, Michael. *The Origins of the English Novel, 1600-1740*. Baltimore: The Johns Hopkins University Press, 1987. A large and challenging work, which includes a readable and rewarding chapter on *Robinson Crusoe*.

Rogers, Pat. *Robinson Crusoe*. London: Allen & Unwin, 1979. A rich source book for the study of Defoe's most famous work. Provides, among many other useful materials, a brief account of Defoe's life, chapters entitled "Travel, Trade, and Empire" and "Religion and Allegory," a full bibliography, and two appendices containing pre-*Robinson Crusoe* accounts of Alexander Selkirk (the castaway who inspired Defoe's fictional character).

Watt, Ian. *The Rise of the Novel: Studies in Defoe, Richardson, and Fielding*. Berkeley: University of California Press, 1964. First published in 1957, Watt's study remains, in spite of numerous challenges, one of the key works in the field of early English fiction. He devotes a long and fascinating chapter to *Robinson Crusoe*.

RODERICK HUDSON

Type of work: Novel
Author: Henry James (1843-1916)
Type of plot: Psychological realism
Time of plot: 1870's
Locale: Chiefly Rome, also Florence and Switzerland
First published: 1876

Principal characters:
Roderick Hudson, a young American sculptor
Rowland Mallet, a young, wealthy art patron
Mrs. Light, a vain and silly widow
Christina Light, her beautiful daughter
The Cavaliere Giacosa, Christina's father
Prince Casamassima, Christina's husband
Sam Singleton, an American painter
Hudson, Roderick's insipid mother
Mary Garland, Roderick's American fiancée

The Story:

Rowland Mallet, expecting to sail for Europe in September, visited his cousin Cecilia in Northampton, Massachusetts. He was an idle bachelor, having inherited money, and he felt that he was leading a useless life. Having a passion for art, he was interested to learn of a young sculptor who lived in the town. On meeting the intense, impetuous Roderick Hudson and seeing proof of his talent, he offered to subsidize the young artist for a period of study in Rome. Rowland gained the assent of Hudson's widowed mother. At a farewell picnic, Rowland had a last talk with Mary Garland, a distant cousin of Mrs. Hudson, who had been visiting in Northampton. Rowland realized that he would not see her for perhaps three years. In their brief acquaintance, she had come to mean a great deal to him, but on the Atlantic voyage, Roderick Hudson told Rowland that he was engaged to Mary.

In Rome that autumn, as Rowland had expected, Roderick responded to the stimulus provided by the art treasures of the city. He assimilated experience readily and became eager to create masterpieces of his own. Rowland was pleased with his role as patron and nourisher of talent. One day, while Roderick sat sketching in the Villa Ludovisi, the two companions observed a trio of passersby—a shabbily appearing man, a middle-aged woman, and a young girl with blue eyes, dusky hair, and perfect features. Roderick was enraptured and yearned to model her, but they did not stop.

Rowland began to introduce Roderick into society. The young and handsome sculptor, attractively impertinent and strident, became a favorite. He spent the days hard at work and the nights in Roman drawing rooms. His first work, a life-sized Adam, drew admirers to his studio. Among them were another sculptor, Gloriani, and a young American painter, Sam Singleton. Gloriani was skeptical of Roderick's staying power, while Singleton was an uncritical worshiper. Roderick frequently grew lyrical about his own brilliant future.

The onset of summer, however, brought Roderick to an impasse. His exuberance and inspiration departed. Rowland Mallet prescribed a change of scenery, and the two left Rome to ramble northward. Roderick desired to spend most of the summer alone.

In England, after a month with no word from Roderick, Rowland dispatched a letter. The reply was unsettling; Roderick had been gambling and was heavily in debt. When the two friends met in Geneva, Roderick admitted debauchery but felt no remorse. He had learned his susceptibility to the beauty and mystery of women.

Back in Rome, Roderick was discontented and worked only by fits and starts. Then one day, the man and woman and the beautiful young girl whom he had observed in the Ludovisi gardens burst into his studio. Madame Light, her daughter Christina, and the Cavaliere Giacosa had come to see the rising young sculptor and his works. Roderick insisted he must do a bust of Christina.

Mrs. Light was a vain, silly widow. She had picked up the old Cavaliere in her European ramblings and now lived solely to marry Christina to a fortune. Christina's beauty was supplemented by wit, will, and education.

During the winter, Roderick worked on his bust of Christina and became enamored of her. Rowland feared her influence on him. She seemed selfish and vicious, a complex person who demanded worship. Meanwhile, Christina's mother was becoming established in Roman society. Roderick took a commission from an American snob to create in marble the ideal of Intellectual Refinement.

The old Cavaliere became Rowland's confidant. Roderick would find his love unrequited, he said. Mrs. Light was determined that Christina should marry a man of wealth and position. Though Rowland and Christina disliked each other, they achieved a certain understanding. Christina confessed that she despised her own egotism and longed for someone to free her from herself. Roderick's adoration continued.

In an effort to cool the relationship, Rowland informed Christina of Roderick's engagement. Roderick's subsequent anger revealed something to Rowland: his friend lacked a feeling heart; he did not mind hurting Mary. Rowland's faith in Roderick's potential had been foolish. The artistic temperament was amoral.

Winter brought a new personage on the scene. Prince Casamassima was seen with the Light entourage. He was Mrs. Light's choice for Christina.

Rowland encountered Christina at various places in Rome, and their exchange of frank confidences continued. Rowland requested her to leave Roderick alone. She seemed to desire Rowland's respect, but when she left Rome briefly, Roderick followed.

Despite Roderick's interlude of riotous living in Naples, Rowland's fondness for him was undiminished. Even when he stopped work on Intellectual Refinement, Rowland tried to understand.

Christina's engagement to Prince Casamassima was announced, but Roderick continued his pursuit. Rowland admitted himself disgusted with people. His good deed had turned sour; Mrs. Hudson and Mary Garland would be hurt to learn the truth about Roderick. His thoughts kept going back to Mary.

Hoping to save the situation, he cabled for Mrs. Hudson and Mary. Roderick greeted Mary in a state of drunkenness. To Rowland, she was more attractive than before.

Although Christina's wedding date was set for June, Roderick's infatuation continued. Rowland was astonished to learn from Madame Grandoni that his own love for Mary Garland was perfectly evident. Then Christina broke off with the prince. Roderick isolated himself in his quarters for a week to contemplate this good fortune. Mrs. Light summoned Rowland to talk sense to Christina. Mrs. Hudson and Mary, still unaware of the complex situation, suffered in silence.

Rowland unwillingly conversed with Christina. Although Prince Casamassima's money did not excite her, she refused to accept Roderick's proposal of marriage. Three days later, Christina and the prince were suddenly and privately married. Simultaneously, a secret came to light: Christina's father had been Mrs. Light's lover, the Cavaliere. Christina had married quickly before such a scandal could cause the prince to break with her.

Roderick, angry, disappointed, and miserable, was ready to leave Rome. He placed himself entirely in Rowland's hands. Rowland agreed when Roderick confessed to his mother and Mary that he was a failure. Mrs. Hudson was appalled to learn that the uncompleted Intellectual Refinement was a five-thousand-dollar commission.

They all went to Europe for the summer. Rowland vaguely hoped that Roderick could still pull himself together. Rowland admired Mary more and more. After an idle, dreary summer, they moved on to Switzerland. Roderick's perceptions of beauty were as acute as ever, but he was unable to do anything constructive.

Rowland pressed the point about Roderick's engagement. Mary did not interest him, but he did not break it off. Roderick saw no point in Rowland's desire to keep his admiration for Mary a secret.

In one of their daily rambles, Roderick and Rowland encountered the Prince and Princess Casamassima. Christina detested her husband. Hitherto petulant and unforgiving of her, Roderick turned to pursuit again. The next day, he asked Rowland for one thousand francs to meet her at Interlaken. He got some money from Mary when Rowland, at the end of his patience, refused the request. He chided Rowland for moralizing, but Rowland admitted his love for Mary.

Roderick then disappeared. A spectacular mountain thunderstorm arose in the afternoon. He had not returned by dawn the next day. Sam Singleton, who had been diligently sketching all the while Roderick had idled, had stopped for a visit. He and Rowland went to look for Roderick. His body lay beneath a high cliff three hours' walk from the inn. He had fallen, apparently, on his way to Interlaken.

Mrs. Hudson and Mary Garland went back to Northampton. Rowland, with his inexhaustible patience, frequently came to call on Mary.

Critical Evaluation:

Roderick Hudson is Henry James's first novel. It came after many short stories, which had developed not only James's technical skills but also many of his thematic interests. It might be said that James was interested in three themes: the problem of young men or women who need help to express themselves fully as human beings; the problem of young Americans, whom he sees as needing the experience of European society, traditions, and institutions; and money, and how money can be used to help promising characters to fulfill themselves.

His belief in the civilizing effects of Europe on young Americans must be understood in the context of the time. He wrote at the end of the nineteenth and the beginning of the twentieth centuries, when America was a less confident country than it became later. His enthusiasm for what Europe could do to polish an American, (intellectually, artistically, socially, and psychologically) must be taken in conjunction with a caveat: Such an encounter can sometimes do harm, particularly since the European ethos is not without flaws that the innocent American may not be able to resist.

This novel manifests, in simpler ways than James's later works, many of these ideas. It is a tale of a young man—Roderick Hudson— of artistic promise who needs the experience of the great world of European art, and who, at first at least, proves able to profit from his experience. He learns to express himself with considerable promise. He seems personally flawed, proud of his gift, but arrogantly unconcerned about how precious it is, and how susceptible he is to the distractions of pleasure, which is readily at hand in the moneyed circles in which Rowland places him. He is sometimes unable and sometimes unwilling to distinguish between the valuable aspects of European experience and its destructive temptations. When Christina Light comes along, he is unable to believe that his love can be resisted. He understands little of the least attractive powers of money and social position. He comes to Rome as an innocent, blessed with talent that others envy, but lacking the self-discipline of the artist or the moral strength of his friend Mallet, who thinks that he can protect Roderick from his lack of character and from a world wiser, older, and more corrupt than he can imagine. It must also be said that Roderick is at some considerable fault, particularly in his self-absorption and self-pity, and his cruel lack of interest in how his conduct affects others. Europe is not responsible for his selfishness. He seems to have no concern for proving worthy of Mallet's help, which goes far beyond financial support, and his treatment of his mother and Mary Garland can hardly be blamed on the evils of European high society. He is a spoiled, arrogant young man, who sadly throws away an artistic gift that lesser artists of his acquaintance in Rome look upon with yearning. Talent, James seems to be saying, will not protect one from a lack of character.

If one has a desire to read a lot of Henry James, this is a good novel with which to begin, although there are certain oddities about James that have to be understood. He is not much interested in complicated plot or adventurous incident. He is interested in character, particularly a young American character of promise meeting the temptations of European high life. On top of that, he is strongly inclined to two technical devices that can be difficult to deal with if a reader is used to fast-moving story. He likes his characters to talk at length and with fineness of thought about their problems. He gives them a capacity for subtle expression and often a muted wittiness than can be missed if read too quickly. He extends this minuteness of expression to his narrative third-person voice, which is allowed, usually within a limited set of parameters, to penetrate the minds of his characters. What James seems to be suggesting is that if his characters could express themselves with the fineness and high intelligence that his narrative voice possesses, they would, thusly, define themselves. Realistic credibility, in short, gives way to depth and subtlety of expression. The secret of this novel, and of the novels that followed it, is the artistic pleasure not in what happens, but in how the problems, mainly moral, are considered by the characters and by the narrator, who is always the most perceptive voice in the novel. It is not simply a matter of what happens; it is equally a matter of how what happens is experienced by all involved.

The conclusion of Roderick Hudson is somewhat banal, but tonally it has a wry and anticlimactic air about it that suggests that James was not going to be an easy novelist, or, indeed, a particularly popular one. The real power of the book is not in its ending but in its contemplation of how people make messes of their lives while attempting to do the opposite. If it seems stylistically and thematically complicated and somewhat spare of plot, it is, compared to the novels that followed, like *Gone with the Wind* (1936).

"Critical Evaluation" by Charles Pullen

Bibliography:

Anderson, Charles R. *Person, Place and Thing in Henry James's Novels*. Durham, N.C.: Duke University Press, 1977. A study of the connection of James's novels to other novels of the nineteenth century. The chapter on *Roderick Hudson* refers to James's life in Rome and discusses the ways that the characters relate to one another.

Edel, Leon. *Henry James: A Life*. New York: Harper & Row, 1985. A valuable study that includes discussion of his work, with substantial comment on *Roderick Hudson*.

Ford, Ford Madox. *Henry James: A Critical Study*. New York: Octagon Books, 1972. Short, readable study of James by a fine novelist.

Lee, Brian. *The Novels of Henry James*. London: Edward Arnold, 1978. A short study of the relation of culture to the individual. Includes a chapter on *Roderick Hudson* that discusses James's enthusiasm for European culture.

McCormack, Peggy. *The Rule of Money: Gender, Class, and Exchange Economics in the Fiction of Henry James*. Ann Arbor: University of Michigan Press, 1990. Discusses how James's characters learn to adjust to the rules of the game in their society. Useful for understanding the mores and practices of a departed era.

THE ROMANCE OF LEONARDO DA VINCI

Type of work: Novel
Author: Dmitry Merezhkovsky (1865-1941)
Type of plot: Historical
Time of plot: 1494-1519
Locale: Italy and France
First published: Voskresshiye Bogi: Leonardo da Vinci, 1901 (English translation, 1902)

Principal characters:
LEONARDO DA VINCI, a Renaissance artist
GIOVANNI BELTRAFFIO, his pupil
CESARE BORGIA, Leonardo's patron
MONNA CASSANDRA, a sorceress
FRANCESCO MELZI, another pupil of Leonardo
MONNA LISA GIOCONDA, a model for a portrait by Leonardo

The Story:

In 1494 the fear of the coming of the Antichrist prophesied in the New Testament began to make itself felt in Italy. Greek and Roman statues, which had recently been excavated and accepted as supreme works of art by such men as Leonardo da Vinci, were considered by the common people to be pagan deities returning to prepare the world for the reign of the Antichrist.

Leonardo da Vinci had become a member of the court of Duke Moro in Milan. Besides acting as chief architect for the duke, he interested himself in teaching his pupils, Giovanni Beltraffio and Andrea Salaino, and in working on whatever caught his fancy. Most of the money he received from the duke's treasury went to buy pieces of amber with insects imbedded in them, old shells, live birds that he studied and then freed, and other curious objects that distracted his attention and kept him from completing his painting, *The Last Supper.*

The student Giovanni was attracted to Monna Cassandra, a beautiful girl who lived in the neighborhood. Unknown to him, she practiced the black arts and was a favorite of suspected witches. The duke of Milan called upon the king of France to help protect and support his dukedom. Louis XII of France, however, soon proved false to his friendship with the duke and overran the duchy. The French forces used a clay statue of a mounted warrior, which Leonardo had not yet cast in bronze, as a target for a shooting contest, and a flood caused the walls on which *The Last Supper* was painted to bulge and crack. Realizing that these two works of art could never be finished, Leonardo decided to leave Milan and go to the court of Cesare Borgia, the son of Pope Alexander VI.

As Borgia's adviser, Leonardo designed many pieces of war equipment and machinery, which Borgia used in his attempt to seize all of Italy for the pope. None of Leonardo's pupils approved of his working for Borgia, whose cruelties and vices made him hated throughout Italy.

One day one of Leonardo's students, a blacksmith named Zoroastro da Peretola, went against his orders and tried to fly in Leonardo's only partly completed airplane. Falling from a considerable height, he received such a jolt that his mind was never again sound. Leonardo left Borgia's services and, with the help of his friend Machiavelli, received a commission from the city of Florence to plan a system of waterways that would divert the course of the Arno River. Machiavelli had underestimated the expense of the work, and Leonardo was soon in trouble with the authorities. The canal project was abandoned, and Leonardo was asked instead to paint a large picture depicting the battle of Anghiari. At that time Michelangelo was also working in

Florence, and a great jealousy had grown up between admirers of the two artists. Leonardo tried to make friends with Michelangelo, but the passionate artist would have nothing to do with the mild Leonardo. Raphael, at that time only a young man, was friendly with both artists. His works were more popular with artistically minded Pope Leo X than those of either of the older men.

During his stay in Florence, Leonardo had begun the portrait of a young married woman of the town named Monna Lisa Gioconda. As she sat for him, day after day, he would amuse her by telling her stories as he worked or converse with her on any subject in order to keep her interested in the dull task of posing. As the months passed, Monna Lisa and Leonardo were more and more drawn to each other. Both were essentially secretive persons who seemed to understand each other intuitively. Months passed into years, and still Monna Lisa came to the studio to pose. No one suspected anything improper of the meetings, but it became a source of amusement in Florence that the gentle artist, who had never before taken an interest in women, seemed to be in love. Monna Lisa's sudden death shocked Leonardo to the bottom of his soul. He had hoped to finish her portrait, to finish this one work at least, but with Monna Lisa's death his hopes fell. He had tried to show in her face the mystery of the universe, for he had found that the mystery of Monna Lisa and the mystery of the universe were one.

As a result of the trouble over the canal and the unfinished picture of the battle of Anghiari, Leonardo da Vinci was dismissed from the service of the city of Florence. He returned to Milan to serve under the new ruler of that city, Louis XII of France. There Giovanni Beltraffio again met Monna Cassandra. One day, she promised to show him the answers to his deepest questions. He was to meet her late that same night. As Giovanni left her, he was shocked to see in her face the expression of the White She-Demon, a specter that had haunted him since childhood.

Before the time for their meeting, however, Monna Cassandra was taken prisoner by the Most Holy Inquisition. Thinking her completely innocent, Giovanni visited all of his old friends in an effort to secure her release. The more he tried to help her, however, the more convinced he became that there were indeed evil spirits who inhabited the forms of human beings and that the White She-Demon was one of them. Unable to prevent Monna's death, Giovanni walked about the streets disconsolately. Suddenly he realized that the strange odor he had been smelling was the scent of burning flesh. Monna and one hundred and twenty-nine others accused as witches were being burned at the stake. Terror-stricken, he almost lost his mind. Later, still haunted by the White She-Demon, Giovanni committed suicide.

The loss of his favorite pupil would have been a more terrible blow to Leonardo if Francesco Melzi had not recently joined his group of students. Melzi, who was to be the true and faithful friend of the old artist, helped him through the final years of his life, especially in that trying period when the death of Louis XII left Leonardo without a patron, but the new French king, Francis I, soon afterward called Leonardo da Vinci to Paris. In 1516 Leonardo and his small group left Italy for France, and the artist was never to see his home country again.

In France he was well treated despite his inability to finish anything he began. He took up the Monna Lisa portrait again and almost finished it to his satisfaction from memory. One day King Francis visited him in his studio. Seeing the portrait, the king purchased it but agreed that Leonardo could keep his beloved portrait until he died.

King Francis did not have long to wait. A few years later Leonardo, old and weak, grew sick and died. His faithful pupil, Francesco Melzi, saw to it that Leonardo received the rites of the Church before his death. He also arranged to have the artist buried in a style which, he hoped, would forever still the whispering tongues that called Leonardo a disciple of the Antichrist to come.

Critical Evaluation:

Dmitry Merezhkovsky is frequently associated with the Symbolist movement of the late nineteenth century. He believed art should be recognized as humanity's highest metaphysical activity. Symbolism elevated idealism above materialism, aesthetics above science, imagination above reason, and subjectivity above objectivity. Drawing examples from ancient Greece, medieval Europe, Renaissance Italy, and Russia, Merezhkovsky argued that all great art is motivated by religious strivings. Greek tragedy was an attempt to place humanity in the cosmos. Gothic cathedrals indicate the desire for ascension. Michelangelo and Leonardo da Vinci were motivated by religious questions to develop a new theology. Likewise, Merezhkovsky considered Symbolist art theurgy, a means to higher truth, and the basis for spiritual revival in Russia. With the artist as spiritual guide, religion becomes a source of unity between artists and people.

The incompatibility of artists and the people became apparent as Symbolism grew as a cultural movement. Within the framework of Friedrich Nietzsche's theory of the superman, Merezhkovsky developed a new theology over the course of several decades. For Merezhkovsky, historical Christianity scorns the world and exalts selflessness, asceticism, and humility. Instead, he admired Christ as a superman who overcame death. He considered the next step in religious consciousness as the development of godmanhood, a process of spiritual evolution occurring in three distinct historical phases. The first humanity is the pre-Christian world of the flesh, depicted in the Old Testament. The second revelation, in the New Testament, revealed that spiritual love is truth. In the third revelation, the Holy Mother, who symbolizes the union of divine spirit and earthly flesh, ends human religious duality. The outcome is apocalyptic; a new humanity is created on earth, the world is transformed, and a new church is born.

Christ and Antichrist, the trilogy of novels in which *The Romance of Leonardo da Vinci* is the second, was Merezhkovsky's attempt to recapitulate the stages of world history and to delineate the features of the godman who would appear at the end. Each work in the trilogy focuses on a titanic figure who epitomized humanity in his own time. Taken together, the three volumes demonstrate Merezhkovsky's conviction that history is a dialectic between the two principles of paganism and Christianity, a dialectic that must ultimately be resolved. The work was written at different stages in Merezhkovsky's spiritual development, so the volumes are not unified and, ultimately, reflect the failure of his religious creation.

The first volume, *The Death of the Gods: Or, Julian the Apostate* (1896), is essentially a Nietzschean tract. Based on the Roman Emperor who attempted to restore paganism, it exalted courage, beauty, and defiance of death. The novel was successful throughout Europe due to its scandalous portrayal of sexuality and violent revelry. Julian embodies the Nietzschean ideal of sensuality. Paganism is the principle of happiness on earth, and it values personal freedom, beauty, sensuality, and prosperity.

The second volume, *The Romance of Leonardo da Vinci*, depicts the resurgence of paganism and an attempted reconciliation with Christianity by a godman. Leonardo harmonizes the principles of pagan beauty and sensuality and Christian spiritual tranquillity. As opposed to his contemporary, Michelangelo, who was ruled entirely by the flesh, Leonardo expresses a desire for ascension. Leonardo's plan for a flying machine indicates both the Christian desire for heaven and the pagan desire for superhuman powers. His paintings illustrate the harmonious combination of divergent elements. Their detailed accuracy stems from the careful observation of the world, but the details serve to recapture the living spirit of the subject. Leonardo combines masculine and feminine elements in himself and finds his feminine counterpart in Monna Lisa. Prefiguring the godman, Leonardo unites perfect love and perfect knowledge, strength and compassion, daring and humility, sensuality and intellect, idealism and practicality, art and science, love of beauty and spiritual yearning. His new religious consciousness was inconsistent; he wavered between Christian humility and pagan ideals of sensuality and personal freedom. Furthermore, his artistic efforts had to submit to political machinations. Leonardo ultimately emerges as a prophet of a new religion, not its fulfillment.

The novel combines stylistic elements typical of the Symbolist period with the copious detail of historical romance. The demonic motifs of the Symbolists, represented by Monna Cassandra and the White She-Devil, express a religious desire to explore evil's place in the divine scheme. The sun and its golden hue, prominent in *The Romance of Leonardo da Vinci*, signified paganism for the Symbolist poets. Images of scientific complexity and technology, such as mathematical calculations, architectural plans, and the camera obscura, reflect the futuristic bent of the art of Merezhkovsky's time. The novel makes no attempt at historical accuracy but does re-create the wealth of art, literature, and politics in Renaissance Italy. The uneasy relationship between art and politics in Renaissance Italy. The uneasy relationship between art and politics also presents a powerful critique of the literature of late nineteenth century Russia.

Although the novel's historical interest and relevant political commentary made it an international success, its characters are not fully developed. The novel is told primarily from Leonardo's point of view, but the narrator frequently interprets the action. *The Romance of Leonardo da Vinci* reads as a vehicle for Merezhkovsky's religious ideas rather than convincing fiction. He did, however, bring Italian Renaissance to the consciousness of Russians.

In later years, Merezhkovsky considered Leonardo a transition figure between the pagan past of art and beauty and the pagan future of science and reason. From this perspective, the pagan elements he represented were destined to grow until they overshadowed the Christian elements. The last novel of the trilogy, *Peter and Alexis* (1905), describes the dissolution of the synthesis prefigured by Leonardo. Christian and Pagan beliefs are represented by noble and idealistic figures, rendering their final incompatibility even more tragic. The novel reflects Merezhkovsky's growing disillusion with the Religious Philosophic Society he founded with his wife, poet Zinaida Hippius, and with the growing social turbulence in Russia. Merezhkovsky initiated a religious search, but did not see its fulfillment.

"Critical Evaluation" by Pamela Pavliscak

Bibliography:

Bedford, Charles. *The Seeker: D. S. Merezhkovsky*. Lawrence: University Press of Kansas, 1975. Explores the religion and ethics of Merezhkovsky. Examines the synthesis of Christianity and paganism attempted in Merezhkovsky's trilogy of historical novels and finds that *The Romance of Leonardo Da Vinci* most successfully combines the two.

Fedotov, Georgy. *The Russian Religious Mind*. 2 vols. Belmont, Mass.: Norland, 1975. Surveys Russian religious thought and practice. Provides valuable background to Merezhkovsky's literary efforts by summarizing contemporary religious beliefs.

Hippius, Zinaida. *Between Paris and St. Petersburg: Selected Diaries of Zinaida Hippius*. Translated by Temira Pachmuss. Champaign: University of Illinois Press, 1975. Merezhkovsky's wife outlines literary events in the lives of both authors and gives valuable insight into their religious and social ideas.

Pachmuss, Temira. *D. S. Merezhkovsky in Exile: The Master of the Genre of Biographie Romancée*. New York: Peter Lang, 1990. One of the few works on Merezhkovsky in English to devote attention primarily to his prose. Defines the genre of biographical romance and considers Merezhkovsky's historical novels as an example of the genre. Includes analysis of narrative structure, point of view, and characterization.

Rosenthal, Bernice G. *Dmitri Sergeevich Merezhkovsky and the Silver Age: The Development of a Revolutionary Mentality*. The Hague: Martinus Nijhoff, 1975. Offers an overview of the historical novels in the context of Merezhkovsky's philosophical thinking. Nietzsche's direct and indirect influence on Merezhkovsky is elaborated. Analysis of narrative structure, important themes, and characters.

THE ROMANCE OF THE FOREST

Type of work: Novel
Author: Ann Radcliffe (1764-1823)
Type of plot: Gothic
Time of plot: Seventeenth century
Locale: France and Savoy
First published: 1791

Principal characters:
ADELINE, a victim of intrigue
PIERRE DE LA MOTTE, her benefactor and a fugitive from justice
MADAME DE LA MOTTE, his wife
LOUIS, their son
THEODORE PEYROU, a young soldier
THE MARQUIS DE MONTALT, a villainous nobleman
ARNAUD LA LUC, a cleric and scholar
CLARA, his daughter
PETER, a loyal servant

The Story:

On a dark and tempestuous night, Pierre de la Motte left Paris to escape his creditors and prosecution by the law. Descended from an ancient house, he was a man whose passions often proved stronger than his conscience. Having dissipated his own fortune and that of his wife, he had engaged in various questionable schemes that brought him at last to disgrace and made this flight necessary. Leaving Paris with his wife and two faithful servants, he hoped to find a refuge in some village of the southern provinces. The departure was so sudden that there had been no time for the couple to say farewell to their son Louis, on duty with his regiment in Germany.

Several leagues from the city, the coachman, Peter, lost his way while driving across a wild heath. La Motte saw in the distance the lighted window of a small, ancient house. He dismounted and walked there in the hope of securing directions from its inmates. A grim-visaged man opened the door at his knock, ushered him into a desolate apartment, and abruptly locked the door behind him. Over the howling of the wind, la Motte could hear rough voices close at hand and the muffled sobbing of a woman.

The door was at last unlocked, and the forbidding ruffian reappeared, dragging by the hand a beautiful young woman of about eighteen. The man put a pistol to la Motte's breast and offered him his choice between death or taking the girl with him. When the girl begged him to take pity on her, la Motte was moved by her tears as much as by his own danger and readily assented. Other men appeared, and the now blindfolded prisoners were taken on horseback to the edge of the heath. There la Motte and the woman were put into his carriage. Followed by the threats and curses of the wild crew, Peter drove rapidly away. The agitated woman, thrust so strangely into the company of la Motte and his wife, gave her name only as Adeline. Not wishing to add to her distress and filled with pity for her, they did not pursue their questioning.

Several days later, the travelers reached the vast forest of Fontanville. The sun was setting when they were awed to see against the ruddy sky the towers of an ancient abbey. Soon after, when a carriage wheel broke and overturned the vehicle, they decided to return to the abbey.

During their explorations, they discovered a suite of apartments still habitable and of more modern date than the rest of the structure. Despite his wife's misgivings, la Motte decided to make the secluded abbey his place of refuge.

Peter, dispatched to a nearby village for provisions and furniture, returned with the report that the ruins were the property of a nobleman living on a distant estate. The country people also claimed that a mysterious prisoner had once been confined there, and although no one knew his fate, his ghost was supposed to haunt the scene of his imprisonment. For seventeen years, the natives of the region had not dared to approach the old abbey.

La Motte was well pleased with all that he heard; before long, he and his household had made their quarters comfortable. La Motte spent most of his mornings out of doors, either hunting or fishing, and his afternoons and evenings with his family. Sometimes he read, but more often he sat in gloomy silence. Only Adeline had power to enliven his spirits when he grew moody and depressed. She had fully recovered from her terrifying experience and had a sweet, lively disposition and diligent habits. After a time, she confided the story of her life to Madame de la Motte, whom she had begun to look upon as a mother.

She was the only child of the poor but reputable Chevalier de St. Pierre. With her mother dead, she had been reared in a convent, after which her father had intended that she should marry. When she refused, he rebuked her for her obstinacy and one day he took her not to his magnificent house in Paris but to that lonely house on the heath. There she had been turned over to the care of brutal keepers. Only the arrival of la Motte, she believed, had saved her from an unknown but terrible fate.

After a month in this forest refuge, la Motte regained a measure of his tranquillity and even cheerfulness, much to the delight of his wife and their ward. Then his mood suddenly changed again. As if he were preyed upon by some guilty secret or deep remorse, he avoided his family and spent many hours alone in the forest. Peter, the faithful servant, tried to follow his master on more than one occasion, but la Motte always eluded his follower and at one particular place disappeared as if the trees and rocks had swallowed him. About that time, Peter brought a report from the village that a stranger was in the neighborhood inquiring for his master. Greatly disturbed, la Motte remembered a trapdoor he had observed in one of the decaying chambers of the abbey. With the hope that it might lead to a place of hiding, he explored the passageway to which the trapdoor gave access and finally came to a room containing a large chest of ancient design. Throwing open the lid, he was horrified to find a human skeleton. Although he told them nothing about the gruesome remains in the chest, he insisted that his family join him in the hidden apartments he had discovered.

When he ventured out of hiding the next day, la Motte saw a stranger in the abbey. He returned quickly to his place of concealment. Their provisions, however, were running low, and at last it was decided that Adeline should reconnoiter the ruins to learn whether the supposed officer of the law had gone away. In the cloisters, she encountered a young man in military uniform. Although she tried to flee, he overtook her and demanded to know the whereabouts of Pierre de la Motte. Adeline's relief was as great as her joy when the stranger turned out to be Louis de la Motte, whose filial affection had drawn him to his father's side. Unfortunately, his growing fondness for Adeline completely destroyed Madame de la Motte's liking for her. To avoid the older woman's coldness, Adeline spent much of her time in the forest, where she composed poems inspired by the beauty of the landscape and her own gentle melancholy.

One day, while she was singing some stanzas of her own composition, a strange voice echoed her. Startled to find a young man in hunter's dress close at hand, she would have fled in fright if the stranger had not paused respectfully on seeing her agitation. Adeline decided to refrain for a time from walking so far from the abbey. On her return, Madame de la Motte added to her confusion by greeting her suspiciously.

About a month later, a party of horsemen arrived at the abbey during a violent midnight storm. When la Motte ignored their knocking, they pushed the decayed door from its hinges and stalked into the hall. Overcome by fear for her benefactor, Adeline fainted. She revived to find the young man of the forest in the room and learned from the conversation that his name was Theodore Peyrou and that his older companion, a chevalier of haughty demeanor, was the Marquis de Montalt, the owner of the abbey, who was staying at his hunting lodge on the edge of the forest. La Motte, who had fled when the knocking began, returned to the room. Immediately, he and the marquis regarded each other in great confusion, and the nobleman put his hand threateningly on his sword. He agreed, however, when la Motte requested a private discussion in another room. Madame de la Motte overheard enough of their conversation to realize that there was some secret between the two men.

The marquis and his retinue departed early in the morning. Returning the next day, the nobleman, after inquiring for la Motte, paid courteous attention to Adeline. When he and la Motte had disappeared into the forest on an errand of their own, Theodore remained with the ladies. Adeline suddenly realized that she was falling in love with the young man. Louis de la Motte prepared to return to his regiment. The marquis continued to visit the abbey almost every day. Adeline met Theodore in the forest, and he promised to meet her again the next evening but was unable to do so when the marquis suddenly ordered him to return to duty.

That night, Adeline dreamed that she was in a strange chamber of the abbey, where a cloaked guide conducted her to a coffin covered with a pall. When her guide lifted the covering, she saw a dead man lying within, blood gushing from his side. The next day, the marquis came for dinner and consented with reluctance to sleep at the abbey. A rearrangement of the private apartments was necessary to accommodate the guests. Adeline retired to a small chamber usually occupied by Madame de la Motte's maid. Behind an arras, she uncovered a door that led into the chamber she had seen in her dream. A rusted dagger lay on the floor; in a moldering bed, she found a small roll of manuscript. On her return to her room, she heard voices coming from the room below. To her horror, she heard the marquis declare his passionate intention to make her his. She retired in great distress of mind, to be aroused again when the nobleman, in evident alarm, left the abbey unceremoniously before daybreak. Later that same morning, the marquis returned and, over Adeline's protests, declared his suit. When she turned to la Motte for aid, he assured her that he was unable to help her, since his safety depended on the nobleman. So great was Adeline's despair that she almost forgot the manuscript she had found in the abandoned room. She had read enough of it, however, to realize that the despairing document had been written by the mysterious prisoner of the abbey, who had been a victim of the marquis. She also learned from Peter that the marquis had a wife still living.

To save the helpless girl, Peter promised to take her to his native village in Savoy. She was to meet him at an old tomb in the forest; but when she arrived at the place of meeting, a strange horseman appeared and despite her struggles carried her to the marquis' hunting lodge. There she managed to escape through a window. Theodore, who had returned from his regiment when he learned of the marquis' evil plans, joined her in her flight. In a carriage that he had waiting they drove all night in the direction of the frontier. At an inn where they stopped for some refreshment, they were overtaken by officers who tried to arrest Theodore in the king's name. Resisting, he received a saber cut in the head. He had almost recovered from his wound when the Marquis de Montalt appeared and ordered his men to seize Theodore on a charge of treason. Theodore, snatching up a sergeant's cutlass, wounded the marquis. During the confusion, Adeline was hustled into a chaise and driven back to the abbey, where la Motte locked her in her room. Anxious for word of Theodore, she was told a short time later that the young officer had been returned under arrest to his regiment.

By the time the marquis was able to travel, his passion for Adeline had turned to hate, and he ordered la Motte to kill the girl. The unscrupulous nobleman's hold over la Motte was strong, for that unhappy man, driven to desperation by his lack of funds, had during his early days at the abbey held up and robbed the marquis, whom he mistook for a chance traveler. Although he was completely in the marquis' power, la Motte refused to stain his hands with blood. Instead, he ordered the faithful Peter to take Adeline to Leloncourt, in Savoy, where she would be safe from the marquis' agents. When her flight was revealed, the nobleman had la Motte arrested for highway robbery and imprisoned.

Shortly after her arrival in Leloncourt, Adeline became ill. Arnaud la Luc, a scholarly clergyman, took her into his home, During her convalescence, she formed a close friendship with his daughter, Clara. Her grief over Theodore was so deep that she never mentioned him to her new friends. Then la Luc's health began to fail, and she and Clara accompanied him to the Mediterranean seacoast. There Adeline encountered Louis de la Motte and learned that he was on his way to Leloncourt on an errand for Theodore. To her great surprise, it was revealed that the man she knew as Theodore Peyrou was in reality the son of Arnaud la Luc. The travelers immediately hastened to Vaceau, where the young officer was being held under sentence of death.

Meanwhile, la Motte had been taken to Paris for trial on the charges brought against him by the marquis. The prisoner was in despair when an unexpected witness appeared in his behalf. The man was Du Bosse, one of the ruffians hired to dispose of Adeline while she was held prisoner in the lonely house on the heath. His story started an investigation, which revealed that Adeline was the natural daughter of the Marquis de Montalt, who had never seen the girl before he met her at the ruined abbey. In the past, one of his agents had always played the part of her father. The marquis was arrested and Adeline summoned to Paris for his trial. With his arrest, other of the marquis' activities came to light. He had ordered the murder of his older brother, whose skeleton la Motte had found in the abbey. The confederate also testified that Adeline was not the nobleman's natural daughter but his older brother's legitimate child, an heiress whom the marquis had tried to conceal from the world. The manuscript Adeline had found provided further evidence of her uncle's villainy. He was sentenced to death for his crimes.

When the extent of the marquis' evil schemes became known, Theodore received a royal pardon and was restored to his military rank. Pierre de la Motte was sentenced to exile in England, and Adeline provided for his comfort and that of his wife in their old age. She buried her father's skeleton, with all respect, in the vault of his ancestors. A short time later, she and Theodore married and went to live at Leloncourt. Clara married Monsieur Verneuil, Adeline's distant kinsman, who had been helpful to her and the la Lucs during the time of their distress over Theodore and la Motte. Before many years had passed, Louis de la Motte came with his bride to a house nearby, and there in Leloncourt the three deserving couples lived out their lives in happiness and prosperity.

Critical Evaluation:

The Romance of the Forest, a popular eighteenth century romance, marks Ann Radcliffe's contribution to the development of the novel genre. In her gothic tales, a damsel in distress must usually endure various trials involving danger, terror, and mystery. Underlying the plot is the opposition of good and evil. Radcliffe may employ such traditional elements of gothic fiction as dungeons, decaying castles, ghosts, and villains, but the conflict she portrays is between virtue and vice, and the novel sets up a fixed system of punishments and rewards. Powers of evil, whether natural or supernatural, are ultimately overruled.

Radcliffe's characters represent varying degrees of good and evil. Adeline, the heroine, is the most virtuous. She does not rebel against the evil forces that seek to destroy her but trusts her safety to divine providence. Her moral strength enables her to triumph despite her feminine vulnerability. Adeline, who faces both physical and emotional isolation, has mysterious origins, and she spends her childhood in a convent, apart from family. Later, her supposed father rejects her and places her in the hands of strangers. Radcliffe does not reveal Adeline's heritage and the facts regarding her father's identity and murder until the close of the novel.

Adeline is also isolated physically. Each time she tries to escape disaster, she is somehow imprisoned. After leaving the convent, she is first locked in a dark chamber with barred windows, then sent away with strangers to live in exile in the abbey ruins of the forest. There she is abducted from a black tomb by the marquis's servant and eventually returned to confinement in the abbey towers.

She escapes these physical barricades only when she flees France to seek asylum in the mountains of Savoy. Her new location is not only at a higher altitude but also on higher moral ground. The darkness of the forest and the plots to abduct her are here replaced by sunlight, open scenery, and the kindness of the la Luc family who assists her. Even here, however, her emotional isolation continues. The la Lucs care for her, but she remains separated from the knowledge of her true identity and from the man she loves.

Theodore, Adeline's lover and rescuer, is a virtuous young man who left home to study for the ministry but found himself ill-suited for the role of a clergyman. He seeks a more active vocation (and perhaps a less devout life) by joining the military and finds himself in service to the villainous Marquis de Montalt. Theodore attempts to save Adeline, but because he leaves his military post and later physically attacks the Marquis de Montalt he is arrested for desertion and assault. He cannot rely on his innocence and virtue to save him because he has broken the law. Theodore faces a death sentence more imminent than the threats Adeline endured, but since Theodore's motives were honorable, he is eventually released from prison and rewarded with the love of the heroine.

Unlike Theodore, who breaks rules to save Adeline, Pierre de la Motte and his wife often commit wrongs for selfish ends. La Motte, who lost the family fortune through self-indulgence, finds that he is capable of ever greater evil—cheating, stealing, and finally attacking and robbing innocent victims—to preserve his own welfare. Thus, he conspires to deliver Adeline into the hands of the marquis to save himself. Yet la Motte is not totally depraved; Radcliffe asserts that his heart was betrayed by "weakness rather than natural depravity." He had fallen victim to the temptations of the "dissipations of Paris." Madame de la Motte too is weak. She at first befriends Adeline but then rejects her when she succumbs to jealously and suspicion. Later, when she learns of the Marquis's plot to abduct Adeline, she acquiesces in the scheme even though she knows that Adeline is innocent of any offenses.

The la Mottes have a capacity for both good and evil. Their natural inclination toward politeness and pity is their redeeming quality, which surfaces when they are called on to save Adeline's life. Radcliffe rejuvenates the couple's moral reputations by using them to resolve the plot, for it is their information that leads to Theodore's acquittal and the marquis's demise. Ultimately, the la Mottes cannot be pardoned as Theodore was because their transgressions are more serious. The couple escapes prison sentences and death penalties, but they must face exile.

The greatest evil is embodied in the character of the Marquis de Montalt, who has no redeeming qualities. Unlike the la Mottes, the marquis is not capable of good impulses. He is the antithesis of Adeline, who possesses no title, birthright or position but is virtuous. The marquis has the appearance of virtue but is evil. His "elegance of manners" merely "veiled the depravity of his heart." He identifies Adeline as his niece and restores her inheritance, but these actions reflect defeat rather than repentance.

Radcliffe's tale presents a picture of a fallen world. Original sin has fostered moral decay, temptation, and death. The wild, overgrown forest resembles the corruption of Eden. The lost manuscript and rusty dagger that Adeline finds in the abbey are symbols of the excesses that eventually destroy the marquis. Even Adeline is affected by her fallen world. She is deceived about her own identity and becomes a victim of those who are less upright. Yet virtue ultimately triumphs, and each character receives a proper reward. Hence, Radcliffe assures her readers, justice, however long delayed, will overtake the guilty.

"Critical Evaluation" by Paula M. Miller

Bibliography:

Bruce, Donald Williams. "Ann Radcliffe and the Extended Imagination." *Contemporary Review* 258 (June, 1991): 300-308. Discusses Radcliffe's use of imagination in shaping her descriptions of landscape to correlate with the development of her heroines. Includes historical information regarding her study of Italian travelogues.

Cottom, Daniel. *The Civilized Imagination: A Study of Ann Radcliffe, Jane Austen, and Sir Walter Scott*. New York: Cambridge University Press, 1985. A scholarly examination of the link between Radcliffe's novels and eighteenth century English society. Cottom focuses on the relationships of the female protagonists and social values.

Durant, David. "Ann Radcliffe and the Conservative Gothic." *Studies in English Literature* 22, no. 3 (Summer, 1982): 519-530. Durant proposes that Radcliffe's gothic fiction is a reaction against romanticism and the irrational. Discusses Radcliffe's heroines and their rejection of the "fallen world."

Ringe, Donald. A. *American Gothic: Imagination and Reason in Nineteenth-Century Fiction*. Lexington: University Press of Kentucky, 1982. In chapter 2, Ringe addresses the use in fiction of the supernatural, dreams, and the psychological motivation. Cites Radcliffe's novel for its use of those traditional elements of the gothic tradition.

Tracy, Ann B. *The Gothic Novel 1790-1830: Plot Summaries and Index to Motifs*. Lexington: University Press of Kentucky, 1981. Includes a synopsis of Ann Radcliffe's major novels, including *The Romance of the Forest*. Includes a very strong introductory chapter, which discusses the common themes and important elements of gothic fiction.

ROMANCE OF THE THREE KINGDOMS

Type of work: Novel
Author: Lo Kuan-chung (c. 1320-c. 1380)
Type of plot: Historical
Time of plot: c. 180-c. 280
Locale: China
First published: *San kuo chih yen-i*, fourteenth century (English translation, 1925)

Principal characters:

LIU PEI, a distant descendant of the royal family of the Han dynasty and the founder of the Shu Kingdom
KUAN YÜ, Liu Pei's sworn brother, later apotheosized as the God of War
CHANG FEI, the sworn brother of Liu and Kuan and a blunt soldier of great prowess
CHU-KO LIANG, chief strategist and eventually the prime minister to Liu Pei and to his weakling successor
TS'AO TS'AO, the founder of the Wei Kingdom, noted for his unscrupulous resourcefulness
SUN CH'ÜAN, the founder of the Wu Kingdom
CHOU YÜ, Sun Ch'üan's brilliant military commander, perpetually piqued by Chu-ko Liang's superior intelligence
CHAO YÜN, a brave general of the Shu Han Kingdom
LÜ PU, an unprincipled and matchless warrior famous for his romantic involvement with the beauty Tiao Ch'an
SSU-MA I, the founder of the all-powerful Ssu-ma family in the Wei Kingdom
CHIANG WEI, Chu-ko Liang's successor

The Story:

When the Yellow Turban rebellion was finally quashed, the many soldiers of fortune who took part in its suppression seized power for themselves, thus precipitating the downfall of the Eastern Han dynasty. Among these the most shrewd and successful politician was Ts'ao Ts'ao, who had already attracted a large following of able strategists and warriors. After the systematic elimination of his many rivals, such as Tung Cho, Lü Pu, Yuan Shao, and Yuan Shu, he ruled over North China as the King of Wei, subjecting the Han Emperor and his court to great indignity.

Liu Pei, who also rose to fame during the Yellow Turban rebellion, was for a long time doing very poorly, despite the legendary prowess of his sworn brothers, Kuan Yü and Chang Fei. It was not until he sought out Chu-ko Liang and made him his chief strategist that his fortunes began to improve. In time he ruled over Szechwan as the King of Shu.

While Liu Pei was beginning to mend his fortunes, the only man who blocked Ts'ao Ts'ao's territorial ambitions was Sun Ch'üan, who had inherited from his father and older brother the rich kingdom of Wu, south of the Yangtze. When Ts'ao Ts'ao finally decided to cross the Yangtze and subdue Wu, Sun Ch'üan and Liu Pei formed an alliance, and the combined strategy of their respective military commanders, Chou Yü and Chu-ko Liang, subjected Ts'ao Ts'ao's forces to a crushing defeat in the Battle of Red Cliff. After this victory Liu Pei went to Szechwan, and the precarious balance of power of the Three Kingdoms was established.

The friendly relationship between Shu and Wu did not last long. Kuan Yü, entrusted with the vital task of governing the province of Hupeh, adjacent to the Wu territory, had antagonized Sun Ch'üan, and in the subsequent military struggle he was killed. Liu Pei now vowed to conquer Wu; against the sage advice of Chu-ko Liang, who wanted to conciliate Wu so as to counter their more dangerous common enemy, Wei, he led a personal expedition against Wu and suffered a disastrous defeat. Liu Pei died soon afterward.

Liu Pei's son and successor was a moronic weakling. Out of loyalty to his late master, however, Chu-ko Liang was determined to serve him and improve the fortunes of Shu. He made peace with Wu and led several expeditions against Wei. These campaigns ended in a stalemate. Overburdened with work and handicapped by the lack of able generals (of the "Five Tiger Warriors" of Liu Pei's day, only Chao Yün had remained, an old fighter as intrepid as ever), Chu-ko Liang could no longer direct his campaigns with his usual brilliance. Moreover, the Wei commander, Ssu-ma I, whose family had become increasingly powerful in the Wei court following the death of Ts'ao Ts'ao, was in many ways his match. Finally Chu-ko Liang died of physical exhaustion.

By that time the Ssu-mas had usurped the power of Wei and had subjected Ts'ao Ts'ao's descendants to as much cruelty and torture as Ts'ao Ts'ao and his immediate successor had subjected the Han emperors. Wu and Shu had weakened. Although Chiang Wei, the Shu general, tried bravely to stem the tide, he was overwhelmed by the numerical strength of the invading Wei forces, under the command of T'eng Ai and Chung Hui. Soon after the death of Chiang Wei, the kings of Shu and Wu surrendered. Ssu-ma Yen, Ssu-ma I's grandson, now ruled as the first Emperor of China.

Critical Evaluation:

Instead of maintaining a single imperial family line from millennium to millennium, as in Japan, China traditionally had a succession of ruling houses, or dynasties, which rose and fell in a cyclical pattern. Whenever a dynasty reached the point of collapse, the field was thrown open for the era's most talented and ambitious soldiers of fortune to form alliances and fight with rival camps in struggles that let to the establishment of a new dynasty. Periods of dynastic change occasionally stretched into decades if no single camp could prevail over all its competitors, as was the case in the time in which this story is set. Ironically, the highly talented first generation of contenders witnessed a protracted stalemate in the struggle. Its members eventually died off, while the much weaker second generation blundered its way into the reunification of the empire.

The bulk of *Romance of the Three Kingdoms* deals with the extraordinary accomplishments and tragic shortcomings of the first generation of strategists and warriors. Epic grandeur suffuses Lo Kuan-chung's novelistic synthesis of historical accounts and folk story cycles. For reasons about which scholars can only speculate, China lacked the sort of grand verse epic found in most of the great ancient civilizations. *Romance of the Three Kingdoms*, however, emerged to an ascendant position as the nation's enduring epic in prose. The epic warrior hero, Kuan Yü, even achieved the status of a deity in the popular mind. By the late imperial age, China housed more temples devoted to the worship of Lord Kuan Yü, God of War, than to any other deity aside from the local Earth God.

Long before his ascent to the throne as the ruler of Shu Han in the southwest, Liu Pei emerged as the most sympathetic contender in the grand struggle. As a humble provincial member of the Liu clan that produced all of the Han dynasty emperors, Liu Pei entered the fray not out of personal ambition but rather as a result of an altruistic yearning to thwart the Machiavellian usurper, Chancellor Ts'ao Ts'ao, and thereby restore the house of Han. Unlike Ts'ao Ts'ao of Wei and Sun Ch'üan of Wu, Liu Pei repeatedly placed the imperative of virtue and benevolence above the dictates of expediency, even when this prevented him from securing various important military objectives. Although the loss of these military objectives resulted in temporary setbacks for Liu Pei from time to time, his principled conduct strengthened the ties of loyalty and dedication that bonded him with his sworn brothers, scholarly military advisers, rank-and-file soldiers, and civilian subjects.

At the levels of elite and popular culture in China, Liu Pei has long been revered as a model of kingly virtue and benevolence. Liu Pei's sworn brothers Kuan Yü and Chang Fei have similarly been celebrated as beacons of martial courage and loyalty, while the military strategist and ministerial adviser Chu-ko Liang has long fired the imagination of Chinese readers and theatergoers as an embodiment of wisdom and shrewd statecraft. These men, however, were not the stick figures of a morality play, but characters whose failings loomed almost as large as their strengths. Kuan Yü's fame for bravery often went to his head, and his arrogant dismissal of Sun Ch'üan's proposal to strengthen the ties between the Shu and Wu with intermarriage led to the deterioration of relations between the two states and to his eventual capture and decapitation at the hands of Sun Ch'üan. Liu Pei placed his personal oath of sworn loyalty to Kuan Yü above the long-term collective interests of restoring the Han dynasty, and, over Chu-ko Liang's strong objections, he led an abortive attack on Wu simply to avenge Kuan Yü's execution. After the ensuing military debacle and chaotic retreat back to Shu, Liu Pei's health failed. When he expressed his deathbed wish that Chu-ko Liang ascend the throne of Shu rather than let it pass to Liu Pei's moronic son, Chu-ko Liang doggedly insisted on serving as the foolish son's adviser, even though he knew that the son's succession would lead to the rapid and irreversible decline of Shu as a serious contender in the struggle to reunite China. Chu-ko Liang thus epitomizes the unwavering dedication to a noble but unrealizable enterprise of the sort that Confucius had long ago linked to the life of virtue.

"Critical Evaluation" by Philip F. Williams

Bibliography:

Hsia, C. T. *The Classic Chinese Novel: A Critical Introduction.* New York: Columbia University Press, 1968. Contains an introductory analysis of *Romance of the Three Kingdoms* that is the best starting point for appreciation of this novel. Insightful regarding the conflict between the claims of statecraft and of personal loyalties.

Lu Hsün. *A Brief History of Chinese Fiction.* Translated by Yang Hsien-yi and Gladys Yang. Peking: Foreign Languages Press, 1976. The section on *Romance of the Three Kingdoms* includes an interesting comparison of the early version of the novel with the finished version.

Plaks, Andrew H., ed. *Chinese Narrative: Critical and Theoretical Essays.* Princeton, N.J.: Princeton University Press, 1977. Two essays compare *Romance of the Three Kingdoms* with other Chinese literary masterpieces.

______________. *The Four Masterworks of the Ming Novel.* Princeton, N.J.: Princeton University Press, 1987. Insightful and in-depth interpretations of *Romance of the Three Kingdoms* and the other three novels of the Ming dynasty.

Rolston, David L., ed. *How to Read the Chinese Novel.* Princeton, N.J.: Princeton University Press, 1990. A pioneering collection of translated essays by major premodern Chinese critics. The essay on *Romance of the Three Kingdoms* provides a vivid sense of how the Chinese interpreted this novel centuries ago.

THE ROMANTIC COMEDIANS

Type of work: Novel
Author: Ellen Glasgow (1873-1945)
Type of plot: Fiction of manners
Time of plot: 1920's
Locale: Richmond, Virginia
First published: 1926

Principal characters:
JUDGE GAMALIEL BLAND HONEYWELL, a widower of sixty-five
ANNABEL, his twenty-three-year-old second wife
MRS. UPCHURCH, Annabel's mother
EDMONIA BREDALBANE, the Judge's sister
AMANDA LIGHTFOOT, the Judge's childhood sweetheart

The Story:

As Judge Honeywell walked home from church on the first Easter morning after his wife's death, he was surprised by his own reactions to the Virginia springtime. He felt quite young, for sixty-five, and life with his wife, now dead, seemed so remote as never to have happened. In fact, he felt relieved, for his first wife had seldom let him lead an existence of his own.

The Judge hospitably looked after Mrs. Upchurch and her daughter Annabel because they were kinswomen of his late wife; but shortly after a memorable Easter morning, he began to think of twenty-three-year-old Annabel in quite another way. His changed attitude began because he was secretly sorry for her. She had been engaged to a young man who had left her almost at the altar. It had hurt her bitterly, as the Judge and her mother knew.

As time passed, Judge Honeywell found himself thinking more and more of Annabel Upchurch and of Amanda Lightfoot, his childhood sweetheart. Unfortunately, the Judge's sister, Mrs. Bredalbane, tried to convince him that falling in love with Amanda would be the sensible thing to do. The Judge promptly closed his mind to Amanda and began thinking more of Annabel, who had asked the Judge if he would help her to open a flower shop.

Soon the Judge had purchased a house with a large garden for Mrs. Upchurch and her daughter, so that Annabel might practice landscape gardening. When he told the girl, he added that he only expected the reward of seeing her happy; but when she left, he kissed her.

By the time that Mrs. Upchurch and Annabel were settled in their new home, the Judge knew he was in love with Annabel, who was more than forty years younger than he. He bought new clothes and had his hair and beard trimmed to lessen the amount of gray which had appeared. He felt that he could give Annabel everything she needed—love, tenderness, security, and wealth.

The number and quality of the Judge's gifts soon made apparent to Annabel and her mother what was on the old man's mind. Annabel thought at first that it would be more suitable for him to marry her mother; however, as she informed her mother, marrying an older man was certainly better than living in an atmosphere of shabby gentility. Annabel decided to visit Amanda Lightfoot. Knowing that Amanda had never married because she had been in love with the Judge, Annabel wished to find out if the older woman still loved him. If she did not, Annabel decided, she herself would marry him, but the older woman almost refused to say anything at all. Annabel was disappointed but secretly relieved. When she arrived home, Judge Honeywell was waiting with a present for her, a sapphire bracelet. Before he left the house, he told her he loved her, and she accepted him.

After the marriage, the Judge and Annabel traveled in Europe and in England. The Judge felt that he was as fine a man as he had been at thirty-five, although his nerves were jarred a little when someone occasionally referred to Annabel as his daughter. That she often danced with young men did not bother him. He felt no envy of their youth; after all, she was his wife.

The Judge was glad to be back in his home in Virginia after the honeymoon. His dyspepsia soon disappeared after he began to eat familiar cooking once more, and he felt at peace to be living in the familiar old house, which had not been refurnished in more than thirty years.

The couple dined out frequently and went to many dances. The Judge, after noting how silly his contemporaries appeared on the dance floor, abstained from any dancing, but he encouraged Annabel to enjoy herself. He always went with her, not from jealousy but because he felt that he had to keep up with her life. It cost him a great deal of effort, for on those evenings he sometimes thought that he had never before known what fatigue was really like.

At home, Annabel had brought changes into the house. While he did not approve, Judge Honeywell said nothing until she tried to change the furniture in his own room. She learned then, although it cost him a ring she had admired, that he would not let her meddle with his own privacy.

When the Judge came down with bronchitis, Annabel proved an able and attentive nurse. During his convalescence, however, she found it difficult to remain at home reading night after night. He, noticing her restlessness, told her to begin going out again, even though he could not go with her. When Annabel went out, her mother or the Judge's sister would come to have dinner and stay with him during the evening.

The passing weeks brought a change in Annabel which many people noticed. Noted for her boisterous spirits and lack of reticence, she surprised them by becoming more vague about her comings and goings. At the same time, they complimented the Judge on how happy she seemed. The compliments made the old gentleman content, for, as he said, Annabel's happiness was what he wanted most.

Slowly, Judge Honeywell began to feel that all was not right in his home. Annabel was distant in her manner. When he talked with his sister and Annabel's mother, both reassured him of his wife's devotion. Still, he knew something was not right. He received proof one day when he found Annabel kissing a young man. Dabney Birdsong belonged to an old family in the community. Annabel had resolved to have him, cost what it might. To the Judge, his greatest sorrow was that it might be only an infatuation which would not make Annabel happy. Annabel, on the other hand, thought if she did not have Dabney, she would die.

Annabel and her lover ran away and went to New York. The Judge followed them to the city. Unable to understand his young wife, he felt sorry for her because she defied convention, and he thought that he himself was to blame for what had happened. After a talk with Annabel he left New York, defeated, to return to Virginia.

The rain and the drafty train gave the Judge a cold that turned into influenza, and he was in bed for several weeks in a serious condition. During his convalescence, he discovered that spring had once more arrived. With the stirring in nature, he felt a resurgence of life in his weary body. Like many an old man before him, the season of freshness and greenery gave him the feeling of youth that he had had on the previous Easter Sunday morning. He found himself beginning to look with new, eager interest at the young nurse who was attending him during his illness.

Critical Evaluation:

Ellen Glasgow has been largely overlooked by students of American literature. Her output was prodigious, and her penetrating analysis of the social history of Virginia from 1850 to 1930, her insight into the position of women, and her brilliant use of ironic characterization are qualities that set her apart from the mass of popular novelists of the first third of the century and necessitate a reevaluation of her work.

It was Glasgow's colleague, James Branch Cabell, who first called her a social historian; reviewing *Barren Ground* (1925), he said that her books, taken collectively, were a "portrayal of all social and economic Virginia since the War Between the States." Other critics and Glasgow herself accepted the label; despite its accuracy, the phrase "social historian" is too narrow for the wide range of Glasgow's talents. She has also suffered from commentary by antagonistic male critics. Never one to accept a "woman's role," Glasgow often attacked those whose writing or person she did not admire. This penchant, as well as her creation of less-than-admirable male characters, has led to some highly questionable commentary about both her life and work. As late as 1971, one critic commented on her "anti-maleness," and then went on to contradict himself: "She continued to pursue the male of her own species with glee." Such unmeasured statements have not helped Glasgow's literary reputation.

Properly, Glasgow should be seen as an early member of the Southern Literary Renaissance. In 1931, she helped to organize a conference of Southern writers at the University of Virginia, attended by William Faulkner, Sherwood Anderson, and Allen Tate, among others. She was always interested in her native Virginia and wrote perceptively about various epochs and social classes. If her view is often an ironic one, it nevertheless helps the reader to see the love-hate relationship that she had with the South. She judges, but with a sympathetic voice.

The Romantic Comedians was published soon after the more famous *Barren Ground* and is, like Glasgow's succeeding work *They Stooped to Folly* (1929), a novel of manners. Like all such works, *The Romantic Comedians* depends for much of its impact on tone and point of view, for neither plot nor characters are unique. The novel relies on the reader's knowledge of similar situations and characters in making its ironic commentary. From the outset, the narrator directs the readers' attitudes. Characters' names satirically reveal inner traits: "Bland Honeywell," "Upchurch," "Bredalbane," "Lightfoot." Judge Honeywell is seen as a slightly ridiculous figure, interested in the outward demonstration of his grief and unable to understand correctly his own emotions: "'I am a bird with a broken wing,' he sighed to himself." This romantic outward show of grief over his dead wife lacked sincerity, for simultaneously, he "felt an odd palpitation . . . where his broken wing was helplessly trying to flutter." Glasgow shows herself to be in the great tradition of Jane Austen and George Eliot, two other ironic critics of society.

Judge Honeywell is portrayed as a man of a bygone era, unable to understand or adjust to new ideas, yet somewhat naïvely excited by the prospect of Annabel's youth and beauty. He has firm values that nevertheless do not alter his self-interested actions. His most endearing characteristic is his willingness to forgive Annabel, but this too he carries to excess, needlessly accepting the guilt for her unhappiness.

Not only is Judge Honeywell satirized but also all the other characters are shown to be romantic or a bit ridiculous. Annabel is deluded by imagining that ultimate personal happiness is attainable and of primary importance. Her amoral attitude does, however, cut through the hypocrisy and moral sham of people like her mother and Amanda Lightfoot. Annabel asserts that perfect ladies "lie as perfectly as they behave." Edmonia Bredalbane carries her "scandalous" behavior to an extreme which, even in its refreshing lack of convention, is shown to be silly. Glasgow reverses the generally accepted roles in the relationship of the Judge and his twin sister; here the woman is emancipated and the man tied by convention.

The theme of the novel is voiced by Mrs. Upchurch who muses on "the popular superstition that love and happiness are interchangeable terms." She notes that both old and young, old-fashioned and modern, are "enslaved" by this illusion. The Judge, Amanda, Annabel, Dabney, "all this company of happiness-hunters appeared to be little better than a troupe of romantic comedians." This attitude seems to be the view of the narrator as well, but Mrs. Upchurch is not always the narrator's mouthpiece. In fact, Mrs. Upchurch's pragmatic morality, which shifts radically depending on the situation, is as often laughed at as the Judge's unyielding system. Mrs. Upchurch, however, has a more realistic view of life than any other character.

Glasgow displays skill not only in the consistency of her tone but also in her use of images to suggest character. The Judge always thinks of Annabel in terms of nature—"fields and streams," "tall wind-blown grasses," the "April mist" in her eyes; yet these very qualities in Annabel—her "natural" freedom and amorality—doom their marriage; wild nature cannot become domestic and maternal. As their relationship deteriorates, he begins to think of her in terms of images of light without heat: She lacks the warmth he craves. She is like "the fire at the heart of an opal"; her head is like "November leaves in the sunlight"; after she runs off with Dabney, she looks alive "not as a flower, but as a jewel."

Although the point of view is most often centered in Judge Honeywell's consciousness, the narrator sometimes inserts commentary to make her attitude more obvious. Usually this is unobtrusive, but occasionally it becomes an affectation of style or a violation of the convention already established. An example would be the phrase, "like most lawyers and all vestrymen" in beginning a comment on the Judge. In general, though, Glasgow's ironic tone is consistent, pungent, and entertaining. The female characters—including the dead Cordelia—each represent a distinctive way of dealing with the role assigned to women in the South of the 1920's. These aspects make Glasgow more than a social historian and suggest a higher place for her in the hierarchy of American letters.

"Critical Evaluation" by Margaret McFadden-Gerber

Bibliography:

Godbold, E. Stanly, Jr. *Ellen Glasgow and the Woman Within.* Baton Rouge: Louisiana State University Press, 1972. A reliable biography with useful comments on Glasgow's major novels. Some criticism.

Holman, C. Hugh. "The Comedies of Manners." In *Ellen Glasgow: Centennial Essays*, edited by M. Thomas Inge. Charlottesville: University Press of Virginia, 1976. Contrasts the comedy of the Queensborough trilogy with the didacticism of earlier realistic novels. Focuses on Glasgow's narrative techniques (influenced by Henry James) and points out similarities and differences among the three novels.

Raper, Julius Rowan. *From the Sunken Garden: The Fiction of Ellen Glasgow, 1916-1945.* Baton Rouge: Louisiana State University Press, 1980. Thoughtful commentary on all major novels. Argues that *The Romantic Comedians* displays a classic comic pattern (subversion of gerontocracy by youth).

Rouse, Blair. *Ellen Glasgow.* New York: Twayne, 1962. Good introduction to Glasgow's fiction. Views Queensborough as the essence of several Virginia towns and suggests tragic overtones within the comedy of *The Romantic Comedians.* Annotated bibliography.

Santas, Joan Foster. *Ellen Glasgow's American Dream.* Charlottesville: University Press of Virginia, 1965. Sees *The Romantic Comedians* along with *They Stooped to Folly* and *The Sheltered Life* (1932) as a progressive study of the limitations of a fading Virginia aristocracy.

ROMEO AND JULIET

Type of work: Drama
Author: William Shakespeare (1564-1616)
Type of plot: Tragedy
Time of plot: Fifteenth century
Locale: Verona, Italy
First performed: c. 1595-1596; first published, 1597

Principal characters:
Romeo, son of the house of Montague
Juliet, daughter of the house of Capulet
Friar Laurence, a Franciscan
Mercutio, Romeo's friend
Tybalt, Lady Capulet's nephew

The Story:

In Verona, Italy, there lived two famous families, the Montagues and the Capulets. These two houses were deadly enemies, and their enmity did not stop at harsh words, but extended to bloody duels. Romeo, son of old Montague, thought himself in love with haughty Rosaline, a beautiful girl who did not return his affection. Hearing that Rosaline was to attend a great feast at the house of Capulet, Romeo and his trusted friend, Mercutio, donned masks and entered the great hall of their enemy as guests. Romeo was no sooner in the ballroom than he noticed the exquisite Juliet, Capulet's daughter, and instantly forgot his disdainful Rosaline. Romeo had never seen Juliet before, and in asking her name he aroused the suspicion of Tybalt, a fiery member of the Capulet clan. Tybalt drew his sword and faced Romeo. Old Capulet, coming upon the two men, parted them, and with the gentility that comes with age requested that they have no bloodshed at the feast. Tybalt, however, was angered that a Montague should take part in Capulet festivities and afterward nursed a grudge against Romeo.

Romeo went to Juliet, spoke in urgent courtliness to her, and asked if he might kiss her hand. She gave her permission, much impressed by this unknown gentleman whose affection for her was so evident. Romeo then begged to kiss her lips, and when she had no breath to object, he pressed her to him. They were interrupted by Juliet's nurse, who sent the young girl off to her mother. When she had gone, Romeo learned from the nurse that Juliet was a Capulet. He was stunned, for he was certain that this fact would mean his death. He could never give her up. Juliet, who had fallen instantly in love with Romeo, discovered that he was a Montague, the son of a hated house.

That night Romeo, too much in love to go home to sleep, stole to Juliet's house and stood in the orchard beneath a balcony that led to her room. To his surprise, he saw Juliet leaning over the railing above him. Thinking herself alone, she began to talk of Romeo and wished aloud that he were not a Montague. Hearing her words, Romeo could contain himself no longer, but spoke to her. She was frightened at first, and when she saw who it was she was confused and ashamed that he had overheard her confession. It was too late to pretend reluctance. Juliet freely admitted her passion, and the two exchanged vows of love. Juliet told Romeo that she would marry him and would send him word by nine o'clock the next morning to arrange for their wedding.

Romeo then went off to the monastery cell of Friar Laurence to enlist his help in the ceremony. The good friar was much impressed with Romeo's devotion. Thinking that the union of a Montague and a Capulet would dissolve the enmity between the two houses, he promised to marry Romeo and Juliet.

Early the next morning, while he was in company with his two friends, Benvolio and Mercutio, Romeo received Juliet's message, brought by her nurse. He told the old woman of his arrangement with Friar Laurence and bade her carry the word back to Juliet. The nurse gave her mistress the message. When Juliet appeared at the friar's cell at the appointed time, she and Romeo were married. Time was short, however, and Juliet had to hurry home. Before she left, Romeo promised that he would meet her in the orchard underneath the balcony after dark that night.

That same day, Romeo's friends, Mercutio and Benvolio, were loitering in the streets when Tybalt came by with some other members of the Capulet house. Tybalt, still holding his grudge against Romeo, accused Mercutio of keeping company with the hateful and villainous young Montague. Mercutio, proud of his friendship with Romeo, could not take insult lightly, for he was as hot-tempered when provoked as Tybalt. The two were beginning their heated quarrel when Romeo, who had just returned from his wedding, appeared. He was appalled at the situation because he knew that Juliet was fond of Tybalt, and he wished no injury to his wife's people. He tried in vain to settle the argument peaceably. Mercutio was infuriated by Romeo's soft words, and when Tybalt called Romeo a villain, Mercutio drew his sword and rushed to his friend's defense. Tybalt, the better swordsman, gave Mercutio a mortal wound. Romeo could try to settle the fight no longer. Enraged at the death of his friend, he rushed at Tybalt with drawn sword and killed him quickly. The fight soon brought crowds of people to the spot. For his part in the fray, Romeo was banished from Verona.

Hiding out from the police, he went, grief-stricken, to Friar Laurence's cell. The friar advised him to go to his wife that night, and then at dawn to flee to Mantua until the friar saw fit to publish the news of the wedding. Romeo consented to follow this advice. As darkness fell, he went to meet Juliet. When dawn appeared, heartsick Romeo left for Mantua.

Meanwhile, Juliet's father decided that it was time for his daughter to marry. Having not the slightest idea of her love for Romeo, the old man demanded that she accept her handsome and wealthy suitor, Paris. Juliet was horrified at her father's proposal but dared not tell him of her marriage because of Romeo's part in Tybalt's death. She feared that her husband would be instantly sought out and killed if her family learned of the marriage.

At first she tried to put off her father with excuses. Failing to persuade him, she went in dread to Friar Laurence to ask the good monk what she could do. Telling her to be brave, the friar gave her a small flask of liquid which he told her to swallow the night before her wedding to Paris. This liquid would make her appear to be dead for a certain length of time; her seemingly lifeless body would then be placed in an open tomb for a day or two, and during that time the friar would send for Romeo, who would rescue his bride when she awoke from the powerful effects of the draught. Then, together, the two would be able to flee Verona. Juliet almost lost courage over this desperate venture, but she promised to obey the friar. On the way home she met Paris and modestly promised to be his bride.

The great house of the Capulets had no sooner prepared for a lavish wedding than it became the scene of a mournful funeral. Juliet swallowed the strong liquid and seemed lifeless. Her anguished family sadly placed her body in the tomb.

Meanwhile Friar Laurence wrote to Romeo in Mantua, telling him of the plan by which the lovers could make their escape together. These letters, however, failed to reach Romeo before word of Juliet's death arrived. He determined to go to Verona and take his last farewell of her as she lay in her tomb, and there, with the help of poison procured from an apothecary, to die by her side.

Reaching the tomb at night, Romeo was surprised to find a young man there. It was Paris, who had come to weep over his lost bride. Thinking Romeo a grave robber, he drew his sword. Romeo, mistaking Paris for a hated Capulet, warned him that he was desperate and armed. Paris, in loyalty to Juliet, fell upon Romeo, but Romeo killed him. By the light of a lantern, Romeo recognized Paris and, taking pity on one who had also loved Juliet, drew him into the tomb so that Paris too could be near her. Then Romeo went to the bier of his beautiful bride. Taking leave of her with a kiss, he drank the poison he had brought with him and soon died by her side.

It was near the time for Juliet to awaken from her deathlike sleep. The friar, hearing that Romeo had never received his letters, went himself to deliver Juliet from the tomb. When he arrived, he found Romeo dead. Juliet, waking, asked for her husband. Then, seeing him lying near her with an empty cup in his hands, she guessed what he had done. She tried to kiss some of the poison from his lips that she too might die, but failing in this, she unsheathed his dagger and without hesitation plunged it into her breast.

By this time a guard had come up. Seeing the dead lovers and the body of Paris, he rushed off in horror to spread the news. When the Capulets and Montagues arrived at the tomb, the friar told them of the unhappy fate which had befallen Romeo and Juliet, whose only sin had been to love. His account of their tender and beautiful romance shamed the two families, and over the bodies of their dead children they swore to end the feud of many years.

Critical Evaluation:

This story of star-crossed lovers is one of William Shakespeare's tenderest dramas. Shakespeare is sympathetic toward Romeo and Juliet, and in attributing their tragedy to fate, rather than to a flaw in their characters, he raised them to heights near perfection, as well as running the risk of creating pathos, not tragedy. They are both sincere, kind, brave, loyal, virtuous, and desperately in love, and their tragedy is greater because of their innocence. The feud between the lovers' families represents the fate which Romeo and Juliet are powerless to overcome. The lines capture in poetry the youthful and simple passion which characterizes the play.

One of the most popular plays of all times, *Romeo and Juliet* was Shakespeare's second tragedy (after *Titus Andronicus* of 1594, a failure). Consequently, the play shows the sometimes artificial lyricism of early comedies such as *Love's Labour's Lost* (c. 1594-1595) and *A Midsummer Night's Dream* (c. 1595-1596), while its character development predicts the direction of the playwright's artistic maturity. In Shakespeare's usual fashion, he based his story on sources that were well known in his day: Masuccio Salernitano's *Novellino* (1476), William Painter's *The Palace of Pleasure* (1566-1567), and, especially, Arthur Brooke's poetic *The Tragical History of Romeus and Juliet* (1562). Shakespeare reduces the time of the action from the months it takes in Brooke's work to a few compact days.

In addition to following the conventional five-part structure of a tragedy, Shakespeare employs his characteristic alternation, from scene to scene, between taking the action forward and retarding it, often with comic relief, to heighten the dramatic impact. Although in many respects the play's structure recalls that of the genre of the fall of powerful men, its true prototype is tragedy as employed by Geoffrey Chaucer in *Troilus and Criseyde* (1382)—a fall into unhappiness, on the part of more or less ordinary people, after a fleeting period of happiness. The fall is caused traditionally and in Shakespeare's play by the workings of fortune. Insofar as *Romeo and Juliet* is a tragedy, it is a tragedy of fate rather than of a tragic flaw. Although the two lovers have weaknesses, it is not their faults, but their unlucky stars, that destroy them. As the friar comments at the end, "A greater power than we can contradict/ Hath thwarted our intents."

Shakespeare succeeds in having the thematic structure closely parallel the dramatic form of the play. The principal theme is that of the tension between the two houses, and all the other oppositions of the play derive from that central one. Thus, romance is set against revenge, love against hate, day against night, sex against war, youth against age, and "tears to fire." Juliet's soliloquy in Act III, scene ii makes it clear that it is the strife between her family and Romeo's that has turned Romeo's love to death. If, at times, Shakespeare seems to forget the family theme in his lyrical fascination with the lovers, that fact only sets off their suffering all the more poignantly against the background of the senseless and arbitrary strife between the Capulets and Montagues. For the families, after all, the story has a classically comic ending; their feud is buried with the lovers—which seems to be the intention of the fate that compels the action.

The lovers never forget their families; their consciousness of the conflict leads to another central theme in the play, that of identity. Romeo questions his identity to Benvolio early in the play, and Juliet asks him, "Wherefore art thou Romeo?" At her request he offers to change his name and to be defined only as one star-crossed with her. Juliet, too, questions her identity, when she speaks to the nurse after Romeo's slaying of Tybalt. Romeo later asks the friar to help him locate the lodging of his name so that he may cast it from his "hateful mansion," bringing a plague upon his own house in an ironic fulfillment of Mercutio's dying curse. Only when they are in their graves, together, do the two lovers find peace from the persecution of being Capulet and Montague; they are remembered by their first names only, an ironic proof that their story had the beneficial political influence the Prince, who wants the feud to end, wishes.

Likewise, the style of the play alternates between poetic gymnastics and pure and simple lines of deep emotion. The unrhymed iambic pentameter is filled with conceits, puns, and wordplay, presenting both lovers as very well-spoken youngsters. Their verbal wit, in fact, is not Shakespeare's rhetorical excess but part of their characters. It fortifies the impression the audience has of their spiritual natures, showing their love as an intellectual appreciation of beauty combined with physical passion. Their first dialogue, for example, is a sonnet divided between them. In no other early play is the imagery as lush and complex, making unforgettable the balcony speech in which Romeo describes Juliet as the sun, Juliet's nightingale-lark speech, her comparison of Romeo to the "day in night," which Romeo then develops as he observes, at dawn, "more light and light, more dark and dark our woes."

At the beginning of the play Benvolio describes Romeo as a "love-struck swain" in the typical pastoral fashion. He is, as the cliché has it, in love with love (Rosaline's name is not even mentioned until much later). He is youthful energy seeking an outlet; sensitive appreciation seeking a beautiful object. Mercutio and the friar comment on his fickleness. The sight of Juliet immediately transforms Romeo's immature and erotic infatuation to true and constant love. He matures more quickly than anyone around him realizes; only the audience understands the process, since Shakespeare makes Romeo introspective and articulate in his monologues. Even in love, however, Romeo does not reject his former romantic ideals. When Juliet comments, "You kiss by th' book," she is being astutely perceptive; Romeo's death is the death of an idealist, not of a foolhardy youth. He knows what he is doing, his awareness growing from his comment after slaying Tybalt, "O, I am Fortune's fool."

Juliet is equally quick-witted, and also has early premonitions of their sudden love's end. She is made uniquely charming by her combination of girlish innocence with a winsome foresight that is "wise" when compared to the superficial feelings expressed by her father, mother, and Count Paris. Juliet, moreover, is realistic as well as romantic. She knows how to exploit her womanly softness, making the audience feel both poignancy and irony when the friar remarks, at her arrival in the wedding chapel, "O, so light a foot/ Will ne'er wear out the everlasting flint!" It takes a strong person to carry out the friar's stratagem, after all; Juliet succeeds in the ruse partly because everyone else considers her weak in body and in will. She is a subtle actress, telling the audience after dismissing her mother and the nurse, "My dismal scene I needs must act alone." Her quiet intelligence makes the audience's tragic pity all the stronger when her "scene" becomes reality.

Shakespeare provides his lovers with effective dramatic foils in the characters of Mercutio, the nurse, and the friar. The play, nevertheless, remains forever that of "Juliet and her Romeo."

"Critical Evaluation" by Kenneth John Atchity

Bibliography:

Battenhouse, Roy W. *Shakespearean Tragedy: Its Art and Its Christian Premises*. Bloomington: Indiana University Press, 1969. Argues that in *Romeo and Juliet*, Shakespeare shows a mistrust of carnal love, which leads the protagonists to suicide and damnation; the suicides in the tomb at the end of the play are an inversion of the Easter story.

Cartwright, Kent. *Shakespearean Tragedy and Its Double: The Rhythms of Audience Response*. University Park: Pennsylvania State University Press, 1991. Examines how audiences respond to Shakespeare's tragedies. Shows how an audience of *Romeo and Juliet* usually identifies strongly with the lovers, although the play compels detachment.

Evans, Robert. *The Osier Cage; Rhetorical Devices in "Romeo and Juliet."* Lexington: University Press of Kentucky, 1966. Explores the style of *Romeo and Juliet*, particularly Shakespeare's use of opposites such as love and violence, darkness and light, and appearance and reality.

Watts, Cedric. *Romeo and Juliet*. Boston: Twayne, 1991. One of the best starting places. Contains information on the history of the play and discusses its themes, sources, and characters.

Wells, Stanley, ed. *The Cambridge Companion to Shakespeare Studies*. Cambridge, England: Cambridge University Press, 1986. All studies of Shakespeare should begin with this book. Includes excellent chapters on the poet's life, the beliefs of Elizabethan England, and reviews of scholarship in the field.

ROMOLA

Type of work: Novel
Author: George Eliot (Mary Ann Evans, 1819-1880)
Type of plot: Historical realism
Time of plot: 1492-1498
Locale: Italy
First published: 1862-1863

Principal characters:
BARDO, a Florentine scholar
ROMOLA, his daughter
TITO MELEMA, an adventurer
TESSA, a peasant
BALDASSARE CALVO, Tito's benefactor
GIROLAMO SAVONAROLA, a Dominican friar

The Story:

Tito Melema arrived in the Florence of the Medicis penniless and unknown, but the sale of some rare jewels in his possession soon brought him into the circle of the wealthy, learned men of the city, among them the blind antiquarian, Bardo. Bardo was a great scholar who continued his annotations of Greek and Roman books through the eyes of his beautiful daughter, Romola. Bardo's only interests in life were his library and museum, and he had reared his daughter in innocence of the outside world. Bardo accepted Tito eagerly, for he was always eager to meet a scholar and a man who had traveled widely. He also told Tito of a son whom he had lost.

Tito's fortune had at last come to him with the sale of all of his jewels except a single ring. He recalled that the money properly belonged to Baldassare Calvo, the man who had been almost a father to him, the man who might now be a slave in the hands of the Turks. If Baldassare were really alive, Tito told himself, he would spend the money for the old man's ransom, but he was not sure his foster father still lived. Tito quickly entrenched himself in the learned society of Florence. At the yearly festival of San Giovanni, patron saint of Florence, Tito, while sitting at a window with a friend, fancied that he saw in the crowd below a monk who gazed upon him with a malicious glance. Also glancing up at Tito from below was the beautiful Tessa, daughter of a milk vendor, whom Tito had met on the day of his arrival in Florence.

Later, as he walked through the crowded streets, he rescued Tessa from some jostling revelers. When he had left her, he met the strange monk who had gazed at him from the crowd earlier in the afternoon. The monk, Fra Luca, gave him a note that had been brought from a pilgrim in the Near East. The note was from Baldassare, who pleaded that Tito should rescue him from slavery. Unwilling to give up his happy life in Florence, Tito ignored his foster father's plea. Tito wondered what was so familiar about the monk's face.

Attracted to the lovely, grave Romola, Tito spent many hours reading and writing manuscripts with her blind father. One day, when Tito had the opportunity to be alone with Romola for a brief moment, he declared his love to her, and Romola shyly confessed her love for him. That same day, Monna Brigida paid a call on her cousin Bardo. When she accidentally mentioned the name of a Dominican monk, Dino, Tito discovered that the lost son of Bardo was not dead but had been banished from his father's house. Tito realized that Fra Luca was Dino, and he feared exposure of his benefactor's slavery. He felt the time ripe for asking the old man for permission to marry Romola. Bardo readily consented.

Tito learned that Fra Luca was dangerously ill at Fiesole. One evening, Romola told him that her dying brother had sent for her. Tito feared that Fra Luca would tell her the story that Tito had hoped would die with him. In despair, he wandered through the city and accidentally met Tessa. In a ribald ceremony that amused the gaping crowd, Tito allowed Tessa to believe that he had really married her. Unwilling to undeceive her, he made her promise to keep the marriage a secret. Meanwhile, Dino died without revealing to Romola the story of Baldassare and the ungrateful Tito. Tito and Romola were married.

Bardo died and left Romola to carry on his scholarly work. Meanwhile, as the Medicis struggled to maintain control of their city, the political situation deteriorated. The Medicis' troubles were made worse by the charismatic preaching of Savonarola, who proclaimed that the impending arrival of the French was God's will. This situation helped to advance Tito's fortunes; he became an interpreter in negotiations with the French. On the day the French king arrived in the city, the soldiers led through the streets a group of prisoners who begged their ransoms from the Florentines. The mocking mob cut an old man loose from his fetters and allowed him to escape into the crowd. The prisoner ran blindly into Tito, who stood with a group of dignitaries on the steps of San Marco. Tito turned and found himself looking into the face of Baldassare Calvo, who then disappeared into the crowd.

Fearing Baldassare's revenge, Tito bought a coat of mail to wear under his clothes. Tito begged Romola to sell her father's library and leave Florence with him. When Romola refused, Tito secretly sold the library. Betrayed by her husband, Romola fled Florence, only to be met outside the city by Savonarola, who persuaded her to honor her marriage vows and return to Florence. In his search for a place to stay, Baldassare came by chance to the house where Tessa and her children by Tito lived with a deaf old peasant woman. The woman gave the old man permission to sleep in the loft. Tessa eagerly confided in Baldassare. She told him that Tito had sent her to live with the old peasant woman, whom he paid well for the care she gave Tessa and his children, and that he had sworn the two women to secrecy. While Baldassare lay in the hayloft, Tito came to see Tessa. Suspecting from her description the identity of the old man, Tito went to his foster father to ask his forgiveness. He had decided that Baldassare should come to live with him and share his comfort, but the old man did not forgive. He lunged at Tito, breaking his knife against the chainmail, and then threatened to expose Tito and ruin him.

At a dinner in Florence, Baldassare appeared to denounce Tito before his political friends. The trembling old man was pronounced mad and sent to prison. During a plague, the jails were emptied to make room for the sick, and Baldassare was released. He spied upon Tito until he learned of Romola. He approached Romola to tell her of Tessa. When he told Romola of Tito's betrayal, she was able to piece together all the suspicions she had felt toward her husband, his long absences from home, his strange moods, and his secret fears. One day, she found little Lillo, Tessa's son, wandering lost in the streets. She took the child to his home, and there she realized that she had discovered Tessa.

The final blow came to Romola when her godfather, Bernardo Del Nero, the only person in the world she still loved, was arrested. The Medicis had been plotting to come back to Florence, and Bernardo was a member of the committee that plotted their return. Romola knew Tito had been a spy for both political factions; he had gained his own safety by betraying others. Romola revealed to Tito her knowledge of Baldassare's story and the truth of the old man's accusation against him. Romola tried to prevent Bernardo's execution by pleading with Savonarola for his release, but the preacher refused to intervene. Disillusioned and sorrowful over her godfather's death, Tito's betrayals, and Savonarola's falseness, Romola left Florence to seek a new life.

Tito also planned to flee Florence, for his double dealings had been discovered. A mob pursued him out of the city. To escape his pursuers, he threw away his money belt. While the crowd scrambled for it, he jumped into the river. Weakly, he pulled himself ashore on the opposite side. There Baldassare, now a starving beggar, found him. In a final effort, the old man threw himself upon his exhausted enemy and strangled him.

After spending many months in another city, Romola returned to Florence to learn of her husband's murder at the hands of an old man who had long been his enemy. Romola understood the justice of Tito's violent end. She found Tessa and the children and brought them to live with her, determined to repair the damage that Tito's deceptions had wrought.

Critical Evaluation:

Of her novels, George Eliot once said, *Romola* stood out as "having been written with my best blood." This is a revealing statement coming from the author of *Middlemarch* (1871-1872) and *The Mill on the Floss* (1860), novels considered by most critics to be superior works. Why did Eliot shower *Romola* with such high praise?

Romola is Eliot's most ambitious historical novel. Readers find themselves transported back to fifteenth century Florence. There, politics and religion intermingled; this is illustrated by the expulsion of the Medicis from power, an act in part inspired by the fervent preaching of Fra Girolamo Savonarola. Eliot spent many months studying Florentine history, both at home and during a trip to Italy in 1861. Her research resulted in a solid and reliable account of the time period that the novel portrays. Unfortunately, her meticulous attention to detail sometimes makes for cumbersome and difficult prose.

In addition to the painstaking re-creation of Italian history, George Eliot presents her readers with a cast of both fictional and historical characters. One of her most intriguing creations is Tito Melema, the young man who quickly curries favor with the Florentine elite. No other George Eliot character manifests the selfishness and deceit of Tito. Eliot's portrayal is of a man with great personal charm. His unmatched skills in manipulating people, language, and politics drives the plot forward and provides the reader with a fascinating study of the devastating effects of rationalization and egotism.

In apparent contrast to the fictional Tito, Eliot portrays the historical Fra Girolamo Savonarola, a Dominican friar whose calls for reform captivated Florence from 1491 to 1498. Savonarola is also a man of great charisma and influence, whose moral convictions are revealed by his religious zeal. Savonarola believes that God is working through him, carrying out heavenly justice through a human channel. Unlike Tito, Savonarola acts with the best of intentions, but he too is unwilling to contemplate the effects of his deeds. Consequently, Tito and Savonarola are revealed to be cut from the same moral cloth. Both men misuse their power and breed mistrust in those who rely upon their judgment. Together, these characters offer a rich resource for reflection on questions of intentionality, morality, human will, and the appropriate use of political power.

In distinction to Tito and Savonarola stand tne two main female characters in the book, Tessa and Romola. Tessa, in particular, seems to represent traits commonly associated with femininity in the nineteenth century. She is beautiful, naïve, and uneducated, and she easily falls prey to the charming and unscrupulous Tito. Unlike Tito, for whom every situation is an opportunity to deceive, Tessa takes everything literally. She is unable to see beyond appearances.

In contrast, Romola is educated and poised but lacks life experience. Like Tessa, Romola is seduced by Tito's magnetism. Unlike Tessa, however, Romola is attracted to Tito's worldliness and scholarly capabilities. He is a man who can understand her dedication to intellectual pursuits. Both Romola and Tessa experience the same disrespectful treatment from Tito and from their culture at large. Only Romola, however, is aware of the strictures placed on her because of her sex. Tessa is happy to perform the duties of wife and mother; Romola recoils under the prohibitions that forbid her to follow her father's path. Romola is continually ignored or punished by a society that refuses to listen to her or take her seriously. Romola shares with George Eliot's other heroines (for example Dorothea Brooke in *Middlemarch* or Maggie Tulliver in *The Mill on the Floss*) a sense of estrangement from her culture.

This particular aspect of the novel—its presentation of an autonomous and capable woman repressed and alienated by her culture—led many of the novel's critics to reprimand its author for using a fifteenth century setting to discuss nineteenth century problems. The historical setting provided Eliot with a contrast that allowed the reader to see with clarity that fifteenth century restrictions were quite relevant to the situation of women in the nineteenth century. Medieval Florence provided Eliot with the perfect opportunity not only to explore and to instruct with regard to women's capabilities but also to illustrate the educational value of history.

The use of history as an instructional guide in *Romola* has led many critics to argue that this work contains Eliot's expression of a nineteenth century philosophy known as positivism. Developed by the French thinker Auguste Comte, positivism espouses the idea that in its growth and development over time, human society has participated in a moral evolution. According to Comte, in the manner that a child grows and learns to develop a sophisticated moral sense, so do cultures. From this perspective, fifteenth century Florence represents the painful transition from societal childhood to maturity. Romola represents this broader change, beginning the novel with a childish naïveté that grows into a moral sense that surpasses even that of the most devoted Christians. Taught the necessity of blind obedience to external authority, Romola struggles throughout the novel to discover her own inner strength and moral vision. Romola's efforts to use her intellect in service of others and to develop a sense of moral duty without God form a major theme in the novel.

Although *Romola*'s blend of history and fiction as well as its thematic explorations of egoism and piety, of religious mysticism and political intrigue, and of duty and rebellion make it a grand artistic achievement, its reception has been less than enthusiastic. Out of the English milieu that is more typical of her work, Eliot seems to lose, among the years that separate her from her subject, some of the acerbic wit and shrewd insight that characterize her other novels. On the other hand, one may say that it is precisely because Eliot attempted to create a work that would embody the philosophical, literary, and historical ideals she valued, that she regarded *Romola* as one of her best works.

"Critical Evaluation" by Susan E. Hill

Bibliography:

Barrett, Dorothea. *Vocation and Desire: George Eliot's Heroines*. London: Routledge & Kegan Paul, 1989. Chapter on *Romola* discusses the influence of Auguste Comte's positivist philosophy on *Romola*. Superb feminist reading of Eliot's novels.

Bonaparte, Felicia. *The Triptych and the Cross: The Central Myths of George Eliot's Poetic Imagination*. New York: New York University Press, 1979. The only book-length study of *Romola*, containing a thorough analysis of the historical, mythic, and classical influences in the novel. Includes discussion of *Romola* in the context of Eliot's other novels.

Bullen, J. B. "George Eliot's *Romola* as a Positivist Allegory." *Review of English Studies* 26 (1975): 425-435. This influential article was the first to examine the question of George Eliot's use of Comte's positivist philosophy in the novel. Contains a lucid and helpful explanation of positivism and a valuable account of its role in the novel.

Eliot, George. *The George Eliot Letters*. 9 vols. Edited by Gordon Haight. New Haven, Conn.: Yale University Press, 1954-1956, 1978. Offers commentary on the dynamics of her writing process. There are also a number of letters from readers that reveal how the novel was received by the public. Most of the letters concerning *Romola* can be found in volumes 4 and 8.

Robinson, Carole. "*Romola:* A Reading of the Novel." *Victorian Studies* 6 (1962): 29-42. A brief and clear exposition of the major themes and ideas in the novel. Suggests that the issue of "philosophical uncertainty" is the key to understanding the text.

ROOM AT THE TOP

Type of work: Novel
Author: John Braine (1922-1986)
Type of plot: Social realism
Time of plot: 1947
Locale: Warley, Yorkshire, England
First published: 1957

Principal characters:

JOE LAMPTON, an ambitious young accountant eager to shed his working-class background by rising to the top in Warley's establishment
ALICE AISGILL, an older woman with whom Joe has an affair
SUSAN BROWN, the attractive but vacuous daughter of Warley's most powerful businessman
JACK WALES, the handsome young son of a rich industrialist, Joe's rival for Susan's affections
MR. BROWN, Susan's father, a self-made man

The Story:

The story of Joe Lampton's rise to prosperity begins in a railway compartment. Joe, slightly hungover and wearing cheap clothes, was leaving his home in Dufton for a job in the municipal government of Warley. Ambitious to escape his working-class background, Joe had used his stint in a German prisoner-of-war camp during World War II to study accounting. The move to Warley gave him the chance to rise into the middle class and even to aspire to wealth.

Joe joined the Warley Thespians, a little theater group, as a way of becoming refined and of mixing with important people. There he met the thirty-four-year-old Alice Aisgill, frustrated at having given up an acting career for an unhappy marriage to a local industrialist. Joe and Alice fell in love and had an affair. Yet, at the same time, Joe was attracted to Susan Brown, the nineteen-year-old daughter of Warley's most important businessman. Joe understood that his future success lay in winning and marrying Susan, yet he could not give up Alice. He tried to have both by continuing his affair with Alice while developing a calculated strategy to woo Susan.

The great obstacle to Joe's future was the presence of Jack Wales. Jack was almost everything that Joe was not: rich, self-assured, a student at a prestigious university, a war hero, and destined for a place in the family firm. Jack was at home in the Leddersford Conservative Club (the haunt of Warley's elite), drove a nice car, and dressed well. Yet, despite his shortcomings, Joe won Susan. Joe knew how to use his sexual attractiveness to get his way. Jack was solid but unexciting and, to Susan's dismay, came with her mother's approval.

At this juncture, Susan's parents decided to act. Mr. Brown had a word with the Warley Treasurer, Joe's superior, and the Treasurer in turn spoke to Joe. Speaking purely hypothetically, the Treasurer told Joe that a good future was in store for him in Warley, that he might expect promotion in local government, but that all this might be lost if he persisted in seeing Susan. The Treasurer advised him to find a suitable girl—that is, a girl of a lower class than Susan—and to get married. Joe was furious as he realized that Warley's establishment had conspired against him, that he might lose his expectations of a good future, and that he had no hope of marrying

Susan. He continued to date her, however, even as his affair with Alice grew more intense. Its intensity enabled Joe to accept Susan's breaking off of their relationship when she found out about his relationship with Alice.

Joe then thought he wanted to marry Alice. The couple went away together on a long weekend and felt like husband and wife. However, knowing that marriage with Alice would prevent his rise in society, Joe reconciled with Susan. Alice developed a serious medical condition that required surgery; while she was in the hospital, Joe and Susan consummated their love. Two months later, the day Alice was discharged from the hospital, Mr. Brown called Joe and ordered him to have lunch with him at the Leddersford Conservative Club. Over lunch, Brown offered to set Joe up in business if he agreed never to see Susan again. Joe indignantly refused to be bought. That was what Brown wanted to hear. He said that Joe and Susan could get married and that the first thing was to fix the date. Joe, puzzled, asked Mr. Brown why he was in such a hurry for them to get married when he had been against their marrying from the start. The reason, Joe quickly learned, was that Susan was pregnant. The lunch ended with Mr. Brown's ordering Joe to break off relations with Alice, who, he said, was "an old whore" who had slept with other young men, including Jack Wales.

Joe told Alice that he no longer loved her and announced his engagement to Susan. In despair, Alice went on a drinking binge and drove her car so fast that it left the road at a curve. The following morning, Joe learned of Alice's death. No one blamed Joe for her death, but he knew that she had committed suicide and that he had been responsible. Guilty with his knowledge, he left work and went to a nearby town to drink away his guilt. He stopped in a pub frequented by homosexuals and allowed a man to buy him drinks. Then he slipped away, had dinner, and drank at another pub. He picked up Mavis, a working-class girl, took her to a secluded place, and had sex with her. On his way home, friends of hers attacked him, but he fought back and escaped. The book ends with Joe's return to Warley, mourning Alice but accepting his future life as Susan's husband.

Critical Evaluation:

Room at the Top is one of several novels and plays of the 1950's by authors who had been born during the 1920's. Other works from this group include the plays *Look Back in Anger* (1956) by John Osborne and *A Taste of Honey* (1958) by Shelagh Delaney and the novels *Saturday Night and Sunday Morning* (1958) by Alan Sillitoe, *Hurry on Down* (1953) by John Wain, and *Lucky Jim* (1953) by Kingsley Amis. This generation of writers came to be called "Angry Young Men" largely because of Osborne's play, although women were also writing. Their themes included the realistic depiction of working-class life and complaints about how little of the social structure government welfare programs had changed. Angry writers rejected both the literary formulas and what they considered to be the deadness of feeling of postwar literature, yet they did not use their writing to espouse causes, as had the authors of the 1930's. Braine neither espoused left-wing causes nor challenged the status quo. John Osborne made Jimmy Porter, the protagonist of *Look Back in Anger*, scream and whine about the mediocrity of the era. Braine, in contrast, gave Joe Lampton self-awareness and made him want to find a place in the existing establishment.

Braine certainly did not write *Room at the Top* with a view to social criticism. He denied that it was the writer's job to pass judgment on either individuals or society. The writer was to say what was, not what should be. Thus, Braine believed that novels should be marked by "a vigorous realism"; in this case, he was careful to describe clearly and to fill his descriptions with brand names. Braine himself thought that what drew attention to *Room at the Top* was its realism, its "true feeling of living in the present, or at least in the just-past Forties." Braine also believed that writers should write from their own experience. Certainly, one of the novel's strengths is its clear presentation of life in the north of England.

The novel's theme is that of the young man who rises in the world by his own exertions. Joe Lampton wants to become what he calls a Zombie, a person who sells himself to the powerful in society in order to find a niche in that society. Unlike others, however, Joe wants to sell himself for the highest price possible. He wants to be a "Grade Two Zombie" with power and wealth, not a Grade Eight or Ten one who has sold himself for a modest, lower-middle-class standard of living. "In business, I ruminated, I'd have to soft-soap people whom I despised, I'd have to steer the conversation towards their favourite subjects, I'd have to stand them meals and drinks. But the game was worth the candle; if I sold my independence, at least I'd get a decent price for it." To achieve his goal, Joe plots out careful, calculating strategies for both his personal relationships and his work life. Yet Braine includes hints, as Joe reflects on the position he has gained, that perhaps the cost of selling himself was too high.

Room at the Top is written in first-person narrative; Joe Lampton narrates the events of his own story, in chronological order, from the vantage point of ten years later. Occasionally, however, Braine has Joe step back and take an objective look at himself. In these passages, Braine uses the third person—not the third person of the outside narrator, however, but rather the voice of Joe Lampton taking a clinical, objective look at himself.

Joe and Alice are the two best-drawn characters. Alice is admirable in her honesty and realism about their relationship. Joe is a somewhat more complex and ambiguous character. He, too, is mostly honest about his own actions, yet he does terrible things. Readers are meant to recognize his amorality, yet they are meant to sympathize with him as well. The other main characters are less well realized. One does not understand why Joe is attracted to Susan Brown, other than for her father's influence, for she is drawn as superficial and vacuous. Jack Wales is a cardboard cutout of the handsome son of privilege. Mr. Brown, although a more real character, partakes somewhat of the stereotype of a self-made man. Joe is drawn to Mr. Brown largely because the two are alike in having shed their working-class backgrounds. When they have lunch, Joe remarks that his father, a staunch member of the British Labour Party, would turn in his grave if he could see Joe at the Conservative Club. Mr. Brown says, "So would mine, lad. But we're not bound by our fathers."

The novel reflects attitudes of its day in its treatment of homosexuals and in its double standard of sexual morality. In the scene in which Joe is in the pub, the homosexuals are discussed in disparaging terms and depicted stereotypically. Throughout the novel, also, women who are sexually active are depicted in less approving ways than men who are sexually active. Despite, and in part because of, these outdated attitudes, *Room at the Top* offers one of the finest depictions of the life of a young man in Great Britain immediately after World War II.

D. G. Paz

Bibliography:

Allsop, Kenneth. *The Angry Decade: A Survey of the Cultural Revolt of the Nineteen-Fifties*. London: Peter Owen, 1958. Although this book was written at the end of the very decade it discusses, it remains the single best study of that period in British literary history. Its chapter on Braine uses interviews with the author.

Braine, John. *Writing a Novel*. New York: Coward, McCann & Geoghegan, 1974. Braine's own explanation of how he crafts fiction, the result of reflections on his teaching of creative writing, provides insights into the development of *Room at the Top*. Essential reading, in which Braine includes examples of how he planned and revised this novel.

Frazer, G. S. *The Modern Writer and His World*. Baltimore: Penguin Books, 1964. Includes a highly negative evaluation of *Room at the Top* and, hence, is useful as a counterweight to more laudatory views. Frazer finds in Braine's work a cheap style, inadequate understanding of the characters of Joe Lampton and Susan Brown, and silliness in thinking that a thirty-four-year-old woman is decrepit.

Lee, James W. *John Braine*. New York: Twayne, 1968. A balanced survey of Braine's background and upbringing in the north of England and a consideration of the four novels that he had published by 1968. The chapter on *Room at the Top* is a good analysis of the novel's themes and literary style. The only book devoted wholly to a study of the author.

Sinfield, Alan. *Literature, Politics, and Culture in Postwar Britain*. Berkeley: University of California Press, 1989. A survey, written from a left-wing perspective, of the relationships between political change and literary production in Britain since 1945. It includes a chapter on left-wing writing.

A ROOM WITH A VIEW

Type of work: Novel
Author: E. M. Forster (1879-1970)
Type of plot: Social realism
Time of plot: Early 1900's
Locale: Florence, Italy, and Surrey, England
First published: 1908

Principal characters:

MISS LUCY HONEYCHURCH, a young Englishwoman
MISS CHARLOTTE BARTLETT, her cousin and chaperon
MR. EMERSON, an Englishman
GEORGE EMERSON, his son
THE REVEREND ARTHUR BEEBE
MRS. HONEYCHURCH, Lucy's mother
FREDDY HONEYCHURCH, Lucy's brother
CECIL VYSE, Lucy's fiancé
MISS CATHERINE ALAN, a guest at the Pension Bertolini
MISS TERESA ALAN, her sister
MISS ELEANOR LAVISH, a novelist

The Story:

Lucy Honeychurch and Charlotte Bartlett were disappointed by the Pension Bertolini and by the fact that their rooms had no view. They were embarrassed at dinner when Mr. Emerson offered to exchange his and his son's rooms, which had views, with theirs. Their unhappiness decreased when the Reverend Arthur Beebe, whom they had known previously, and who had been appointed rector of Lucy's home parish, joined them at dinner. After dinner, he managed to convince Charlotte that the exchange of rooms would not put them under any obligation to the Emersons. The change, although effected, merely confirmed Charlotte's opinion that the Emersons were ill-bred.

At Santa Croce Church, Lucy met the Emersons, who guided her to the Giotto frescoes that she had come to see. She found that she was more at ease with Mr. Emerson than she had expected, although his rejection of artistic and religious cant and his concern about his son confused her.

Late one afternoon, Lucy declared that she would go for a walk alone. She bought some photographs of paintings that she had seen and then walked through the Piazza Signoria. As she did so, she passed two men arguing over a debt. One stabbed the other; the stricken man, bleeding from the mouth, died at her feet. At the same moment, she saw George Emerson watching from across the square. As he reached her side, she fainted. After she had recovered, she sent him to get her photographs, which she had dropped. Disturbed because they were covered with blood, he tossed them into the Arno on the way home. When Lucy asked why he had thrown the pictures away, he was forced to tell her. He felt that something very significant had happened to him in the piazza. Lucy stopped with him near the pension. She leaned beside him over the parapet and asked him to tell no one that he had been there. Perturbed by their enforced intimacy, she was puzzled and amazed when George said that the murder would make him want to live.

In a large party, the visitors at the pension, together with a resident English chaplain, drove toward Fiesole. Lucy, excluded from Miss Lavish's conversation with Charlotte, asked one of their drivers to direct her to the clergyman. Instead, he led her to George. Lucy found at the end of the path a terrace covered with violets. While she stood there, radiant at the beauty of the place, George stepped forward and kissed her. Charlotte, whom neither had seen at first, called her cousin back.

Charlotte told Lucy that George was a cad and that obviously he was accustomed to stealing kisses. She took advantage of Lucy's need for sympathy to indicate that George's way of life, as she saw it, was merely brutal. In the morning, the women took the train for Rome.

Back at her home in Surrey, Lucy became engaged to Cecil Vyse, whom she had visited in Rome. When Mr. Beebe came to the house for tea, he was perturbed by the news of the engagement. Returning from a party with Lucy and Mrs. Honeychurch, Cecil saw a pair of ugly villas that had been put up by a local builder. When the village residents became alarmed as they considered the type of person who might rent them, they were assured that Sir Harry Otway had bought the houses and intended to lease them only to suitable tenants. Lucy suggested the Misses Alan whom she met in Florence. After seeing the villas, Cecil and Lucy walked on through the woods. By a pond where Lucy had bathed as a child, Cecil, for the first time, asked if he might kiss her. Their embrace was not successful and only reminded Lucy of the Emersons, whom she then mentioned to Cecil.

Shortly before the Alans' occupancy had been arranged, Cecil met the Emersons in London and suggested that they take one of the villas. Not connecting them with Lucy, he hoped thereby to disrupt the local social order. After the Emersons had moved into their house, Mr. Beebe took Freddy Honeychurch to meet them. The boy immediately asked George to go swimming with him. Together with Mr. Beebe they swam and raced gaily at the pond in the woods. There Lucy came upon George again. Although he greeted her joyously, she bowed stiffly and moved on with her mother and Cecil.

While George was visiting the house one Sunday, Cecil loftily refused to play tennis. Lucy, George, Freddy, and a friend of his played while Cecil read. After the game, Cecil read aloud from the novel he was holding. Written by Miss Lavish, it contained a scene describing George and Lucy's kiss. Cecil was ignorant of this fact, but George and Lucy were profoundly moved. On the way into the house, George again kissed her. Charlotte was staying in the house at that time, and Lucy was furious that she had betrayed her to Miss Lavish. Together they went to George, and Lucy asked him to leave. Before he obeyed, he told Lucy that he loved her and that it would be disastrous for her to marry Cecil, who was incapable of intimacy with anyone.

Although she denied to herself that she was attracted to George, Lucy broke her engagement to Cecil that evening. In the meantime, Mr. Beebe received a letter from the Misses Alan, who were planning to visit Athens. To escape her confusion, Lucy decided that she must go with them, and Charlotte joined Mr. Beebe in persuading Mrs. Honeychurch to let Lucy go. Lucy, afraid that George would hear of her rejection of Cecil and return to see her, hoped in this manner to avoid another meeting with him.

As Lucy was returning from a day in London with her mother, Charlotte came out of Mr. Beebe's house and asked them to go with her to church. Lucy declined, went into the house, and awaited their return. There she found Mr. Emerson in the library. George, feeling utterly lost, had gone to London. Lucy finally admitted that she was not to marry Cecil, but when Mr. Emerson revealed his intuitive knowledge that she loved George, she became angry and wept. Although she gradually perceived that all he said was true, she was upset at the prospect of distressing everyone afresh if she acted on her new knowledge. Strengthened by Mr. Emerson's passion, sincerity, and confidence, however, she promised to attempt to live the truth she had learned.

With her family opposing the marriage but not insistently, Lucy married George. They spent their honeymoon in the Pension Bertolini, where they wonderingly realized that subconsciously Charlotte had been on their side. She had known that Mr. Emerson was in Mr. Beebe's house, and she also must have realized how he would speak to Lucy when they met there.

Critical Evaluation:

E. M. Forster and Virginia Woolf were the literary leaders of the Bloomsbury Group, a circle of intellectuals who gathered regularly in London in the first two decades of the twentieth century to discuss art and aesthetics. The circle also included the economist John Maynard Keynes, the painters Vanessa and Clive Bell, and the philosopher and critic Lytton Strachey. From the group's wide-ranging discussions, Forster often received ideas about art that he later incorporated into his fiction. Forster became noted for his deft style, complex characters, and important themes.

Although he is best remembered for his acknowledged masterpieces *Howards End* (1910) and *A Passage to India* (1924), Forster's earlier novels and short stories often point in the direction to which his later fiction turned. These earlier works are usually concerned with how people living in a modern world lack the passion necessary for a complete life. To make his point, Forster often contrasts the passionate intensity of people in southern European countries with the flaccid people of his native land. Typically, a character in one of these stories travels from England to Greece or Rome and there undergoes a revelation. In Forster's famous short story "The Road from Colonus" (1903), for example, Mr. Lucas discovers passion at an idyllic spring in Greece. His daughter forces him to return to England, however, and he subsequently dies a miserable and lonely old man. In *A Room with a View*, on which Forster was working as he finished "The Road from Colonus," Lucy Honeychurch discovers the passion of Italy. Lucy's fate is more fortunate than Mr. Lucas'. Although she initially rejects the passion that Italy represents (indeed, she is shocked by it), she later comes to accept it as a fundamental part of life. The novel consequently ends happily with her in George Emerson's arms as they honeymoon in Florence.

Forster struggled to write *A Room with a View*. Although he initially conceived it and started taking notes during a trip to Italy in 1902, he did not complete the novel until 1908, after he had already published two other novels, *Where Angels Fear to Tread* (1905) and *The Longest Journey* (1907). His struggles with *A Room with a View* stemmed partially from the book's odd structure—the first half is set in Florence, while the majority of the second half is set in the English countryside of Surrey, with a brief return to Florence in the final chapter. Furthermore, Forster was undecided as to whether he wanted the novel to end happily or tragically. He opted for the happy end to ensure that his theme of personal growth would be clear to his readers.

It is perhaps most useful to read *A Room with a View* symbolically in order to understand Forster's primary theme. In such a reading, Lucy Honeychurch is a person intended to serve as an example for the reader and one with whom the reader may identify. Charlotte Bartlett and Cecil Vyse represent the forces of oppression that try to stifle Lucy's growing sense of passion. The Emersons represent the forces of good, encouraging her to follow her inner conviction that passion is essential to life. Lucy initially obeys the dictates of Charlotte and Cecil, which is no great surprise because they are the voices of English convention. When she chooses later to listen to Mr. Emerson (who knows instinctively that she and his son are in love), Lucy ignores the voices of convention and decides to follow her heart and marry George. Consequently, Lucy grows into a whole person, one who recognizes the necessity of passion in her life. At the beginning of the novel, Lucy complains that her room in Florence lacks a view, that she cannot "see." By novel's end, she "sees" very well indeed, having gained insight into human nature and herself.

Throughout his novel, Forster continually juxtaposes staid Christianity—represented by the Reverends Cuthbert Eager and Arthur Beebe—with the richness of pagan myth. To Forster, Pan, the Greek god of fertility and vigor, represented the passion missing from the daily lives of most people. Consequently, his early short stories and novels are replete with symbols that point to Pan's importance. A scene central to *A Room with a View* can serve as an example. Near the Honeychurch residence is a small pond, nicknamed the Sacred Lake, and after George and his father move into the neighborhood, Lucy's brother impetuously invites George and the Rev. Beebe for a swim, to which they agree. During the course of their riotous skinny-dipping, which seems governed by Pan himself, the three men engage in a celebration of life that does not end until Lucy, her mother, and Cecil happen by the pond. Forster intends for his readers to contrast the pure, free passion evident in this scene with the artificial existence found in the next chapter, in which Lucy feels stifled by her mother and her fiancé Cecil, and to conclude—as Lucy does later in the novel—that such displays of passion are essential for a full life.

Although reviews were generally flattering, sales of *A Room with a View* disappointed Forster. Enough copies sold, however, for his publisher, Edward Arnold, to agree to publish his next novel, *Howards End*. This work proved to be a qualified critical and financial success and assured Forster's reputation as a writer of importance.

"Critical Evaluation" by Jim McWilliams

Bibliography:

Dowling, David. *Bloomsbury Aesthetics and the Novels of Forster and Woolf*. New York: St. Martin's Press, 1985. Demonstrates the iconographic significance of the paintings mentioned in the novel. Analyzes the change that Lucy Honeychurch undergoes through her meetings with the Emersons. Points out Cecil Vyse's attempts to place her on a pedestal.

Furbank, P. N. *E. M. Forster: A Life*. New York: Harcourt Brace Jovanovich, 1978. Definitive biography: detailed, well-written, and copiously illustrated. Demonstrates how a trip Forster made to Florence in late 1901 inspired him to attempt a novel about English tourists in Italy. Recounts his subsequent struggles in writing *A Room with a View* and summarizes the novel's critical reception.

Kelvin, Norman. *E. M. Forster*. Carbondale: Southern Illinois University Press, 1967. Praises the social comedy in *A Room with a View* but sees Mr. Emerson, a humanist like Forster himself, as the novel's central character. Shows how Mr. Emerson controls the plot and other characters.

Land, Stephen K. *Challenge and Conventionality in the Fiction of E. M. Forster*. New York: AMS Press, 1990. Explains how *A Room with a View* fits into a pattern established by Forster's other novels by positioning Lucy as the heroine, Charlotte and Cecil as villains, George as a challenger, and Miss Lavish as a "rebel woman." Argues that the novel's conclusion is unsatisfying.

Rosecrance, Barbara. *Forster's Narrative Vision*. Ithaca, N.Y.: Cornell University Press, 1982. Analyzes the quirky narrative voice in *A Room with a View* and concludes its effects on a reader are primarily comic; points out that the voice functions as a type of stage manager.

ROOTS
The Saga of an American Family

Type of work: Novel
Author: Alex Haley (1921-1992)
Type of plot: Historical realism
Time of plot: 1750-1900's
Locale: The Gambia and the American South
First published: 1976

Principal characters:
KUNTA KINTE, an African who is enslaved
BELL, Kunta's wife
KIZZY, Bell and Kunta's daughter
CHICKEN GEORGE, Kizzy's son
TOM, Chicken George's son
ALEX HALEY, Kunta Kinte's descendant

The Story:

In the spring of 1750, Kunta Kinte was born in Juffure in The Gambia, Africa. His father was Omoro; his mother, Binta. Kunta learned the Mandinka village's customs and its religion—Islam. At five years of age, he graduated to the second *kafo*, donning clothes, attending school, and herding goats. He learned that some people in Juffure were slaves and that *toubob*—white people—sometimes captured Africans and sold them into slavery.

At ten years of age, he entered the third *kafo*, when boys received manhood training, learning how to hunt, use their wits, and make war. They studied sacred writings—the Koran, the Pentateuch, and the Psalms. The boys then were circumcised and sent back to the village as men. Kunta moved from his mother's hut into his own. He, his younger brother, Lamin, and some friends went to hunt for gold. He listened to the Council of Elders discussing village business.

One day after sentry duty, Kunta looked for wood for a drum. Some *toubob* and their black assistants ambushed and captured him. He and people from other tribes were shackled in a ship's hold, where many died. The stench of vomit, urine, feces, and death was overwhelming. Kunta became very ill, but survived the four-month journey.

Sold to a white man, Kunta could not understand why other black men did not free him. He ran away, but was recaptured by men and dogs. Kunta worked in the fields and watched the ways of both *toubob* and black people in this new land, where tobacco and butchered hogs offended his Muslim nose. Kunta's master called him Toby. He secretly learned some *toubob* words and pretended to obey, but when his leg irons were removed, he again ran away. Again he was captured; again he ran. This time he was shot. He recovered and ran again; his captors cut off half of his foot.

A *toubob* man of medicine and a black woman, Bell, helped Kunta's foot heal. A man called Fiddler befriended him and began teaching him English. When Kunta was well enough, he helped the gardener, taking over his duties after the old man became ill. The Fiddler told Kunta he was in Virginia; the old gardener talked about slavery and about the rebellion against the king. The slaves discussed white people's fear that the English would encourage slaves to fight their masters. The gardener also talked about their owner, whose wife and baby had died. Massa Waller had bought Kunta from Waller's brother.

Kunta became Waller's driver, taking the doctor to call on patients, friends, and relatives. At Waller's parents' plantation, Kunta met another African. Kunta realized that, although keeping his dignity, he was losing his African identity. Partly because the old African encouraged him to have children, Kunta considered marrying. He and Bell spent time together and finally "jumped the broom." Marriage agreed with him; Bell told him what she had read in the master's newspaper (although slaves were forbidden to read), and Kunta told her about Africa. Kunta and Bell had a daughter, Kizzy. Massa Waller's niece, Anne, adored her, infuriating Kunta. Kunta began teaching Kizzy Mandinka, although Bell feared it would endanger the child.

News of slave uprisings interested Kunta and his friends, partly because revolts so terrified white people. Kizzy loved a slave named Noah, who ran away. When caught, he confessed that Kizzy had forged his pass. Waller sold Kizzy; Kunta and Bell never saw her again.

Tom Lea, a North Carolinian, bought Kizzy and raped her repeatedly. She had a son, George. Kizzy and Lea's other slaves—Malizy, Pompey, and Sarah—cared for George. Kizzy taught George about his grandfather. George began spending time with Mingo, a slave who trained fighting cocks. Finally, Lea had Mingo build George a shack and train him as an assistant. Upset, Kizzy burst out with the truth about George's father's identity.

George became such an excellent rooster trainer that he was called Chicken George. Chicken George married Matilda, a girl from a neighboring plantation, and Massa Lea bought her. The couple had eight children. Chicken George began saving to buy the family's freedom, but Massa Lea lost him in a chicken fight. By the time Chicken George returned from England, Massa Lea had sold Matilda and their children to the Murrays.

Chicken George and Matilda's son Tom, a blacksmith, began saving to buy his grandmother and the other Lea slaves, except Uncle Pompey, who had died. When Chicken George returned to Lea's farm, he found Kizzy and Sarah dead also. He got his father drunk and found his hidden manumission paper, then tracked down his family, including new in-laws and grandchildren. He stayed briefly on the Murray farm, telling his grandson about their African ancestor, but left because of the law that a freed slave could stay in North Carolina only sixty days.

When the Civil War began, a white boy, George Johnson, came begging for food; Murray made him an overseer. The family, who liked his honesty and hard work, taught him his job. George left and returned with his pregnant wife, Martha, who was so weak their baby was born dead.

Despite the Emancipation Proclamation, freedom came only with the war's end in 1865. Chicken George returned and took the family, with other freed people and the Johnsons, to Tennessee. Matilda died; a few years later Chicken George fell into a fire and was killed. Tom and his wife Irene's daughter Cynthia married Will Palmer, who managed a lumber mill. They told their daughter, Bertha, the story of the African. At college, Bertha met Simon Alexander Haley. They married and had a son, Alex Haley.

As a boy, Haley listened to relatives talk about their ancestor, Kunta Kinte. He used his journalistic skills, developed in the Coast Guard, to track down his ancestors. *The Reader's Digest* financed his search, which took him to the Gambian village of Juffure, where a *griot*—an oral historian—told the Kinte family's story. When the *griot* told about young Kunta Kinte who went out to cut wood and was never seen again, Haley knew he had finished his ancestor's tale. Haley and the Mandingos were ecstatic. Haley found records of the ship on which Kunta was transported and of Kunta's sale from John to William Waller. Haley spent ten nights on a plank in a freighter's hold to get a hint of his ancestor's experience.

Critical Evaluation:

Alex Haley's *Roots: The Saga of an American Family* has been both lauded for giving African American people a sense of identity and condemned for amateurish style and sloppy scholarship. It deserves both the praise and the criticism. Haley called it a "novelized amalgam" of factual history and of fiction.

Spawning perhaps the most important television miniseries of the late twentieth century, *Roots* reminded black Americans of the value of their African heritage and the strength of their ancestors, who endured the grueling journey from Africa and the agony of slavery. The book prompted many African Americans to search for their own heritage. In short, it promoted black pride. The book and miniseries also made white Americans more aware of their ancestors' culpability for the plight of their black compatriots. In the light of history, especially when based on fact and presented so vividly, black anger made more sense.

Critics have pointed out that almost all of the black characters are strong and noble, and almost all of the white characters are weak, evil, foolish, or all three. For example, Kunta Kinte's father, Omoro, is brave, handsome, respectable, and perfect as a role model for his four healthy sons, while the slave traders and owners (who include most white characters in the book) beat, shackle, rape, and mutilate people.

Roots is also criticized for its adolescent style. Haley includes some references to sex, including masturbation, to aim for mature audiences, but the work is generally most appropriate for high school readers. The style is often amateurish, and the book lacks the subtlety and complexity of character to make it great literature. For example, in chapter 67, after a fight with Bell, Kunta Kinte has the following reverie:

> It pained him to think how grievously he had underestimated her and the other blacks.
> Though they never showed it except to those they loved, and sometimes not even then, he realized at last that they felt—and hated—no less than he the oppressiveness under which they all lived. He wished he could find a way to tell her how sorry he was, how he felt her pain, how grateful he was to feel her love, how strong he felt the bond between them growing deep within himself.

Historical references are often clumsy, and Haley has been roundly criticized for sloppy scholarship, such as having Kunta Kinte working in huge cotton fields in Virginia, where almost no cotton was grown; having Mandinka people kiss children, a use of the mouth they would have considered dirty; and having Chicken George not know he was free after going to England and being in New York.

The book also becomes much less interesting near the end, when Haley briefly chronicles his last few ancestors. His final chapter, which describes his research, would be more appropriate as an introduction or an epilogue. *Roots* is not a particularly well-written book. It has not received much scholarly or critical attention. It is, however, an extremely important work in American culture for its attention to slavery and African heritage.

M. Katherine Grimes

Bibliography:

Arnez, Nancy L. "From His Story to Our Story: A Review of *Roots*." *The Journal of Negro Education* 46 (Summer, 1977): 367-372. Sees the book as a gift to African Americans, restoring their heritage. Believes that it and the television miniseries of the same name have helped white Americans to understand the horrors of slavery.

Baldwin, James. "How One Black Man Came to Be an American." *New York Times Book Re-*

view, September 26, 1976, 1-2. This important African American writer compliments Haley's re-creation of Kinte's Africa. Emphasizes the impact of generations on following ones and history's effects on individuals.

Cooke, Michael G. "Roots as Placebo." *Yale Review* 67 (Autumn, 1977): 144-146. Criticizes Haley's writing as adolescent, neither subtle nor complex. Asserts that its magic comes from sentimentality, from promising more than it delivers, and from a placebo effect: It pretends to deal with U.S. disease and a strong cure, but is too mild to heal.

Courlander, Harold. "Kunta Kinte's Struggle to Be African." *Phylon: The Atlanta University of Race and Culture* 47 (December, 1986): 294-302. Questions Haley's scholarship. Asserts that Kinte, although unbelievable, is "an unreconstructed African."

Stein, Howard F. "In Search of *Roots*: An Epic of Origins and Destiny." *Journal of Popular Culture* XI (Summer, 1977): 11-17. Asserts that discussing *Roots* would help race relations in the United States; therefore, it is not just about the past but also for the future. Says that Kunta Kinte learned "other ways of fighting slavery than fleeing it," but also thinks that Haley stereotyped black people as strong and white people as evil.

THE ROPE

Type of work: Drama
Author: Plautus (c. 254-184 B.C.E.)
Type of plot: Comedy
Time of plot: Late third century B.C.E.
Locale: Cyrene, in Libya
First performed: Rudens, late third or early second century B.C.E. (English translation, 1694)

Principal characters:
DAEMONES, an aged Athenian
PALAESTRA, his daughter
AMPELISCA, a slave woman
PLESIDIPPUS, a young man in love with Palaestra
LABRAX, a procurer
CHARMIDES, an aged Sicilian, his guest
GRIPUS, a servant of Daemones
TRACHALIO, a servant of Plesidippus

The Story:

Daemones, an old Athenian exiled from Athens, had come to Cyrene to spend his waning years. He was a kindly man, and his exile had come about as a result of his excessive generosity to others and consequent indebtedness, rather than from any sort of dishonorable activity on his part. Nor were his impoverishment and exile his only misfortunes. Some years before, his daughter Palaestra, then a girl, had been stolen from him and sold by the thief to the procurer Labrax, who brought her, unknown to her father, to Cyrene. There she was reared and educated by Labrax, and there, as she approached maturity, the young Plesidippus saw her and fell in love with her. Wanting to secure her freedom, he arranged to buy her from Labrax for thirty minae. He gave the procurer a retainer and bound him by oath to turn Palaestra over to him when he paid the full sum agreed upon.

Labrax was as unscrupulous as his profession would suggest. When the Sicilian, Charmides, suggested that the procurer could get a much better price out of his women by taking them to Sicily, Labrax decided to ignore his contract. He contrived to get Plesidippus out of the way by arranging to meet him before the Temple of Venus for a sacrificial breakfast. The night before, however, he moved Palaestra and her fellow slave, Ampelisca, together with all his belongings aboard ship. Then, accompanied by Charmides, he set sail. A storm arose during the night, wrecking the ship, casting Labrax and his guest on the rocks, and permitting Palaestra and Ampelisca to escape in a small boat. The two young women landed near the Temple of Venus, not far from the house of Daemones. After asking sanctuary of the priestess, they went inside.

A short time later Ampelisca was sent to Daemones' house for water. On her way, she encountered Plesidippus' servant, Trachalio, who had come to the temple looking for his master. She sent him inside to see Palaestra. While she was waiting for the servant of Daemones to bring her the water, however, she spied Labrax and Charmides, whom she had believed dead, laboriously making their way to the temple from the place where the sea had washed them up on the rocks. Terrified, she hastened back to the temple to warn her friend.

When Labrax and Charmides arrived, wet and tattered, they devoted most of their remaining energy to mutual recriminations for their plight until the procurer learned from a servant that his two slaves were not drowned but were inside the temple. He rushed in, intent on saving at least that much of his property, and attempted to drag the two slaves away from the statue of Venus at whose feet they had sought sanctuary. Trachalio witnessed this violence and came out, calling for aid for the outraged suppliants. Daemones heard him and brought his servants to the slaves' assistance. Labrax was soundly beaten, but without quelling his determination to get back his two slaves. Then, while Daemones' men held the struggling procurer, Trachalio went to find Plesidippus and bring him to the temple. On his arrival the young Athenian, angry at the outrageous trick Labrax had nearly succeeded in playing on him, dragged the scoundrel to justice.

Daemones took the two young women home with him; on the previous night he had dreamed that he had prevented a she-ape from stealing the fledglings from a swallow's nest. He believed that the episode with Labrax was in some way a fulfillment of that dream and that the slaves, therefore, were somehow important to him. He had no sooner escorted the two young women inside the door than his wife, jealous of their youth and beauty, created an intolerable furor on the grounds that he had brought harlots into the house.

Meanwhile, Daemones' servant, Gripus, was making his way home from a morning's fishing, elated at having pulled up in his nets a large container which, unknown to him, had been lost by Labrax the night before and which contained, in addition to the procurer's own wealth, certain tokens that would help Palaestra to identify her parents if she should ever encounter them. Gripus intended to keep the contents of the container for himself, but on his way home Trachalio overtook him, recognized the container, and raised such a clamor that Daemones was finally brought out to arbitrate between them. Trachalio told the old man whose container it was and said that it contained, among other things, the identifying trinkets of Palaestra. To test Trachalio's story, Daemones asked Palaestra to describe the trinkets. Her description both fitted the contents of the container and revealed that the slave was Daemones' long-lost daughter. Father and daughter, united in great joy, ignored Gripus' claims to ownership of the remainder of the container's contents and went into Daemones' house.

By that time the case of Labrax had been tried by the court, and it had been decided that the procurer had no legal title to Palaestra, for she had been born free. Ampelisca, however, was adjudged rightfully his, and he returned to the temple to look for her. Overhearing Gripus grumbling about the container, he questioned him and to his joy learned that it had been recovered. Promising Gripus a talent of silver for identifying the container's present possessor, he was directed to Daemones, who, scrupulously honest, returned it willingly. The procurer was about to go off when Gripus protested that the talent of silver had not yet been paid. Although Labrax had sworn on the altar of Venus to give the money to the servant, who wanted to buy his freedom, Gripus would have had nothing for his pains if Daemones had not intervened. The old man suggested that Labrax give Gripus only half a talent and give Ampelisca her freedom for the remainder. To this suggestion Labrax agreed. Even Gripus was content with it when he learned that Daemones was willing to give him his freedom for the half talent.

One of the first things that Daemones did in his newly recovered status as father was to betroth his daughter to Plesidippus. In addition, he agreed to encourage the young man to give Trachalio his freedom and permit him to marry Ampelisca if she were willing. Then everyone, including Labrax, had a hearty dinner with Daemones.

Critical Evaluation:

The Rope is one of Plautus' longer plays. Some scholars think that it is also his finest play. In some respects, it is not a typical play. For one thing, the setting, on the African seacoast, is distinctly exotic, compared to the typical urban settings of much Roman comedy. In general tone, the play is more poetic than the Plautine comedies, which tend to be raucous. The emotions are serious in this play, with an ending that reintegrates all the characters, even the villainous pimp. The storm and the shipwreck and the final universal forgiveness evoke the atmosphere of romance so familiar in plays such as *The Tempest* (1611-1612), by William Shakespeare.

In other ways, *The Rope* has some typical elements. As the prologue reminds the audience, Plautus' play is based on the Greek play by Diphilus, who named the town Cyrene. This is a reminder to any audience of the standard practice of Plautus' times; the Roman playwrights translated the Greek originals, creating a category called *comoediae palliatae*, that is, comedies in Greek dress. The translation is from Greek to Latin and includes changes in the details of locale and customs. This must have enabled the Roman dramatists to enjoy at least two advantages: They could amuse their audiences with the essential comic tool of incongruity achieved with anachronisms, and, if their satire and jokes gave offense, they could always claim they were poking fun at the Greeks, not at their Roman audiences.

Greek New Comedy, the most influential comedic formula in Western literature, has survived for thousands of years and continues to appeal to audiences today primarily through its transmission in the works of Latin playwrights, including Plautus. Certain aspects of *The Rope* are typical of this traditional comedy: the kidnapped child, the tokens of high birth, the villain, the thwarting of young love, the recognition scene, and the reuniting of families.

Plautus is known for creating memorably clever servants who engineer much of the comic action. In this respect, the servants in *The Rope* are typical, for Trachalio and Gripus provide most of the comedy. It is not unusual for memorable characterizations and speeches, such as Gripus' daydream of power and wealth, or the dialogue of the fishermen, to have little to do with the action; however, they can distinguish a play.

A distinctive aspect of *The Rope*, in keeping with its air of romance and fantasy, is the mystical element, much stronger here than in most of his other surviving works. The mystical element begins with the setting, which has two human habitations: Daemones' humble farmhouse and the temple of Venus. The prologue is spoken by Arcuturus, a bright star in the constellation, who, before telling the tale, provides a strong clue to its moral nature. The gods, he informs the audience, watch closely over human affairs, and they keep track of the good and the evil. He and other stars report back to Jove so that Jove may "confer prosperity" on the deserving.

In the story which follows, the gods do not directly arrange matters; still, a spiritual element pervades. The two women, miraculously saved from the storm and shipwreck, arrive at the temple of Venus. A minor character in the play, the Priestess of Venus, provides them with shelter and refuge. The temple becomes a focal point in the action, as the pimp tries to reclaim his "property" and the women fight him off.

In that respect, the women may be said to be "reborn" because of the storm, from their pathetic state as slaves to free women. Their rebirth, as one scholar has observed, takes on a mythic note: The goddess Venus was born from the tempestuous sea. Different versions of her birth have her coming either from the foam or from a shell. This play may well be the first literary allusion in classical literature to the Venus-rising-from-a-shell version. Another mystical element is Daemones' dream of the ape and the fledglings in the swallow's nest. The dream inspires him to protect the two slaves.

An indirect allusion to rebirth continues in the matter of the container that is recovered from the sea. The tug of war between the servants—which includes the rope referred to in the title—while a fine bit of comic business, also brings in the box containing the proof that

Palaestra is Daemones' daughter. Curiously for a young female character in similar comedies, Palaestra is more concerned with her identity with and finding her family than she is interested in her hardworking, faithful lover, Plesidippus. When the box also survives the storm and reappears, her fond wish is granted, for Daemones recognizes his long-lost daughter, and the family, so long separated and broken, is reunited and whole again.

Plautus' plays seemed to have been very popular in his lifetime and later. The plays are so popular, in fact, his name has been attached to about a hundred plays. Whether or not he wrote that many, over the years about twenty complete ones that have survived have come to be accepted as his. To describe a typical Plautine comedy or even a typical New Comedy is, therefore, to describe the comedy on the basis of incomplete knowledge. Many plays have not survived, or have not yet been discovered.

The surviving plays of Plautus have not always pleased and delighted audiences. In the Middle Ages in Europe, for example, he was considered too boisterous. Although Latin scholars have appreciated his enormous talent for colloquial Latin and his wordplay, not all have respected his work. Much of it has seemed too lighthearted and superficial; the works are amusing, but they lack significant social commentary.

The Rope is an interesting example of his work because it has the trademark humor, comic characters, plot elements, and more. The myth of Venus' rebirth, a story that balances the destructive power of the sea with its benign, productive power, weaves throughout the play. This allusion flavors the conventional comedic story of family loss and reunion with a spirituality unusual in Plautus' extant comedies.

"Critical Evaluation" by Shakuntala Jayaswal

Bibliography:

Arnott, W. Geoffrey. *Menander, Plautus, Terence*. Oxford, England: Clarendon Press, 1975. An introductory survey of New Comedy. Brief comparisons suggest the similarities and differences between the Greek playwright and his Latin successors.

Duckworth, George. *The Nature of Roman Comedy: A Study in Popular Entertainment*. Princeton, N.J.: Princeton University Press, 1952. The classic study on the subject of Roman comedy. Provides a comprehensive introduction to Latin playwrights, including Plautus.

Konstan, David. "*Rudens*: City-State and Utopia." In *Roman Comedy*. Ithaca, N.Y.: Cornell University Press, 1983. Examines the plays of Plautus and Terence in the light of the cultural system in the ancient city-state society. Sees the theme of this play as an attempt to extend the boundaries beyond the city-state to include heaven and nature.

Leach, Eleanor Winsor. "Plautus' *Rudens*: Venus Born from a Shell." *Texas Studies in Literature and Language* 15, no. 5 (1974): 915-931. Analyzes the use of myth in Plautus' play. Sees the play as a reenactment of the birth of Venus, with her restorative powers, from the chaotic sea.

Segal, Erich. *Roman Laughter: The Comedy of Plautus*. Cambridge, Mass.: Harvard University Press, 1968. Organized by topics. Presents an argument about Plautus' comedy as a whole: His comedy was meant to make the Romans laugh by reversing Roman values on stage.

ROSENCRANTZ AND GUILDENSTERN ARE DEAD

Type of work: Drama
Author: Tom Stoppard (Tomas Straussler, 1937-   )
Type of plot: Existential
Time of plot: 1600
Locale: Denmark
First performed: 1966; first published, 1967

Principal characters:
ROSENCRANTZ, a courtier to the Danish throne
GUILDENSTERN, a courtier to the Danish throne
THE PLAYER, an actor and manager of a troupe of traveling players
ALFRED, one of the players
TRAGEDIANS, actors in the troupe of traveling players
HAMLET, prince of Denmark
CLAUDIUS, king of Denmark and Hamlet's uncle
GERTRUDE, queen of Denmark and Hamlet's mother
POLONIUS, advisor to the king
OPHELIA, his daughter

The Story:

In nondescript surroundings, Rosencrantz and Guildenstern gambled at tossing coins. Rosencrantz kept winning but remained calm about his unusual lucky streak. Guildenstern reflected uneasily about this apparent suspension of the laws of probability, which caused him to begin questioning the nature of the reality into which he and Rosencrantz had been plunged. They had no memory of past events, except for a vague recollection of having been sent for. Dismayed at being unable to account for themselves or their situation, they felt stranded and without direction.

Their speculations were interrupted by the arrival of a band of motley players on their way to the Danish court. The principal player greeted Rosencrantz and Guildenstern enthusiastically, for he hoped they would pay for a performance. The Player informed them that his company did on stage what other people did off stage. Guildenstern was offended by this suggestion of a lewd performance. He requested that the players perform something more traditional.

Hamlet and Ophelia passed by; Hamlet was disheveled and Ophelia distraught. They were followed by Claudius and Gertrude, who seemed to know who the courtiers were but were unable to distinguish between them. Claudius told them that Hamlet had been transformed and that they were to "glean" what afflicted him. Gertrude promised them a royal reward. The king's advisor, Polonius, told Claudius and Gertrude that he knew the cause of Hamlet's lunacy.

Rosencrantz and Guildenstern were disquieted by all this activity. Guildenstern remarked that they were caught up in events beyond their comprehension. Guildenstern pretended to be Hamlet while Rosencrantz practiced the art of "gleaning." Then they overheard Hamlet telling Polonius that he could be the same age as Hamlet if he could walk backwards like a crab. Polonius left in a state of confusion. Hamlet greeted them as two old friends, but he, too, confused their identities. They attempted to "delve" into the cause of Hamlet's lunacy, but discovered nothing except that Hamlet could tell a hawk from a handsaw when the wind was southerly. Hamlet left the courtiers and then returned with the tragedians and Polonius. Hamlet planned to have the players enact "The Murder of Gonzago" for the Danish court. The Player left to study the extra lines written by Hamlet.

After Claudius and Gertrude questioned Rosencrantz and Guildenstern and discovered that they had been unsuccessful as spies, they determined that Polonius was to spy on Hamlet and Ophelia. Claudius decided that he must send Hamlet to England. Rosencrantz and Guildenstern were completely confused by the events they had witnessed. The tragedians rehearsed the play to be performed before the court, and Rosencrantz and Guildenstern, though without realizing it, witnessed an enactment of their own fate, death at the hands of the king of England.

Claudius was displeased by the play. On the way to hide the body of the murdered Polonius, Hamlet dragged the corpse past Rosencrantz and Guildenstern. Then Claudius gave Rosencrantz and Guildenstern the task of escorting Hamlet to England. Rosencrantz and Guildenstern found themselves on board a ship headed for England. Guildenstern summarized their situation: They were Rosencrantz and Guildenstern bearing a letter from one king to another and they were taking Hamlet to England. They rehearsed their audience with the king of England and in the process discovered that the letter given to them by Claudius condemned Hamlet to death. Once again, they were terribly disconcerted.

They heard music coming from barrels on the ship's deck and discovered that the tragedians were on board as well. The Player told them the play had offended the king. Guildenstern struggled to discover a pattern in these events. Pirates attacked the ship. After the skirmish, Rosencrantz and Guildenstern discovered that Hamlet was missing. Having a letter to the English king but no Hamlet made them very uneasy. Once again, they rehearsed their audience with the king of England. When they came to the part about the letter, they discovered that the letter condemned not Hamlet, but them, to death. Guildenstern was enraged by the senselessness of their situation and by the Player's calm reaction to their impending deaths. He snatched up the Player's dagger and stabbed him in the throat. The Player died in a theatrical manner. The tragedians, who were watching with interest, applauded with enthusiasm. The befuddled Guildenstern examined the Player's dagger and discovered that it had a retractable blade. The Player modestly evaluated his performance as merely competent, informing the courtiers that enactments of death, not death itself, were all that people really believed in. Resigned to his fate, a weary Guildenstern reflected that death is essentially absence. Rosencrantz declared that he was relieved to be done with it. With these words, he disappeared. Still puzzled by the circumstances of his existence, Guildenstern ceased to exist. The ambassador from England returned to the Danish court and announced that "Rosencrantz and Guildenstern are dead."

Critical Evaluation:

Tom Stoppard's plays revolutionized twentieth century theater with their combination of comic wit and serious themes. His first major dramatic work, *Rosencrantz and Guildenstern Are Dead*, was first performed on April 11, 1966 at the Old Vic Theatre, London, by the National Theatre Company. That same year, the work received the Play and Players Award for best new play in England, and in 1968 it received the Antoinette Perry (Tony) Award for best play and the New York Drama Critics Circle Award for best play. In the years that followed, Stoppard's work ranged from a collaboration with Terry Gilliam (of Monty Python fame) on the screenplay of *Brazil* (1985, Los Angeles Critics Circle Award for best original screenplay) to screen adaptations of works by Vladimir Nabokov, Graham Greene, and E. L. Doctorow. A prolific and brilliant writer, Stoppard also continued to write plays, including *Travesties* (1974) and *The Real Thing* (1984).

In William Shakespeare's *Hamlet*, Rosencrantz and Guildenstern, the two courtiers summoned by Claudius to spy on Hamlet, bear to the English king the order for their own execution. As characters, they remain undefined, functioning in tandem as ciphers for a sort of banal treachery, their services purchased by the promise of reward. As spies they prove clumsy and inept. As foils for Hamlet, they are beheaded by the English king.

In *Rosencrantz and Guildenstern Are Dead*, Stoppard turns *Hamlet* inside out by retelling the story from the courtiers' point of view, a very different one indeed. The Player reminds the confused courtiers that there is a design in all art, a finality toward which all events point. This is appropriate for the characters in *Hamlet*, who sweep across the stage with a sense of sureness and identity, but it totally bewilders Rosencrantz and Guildenstern, who have no memory of the past nor comprehension of the future. Although they struggle to make sense of their situation, for them existence is episodic and without pattern. The vaguely menacing Player informs them that all events lead to death, "the bad end unhappily, the good unluckily." In response to Guildenstern's inquiry, "Who decides?," the Player responds, "It is written." Rosencrantz and Guildenstern are unaware of their fictive existence. They must fill in the time between their brief appearances in *Hamlet* until they meet death at the hands of the English king. Thus we find them tossing coins on the road to Elsinore. When they encounter the tragedians on their way to court, it is as part of the *Hamlet* script, which defines and controls them.

Stoppard imparts individual quirks of character to the virtually indistinguishable Rosencrantz and Guildenstern of Shakespeare's play. The simple and uninquiring Rosencrantz and the perpetually perplexed Guildenstern charm the audience. Their efforts to extricate themselves from a situation beyond their comprehension engenders uncomfortable laughter, for the audience is aware of their fate and the futility of their situation. Rosencrantz and Guildenstern engage the audience's sympathy because they have ceased to be nonentities; moreover, their plight mirrors the confused alienation present in much of modern life. It is this realization that contributes to the poignancy of the announcement of their deaths by the English ambassador at the end of Stoppard's play, which is in sharp contrast to the feelings engendered by their deaths in *Hamlet*.

Stoppard has given the existential dilemma a new twist. For Rosencrantz and Guildenstern, essence precedes existence. The course of their lives has been predetermined; consequently, choosing between alternatives is meaningless. For them, alternatives do not really exist. Guildenstern is vaguely aware that the reality they inhabit is of a different order when the tossed coin invariably comes up heads in defiance of the laws of probability. The Player, who provides the bridge between *Hamlet* and *Rosencrantz and Guildenstern Are Dead*, understands the situation perfectly. He has been through all this before, his memory of events unimpeded by a scripted death. He knows not only the fictional nature of his existence but the fate of the doomed courtiers. The unfortunate Rosencrantz and Guildenstern mistake themselves for real people, which is why their search for meaning elicits sympathy from an audience that shares the Player's knowledge of the senseless deaths awaiting them.

Unlike Rosencrantz and Guildenstern, the audience exists in a reality where choice appears to affect outcome. Knowing that Rosencrantz and Guildenstern are unaware that they share a predetermined end suggests the notion that humankind might be in the same boat, a metaphor that Stoppard employs in the third act. Because they are free to move about and improvise on board the boat that bears them to England, Rosencrantz and Guildenstern share the illusion of freedom as they move toward their rendezvous with death.

Rosencrantz and Guildenstern Are Dead contradicts Arthur Miller's contention that attention must be paid to the tragedy of the common man. Stoppard's play suggests that the ennobling qualities of tragedy may be limited to principal characters. Hamlet goes to his death secure in the knowledge that he has acted within the scope of a provident deity. But Rosencrantz and Guildenstern cease to exist without having acquired the wisdom of experience or the dignity of meaning. For Stoppard their comic search for meaning within an incomprehensible context more closely parallels the human condition than does the dramatic death of a tragic hero. When Rosencrantz and Guildenstern simply cease to exist, the audience is moved by their absence, for Stoppard has endowed them with a humanity that transcends the pointlessness of their existence. In this sense their fictive lives parallel Stoppard's work, wherein comedy is to be taken seriously, and tragedy is leavened with comic wit.

David Sundstrand

Bibliography:

Brassell, Tim. *Tom Stoppard: An Assessment*. New York: St. Martin's Press, 1985. An excellent discussion of Stoppard's themes that includes a chapter on *Rosencrantz and Guildenstern Are Dead*.

Corballis, Richard. *Stoppard: The Mystery and the Clockwork*. Oxford: Amber Lane Press, 1984. Corballis suggests that, with the death of tragedy in the twentieth century, Hamlet had to be redefined and that Guildenstern is the existential hero.

Hunter, Jim. *Tom Stoppard's Plays*. New York: Grove Press, 1982. Hunter discusses Stoppard's work from the perspective of staging, playing, talking, and thinking. Also provides a study guide with page references to listed discussions.

Jenkins, Anthony. *The Theatre of Tom Stoppard*. Cambridge, England: Cambridge University Press, 1987. Thematic interpretations of Stoppard's work, with an interesting discussion of *Rosencrantz and Guildenstern Are Dead* that explores their plight as a game where the rules are not understood by all the players.

Schlueter, Jane. *Metafictional Characters in Modern Drama*. Columbia: Columbia University Press, 1979. Includes the chapter "Stoppard's Moon and Birdboot, Rosencrantz and Guildenstern," an excellent discussion of the way in which Stoppard handles characters who move between different fictive realities.

ROSMERSHOLM

Type of work: Drama
Author: Henrik Ibsen (1828-1906)
Type of plot: Social realism
Time of plot: Mid-nineteenth century
Locale: Small coastal town in western Norway
First published: 1886; first performed, 1887 (English translation, 1889)

Principal characters:
JOHANNES ROSMER, a former clergyman
REBECCA WEST, his friend
RECTOR KROLL, the schoolmaster
ULRIC BRENDEL, a disillusioned liberal
PETER MORTENSGARD, a publisher
MADAM HELSETH, housekeeper at Rosmersholm

The Story:

Since the death of his wife, Beata, Johannes Rosmer had turned more and more to his friend, Rebecca West. Rosmer had had an unhappy marriage with an unsympathetic, neurotic wife who had taken her own life in a millpond. Rebecca had been her friend, as well as the husband's. Beata's brother, Rector Kroll, the schoolmaster, was also Rosmer's close friend.

Rector Kroll called on Rosmer to get him to join a political drive against the new liberal party that was gaining power in the village. The party was controlled by Peter Mortensgard, publisher of the *Beacon*, a paper Rector Kroll considered radical and dangerous because it criticized the conservative party, which he represented. Kroll was disappointed to learn that Rosmer no longer held his former static views on politics and social structures but, instead, supported the liberals. Rosmer's real concern was not with politics at all, but only with encouraging people to ennoble their souls; he felt the new party was a step toward this goal. Rebecca supported him in his belief.

While they talked, Madam Helseth, the housekeeper, announced Ulric Brendel, a self-styled genius who was going to the village to offer his services to the liberal party. Brendel was in rags and obviously without any means of livelihood, and to Rector Kroll he epitomized the liberals. To Rosmer and Rebecca, however, Brendel was a man living and working as his conscience directed, and they helped him with clothing and money.

This act turned Kroll against them. He now turned on Rosmer savagely and accused him of betraying his class. Rosmer had been a clergyman, and Kroll attempted to plead with him from a religious point of view, but Rosmer claimed that he had also renounced the church and become a freethinker. He felt that people were growing so bitter in political struggles that they must be brought back to tolerance and good will. It was his hope that he could aid in this task by renouncing his way of life and working with the new leaders.

Kroll then accused Rosmer of living in sin with Rebecca, even though he had defended Rosmer and Rebecca when town gossips had whispered about them. He accused Rebecca of influencing Rosmer in his new attitude and suggested that she had been responsible for the suicide of Rosmer's wife. He said his sister had believed that Rosmer wished to wed Rebecca, and for that reason she had drowned herself. Kroll maintained he had not spoken up before because he did not know that Rebecca was an emancipated woman, and he had not believed her capable of such actions. His worst thoughts about Rosmer and Rebecca were confirmed when Peter Mortensgard appeared at Rosmer's home in answer to a note Rebecca had written him in Brendel's behalf. When Kroll left, he promised to inform the town of Rosmer's treachery.

Mortensgard had come to solicit Rosmer's aid in the liberal cause, but when he learned that Rosmer had left the church, he did not want the former clergyman's help. He needed Christians, not freethinkers, as he himself was, and so Rosmer was left with no one to support. Mortensgard, too, slyly accused Rosmer and Rebecca of indiscretions and of causing the death of Rosmer's wife.

From that time on Rosmer began to feel guilty about his part in her death and feared that he had not concealed his true feelings for Rebecca from his wife. Determined not to let the past rule his life, he asked Rebecca to marry him. She fled from him sobbing, swearing that she could never marry him, that if he ever asked her again she would die the way his wife had died.

Kroll did his work well. The paper supporting his party accused Rosmer of betraying his class to gain favor with the liberals. The article linked Rebecca and Rosmer in a debasing way. Rosmer wanted to fight back, if only to free people's minds from pettiness and mass thinking, but he felt that he could not accomplish this task because he no longer felt innocent of his wife's death; only the innocent could lead others.

Rebecca decided to give him back his purity of conscience. In Kroll's presence she told Rosmer that she alone was responsible for his wife's suicide. She said that she had come to Rosmersholm for the sole purpose of converting Rosmer to the liberal party. She knew that Brendel had once had great influence over Rosmer, and she hoped to renew that influence and win him to the emancipators. With victory in sight, his wife was a stumbling block. To overcome that obstacle, she made that sick woman believe that she was going to have a child by Rosmer. In desperation the wife threw herself into the millpond. Rebecca's love for Rosmer made her confess so that he could clear his own conscience of all guilt. Kroll and Rosmer left her alone after her confession, and she prepared to leave Rosmersholm forever.

While she packed, Rosmer returned and told her his old friends had persuaded him that the task of ennobling people's minds was not for him, or for anyone. He told her that he knew she had only used him to attain her own goals. Then she made her greatest confession to him. She said that she had first been moved by physical passion. She had plotted to get rid of his wife. Then, after the suicide, Rebecca had come to feel such deep and quiet love for Rosmer that it had taken her spirit from her. He had ennobled her soul.

Rosmer could not quite believe her story; he feared that she was again using him for her own purposes. As they talked, Brendel appeared and told them that he was leaving town, that his genius was gone, and he was bankrupt. He told them, too, that Mortensgard was the only one who could win their cause, for he was without ideals. Only those without ideals could gain a victory. He said also that Rosmer could gain victory if the woman who loved him would convince him of her loyalty. After Brendel left them, Rosmer asked Rebecca to prove that he had ennobled her soul. The price was high. He asked her to throw herself into the millpond as she had caused his wife to do. Only her self-inflicted death could give him back his faith in himself, she agreed to his plan. Since they no longer believed in a judgment after death, they must punish themselves for their love. At the last minute, Rosmer decided to join Rebecca in death. They stood with their arms entwined, then threw themselves into the pond.

Critical Evaluation:

The last of Henrik Ibsen's social dramas, *Rosmersholm* gives readers a glimpse of the psychological studies he was to write later. In this play, Ibsen continues the attempt to arouse his readers to raise themselves above the mass, not to be pulled down to the level of the popular majority. This work is written with the dramatist's usual skill and ranks with his other great plays.

Rosmersholm is literally the home of Rosmer, but in keeping with the temper of the play, the title actually signifies a spiritual homecoming for Johannes Rosmer. His life, both personal and political, is stormy. Almost without realizing it, he finds himself associated with unpopular political causes and movements by his friendship with Brendel and Mortensgard. In a similar vein, his relationship with Rebecca West, after Beata's suicide, further alienates him from the mainstream. Former friends and colleagues—notably Rector Kroll—desert him, forsake him, and betray him. His admission of religious lapse only exacerbates the situation. When all of his life seems to tumble about him like a house of cards, Rosmer seeks reassurance by asking Rebecca to make the ultimate sacrifice of her life. At the decisive moment, Rosmer elects to join her in suicide. In so doing, Rosmer finds his home—his spiritual home, Rosmersholm—that had formerly eluded him.

In reality, Rosmer only toys with politics. He does not have the committed revolutionary's dedicated zeal; he is not capable of the self-sacrifice involved in giving himself over to a cause. His loyalties are divided between public issues and personal gratification. In the end, he chooses the latter, an important decision signifying a shift in Ibsen's focus and emphasis. Ibsen's earlier work deals with social issues of consequence to masses of people. *Rosmersholm* is a transitional piece that marks a change from social issues, which are a feature of his earlier dramas, to personal and individual concerns, which characterize Ibsen's later dramas.

Still, *Rosmersholm* is a politically charged play, for Rosmer's social ostracizing is more a consequence of his political philosophy than of his presumed unconventional lifestyle. In fact, the latter is attributed to the former, and much of the action in the play revolves around political philosophy and meetings with political figures, creating an onus from which even Rebecca is not exempt. The liberal-versus-conservative argument is the fulcrum of the conflict, with the issue of the so-called emancipated woman—Rebecca—serving as a microcosm of the entire macrocosm of the dispute. Rosmer's loyalties are thus ground between the Scylla of public principle and the Charybdis of personal passion. Ibsen offers the only logical possible solution to the dilemma: in effect, a mutual suicide pact. The inevitability of this conclusion is not clear from the start; it only emerges in the unfolding of the play. As a consequence of such subtlety, the dramatic dimensions of *Rosmersholm* are enhanced to tragic proportions, making the play, despite its ambivalent stance, a genuine classic of its kind.

Bibliography:

Durbach, Errol. *"Ibsen the Romantic": Analogues of Paradise in the Later Plays.* Athens: University of Georgia Press, 1982. A tracing of romantic elements in Ibsen's later plays. The section on *Rosmersholm*, a play that Durbach considers bleak and depressing, discusses how joy nevertheless can be found in the midst of despair.

Holtan, Orley I. *Mythic Patterns in Ibsen's Last Plays.* Minneapolis: University of Minnesota Press, 1970. An overview of the mythic content in Ibsen's last seven plays, Holtan's study contains a good discussion of the echoes from ancient Scandinavian mythology that can be heard in *Rosmersholm*.

Johnston, Brian. *The Ibsen Cycle: The Design of the Plays from "Pillars of Society" to "When We Dead Awaken."* Boston: Twayne, 1975. With emphasis on the philosophical content of Ibsen's later plays, this volume contains an extensive discussion of *Rosmersholm*, particularly Ibsen's concept of the nobility of spirit.

Meyer, Michael. *Ibsen: A Biography*. Garden City, N.Y.: Doubleday, 1971. A standard biography of Ibsen, it contains a good discussion of both the play itself and its place in Ibsen's canon, in which, according to Meyer, it marks the transition from a concern with matters of society to a focus on the internal life of individuals.

Weigand, Hermann J. *The Modern Ibsen: A Reconsideration*. New York: Henry Holt, 1925. Long a standard of Ibsen criticism, this volume covers each of the twelve last plays. The section on *Rosmersholm* offers a detailed and incisive explication, with emphasis on the psychological motivations of each of the characters, and serves as an excellent introduction for the general reader.

ROUGHING IT

Type of work: Fictionalized autobiography
Author: Mark Twain (Samuel Langhorne Clemens, 1835-1910)
First published: 1872

Roughing It is a partly fictional account of Mark Twain's travel to the Nevada Territory and to California, his varied life there, colorful personalities encountered, and his visit to the Hawaiian Islands (then called the Sandwich Islands). Interspersed throughout are factual and semifactual journalistic reports, as well as tall tales. The book covers Mark Twain's stagecoach trip with his brother Orion Clemens, the newly appointed secretary of the Nevada Territory, from St. Joseph, Missouri, to Carson City, Nevada (July to August, 1861); Twain's unsuccessful efforts to stake a timber claim and to prospect for silver (until August, 1862); his reporting and freelance writing for the *Territorial Enterprise* of Virginia City, Nevada (until May, 1864); his reporting for the *San Francisco Morning Call* (1864 to 1865); his trip to Hawaii (March to August, 1866); his work in San Francisco (until December, 1866); and his return to the East Coast through the isthmus of Panama (December, 1866 to January, 1867).

Between the time of his return to the United States and the publication of *Roughing It*, Mark Twain enjoyed a varied life. Details of his trip in 1867 to Europe and the Holy Land were converted into his best-seller *The Innocents Abroad*, published in 1869. Soon after Mark Twain married Olivia Langdon of Elmira, New York, his publisher persuaded him to follow up on the success of *The Innocents Abroad* with an account of his earlier travels in the Far West. Promising to deliver a manuscript in January, 1871, Mark Twain wrote furiously for a time but was interrupted by his father-in-law's death and his wife's illness. He then grew so dissatisfied with his writing that he extensively revised and padded the work with additional source material, partly by including some of his own western journalistic pieces, to make a substantial book—for he always felt that it was necessary for a subscription book to be both a critical and a financial success. The final version, delivered in November, 1871, was flawed and uneven, but when it appeared in the United States and London in February, 1872, *Roughing It* was a success. Critical opinion regards *Roughing It* as his best travel book, along with *The Innocents Abroad*. Furthermore, since *Roughing It* reveals a great deal about the United States at a crucial period in its history (*The Innocents Abroad* mainly relates the responses of a set of unrepresentative American tourists in the Old World), it is a more significant cultural document.

The seventy-nine chapters of *Roughing It* fall into six separate and uneven parts. Getting to Carson City occupies chapters 1 through 20. Mark Twain's wandering, timber work, and efforts at mining are covered in chapters 21 through 41. After this, he describes his work as a reporter in Virginia City, Nevada, and his renewed attempts to strike it rich, this time in the California mine fields. The parts concerning the Hawaiian Islands (chapters 62 through 77) betray both haste and padding, and represent little in the way of "roughing it." Ever desirous to swell his production, Twain added three appendices: "Brief Sketch of Mormon History"; "The Mountain Meadows Massacre," about the Mormon slaughter of a California-bound wagon train in September, 1857; and "Concerning a Frightful Assassination That Was Never Consummated," about the alleged near-murder in 1870 of Conrad Wiegand, a naïvely idealistic, whistle-blowing journalist from Gold Hill, Nevada. The first American edition of *Roughing It* was published in one volume; when it was reprinted as part of *The Writings of Mark Twain* in 1899, it was divided into two volumes. Chapter 42, the first chapter of the second volume, begins most abruptly with "What to Do Next?", stalls by adding an autobiographical sketch, and seems to reveal not merely the unnamed narrator's uncertainty but perhaps Mark Twain's as well.

An excellent way of enjoying *Roughing It* is to notice how skillfully the narrator traces his evolution from a tenderfoot to an oldtimer. After naïvely dreaming of "Indians, deserts, and silver bars," he gladly agrees to accompany his brother to Nevada and plans to have fun in the Far West for three months. Mark Twain, who always loved numbers and arithmetic, regularly records distances covered and successive stops during their glorious, twenty-day stagecoach trek. For example, he reports that on the tenth day they arrive at Green River, then proceed to Fort Bridger, 1,025 miles away; next, a two-day stop at Salt Lake City, with 600 final miles to go. Early in the going, they discard unneeded items of fancy dress, they ineptly strap on weapons, and they stand in awe of Homeric stagecoach drivers, picturesque way stations, and colorful workers.

Four episodes combine to demonstrate the foolishness of Mark Twain's Eastern training. A coyote, "not a pretty creature, or respectable," is observed; he stays just out of pistol range, teases a town-bred dog with his "fraudful smile" only to outrun him, and thus becomes a symbolic King of the West—scrubby-looking, perhaps, but certainly in charge of the situation (chapter 5). Later, the narrator is persuaded by an auctioneer to buy a horse, the "Genuine Mexican Plug," which immediately bucks him off, darts away, throws other riders, and is finally given away to a passing emigrant more ignorant than its unhappy owner (chapter 24). (Here, Twain parades his genius at describing animals, as he will do again in chapter 61, which features the biography of Tom Quartz, a pocket-miner's cat.) Caught overnight in a Nevada snowstorm later, the narrator and two friends find their book-learning of no use: they cannot start a fire by discharging their pistols, and their horses do not stand loyally by (chapters 32 to 33). In "The Great Landslide Case," which is often anthologized separately, conniving Westerners relish fooling a pompous Eastern attorney into thinking that his client must lose his ranch when a neighbor's ranch has slid downhill intact and buried it (chapter 34). Mark Twain gradually recasts his narrator—first as a prospector and then as a journalist. In both endeavors the fellow sheds his greenhorn personality and grows pro-Western and knowledgeable—though often remaining humorously unsuccessful in his new pursuits. So mature and acclimated does he eventually become that he can simultaneously appreciate Western storytellers and report their vernacular style a bit superciliously. When, for example, the miner Scotty Briggs goes to a Virginia City parson at his "gospel-mill" to arrange for his lamented partner Buck Fanshaw's funeral, their conversation is a mixture of colorful Western slang and sacerdotal locutions. The episode spoofs both men's speech patterns, even while remaining aware of Scotty's total and utter sincerity (chapter 47).

Western topics covered in the chapters preceding the narrator's Hawaiian junket are quite varied and include criticism of the Western jury system, respect for education and professionalism, grudging admiration for a burly sea-captain's hanging of his black mate's killer, proof of flush-time vices (gambling, crime, brothels, jails, and "the birth of the 'literary' paper"), and praise of Chinese laborers for their many admirable traits and their contempt for the politicians and policemen who abuse them. Mark Twain surely reveals his writer fatigue when he invites the reader to skip chapter 52, which he announces will discuss silver mines in detail. The chapter that follows is graced with one of his most lovable literary triumphs—the story of Jim Blaine's grandfather's ram. Admirers get Jim "comfortably and sociably drunk" and then invite him to talk about the ram. Jim drones on and on, with each topic reminding him of another: a woman who loans her glass eye to a friend, a coffin-peddler's bewigged wife, a deacon whose first wife's daughter married a missionary and "died in grace—et up by the savages," a dog that upsets Calvinistic theories of predestination by nimbly avoiding an accident that cripples a fated human victim, a man "nipped" by a carpet-weaving machine that speedily turned him into a fourteen-yard rug, and so on. Old Jim discusses no fewer than twenty-seven named characters but nods off without ever getting to that ram.

Mark Twain enjoys the Hawaiian Islands because he can respond to their pristine scenery, criticize soul-deadening missionary work there, visit sites of historic importance, describe native tattoos and poi and hula dances, and report how he generously guarded lady bathers on whose clothes he sits to prevent their being stolen. He probably expends too many words on Hawaiian politics, which seems dated and somewhat stale now. But his thrilling description of volcanic eruptions—a stylish set piece reminiscent of several in *The Innocents Abroad*—is positively Miltonic. With fatigue clearly evident, he closes *Roughing It* with quick accounts of lecturing about Hawaii back in Nevada and California, and then returning aboard a cholera-infected steamer to New York, where he lugubriously notes many changes. Children he once knew now sport "whiskers or waterfalls," while many grown friends have been jailed or hanged.

Roughing It defies easy categorizing. Above all, it is a touched-up autobiography, the main purpose of which is to be a vehicle for Mark Twain's boastful account of his troubled maturation under Western skies. It is also a travel narrative that satirizes sentimental examples of the moribund genre even while it is a pioneering example of what eventually became known as new journalism or the nonfiction novel. Above all it is a mini-anthology of delightful Western tall tales and anecdotes. Twain wrote three more travel books after *The Innocents Abroad* and *Roughing It*: *A Tramp Abroad* (1880), *Life on the Mississippi* (1883), and *Following the Equator* (1897). The first part of *Life on the Mississippi* contains some of his best reminiscences, but the second part, as well as the other two travel books, betray a strained falling-off in quality. *Roughing It*, flawed though it is, remains universally regarded as one of the most durable books in its genre ever written.

Robert L. Gale

Bibliography:

Gale, Robert L. *Plots and Characters in the Works of Mark Twain.* 2 vols. Hamden, Conn.: Archon Books, 1973. Includes a summary of the events in *Roughing It* and detailed identifications of 177 persons figuring in the action.

Gerber, John. *Mark Twain.* Boston: Twayne, 1988. A concise introduction to *Roughing It*, with discussion of the composition, autobiographical elements, narrator's inconsistency, comic styles and devices, excessive exposition and description in the second volume, and resemblances to *The Innocents Abroad.*

Gunn, Drewey Wayne. "The Monomythic Structure of *Roughing It.*" *American Literature* 61 (December, 1989): 563-585. Sees *Roughing It* as an archetypal journey story: The hero leaves home, is challenged by obstacles, and gains self-knowledge.

Rasmussen, R. Kent. *Mark Twain A to Z.* New York: Facts On File, 1995. Contains a chapter-by-chapter synopsis of *Roughing It* that includes numerous cross-references to separate analytical essays on characters, places, and events mentioned in the text. Also offers a clear explanation of the relationship between episodes in the book and events in Mark Twain's own life.

Rogers, Franklin R. "The Road to Reality: Burlesque Travel Literature and Mark Twain's *Roughing It.*" *Bulletin of the New York Public Library* 67 (March, 1963): 155-168. Argues that Twain conflates the sentimentalist and the realist from burlesque travel literature into one persona, who begins as the romanticizing tenderfoot and emerges as the seasoned oldtimer. The book also reflects the disillusionment of post-Civil War writers.

Smith, Henry Nash. "Mark Twain as an Interpreter of the Far West: The Structure of *Roughing It*." In *The Frontier in Perspective*, edited by Walker D. Wyman and Clifton B. Kroeber. Madison: University of Wisconsin, 1957. Discusses the inconsistent voices of Twain's narrator, the naïve tenderfoot changing into oldtimer, satirist and parodist, observant reporter, custodian of official values, pompous moralist, and short-story teller.

ROXANA

Type of work: Novel
Author: Daniel Defoe (1660-1731)
Type of plot: Picaresque
Time of plot: Eighteenth century
Locale: England and Europe
First published: 1724

Principal characters:
ROXANA, a courtesan
AMY, her maid
MR. ——, her landlord
THE PRINCE DE ——
A MERCHANT

The Story:

Born in France, from which her parents fled because of religious persecution, Roxana grew to adolescence in England. At the age of fifteen, she married a handsome but conceited man. After seven years of marriage, during which time her husband went through all of their money, Roxana was left penniless with five children.

She appealed for aid to her husband's relatives, all of whom refused her except one old aunt, who was in no position to help her materially. Amy, Roxana's maid, refused to leave her mistress, although she received no wages for her work. Another poor old woman whom Roxana had aided during her former prosperity added her efforts to those of the old aunt and Amy. These good people managed to extract money from the relatives of the children's father. All five of the little ones were given over to the care of the poor old woman.

Roxana was penniless and at the point of despair when her landlord, after expressing his admiration for her, praised her fortitude under all of her difficulties and offered to set her up in housekeeping. He returned all the furniture he had confiscated, gave her food and money, and generally conducted himself with such kindness and candor that Amy urged Roxana to become the gentleman's mistress should he ask it. Roxana, however, clung to her virtuous independence. Fearing that the gentleman's kindness would go unrewarded, Amy, because she loved her mistress, offered to lie with the landlord in Roxana's place. This offer, however, Roxana refused to consider. The two women talked much about the merits of the landlord, his motive in befriending Roxana, and the moral implications of his attentions.

When he came to take residence as a boarder in Roxana's house, he proposed, since his wife had deserted him, that he and Roxana live as husband and wife. To show his good faith, he offered to share his wealth with her, bequeathing her five hundred pounds in his will and promising seven thousand pounds if he left her. There was a festive celebration that evening and a little joking about Amy's offer to lie with the gentleman. Finally Roxana, her conscience still bothering her, yielded to his protestations of love and slept with him.

After a year and a half had passed and Roxana had not conceived a child, Amy chided her mistress for her barrenness. Feeling that Mr. —— was not her true husband, Roxana sent Amy to him to beget a child. Amy did bear a child, which Roxana took as her own to save the maid embarrassment. Two years later, Roxana bore a daughter who died within six months. A year later, she pleased her lover by bearing a son.

Mr. —— took Roxana with him to Paris on business. There they lived in great style until he was robbed and murdered for the jewels he carried on his person. Roxana managed to retain the gentleman's wealth and secured it against the possible claims of his wife, who was still living.

In France, the Prince de —— hoped to make amends to Roxana for the murder of her protector by lavishing gifts upon her and flattering her beauty until she consented to be his mistress, this time allowing her virtue to be sullied not because of poverty but through vanity. In order to suppress gossip, Roxana pretended that she had gone back to England on business, confined herself to her quarters, and instructed Amy to admit only Prince de ——.

Roxana's new lover showered her bountifully with gifts. When she bore him a son, he promised to acknowledge the child as his own and to provide adequately for it. After the birth of the child, Roxana thought that she recognized her husband, a member of the gendarmes. Amy visited the man and found him to be the same worthless scoundrel who, years before, had abandoned his wife and five children. When the prince had to go to Italy on an official assignment, he took Roxana with him. They remained there for two years. She bore another son who lived only two months. Then the prince's wife died, and he, repenting his sins, parted from Roxana, who had been his faithful mistress for eight years.

Roxana and her maid sailed for England after engaging a merchant to handle Roxana's wealth. Roxana had to go to Holland to receive her money from the merchant. The merchant arrived in Holland from Paris and took lodgings in the same house. He and Roxana became well acquainted. The merchant wanted to marry her, but she, too avaricious and calculating to risk her wealth for a mere caprice of love, suspected his motives. She did allow him to seduce her, however, for she felt that she owed him some token of gratitude for his assistance. She was already pregnant when they parted.

Returning to London, Roxana settled her financial affairs and bore her son. She established herself in a handsome apartment and was courted by numerous fortune hunters, but her philosophy, as she chose to call it, would not permit her to marry anyone. As a wife, she would have to share her wealth; as a mistress, she received riches, and she was determined to amass a fortune.

Roxana gave lavish parties, which were attended by many fashionable people of London. Soon her name became famous. Her purpose was fulfilled when a rich lord offered her a substantial income if she would become his mistress. She retired from society, took a new apartment, and saw only the lord. She passed several years in this fashion. By that time, she was fifty years old. Tiring at last of her lover, she began to see her friends again.

With Amy's help, she began to live a different kind of life so that eventually she could assist her children. She took a room in another part of the city with a Quaker lady. Amy let people believe that her mistress had gone to Europe.

By chance, Roxana met the merchant whom she had known in Holland and whose son she had borne. The merchant renewed his suit. Although Amy sent word from Europe that Prince de —— was trying to find Roxana and wished to marry her, Roxana, having learned that her husband was dead, accepted the merchant's proposal. The pair planned to return to Holland and take residence there. They would declare themselves eleven years married in order to legitimize their son.

One of Roxana's legitimate daughters had by chance been her maid while Roxana lived in London. At first, the mother had tried to help her daughter by giving her, through Amy, money and advantages above her station. When the girl began to suspect that her mistress was her mother, Roxana was distressed, for she would be undone should her past be revealed. When

Amy, infuriated with the prying girl, threatened to murder her, Roxana, after many years' friendship, dismissed her faithful maid. At last, however, the persistent daughter's inquiries were silenced, and Roxana was able to go to Holland with her husband.

Critical Evaluation:

The Fortunate Mistress: Or, A History of the Life and Vast Variety of Fortunes of Mademoiselle de Beleau, Afterwards Call'd the Countess de Wintselsheim, in Germany, Being the Person Known by the Name of the Lady Roxana, in the Time of King Charles II, commonly known as *Roxana*, is the last novel in Daniel Defoe's series of great fictional works written between 1719 and 1724, which included *Robinson Crusoe* (1719), *Moll Flanders* (1722), and *A Journal of the Plague Year* (1722). Like its predecessors, it reflects the author's preoccupation with economic individualism and middle-class values as well as his dissenting Protestant orientation. Like other Defoe novels, *Roxana* is written in Defoe's characteristically robust style. At the same time, this prose work is unique, as it departs from the earlier novels to some degree in its point of view, its thematic variations, and its plot structure.

In *Roxana*, as in all of his works of fiction, Defoe is preoccupied with his characters' struggles for economic independence; Roxana, like Robinson Crusoe and Moll Flanders, is faced with poverty and starvation, but through her ambition, practicality, and shrewd business sense she overcomes tremendous obstacles, eventually amassing a fortune. Roxana and her predecessors are fiercely individual entrepreneurs. In order to stress their independence, Defoe typically isolates his heroes and heroines in some drastic way—Crusoe is shipwrecked; Moll and Roxana are social outcasts as a result of their criminal careers. Given these dire circumstances, Defoe shows how sheer necessity operates to make his characters act as they do.

Roxana is driven to a variety of criminal activities when she and her five children are abandoned by a worthless husband. Defoe had more than ample factual evidence upon which to draw such a portrait. It was during his age that modern urban civilization had first devised large police forces, detective networks complete with organized informant systems, and a complex court system for handling the huge new criminal population. Not only in his fiction but in countless journalistic pieces and pamphlets, Defoe argues passionately for the repeal of inhumane debtor's laws, which he recognized as the cause of so much crime and injustice. As he argues in one eloquent plea, "Necessity will make us all Thieves." At least partly connected with this intense social concern was Defoe's Protestant background. He did not believe in the religious tenets of Puritanism, but Defoe inherited its conception of human existence as a continual struggle, its habit of viewing everyday events as charged with moral significance, and its tendency toward introspection.

In *Roxana*, Defoe's social conscience and ethical underpinnings combine to produce a unique, and in many ways brilliant novel, which is difficult to classify. On the surface, the work resembles a picaresque tale and shares many features with other works of that category. In other ways, however, *Roxana* is radically different from a traditional picaresque narrative, most significantly in the depth of its characterizations and in the implications of its plot. A picaro is typically the tool through which the author presents a series of comic episodes for the purpose of satirizing society and human folly. Defoe's heroine is a multidimensional individual. Roxana is a woman shaped by her environment and is constantly striving to get the better of it. In contrast to the picaro, whose misadventures never pose a serious threat to his or her life, Roxana's danger is real. She need only be apprehended to run the risk of hanging. Roxana's fears, pains, pleasures, and ambitions make her a human and sympathetic heroine. This quality of realism is further heightened by Defoe's distinctive style, which shows all the influences of his journalist's profession. He has a reporter's eye for detail, and he crowds his scenes with particulars, all described in plain, straightforward prose. His objective, unadorned language creates a powerful effect of verisimilitude. Defoe always insisted that his fictions were not romances (what one in contemporary times might also call adventure stories). Defoe's social and moral orientation, coupled with his wonderful capacity for "lying like the truth," place *Roxana* far beyond the realm of typical eighteenth century romances.

There is a strongly autobiographical flavor to all of Defoe's novels, which results largely from the author's close identification with his main characters. In its beginning sections, *Roxana* is no exception. Later in the narrative, a curious thing begins to happen. As Defoe develops Roxana's character—which he modeled closely on the actual careers of several real-life criminals—she begins to act in ways of which he cannot approve, and he loses his sympathy and close imaginative identification with her. This shifting sympathy occurs repeatedly throughout the novel and results in a curious vacillation on the author's part between admiring and approving of his heroine and being deeply shocked at her behavior. The basic reason for Defoe's ambivalence toward Roxana lies in the fact that in this novel, the same basic theme used in *Moll Flanders*—that of the innocent woman being corrupted by the pressures of poverty—is carried to much greater lengths. Moll is to be forgiven because she abandons her life of crime once she has gained sufficient wealth to be independent. Roxana continues her illicit activities long after the demands of economic necessity are met.

Roxana also differs from its author's other works in the relative tightness of the plot, which is particularly unified by the threat of possible exposure and consequent ruin for the heroine. This threat is reinforced so often and the daughter is so persistent a presence in the later narrative that exposure seems, indeed, the only natural conclusion to which the plot can proceed—but it does not. Defoe is not willing to have his heroine hanged any more than he can in right conscience allow her to live happily ever after. This conflict between sympathy and justice generates much of the dramatic tension in the novel. The solution to which Defoe resorts at the end of the novel solves not only the problem of plot but that of the author's shifting attitude toward Roxana. In an insightful psychological twist, he imposes Roxana's punishment in the form of haunting guilt over her daughter's murder and consuming fear that her evil past will be revealed. Therefore, at the end of the novel, Roxana suffers the fate of Tantalus. Surrounded by wealth and friends, she can never enjoy them. Her peace is poisoned, as she realizes that the simple pleasures of her friend the Quaker woman are forever unattainable for herself.

"Critical Evaluation" by Nancy G. Ballard

Bibliography:

Backscheider, Paula R. *Daniel Defoe: Ambition and Innovation*. Louisville: University of Kentucky Press, 1986. Provides biographical data and critical interpretations of Defoe's novels.

Bell, Ian A. *Defoe's Fiction*. New York: Barnes & Noble Books, 1985. Studies the elements of Defoe's writing style and characters. Discusses the character Roxana.

Boardman, Michael M. *Defoe and the Use of Narrative*. New Brunswick, N.J.: Rutgers University Press, 1985. Provides a discussion on Daniel Defoe's technique of storytelling. Focuses on how Defoe structures his stories.

Novak, Maximillian. *Realism, Myth and History in Defoe's Fiction*. Omaha: University of Nebraska Press, 1983. An excellent starting place. Discusses the author's use of realistic characters such as Moll Flanders and reveals the myth of female inferiority, discussing how Defoe overcomes that myth.

Richetti, John J. *Daniel Defoe*. Boston: Twayne, 1987. Looks at the process of writing and development of a plot and its characters, using *Roxana* and *Moll Flanders* as examples.

Starr, G. A. *Defoe and Causitry*. Princeton, N.J.: Princeton University Press, 1991. Discusses the character and morality of Roxana, and how she created her many problems by her own choices and decisions.

RUBÁIYÁT OF OMAR KHAYYÁM

Type of work: Poetry
Author: Edward FitzGerald (1809-1883)
First published: 1859

Although Edward FitzGerald was a friend of such writers as Alfred, Lord Tennyson, and Thomas Carlyle, FitzGerald himself published few works. His principal one was a translation of the rubáiyát (quatrains) of a twelfth century Persian mathematician-astronomer, Omar Khayyám. Barely noticed when it first appeared in 1859, the work became popular on both sides of the Atlantic soon after Dante Gabriel Rossetti found a copy of the book and urged his friends to read it. A second edition appeared nine years after the first, expanded from 75 quatrains to 110. FitzGerald continued to make changes in a third and fourth edition, finally reducing the work to 101 quatrains.

It is widely acknowledged that the poem is much more than a translation. FitzGerald freely adapted the original quatrains, adding many of his own images and giving disconnected stanzas a unity of theme, tone, and style. He stayed with the four-line stanza of the original *Rubáiyát*, rhyming on all but the third line, though in a few instances all four lines rhyme. The result, known as the Rubáiyát stanza, employs an iambic pentameter line (ten syllables, five of them accented) and is crafted so that the third line, FitzGerald explained, "seems to lift and suspend the Wave that falls over the last." The final line usually gives the quatrain an epigrammatic force. FitzGerald also combined parts of some quatrains and arranged the whole collection into what he called "something of an Eclogue," a poem with a rustic setting that uses dialogue or soliloquy. He also gave the poem a framework appropriate to its astronomer author, opening at dawn and ending at nightfall on the same day, when the moon has risen and the narrator, who identifies himself along the way as "old Khayyám," is no more.

The poem begins not only at the break of a new day but also on New Year's Day, which occurred in Khayyám's time at the vernal equinox, the beginning of spring. This season provides the poet with useful symbols—the grape, the rose, the nightingale, and the verdant garden—and the spring setting inspires the poet to ponder the mystery of creation, life's brevity, the futility of trying to understand life's purpose, and the wisdom of enjoying life while it lasts.

As the sun drives out the night, the poet bids his companion to rise and accompany him. This companion is addressed later as "Love" and is the famous "thou" whom the poet finds "enow" (enough) in the wilderness along with a book of verses and a loaf of bread. She acts as a foil to the poet's meditations on their journey through the day, and this artful device gives the impression that the poet is addressing the reader as a familiar person. The narrator's voice becomes the principal unifying element in the poem. By the eleventh stanza (in the first edition), the personal element has been established, and one cannot resist the poet's invitation to "come with old Khayyám."

Eager to begin the day, the poet says he may have heard a voice within the tavern chiding the drowsy ones for tarrying outside. He has seen others waiting impatiently to enter the tavern, impatient because time is wasting and, when they are dead, they shall not return. The tavern, which symbolizes for the poet the world at large, is a place where one's cup is filled with the "Wine of Life," and one had better hurry to drink it, for the wine keeps draining away slowly. If the rose dies, others will take its place, the companion answers, implying that spring renews life, but the poet makes it clear that the rose symbolizes people who will be gone forever.

Put such thoughts away, old Khayyám urges, and go with him to the garden, where the names of kings and slaves are forgotten, where one can see, in the natural setting, images that teach how to enjoy the brief stay on earth. There, all the poet sees reminds him that life is short; everyone becomes dust and never returns. One is therefore well advised to live today and not worry about yesterday or tomorrow. In this verdant setting, the poet is reminded of the cyclic nature of life. Spring renews the earth, but the rose and the hyacinth are nurtured by the buried bodies of those who have come and gone. No one is exempt, not the hero, the sultan, or Caesar himself.

The poet's skepticism regarding the usefulness of learning is brought to light as he recalls how little he learned from "Doctor and Saint." All he learned from them is that the individual has no control over his or her existence. One is but a pawn in the hands of a seemingly whimsical Creator. In this way, the individual is no different from nature's abundant manifestations: the rose, water, and wind. Although humans can reason, compute, ask questions, and seek causes, reason cannot penetrate the veil that separates the living from the dead. Futile is the search for life's purpose and futile is the hope for existence in the afterlife—if, indeed, there is an afterlife. All the poet has learned is that wine is the best antidote for reason's inability to see into the darkness.

Wine offers the hedonist a quick escape from a meaningless life, but the grape also, for old Khayyám, symbolizes nature's abundant resources and, as such, offers a way of escaping *into* life, abandoning the arid, futile speculations of saint and Sufi (mystic). The tavern is a haven in which the weary traveler may find respite from the knowledge that life is brief and one is doomed to join those countless numbers who have sunk beneath the earth, never to return. Grimly, the poet sees that humans are like bubbles in the wine that the Eternal Saki pours, desert travelers in a Phantom Caravan.

Reminded of his own intellectual abilities and accomplishments, the poet dismisses their significance. Though he could calculate and use logic, he has abandoned reason and has put his faith in wine, which is all in which he was ever rich. This potent liquid confutes warring sectarians and transmutes life's base metal into gold. The only certainty, the poet has discovered, is that life is brief and once one is dead, one is dead forever. Heaven and hell are within the individual, who is in the hands of an unknowable master. Using his reason to refute reason's power to understand the meaning of existence, old Khayyám explains that it is absurd to think that the individual is punished in heaven for being made imperfect or expected to repay God in "pure gold" for an existence that was "dross-alloyed." It is equally absurd to think that God would sue to collect a debt from one who had no part in making the contract.

These thoughts remind the poet of an earlier experience, a dream or a fantasy, in which he found himself in the house of a potter surrounded by pots of all shapes and sizes, a loquacious lot that had the same concerns many humans have, the purpose of their existence, why some are misshapen and others are not, and who the Potter is. These vessels, it seems, were made to hold wine, the spirit of life, and they eagerly await the winebearer. They, too, come to the same realization that old Khayyám himself has: Wine enables one to endure a life of unanswered questions. The poet acknowledges that his devotion to the potion has tarnished his reputation. He even repented, but when spring returned, his penitent spirit vanished, and he returned to the grape.

The plaintive voices of the vessels bring to mind once again the vanishing rose, youth, and spring itself, and though spring will return, one day the poet will not. This melancholy thought makes him wish he could spring forth from the ground like the harvest, rewrite what Fate has written for him, or obliterate Fate altogether. Addressing his companion, he says that if they could re-create the world, they would surely mold it closer to their hearts' desire. The passage of time, however, is inexorable. Often, he says, the moon will wax and wane, returning again and again. On one of those rounds, in the darkness of night while other guests are "star-scattered on the grass," it will be discovered that he is gone.

The day's journey from morning to evening, from the bedchamber to a pleasant garden, is also a journey through the mind of a philosophical poet pondering the mystery of human existence. In the lush garden that reminds him of nature's poignant beauty, of creation, and of the remorseless finality of death, the poet cannot find a satisfying, rational answer to his questions. Answers, if they exist, lie beyond the power of human reason. Impatient with the explanations of others, the poet concludes that it is best simply to live for today and drink oneself into oblivion.

As we have seen, however, wine, the tavern, and intoxication have symbolic value for the poet. In one sense, the tavern represents the world at large and includes the garden to which the poet and his companion journey. Wine, representing life itself, or the spirit, impels one, not *from* life, but *into* it. Commitment to the grape represents commitment to living intensely in the moment, becoming intoxicated by the spirit of life. In that state, one becomes oblivious to those questions that baffle saint and doctor alike. One escapes from the world of futile rationality into a world of sensory awareness.

FitzGerald considered Omar Khayyám a "material Epicurean," yet FitzGerald's translation suggests that Khayyám offered something beyond a refinement of life's pleasures, beyond a refined enjoyment of wine, women, and song. Without pushing the symbols too far, one could find the rose to be more than a dying flower that reminds one of life's brevity and the wine to be more than a temporary escape into oblivion. Clearly, old Khayyám of the quatrains sees in the rose a beauty that sustains life and reminds one of that nature which restores and enriches. Clearly, too, he sees the tavern as a metaphor of the larger world of nature, and he believes, finally, that the power of wine to intoxicate is the individual's only and best reward.

Bernard E. Morris

Bibliography:

Avery, Peter, and John Heath-Stubbs. Introduction to *The Rubái'yát of Omar Khayyám*, translated by Avery and Heath-Stubbs. New York: Penguin Books, 1981. Avery and Heath-Stubbs stay close to the original in their translation of 235 quatrains. Their introduction broadens our understanding of Omar Khayyám, and the translations, attractively illustrated, enhance our appreciation of Khayyám's *Rubáiyát* without diminishing FitzGerald's achievement.

Bowen, John Charles Edward. *A New Selection from the Rubáiyát of Omar Khayyám*. Warminster, England: Aris & Phillips, 1976. The chief value of this work is that it includes a literal translation of the quatrains Bowen renders into verse and, along with Bowen's, many of FitzGerald's translations from the first and fourth editions. One is therefore able to compare four different versions of some of the quatrains.

Dashti, Ali. *In Search of Omar Khayyam*. Translated by L. P. Elwell-Sutton. New York: Columbia University Press, 1971. Dashti describes the character of Omar Khayyám by studying him through the eyes of Khayyám's contemporaries' writings. On the basis of this portrait, Dashti authenticates thirty-six quatrains with some confidence, translates them along with other quatrains, and examines their literary style.

Untermeyer, Louis, ed. *Rubáiyát of Omar Khayyám: Translated into English Quatrains by Edward FitzGerald*. New York: Random House, 1947. Although FitzGerald's inimitable translation is often printed, this edition (of all but the second edition) has a fine introduction by Louis Untermeyer and contains FitzGerald's prefaces and notes together with attractive illustrations.

Yogananda, Paramhansa. *The Rubáiyát of Omar Khayyám Explained.* Nevada City, Calif.: Crystal Clarity, 1994. This contemporary mystic interprets the *Rubáiyát* as an allegory of the human spirit, not as the work of a hedonist. Though his reading contrasts sharply with FitzGerald's, Yogananda nevertheless uses the first edition of FitzGerald's translation as his text.

RUBYFRUIT JUNGLE

Type of work: Novel
Author: Rita Mae Brown (1944-   )
Type of plot: Social realism
Time of plot: Early 1950's through late 1960's
Locale: Pennsylvania, Florida, and New York City
First published: 1973

Principal characters:
MOLLY BOLT, the narrator and main character
CARRIE, Molly's mother by adoption
CARL, Molly's father by adoption
LEROY DENMAN, Molly's cousin and friend
LEOTA B. BISLAND, Molly's first love

The Story:

Molly Bolt at age seven was already tough and lively. She had taught herself to read at age three and was brighter and more assertive than most children in Coffee Hollow, Pennsylvania. When a classmate, "Broccoli" Detwiler, peed in front of her, she noticed that his penis looked different from others she had seen (he was uncircumcised) and immediately decided they could make money by showing it off to classmates after school for a nickel a look. The project was a big hit, and Molly realized that money conveyed power and popularity. When little Earl Stambach told the teacher and the teacher contacted the parents, Molly's mother, Carrie, angrily berated Molly for thinking she was clever. She tried to belittle her by yelling that Molly was not even her daughter, that she was a bastard. Molly's response was immediate: "I don't care. It makes no difference where I came from. I'm here, ain't I?"

Molly Bolt continued to live by this principle of self-assertion throughout her life. She learned to accomplish her goals in whatever way she needed, whether or not that meant following the restrictive views of others. She retaliated against Earl Stambach's tattling by tricking him into eating rabbit droppings that he thought were raisins and then blackmailing him into ceasing to tattle against her.

Leroy was Molly's cousin and close friend. When his mother died of cancer, Molly saw that their families built their views on a rigid standard that did not actually fit their actions. Except for her father, Carl, most of the extended family tried to ignore realities that did not match their pretended standards of human behavior. After the funeral, Carl hugged the grieving husband in sympathy, yet this sympathy contradicted the entrenched idea that men should not hug men. Molly saw that there were times when rules needed to be broken.

School and homelife provided Molly with many opportunities to learn about hypocrisy and how to circumvent rules. During a Christmas play in which Molly had been assigned the role of the Virgin Mary, a snobbish classmate improvised throughout the presentation to give herself a larger role. Molly ended up kicking her off the stage, much to the shocked delight of the audience. At home, when Carrie decided that Molly was too much of a tomboy and insisted she stay indoors and do household chores, Molly retaliated by locking her in the cellar. Molly saw such actions as necessary to preserve her independence and her right to be herself.

When Molly was in the sixth grade she developed a crush on her friend Leota B. Bisland. They spent time together after school kissing each other, and one night at Leota's house they learned that touching bodies in other ways was even more fun. Rather than feel ashamed that her first love experimentation had been with another girl, Molly recognized that love did not always follow society's norms. Years later, when Molly visited Leota as an adult, she found that Leota was married to a man and denied having any lesbian thoughts. Molly, on the contrary, had had sex with both women and men and was not willing to label herself or condemn herself for her actions.

Molly, Carrie, Carl, and cousin Leroy and his family moved to Florida in search of greater economic opportunity. Molly made friends at school because of her sense of humor and her quick brain. Leroy had a sexual friendship with an older boy but could not face the fact that this might mean he was a homosexual. Molly told him not to worry about labels. She and Leroy had sex together, and Molly had affairs with other boys at school, but she also had an affair with her classmate Carolyn Simpson. Carolyn, like Leroy, could not accept feelings that contradicted social customs, and she bowed to the social norms.

At college in Gainesville, Florida, Molly encountered the same patterns. She fell in love with her roommate, Faye, but when others learned of their affair Molly was chastised by the dean of women students (herself a closeted lesbian), sent to a psychologist to be "cured," and would have been kicked out of school had she not been within a few weeks of graduation. Faye, fearing that her rich parents would cut off their financial support, deserted Molly and acquiesced to social pressure. When Molly returned home, Carrie kicked her out of the house, saying she was "a dirty queer."

Molly hitchhiked her way from Florida to Greenwich Village in New York City, where she had heard there was more acceptance of varied lifestyles. Lacking money, she stayed the first night in a deserted car on the street. Calvin, a young homosexual man who had been using it as a sleeping space too, came to the car. He led Molly to a restaurant, where a friend gave them free food, and then took her to a man who paid her $100 for throwing grapefruit at him when he was naked. Molly was continuing to learn that there are many different kinds of people and many ways to survive. She rented a small apartment, worked at a movie theater and later a restaurant and other places, and enrolled in a local university to study filmmaking.

During her years as a part-time student and full-time worker, Molly encountered several lesbian women and saw that there were many versions of lesbian lifestyle. One of her lovers was Holly, a tall black woman who was being supported financially by an older wealthy lesbian. Molly rejected such a situation for herself, preferring self-sufficiency. She had an affair with the forty-one-year-old Polina Bellantoni and briefly during that time also with Polina's sixteen-year-old daughter Alice. Polina was also having an affair with Paul, an extremely unattractive man, and Molly learned that when Polina and Paul had sex they verbalized scenarios of themselves as the opposite gender. At the same time, Polina claimed that she was heterosexual and that Molly was perverted.

Near the end of her college years, Molly revisited her rural town in Pennsylvania, where Leota, now married, denied that there had been any childhood romance. Later Molly went to Florida to see Carrie and make a film of her for her senior filmmaking project. Leroy was there with his wife and children. He envied Molly's courage in living her life. Carrie claimed that she had never disowned Molly, and Molly accepted Carrie as what she was. When Molly showed her documentary film with the films of rape and violence made by her classmates, no one acknowledged her work. Molly vowed to become a filmmaker who gave women visibility—"then watch out world."

Critical Evaluation:

Rita Mae Brown created a fictional character to teach the necessity of the acceptance of diversity, and she made the story entertaining and compelling with the use of youthful slang and Molly's bravado wit. *Rubyfruit Jungle* was first published in 1973 by a small feminist publishing house, Daughters, Inc., and the book went through seven printings before 1977. When Bantam Books bought the rights and published the novel in 1977 (with repeated subsequent printings), it became a mainstream best-seller.

Rubyfruit Jungle was the first lesbian novel with a positive view of homosexuality to be published by a major press, and it became a classic in contemporary lesbian literature and brought Rita Mae Brown national recognition. As a *Bildungsroman* novel of personal development, *Rubyfruit Jungle* is often compared to Mark Twain's *Adventures of Huckleberry Finn* (1884) and the picaresque tradition of a character on a journey of self-discovery. In this coming-of-age novel, Brown emphasizes the importance of the individual spirit while at the same time showing the influence of society in shaping the individual and providing challenges to the individual's freedom. In many ways Molly Bolt is an outsider who moves from innocence to experience as she learns to exist in a hostile world. The novel was also seen as a contribution to, and product of, the emerging women's movement. Molly's odyssey shows the need for mutual respect among all classes, races, and genders. Her story is lesbian, but her determination applies to many other struggles.

Critics have often noted that Brown is a Southern writer with a keen sense of place. Carol M. Ward wrote that the four sections of the novel, which show changes in time, location, and sexual partners, all reveal transformations in Molly. Brown contrasts rural and natural with city and artificial environments, and she structures Molly's journeys in such a way as to contrast North and South. Molly herself often expresses criticism of the artificial boundaries that separate.

Molly's family was always poor, and Molly constantly struggles to have enough money to pursue her dreams, sometimes simply for enough to survive. Her father Carl encouraged her to make of her life something different from the trap he felt his life to be. Carrie, bitter about the economic restrictions that she had endured, was jealous of Molly's ambition and her ability to act on her needs. When Molly returns from exile to see her, however, Carrie is clearly pleased at Molly's successes, which allows Molly to be reconciled and to accept the mother-daughter relationship. The film Molly makes is a tribute to that love and to the resilience of the human spirit, just as the film's negative reception in New York is symbolic of society's inability to see the value of that spirit.

Rita Mae Brown fought for women's rights from a young age, writing essays and lesbian poetry while active in feminist politics. Her other novels, including her several volumes of detective fiction, have presented a variety of characters and situations. *Rubyfruit Jungle* remains her most influential work, her most widely read and widely acclaimed literary success. Molly Bolt is a daring, uninhibited heroine, and her wit and determination make her a character who reflects the eternal longing for a better world.

Lois A. Marchino

Bibliography:

Alexander, Delores. "Rita Mae Brown: 'The Issue for the Future Is Power.'" *Ms.* 3 (September, 1974): 110-113. In this article, published shortly after the publication of *Rubyfruit Jungle*, Alexander discusses Brown's writing and her position on the contemporary women's movement.

Chew, Martha. "Rita Mae Brown: Feminist Theorist and Southern Novelist." In *Women Writers of the Contemporary South*, edited by Peggy Whitman Prenshaw. Jackson: University Press of Mississippi, 1984. Chew examines the connections between Brown's political essays and her fiction. She places Brown in the context of Southern writers who are political activists.

Fishbein, Leslie. "*Rubyfruit Jungle*: Lesbianism, Feminism, and Narcissism." *International Journal of Women's Studies* 7 (March/April, 1984): 155-159. Concentrates on the novel in relation to lesbian and feminist issues. Sees Brown as a strong voice in lesbian literature.

Harris, Bertha. Review of *Rubyfruit Jungle*, by Rita Mae Brown. *Village Voice Literary Supplement*, April 4, 1974, 34-35. Early and sympathetic review of the novel by another writer of lesbian novels. Harris discusses it among works from the feminist publishing house Daughters, Inc.

Ward, Carol M., ed. *Rita Mae Brown*. New York: Twayne, 1993. An excellent full-length discussion of Brown and her works arranged according to individual books. Includes a discussion of *Rubyfruit Jungle* in the chapter "The Grand Canyon Between First Person Narrative and Third Person Narrative." Also contains an extensive selected bibliography of reviews and criticism about the novels.

R.U.R.

Type of work: Drama
Author: Karel Čapek (1890-1938)
Type of plot: Social satire
Time of plot: The future
Locale: An unnamed island
First published: 1920 (English translation, 1923); first performed, 1921

Principal characters:
HARRY DOMIN, the general manager of Rossum's Universal Robots
HELENA GLORY, his wife
DR. GALL, a scientist
MR. ALQUIST, the head of the works department of R.U.R.
PRIMUS, a robot
HELENA, a robot

The Story:

The Rossum Universal Robot Factory had perfected mechanical men and women. The formula had been developed originally by old Rossum, but it had been left to his son, an engineer, to manufacture the robots. Robots knew no joy, no desire to take a solitary walk, no personal wish of any kind. They were highly developed, with mechanisms devised for only one purpose: work.

The robots manufactured by Rossum's Universal Robot Factory were so lifelike, however, that when the president's daughter, Helena Glory, called at the factory and was shown around by Harry Domin, general manager, she could hardly believe that the robots were not human. Helena had been sent by the Humanity League on a mission to gain better living conditions for the robots. Helena knew that when the robots began to act strangely, as they sometimes did, they were destroyed and their parts were used to make new robots. She was dismayed to find that the robots she met and talked with in the factory did not care whether they were killed or starved. They thought of nothing but their work. They talked rationally, answering her questions, but they seemed to have no desires or feelings beyond their given jobs. Domin and the other executives were willing to have her preach to the robots all she wished.

In the warehouses there were hundreds of thousands of robots waiting to be shipped all over the world. Domin tried to convince Helena of the rightness of the new era. Now, humanity was no longer effective. People were too imperfect, too expensive, too long children. Although Domin could not agree that robots should be freed and allowed human rights, he admitted that sometimes they acted queerly. Often one would gnash its teeth, throw things about, and then stand still. The attack was similar to epilepsy, and the robot would have to go to the stamping-mill to be destroyed. Helena believed these were signs of developing a soul. The managers were working on a pain-nerve. They thought that if the robots were to feel pain, these attacks could be foreseen and treated.

The executives tried also to convince Helena of the virtue of robots by pointing out to her that the prices of all manufactured and farm goods had dropped almost to nothing. Where Helena could see only the millions of humans out of work, the managers could see a world in which no human being had to work. People could then sit back and enjoy the labors of mechanical workers. Only Mr. Alquist, head of the works department, disagreed with that notion.

Alquist could see the joy that people found only in working and creating. The others quickly voted him down.

Without prior warning, Domin told Helena that he loved her and could not bear to lose her. Puzzling even herself, she accepted him. Ten years passed. The managers tried to keep from Helena the news that the robots were causing trouble. All over the world small groups of robots had revolted against their masters. Some governments had turned the robots into soldiers and terrible wars had been fought. Learning of these revolts, she begged Domin and the others to close the factory while there was still time. The men laughed at her fears. They had a gunboat standing by which would protect them from any rebels in the warehouses. Only Alquist agreed with Helena. He even prayed that God would destroy the robots and let humanity return to work. He knew, as Helena did, that people had stopped reproducing; there had been no births recorded in the past week.

Dr. Gall, the physiologist, began to fear the results when he learned that some of the more intelligent robots, according to their different grades, had begun to feel pain and to have heart flutters. They had also begun to show definite signs of hating and loving. The R.U.R. shareholders, however, were making too much money, and world governments were growing too powerful with robot soldiers, to permit their discontinuation, even if Domin and the others had accepted Helena's and Alquist's views. Feeling that the end was near, Dr. Gall could only warn Helena to look out for herself. The scientist believed they were all doomed.

The only weapon the managers could use against the robots, should they rebel, was the secret of their manufacture, the secret that promised to end a world organization of robots. As soon as the current trouble was over, each country would begin to manufacture its own robots. The differences in language and customs would prevent a world union in the future.

The trouble soon grew into a real danger. A mail boat arrived with leaflets announcing that the world organization ordered all robots to kill every man, woman, and child in the world. The robots claimed that humanity had become a parasite, that robots were now smarter than humanity and must rule the world. The orders were to be carried out immediately.

After a gallant fight the humans in the factory were overpowered. Even when he knew death was near, Domin had no regrets. He had wanted to free humanity from the restrictions of an unfair social system, from poverty, from the slavery of working for another; something had gone wrong. Somehow the robots had begun to care about the things that people cared about. The mystery was solved when Helena confessed that she had persuaded Dr. Gall to give the robots souls. She had hoped that if the robots were more like human beings both groups could understand each other better. Now the robots were so human that they acted like humans. This similarity included killing.

The only hope was to persuade the robots that they dare not kill the men who knew the secret of their manufacture. Domin preferred death rather than to give up his dream, but the others, hoping to use the formula in their bargaining, outvoted him. Then they learned that Helena, hoping to put an end to the factory and to help children be born again, had burned the formula.

All the humans were killed except Alquist, spared by the robots because he also worked with his hands. Alquist, unable to duplicate the formula, could not save the robots, who were dying by the millions. Before long they would be extinct. The irony was that Alquist needed human beings to study and experiment with in order to rediscover the formula, but there were no humans left.

One day Alquist decided that there was hope. Primus, a robot, and Helena, a robot made in Helena's image, exhibited all the symptoms of love. At first Alquist planned to dissect them, to see what made them feel human love. When he learned that they were willing to die for each other, but that they would not be parted, he knew that he need search no longer for the secret of robot life. Their love would bring forth new life, and the world would know humanity once more.

Critical Evaluation:

Early translations of *R.U.R.* gave the word "robot"—derived from the Czech word for forced labor—to the English language. Subsequent users have, however, shifted its meaning. Rossum's robots are slaves manufactured from artificial flesh and blood, but the word is currently applied in industry to refer to machines that mimic the actions of a human limb. The shift in meaning was begun when Fritz Lang's film *Metropolis* (1926) extended the term to embrace a humanoid creature made of metal. It was taken a stage further when some science fiction writers who wished to discriminate between humanoid machines and humanoids made of artificial organic materials—and who were more familiar with *Metropolis* than *R.U.R.*—chose to restrict the term "robot" to metallic humanoids while calling fleshy humanoids "androids."

The fact that people associate the term "robot" with machinery has led some commentators to interpret *R.U.R.* as an allegory about mechanization. It can, indeed, be decoded in this way but that was certainly not what Karel Čapek intended. He used a very similar plot in the novel *War with the Newts* (1936), in which the role played by Rossum's robots is played by a newly discovered race of intelligent animals. A novel that does feature marvelous machinery, *The Absolute at Large* (1922), proceeds in a rather different manner. It is true that Čapek was suspicious of the march of technology, but he was far more suspicious of the follies and mistaken ambitions of human beings, as can easily be seen in *The Insect Play* (1921), a satire he wrote with his brother Josef shortly after writing *R.U.R.*

R.U.R.'s primary target is the attitude of mind that Harry Domin represents: that human beings are—or ought to be—eager to be released from the burden of labor, for which they are in any case ill-adapted by virtue of their appetite for play and other diversions. Labor, according to Domin, ought instead to be done by beings specifically adapted to that task: beings without ambition or distraction, and hence without any rights to enable them to pursue ambitions or distractions. This description can far more readily be applied to the attitude of the leisured classes toward the servant classes, whose labor supports the leisured classes' lifestyle than it can to the relationship between humanity as a whole and machinery. The common view in Čapek's day—as exemplified by the imagery of *Metropolis*—was not that machines were slaves but rather that the majority of people were in the process of becoming slaves of machinery.

If *R.U.R.* is seen as a political allegory, Čapek's drama is a call for the recognition that those who are condemned to eternal labor actually have the same needs and desires as those who remain free, and a warning that willful blindness to those needs and desires will eventually provoke violent rebellion. Through the character of Alquist, the author adds to this proposal the further judgment that the leisured classes are mistaken in their assessment of their own needs, because people who do not labor at all are forsaking their own creativity; creativity is not expressed without work. Creativity, not idleness, is humanity's most precious possession.

The "souls" that Dr. Gall imports into the robots at Helena's request are metaphorical. What the robots have actually been given is a means of feeling, not in the sense that emotions that were not there before have been grafted on, but in the sense that a potential that was always there has now been activated. While the robots remain robots (that is, laborers), however, this release of feeling can only be turned to destructive ends. Ironically, the rebellion of the robots is hardly necessary, given that their masters—having forsaken their creativity—have ceased even to practice the most fundamental creative act of reproducing themselves. The world within the play gets twisted so far out of shape that a new beginning is required before a new order may be secured. That new beginning is—as, in Čapek's view, it must be—the rediscovery of the power of love by those whose feelings had previously been channeled into hatred. It is the robots rather than their masters, according to Čapek, who retain this potential; Harry Domin's love for Helena, and hers for him, have been wasted in secret conflict.

Čapek was active in politics for a little while after the creation of the state of Czechoslovakia in the wake of World War I, but preferred to make use of his talents and energies as a writer. He did not survive to experience the country's annexation by Hitler, although his brother Josef was to die in a concentration camp. Answering critics, Čapek denied that his view of the world was entirely cynical and pessimistic, but such works as *R.U.R.* and *War with the Newts*—both of which feature the extinction of the human race—seem to some observers to undermine his denial. It is important to notice, however, that the "humans" who are swept away in these allegories are humans who have lost sight of their own humanity, and that they are succeeded by other beings who have discovered the real meaning of "humanity," and have therefore become human beings.

Seen in this light, Čapek's works—*R.U.R.* in particular—are certainly awful warnings, but they are not despairing. After its fashion, *R.U.R.* seeks to help its audiences recover their authentic humanity which, as members of the leisured theater-going classes, they may perhaps be in danger of losing.

"Critical Evaluation" by Brian Stableford

Bibliography:

Čapek, Karel. *Toward the Radical Center: A Karel Capek Reader*. Edited and introduced by Peter Kussi. Translated by Norma Comrada, et al. Highland Park, N.J.: Catbird Press, 1990. Includes a brief but informative biography. Evaluates existing translations of Čapek's works and provides many new translations, including *R.U.R.* Discusses Čapek's philosophy, politics, and use of language.

Harkins, William Edward. *Karel Capek*. New York: Columbia University Press, 1962. Best introduction to *R. U. R.* Only book-length critical study of Čapek's work written in English, discussing philosophy, artistic structure, theme, character, literary influences, and innovations in form.

King, Sharon D. "A Better Eve: Women and Robots in Capek's *R.U.R.* and Pavlovsky's *El Robot*." In *Women in Theatre*, edited by James Redmond. Cambridge, England: Cambridge University Press, 1989. Interesting, detailed analysis of the character of Helena, including discussion of male-female roles and attitudes about childbirth and sterility.

Matuska, Alexander. *Karel Capek: An Essay*. Translated by Cathryn Alan. London: Allen & Unwin, 1964. Clear introduction to life and philosophy for new readers. Discusses *R. U. R.* as an analysis of human nature and of labor.

Wellek, Rene. *Essays on Czech Literature*. The Hague: Mouton, 1963. Divides Čapek's writing into three periods, discussing changes in style and subject matter. Evaluates the play's theatrical qualities, traces popularity, and analyzes the play's emphasis on the dangers of mechanization.

RUSLAN AND LYUDMILA

Type of work: Poetry
Author: Alexander Pushkin (1799-1837)
Type of plot: Mock-heroic
Time of plot: Late tenth century
Locale: Russia
First published: Ruslan i Lyudmila, 1820 (English translation, 1936)

Principal characters:
RUSLAN, a knight
LYUDMILA, Kievan princess, Ruslan's bride
CHERNOMOR, an evil sorcerer
THE FINN, a benevolent sorcerer
NAINA, a witch
ROGDAY,
FARLAF, and
RATMIR, Ruslan's rivals
VLADIMIR, Prince of Kiev

The Story:

As Vladimir and his warrior retinue feasted in celebration of Lyudmila's marriage, the amorous bridegroom Ruslan plucked at his mustache and waited impatiently for the ceremonies to end. Just as uneasy were his rivals Rogday, Farlaf, and Ratmir, who sat brooding over their love for Lyudmila and their hatred of Ruslan. Finally the newlyweds retired to the bridal chamber, and soon only the rustle of discarded clothing and lovers' murmurs were to be heard—until suddenly, in a flash of lightning, a roll of thunder, and a puff of smoke, Lyudmila vanished. A frustrated and puzzled Ruslan was left to explain the mysterious disappearance of his bride. Vladimir blamed Ruslan for failing to protect her, and offered Lyudmila's still virginal hand to whichever knight succeeded in bringing her back. The four young men at once mounted their horses and galloped off, but soon parted ways.

A dejected Ruslan found himself at the cave of the Finn, a serene old hermit who greeted him by name. He explained that it was the sorcerer Chernomor who had spirited Lyudmila away for his own lustful ends, but that Ruslan need not fear—his bride would remain unharmed and he would gain her back in the end. He also told Ruslan his own story of love and misplaced enchantment and warned that his old love Naina, now a witch, would turn her malice on him too. Ruslan, emboldened by hope, continued his quest.

Meanwhile Rogday had decided to first do away with Ruslan and then pursue Lyudmila. After chasing down the cowardly Farlaf by mistake, then leaving in amused disgust, Rogday encountered an old woman who directed him further; this same old woman, promising that the girl would not escape, advised Farlaf to go home and bide his time.

Lyudmila had awakened to find herself in Chernomor's castle, in a splendid chamber hung with precious brocades and redolent of incense. Wandering through the enchanted gardens, utterly alone, she contemplated throwing herself from a bridge or starving herself rather than eating the sumptuous dinner miraculously set before her—but in both cases thought better of it. At nightfall, she waited in terror to see what would befall her; her door opened to reveal a procession of slaves carrying a long gray beard on pillows, and at the end of the beard pompously strode Chernomor, the hunchbacked dwarf. Lyudmila leapt from her bed, snatched off the dwarf's cap, shook her fist, and screamed so deafeningly that the entire parade fell into confusion and Chernomor tangled himself in his own beard. The slaves scooped him up and carried him off to untangle him.

Far away, after a bloody battle by moonlight, Ruslan managed to unhorse Rogday and hurl him into the river, where he was immediately pulled to the bottom by a mermaid. Lyudmila, meanwhile, discovered that wearing Chernomor's cap made her invisible.

Ruslan, disarmed in the struggle with Rogday, wandered gloomily among ruins of an old battleground; although he found himself a new mail shield and a new lance, he could not find a proper sword. That same night he encountered an enormous, helmeted head which he took at first for a hill. Ruslan, after an exchange of insults, struck the head and it rolled away to reveal a magical sword. The enchanted head was that of Chernomor's giant brother, who had been betrayed by the dwarf. It revealed Chernomor's secret—that all his magical power resided in his beard.

As Ruslan proceeded north, overcoming witches, giants, and various spirits, Ratmir was distracted from his pursuit of Lyudmila by an magical castle and twelve voluptuous maidens. Lyudmila teased her captors by leaving traces of her invisible presence, until Chernomor managed to trick her into showing herself—he took the form of Ruslan. As she fell into an enchanted swoon, he began to paw her, but the sound of a horn interrupted him. Ruslan had arrived.

Chernomor flew to the attack, but Ruslan grabbed his beard and held on as they soared over mountain, forest, and sea. Ruslan finally forced the dwarf back to the castle, where he cut off the beard, packed the dwarf behind his saddle, and galloped up to find Lyudmila. The voice of the Finn advised Ruslan to take the sleeping girl back to Kiev, where she would recover. On the way back Ruslan met his former rival Ratmir, now a fisherman leading an idyllic life with the young wife who had wooed him away from the maidens. Naina, however, now led treacherous Farlaf to the sleeping Ruslan's camp, where Farlaf ran the knight through with his sword and carried Lyudmila off to Kiev to claim his prize. As Ruslan lay dying, the city waited for the enchantment to lift, but to no avail. Meanwhile, a crisis was at hand—Kiev was under attack by nomad raiders.

The wise Finn then went to a magical spring where he fetched water of death to close Ruslan's wounds, and water of life to restore him. Ruslan arrived in time to rally the Kievans, defeat the Pechenegs, and revive Lyudmila. The city rejoiced, Farlaf confessed and was pardoned, and the couple lived happily ever.

Critical Evaluation:

When *Ruslan and Lyudmila* appeared in 1820, it made a sensation in Russian literature. It also made young Alexander Pushkin's name, and it helped make Russian a literary language. Given the fact that Russia had had a written language—and writers—for centuries, that might seem an odd statement. It was, nevertheless, Pushkin who demonstrated the range and flexibility of contemporary Russian. Pushkin showed that it could accommodate formal and informal diction alike, that it was an instrument that could be played in any number of styles.

With its victory over Napoleon Bonaparte, the Russian Empire was an indisputable military and political power on the European scene. Many Russian writers thought, however, that they did not yet have a culture, let alone a literary culture, of their own, and consciously set about to create one. That meant that in Russia, Western literary movements such classicism, sentimentalism, and Romanticism—themselves, by the late eighteenth century, not so neatly divided—

were all telescoped into a few decades. A question that faced Russian writers was whether western European literary models were the right models. The question of language was a question of cultural identity. The Slavophile camp looked nostalgically back to a mythic pre-Petrine Slavic past. The Westernizers favored adapting the western European literary legacy. In the arguments over the direction Russian literature was to take, Pushkin came down on the side of the Westernizers, *Ruslan and Lyudmila* was, in its own lighthearted way, a blow to the cause of the Slavophiles. Who, after this brilliant mock-epic, could possibly write a serious Slavic epic?

For all its nearly three thousand lines, its six cantos plus an epilogue, the poem moves along at a sprightly, dancing pace. Pushkin's choice of iambic tetrameter, a relatively short line, is one reason for this. Another is Pushkin's particular genius at varying his rhyme scheme to advance or retard the movement. The basic verse form of the poem is an alternating quatrain (*abab*), but Pushkin also uses enveloping rhyme (*abba*), occasional couplets, and a five- or six-line unit. Add to that the fact that all Russian words, long or short, have only one accent (unlike English, which has primary and secondary accents on longer words), and the result is that even very formal poetry in Russian is less likely to have the monotonous, jingling quality of serious English poetry at its worst. Pushkin has a pattern at work, but it is a fluid and shifting one that corresponds to changes in action or narrative tone.

Pushkin seems to have borrowed from everyone, from high literature and low, in writing the poem. Russian folktale, song, epic, and popular literature have their influence, as does, for example, Ludovico Ariosto's *Orlando Furioso* (1516). *Ruslan and Lyudmila* is a work of dazzling originality, a piece that is at home in the Western tradition and is at the same time unmistakably Russian.

On the one hand, Pushkin draws on native Russian sources that tell of an exotic, heroic, even barbarous past. Vladimir did rule in Kiev and Novgorod in the late tenth century, and the grim battlefield where Ruslan rummages among the bones of long-dead warriors recalls a famous passage from Russian chronicles. A warrior named Rokhday is listed as a guest at one of Vladimir's famous feasts. The name Ruslan comes from historical sources. Finns were famed as sorcerers in those times. The magic cap, the "living water" and the "dead water," and the enchanted head all appear in folktale and epic. Furthermore, in the 1828 edition, Pushkin added a prologue straight out of the folktale tradition:

> There is a green oak by the bay,
> And on that oak a golden chain,
> And day and night a learned cat
> On that chain length paces round.

Like a storyteller closing the circle in traditional fashion, he ends the poem with the same words that end his prologue.

Despite all this, there is no direct plot link connecting *Ruslan and Lyudmila* with the Russian folk epics. Such epics involve trials undertaken by pure-hearted knights seeking to rescue virtuous maidens. These epics, ironically, come straight out of Western chivalric romance, not Russian tradition.

Puskin's audience were the young women and men of the St. Petersburg salons, to whom the poem's playful combination of innocence, eroticism, and wit would certainly appeal. Lyudmila's charm and common sense have more to do with nineteenth century sensibility than with tenth century mores. The narrator might as well be talking about a young lady of his acquaintance. So, too, in Ruslan and Ratmir's encounter; Ruslan greets his former rival as "dear prince" and continues to chat as if they had just seen each other at the theater the week before. The narrator undercuts Ruslan's sense of injured honor and manhood—which in traditional epic was grounds for war—by comparing his feelings to those of a rooster whose favorite hen has just been snatched away by a passing vulture. This and other digressions give the poem a casual, insouciant tone that prevents the reader from taking any of what otherwise might be serious or even tragic themes—sorcery, betrayal, abduction, murder—seriously. It has also prevented many scholars from assigning too much weight to Pushkin's most buoyant and fanciful work.

Jane Ann Miller

Bibliography:

Bayley, John. *Pushkin: A Comparative Commentary*. Cambridge, England: Cambridge University Press, 1971. Devotes a number of pages to *Ruslan and Lyudmila* and its impact. Discusses the poem also in the context of Pushkin's later fairy tales in verse.

Briggs, A. D. P. *Alexander Pushkin: A Critical Study*. New York: Barnes & Noble Books, 1983. An excellent introduction to Pushkin's work. Especially good at explaining formal aspects of Pushkin's poetry to readers who do not speak Russian.

O'Bell, Leslie. "Young Pushkin: *Ruslan and Liudmila* in Its Lyric Context." *The Russian Review* 44, no. 2 (April, 1985): 139-155. Discusses the poem in light of Pushkin's earlier lyrics and takes issue with the common critical evaluation of the poem as sparkling entertainment but less-than-profound poetry.

Pushkin, Alexander. "Ruslan and Lyudmila." In *Collected Narrative and Lyrical Poetry*. Translated by Walter Arndt. Ann Arbor: Ardis, 1984. Includes a look at Pushkin's sources, with special attention to the vogue for Gothic tales and translated ballads. Discusses contemporary reaction to the poem.

Vickery, Walter. *Alexander Pushkin Revisited*. Rev. ed. New York: Maxwell Macmillan International, 1992. The chapter "Early Verse and *Ruslan and Lyudmila*" also gives a good overview of the state of Russian literature when Pushkin entered the scene.

THE SACRED FOUNT

Type of work: Novel
Author: Henry James (1843-1916)
Type of plot: Psychological realism
Time of plot: 1890's
Locale: Newmarch, a British country estate, and the train from Paddington Station to Newmarch
First published: 1901

Principal characters:
THE NARRATOR
GILBERT LONG and
GUY BRISSENDEN, former acquaintances of the narrator
GRACE BRISSENDEN or MRS. BRISS, his wife,
FORD OBERT, a painter,
MRS. MAY SERVER and
LADY JOHN, houseguests at Newmarch

The Story:

The nameless narrator encountered two former acquaintances, Gilbert Long and Grace Brissenden, both of whom were also going to the party at Newmarch, and both of whom appeared considerably changed to the narrator. Long, who had previously struck the narrator as a handsome clod, seemed suddenly to have become clever, and Mrs. Brissenden, who was supposedly at least forty, seemed to have grown younger, or at least not to have aged. In conversation with Mrs. Briss, as she was called, the narrator received the idea for what was to become his theory, that Gilbert Long's intellectual improvement was the result of his having entered into a relationship with a clever woman, identified by Mrs. Briss as Lady John, another guest at Newmarch. Lady John was coming on a later train with Guy Brissenden, her screen, as that gentleman's wife intimated, for her affair with Long.

Arriving at the party, the narrator failed, just as he had initially failed to recognize Mrs. Briss, to recognize Guy Brissenden, who, although only in his late twenties, looked older now than his wife. Guy appeared, in fact, "quite sixty." This discovery completed the narrator's theory that as one party to a relationship gains, either physically or intellectually, the other loses, is drained by the "sacrificer" until quite depleted. The narrator communicated this theory to Ford Obert, who had assumed Mrs. Briss to be considerably younger than her husband.

The narrator attempted to corroborate his theory. His discovery that Lady John was as witty and superficial as ever led him to reject her, in a conversation with Mrs. Briss, as Long's "victim," for the partner to such a relationship would of necessity lack her former attributes. At this juncture, the two conspirators discovered in colloquy two figures who proved to be Briss and May Server, the latter presumably using Briss as a screen, just as Lady John was formerly said to have done. Mrs. Briss happily proved to be the very woman for whom they had been looking to serve as the replacement for the now unacceptable Lady John. Mrs. Server was "all over the place," flitting from man to man in an attempt to mask the loss of her faculties. So Mrs. Briss confided to the narrator in their next interview. Her description tallied remarkably with that given the narrator by Ford Obert, who saw Mrs. Server greatly changed from the self-possessed woman she had been when she sat for him to have her portrait painted. By this time, the narrator, on the grounds of both Mrs. Briss's and Obert's testimony and of an encounter with

Mrs. Server herself, had come around to accepting Mrs. Briss's account, but his tender feeling for Mrs. Server, his sense that he and his collaborator were poking into a matter that was none of their business, and perhaps also his pique that Mrs. Briss was beating him at his own game, prevented him from acknowledging to her fully the degree of conviction to which she had brought him.

The amount of data with which the narrator was confronted becomes prodigious, but the theory expands to accommodate all of it: Lady John made up to Briss to conceal the fact that she is in love with Long; Mrs. Server's single appearance with Long (the point is actually made by Mrs. Briss) was the exception that proves the rule; Mrs. Server's avoidance of the narrator, out of all the men at the party, indicated her awareness that he was on to her predicament. (It never struck him that she could find his inquisitiveness obnoxious.) Mrs. Server's frequent juxtaposition with Briss was less Mrs. Briss's postulated screen than the mutual tacit commiseration of the two victims, each conscious of the other's depletion. (The narrator's hypothesis was that victims know of their condition while victimizers do not.) A conversation with Briss, who told the narrator that Mrs. Server had nothing to say and who confessed a certain terror of and yet fascination with her, confirmed the narrator's view of their condition and mutual relation—although Briss's confusion might as easily have been sincere, and Mrs. Server's evidently morbid state could not be attributable to the loss of her three children. Briss, however, could have been covering an actual affair that he was having with Mrs. Server, one that prompted him to send Briss off in pursuit of her. Next, the narrator himself engaged in talk with Mrs. Server, hinting in a veiled manner at her relation with Briss and gleaning that she took comfort in his awareness of her plight and his tolerant sympathy. Mrs. Server's participation in the dialogue was, however, so vague and so slight that in "truth" she gave evidence of everything or nothing.

Lady John then confronted the narrator with the fact that his supersubtlety and passion for reading meanings into everything had put the rest of the company in great upset, and she chastised him for sending Briss off to Mrs. Server when it was perfectly obvious to everyone the loathing that she inspired in him. The narrator, in an elaborate subterfuge, attempted to convince Lady John that as long as Long was in love with her and he himself with Mrs. Server, she ought to relinquish Briss so that the narrator might at least have the pleasure of seeing the woman he loved, Mrs. Server, get the man she loved, Briss. Their conversation was halted when they saw Mrs. Briss and Long deep in talk, a fact that led the narrator to speculate that Lady John benightedly and jealously had conceived a liaison between the two, whereas he, by dint of his "superior wisdom," knew them now to have come to a knowledge, and by the very agency of his inquiries, of their "bloated" or victimizing conditions, and to be joining together for mutual protection. As their talk ended, Mrs. Briss approached him and briefly informed him that she wished to speak to him later in the evening, after the other guests had retired.

The narrator's theory began to crumble. First, Ford Obert appeared to inform him that Mrs. Server was no longer in her drained condition and that the man, whoever he was, was out of the question, since she has given him up. To top this blow, Mrs. Briss arrived to demolish what was left of the narrator's theory. There was nothing in what he said, she informs him, and she had speculated along his lines only while under his spell. Mrs. Server was not the woman because there was no woman. Gilbert Long, as her conversation with him had amply testified, was as stupid as he ever had been. As a matter of fact, he and Lady John were lovers, a fact that squared perfectly with his theory because she was not drained (there being very little to drain) nor he improved. Moreover, she had it from Briss that Lady John and Long were intimate. What the narrator had thought he had seen is simply his insanity. Finally, to clinch her argument, to explain, in fact, her wriggling and self-contradiction throughout the course of the interview, Mrs. Server had not been using Briss as a screen; she had—and this from Briss's own lips—been making love to him. Also, Mrs. Server was sharply perceptive. At the narrator's amazed gasp, Mrs. Briss asked if that was not the very thing he had maintained. She then told him he was crazy and bid him good night. The narrator could only wanly observe that she had had the last word.

Clearly disinvited, he would have to leave. The facts toward which the narrator had worked, then, were finally unknowable. Whether Mrs. Briss was telling the truth at the end, lying in collusion with Long to protect their status, or attempting to shield the fact that she was actually carrying on an affair with Long, could not be resolved. The theory, it seemed, had rested on the unstable base of the narrator's ego.

Critical Evaluation:

Critical interest in *The Sacred Fount* centers on the credibility of the inquisitive and sometimes intrusive unnamed narrator who tells the story of a weekend gathering at an English country manor. From his perspective, the guests who gather at Newmarch all have hidden lives, and he is determined to discover the truth about them. He is particularly obsessed with determining how Grace Brissenden can have grown younger as a result of her marriage, while her husband seems to have withered. Equally intriguing to him is the fact that the same pattern seems to have affected two other characters who are not supposed to be attached in any way: Gilbert Long, who has suddenly become interesting and exciting after being considered a dullard for years, and May Server, once a vibrant creature but now exhausted and near the point of a breakdown. The qualities of such relationships intrigue the narrator, and he spends all of his time concocting theories about romantic relationships (including a number of illicit affairs among the various characters) that can account for the changes he has observed. The narrator commits himself to discover "the sacred fount," that source of inspiration from which people such as Grace Brissenden and Gilbert Long draw their power.

Viewed in this fashion, the novel is a kind of detective story in which the narrator serves as the sleuth. The problem, however, is not so simple as who did it. Far from being the insightful Sherlockian figure of typical detective fictions, Henry James's narrator often finds himself making assumptions that are not shared by others. In fact, as he learns at the end of the story, his conclusions about a number of characters are off the mark, assuming that Grace Brissenden's final indictment is to be believed. Whether she is simply setting the narrator straight so that he will quit his meddling, or creating an elaborate fiction to preserve the reputations of the party at Newmarch, is also not clear. The narrator in *The Sacred Fount* is either a perceptive observer of society, capable of detecting meaning and motive in the slightest gesture, or a hopelessly deluded intruder whose incessant pursuit of evil wrecks the lives of those he believes he is protecting. *The Sacred Fount* does not reward the reader with the certainties of detective fiction, in which the truth is discovered. Rather, *The Sacred Fount* is a lesson on the inability of one mind to know the truth.

Critical opinion about the narrator has been divided. Some have seen James's narrator as a sensible, sensitive figure who reveals the sordid details of the lives of people who are supposedly respectable. If this is who the narrator is, then he is a speaker through whom James is satirizing the British upper classes. Other critics, however, have suggested that the narrator is completely untrustworthy, even to the point of being insane. His intrusions and wild speculations lead to nothing but trouble, and his expulsion from Newmarch at the end of the novel is fit punishment for someone who is no better than the snake in Paradise.

The novelist has not made it easy for readers to determine which view to take. Like many of James's later novels, *The Sacred Fount* is obscure and difficult to read. The writer's decision to maintain the point of view inside the consciousness of a narrator who is himself not clear about the implications of what he sees going on around him, and who is prone to find sinister meaning in even the most innocent or innocuous word or gesture, leads some readers almost to despair. James relies on this obscurity to create the effect he wishes to produce on his readers. It suggests the opacity of humanity, attempting to glimpse what lies beneath the surface statements, movements, gestures, and actions that characterize the observed lives of others. No one, James asserts, can really know for sure what another human being is really like, because the outward signs of behavior are often masks deliberately constructed to hide the true feelings and motivations of men and women who do not wish to reveal themselves as they really are.

The issue is not only social, but epistemological: If James is right in his view of human nature, then human existence is solipsistic, and no person can ever really know another. Far from being a distraction, then, the obscurity created by the novelist—the work's "inaccessibility," to use critic R. P. Blackmur's term—is the work's greatest strength. In this case, technique reinforces theme.

The lesson of the novel is not simply epistemological, however; the work is also a cautionary tale about the limits of fiction. As he illustrates in other works as well as this one, James believes that the function of the novelist is much like that of the narrator in *The Sacred Fount*: to penetrate the layers of opacity that obscure a person's true self to lay bare human personality in all its complexities. Such examinations are fraught with danger, since the act of revelation can invade not only the privacy of individuals on a social level but also the psychological integrity of individuals subjected to such scrutiny. How successful a novelist can be in revealing human character without violating the integrity of those portrayed or misrepresenting them is one of the key questions addressed in this haunting and perplexing tale.

Laurence W. Mazzeno

Bibliography:

Blackall, Jean Frantz. *Jamesian Ambiguity and "The Sacred Fount."* Ithaca, N.Y.: Cornell University Press, 1965. Uses the novel as the principal example to illustrate the novelist's handling of ambiguity in his fiction. Calls the work an "intellectual detective story" in which the reader, not the narrator, is cast in the role of the detective, tasked to determine where truth lies in this complex tale of social relationships.

Gargano, James W., ed. *Critical Essays on Henry James: The Late Novels*. Boston: G. K. Hall, 1987. Includes excerpts from three reviews by James's contemporaries, and a twentieth century essay justifying the novelist's narrative method and defending the sanity of the narrator.

Jones, Granville H. *Henry James's Psychology of Experience: Innocence, Responsibility, and Renunciation in the Fiction of Henry James*. Hawthorne, N.Y.: Mouton, 1975. Psychological analysis of James's major fiction. Extensive discussion of the narrator's role in *The Sacred Fount*; provides useful commentary from earlier critics of the novelist's complex method of presenting his story.

Kappeler, Susanne. *Writing and Reading in Henry James*. New York: Columbia University Press, 1980. A major section of this study is devoted to an examination of *The Sacred Fount*; explores the function of the narrator, who serves not only to record but also to interpret experience. Claims James breaks down traditional barriers between writer, critic, and reader.

Sicker, Philip. *Love and the Quest for Identity in the Fiction of Henry James*. Princeton, N.J.: Princeton University Press, 1980. Concentrates on the psychological dimensions of the novel. Believes the source of the ambiguity lies in James's "presentation of two differing views of identity." Discusses the role of the narrator. Claims the novel reveals James's vision of love in human relationships.

THE SAGA OF GRETTIR THE STRONG

Type of work: Folklore
Author: Unknown
Type of plot: Adventure
Time of plot: Eleventh century
Locale: Iceland, Norway, and Constantinople
First transcribed: Grettis Saga, c. 1300 (English translation, 1869)

Principal characters:
GRETTIR THE STRONG, an outlaw
ASMUND LONGHAIR, his father
ILLUGI, his youngest brother
THORBJORN OXMAIN, Grettir's enemy
THORBJORN SLOWCOACH, Oxmain's kinsman, killed by Grettir
THORIR OF GARD, an Icelandic chief
THORBJORN ANGLE, Grettir's slayer
THORSTEINN DROMUND, Grettir's half brother and avenger

The Story:

Grettir the Strong was descended from Onund, a Viking famed for enemies killed in war and the taking of booty from towns plundered on far sea raids. In a battle at Hafrsfjord, Onund lost a leg and was thereafter known as Onund Treefoot. His wife was Aesa, the daughter of Ofeig. Thrand, a great hero, was his companion in arms. During a time of great trouble in Norway, the two heroes sailed to Iceland to be free of injustice in their homeland, where the unscrupulous could rob without fear of redress. Onund lived in quiet and plenty in the new land, and his name became renowned, for he was valiant. At last he died. His sons fought after his death, and his lands were divided.

Grettir of the line of Onund was born at Biarg. As a child he showed strange intelligence. He quarreled constantly with Asmund Longhair, his father, and he was very lazy, never doing anything cheerfully or without urging. When he was fourteen years old, grown big in body, he killed Skeggi in a quarrel over a provision bag that had fallen from his horse, and for that deed his father paid blood money to the kinsmen of Skeggi. Then the Lawman declared that he must leave Iceland for three years. In that way the long outlawry of Grettir began.

Grettir set sail for Norway. The ship was wrecked on rocks off the Norwegian coast, but all got safely ashore on land that belonged to Thorfinn, a wealthy landsman of the district. Grettir made his home with him for a time. At Yuletide, Thorfinn, with most of his household, went to a merrymaking and left Grettir to look after the farm. In Thorfinn's absence, a party of berserks, or raiders, led by Thorir and Ogmund, came to rob and lay waste to the district. Grettir tricked them by locking them in a storehouse. When they broke through the wooden walls, Grettir, armed with sword and spear, killed Thorir and Ogmund and put the rest to flight. Sometime before this adventure, he had entered the tomb of Karr-the-Old, father of Thorfinn, a long-dead chieftain who guarded a hidden treasure. For his brave deed in killing the berserks, Thorfinn gave him an ancient sword from the treasure hoard of Karr-the-Old.

Next Grettir killed a great bear which had been carrying off the sheep. In doing so he incurred the wrath of Bjorn, who was jealous of Grettir's strength and bravery. Then Grettir killed Bjorn and was summoned before Jarl Sveinn. Friends of Bjorn plotted to take Grettir's life. After he killed two of his enemies, his friends saved him from the wrath of the jarl, who had wished to banish him. His term of outlawry ended, Grettir sailed back to Iceland in the spring.

At that time in Iceland, young Thorgils Maksson, Asmund's kinsman, was slain in a quarrel over a whale, and Asmund took up the feud against those who had killed him. The murderers were banished.

When Grettir returned, Asmund gave him the welcome that was his due because of his fame as a brave hero. Shortly after his return, Grettir fought with some men after a horse fight. The struggle was halted by a man named Thorbjorn Oxmain. The feud might have been forgotten if Thorbjorn Oxmain's kinsman, Thorbjorn Slowcoach, had not sneered at the hero.

Word came that a fiend had taken possession of the corpse of Glam, a shepherd. At night Glam ravaged the countryside. He could find no man with whom he could prove his strength, so Grettir went to meet Glam. They struggled in the house of Thorhall and ripped down beams and rafters in their angry might. At last Glam fell exhausted. Defeated, he predicted that Grettir would have no greater strength and less honor in arms from that day on and that he would grow afraid of the dark. Grettir cut off Glam's head and burned the body to destroy the evil spirit that possessed the dead shepherd.

Grettir decided to return to Norway. Among the passengers on the boat was Thorbjorn Slowcoach; they fought, and Grettir killed his foe. The travelers landed on a barren shore where they were without fire to warm themselves, and Grettir swam across the cove to get burning brands at an inn where the sons of Thorir of Gard, an Icelandic chieftain, were holding a drunken feast. He had to fight to get the fire he wanted; in the struggle, hot coals set fire to the straw on the inn floor and the house burned. Charged with deliberately setting fire to the inn and burning those within, Grettir went to lay the matter before the king. To prove his innocence of the charge of willful burning, he was sentenced to undergo trial by fire in the church, but the ordeal ended when Grettir became angry and threw a bystander into the air. The king then banished him from Norway, but because no ships could sail to Iceland before the spring, Grettir was allowed to remain in the country that winter. He lived some time with a man named Einar, on a lonely farm to which came the berserk Snaekoll, a wild man who pretended great frenzy during his lawless raids. Grettir seized him in his mad fit and killed the robber with his own sword. Grettir fell in love with Einar's beautiful daughter, but he knew that Einar would never give his child to a man of Grettir's reputation. Giving up his suit, he went to stay with his half brother, Thorsteinn Dromund. They were men of the same blood, and Thorsteinn swore to avenge Grettir if ever he were killed.

Grettir's father, Asmund, died. On his deathbed he said that little good would come of his son. Grettir's time of bad luck in Iceland began. Thorbjorn Oxmain killed Atli, Grettir's brother, in revenge for the slaying of Thorbjorn Slowcoach, and Thorir of Gard, hearing that his sons had been killed in the burning of the inn, charged Grettir with their murder before the court of the Althing. By the time Grettir returned, he had been proclaimed an outlaw throughout Iceland. He had little worry over his outlawry from the inn burning. Determined to avenge his brother, he went alone to Thorbjorn Oxmain's farm and killed both the man and his son. Grettir's mother was delighted with his deed, but she predicted that Grettir would not live freely to enjoy his victory. Thorir of Gard and Thorodd, Thorbjorn Oxmain's kinsman, each put a price of three silver marks upon his head. Soon afterward Grettir was captured by some farmers, but he was released by a wise woman named Thorbjorg.

Avoided by most of his former friends, who would no longer help him, Grettir went far north to find a place to live. In the forest, he met another outlaw named Grim, but a short time later, he was forced to kill his companion because Grim intended to kill him for the reward offered for Grettir's head. About that time there was a fear of the dark growing upon Grettir, as Glam had prophesied. Thorir of Gard hired Redbeard, another outlaw, to kill Grettir, but Grettir discovered the outlaw's plans and killed him instead. At last Grettir realized that he could not take any forest men into his trust, and yet he was afraid to live alone because of his fear of the dark.

Thorir of Gard attacked Grettir with eighty men, but the outlaw was able to hold them off for a time. Unknown to him, a friend named Hallmund attacked Thorir's men from the rear, and the attempt to capture Grettir failed. Nevertheless, Grettir could not stay long in any place, for all men had turned against him. Hallmund was treacherously slain for the aid he had given Grettir; as he died, he hoped that the outlaw would avenge his death.

One night a troll woman attacked a traveler named Gest in the room where he lay sleeping. They struggled all night, but at last Gest was able to cut off the monster's right arm. Then Gest revealed himself as Grettir. Steinvor of Sandhauger gave birth to a boy whom many called Grettir's son, but he died when he was seventeen years old and left no personal saga.

Thorodd then tried to gain favor by killing Grettir, but the outlaw soon overcame him and refused to kill his enemy. Grettir went north once more, but his fear of the dark was growing upon him so that he could no longer live alone even to save his life. At last, with his youngest brother, Illugi, and a servant, he settled on Drangey, an island which had no inlet so that men had to climb to its grassy summit by rope ladders. There Grettir, who had been an outlaw for some sixteen years, was safe for a time, because no one could climb the steep cliffs to attack him. For several years he and his companions lived on the sheep which had been put there to graze and on eggs and birds. His enemies tried in vain to lure him from the island. At last an old woman cut magic runes upon a piece of driftwood which floated to the island. When Grettir attempted to chop the log, his ax slipped, gashing his leg. He felt that his end was near, for the wound became swollen and painful.

Thorbjorn Angle, who had paid the old woman to cast a spell upon the firewood, led an attack upon the island while Grettir lay near death. Grettir was already dying when he struck his last blows at his enemies. Illugi and the servant died with him. After Thorbjorn had cut off Grettir's head as proof of the outlaw's death, Steinn the Lawman decreed that the murderer had cut off the head of a man already dead and that he could not collect the reward because he had used witchcraft to overcome Grettir. Outlawed for his deed, Thorbjorn went to Constantinople, where he enlisted in the emperor's guard. There Thorsteinn Dromund followed him and cut off the murderer's head with a sword which Grettir had taken, years before, from the treasure hoard of Karr-the-Old.

Critical Evaluation:

One of the most famous of all Norse sagas is the story of Grettir, hero and outlaw of medieval Iceland. Grettir, born about 997, was descended from Vikings who colonized Iceland in the second half of the ninth century, after they had refused to acknowledge Harold Fairhair as their king. Grettir emerges from his mist-shrouded, lawless world as a man so memorable that his story was handed down by word of mouth for more than two hundred years after his death. By the time his story was finally committed to writing, it had absorbed adventures of other folk heroes as well; but in the main, the saga is true to the political and social history of the age.

The Grettir of *The Saga of Grettir the Strong* is barely civilized, barely Christian, often childish in his behavior, careless of life and limb. This strong man of the north is formed by his homeland and by his heritage. Both good and evil are combined in his character. He is proud and compulsive in his behavior, and it sometimes appears that he is fighting the same battle over and over again, though the antagonists are always different. His strength is his weakness in that he needs to prove this strength continuously.

The Icelandic society into which Grettir is born was a stable one; except for the introduction of Christianity in 1000 and its ameliorating effects, the customs of the Norsemen remained much the same on into the eighteenth century. In this land of ice and bone-chilling cold, with its steep cliffs rising straight up from the sea and where only a small part of the land is arable, Grettir is born. It is a land of superstitions where trolls, who were demoniacal creatures, could possess one's soul. The saga of Grettir invites the reader to speculate on the possibility that Grettir may be possessed. He is certainly cursed.

Grettir's father does not like him, and his mother dotes on him. Psychologists could point to this fact alone and write a profile that would convince the reader that Grettir's daring and sometimes foolhardy deeds were all done in an effort to please his father.

Grettir is lazy. He does not want to work, and this is partly the reason his father dislikes him. When he is ten years old, his father sends him to care for the geese. He does not want to work and considers this chore beneath him in any case, so he wrings the goslings' necks and breaks the wings of the geese—a senselessly cruel exercise in evil. Refusing to conform to the work ethic, even when he grows into a man, Grettir is never able to accept parental or social authority.

A descendant of Onund Treefoot, who had sailed the seas looting and exploring, with his life constantly endangered by both the elements and his foes, Grettir is brave. The life of the sea was one of uncertainty and frustrations, especially in the tenth and eleventh centuries. Supplies were often inadequate. Hunger was a constant companion. Thus it is with Grettir in the uncharted seas of his life.

There were no family names in the Icelandic culture. Each person had one name and was further identified by his or her birthplace, a patronymic, or by a nickname such as "the Strong." Perhaps it was necessary for Grettir to do some of the foolhardy things he did in order to maintain his identity.

The translation of Grettir's saga by Denton Fox and Hermann Palsson is straightforward and carries the reader through the prologue of Onund Treefoot, Grettir's great-grandfather, to Grettir's story, and on to the epilogue in which the story of Grettir's half brother, Thorsteinn, is told. Thorsteinn avenges his brother's death in Byzantium, and that is another claim to fame for Grettir. He is the only Icelander who was ever avenged there. This translation is excellent. The shape of the land, its creatures, and its customs are conveyed by the language used. The reader feels the despair of this sorely tried hero. He or she sees the bleak, cold country and shivers as Grettir swims across the channel to get fire for his shipwrecked companions and rises ice-encrusted from the sea.

In Norway, where Grettir flees when he was first outlawed, groups of robbers and outlaws, called berserks, often came charging out of the forests demanding a farmer's possessions. One bloody episode involving the berserks is memorable because Grettir saves the farmer's daughter from them. Grettir runs toward a berserk, who is still on his horse, and kicks the end of his shield so hard that it is driven into the villain's mouth, causing his lower jaw to dangle down to his chest; then Grettir cuts off his head. Despite Grettir's many less-than-noble qualities, his bravery and willingness to defend the less powerful are heroic.

Grettir is always a champion of the afflicted, particularly those assailed by trolls and other supernatural beings. Perhaps this is because Grettir is cursed by a troll man whom he kills. After the curse, Grettir acknowledges that it is even harder than before for him to maintain his self-control. His fears of the dark and of being alone also date from this ill-fated encounter. His death is brought about by witchcraft, which was later outlawed by the Althing, or General

Assembly of Iceland, which met yearly to hear complaints. The chieftains were the members of the Althing, and their consensus was that a man who ignobly killed a dying man through witchcraft was a coward. The man who killed Grettir was also outlawed by the Althing.

The saga ends with the beautiful story of Grettir's half brother, Thorsteinn, and Spes, the charming Byzantium woman who ransoms Thorsteinn from prison where he has been incarcerated for killing Grettir's murderer. *The Saga of Grettir the Strong* well deserves its place with other masterpieces of world literature. The reader is moved at the tragic life and death of this giant of a man, who even as a child was mean enough to kill goslings, yet who risked his life to swim across a river so Steinvor and her daughter could go to Christmas Eve Mass.

"Critical Evaluation" by V. Addington

Bibliography:

Andersson, Theodore M. *The Icelandic Family Saga: An Analytic Reading*. Cambridge, Mass.: Harvard University Press, 1967. Unlike the many saga studies which focus on history and origin, this book examines the sagas as narrative. Chapters on structure, rhetoric, and heroic legacy are followed by insightful commentary.

Arent, A. Margaret. "The Heroic Pattern: Old Germanic Helmets, *Beowulf*, and *Grettis Saga*." In *Old Norse Literature and Mythology*, edited by Edgar C. Polomé. Austin: University of Texas Press, 1969. Discussion of the pictorial ornamentations found on Germanic helmets, and how the cultural and religious themes depicted on typical helmets shed light on the literature. Twenty-seven illustrations.

Hastrup, Kirsten. "Tracing Tradition: An Anthropological Perspective on *Grettis Saga Ásmundarsonar*." In *Structure and Meaning in Old Norse Literature*, edited by John Lindow et al. Odense, Denmark: Odense University Press, 1986. Traces the perception of Grettir the Strong by Icelanders over the past seven hundred years, showing how the meaning of the outcast-hero has changed.

Hume, Kathryn. "The Thematic Design of *Grettis Saga*." *Journal of English and Germanic Philology* 73, no. 4 (October, 1974): 469-486. Explains the puzzling contrasts in Grettir's character and the narrative tone between different episodes. The theme of the unacceptability of the heroic in a modern society accounts, Hume demonstrates, for the differences.

Schach, Paul. *Icelandic Sagas*. Boston: Twayne, 1984. Contains a brief but excellent introduction to this saga, including a discussion of its authorship, structure, and themes of intergenerational conflict and tragic isolation. Other sections provide historical and literary contexts, a chronology, and a bibliography.

THE SAILOR WHO FELL FROM GRACE WITH THE SEA

Type of work: Novel
Author: Yukio Mishima (Kimitake Hiraoka, 1925-1970)
Type of plot: Psychological realism
Time of plot: After World War II
Locale: Yokohama, Japan
First published: Gogo no eikō, 1963 (English translation, 1965)

Principal characters:
Noboru Kuroda, an adolescent male
Fusako Kuroda, his widowed mother
Ryuji Tsukazaki, second mate of a tramp vessel
Chief, anonymous leader of a band of boys to which Noboru belongs

The Story:

Part 2. Noboru, a precocious boy of thirteen, convinced of his own genius, spent much of his time in his bedroom, looking out over Yokohama Bay and listening to the sound of ships' horns. His personal philosophy, like that of the German pessimist Arthur Schopenhauer, comprised distrust of authority and women, concentration on death and nihilism, and faith in universal order. One night he discovered a peephole in his bedroom wall through which he was able to observe his mother's boudoir. Several days later, his mother, Fusako, who was only thirty-three years old and had retained much of her beauty, invited a sailor named Ryuji to dinner, and they passed the night in lovemaking. Noboru, through his peephole, observed their most intimate moments. At first, he found nothing objectionable, merely a verification of his philosophy of universal order. In his mind, he was encroaching on the mother, the mother on the man, the man on the sea, and the sea on the boy in a purposeful design.

Superficially, Fusako, as the wealthy proprietress of an exclusive male boutique, had nothing in common with Ryuji, the rough sailor. About her own age, he had always lived as a loner, hating both the land and the sea as types of a prison. From his youth, he had cherished the illusion of a special destiny leading him to glory. Becoming a sailor to escape a boring life such as his father had led, Ryuji had not, like the conventional seafarer, engaged in easy and frequent sex. His image of perfect love consisted of idyllic courtship ending in death.

On the morning after Noboru's spying on his mother, he told her that he was going swimming, but instead he spent the day denouncing the insignificance of ordinary life with a band of six schoolfellows, all top students. They were ranked according to leadership; their chief was number one, and Noboru number three. In boasting of his spying exploits, Noboru portrayed the sailor as a hero, a man dominating a woman, but the chief disagreed on the grounds that such a relationship was unimportant. He had inculcated as a principle that the band should remain absolutely apathetic concerning all things sexual. By means of a therapy of showing pictures that portrayed every physical aspect of intercourse, he had made the band completely dispassionate. Part of their ritual at this meeting consisted of killing a kitten as a symbol of the emptiness of existence. Selected as executioner, Noboru bashed the kitten against a log. The boys stripped off the animal's skin and dissected its organs in order to experience the sensation of absolute nakedness. Noboru compared the nakedness of the kitten with the nakedness of his mother.

A chance meeting with Ryuji on his way home turned Noboru's rapture into embarrassment. Since he had told his mother that his destination was elsewhere in the city, he was forced to admit his deception to the sailor, who good-naturedly promised not to expose his lie. Instead of feeling gratitude, Noboru looked down upon Ryuji as a fawning adult, seeking to ingratiate himself. As they talked about sailing and the sea on their way to Noboru's home, however, he had another change of heart, impressed by the sailor's masculinity and experience. Fusako was similarly attracted by Ryuji's manliness, but she struggled against being trapped in the conventional role of a grieving woman deserted by a sailor lover.

During their final encounter before his next voyage, Ryuji had the fantasy that one of their kisses was the kiss of death and that Fusako should, therefore, feel that their parting was like dying happily. Previously, in his dreams, he had associated the notion of final glory with abandoning a woman. Their actual farewell on the docks, however, was formal, without emotion on either side.

Part 2. When Ryuji returned to Yokohama in time for the New Year festivities, Fusako took him straight to her home. During his absence, she had been chaste, dissipating her energies through work and exercise. By this time, Ryuji, having reached the age of thirty-three, had realized that his dream of a grand future would never come to pass and considered giving up the sea. Although the sea represented freedom, it also involved a monotonous existence with no tangible glory. In the midst of indecision, he asked Fusako to marry him, at the same time offering to give her all of his money, whether or not she accepted his proposal. Fusako, touched by this artless generosity, agreed immediately.

After the holidays, when Noboru rejoined his band in an enormous abandoned crate on the harbor front, he expressed his disgust at Ryuji's decision to settle down as a landsman. The chief first asked whether he would like to participate in turning the sailor back into a hero, but then without saying more on the subject, he launched into a generalized diatribe against fathers and father figures, boasting that he was capable of making his own world die, an achievement equivalent to glory.

Ryuji took up permanent residence with Fusako, and, soon after, she informed Noboru of their imminent marriage. Conditions in the household grew tense. Fusako discovered the existence of the peephole and angrily confronted Noboru. Expecting Ryuji to administer bodily punishment, she was shocked when he merely delivered a verbal rebuke. Noboru was even more upset by this placid reaction, which completely shattered his image of the sailor as hero and glory-figure. Angrily, he asked the chief to call an emergency meeting of the band to discuss the situation. They decided that Ryuji's example represented an affront to order and that he had to be eliminated. They decided that he should be drugged and then disemboweled in line with their previous ritual with the kitten. They had no fear of consequences, since none had reached the age of fourteen, and the penal code clearly stated that acts of juveniles under that age were not punishable by law.

On the day of execution, Noboru succeeded in delivering Ryuji to the appointed meeting place under the pretext that his companions wanted to hear tales of the sea. Ryuji willingly began a narrative combining nautical and personal reminiscences. Although sensing that something was not quite right, he unhesitatingly drank a cup of poisoned tea that was offered to him. It had an odd taste, a sensation he associated with the bitterness of glory. His romantic association of love, death, and glory vanished with him into nothingness.

Critical Evaluation:

Widely regarded as one of the most philosophical and thought-provoking novelists of the post-World War II period, Yukio Mishima produced twenty-five major works of fiction, concentrating on contemporary Japan, but embracing universal literary and philosophical themes.

These themes he presented in such dichotomies as art and nature, literature and life, asceticism and hedonism, mind and body, and Eastern and Western culture. His portrayals of art and beauty, love and death, nearly always involved some shocking exposure of deviant sexuality, such as Noboru's voyeurism. Unlike conventional authors, Mishima sought to remain in the public eye, advertising both his aestheticism and his political conservatism. As a final act of staged publicity, he committed suicide in full military regalia watched by thousands on television.

The original Japanese title *Gogo no eikō*, literally meaning "towing in the afternoon," conceals a pun on eikō, which stands for "glory" as well as "towing." Since this pun cannot be translated into English, Mishima selected the English title which the novel now bears from a list devised by his translator. It presumably means that Ryuji, by abandoning the sea, had deviated from his destined role in the universal order and had therefore fallen from an approved position. Throughout the novel, the sea is a metaphor for woman, sex, glory, and death, elements which are continually interwoven.

Events are narrated from the perspective of only two characters, Ryuji and Noboru. They are foils for each other, Ryuji representing bodily development and romantic optimism, and Noboru standing for intellect, youth, and carnal nihilism. Ryuji may be seen as an idealistic figure, hopelessly obsessed by the trinity of the sea, feminine beauty, and death. These elements are united in his recurrent dream of a man lured by a perfect woman into a passionate embrace in which a kiss of death is accompanied by the sound of the sea. Ryuji's quest for glory, with which this dream is associated, is by itself highly romantic, but his actions fall sadly short of his mission. The high degree of erotic satisfaction provided by Fusako compensates for his lack of fulfillment, but it leads to his abandoning the sea, a further retreat from his vision of glory. His death, moreover, does not represent a tragic resistance to destiny or, as he fantasized it should be, a glorious and triumphant finale to a storm-tossed career. It comes instead as the result of the commonplace act of drinking a cup of tea. Since each member of the band has been instructed to bring a knife to the meeting place, it is clear that Ryuki's body, like that of the kitten, will be dissected after his death. At this moment, the figure of Ryuki symbolizes the pessimistic philosophy of Schopenhauer instead of the romantic optimism that had until then been associated with him.

Noboru, who is Ryuki's antithesis, observes and criticizes him, and eventually starts in motion the machinery leading to Ryuki's destruction. At first, Noboru highly approves of the sailor when he finds him in bed with his mother. For him, the sight is "like being part of a miracle." He admires the sailor's muscular body and sexual prowess, but when the latter exchanges the sea for a subordinate position in Fusako's boutique, Ryuki is converted from his mother's conqueror into her ally. Although seeing himself as the instrument of Ryuji's destruction, Noboru is forced to turn to the chief for energy to carry out the actual deed. Noboru's antagonism toward Ryuji is linked with his personal development and his coming-of-age. In part 1, his bedroom door is locked by his mother at night, a sign of childhood dependence; in part 2, on the advice of Ryuji, it is left unlocked. This symbolizes both Noboru's emancipation and the role he will play in Ryuji's ultimate demise. It also represents a choice in life between retreating to a safe haven and taking arms against turbulent reality. Noboru clearly indicates these alternatives when he wonders whether there is any way that he could remain in the room and at the same time be out in the hall locking the door.

Although the characters of the novel lend themselves to a psychological interpretation, the key elements in the plot are implausible from a realistic perspective, particularly the thirteen-year-old boy's commitment to nihilistic philosophy, the contemplated marriage between the rough sailor and the wealthy owner of a luxury boutique, and the effortless massacre of the sailor as the joint act of a group of schoolboys. On this level, the novel is best understood as an exquisitely wrought allegory, expounding the doctrines of nihilism.

A. Owen Aldridge

Bibliography:

Napier, Susan J. *Escape from the Wasteland: Romanticism and Realism in the Fiction of Mishima Yukio and Ōe Kenzaburō*. Cambridge, Mass.: Harvard University Press, 1991. Does not treat *The Sailor Who Fell from Grace with the Sea* separately, but offers many insights and suggestions.

Petersen, Gwenn Boardman. *The Moon in the Water: Understanding Tanizaki, Kawabata, and Mishima*. Honolulu: University of Hawaii Press, 1979. Provides a lucid interpretation of the sexual and aesthetic elements in the novel.

Ueda, Makoto. *Modern Japanese Writers and the Nature of Literature*. Stanford, Calif.: Stanford University Press, 1976. Discerning analysis by a Japanese scholar of Mishima's fiction.

Viglielmo, Valdo H. "The Sea as Metaphor: An Aspect of the Modern Japanese Novel." In *Poetics of the Elements in the Human Condition*, edited by Anna-Teresa Tyrnieniecke. Dordrecht: Reidel, 1985. Volume 19 of the Series Analecta Husserliana. An ingenious and credible interpretation of the multiple meanings of the sea.

Wolfe, Peter. *Yukio Mishima*. New York: Continuum, 1989. The best criticism in English of the novel, portrayed as "a work of warped genius" that "opens exciting realms of response, but only to slam them shut."

SAINT JOAN

Type of work: Drama
Author: George Bernard Shaw (1856-1950)
Type of plot: Historical
Time of plot: Fifteenth century
Locale: France
First performed: 1923; first published, 1924

Principal characters:
JOAN, the Maid, a teenage French country girl
CHARLES, THE DAUPHIN, heir to the French throne
ARCHBISHOP OF RHEIMS, a political prelate
"JACK" DUNOIS, a French general
PETER CAUCHON, the bishop of Beauvais
EARL OF WARWICK, an English nobleman
STOGUMBER, an English chaplain

The Story:

At Vaucouleurs castle, Robert de Baudricourt was berating his steward for claiming that the hens had stopped laying. The steward insisted they would not lay until Robert talked to Joan, the Maid, who demanded to see him. Robert finally admitted Joan. She promptly requested a horse, armor, and some soldiers to take her to the dauphin. She had already persuaded several soldiers to accompany her and convinced them that God had sent her to save France from the English occupying force. Robert yielded, and the hens immediately began laying again.

At Chinon, the archbishop and the Lord Chamberlain were complaining about the dauphin's irresponsibility. Bluebeard, a nobleman, told about a cursing soldier who had died after being cautioned by an angel dressed as a soldier. Charles appeared, looking browbeaten but excited about Robert's surprise. Almost everyone advised Charles not to see Joan, but he insisted. They then decided that Bluebeard would pretend to be Charles, to see if Joan could pick out the real dauphin; the archbishop cynically remarked that such seeming miracles could be as useful as real ones. When Joan entered, she immediately spotted Charles and told him that she was sent by God to help him drive the English from France and to crown him king. Charles, full of doubts, tried to escape her but finally yielded and gave Joan command of the army. Cheering, the knights prepared to head for Orléans.

Two months later at Orléans, Dunois' French forces had still not attacked the English because the east wind was preventing their ships from going up the river. When Joan arrived, Dunois explained the military situation. Joan grasped the problem immediately and agreed to pray for a west wind to make the French attack possible. As she spoke, a page sneezed and everyone suddenly noticed that the wind had changed. Joan, overwhelmed by this sign, rushed with Dunois into battle.

In the English camp, Chaplain Stogumber and the Earl of Warwick considered France's recent military victories. Stogumber resented seeing Englishmen beaten by French "foreigners." Warwick complained that people were beginning to define themselves by their country, rather than by local allegiances—a danger to both feudal lords and the Church. Warwick therefore hoped to collaborate with Bishop Cauchon, who represented the rival Burgundian faction in France. When Cauchon arrived, he and Warwick agreed that neither felt happy about the imminent crowning of Charles, that they preferred to limit his future progress, and that capturing Joan offered the best chance of success. The three men then debated the precise nature of Joan's threat and the possible remedies. Cauchon considered her a heretic for her belief that God communicated with her directly; if people insisted on their own interpretation of God's will rather than that of the Church, there would be religious and social chaos. His ideal solution was to compel Joan to abandon her heretical belief. In Warwick's opinion, Joan was spreading a secular belief that he defined as Protestantism and that he considered dangerous to the feudal social structure—the idea of "nations" under autocratic kings who would hold their power directly from God. Warwick and Cauchon, who defined Joan's belief as nationalism, agreed that Joan must at least recant her heresy; if she could be thoroughly neutralized they were willing to spare her life, but Stogumber was prepared to burn her as a witch.

At Rheims Cathedral, Charles had just been crowned king of France. Joan wondered to Dunois why everyone suddenly seemed to hate her. She said that once she conquered Paris, she would return to the country. Dunois expressed doubts about more fighting, but Joan insisted that her "voices"—the saints' voices she heard and obeyed—told her she must continue. When Charles and others arrived, Joan suggested that she return to her father's farm. Everyone seemed much relieved, but it was obvious that she wanted to continue fighting for France. When the archbishop came, he counseled that her stubborn confidence in her own beliefs would lead to her destruction. Dunois revealed that the English had offered a reward for whoever captured Joan. Joan finally realized that, if she were captured, none of her old supporters would try to save her.

In May, 1431, Joan was about to be tried for heresy in Rouen. Stogumber and a French priest complained that many charges had been dropped, but the Inquisitor and Cauchon insisted that the crucial ones remained. Warwick revealed that English soldiers were guarding the site, ready for trouble. Soldiers brought Joan into court. When questioned, Joan did not understand the charges, insisting that she loved the Church and therefore could not be a heretic. Some suggested that she be tortured to make her confess, but the Inquisitor refused. Joan continued to assert that everything she had done had been at God's command and that she had to trust her own judgment of what God wanted of her. Her insistence on her own judgment condemned her as a heretic. Several people begged her to recant, and, when she realized the punishment was death, she did so. When she learned, however, that her alternative punishment would be life in prison, she denied her recantation and chose death at the stake. English soldiers led her away and executed her. Those who saw her die, including Stogumber, were transformed.

In 1456, Charles was reading in bed when Ladvenu, who had helped Joan at the trial, brought word that Joan's verdict had been overturned: The judges had been ruled corrupt and Joan declared innocent. Several people from twenty-five years earlier, including some who had died in the meantime, appeared, including Joan, Cauchon, Dunois, an English soldier who had given Joan a makeshift cross, Stogumber, and Warwick. They revealed their subsequent fates. A twentieth century man appeared, announcing Joan's canonization in 1920. Strangely, no one wanted a living Joan, and, one by one, the ghostly spirits disappeared. Alone, Joan wondered when this world would be ready to receive God's living saints.

Critical Evaluation:

Like most of George Bernard Shaw's dramatic works, *Saint Joan* has a didactic purpose. By the 1920's, Shaw had become disillusioned about many political programs, including aspects of his own Fabian Socialism, and he had developed the concept of the "evolutionary appetite" or Creative Evolution. According to this belief, the Life Force itself needs to keep evolving and developing, thereby producing individuals who, by embodying new ideas, force humanity to the next evolutionary stage; such individuals include Jesus, Mohammad, Oliver Cromwell, and Saint Joan. New concepts necessarily threaten the existing social order, and people in power often try to suppress the ideas by killing those who embody them. Nevertheless, such powerful evolutionary ideas eventually triumph, as they must if humanity is to fulfill its destiny.

Shaw believed that Joan forced the people of her time to confront two central tenets of modern consciousness—Protestantism and nationalism, both of which give greater scope to individual conscience. He discussed this theme at length in the preface (nearly half as long as the play itself) and presented it most explicitly in the confrontation between Warwick and Cauchon in scene iv. This scene was criticized for being too wordy and for its implausibility. After all, intelligent medieval people, for whom the social structure of feudalism and the power of the Catholic church were completely self-evident, might well struggle with the exact nature of Joan's threat, but there would have been no need for them to explain their fundamental worldviews to each other in such detail. Anticipating this criticism, Shaw insisted that twentieth century audiences, who were profoundly ignorant of history, had to have the medieval perspective spelled out for them if the play were to make any sense.

Joan's trial (scene vi) also drew criticism for compressing historical events, for blending comedy (Stogumber's extraneous charges) and tragedy (Joan's excommunication and death), as well as, occasionally, for the uninspired poetry of Joan's last speeches. Yet, these two scenes display one of Shaw's greatest strengths—his ability convincingly to express points of view completely different from his own. In the preface, he insisted that Joan received a fair trial from Cauchon and the Inquisitor; he therefore gave these men wonderfully persuasive speeches, even though the characters embodied what Shaw considered doomed ideas. Shaw's Joan dies because she is, in truth, a heretic from the prevailing system of thought. With typical Shavian perversity, her heresy is the necessary precondition for her sanctity.

Chronologically, *Saint Joan* followed the despairing play about war (*Heartbreak House*, 1913-1919) and his massive five-play cycle about Creative Evolution (*Back to Methuselah*, 1921), which reflected Shaw's disgust with the postwar world and traced human life from the Garden of Eden to the year 31,920. Compared with these two works, *Saint Joan* is simple and direct, and it reflects real affection for its heroine. Like the earlier plays, however, it also reflects contemporary issues that concerned Shaw. Shaw chose, for example, to contemplate Joan's era from the perspective of one who had observed the horrors of trench warfare; the implicit comparison of old cruelties with new ones allowed him to present Warwick and Cauchon more sympathetically. Shaw also implied that society still persecutes anyone who resists the prevailing orthodoxy. Thus, in the preface, he equated the twentieth century belief in science and medicine with the unthinking medieval faith in the Church, noting the modern condemnation of those who refused inoculations. In the epilogue, he had Cauchon wonder if Christ (and, by extension, any truly original but disruptive individual) "must perish in torment in every age to save those that have no imaginations." He questioned traditional gender roles by focusing on a heroine who sensibly rejected them, and he used Stogumber's mindless English chauvinism to criticize British imperialism, especially in his own native Ireland.

Structurally, this historical play presents a mixture of romance, tragedy, and farce; the combination of styles underscores Shaw's ironic approach to his subject. The first three scenes, in which Joan moves from triumph to triumph, have a fairy-tale quality that vanishes as the forces of conventionality converge to destroy her. Both the inevitability and the cruelty of her approaching death make the last three scenes dark indeed. The epilogue, by contrast, turns her suffering into a cosmic joke. First, her just conviction is overturned in a politically motivated show trial. Then, her former friends and enemies, living and dead, gather in Charles's dream to consider their past actions with detached amusement. Finally, a ridiculous man in twentieth century clothing appears, rather like a space alien, to inform the people of 1456 that Joan the heretic has become a saint. When Joan suggests a miracle to make her live again, however, everyone flees in panic. For ordinary humans, Shaw sardonically implied, the only good saint is a dead one.

Susan Wladaver-Morgan

Bibliography:

Hill, Holly. *Playing Joan: Actresses on the Challenge of Shaw's Saint Joan*. New York: Theatre Communications Group, 1987. Consists of twenty-six interviews with actresses who have played the role of Joan, sometimes in languages other than English. Partly anecdotal, the collection provides insight into the varied interpretations of the play.

Holroyd, Michael. *1918-1950: The Lure of Fantasy*. Vol. 3 in *Bernard Shaw*. New York: Random House, 1991. Part of Holroyd's magisterial biography of Shaw. Provides a brief analysis of *Saint Joan* as well as a great deal of information on the circumstances surrounding its creation and production. Also includes an excellent analysis of the development of Shaw's ideas.

Nightingale, Benedict. *A Reader's Guide to Fifty Modern British Plays*. Totowa, N.J.: Barnes & Noble Books, 1982. Considers Shaw and thirty-three other British playwrights and thus provides a historical, comparative context for Shaw's work. Includes a concise analysis of *Saint Joan* and four other Shaw plays.

Tyson, Brian. *The Story of Shaw's "Saint Joan."* Kingston, Ontario: McGill-Queen's University Press, 1982. Detailed scene-by-scene analysis of the play based on examination of Shaw's original manuscript in the British Museum. Covers Joan's miracles in one chapter, then focuses on the Warwick-Cauchon confrontation, the trial, and the epilogue.

Weintraub, Stanley, ed. *Saint Joan: Fifty Years After, 1923/24-1973/74*. Baton Rouge: Louisiana State University Press, 1973. A collection of twenty-five essays that analyze Joan from Marxist, feminist, Irish nationalist perspectives and many other perspectives (including a consideration of Joan as a 1920's flapper). Authors include T. S. Eliot and Luigi Pirandello.

ST. PETER'S UMBRELLA

Type of work: Novel
Author: Kálmán Mikszáth (1847-1910)
Type of plot: Comic realism
Time of plot: Second half of nineteenth century
Locale: Hungary
First published: *Szent Péter Esernyöje*, 1895 (English translation, 1900)

Principal characters:
PÁL GREGORICS, a wealthy bachelor
ANNA WIBRA, his housekeeper and cook
GYURY or GYÖRGY WIBRA, the illegitimate son of Anna Wibra
JÁNOS BÉLYI, a priest in Glogova
VERONICA BÉLYI, his sister
WIDOW ADAMECZ, the priest's housekeeper
JÁNOS SZTOLARIK, a lawyer
JÓNÁS MÜNCZ, a Jewish merchant

The Story:

When the new priest, young János Bélyi, arrived in Glogova, prospects for an enjoyable life were extremely dim. The little Hungarian town was a forlorn place where impoverished peasants lived out their lives trying to get as much as possible out of the poor soil. No provisions were made for the priest's subsistence, and church property was almost nonexistent. While the priest was contemplating the fact that he would have to eat less and pray more, the situation became more critical with the arrival of his little baby sister. His parents had died and somebody had decided to send little Veronica to her nearest relative, the priest; thus, a little baby in a basket was suddenly put at the doorstep of his modest home. In order to find a solution to his problems, he took a prayerful walk.

A heavy rain began to fall. Suddenly he remembered the baby, still lying in front of his house, and he was certain the child would be soaking wet before he could arrive. To his surprise he found her completely dry, protected by an old red umbrella. The priest could not imagine who had been so kind to his little sister; however, the townspeople soon found all sorts of explanations. Since the only stranger who had been seen lately was an old Jew, the peasants came to the conclusion that St. Peter had come to show his mercy for the poor child.

At the next funeral on a rainy day the priest used the red umbrella. The men carrying the coffin stumbled, and the supposedly dead man, who was merely in a trance, became very much alive. To the villagers this incident was another sign of the supernatural character of the umbrella. As a result of the umbrella, the priest's conditions improved rapidly, and all kinds of gifts arrived at his house for the baby who had caused St. Peter to come to Glogova. Even Widow Adamecz offered her services as housekeeper free of charge, additional proof of the miraculous power of the umbrella to all who knew the money-conscious widow.

In the beginning the priest tried to resist continuous requests for the presence of the umbrella during church ceremonies, but his parishioners felt so offended when he refused that he finally gave in and used the umbrella on all occasions. Pilgrims came from far away to look at the umbrella, and brides insisted on being married under it. Soon the town felt the need for building an inn that carried the name Miraculous Umbrella. The priest wondered how the umbrella came to Glogova; he was to wait many years for an answer.

In the town of Besztercebanya lived a wealthy bachelor, Pál Gregorics. A spy during the war, he had been seen many times with a red umbrella. Pál Gregorics was in love with his housekeeper, Anna Wibra, who gave birth to an illegitimate son, Gyury Wibra. The townspeople observed how Pál Gregorics devoted all of his time to the child. Pál's two brothers and his sister did not like the possibility that they might someday have to share Pál's estate with an illegitimate child. For this reason Pál, afraid that his relatives might try to harm young Gyury, decided to trick them by pretending he did not care for the boy, and he sent Gyury to a distant school. To deceive his brothers and sister, he acted as if he had invested all of his money in several estates which required inspection from time to time, but in reality he visited his son.

Despite great love for his father, Gyury reproached Pál for making himself a laughingstock by always carrying the old red umbrella. Pál disregarded the complaints and promised his son he would one day inherit the umbrella. When Pál felt he was going to die, he asked his lawyer János Sztolarik to prepare his will. Mysteriously, he asked two masons, under strict order of secrecy, to break a wall in order to place a caldron into the wall and finish the masonry as it had been before. Although he had told his housekeeper to notify Gyury of his illness, she failed to do so, and Pál Gregorics died, without seeing his son, with the red umbrella in his hands.

When Sztolarik read the will, Pál's brothers and sister were horrified to hear nothing about the rich estates which their brother supposedly owned. They spent much time and money to find out what Pál had done with the money. They suspected a secret bequest to Gyury, but investigators reported that the boy was studying and living on a meager income. Finally they discovered the two masons, who revealed for a large sum of money the secret of the caldron in the wall. Certain they had found the answer to their riddle, they bought the house, which had been willed to Gyury, for an extremely high price. When they broke the wall open, they found the caldron filled with rusty nails.

Soon afterward Gyury completed his education and became a lawyer in Besztercebanya. He had heard about the frantic search for his father's estate, and he began to wonder where it could be. The first clue was given by the dying mayor, who told how Pál Gregorics had carried secret documents in the hollow handle of his umbrella during the war. Gyury's suspicion was confirmed when his mother told him how Pál, even in death, was still clutching the umbrella. The search for the umbrella then began. Gyury's investigations pointed to an old Jew, Jónás Müncz, who had bought for a few coins those odds and ends belonging to his father that the relatives did not want. Further inquiries established that the Jew had died but that his wife owned a small store in Babaszek. Gyury and his coachman hurried to that town. An interview with Frau Müncz revealed that her husband had been fond of the umbrella and had carried it around at all times. Gyury heard from Frau Müncz's son that the old Jew had been seen putting the umbrella over a little baby in Glogova.

As he was about to leave for Glogova, Gyury found a lost earring for which, according to the town crier, the mayor was searching. Returning the earring to the mayor, he was introduced to its owner, a young and extremely beautiful woman. Furthermore, he learned she was Veronica Bélyi, sister of the village priest in Glogova. She had been on her way home when an accident damaged her vehicle.

Gyury gladly offered to conduct Veronica and her traveling companion in his carriage, but the two women decided that it was now too late for departure, and Gyury agreed to postpone his trip until morning. During a party in the mayor's house, Gyury heard about the miraculous umbrella in Glogova and realized that the umbrella he was seeking was identical with the priest's umbrella. Throughout the night he could hardly sleep from thinking how near and yet how far away the umbrella was. During the night he dreamed that St. Peter advised him to marry the priest's sister; thus he would have a beautiful wife and a legal claim on the umbrella.

On the trip to Glogova, Gyury considered the advantages of the suggestion offered to him in his dream, but he was afraid Veronica might not love him. The carriage broke down not far away from the town. Searching for some wood needed for repair, he heard faint cries for help; a man had fallen into a deep hole. After several attempts he succeeded in lifting out the unfortunate man, who turned out to be the priest of Glogova; he had fallen into the hole while waiting for Veronica on the previous night. Deeply grateful, the priest wanted to know whether there was anything he could do for his rescuer. Gyury told him he had something in his carriage belonging to the priest. The priest was surprised to find his sister in the vehicle; he informed Veronica of his promise, and she became engaged to Gyury.

In Glogova the young man had a conversation with the lawyer Sztolarik, who had heard from Gyury about his successful search. The lawyer was concerned because he felt that Gyury could not be sure whether love for Veronica or for the umbrella was the primary motive for his marriage. Veronica, overhearing the conversation, ran away heartbroken.

Gyury was eager to see the umbrella, which the priest gladly showed him; but the old handle had been replaced by a new one of silver. Gyury's last hope for recovering the old handle was crushed when the priest's housekeeper informed him that she had burned it. Meanwhile, the priest began to worry about the absence of his sister. Hearing of her disappearance, Gyury was also greatly upset. Suddenly he realized that he could overcome the loss of the umbrella, but not the loss of Veronica. Church bells gave the fire alarm signal, and everybody in Glogova appeared for the search. When Gyury found Veronica and told her about the burned handle, she recognized his greater love for her, and she and Gyury were married in the grandest wedding Glogova had ever seen. Although Gyury never knew whether the handle contained the key to his inheritance, the umbrella remained a treasured relic in his family.

Critical Evaluation:

Kálmán Mikszáth was a country squire, lawyer, magistrate, journalist, member of parliament, and novelist; his forte, however, was undoubtedly the ability for superb storytelling. He draws his characters with the certainty of a man who knows and understands the people about whom he writes, mainly the Hungarian peasantry. The ease with which he transforms everyday life into unusual stories reminds one strongly of Guy de Maupassant; his sense of humor, as demonstrated in this novel, makes reading a pleasure. The author became a member of the Hungarian Academy and of the Hungarian Parliament, but his parliamentary speeches will be long forgotten while the hilarious episodes of *St. Peter's Umbrella* will be still remembered.

Sometimes called the Hungarian Mark Twain, Mikszáth established his fame as a short-story writer before he turned to writing novels, the first of which was *St. Peter's Umbrella*. Like much of Twain's work, the novel reveals a bittersweet, jauntily pessimistic tone in Mikszáth's attitude toward the human condition. Although Mikszáth wanted to believe in essential human goodness, he was empirically convinced that human flaws and failings were innate and ineradicable. Thus, the well-meaning priest becomes party to a heretical superstition about the umbrella. So, too, the otherwise inoffensive brothers and sister of Pál Gregorics become greedy vultures who begrudge Gyury a share of his father's estate.

Yet, for all this, *St. Peter's Umbrella* is not a Dickensian tale of unrelieved gloom but a lighthearted fable with the makings of a modern legend—literary rather than folk in its origins, for it does not stem from the ethnic lore of Hungary. The unifying factor in the story is the umbrella, a symbol of protection from inclement weather. As the plot unfolds, the umbrella gains additional symbolic significance: It mysteriously appears in Glogova, bringing good fortune. It becomes even more intriguing as the object of Gyury's search. Hence, the umbrella is the stuff from which fable and legend are made. In fact, throughout the novel, Mikszáth follows the conventions of Hungarian fables and consequently invests the story with an air of authenticity.

The aura of authenticity in *St. Peter's Umbrella* is so strong that the improbable coincidences are often overlooked. How likely is it that a passerby would place an umbrella over an untended baby in a rainstorm? How likely is it that a putative corpse being buried on a rainy day by a priest with an umbrella should prove to be very much alive? How likely is it that Gyury would find the widow of Jónás Müncz? How likely is it that Gyury would find a lost earring, which coincidentally belonged to Veronica Bélyi, sister of the priest who possessed the umbrella for which Gyury was searching? How likely is Gyury's falling in love with Veronica? It is a tribute to Mikszáth's storytelling powers that the reader never asks such questions, enjoying the fable on its own terms.

Bibliography:

Reményi, Joseph. "Kálmán Mikszáth: Novelist and Satirist." *Hungarian Writers and Literature*. New Brunswick, N.J.: Rutgers University Press, 1964. Pages 154 to 164 introduce Mikszáth's works. Establishes a context for Mikszáth's works.

Scheer, Steven C. *Kálmán Mikszáth*. Boston: Twayne, 1977. A good starting place in the study of Mikszáth's life and work. Bibliography.

ŚAKUNTALĀ

Type of work: Drama
Author: Kālidāsa (c. 100 B.C.E. or 340 C.E.-c. 40 B.C.E. or 400 C.E.)
Type of plot: Love
Time of plot: Golden Age of India
Locale: India
First performed: Abhijñānaśākuntala, c. 45 B.C.E. or c. 395 C.E. (English translation, 1789)

Principal characters:
Śakuntalā, the beautiful daughter of a Brahman and a nymph
Kanwa, Śakuntalā's foster father and a wise hermit
Dushyanta, the king of India, in love with Śakuntalā.
Mathavya, the court jester

The Story:

Dushyanta, the king of India, was hunting one day when his chariot took him into the sacred grounds of a religious establishment. A hermit stopped the king and reminded him that he had sworn to protect the religious people who lived there. The king left his chariot and wandered through the hallowed groves. As he walked, he heard voices and saw three young women passing through the grove to water the plants growing there. When a bee, angered by their presence, flew at her, Śakuntalā, not knowing that the king was anywhere near, playfully called on Dushyanta to rescue her.

Dushyanta, stepping from his hiding place, announced himself, not as the king, but as the king's representative appointed to oversee the safety of the grove and its inhabitants. While they talked, Dushyanta learned that Śakuntalā was no ordinary maid, but the child of a Brahman and a water nymph. Dushyanta fell in love with her. Śakuntalā also felt the first pangs of love for the king and believed that the Hindu cupid had struck her with his five flower-tipped arrows.

Mathavya, the king's jester, complained to his master that too much time was being spent in hunting and that the life was too hard on him. Ostensibly to humor the jester, but actually to have more time to seek out Śakuntalā, the king called off any further hunting and ordered his retinue to camp near the sacred grove in which Śakuntalā lived with her foster father, a hermit-wiseman named Kanwa. A short time later word came to the camp that the king's mother wished him to return to the capital to take part in certain ceremonies, but Dushyanta was so smitten with love for Śakuntalā that he sent his retinue back while he himself, in the hope of seeing Śakuntalā again, remained at the sacred grove.

After their first meeting, both the king and Śakuntalā had languished with love. At last Dushyanta found excuse and opportunity to revisit the grove, and there he met the woman again. Both were clearly in love, but neither one knew how to tell the other. One of Śakuntalā's attendants finally conceived the idea of having her send a love note to the king. As Śakuntalā wrote the note, Dushyanta heard her speaking the words aloud. He stepped from his place of concealment and told her of his determination to make her his consort and the head of his household, above all his other wives. Śakuntalā left, telling him that she would have to talk over the subject of marriage with her attendants, for her foster father, Kanwa, was absent and so could not give his consent.

Sometime later a scurrilous and eccentric sage came to the sacred grove. He felt himself slighted by Śakuntalā, who had not heard of his arrival and so did not accomplish the rites of hospitality to suit him. In his anger he called down a curse upon the woman, although she did not know of it. The curse was that her lover should not remember her until he saw once again the ring of recognition that he would give her. The attendants who heard the curse were afraid to tell Śakuntalā for fear she would become ill with worry.

Before Dushyanta left the sacred grove to return to his palace, Śakuntalā agreed to a secret marriage and became his wife, but she decided to remain at the grove until the return of her foster father. Before he left, the king gave her a ring, as a sign of her new status. Not long after the king's departure, Kanwa returned. Having the gift of omniscience, he knew all that had taken place, and, as Kanwa reentered the sacred grove, a supernatural voice told him that Śakuntalā should give birth to a son destined to rule the world. Kanwa, thus assured of the future, gave his blessing to the union of Śakuntalā and the king. He had his people make the necessary preparations for sending the bride to her husband, to appear as the royal consort.

When the time came for her departure, Śakuntalā was filled with regret, for she loved the sacred grove where she had been reared. In addition, she had premonitions that her future was not to be a happy one. Kanwa insisted, however, that she make ready to leave, so that her son could be born in his father's palace.

When the hermits of the sacred wood appeared in Dushyanta's presence with Śakuntalā, the curse proved true, for King Dushyanta failed to remember Śakuntalā and his marriage to her. The hermits, feeling that they had done their duty in escorting Śakuntalā to her husband, left her in the king's household. Śakuntalā, heartbroken at her husband's failure to remember her, looked for the ring of recognition he had given her. The ring had been lost during the journey from the sacred wood to the palace.

Not long after Dushyanta had sent Śakuntalā from his presence, his courtiers came to tell him that a strange, winged being had flown into the palace gardens, picked up Śakuntalā, and carried her away into the heavens. The king was much disturbed over the event, but resolved to put it from his mind. Later the ring of recognition, bearing the king's crest, was discovered in the hands of a poor fisherman; he had found it in the belly of a carp. The ring was carried to Dushyanta; no sooner had he set eyes upon it than he remembered Śakuntalā and their secret marriage, for the sight of the ring removed the curse.

Remembrance of Śakuntalā did him no good; when she had been snatched from the palace garden, she had been lost to mortal eyes. Dushyanta grew sad and refused to be comforted. Meanwhile the nymph who had stolen Śakuntalā from the palace garden kept watch and took note of the king's unhappiness. Finally she took pity on him and had the chariot of the god Indra sent down to earth to convey King Dushyanta to heaven for a reunion with Śakuntalā.

In heaven the king found a young boy playing with a lion. He was amazed to see what the child was doing and felt a strong attraction for him. While he watched, an amulet fell from the child's neck. The king picked it up and replaced it on the boy's shoulders, much to the surprise of the boy's heavenly attendants, for the amulet was deadly to all but the child's parents. Dushyanta, recognized as the true father, was taken to Śakuntalā, who readily forgave her husband, for she had heard the story of the curse. The gods, happy to see the pair reunited, sent them back to earth, along with their little son Bharata, to live many years in happiness together.

Critical Evaluation:

The greatness of the drama lies in its tremendous lyric power. The play was originally written in a combination of verse and prose, a form that most modern translators from the original Sanskrit have striven to emulate, although not always successfully. While almost nothing is known of Kālidāsa, legend has it that he was the son of a good family of high caste, but that he was abandoned as a baby and reared as a common laborer. In spite of that handicap, says the legend, he became a great poet and dramatist, as well as the favorite of an Indian princess.

The story of Śakuntalā stems from an ancient Hindu legend, recounted in book 1 of the *Mahabharata* (200 B.C.E.-200 C.E.). When Kālidāsa dramatized this well-known legend, he was not presenting an unfamiliar tale, but artfully retelling an old one. Greek writers had the Iliad and the Odyssey (both c. 800 B.C.E.) for their sources; Indian writers went to the two great Hindu epics, the *Mahabharata* and the *Ramayana* (third century B.C.E.) for theirs. In the West and in the East, writers usually adhered to the main storyline of the original but varied the plot structure slightly and added subplots and details of psychological insight. The advantages of working within an accepted cultural framework are immediately evident. The audience instantly recognizes the story, correctly identifies allusions in it, and knows the story's place in the larger mythological context, freeing the writer from lengthy description and explanation. The writer may concentrate on intricacies of plot and on the characters' spiritual and psychological development.

In addition to this common use of tradition, there are crucial differences. The first is material: The content of the two mythologies of East and West is vastly different. More important is a subtle and complex difference in dramaturgy. Aristotelian Western drama places top priority on plot (imitation of action); characterization, setting, and other embellishments are subordinate to the action. Sanskrit drama, however, emphasizes *rasa* (a dominant emotion or flavor, a "sympathy"). It imitates emotion; the action is thus subordinated to the progressive evocation of an emotional state. Hence, priorities are shifted from action to feeling, from an accumulation of episodes to a series of moods, a movement from plot to dominant emotion.

In *Śakuntalā*, the dominant emotion is love, in all its varieties and flavors. Śakuntalā fares badly at the hands of the gods and of human beings in order to intensify the depiction of her emotional state, to bring out in stark relief the multifaceted depths of her love. Śakuntalā's love—its intensity, its depth, its breadth—is what *Śakuntalā* is all about. The play examines an emotional state so compelling that it overwhelms all other considerations.

Herein lies the core of Sanskrit drama at its best in Kālidāsa's masterpiece: Feeling takes precedence over rationality. The Western reader must therefore adjust to the Hindu scale of dramatic values instead of imposing Western standards upon a non-Western play. The rewards of reading *Śakuntalā* in the appropriate cultural context are well worth the effort.

Bibliography:

Bose, Mandakranta. *Supernatural Intervention in "The Tempest" and "Śakuntalā."* Salzburg: Institut für Anglistik und Amerikanistik, Universitat Salzburg, 1980. Explains the basis for comparing these two works; focuses on the important structural function of supernatural forces in them, noting how the structure of society in which they live affects the writers' use of such mythic devices in their dramas.

Harris, Mary B. *Kālidāsa: Poet of Nature*. Boston: Meador Press, 1936. Thematic study of Kālidāsa's use of nature in his plays. Concentrates on analysis of *Śakuntalā* and the writer's other major dramatic works. Analyzes several of Kālidāsa's nondramatic writings.

Krishnamoorthy, K. *Kālidāsa*. New York: Twayne, 1972. Introduction to the writer and his works. Describes *Śakuntalā* as a play about the raptures and torments of love, highlighting important Indian values: "duty, property, love, and spiritual good."

Miller, Barbara Stoler, ed. *Theater of Memory: The Plays of Kālidāsa*. New York: Columbia University Press, 1984. Excellent introduction to the writer's major dramatic works; commentary on *Śakuntalā* emphasizes its major themes and the playwright's mastery of dramatic techniques. Bibliography of secondary sources.

Wells, Henry W. "Theatrical Techniques on the Sanskrit Stage." In *The Classical Drama of India*. New York: Asia Publishing House, 1963. Examines the theatrical qualities of *Śakuntalā*, focusing on construction of scenes, dialogue, and development of dramatic tensions that reach a climax in the final act.

SALAMMBÔ

Type of work: Novel
Author: Gustave Flaubert (1821-1880)
Type of plot: Historical
Time of plot: Third century B.C.E.
Locale: Carthage
First published: 1862 (English translation, 1886)

Principal characters:
HAMILCAR, Suffete of Carthage
SALAMMBÔ, his daughter
MATHÔ, a Libyan chief
SPENDIUS, a Greek slave
NARR' HAVAS, a Numidian chief

The Story:

Inside the walls of Carthage a vast army of mercenaries gathered in the gardens of Hamilcar. There were Ligurians, Lusitanians, nomadic barbarians from North Africa, Romans, Greeks, Gauls, and Egyptians. A feast for these thousands of hired warriors was in preparation. Odors of cooking food came from Hamilcar's kitchens, and the Council of Elders had provided many oxen to roast over the open fires in the gardens. The men, tired from their defeat at the hands of the Romans and weary from the sea journey over the Mediterranean, waited with ill-concealed impatience for the feasting to begin.

More than that, they were in an ugly mood because they had not been paid. Hamilcar, their beloved leader even in defeat, had promised them their pay many times. The city elders, however, parsimonious and afraid of this huge assembly of fierce foreigners, withheld their pay. Offers of token payment had been angrily refused.

While the revelry was at its height, many men were emboldened by drink and began to pillage the palace of Hamilcar. In a private lake, surrounded by a heavy hedge, they found fish with jewels in their gill flaps. With joy they ruthlessly tore off the gems and boiled the sacred fish for their feast. The slaves brought new foods and fresh casks of wine for the drunken revelers. Then above them on a high balcony appeared Salammbô, the priestess of the moon goddess and daughter of Hamilcar. Her great beauty stilled the wild barbarians. She called down a malediction on their heads and in a wailing refrain lamented the sad state of Carthage.

Among those who watched the young girl, none was more attracted than Narr' Havas, a Numidian chief who had been sent by his father to Carthage to serve with Hamilcar. Although he had been in Carthage six months, this was his first sight of Salammbô. Also watching her keenly was Mathô, a gigantic Libyan. He had heard of Salammbô and already loved her. With Mathô was Spendius, a former Greek slave who, tricky and shrewd, played the jackal to brave Mathô. Spendius had been long in service to Carthage, and he whispered the delights of Salammbô to his master.

The elders gave each soldier a piece of gold if he promised to go to Sicca and wait for the rest of his money to be sent to him. The gold and the solemn promises enticed many, and finally all the mercenaries and barbarians joined the march to Sicca. Many of their leaders distrusted the words of the elders, but they were sure of better treatment when Hamilcar returned to Carthage.

Mathô lay in his tent all day long at Sicca. He was in love, and since he had no prospect of ever seeing Salammbô again, he despaired. Finally the wily Spendius profited greatly by Mathô's inaction, ingratiating himself with Mathô.

At Sicca the enormous Hanno appeared in his costly litter. Hanno, one of the Council of Elders, was tremendously fat; the fat on his legs even covered his toenails, and his body was covered with weeping sores. He pompously addressed the crowd, telling them of Carthage's intent to pay later and urging them all to return to their homes. The Gauls and the Campanians and the rest, however, understood not a word of Hanno's address, which was in Punic. Spendius leaped up beside Hanno and offered to translate. Falsely he told the soldiers that Hanno was exalting his own gods and reviling theirs. The mob became unruly, and Hanno barely escaped with his life.

Soon the inflamed barbarians were on the march again, this time to besiege Carthage. At their head rode Mathô, Narr' Havas, and Spendius, now a leader. The mob camped at the gates of Carthage. The city sent Gisco, a famous warrior, to deal with them. In fear the Carthaginians raised a little money and began to pay the soldiers. They felt powerless without Hamilcar. The payment was slow. Gisco had insufficient funds, and many barbarians claimed more pay than they merited.

As the unrest grew, Spendius went to Mathô with a project of his own. He was sure he had found a way into the city, and if Mathô would follow his lead and help him in his own private errand, he would take Mathô to Salammbô. Outside the walls Spendius had found a loose stone in the pavement over the aqueduct that supplied the city with water. With his giant's strength, Mathô lifted the stone, and the two swam with the current in the darkness until they came to a reservoir inside the city itself. Then Spendius revealed his project. He and Mathô were to steal the zaïmph, the mysterious veil of Tanit, goddess of the moon. The Carthaginians put their trust in Tanit and Tanit's strength lay in the veil, so Spendius hoped to demoralize the city. Mathô was fearful of committing sacrilege, but he was obliged to take the veil in order to see Salammbô.

While the female guards slept, the two stole into Tanit's sanctuary and Mathô seized the veil. Then quietly Spendius led the trembling Mathô, who wore the sacred robe, into Salammbô's sleeping chamber.

As Mathô advanced with words of love to Salammbô's bed, the terrified girl awoke and shouted an alarm. Instantly servants came running. Mathô had to flee, but while he wore the sacred veil no one dared to lay a hand on him. Mathô left the city and returned to the barbarians with his prize.

Hamilcar returned to Carthage in time to organize the defense of the city, and the siege melted away. The barbarians were short of food, so they marched to Utica to demand supplies. Only loosely bound to Carthage, Utica was glad to harass Carthage by aiding its enemies. Newly supplied with arms and food, the barbarians were a more formidable host. Hamilcar, however, had brought his army out of Carthage and joined the battle on the plain. Although the Carthaginians were few in number, they were disciplined and well led. They engaged the barbarians several times, always indecisively. Finally, by a stroke of luck, the army of Hamilcar was trapped, and the barbarians surrounded the city's defenders.

Meanwhile Salammbô was goaded by the high priest into retrieving the sacred veil. Disguised and with a guide, she made her way into the barbarian camp, under priestly injunction to do whatever might be necessary to reclaim the robe. Finding Mathô's tent, she went in and asked for the veil, which hung among his trophies of war. Mathô was thunderstruck and stammered eager protestations of love. Remembering the commands of the priest, Salammbô submitted to Mathô. While the Libyan slept, she took the veil and went unmolested into her father's camp.

Hamilcar noticed immediately that the thin golden chain linking her ankles was broken, and in his shame he promised her to Narr' Havas, who had long since deserted the barbarians and returned to help Hamilcar. The marriage, however, was delayed until after the final defeat of Hamilcar's enemies. Hamilcar, wary of the stalemate in the battle, led his followers back to Carthage, and the barbarians again laid siege to the city. Spendius sought to end the siege by breaking the aqueduct. Thirst and famine threatened the city from within. When pestilence broke out, the children of Carthage were burned in sacrifice to Moloch. Moloch was appeased, and torrential rains saved the city.

With help from his allies, Hamilcar began to reduce the forces of the enemy. A large part of the army was trapped in a defile in the mountains and left to starve. Mathô was taken prisoner.

On the wedding day of Narr' Havas and Salammbô, Mathô was led through the city and tortured by the mob. Still alive but with most of his flesh torn away, he staggered up to the nuptial dais of Salammbô. There he fell dead. Salammbô recalled how he had knelt before her, speaking gentle words. When the drunken Narr' Havas embraced her in token of possession and drank to the greatness of Carthage, she lifted a cup and drank also. A moment later she fell back on the wedding dais, dead. So died the warrior and the priestess who by their touch had profaned the sacred robe of Tanit.

Critical Evaluation:

Salammbô is one of the great historical romances of French literature. Following Théophile Gautier's "One of Cleopatra's Nights" (1838) and *The Romance of a Mummy* (1858), which were set in different eras of Egypt's remote history. Gustave Flaubert's novel brought a new level of sophistication to the French historical novel. Many French writers were fascinated by the ancient history of the lands surrounding the Mediterranean. French historical novelists were particularly entranced with decadence, which makes for entertaining reading and into which the great empires of the ancient world had fallen before being sacked by barbarians. Although in Flaubert's novel the barbarians lose, the book strongly implies that Carthage will soon fall as a result of its moral decline.

Decadence was not only a topic; it became a writing style. Gautier defined a decadent style in writing in his introduction to the posthumous third edition of Charles Baudelaire's *Flowers of Evil*, which had first been published in 1857—the year in which Flaubert visited Tunisia to collect material for *Salammbô*. Flaubert, however, was not at all interested in decadent style. He had recently completed the profoundly antiromantic *Madame Bovary* (1857), and he approached his new task in the same careful, literal-minded, scrupulous manner. He stated that his intention was "to perpetuate a mirage by applying to antiquity the methods of the modern novel." The Carthage that he desired to reproduce in the pages of his novel might have been trembling on the brink of decline, but Flaubert had no wish to submit his powers of description to the glamour of its decay. The novel, nevertheless, may be considered to betray its author's intentions, in that its lush, sensuous, and exuberant description lend glamour to an extremely unglamorous dirty little war.

No one else ever managed to combine the lush exoticism of the ancient world with such brilliantly detailed and realistic descriptions as are found in *Salammbô*. The fact that Carthage, unlike Rome or Alexandria, had been so obliterated by its conquerors that nothing substantial survived for modern contemplation makes Flaubert's feat of re-creation all the more remarkable. Continued scholarly reports have added much information to those that Flaubert studied relentlessly, but it is improbable in the extreme that anyone will ever manage to draw them together into an image as sharp, as rich, and as clear as the one that Flaubert constructed.

The tale told in *Salammbô* is a very violent one that includes several episodes of hideous cruelty. These are brought to a climax in the extraordinary concluding passage, in which Mathô is virtually torn apart by the citizens of Carthage as he makes his way to the place where Salammbô and her husband are celebrating their wedding day, there to have his heart torn out. This end is symbolic as well as literal: Salammbô has already torn his heart out. It was her dazzling erotic allure rather than the cunning encouragements of Spendius that overwhelmed Mathô's fear of committing sacrilege and gave him the nerve to steal the veil of Tanit. Flaubert was always fascinated by the femme fatale. He produced his own account of the story of Salomé, who asked for John the Baptist's head on a platter, in "Hérodias" (1877), and his *The Temptation of Saint Anthony* (1874) includes an archetypal femme fatale figure in Ennoïa. As he does in *Salammbô*, however, he implies in these works that there is no real triumph to be gained in seducing men to their doom, and that both parties to any such transaction are ruined by it.

The mirage that Flaubert perpetuates in his plot is not so much an image of lost Carthage, seeming to hover above the desert sands, but rather an illusion of the power of human emotion. *Salammbô* relentlessly smashes the idols of romantic fiction: true love, honor, cunning, bravery in battle, and other such staples of public and individual mythology all are shown to be nonsense. Few of the later writers who imitated *Salammbô*, however, retained Flaubert's clear-sighted awareness of where the mirage ends and the desert begins.

The distinction between civilization and barbarism, which seemed so clear to the Greeks and Romans—and to many later writers who looked back with regret on the collapse that brought about the Dark Ages—is deliberately blurred in *Salammbô*. The barbarians fight Carthage's—civilization's—battles, but they do not get paid for it. When they demand reparation their forces are riven by internal dissent and eventually split by the offer of selective bribes. In courage and honesty of emotion, if not in table manners, they often outshine the Carthaginians. Their strike is broken with an amoral cynicism that the captains of industry of contemporary times can only emulate. Narr' Havas never gets to enjoy his promised bride; readers are not told whether he ever gets to collect all his back pay, but one is inclined to suspect that he does not. *Salammbô* agrees with many other fictitious accounts of the classical world in presuming that civilization won its temporary victory by offering promises of leisure and luxury that it could not keep. Flaubert, however—unlike most of the novelists who contemplated the decadence of the ancient world—was cynical, or realistic, enough to suppose that the bankruptcy that eventually brought about the fall of civilization was actual as well as merely moral. Flaubert was one of Western civilization's great demythologizers; *Salammbô* explores the mythologies of the romantic war story.

"Critical Evaluation" by Brian Stableford

Bibliography:

Brombert, Victor. *The Novels of Flaubert: A Study of Themes and Techniques*. Princeton, N.J.: Princeton University Press, 1966. Chapter 3 discusses "*Salammbô*: The Epic of Immobility."

Culler, Jonathan. *Flaubert: The Uses of Uncertainty*. Rev. ed. Ithaca, N.Y.: Cornell University Press, 1985. *Salammbô* is discussed in chapter 3.

Green, Anne. *Flaubert and the Historical Novel: Salammbô Reassessed*. Cambridge, England: Cambridge University Press, 1982. A detailed study of the text and its literary context.

Sherrington, R. J. *Three Novels by Flaubert: A Study of Techniques*. Oxford, England: Clarendon Press, 1970. Chapter 4 is a 78-page analysis of *Salammbô*.

Spencer, Philip. *Flaubert*. Winchester, Mass.: Faber & Faber, 1952. One of surprisingly few comprehensive biographical and critical studies of the author in English; probably the best general introduction to the man and his works.

SAMSON AGONISTES

Type of work: Drama
Author: John Milton (1608-1674)
Type of plot: Tragedy
Time of plot: c. 1100 B.C.E.
Locale: Palestine
First published: 1671

Principal characters:
SAMSON, a Hebrew champion, one of the Judges
MANOA, his father
DALILA, a Philistine woman, Samson's wife
HARAPHA, a Philistine giant
CHORUS OF HEBREW ELDERS

The Story:

Samson, eyeless in Gaza, had been given a holiday from his labors during the season of a Philistine religious festival. He sat alone before the prison, lamenting his fallen state. His hair had grown long again and his physical strength had returned, but to him life seemed hopeless. He wondered why God had chosen him, who seemed destined to live out his days as a miserable, blinded wretch, but he nevertheless blamed his misfortunes on himself. He should not have trusted in his strength without also seeing to it that he gained the wisdom to protect him from the wiles of Philistine women. He mourned also the blindness that made him live a life that was only half alive.

A chorus of Hebrew elders joined him. They recalled his past great deeds and spoke of the present state of Israel, subject to Philistine rule. Samson accused his people of loving bondage more than liberty because they had refused to take advantage of the victories he won for them in the days of his strength. Manoa, Samson's aged father, also came to see his son, whose fate had given him great distress. He brought news that plunged Samson still deeper into his depression: The Philistine feast was being given to thank the idol Dagon for delivering the mighty Hebrew into the hands of his enemies. Samson realized then the dishonor he had brought to God, yet he was able to find hope in the thought that the contest now was between Jehovah and Dagon. He foresaw no good for himself, cast off by God, and he prayed only for speedy death.

As the chorus mused over God's treatment of his chosen ones, Dalila approached. When she offered Samson help as recompense for her betrayal of him, he scorned her. She tried to excuse herself, pleading weakness and patriotism, but Samson refused to compound his sins by yielding to her again; he was regaining spiritual as well as physical might. He again accepted his position as God's champion when Harapha, a Philistine giant, came to gloat over his misfortune. It was too bad that Samson was now so weak, said Harapha; had he met him sooner he would have won great honor by defeating him. Harapha could not defile himself by combat with a slave. Samson, enraged, invited Harapha to come within his reach. The giant refused to accept the challenge, however, saying that such a contest would be beneath his dignity, and left.

When a public officer came to summon Samson to the feast, the blind man refused to go. His presence there would violate Hebrew law, and he had no desire to have the Philistine mob make sport of his blindness. As Samson told the chorus why he would not go, however, he felt a sudden inner compulsion to follow the messenger. He sensed that the day would mark some remarkable deed in his life. When the officer brought a second, more imperative summons, Samson accompanied him.

Manoa, returning with the news that he had been able to persuade the Philistine lords to ransom his son, gladly planned to sacrifice his patrimony and spend his old age caring for Samson. As he was speaking of his hopes that Samson would recover his sight, horrible shouting broke out in the temple. A Hebrew messenger, fleeing the awful spectacle, told Manoa and the chorus that he had just seen Samson pull the temple down upon himself and thousands of Philistines. Manoa decided that Samson had conducted himself like Samson, and had heroically ended a heroic life.

Critical Evaluation:

Samson Agonistes is John Milton's profound treatment of a biblical story in the form of the classical Greek tragedy. The play, published with *Paradise Regained* in 1671, was not designed for the stage (such a play is known as a closet play); the author modeled his work on Greek tragedy because he found it "the gravest, moralest, and most profitable of all other poems." The story of Samson is one of the most dramatic episodes in the Old Testament; the parallels between the life of the blind Hebrew hero and Milton's own must have encouraged him to base his last work on the story of the man singled out before his birth as a servant of God. Milton opens his play during Samson's imprisonment. He refers frequently to the biblical accounts of the events of Samson's youth, but the episodes that make up most of the play are his own creation. Each affects Samson's character, renewing his faith in God and influencing his decision to go to the Philistine temple to die.

Samson Agonistes is a powerful and moving drama. The poetry is majestic and simple, different from the rich verse of *Paradise Lost* (1667) and *Paradise Regained* but perfectly suited to the subject. The play is the masterpiece of an old man, one who has suffered like Samson and who has, in his own way, triumphed over suffering. *Samson Agonistes* was published in the same volume as *Paradise Regained*, three years before Milton's death, so tradition has ascribed its composition to the late years of his life and has marked the drama as the last of his three great poems. More recently, however, various theories have placed the date of the work as far back as the 1640's. Generally, support for the earlier date of composition is related to the critical opinion that the artistry of *Samson Agonistes* is of a lower order than that of *Paradise Lost* and *Paradise Regained*. In other words, by placing *Samson Agonistes* at a greater chronological distance from the other poems, it is easier to support a theory that it is an inferior work of art. It is certain from manuscript evidence that as early as the 1640's Milton had planned a series of five Samson plays; so it is by no means impossible that at least a first draft of *Samson Agonistes* was written at that time. The traditional view that *Samson Agonistes* belongs to the end of Milton's canon is still widely held, and whether the drama was written shortly before publication or nearly thirty years earlier, scholars know that it was initially conceived long before it appeared.

Perhaps the origin of the view that *Samson Agonistes* is inferior to Milton's other major poems lies in Samuel Johnson's criticism of its tragic form. Ever since he said that the play has a beginning and an end but no middle, critics have been addressing themselves to the problem of viewing the poem as a classical Greek tragedy. Milton set the stage for later arguments by prefacing the poem with an essay discussing Aristotle's concept of tragedy and extolling classical tragedy. By harking back to the ancients as his models rather than his own Elizabethan predecessors, he hoped to reestablish the "classical" pattern of tragedy, purging the abuses into which the genre had fallen through the English habit of mixing comedy and low-born persons into the plot of a tragic play. The difference between Milton and the ancients is also established in the prefatory essay, however, when he says that *Samson Agonistes* was never meant for the stage. Those who have sided with Johnson have found that in spite of Milton's attempt to follow the classical pattern, the play is flawed by the static and lifeless quality they see in the central episodes.

What the drama lacks, however, is not life, but action. All the famous acts of the protagonist have occurred either in the past or "offstage." Samson's actions as the hero of the Israelites and his subsequent fall are over before the poem begins, and his final triumph over the Philistines is narrated, not shown. There is no physical action during the episodes with Manoa, Dalila, and Harapha, but there is much psychological action. These episodes provide readers with the background of Samson's present dilemma and reveal the progressive revitalization of Samson's willingness to fulfill his role as the hero and deliverer of his people. The three episodes in the middle of the play may be seen as temptations to betray his faith, fortitude, and patience. The action of the drama may be seen as the psychological process by which Samson meets and overcomes these temptations. Through these episodes, which some have found dramatically empty, Samson moves from despair to courage and to the final heroic act of self-sacrifice. Johnson's critical mistake was in not accepting inner conflicts and resolutions as action.

Beyond the structural problems that complicate *Samson Agonistes'* claim to being a tragedy, there is an additional difficulty arising from the basic difference in theological perspective between Milton and his Greek counterparts. The question is whether it is possible to write such a thing as Christian tragedy. Is it possible, within the Christian view of the human experience as a comedy, to have an ultimately tragic event? One of the paradoxes in the drama then is that while the play ends with death, it is a death-in-victory, like that of Jesus Christ. Therefore, it may be argued that the play is not a tragedy.

In a sense, the tragedy has already taken place before readers meet Samson "eyeless in Gaza." Samson has already fallen, and the fall was precipitated by hubris, his tragic flaw of excessive pride. Samson's death results from a conscious willful act, not from a flaw or from an act of the indifferent Fates. Through his death Samson triumphs over his enemies and fulfills his destiny. This victorious tragedy, too, has parallels among the classics. Certainly the Oedipus cycle presents the similar pattern of a protagonist who falls first through a flaw and then later, in a tragedy resulting from the first fall, transcends the disaster of death with a spiritual victory.

Granting the classical parallels in Milton's poem, readers are left with the issue of fitting tragedy into Milton's Christian view of history. Critics are right to say that tragedy is not ultimately possible for a Christian hero in a Christian universe. That is not to deny, however, that tragedy may exist in human terms. Thus, on one level the deaths of Samson and Christ are tragic, but the paradox of the Christian faith is that one who loses his life shall find it. Although individual tragedies can exist, they are ultimately subsumed in the larger cosmic framework of the divine design. That is, they become a part of a larger pattern in which death is followed by resurrection. Hence, readers can see Milton's tragic poem as the union of a biblical theme and a classical literary form, just as *Paradise Lost* is the union of the classical epic form and the Christian vision of creation.

"Critical Evaluation" by Timothy E. Bollinger

Bibliography:

Crump, Galbraith M., ed. *Twentieth Century Interpretations of "Samson Agonistes."* Englewood Cliffs, N.J.: Prentice-Hall, 1968. Assembles seven seminal articles and eight shorter selections of critical commentary. Following an introductory critical survey, the selections offer a wide range of literary criticism dealing with the tragedy's biographical significance, structure, style, themes, and genre.

Hanford, James Holly, and James G. Taaffe. *A Milton Handbook*. 5th ed. East Norwalk, Conn.: Appleton-Century-Crofts, 1970. Presents an overview of the tragedy and a survey of previous criticism. An excellent starting point. Bibliography.

Hunter, William B., ed. *Milton's English Poetry*. Cranbury, N.J.: Bucknell University Press, 1986. Reprints articles on Milton's poetry from *A Milton Encyclopedia*, written by distinguished scholars. The long entry on *Samson Agonistes* provides a detailed survey of the numerous important critical issues and controversies associated with the tragedy.

Low, Anthony. *The Blaze of Noon: A Reading of "Samson Agonistes."* Ithaca, N.Y.: Columbia University Press, 1974. Offers a scholarly analysis of origins, style, and characters of the tragedy. The extended scholarly discussion is developed with the general reader in mind; the book is accessible and erudite.

Wittreich, Joseph. *Interpreting "Samson Agonistes."* Princeton, N.J.: Princeton University Press, 1986. A challenging but highly informative book, it surveys the biblical and Renaissance traditions related to Milton's tragedy. Furnishes a comprehensive assessment of modern criticism.

SANCTUARY

Type of work: Novel
Author: William Faulkner (1897-1962)
Type of plot: Melodrama
Time of plot: 1929
Locale: Mississippi and Memphis, Tennessee
First published: 1931

Principal characters:
Popeye, a racketeer
Horace Benbow, a lawyer
Temple Drake, a woman raped and kidnapped by Popeye
Tommy, a moonshiner killed by Popeye
Lee Goodwin, a moonshiner accused of Tommy's murder
Ruby Lamar, Goodwin's woman
Reba Rivers, the madam of a Memphis bawdy house
Gowan Stevens, a college student

The Story:

Horace Benbow, on his way to Jefferson one afternoon, stopped to drink from a spring on the Old Frenchman place. When he rose, he saw an undersized man in a black suit watching him; the man's hand was in a pocket that held his gun. Satisfied at last that the lawyer was not a revenue officer, Popeye led Benbow to the gutted ruins of a plantation house. That night the lawyer drank moonshine and ate with Popeye, several moonshiners, and a blind and deaf old man, the father of Lee Goodwin, one of the moonshiners. They were fed by Ruby, Goodwin's woman. Later, Benbow was given a lift into Jefferson on a truck loaded with whiskey on its way to Memphis.

The next afternoon, at his widowed sister's home, Benbow watched her walking in the garden with young Gowan Stevens. Stevens left that evening after supper because he had a date with a woman at the state university the following night. The woman was Temple Drake.

After a dance, Stevens got drunk. He awoke the next morning in front of the railroad station. A special train taking university students to a baseball game had already left. Driving rapidly, Stevens caught up with the train in the next town. Temple jumped from the train and climbed into his car. Disgusted with his disheveled appearance, she ordered him to drive her back to the university. Stevens insisted that he had promised to drive her to the game. On the way, he decided to stop at Goodwin's place to buy more whiskey.

Stevens wrecked his car when he struck a tree across the lane leading to the house. Popeye took Temple and Stevens to the house. Temple went into the kitchen, where Ruby sat smoking and watching the door. When Temple saw Stevens again, he was drunk. Then Popeye refused to drive them back to town. Temple was frightened. Ruby told Temple to go into the dining room to eat with the men.

One of the men tried to seize her, and Temple ran from the room and hid in a back room. Tommy, one of the moonshiners, followed her with a plate of food. The men began to quarrel, and Stevens was knocked unconscious and carried into the house. Goodwin and a moonshiner named Van tussled until Popeye stopped them. When Van found Temple in one of the bedrooms, Goodwin knocked him down.

Then began a series of comings and goings in the bedroom. Ruby came to stand quietly in the darkness. Later, Popeye appeared and stood silently over the girl. After he had gone, Goodwin entered to claim a raincoat in which Temple had wrapped herself. Popeye returned once more, followed noiselessly by Tommy, who squatted in the dark beside Ruby. When the men finally left the house to load the truck for its run to Memphis, Ruby took Temple out to the barn and stayed with her until daylight.

Stevens awoke early and started out for the nearest house to hire a car. Feeling that he could not face Temple again after his drunken night, he paid a farmer to drive to the house for Temple, while he thumbed a ride into town. Learning that Stevens had already gone, Temple went into the kitchen with Ruby. When she left the house again, she saw the shadowy outline of a man who was squatting in the bushes and watching her. She returned to the house. Seeing Goodwin coming toward the house, she ran to the barn and hid in the corncrib. Watching, Popeye saw Goodwin looking from the house toward the barn. In the barn, Popeye found Tommy at the door of the corncrib. While Tommy stood watching Goodwin, Popeye shot him. Popeye raped Temple with a corncob and kidnapped her. A short time later, Goodwin told Ruby that Tommy had been shot. He sent her to the nearest house to phone for the sheriff.

Benbow stayed with his sister for two days. When Goodwin was brought in, charged with Tommy's murder, Benbow agreed to defend the prisoner. Goodwin, afraid of Popeye, claimed only that he had not shot Tommy. It was Ruby who told Benbow that Popeye had taken Temple away in his car.

Benbow attempted to trace the woman's whereabouts. State Senator Snopes told him that Judge Drake's daughter was supposed to be visiting an aunt in Michigan after an attempted runaway marriage.

A week before the opening of the court session, Benbow met Senator Snopes again. For a price the politician was willing to reveal that Temple was in Reba Rivers' bawdy house in Memphis. Benbow went at once to see the girl. Temple, although reluctant to talk, confirmed many details of Ruby's story. The lawyer realized that without Temple's testimony he could not prove that Goodwin was innocent of Popeye's crime.

One morning, Temple bribed Reba's black servant to let her out of the house to make a phone call. That evening she managed to sneak out again, just as a car with Popeye in it pulled up at the curb. When she refused to go back to her room, he took her to the Grotto, where Temple had arranged to meet a young man called Red, whom Popeye had taken to her room. At the Grotto, she danced with Red while Popeye played at the crap table. She begged Red to take her away with him. Later in the evening, two of Popeye's henchmen forced Temple into a car waiting outside. As they drove away, Temple saw Popeye sitting in a parked car.

Red's funeral was held in the Grotto. For the occasion, the tables had been draped in black, and a downtown orchestra had been hired to play hymns. Drinks were on the house. The night before the trial, Benbow learned from Reba Rivers that Popeye and Temple had left her house. Ruby took the witness stand the next day, and she told the story of Tommy's murder. She and Benbow spent that night in the jail cell with Goodwin, who was afraid that Popeye might shoot him from one of the buildings across the street.

Temple, located through the efforts of Senator Snopes, was called to testify the next morning. She indicated that Goodwin was the man who had attacked her on the day of Tommy's murder. Goodwin was convicted. That night a mob dragged the prisoner from the jail and burned him. Popeye, on his way to Pensacola, was arrested for the murder of a policeman in Birmingham. The murder had occurred the same night that Red was shot outside the Grotto. Popeye made no defense, and his only claim was that he knew nothing about the Birmingham shooting.

Convicted, he was executed for a crime he had not committed. Judge Drake took his daughter to Europe. In Paris' Luxembourg Gardens with her father, listening in boredom to the band, Temple sat in quiet, sullen discontent.

Critical Evaluation:

William Faulkner, who was awarded the Nobel Prize, the Pulitzer Prize, and two National Book Awards, may be the best fiction writer in America. Unsuccessful in his early attempts at poetry, Faulkner began selling his short stories to national magazines. This enabled him to support his family, in a manner of speaking, as he pursued fame. His first published short story, "A Rose for Emily," was his favorite and it is perhaps his most often anthologized. *Sartoris* (1929), whose plot retells events in Faulkner's grandfather's life, was rather successful and so the soft-spoken Southerner began to discover his "own postage stamp of soil," Yoknapatawpha County (based on his hometown of Oxford, Mississippi and its environs).

Faulkner is known for the complexities of his novels, which are usually not told chronologically. Rather, the story of events is filtered through one or more observers who interpret these actions in the context of their own biases, needs, and confusions. In Faulkner's world, the reader is often a witness at second hand. *Sanctuary* is an example of this element of his work. Although Faulkner claimed that he wrote *Sanctuary* as a cheap, lurid tale to make money, critics have come to recognize that it is as significant to his canon as *Light in August* (1932) or *The Sound and the Fury* (1929), which focus on the nature of evil and the influence of past actions on the present. As in other Faulkner works, the story of *Sanctuary* is told by a seemingly innocent bystander (Horace) who becomes enmeshed in the drama.

In one draft, Faulkner's tale focused almost totally on Horace Benbow, whose incestuous love of his sister becomes transferred first to a married woman he eventually marries (Belle), and then to her daughter (whose sexual adventures lead Horace to see her as a twin of Temple Drake). Faulkner revised the book to focus more clearly on Temple and her encounter with her evil. Horace's judgment of her and her actions affect the reader's reactions as he struggles to find justice in the courts and as he strives to find Temple's basic decency, her goodness. Readers see everything through Horace's scornful, twisted, and disillusioned psyche. He is a witness corrupted by knowledge, and Temple is witness and victim. She becomes a victimizer as well when she testifies against Lee Goodwin. Together she and Horace are guilty of complicity in evil. To see evil, Faulkner implies, is to be corrupted by it.

The characters seem trapped in a past action that hovers over their present circumstances. For the idealistic Horace, as for Temple, that singular past action will continue to define him as he struggles against the unyielding, senseless evil and meaninglessness of modern life. For Temple, this past is her rape and her witnessing of Tommy's murder at the hands of Popeye. To Horace, it is his idealistic yet self-centered and pathetic love for his sister, wife, and stepdaughter, all of whom flaunt their sexual escapades. Horace's disillusioned despair will haunt him as long as he lives.

Readers see the story through Horace's eyes, and so are influenced to believe that women are the source of all evil. At first idealistic and irrational, Horace imbues women and the law with every virtue. Later, disillusioned, he declares, almost gleefully, that the "inherent evil" of women has corrupted even the courts of justice. He could thereby believe that Popeye's rape of Temple was her fault.

If Faulkner's characters are destined to suffer the violent fates they meet, it is not through external forces, but rather through their own inner demons, that they become so destined. In every case, the characters' internal evil emerges to vanquish others and then themselves. So,

Temple's rape releases her carnal corruption, which in turn leads to the deaths of four men—Tommy, Red, Lee, and Popeye—and to the disillusionment of Horace and of her boyfriend Gowan Stevens. Though she senses that something is wrong, Temple does not comprehend her fate. She is aware only that "something is happening to [her.]" Temple never seems to suspect that she is the cause of the evil that befalls her. This lack of insight characterizes most evil people. Like Popeye, Temple seems to have no conscience, no sense of right and wrong.

Popeye is not just a bad man. He has been called the epitome of pure evil, while other readers say he is simply amoral. Like other evil men in Faulkner's works, Popeye is described as if he were a robot. He has rubber knobs for eyes; his frame is angular, like a lamp; he has a permanent sneer on a face that looks like melted wax; and he is inhuman—he has such a delicate stomach he cannot drink the whiskey he sells, and he is unable to have sex. Yet his evil seems less severe than Temple's.

Sanctuary may be more than just a horrific tale of murder and rape. Faulkner's characters and their vile actions may symbolize Faulkner's vision of the rape and corruption of the South by the mechanized industries, politicians, and fortune-hunters who descended upon it after the Civil War. Faulkner indicates that evil has a power stronger than that of goodness, that this evil is made possible by the weakness of good men and women who hide in their private illusions of justice and goodness.

"Critical Evaluation" by Linda L. Labin

Bibliography:

Bassett, John, ed. *William Faulkner: The Critical Heritage*. London: Routledge & Kegan Paul, 1975. Ninety-four critical reviews and essays on Faulkner including eight on *Sanctuary*, all written within two years of the publishing of *Sanctuary*.

Brooks, Cleanth. *William Faulkner: The Yoknapatawpha Country*. New Haven, Conn.: Yale University Press, 1963. Contains chapters on most of the Faulkner novels and a section comparing *Sanctuary* and *Requiem for a Nun*, calling them Faulkner's discovery of evil. One of the most helpful and accessible books for information on Faulkner.

Clarke, Deborah. *Robbing the Mother: Women in Faulkner*. Jackson: University Press of Mississippi, 1994. Argues that female sexuality threatens a male-dominated cultural order in *Sanctuary*. Delineates women in Faulkner's novels and finds women treated poorly. Some reference to the women in Faulkner's life.

Dowling, David. *William Faulkner*. New York: St. Martin's Press, 1989. Includes a chronology and sections describing the major works completed during different periods in Faulkner's life. History of Yoknapatawpha County, extended bibliography, and index. Finds *Sanctuary* to be the darkest of all of Faulkner's novels and compares it to the other Faulkner novels of the 1930's.

Page, Sally R. *Faulkner's Women: Characterization and Meaning*. Deland, Fla.: Everett/Edwards, 1972. A survey of the women characters in Faulkner's novels, with attention to their individuality and the stereotypes they represent. Finds that Faulkner depicts women favorably.

SANINE

Type of work: Novel
Author: Mikhail Artsybashev (1878-1927)
Type of plot: Philosophical
Time of plot: 1906
Locale: Russia
First published: *Sanin*, 1907 (English translation, 1915)

Principal characters:
VLADIMIR PETROVITCH SANINE, an individualistic young Russian
LIDA PETROVNA, his sister
MARIA IVANOVNA, his mother
CAPTAIN ZARUDIN, in love with Lida
DR. NOVIKOV, also in love with Lida
SINA KARSAVINA, briefly the mistress of Sanine
YURI SVAROZHICH, in love with Sina Karsavina

The Story:

During the formative years of his life, Vladimir Petrovitch Sanine was away from the influence of his family and their home. When he returned as a young man to his mother's house in a provincial garrison town, he came as a person believing only in himself, his strength, and the desirability of following his inclinations wherever they might lead him. His mother, Maria Ivanovna, could not understand her son. His sister Lida, however, found him strangely attractive, even though she distrusted and feared his thinking and its influence.

Lida, having many admirers among young civilians and the junior army officers, was the belle of the little garrison town. Her two most serious admirers were Dr. Novikov, who wished sincerely to marry her but was awkward as a suitor, and Captain Zarudin, a brutal and lascivious army officer who wished only to make a sexual conquest and was well on his way to success with the young woman. Sanine, giving the same freedoms to others as he believed in for himself, made no serious attempt to interfere in his sister's affairs.

Before long Sanine was caught up in the social life among the young intelligentsia of the town. Among those in the group were Sina Karsavina and Yuri Svarozhich. The former was a pretty young schoolteacher of strong emotions who found herself drawn strangely to Sanine, although she was very much in love with Yuri, a young student who had been exiled to the provinces for his part in revolutionary activities. Although attracted to Sina, Yuri felt that his political duties and ambitions would be hampered if he were married. As a result of his beliefs in political duty, and as a result of bashfulness as well, he tried to avoid becoming emotionally involved with the young schoolteacher.

As the weeks passed, Lida was drawn closer to Captain Zarudin. So strong was his physical attraction that she refused a proposal of marriage from Dr. Novikov, whose jealousy almost became hate. Soon afterward, Lida became Captain Zarudin's mistress. Discovering that she was pregnant, she turned for help to her lover, only to learn that he was now finished with her, having made his conquest. Lida was distraught and thought of drowning herself, but she was found by her brother in time. He convinced her that she needed to live and that she should become Dr. Novikov's wife. Having his sister's agreement, Sanine went to Dr. Novikov, who was about to leave the town. Little persuasion was needed, even with a knowledge of the facts, to get the doctor's agreement to marry Lida.

About this time Captain Zarudin had a visitor from St. Petersburg. When Captain Zarudin and his friend paid a visit to the Sanine home so that the officer might show off the beautiful woman he had seduced, Sanine ordered the captain to leave the house and suggested further that he leave town. Captain Zarudin, true to the code of his corps, challenged Sanine to a duel. Sanine believed that dueling proved nothing, and so refused the challenge. He learned that his sister, on the other hand, expected him to fight the duel. Realizing that his sister, like his mother, was a conformist to opinion and tradition, Sanine felt alienated from them because of their attitudes and their failure to understand his ideas.

Even more angered by the refusal of his challenge, Captain Zarudin feared that his failure to avenge his honor might put him in a disgraceful position with his brother officers. That he had disgraced himself in some people's eyes by his treatment of Lida did not enter his mind. One evening, as Sanine and some friends were strolling along the boulevard, they unexpectedly met Captain Zarudin and several of his brother officers. Captain Zarudin spoke harshly to Sanine and threatened him with a riding crop. In self-defense, Sanine knocked down the officer with his fist. Captain Zarudin, not much hurt physically but humiliated by the indignity of the blow, almost went out of his mind. Taken back to his quarters, he refused to see even his friends or his orderly.

After the brief but violent encounter, Sanine walked home with a Jewish friend, Soloveitchik. The two sat for a long time discussing human life and its meaning. Sanine refused to accept any blame for his behavior, although he might have ruined Captain Zarudin's career and life. The Jew asked Sanine if a man who worried and thought too much might not be better off dead. Sanine replied that a man or woman who could not enjoy life was already dead. Shortly afterward, he left. On his way home he met Captain Zarudin's orderly, who informed him that the officer had committed suicide by shooting himself. The next morning word came, too, that Soloveitchik had hanged himself. The two sudden deaths caused a great furor in the little town, but Sanine steadfastly refused to admit that he was in any way responsible.

One morning Yuri received a letter from Sina asking him to meet her at a monastery near the town. He met her as requested, and a tender but awkward love scene ensued. Yuri hated to admit he needed the woman, and his conscience bothered him in strange ways. When Sina was suddenly called back to town that evening, Sanine, who was also visiting at the monastery, offered to escort her. On the way both Sanine and Sina were overcome by their emotions, and she surrendered to him. Though she was upset afterward, she decided that the best thing for her to do was to forget what had happened. In the meantime Yuri's sister tried to persuade her brother to marry. The problems that marriage raised for him were so great that the young man could not face them, and he shot himself. At the funeral Sanine was asked to say a few words, and he declared that there was one fool less in the world. His response horrified everyone. Soon afterward, Sanine left the town again by train. Early one morning, as the train was crossing the plains, he jumped off to glory in the beauty of an autumn sunrise.

Critical Evaluation:

Sanine centers on the title character and the profound effect he produces on his family and acquaintances. At the end of the novel, Sanine vanishes into the limbo from which he originated. The hero exists in a vacuum; little information is given about his past activities or his future plans. His physical presence is powerful, however, as is made clear by repeated mention of his prominent muscles and mocking eyes. By limiting Sanine's existence to the novel's present,

Mikhail Artsybashev demonstrates Sanine's appreciation of life's immediacy. Sanine is a mouthpiece for the author's views and a didactic figure who considers it his duty to become involved in the lives of others and to demonstrate his convictions. Anarchical individuality guides his philosophy. For Sanine, Christianity has left humans ill-equipped for everyday living because Christianity directs attention inward. Its emphasis on humility deprives the underprivileged of the will to protest against the established order. Abstractions of law, morality, and government, in turn, which are also founded on hierarchical authority, suppress self-will. The development of egoism, and the denial of any higher power, will, and should, in Sanine's view, lead to the rejection of domination.

Sanine consistently critiques intellectual achievement. Life is sensations, emotions, and sensual pleasure, but thought is empty conceptions and vain speech, powerless against the mystery of life and death. Sanine excepts literature, with its potential to ameliorate the human condition, from his contempt for intellectual activity. Nature, on the other hand, is a constant presence in the novel. Artsybashev shows the cyclical quality of life in the change of seasons. Although his style is cumbersome, the pictorial quality of Artsybashev's natural scenes reveals a sensitivity to color and detail. Sanine's intense physical response to nature demonstrates his pagan enjoyment of the earth.

The technology student, Svarozhich, acts as a foil to Sanine and demonstrates unnatural living. The two represent opposite camps among the Russian intelligentsia, which is emphasized by Sanine's and Svarozhich's both having their own followers. Sanine's behavior testifies to physical joy, and Svarozhich's thoughts reveal profound pessimism. Like Sanine, he was formerly active in revolutionary circles. Svarozhich, however, spent six months in prison and remains under police surveillance. Obsessed with the futility of human endeavor and engaging in the morbid introspection typical of Fyodor Dostoevski's characters, he toys with the idea of suicide throughout the novel and eventually kills himself.

Sanine considers Svarozhich a representative of the second phase of human development, characterized by the reevaluation of human desires. Svarozhich's agonizing self-scrutiny abstracts him from natural impulses. According to Sanine, humans should give themselves freely to pleasure and enjoy love without fear or constraint. Sanine addresses his judgement to Karsavina, with whom Svarozhich has failed sexually and whom Sanine is seducing. When asked to say a few words at Svarozhich's grave, Sanine declares that Svarozhich lived foolishly and died an idiotic death. Soloveichik's pacifism, which Artsybashev associates with Judaism, and subsequent suicide put him in the same psychological category as Svarozhich. The ingratiating Soloveichik was probably intended to critique the doctrine of nonresistance to evil.

Although Artsybashev focuses primarily on young representatives of the middle class, he also portrays the military. The military's status as a select and autonomous caste in Russian society was a central public concern. Unlike his literary predecessors, he shows soldiers stationed in remote provinces during peacetime. The soldiers are arrogant and vain, holding others in contempt and pursuing false honor. In the novel, soldiers, as do intellectuals, lead incomplete existences. Compared to Sanine, who is sexually desirous but also appreciative of women, Zarudin is consistently lascivious and callous to women. After he is humiliated by Sanine's blow, he is abandoned by his fellow officers and confronted with the spiritual bankruptcy of his existence. Recalling his rejection of Lida, he regrets the suffering he caused her and vows to renounce his former ways. Renunciation proves impossible, however, and his life ends in suicide.

The rash of suicides at the end of the novel suggests social instability. Each suicide represents a significant element of Russian society at the turn of the century. The army enables the government to maintain the status quo, the student body questions autocratic rule, and the Jews take the blame for public discontent. Zarudin realizes his military life was empty, Svarozhich fails to justify his own existence, and Soloveichik finds his continual suffering intolerable. Those who remain alive by the end of the novel are generally the mediocre. Sanine is the only character who is not paralyzed with inadequacy by the end of the novel.

The structure of the novel is chronological, punctuated with long diatribes, primarily initiated by Sanine. Psychological motivation is scant. Characters are sketched primarily as vehicles for Artsybashev's debate. Given Sanine's advocacy of primal response to the world, he and the other characters exhibit little emotional reaction to events. Artsybashev relies heavily on coincidence to bring Sanine into situations in which his behavior can be demonstrated or his views expressed at length. Given the complex character groupings and Sanine's involvement with them all, narrative momentum often flags.

Artsybashev gained wide notoriety with *Sanine*, mainly because of its polemical content. Publishers in several countries were quick to respond to the public demand for titillating reading. Translations appeared throughout Western Europe within a year of its publication in Russia. Artsybashev's alleged affront to public morality resulted in a number of court cases, myriad literary imitations, and an avalanche of reviews. The novel's graphic violence and sexuality, not its literary or philosophical merits, attracted most of the attention.

The novel reflects the Russian intelligentsia's disenchantment with public ideals, particularly after the failure of the 1905 Revolution, and the extreme sexual freedom of the times. Other controversial issues, such as abortion, incest, and women's rights, are debated in the text.

Artsybashev's work also represents the spiritual questions of the time. *Sanine* is frequently viewed as a vulgarization of Dostoevski's *Notes from the Underground* (1864) since it features an amoral, cynical, antihero who rationalizes his behavior in long-winded discussions. For the most part, Sanine's behavior fails to provide the model Artsybashev intended. His critique of intellectual discussion takes the form of intellectual discussion, and his arguments lapse into sensationalism. Despite these problems, *Sanine* embodies contemporary debate and suggests the bankruptcy of empty convictions and false priorities.

"Critical Evaluation" by Pamela Pavliscak

Bibliography:

Engelstein, Laura. *The Keys to Happiness: Sex and the Search for Modernity in Fin-de-Siècle Russia*. Ithaca, N.Y.: Cornell University Press, 1992. Surveys popular culture in early twentieth century Russia. Elaborates Artsybashev's role as literary innovator.

Luker, Nicholas. *In Defense of a Reputation: Essays on the Early Prose of Mikhail Artsybashev*. Nottingham, England: Astra Press, 1990. A balanced consideration of Artsybashev's major novels and a thorough summary of earlier criticism of Artsybashev's works, most of which are available only in Russian. Emphasizing the careful structure of *Sanine*, Luker makes a convincing case for considering Artsybashev a serious author.

Phelps, William. *Essays on Russian Novelists*. New York: Macmillan, 1911. A contemporary account of the sensation *Sanine* made abroad as an affront to morality and as a pagan appreciation of nature.

Rosenthal, Bernice G., ed. *Nietzsche in Russia*. Princeton, N.J.: Princeton University Press, 1986. Collection of essays about the influence of Friedrich Nietzsche on Russian authors in the late nineteenth and early twentieth centuries. Several essays discuss Artsybashev, including one that considers Sanine as a Nietzschean superman.

Todd, William Mills, ed. *Literature and Society in Imperial Russia, 1800-1914*. Stanford, Calif.: Stanford University Press, 1978. Examines the relations between Russian literature and mass readership. *Sanine*'s success is considered in the broader context of works read by the middle classes.

SAPPHO

Type of work: Novel
Author: Alphonse Daudet (1840-1897)
Type of plot: Naturalism
Time of plot: Nineteenth century
Locale: Paris
First published: Sapho, 1884 (English translation, 1886)

Principal characters:
JEAN GAUSSIN, a student
FANNY LEGRAND, his mistress
IRÈNE, his fiancée
BOUCHEREAU, a famous physiologist
DÉCHELETTE, a wealthy engineer
LAGOURNERIE, a poet
DE POTTER, a composer
ROSA, de Potter's mistress
FLAMANT, a convict engraver
CÉSAIRE, Jean's uncle

The Story:

Déchelette, a vigorous but aging engineer, spent all but two months of the year on construction projects far from Paris. Each summer, however, he returned to the carefree city to compress into two months enough pleasure to make up for his enforced absences. Jean Gaussin, a young student from the south of France, attended one of Déchelette's masquerade parties. Jean was bewildered at the extravagant ball. Unhappy and lost, he wandered into a gallery, where he found a woman dressed as an Egyptian. When he was ready to leave, the woman stopped him and asked him to take her to his room. In this way, he became her lover. Her name, she told him, was Fanny Legrand.

She continued to come to his room frequently. When he finally visited her apartment, he was astonished at the luxury of the place. In the morning before he arose, the servant announced a visitor. Fanny went into another room to see the early caller, and Jean was horrified to overhear a violent quarrel. Fanny was shouting insults and curses at the man in the language of the gutter. Finally, the man began to sob and pressed money on Fanny. He begged her not to dismiss him, whatever else she did. Jean went back to his classes much disturbed.

Unable to end the affair, he rented an apartment and set up housekeeping with Fanny. She proved to be a capable housewife and a demanding mistress. Jean felt settled and at ease. He made good progress in his consular studies. The following summer, he met Déchelette and Caoudal, a sculptor, at a café and learned the past history of his mistress. Twenty years before, she had lived with Caoudal and had been the model for his well-known figure of Sappho. She had lived with Déchelette at various times, and LaGournerie, the poet, had kept her for some years. Jean felt nauseated when he came to understand that she owed her imaginative diction to LaGournerie, her graceful gestures to Caoudal, her ample spending money to Déchelette. One of her latest lovers had been Flamant. The poor man, an engraver, had counterfeited some banknotes and had been sentenced to prison. Jean learned that Fanny was nearly forty years of age, almost twenty years older than he.

When he confronted Fanny with his knowledge, she readily admitted her past. When she protested her love for him alone, Jean asked for her box of keepsakes. From her letters, he traced her history of loose love for nearly thirty years. The farewell letter from Flamant asked Fanny to look after his young son. Jean suspected that the child was also Fanny's. Despite this knowledge, Jean could not leave his mistress after Fanny meekly submitted to his reproaches. They continued to live together.

Césaire, Jean's uncle, came to Paris with news that Jean's family had been ruined by failure of the grape crop, and that he had been sent to Paris to collect an old debt of eight thousand francs. With Fanny's help, Césaire collected the money but soon lost it gambling. Fanny volunteered to get more money from Déchelette. Jean and Césaire awaited her return anxiously. Jean tortured himself by imagining how she would get it. After some hours, Fanny returned with the money. Césaire left for home, loudly asserting Fanny's goodness and promising to keep silent about Jean's loose life.

With the decline in the Gaussin fortunes, Jean and Fanny decided to separate. Fanny went to work managing an apartment for Rosa, the mistress of the wealthy composer, de Potter. She and Jean were together each Sunday on her day off. After reckoning his decreased allowance, Jean found that they could take a small hut in the country. He was sure they could exist there for another year, and then he would be through with his course of study. Jean, however, hated their life in the country. The grumbling old servant that Fanny had hired previously, now gone, was revealed to have been her stepmother. Her father, a dissolute cab driver, came to visit them. Flamant's child, a savage boy six years of age, lived with them. Jean counted on an appointment to a consular office to break away from Fanny.

On his trips into town, he became acquainted with Bouchereau, the eminent physiologist. Then he met and fell in love with Bouchereau's niece, Irène. Jean hoped that he would receive an appointment in South America and that Irène would go with him as his wife. As he was gradually permitted to see Irène more often, Jean became troubled. Her innocent enjoyment of simple things was disturbing, for he had become so satiated with his experienced courtesan that other women had little attraction for him. When he told Fanny of his approaching marriage, a furious quarrel broke out.

Shortly afterward, Jean met de Potter, who congratulated him on his approaching marriage. De Potter's story was a horrible warning to Jean; the composer had never been able to get away from his mistress, and the attraction of her flesh had held him fast for many years. De Potter's wife rarely saw him; his children were almost strangers. De Potter was bitter about his wasted life, but he could not leave the aging Rosa, whom he supported in luxury.

Despite de Potter's example, despite his engagement to Irène, Jean resolved to keep Fanny. On the eve of his departure for his post in South America, he broke his engagement to Irène and wrote to Fanny to join him in Marseilles. Waiting with tense expectancy in a hotel room in the Mediterranean port, Jean received a letter from Fanny. She had gone back with Flamant on his release from prison. Fanny was too old to go traveling about. She could not leave her beloved Paris.

Critical Evaluation:

Already a noted novelist and an acknowledged leader in the naturalist movement before he wrote *Sappho*, Alphonse Daudet chose for his sixth novel a subject of great personal interest. Having been engaged himself in a lengthy affair with a Parisian courtesan, the novelist dramatizes in *Sappho* the bohemian lifestyle characteristic of the denizens of certain sections of the city. This subject was of great interest to contemporary readers, whose curiosity was aroused by tales of young men caught up in the web of sex and degradation. French readers were insatiable in their appetite for stories of *collages*, relationships between unmarried lovers, especially when the woman was one of ill repute. Despite its reputation as a salacious work, Daudet's novel contains little to satisfy the baser interests of readers; instead, he handles the relationship between the young Jean Gaussin and the older Fanny Legrand with sensitivity and decorum not normally associated with writers of naturalistic fiction.

As one might expect, the central interest in the novel is in the relationship between Jean and the worldly wise courtesan who seduces him and leads him into the relationship that will govern his life for years to come. Daudet has often been commended for his ability to create strong female and weak male characters, and for his penetrating insights into love relationships. Drawing on his personal experiences for this novel, he is particularly successful in delineating his protagonists. Nevertheless, Jean is not simply a fictionalized portrait of the artist as a young lover. Instead, Daudet gives him little of the artistic sensitivity that his creator possessed, instead providing him the kind of career aspirations more common among young men in France in the late nineteenth century. Bound for a career in the diplomatic service, Jean is initially fascinated with the lifestyle represented by Fanny; he pursues her initially merely to fulfill some juvenile romantic fantasy. He does not realize the power of such a woman until it is much too late to avoid her clutches.

Fanny Legrand is one of those "vampire" characters who fascinated nineteenth century readers throughout Europe. Like the figure in Gothic legend that gives the name to the term, Fanny metaphorically draws her life from her lovers: Her manners, her imaginative language, even her money come from the men with whom she has consorted. Jean finds that he, too, is being sucked dry by his relationship with the courtesan, but he is powerless to flee from her. Like a vampire, she has mesmerized him with her fatal attractiveness; although he is aware on an intellectual level that he should break off his relationship with her, he finds he does not have the emotional strength to do so. Even when he becomes engaged to another, he remains drawn to Fanny; his desperate plea at the end of the novel that she join him on his journey to South America shows the hold she possesses over him. Fanny, too, depends on such relationships for her own strength, just as she depends on the milieu in which she lives to keep up her lifestyle; like the vampire who cannot stray too far from his coffin, Fanny cannot leave the confines of Paris lest she lose her powers. Unable to go with Jean, she sends him an ironic letter in which she sets him free with "A kiss, the last one, on your neck."

Within her sphere, Fanny is a powerful creature whose animal magnetism draws men to her and causes them to lose their sensibility as they satisfy their sensual desires. Daudet's portrait of his heroine is psychologically convincing, displaying his exceptional ability to render human emotion and motivation.

Although Daudet espoused the tenets of naturalism, in *Sappho* he does not always adhere strictly to the notion that the writer must become a transparent chronicler of events. Instead, the novel contains numerous authorial comments intended to tell readers how to react to situations and characters. For example, when Jean finds he cannot escape the hold which Fanny has over him, he declares that he loves her. At this point, Daudet observes: "There is in certain words that we ordinarily use a hidden spring which suddenly opens them down to the base . . . Love is one of these words. Only for those for whom its clearness has once been felt, translated in its entirety, will understand the delightful anguish in which Jean lived." Such authorial intrusion is reminiscent more of Anthony Trollope and Charles Dickens than of Émile Zola and other proponents of objectivity in fiction.

Daudet introduces such passages deliberately, because he wishes that *Sappho* be more than a mere portrait of French life as he has experienced it. His dedication for the novel makes his authorial intentions clear: "For my sons when they are twenty." The novel is Daudet's lesson about the pitfalls that await young men whose very nature makes them susceptible to the charms of women like Fanny. The novel reveals the secret of man, that he is vulnerable in his sensuality rather than in his capacity for love. The didactic nature of the work has been commented on by critics since the novel appeared in 1884. Unquestionably, the novelist meant the work to be instructive; while it offers no strong moralistic statement, *Sappho* provides a lesson for those who have not yet had the experiences he chronicles.

"Critical Evaluation" by Laurence W. Mazzeno

Bibliography:

Dobie, G. V. *Alphonse Daudet*. New York: Thomas Nelson, 1949. Biographical study with critical commentary interspersed in the story of Daudet's career. Discusses the novelist's attempt to create a believable story of an ordinary man in love with a Parisian courtesan. Claims *Sappho* is Daudet's greatest contribution to the naturalist movement.

Gosse, Edmund. *French Profiles*. Freeport, N.Y.: Books for Libraries Press, 1970. Overview of Daudet's career. Remarks on the particular strengths of *Sappho*, the novelist's contribution to a French tradition that highlights the "obsession of the feminine."

Matthews, Brander. *The Historical Novel, and Other Essays*. New York: Charles Scribner's, 1901. Sensitive commentary on the novel's theme, and a useful discussion of its place in Daudet's canon. Emphasizes the moral qualities of the work.

Roche, Alphonse. *Alphonse Daudet*. Boston: Twayne, 1976. Intended for general readers, offers an introduction to the writer's major works. Discusses Daudet's handling of the relationship between his principal characters in *Sappho*; comments on the publication history of the novel; remarks on the stir created by its appearance in nineteenth century France.

Sachs, Murray. *The Career of Alphonse Daudet*. Cambridge, Mass.: Harvard University Press, 1965. Discusses Daudet's place as a major figure in French literature. Analyzes the novelist's handling of the love relationship in *Sappho*, calling it exceptionally well done and psychologically realistic.

SAPPHO

Type of work: Drama
Author: Franz Grillparzer (1791-1872)
Type of plot: Tragedy
Time of plot: Sixth century B.C.E.
Locale: Lesbos, Greece
First performed: 1818; first published, 1819 (English translation, 1928)

Principal characters:
SAPPHO, the renowned Greek poet
PHAON, a young man loved by Sappho
MELITTA, Sappho's young and beautiful slave
RHAMNES, an elderly male slave owned by Sappho

The Story:

Sappho, beloved by all and treated as if she were the queen of her native island of Lesbos, went to Olympia to compete for the prize to be awarded for poetry and song. As the result of her genius, she won the laurel wreath accorded the victor and returned in triumph to her island home. To the surprise of those on Lesbos, she brought back with her a handsome, pleasant, but very young man named Phaon, with whom she had fallen deeply in love. Phaon, having heard the poems of Sappho read in his father's home, had great admiration for the poet before he journeyed to Olympia to compete in the games as a charioteer. There he and Sappho had met and fallen in love.

Phaon, a young man of simple tastes, was almost overwhelmed by Sappho's home, her way of life, and her place of importance on the island. Sappho, deeply in love with Phaon, tried to make him comfortable and at ease in his new environment by constantly expressing her love for him and telling him how much he meant to her happiness.

In Sappho's household was a beautiful young female slave named Melitta, who had been taken into Sappho's home as a small child. For some years, the girl had been very close to her mistress. When Sappho returned from Olympia, she suddenly realized that the child had become a woman. This realization caused Sappho some pangs, for it brought home the fact that Sappho herself was no longer young. For the first time, the poet wished she were younger again, for the sake of Phaon.

One day, Phaon, who still was ill at ease in the luxurious household of his mistress, found refuge in a grotto from the noisy merrymaking of Sappho's guests. While he was enjoying the silence of the place, Melitta wandered nearby, having been sent to the gardens to pick some flowers. As she walked along, she voiced her grief at being a slave in a foreign land, lonely for a home and family. Phaon, hearing Melitta's lamentations, was greatly moved, for he too was lonesome in a strange land. He went to the slave and tried to cheer her. This led to a kiss, which was observed by Sappho as she came looking for Phaon. Upset, she did not reveal her presence and left Phaon to himself for a time. Later, she found him asleep in the grotto and awakened him with a kiss. As he awoke, Phaon murmured Melitta's name. Fully awake, he told Sappho of a dream in which he saw himself in love with Melitta, who had usurped the place of Sappho. Sappho told him not to believe in lying dreams.

Although she concealed the fact from him, Sappho's pride was badly hurt by his account of the dream and by the kiss she had seen him bestow upon Melitta. Coming upon Melitta, Sappho accused the slave of maliciously trying to steal Phaon's love. After heated words had passed between the mistress and Melitta, Sappho drew a dagger and threatened Melitta's life. Phaon's appearance saved the woman from injury at Sappho's hands. Phaon then announced his love for the slave and accused Sappho of trying to weave magic spells with her poetry to make him believe he loved her.

Later that day, Sappho called her most trusted slave, Rhamnes, to her and commanded him to take Melitta away from Lesbos to Chios, across the sea, to be placed in the household of one of Sappho's friends. That night, Rhamnes tried to lure the woman from her quarters to a boat on the beach. Melitta, suspecting a trap, protested. Phaon, fearful for Melitta's safety, had remained awake and had heard Rhamnes enter Melitta's quarters. When he discovered Rhamnes' trickery, he made him relinquish Melitta.

Alarmed by what had happened, Phaon decided to flee Lesbos and Sappho's household. Taking Melitta with him, he embarked in the boat Rhamnes had planned to use in spiriting the young beauty away.

As soon as he was free of the threat of Phaon's dagger, Rhamnes sounded the alarm and told of Phaon's flight with Melitta. Planning revenge, Sappho called the people of the island to her and promised a handsome reward of gold for the return of the fugitives. Spurred by the reward and their love for Sappho, the islanders hurried after Phaon and Melitta. When they came up with the fugitives upon the sea, Melitta was struck on the head by an oar during the struggle. Phaon then yielded to their captors.

Back in Sappho's house, Phaon demanded to know why she should be given the privilege of judging him, as if she were a queen. The islanders told him that they regarded her as their queen. When Sappho demanded the return of Melitta, Phaon said that, in threatening the slave's life, Sappho had relinquished all her rights to the girl. Sappho then accused Phaon of being a deceiver in love. Phaon defended himself by saying that he had been mistaken in his love, that the love he had felt for Sappho was love of her genius. He added that he had really loved her as a goddess, not as a woman, not knowing the difference until after he had met and fallen in love with Melitta.

Sappho was disturbed by what had happened and by what Phaon had said. At first, thinking that she was being asked too great a price for having poetic gifts, she wished to disown her genius in order to live and love as an ordinary woman. She left the company to think in solitude. As she looked out across the sea, her lyre suddenly clanged loudly, as if warning her, and she decided not to try to escape the genius given her by the gods. She asked the gods only to keep her from being an object of men's derision. Returning, she forgave the young lovers with a kiss and then walked to an altar of Aphrodite which stood on a cliff overlooking the sea. Calling upon the gods to take her to them, Sappho hurled herself over the brink into the water below. Phaon and Sappho's people ran to rescue her, but they were too late. The ocean currents had dashed her to her death against the rocks.

Critical Evaluation:

Like so many of his contemporaries in the Romantic movement, Franz Grillparzer found early inspiration for a number of his creative works in classical mythology. For centuries, the tale of the Greek poet Sappho's unrequited love for the young Phaon had served as the subject for works that emphasized the comic qualities inherent in the story of an older woman attempting to secure the love of a younger man. Grillparzer found something else entirely in the tale. For him, the story of Sappho and Phaon was appealing because it permitted him to explore a topic of personal interest: the fate of artists in a world that does not understand or appreciate them.

Structurally, *Sappho* follows closely the form of Greek tragedy. Grillparzer is careful to observe the classical unities (a practice he abandons in later works), concentrating the dramatic action on the climactic scenes in which Sappho confronts her lover, Phaon, and his new beloved, Melitta. Through this series of altercations, and through the skillful presentation of much-needed background material in a series of lengthy speeches by a number of characters, the playwright vivifies the central conflict in his drama. Neither the conflict nor its resolution are classical, however; instead, in *Sappho* Grillparzer dramatizes the conflict the Romantic artist faces in dealing with those who are unable to understand or appreciate the psychological demands placed on those who have the power to create art. The heroine desperately wants to synthesize her desires for a normal life as a wife and lover with her vocation as a poet. Unfortunately, her beloved Phaon sees her only in the latter role, revering her as an artist but transferring his love to the younger Melitta. The heroine's decision to end her life when she finds she cannot keep Phaon as her lover is carried out as a means of demonstrating that she has the will to determine her own fate.

The central critical issue in Grillparzer's play revolves around an important issue that has both technical and moral overtones: whether the dramatic action justifies the ending. More than one critic has observed that the choice Grillparzer has given his heroine seems forced, and her fate too extreme. She seems to love Phaon deeply, and his failure to return that love leaves her desolate. Nevertheless, her status as a poet is in no way diminished by this rejection; she should be able to go on without him, still revered for her artistry, which everyone recognizes. The play suggests, however, that Sappho does not wish to settle for one or the other option: She wishes to have both her fame as an artist and her life as a wife to the man she loves. As a result, some critics have dismissed her as unbalanced, which may be normal for a poet but is unsatisfactory in terms of dramatic characterization.

While such a reading can be plausibly constructed from the text, it does not do justice to Grillparzer's understanding of his character or the tradition in which he is working. As a Romantic tragedy, *Sappho* shares affinities with other great works in the tradition. Comparisons with Johann Wolfgang von Goethe's *Faust* (1808-1832) and Percy Bysshe Shelley's *The Cenci* (1819) are not inappropriate. More noteworthy are what the play shares with the greatest of all Romantic love stories, *Tristan and Isolde* (Richard Wagner's opera, 1857-1859). The love triangle in Grillparzer's play is an ironic reversal of the legend, in that Grillparzer gives to his aging heroine the qualities that the young lovers in the medieval tale possess: a fine sensitivity for life that allows them to rise above the mundane, and an artistic temperament that makes their love greater than the simple sensual affairs of mere mortals. The story in *Sappho* also parallels an even more famous love triangle, that of Arthur, Guinevere, and Lancelot in the Arthurian legends. In all of these cases, the lovers find no optimal means of compromising their feelings.

The common thread that unites these tragedies, and which runs through all of Romantic literature, is the struggle of the hero to transcend the limitations of time. Certainly this is the case with Grillparzer's Sappho. The poet realizes that she is growing older; she can understand Phaon's desire to take a younger bride in Melitta, but she is unable to accept it. On more than one occasion, she makes it clear that her efforts to keep her lover are motivated by her desire to stop time. In her art, she has been able to do that; the poems she produces are monuments that will transcend time, providing pleasure and insight not only to her contemporaries but also to generations who will follow her. They are not Sappho herself, of course; although she lives through her art, she cannot be fully actualized as a person except through human love. When Sappho realizes that she cannot arrest time, she chooses what, for her, seems the only possible option: She determines for herself when the moment of death will come, demonstrating—in a

Romantic statement—that she is in control of her life just as she is in control of her art. Whether or not this choice seems believable to readers of subsequent generations, it represents accurately the Romantic attitude that places the greatest value on the integrity of the self and the right of choice.

"Critical Evaluation" by Laurence W. Mazzeno

Bibliography:

Coenen, Frederic. *Franz Grillparzer's Portraiture of Men*. Chapel Hill: University of North Carolina Press, 1951. Focuses on the depiction of Phaon and Rhamnes in *Sappho*. Calls the former a "delightfully youthful figure" who grows in self-knowledge during the drama; asserts the latter figure is better drawn than most servants in similar dramas.

Thompson, Bruce. *Franz Grillparzer*. Boston: Twayne, 1981. Surveys Grillparzer's poetry, prose, and drama. Reviews the critical reception of *Sappho*, and examines the author's handling of the psychological dimensions of his heroine. Concludes the work is an example of Grillparzer's treatment of the theme of the artist's tragedy.

Wells, George A. *The Plays of Grillparzer*. London: Pergamon Press, 1969. Excellent scholarly analysis of *Sappho*, summarizing earlier critical opinion and providing detailed examination of character, plot, and structure. Notes the technical advancements over Grillparzer's earlier work.

Yates, Douglas. *Franz Grillparzer: A Critical Biography*. Oxford, England: Basil Blackwell, 1946. Insightful study of the writer's major works, organized chronologically to show his development as a dramatist. Chapter on *Sappho* examines Grillparzer's intentions and his handling of the theme of the artist's tragedy.

Yates, W. E. *Grillparzer: A Critical Introduction*. Cambridge, England: Cambridge University Press, 1972. Provides brief sketch of Grillparzer's life. Analyzes his works, focusing on themes such as love, duty, and the role of the artist. Describes the genesis of *Sappho* and provides extensive discussion of character development, showing how the heroine achieves self-knowledge through her tragedy.

SARTOR RESARTUS

Type of work: Philosophical
Author: Thomas Carlyle (1795-1881)
First published: serial, 1833-1834; book, 1836

Many scholars of Thomas Carlyle refer to *Sartor Resartus* as fiction, but readers who think of the nineteenth century novel when they think of fiction would hardly agree. Although *Sartor Resartus* does have a putative hero, Diogenes Teufelsdröckh, whose life and opinions become the substance of the book, he is only the mouthpiece through whom Carlyle unleashes a torrent of criticism about the materialism and philosophical rationalism of his age. Writing about the German humorist Jean Paul Richter, Carlyle observes that "every work, be it fiction or serious treatise, is embaled in some fantastic wrappage," and he refers to Richter's "perfect Indian jungle" of a style. This precisely describes Carlyle's prose as well.

Sartor Resartus is divided into three books of eleven, ten, and twelve chapters, respectively. The title means, literally, The Tailor Retailored, and the whole work elaborates a long metaphor suggested by Jonathan Swift's question in the second book of *A Tale of a Tub* (1704): "What is Man himself but a *Micro-Coat*, or rather a compleat Suit of Cloaths with all its Trimmings?" In Carlyle's view, civilization—that is, religion, government, and all the other institutional garments that human beings weave to clothe themselves—is frayed and shabby and needs retailoring. For the transcendentalist Carlyle, clothes also become the shroud of matter by which all spirit makes its appearance in this world of sensible experience.

Carlyle adopts the conventional apprenticeship novel to his own purposes in *Sartor Resartus*. His chosen hero, the young man who goes out into the world and meets its challenges, has the fantastic name of Diogenes Teufelsdröckh, or Born-of-God Devil's-Dung. This improbably named character becomes professor of Allerley-Wissenschaft at the University of Weissnichtwo, or Professor of Things in General at the University of Know-Not-Where.

Carlyle's complicated narrative begins with praise for "deep-thinking Germany" and its Idealist tradition in philosophy, its expounding of a transcendental super-sensible realm closed off from the five senses. This admiration for German thought permeates *Sartor Resartus*, appearing not only in Teufelsdröckh's nationality, but also in the repeated German phrases and in the penchant for beginning nouns with capital letters. Given this predilection, the narrator responds eagerly to the arrival of Professor Teufelsdröckh's new book on the origin and influence of clothes.

After months of perusing Teufelsdröckh's opus, the narrator unexpectedly receives a letter from Teufelsdröckh's associate, Herr Hofrath Heuschrecke (Mr. Councilor Grasshopper), announcing that he is sending materials for a "Life and Opinions of Herr Teufelsdröckh." Before these materials arrive, however, the narrator muses on the character of Teufelsdröckh and on passages from the volume on clothes. In book 1, chapter 5, for instance, Carlyle attacks one of his favorite targets, Enlightenment rationalism, when his narrator quotes Teufelsdröckh's sneer at the "Cause-and-Effect Philosopher."

A chapter on "The World out of Clothes" stresses the inadequacy of rational systems, praising Teufelsdröckh's broad, intuitive approach to understanding the spiritual basis of nature, an infinitely complex system, but one that faith convinces us reveals a plan. We live as in a dream, perceiving only in "rare half-waking moments" the spiritual reality behind the mask of matter in the creation.

This same theme is pursued in a chapter that renounces "vulgar Logic" in favor of "Pure

Reason"; that is, logic views man simply as an "omnivorous Biped that wears Breeches," whereas Pure Reason, or direct, unmediated intuition, apprehends in humans "A Soul, a Spirit, and divine Apparition." Yet matter should not be denigrated, for it is everywhere the manifestation of Spirit. Science threatens our reverence for Spirit, however, because its curiosity about matter dampens our sense of wonder at the mystery of existence.

Book 1 ends with the narrator's receipt of six large paper bags stuffed with Teufelsdröckh's manuscripts. The narrator's subsequent absorption in the story of the philosopher's life and opinions will form the substance of book 2, told mostly in long passages quoted from Teufelsdröckh's papers.

The hero's origins in the village of Entepfuhl (Duck Pond) are mysterious; an enigmatic stranger brings the infant in a basket to a childless, aging couple, Andreas and Gretchen Futteral. The young Diogenes' childhood is idyllic, his intellectual development prodigious. In his adolescence, he loses both Andreas and Gretchen, but in learning the puzzle of his birth, he miraculously discovers his individuality: "*I was like no other*," he exults. His university experience disillusions him, and the narrator digresses to blister one of Carlyle's favorite targets, the barrenness of rationalism. But Teufelsdröckh's youthful skepticism is a natural rite of passage, for "first must the dead Letter of Religion own itself dead, and drop piecemeal into dust, if the living Spirit of Religion, freed from this its charnelhouse, is to arise on us, newborn of Heaven, and with new healing under its wings." This passage well illustrates Carlyle's unrelieved practice of narrating by metaphor.

After the young Teufelsdröckh leaves the university, he follows a ragged course. He flounders in a legal career before suffering through his first great love interest, the collapse of which turns him into a Byronic pilgrim wandering in the mountains. At this point in book 2, Carlyle subjects his hero to an ordeal of religious despair that the hero fights his way through. Chapter 7, "The Everlasting No," finds Teufelsdröckh mired in spiritual sloth but still clinging to his belief in a transcendent Truth and the demands of Duty. Finally, he rouses himself and looks outward at the world, the "*Not-me*," finding great relief in this escape from the burden of solipsism, or absorption in self.

In chapter 8, "Centre of Indifference," the revitalized Teufelsdröckh plunges into the give-and-take of great events and great scenes, and Carlyle expands on one of his favorite themes, the importance of the great man in shaping history. This was a topic on which he was to write at length in *On Heroes and Hero-Worship* (1841). By chapter's end, Teufelsdröckh has banished spiritual pride and can ask himself, "Pshaw! what is this paltry little Dog-cage of an Earth; what art thou that sittest whining there?"

Chapter 10, "The Everlasting Yea," relates Teufelsdröckh's emergence whole on the far side of the slough of despond. He reports that "Annihilation of Self . . . had been happily accomplished; and my mind's eyes were now unsealed, and its hands ungyved." He suddenly enjoys knowledge of a living universe full of the immanent God, a nature he calls the "Living Garment of God." This mystical breakthrough inspires in him infinite love and pity for his fellow human beings, and it frees him from Calvinist fretting about Original Sin. The insight he achieves owes a debt to Goethe's *Faust* (part I, 1808): People's unhappiness derives from the source of their greatness, their finite soul's striving for the infinite. Once they overcome their preoccupation with happiness and turn their attention to God, they shall achieve peace. Carlyle's famous command is "Close thy *Byron*; open thy *Goethe*." In an apostrophe to Voltaire, Teufelsdröckh tells Voltaire that his work is over; Christian superstition is dead. These three chapters are the centerpiece of *Sartor Resartus*, and they conclude resoundingly: "Work while it is called To-day, for the Night cometh wherein no man can work."

The remaining chapters return to the same ideas, fashioning them in different metaphors. "Incident in Modern History" celebrates the life of George Fox (1624-1691), founder of the Society of Friends (Quakers). "Church Clothes" elaborates on a conceit in which government appears as the outer skin of society, and religion becomes "the inmost Pericardial and Nervous Tissue, which ministers Life and warm Circulation to the whole." Utilitarians, or "Motive-Millwrights," take a couple of punches in "Symbols," a chapter that also lauds as the highest of all symbols the artist or poet who emerges as a prophet in whom "all men can recognise a present God." Jesus is cited as "our divinest Symbol." Clearly, Carlyle aspired to be the artist-prophet of his age.

Liberal, rationalist contempt for the church and its hierarchical authority is condemned in "The Phoenix," which predicts that a saving remnant will revitalize the institution. This revitalization is enabled by the "organic filaments" which connect the dying elements of the old generation to the elements being born in the new generation. Humankind is a unity that gives sequence and continuity to life. The new age will need new titles, but kings will remain kings. The true basis for organizing society will always be hero worship, which elevates great individuals to their proper positions. Even with the old religion in retreat, there remain "Fragments of a genuine Church-*Homiletic*" scattered amid "this immeasurable froth ocean we name *Literature*." Paramount among the prophets of literature is Goethe.

One of Carlyle's longest chapters is "Natural Supernaturalism"; in this chapter, he sneers at science as petty in the face of the miracles that we witness daily: "the true inexplicable God-revealing Miracle lies in this," he insists, "that I can stretch forth my hand at all." God's presence shines throughout the universe, and each of us lives as a ghost, "a shadow-system gathered round our Me." We come into this world and take a bodily shape before disappearing again, "through Mystery to Mystery, from God and to God."

A chapter entitled "Circumspective" expounds a semiotics of spirit, and "The Dandiacal Body" contrasts, rather meanly, the sect of self-absorbed dandies whose "*Fashionable Novels*" constitute their sacred books, with the "Poor-Slaves," that is "Rhizophagous," or potato-eating, Irish-Catholic peasantry. Two final chapters, repeating the same metaphors, conclude the hyperbolic musings of Carlyle's modern Diogenes.

Two years after Carlyle published *Sartor Resartus*, the American Transcendentalist Ralph Waldo Emerson published his famous meditation *Nature* (1836), in which he announced his own version of the Idealism that Carlyle celebrated; in "Self-Reliance" (1841), Emerson gave his most eloquent testimony in support of Carlyle's hero-worship. In their fierce defense of a super-sensible realm of Spirit, their condemnation of the positivism of their times, and their proclamation of the individual's freedom to achieve greatness through efforts of the will, these two sages contributed greatly to nineteenth century intellectual history.

Frank Day

Bibliography:

Kaplan, Fred. *Thomas Carlyle: A Biography*. Ithaca, N.Y.: Cornell University Press, 1983. Comprehensive biography. Presents Carlyle's circumstances while writing *Sartor Resartus* and his dealings with publishers, and vividly depicts Carlyle's relations with notable figures such as Harriet Martineau and John Stuart Mill. His affinities with American readers emerge clearly. Many illustrations.

LaValley, Albert J. *Carlyle and the Idea of the Modern*. New Haven, Conn.: Yale University Press, 1968. Studies Carlyle's prophetic writings in relation to William Blake and such other prophets of his day as Friedrich Nietzsche and Karl Marx. Stresses the fact that *Sartor Resartus* presents Christianity as exhausted and asserts that the self will be the new basis of religion.

Levine, George. *The Boundaries of Fiction: Carlyle, Macaulay, Newman*. Princeton, N.J.: Princeton University Press, 1968. Pointing to the use in *Sartor Resartus* of symbols and images, and to its satire and didacticism, Levine treats it not as a novel but as a "confession-anatomy-romance" in Northrop Frye's system of classification.

Seigel, Jules Paul, ed. *Thomas Carlyle: The Critical Heritage*. London: Routledge & Kegan Paul, 1971. A collection of contemporary reviews. John Sterling praises the "genius and moral energy" of *Sartor Resartus*; Alexander Hill Everett calls the book a "philosophical romance"; and Nathaniel Frothingham admires its "humane cast of thought."

Tennyson, G. B. *Sartor Called Resartus*. Princeton, N.J.: Princeton University Press, 1965. Invaluable study of *Sartor Resartus*. Includes chapters on the book's German background and on its composition, structure, texture, and style. The final chapter illustrates the book's philosophy in the context of the period. Appendix includes a chronology of the composition of Carlyle's works.

SARTORIS

Type of work: Novel
Author: William Faulkner (1897-1962)
Type of plot: Psychological realism
Time of plot: Immediately following World War I
Locale: Mississippi
First published: 1929

Principal characters:
Young Bayard Sartoris, a self-destructive veteran
Aunt Jenny Depre, his caustic aunt
Old Bayard Sartoris, his irascible grandfather
Narcissa Benbow, a friend of Jenny who reluctantly falls in love with young Bayard
Horace Benbow, her effete and absent-minded brother, also a veteran
Simon Strother, a black retainer of the Sartoris family
Byron Snopes, a Peeping Tom and Narcissa's secret admirer

The Story:

Shortly after the conclusion of World War I, Will Falls, an ancient veteran of the Civil War, came to visit old Bayard Sartoris in his Jefferson, Mississippi, bank, bringing a pipe that had belonged to John Sartoris, Bayard's father and a colonel in the Confederacy. John's heroic ghost seemed to fill the room as they reminisced.

The bank day over, Simon Strother, a Sartoris family servant, came to drive old Bayard home in the family carriage and reported that Bayard's grandson, also named Bayard, was seen arriving on a train that afternoon. Young Bayard was a Royal Air Force pilot along with his twin brother John. John had died foolishly in the skies over France. Juxtaposed with young Bayard's reported sighting was another story of the past, this one about a third Bayard Sartoris, who fought in the Civil War. Colonel John Sartoris' brother died vaingloriously in the service of Jeb Stuart. His Civil War exploits had, as had his brother John's, become part of the Sartoris family legend. The repository of the Sartoris legends was eighty-year-old Aunt Jenny Depre, who kept house for the Sartorises. The sister of John and Bayard Sartoris of the Civil War, she alternated between paying homage to and scoffing at the deeds of her brothers. A no-nonsense person with an acidic tongue, she attributed the violence and foolishness of the World War I generation of brothers to the same streak of Sartoris bullheadedness that ran through the Sartoris men of the Civil War.

Safely returned home to the care of Aunt Jenny and his grandfather, young Bayard still could not find peace. He was filled with guilt over his brother's death and was driven to self-destructive behavior. He foolishly tried to ride an untrained stallion and was thrown. Rather than return home, he became drunk with some country folks and then serenaded all the eligible ladies in town, including Narcissa Benbow. He also raced recklessly through the county in an automobile, running wagons off the road. Although warned to avoid the automobile because of a bad heart, the elder Bayard rode along, ostensibly to restrain his grandson's recklessness but really, according to Miss Jenny, because, as another Sartoris male, he desired the same thrill of danger as his grandson. Narcissa Benbow was Jenny's friend and formerly had been in love with Bayard's brother John. Visiting one day, she confided to Jenny that she had been receiving anonymous and obscene love letters. For all of her ladylike decorum, however, she was secretly flattered by the letters. The sender, Byron Snopes, was a stealthy, animalistic bookkeeper at the Sartorises' bank, who dictated his missives to a schoolboy, as if they were business correspondence. The boy blackmailed Snopes into giving him an air rifle.

Narcissa welcomed home another returning veteran, her brother Horace Benbow. A noncombatant during the war, he had served in the YMCA and had learned glassblowing in Italy. Impractical and absent-minded, his love of beauty was a thin disguise for his cowardice. He adored his sister, even naming one of his glass vases after her, but he fell out of favor with her when he resumed an affair with Belle Mitchell, a discontented married woman.

A third returning veteran was Caspey Strother, son of Simon, who had come to believe that, given their equal status in France, blacks need no longer accept a servile position in Southern society. Caspey's war tales were exaggerated, and the only real wounds he suffered were in a crap game. Old Bayard regarded Caspey's notions of his rights as insolent. In the meantime, old Bayard had developed a wen on his face, which, much to Aunt Jenny's exasperation, he allowed Will Falls to treat with an ancient Indian remedy. Fearful that Bayard would get blood poisoning, she took him to a pretentious but ineffectual specialist. Falls's salve ultimately worked perfectly, much to the dismay of Jenny and the doctors. Eventually, young Bayard had an automobile accident in which he broke his ribs. Narcissa, with conflicting feelings of attraction and revulsion, read to him as he recovered, although he had no interest whatsoever in books. The relationship developed further until they agreed to marry. On the eve of the wedding, Byron Snopes broke into Narcissa's bedroom, stole the anonymous letters he had written her, robbed the Sartorises' bank, and left town.

Simon got into trouble with his church congregation, which had entrusted him with money being collected to build a new church building. Simon had given the money away to a mistress, claiming, in imitation of his employer, that he had lent the money out. He assured the congregation that the elder Bayard would restore the money, much to his employer's outrage. Young Bayard found a momentary contentment in marriage, Narcissa's pregnancy, and the rhythms of seasonal plantation life. He and Narcissa watched the sharecroppers make sorghum molasses, went possum hunting with Caspey, and shared Thanksgiving dinner with family and friends. Memories of his twin brother, however, drove him to despair again. Driving recklessly off the road one December day, he caused his grandfather to die of a heart attack. Ashamed of his conduct, he did not return home but escaped into the country to stay with the MacCallums, with whom he and his brother had often hunted. This return to a wholesome life close to the earth reminded him of better times, but it could not restore his spirits. On Christmas eve he left the MacCallums', spent the night and Christmas morning with a black sharecropping family, and then took a train away from his home forever.

At the conclusion to the novel, Narcissa received a letter from Horace, who had gone off to live with Belle. Jenny and she also received, from various parts of the country, Bayard's requests for money. Bayard eventually agreed to test-fly a dangerously designed airplane and was killed on the day his son was born to Narcissa. Jenny announced that the child's name must be John, but in an effort to evade the Sartoris heritage of violence and self-destructiveness, Narcissa insisted on naming the child Benbow Sartoris. Simon Strother was eventually murdered as the result of his adulterous affair. Jenny tended to Simon's and the Sartoris men's graves. Picking up the pieces left behind by the destructive Sartoris men seemed to be her lot in life, a role that she stoically accepted.

Critical Evaluation:

The juxtaposition of modern themes and the mythology of a Southern family's past resulted in William Faulkner's first important novel. He had written two prior books, *Soldier's Pay* (1926) and *Mosquitoes* (1927), whose modernism was fairly typical of their time, but they lacked the rich texture of *Sartoris*. In this novel, Faulkner imparts to his alienated modern heroes a long tradition of Sartoris glory and vainglory. His dramatization is deepened by positioning it in the context of Southern history and by creating a strong sense of place.

Some critics see family history as a burden that young Bayard must bear, an impossibly high standard to which he must aspire. Others argue that, in the modern, mechanized world, Bayard is prevented from shouldering that burden and following in the heroic footsteps of his ancestors. In either case, his life epitomizes the despair so often associated with modern protagonists. Lacking meaning in their lives, the protagonists of many modern novels find themselves alienated from their society and from life itself.

Sartoris is about the South's entering the modern world, taking one last backward glance into the past as it does so. The novel displays a double consciousness about the Southern past. From the beginning, when Will Falls visits old Bayard, the influence of the Civil War and the heroic Sartoris legend pervades the book. Various devices, such as narrative commentary, the reminiscences of Falls and Aunt Jenny, and the opening of the chest in the attic containing Sartoris relics, combine to underscore the past's influence on the present. The novel's attitude toward the past is a mixture of romantic nostalgia and modern skepticism. Miss Jenny, for example, speaks tartly of the antics of the male line of her family even as she keeps their legends alive. She is simultaneously contemptuous and tender.

The novel is not only concerned with romanticized views of the Southern past but with romantic notions generally. Faulkner depicts the romantic attitudes of a variety of characters, and he employs satire to undercut those notions. For instance, the idealized brother-and-sister relationship of Horace and Narcissa is undermined by both her willingness to keep Snopes's obscene letters and his sordid affair with a married woman. In *Sartoris*, Faulkner seems eager to explore the many possibilities of his fictional world. In fact, one of the problems noted by critics of this work is that in it, he tries to do too much. There are too many stories, and they are only superficially related to each other. The novel has been called episodic and lacking a center. The first draft of the book, called *Flags in the Dust*, was even longer and had to be edited before a publisher would agree to print it. The material is so rich that Faulkner revisits many of the same characters, or similar ones, in later novels. He later devoted a trilogy of novels (*The Hamlet*, 1940; *The Town*, 1957; and *The Mansion*, 1959) to the wily Snopes family. He writes of Horace and Narcissa in *Sanctuary* (1929). He returns to common people such as V. K. Suratt (who later becomes V. K. Ratliff) and the MacCallums in various novels. He also returns to black characters in books such as *The Sound and the Fury* (1929) and *Go Down, Moses* (1942). For all its artistic flaws, *Sartoris* is exciting because of the richness of its material and the tangible enthusiasm of its author as he discovers the characters and the setting that will occupy him for the rest of his career.

William L. Howard

Bibliography:

Hoffman, Frederick J. *William Faulkner*. 2d rev. ed. Boston: Twayne, 1966. A basic study of Faulkner's work and life. Notes that *Sartoris* is the beginning of his great novels about his own "postage stamp of native soil," Yoknapatawpha County and shows a deeper insight into the cultural context in which his characters operate than his previous novels had.

Howe, Irving. *William Faulkner: A Critical Study*. 3d ed. Chicago: University of Chicago Press,

1975. Divided into two parts, one addressing Faulkner's "world and his work" and the other evaluating his achievement in the major novels. *Sartoris* is treated as an apprentice work.

Millgate, Michael. *The Achievement of William Faulkner*. New York: Random House, 1966. Includes a chapter on Faulkner's career, separate chapters on each of his novels, and a chapter assessing his achievement. Sees *Sartoris* as a bridge between his apprenticeship and his mature novels. Notes that, in this novel, Faulkner successfully captured the spirit of a place for the first time.

Tuck, Dorothy. *Crowell's Handbook of Faulkner*. New York: Thomas Y. Crowell, 1964. An excellent source for basic information about each of Faulkner's novels. Provides a synopsis of *Sartoris* as well as essays on the history of Yoknapatawpha County and Faulkner's style of writing.

Vickery, Olga W. *The Novels of William Faulkner*. Rev. ed. Baton Rouge: Louisiana State University Press, 1964. Treats Faulkner's novels separately, then discusses themes that pervade a number of them. Sees *Sartoris* as about mythmaking and the deflation of myths.

THE SATANIC VERSES

Type of work: Novel
Author: Salman Rushdie (1947-   )
Type of plot: Fantasy
Time of plot: Late twentieth and early seventh centuries
Locale: London, India, and Jahilia
First published: 1988

Principal characters:
GIBREEL FARISHTA, an Indian film star
SALADIN CHAMCHA, an English actor, the man of a thousand and one voices
PAMELA LOVELACE, his wife
ALLELUIA CONE, a mountain climber, Gibreel's lover
MAHOUND, a pejorative Christian name for the prophet Mohammed
HIND, queen of Jahilia
THE IMAM, an exiled religious figure
AYESHA, a young woman who leads her followers on a fatal pilgrimage to Mecca
ZEENY VIKAL, a medical doctor, art critic, and political activist
SALMAN, Mahound's scribe
BAAL, a satirist

The Story:

Odd-numbered Chapters. Around New Year's Day, just before dawn, Sikh terrorists destroyed an Air India jumbo jet in flight. Two passengers miraculously, or fantastically, fell safely into the English Channel, the one flapping his arms and singing, the other desperately, doubtfully clinging to his companion. Forty-year-old Gibreel Farishta, née Ismail Najruddin, was a poor orphan who had grown up to become India's biggest film star. "Fortyish" Saladin Chamcha, née Salahuddin Chamchawala, the estranged Anglophile son of a prominent Bombay businessman, was also an actor, master mimic, and costar of the popular English television series *The Aliens*. The two men interpreted their salvation differently, and, once ashore, they were given very different receptions. Unable to prove his identity and having already begun to assume a goatlike appearance and smell, Chamcha was arrested and verbally and physically abused by racist police officers. Gibreel, dressed in the clothes of his host's (Rosa Diamond's) late husband, was allowed to go free.

Chamcha's situation worsened. Escaping from a migrants-only ward of the mental hospital, where he had been committed once the police discovered that he was what he claimed to be, a British citizen, he found himself without a wife. He had returned home to find his very proper-sounding and proper-looking English wife, Pamela Lovelace, in bed with another man, Jamsheed Joshi. He was also without a job, the role of Maxim Alien having been cut by the show's Thatcherite producer, Hal Valence. With "Jumpy" Joshi's help, he secured temporary lodgings in the kind of immigrant neighborhood that he had spent much of his life trying to avoid. As his anger and helplessness grew, so did Chamcha. Local activists transformed the satanic-looking eight-foot-tall satyr into an immigrant hero. Not until he vented his rage in a local nightspot, where Asians, West Indians, and others danced alongside wax effigies of third world heroes and their English oppressors (including Margaret Thatcher), was he able to resume his earlier form.

Gibreel, meanwhile, fared much better. Transformed into his namesake, the Angel of the Recitation, he sought refuge in the bed of his English lover, the fair-skinned climber of Mount Everest, Alleluia Cone (originally Cohen), whom he had met immediately after his near fatal illness several months earlier and before his mysterious disappearance from Bombay. Spurned by England and his English wife alike, Chamcha, transmogrified into Shaitan as well as the angel Azraeel, avenged his fall from grace by destroying Gibreel's happiness, undermining his faith in Alleluia Cone, and thus pushing Gibreel one step closer to madness. Leaving Alleluia did not mean Gibreel could leave behind the dreams that had been troubling him since his recovery from the Phantom Bug. From her home, he walked straight into a nightmarish London beset by racial strife and police cover-ups that left several people dead, including Pamela and her lover. Chamcha nearly died trying to save the Bangladeshi couple with whom he had stayed earlier but was saved by Gibreel, despite his realizing that it was Chamcha who had scripted his break-up with Alleluia.

Chamcha's life improved. He survived a heart attack, returned to Bombay, and became reconciled not only with his dying father but also with India, to the point of taking an interest in local politics, or at least in one political activist, Zeeny Vikal. Gibreel's fortunes, meanwhile, took a downward turn. His films bombed; his cynicism grew. A chance encounter ended with Gibreel's shooting the stuttering film producer and erstwhile good Samaritan Whisky Sisodia and then throwing Alleluia Cone off a high-rise roof in a virtual replay of his former mistress Rekha Merchant's suicide two years earlier. After telling his tale, Gibreel then killed himself, with Chamcha looking helplessly on.

Even-numbered Chapters. Gibreel had troubling dreams. In the first, Abu Simbel, leader of Jahilia (pre-Islamic Arabia) offered to make a deal with Mahound: He will accept the new monotheistic religion if Mahound will grant subordinate but still divine status to three local goddesses. After consulting the angel Gibreel, Mahound accepted the offer. Later, however, after the number of his followers had grown, Mahound claimed that the concession had been the work of Shaitan and that the verses in the revelation conceding semidivine status to the three goddesses were satanic in origin and effect and therefore had to be corrected. In the second, an exiled Imam (based upon the Ayatollah Khomeini) returned to Desh (Iran) and commanded Gibreel to defeat Ayesha (a version of the whore of Babylon, or, alternately, the Great Satan, the United States). In the third, Mahound completed his conquest of Jahilia, ordering the closing of its most famous brothel and the executions of its prostitutes, who had adopted the names of Mahound's twelve wives. In the fourth, the angel Gibreel ordered a young woman, Ayesha, to lead a group of pilgrims to the sea and on to Mecca. When the sea failed to part, as the angel had told her it would, all but a few pilgrims drowned.

Critical Evaluation:

The Satanic Verses elicited that harshest of reviews, a death sentence, from Iran's Ayatollah Ruhollah Khomeini, whose familiarity with the novel was apparently limited to second-hand reports of Gibreel's "blasphemous" dreams. The *fatwā*, issued on February 14, 1989, had less to do with Salman Rushdie and his novel than it did with the power struggle then going on in Iran between hardliners such as Khomeini and moderates. The author and his book suffered greatly as a result. Rushdie has effectively been made hostage to a new form of international terrorism backed by the promise of financial and heavenly rewards for the assassin. He had to go into hiding. His novel, when not either burned or banned, has been discussed almost exclusively on the *fatwā*'s terms.

In its intricate and provocative exploration of postmodern and postcolonial sensibilities, *The*

Satanic Verses celebrates and extends what one character calls "the eclectic, hybridized nature of the Indian artistic tradition." Its multiplicity of styles and stories, its blurring of the boundary separating reality from dream, fact from fiction, its "pitting levity against gravity," and its allowing characters' names to migrate, as it were, from one narrative to another, do more than confuse some readers and entertain others. Metaphorically, such techniques work much the same way as the novel's intertextuality does in drawing on a wide variety of ceaselessly metamorphosing texts, the Koran, the Bible, the *Mahabharata* (200 B.C.E.-200 C.E.), and the *Odyssey* (c. 800 B.C.E.) on the one hand, Hindi films and British television shows on the other. "Democracy can only thrive in a turbulent environment," Rushdie has noted, and *The Satanic Verses* is a narratively turbulent novel in which pyrotechnic style is put to political purpose as Rushdie considers both the chances for and challenges to democracy in an increasingly intolerant and multicultural world. Not even a writer as ambitious as Rushdie can hope to be completely democratic.

Rushdie has written that the telling of one story in effect censors the telling of others. Rushdie can, however, imply the existence of these other tales and, more important, make clear what happens in a world ruled by a "terrifying singularity" where "And, or, maybe" has no place, no voice.

The stasis and "purity" of Mahound's "Rule" and "the Untime of the Imam" (Khomeini's "revolt against history"), Rushdie believes, perverts one of Mohammed's greatest achievements, his having situated himself in the actual historical circumstances of his time and place. *The Satanic Verses* may be critical of religion, but it is not antireligious and certainly not blasphemous. "Fact is," the stuttering but good-hearted Whisky Sisodia tells Chamcha, "religious fafaith, which encodes the highest ass ass aspirations of human race, is now, in our cocountry, the servant of lowest instincts, and gogo God is the creator of evil." The novel views these aspirations in secular terms and religious movements—whether Islam in the early seventh century or Muslim and Hindu fundamentalism in the late twentieth—as responses to specific economic and political problems. Rushdie is, however, equally critical of the West, whose freedoms he embraces but whose racism he deplores in all its forms. These range all the way from physical assaults to more subtle variations on the old Asian theme. Chamcha learns from another transmogrified immigrant: "They have the power of description, and we conform to the pictures they construct." The most insidious form of racism is the creation of the mono-culture of multinational capitalism, what Rushdie only half-jokingly calls "The Coca-colonization of the planet."

Metamorphosis at all levels is at the heart of *The Satanic Verses*. The questions it asks—"Who am I?" and "How does newness come into the world?"—may be old, but Rushdie gives them a new urgency as he ponders "the migrant condition." Rushdie has argued that mass migration has created radically new types of human beings: people who root themselves in ideas rather than places, in memories as much as in material things. Such people have been obliged to define themselves, because they are so defined by others, by their otherness. In a melting pot, strange mixes are made. *The Satanic Verses* succeeds on many fronts—managing to be at once narratively compelling, stylistically flamboyant, psychologically insightful, and sociopolitically relevant—and it succeeds most in that it creates a space where postcolonial and postmodern sensibilities intersect, where the migrant condition becomes a metaphor for all humanity.

Robert A. Morace

Bibliography:

Brennan, Timothy. *Salman Rushdie and the Third World: Myths of the Nation*. New York: St. Martin's Press, 1989. Discusses both the strengths and weaknesses of Rushdie's cosmopolitanism and the ways in which his fiction draws on Third World materials but does not adequately represent Third World concerns.

Harrison, James. *Salman Rushdie*. New York: Twayne, 1992. A good general introduction to Rushdie; separate chapters on the novels, Rushdie's biography, and India.

MacDonogh, Steve, ed. *The Rushdie Letters: Freedom to Speak, Freedom to Write*. Lincoln: University of Nebraska Press, 1993. In addition to the letters to Rushdie written by twenty-seven prominent writers, the volume includes essays by Rushdie and Tom Stoppard and Carmel Bedford's compilation, "Fiction, Fact, and the Fatwā."

Rushdie, Salman. *Imaginary Homelands: Essays and Criticism 1981-1991*. New York: Penguin, 1991. Several essays deal specifically with *The Satanic Verses* and the *fatwā*; many others, no less relevant, deal with various postcolonial topics.

Said, Edward. *Culture and Imperialism*. New York: Knopf, 1993. Although it includes no extended discussion of Rushdie and his novel, Said's book is required reading for anyone hoping to understand *The Satanic Verses* in the postcolonial context.

SATIRES

Type of work: Poetry
Author: Nicolas Boileau-Despréaux (1636-1711)
First published: Satires 1-7, 1666; 8-9, 1668; 10, 1694; 11, 1698; 12, 1711 (English translation, 1711-1713)

The name of Nicolas Boileau-Despréaux, or more usually Nicolas Boileau, is often linked only to *The Art of Poetry* (1674), his critical treatise setting down the rules and unities of French classicism. He received the mantle of prophet and lawgiver for that movement, which is something of a false emphasis. *The Art of Poetry* was a summary and compendium of standard poetic practices, of the rules French literature had been operating under for the entire century.

The modern student of literature may not realize the importance of Nicolas Boileau in the development of literary taste. The subjects of Boileau's satires resemble those of his classical predecessors and of his contemporaries in seventeenth century France. Modeling his work on the giants of the past, most noticeably Juvenal, Boileau attacks contemporary fashion and its excesses with a vitriol exceeding that of many less perceptive and less daring satirists. While only a dozen of his writings are formally designated satires, the satiric point of view colors all his writings, including *The Art of Poetry*.

The influence of Boileau on the development of literature should not be underestimated. For more than a hundred years Boileau was upheld as something like a literary dictator of Europe. His influence extended over England during the late seventeenth and throughout the eighteenth centuries. His work established on the Continent and in England a feeling of reverence for the authors of Greece and Rome. His support of the ancients over the moderns in his discussion of literary merit may seem strange, since on numerous occasions he expressed great admiration for his contemporaries Jean Baptiste Racine and Molière. He was nevertheless a vigorous defender of the classical methods of balance and restraint, contrasting their reserve with what he found to be the silly exuberances of most contemporary writing (especially the multivolume romances that were exceptionally popular in France). His pronouncements on the necessity to "follow nature"—which, in turn, meant to follow the practices of the great classical writers whose works mirrored nature—became dogma for authors both in France and abroad for the next century.

Despite his great influence on European ideas of what literature should be, Boileau may be best remembered as a practitioner, not a theoretician, of French verse. His *Satires* are a notable example of the skill with which he returned French poetry to a character of imitation of nature. Seventeenth century poetry had turned chiefly to the burlesque and heroic styles, which were highly conceited and artificial. With the *Satires*, written with common sense as a norm and the expression of truth as a goal, Boileau did much to purify his medium.

He had a genius for satire and ample opportunity to find subjects for his verse in the brilliant and sophisticated court of Louis XIV, the Sun King. The monarchy had become absolute in France, and the ideal of the courtier—the aristocratic, gracious, elegant, witty, refined, accomplished man—afforded ideal occasion for a satirist to comment upon the vanity, ambition, intrigue, and posturings that invariably accompany competition for royal favor.

Boileau was presented to the king in 1669. Despite his trenchant criticisms of the vices and foibles of society, he remained in favor at the court for thirty years. Not only was his frank and courageous outspokenness notable, but his benevolence, generosity and kindliness were as well. Accordingly, his satirical writings are not stinging lashes of vice, as with Juvenal, but a gentler ridiculing of humanity's failings. His twelve satires touch on many facets of the fashionable life of his times and give a lively indication of what it was like to live in seventeenth century Parisian society.

The second, seventh and ninth satires are concerned with the art and craft of the satirist and with Boileau's own fortunes in that calling. Boileau liberally criticizes his fellow poets and makes no pretense of acceding to public opinion about the merit of any writer. However high a poet's fashionable reputation may be, if he cannot rhyme Boileau says so. He attacks many of his contemporaries, but seldom drops into *ad hominem* criticism. Moreover, time has proven his opinions to be remarkably just: The names that receive most of Boileau's scorn have become as obscure to the present day as their poetry is mediocre. Likewise, those whom he praised remain as the outstanding seventeenth century French authors.

Satire 2, addressed to Molière, laments the difficulties of finding rhymes without having them tyrannize over the sense in a poem. In mock despair, and in perfectly-rhymed Alexandrines, Boileau rehearses the poet's plight, the necessity of either glib and vapid epithets to match a rhyme, or else wrenched syntax and broken phrases. In the seventh satire, Boileau discusses a tentative plan to banish satire from his writing, saying it is a malicious style that makes the author many enemies. He would much prefer to write poems of praise. Alas, however, all his poetic powers desert him at such an attempt; his talent, he concludes, lies in the exposure of folly, and a satirical poet he will have to remain. The ninth satire has a similar tone: The author affects to scold himself for his feeble efforts to reform the city by his verse. He points out the vanity of any hope for esteem of his work and says that the fools he castigates are not even worth spilling ink over. As the poem develops, it shifts subtly into an ironic ridicule of all the people who are the just subjects of the satirist's pen, and becomes a triumph, not a reproach, to Boileau.

Another group of satires is directed toward the life of the city, with its would-be aristocrats and pseudosophisticates. Satire 1 demonstrates how the poet is abused and neglected in the city, while the lackey, the toady, the pedant are all exalted, and all vices flourish. Satire 6 continues this theme with an account of the noise, dirt, confusion, and crime that surround the city dweller. These two were originally composed as one poem, in imitation of Juvenal's Satire 3. Boileau's third satire tells the uproarious tale of a feast given by a gourmand who pretends to be a gourmet and of the ridiculous pretensions to elegance and erudition of the host and his country-bumpkin guests. The execrable repast is reduced to shambles by a hair-pulling scuffle between the guests: one an absurdly aspiring poet, the other an absurdly aspiring literary critic.

Satires 5 and 6 catalog the excesses of the town by an inquiry into what constitutes true nobility and true honor. In Satire 5, hereditary nobility is ridiculed, along with its trappings of heraldry and elaborate equipage. Boileau shows how the bearer of a name famous of old for courage and daring may be an arrogant coward, retaining nothing of the virtue of his ancestors. On the other hand, a truly valorous man who is of humble descent ought to be able to adopt Achilles, Alexander, or Caesar for his ancestors, the author says, since he behaves like them. Ancient days, when nobility was a valid indication of virtue, are contrasted to the present, whose wretched aristocrats are so deep in debt that they must barter their titles for enough gold to maintain the ostentation considered essential for a peer. Satire 11 exposes similar abuses of the ideal of honor. This was written considerably later than the preceding poems, in 1698, at a time when Boileau's family was engaged in a lawsuit over the validity of their own hereditary title to the nobility (which was finally proven to be false). Various erroneous ideas about honor are shown: ambition, avarice, vanity. For Boileau, honor resides ultimately only in justice, and he castigates the inability of the self-interested and contentious to understand or practice justice.

To this point, the satires have all been directed against the specific failings of people, their personal failings and vices. In Satires 4 and 8, Boileau takes a broader view and attacks the condition of being human. Satire 4 argues that all people are mad, but all believe that they are sane. The theme developed is the perennial one of one's ability to see the mote in another's eye but not the beam in one's own. All are mad in their attachment to something: learning, refined manners, religion, atheism, wisdom, money, gambling, poetry. He concludes that it is probably better for people to be mad and happy than coldly reasonable with nothing to give them joy. Satire 8 takes a sharper tone on the same subject, the universal folly of humanity. Boileau adopts a mordant disdain for all human accomplishments, comparing people to beasts and finding the latter more humane in their activities. Depravity and corruption are everywhere, and even one's capacity for reason is so abused and ignored as to set one beneath the irrational animals. These two broader-ranging satires approach a kind of misanthropy not seen in the witty ridicule of foppery and the vanities of the others. All the poems, however, are in the traditional voice of the satirist, who is the gadfly of society, attempting to correct humanity's faults by turning on them the bright clear light of reason and common sense.

Another time-honored subject for the satirist is woman, and she has her place in the Boileau canon. His Satire 10 on women is the longest of the twelve. Not published until 1693, it is prefaced by an apology to the fair sex for the unkind portraits drawn therein, suggesting that since they are such near-perfect creatures, they cannot surely resent a well-meaning attempt to refine them a trifle more. The poem is a dialogue between Boileau and a friend, Alcippes, who has decided to take a wife. Boileau depicts the consequences of marrying various kinds of women: the adulteress, the coquette, the card-player, the penny-pincher, the shrew, the hypochondriac, the pedant, the falsely-pious. All these character vignettes are artfully and vividly portrayed and have a devastating effect upon the poor lover, Alcippes. When he vows his lady is none of these, the poet declares that he has not told a quarter of the vices women can have. The confused would-be bridegroom protests that in any case he can always divorce her if she should be so bad. Boileau then triumphantly adduces woman's final villainy: Once her claws are in a man she will never let him go.

The twelfth and last of Boileau's satires is quite different from the others. The satire is a serious attack on the problem of ambiguity in language deliberately used for evil ends. The meaning of *equivoque* (ambiguity, duplicity), expands through the poem, not only to indicate verbal ambiguity but also confusion of intentions, thoughts, expressions—all sorts of misconceptions of the human mind and, most seriously, the way these have altered and corrupted Christianity from its original purity and holiness. As a theological argument, the poem attacks everything that Boileau considered heresies, particularly Jansenism and Jesuitism. The sincerity of this piece is beyond doubt, for Boileau was all his life a good Catholic; but its poetic power is perhaps less than in some of the earlier pieces. For several years after its composition, the poem was not permitted publication.

Taken as a whole, the satires of Boileau are characterized more by a genial gaiety than any deep bitterness or spite toward their victims. There is malicious wit, but no indignant rage, and the butt of the joke is ridiculed rather than condemned. In all, the *Satires* are a delightful account of one man's view of a fascinating and glamorous era of French civilization.

"Critical Evaluation" updated by Laurence W. Mazzeno

Bibliography:

Haight, Jeanne. *The Concept of Reason in French Classical Literature: 1635-1690*. Toronto:

University of Toronto Press, 1982. Examines Boileau's efforts to associate reason with socially accepted behavior in seventeenth century France. Describes the connection between aesthetics and sociology in Boileau's writing.

Moriarty, Michael. *Taste and Ideology in Seventeenth-Century France*. Cambridge, England: Cambridge University Press, 1988. Explores the connection between Boileau's literary taste and his political ideology. Explains why Boileau's association of taste with an admiration for high culture caused him to reject representations of popular culture.

Pocock, Gordon. *Boileau and the Nature of Neo-Classicism*. Cambridge, England: Cambridge University Press, 1980. Examines the general themes and structures in the satires. Stresses Boileau's creative imitation of Horace and other classical Roman satirists.

White, Julian E. *Nicolas Boileau*. New York: Twayne, 1969. Introduction to Boileau's literary career and a fine annotated bibliography of important critical studies on his work. Examines his satires within the classical tradition of comedy of manners and describes Boileau's originality as a satiric poet.

Yarrow, P. J. *The Seventeenth Century: 1600-1715*. Vol. 2 in *A Literary History of France*. New York: Barnes & Noble Books, 1967. Traces the general evolution of French neoclassical literature during the seventeenth century. The chapter on Boileau describes the unity of his aesthetic and moral vision as expressed in his satires and in his theoretical writings.

SATIRES

Type of work: Poetry
Author: Juvenal (Decimus Junius Juvenalis, c. 60-c.130 C.E.)
First published: Saturae, 100-127 (English translation, 1802)

Juvenal is one of the greatest satirists and moralists of the world. Examination of the poet's influence on writers of generations succeeding his own bears out such an assessment. Often imitated, and even more frequently quoted, Juvenal has been venerated as one of the great practitioners of satire and one of the most penetrating commentators on the human condition.

The reaction to Juvenal has not been universally laudatory. More than one commentator has objected to his seemingly unmitigating attack on the evils of his age; his undisguised misogyny has also come under fire. Like his contemporary and friend, the epigrammatist Martial, he seems to have nothing good to say about anything associated with Rome or its citizenry. He vilifies the court of the emperors, the Roman nobility, a host of professions, and even the common citizens, whose lives he sees being wasted in the vain pursuit of pleasure and wealth. Whether addressing specific vices (such as those he criticizes in satires 4 and 6) or the general ills of humankind (the subject of his famous satire 10), Juvenal seems too unsparing in his portrayal of vice and corruption; seldom (some might say never) does he have a good word for anyone or any institution. As succeeding generations have noted, the evils he exposes are not unique to the Roman empire; avarice, sycophancy, lewdness, and self-centeredness exist in every society, and Juvenal's satires speak to readers of any age who can see the analogies between the satirist's times and their own.

The angry stance Juvenal takes in his poems has spawned a tradition of satire that has run for nearly two thousand years through European literature. Perhaps more than any other figure, he is the source of inspiration for the greatest of English satirists, Jonathan Swift. Juvenal and Swift have often been misunderstood because the negative tone of their writings obscures their writings' positive moral instruction, something that characterizes the work of the best satirists. Juvenal writes not simply to criticize, but to instruct, hoping that by exposing the foibles of humankind he might inspire thoughtful people to mend their ways and improve their lives.

Juvenal was born in Aquinum, southeast of Rome, also the birthplace of St. Thomas Aquinas. Few facts about him have survived outside those provided by his own writing, although a biography written in the fourth century said that he was the son of a freedman and practiced rhetoric until middle age for his own amusement—perhaps until he took up poetry. As a satirist, the vices of his age gave him material.

Born during the reign of Nero, he lived under nine other emperors, including Otho, of whom he was especially critical, and tyrannical Domitian. Juvenal's pictures of life in Rome are gloomy and bitter. He feared the growing power of the moneyed classes, the traders, and the freedmen. He disapproved of the softening influences of Greek and Eastern cultures and the vices they introduced. Some scholars have accused him of dwelling on vice for the pleasures he took in writing about immorality; his own claim was that he wrote to exalt virtue and encourage people to seek it.

He explained his choice of medium in his first satire. Having no desire to rewrite old plays or endless epics, and having seen a barber become wealthier than a partrician and an idiotic Egyptian advance himself at the expense of the Romans, he declared that "it is difficult not to write satires." His writing was little appreciated during his lifetime. Indeed, his satires disappeared for several centuries. Rediscovered, Juvenal was esteemed as an epigrammatist and social historian because of his vivid pictures of Latin life.

Sixteen satires, totaling 3,775 lines, made up the total preserved work of Juvenal. The poems vary in length from the little more than sixty lines of the unfinished satire 16, which deals with the prerogatives of a soldier, to the 661 lines of satire 6, directed against women, which is long enough to fill a papyrus roll by itself. His first book, containing 690 lines in all, includes his first five satires, of which satire 1, appropriately, explains why he turned to this form of literary activity. He declares that he began writing to pay back the many poets who have bored him, from crude Cordus, with his lengthy epics, to the writers of comedies and elegies. Since depravities on every side "rate the midnight oil of Horace," he bade the writer of satires to "set sail." Pondering, however, the advice of those who had warned him against the wrath of rulers, he declared his intention to dedicate his attention to the dead, those whose ashes lie along the roads outside Rome.

Satire 2, directed against effeminate men, put into circulation the familiar proverb that "one rotten apple spoils a whole barrel." This work describes the pretty boys with their long hair and their togas of pastel colors.

The whole of Rome was his target in satire 3. Hearing that his friend Umbritius was moving to Cumae to escape the vices of the capital, Juvenal commended his decision: "After all, it is something even in a lonely corner to make yourself the landlord of a single lizard."

In satire 4 he considers those able to escape the consequences of any crime because they are wealthy or highborn. In satire 5, he inveighs against stingy patrons and clients who have no sense of shame. He described the tasteless food provided for clients who came to the rich man's table, contrasting this fare with the delicious banquets served when only a few friends are invited in to dine.

The approaching marriage of Postumus gives the poet a motive for a coarse diatribe against the women of Rome in satire 6. In primitive times, he asserts, chastity existed on earth, but not among the Roman matrons of his time. He describes their beauty aids, their aimless lives, their extravagances, and their pretense to culture. Some even go as far as to forget their sex in their desire to be gladiators. He proposes a remedy: End the evils of an extended peace and the luxury that has taken the place of frugality and self-sacrifice.

Satire 7 laments the evil plight of men of culture when poets and historians cannot make a living and teachers, after years of preparation, get less money in a year than a successful jockey after one race. Blood is no reason for expecting respect, says Juvenal in satire 8. Retraced a few generations, even the noblest blood is mixed with the common. Deeds are more important. The brief satire 9 is a poem on pimps and informers. It is followed by the famous satire 10, adapted in 1749 by Samuel Johnson with the title *The Vanity of Human Wishes*. The poem states that few human beings know what is good or bad for them. Most people wish for health or honor. Students of rhetoric crave eloquence, the ruin of Demosthenes and Cicero. The ambitions of Alexander and Xerxes were their undoing. People desire long life, which brings ills, or beauty, which causes unhappiness. If people were wise, they would let the gods make the decisions. As Johnson translates it: "So raise for good the supplicating voice,/ But leave to Heaven the measure and the choice." If people must pray, they should ask for a healthy mind in a healthy body and a spirit reconciled to trouble or death.

Extravagance is the theme of satire 11, sent to Persicus along with an invitation to dinner. Many in Rome beggar themselves for pleasure, says Juvenal, but at Juvenal's table, his friend will eat what he can afford, simply served, and without lavish entertainment.

In a more mellow vein, Juvenal devotes satire 12 to his joy that his friend Catullus has been rescued after a shipwreck. His ceremonies of thanksgiving, however, are to be simple. He will not offer rich treasures to the gods as some legacy hunters have done. Then, not able to remain benevolent long, he ends with a jibe at Pacuvius, who profits from the misfortunes of others.

Calvinus, who complained loudly at being defrauded, is satirized in satire 13, and the avaricious Fuscinus in satire 14 is urged to provide a better example to his children. Satire 15 differs from the preceding, being in effect a parable about the rivalry of neighboring towns. Once one was kind to another; now vipers are less cruel to their fellows. Pythagoras, should he return, would be certain the beasts of the fields are superior to humans.

The final, unfinished, satire 16 represents a departure for the poet. He lists the special advantages that soldiers have over everyone else. The work breaks off with an unfinished sentence, in the middle of a line, without leaving the reader sure whether Juvenal really intends, for a change, to praise, or whether he is preparing to deflate, the military. There is no explanation of why Juvenal failed to finish the poem. Perhaps there is some truth in the story that he was either summarily banished or sent on a mission from which he never returned.

Bibliography:

Coffey, Michael. *Roman Satire*. London: Methuen, 1976. Groups the major satirists according to various traditions. Examines Juvenal's *Satires* with discussion of prevalent themes and such stylistic considerations as imagery and rhetoric. Extensive notes.

Duff, J. Wight. *Roman Satire: Its Outlook on Social Life*. Hamden, Conn.: Archon Books, 1964. Surveys the major satirists in terms of the larger social context. Final chapter explores Juvenal's anger, outspokenness, evocative dramatization, and use of detail.

Green, Peter. *The Shadow of the Parthenon*. Berkeley: University of California Press, 1972. Includes the essay, "Juvenal and His Age," which discusses the elusiveness of the writer and his obsession with avarice and luxury. Explores the difficulty of finding an overall structure or order for the sixteen *Satires*.

Highet, Gilbert. *Juvenal the Satirist*. Oxford, England: Clarendon Press, 1954. Provides a definitive volume on Juvenal's life and work. The bulk of this scholarly tome analyzes the sixteen *Satires* and looks at their influence and appraisal through various later ages. Useful indexes to persons, places, things, and passages in the works.

Knoche, Ulrich. *Roman Satire*. Translated by Edwin S. Ramage. Bloomington: Indiana University Press, 1975. In chapter on Juvenal, Knoche calls him the most serious of the satirists, focusing on social conditions rather than individuals. Included are summaries of the *Satires* and evaluations of modern editions.

SATIRES

Type of work: Essays
Author: Lucian (c. 120-c. 200 C.E.)
First transcribed: Nekrikoi dialogoi (*Dialogues of the Dead*, 1684), *Enalioi dialogoi* (*Dialogues of the Sea Gods*, 1684), *Theōn dialogoi* (*Dialogues of the Gods*, 1684), *Hetairikoi dialogoi* (*Dialogues of the Courtesans*, 1684), second century

Although Lucian was but one of many satirists who attacked the excesses of the Roman empire in the second century, he has the distinction of being one of the most influential of all practitioners of the genre. His works often seem motivated by personal animosity and inspired by self-serving principles, but he rises above invective to achieve a vision of humanity that has inspired countless writers who have followed him. Best known for his development of the satiric dialogue, in which characters reveal their own deficiencies as they defend themselves, Lucian managed to make from the many foibles and hypocrisies of his own day material for timeless analysis of humankind's greatest follies.

Condemned by Christian writers (and ultimately by the Catholic church) as an atheist for his scathing portrait of the deities in *Dialogues of the Gods*, he fell into disrepute in the West for more than a millennium; however, with the rediscovery of classical writings in the Renaissance, Lucian's reputation grew rapidly, and by the sixteenth century he had become one of the most widely read and influential satirists of all time.

The list of literary figures indebted to Lucian is long and contains the names of some of the most distinguished writers in the European tradition. Desiderius Erasmus and Thomas More fell under his spell. The rhetoricians and the dramatists of Renaissance England found his works compelling subjects for study. His satires, especially his work about Timon the misanthrope, inspired a number of works during this period, including plays by Ben Jonson, Francis Beaumont, and John Fletcher. William Shakespeare borrowed from Lucian not only for *Timon of Athens* (c. 1607-1608) but also for the famous graveyard scene in *Hamlet* (c. 1600-1601). John Dryden found him a useful mentor and wrote a brief biography for an edition of Lucian produced at the end of the seventeenth century. Lucian's *True History* is the model for Jonathan Swift's *Gulliver's Travels* (1726), the greatest of all English satires. In France, both François Rabelais in the sixteenth century and Voltaire two centuries later found inspiration in his writings. Prolific and caustic, Lucian fulfills admirably the role of the satirist, using humor and invective to promote social change.

The satires of Lucian are directed not so much against social customs and manners as against the ideological attitudes of men in the Roman empire. Of a conservative spirit, Lucian wanted to recall people to old ethical standards and values by exposing the shams and affectations of religion, philosophy, pedantry, and superstition. So vehement does he become in his attacks, it often seems that he is condemning not only the abuse of the thing but also the thing itself, particularly in the satires on philosophy.

The *Dialogues of the Gods* is composed of twenty-six conversations among the Olympian deities. Their own words condemn them, for in their bickering, gossip, complaints, and flatteries they show themselves to be as prideful and ignorant as human beings, and as much enslaved by their ignoble passions, so that they are not at all worthy of the awe and reverence that the mortals on earth accord them. Hera nags at Zeus because of his myriad love affairs; Asclepius and Herakles argue over precedence in seating at the dinner table; Hermes whines over all his work as messenger to the gods; Zeus scolds Helius for giving the sun-chariot to Phaeton; Apollo and

Hermes chat about the similarity of the twins Castor and Pollux; Ares whispers sedition behind Zeus's back; the Judgment of Paris is enacted. Each vignette develops its own little drama, and through them Olympus is lowered to the level of the common marketplace.

The *Dialogues of the Sea Gods* follows the same pattern. Poseidon comforts his son Cyclops after Odysseus has duped and blinded him; the river Alpheus rehearses his protestations of love for the river Arethusa; the metamorphoses of Proteus are marveled at by his friends as if he were a circus magician; nymphs and Nereids talk about their lovers and gossip about one another.

The satire in the *Dialogues of the Dead* is more penetrating and mordant. The residents of the Underworld, newly dead and long-dead, live together in uneasy fellowship. They still dispute over the petty things that concerned them when they were alive. Men who on earth were highly honored, fabulously wealthy, physically beautiful, are leveled to dry and uniform bones, but still they squabble over reputation, appearances, precedence. Cynics argue with epicureans, the once-poor taunt the once-rich, and Charon prays for war or plague on earth so he may collect more fares on his ferry. Achilles learns there is no glory on the far side of the Styx, but Alexander the Great tries unsuccessfully to impress his magnificence on his fellow shades. Menippus, the cynic philosopher, thrives in Hades because all his earthly activities were directed against the vanities that people lose at death. Socrates and Diogenes appear, also Agamemnon, Ajax, Tiresias, Menelaus, Paris—soldiers, courtiers, kings, and philosophers reduced to wandering shades who can do nothing but talk of the past.

Menippus the Cynic was one of Lucian's favorite characters, and he is frequently used as a touchstone for satirizing pretentiousness in philosophy and religion. In the dialogue that bears his name, Menippus tells his friend of a necromantic experiment he made in order to visit Hades. Troubled by the great discrepancy between the licentious freedom of the gods—as the poets describe them committing murders, rapes, incest, usurpations—and the strict laws forbidding mortals to engage in the same activities, Menippus goes to the philosophers to have the situation explained to him. He discovers them to be as helpless and vicious as ordinary people, and sometimes even more ignorant. Finally he decides to seek out the seer Tiresias in Hades and ask him how one should live. With the help of a Chaldean soothsayer, Menippus gains entrance to Hades; he sees the judgment of the dead and their punishments. In the Acherusian Plain of Hell he sees the common dead and the demigods, all indistinguishable, all reduced to dusty bones. Men who were kings on earth occupy, in Hades, the same allowance of space as beggars, and they are forced to tutor or sell fish or cobble shoes. The philosophers indefatigably carry on their learned disquisitions. While Menippus is in Hades, an assembly is called, which he attends. A decree is sent out against rich men on earth, that their souls after death be sent to inhabit asses for a quarter-million years, to learn humility. Finally finding Tiresias, Menippus explains his dilemma. The sage tells him the life of the ordinary person is best; one should shun clever logic and metaphysical speculation, live cheerfully, and work productively. Convinced, Menippus returns to earth.

In a companion piece to this satire, Menippus tells a friend of an aerial expedition he made to visit Heaven. After observing the vices and follies of mortals, and their ignoble goals and contemptible behavior, he vows to find a worthier occupation: to discover the divine order of the universe. When he observes the workings of the stars and the nature of earth, however, he can make no sense out of them. Again he goes to the philosophers, only to find them as confused as himself but too proud to admit it. Menippus then fashions a pair of wings for himself, one from an eagle, the other from a vulture, and from the top of Mount Olympus launches himself heavenward, hoping to get some firsthand information about the universe. A rest stop at the moon and a chat with Empedocles, whom he finds there, enables him to look down on the entire earth and its inhabitants going antlike and self-importantly about their affairs. All their crimes are revealed to him. Continuing on, he arrives in Heaven, is admitted to the presence of mighty Zeus, and explaines his mission. The god, forgoing his mighty mien, quizzes Menippus about weather conditions, the price of wheat, social news, and Zeus's own popularity among the people. Menippus is invited to a banquet, at which Zeus denounces to the company those philosophers about whom Menippus has been complaining. The gods decide to annihilate them all in four months' time. Menippus is returned to earth and deprived of his wings, for the gods cannot have mortals disturbing them whenever the mortals' fancy moves them. Finishing the narrative to his friend, Menippus goes off to tell the philosophers of the doom pronounced on them.

Another story of a journey is the dialogue of Charon and Hermes. Tired of his ferryman work, Charon takes a holiday to visit the earth and see what life is like, because he has long been impressed at how the dead so lament the loss of it when he conducts them to the underworld. Charon persuades Hermes to assist him, and the two pile up four mountains to give Charon a view of the world from a good vantage point. The greatest cities seem to him nothing but little animal dens. A charm of Hermes sharpens Charon's eyesight enough to see all human activities. He observes people striving for fame, glory, power, and wealth, never thinking of the death that broods over them, even as Charon broods. Solon, a wise man, is the only one aware of mortality, and Charon watches him vainly trying to warn King Croesus to take less interest in his gold. Charon, who has heard the dooms of many mortals pronounced by the Fates, watches the mortals and comments on the vanity of their strivings. He looks at the ostentatious tombs that the great provide for themselves and derides this worldly display. He asks to be shown the cities of Babylon, Ninevah, and Tyre, but Hermes tells him they have all been long destroyed. Wonderingly, Charon concludes that people are utter fools: Nothing they do either comes with them after death or endures after them on earth.

Philosophy receives another drubbing in another dialogue. Zeus auctions off philosophers: Pythagoras, Diogenes, Heraclitus, Socrates, Democritus, Epicureans, and Stoics. Various dealers question them and bid on them. Philosophy is sold as if it were any other commodity. In another dialogue, the philosophers, granted a day's respite from Hades, come up to earth to murder Lucian for his cavalier treatment of them. Lucian protests that he is a faithful admirer of philosophy and proposes that his case be formally tried, with Philosophy herself as the judge and the several philosophers as the jury. Philosophy agrees and brings her waiting-ladies, Virtue, Temperance, Justice, Culture, and Truth. The trial opens with Diogenes speaking for the prosecution. He accuses Lucian of ridiculing, parodying, and scorning philosophy, and of teaching his audiences to flout and jeer at philosophy also. Lucian replies that he never abused the true philosophers, but only those who corrupt the doctrines, the hypocrites who want to be honored as philosophers but behave like rogues. He describes the corruptions of philosophy he sees around him in the world, and he appeals at last to Truth to confirm his words. Truth and Philosophy agree, and even the philosophers are convinced; they acquit Lucian. Together they decide to separate the true practitioners and punish the false ones. They call all who claim to be philosophers to the Acropolis, to make their defense before Virtue, Philosophy, and Justice. Very few appear. Then Lucian calls out that gifts are to be distributed to philosophers, and a horde rushes in to receive the gifts. The latter group look more like philosophers than the honest ones. When Lucian takes a fishing rod baited with gold and figs and dangles it over the city, he catches a variety of specimens, all described according to the branch of philosophy they claim to represent, all like monstrous fish. There are so many of them that Philosophy decides to send Lucian out with Exposure to crown or brand them all as needed.

Lucian's other satires are numerous and equally pointed. In another, a cobbler's rooster turns out to be a reincarnation of Pythagoras. The cobbler complains about the injustice of his poverty, and the bird answers, showing the misery that often accompanies riches and the vices of wealthy men. The cobbler, Mycyllus, learns to be content with his station in life. The gods are again satirized and their dignities punctured in more dialogues. Further dialogues inspect superstitions and prejudices. Still not through, Lucian again attacks, in additional dialogues, philosophy, oratory, the gods, egotists, and parasites. Lucian's satire occasionally becomes so personal and venomous that it seems more a venting of spleen than a social corrective. It is always vivid and entertaining, however, and often uncomfortably just.

"Critical Evaluation" updated by Laurence W. Mazzeno

Bibliography:

Allinson, Francis G. *Lucian: Satirist and Artist*. New York: Longmans, Green, 1927. Excellent on the topic of the supernatural in Lucian, discussing his work in terms of its treatment of the ancient gods, superstition, and Christianity. Spells out the major influences on Lucian.

Baldwin, Barry. *Studies in Lucian*. Toronto: Hakkert, 1973. Traces the scant evidence concerning Lucian's life and speculates on who may have been Lucian's important friends and enemies. Strong emphasis is placed on Lucian's satire in comparison with that of other notable contemporaries. Stresses Lucian's intense involvement with "fashions and living issues" of his time.

Craig, Hardin. *The Written Word, and Other Essays*. Chapel Hill: University of North Carolina Press, 1953. The essay on "The Vitality of an Old Classic: Lucian and Lucianism" is a graceful appreciation of the best features of Lucian. The discussion of Lucian's skill with the dialogue is excellent.

Jones, C. P. *Culture and Society in Lucian*. Cambridge, Mass.: Harvard University Press, 1986. Three appendices and a seventeen-page bibliography. Separate chapters discuss, among other topics, Lucian's inconsistent treatment of philosophy, the "concealed victims" of the satires, and the gods and oracles.

Robinson, Christopher. *Lucian and His Influence in Europe*. London: Duckworth, 1979. Studies the literary features of Lucian's work, showing how Lucian was a product of the golden age of Rome and demonstrating how innovative he was. Lucian's ingenuity and humor are stressed, and his influence on later writers clarified.

SATIRES

Type of work: Poetry
Author: Persius (Aulus Persius Flaccus, 34-62 C.E.)
First published: Saturae, first century (English translation, 1616)

The *Satires* of Persius belong to a rich tradition in Roman literature. According to an ancient biography attached to the manuscripts of the *Satires*, Persius was born into an affluent family associated with Rome. His short life spanned the reigns of Tiberius, Caligula, Claudius, and Nero, a time characterized by increasing constraints on literary and personal freedom. Although Persius preferred a quiet domestic life to the busyness of urban literary and intellectual circles, he nevertheless shared friendships with many influential writers of his day, including the epic poet Lucan, the lyric poet Caesius Bassus, and, to some degree, the philosopher and politician Seneca.

It is impossible to understand Persius' intent in composing the *Satires* without a proper understanding of the philosophy of Stoicism, which so influenced his opinions. When sixteen years of age, Persius became the student of Lucius Annaeus Cornutus, an important Stoic philosopher and a freedman of Seneca's family. Stoicism was the preeminent philosophy among Roman writers and intellectuals, and its proponents were often at odds with the mechanisms of the imperial political regime. The basic tenet of Stoicism is that one should live a virtuous life with the soul in accord with the principle of divine reason; denial of passions that disrupt the soul and living free from extremes are of fundamental importance. Thus Persius, combining a philosophical conviction with poetic skills in satire, sought to expose and criticize those vices rampant in his own society.

In the first satire, Persius diagnoses the decay of Roman literary tastes concurrent with a decline in morality. He presents this satire as a dialogue between himself and a friend. The argument ensues after Persius recites a line of "superior" poetry, probably from Gaius Lucilius (a founder of Roman satire), and his friend remarks that too few people in Rome would spend time reading such fine literature. Persius responds that he is not concerned with the tastes of most Romans, and initiates his critique along Stoic lines.

To his friend's argument that one should be recognized for one's learning, Persius promptly suggests that the real benefit of knowledge is private, by which he implies that improvement of the soul is the goal. Persius notes that praise is most often mere remembrance in gossip. The friend accuses Persius of being prudish, but Persius responds that he is desirous of honest praise only, not that secured by favor or bribery.

Persius then sharpens his criticism of the writing produced in his own time. He complains that it is artificial and obsessed with rhetoric as a justified end, and that grandiose heroic acts are composed by writers who could not muster the attention to describe a mere grove in fine detail. The criticism of rhetoric—which succeeds only when passions are inflamed and people dragged along—is especially important, because rhetorical precision was of fundamental importance for public life under the emperors. Although Persius does not—and could not—criticize the increasing constraints on freedom of speech, he does manage to criticize its outcome.

Persius argues against other literary habits in vogue at that time, which he believed threatened direct and honest writing. Eventually he agrees to keep quiet, but only after he recalls Gaius Lucilius' observation that humanity has a great propensity for foolishness. This satire concludes with a petition from Persius for his readers to join him in celebration of superior writers and abandon the poor tastes of their society. The first satire is thus marked by the nostalgia common when a person attempts to distinguish good literature from inane competition, but it further carries the serious conviction of Stoic philosophy.

The second satire is critical of the hidden intentions behind most prayers. Persius wrote it to commemorate the birthday of a friend, Plotius Macrinus, and immediately names Macrinus as one who offers genuine prayers. Most men, Persius argues, offer the most selfless prayers in public and, in private, wish for the opposite: A man may publicly petition for his uncle's good health, while he privately waits for his death and the inheritance. Persius insists that Jupiter (the king of the gods in the Roman pantheon) finds no pleasure in these petitions nor the scant offerings traditionally given to secure the god's favor.

Persius turns his criticism from this depravity of saying one thing and intending another to human inconsistencies. He strikes quickly at superstitious beliefs and, in a superbly constructed point, takes aim at the person who eats lavishly but prays for health, and the man who makes expensive sacrifices but prays for wealth. Finally, he attacks the belief that the gods are subject to the same desires as humanity, and may thus be bribed accordingly. The second satire closes with a recommendation to cultivate a soul of noble generosity and integrity and not offer vain sacrifices with petitions for shallow gain.

The third satire condemns living without the benefits of a philosophical attitude and restraint, and reveals the appalling consequences of such a life. The poet seems to include himself among those who live poorly when they know better, but such self-criticism is typical of Stoic ethics.

The poem begins with a call to awaken from sleep, a metaphor that must not be overlooked. Persius notes all the common excuses given for procrastination, but his interlocutor reprimands such inactivity as mere childishness, which is not suitable as one matures. He warns that to continue on a path of indolence is to spoil one's opportunity to achieve a virtuous life. It is especially wicked for the person who encounters philosophy and learns to distinguish proper living from poor to neglect such duties. Thus, one must construct a plan for one's life, and not live subject to the whims of each day.

From line sixty-three to the end, the third satire turns to those people who have not yet enjoyed the benefits of a philosophical life, and Persius makes a conservative and dire observation regarding their immanent eternal slavery to ignorance. He insists that one must learn the general issues at stake in philosophy as soon as possible and dedicate one's life to them. The list of issues Persius provides reveals his own conviction in Stoicism's necessity, and he reflects on the ill treatment a philosopher receives from the common people. Persius does not offer a solution to this ridicule nor criticize the foolishness of the crowd, but implies their lives are deprived of true virtue and joy.

Persius concludes the third satire with a story of a man fallen ill, who returns to his poor habits once cured by his doctor and dies indulging in his lavish behavior. The third satire closes by arguing that those base impulses that stir the person to indulge in desires are a clear sign that although perhaps one is not yet gravely ill, symptoms do exist that only the sober life may rectify.

The fourth satire is the shortest, fifty-two lines. In it, Persius turns his attention to self-examination and opens with a criticism of those who put more stock in public affairs than in the virtuous improvement of their own lives. He initially addresses the poem to Alcibiades, the Athenian statesman, playboy, and maverick student of the philosopher Socrates. Alcibiades, the ward of the Athenian statesman Pericles, was blessed with an excellent upbringing and skill in speaking, but never knew his own psychological pitfalls. Persius' criticism is directed at both this type of person and the multitude who ignorantly follow such a person, passionately stirred up by his charms.

The poem then turns to a more general lament over the human habit to criticize and gossip about others while knowing so little of oneself, along with the fault that Persius terms "covering a secret wound behind a golden belt," the confusion of the public opinion of a person with the real person. The fourth satire closes with advice to shun the opinions of the crowd and hold oneself accountable to high personal standards. The final image is succinct and compelling: One should tend to one's own house, having realized how empty it is.

The fifth satire is the longest, at 191 lines. As does the second satire, it closely imitates Horace with respect to style and theme. The poem is dedicated to Persius' friend and mentor, Lucius Annaeus Cornutus, whose influence the poet joyfully recognizes in all aspects of his life. Persius first recalls his study under Cornutus at sixteen years of age, when he performed his coming-of-age ceremony and found himself at the mercy of adolescent temperament. He accredits Cornutus' teaching with saving his soul and setting straight his ethical standards. Persius respectfully suggests that they were fated to meet each other.

The remainder of the fifth satire turns with a critical eye to the vices of other people. Persius argues that each person is distinguished by his or her particular desires, and laments that so few follow the proper path of the Stoic's life, as Cornutus did. He offers that all people seek liberty, but few understand the genuine object of freedom; therefore, most people are slaves to their passions. The Stoic knows the best remedy: One must dedicate oneself to proper living, distinguish truth, and employ reason to live a moderate and self-controlled life, freed from inane desires that weaken the soul, especially the vices of avarice and lust. Persius satirizes those people whom he is accustomed to criticize: candidates for office who seduce the mob, the superstitious, and, finally, ignorant soldiers. The poem closes abruptly, following his list of senseless activities that bind the soul into some form of slavery.

The sixth satire is addressed to the lyric poet Caesius Bassus. In it, Persius assesses the virtues of moderate living and the difficulty such a life may cause for those not so inclined. Persius remarks that he has a good life, keeps at his estate away from the crowd, and meets his daily needs without great concern for hoarding wealth or, conversely, indulgence in trivial expenditures.

Persius turns his criticism toward common arguments against his way of life, most notably those offered by the fault-finding troublemaker (he uses the name "Bestius," taken from Horace) or the heir who threatens to neglect proper funeral rites—which the Romans perceived as a dishonor and threat to one's final rest—unless his avarice is fed. To this heir, Persius offers a discussion that meanders in presentation, but essentially argues that he would not presently starve himself that someone in the future may grow fat. In this way, Persius presents the Stoic emphasis on moderation. The poem closes with a satiric encouragement of vice, by which he emphasizes the imminent danger of such a life.

Persius' style is difficult and, as mentioned before, often imitates Horace. His moderate lifestyle, distant from the rigors of urban demands, helped to establish a secure, if not grand, reputation for him. Persius' contributions are important to the legacy of Roman satire and reveal much about his society and the nature of philosophical and literary protest in imperial Rome. They further present a fine study of Stoicism's potential influence on the young, and their insistence on moderation attracted many subsequent writers, most notably the seventeenth century English poet John Dryden, who made one of the earliest translations.

Stephen C. Olbrys

Bibliography:

Coffey, Michael. *Roman Satire*. New York: Barnes & Noble Books, 1976. Places Persius within his literary and historical context; chapter 6 offers a particularly thorough summary. Introduces basic issues of classical scholarship at stake in Persius.

Morford, Mark. *Persius*. Boston: Twayne, 1984. Superbly detailed explanation of the *Satires* and a discussion on Persius' style and influence. Includes a copious bibliography of primary and secondary sources, interesting notes, a chronology, and an index. The best book for a beginner's study of Persius.

Nisket, R. G. M. "Persius." In *Satire: Critical Essays on Roman Literature*, edited by J. P. Sullivan. Bloomington: Indiana University Press, 1968. Studies Persius and the *Satires* within their literary context. Thought-provoking source for a thorough introduction to Persius.

Reckford, K. J. "Studies in Persius." *Hermes* 90, no. 4 (October, 1962): 476-504. A fine, although technical, overview of aspects in Persius' literary technique and influences. For more advanced study of the *Satires*.

Rudd, Niall, trans. *The Satires of Horace and Persius*. New York: Penguin, 1973. A superior translation in blank verse of the *Satires*. The introduction provides useful information for beginning students of Persius' life and craft. Includes notes to the translation.

SATIROMASTIX
Or, The Untrussing of the Humourous Poet

Type of work: Drama
Author: Thomas Dekker (c. 1572-1632)
Type of plot: Satire
Time of plot: c. 1100
Locale: England
First performed: 1601; first published, 1602

Principal characters:
WILLIAM RUFUS, king of England
SIR WALTER TERRILL, his noble follower
CAELESTINE, Sir Walter's bride
SIR QUINTILIAN SHORTHOSE, the bride's father
MISTRESS MINIVER, a wealthy widow
SIR VAUGHAN AP REES, a Welshman, suitor of the widow
SIR ADAM PRICKSHAFT, another suitor of the widow
CRISPINUS, a poet
DEMETRIUS, another poet
HORACE, the humorous poet
ASINIUS BUBO, Horace's admiring follower
CAPTAIN TUCCA, a roaring roisterer

The Story:

While Sir Quintilian Shorthose supervised the preparations for the marriage of his daughter Caelestine, Sir Adam Prickshaft, Sir Vaughan ap Rees, and Mistress Miniver came to share in the festivities. All three knights were enamored of the widow. When the bridal party entered, Sir Walter Terrill, the groom-to-be, announced that King William Rufus would grace the wedding with his presence. The groom had sent to the poet Horace for a wedding song.

Horace was laboring by candlelight, surrounded by books, when his admiring friend Asinius Bubo visited him. Bubo warned that Crispinus and Demetrius planned to put Horace in a play as a bricklayer. To the great embarrassment of Horace, Crispinus and Demetrius entered and accused him of unfair attacks on them.

Soon Blunt, accompanied by Captain Tucca, came to get the wedding verses, but Horace confessed he had not been able to finish them in the three days allotted him. Captain Tucca blasted Horace with a stream of Rabelaisian abuse for writing satires about him. Quivering with fear, Horace apologized and promised future good behavior. The captain tipped him generously, and the visitors left.

The three knights urged Mistress Miniver to choose one of them for her second husband, but their talk was interrupted by the arrival of King William Rufus and his train. The king greeted the bride with a kiss, obviously taken with her beauty and charm. During the dance he managed to single her out frequently, engaging in risque banter. When the ladies withdrew, the king dared Sir Walter to postpone the wedding night and to trust his bride at court alone with the king. Goaded with lack of faith in her, Sir Walter unwisely promised to send her.

In spite of Horace's love letters purchased by Sir Vaughan, the widow refused him, favoring Sir Adam. Enraged, Sir Vaughan asked Horace to write a satire on baldness, since Sir Adam was bald. Sir Quintilian, needing a messenger to speak for him, turned to raucous, foul-mouthed Captain Tucca. The captain also agreed to carry rich gifts to the widow from Sir Adam. However, Captain Tucca wooed for himself. Later, the captain was shown a new series of satirical epigrams by Horace of which the captain was subject.

Sir Vaughan entertained the widow at a banquet, at which Horace read his satire on baldness. Mistress Miniver announced she could never be "enameled" of a baldheaded man again. Captain Tucca burst in and threatened Horace; Sir Vaughan drove him out, but Mistress Miniver called after the captain, demanding that he return the money she had lent him. Sir Vaughan rushed after the captain to punish him. Bubo showed Horace a challenge left by the fire-eating Captain Tucca.

Captain Tucca promised Sir Adam he would have Crispinus and Demetrius praise baldness in verse. Bubo and Horace came to the captain for a parley, and the three made peace again. Captain Tucca convinced Sir Vaughan that borrowing the money had been part of his plan to help the knight win the widow. At the next gathering of the widow's friends, Crispinus read his praise of baldness; then Captain Tucca aroused the whole group to take Horace to court and punish him for his sharp satires.

Sir Walter, Sir Quintilian, and Caelestine lamented her danger, and Sir Quintilian proposed that she drink poison. Grief-stricken, Sir Walter consented to the loss of his wife in order to save her honor. When revelers came to escort the couple to court, Sir Walter announced his wife's death and requested that they go with him in procession to the king.

King William Rufus, laughing at the gullibility of Sir Walter, waited eagerly for the coming of the bride. Sir Walter, dressed in black, escorted the body into the king's presence. Seeing Caelestine lifeless, the king cried out in horror. Sir Walter accused the king of tyranny and explained that Caelestine had chosen to die rather than to lose her honor; Sir Walter's oath was kept by his bringing her body to the king. Shame overcame the repentant monarch. Caelestine revived, and Sir Quintilian told how he had given her a potion which gave the appearance of death, though both Sir Walter and she had believed it poison. The king restored the wife unharmed to her husband.

Crispinus offered an interlude for comic relief after the seriousness of the situation. Captain Tucca led Horace and Bubo, both wearing horns, into the royal presence. Bubo was made to swear he would abandon Horace and his poetry; upon swearing this, he was released. Horace, crowned with nettles instead of laurels, promised at great length to reform as a writer and to give up sour criticisms and complaints. Captain Tucca announced that he and Mistress Miniver were to be married. The disgruntled knights accepted defeat, and Captain Tucca promised to repay them what they had given him for their wooing of the widow. A dance followed, and all ended happily.

Captain Tucca delivered an epilogue promising future theatrical battles between Horace and the poetasters.

Critical Evaluation:

Satiromastix owes its fame to its attack on Ben Jonson. Apparently the play was patched up in some haste in order to reply to Jonson's *Poetaster* (1601), which caricatures Thomas Dekker and John Marston. The literary community of Renaissance London was a relatively small but highly active arena, in which personal and professional egos frequently collided. Clashes such as the "Harvey-Nashe Controversy" and dueling pamphlets and verses were numerous. Conflicts were even more frequent among the playwrights and actors.

During the 1599-1600 theatrical season, London experienced a War of the Theaters, in which rival stage companies sniped at one another through increasingly sharp and satirical attacks written into their new productions. The playwright who became the acknowledged leader in these attacks was Ben Jonson. Already known as a satirist, his highly unflattering portraits of his fellow dramatists reached a climax in *Poetaster*, in which he singled out Thomas Marston (as Crispinus) and Thomas Dekker (as Demetrius Fannius) for special attack. Jonson scored points against the two as being incompetent as writers, unlearned as scholars, and unsuccessful as businessmen. The two writers, with Dekker apparently doing most of the composition, responded with *Satiromastix*, which contained their own powerful assault on Jonson.

This particular aspect of the play—its intensely topical, transitory, and highly specific satire—has caused problems for critics and scholars since the initial production in 1601; they frequently cite Dekker's "unbalanced" dramatic structure, which restricts the main plot to a relatively few scenes, while allowing a subplot and the satirical lampoon on Jonson to overwhelm the action.

There are three plot lines in *Satiromastix*. The first centers on the marriage of Sir Walter Terrill and his bride Caelestine. At their wedding feast, the young couple is accosted by William Rufus, king of England, who demands that Caelestine spend her wedding night at his palace. He clearly intends to seduce the young bride, but because of his royal rank, his request cannot be denied. Caelestine's father gives her a drug that causes her to fall into a swoon that mimics death. Her supposedly lifeless body is delivered to William Rufus, who, when told she took poison to preserve her honor, is overcome by guilt. He confesses his ignoble intentions and begs forgiveness, at which point Caelestine revives. This, supposedly the major action of the play, is stretched throughout five acts, with the story being told in small bits and pieces often interrupted by other activity.

The secondary plot concerns the wealthy widow, Mistress Miniver, who is being wooed by an assortment of suitors. Through an increasingly bawdy and suggestive string of puns and other wordplay, this comedic subplot becomes the major force of the play.

Finally, there is the attack on Jonson, known as the poet "Horace." Horace is introduced into the action when Sir Walter hires him to compose wedding verses for his own marriage to Caelestine. Later, Mistress Miniver's suitors also employ Horace to write letters and epigrams for themselves. Horace is a hack, and not a very good one at that.

Dekker vigorously assaults Horace (that is, Jonson) for a variety of faults and failings, including poetic incompetence, moral and artistic bankruptcy, personal cowardice, and physical ugliness. Specifics of Jonson's own past—his early career as a bricklayer, his notorious ill temper, even the fact that he once killed a fellow actor in a duel and was tried for manslaughter—are made attributes of Horace, who is portrayed as a bumbling, bragging artistic fraud. In an especially telling stroke, Dekker lifts the character of Captain Tucca, who was created by Jonson in *Poetaster*, uses this figure, already closely associated with Jonson and his work, to attack Jonson. The bombastic captain, who carried much of the assault on Dekker and Marston in *Poetaster*, has his character completely reversed and his strokes are aimed at Jonson, his creator.

The attacks on Jonson are meant to answer to charges in *Poetaster. Satiromastix* may actually have preceded Jonson's play in production, thus serving as a first strike in the War of the Theaters. Dekker's play is uninhibited and unreserved in its unflattering portrait of Jonson and, while *Satiromastix* is considerably inferior to *Poetaster* in artistic achievement, it seems to have been an effective response to Jonson, for Jonson attempted no answer to Dekker.

The successful satirical attacks on Jonson weaken *Satiromastix* as a drama. Critics generally agree that Dekker, or Dekker and Marston as collaborators, took an almost-completed work by

Dekker and adapted it into a response to *Poetaster*. The result was a series of individually well-written satirical scenes that, hastily inserted into the play, disrupt the dramatic progress and development. By the final act, the attacks on Horace almost completely dominate the stage, reducing the resolution of the story of Sir Walter and Caelestine to a rapid summary quickly and not quite convincingly presented.

In *Satiromastix* Dekker creates one of his typical dramas, a tragicomedy that combines an intriguing plot with a fairly light examination of moral and ethical issues. This play is loosely connected to two extensive subplots. These subplots are overlaid with an extensive, highly personal assault on Ben Jonson as a person and as a writer. The result is an interweaving of some excellent, telling satire with a conventional drama.

"Critical Evaluation" by Michael Witkoski

Bibliography:

Champion, Larry S. *Thomas Dekker and the Traditions of English Drama*. New York: Peter Lang, 1985. A good, general overview of Dekker's writings and a helpful guide to his place in the dramatic literature of the time.

Hoy, Cyrus Henry. Introduction to *The Dramatic Works of Thomas Dekker*, edited by Fredson Bowers. Cambridge, England: Cambridge University Press, 1980. A well-rounded survey of Dekker's stage works, with emphasis on their composition and production. It is helpful to have the dramas and their critical examination so closely connected.

Kernan, Alvin. *The Cankered Muse*. New Haven, Conn.: Yale University Press, 1959. A study of the rival theatrical companies and playwrights of Elizabethan London and the impact of their controversies on the dramas of the period.

Logan, Terence P., and Denzell S. Smith, eds. "Thomas Dekker" in *The Popular Schools*. Lincoln: University of Nebraska Press, 1975. A sourcebook for additional information about Dekker and his plays.

Price, George. *Thomas Dekker*. New York: Twayne, 1969. Covers Dekker's life and work and is especially good in placing him within the context of his times. Valuable for those beginning to study Dekker.

THE SATYRICON

Type of work: Short fiction
Author: Petronius (Gaius Petronius Arbiter, c. 20-c. 66 C.E.)
Type of plot: Satire
Time of plot: First century
Locale: Italy
First transcribed: c. 60 (English translation, 1694)

Principal characters:
ENCOLPIUS, the narrator
ASCYLTUS, his friend
GITO, their attendant
EUMOLPUS, a poet
TRIMALCHIO, a wealthy vulgarian

The Story:

Encolpius railed at the growth of artificiality in modern rhetoric and the ill-prepared students who came to the school. Agamemnon, the professor, agreed with him but placed the blame entirely on parents who refused to make their children study. Weary of the dispute and far gone in drink, Encolpius fled the school. An old woman, who made indecent proposals to him, showed him the way back to his inn.

Gito, his sixteen-year-old slave, had prepared supper, but the comely boy was crying: Ascyltus had made violent love to him. Encolpius was soothing the boy with caresses and tender words when Ascyltus broke in on them. A quarrel ensued between the two friends as to who should enjoy Gito's favors. The dispute was settled only when all three agreed to pay a visit to Lycurgus, a rich friend of Ascyltus. Lycurgus received them most cordially and introduced them to Lichas, his friend. Lichas, completely taken with Encolpius, insisted that Encolpius and Gito come home with him. On the way, Tryphaena, a beautiful woman attached to Lichas' entourage, made surreptitious love to Encolpius, who resolved to have little to do with Lichas. When the party arrived at Lichas' villa, Tryphaena deserted Encolpius for the bewitching Gito. Smarting under her desertion, Encolpius made love to Doris, Lichas' attractive wife. All went fairly well until Gito tired of Tryphaena. Then she accused both Gito and Encolpius of making improper advances, and the two returned in haste to Lycurgus' house.

Lycurgus at first supported the two adventurers, but as the jealous Lichas increased his complaints, Lycurgus turned against the pair. At the suggestion of Ascyltus, the three set out again to seek what love affairs and plunder they could find. They were well supplied with gold, for Encolpius had thoughtfully plundered one of Lichas' ships before leaving.

A fair was in progress at a nearby small town. There they came upon a groom who was saddling a rich man's horse. When the groom left for a moment, Encolpius stole the rich man's riding cloak. Soon afterward Ascyltus found a bag of coins on the ground. The two friends hid the gold by sewing it under the lining of Encolpius' threadbare tunic. Just as they finished, the rich man's retainers gave chase to recover the riding cloak. Dashing through a wood, Encolpius was separated from his friend and lost the tunic. They met again at a market. There they saw the tunic up for sale with the pieces still hidden in the lining. When they offered to trade the riding cloak for the tunic, the bystanders became suspicious and tried to make the two friends appear before a judge. Dropping the riding cloak and seizing the tunic, they fled.

After telling Gito to follow later on, they set out for the next town. Seeing the dim forms of two comely women hurrying through the dusk, they followed them unobserved into an underground temple. There the two men saw a company of women in Bacchanalian garb, each with a phallic emblem in her hand, preparing to worship Priapus. They were discovered by the horrified women and chased back to their inn.

As they were dining with Gito in their rooms, the maid of one of the women whom they had followed to the sacred rites came in and begged them to listen to her mistress, who was a respectable matron. Even though Encolpius swore never to tell of the forbidden rites, the matron had the three seized and taken to her villa. The men were bound and given powerful love potions, and then all the women of the household made love to them. After escaping from the love-maddened ladies, Encolpius had to rest for three days; Gito seemed little affected.

Next the three attended a huge banquet given by Trimalchio, a rich and vulgar freedman. After hours of eating and drinking, they were glad even for the respite of storytelling. Trimalchio started off with a boring elucidation of the signs of the zodiac, and many of the guests told pointless anecdotes. From Niceros, however, they heard an absorbing tale. While still a slave, Niceros was staying at an inn where he was in love with the landlord's complaisant wife, Melissa. One day he induced a soldier to go for a walk with him. When they came to a graveyard, the soldier took off his clothes and threw them beside the path. Making a magic circle around the clothes, he straightaway turned into a wolf and went howling away. When Niceros saw to his horror that the clothes had turned to stone, he hurried home to Melissa. She told him that a wolf had just come into the yard and killed some sheep. A servant drove a spear through the animal's neck but the wolf escaped. Niceros ran back to the cemetery, where he found that the stone clothes had dissolved in blood. In the morning he went to the soldier's room. There a physician was stanching the blood from a wound in the soldier's neck.

Encolpius, Ascyltus, and Gito were finally so stuffed and bored they could stand no more. To their relief, the company moved outdoors to exercise. They learned from the conversation that another banquet was to follow, this one given by Trimalchio's wife. They left hurriedly. Following another quarrel over Gito, Encolpius and Ascyltus parted company. To the distress of Encolpius, Gito elected to go with Ascyltus.

After sorrowing uselessly for days, Encolpius fell in with an old man, the poet Eumolpus. When the two went to the baths to cement their friendship, Encolpius was overjoyed to find Gito acting as attendant for Ascyltus, who was in another room. Gito confessed that he really liked Encolpius better; in a happy mood, Encolpius took the boy back to his apartment.

Matters would have been smoother for Encolpius if he had not tried to make love to Circe. As a result of his past tribulations and hardships, he had no strength for her ardors. Suspecting him of trifling with her, she raised such an outcry that Encolpius judged it wise to leave town.

On Eumolpus' advice, the comrades embarked secretly at night on a ship lying in the harbor. In the morning, Encolpius discovered to his chagrin that they were aboard Lichas' ship. The owner and Tryphaena were aboard. Eumolpus tried to disguise Encolpius and Gito with burnt cork. Nevertheless, their subterfuge was discovered, and for awhile it looked as though they would be flogged. Lichas, however, remembered his old attraction to Encolpius, and Tryphaena was smitten anew with Gito; so they were spared.

When Lichas' ship was wrecked in a storm, the three comrades got ashore at Croton. Eumolpus posed as a rich landowner, and Encolpius and Gito passed as his slaves. By cleverly deluding the inhabitants, they lived luxuriously as guests of the town. After a year suspicion grew as to Eumolpus' supposed wealth. Seeing an end to their pleasant stay, Encolpius and Gito escaped just in time. The aroused townspeople used Eumolpus as a scapegoat. They decked him out with boughs and sacred vestments, led him through the city, and hurled him down a cliff.

Critical Evaluation:

The Satyricon is a mere fragment of an extremely complex medley of stories that, in the complete version, perhaps were part of a mock-epic prose romance. Attached to the manuscript of *The Satyricon*, which was discovered in 1663 at Trau in Dalmatia, was a scribe's note describing the contents as taken from the "fifteenth and sixteenth books." If this information is correct, the original work must have been enormously long. For centuries, scholars have disputed the purpose, scope, and meaning of the whole work. Not even the name of the author is accepted for certain. By tradition, *The Satyricon* is attributed to Gaius Petronius—better known as Petronius Arbiter, the arbiter of the court of Nero. Tacitus' famous description of the death of Gaius Petronius seems to correspond well with the reader's perception of the writer of such a book: a refined voluptuary, clever but cynical, practical, sophisticated in his knowledge of the pleasures and vices of ancient Rome. Apart from Tacitus' brief account concerning Petronius, nothing is known for certain about the origin or reception of his book, and the fragment that remains has often been misinterpreted.

One major problem in reading *The Satyricon* in English is that many translations, particularly those of the nineteenth and early twentieth centuries, are corrupt. Some translators, because of prudery, have cut from the text whole portions that they consider offensive. Others have interpolated sections that are clearly not Petronius'; these additions, for the most part, err in the opposite direction: They are passages of deliberately and crudely obscene material that surpass in indelicacy the author's refined erotic language. In general, the best translation of *The Satyricon* is by William Arrowsmith, whose vigorous, honest, and sensitive version closely approximates the qualities of the Latin original. Readers of Latin may examine with confidence the modern scholarly editions by Alfred Ernout and E. T. Sage, or the older but still useful edition by W. D. Lowe. The reader, however, must be cautioned about poor English translations that markedly alter the content or misconstrue the tone of the Petronius model. These inadequate translations, for the most part, cut out all or most of the poetical selections. A simple test to determine whether or not a given translation is faithful to the source is to check Eumolpus' long verse passage entitled "The Civil War"; accurate translations will include the whole passage, although the poem, allusive and rhetorically pompous, may seem tedious to some readers.

In its context, Eumolpus' poem imitates or parodies heroic style. Petronius delights to parody conventions of language or literary form. The title of his work has been variously translated as "medley" (from *satura*, a mixed dish, from which the word "satire" is derived) or as "satyr-book" (from *saturika*, that is, concerned with satyrs and hence lecherous). From the fragment that exists, *The Satyricon* may be taken in both senses, as a Roman "satire"—a farrago of mixed stories using a multitude of styles—and as a book of comic-erotic adventures pleasing to satyrs. Within the main plot concerning the adventures of Encolpius are interwoven many stories or parts of stories, in the manner of popular Greek tales (or of their imitated Roman counterparts, of which Apuleius' early second century *The Golden Ass* is a famous example). The most remarkable of the stories is Eumolpus' "The Widow of Ephesus," a cynical narrative that has served many later writers and dramatists including—to choose only English authors—George Chapman and Christopher Frye. Although Eumolpus' story may be extracted from the plot as a perfect short piece, in the context of the action (Encolpius, Gito, and Eumolpus are aboard the ship of their enemies, Lichas and Tryphaena), the anecdote takes on additional ironic meanings. Similarly, the stories that abound within stories of *The Satyricon* acquire richer tones of irony, satire, or comedy, depending upon the context at the moment. Petronius' chief device is parody, to either amuse or ridicule, and the stories furnish ample subjects for literary and social burlesques.

Although *The Satyricon* belongs to the genre of Menippean satire—a mixture of verse with prose, philosophy with low comedy, romance with realism—the word "satire," as it is commonly understood, should not be applied to the book. Troubled by Petronius' outspoken and often coarsely erotic subject matter, some prudish commentators have attempted to apologize for the work on the grounds of its supposed moral satire. To be sure, the picture of Roman manners and morals that the author provides is one of vulgarity and excess. Petronius, however, is neither a Christian moralist nor, for that matter, a moralist in the stamp of Juvenal. Far from ridiculing the corruption of contemporary morals, he approaches his subject with amused tolerance. Even the great scene of Trimalchio's banquet, widely regarded as a keen satire upon Roman debauchery, may be seen in a different light as a comic burlesque upon vulgar ostentation. The tone of Petronius' irony is sprightly rather than censorious. If the author has a moral argument to demonstrate, he skillfully conceals it.

Similarly, any notion that *The Satyricon* is intended as a social satire—one concerned with the degradation of Roman culture—must be examined cautiously in terms of Petronius' moral ambivalence. Although his major characters are clearly homosexual (some are less clearly bisexual) and parasitical, they are not treated as objects of ridicule; instead, they are shown as amusing rogues, foolish or crafty, successful or unfortunate. The main character, Encolpius (whose name is roughly translated as "the crotch") is easily misled, especially by the guiles of his homosexual partner, the sixteen-year-old, narcissistic Gito; Encolpius is cheated and abused by his rival for Gito's affections, the devious Ascyltus; another rival is the old pederast Eumolpus, the poet. In the world of *The Satyricon*, homosexual intrigues are taken as a norm and are treated casually. As a youth, Trimalchio began to earn his fortune through his sexual compliance with his master. To be evenhanded, Petronius treats heterosexual relations with the same casual tolerance. His women are as sexually assertive as the men. Quartilla, Tryphaena, Circe, Chrysis, Corax—all are aggressive, earthy, lusty types quite the equal of their lovers. Yet the reader should not conclude from the evidence of Petronius' story that he judges Roman society harshly. Rather, he takes men and women as he finds them, observes their habits with cool, realistic detachment, and—in the section dealing with obscenity, following the Circe episode—refutes the charges that his book is obscene. The matter rests ultimately with the reader, who may regard Petronius' fragment as a work either of social criticism or of mock-epic romance.

Judged from the second point of view, *The Satyricon* describes the fortunes of Encolpius, who has apparently aroused the wrath of the sex-god Priapus. Throughout the book, the god's vengeance pursues his hapless victim. Against his will, Encolpius must take part in the orgy of Quartilla, priestess of the cult of Priapus; with Circe he is humiliated by his impotence. He always tries to free himself from blame but only manages to offend Priapus more seriously (as when he kills a pet goose sacred to the god). Encolpius' adventures may be understood as a parody of Odysseus' in the Homeric epic. Just as Odysseus outraged the god Poseidon and suffered from mistreatment as a consequence, so Encolpius apparently is tormented by Priapus. If the comparison drawn from the fragment is apt, the complete *Satyricon* must have been a prose mock-epic of great scope and richness, recalling the later James Joyce's *Ulysses* (1922), which, modeled upon the *Odyssey* (c. 800 B.C.E.), parodies heroic and literary conventions. *Ulysses* and *The Satyricon* are replete with puns, verbal games, and innovative stylistic techniques, and, through myth and symbolic action, create their own moral universe.

"Critical Evaluation" by Leslie B. Mittleman

Bibliography:

Auerbach, Erich. "Fortunata." In *Mimesis: The Representation of Reality in Western Literature*. Translated by Willard R. Trask. Princeton, N.J.: Princeton University Press, 1968. A masterly study of Trimalchio's banquet that contrasts Petronius' treatment of *fortuna* with Homer's.

Bagnani, Gilbert. *Arbiter of Elegance: A Study of the Life and Works of C. Petronius*. Toronto: University of Toronto Press, 1954. Includes discussions of the date and authorship, Roman propaganda literature, the language of *The Satyricon*, and a comparison of Alexander Pope and Petronius.

Slater, Niall W. *Reading Petronius*. Baltimore: The Johns Hopkins University Press, 1990. Explores the humor of *The Satyricon* through an initial linear reading, two readings focusing on various language systems and on Petronius' comedic purpose, or lack thereof.

Sullivan, J. P. *"The Satyricon" of Petronius: A Literary Study*. Bloomington: Indiana University Press, 1968. Discusses authorship and date of *The Satyricon*, Petronius' choice of form, satire, criticism, and parody in the work, the author's humor, and sexual themes.

Todd, Frederick Augustus. "*The Satiricon* of Petronius." In *Some Ancient Novels: "Leucippe and Clitophon," "Daphnis and Chloe," "The Satiricon," "The Golden Ass."* Freeport, N.Y.: Books for Libraries Press, 1968. In his contrast of *The Satyricon* with earlier classical romances, Todd declares Petronius' work to be unique in his use of common, highly individualistic characters, realistic scenes, and lack of rhetorical flourish. He points out that Petronius suits the language to the character and is one of the chief sources for information about spoken Latin.

SAUL

Type of work: Drama
Author: Vittorio Alfieri (1749-1803)
Type of plot: Tragedy
Time of plot: Eleventh century B.C.E.
Locale: Gilboa, Israel
First published: 1788 (English translation, 1815); first performed, 1794

Principal characters:
SAUL, the aging king of Israel
DAVID, the exiled commander of Saul's forces
JONATHAN, Saul's son and friend of David
MICHAL, Saul's daughter and David's wife
ABNER, Saul's cousin and present commander of his forces
AHIMELECH, the priest of Nob

The Story:

After his famous victories over the Philistines, which began with his triumph over the giant Goliath, David had risen to great power in Saul's kingdom. He had become the best friend of Saul's son and heir, Jonathan, had entertained Saul with his music, and had married Saul's daughter, Michal. David's success and popularity, however, had made Saul so jealous and envious that he drove David from Israel and threatened to kill him if he returned from exile. Saul had fallen from favor with God (Jehovah) when he failed to execute the captured Amalekite king, Agag, but he did not blame himself. Instead, in his madness he came to fear that David was scheming to assassinate him.

Knowing of the upcoming battle with the Philistines, David slipped back to the Israelite camp in the night and met with Jonathan and his wife, whom he had not seen for a long time. Jonathan informed him that Abner, the king's cousin and a conniving courtier, was deceiving the insane king and encouraging him to kill David. David's plan was to abase himself before Saul and beg his pardon, although he knew he had done no wrong.

When Saul appeared, he complained about his age and the loss of his champion, but Abner insisted that David was the cause of Saul's misfortunes, along with the now dead priest, Samuel, who had anointed David. The confused Saul had come to hate David, but he still admired his qualities of character, and in a dream Samuel had offered David a crown, but he refused it and placed it back on Saul's head. Michal and Jonathan appeared before Saul to announce David's return, and David convinced Saul of his innocence by presenting a piece he cut from Saul's robe when he was in a cave at En Gedi, his point being that he could easily have killed the king then if he had wanted to.

David showed his modesty and his good sense by appealing to Abner to continue in his role as commander, and he offered to act as his subordinate. When Saul became suspicious of David's sword, which had been given to him by priests at the temple, David sang to him as in the old days, and the king was at ease for a while. Then the king once again flew into a rage against David and the priests, and Jonathan could not convince his father of his friend's innocence, so David had to hide.

The priest Ahimelech then appeared to warn Saul, but the furious king ordered Abner to kill him and to massacre the other priests and their families at Nob as well. After that, David could not fight against the Philistines because the kingdom had become contaminated by Saul's sinfulness and violence. In the battle the Israelites were soundly defeated and Jonathan was killed. Michal came to her father as the enemy approached, but he was hallucinating, seeing in her his old enemy Samuel and appealing for the return of David, even if it would mean his own death. At last, Saul ordered Abner to take care of his daughter Michal and, left alone as the Philistines appeared, killed himself by falling on his sword.

Critical Evaluation:

Regarded as one of Italy's major poets, Vittorio Alfieri helped define the Italian drama of his age, particularly the tragedy, of which he wrote nineteen between 1776 and 1786. *Saul* was written in 1782. Alfieri also wrote an engaging autobiography, one that accounts for various love affairs in which he engaged while traveling throughout Europe, and his published writings include a treatise on tyranny, several comedies, lyric poetry, and satires. His best work, however, is in the genre of tragedy, and *Saul* is generally considered his best play.

In the late eighteenth and throughout the nineteenth centuries Alfieri was admired as one of Italy's foremost Romantic writers, an opponent of tyranny, a spokesman for Italian political unity and identity, and a libertarian. Although he was not inclined toward religious subjects for his work, his reading of the Bible in 1782 led him to write *Saul* with great rapidity. His personal inclination toward depression (melancholy) and his sense of his own aloneness may be detected in Saul, for whom he creates genuine stature as a tragic hero. In 1793, Alfieri himself appeared in the title role.

Although Alfieri's acquaintance with William Shakespeare's tragedies was not extensive (he knew them mostly in French translation), *Saul* is somewhat reminiscent of *King Lear* (c. 1605-1606). In both plays one encounters the motif of an aging monarch who turns against his own best interests, including the good of his people and even his own children, and in the process goes mad and brings destruction on himself and his kingdom. Lear is manipulated by two of his daughters, Saul by his cousin, the "perfidious" Abner, who is ambitious and deeply envious of David.

Although he is a victim of Saul's insanity, David, for all of his obvious virtue and strength of character, is not especially appealing. David, who opens the play with a soliloquy in which he states his determination to fight the Philistines even if Saul would have him executed, is courageous to the point of audacity. David seems perhaps too aware of his heroism. In Act II he directly confronts the unstable king, and he boldly demonstrates his innocence. In the third act he also shows his compassion by singing to soothe Saul's troubled mind.

The four substantial lyrical poems sung by David that Alfieri inserts into Act III, scene iv, are noteworthy in their own right. The remainder of the tragedy is composed in unrhymed hexameters, a conventional meter in Italian and French plays, and it is typically translated into English as blank verse (unrhymed iambic pentameter). Alfieri's style in the plays has been characterized as "severely simple," which is somewhat surprising for a lyric poet. Extensive descriptive passages and metaphoric language are not common in his dramatic writing, so the lyrics in the third act of *Saul* are exceptional. A note to the play indicates that if the actor portraying David is not also a capable singer, then an instrumental passage before each stanza would be appropriate, followed by David reciting "with majesty and gravity."

Perhaps in an effort to build sympathy for David, Alfieri elaborates on his love for Michal, but the result is that while one may feel compassion for her, one is not quite convinced that their separation has been or will be as painful for him. At the end of the first act, David confidently informs Michal, "I am impell'd/ By a sure instinct; I at random act not." When he suddenly appears before Saul in Act II, the king himself says, "In thee speaks a God." Even his proper, devout humility ("Saul gave my life; Saul takes that life away") seems somehow too pat. "O virtue of a David!" Jonathan exclaims in Act I, "God's elect/ Thou art assuredly." Near the end of the play, when he and Michal share a "last embrace," David is moved, but his grief is slight and fleeting compared to hers.

Against the confidence and boldness of the mighty, youthful, and perhaps overly virtuous David, Alfieri constructs the deeply flawed Saul, a type of Romantic hero who recalls Christopher Marlowe's overreachers such as Faustus and Tamerlane. Johann Wolfgang von Goethe was to refashion the type in *Faust* (1808); Percy Bysshe Shelley's Prometheus and several of George Gordon, Lord Byron's protagonists were to epitomize it in the next century. Saul's heroism resides in the fact that he has defied God in sparing the Amalekite king, Agag. In the process he has incurred the wrath of Samuel and other priests. The proper response would have been to act as Abraham did with his son Isaac, as David implies in the third scene of Act II. Even his pursuit of David, the Lord's anointed, has heroic implications, as it, too, suggests Saul's defiance.

What makes Saul a captivating character for a playgoer, however, is his psychological complexity. Unlike the conventionally heroic David, whose weaknesses are not hinted at in the play, Saul is human and vulnerable. When he appears at the start of Act II, his mind seems lucid as he admires the beauty of the dawn but laments his age and loss of strength. "How many years," he asks Abner, "have pass'd now, since a smile/ Was seen to play on my lips?" Saul clearly perceives his own mental disorder: "I am a burden to myself and others;/ In peace I wish for war, in war for peace." He sees that God has rejected him, and he even detects that Abner can be "hostile, invidious, crafty, and a traitor."

Saul's inability to resist the ministrations of David may suggest that he is as open to the potential for good as he is to the potential for evil in the form of Abner, and it is fairly easy to understand his jealousy over David's heroism. When Jonathan reasons with him about David, Saul confesses, "A strange inexplicable mystery/ This David is to me. . . . he pleased/ My eyes; but never, never won my heart." Even his son's assurance as to David's virtue and trustworthiness cannot untangle Saul's feelings of mixed love and hatred.

Ultimately, perhaps, it is Saul's inability to deal with the spiritual and moral arrogance of the self-righteous that undoes him. When the priest Ahimelech scorns him—"thou art but a crown'd heap of dust"—and repeats his threat, "tremble, Saul," Saul gives vent to his mad craving for vengeance and orders the priest's execution along with that of the other priests and their families at Nob. Ahimelech's courage is admirable but conventional, the typical attitude of the willing martyr: "No king can hinder me/ From dying like a just man; whence my death/ Will be as welcome as it is illustrious."

When he reaches out to Jonathan in Act IV ("Jonathan,/ Lov'st thou thy father?") and to Michal at the end of the play, Saul shows another facet of his character, that of the caring but hurt father. Even as his son prepares to fight by his side (to the death, although the play makes no mention of that), Saul says, "I have no children." His last concern is for Michal's safety, which he regards as assured so long as she is presented not as Saul's daughter, but as David's wife.

Not a religious man himself, Alfieri portrays sinful Saul as the sympathetic "tragic hero" and virtuous David as a traditional but unappealing "epic hero." Not surprisingly, his depiction of God, as seen by David, Ahimelech, and Saul, is of the foreboding Lord of wrath, judgment, and vengeance. David points out to Jonathan in the first act that "in the fierce career/ Of His retributory punishments,/ He hath involved the guiltless with the guilty." God, says Ahimelech, "writes His vengeance in adamant." Left alone at the end, Saul asks, "Inexorable God,/ Is Thy retributory wrath appeased?"

Ron McFarland

Bibliography:

Betti, Franco. *Vittorio Alfieri*. Boston: Twayne, 1984. Major portion of a chapter reflects on Saul's nobility gained through struggle, on the "touching figure of Michal," and on the theme of the past (Saul's age versus David's youth). Notes that in his suicide, Saul demonstrates the power of his will as a hero—neither the Philistines nor God can take credit for striking him down.

Bondanella, Peter, and Julia Conaway, eds. *Dictionary of Italian Literature*. Westport, Conn.: Greenwood Press, 1979. Giancarlo Maiorino's brief entry on Alfieri is useful. Concludes with comments on Saul, whom he sees as "the only character capable of expressing the superhuman passions of Alfieri himself."

Hallock, Ann H. "The Religious Aspects of Alfieri's *Saul*." *Forum Italicum* 18 (Spring, 1984): 43-64. Most thorough commentary on the play in English. Summarizes previous criticism from autobiographical, politico-philosophical, and psychological perspectives, but argues that the fundamental question of the play is "the nature of man without God."

Hillary, Richard B. "Biblical Exegesis in Alfieri's *Saul*." *South Atlantic Bulletin* 38 (March, 1973): 3-7. Focuses on Old Testament concept of sin as it relates to Saul's insanity.

Wilkins, Ernest Hatch. *A History of Italian Literature*. Revised by Thomas G. Bergin. Cambridge, Mass.: Harvard University Press, 1974. Chapter on Alfieri sets him and his work in the context of Italian literature and includes comments on *Saul*.

THE SCARLET LETTER

Type of work: Novel
Author: Nathaniel Hawthorne (1804-1864)
Type of plot: Psychological realism
Time of plot: Early days of the Massachusetts Colony
Locale: Boston
First published: 1850

Principal characters:
HESTER PRYNNE, a woman convicted of adultery
ARTHUR DIMMESDALE, a minister of the community
ROGER CHILLINGWORTH, a physician and Hester's husband
PEARL, Hester's daughter

The Story:

On a summer morning in Boston, in the early days of the Massachusetts Colony, a throng of curious people had gathered outside the jail in Prison Lane. They were there looking for Hester Prynne, who had been found guilty of adultery by a court of stern Puritan judges. Condemned to wear on the breast of her gown the scarlet letter "A," which stood for adulteress, she was to stand on the stocks before the meetinghouse for three hours so that her shame might be a warning and a reproach to all who saw her. The crowd waited to see her ascend the scaffold with her child—the proof of the adultery, Hester's husband being absent—in her arms.

At last, escorted by the town beadle, the woman appeared. She moved serenely to the steps of the scaffold and stood quietly under the staring eyes that watched her public disgrace. It was whispered in the gathering that she had been spared the penalty of death or branding only through the intercession of the Reverend Arthur Dimmesdale, into whose church she had brought her scandalous sin.

While Hester stood on the scaffold, an elderly, almost deformed man appeared out of the forest. When her agitation made it plain that she had recognized him, he put his finger to his lips as a sign of silence.

Hester's story was well-known in the community. She was the daughter of an old family of decayed fortune; when she was young, her family had married her to a husband who had great repute as a scholar. For some years, they had lived in Antwerp. Two years later, the husband had sent his wife alone across the ocean to the Massachusetts Colony, intending to follow her as soon as he could put his affairs in order. News had come of his departure, but his ship was never heard of again. The young, attractive widow had lived quietly in Boston until the time of her disgrace.

The scaffold of the pillory on which Hester stood was situated next to the balcony of the church where all the dignitaries of the colony sat to watch her humiliation. The ministers of the town called on her to name the man who was equally guilt; the most eloquent of those who exhorted her was the Reverend Arthur Dimmesdale, her pastor. Hester refused to name the father of her child, and she was led back to the prison after her period of public shame had ended.

On her return to prison, Hester was found to be in a state of great nervous excitement. When at last medical aid was called, a man was found who professed knowledge of medicine. His name was Roger Chillingworth, he told the jailer, and he had recently arrived in town after a year of residence among the Indians. He was the stranger who had appeared so suddenly from the forest that afternoon while Hester stood on the scaffold, and Hester had recognized him immediately as her husband, the scholar Prynne. His ship had been wrecked on the coast, and he had been captive among the Indians for many months. When he was brought to Hester, he too asked her to name the father of her child. When she refused, he told her he would remain in Boston to practice medicine and that he would devote the rest of his life to discovering the identity of the man who had dishonored him. He commanded Hester not to betray the relationship between them.

When Hester's term of imprisonment was over, she found a small house on the outskirts of town, far removed from other habitation. There, with her child, whom she had named Pearl, she settled down to earn a living from needlework, an outcast from society. She still wore the scarlet emblem on the breast of her sober gowns, but she dressed her child in bright, highly ornamented costumes. As she grew up, Pearl proved to be a capricious, wayward child, hard to discipline. One day, Hester called on Governor Bellingham to deliver a pair of embroidered gloves. She also wanted to see him about the custody of Pearl, for there was a movement afoot among the strict church members to take the child away from her. In the garden of the governor's mansion, Hester found the governor, Dimmesdale, and old Roger Chillingworth. When the perverse child refused to repeat the catechism, the governor thought it necessary that she be reared apart from her mother. Dimmesdale argued persuasively, however, and in the end Hester was allowed to keep Pearl, who seemed to be strangely attracted to the minister.

Roger Chillingworth had become intimately acquainted with Arthur Dimmesdale as both his parishioner and his doctor, for the minister had been in ill health ever since the physician had come to town. The two men lodged in the same house, and the physician came to know Dimmesdale's inmost thoughts and feelings. The minister was much plagued by feelings of conscience and guilt, but when he incorporated these ideas in generalities into his sermons, his congregation only thought more highly of him. Slowly the conviction grew in Chillingworth that Dimmesdale was Pearl's father, and he conjured up for the sick man visions of agony, terror, and remorse.

One night, unable to sleep, Dimmesdale walked to the pillory where Hester Prynne had stood in ignominy. He went up the steps and stood for a long time in the same place. A little later Hester, who had been watching at a deathbed, came by with little Pearl. The minister called them over, saying when they were there before he had lacked the courage to stand beside them. As the three stood together, with Dimmesdale acknowledging himself as Pearl's father and Hester's partner in sin, Roger Chillingworth watched them from the shadows.

Hester Prynne was so shocked by Dimmesdale's feeble and unhealthy condition that she determined to see her former husband and plead with him to free the sick minister from his evil influence.

One day, she met the old physician gathering herbs in the forest and begged him to be merciful to his victim. Chillingworth, however, was inexorable; he would not forgo his revenge on the man who had wronged him. Hester thereupon said that she would tell Arthur Dimmesdale their secret and warn him against his physician. A short time later, Hester and Pearl intercepted Dimmesdale in the forest as he was returning from a missionary journey to the Indians. Hester confessed her true relationship with Chillingworth and warned the minister against the physician's evil influence. She and the clergyman decided to leave the colony together in secret, take passage on a ship then in the harbor, and return to the Old World. They planned to leave four days later, after Dimmesdale had preached the sermon on Election Day, when the new governor was to be installed.

Election Day was a holiday in Boston, and the port was lively with the unaccustomed presence of sailors from the ship in the harbor. In the crowd was the captain of the vessel, with whom Hester had made arrangements for her own and Dimmesdale's passage. That morning, the captain informed Hester that Roger Chillingworth had also arranged for passage on the ship. Filled with despair, Hester turned away and went with Pearl to listen to Dimmesdale's sermon.

Unable to find room within the church, she stood at the foot of the scaffold where at least she could hear the sound of his voice. As the procession left the church, everyone had only words of praise for the minister's inspired address. Dimmesdale walked like a man in a dream, and once he tottered and almost fell. When he saw Hester and Pearl at the foot of the scaffold, he stepped out of the procession and called them to him. Then, taking them by the hand, he again climbed the steps of the pillory. Almost fainting, but with a voice terrible and majestic, the minister admitted his guilt to the watching people. With a sudden motion, he tore the ministerial band from across his breast and sank dying to the platform. When he thus exposed his breast, witnesses said that the stigma of the scarlet letter "A" was seen imprinted on the flesh above his heart.

Chillingworth, no longer able to wreak his vengeance on Dimmesdale, died within the year, bequeathing his considerable property to Pearl. For a time, Hester disappeared from the colony, but she returned alone years later to live in her humble thatched cottage and to wear as before the scarlet emblem on her breast. The scarlet letter, once her badge of shame, became an emblem of her tenderness and mercy—an object of veneration and reverence to those whose sorrows she alleviated by her deeds of kindness. At her death, she directed that the only inscription on her tombstone should be the letter "A."

Critical Evaluation:

Since its publication in 1850, *The Scarlet Letter* has never been out of print, nor indeed out of favor with literary critics. It is inevitably included in listings of the five or ten greatest American novels, and it is considered the best of Nathaniel Hawthorne's writings. It may also be the most typical of his work, the strongest statement of his recurrent themes, and an excellent example of his craftsmanship.

The main theme in *The Scarlet Letter*, as in most of Hawthorne's work, is that of sin and its effects both on the individual and on society. It is frequently noted that Hawthorne's preoccupation with sin springs from the Puritan-rooted culture in which he lived and from his knowledge of two of his own ancestors who had presided over bloody persecutions during the Salem witchcraft trials. It is difficult for readers from later times to comprehend the grave importance that seventeenth century New Englanders placed on transgression of the moral code. As Yvor Winters has pointed out, the Puritans, believing in predestination, viewed the commission of any sin as evidence of the sinner's corruption and preordained damnation. The harsh determinism and moralism of those early years had softened somewhat by Hawthorne's day, and during the twelve years he spent in contemplation and semi-isolation, he had worked out his own notions about human will and human nature. In *The Scarlet Letter*, Hawthorne proves to be closer to Paul Tillich than to Cotton Mather or Jonathan Edwards. Like Tillich, Hawthorne saw sin not as an act but as a state—what existentialists refer to as alienation and what Tillich describes as a threefold separation from God, other humans, and self. Such alienation needs no fire and brimstone as consequence; it is in itself a hell.

There is a certain irony in the way in which this concept is worked out in *The Scarlet Letter*. Hester Prynne's pregnancy forces her sin into public view, and she is compelled to wear the scarlet "A" as a symbol of her adultery. Yet, although she is apparently isolated from normal association with "decent" folk, Hester, having come to terms with her sin, is inwardly reconciled to God and self; she ministers to the needy among her townspeople, reconciling herself with others until some observe that her "A" now stands for "Able." Arthur Dimmesdale, her secret lover, and Roger Chillingworth, her secret husband, move much more freely in society than she can and even enjoy prestige: Dimmesdale as a beloved pastor, Chillingworth as a respected physician. Yet Dimmesdale's secret guilt gnaws so deeply inside him that he is unable to make his peace with God or to feel at ease with his fellow citizens. For his part, Chillingworth has permitted vengeance to permeate his spirit so much that his alienation is absolute; he refers to himself as a "fiend," unable to impart forgiveness or change his profoundly evil path. His is the unpardonable sin—unpardonable not because God will not pardon, but because his own nature has become so depraved that he cannot repent or accept forgiveness.

Hawthorne clearly distinguishes between sins of passion and those of principle. Even Dimmesdale, traditional Puritan though he is, finally becomes aware of the difference:

> We are not, Hester, the worst sinners in the world. There is one worse than even the polluted priest! That old man's revenge has been blacker than my sin. He has violated, in cold blood, the sanctity of a human heart. Thou and I, Hester, never did so.

Always more concerned with the consequences than the cause of sin, Hawthorne to a remarkable extent anticipated Sigmund Freud's theories of the effects of guilt. Hester, whose guilt is openly known, grows through her suffering into an extraordinarily compassionate and understanding woman, a complete person who is able to come to terms with all of life, including sin. Dimmesdale, who yearns for the relief of confession but hides his guilt to safeguard his role as pastor, is devoured internally. Again like Freud, Hawthorne recognized that spiritual turmoil may produce physical distress. Dimmesdale's health fails and eventually he dies from no apparent cause other than guilt.

The characters in *The Scarlet Letter* are reminiscent of a number of Hawthorne's shorter works. Dimmesdale bears similarities with Young Goodman Brown who, having once glimpsed the darker nature of humankind, must forevermore view humanity as corrupt and hypocritical. There are also resemblances between Dimmesdale and Parson Hooper in "The Minister's Black Veil," who continues to perform the duties of his calling with eloquence and compassion but is permanently separated from the company of men by the veil that he wears as a symbol of secret sin. Chillingworth shows resemblances with Ethan Brand, the limeburner who found the unpardonable sin in his own heart: "The sin of an intellect that triumphed over the sense of brotherhood with man and reverence for God, and sacrificed everything to its mighty claims!"

Hawthorne's craftsmanship is splendidly demonstrated in *The Scarlet Letter*. The structure is carefully unified, with three crucial scenes—at the beginning, middle, and end of the action—taking place on the scaffold. The scarlet "A" itself is repeatedly entwined into the narrative as a symbol of sin and shame, as a reminder of Hester's ability with the needle and her capability with people, and in Dimmesdale's case, as evidence of the searing effects of secret guilt. Hawthorne often anticipates later developments with hints or forewarnings: There is, for example, the suggestion that Pearl lacks complete humanity, perhaps because she has never known great sorrow, but at the end of the story when Dimmesdale dies, Hawthorne writes, "as [Pearl's] tears fell upon her father's cheek, they were the pledge that she would grow up amid human joy and sorrow, nor forever do battle with the world, but be a woman in it."

Hawthorne's skill as a symbolist is fully in evidence. As one critic has noted, there is hardly a concrete object in the book that does not do double duty as a symbol, among them the scarlet letter, the sunlight that eludes Hester, the scaffold of public notice, the armor in which Hester's shame and Pearl's selfishness are distorted and magnified. The four main characters themselves serve as central symbols in this, the greatest allegory of a master allegorist.

"Critical Evaluation" by Sally Bruckner

Bibliography:

Baym, Nina *"The Scarlet Letter": A Reading*. Boston: Twayne, 1986. Full-length critical introduction that examines the setting, characters, and themes. One fascinating chapter treats the scarlet "A" as a character. Includes a chronology and extended bibliography.

Bloom, Harold, ed. *Nathaniel Hawthorne's "The Scarlet Letter."* New York: Chelsea House, 1986. Part of the Modern Critical Interpretations series. Offers seven fascinating, fairly sophisticated critical essays written after 1962. Contains several approaches to the work as not a novel but as a typical American romance.

Colacurcio, Michael J. *New Essays on "The Scarlet Letter."* New York: Cambridge University Press, 1985. Offers serious students a brief review of the different critical approaches brought to the novel from the time of its publication to the 1980's.

Gerber, John C., ed. *Twentieth-Century Interpretations of "The Scarlet Letter": A Collection of Critical Essays*. Englewood Cliffs, N.J.: Prentice-Hall, 1968. Twenty essays for the beginning student that explore background, form, techniques, and interpretations. Includes a useful chronology that pairs dates in Hawthorne's life with historical events.

Gross, Seymour, ed. *A "Scarlet Letter" Handbook*. San Francisco: Wadsworth, 1960. A discussion of Hawthorne's earlier fiction, followed by a collection of brief essays on themes, characters, symbolism, and structure. Includes topics for discussion and student papers and an annotated bibliography.

Turner, Arlin. *The Merrill Studies in "The Scarlet Letter."* Columbus, Ohio: Charles E. Merrill, 1970. Essays for the general reader, including pieces on Hawthorne's process of composition, reviews of the novel dating back to its publication in 1850, nineteenth century commentary, and a sampling of twentieth century approaches.

THE SCHOOL FOR HUSBANDS

Type of work: Drama
Author: Molière (Jean-Baptiste Poquelin, 1622-1673)
Type of plot: Comedy of manners
Time of plot: 1660's
Locale: Paris
First performed: 1661; first published, 1661 as *L'École des maris* (English translation, 1732)

Principal characters:
SGANARELLE, a gentleman of means
ARISTE, his brother
ISABELLE, Sganarelle's ward
LÉONOR, her sister and Ariste's ward
VALÈRE, Isabelle's lover

The Story:

Léonor and Isabelle, orphaned on the death of their father, were committed by his deathbed wish to the guardianship of his friends, Sganarelle and Ariste, with the additional charge that if Sganarelle and Ariste did not marry the young women then the guardians were to provide suitable husbands for their wards. The two brothers had different ideas about the upbringing of the orphans. The elder, Ariste, chose to conform to the fashions of the day but without going to extremes. He gave his ward, Léonor, the opportunity to attend balls and dances and meet the gallants of the city. Although he himself wished to marry her, he loved Léonor sufficiently to leave the choice to her. Sganarelle, however, thought all this was foolish. Where Ariste hoped to govern only by affection, Sganarelle believed in the effectiveness of severity. He confined Isabelle strictly to her quarters and to household duties, thus keeping her from meeting any eligible young men. Determined to marry her himself, he hoped to discipline her to that end. When Sganarelle scoffed at his brother's leniency and predicted that he would in the end be tricked by so young a wife, Léonor declared that if she married her guardian she would be faithful to him, but that if she were to be Sganarelle's wife she would not be answerable for any of her actions.

Meanwhile, Valère, Sganarelle's new neighbor, had fallen in love with Isabelle, whom he had seen at a distance, and Isabelle reciprocated his love; however, with no means of communication neither knew the true feelings of the other. Isabelle finally worked out a plan to test Valère. She told Sganarelle about Valère's attentions and, knowing her guardian would then angrily accost Valère, declared that they were distasteful to her. Sganarelle asked Valère to cease molesting his ward and told him that, even though Isabelle knew of Valère's hopes, his was an unrequited passion, that her only wish was to find happiness in marrying her guardian. Valère sensed in this message something more that Isabelle hoped to convey to him.

Sganarelle told Isabelle that Valère had been crushed by her harsh message. Isabelle, under the pretense of returning a letter which, according to her story, an accomplice of Valère's had thrown into her chamber, persuaded her guardian to deliver the note. Actually, it was a love letter that she had written to Valère. Sganarelle, taking her request as a touching example of model womanly behavior, delivered the letter, which told of Isabelle's resolve to get free of her prison at any cost during the six days remaining before her enforced marriage to her guardian. Valère, making use of Sganarelle to take back to Isabelle words showing the sincerity of his attachment, declared that his only hope had been to make her his wife and that, although he now realized the hopelessness of his suit, he would always love her. First he flattered Sganarelle as an opponent no one could possibly displace, and he showed himself so completely crestfallen and hopeless in surrendering all thought of winning his fair prize that Sganarelle even came to feel a little sorry for his rival.

Isabelle, trying to trick her guardian into appearing despicable in the eyes of her lover, pretended to fear an attempt by Valère to force her from her chamber and carry her off before her marriage to Sganarelle. Bursting with pride at what he considered the womanly discretion of his ward, discretion obviously reflecting his own wisdom in her upbringing, Sganarelle offered to return to Valère and berate him for his bold and mischievous scheme. All turned out as Isabelle hoped. In reply, Valère declared that if what Sganarelle reported were possibly true, then his passion was indeed hopeless. Sganarelle, to make matters perfectly clear, took Valère directly to Isabelle to hear the cruel decision from her own lips. By words that could be understood two ways, Isabelle and Valère declared their love for each other under the nose of their dupe. Then on Isabelle's order Valère departed, promising that in three days he would find a way to free her from her jailer. Sganarelle, however, could not wait three days. Overjoyed at the exhibitions of what he took to be his ward's fond regard for him, he was eager to consummate the marriage. He told Isabelle the ceremony would be performed the next day.

Isabelle realized that her last resource was to commit herself unreservedly to her lover at once, but as she prepared for flight Sganarelle saw her and informed her that all preparations had been made for their union. Isabelle trumped up a story that she was about to leave the house to spend the night with a worthy friend, Lucrece, because Léonor, in desperation, had asked for the use of Isabelle's room that night. Against her better judgment, she declared, she had consented and had just locked her sister in. Isabelle pretended that Valère had really been Léonor's lover for more than a year, but had abandoned her when he became infatuated with Isabelle. She said that Léonor, hoping to win back his love, planned to meet him in the lane near the house. Sganarelle, declaring this plan immodest, wanted to drive Léonor out of the house at once. Isabelle restrained him, however, and persuaded him to let her take the message to Léonor, after insisting that Sganarelle must hide himself and promise to let her sister leave without his speaking to her. Sganarelle agreed, secretly pleased at the thought of his brother's discomfiture over the wanton doings of his ward.

Isabelle, pretending to be Léonor, left the house. Curious, Sganarelle followed. He saw Valère and Isabelle meet and, after declaring their love, enter Valère's house. Thinking that Léonor was with Valère and wishing to keep scandal from touching Isabelle through her sister, he hurriedly called a magistrate and urged him to marry the pair. The magistrate was to wait, however, until Sganarelle could return with the bride's guardian to witness the ceremony.

Ariste, although he could not believe his ears when Sganarelle gloatingly insisted that Léonor was with Valère, was induced nevertheless to accompany his brother. Valère, who had hidden Isabelle in a separate room, had the magistrate prepare a formal contract, to be signed by all parties present, indicating their consent to the marriage. Still under the delusion that the bride to be was his brother's ward Léonor, Sganarelle agreed to the wedding; Ariste, placing the desires of his supposed ward above his own dreams, assented also.

Meanwhile, Léonor returned early from the ball she had attended. Ariste gently chided her for not confiding in him her love for Valère, but Léonor, amazed, protested that she loved only Ariste, her beloved guardian, whom she was ready to marry immediately. Angered, Sganarelle realized too late the trick played on him by Isabelle. All women, he declared, were to be disbelieved and shunned. In the schooling of husbands it was he and not his brother Ariste who had failed.

Critical Evaluation:

Molière's theatrical troupe first performed his three-act comedy *The School for Husbands* in 1661. Molière assigned to himself the role of Sganarelle. At first glance, it may seem odd that Molière chose to play the role of an unsympathetic and egomaniacal character, but Sganarelle is a wonderful comic role. In all except one scene in this verse comedy Sganarelle dominates the stage, although his ability to dominate other characters proves to be illusory. Sganarelle is such a thoroughly unpleasant person that the audience wants to see him fail.

From the very beginning of this comedy Molière contrasts Sganarelle's irrational attempts to limit the actions of Isabelle with the more enlightened and tolerant attitude of his older brother, Ariste, toward his fiancée, Léonor. *The School for Husbands* begins with a dialogue between Sganarelle and Ariste. Sganarelle affirms that he has no interest in learning what others may think of his strange and inflexible behavior, but he grants to himself the right to criticize others. This hypocrisy immediately creates an unfavorable opinion of Sganarelle in the minds of Molière's readers. There is also a marvelously ironic use of role reversal between these two brothers. Although Ariste is twenty years older than his brother, it is he and not Sganarelle who wears fashionable clothing and appreciates modern attitudes toward tolerance. Ariste does not object that Léonor spends money buying clothing for herself because this brings her pleasure, and Ariste is so well-to-do that he need not worry about such expenditures. He has no desire to "tyrannize" Léonor, and he is mature enough to realize that it would be better for him if she were to marry someone else rather than marry Ariste against her will. Ariste has no desire to be miserable in his marriage. Unless Léonor freely agrees to marry him, Ariste prefers to remain a bachelor. Ariste's ideas on marriage are eminently sensible, and he realizes that a marriage which is not based on equality and respect is doomed to unhappiness. Sganarelle, however, mocks Ariste's belief that a husband will be loved by his wife only if he respects her freedom and dignity. This comedy illustrates Ariste's wisdom and Sganarelle's folly.

Fate and a woman soon bring about Sganarelle's defeat. A very reasonable man named Valère loves Isabelle, but he does not realize that Sganarelle also hopes to marry her. As a result of his innocence and trust in the basic goodness of others, Valère speaks to Sganarelle of his passion for Isabelle. Valère correctly assumes that Isabelle has no desire to marry such a repulsive and insensitive man as Sganarelle. With supreme overconfidence Sganarelle repeatedly makes the same mistake without realizing how his actions and comments will be interpreted or used by other characters. In the second act, he tells Valère that Isabelle wants nothing to do with him, but Valère correctly interprets this remark as a confirmation of her love for him. Sganarelle, being so sure that he cannot be fooled, is fooled. Sganarelle, who considers himself to be clever, falls for a trap prepared by Isabelle. She speaks of her anger (feigned) that Valère has thrown through her bedroom window a rock to which a love letter had been attached. She asks Sganarelle to return this letter unopened to Valère, and Sganarelle willingly delivers a love letter to Valère. Sganarelle's inflexibility and delusionary perception of reality leads to his unintentionally serving as the intermediary who helps to convince Valère of Isabelle's love for him. By an ironic twist of fate the thoroughly unpleasant Sganarelle brings about the happy ending.

The third act in *The School for Husbands* contains many different levels of irony. As a result of his extreme vanity, Sganarelle does not realize that it is in his own self-interest to be flexible. He ensures his own failure, and the happiness of the two sympathetic couples, when he arranges for a notary to come to his house in order to prepare a marriage contract. The notary is delighted to have this new business, and he does not care who marries whom as long as he is paid. Molière's spectators realize that Sganarelle's perverse plan cannot succeed. Readers and theatergoers alike are amused in the third act when the self-righteous and ridiculous Sganarelle again criticizes Ariste for his complete faith in his fiancée, Léonor. Like Valère and Isabelle, Ariste also refuses to believe Sganarelle's preposterous claims. Ariste is trusting enough of the love that he and Léonor feel for each other that he dismisses Sganarelle's absurd charge that Léonor wishes to marry Valère.

While Sganarelle is busy berating his brother, Ariste, Valère marries Isabelle, and it is clear to the audience that Ariste and Léonor will soon get married. Once the cooperative notary has finished composing the marriage contract for Valère and Isabelle, he can render the same professional service for Ariste and Léonor. Léonor's servant Lisette speaks the last words in this comedy. After having listened to Sganarelle's irrational criticism of women, Lisette expresses the hope that men can profit from the moral lessons taught in this comedy. Men who respect women's freedom will attain happiness and true joy, whereas fanatics such as Sganarelle will never find pleasure in marriage.

"Critical Evaluation" by Edmund J. Campion

Bibliography:

Ciccone, Anthony A. *The Comedy of Language: Four Farces by Molière*. Potomac, Md.: J. Porrua Turanzas, 1980. Discusses comic uses of language and levels of irony in *The School for Husbands*. Examines the contrasts between the behavior of Ariste and Sganarelle.

Gaines, James F. *Social Structures in Molière's Theater*. Columbus: Ohio State University Press, 1984. Explores the differences between noble and middle-class values in Molière's comedies. Contrasts Sganarelle's obsessive desire to dominate his fiancée with the more enlightened views of his brother, Ariste.

Howarth, W. D. *Molière: A Playwright and His Audience*. Cambridge, England: Cambridge University Press, 1982. Discusses performances by Molière's troupe and the critical reception of his comedies by Parisian theatergoers of his era. Explores Molière's creative uses of theatrical conventions in order to create witty farces and comedies.

Hubert, Judd D. *Molière and the Comedy of Intellect*. Berkeley: University of California Press, 1962. Contains an excellent introduction to the evolution of Molière's skill as a comic playwright. The chapter on *The School for Husbands* examines the antithetical attitudes of Sganarelle and Ariste and discusses the nature of Sganarelle's self-imposed isolation from society.

Wadsworth, Philip A. *Molière and the Italian Theatrical Tradition*. York, S.C.: French Literature Publications Company, 1977. Discusses Molière's creative imitation of Italian theatrical tradition in his early farces. Contrasts Sganarelle's inflexibility with the more reasonable behavior of Ariste.

THE SCHOOL FOR SCANDAL

Type of work: Drama
Author: Richard Brinsley Sheridan (1751-1816)
Type of plot: Comedy of manners
Time of plot: Eighteenth century
Locale: London
First performed: 1777; first published, 1780

Principal characters:
SIR PETER TEAZLE, an elderly nobleman
LADY TEAZLE, his young wife
MARIA, Sir Peter's ward
SIR OLIVER SURFACE, Sir Peter's friend
JOSEPH SURFACE and
CHARLES SURFACE, Sir Oliver's nephews
LADY SNEERWELL, Lady Teazle's friend
ROWLEY, Sir Peter's servant

The Story:

Lady Sneerwell, who in her youth was the target of slander, had set her life upon a course to reduce the reputations of other women to the level of her own. Aided by her intimate, Snake, she intrigued to involve the Teazles in scandal, to bring Joseph Surface's true character to light, to wreck the love between Charles and Maria, and to gain Charles for herself along with Sir Oliver's fortune. To her the world consisted of nothing but scandal and scandalous intrigues, and she did her best to make her vision a reality. She was not successful, however, when she abused Charles Surface to Sir Peter Teazle's ward Maria, who refused to listen to her. Instead, Maria trustingly confided in Lady Candour, whose defense of a reputation ensured its complete annihilation.

Sometimes Sir Peter Teazle pondered the wisdom of his marriage to Lady Teazle, doubting the judgment of an old bachelor in marrying a young wife. Lady Teazle was a country-bred girl who was enjoying London life extravagantly and to the full. Sir Oliver Surface was concerned about his two nephews, his problem being the disposal of his great fortune. Sir Oliver had been abroad for the past fifteen years and felt that he did not know their real natures; he hoped by some stratagem to catch them unawares and thus be able to test their characters.

One day, Sir Peter and Lady Teazle quarreled because Sir Peter violently objected to her attendance at the home of Lady Sneerwell. Lady Teazle accused Sir Peter of wishing to deprive her of all freedom and reminded him that he had promised to go to Lady Sneerwell's with her. He retorted that he would do so for only one reason, to look after his own character. When he arrived, Lady Sneerwell's rooms were full of people uttering libelous remarks about their enemies and saying even worse things about their friends. Sir Peter escaped as soon as possible.

When the rest of Lady Sneerwell's guests retired to the card room, leaving Maria and Joseph alone, Joseph once more pressed his suit. He insinuated that she was in love with Charles and was thus running counter to Sir Peter's wishes. Lady Teazle walked in just as Joseph was on his knees avowing his honest love. Surprised, Lady Teazle told Maria she was wanted in the next room. When she asked Joseph for an explanation, he told her that he was pleading with Maria not to tell Sir Peter of his tender concern for Lady Teazle.

Sir Oliver consulted Rowley, Sir Peter's shrewd and observing servant, in an attempt to learn more about his nephews' characters. Rowley himself believed that Joseph did not have as good a character as his reputation seemed to indicate and that Charles had a better one. Sir Peter was also consulted. He declared that he was ready to stake his life on Joseph's honor. He was much put out, therefore, when Maria once more refused to marry Joseph.

Sir Peter, Sir Oliver, and Rowley planned to test the worthiness of the nephews. Charles, as usual, was in dire need of money. Since a moneylender named was going to see Charles, Sir Oliver was to accompany him as Mr. Premium, a man who could supply the money Charles needed.

When they arrived at Charles's lodging, a drinking party was in progress. Some of the guests were at games of dice. Sir Oliver was not at all impressed with Trip, Charles's footman, who gave himself the airs of a fashionable man about town. Upon investigating, Sir Oliver discovered that Charles had, with the exception only of the portraits of his ancestors, turned his inherited possessions into cash. Convinced that Charles was a scamp, Sir Oliver, still calling himself Premium, agreed to buy the paintings, and he purchased each picture as presented except his own, which Charles would not sell for any amount of money. Sir Oliver was pleased by this fact and on that ground discounted Charles's reputation for extravagance. Charles received a draft for eight hundred pounds for the portraits and immediately sent one hundred pounds to Mr. Stanley, a poor relation in even more straitened circumstances than he was.

During an assignation between Joseph Surface and Lady Teazle in Joseph's library, he advised her to give her husband grounds for jealousy rather than to suffer his jealousy without cause. He argued that to save her reputation she must ruin it and that he was the man best able to help her. Lady Teazle considered such a doctrine very odd.

While they were talking, Sir Peter arrived unexpectedly, and Lady Teazle hid behind the screen that Joseph ordered placed against the window. Joseph pretended to be reading when Sir Peter walked in. The purpose of Sir Peter's call was to inform Joseph of his suspicions that Lady Teazle was having an affair with Charles; he also showed Joseph two deeds he had brought with him, one settling eight hundred pounds a year on Lady Teazle for her independent use, the other giving her the bulk of his fortune at his death. Joseph's dissimulation before Sir Peter and Sir Peter's generosity to her were not lost on Lady Teazle. When Sir Peter began to discuss Joseph's desire to wed Maria, Lady Teazle realized that Joseph had been deceiving her.

Below stairs, Charles inopportunely demanded entrance to the house to see his brother. Not wishing to see Charles, Sir Peter asked where he could hide. Sir Peter caught a glimpse of a petticoat behind the screen, but Joseph assured him that the woman was only a French milliner who plagued him. Sir Peter hid in a closet, and Lady Teazle remained behind the screen.

When Charles came in, he and Joseph discussed Lady Teazle and Sir Peter's suspicion that Charles was her lover. Charles mentioned that he believed Joseph to be her favorite and recounted all the little incidents that led him to think so. Embarrassed by this turn in the conversation, Joseph interrupted to say that Sir Peter was within hearing. Placed in a difficult position, Charles explained to Sir Peter that he was merely playing a joke on Joseph. Sir Peter knew a good joke on Joseph, too, he said; Joseph was having an affair with a milliner. Charles decided that he would have a look at the milliner and threw down the screen. Joseph was undone because Lady Teazle refused to agree with any excuses he made. She angrily informed her husband of the whole nature of Joseph's intentions and departed. Sir Peter followed her, leaving Joseph to his own conscience.

Sir Oliver, masquerading as Mr. Stanley and badly in need of assistance, gained admittance to Joseph's apartment. Joseph refused to help Mr. Stanley, saying that he received very little money from Sir Oliver and claiming that he had advanced all his funds to Charles. After Sir Oliver left, Rowley, who was a party to the whole scheme, came to tell Joseph that Sir Oliver had arrived in town.

Sir Oliver went again to see Joseph. Still believing that his uncle was Mr. Stanley, Joseph was showing him out just as Charles entered. Charles, surprised to see Mr. Premium in his brother's apartment, also insisted that he leave, but at that moment Sir Peter Teazle arrived and addressed Sir Oliver by his right name. Both Sir Oliver and Sir Peter were now aware of Joseph's real character. Charles, promising to try to reform, got Maria and his uncle's inheritance as well. Lady Sneerwell was exposed by Snake, who was paid double to speak the truth, and Lady Teazle returned her diploma to the School for Scandal of which Lady Sneerwell was president. Everyone was happy except Lady Sneerwell and Joseph Surface.

Critical Evaluation:

First performed at London's famous Drury Lane theater in 1777, *The School for Scandal* was staged a total of 261 times before the end of the eighteenth century and has been revived hundreds of times since, making it one of the most enduringly popular comedies in the English language. Accounting for the play's popularity is not difficult: Richard Brinsley Sheridan, who had succeeded the Great David Garrick as manager of Drury Lane in 1776, was blessed with a keenly theatrical imagination and an instinctive sense of how best to please an audience. These talents are nowhere more evident than in *The School for Scandal*, which is, above all else, first-rate theater—a play graced by sparkling dialogue, a cast of memorable characters, and a complex plot that combines elements of high comedy, intrigue, and genuine feeling.

The ingredients that guarantee success on the stage, however, do not always guarantee critical esteem. Although critics have over the years had a great deal to say about William Shakespeare's *Twelfth Night* (c. 1600-1602) and Ben Jonson's *Volpone* (1605), they have had relatively little to say about *The School for Scandal*. Most discussions of the play, in fact, have focused not so much on literary analysis as on the question of Sheridan's success in rebelling against the sentimental comedies of his day and in recovering the spirit of such earlier Restoration comedies as William Congreve's *The Way of the World* (1700). Unfortunately, when measured against these earlier plays, *The School for Scandal* has usually been found inferior—a comedy, as one critic trenchantly put it, in which the Restoration is unrestored.

It might be best to begin study of the play with the general disclaimer that *The School for Scandal* is not only a Restoration comedy, it is another kind of comedy altogether—moral rather than satiric, basically humane and optimistic rather than hard-edged and cynical. It is a comedy written for an audience whose basic assumptions about art, theater, and human nature made it radically different from the audience of Congreve's day.

The School for Scandal has been called a middle-class morality play, and in a sense it is. At play's end, good characters are rewarded and bad characters ("evil" is really too strong a word) are routed, thus providing the audience with two useful object lessons: Honesty and benevolence will, in the end, win out over duplicity and selfishness, and, as the surname of the brothers Charles and Joseph suggests, surface appearances are not always trustworthy indicators of inner character. It would be wrong, however, to assume that Sheridan was a moralist using comedy merely as sugar coating. His primary goal in *The School for Scandal* was, without doubt, comic delight rather than moral instruction.

Although Sheridan's dialogue in *The School for Scandal* has often been celebrated, language in the play is less important as a source of comedy than are plot and character. Creating interesting characters and placing them in situations that compel them to respond in particularly telling ways allows Sheridan to examine what writers of social comedy from Aristophanes to Woody Allen have never tired of examining: the abiding, perhaps even necessary, inconsistency in human society between surface and substance, appearance and reality, truth and fiction.

Lady Sneerwell and the members of her scandalous school are masters of social illusion. As a former victim of scandal herself, Lady Sneerwell understands only too well how fragile a thing reputation is. More to the point, perhaps, she has achieved an even more profound intuition: She has come to understand how all reputation—good or bad—is, from a purely social (rather than moral) perspective, a fiction, a contrivance of opinion. This understanding enables her to fashion the scheming hypocrite Joseph Surface into an admired man of sentiment and his good-hearted, although slightly profligate, brother Charles into a notorious libertine. That Joseph is by nature selfish and mercenary and Charles humane and generous is largely irrelevant within the sophisticated world of London high society, where surface is all that matters.

If *The School for Scandal* were another kind of comedy, Lady Sneerwell and her scandal-mongering friends, Mrs. Candour, Crabtree, and Sir Benjamin Backbite, might be allowed to hold the stage. Their antics, as amply demonstrated in Act II, scene i, amount to little more than niggling gossip. The Widow Ochre may use too much makeup and Miss Sallow may try "to pass for a girl at six-and-thirty," but these are relatively minor instances of affectation and the point remains amusement rather than pain. Even the somewhat more serious matter of Lady Teazle's corruption by the school is played largely for laughs, and the prevailing tone throughout these scenes is one of childish naughtiness rather than true wickedness. A more concrete check on the goings-on is provided by the presence of Sir Peter and his young ward, Maria, both of whom display comically exasperated (but morally legitimate) dismay at the behavior of the scandalous characters.

Sheridan knew his audience, and he understood that moral comedy can flirt with sin but must never embrace it. Thus when the various schemes of Lady Sneerwell and Joseph proceed beyond the realm of detached amusement and begin to threaten the happiness of morally superior characters, the plot quickens toward resolution. This resolution comes about through the introduction of an outsider, Sir Oliver Surface, whose ability to penetrate social façades enables him to function as a kind of moral catalyst, and through two expertly crafted scenes in the fourth act. In the auction scene, Charles is shown to be a kind and generous man whose worst fault seems to be a fondness for cards and good company; in the famous screen scene that follows, Joseph is fully revealed as a smooth-tongued hypocrite. When the screen, that conventional yet effective stage device that both symbolizes and comments on the discrepancy between social fiction and moral truth, comes tumbling down, revealing a thoroughly abashed Lady Teazle, the audience can only respond with applause. Lady Teazle will soon resign her place in Lady Sneerwell's school, and Sir Peter will soon accept Charles as a proper husband for Maria, leaving Lady Sneerwell and Joseph with only each other—which seems perfectly appropriate punishment for them both.

"Critical Evaluation" by Michael Stuprich

Bibliography:

Auburn, Mark. *Sheridan's Comedies: Their Contexts and Achievements*. Lincoln: University of Nebraska Press, 1977. Perhaps the best of the very few full-length studies of Sheridan and his work. First-rate discussion of *The School for Scandal*.

Danziger, Marlies K. *Oliver Goldsmith and Richard Brinsley Sheridan*. New York: Frederick

Unger, 1978. A good place to begin study of Sheridan and his work. Contains an excellent discussion of *The School for Scandal* and a useful bibliography.

Loftis, John. *Sheridan and the Drama of Georgian England*. Oxford, England: Basil Blackwell, 1976. Carefully researched and rewarding study by a leading scholar in the field. Places Sheridan's work firmly in the context of late eighteenth century theater and dispels many of the myths surrounding *The School for Scandal*. Highly recommended.

Schiller, Andrew. "*The School for Scandal:* The Restoration Unrestored." *Publications of the Modern Language Association* 71 (September, 1956): 694-704. In this classic article, Schiller attacks the idea that *The School for Scandal* recaptures the spirit and substance of Restoration comedy. Schiller considers *The School for Scandal* "a kind of bourgeois morality play."

Worth, Katharine. *Sheridan and Goldsmith*. New York: St. Martin's Press, 1992. Worth is at her best in this slender but worthwhile book when discussing the plays of Sheridan and Goldsmith in the context of eighteenth century theatrical traditions and practices. Very good chapter on *The School for Scandal*.

THE SCHOOL FOR WIVES

Type of work: Drama
Author: Molière (Jean-Baptiste Poquelin, 1622-1673)
Type of plot: Comedy of manners
Time of plot: Seventeenth century
Locale: France
First performed: 1662; first published, 1663 as *L'École des femmes* (English translation, 1732)

Principal characters:
ARNOLPHE (M. DE LA SOUCHE), a wealthy man
AGNÈS, his ward
HORACE, Agnès' lover
CHRYSALDE, Arnolphe's friend
ENRIQUE, Chrysalde's brother-in-law
ORONTE, Horace's father

The Story:

As Arnolphe told his friend Chrysalde, if a man were not to be made to look like a fool by his wife, he must choose a wife who is ignorant of the ways of the world and in no danger of being admired by other men. Arnolphe, famous for his bitter ridicule of other men who were put to shame by the unfaithfulness of their wives, was determined that he would not find himself in a like position. For that reason, he proposed to marry Agnès, his young ward, whom he had protected from society. He thought her such an ignorant girl and such a fool that she would make a perfect wife.

Agnès had been put in his care by her widowed foster mother. The girl had her early training in a convent to which Arnolphe sent her. Later she lived in a small cottage on his estate. Her life was secluded, in order that she might be kept safe from learning and from outside influences until she reached an age for marriage. On a whim, Arnolphe had changed his name to Monsieur de la Souche, but Agnès was not aware of this fact. Neither was she aware of Arnolphe's plan to marry her.

Before Arnolphe could inform Agnès of his wishes, Horace, the son of his friend Oronte, told him that he was in love with her. Horace, knowing only that Agnès was the ward of one de la Souche, did not realize that Arnolphe and de la Souche were the same man. Horace asked Arnolphe not to tell anyone of the love affair because it must be kept a secret from both de la Souche and Horace's father. Arnolphe could only smother his rage in silence as he listened to the tale of Agnès' duplicity. Even though she was not aware that Arnolphe planned to make her his wife, he already felt that she was faithless to him and had shamed him. He thought he must accuse her of sinning against him and must also tell her his plans immediately.

Agnès did not react as he had anticipated. In her innocence, she told him of the pleasure she found in Horace's company. Arnolphe was relieved to learn that she had given her lover only kisses, for she was so innocent that she had once asked if babies came from the ear. He ordered her not to see Horace again, even to slam the door in his face or throw stones at him if he attempted to see her. In addition, he lectured her on the role of women, wives in particular, and gave her a book of maxims to study so that she might be better prepared for marriage. The maxims expressed Arnolphe's ideas exactly since they, too, saw wives as the complete possessions of their husbands. Arnolphe told Agnès that he intended to marry her, but she misunderstood him and thought he meant to give her in marriage. She was happy because she thought she would be married to Horace.

Arnolphe learned from Horace that Agnès had obeyed orders and thrown a stone at him, but he learned also that she attached a letter to the stone. In the letter she had professed her love for Horace, and the young man was delighted. Still not knowing that his supposed friend was in reality Agnès' guardian, Horace asked Arnolphe for help in rescuing her from de la Souche.

Arnolphe decided to marry Agnès at once and sent for the notary. He was doubly miserable, because he felt betrayed and because he really loved the girl. Thus he was enraged when he learned of Horace's plan to gain admittance to Agnès' room, and he ordered his servants to set upon Horace with clubs as he tried to climb to Agnès' window. He was horrified, however, when the servants told him that they had beaten Horace too hard and had killed him.

Even though he hated the young man, Arnolphe was relieved to see Horace alive and not seriously injured. Horace told him that he had pretended to be dead so that his attackers would leave him. Agnès, swearing that she was never going back to her prison cottage, had slipped out during the uproar. Horace, with no place to take the girl, asked Arnolphe to help him by hiding the girl until they could be married. Arnolphe hid his face as he met Agnès, and it was not until after Horace had gone that she recognized Arnolphe as de la Souche. Still, her innocence made her unafraid, and she told Arnolphe that Horace was more to her liking for a husband than he was. Swearing that she would have no one but Horace, she refused to consider marrying Arnolphe in spite of his alternate threats and promises. At last Arnolphe declared angrily that he would send her to a convent, and he had his servants lock her up until a carriage could be secured.

Horace, ignorant of these developments, went again to his friend Arnolphe, this time in great agitation. His father, Oronte, had arrived for a visit with his friend Enrique, the brother-in-law of Chrysalde. It was Oronte's purpose to marry Horace to Enrique's daughter, and Horace asked Arnolphe to persuade Oronte not to force the marriage. Although he promised to help Horace, Arnolphe did exactly the opposite. He told Oronte that a father should never give in to a son but should make him bow to a parent's wishes. He insisted that Horace and Enrique's daughter be married at once. Then Horace learned that Arnolphe was in reality de la Souche and knew that he had been betrayed.

Arnolphe had Agnès brought before the gathering because he wanted to witness her grief and Horace's as they were separated forever. He was disappointed; to his astonishment, he learned that Agnès was Enrique's daughter. Enrique, years before, had secretly married the sister of Chrysalde. After her death, Enrique, forced to flee the country, had left his small daughter with a country woman. Too poor to provide for the child, the woman had in turn given Agnès to Arnolphe. Enrique had only recently learned of her whereabouts. As soon as he learned that she was with Arnolphe, he had arranged her betrothal to the son of his friend Oronte. Thus the lovers were united with the blessing of everyone but Arnolphe, who could only sputter and wring his hands. He had truly been betrayed.

Critical Evaluation:

The School for Wives was probably the most popular success of Molière's controversial career. Molière himself played Arnolphe, the middle-aged theorist of marriage, and Armande, his bride of less than a year, portrayed the ingenue, Agnès. Although the motif of the play is an old one and appears in Italian and Spanish tales, it is a fact that the problem of the ardent middle-aged lover and the bride half his age whom he has trained from girlhood was Molière's own. Perhaps this is why, in the last act, when Arnolphe pleads with the girl for her love, the comedy seems to drop away, exposing an agonized and aging man speaking desperate and moving words. The play is very funny, but it rings with truth and psychological realism beneath the humor and absurdity.

The School for Wives was Molière's first five-act comedy in verse, and generally its tone is realistic; the farcical action is confined, for the most part, to the servants. Although influenced by the traditional French farce and the Italian *commedia dell'arte*, the play is essentially a comedy of character, with an overlay of the comedy of manners. The theme is the old one that love conquers all and that the heart will always understand its own desires and will recognize the heart and soul destined to be joined with it. In an age of arranged marriages and subsequent philandering, Molière's conviction that marriage should be based on love would have been radical if it had not been integrated into the absurdities of the comedy.

The subsidiary themes of the play are that a young woman has a right to decent education commensurate with her intelligence and curiosity and that any attempt to keep her ignorant is in contempt of her privileges as a human being. At the beginning of the play, Arnolphe sympathetically presents his position: He is so exasperated by feminine coquetry that he feels the only safety is in marrying a fool. His greatest mistake is in carrying his attitude to ridiculous and wrongheaded extremes. With the single-mindedness of a pedant, he constructs a complete scheme for rearing the girl in a convent from the age of four so that she will be entirely untrained in the ways of the world. His pride in his scheme warns the audience of his eventual and inevitable downfall.

The play is witty and amusing, but contains a surprisingly small amount of action. Mostly, it consists of speeches, many of them long and drawn out, the audience hearing about the action more than witnessing it. To Molière's contemporaries, however, such a comedy was subject to certain rules of decorum; all violent action was banned from the stage and the audience's imagination filled in what was necessary. Although the play is often static, it is never dull; *The School for Wives* is one of Molière's most delightful comedies.

Agnès is one of the most fascinating characters in any Molière comedy; if she sins, it is through lamblike ignorance and innocence, and her gradual awakening is a marvel of character portrayal. The revelation of her slowly developing temperament, all the stronger for its innocence and naïveté, is as touching as it is charming. At the same time, the pedant's personality undergoes a transformation, for he finds that he discovers, in spite of himself, the true nature of love. He, who had dismissed love and all of the accompanying nonsense as beneath him, finds that he is hopelessly in love with the girl he created. He has no choice but to eat his words and to suffer the consequences of his stupidity and blindness. His awkward gropings toward the manners and words of love become both his own punishment and the delight of the audience.

The moral point of the play rests in the fact that Arnolphe deliberately sought to confine a human being, to unnaturally limit her development. Under the pretense of keeping her "simple," he made her into a charming freak. The struggle is between the spontaneous and the rigid, a struggle which lends itself perfectly to comedy. The more Arnolphe treats life mechanically, the more his efforts backfire, for life reacts spontaneously to make the outcome of his elaborate schemes the opposite of his intentions. Always, in Molière's plays, nature is held up as a better guide than authority; human nature and human emotions must be allowed to take their own course. It is always the extreme position which causes unhappiness and eventual disaster. If human beings would avoid absurd obsessions, life would be smoother and more joyous for everybody concerned. However, of course, it would be duller, for it is this all-too-human tendency of people to embrace extreme points of view and absurd attitudes that provides

Molière with his most brilliant comic creations.

Molière uses several clever devices to enliven his essentially simple plot. One is the fact that Arnolphe has taken the name of de la Souche. This allows Horace to make him the confidant of successive attempts to get Agnès out of old de la Souche's clutches. The complications of this misunderstanding are both absurd and hilarious. Another delightful and clever contrivance is the grotesque scurry of the denouement. The final scene of Act V is filled with rapid-fire patter in which Chrysalde and Oronte, Horace's father, newly arrived on the scene with a person called Enrique, who has spent the last fourteen years in America, explain to all concerned that the rustic Agnès is actually Chrysalde's niece and the daughter of this Enrique. Enrique is a perfect and totally implausible *deus ex machina*, standing by dumb as a fish until just before the curtain falls to remark in three lines that he has no doubts about the identity of his daughter and consents to her marrying Horace. It is a daring and absurd conclusion to the play, but it provides the necessary happy ending for the young lovers, and leaves Arnolphe sadder but wiser.

There is much excellent comedy in *The School for Wives*, the frenzy of Arnolphe, the leg-pulling by Chrysalde, an absurd notary babbling in legal jargon, a saucy maid named Georgette, and the irony of the old man trying to win the love of a girl he tried to lock away from all eyes but his own. Chrysalde, in particular, is a satirist with a sense of humor, who tries with a long merry tirade to laugh Arnolphe out of his obsession. The contrasts and contradictions of human behavior provide the basic, and often subtle, humor of the play, but Molière is never above farce, as in the opening scene when Alain and Georgette first refuse to let their master through the gate and then quarrel about which of them is to do it. As is often the case in Molière's comedies, as well as in real life, the people in the play assume different guises, they adopt different faces as they need them, they remove their masks and then invent new ones. The cloak of politeness falls, and the chaos beneath is hilariously revealed.

"Critical Evaluation" by Bruce D. Reeves

Bibliography:

Calder, Andrew. *Molière: The Theory and Practice of Comedy*. London: Athlone Press, 1993. Examines connections between dramatic theory and theatrical performances of Molière's comedies. Discusses conflicts between ridiculous and sympathetic characters and the role of moral judgment in *The School for Wives*.

Guicharnaud, Jacques, ed. *Molière: A Collection of Critical Essays*. Englewood Cliffs, N.J.: Prentice-Hall, 1964. Contains numerous essays originally written by major critics in English or translated from French into English for this volume on Molière's comedies. Explores satire, parody, comedy of manners, and wit in Molière's comedies.

Hall, H. Gaston. *Comedy in Context: Essays on Molière*. Jackson: University Press of Mississippi, 1984. Contains twelve essays by an eminent Molière specialist. Examines comic images, social satire, and parody in *The School for Wives*.

Palmer, John. *Molière: His Life and Works*. London: G. Bell and Sons, 1930. A well-documented biography of Molière's career as a playwright, actor, and director of a theatrical troupe. Discusses the perverse nature of Arnolphe's failed attempt to dominate Agnès and his specious reasoning in *The School for Wives*.

Walker, Hallam. *Molière*. Updated ed. Boston: Twayne, 1990. Contains an excellent general introduction to Molière's comedies and an annotated bibliography of important critical studies on Molière. Examines images of marriage and the exploitation of women in *The School for Wives*.

SEA GARDEN

Type of work: Poetry
Author: H. D. (Hilda Doolittle, 1886-1961)
First published: 1916

The poet Hilda Doolittle, born into a Moravian family in Bethlehem, Pennsylvania, was living in England when her first book, *Sea Garden*, was published. Restless by nature, she had left Bryn Mawr College after one year as a student and proceeded to educate herself in classical literature. Her former fiancé, the poet Ezra Pound, had helped initiate her attraction to the Greeks, and she soon followed him to London, where he was making a name for himself in bohemian and literary circles. It was Pound who, reading Doolittle's first poems in a London café, signed them at the bottom, "H. D. Imagiste," thus founding the Imagist movement in poetry and launching his friend's career under the more aurally pleasing pseudonym of her initials.

The principles of Imagism, as set forth by Pound, emphasize great concentration of language and subject matter. Like a Japanese haiku, the Imagist poem eschews verbiage and gives the reader a concrete and discrete image—or series of images—on which to focus. H. D.'s particular brand of Imagism blends her fascination with the world of classical antiquity and mythology with a drive toward both passion and austerity. The speaker is always a presence in her poems, and the speaker's relationship to the thing described is what the poem primarily conveys.

Sea Garden collects H. D.'s early Imagist poems. A slim volume, it is highly cohesive in its theme: enough so as to be an Imagist long poem. The predominant motif is the meeting and mating of contrary elements on an unearthly middle ground "where sea-grass tangles with/ shore-grass" ("Hermes of the Ways"). The emblems of this encounter are the flowers whose names and descriptions fill the book: "Sea Rose" (the first poem), "Sea Lily," "Sea Poppies," "Sea Violet," and "Sea Iris." Along with the flowers are invocations to mostly unnamed gods, goddesses, and godlike mortals, and poems describing the destructive and regenerative powers that natural forces (wind and water, primarily) have over natural objects such as trees, cliffs, and especially flowers.

The two powers, destructive and regenerative, are synonymous in H. D.'s philosophy and throughout *Sea Garden*. An example of the book's pairing of these two opposite ends of one thing is in a poem near the center of the volume, "Sheltered Garden." In this poem, the speaker "gasp[s] for breath," trapped in a mazelike garden of "scented pinks" that she likens to "pears wadded in cloth" or "melons smothered in straw." "It is better to taste of frost," she continues,

> the exquisite frost—
> than of wadding and dead grass.
> For this beauty,
> beauty without strength,
> chokes out life.

"O to blot out this garden," the poem ends, "to forget, to find a new beauty/ in some terrible/ wind-tortured place."

Critics and biographers of H. D. have focused extensively on her bisexuality and on the powerful influence of Sigmund Freud, a patriarch of psychoanalysis, who treated her in 1933 and again, briefly, in 1934. *Sea Garden* predates her analysis, and the reader can find in these poems the intense quest for an authoritative voice and the effort to recover the fragments of a more unified self that would bring H. D. to Freud nearly two decades later. As did Freud, H. D. had archaeological interests. Much of her poetic career was occupied with the attempt to invoke and inhabit the lost voices of an ancient past. Freud theorized that a matriarchal civilization once existed, predating the patriarchal world of history. The traces of this matriarchal world are all but lost. H. D. gestures toward such a civilization in poems such as "The Shrine," addressed to an unnamed, neglected goddess, a goddess of the sea whom "landsmen" call "useless" and blame for shipwrecks. "The Shrine," whose narrator could be female or male, reads at points like a protest against men's denigration and trivilization of female strength.

The motif of resuscitation informs virtually all the poems, which repeatedly address themselves to some neglected, nearly extinct iconic figure. The first such figure is the sea rose, "marred and with stint of petals," but far more "precious" than the ordinary garden rose or spice rose. "Can the spice-rose," asks the ending, "drip such acrid fragrance/ hardened in a leaf?" Questions like these hint that the speaker—and, by extension, the writer—are revolutionaries, women who reject traditional roles, refusing to write "pretty" verses. The speaker will prefer, even revere, the bitter and attenuated over the lush and sweet and the blasted cliff over the fragrant forest. If she must be "wind-tortured" in the process of choosing such a preference, she will welcome that torment. In the end, the beaten thing (such as the goddess of "The Shrine") triumphs: "Yet though the whole wind/ slash at your bark,/ you are lifted up" ("Sea Lily").

The sea garden is a mythological realm, beyond this world yet filled with this world's passions. It is like the realm of the Greek gods. Its inhabitants are often androgynous, or of undesignated gender. In one of the late poems, "Prisoner," one prisoner addresses another, with whom he or she has fallen in love. Both seem to be prisoners of war. In the world of the sea garden, a world of water rather than land, radical combinations are possible, and the bounds of gender itself are in question. In an early poem, "The Contest," the speaker addresses a warrior or wrestler with a "male torso" in the first two sections. In part 3, the wrestler seems to answer back, describing the speaker's posture and "slight breast." Neither speaker is named, and gender remains uncertain despite the not-entirely conclusive markers. The poem is on a high level of abstraction; the contest, apparently between two people, reads as a counterpoint of images.

It is such a purification, a stripping-away, toward which these poems constantly strive. The sea-flowers themselves, subjected to the battering of the waves, barely survive. What remains of them is curiously splendid. Austerity, in H. D.'s Imagism, often shades into luxuriance. Many of these spare poems are thick with flower names, descriptions of jewels, and descriptions of the face and body of the beloved. H. D. uses a lush and often esoteric vocabulary reminiscent of such late-nineteenth century aesthetes as Walter Pater and Oscar Wilde. She also shares their love of things Hellenic, their aura of sexuality, and their fascination with religious arcana. Her Poundian influence, and her own literary inclination, however, always lead her back to simplicity, to the thing itself. The figure of the erotic martyr, who appears in H. D.'s poems and in the work of many authors of the late nineteenth century, represents the desire for purification, divestment, or stripping-away rather than histrionic display.

"Spare us from loveliness," the speaker keeps crying in the poem "Orchard." Ambivalence about beauty drives the early work of H. D. to a continual refinement of imagery. That refinement is represented by nature at its barest, and the action of the wind on land. In a poem such as "The Cliff-Temple," the action of the wind is like the action of the poet on her own language, continually breaking things down, working to reveal essences. High places and unattainable gods are contrasted with forest underbrush and fallen fruit, as the poet reminds herself to flee from luxury toward the difficult. The higher she climbs, the more removed is her goal. "O poplar," she cries in "Mid-day," an early poem,

you are great
among the hill-stones,
while I perish on the path
among the crevices of the rocks.

This despairing ending is revised in later poems. "The Cliff-Temple" ends with the speaker's almost matter-of-fact recognition that the journey will never end, nor the object be attained.

Over me the wind swirls.
I have stood on your portal
and I know—
you are further than this,
still further on another cliff.

In *Sea Garden*, H. D. seems to be writing about her own career; the poems are all, in one way or another, about their own composing. Any extraneous matter has been eliminated, and even those poems that, according to biographer-critics, arose from the events of H. D.'s life seem to bear no relationship to anything in the external world. Her experience has been impersonalized, made into metaphors of poetic inspiration and poetic quest.

In the final poem of the volume, "Cities," the poet broadens her scope. The book's messianism, which is, in all but this poem, purely individual—the dream of a muse who comes to stay—culminates in the vision of a New Jerusalem for an entire community. An unnamed "we" (the reader presumes a society of artists) conspire to eradicate banality and resurrect the beauty of a forgotten era. The poem describes an ugly urban maze erected by the "maker of cities" above the old, gorgeous city of "arch upon perfect arch,/ of pillars and corridors that led out/ to strange court-yards and porches." The speaker wonders about the maker's motives, concluding that both he and the old city's inhabitants were put off by its splendor:

For alas,
he had crowded the city so full
that men could not grasp beauty,
beauty was over them,
through them, about them,
no crevice unpacked with the honey

The new city, posits the speaker, was intended to foster human striving after beauty by removing it from reach but keeping it in sight. This same intention informs many of the poems in the volume. The poet repeatedly seeks to escape beauty and strive for the transcendent. In the context of "Cities," however, the idea has elitist and misanthropic implications: The speaker describes the new inhabitants as larvae, "disfigured, defaced," sleeping in their cells, crawling out "to attack our frail strength." "We," on the other hand, the few remaining former citizens, are bees who still hoard traces of honey, whose task it is to "recall the old splendour,/ await the new beauty of cities." Twice the speaker addresses the ugly new citizens with the very phrase the "landsmen" used against the goddess in "The Shrine": "You are useless."

Although a feminist interpretation is possible (the old city, with its feminine architectural shapes, is a matriarchal civilization, while the new one is a repressive patriarchal one), the inhabitants of the two cities are distinguished not by gender but by beauty and its appreciation. "We protect our strong race," says the speaker. The reader, who may detect in the poem the same elitist nostalgia that often informs the work of other famous modern poets such as T. S. Eliot and W. B. Yeats, may interpret the poem in terms of elitism rather than feminism. A certain tone running through the volume, one of self-dramatization and self-aggrandizement, culminates in this vision of a heavenly home for lovers of beauty.

The exacting reader may find the sea garden an airless and insular place, but there is no question of the beauty of its highly concentrated imagery, of its rhythms and assonances, of its short, incantatory lines, or of H. D.'s singular achievement in defining the poetic movement known as Imagism. It is a strong first volume by a poet who would move on to greater accomplishments. *Sea Garden* defines at the outset a career marked by restlessness and a perpetual, mystical questing.

Natania Rosenfeld

Bibliography:

DuPlessis, Rachel Blau. *H. D.: The Career of That Struggle*. Bloomington: Indiana University Press, 1986. A succinct summary of H. D.'s life and work from a feminist viewpoint. Includes a useful bibliography.

Friedman, Susan Stanford. *Psyche Reborn: The Emergence of H. D.* Bloomington: Indiana University Press, 1981. An extensive study of H. D.'s development and influences, with a feminist and psychoanalytic focus.

Friedman, Susan Stanford, and Rachel Blau DuPlessis, eds. *Signets: Reading H. D.* Madison: University of Wisconsin Press, 1990. A volume of reminiscences, tributes, and essays by friends, scholars, and poets.

Guest, Barbara. *Herself Defined: The Poet H. D. and Her World*. New York: Quill, 1984. An eminently readable, fascinating biography with fictional embellishments by an avant-garde poet who has read and researched H. D. with care and understanding.

H. D. *Collected Poems, 1912-1944*. Edited by Louis L. Martz. New York: New Directions, 1983. Vital for the serious reader of H. D., this book begins with all of *Sea Garden*. The introduction gives a good overview.

THE SEA OF GRASS

Type of work: Novel
Author: Conrad Richter (1890-1968)
Type of plot: Regional
Time of plot: 1885-1910
Locale: Southwestern United States
First published: 1936

Principal characters:
COLONEL JIM BREWTON, a pioneer rancher
LUTIE, his wife
HAL, his nephew
BRICE CHAMBERLAIN, a lawyer
BROCK, Lutie's son by Brice Chamberlain

The Story:

Hal Brewton never forgot the day he stood on the railroad platform at Salt Fork, where he waited to meet Lutie Cameron, who was arriving from St. Louis to marry his uncle, Colonel Jim Brewton, the owner of the vast Cross B Ranch. At the time of the story, Colonel Brewton was involved in a range war with nesters coming to rip the sod from the grazing lands in order to raise wheat.

On the day of Lutie's arrival, two of the colonel's cowhands were being tried for shooting at a homesteader on the Brewton range. Although the colonel's lawyer, Henry McCurtin, won the case, the opposition lawyer, young Brice Chamberlain, protested indignantly that the victory would not be permanent. Colonel Brewton was contemptuous of the lawyer's warnings.

Lutie Cameron was a lovely woman, too lovely for that still-wild territory. When men saw her, she won them completely. Only Hal refused to be moved by her charm. All that winter in an academy at Lexington, Missouri, he thought of her as part of the destruction coming from the East to destroy the sea of grass he loved.

The following summer, he returned to a changed ranch house. Lutie had filled it with furniture and flowers and had planted a row of cottonwoods and tamarisks about it. Guests from the whole territory came and went. Officers from the Army posts, officials of the railroad companies, and neighboring ranchmen all found ample welcome at the home of Colonel and Mrs. Brewton.

The old-timers who had known the colonel before he had married Lutie hoped that she would settle down after having children. The babies were born, two boys and a girl; however, Lutie did not become any calmer. The third baby was scarcely in its cradle before she was dancing with Brice Chamberlain as her favored partner. Colonel Brewton ignored the gossip that was whispered about Lutie.

Local politics concerning homesteading rights shifted with the administration in Washington, D.C., for the territory depended upon appointments to its judicial staffs. For a while, Brice Chamberlain had influential support from the government. Then, during another administration, the forces that backed Colonel Brewton were in power, and the incoming tide of settlers seemed to be checked. Hal read of the change with great pleasure, but when he returned to Salt Fork, he discovered that Chamberlain was still in his law office on the Salt Fork plaza. He learned that hundreds of settlers were waiting nearby for a change in government that would permit them to stake claims upon the miles of land held by men like Colonel Brewton.

Lutie then calmly announced that she was leaving her husband and children. She explained that she had had enough of the flat grass country and the fighting between ranchers and homesteaders. She claimed she would be able to get possession of her three children, Jimmy, Brock, and Sarah Beth, later, by court action.

The town was informed that Mrs. Brewton was leaving for a visit in St. Louis. Most of the people knew better. Their feelings were confirmed when they saw Brice Chamberlain with a bag packed, ready to head East on the same train; but the colonel paced the station platform, a gun belt buckled under his broadcloth coat. Chamberlain did not board the train.

A few days later, the colonel sent Hal to Denver, to give Lutie a thousand dollars—he knew that his wife's cowardly lover had no intention of following her—but Hal could find no trace of Lutie in Denver. At the same time, a new administration appointed Chamberlain a judge of the district court. Back in Salt Fork, Hal saw the white-covered wagons of the emigrant trains moving westward into the range country. When Colonel Brewton planned to run the homesteaders off his land, a troop of cavalry from Fort Ewing was sent to guard him until all chances of his stopping the land grabbers were gone.

Studying for his medical degree, Hal spent three more years away from Salt Fork. When he returned, he discovered that his sea of grass had been hopelessly despoiled. His uncle seemed much older. The Brewton children were growing up wild, for their mother had never sent for them.

One day, Hal saw Jimmy and Brock fighting in the dusty Salt Fork street. Then a nester among the onlookers called out that he was betting on the Chamberlain brat. So Hal heard for the first time the rumor that Brock was not his uncle's son. Hal fired at the nester but missed. When Colonel Brewton appeared, the crowd, even the jeering nesters, grew quiet.

As young Brock grew older, he became the image of Brice Chamberlain. It was obvious that he realized the truth and resented it. He took to gambling, drinking, and barroom brawling. At last, he was caught cheating in a card game. For that disgrace Colonel Brewton could not forgive him, but he continued to indulge the boy and pay his debts. By that time, Hal was practicing medicine in Salt Fork. He was glad when Sarah Beth, who had been away at school, returned and began to look after her father.

One day, Brock shot and killed Dutch Charley, who had accused Brock of using a woman to help him cheat at cards. Brock was locked up, but Brice Chamberlain soon got him out of jail. When Brock returned home, he defied Colonel Brewton and said he was leaving the Brewton ranch to go to work for Brice Chamberlain's interests. This last blow to the colonel's pride permanently wrecked his health.

Brock now took the name of Chamberlain, an act that cut the old colonel still more. Brock began to ride wild, shooting up towns and staging reckless holdups. He became the talk of the Southwest for his daring lawlessness. At last, he was trapped by a posse of homesteaders and held at bay in a cabin by twenty or thirty vigilantes.

That same day, Lutie Brewton unexpectedly returned. She was fifteen years older, but she still carried herself with quiet self-possession. Lutie immediately assumed her place in her household as though she had been away fifteen days, not fifteen years.

Meanwhile, the colonel rode out to the cabin where Brock was holding off the sheriff and the armed and angry nesters. With Hal, who had been summoned to attend a wounded deputy, he broke through to Brock, who lay dying from a bullet wound in his lung. They brought his body back across desolate country scorching in raw sunlight, with nesters' families huddled about sagging shacks and plows rusting in fields where wheat would not grow in hot, rainless summers. Sand was beginning to drift among dugouts and rotting fence posts.

Brock was buried on the Brewton ranch. The stone inscribed with the name "Brock Brewton" was the old colonel's challenge to all gossip and speculation around Salt Fork. He and Lutie took up their life where she had broken it off years previously, and no one ever dared ask either the colonel or his wife where she had been. It seemed to Hal that the colonel had found peace at last.

Critical Evaluation:

The use of Hal Brewton as the narrator in *The Sea of Grass* is extremely clever. He reminisces from the vantage point of being Salt Fork's physician. He has seen many changes in the nearly fifty years he has lived there. He is the nephew of Colonel Jim Brewton, whose stoicism he admires, and hence he is sympathetic both to him and more gradually to Lutie, whose beauty captivates him. He is Brock's cousin—nominally, at least—and therefore he narrates events in that conflicted youth's short life with muted emotion. Best of all, since Conrad Richter chose to present a quarter-century's salient events in the lives of his triangle of central characters—Lutie, Brewton, and Brock—it is useful to have Hal periodically leave Salt Fork for schooling in the more settled East, so that, upon each return, he can observe dramatic changes and record them more emphatically. His objectivity, however, is tinged with melancholy; therefore his prose has lyric overtones, and his narration is often a kind of elegy. At the end of chapter 14, Hal imagines that Lutie is recalling Brock in her mind's eye as a yellow-haired baby again "in the candlelight of a world that had vanished like last year's snow." Richter, who was a well-read author, assuredly wants his readers to hear echoes in these lines of the fifteenth century French poet François Villon's most famous line: "Mais où sont les neiges d'antan?" (But where are the snows of yesteryear?). Several critics have noted that Richter may also have been inspired to employ the kind of narrator he did by reading Willa Cather's novel *A Lost Lady* (1923), the narrator and heroine of which are very much like those in *The Sea of Grass*.

This short novel is compactly structured, with three numbered parts of almost exactly equal lengths. Each part, however, has a different number of chapters, perhaps to indicate the fact that separate dramatic segments presented in them carry different weights of import. Part 1, called "Lutie," has five chapters; part 2, "The Colonel," seven chapters; and part 3, "Brock," three. Chapter 6, the shortest in the book, is also the most static. In it, Lutie leaves the town by train, and everyone else, including her husband, waits to see whether Brice will board it with her. However, nothing happens. The bleat of lambs in the shipping pen, though, reminds Hal of Lutie's three abandoned children. Chapter 15, the last, is also the longest. It skillfully ties up every plot strand in paragraph after paragraph, often out of chronological order for heightened effect. This chapter presents a memorable contrast between the Old West and the new: Lutie rather frenetically insists that Hal escort her to Mass before asking him for details about Brock, who earlier has derisively noted that the only thing not riddled with bullets from the posse's guns in his wretched hideout is a portrait of Christ.

Each of the three parts dramatizes a different kind of failure. Lutie, in part 1, fails her husband—for whatever reasons—leaves him for her paramour, but fails to find happiness with this man, or even to set up a brief residence with him. The colonel, in part 2, prepares his loyal ranch hands to fight the "army" of nesters but fails to do so. Brock, in part 3, pursues a life with drinkers, town women, gamblers, and gunslingers, all of whom fail him, and he ends up being killed. The only other significantly active character, Brice Chamberlain, relates to Lutie, the colonel, and Brock, but remains busy only in the shadows. He succeeds materially and professionally by failing Lutie, by legalizing the cause of the ruinously encroaching nesters, and by failing his son Brock. This novel, however, is less about failure than it is about Colonel

Brewton's achieving tragically heroic stature through steady and responsible action. When Lutie leaves him, he tries to send her money for at least temporary help, and at the end he quietly welcomes her back into his life. (What marital success they may achieve is left to the reader to decide.) When the president sends the army to guard the nesters' encampment, Brewton, a former soldier, puts loyalty to the expanding nation foremost. When Brock is dying, Brewton races straight to him, offers what comfort he can, and buries him—on his land and as his son. Richter presents Brewton's reverence for the land sympathetically, but he shows it to be impractical in the face of inexorable Western settlement. Hence, there are two morals: One is romantic, the other realistic. The romantic moral is that population explosions hurt nature. The realistic moral is that old ways must yield to the new.

Richter augments the unity of *The Sea of Grass* by repeating key words in describing characters, setting, and action. Lutie is lithe, slender, sparkling, with her head erect, and redolent of violet perfume. Almost monotonously, she is called "gay"—before that word lost its nonsexual meaning. Brewton is massive, dark, arrogant, implacable. His ropy, wine-dark hand and neck veins expand when he is outraged. Feisty Brock has feather blond hair and quick hands, whether he is playing the piano, dealing cards, or shooting. Richter stresses Brice's blue eyes, blond hair, long legs, and brown-checked Eastern suit.

Musical motifs of imagery also ripple through the text. Most of the numerous similes and metaphors appropriately derive from natural elements. Thus, Brewton is likened to a stallion, a steer, granite; his eyes are fiery, stormy. The nesters, who are regularly demeaned by being depicted in dirty clothes, resemble a plague almost biblical in its advance and devastation. The most frequently repeated metaphor is naturally the one comparing the almost limitless prairie to a rippling sea, a sea of grass. Ultimately, this proves to be a sad metaphor, because in time the grass—which Brewton and Hal love but which Lutie hates and hides from—will be, unlike the sea, gone.

"Critical Evaluation" by Robert L. Gale

Bibliography:

Barnes, Robert J. *Conrad Richter*. Austin, Tex.: Steck-Vaughn, 1968. Considers only Richter's fiction that has the Southwest as a setting. Especially valuable for its discussion of Richter's style and his use of deliberately repeated details in *The Sea of Grass*.

Estleman, Loren D. *The Wister Trace: Classic Novels of the American Frontier*. Ottawa, Ill.: Jameson Books, 1987. Analyzes *The Sea of Grass* as a prose poem about change and loss.

Gaston, Edwin W., Jr. *Conrad Richter*. Updated ed. Boston: Twayne, 1989. The best and most extensive treatment of Richter's plain life and creative versatility. The section on *The Sea of Grass* concerns its origins, plot, point of view, contrasting characters, themes (parenting and alienation, historical change, unity of people and nature), and relation to other fiction by Richter.

LaHood, Marvin J. *Conrad Richter's America*. The Hague: Mouton, 1975. Highly academic treatise. Section on *The Sea of Grass* emphasizes the central characters and their different reactions to the land.

Pilkington, William T. "Conrad Richter." In *Fifty Western Writers: A Bio-Bibliographical Sourcebook*, edited by Fred Erisman and Richard W. Etulain. Westport, Conn.: Greenwood Press, 1982. Presents a brief biography of Richter, discusses his major themes, and surveys the extensive criticism of Richter. Analyzes *The Sea of Grass* as a historical and mythical drama of old and new ways, with Lutie as a reconciling influence.

Richter, Harvena. *Writing to Survive: The Private Notebooks of Conrad Richter*. Albuquerque: University of New Mexico Press, 1988. A fascinating weaving together of passages from Richter's many notebooks and his devoted daughter's intelligent commentary thereon. Includes a complete bibliography of Richter's novels, short stories, short-story collections, nonfictional works, articles, and book reviews.

THE SEA-WOLF

Type of work: Novel
Author: Jack London (1876-1916)
Type of plot: Adventure
Time of plot: 1904
Locale: Pacific Ocean and the Bering Sea
First published: 1904

Principal characters:
HUMPHREY "HUMP" VAN WEYDEN, an unwilling sailor aboard the *Ghost*
WOLF LARSEN, the captain of the *Ghost*
MUGRIDGE, the ship's cook
MAUD BREWSTER, a survivor picked up at sea

The Story:

When the ship in which he was a passenger sank in a collision off the coast of California, Humphrey Van Weyden was picked up by the crew of Wolf Larsen's ship, the *Ghost*, a sailing vessel headed for seal hunting ranges in the Bering Sea. Wolf Larsen was a brute. Van Weyden witnessed the inhuman treatment of a sick mate, who died shortly afterward. He saw a cabin boy badly beaten. In his own interview with the captain, he fared little better. Instead of promising to help him return to San Francisco, Wolf demanded that Van Weyden sign as cabin boy and stay with his ship.

The crew set to work taking in the topsails and jibs. From that moment Hump, as the crew called Van Weyden, learned things the hard way. He had to get his sea legs, and he had to learn the stoic indifference to pain and suffering that the sailors seemed to have mastered already. As cabin boy, he peeled potatoes and washed greasy pots and pans. Mugridge, the cook, abused him and robbed him of his money. Only one man, Louis, seemed to share Hump's feelings about the captain and his ship. Louis predicted that many deaths would result from the voyage. He said that Wolf Larsen was a violent, dangerous man and that the crew and seal hunters were vicious outcasts. Wolf did seem mad. He varied from moods of wild exultation to spells of extreme depression. In his cabin were classic books of literature, and when he spoke, he could use either excellent English or the lingo of the sailors. Sometimes he amused himself by arguing with Hump. He claimed that life was without meaning.

During a southeaster, Hump badly dislocated his knee, and Wolf unexpectedly allowed Hump to rest for three days while he talked to him about philosophy and literature. When Hump returned to the galley, the cook was whetting his knife. Hump obtained a knife and began whetting it also. Hump's actions so frightened the cowardly cook that Hump was no longer the victim of the cook's abuse.

Louis talked of the coming season with the seals. Moreover, he hinted that trouble would come if the *Macedonia*, a sealing steamer, came near. Captained by Death Larsen, the brother and enemy of Wolf, the *Macedonia* was a certain menace. As a prelude to things to come, an outbreak of fury took place aboard the *Ghost*. First, Wolf Larsen and the mate beat a seaman named Johnson to a pulp because he complained of ill treatment; then Leach, the former cabin boy, beat the cook. Later, two hunters exchanged shots, severely wounding each other, and Wolf beat them because they had crippled themselves before the hunting season began. Afterward, Wolf suffered from one of his periodic headaches. To Hump, life on shipboard was a tremendous experience in human cruelty and viciousness.

A few days later, the men tried to mutiny. In the row that followed, Johansen, the mate, was drowned, and Wolf was nearly killed. While Hump dressed Wolf's wounds, Wolf promoted him to mate in Johansen's place. Leach and Johnson would have killed Wolf in a second, but he remained too wary for them. At the seal hunting grounds, a terrific storm cost them the lives of four men. The ship itself was beaten, its sails torn to shreds and portions of the deck swept into the sea.

When Leach and Johnson deserted in a small skiff, Wolf started out in pursuit. On the morning of the third day, an open boat was sighted. The boat contained a young woman and four men, survivors from a sinking steamer. Wolf took them aboard, planning to make sailors of the men as he had of Hump. Shortly afterward, the *Ghost* overtook Johnson and Leach. Refusing to pick them up, Wolf let them struggle to get aboard until their small craft capsized. He watched them drown without comment and then ordered the ship's course set for a return to the seal hunting grounds.

The woman survivor was Maud Brewster, a rich woman and a poet. She was weak physically, as Hump had been. Wolf resented the intimacy that sprang up at once between Maud Brewster and Hump. He took out his resentment by deciding to give the cook the first bath the cook had ever been known to take. At Wolf's orders, Mugridge was thrown into the water with a tow rope slung about his middle. At first, the cook fled madly about the ship, causing one man to break a leg and another to be injured in a fall. Then Mugridge was thrown into the sea. Before Wolf was ready to bring Mugridge back aboard ship, a shark bit off the cook's right foot at the ankle. Dragged aboard, Mugridge in his fury tried to bite Wolf's leg, and Wolf almost strangled him. Then Hump bandaged the wounded man's leg. Maud Brewster looked on and nearly fainted.

The *Macedonia* appeared one day and robbed Wolf's hunters of their day's catch of seals by cutting off the line of approach to the *Ghost*. In revenge, Wolf set his men to work capturing hunters from the *Macedonia*. When the *Macedonia* gave chase, Wolf sailed his ship into a fog bank. That night, Wolf tried to seize Maud, but Hump, awakening, ran his knife into Wolf's shoulder. At the same time, Wolf was overcome by one of his headaches, this seizure accompanied by blindness. Hump helped the captain to his bunk, and under the cover of darkness, he and Maud made their escape in an open boat. After days of tossing about on the open sea, they came to a small island. Using supplies they had taken from the *Ghost*, they set about making themselves houses and gathering food for the coming winter. One morning, Hump saw the wreck of the *Ghost* lying offshore. Going aboard, he discovered Wolf alone, his crew having deserted him to go aboard Death Larsen's ship. Wolf seemed nearly insane and had only a desire to sleep. Hump stole some pistols and food, which he took to the island. Hump, planning to repair the masts of the *Ghost*, began work on the crippled ship. That night, Wolf undid all Hump's work and cast the masts off the vessel.

Hump and Maud began anew to refit the ship. One day, Wolf attempted to murder Hump, but during the struggle, he had one of his spasms and fainted. While he was still unconscious, they handcuffed him and shut him in the hold.

Then they moved aboard the *Ghost*, and the work of refitting the vessel went forward. Wolf had a stroke that paralyzed the right side of his body. Hump continued to repair the vessel. At last, it was able to sail. Wolf next lost the use of his muscles and lay in a coma. When he died, Hump and Maud buried him at sea. By that time they were deeply in love. When a United States revenue cutter discovered them one day, they felt that their dangerous odyssey was at an end. They were, however, about to begin another journey together.

Critical Evaluation:

Jack London's talent for creating adventure stories made him one of the most popular writers of his time. His familiarity with adventure came from his own experience. He began making his own living at the age of fourteen. By the time he was able to live as a writer (with the publication of his collection of stories, *The Son of the Wolf*, 1900), London had worked a variety of menial jobs. He had been a seaman, a waterfront fighter, a coal shoveler, an oyster pirate, a wage slave in a laundry, and a gold prospector in the Klondike, to name a few. He also spent thirty days in prison for vagrancy. London lived the seafaring life, and *The Sea-Wolf* portrays a vivid picture of the life on a sealing ship—from the technical details of steering a vessel in a blinding storm to violent encounters between seamen.

The Sea-Wolf is more than a simple adventure tale. It reflects philosophical ideas prevalent in London's time. In order to educate himself and improve his prospects, London read voraciously in all subjects. From Charles Darwin's *On the Origin of Species by Means of Natural Selection* (1859), London learned that in nature, living is a constant struggle, and organisms that have the ability to adapt to their environment survive. The works of nineteenth century philosopher Herbert Spencer taught him that human life is a matter of the survival of the fittest. The individual most likely to survive and dominate others would be much like the "superman," the man of superior intellectual and physical abilities who follows an amoral code as described by nineteenth century German philosopher Friedrich Nietzsche, another favorite of London. *The Sea-Wolf* portrays a struggle between civilization and raw nature. In the untamed, natural arena of the sea these two competing philosophies, embodied in Humphrey Van Weydon and Wolf Larsen, come into conflict.

The violently competitive environment on the *Ghost*, in which men struggle to establish their place in a pecking order based on physical strength, intimidation, courage, and aggression, seems to validate the world view described by Spencer and Nietzsche. Larsen is close to the Nietzschean superman. Larsen is extraordinarily strong, with a body that strikes Humphrey with awe: "God made you well," he tells Larsen. Larsen may not be as learned as the formally educated Humphrey, but he impresses Humphrey by his breadth of knowledge, his thirst for reading in all subjects, and his keen understanding of human nature. He is an ardent individualist who follows the amoral code that suits him and the life he has led. To him human life has no individual value; for every one that dies many more are born. It is the nature of life to replenish itself. It is also the nature of life to kill so it can survive, to subdue the weak so it can remain strong. Larsen's uncompromisingly naturalistic code is realized in his cruel treatment of his men—dragging Mugridge the cook overboard, brutally beating two seal hunters, and allowing Johnson and Leech to drown.

London, however, cannot adhere completely to the philosophy of might makes right. In his wolf stories (*Call of the Wild*, 1903, and *White Fang*, 1906), the law of nature, of survival of the fittest, dominates. In the social world in which humans interact, however, London was convinced that brutality could not be the only norm. During his time on the *Ghost*, Humphrey fights to live by his civilized moral beliefs—the dignity of the individual, the need for compassion, and the value of human life. In frequent philosophical arguments with Larsen, Humphrey attempts to defend this moral code against Larsen's naturalistic beliefs. The brutal environment of the *Ghost* wears him down almost to the point of rejecting his moral code. Humphrey's love for Maud Brewster, however, encourages him to continue his moral struggle.

With Maud's appearance it seems that London sought to pander to the contemporary taste for sentimentalism, injecting feminine romance into his masculine adventure tale. Maud is a conventional female literary figure. Physically weak but morally courageous, she represents the humanistic values of a more civilized world. Under Maud's domestic influence, Humphrey's commitment to live morally is renewed. Humphrey becomes Maud's protector. They flee the *Ghost*, braving the open sea, in order to save Maud from Larsen's physical advances.

Although Humphrey is triumphant in the end, *The Sea-Wolf* does not completely reject Larsen's code. Larsen is London's most intriguing character, appealing and repugnant. He is an interesting combination of physical and mental power. His presence causes the book's most exciting dramatic scenes. Just as Larsen predicted, Humphrey's tenure on the *Ghost* makes him a better man. He becomes morally, mentally, and physically stronger, learning to be courageous and ingenuous in his effort to stay alive. At first sheltered and weakened by his upper-class privilege, Humphrey's nature is toughened through contact with Larsen's potent individualism.

Humphrey's humanism, however, has no influence on Larsen's brutal naturalistic philosophy. The once physically powerful man is made blind, deaf, and dumb by a brain tumor. His muscles slowly degenerate, leaving him paralyzed. In life he intentionally cut himself off from humanity through his excessive individualism and lack of compassion. Fittingly, he spends his last few hours in complete isolation, unable to see, hear, speak, or move.

The Sea-Wolf seems to demonstrate Darwinian principles. The balance that Humphrey has struck between body and spirit, rugged individualism and humanistic compassion, allows him to adapt to his changing environment more successfully than Larsen. The fittest survives.

"Critical Evaluation" by Heidi Kelchner

Bibliography:

Labor, Earle. *Jack London*. Boston: Twayne, 1974. Praises London's convincing portrayal of Wolf Larsen and of Humphrey's transformation from a weak, rich socialite to a dynamic he-man.

London, Jack. *Novels and Stories*. Notes and chronology by Donald Pizer. New York: Literary Classics of the United States, 1982. Uses text from the first editions. Includes notes on the texts, historical and geographical notes, maps, and notes on the stories.

Lundquist, James. *Jack London: Adventures, Ideas, and Fiction*. New York: Frederick Ungar, 1987. Suggests that the quality of London's stories arises from the risks he took and from his colorful personal experience. Traces London's intellectual leanings.

Pattee, Fred Lewis. *The New American Literature, 1890-1930*. New York: Cooper Square Publishers, 1968. Chapter 9 discusses the influence that London's life had on his writing.

Sinclair, Andrew. *Jack: A Biography of Jack London*. New York: Harper & Row, 1977. Discusses the biographical detail in *The Sea-Wolf*. Describes London's marriages and affairs.

THE SEAGULL

Type of work: Drama
Author: Anton Chekhov (1860-1904)
Type of plot: Impressionistic realism
Time of plot: Nineteenth century
Locale: Russia
First performed: 1896; revised, 1898; first published, 1904 as *Chayka*, (English translation, 1909)

Principal characters:
IRINA ARKADINA, an actress
KONSTANTIN TREPLEV, her son
PYOTR SORIN, her brother
ILYA SHAMRAEV, manager of his estate
POLINA, his wife
MASHA, their daughter
NINA ZARETCHYN, a young actress
BORIS TRIGORIN, an author
YEVGENY DORN, a doctor
SEMYON MEDVEDENKO, a schoolmaster

The Story:

One day Konstantin Treplev killed a seagull and laid it at the feet of Nina, the beautiful young actress with whom he was hopelessly in love. He told her that unless she could love him, he too would be lying dead at her feet. Nina, however, was not in love with Konstantin; she was infatuated with Trigorin, the famous novelist, who in turn was in love with Irina Arkadina, an actress and Konstantin's mother.

Konstantin hated Trigorin, looking upon him as a purveyor of empty phrases, a writer entirely different from what he himself hoped to become. Konstantin's ambition was to create new and more expressive literary forms, and he had written a play in which Nina had consented to appear. The performance, which was staged in the open air on the estate of Pyotr Sorin, Konstantin's uncle, was not exactly a success, although it possessed unquestioned literary merit. Madame Arkadina and Trigorin, who were present, refused to take the production seriously. Trigorin was most impressed by the performance of nineteen-year-old Nina in the principal role.

Madame Arkadina's behavior at her son's play was typical of her attitude toward Konstantin in every aspect of their relationship. As a famous actress, whose popularity depended upon her keeping her youth and good looks, she naturally was not overjoyed at the constant reminder that she was the mother of a twenty-five-year-old son. Consequently, she kept Konstantin in the country, where he would not be seen and thus be associated with her in the public mind. Moreover, she gave him little or no money to spend, so that he was forced to wear the same suit for years until it was threadbare. Her brother, Pyotr Sorin, had taken his sister to task on several occasions for her stinginess, but she had pleaded poverty, meaning, of course, that she preferred to spend her money on herself.

In spite of the way she treated him, Konstantin was greatly attached to his mother, so much so that he developed a morbid, unhealthy attitude toward his work and life in general. Occasionally he would lose his temper and quarrel violently with his mother. When he did so, she would burst into tears, and Konstantin would be overcome promptly by feelings of remorse.

Konstantin was not the only unbalanced individual on the Sorin estate. Another was Masha, the daughter of Pyotr Sorin's manager, who was as hopelessly in love with Konstantin as he was with Nina. Although she was only a young girl, she dressed habitually in black—in mourning, as she said, for her chronic unhappiness. Semyon Medvedenko, the schoolmaster, was in love with her, but he had only twenty-three rubles a month on which to support his mother, two sisters, and a brother. After two years, giving up all hope that Konstantin would ever notice her, Masha decided to marry Semyon. She bore him a child, but she was so indifferent to it that the schoolmaster had to take care of the baby in addition to his other responsibilities.

Konstantin, like most young writers, knew many people who were willing to offer him advice on how he should write, and what he should write about. Among these advisers was Yevgeny Dorn, the local doctor, who had never written a line in his life, but who had theories about how it should be done. His idea was that Konstantin spent entirely too much time worrying about literary form, whereas literature was not a matter of form, good or bad, but of spontaneous ideas. Another dispenser of advice was the old man, Pyotr Sorin. He suggested that his nephew write a story called *The Man Who Wished*, based on Sorin's own life. He maintained that when he was young he had wished to become an author, but had failed. Then he wanted to become an orator, but he spoke abominably. Finally he wanted to marry, but he never did. When Sorin was reminded that he also wished to become State Councilor and succeeded, he roared with laughter, claiming that he had achieved the post without any effort of his own. The most complete analysis of the writer's art was made by the novelist, Trigorin. One day, while he was taking notes on the personal habits of the neurotic Masha, he was interrupted by Nina, who expressed the view that a writer's life must be a very fascinating one. He told her that writing was merely a violent obsession which lays hold of a man and places him on a treadmill from which there is no escape. Against his will, almost, the writer of fiction was compelled to utilize everything in his experience for his next story. Even the seemingly trivial incident of the seagull which Konstantin had shot, Trigorin viewed as material for a story. He began to see Nina herself as the seagull and himself as the hunter. He realized that Madame Arkadina would be furiously jealous of his interest in the younger woman. Fate played into his hands when Nina promised to run away from home and join him in Moscow.

For nearly a year Nina was Trigorin's mistress in Moscow. After she bore him a child that died, Trigorin deserted her. Even her acting career was unsuccessful, consisting largely of a tour of country towns. All that time Konstantin followed Nina about, but the only encouragement he got was an occasional letter which showed that Nina's spirit was near the breaking point.

At last, worn out and hungry, she came to the Sorin estate, which awakened in her, memories of her happy girlhood. Konstantin urged her to stay with him or to allow him to go away with her, but she refused. She had accepted an engagement for the winter with a second-rate repertory company at Eltz, and there she intended to go as the next step in her career as an actress. Out of her suffering she had realized that in any art it was not the honor and glory which mattered—it was perseverance. Konstantin did not have that kind of strength, and when Nina, the seagull, flew out of his life forever, he locked himself in his room and put a bullet through his head.

Critical Evaluation:

The Seagull was based on an event in Anton Chekhov's life. One afternoon, while he was taking a walk with his friend, Ilya Levitan, the landscape painter, he saw Levitan shoot a seagull which was flying over the river. Later, the moody painter, feeling he was scorned by the woman he loved, threw the dead seagull at her feet and threatened to kill himself. The play Chekhov made from this incident is perhaps the most elaborate and realistic analysis of the life of the artist ever presented in dramatic form; but all that almost any other dramatist would have selected as the material for his play takes place in Moscow between the third and fourth acts. What the audience sees is the effect of what has taken place, and in this lies the essence of what Chekhov has contributed to the art of the theater.

The first production of *The Seagull* on October 17, 1896, was a total disaster. The critics dismissed it as inept and even absurd, and Chekhov, who had fled the theater before the final curtain, accepted their verdict. One audience member, critic-playwright Vladimir Nemirovich-Danchenko, did not agree and determined to mount a second production of the play. Danchenko, who was at that time organizing the Moscow Art Theatre with Constantine Stanislavski, convinced his partner that the new Chekhov play had great potential and then talked the playwright into allowing *The Seagull* a second chance. Their production of the play in 1898 was an enormous artistic, critical, and commercial success and led to that collaboration of playwright and theater which established the Moscow Art Theatre as one of the world's greatest, and stimulated the writing of Chekhov's last three dramatic masterpieces, *Uncle Vanya* (1899), *The Three Sisters* (1901), and *The Cherry Orchard* (1904).

For all of the controversy provoked by the play, it is the most conventional of Chekhov's major plays. *The Seagull* is structured around romantic triangles—Arkadina-Trigorin-Nina, Konstantin-Nina-Trigorin, and, to a lesser extent, Masha-Konstantin-Medvedenko—activated by spite and jealousy, composed of incidents characteristic of popular melodrama—a failed suicide, a seduction and abandonment, a dead child, a successful suicide—and climaxed by an "obligatory scene" in which the main characters meet and resolve their conflicts in a face-to-face confrontation.

Chekhov's handling of this orthodox plot, however, is revolutionary and previews the formula he perfected in his last three masterworks. Konstantin's two suicide attempts and the melodramatic consequences of Nina's affair with Trigorin happen offstage. Chekhov deformalizes the play by undercutting the most intense moments with trivial details and apparently arbitrary bits of stage business—small talk, irrelevant comments and interjections, unexpected comical gestures, characters standing with their backs to the audience, and a game of "Lotto" while Konstantin prepares his suicide.

These deviations from traditional techniques are not merely novel stage gimmicks, however, but reflect Chekhov's basic dramatic and thematic purposes. He was not interested in theatrical action or excitement as such, but in the effects such incidents have on his people. Reality, he felt, does not consist of a series of dramatic climaxes, but is, rather, a mundane process of day-to-day living in which the crucial events happen unobtrusively in the background. The important thing, therefore, is to explore and dramatize their continuing effects on the characters. Thus, even in the last plays, Chekhov does not abandon conventional dramatic structure but mutes it in order to concentrate on what he believed to be more important: real people living real lives.

The Seagull does, however, differ thematically from his later plays; it is the work in which Chekhov makes his definitive statement about the nature of creativity and the role of the artist in society. As both a practicing physician and a creative artist, Chekhov had experienced great difficulty in reconciling the objective, practical world of medicine with the subjective, aesthetic environment of literature and theater. He had already analyzed the problem extensively in his fiction—notably in "A Boring Story" (1889), "The Grasshopper" (1892), and "The House with an Attic" (1896), but *The Seagull* was his final, comprehensive exploration of the subject. Thus, it has a thematic clarity and rhetorical directness that differentiates it from its successors.

This is not to say that *The Seagull* is more simple or obvious than the other works. The four major characters are exceedingly complicated; their relations to one another are subtle, ambiguous, and contradictory, and, although they are given ample opportunity to dramatize these complexities, it is for the audience to attempt the synthesis. Moreover, as completely individualized as the characters are, they embody basic attitudes toward life and art which are crucial to a final understanding and appreciation of the play.

Konstantin Treplev has three roles that he cannot reconcile—son, lover, and creative artist. His feelings about his mother are deep and ambivalent; he passionately craves her affection, yet he finds himself in an unequal competition with her; he desperately wants her to approve his creative efforts, yet consciously advocates artistic notions that are antithetical to hers; he is fully aware of her egotism, pettiness, selfishness, and cruelty, yet he clings to a vision of her as a tender, considerate young mother.

Konstantin's relationship to Nina is equally unrealistic. At best theirs was an adolescent boy-girl flirtation; there is no indication that she has ever been serious about him. In the early scenes of the play, as Konstantin tries to court her, she puts him off. Konstantin cannot see this; he insists on projecting his romantic fancies onto her and feels betrayed when she fails to respond. His sentimental longing for her is not unlike Masha's crush on him, and he has no more chance with Nina than Masha has with him.

As an artist Konstantin has two functions in the play: He is both a creative writer striving to find his own personal voice and a representative of the Symbolist movement. Thus, Chekhov can use him to comment on literary fashion while also developing his unique story. Although Arkadina speaks as much out of vindictiveness as conviction, her comments about Konstantin's play—"decadent raving," "pretensions to new forms"—echo opinions Chekhov expressed in his own correspondence. Yet Konstantin is completely sincere in his advocacy of the new forms, and thus represents a perennial artistic type, one who seeks to revolutionize the arts by finding new forms, not realizing, as Konstantin finally does, that form without content is pointless.

One of the many ironies in the play is the fact that the rival writers, Konstantin Treplev and Boris Trigorin, have the same problem: they have no real direction and nothing to say. If Treplev is the abstract writer who, in an effort to capture essences in his writing, loses all humanity, Trigorin is the slick writer whose vision cannot go beyond the everyday lives of his trivial characters. He is in a permanent rut, and he knows it. Commercial success and the adulation of Arkadina and Nina are meaningless to him because he is honest enough to know that his work is frivolous when compared to that of truly serious writers.

Writing has, for Trigorin, almost become an unsatisfying but necessary compulsion. He carries his notebook with him and is constantly jotting notes until the audience gets the feeling that he only observes, never lives. When the dead seagull is presented to him, he makes notes for a story. Trigorin then acts out his story with Nina; life copies art and both are bereft of real intensity. Perhaps his affair with Nina is not merely a casual seduction, but a vain attempt at direct experience. Trigorin would be a villain were he not so weak; he arouses contempt and pity, not anger. Like Konstantin, he needs others to support his deflated ego, but, unlike his rival, he lacks the strength even to kill himself.

Arkadina is a more complex figure than she seems at first glance. She, too, is an artist, but, as a performer, she has no interest in the opinion of posterity, nor, for that matter, does she have much interest in any aspect of the future. She sees herself as a beautiful young actress and clings tenaciously to that image in the face of reality. Her casual dismissal of time reveals an obsession with it. Arkadina is deeply insecure and very much afraid of age, sickness, poverty, and death. This fear shows in her suppression of all references to such things; her hostility toward her sick older brother, Sorin; her jealousy and fear of the truly young, especially Nina; her apparent flightiness; her domineering treatment of all underlings, including Trigorin; her stinginess; and, most of all, her attitude toward Konstantin. He is right in his belief that the major reason for her hostility toward him is that he reminds her that she is a middle-aged woman.

It is, however, through Nina, the seagull of Trigorin's unwritten short story, that Chekhov makes his definitive statement about creativity, and it is in her climactic interview with Konstantin that the major issues of the play are resolved. Although their external situations differ, they have both reached the crucial points in their artistic careers: They know what they can and must do if they are to realize their potentials.

Even though some of his stories have been published, Konstantin has received neither the critical acclaim nor the personal satisfaction he desires, and he understands why: His search for new forms has led him into an artistic cul-de-sac. "Good literature," he muses, "is not a question of forms new or old, but of ideas that must pour freely from the author's heart." Konstantin's basic problem is that he has nothing to say "from the heart" and he knows it.

Konstantin has not been stimulated by success, and Nina has been hurt, but not defeated, by failure. She is almost ready to realize herself, but one final obstacle remains: She must get rid of her obsessive identification with the seagull of Trigorin's story. Therefore, Nina has returned to Sorin's estate, not to see Konstantin as he desperately hopes, but to complete the purgation of this obsession by returning to its place of origin. To remain identified with the dead bird is to accept defeat; to free herself from it is to free herself from Trigorin's personal influence and his destructive attitudes. As she talks to Konstantin, she visibly shakes off the last vestiges of these pernicious influences. She has gone from the stagestruck girl of the first act, who viewed acting as a way to "fame, resounding fame," to the mature woman who understands that the essential thing is the creative act itself: "One must know how to bear one's cross, and one must have faith," she proclaims: "When I think of my calling I do not fear life."

Konstantin has no such calling, and he is plunged into the final despair by her visit. Frustrated by his attempts to reach his mother, convinced that he will never write anything of value, all hopes for his relationship with Nina dashed, Konstantin kills himself. Nina, on the other hand, begins her life as a complete woman and a committed actress—to become, perhaps, a great one.

"Critical Evaluation" by Keith Neilson

Bibliography:

Bristow, Eugene K., ed. *Anton Chekhov's Plays*. New York: W. W. Norton, 1977. An anthology of Chekhov's major plays, accompanied by thirteen critical articles. Of special interest is Thomas G. Winner's "Chekhov's *Sea Gull* and Shakespeare's *Hamlet:* A Study of a Dramatic Device."

Hingley, Ronald. *Chekhov: A Biographical and Critical Study*. New York: Barnes & Noble Books, 1950. A thoughtful study of all aspects of Chekhov's art, emphasizing his life. Chapters on Chekhov's connections with the Moscow Art Theater and his approach to drama are of special significance for understanding of *The Seagull.*

Jackson, Robert Louis, ed. *Chekhov: A Collection of Critical Essays*. Englewood Cliffs, N.J.: Prentice-Hall, 1967. Of the sixteen essays, nine are devoted to the theater of Chekhov, including the editor's "*The Seagull*: The Empty Well, the Dry Lake, and the Cold Cave."

Magarshak, David. *Chekhov the Dramatist*. New York: Hill & Wang, 1960. A thorough discussion of all Chekhov's plays on such topics as plays of direct action, transition, and plays of indirect action. References to *The Seagull* place the play in a proper perspective within the playwright's general dramatic output.

Valency, Maurice. *The Breaking String: The Plays of Anton Chekhov*. London: Oxford University Press, 1966. One of the best treatments of Chekhov's plays. Analyzes the general aspects of Chekhov's approach to theater and provides detailed discussion of all plays, including *The Seagull*.

A SEASON IN HELL

Type of work: Poetry
Author: Arthur Rimbaud (1854-1891)
First published: Une Saison en enfer, 1873 (English translation, 1932)

A Season in Hell might never have been accepted into the canon of great literature if not for the earlier poems of Arthur Rimbaud. These works, which are filled with beautiful imagery and Greek myth and adhere to academically orthodox structures and meters, had established Rimbaud as a significant force in the world of poetry. The wildly experimental *A Season in Hell* largely disposed of meter and structure. This epic prose poem jumps, leaps, and bounds toward and away from meaning and a discernible story line as Rimbaud takes a whim or a dream forward and as he takes a reflective step back. The imagery is there, constantly and consistently, but the juxtaposition of images and thoughts is open to a wide range of interpretation. Thus *A Season in Hell* can be counted among the more abstruse works of great poetry.

The poem reflects the tumultuousness of Rimbaud's life and concerns his attempts to find meaning in his life. He is alienated and alone, unhappy and misunderstood. This poem coincides so neatly with Rimbaud's life that it might as well be called an autobiography as a poem, though at times an exaggerated and wildly creative construction of an autobiography.

After a view of past, present, and future in the first chapter, Rimbaud takes the reader through his life, which he describes as the search for the innocence of his childhood, lost by that time. This theme lies at the heart of the work. Rimbaud wants to return to a child's capacity for wonderment and constant exhilaration with life as something new, unknown, beautiful, incomprehensible, and fantastic. Rimbaud is now too old to witness the world that way or to live as a child, but the poem explains his longing to return to that childlike state of fascination as he details his difficult time in adulthood, his own personal "season in hell."

The chapter titled "Delirium I" is the confession of Rimbaud's companion in hell. Presumably the companion is Paul Verlaine, who had helped Rimbaud to be published in Paris and who had been Rimbaud's homosexual lover for the two years immediately preceding the writing of *A Season in Hell*. Shortly before the work was published, Verlaine shot Rimbaud in the wrist, and Rimbaud was forced to have him arrested. Much can be gleaned from the poem about Verlaine, about Rimbaud himself, and about the relationship between them. Apart from suggesting personal difficulties, the poem conveys a general tone of discontentedness with modern Christianity, feelings of forlorn sadness, and an inability to connect with others.

In the chapter titled "Alchemy of the Word" Rimbaud examines his own poetry. He expresses hope that through poetry he can be saved. He illustrates his sense of poetics, declaring: "I invented the color of the vowels!—*A* black, *E* white, *I* red, *O* blue, *U* green . . . I reserved translation rights . . . I wrote out silences and the nights. I recorded the inexpressible. I described frenzies." Then he offers a section of poems, apparently written before the rest of the text and quoted from memory. Some of these show discrepancies, either deliberate or as a result of being misquoted with earlier versions of the poems. Rimbaud then recounts his hallucinations and explains his quest visions. He did all he could to see beneath the obvious and to find deeper meaning and hope, but he was no more able to find meaning through art or intoxication than through love.

This poem is a confessional. In it Rimbaud focuses on the plight of the individual who wants to extrapolate truths that are common to everyone. From Rimbaud's perspective, everyone seeks to procreate and to create art, but all are unable to reproduce themselves, all are unable to replicate their visions perfectly. Instead, they are continually stranded in their seeking for what is impossible to attain. This idea is related to the Christian ethic and the knowledge that a mortal seeking perfection can never attain that lofty goal and will consequently suffer all through life.

To understand *A Season in Hell* and Rimbaud's other works it is important to know that all his poetry was written between his sixteenth and twentieth years. By 1869, Rimbaud was writing as a seasoned scholar and an experienced man. In the style of the very few artists completely driven by their need to be artists, Rimbaud gave his life to the derangement of his senses in order to have visions and thus to produce poetry. He wandered throughout Europe and offered himself up to every possible experience, hoping that by living to the fullest extent possible he could open his mind to understanding life, the human experience, and his place in it.

Rimbaud hoped with his poetry to find salvation or happiness for himself. Much of *A Season in Hell* deals with his personal thoughts on the subjects of Christianity and his attempted flight from it. As a pagan, he could live an unrestricted life, but the undercurrent remained. Even his greatest voicings against Christianity serve to mark his connection to it.

The poem's ending does not appear happy, but, like the rest of this complicated and sometimes contradictory prose poem, it is open to interpretation. Soon after the publishing of *A Season in Hell*, Rimbaud abandoned all writing and moved to Africa. He never wrote poetry again.

Beaird Glover

Bibliography:

Bloom, Harold, ed. *Arthur Rimbaud.* New York: Chelsea House, 1988. An extended selection of criticism of Rimbaud that considers his work from his early free verse poems to *A Season in Hell.* Includes many slants on the possible meanings, aesthetics, poetics, and interpretations of Rimbaud's work.

Chadwick, Charles. *Rimbaud.* London: Athlone Press, 1979. Includes a biographical section followed by a chronological account of Rimbaud's poems. More than pure criticism, this offers an account of the happenings during Rimbaud's life at the time of writing and publishing *A Season in Hell.*

Fowlie, Wallace. *Rimbaud.* Chicago: University of Chicago Press, 1965. Two large sections, one concerned with biography, the other with poetry. A chapter is devoted in each part to examination of *A Season in Hell.* Also includes a bibliography and index of names used in Rimbaud's work.

Hackett, C. A. *Rimbaud.* London: Bowes and Bowes, 1957. Removes Rimbaud from much of the myth and legend that surround him and considers his work from a literary and human aspect. Traces Rimbaud's growth and maturity as a poet, with reference to style and technique as the poet's life and work changed.

Starkie, Enid. *Arthur Rimbaud.* New York: W. W. Norton, 1947. A large book with illustrations. Devotes much space to *A Season in Hell* and the circumstances of Rimbaud's life surrounding it. Many passages are in French and are not translated.

A SEASON IN RIHATA

Type of work: Novel
Author: Maryse Condé (1937-   )
Type of plot: Psychological realism
Time of plot: Late twentieth century
Locale: Rihata and Farokodoba, Africa
First published: *Une Saison à Rihata*, 1981 (English translation, 1988)

Principal characters:
ZEK, a forty-three-year-old manager of a bank agency
MARIE-HÉLÈNE, his wife
MADOU, Zek's younger half brother and minister for rural development
VICTOR, a man who kills Madou
MUTI, Victor's aunt
PRESIDENT TOUMANY, a dictator
SORY, a singer
DAWAD, the regional secretary
CHRISTOPHE, Zek and Marie-Hélène's nephew
SIA, Zek and Marie-Hélène's oldest daughter

The Story:

For two days, the residents of Rihata had been awaiting the arrival of Madou. When he arrived in Rihata to commemorate the anniversary of President Toumany's overthrow of the previous government, Zek and several local officials greeted him at the airport and took him to a reception in his honor. Afterward, Madou went to Zek's home and told Zek's wife, Marie-Hélène, that he planned to leave Rihata for the village of Farokodoba soon to meet with officials from a neighboring country as a representative of President Toumany.

Madou and Inawale, his chauffeur, arrived in Farokodoba. While Madou negotiated with the men representing Lopez de Arias, the leader of the neighboring country, Inawale wandered around the village, followed by a man named Victor. Victor convinced Inawale to go to a bar with him and put a drug in Inawale's drink. Victor stole Inawale's money and gun, after trying to find out from him why Madou was in the village. Victor and two of his friends who had been at the bar went to see Muti, Victor's aunt, and told her what Victor had done to Inawale. Muti was angry because she suspected that the police would soon be looking for them. Her concerns proved to be justified. She was arrested after a Toumany supporter told Madou of Muti's relationship with the individual who drugged and robbed Inawale. When Victor found out that Muti had been arrested and taken to Rihata, he went there to assist her.

Upon arriving in Rihata, Victor went to a bar. By coincidence, Zek entered the same bar. When Victor discovered his relationship to Madou, he followed Zek out of the bar. Victor told Zek that he was heading to N'Daru, the capital, to see his brother, but that he needed a place to stay overnight. Zek allowed him to stay in his garage. The following morning, Victor learned from Christophe, Zek's nephew, the location of Madou's residence. After leaving Zek's home, Victor headed to another bar. A procession of vehicles passed by the bar, and Victor found out that people involved in the assault against Inawale were being taken to N'Daru in the procession. Victor headed back to Zek's house and saw Madou and Marie-Hélène talking with each other. Victor decided to kill Madou in retribution for Muti's arrest.

On Saturday, the market day, Zek, Christophe, and several public officials attended the name-giving ceremony for Sory's newborn son. Sory had also invited Victor because it was customary to invite strangers to such events. Sory sang a song about greedy government officials, which offended Dawad, the regional secretary. Angry over Sory's song, Dawad had Sory arrested several days later. Madou attended a play supporting President Toumany that was put on by the ruling party's youth. During the performance, the lights went out and tracts criticizing President Toumany were placed on chairs. When the lights were turned back on and Madou saw a tract on his seat, he tore it up and left while the police searched for the culprits.

The next day, the police brought three men who allegedly were responsible for the tracts to the police station. That day, Madou went to Zek's home to see Marie-Hélène but found out from her daughter Sia that Marie-Hélène was at the hospital giving birth. When Madou went back to his villa, Victor was waiting for him with a gun. During the confrontation between Madou and Victor, Marie-Hélène's son was born; Zek named him Elikia, which meant hope in his native language. When he went home from the hospital, Zek learned from his neighbor that Madou had been shot.

Victor was arrested immediately after shooting Madou. Marie-Hélène was discharged from the hospital, and Zek arrived to pick her up. When she and Zek went home, she began to think about what had happened to Madou. She wanted him to live because of their past romantic relationship and his promise to assist Zek in obtaining a position as an embassy attaché.

Victor, Sory, and other individuals accused of antigovernment activities were transported to the police station in N'Daru to await trial. Marie-Hélène visited Madou in the hospital and told him she had a son. He felt a sadness, for the happiest periods of his life had been with her. Later, she returned to the hospital with Sia. Madou felt that Sia loved him and understood the relationship he had with her mother. When Madou's wife entered later that day, he convinced himself before he died that he had been a good husband for providing her with food, shelter, money, and clothes.

When Zek heard on the radio of his brother's death, he had mixed feelings. Zek decided he could forgive and forget about his brother's affair with his wife now that he was dead; yet he also lamented that he might never obtain a position as an embassy attaché. Zek went to his wife's bedroom and told her the news about Madou. President Toumany decreed a national mourning period and ordered the execution of all those involved with Madou's death. He believed that he could use Madou's death to his advantage to destroy enemies of the government and bring forth allies. Ironically, the president decided to appoint Madou as prime minister of the country, although he was dead.

Critical Evaluation:

A native of Guadeloupe who also lived in Africa, Maryse Condé received a Ph.D. in comparative literature from the Sorbonne in France. Her later novels include *Heremakhonon* (1982), *Segu* (1987), *The Children of Segu* (1989), *I, Tituba, Black Witch of Salem* (1992), *Tree of Life* (1992), and *Crossing the Mangrove* (1995). Because of her exploration of race and experimentations in narrative technique, she has been compared to the Caribbean writer Aimé Césaire, as well as to William Faulkner. Noting the influence of Faulkner and Césaire on her work, she points out in an interview:

> As far as *Crossing the Mangrove* is concerned, I had in mind and in fact on my desk was Faulkner's *As I Lay Dying* [1930]. It is strange that when I think of intertextuality, I have in mind two American writers [William Faulkner and Philip Roth]. I don't have any French writers in my mind. I don't

> have any Latin American writers in mind either. And I don't have any West Indian writers except Césaire, who is in everybody's mind.

The major theme of *A Season in Rihata* is the power of the past to influence and affect the lives of individuals in the present. Marie-Hélène seeks to resolve her guilt over the affair with Madou and a romantic relationship she had with Olnel, a Haitian man with whom her sister Delphine fell in love while they were students in France. Delphine, Christophe's mother, commits suicide when she realizes that Olnel, the father of her child, will never marry her. Christophe seeks to order his present world by finding out information regarding his biological mother and father so that he can have a sense of self and identity. Zek, too, is haunted by the past, feeling as if some failure within himself led to his wife's affair with his half brother. Madou tries to come to terms with his past and his guilt over the affair with Zek's wife and over the fact that several of her children may be his.

Another central theme is the search for fulfillment, expressed through the metaphor of motherhood. Throughout *A Season in Rihata*, characters seek out a mother figure to provide comfort and nurturing. Christophe is constantly searching for information about Delphine, but no one wants to provide him with it because the past is too painful. Marie-Hélène seeks a mother figure in the form of the African continent. She initially desires to leave her native Guadeloupe; she regards it as a "sterile womb" after her sister's death and, as a consequence, "Africa, Mother Africa, had appealed to her imagination and raised her expectations." Madou also seeks a mother figure. When he has been shot and is lying in the hospital, he regresses to an earlier womblike state: "He was lying in his mother's womb, far from the sound and the fury that the assassination attempt had triggered. He had returned to a time before childhood, before the creation of the world, before desire and sin. It was Eden." In this novel, the quest for the mother is symbolic of the desire for peace, security, love, and innocence, but often that quest is unfulfilled.

A third significant theme is political corruption in the emerging postcolonial world. Condé presents the ironic predicament in which the residents of Rihata find themselves: The black Africans who run the country are just as corrupt as the white Europeans who once ruled them, if not more so. Marie-Hélène expresses this sentiment in recounting her time in Rihata: "To think that twenty years earlier they had set the world to rights, talked about happiness for man and liberation for women. Now [she and Olnel] were both in countries largely destroyed by dictators, and they were compromising. Yes, compromising! What had gone wrong? What part of them had died with their youth?" She, Zek, and Madou all recognize the personal and political corruption that has marred the dream of a truly free and independent African state.

Condé successfully treats a number of compelling issues in this novel. She examines both the public and private lives of individuals living in a period of turmoil and change. Her success in dealing with such sensitive issues can be attributed to her narrative technique, for she tells the story from the viewpoints of the primary characters, enabling the reader to comprehend the complex nature of human desire, motivation, emotion, and thought. Exploring the reactions to postcolonial Africa from the perspectives of characters of different genders, educational backgrounds, and political views, Condé presents a moving, realistic, and unforgettable portrayal of life. Her work spans the past and the present, the Caribbean, Africa, and Europe, and the personal and the public realms of life in a well-crafted and thoroughly believable study of the human condition.

Sharon Lynette Jones

Bibliography:

Hewitt, Leah D. "Inventing Antillean Narrative: Maryse Condé and Literary Tradition." *Studies in Twentieth Century Literature* 17, no. 1 (Winter, 1993): 79-96. A thoughtful analysis of themes in Condé's works, including *Heremakhonon* and *A Season in Rihata*. Also examines Condé's narrative technique, pointing out the similarities between Faulkner's *The Sound and the Fury* (1928) and Condé's *Crossing the Mangrove*.

Larrier, Renée. "Maryse Condé." In *Encyclopedia of World Literature in the Twentieth Century*, edited by Steven R. Serafin and Walter D. Glanze. Rev. ed. Vol. 5. New York: Continuum, 1993. Informative overview of Condé's life and works. Examines the major themes and narrative techniques in her novels.

Ngate, Jonathan. "Maryse Condé and Africa: The Making of a Recalcitrant Daughter?" *A Current Bibliography on African Affairs* 19, no. 1 (1986-1987): 5-20. Useful analysis of Condé's works and their relationship to Africa, including the use of Africa as a setting for *A Season in Rihata*.

Smith, Arlette M. "The Semiotics of Exile in Maryse Condé's Fictional Works." *Callaloo* 14, no. 2 (1991): 381-388. Well-argued examination of biological mothers, adoptive mothers, and the seductress figure in *A Season in Rihata* and other works. Suggests that the metaphors may represent Condé's own conflict as an Antillean reconciling her African roots and Western values.

Taleb-Khyar, Mohamed B. "An Interview with Maryse Condé and Rita Dove." *Callaloo* 14, no. 2 (1991): 347-366. Provides invaluable insight into Condé's approach to literature.

THE SEASONS

Type of work: Poetry
Author: James Thomson (1700-1748)
First published: 1730; final version, 1746

A cycle of four long poems in blank verse with a brief concluding hymn, *The Seasons* celebrates the magnificence and harmony of nature as a manifestation of the Supreme Being. It embodies literary, philosophical, and theological ideas characteristic of the eighteenth century, yet it also prefigures the Romantic movement of the nineteenth century, particularly in its depictions of storms and wilderness. It enjoyed extraordinary popularity and influence in both centuries, and its impressive, picturesque landscapes made it a favorite text for illustration.

The poem evolved gradually, beginning with a short piece called "Winter," published in 1726. As he expanded and revised the work, James Thomson adopted the *Georgics* of the ancient Roman poet Vergil as his literary model, finding there a precedent for his subject matter (nature), his four-part structure, and his elevated style. Standing in the middle ground between the pastoral and the epic, "georgic" verse was expected to use lofty diction in celebrating the earth's bounty. Whereas pastoral poetry uses nature artificially as stage scenery for the philosophizing of urbane shepherds, georgic poetry draws inspiration from the noble labors of the farmer. Thomson by no means restricts himself to the farm, however; he seeks in untamed nature a special quality that fascinated his age: the "sublime," the paradoxically uplifting experience of awe and even of terror.

Each of the four poems opens with conventional elements: an invocation to the poet's muse and an elegant address to his patron. Thereafter, each loosely adheres to a different structural principle. The first poem, "Spring," celebrates the influence of the season over the whole Chain of Being, starting with the lowest, inanimate matter, and ending with the highest of beings on earth, "Man." Thomson prefers not to depict nature for its own sake but to do so for what it teaches, and many of its glories become occasions for edifying digressions. After describing the breezes warming the soil, the poet argues for the dignity of his theme, for agriculture crowns the British empire as it once crowned the Roman empire. Describing a rainbow after a spring shower, he contrasts the scientific theory of Sir Isaac Newton with the dumb amazement of the ignorant swain. The thought of the virtues in herbs provokes a long discussion of humanity's lost innocence. In days of old, reason governed passion and even the lion was gentle, but, since the Flood, afflictions have beset humanity. Yet, humankind still neglects the "wholesome Herb" and consumes the flesh of harmless animals. Some readers have criticized the looseness that results from this circuitous method, and no doubt the long, cumulative process of composition worked against the development of a rigid structure, but this lack of architecture reflects Thomson's sense of nature, for the poem possesses an underlying coherence that may be discerned only intermittently beneath the wonderful variety of the surface.

Birds follow vegetation; the poem relates how, infused with love from the "Source of Beings," they mate and build nests, brood over their eggs, and at last teach their offspring the art of flight. This springtime diffusion of amorous passions dominates the rest of the poem, but it refuses to conduct—out of respect for female readers, says the poet—a detailed discussion of animals, and gives rise instead to a lecture on the torments that befall youthful lovers and the happiness of those who join in marriage and bring forth a delightful "human blossom." Moralizing or "didactic" verse of this kind (besides being sanctioned by Thomson's literary model) was considered to be an integral part of the "topographical" poem, in which an impressive landscape becomes the occasion for profound and edifying meditation. Indeed, *The Seasons* inseparably intertwines description and didacticism, arguing throughout that our experience of nature inspires feeling, feeling inspires thought, and thought inspires praise of God.

"Summer," the longest of the four poems, traces a single day from morning to night, but it also uses the eye of imagination to describe the harsh climate of the tropics. The sun rules majestically over the summer day. All beings are its courtiers; his reign extends even to shining metals and gems that lie within the earth; ponds and oceans glitter with the sun's reflected light, yet nothing equals it. Having stirred the reader's wonder at the power of the sun, Thomson uses it for his devotional purpose: How, then, should he sing of God, its source? Yet, if men were silent, all creation would praise Him. The theology of *The Seasons* has been a topic of controversy: Some interpret its God as deist, a Supreme Being who has revealed himself only in his creation. Here, however—and at the end of "Summer"—Thomson insists that the human mind cannot fathom the Deity, and his poem echoes passages from Scripture that imply a traditional Christian position, despite the absence of references to Jesus Christ. His concern with the limitations of the human perspective reemerges in a subsequent passage when he emphasizes that, although science reveals that nature seethes with innumerable microscopic life-forms, as these lives are to us, so are we to the vast plan that comprehends all things.

The centerpiece of this poem is a reverie at noontime, when the poet retires in fancy to a grove and enjoys an idyllic landscape with a waterfall. The view is clearly idealized. Composed and almost framed, such landscapes show the influence of Renaissance artists such as Nicolas Poussin, Claude Lorrain, and Salvator Rosa. From within this dream setting, the imagination travels yet further to the jungles, groves, and savannahs of tropical lands. From a mountaintop in Africa, the poet watches a prodigious storm gather and break, washing over the continent and replenishing its rivers, and then recites the horrible fates that befall the people of the "torrid zone," impressing the reader with the awesome and sublime power of nature. Returning to England, another storm occasions two narrative episodes about lovers. The first issues a warning: Though innocent Celadon feared nothing, lightning slew his beloved Amelia. After the storm subsides, the poet recalls Damon, who could not resist watching his beloved Musidora as she bathed, but at last fled, leaving her a pledge of his honor, which she found and welcomed.

Patriotic sentiment represents another major theme in *The Seasons* that has a precedent in Vergil's *Georgics*. The earth's bounty testifies not only to the goodness of the Creator but also to the glory of the state and the empire. The afternoon portion of "Summer" is spent walking in the valley of the Thames, where the countryside's prosperity inspires the poet to enumerate its great kings, adventurers, soldiers, statesmen, philosophers, poets, and, finally, its beautiful women.

"Autumn" opens with an extended passage in praise of "industry," or labor. The sun's entry into Virgo and Libra (the scales) brings cloudy skies and ripe crops, and the keynote of this poem is harmony, not only nature's harmony within itself but also the human obligation to balance enjoyment of the earth's riches with self-discipline and virtue. Industry has lifted humanity out of primitive barbarism and has produced civilization; with civilization has come justice, the polity, and commerce. Thomson, however, only touches upon modern luxuries before turning the reader's attention to the tale of a poor and virtuous gleaner, an adaptation of the biblical book of Ruth. One day, when the maid Lavinia is gleaning the fields of Palemon, a young nobleman notices her and falls in love. Amazed by her likeness to his old patron Acasto, he learns that she is in fact Acasto's daughter, and he makes her his wife.

Thomson then returns to a subject raised earlier in "Spring," namely, the morality of hunting. The peaceful muse spurns the hunter's triumph over the helpless hare or stag. Thomson is lenient, however; in "Spring," he had conceded that skillful fishing was humane, and here he consents to hunting the "robber fox." After describing a vineyard and the various tasks involved in wine-making, the poet discusses precipitation and the origin of lakes and rivers. The 1730 version of the poem endorsed the old, erroneous "percolation" theory, which stated that sand and gravel draw the ocean's saltwater up to mountain springs, removing salt in the process. Later, Thomson inserted lines setting forth the condensation theory of astronomer Edmond Halley and shows the entire system of precipitation and drainage working harmoniously, demonstrating that science sustains rather than opposes faith in Providence. Nevertheless, scientific "Reason" needs to be informed by "Imagination," and later in the poem, in a sequence reminiscent of John Milton's *Il Penseroso* (1645), a fit of "philosophic melancholy" descends upon the poet. Let others pursue a life of activity; the poet's supreme pleasure is a simple rural retreat, where he can study nature and be caught up in philosophic rapture.

As in "Summer," the emphasis in "Winter" is on the season's extremes, and Thomson exploits the possibilities for sublime effects. This poem also, however, exalts the indoor pleasures of study and the contemplation of history, proceeding toward the final moral: When winter seems to have ruined everything and only human virtue survives the universal wreckage, spring returns and life awakens again, renewing hope.

Winter approaches with fierce storms of winds, hail, and blinding snow; an unfortunate swain loses his way and perishes while his family waits at home. This introduces a passage reflecting on the many miseries of human life, but the universal theme soon becomes the occasion to comment on a contemporary political problem. In 1729, a parliamentary committee had been appointed to investigate allegations of torture in English jails. Thomson's plea on behalf of the abused prisoners is personal; nine members of the committee, whose unspoken purpose was to score points against the Whig government of Sir Robert Walpole, were subscribers to *The Seasons*.

"Winter" draws the reader into scenes of the utmost desolation: Wolves descend from the mountains, hunting down horses and bulls and even snatching infants out of their mother's arms. These horrors, however, enhance the appeal of the contemplative life that dominates the center of the poem. Although Thomson praises the simple virtue of the Swiss peasants known as Grisons, he would himself retire to more sophisticated and urbane pastimes, meditating on the heroes of ancient Greece and Rome. Their "ancient shades" parade before his eyes, and after them march the great English poets, with Thomson's revered contemporary Alexander Pope in the rear. The last portion of the poem returns to desolation, a shipwreck in the Northwest passage and the Siberian wasteland, to prepare for the final note of life's resurrection. Frost, though seemingly ruinous, actually renovates the earth, and winter gestates the new life of spring.

The short, exuberant finale, "A Hymn on the Seasons," echoes Psalm 148 in its praise of God for revealing himself in his creation, though Thomson emphasizes each season as a distinct manifestation of God. The hymn functions as a synopsis of the devotional theme of the whole poem. In the end, however, when human words and voices fail, only "expressive Silence" remains.

Matthew Parfitt

Bibliography:

Campbell, Hilbert H. *James Thomson*. Boston: Twayne, 1979. A convenient introduction to Thomson's life and works, with extensive commentary on *The Seasons*. Includes an annotated bibliography.

Cohen, Ralph. *The Unfolding of "The Seasons."* Baltimore: The Johns Hopkins University Press, 1970. An exhaustive full-length study of the poem, arguing that the poem's literary merits and historical significance have been underestimated.

McKillop, Alan D. *The Background of Thomson's "Seasons."* Minneapolis: University of Minnesota Press, 1942. An essential study of the numerous sources and rich intellectual culture that are reflected in *The Seasons*. Includes a valuable bibliography.

Sambrook, James, ed. Introduction to *James Thomson, "The Seasons."* New York: Oxford University Press, 1981. This authoritative critical edition offers a clear presentation of the complicated series of revisions that produced the final work. The introduction surveys the poem's principal subjects and the history of its composition and publication.

Spacks, Patricia Meyer. *The Varied God: A Critical Study of Thomson's "The Seasons."* Berkeley: University of California Press, 1959. A readable study of the significance of Thomson's revisions, showing how the moral and devotional purposes emerged.

SEATONIAN POEMS and A SONG TO DAVID

Author: Christopher Smart (1722-1771)

Principal published works: On the Eternity of the Supreme Being, 1750; *On the Immensity of the Supreme Being*, 1751; *On the Omniscience of the Supreme Being*, 1752; *On the Power of the Supreme Being*, 1754; *On the Goodness of the Supreme Being*, 1755; *Hymn to the Supreme Being, on Recovery from a Dangerous Fit of Illness*, 1756; *A Song to David*, 1763

Christopher Smart's Seatonian poems won prizes at Cambridge University from 1750 to 1756. These poems cover the attributes of the "Supreme Being" to whom they are addressed: his Eternity, Immensity, Omniscience, Power, and Goodness. The poems are Miltonic not only in the structure of the verse but in the largeness of vision they conjure up. The second of these in particular, "On the Immensity of the Supreme Being," is a landmark of Miltonic adaptation. It begins with an avowal that God is best praised by that poetry which, like nature itself, acknowledges "the grand thanksgiving" of creation. Its prevailing tone is humility; the center of the poem is God and not human beings. It is, in fact, a poem about human imperfection opposed to the plenitude of the created universe, and in this respect it is quite unlike the mainstream of eighteenth century poetry.

The beauty of the earth is praised for the evidence it gives of the nature of the deity. "Astonish'd into silence," the poet reflects on the variety, beauty, and multiplicity of creation, finding even in the bottom of the sea the evidence of a divine intention in

> th' unplanted garden round
> Of vegetable coral, sea-flow'rs gay,
> And shrubs of amber from the pearl-pav'd bottom.

Like the other Seatonian poems, this suggests that the works of civilization are far inferior to those of nature.

Smart's "Hymn to the Supreme Being" was written, as he said, to express his thanks for recovering from a dangerous illness. He begins by relating the sickness of David, a figure ever-present in his mind. For Smart, David stands not only for the figure of the psalmist but for the man who is both "the sovereign of myself and servant of the Lord." When he compares the sickness of David with his own illness, he sees that he has very little to recommend him to the special care of heaven. In going over his life he addresses himself constantly to the great themes of waste and sorrow. He finds that he has no special title to mercy, much less to divine notice, but it is his discovery of this fact that both casts him down and lifts him up. His penitence and his union with a world of sinners, which he sums up as the "contrite heart," are the whole of the defense he offers of his past life. The poem is both a thanksgiving for and a praise of charity; it makes clear that the beneficiary is such only by the grace of heaven.

The figure of David is preeminent in Smart's "A Song to David," a poem that is both a biography and a spiritual celebration of its subject. Smart begins by pointing out the excellences of David's character, which won for him material rewards. He outlines the courage and intelligence of his hero "arm'd in gallant faith." Yet above all other issues, and infinitely more meaningful than David's success as a warrior and a politician, is David's piety. It is his consecration to his religion that Smart particularly admires, and the poem is in substance in praise of this. The goodness of David he explains by reference to those occasions when the king showed mercy to his enemies: "To pity, to forgive, to save." Beyond this, according to the poet, is the perpetual prayer of David, the purity of his devotion, his fasting and fear of the Lord.

Whether in warfare or in the employments of peace he is the paradigm of the virtuous man and the consecrated leader.

Like Milton, Smart appreciates in David another quality, that of poetic creativity. David as king elicits Smart's praises. David as the man of "perpetual prayer" draws his admiration, but David as the figure of the artist is perhaps even more central to the poet's vision. Smart writes of the "invention" of David, his capacity to make the form and the language of the Psalms convey the richness of his responses. He praises, too, the "conception" of the poet-king, his powers of imagination. His emotional quality is mentioned last, the "exaltations" that the poet, above all other men, manages to achieve and to express. David is in fact the model of the poet: He begins in contemplation and ends in creation. In this he repeats, indeed acts out, the first process of all, the creation of the world itself.

Thereafter Smart returns to the character of David, which he compiles from the stories of his reign as well as from the Psalms themselves. It is both the character of a man that is described and that of a symbol. The first of the allegorical qualities of soul that Smart attributes to David is serenity; it intimates the wish of the king for peace in his kingdom and on earth. The next of these is strength, to persist against the great odds of a divided people and hostile external forces. Smart then writes about the constancy, joy, and wisdom of his hero, in terms which may be taken to reveal Smart's consciousness of his own tragic lack of these qualities. Writing shortly after a prolonged attack of insanity, in despair over his private and artistic life, Smart put into this poem a deep sense of the need for these qualities in life as in art.

One of the great themes of Smart's work as a whole is the appreciation of created things. This theme is explicitly connected to the idea of God as he is revealed by the things he has made. "A Song to David" leaves his first subject, the king himself, and turns to a lengthy consideration of this favorite and recurring theme. Smart himself can best convey the depth of his feelings for the plenitude of the created world:

> Trees, plants, and flow'rs——of virtuous root;
> Gem yielding blossom, yielding fruit,
> Choice gums and precious balm;
> Bless ye the nosegay in the vale,
> And with the sweetness of the gale
> Enrich the thankful psalm.

The "thankful psalm" is a good description of the essential character of Smart's work as a whole. He continually seizes upon the variety, beauty, and intelligibility of creation and, as critics have pointed out, he does not spend as much poetic energy in contemplating his own condition as he does praising what he perceives by his senses. Smart praises the world of water and that of land, that of sky, and that of earth. He uses the ancient conception of the chain of being to give form to the feelings he tries to convey: From the world of shells and fishes to that of higher life he gives an outline of the harmonic order of the universe. Very little escapes this great catalog, not even those inanimate things at the base of the pyramid of Being. After this interlude of praise, Smart returns to his ostensible subject, the Hebrew poet and king.

The height of David's achievement is summarized in Smart's concept of Adoration, the act of submitting the mortal to the immortal. This concluding section of the poem is a vital link in connecting two subjects: the Hebraic tradition and the Christian. In a long and orchestral ending, Smart relates the qualities of David to those of Christ, and here the figure of the warrior and poet emerges as the forerunner of an even greater figure.

This outline would seem to indicate that Smart was almost totally involved in matters of religion; that his own religious mania succeeded, in spite of himself, in coloring all of his writing. The fact is that Smart found time to translate Horace and to provide a translation of the Roman poet of such high quality as to ensure its continuing use. Translation was a great eighteenth century craft, if not indeed an art, and Smart shows the same familiarity with the classical spirit as that shown by Alexander Pope and other masters of paraphrase. The *Odes* of Horace are simply and cleanly translated. Perhaps their most significant contribution is the expression of classical thought in enlightenment language.

Besides his religious poetry and his translation, Smart was able to work in minor veins of poetry. His poem "Of Jeoffrey, His Cat" is certainly slight, but it is strong evidence of Smart's ability to observe and to deduce: The cat is shown not with the automatic stare of everyday but as Smart sees it, "wreathing his body seven times round with elegant quickness." In many other minor poems Smart concentrates on his appreciation of the qualities of the senses. He writes about music in "On Gratitude" and celebrates the "Voice & Lyre" just as, in the religious poems, he celebrates all those things that bring beauty to life. In "An Epistle to John Sherratt, Esq." Smart writes that of all the offerings he can conceive of, none so delights the mind as "gratitude expres'd in song." This thankfulness for the rewards of the senses is a constant theme in his work, and he relates it with equal constancy to the intention of God in creating a world full of aesthetic and moral delight. In another poem he writes that "the sweets of Evening charm the mind." This is quite un-Miltonic in language and tone but very much related to Milton's consciousness of the nature and meaning of all things experienced by the mind. "Every thing that grows," Smart writes in this poem, is a reminder of "superior natures" and the highest sphere of imagination. In his work, whether it is about figures from history or the experiences of everyday life, he reiterates the constant theme of thankfulness for the variety and beauty of life. He reiterates, too, something substantially Miltonic: the conviction that all this beauty means something and that it is a key to an understanding of the nature of life itself.

Bibliography:

Ainsworth, Edward G., and Charles E. Noyes. *Christopher Smart: A Biographical and Critical Study.* Columbia: University of Missouri Press, 1943. Scholarly study of the writer's life, offering critical analyses of the major works. Contains illuminating commentary on the Seatonian poems and on *A Song to David.* Especially useful for a discerning reaction to Smart's work by his contemporaries.

Anderson, Frances. *Christopher Smart.* New York: Twayne, 1974. Study intended for general readers. Sketches the poet's life and gives some historical background to illuminate his accomplishments. Contains a brief discussion of the Seatonian poems and a chapter on *A Song to David*; stresses Smart's conscious imitation of the biblical psalmists in both.

Binyon, Laurence. *The Case of Christopher Smart.* London: Oxford University Press, 1934. Critical analysis of the poet's works, aimed at establishing his place among the important poets of his century and in British literary tradition. Includes an especially thorough examination of *A Song to David.*

Broadbent, J. B., ed. *A Song to David.* Cambridge, England: Rampant Lions Press, 1960. Critical edition of the poem with extensive commentary on the structure and analysis of Smart's technical skill and thematic aims.

Dearnley, Moira. *The Poetry of Christopher Smart.* New York: Barnes & Noble Books, 1969. Includes lengthy chapters on *The Seatonian Poems* and on *A Song to David.* Stresses the poet's intense religious feelings, which inspired all his writings. Also provides commentary on the structure of *A Song to David.*

THE SECOND MRS. TANQUERAY

Type of work: Drama
Author: Arthur Wing Pinero (1855-1934)
Type of plot: Social realism
Time of plot: 1890's
Locale: London and Surrey, England
First performed: 1893; first published, 1895

Principal characters:
AUBREY TANQUERAY, a London socialite
CAYLEY DRUMMLE, his friend
PAULA, Aubrey's second wife
ELLEAN, Aubrey's daughter by a former marriage
CAPTAIN HUGH ARDALE, Ellean's suitor
MRS. ALICE CORTELYON, the Tanquerays' neighbor in Surrey

The Story:

Aubrey Tanqueray, a wealthy widower, was to be married to Paula Ray, a woman younger than he and of questionable character. Aubrey's first wife had not contributed a great deal to his happiness. A daughter, Ellean, had been born to the Tanquerays shortly before the first Mrs. Tanqueray died of a fever, the only warmth, in the opinion of one of Aubrey's friends, ever to have come to the woman's body. Ellean had spent most of her life in a convent and was planning to take final vows.

Cayley Drummle, a friend, discussed with Aubrey the inadvisability of marriage between different social classes, but Aubrey, intent upon having warmth and companionship in his home life, was resolute in his determination to marry Paula. Aubrey had momentary misgivings, however, when Paula appeared late at night at his apartment. Such conduct did not become a lady, Aubrey charged; it would cause talk among the servants. Paula's opinion, indicative of her treatment of domestics, was that servants were merely machines to do chores and to appear for testimony in the divorce courts. Despite her glib pretenses, Paula, too, felt somewhat unsure about the social abyss which she and Aubrey were attempting to bridge. While she went to put on her cloak, Aubrey, reminded by his servant that he had not opened the day's mail, read a letter from Ellean in which she told him that she had communed with the spirit of her mother, who had admonished her to return to Aubrey in his loneliness. Perplexed, he was unable to foresee happiness between his daughter and his wife-to-be.

Two months after their marriage the unhappiness of the Tanquerays in their domestic life was apparent to all their friends. Paula was bored with the inactivity of country life at Aubrey's house in Surrey. He was apprehensive over Ellean and Paula's incompatibility. Both women wondered why their neighbors did not call on them.

Ellean, after her arrival, became a barrier between her father and stepmother because of her life in the convent. Although Aubrey tried to throw the two women together, they soon showed that they had nothing in common. When Cayley Drummle, visiting on an adjoining estate, came for a call, he was the confidant of both Paula, who expressed her wishes for the life she had known before her marriage, and of Aubrey, in his expressions of keen disappointment over Ellean's lack of interest in meeting eligible young men.

Benevolent Drummle encouraged Mrs. Cortelyon, his hostess and Aubrey's long-time friend, to call on Paula. Although Aubrey saw through Drummle's efforts, he appreciated Mrs. Cortelyon's visit and her invitation to have Ellean as her guest in Paris during the Easter vacation.

Paula resented Mrs. Cortelyon's attentions to Ellean, who made no attempt to conceal her preference for a member of her father's social set. Mrs. Cortelyon made the situation more awkward when she courteously and straightforwardly told Paula that her memories of Aubrey's first wife could never be erased by the presence of another woman in the Tanqueray house.

Feeling excluded from her husband's life, Paula spitefully sent a letter to Sir George and Lady Orreyed, the latter a friend of Paula's in her former way of life. Aubrey had earlier forbidden an invitation to the Orreyeds because he did not wish to have Ellean associating with people as boisterous and unconventional as they were.

Ellean went to Paris with Mrs. Cortelyon, and the Orreyeds came to visit the Tanquerays. During their visit they insulted their host and hostess because of the limited supply of liquors, broke furniture in the heat of a marital squabble, and lolled about in unbecoming positions. Their crudeness was offensive to Paula, but having invited them she could not, under the circumstances, ask them to leave; she could only hate them.

Although Aubrey's purpose in marrying Paula had been partly to show her kindness, he was unable to do so because Paula, always on the defensive, would not accept his attentions. Drummle, having known Paula in her former situation, was seemingly capable of mellowing her. It was he who, on learning that Paula had intercepted letters from Mrs. Cortelyon and Ellean to Aubrey, convinced her that such conduct was only breeding much of the unhappiness that she was enduring.

Paula gave the letters to Aubrey, who forgave her maliciousness in keeping the correspondence from him. After Aubrey told her of his disappointment and frequent embarrassment because of her common jokes and paltry cynicism, Paula admitted that she had not been fair to him and Ellean, and she asked for another chance to prove herself when Ellean should return from Paris and London.

Mrs. Cortelyon and Ellean returned soon afterward, the older woman anxious because she had not heard from Aubrey regarding his reaction to Ellean's romance with Captain Hugh Ardale. The courtship had been the subject of the letters Paula had intercepted.

Deeply in love with Ardale, a British soldier stationed in India, Ellean approached Paula to share the story of her good fortune. Paula repulsed Ellean at first, saying that the girl was being kind only because she was soon to be married. Then, after confessing her bitter jealousy, Paula reconciled with Ellean, and Paula was happy in Ellean's new-found happiness.

Ardale, who had accompanied Ellean and Mrs. Cortelyon home from Paris, came to the Tanqueray house from a nearby hotel. Paula, after telling Ellean that she and Ardale had met before, said that she wanted to talk with him about Ellean. Alone, Paula and Ardale recalled the time when she had been his mistress. When Paula told him that Aubrey must be informed of Ardale's past, Ardale threatened suicide if Paula interfered to prevent his marriage to Ellean.

Told of Paula and Ardale's past relations, Aubrey would not allow Ellean to see Ardale again. Shocked by her father's attitude, Ellean guessed that Paula had influenced Aubrey against Ardale. When Ellean pressed Paula for an explanation, Paula could not bring herself to divulge her past life to her stepdaughter. Ellean then told Paula that she could surmise what Paula had told Aubrey and that she had known from their first meeting that Paula was not a good woman.

Ardale sent a note to Paula, telling her that he was going back to Paris to await any word that she or Aubrey would want him to have, and asking that they explain the situation to Ellean. After Aubrey had read the note, at Paula's request, they discussed philosophically what the future might hold for them together. Paula said that the only great distances in the world were those that people carry within themselves, the distances that separate husbands and wives, and she predicted that Aubrey would tire of her in the future.

Drummle returned to discuss with Aubrey the affair of Ellean and Ardale. As the men talked, Ellean appeared and asked her father to go quickly to Paula. The girl told Drummle that when she had gone to Paula's room to apologize for her unkind remarks, she had heard a body falling. Entering the room, she had found Paula dying. Ellean said that she, in her unkindness, had helped to kill Paula.

Critical Evaluation:

The Second Mrs. Tanqueray is considered by many to be the first truly modern English play. Presenting a genuine social problem, this drama pictures people as they are in terms of their social prejudices and the difficulties arising from those biases. Other contributions that this play made to realistic English drama are the dramatist's use of actual place names in London and Surrey, the more logically motivated action, and the exactness of stage directions and sets.

The Second Mrs. Tanqueray is one of the best examples in theatrical history of the play whose production was timely. Had it been written a few years earlier, it is doubtful that it would have gained a production or, if it had, that it would have met with anything but hostility and commercial failure. Presented even a few years later, after the early works of George Bernard Shaw and his realistic contemporaries, it is unlikely that its iconoclasm would have set it apart or that it would have enjoyed the instant masterpiece status accorded it by many of the best critics. In 1893, some of the Victorian moral rigidity began to give way to the more casual Edwardian lifestyle, and the influence of the new Continental theater was first being felt. The moment was ripe for a play that challenged Victorian social and moral postures, but did not, finally, repudiate those attitudes and values.

Critics who have written about the play at some remove from the propitious time of its arrival, however, have been more harsh in their appraisals. The most serious shortcoming of the play is that, seen from a modern perspective, the play is too serious for a conventional well-made play, but still lacks true depth because Pinero fails to pursue the moral and psychological implications of the characters and situations to their logical conclusions. In other words, Pinero has the material for a potentially important serious play, but, for reasons of personal taste or commercial wariness, backed off and imposed a contrived but socially conventional conclusion on his play. To be specific, is the suicide of the heroine, Paula Tanqueray, the inevitable result of her character and circumstances, or is it simply a means by which Pinero sentimentally extricates himself from a situation too morally ambiguous for Victorian audiences to accept?

If the suicide can be justified, it must be seen as the result of an accumulation of factors: Paula's disillusionment with Aubrey and the realization that, although he loves her, he neither respects her nor considers her morally fit to associate with his daughter; her boredom with rural life and recognition of the fact that she will never be accepted by Aubrey's friends; her discovery that she has outgrown her old world, but has no new one to enter; lingering pain over her earlier breakup with Hugh Ardale, which is renewed by his return; her loss of Ellean's potential love; and, finally, her own feeling that she is getting old and will soon have nothing left. Aubrey vows another "fresh start," but Paula knows better.

One can explain the motivation behind Paula's actions, but her behavior is not always dramatically convincing. She is too naïve and eager, for a woman of the world, in her dealings with Ellean; her haughty and self-defeating handling of Mrs. Cortelyon seems artificial; her treatment of Aubrey frequently seems arbitrary and unnatural; and her moralistic decision to confess her previous affair with Ardale to her husband cannot be justified. Thus, the suicide is not the only problem in the play. In spite of some powerful and probing characterization, Paula's behavior too often seems to be necessitated by the shape of the plot rather than the nature of the character.

Other characters also suggest complexities greater than those usually encountered in well-made plays. How much of Aubrey's love for Paula is genuine emotion and how much of it is rooted in an idealistic, moralistic desire to save and uplift a lost soul? How much influence does his deceased first wife have on the Tanqueray household and especially on Ellean? And what about the relationship between Aubrey and his daughter? Is it completely within the normal father-daughter pattern? None of these provocative suggestions, however, is followed through. They remain tantalizing hints on the edge of the action, clues to character depths and complexities which are never explored.

Thus, however good *The Second Mrs. Tanqueray* may be, the reader constantly feels that it could have been much better. It is probably too much to expect Pinero to be an English Henrik Ibsen. Perhaps it is sufficient to say that, along with Henry Arthur Jones, he brought a new seriousness to the British theater and that, because of their lead, a new period of intense creativity was ushered onto the English stage.

Bibliography:

Downer, Alan S. *The British Drama: A Handbook and Brief Chronicle*. New York: Appleton-Century-Crofts, 1950. Examines works by Arthur Wing Pinero; also examines his life. Sees Pinero as a Victorian playwright with notable and innovative ideas.

Fyfe, Henry Hamilton. *Sir Arthur Pinero's Plays and Players*. New York: Macmillan, 1930. Examines the motivations of Paula Tanqueray and other key players. Also discusses the play's plot, dialogue, and setting. Good for a comparison of Pinero's other characters and dramatic works.

Grove, Arnold. "The Future of the English Drama." In *The Renascence of the English Drama: Essays, Lectures, and Fragments Relating to the Modern English Stage, Written and Delivered in the Years 1883-94*, edited by Henry Arthur Jones. Freeport, N.Y.: Books for Libraries Press, 1971. Claims dramatic works such as Pinero's can never record true realism such as pain, suffering, and disease.

Knight, G. Wilson. *The Golden Labyrinth: A Study of British Drama*. New York: W. W. Norton, 1962. Believes that Pinero handled sexual irregularities in man and woman with honesty in *The Second Mrs. Tanqueray*. Also claims Pinero was bound up in technicalities in a play, which he seemed to manage well. Places Pinero in context of other playwrights.

Salerno, Henry F. Introduction to *The Second Mrs. Tanqueray. English Drama in Transition: 1880-1920*. New York: Pegasus, 1968. Quite helpful as a critical analysis. Places dramatic work into context of the times as well as Pinero's interests when he wrote it.

THE SECOND SEX

Type of work: Social criticism
Author: Simone de Beauvoir (1908-1986)
First published: Le Deuxième Sexe, 1949 (English translation, 1953)

The Second Sex is considered a pioneering treatment on the subject of women's personal and social freedom. A prolific writer, Simone de Beauvoir was most famous for *The Second Sex* because of its profound impact upon the feminist movement. Though some feminists have quarrels with the study, most continue to recognize it as a significant, perhaps even definitive, tract in the history of the women's movement. The essays have been criticized by nonfeminist critics too, with some justification. At times the work suffers from imprecise data and oversimplified generalizations. Generally, though, the work is considered one of substance, and more recent editions have corrected many statistical errors.

The text, drawing upon a voluminous number of studies in order to explain the past and present condition of womankind, is not merely a biological and historical treatment. It is also an argument against the received views on the nature of women and an appeal for change. The work has two controlling ideas: First, borrowed directly from Jean-Paul Sartre, is the author's famous notion of the other, a phenomenon that occurs because woman sees herself only in relationship to man, while man does not recognize woman as an entity separate from himself. The second major idea is the claim that woman is conditioned from birth to perform the role of a woman: thus, what is perceived as feminine nature is not innate but an artificial invention.

The study is divided into two parts: Book 1 treats "Facts and Myths," and book 2 "Woman's Life Today." In the first book, physical and historical facts that have contributed to the domination of women are cited in an attempt to show how these facts are related to myths about the nature of women. The myths are a product of male domination, although women contribute to their own situation by accepting and internalizing the myths. The social, biological, and cultural survey begins by tracing the development of women throughout history. Behaviors were inculcated into codes or mythologies as a result of woman's physical disadvantage in the division of labor, superstitions surrounding woman's bodily functions, and woman's functions involving reproduction and child care. The author also draws examples from literature, archetypes, and conventions in art to identify the way man has sought to define the concept of femininity throughout the ages and thus perpetuate false beliefs about women.

De Beauvoir also points out that an existential viewpoint allows an understanding of how biology, economics, and popular wisdom have enabled male domination to flourish. In existential philosophy, man discovers himself by identifying with something else, and thus he transcends alienation. Woman experiences alienation far less affirmatively because she is prevented from discovering her autonomous, creative self by man, who regards her as his property. Specifically, man's role as warrior allows him to claim supremacy. Later cultural myths, especially the paradox of man's declaring respect for woman while declaring her inferiority, enables patriarchy to continue. The misogyny of the Jewish religion's being firmly inculcated into Christian ideology also contributes significantly to female oppression. This misogyny, reinforced by the Church fathers, lasted until the Renaissance, when there occurred a slight improvement with the advent of humanism. Throughout history, contradictions in woman's image abound. For example, there is the idea that woman can be both perfect and evil, an idol and a servant, the source of truth and the source of untruth. Examples of such contradictions are comprehensive. Specifically, the author thoroughly covers the phenomenon of woman as myth in five authors: Henri de Montherlant, D. H. Lawrence, Paul Claudel, André Breton, and Stendhal. From her examples, the ideal woman as protagonist incorporates perfectly the myths of the other. In daily life, societies and individuals define myths according to their needs, and, the essayist reiterates, myths, based upon the point of view of men, are reinforced with women's acquiescence.

The contradictions found in the image of woman are admirably exposed, and ample illustrations support the concept that woman is doomed by the culture's embracing of the idea of the incarnation of man's wishes and desires. This phenomenon keeps woman in a state of perpetual passivity. Usually, her situation disallows her the avenue of transcending her fate, but an awareness of the facts should aid in understanding the problem, thus avoiding perpetuation. Unfortunately, as is pointed out, exposition of the problem alone does not provide a solution.

Focusing on feminine experience and behavior predominately in twentieth century France, the second part of *The Second Sex* first traces the development of the female through life stages. Again, the antideterministic postulate from the first section, that woman is made, not born, is reemphasized. The idea of how woman's lack of choice forces her into social roles and psychological complexes created by history and myth is further expounded. First, the author, in admirably succinct statements, describes the adolescent response in both male and female to sexual drive. As far as sexual initiation, feminine sexuality is far more complicated than male sexuality. The young girl both fears and desires male attention. Her experiences involve not only the erotic drive but also factors resulting from her situation.

As an adult, woman may adopt an image from the various roles males have foisted upon her, such as wife, mother, or prostitute. In the married state (the most accepted role), despite the appearance of equality in the institution of marriage, an inequality prevails, and the inequality has its roots in the husband's role as productive worker and the wife's role as mother. As long as the man holds the economic responsibility, the union is a farce. The author shows her dedication to objectivity most profoundly. She characterizes women in marriage as far less than blameless. The concept of marriage as the only avenue for women has been so thoroughly internalized that women accept it without question as the only means open for them. The effect is that women eschew freedom, the fundamental right of human beings. The end result is marital unhappiness and sometimes adultery. Adultery is a pastime that helps society cope, but adultery does not solve society's problems. In order to reshape their destiny, women will have to pursue endeavors other than escapist ones. Their salvation depends, the author rather ironically contends, upon a male liberator. The rather glum depiction of married life, although insightful at times, is supported mostly by evidence from literature, including letters and diaries, which are subjective. Those women who avoid marriage and choose prostitution are even more unhappy than their married sisters, because prostitution also is enslavement. Economically, marriage and prostitution are similar. The greatest difference between the two oppressed states is that the married woman is respected while the prostitute is reviled. The author uses the word *hetaera* to designate all women, married and unmarried, who use their bodies as capital. In the *hetaira* (a prostitute of the upper classes in ancient Greece), the concept of woman as myth is complete.

Married or unmarried love both give rise to various mental aberrations. Romantic love is always disappointing, and when love is not attained at all, women may turn to adore divinity. The love of the divine has the same effect upon women as romantic love and can only end in failure. Narcissism is the result of frustration and aggression. Possessiveness and jealousy are other painful effects.

Disappointment in the sexual experience with men, the sheer difficulties in obtaining men, affection, and protection may create a situation for the development of lesbian tendencies. No clear boundaries exist, despite mythology to the contrary, between lesbian women and women who are not lesbian, and the behavior itself in not an aberration. To be free, woman must give up the idea of traditional love, and must cease to be a parasite. True love should allow for limitations. It should eschew worship, and essentially, become an interrelation, with both woman and man embracing their true selves. It is only with gainful employment that woman can find herself. Effort is the behavior most needed by women to assure their independence, and women may face myriad problems as a result, such as being torn between their profession and their sexual life.

As far as the formative years in childhood, the author first points out the disparity in the treatment of sons and daughters. The basic argument is that while a mother's influence on a son may be negative and ambiguous, the important quality is that no distinction is made for the son between his existence as a human being and as a human being who works. "Humanity is male," the author asserts. For the girl, a huge gap exists between her existence as a human being and her existence as a human being whose vocation is being female. To survive in the role of such artificiality, the girl must relinquish her childhood image of autonomy and accept the role of submission. In a society in which the community assumes much of the responsibility for raising the child, contradictory phenomena such as the role imposed on girls would dissolve in the face of examples of women who have escaped the role of submission. Girls would see women with careers. Thus, the traditional family perpetuates inequality.

Aging receives careful thought. First, aging means different things to men and women. Women, depending upon their self-image for identity, suffer substantially since erotic attractiveness is what provides them their life's opportunities. At some point during maturity, some women go through a stage in which they attempt to grasp a last opportunity by joining sects, clubs, charities, having another child, or obtaining a lover. During old age, the wisdom of a woman may be bitter or amused, but it will always be negative.

The condition of woman has remained much the same throughout history, and this condition is what is known as the "character" of woman. Woman's character is not determined by hormones nor a predetermination in the brain but rather is shaped by her situation. Like other oppressed people, such as slaves, women are considered childish, devious, and emotional. Women may rise above their situations by way of collective effort.

In conclusion, Simone de Beauvoir calls upon both men and women to recognize each other as peers. Throughout the study, the author has demonstrated that if man has enjoyed superiority to woman, it is not solely because of his greater physical strength and his freedom from the duties of rearing offspring. It is also a result of his involvement in gainful employment, the constructing and revising of the world itself. When woman realizes that the world is not solely the domain of the male, then she is truly capable of being free, and will be able to engage in work, thus losing her passivity and all the characteristics that follow from the artificial feminine role. *The Second Sex* is an important social analysis that still commands respect as a cogent, insightful treatment of many of the major problems in the history of the sexes.

Dorie LaRue

Bibliography:

Bieber, Konrad. *Simone de Beauvoir*. Boston: Twayne, 1979. A comprehensive, factual, and general presentation of De Beauvoir's life and works, including a lucid overview of *The Second Sex*. Has good general bibliography.

Brosman, Catharine Savage. *Simone de Beauvoir Revisited.* Boston: Twayne, 1991. Introduces readers to the vocabulary and existential concepts of de Beauvoir's philosophy. Important, succinct explication of *The Second Sex.*

Hatcher, Donald L. *Understanding "The Second Sex."* New York: Peter Lang, 1984. Primarily a summary with comments on the essays. Excellent for those with no background in existential philosophy.

Marks, Elaine, ed. *Critical Essays on Simone de Beauvoir.* Boston: G. K. Hall, 1987. Twenty-seven essays by specialists, edited by a well-known feminist. Entertaining and balanced.

Schwarzer, Alice. *After "The Second Sex": Conversations with Simone de Beauvoir.* Translated by Marianne Howarth. New York: Pantheon Books, 1984. Interviews with de Beauvoir and Sartre. Lively insights into *The Second Sex* and de Beauvoir's relationship with Sartre.

THE SECOND SHEPHERDS' PLAY

Type of work: Drama
Author: The Wakefield Master (c. 1420-c. 1450)
Type of plot: Mystery and miracle play
Time of plot: The Nativity
Locale: Bethlehem and surrounding country
First transcribed: Secunda Pastorum, fifteenth century

Principal characters:
FIRST SHEPHERD
SECOND SHEPHERD
THIRD SHEPHERD
MAK, a rascal
GILL, Mak's wife
AN ANGEL
MARY

The Story:

On the night of Christ's birth, a cold and lonely shepherd stood in the countryside near Bethlehem watching his flocks and bemoaning his lot in life. He was joined by another shepherd, who added his lamentations to those of the first and pointed out that his lot was worse because he was married. The second shepherd complained that his wife, a fat, shrewish person, had once been a sweet and charming girl, but that marriage had changed her.

While they grumbled, a third shepherd joined them. His chief complaint was the weather, for he thought that never, since Noah's flood, had the season been so bad. To ease their unhappy lot, the three began to sing a song. After they had sung, Mak came into the field to join them. Mak was not very welcome, for he had a reputation as a thief, and the shepherds were somewhat fearful that he would steal something from them. Mak begged them to let him stay and told a sad story of being hungry and unwelcome at home, even though he worked hard to give his wife what she wanted. The three shepherds gave in and bade him lie down and spend the night with them.

After the three shepherds had fallen asleep, Mak arose and prepared to steal a sheep, first casting a spell over the shepherds to keep them from awakening. He went to the fold, selected a fat ewe, and made off with it to his house. Not daring to kill the sheep, lest the noise make the theft known, Mak and his wife Gill decided to hide the sheep in the cradle if anyone came. In the meantime, Mak went back to finish out his night's sleep with the shepherds and cover up his guilt.

The next morning, Mak awakened with the shepherds, made them note that he was taking nothing with him, and started off toward his home. Not long after he reached home, the shepherds, who had missed their ewe, went to Mak's house to see if he or his wife had stolen the animal. According to plan, Mak and Gill hid the sheep in the cradle, and Gill pretended to have given birth to a son the night before. Although the accusers hunted all over the house, they found no sign of the sheep, not even a morsel of meat. After asking Mak's pardon and bidding good health to the new child in the cradle, the shepherds left. Scarcely had they gone, when they remembered they had left no gifts for the baby. Returning to the house with a little gift, they looked in the cradle and discovered their stolen sheep. Mak and Gill tried to explain the presence of the sheep by telling how an evil spirit had taken their child and replaced it with the ewe. The shepherds were not taken in by the story, tossed Mak in a sheet for punishment, and then departed with their sheep.

When the shepherds returned to the fields, an angel appeared to them and told them of the birth of the Savior, who would overthrow the devil and restore the glory that had been lost to man through Adam's Fall. The shepherds, following the commands of the angel, made ready to visit the Christ child as it lay in a manger in Bethlehem, only a short distance away. They considered themselves lucky to have an opportunity to see the Messiah, who had been prophesied in ages past.

Upon their arrival in Bethlehem, where they were led by the star, the three shepherds went to the stable where Mary and the Child were housed. The first shepherd, after greeting both the Mother and the Child, offered his gift of a bob of cherries. The second shepherd, not to be outdone as a giver of gifts, made a little speech filled with respect and gave the Child a little bird to play with. The third shepherd also made a little speech of reverence and then gave his gift, a ball. He urged the Child to grow up and play at tennis.

After the shepherds had given their gifts, Mary thanked them for the presents they had brought and the reverence they had done. She also bade them spread the news of Christ when they left. The three shepherds departed to sing the good tidings to the world.

Critical Evaluation:

The Second Shepherds' Play is one of the best of the medieval mystery plays. Unlike the medieval morality play, which was allegorical in method and restricted to a few topics concerning salvation, the mystery play had much greater range in subject matter and characterization. Although originally limited to the dramatization of biblical events, mystery plays increasingly treated stories from Scripture and Church history with a good deal of latitude. The primary aim of this form of drama was the elucidation of biblical and traditional wisdom for the laity, but from the mystery play emerged the elements of Renaissance drama. In this evolutionary process, a group of plays called the Towneley cycle was very important and, of the Towneley plays, the most influential was *The Second Shepherds' Play*.

The mystery play had its origin in an antiphonal part of the Mass for Easter called the *Quem quaeritis* (Whom do you seek?), which was the forerunner of liturgical innovations that used dialogue, adapted from Scripture, to enliven the worship. As the dialogues expanded, they were moved out of the Mass proper, where they were becoming a distraction, to other services like matins. When the practice was extended to Christmas and other feasts, the range of subjects and the scope of the dialogues were correspondingly amplified.

Eventually, the dialogues began to incorporate materials that were irrelevant, sometimes even inappropriate, to the liturgy. These rudimentary plays were removed from the church to the courtyard and finally to the marketplace, where they slipped out of clerical control. Responsibility for the productions was assumed by the civil authorities and delegated to appropriate guilds; the Noah plays, for example, were assigned to shipbuilders. There followed a slow process of secularization, although biblical themes survived into the sixteenth century.

Early in the fourteenth century, it became customary to perform the plays on the feast of Corpus Christi. Many towns, especially in the north of England, developed cycles of plays covering the whole range of biblical history. The largest extant group is the York cycle, but there were impressive collections at Norwich, Coventry, Newcastle, Chester, and elsewhere.

The Wakefield cycle was the most impressive, partly because of the enormously talented contributions of a gifted playwright known only as the Wakefield Master. Also called the

Towneley cycle, because the manuscript was long at Towneley Hall in Lancashire, this group of plays developed in three parts. The first part is a series of rather simple plays, some of which seem to have been borrowed from the York cycle. The second part is a group of plays that were incorporated into the cycle in the early fifteenth century. The third part, added before the mid-fifteenth century, was the work of the Wakefield Master, who contributed several plays in a characteristic nine-line stanza and revised several others. *The Second Shepherds' Play* is the most distinctive of the master's additions.

The historical importance of the work is in its departure from the devotional thrust of the mystery play. It is true that the mystery play had long accommodated extraneous secular material as it developed into a more elaborate dramatic structure. It is even true that the humor, in the situation and in language, had frequently become coarse. What is striking about *The Second Shepherds' Play* is basically a matter of proportion and individual talent. In this play, the secular component completely overwhelms the biblical. Although the focus of the play is on the Nativity and it concludes with a devout pageant, the intrigues among the shepherds, which dominate most of the play, are only tangentially related to the Nativity and are hugely entertaining in their own right.

In many mystery plays, the action moves quickly and easily between devotion and vulgar farce. *The Second Shepherds' Play* is more neatly divided and better controlled. The first part of the drama deals with the experiences of the shepherds, particularly with the conniving of Mak and his wife Gill. The dialogue of the three shepherds, as they complain of their lot, is full of cynical, comical reflections on their human situation. The plot of this section is simply the duping and their discovery of it. The tone is lighthearted, no great harm is done, and all is an excuse for good-humored repartee. The stanza of nine lines of different lengths accommodates short set speeches as well as rapid, witty interchanges.

The second part of the play, by way of contrast, involves the shepherds in gift-giving in the Christmas tableau. Ostensibly it is only connected to the first part by the presence of the same shepherds. Yet there are some surprising continuities. Despite the seriousness of the event, the poet maintains the same light touch and sensitivity to the mundane concerns of humankind. The tone, however, does not interfere with the solemnity of the scriptural occasion and with the appropriate decorum. Rather, the pageant gains a vitality all too often lacking in religious representations.

There is yet another connection between the two plots insofar as the story of Mak is a sort of secular parody of the Nativity. In the farcical plot, the shepherds do not give their gifts willingly but are conned out of them. When they finally approach the cradle, it is surrounded by the duplicitous Mak and Gill rather than Joseph and Mary, and the cradle contains not the Lamb of God but a real sheep. The main events of the play are a playful, but ultimately not blasphemous, secularization of the Christmas story. The Wakefield Master has infused the Nativity into a pedestrian comedy and then transferred the joyous vitality of the farce to its solemn conclusion, thus stretching the mold of the mystery play in an unprecedented manner. As a result, *The Second Shepherds' Play* shares more with the kind of comedy that was to follow in the Renaissance than it does with its contemporaneous liturgical antecedents and neighbors.

"Critical Evaluation" by Edward E. Foster

Bibliography:

Carpenter, Nan Cooke. "Music in the *Secunda Pastorum*." In *Medieval English Drama: Essays Critical and Contextual*, edited by Jerome Taylor and Alan H. Nelson. Chicago, Ill.:

University of Chicago Press, 1972. Asserts that music is an important element in the play's structure and a means of underscoring thematic statements.

Kinghorn, A. M. *Mediaeval Drama*. London: Evans Brothers, 1968. Devotes several pages to analysis of the play, noting its humor, freshness, and realism.

Nelson, Alan H. "Some Configurations of Staging in Medieval English Drama." In *Medieval English Drama: Essays Critical and Contextual*, edited by Jerome Taylor and Alan H. Nelson. Chicago, Ill.: University of Chicago Press, 1972. Examines scholarly understanding of the use of pageant wagons for the staging of mystery plays and discusses the unlikelihood of the plays' being staged in processions. Includes early illustrations.

Robinson, J. W. *Studies in Fifteenth-Century Stagecraft*. Kalamazoo, Mich.: Medieval Institute Publications, Western Michigan University, 1991. One chapter contrasts the work of the Wakefield Master with that of the York realist. Examines *The Second Shepherds' Play* in detail, looking at structure, characterization, humor, and number imagery, among other topics.

Ross, Lawrence J. "Symbol and Structure in the *Secunda Pastorum*." In *Medieval English Drama: Essays Critical and Contextual*, edited by Jerome Taylor and Alan H. Nelson. Chicago, Ill.: University of Chicago Press, 1972. Argues for a unity that goes beyond the structural parallels of the two parts to examine parallels in their language and the symbolic implications of the shepherds' gifts.

THE SECRET AGENT
A Simple Tale

Type of work: Novel
Author: Joseph Conrad (Jósef Teodor Konrad Nałęcz Korzeniowski, 1857-1924)
Type of plot: Psychological realism
Time of plot: 1880's
Locale: London
First published: 1907

Principal characters:
Mr. Verloc, a foreign secret agent
Winnie, his English wife
Stevie, her weak-minded brother
The Assistant Commissioner, a London police official
Chief Inspector Heat
Mr. Vladimir, First Secretary of an unnamed embassy
Michaelis and
Ossipon, anarchists

The Story:

Mr. Verloc was on his way to a certain foreign embassy, summoned there, to his astonishment and unease, at the unseemly hour of eleven in the morning. Ambling down the street, bulky and stolid, Mr. Verloc did not look very much like the agent provocateur that he was supposed to be. He kept an obscure and ill-patronized little shop, behind which were quarters for his family. There he often entertained a group of London anarchists from whom he had carefully kept the secret that he was an embassy agent. He grumbled inwardly as he approached the embassy, thinking how awkward it would be if any of his anarchist friends were to detect him in the act of entering such a place.

His appointment with Mr. Vladimir did nothing to improve his mood. In fact, his discontent had deepened almost to a state of terror by the time of his departure. Mr. Verloc had allowed himself to get comfortable, if not lazy, in the years since he had settled in England as the agent of a foreign power; he had never contemplated the possibility that he might lose his job. Now he found himself being roundly abused and insulted for what First Secretary Vladimir was pleased to call his fatness, his slothfulness, and his general inefficiency. He had even been threatened with dismissal if he did not promptly promote some incident to upset English complacency. In short, Mr. Vladimir demanded a dynamite outrage within a month and further specified that it must be directed against some monument of learning and science—preferably the Greenwich Observatory.

Badly shaken, Mr. Verloc made his way back to his shop in Soho. Rejoining his household in the room behind it, he managed to resume his usual demeanor of stolid reserve. When, soon after, his anarchist friends paid one of their calls, he betrayed nothing to them of the frustration and fear that lurked behind his impassivity. He was not so successful with his wife. She was able to keep her own counsel, but she missed very little of what went on about her.

Younger than her husband, Winnie Verloc had married him for security rather than for love. It was not even her own security that she was concerned about but that of her unfortunate brother, whose passionate protector she had been ever since the days of their childhood. Now physically mature, Stevie had remained childlike in other ways; he was easily excited and inarticulate, although generally softhearted and trusting. One of the people he trusted most was Mr. Verloc. His sister had done a great deal to bring about this state of affairs; his mother, who was also being supported by Mr. Verloc, had assisted Winnie in impressing upon Stevie the idea that Mr. Verloc was good, that his wishes must be instantly carried out, and that he must be spared the slightest annoyance. Meanwhile, Mr. Verloc serenely went his own way; insensitive to this anxious maneuvering to keep Stevie in his good graces, he largely ignored his brother-in-law even while tolerating his presence in the Verloc household.

To consolidate her son's position still further, the mother of Stevie and Winnie decided that before Mr. Verloc could tire of supporting both of his wife's relatives, she would move to an almshouse. Stevie missed her and began moping. Seeking a remedy for her brother's moodiness, Winnie seized upon what seemed to her a happy expedient. The long walks of her husband, mysterious of purpose and destination, gave Winnie an idea. Finding the right moment to make her request, she persuaded her husband to take Stevie with him. To Winnie's gratification, this experiment soon became an established practice. With things apparently going so well, she saw no reason to object when Mr. Verloc made a rather unexpected proposal regarding Stevie. Since Stevie was fond of Michaelis, an elderly anarchist who frequently visited the house, why not let the brother spend a few days with Michaelis at his retreat in the country?

Apparently pleased with this development, Stevie left to visit Michaelis, and the next few days passed without incident in the Verloc household. Late one afternoon, however, Mr. Verloc came home from one of his walks more upset than Winnie had ever seen him. He had withdrawn all of their money from the bank, and he mumbled vaguely about the necessity of leaving the country. Winnie tossed her head at this—he would go without her, she declared tartly. Mr. Verloc morosely ignored her wifely urgings that he eat his supper and change his slippers. He did not ignore, however, a distinguished-looking stranger who turned up presently and took Mr. Verloc away. Winnie failed to recognize this caller as the Assistant Commissioner of London Police.

During their absence, a second stranger arrived. Winnie became more and more apprehensive upon learning that he was Chief Inspector Heat. When Heat learned that he had been forestalled by his superior, he showed Winnie a cloth label bearing Stevie's name and address. Recognizing it as an identification tag placed in her brother's coat, she asked wildly where Heat had found it. The return of Mr. Verloc, alone, interrupted their conversation. After Heat had taken Mr. Verloc into another room, Winnie tried to overhear what they were saying. Almost mad with grief, she heard her husband tell how he had trained Stevie to take part in a bombing attempt upon the Greenwich Observatory. Stevie, however, had stumbled in the fog, exploding the bomb prematurely and blowing himself to bits.

After Heat left, Winnie faced her husband. White-faced and rigid, she hardly listened to his faltering explanation or his plan to turn state's evidence on the promise of a lighter penalty. When, exhausted, he finally dropped on the couch, she seized the carving knife and stabbed him in the heart. Winnie ran aimlessly out into the dark and stumbled upon Comrade Ossipon, one of her husband's anarchist associates who had eyed her from time to time with admiration. After promising to help her, he discovered, with consternation, what had occurred and that he might be implicated in the affair. Coaxing her onto a boat train, Ossipon waited until it started to move; then he leaped off. With him, he took the money that Winnie had entrusted to his care.

A week passed. Ossipon did not enjoy his possession of Winnie's money; he felt heavily burdened by gloom and guilt. The feeling deepened as he read a newspaper report of the suicide of a female passenger from a cross-channel boat. He was convinced that the last words of the dispatch would always haunt him since he alone knew the truth about Winnie Verloc's death, a deed that the newspaper called a mystery of madness or despair.

Critical Evaluation:

Although Joseph Conrad's literary reputation has been built largely on his nautical tales, such as *Lord Jim* (1990), *Heart of Darkness* (1902), and *Nostromo* (1904), *The Secret Agent* marks a new creative direction for Conrad. It is a rather straightforward, realistic novel set in the heart of London, a city characterized by its filth, immorality, and despair. The novel has been identified as the prototypical serious spy novel. In the "Author's Note" written in 1920, thirteen years after the novel's original publication, Conrad acknowledges that he had been criticized "on the ground of sordid surroundings and the moral squalor of the tale." Populated by wretched political figures who believe in nothing but the absolute destruction of all principles and institutions, the world of the novel focuses upon the anarchical political plots disturbing 1880's England. The human condition, however, is of greater concern to Conrad.

A failed bombing of the Greenwich Observatory in 1894 served as the author's inspiration for the plot. Conrad recounts that he and fellow writer Ford Madox Ford recalled that one of the revolutionaries was "blown to bits for nothing even most remotely resembling an idea, anarchistic or other." Ford's casual observation, "Oh, that fellow was half an idiot. His sister committed suicide afterwards," prompted Conrad's creation of Winnie Verloc and her half-witted brother, Stevie. Conrad admits that Mrs. Verloc is the imaginative center of his story. She and the city of London provide him with the appropriate forum for the discussion of lives of "utter desolation, madness and despair."

A mark of Conrad's fiction is his use of a controlling symbol that unifies the work. A symbolic scene also often functions as an expression of Conrad's themes. As the author pondered how he might bring together his ideas regarding politics, modern life, and the individuals caught up in it all, Conrad reports, "the vision of an enormous town presented itself, of a monstrous town . . . a cruel devourer of the world's light." London embodied for him the fragmentation, the isolation, the loneliness, and the inhumanity of contemporary society. The cab ride through the city as Winnie Verloc and Stevie accompany their mother to the almshouse is the scene that manifests all those qualities. The cabman's cruelty to his half-starved horse, Stevie's inappropriate outrage, and the indifference with which Winnie allows her mother to enter a life of loneliness and poverty point to Conrad's principal ideas. Other repeated symbols figure in the novel: the grotesque obesity of the main characters as a marker of immorality (only the Assistant Commissioner and Stevie—men somehow unaffected by the city's corrupting influences—are described as thin); the reference to human beings as body parts; Stevie's dismemberment; Stevie's endlessly drawing concentric circles, ironically the symbol of perfection.

Conrad's use of irony is another striking element in the novel. In many of his previous works, Conrad created a narrator—often similar to the *Heart of Darkness*'s Marlow figure—through whom he could speak. This narrator was merely a detached observer of the events he describes, uninvolved and distant from the people and events of the story, enabling him to judge them. In *The Secret Agent*, the narrator's ironic tone allows him that distance. In the "Author's Note," Conrad observes that the "ironic treatment alone would enable me to say all I felt I would have to say in scorn as well as in pity." In mock-heroic language, he portrays the absurdity of the anarchists as they hold their regularly scheduled meetings in the security of Verloc's rather respectable and bourgeois household, accept their financial dependence upon generous aristocratic gentlewomen, and remain unaware of their absolute ignorance of the world they are supposedly out to save. This ironic scorn is not as appropriate in dealing with Winnie Verloc. In her case, Conrad uses distance and detachment, which prohibit the narrator from slipping into Dickensian sentimentality as she sacrifices her only love and hope for happiness—ironically with a young butcher, a foreshadowing of the role Winnie plays at the end of the novel—in exchange for her mother's and brother's security. Even in Winnie's despair after murdering her husband, irony controls emotions. Comrade Ossipon, finally realizing that Winnie has killed Verloc and that Verloc has not been blown up as Ossipon thought, remarks how much she resembles her brother, whom he regards as degenerate. The idiot boy and his mad sister do not find a savior. Disgusted and fearful, Ossipon jumps from the moving train carrying Winnie to the Paris ferry, consigning her in her despair and utter loneliness to suicide. This story is told with a scrupulousness that appeals to judgment, not sentiment.

Conrad's greatest achievement in *The Secret Agent* is his vision of the human condition. His nineteenth century London teems with life and activity but is absolutely devoid of meaning and community. The Verlocs live in a tiny triangular island in a deserted Soho street cut off from the surrounding neighborhood. Although married for seven years, Winnie has never inquired into her husband's comings and goings, his friends, or his activities. She deems that life does not warrant too much looking into. Husband and wife hardly speak. Keeping Stevie quiet and occupied are of major concern to her. Winnie's mother wishes most to keep out of the way of Mr. Verloc, even to the point of consigning herself to the almshouse. There is no sense of social interaction, of communication, or of community. When in desperation Winnie seeks someone who might aid her escape from the gallows after she has killed her husband, Winnie realizes her absolute aloneness in the world. She has no one to whom she can turn. Only coincidentally does she encounter Ossipon, who is on his way to visit the woman he thinks has been recently widowed by the unfortunate accident in Greenwich Park. Ostensibly, he seeks to console, in truth he is looking for someone to support him. The one person Winnie thinks will help her only exploits her. Conrad's point in presenting this vision of modern life as fragmented and isolated is not to confirm it as the only possibility. Instead, he wishes to assert, through negative example, the ideal of a unified community.

"Critical Evaluation" by Laura Weiss Zlogar

Bibliography:

Fleishman, Avrom. *Conrad's Politics: Community and Anarchy in the Fiction of Joseph Conrad*. Baltimore: The Johns Hopkins University Press, 1967. The chapter on *The Secret Agent* discusses Conrad's portrayal of the modern world in fragmentation and his advocacy of social order and human community.

Guerard, Albert J. "Two Versions of Anarchy." In *Conrad the Novelist*. Cambridge, Mass.: Harvard University Press, 1966. Discusses Conrad's use of an elevated, ironic style, his narrative stance, and his aesthetic plan in *The Secret Agent*.

Hay, Eloise Knapp. *The Political Novels of Joseph Conrad: A Study*. Chicago: University of Chicago Press, 1963. Discusses how Conrad caricatures the aristocracy and mocks revolutionaries. Points out that Winnie Verloc suffers and faces despair alone, her condition made worse by anarchists.

Karl, Frederick R. *A Reader's Guide to Joseph Conrad*. New York: Farrar, Straus & Giroux, 1969. Examines the novel's moral purpose, its characters, and its style. Argues that the book's concern is the moral corruption of all people. A good starting place.

Tillyard, E. M. W. "*The Secret Agent* Reconsidered." In *Conrad: A Collection of Critical Essays*, edited by Marvin Mudrick. Englewood Cliffs, N.J.: Prentice-Hall, 1966. Discusses Conrad's use of irony to create a necessary distance between the reader and the horrible lives of the characters.

SEEING THINGS

Type of work: Poetry
Author: Seamus Heaney (1939-   )
First published: 1991

A collection of poems that are united by the theme of the movement between two worlds, *Seeing Things* is Seamus Heaney's tenth book of poems. The first and last poems in the book are translations; the opening poem is a translation of the "Golden Bough" passage from book 6 of the *Aeneid* (30-19 B.C.E.) that deals with obtaining the fruit on that bough to gain entrance to the underworld. The ending poem is a translation of a section in canto 3 of Dante Alighieri's *Inferno* (c. 1320). It deals with crossing over to the underworld on Charon's boat. So the two translations that frame the book deal with access to the wonders and knowledge to be gained in another world. The poems in the book are clearly related to this introduction and conclusion. They speak of ordinary things, which are rendered in illuminating detail, that can lead to moments of transcendence or a crossing between two different worlds.

Seeing Things is divided into two distinct sections. In part 1, the lyrics are connected to the translations that deal with the entrance into another world; this is especially so in the first poem, "The Journey Back." The one who has returned from the other world is not an epic hero like Aeneas or Odysseus but a modern poet who celebrated the ordinary world, Philip Larkin. Upon his return, he finds that "not a thing had changed." The dreary world of the street remains unaltered. He is also "Still my old self. Ready to knock one back." He may remain ordinary, "a-nine-to-five man," but he had "seen poetry." He had dwelt for a while in a world that is ruled by the imagination rather than the nine-to-five world. So there is some traffic between two very different worlds. It is a perfect introductory poem to the sequence.

"Markings" is a series of short poems on marking off things or defining them. For example, the first section speaks about the soccer field marked off by "four jackets," and the description is of an everyday event. It acquires a dream state as "Some limit had been passed," and the participants enter a world in which time is "extra, unforeseen and free." The terms come directly from the world of soccer, but they convey the sense of a magical moment beyond the confines of the ordinary world.

"Three Drawings" deals with common activities such as soccer and fishing; however, in stanzas 4 and 5 of "The Point" the ordinary game is, once more, transformed as the speaker asks the question: "Was it you/ or the ball that kept going/ beyond you, amazingly/ higher and higher/ and ruefully free?" The freedom echoes "Markings," but now it is impossible to separate the boy and the ball; they have become one. It is a rueful freedom that evades capture and goes beyond the control of the boy or anyone else.

"Man and Boy" crisscrosses the worlds of father and son in its second section. A mower tells a boy to inform his father about his completed work on mowing the meadow. The boy becomes the poet's father who runs "at eye-level with weeds and stooks" to experience his father's death. The poet speaks of connecting with the "heat" and "quick legs" of that boy. The boy of the poem becomes the father carrying the boy who is now the poet. The generations are encapsulated in the crossing roles. The poet is the adult sympathizing with his then younger father. He is then turned into a child who is now described as "a witless elder escaped from the fire." The events that are described are commonplace, but the continual shifting of roles, a motion from one world to another, haunts human experience and is filled with wonder.

The title poem of the collection is divided into three parts. The second section, perhaps the most interesting, begins with a Joycean word, "Claritas." Joyce uses it in *A Portrait of the Artist as a Young Man* (1914-1915) as one of the elements that is necessary for beauty; it is a "radiance," a revelation of the thing itself. Heaney then describes a scene of Jesus being baptized represented in a stone façade of the cathedral: "lines hard and thin and sinuous represent/ The flowing river." The scene is directly portrayed in its "utter visibility." However, the stone is "alive with what's invisible." Heaney then evokes an imaginative world of "stirred sand-grains" and "unshadowed stream"; the scene is created by the imagination rather than what is observed. The ending of the poem evokes another magical world beyond the façade on the cathedral but related to it. The heat is alive as it "wavered on the steps," and the "air we stood up to our eyes in wavered/ Like the zigzag hieroglyph for life itself." The most ordinary thing in this world, the air, suddenly becomes alive and capable of symbolizing "life itself." It is a stunning poem and a perfect example of the method of the book as a whole.

"Pitchfork" is a detailed description of an ordinary farm tool; however, it reveals a world beyond it as well. The speaker of the poem asks an imagined observer to "see the shaft of a pitchfork sailing past/ Evenly, imperturbably through space." It is being controlled and aimed by the worker. That movement into space reveals a place where "perfection" can be imagined "Not in the aiming but the opening hand." The completion of this simple act leads to images of generosity and a "perfection" that can only be achieved by no longer trying to reach it or aim at it. This state clearly suggests the Zen achievement of mastery by not desiring.

"The Skylight" is another poem that plays with opposing perspectives. The woman in the poem desires "skylights" to open the roof and her world while the male speaker likes it "low and closed." He gives in, and, when the slates are removed, "Sky entered and held surprise wide open." The speaker is not disgruntled by this change but transformed. He describes his new condition as a sick man who "Was lowered through the roof, had his sins forgiven,/ Was healed, took up his bed and walked away." The poem is humorous in tone, and while the speaker is renewed, he no longer is in possession of his snug room, as he is displaced after the transformation.

"Fosterling" is the last poem in the first part of the book. The speaker describes his affection for a picture of windmills with "heavy greenness" and filled with "in-placeness." The image of "heaviness" is transferred in the second stanza to the poet's own "heaviness of being." Poetry is now not "the music of what happens" as Heaney called it earlier but "the doldrums of what happens." He speaks of having waited fifty years to "credit marvels," but with this faith all is transformed. The images are now of brightness and lightness; it is a time to be "dazzled." Faith in a world and experience beyond the ordinary transforms his perspective and opens a new world to him.

Part 2 is called "Squarings." The second poem in the "Lightenings" section is a definition of "Lightenings." The speaker poses a few obvious definitions such as "illumination," and then moves to a higher one. It is "A phenomenal instant when the spirit flares/ With pure exhilaration before death." This is immediately exemplified with the story of the good thief next to Christ on the cross. He is to be transported into a new world by the command of Jesus; however, he is still "untranslatable," since he remains "body racked." He aches for the transformation and has "nail craters" on his brain rather than his hands. The desired transformation is achieved by language, by the italicized words of Christ: "This Day thou shalt be with Me in Paradise." These words concentrate on the translation from one state to another by the means of language, the material of the poetic imagination.

Poem 18 plays with two types of life: bondage and freedom. A rope-man appears to a group of farmers with his wares to sell. He lives a life free of obligations and confinement. As a result, his life on the road "menaced them with freedoms/ They were going to turn their backs on." When the circle formed by seller and buyers breaks up, the farmers see the rope-man's "powerlessness" along with his supposed freedom. He breaks the magic circle that had been established and starts "loading." His freedom is only an illusion; his only power comes from his brief connection with those who have rejected freedom for a settled domestic life.

The second section of "Lightening" deals with an important element in Heaney's poetry. It describes a reroofing in elaborate detail. The verbs dominate: "roof it," "relocate the bedrock," "sink every impulse." There is an important turn in the last stanza. The poet-speaker demands that his place and art "Secure/ The bastion of sensation." It must deal with images, not ideas. So the last commands are: "Do not waver/ Into language. Do not waver in it." The differences between the two are worth noting. To waver "into" language is to move away from things. To waver "in it" is to wallow in words and not what they are emblem of; it is to create an art that has no essential connection to the world.

Poem 8 is one of the best examples of the movement between two worlds. It describes an event recorded in the "annals" when a magical ship appeared to the monks of Clonmacnoise. The "anchor" of the ship "hooked itself on the altar rails." A crewman tries to release the anchor but fails to do so. The abbot then asks the monks to help because "This man can't bear our life here and will drown." The monks manage to free the ship "and the man climbed back/ Out of the marvellous as he had known it." An ordinary world is, to this mysterious traveler, "marvellous." What creates this sense of wonder is a change in perspective from one world to another. The poem is, perhaps, the most direct example of a movement between two worlds, a theme that dominates the book as a whole.

Poem 48 is the last in the sequence, and it unites many of the diverse worlds that had been explored in the earlier poems. The poem plays with time and human knowledge of it. For example, what one anticipates in the future soon becomes the past, and one can only understand the present by the past. There is, apparently, a continual movement between states of time. After this definition, the poem shifts to images of a time "when light breaks over me" as it did on one occasion in the past. When that moment of illumination returns, "I'll be in step with what escaped me." The future is now united with present and past in a moment of true understanding and an obliteration of the earlier separateness. The book continually plays with different worlds that remain separate and distinct, and it is no accident that the last poem shows them coming together.

Seeing Things is one of Seamus Heaney's best book of poems. It also has an important place in Heaney's work as a whole. He began by writing poems about his rural background, then explored the political divisions that exist in Northern Ireland in his middle period, and in this work returns to a world of things. If those "things" are truly seen, they will be found to suggest other worlds and experiences related to but beyond them. It is his most rooted and his most transcendent book. It also shows Heaney's refusal to be tied to one style or subject; he is continually renewing his style and his art.

James Sullivan

Bibliography:

Baley, John. "Seeing Things." Review of *Seeing Things*, by Seamus Heaney. *New York Review of Books* 39 (June 25, 1992): 14-16. An overview of the work and its context in Heaney's oeuvre.

Burris, Sidney. *The Poetry of Resistance: Seamus Heaney and the Pastoral Tradition*. Athens:

Ohio University Press, 1990. The first full-length study of Heaney's work. Notes and index.

Hirsch, Edward. Review of *Seeing Things*, by Seamus Heaney. *The New York Times Book Review* 97 (May 17, 1992): 7. A short review hailing the latest book by the Nobel laureate.

Morrison, Blake. *Seamus Heaney*. London: Methuen, 1982. A good first reference for Heaney's life and works.

Salamagundi 80 (Fall, 1988). The entire issue is devoted to Heaney. Studies, a bibliography, an interview, and more.

SEIZE THE DAY

Type of work: Novel
Author: Saul Bellow (1915-)
Type of plot: Domestic realism
Time of plot: 1950's
Locale: New York City
First published: 1956

Principal characters:
TOMMY WILHELM, the desperate protagonist
DR. ADLER, Tommy's father
DR. TAMKIN, Tommy's "mentor"

The Story:

Tommy Wilhelm descended from the twenty-third floor of the Gloriana Hotel and entered the lobby in search of his father. At the reception desk he collected the mail, bought a newspaper, and was told that his father, Dr. Adler, was already in the dining room having breakfast. Tommy was bracing himself to meet his father; a host of recollections burst upon him. He was painfully aware of his father's contempt for him. The old man—now in his seventies—considered Tommy a failure.

In his middle forties, his marriage on the rocks, Tommy did not consider himself a failure, although his personal life was in shambles. Besides walking out on his wife, he had lost his job at Rojax, was running into debt, and was learning about alimony payments. Tommy understood, vaguely, that part of his problem was that he was a dreamer, a man who trusted too many people and who had too little common sense.

He remembered his first failure, that of trying to be an actor in Hollywood. He had trusted a so-called talent scout named Maurice Valence. He had dropped out of college and gone off to California on Valence's prompting. Tommy should have known that Valence was too anxious to assert his legitimacy, and that, far from having a connection with the film business, he was just a fast-talking con artist who organized a ring of call girls. This first failure—one of many Tommy was to endure over the years—was the beginning of his father's low opinion of him.

His father, Dr. Adler, was having breakfast with a man named Perls, and Tommy suspected that the old man was trying to avoid him or to avoid being alone with him. Adler introduced Tommy to Perls and the conversation eventually centered on Tommy. His father was bragging about Tommy's being an important man at Rojax, and Tommy suddenly realized that his father was trying to promote himself as a father rather than praise Tommy as a son. Tommy was aggrieved as he heard himself reviewing his life story to this stranger. He was especially sensitive to Perls's and Adler's suspicions about Tommy's association with Dr. Tamkin. Tamkin, they declared, was either crazy or a crook, and Tommy was foolish for even talking to him, much less trusting the fellow. Tommy defended Tamkin, but in his heart he feared he had blundered in giving Tamkin power of attorney over his funds.

Laughing over Tamkin's schemes, Perls left the dining room. Alone with his father, Tommy spoke of his personal suffering—his marital problems and his impending financial ruin. By all this his father was unmoved, impatient with this apparent show of weakness and failure in his son. Adler rebuked Tommy, blaming him for his problems and advising him to develop a better sense of self-discipline.

Finally, when Tommy asked for some money, even in the form of a loan, Adler refused, insisting that he did not want to get involved with Tommy's problems: He simply wanted to be let alone.

On the way out Tommy met Dr. Tamkin. Like Maurice Valence, Tamkin was a fast-talking con artist, but unlike Valence, Tamkin raised the con to a transcendent level. His palaver was incessant, a convincing mixture of psychological insight and crass trickery. He had convinced Tommy to invest his last seven hundred dollars in the commodities market and to make Tamkin the custodian of the funds. The chief commodity, lard, was now falling, and Tommy was sickened at the thought that he would soon be bankrupt. Meanwhile Tamkin comforted, cajoled, and wheedled. He lectured Tommy on the evils of money and of the pursuit of money, which was a form of aggression. Tamkin patronized Tommy, telling him that neither Tamkin nor Tommy needed the money, that it was all a game. Tamkin seemed to offer Tommy sympathy and understanding. Tommy's head distrusted Tamkin and his wiles, but Tommy's heart accepted the possibility of Tamkin's being honest.

Tommy and Tamkin were soon sitting in the commodities office, watching the numbers flash on the board. All the while, Tamkin was talking and talking. Despite all of his lies, falsehoods, and chicanery, Tamkin hit upon a truth. Seeing Tommy's agony of spirit, Tamkin advised him not to "marry suffering," to cease blaming himself and complaining of his wife's emasculating influence, and to try to be happy. Tommy needed to live for the here and now, to "live for today."

By the afternoon, lard had fallen and Tommy, staring at the commodities board in the brokerage office, saw himself wiped out. He looked for Tamkin, searching him out even in the bathroom, but the old charlatan was gone, disappeared, and Tommy found himself alone, holding back tears.

In the final section, Tommy made a desperate appeal to his father for help. He found the old man in a steam room, enjoying the pleasures of a rubdown. Trying to keep his self-respect, Tommy pleaded for help, not just money this time, but for a kind word, a sense of understanding, comfort. None of these was his father able to give. In fact, Adler became irate. Furious, he called Tommy a slob and told him to get out of his life. Angry and hurt, Tommy went out, and received his final rebuff from his ex-wife, Margaret. On the phone she scolded him for sending his child-support check late and added further abuse to his father's caustic rejection. Overwhelmed, Tommy wandered at last into a funeral chapel. There, unknown to the mourners, he wept aloud for the dead, weeping for himself and for the death of love and human sympathy.

Critical Evaluation:

Seize the Day presents a character who is caught up in the impersonal American quest for money and success, yet who cannot ignore his own need for personal respect and compassion. A middle-aged Tommy is faced with the need to make money and to avoid looking like a failure, yet he longs for the solace of his father's approval. Tommy wants to listen to his heart, to trust even when that trust is foolish, as in his relationship with Dr. Tamkin. Tommy is an example of the long-suffering sensitive victim who, despite life's hardships, remains basically noble in a fragmented world. Tommy's plight is darkly comic—the poor soul who succumbs to the wiles of the fast-talking con artist and who is ultimately bereft of everything.

Tommy is a representative example of Saul Bellow's typical hero, a man trapped in the contradiction between desire and limitation, aspiration and ability. Such a hero experiences a conflict between head and heart. He is unable to reconcile the disparity between knowing and feeling. Tommy knows, for example, that Tamkin is not to be trusted, but he wants in his heart to trust him. Tommy sees his father's mean-spiritedness and contempt, but he wants his father's sympathy nevertheless.

Characteristically, Bellow depicts this contradiction not in naturalistic terms, as in the works of many of his contemporaries, but from a distinctly comic point of view. In this connection it is interesting to note that Bellow himself translated from the Yiddish the famous short story by Isaac Bashevis Singer, "Gimpel the Fool" (1953), a work spiritually akin to Bellow's point of view. Gimpel is the *schlemiel*, the loser with a soul, whose place in heaven is assured by his genuine humility, his acceptance of the essential holiness of life. Bellow's typical hero is, like Tommy Wilhelm, an intellectual *schlemiel*, aggrieved by the madness of contemporary life but unable to submit to it with the serenity of Gimpel. Tommy suffers, like Gimpel, not only because the world is pitiless and mad, but also because he refuses to accept its madness, striving, instead, for some humanistic ideal. He wants sympathy; he demands it as a human being. He is thwarted by his father's heartlessness and by Tamkin's deceit.

Seize the Day is rich in character portrayals. Tamkin is a mix of the comic and the villainous. He cheats Tommy not only out of his money but also out of his beliefs in the possibility of honesty. Dr. Adler, whose name in German means "eagle," is a kind of predator, preying on his son's weakness as a way of nourishing his own self-image. Lofty, aristocratic, fiercely aloof, Adler has divorced himself from human feelings.

In its concision, its taut depiction of character and event, and in its total immersion in its New York locale, *Seize the Day* is one of Bellow's outstanding novels. It serves as a good introduction to his work, containing the essential theme of the hero in moral conflict with the values of his society and told in a prose that combines erudition with slang, the analytically precise with the casually colloquial.

Edward Fiorelli

Bibliography:

Braham, Jeanne. *A Sort of Columbus*. Athens: University of Georgia Press, 1984. Examines Bellow's novels as centering on the theme of discovery and how his heroes pursue a personal vision tempered by, yet transcending, the American experience.

Clayton, John. *Saul Bellow: In Defense of Man*. 2d ed. Bloomington: Indiana University Press, 1979. Discusses Bellow's characters as alienated and paranoid, yet acting in such a way as to affirm the brotherhood of man.

Newman, Judie. *Saul Bellow and History*. New York: St. Martin's Press, 1984. Provides a summary of critical opinions of Bellow's religious and psychological views of life. Sees Bellow as a novelist concerned with the effect of history on his protagonists.

Pifer, Ellen. *Saul Bellow Against the Grain*. Philadelphia: University of Pennsylvania Press, 1990. Argues that each of Bellow's heroes is in conflict with himself. The conflict between reason and religion ends with the hero's affirmation of a metaphysical or intuitive truth.

Trachtenberg, Stanley, comp. *Critical Essays on Saul Bellow*. Boston: G. K. Hall, 1979. A compendium of the most significant critical essays about Bellow's novels.

SEJANUS HIS FALL

Type of work: Drama
Author: Ben Jonson (1573-1637)
Type of plot: Tragedy
Time of plot: First century C.E.
Locale: Rome
First performed: 1603; first published, 1605

Principal characters:
EMPEROR TIBERIUS
SEJANUS, his corrupt favorite
EUDEMUS, a physician and beautician
LIVIA, Tiberius' daughter-in-law
ARRUNTIUS, a righteous and indignant Roman citizen
SILIUS,
SABINUS,
CORDUS, and
LEPIDUS, noble Romans hostile to Tiberius' corrupt government
MACRO, a fiendish tool of the emperor

The Story:

Silius and Sabinus, respectable Roman citizens of the old stamp, met and discussed the corruption of Tiberius' court. Both admired Agrippina, the widow of Germanicus. Although conscious of the prevalence of spies controlled by the emperor's loathsome favorite Sejanus, they showed no personal fear. Arruntius and the historian Cordus, men of their kind, joined them. Two of Sejanus' spies watched and planned to entrap these men devoted to freedom. Sejanus entered with a group of hangers-on and suitors. Arruntius and his friends observed the favorite with scorn. One of Sejanus' followers presented a suit from Eudemus, the physician of Livia, wife of the emperor's son Drusus. Sejanus sent for Eudemus privately and laid plans with him for the seduction of Livia.

When Tiberius, followed by Drusus, made a public appearance, Sejanus bathed him in fulsome flattery, to the disgust of Arruntius and his friends. The emperor answered with a devious, hypocritical speech. After his departure, Drusus and Sejanus clashed, and Drusus struck him. Sejanus remained alone, promising himself to add revenge to his ambitious motives for the destruction of Drusus. Having found Livia a willing victim of corruption, Sejanus plotted with her and Eudemus to poison Drusus. Sejanus worked on the fears of Tiberius to persuade him to destroy Agrippina and the sons of Germanicus, who after Drusus were heirs to the Empire; he also warned the emperor of the danger of Silius, Sabinus, and others. Tiberius consented to call the senate and to allow Sejanus to handle the destruction of Silius, his wife Sosia, and Cordus, leaving Sabinus and Arruntius for the future.

Arruntius and his friends, hearing that Drusus was dying, recalled the public blow given to Sejanus. Later, the senate convened, with Drusus' death on all lips. Tiberius entered, to the amazement of the senators, who had assumed grief would keep him from a political function. Tiberius delivered one of his hypocritical orations, punctuated by low-voiced comments from the undeceived Arruntius and his friends. Suddenly, without preliminary warning, Sejanus' puppets accused Silius of treason. Recognizing the tyrant's trap and his own hopeless situation, Silius recalled his important services to Rome in peace and war, formally accused Tiberius of fraudulent conduct, and, mocking the tyrant's power, stabbed himself. Tiberius hypocritically expressed regret that he was thus deprived of an opportunity to show mercy to an erring subject. Cordus was next accused and sentenced to prison. His books, histories of the Roman Republic, were sentenced to be burned. Arruntius growled at the senate's "brainless diligence" in attempting to destroy truth by book-burning.

At the conclusion of the senate meeting, Tiberius and Sejanus planned future moves to strengthen their hands; flushed with power and triumph, however, Sejanus made a major mistake by asking to be allowed to marry Livia. Startled into suspicion, the emperor grunted ominously, then launched into a devious speech pointing out the dangers of such a match. Sejanus hastily withdrew his request but, still blinded by overconfidence, he urged Tiberius' retirement to Capri. Alone, he gloated over past successes and looked toward future triumphs, including the overthrow of the emperor himself. Tiberius, thoroughly suspicious, began to work with a new tool, the villainous Macro, to undermine Sejanus. While the emperor retired to Capri, Macro began his work by advising Caligula, one of the sons of Germanicus, to go and surrender himself to Tiberius, saying that he feared the plots of the powerful Sejanus.

The next victim of Sejanus was Sabinus. Arruntius was moved to wonder why Jove did not strike down the impious and ruthless favorite. Sejanus, having reached a dangerous state of intoxication with his own greatness, thought himself superior not only to men but also to gods. Ominous events occurred, but Sejanus scorned superstition and remained confident of success in his march to absolute power. Macro, with authority from Tiberius, caused the senate to convene again, apparently to confer new honors on Sejanus. Macro himself remained in the background but assumed control of the guards. As the senators gathered for the session, Arruntius and Lepidus, a good old Roman unspotted by corruption, stood aside to observe the flatterers eager to get close enough to Sejanus to give his ears confidential whispers. Great rivalry followed to see who could sit close to him during the proceedings. When the senators were seated, a letter from the emperor was read aloud to them. Bit by bit this masterpiece of political deviousness shifted the majority of the hearers from fulsome support of Sejanus to suspicion, fear, and hostility. Flatterers who had clamored to get near the favorite hastily shifted their seats, all but a gouty one who struggled in vain to rise, much to the delight of Arruntius at seeing gout keep the flatterer "miserably constant." Macro entered, supported by the guards, and dragged Sejanus from his seat, heaping violent personal indignities on him. Sejanus was hurried away to execution. Later reports told of his body's being torn to pieces by the mob. Most horrible of all, the children of Sejanus were torn from his divorced wife, Apicata, and were killed. In agony and fury, Apicata accused Livia and Eudemus of poisoning Drusus. Their death sentences were foretold.

Arruntius and Lepidus knew that Rome had but exchanged one instrument of evil for another, as Macro was no improvement on Sejanus, and the venomous, reptilian emperor remained untouched. Arruntius, however, delivered a valedictory prophecy to all tyrants and, using the fall of Sejanus as example, warned of the inevitability and terror of their destruction.

Critical Evaluation:

Ben Jonson, the author of *Sejanus His Fall*, was perhaps the foremost comic dramatist of the Elizabethan and Jacobean periods after William Shakespeare. Jonson was the primary purveyor of the "comedy of humours," in which a character possessed with a mania or obsessive trait drives the social order into comic disorder. Later in his career, Jonson wrote dark, moral comedies tinged with irony. *Volpone: Or, The Fox* (1605) and *The Alchemist* (1610) are two of Jonson's comic masterpieces.

Although Jonson is known primarily for his comedies, he ventured into tragedy. In his theory of tragedy, Jonson was a classicist. Classical tragedy focuses on the unities of time, place, and action. The classical tragedy should take place in a one-day period, be located in one place, and follow a few characters through a singular plot line. Classical tragedies have a chorus or group of characters who comment on the action, and they refrain from violent action onstage. Also, the classical hero is a noble person who falls after an error in judgment or as a result of some character flaw.

Sejanus His Fall was Jonson's first attempt at tragedy. It was performed in 1603 by the King's Men at the Globe Theatre. According to some sources, Shakespeare may have played the part of Tiberius. *Sejanus His Fall*, however, is far from a classical tragedy. In his preface to the play Jonson apologizes for not upholding the unity of time, but Jonson does more than break with this one unity. Instead of focusing on one day, the action in *Sejanus His Fall* spreads over several months. The locales change frequently. The cast is an assortment of characters caught in multiple sequences. The play lacks a chorus, and violent actions are graphically depicted on stage. Jonson could not hold to classical principles, and entertain Elizabethans, in writing his tragedy. Ironically, the play was not well received and was misunderstood by its contemporary audience. Today, it is seldom revived.

Nevertheless, *Sejanus His Fall* is worthy of critical acclaim. It is modern in its investigations of the machination of power, and it is deeply rooted in the primitive traditions of tragedy, which focus on the ritualistic dismemberment of a scapegoat figure. The greatness of the play does not lie in character portrayal, for Tiberius is the only character with complexity. Sejanus has no richness to his personality; he is not an interesting villain. The good characters, such as Lepidus and Arruntius, function primarily as choral commentators, comparing the past with the present; they are either ineffectual or impotent. Rather, our interest is drawn to the contest between two supreme Machiavellians, Tiberius and Sejanus, and to Jonson's suggestion that a corrupt and decadent society will inevitably produce a Tiberius and a Sejanus.

Jonson's drama brings the history of the Roman Empire into a thoroughly modern framework. His story is of a totalitarian machine ruled by a treacherous bureaucracy that is based on fear, betrayal, and deception. His characters lack psychological depth because they have no sense of self. They are victims of a historical process in which the machinery of the state turns the people against themselves. The times are out of joint, and there are no heroes or antiheroes to set them right. No grand avenger who upholds a sense of personal honor ever arises to redress the wrongs of Tiberius. Germanicus is mourned, but none of his kin has the will or drive to seek retribution. Agrippina is so crushed that she can only tell her sons to suffer nobly. Even a hesitant avenger would be welcome in the cold world of spies. The state apparatus controls the populace thoroughly by means of fear of reprisal and the expediency of self-interest. There is not even a strong villain, for example a Richard III, to gloat.

Rome is ruled by Sejanus, a petty politician who lives in a world where evil is reduced to the trivial. Living in a world of soulless men who are forever seeking to follow the political tide, Sejanus uses uncertainty to control his followers. His supporters are honored one day and murdered the next. His network of spies has made the populace afraid. The emperor, the legitimate authority, hides behind his henchman, Sejanus. The honorable soldier, Silius, who fought for emperor and country, is discarded. Senators are fearful and silent. The good citizen, Lepidus, ignores the terror in order to save his own life. Even the gods are silent. Jonson has vividly depicted the totalitarian state.

In this society even ostensibly free men are bought and sold. Sejanus puts political policy above blood ties. Macro sells out his own family. Honor, glory, family, kinship, loyalty, public responsibility—nothing has any meaning in the world of the treacherous bureaucracy. Power is centralized in a figurehead who passes out favors liberally and destroys his enemies. He, too, is a part of the system and just as replaceable as those he eliminates.

This usurpation of the body politic leads to the destruction of individuality. The individual becomes a subject of the power structure. In the play's imagery, the loss of the sense of self is seen in the fragmentation of the body. Faces are depicted as shifting; tongues are described as cleft; people's lips are divided from their hearts. The body of the individual and the body politic suffers a condition in which body parts are out of control. The body also becomes a saleable commodity in a prostituted world order of deceptive transactions. Sejanus, once a male prostitute, figuratively prostitutes the whole body politic. In the end, the body imagery in the play is pronounced in the dismemberment of Sejanus, as the mob tears him to pieces in the reenactment of the ancient ritual of the expulsion of a scapegoat. In Jonson's bleak tragedy, however, expelling the source of evil is not enough. The whole system of the state is caught in a mechanism of repetition, evoking the traditional motif of the wheel of fortune. One devious bureaucrat replaces another.

Two traditional conventions inform the play: In addition to the motif of the revolving wheel of fortune is the classical idea of *hubris*. Together they cause Sejanus' fall. He falls when he is at the summit of success; his decline begins in Act III when he suggests to Tiberius the marriage to Livia. These two somewhat contradictory ideas are suggested within the play: that Sejanus' fall was fated because everyone will eventually fall; and that Sejanus' pride, in his desire to become a god, caused his fall.

The great pessimism of *Sejanus His Fall* lies in the knowledge that Sejanus' downfall will lead to neither a personal renewal nor a cleansing of the state. Rome without Sejanus will be no less corrupt than Rome with him. Jonson has created in this play a nightmare world in which the body politic is in pieces and the state mechanism of treachery leads to a vicious circle of violence and suppression. Considered a minor and obscure work of Jonson, *Sejanus His Fall* remains powerful drama, rooted in ancient ritual and contemporary in its view of repressive totalitarian states.

"Critical Evaluation" by Paul Rosefeldt

Bibliography:

Barrish, Jonas A. Introduction to *Sejanus*, by Ben Jonson. New Haven, Conn.: Yale University Press, 1965. Argues that Jonson moves between closet drama and popular theater but shows a departure from other contemporary playwrights by remaining faithful to his sources. Also shows how Jonson coats his history in a morality play format and reduces his characters to moral types.

Engel, Wilson F. "The Iron World of *Sejanus*." *Renaissance Drama* 11 (1980): 95-114. Shows how Jonson used a diverse collection of classical sources but wove them into a dynamic and coherent plot, producing a drama that vividly depicts the viciousness of a political age.

Lever, J. W. *The Tragedy of State*. New York: Methuen, 1971. Devotes a chapter to Roman tragedy, covering Jonson's *Sejanus His Fall*. Jonson is seen as different from other playwrights of his time in his concern for the political instead of a concentration on heroic personalities.

Platz, Norbert. "'By Oblique Glance of His Licentious Pen': Ben Jonson's Christian Humanist Protest Against the Counter-Renaissance Conception of the State in *Sejanus*." In *Recent Research on Ben Jonson*. Salzburg, Austria: Institut für Englische Sprache und Literatur,

Universität Salzburg, 1978. Shows how Jonson used Roman source material to present an analysis of Elizabethan government. The play also shows how the failure to follow Christian humanist principles adversely affects the state.

Sweeney, John G., III. "*Sejanus* and the People's Beastly Rage." *English Literary History* 48 (1981): 61-82. Shows how Jonson wrote a play that distances itself from the audience and does not give the viewers any characters with whom they may identify.

THE SELF-TORMENTOR

Type of work: Drama
Author: Terence (Publius Terentius Afer, c. 190-159 B.C.E.)
Type of plot: Comedy
Time of plot: Fourteenth century B.C.E.
Locale: The countryside near Athens
First performed: Heautontimorumenos, 163 B.C.E. (English translation, 1598)

Principal characters:
CHREMES, an old man
SOSTRATA, his wife
ANTIPHILA, his daughter
CLITIPHO, his son
CLINIA, a youth
MENEDEMUS, his father
SYRUS, Clitipho's servant
BACCHIS, a courtesan, Clitipho's mistress

The Story:

While Chremes' wife Sostrata was pregnant, Chremes had told her that if the child should be a girl she was to destroy it. Sostrata agreed, but when the baby did turn out to be a daughter the poor woman did not have the heart to carry out her husband's command by herself. Instead, she gave the child to a poverty-stricken Corinthian woman then living in Athens, who was to leave the child outside to die. Out of superstition, she also gave the woman a ring for her finger to accompany the child when it was left exposed.

The old Corinthian woman failed to carry out her instructions. Naming the child Antiphila, she reared the girl as her own. Antiphila grew up, well-mannered and comely, and she was believed by everyone to be the old woman's own daughter.

Clinia, the son of Menedemus, saw Antiphila and fell desperately in love with her. Fearing the disapproval of his strict father, Clinia began living with her in secret as though she were his wife. Menedemus at last discovered the affair, and by constantly chiding his son and accusing him of unmanly indolence, he finally caused the young man to go to Asia and serve in the wars under the Persian king.

Shortly after Clinia had left Athens, Menedemus came to realize that he had been unjust and cruel in his severity. To punish himself he sold all his possessions in Athens, purchased a farm in the country, and began working both himself and his servants almost beyond endurance. Three months after his departure, Clinia returned, no longer able to tolerate his separation from Antiphila. Unaware of his father's change of heart, he kept his return secret from Menedemus and was entertained by Clitipho, a boyhood friend and the son of Chremes. As soon as Clinia had arrived, Clitipho sent his two slaves, Dromo and Syrus, into Athens to bring Antiphila to her lover. On the same day Chremes had learned from Menedemus how much he wanted his son to return and how generous he was determined to be to the young man when the opportunity did finally present itself. In fear of making Clinia audacious in his demands on Menedemus, however, Chremes refrained from telling the young man about his father's change of feeling.

That evening Syrus returned, bringing both Antiphila and a high-priced courtesan, Bacchis, as well. Clitipho, unknown to his father, had previously become deeply infatuated with Bacchis, and the cunning and bold Syrus had decided that the youth's desire to see his mistress could be satisfied if Bacchis were introduced to Chremes as Clinia's mistress and Antiphila were to pretend to be a member of the courtesan's retinue.

Early the next day, Chremes went to Menedemus and told him of Clinia's arrival. The old man, overjoyed at the news, wanted immediately to give his son full control over all his possessions. Chremes, however, counseled against such a move on the same grounds that he had refrained from telling Clinia of his father's change of heart. Moreover, Chremes believed Bacchis to be Clinia's mistress, and he knew that her extravagant mode of living would quickly drain any admirer of all his possessions. The festivities of the night before alone had cost Chremes dearly. What he did advise was that Menedemus should receive Clinia warmly, pretend to be ignorant of his affair with Bacchis, and allow himself to be tricked out of relatively small sums from time to time. This procedure, Chremes thought, would both keep Clinia at home and forestall the ruin of Menedemus.

Meanwhile, Syrus was hatching a plot to trick Chremes out of the ten minae that Bacchis had demanded as the price of her sojourn with Clitipho. The servant was gratified and amused when Chremes gave him apparent sanction for his deception by asking Syrus to contrive a way to deceive Menedemus into believing that Bacchis was not Clinia's mistress. Syrus, agreeing, cunningly proceeded with his own plot by telling Chremes that Antiphila's mother had borrowed ten minae from Bacchis, leaving Antiphila as a pledge for the money. The old woman having presumably died, Antiphila needed the money to purchase her freedom.

At that moment, however, Sostrata, Chremes' wife, was discovering by means of the ring that Antiphila was her abandoned daughter. When this fact was revealed to Chremes, his first reaction was to chide his wife; but he was really pleased to recover his daughter now that his condition had improved financially.

At last Syrus hit upon a plan for deceiving both fathers by telling them the truth. He proposed that Bacchis and her retinue should be moved to Menedemus' house on the pretext that she was Clitipho's mistress and that her affair with Clitipho must be concealed from Chremes. In addition, Antiphila was to be passed off as Clinia's mistress, and Clinia was to ask his father for ten minae to provide for the wedding. Chremes refused to allow another to ransom his daughter for him, however, and gave Clitipho the ten minae. The rest of the plot proved acceptable as well, and Bacchis and her servants were moved to Menedemus' house.

Menedemus assumed that what he was told regarding Bacchis and Clitipho was designed to deceive him, but when he saw the two entering a bedchamber together without a word of protest from the observing Clinia, he grew troubled and told Chremes what he had seen. He also pointed out that Clinia had made no effort to get money out of his father and had seemed highly pleased when Menedemus agreed to his marriage with Antiphila. Thus, the whole truth came out. Chremes, infuriated at first, threatened to settle the whole of his property on Antiphila. The sudden prospect of being left penniless led Clitipho to reflect seriously on his mode of life, and he promised to abandon all courtesans and marry a virtuous woman. Under the gentle persuasion of Menedemus and Sostrata, Chremes finally agreed to let Antiphila marry Clinia, and in the end he promised to forgive even Syrus.

Critical Evaluation:

Although *The Self-Tormentor*, based on an earlier play by Menander, takes its primary force from its intricate plot, it is, like several of Terence's comedies, in some sense a problem play. The problem is whether undeviating strictness or affectionate tolerance is the best mode of rearing children. Menedemus begins by finding the apparent excesses of his son intolerable.

Since his uncompromising reaction results in the loss of his son, his is clearly not the way Terence would recommend. Neither, however, is the old man's swing to the opposite extreme after his son leaves home. The implicit moral is that a flexible moderation between strictness and tolerance is best in rearing a son.

In the prologue to *The Self-Tormentor*, Terence explains that he turned the single plot of his source, a play by the Greek dramatist Menander, into a double one. *The Self-Tormentor* is certainly complicated. Admittedly, the comic effect depends on confusing the audience almost as much as the characters, but there should be an underlying sense that the playwright remains in control. This may not be the case with *The Self-Tormentor*, which is difficult to follow.

The play also has structural weaknesses. For example, in most Roman comedies, the plans formulated by the clever slave dominate the action, but here, Syrus' schemes are not really productive. Terence seems to shift direction in the last part of the play, when he depends upon Sostrata, not Syrus, to bring about a restoration of order. If, as seems clear, the play was popular with Roman audiences, the reason must be its interesting characters, recognizable conflicts, and universal themes.

Terence's double plot operates through the skillful pairing of characters. There are two fathers, Menedemus, the title character, who believes that he has failed as a parent, and Chremes, who has complete faith in his own wisdom. Chremes must, in the tradition of comedy, be brought to self-knowledge, and Menedemus, who has already recognized his error, must be reunited with his son.

The two pairs of lovers are also contrasted. Clinia and Antiphila are both virtuous, idealistic, and capable of devotion. Only in birth and wealth are they unequal. That problem, in a comedy, is easily solved. Using a stock plot device, Terence arranges to have the young woman of good character but inferior station be recognized as the child of respectable parents. The only difference here is that this conventional recognition occurs in the middle of the action, rather than at the end.

Unlike Clinia and Antiphila, Clitipho and Bacchis have no intention of marrying each other. As Bacchis admits to Antiphila, she is essentially a businesswoman, who uses her beauty and her charm in order to attain financial security. Clitipho will remain her lover only as long as he can pay. Besotted as he is, Clitipho understands the temporary nature of their relationship. At the end of the play, he does not object to being married off to an appropriate woman, as long as she is someone he likes.

Although each father quarrels with his son, it is ironic how much the sons resemble their fathers. Menedemus and Clinia are both men of principle. Clinia left home because he would not abandon the woman he loved, and Menedemus punishes himself because he knows that he violated his own standards of right and wrong. Similarly, Clitipho and Chremes are both less than honest. Clitipho deceives his father, and Chremes misleads his friend and neighbor. Both father and son are also impressed with their own cleverness. Neither of them realizes that one who is willing to lie to others may himself be deceived. Neither Chremes nor Clitipho is an evil person. Throughout the play, Chremes believes that he is acting in the best interests of Menedemus, and though he is anxious to keep his mistress nearby, Clitipho is also motivated by his desire to help his friend Clinia.

Though the young men are very different in some ways, they are alike in one important quality. Both of them love their fathers and will do almost anything to heal a breach with them. One reason for Clinia's return is surely his desire to make up matters with his father. As for Clitipho, when he is disinherited, he may regret being deprived of money and property, but he is devastated by the horrible suspicion that if Chremes could so easily reject him, it may be that he is not his father. The pain of losing a mistress is nothing, he realizes, when compared to the anguish he would suffer if he lost Chremes as a father.

Most analyses of *The Self-Tormentor* have emphasized the theme of father-son relationships. However, unlike most other Roman comedies, this play has a strong but not shrewish female character, whose relationships with her husband and her offspring are of crucial importance. While she remains offstage during the first half of *The Self-Tormentor*, undoubtedly quite busy entertaining the three guests who have been foisted upon her, when Sostrata finally enters, she takes charge of the play. She knows how to manipulate Chremes. First, with abject apologies, she admits her disobedience. When her girl child was born, she says, she failed to kill her, as Chremes had ordered, and now their daughter has reappeared in the person of Antiphila. Then Sostrata stands submissive while Chremes first scolds her, then excuses her, since as a woman she cannot help being ignorant and excessively emotional. Then, as Sostrata expected, Chremes changes his mind. It would be nice, he thinks, to have a daughter. Sostrata gets her way. Sostrata is again a pivotal figure in the final scene of the play, first pleading with Chremes to take back their son, then speaking for Clitipho, who seems to have some foolish notion of arguing with his father. On her son's behalf, Sostrata agrees to a marriage; on her husband's behalf, she approves of the woman he likes.

In other ways, then, *The Self-Tormentor* more than makes up for its flaws. Within the context of the always difficult father-son relationships, Terence finds a way to warn against pride and hardheadedness, rashness and debauchery. His audiences may even have left the theater with some increased respect for matrons such as Sostrata.

"Critical Evaluation" by Rosemary M. Canfield Reisman

Bibliography:

Brothers, A. J. "The Construction of Terence's *Heautontimorumenos*." *Classical Quarterly* 30, no. 1 (1980): 94-119. Proposes a solution to a major critical problem by looking at the functions of Bacchis and Antiphila in the plot. A well-reasoned essay.

Duckworth, George E., ed. *The Complete Roman Drama*. 2 vols. New York: Random House, 1942. A classic edition. Duckworth's general introduction remains one of the best overviews of Roman drama. The introduction to *The Self-Tormentor* incorporates explanations of character motivation into a detailed plot summary.

Forehand, Walter E. *Terence*. Boston: Twayne, 1985. One of the most readable studies of the playwright, with a systematic examination of each of his plays. Particular attention is given to the complicated plot of *The Self-Tormentor* and to the effective pairing of the characters. Annotated bibliography of secondary sources.

Goldberg, Sander M. *Understanding Terence*. Princeton, N.J.: Princeton University Press, 1986. In the chapter "The *duplex comoedia*," *The Self-Tormentor* is carefully analyzed. The author concludes that despite its convolutions, the play is essentially simple, designed for one purpose: that of "unmasking Chremes' hypocrisy." Bibliography.

Norwood, Gilbert. *The Art of Terence*. Oxford, England: Basil Blackwell, 1923. The opinions expressed in this work have provided the basis for almost all later criticism. Even when Norwood has been judged to be wrong, he still is given credit for originality and brilliance. Should not be overlooked by any student of classical comedy.

EL SEÑOR PRESIDENTE

Type of work: Novel
Author: Miguel Ángel Asturias (1899-1974)
Type of plot: Historical realism
Time of plot: Early twentieth century
Locale: Guatemala
First published: 1946 (English translation, 1963)

Principal characters:

The President, a cruel dictator
The Zany, a retarded beggar
Colonel José Sonriente, killed by the Zany
General Eusebio Canales, falsely implicated in the death of Colonel Sonriente
Camila, General Canales' daughter
Miguel Ángel Face, the President's confidential adviser
Fedina de Rodas, a young mother

The Story:

The Zany and his fellow homeless beggars lay sleeping in the shadow of the cathedral as night fell. Too poor to pay fines, they were generally undisturbed by the police, but Colonel Sonriente decided to amuse himself by tormenting the Zany, whose one comfort in his miserable life was memories of his mother. When the colonel awakened him by shouting, "Mother!" in his ear, the Zany jumped up and beat the colonel to death.

The beggars were rounded up by the police and tortured to reveal the identity of the murderer. Strangely enough, the correct answer, the Zany, did not seem to satisfy the police. Clearly, the authorities wanted to blame the crime on someone else.

Meanwhile, the Zany fled through the streets of the city until he fell and broke his leg. He was attacked by a buzzard and would have died if not for the intervention of a mysterious, strikingly handsome man named Miguel Ángel Face.

Ángel Face was an unofficial adviser to the President, a ruthless tyrant. The President informed Ángel Face that he had a job for him, but a rather tricky one. A political enemy of the President, General Canales was to be implicated in the murder of Colonel Sonriente, but it did not suit the President's purposes to have him arrested. Rather, Ángel Face was to force the general to become a fugitive by telling one of his servants that the police were on their way to arrest him.

After the general had duly fled, Ángel Face, aided by the thugs Vasquez and Rodas, raided the general's house and kidnapped his daughter, Camila. The smooth-talking Ángel Face assured Camila that he had helped the general escape out of the goodness of his heart and that he had hidden her away in a neighborhood inn to protect her from her father's enemies. Whatever his original intentions, this "line" soon came close to being the truth, for Ángel Face found himself facing a totally new emotion and motivation: love.

Rather than abusing Camila, Ángel Face became worried about her welfare. He tried to find a place for her to stay, starting with her uncle, Don Juan Canales. Here, however, Ángel Face began to learn the consequences of living in a nation ruled by a tyrant, a tyrant for whom Ángel

Face himself worked. Camila's uncle refused to help his niece for fear of being added to the President's list of enemies. Ángel Face was left with a defenseless, innocent girl for whom his affections and concern were growing by the hour.

In the meantime, the police had made their official raid on General Canales' house. Finding no one there, they declared the general to be a fugitive fleeing the consequences of his crime and also began to arrest persons suspected of helping him to escape (even though the plot to allow him to escape had been the President's).

One of those arrested was Fedina de Rodas, wife of one of Ángel Face's henchmen. Fedina was thrown in prison along with her baby. Worse than her brutal torture was the suffering of her baby, who starved to death in her arms. Fedina was finally released from prison and forced to earn her living in a house of prostitution. All this befell Fedina despite the fact that she knew nothing of the general's escape or of his whereabouts.

At that moment, in fact, the general was far from the city, hiding in a deserted hut in the countryside. Eventually he began to meet some of the peasants living nearby, almost all of whom had suffered greatly at the hands of the wealthy and powerful. Hearing their tales of exploitation, the general gradually realized what a corrupt political system he had spent his life serving. Eventually the general escaped into the marshland, vowing to return and fight for the people.

Back in the city, Ángel Face felt himself falling more and more in love with Camila. After nursing her through a near-fatal illness, he married her and they set up house in the city. However, their happiness was marred by two factors. Camila's father, General Canales, had died (probably poisoned) on the eve of leading a band of rebels against the President, and Ángel Face had fallen into disfavor with the President because of his marriage to the daughter of the President's old enemy.

Indeed, the President took his inevitable revenge. He first ordered Ángel Face to go to Washington, D.C., on government business but had him arrested on the way. Camila never saw her husband again. At the end, Ángel Face languished in prison, tortured by false rumors that his wife had become the President's mistress.

Critical Evaluation:

Miguel Ángel Asturias was a leading figure in the phenomenon that has come to be known as the "Boom," the relatively sudden emergence of a large number of immensely talented fiction writers from Latin America. Who started the Boom and who is its most important figure are topics disputed by scholars, but the fact that Asturias published his most famous novel, *El Señor Presidente*, in 1946, before many of his Latin American colleagues had even begun to write, and the fact that he won the Nobel Prize in Literature in 1967 indicates that he should be thought of as one of the earliest and one of the best Boom writers.

Although the Boom was not a school of writers with a set of goals in common, at least two major tendencies appear in much of their fiction. For one, Boom writers are among the most innovative of the twentieth century, blazing technical and stylistic trails. The way they write often seems as important to them and as interesting to the reader as that about which they write. However, they also take their subjects very seriously. The subject they address more than any other is politics, especially the relationship between the government and the governed. On both of these counts, Asturias shows himself to be a central figure in the Boom, and no better example than *El Señor Presidente* exists in his writing.

Asturias' theme is the most common one in Latin American political fiction: the relationship between the powerful and the powerless, victimizer and victim. In every case, Asturias', and hence the readers', sympathies lie with the poor, weak victims of a political structure that rewards greed and cruelty and leaves everything else a waste.

At the top of the political-military power structure of Guatemala (never named in the novel) is the President (based on Manuel Estrada Cabrera), who rules by terror and coercion. He perceives anyone with strength, talent, and the potential to be popular with the citizenry as an enemy and ruthlessly destroys him. Often this destruction, as in Ángel Face's case, takes some time in coming, and, before it arrives, the victim may believe himself to be favored by the President. To rise in the ranks, however—even by being especially loyal and useful to the President—is to acquire power. Those who live by power fear nothing so much as others with power. Thus, even the President's closest advisers and supporters are threats to his power and are always, ultimately, in danger of his wrath.

Fear pervades the tyrannical power structure of Guatemala, therefore, and its irrational nature is seen in the fact that not one of those arrested, brutalized, and often killed by the authorities poses a real threat to the President or, indeed, has done anything that could be interpreted as treasonous or even unpatriotic. This is true of Ángel Face, who rose to a position of power because of his loyalty to the President, of Camila, and of Fedina, whom the authorities know is innocent even before she is thrown in prison and tortured, and even of General Canales, for whose supposed treachery the President offers not a shred of evidence.

A few gleams of thematic light do penetrate this dark world of fear and oppression. Mothers still love their children. Persons of honor are still willing to die for the truth (as "Mosquito" does early in the novel when he refuses wrongly to implicate the general in Colonel Sonriente's death). Compassion and mercy still exist, although these are more frequently found among the poor and powerless than among those who have taken their lessons from the President and make their way by force and intimidation.

The character who offers the most hope is Ángel Face. He has risen to a position of great power and importance, and he has the intelligence and talent to rise higher. Instead, knowing the dangers he faces, he chooses love and compassion.

Rather than moving the novel in an optimistic direction, though, Ángel Face's experience underscores the hopelessness of the situation. Clearly, the President wins out over everyone. Asturias holds out no promise for a better tomorrow. By the end of the novel, Guatemala is shown to be a society with two classes. In one class is the President, wielding all the power; in the other is everyone else.

Asturias began writing *El Señor Presidente* in the 1930's, in the midst of what has come to be called the Age of Modernism. Modernist novelists characteristically use much ambiguity, subtlety, and psychological penetration, qualities almost totally absent from Asturias' novel. Indeed, his themes are obvious, and even his major characters tend to be one-dimensional. Rather than being faults, however, these are deliberate technical strategies.

Asturias lived in the dark world that he writes about, and his desire to announce the horror of that world is too great to allow for such technical niceties as ambiguity. Evil is clearly evil in Asturias' novel and good clearly good, and the characters align themselves under one or the other heading. Even those characters who change over the course of time (especially Ángel Face and General Canales, who come to realize and react against the horrors of the government they serve) do so in easily perceived ways and stages. Even the passages in which realism seems to give way to the fantastic (the one in which the streets "chase" the Zany, for instance, and the one in which the chaotic deliriums of characters under torture are described), Asturias is trying to convey plainly the evils of tyranny. This often imparts the feeling of a parable to this otherwise grimly realistic novel.

El Señor Presidente is not always a pleasant reading experience, but no reader can confuse Asturias' message: Power wielded by a single individual corrupts and destroys.

Dennis Vannatta

Bibliography:

Calan, Richard. *Miguel Ángel Asturias*. New York: Twayne, 1970. Calan devotes two lengthy chapters to *El Señor Presidente*. "*El Señor Presidente*" is an overview of the major themes and technical strategies in the novel. In "Babylonian Mythology in *El Señor Presidente*," Calan argues that Asturias relies on themes and imagery derived not just from Mayan mythology, as scholars have long noted, but also from Babylonian mythology.

Campion, Daniel. "Eye of Glass, Eye of Truth: Surrealism in *El Señor Presidente*." *Hispanic Journal* 3 (Fall, 1981): 123-135. Campion's essay is a helpful analysis of Asturias' style in the novel.

Himelblau, Jack. "Chronological Deployment of Fictional Elements in Miguel Ángel Asturias' *El Señor Presidente*." *Hispanic Journal* 12 (Fall, 1991): 181-209.

Martin, Gerald. "Miguel Ángel Asturias: *El Señor Presidente*." In *Landmarks of Modern Latin American Fiction*, edited by Philip Swanson. London: Routledge, 1990. Martin's essay is a fine overview of the central issues in the novel.

Prieto, René. *Miguel Ángel Asturias' Archaeology of Return*. New York: Cambridge University Press, 1993. Prieto discusses the novel in a broader context of Asturias' life and work. Specifically addressed are surrealism, sexuality, and Dionysian elements in the novel.

SENSE AND SENSIBILITY

Type of work: Novel
Author: Jane Austen (1775-1817)
Type of plot: Domestic realism
Time of plot: Early nineteenth century
Locale: England
First published: 1811

Principal characters:
ELINOR DASHWOOD, a young woman of sense
MARIANNE DASHWOOD, her sister
JOHN DASHWOOD, her brother
FANNY DASHWOOD, his wife
EDWARD FERRARS, Fanny's brother
SIR JOHN MIDDLETON, a Dashwood relation
COLONEL BRANDON, Sir John's friend
JOHN WILLOUGHBY, a young man with whom Marianne falls in love
LUCY STEELE, a young woman who attracts Edward for a time
ROBERT FERRARS, Edward's brother

The Story:

When Mr. John Dashwood inherited his father's estate, it was his intention to provide comfortably for his stepmother and his half sisters. His wife, Fanny, had other ideas, however, and although she was independently wealthy, she cleverly prevented her husband from helping his relatives. When Fanny's brother, Edward Ferrars, began to show an interest in Elinor, John's half sister, Fanny was determined to prevent any alliance between them. She made life so uncomfortable for the older Mrs. Dashwood and her daughters that the ladies accepted the offer of their relative, Sir John Middleton, to occupy a cottage on his estate.

Mrs. Dashwood, Elinor, and Marianne were happy in the cottage at Barton Park. There they met Colonel Brandon, Sir John's thirty-five-year-old friend, who was immediately attracted to Marianne. She considered him too old and rejected his suit. Instead, she fell in love with John Willoughby, a young man visiting wealthy relatives on a neighboring estate.

Once, while the young people were preparing for an outing, Colonel Brandon was called away in a mysterious fashion. Elinor and Marianne were surprised later to hear that he had a daughter; at least that was the rumor they heard. Willoughby seemed determined to give Marianne a bad impression of Colonel Brandon, which displeased Elinor. Shortly after the colonel's sudden departure, Willoughby himself left very suddenly and without explanation. Elinor could not help being concerned about the manner of his departure, particularly since he had not made a definite engagement with Marianne.

A week later, Edward Ferrars appeared at the cottage for a visit. Elinor was strongly attracted to him, but Edward seemed no more than mildly interested in her. After a short stay, he left the cottage without saying anything to give Elinor hope. Meanwhile, Sir John had invited to his home Miss Lucy Steele and her sister, two young ladies whom Elinor thought vulgar and ignorant. She was therefore stunned when Lucy told her that she was secretly engaged to Edward Ferrars, whom she had met while he was a pupil of Lucy's uncle. According to Lucy's story, they had been engaged for four years, but Edward's mother would not permit him to marry. Since Edward had no money of his own and no occupation, they were forced to wait for Mrs. Ferrars' consent before they could announce their engagement. Concealing her unhappiness at this news, Elinor told Lucy that she would help in any way she could.

A short time later, Elinor and Marianne were invited to London to visit friends. Marianne immediately wrote to Willoughby to inform him that she was near. Although she wrote two or three times, she had no reply. One day, she met him at a social event. He was with another young lady and treated Marianne courteously but coolly. The next morning, Marianne received a letter from him telling her that he was sorry if she had misunderstood his intentions and that he had long been engaged to someone else. All of her friends and relatives were furious with Willoughby. Although she was heartbroken, Marianne continued to defend him and to believe that he was blameless. She was comforted by Colonel Brandon, who was also in London.

The colonel privately told Elinor Willoughby's story. The colonel had a ward, a young girl some believed to be his daughter, who was in reality the daughter of his brother's divorced wife. The colonel had had to leave Barton Park so suddenly because he had learned that his ward had been seduced and then abandoned by Willoughby. When Elinor told Marianne the news, her sister received it with such sorrow that Elinor feared for her health. Colonel Brandon continued to be kind to Marianne, and it was obvious to everyone that he loved her deeply.

The young women stayed on in London. A little later, their brother John and his wife took a house there. When the Misses Steele also arrived in town for a visit, Edward's mother learned at last that he and Lucy were engaged. Angrily, she settled what would have been Edward's inheritance on her other son, Robert, leaving Edward and Lucy with no means of support. Edward planned to study for the ministry, and Elinor arranged with Colonel Brandon that he become a curate on his estate so as to enable Edward and Lucy to be married.

Before Elinor and Marianne returned home, they visited Cleveland, an estate between London and Barton Park. There Marianne became ill with a severe cold. Because she was anxious to see her mother, Colonel Brandon went to fetch Mrs. Dashwood. Before they returned, Willoughby, having heard of Marianne's illness, called at the house. He admitted to Elinor that he had treated Marianne so shamefully because he had no money of his own and because his wealthy relative had learned of the affair with Colonel Brandon's ward; as a result, his relative had cut off his allowance, and he had renounced Marianne to marry a wealthy young woman. He declared that he still loved Marianne and wished her to know his story so that she would not think too harshly of him.

Marianne recovered from her illness and returned home with her mother and Elinor. After Elinor told her Willoughby's story, Marianne continued to sorrow for him, but she no longer loved him.

After their return, Elinor learned from a servant that Mr. Ferrars and Lucy had been married. She assumed that Edward had married Lucy. Soon Edward appeared at the cottage and told the Dashwoods that the unscrupulous Lucy had married his brother instead of him, since their mother had disinherited Edward in favor of Robert. Edward had come to ask Elinor to marry him, and he had no trouble in gaining her consent as well as that of her mother. It remained only for him to secure a living. He went to London to seek his mother's forgiveness. Because Mrs. Ferrars had repudiated her son Robert after his marriage to Lucy, she felt a need for affection from one of her children. After much weeping and pleading, which failed to move Edward in his determination to marry Elinor, Mrs. Ferrars gave her consent to the wedding. After their marriage, they moved into the parsonage that Colonel Brandon had promised Edward some months before.

The colonel continued his quiet and gentle courtship of Marianne. At last, she recognized his true worth, and they were married. When they moved to his estate, the two sisters were near each other once more. Fanny and John were so pleased to be related to the colonel that Fanny even forgave Edward for marrying Elinor. Mrs. Dashwood was delighted at the good fortune of her children, and the families lived in peace and contentment.

Critical Evaluation:

Jane Austen wrote this novel during an important transition in English cultural history when the sensible eighteenth century enlightenment ideas were giving way to the more sensitive romantic ideas of the nineteenth century. In *Sense and Sensibility*, she creates the two Dashwood sisters, Elinor and Marianne, to embody the extremes of relational and romantic personality. The story may sometimes seem to fit a predictable formula, in which common sense is pitted against emotional sensitivity, but Austen also makes keen observations about the way to go about attaining happiness.

The cool, rational elder sister, Elinor, falls deeply in love with her brother-in-law, quiet, reserved Edward Ferrars. Elinor's sister-in-law Fanny regards Elinor as too poor for her wealthy brother, but he scorns his family's expectation that he marry a rich heiress. Edward loves Elinor and he avoids her only because he has secretly and foolishly engaged himself to Lucy Steele. This longtime clandestine engagement pains him when he realizes that he never loved Lucy. His gentleman's code of conduct, however, does not allow him to break his engagement, so he expects to have to marry Lucy even after he falls in love with Elinor. Elinor for her part is resigned to the prospect of often meeting Edward and Lucy as a married couple.

Lucy is a brilliantly portrayed character: a charming, intelligent, but completely heartless young woman who uses Edward to secure a position in upper-class society. As soon as Edward is disinherited by his angry mother and his brother Robert has better financial prospects, she shifts her affections and hopes to Robert.

Only because Lucy abandons honorable Edward does he become free to propose to Elinor. These lovers, who have been guided by prudence and respect for social conventions, are finally united and win the happiness they desire because they have honored the sensible values of society.

Meanwhile, the passionate, sensitive Marianne plunges into love with handsome, charming John Willoughby after he gallantly rescues her when she falls down a steep hill. He seems to be the perfect romantic hero. Everyone who sees them together agrees they seem perfectly matched in taste, values, and temperament. The two ignore rules of social conduct by spending many hours together and disregarding others. Marianne visits his home without a chaperone, and their ardent behavior misleads others into believing they are engaged even when they are not. After Marianne is abandoned by her seemingly ideal lover, it is long before she can accept what Willoughby has done. Her first response is to become depressed and dangerously ill, and only slowly does she regain her health and will to live.

Courtship is the theme of all Jane Austen's novels, but in *Sense and Sensibility*, the young ladies and gentlemen in love face dangerous challenges. Both Elinor's and Marianne's love affairs are threatened by mercenary forces intent on destroying their prospects of marriage. The obstacles to a marriage between reserved, sensible Elinor and Edward are his family's greed and pride, as well as his earlier indiscretion in engaging himself. Passionate, romantic Marianne and Willoughby, after an intense attraction that causes them to ignore the barriers between them, suffer and end up bitterly regretting their behavior. Willoughby regrets having abandoned Marianne, "his secret standard of perfection in women," while she regrets having indulged her impulsive, irrational feelings for him.

Certainly, Austen is commenting on the relative value of sense and sensibility in the face of crisis, and clearly she prefers sense. The story vindicates sensible Elinor as a thoughtful, considerate person, who even while suffering from her own disappointed love, nurses and consoles her sister. Even while suffering, she can have the satisfaction of acting correctly, whereas Marianne is forced to condemn herself harshly for her past thoughtless self-absorption, her rudeness to others, her neglect of the rules of good conduct, and her self-destructiveness. Only after coming to this realization can Marianne find happiness with sensible Colonel Brandon, a steady, rational, kind older man.

In this novel, Austen critically examines the changing social values of England in the early 1800's. As Great Britain's colonial empire and industrial revolution created greater wealth and power in the early nineteenth century, traditional country values gradually gave way to newer, more cosmopolitan values. In the novel, plain-speaking, old-fashioned characters like Sir John Middleton and his mother-in-law, Mrs. Jennings, seem at first rather vulgar and naïvely cheerful in their teasing about romance and enthusiasm for dinners and dances. In crisis situations, however, they prove to be good friends who care for the feelings of others and offer valued help to those in need. Mrs. Jennings' true affection for Elinor and Marianne becomes clear when she nurses Marianne through her serious illness.

In contrast to these simple, countrified types, Edward's mother, the elegant, sophisticated, and wealthy Mrs. Ferrars, and her daughter, Mrs. Fanny Dashwood, seem coldly calculating and cruel in their relations with others. They break promises and cast off needy relatives. Those aspiring to the wealth and sophistication of the Ferrars, such as Lucy Steele and Lady Middleton, also act in needlessly cruel and thoughtless ways. By contrasting old-fashioned manners with newer ones, Austen suggests that traditional ways are more trustworthy in times of need. She herself preferred life in a small country village and detested living in the elegant resort town of Bath, where sophisticated, leisured people gathered.

Austen's style adds a dramatically ironic dimension to the novel. Key characters reveal themselves in crisp, natural dialogue, at the same time showing readers that they do not completely understand themselves and their own values. Early in the story, Marianne declares to Elinor, "I have not known [Willoughby] long, indeed; but I am much better acquainted with him than I am with any other creature in the world, except yourself and mamma." Jane Austen observes, "Marianne Dashwood was born to an extraordinary fate. She was born to discover the falsehood of her own opinions, and to counteract, by her conduct, her most favourite maxims."

"Critical Evaluation" by Patricia H. Fulbright

Bibliography:

Butler, Marilyn. *Jane Austen and the War of Ideas*. Oxford, England: Clarendon Press, 1987. Argues that this "unremittingly didactic" novel intends to oppose Marianne's idealistic values with the decisive correctness of Elinor's cautious civility. Asserts that Austen complicates this effort, however, by making Marianne too sympathetic.

Lauber, John. *Jane Austen*. New York: Twayne, 1993. A good basic discussion of the novel that uses the terms "sense" and "sensibility" to interpret and evaluate the characters' positive and negative qualities. Describes the novel as Austen's most passionate and darkly satirical. Contains a useful chronology and a short annotated bibliography.

Moler, Kenneth. *Jane Austen's Art of Allusion*. Lincoln: University of Nebraska Press, 1968. Considers the novel in relation to its literary antecedents, finding that Austen takes the conventional contrast of sense and sensibility and reworks it to show that both sides of the dichotomy have limitations. Asserts that the "sensible" Elinor is as much in need of self-knowledge as Marianne.

Mudrick, Marvin. *Jane Austen: Irony as Defense and Discovery*. Princeton, N.J.: Princeton University Press, 1952. Important early study of Austen's style and tone. Finds in *Sense and Sensibility* a youthful parody of romance dissolving uncomfortably into a mature, serious consideration of personal morality. Argues that Marianne is sacrificed to the restrictions of social propriety.

Wiltshire, John. *Jane Austen and the Body*. Cambridge, England: Cambridge University Press, 1992. Argues that the "bodily condition" of Austen's heroines is as meaningful as their words and manners. Contrasts Marianne's "expressive" body (her exuberant health, dramatic illness, and quiet recovery) with Elinor's "nearly silent" body. Includes a useful bibliography.

A SENTIMENTAL EDUCATION

Type of work: Novel
Author: Gustave Flaubert (1821-1880)
Type of plot: Naturalism
Time of plot: Nineteenth century
Locale: France
First published: *L'Éducation sentimentale*, 1869 (English translation, 1898)

Principal characters:
FREDERIC MOREAU, a young student
MONSIEUR ARNOUX, a businessman
MADAME ARNOUX, his wife
MONSIEUR DAMBREUSE, a banker
MADAME DAMBREUSE, his wife
ROSANETTE, a mistress of many
DESLAURIERS, Frederic's friend
LOUISE ROQUE, Frederic's neighbor

The Story:

In 1840, the boat down the Seine to Nogent had among its passengers Frederic Moreau, who was returning home after finishing his course at the Collège de Sens and who had the prospect of a long vacation before beginning his law studies. Seeing on the boat an older man whose conversation was eagerly followed by a group of admirers, Frederic drew closer to hear what was being said. In a most worldly fashion, Monsieur Arnoux was holding forth on the subject of women. He noticed Frederic in the circle, and, after making the young man's acquaintance, the two promenaded for some time on deck. Arnoux invited Frederic to call when he arrived in Paris. Frederic went up to the first-class deck to sit and reflect on his homecoming. There he saw a woman knitting, whom Frederic thought the most beautiful woman he had ever seen. She was a little older than he and had a demure manner; she never once looked directly at him, though they were alone on the deck. Frederic moved several times to see her from different angles. Finally she dropped her ball of yarn. When Frederic retrieved it, her murmur of thanks was pleasant to hear. A few minutes later, a little girl approached, and he knew the child was her daughter. Then Arnoux appeared on deck and Frederic learned that the woman was his wife. When the boat docked, he watched them drive away.

Madame Moreau, a widow, was glad to see her son, for she had placed all her hopes in his future career in diplomacy. As soon as he decently could, Frederic went out to meet his friend Deslauriers, a young man who was also planning a legal career. The two friends discussed at great length their plans for their life in Paris in the fall.

When the time came for Frederic to leave for Paris, a neighbor of the Moreaus, M. Roque, gave him a letter for M. Dambreuse, a rich Paris banker. Mme Moreau advised her son to call on Dambreuse as soon as he could, for the banker would be able to be of great help to a young lawyer. Bidding good-bye to his relatives and Louise Roque, a girl who had become his special friend during the summer, Frederic left for Paris and his studies at the university.

Deslauriers and Frederic took an apartment together and began to attend lectures in law. Frederic found great difficulty in keeping his mind on his studies, however, for he thought most of the time of Mme Arnoux. He finally received an invitation to the Arnoux store, a large establishment dealing in paintings and other works of art. He was patient enough to become intimate with Arnoux, and he hoped that eventually he would meet his wife.

One night, Arnoux invited Frederic to a masquerade ball, at which Arnoux introduced him to Rosanette, an attractive woman whom her friends called la Maréchale. Frederic was sure that Rosanette was Arnoux's mistress. He was glad to learn about the liaison, thinking that bettered his chances of becoming friendly with Mme Arnoux.

When Frederic was finally invited to dine at the Arnoux home, he was happy to learn that Mme Arnoux remembered him perfectly. She was a friendly woman, but as time went on Frederic saw little chance of ever becoming more intimate with her. Even when he was regularly included in gatherings at their country house, he made no progress. Frederic finally had to conclude that his friends were right; Mme Arnoux was a good woman.

So great was his preoccupation with the pursuit of Mme Arnoux that Frederic failed his examinations that spring. Before he left for home he called at the Dambreuse home, where he was well received. He vowed to study hard, to forget about Mme Arnoux, and to try his luck in public life under the sponsorship of M. Dambreuse. For a time, Frederic studied diligently and cultivated the Dambreuse family; he went only occasionally to see Mme Arnoux. Having passed his examinations, he was admitted to the bar.

Before leaving Paris, he was included in a picnic in honor of Mme Arnoux's birthday. During the party she seemed put out with her husband. Arnoux shrugged off his wife's pique and sent her back to the city with Frederic. As they left, Arnoux gave his wife a bouquet, which she surreptitiously threw away. Thinking she had dropped it, Frederic picked it up and gave it to her in the carriage. As soon as they had started the trip, she begged him to throw the flowers out the window. Never before had Frederic felt so close to her.

At Nogent, Frederic received bad news. His mother's income had dwindled considerably because of the troubled politics of monarchial France, and she had been forced to sell some of her lands. Henceforth she would have only enough to live frugally. A worse blow fell when Frederic's rich uncle in Le Havre announced that he would not leave his wealth to Frederic. Feeling that he was ruined, with no income and no expectations, Frederic resigned himself to a dull life in Nogent and spent three years in almost complete idleness. His only friend was Louise Roque, who had grown into an attractive woman.

At last a telegram arrived to announce that the uncle in Le Havre had died intestate and that Frederic was his only heir. Despite his mother's remonstrances, Frederic hastily prepared to return to Paris. He declared his love for Louise before he left, but all the while he was thinking of Mme Arnoux.

In Paris, Frederic took a fashionable apartment and settled down to a life of ease. He again became an intimate of the Arnoux household and renewed his friendship with Deslauriers. He agreed to furnish the money to found a journal of political opinion, his intention being to give employment to Deslauriers and at the same time to control a paper that would support his own future career in politics. When he learned that Arnoux was pressed financially, he lent money to him on the strength of Arnoux's promise to repay the debt in a few days. Arnoux never repaid the money, however, and out of disappointment Deslauriers broke off their friendship. Frederic consoled himself by his increasing intimacy with Mme Arnoux.

Little by little Arnoux lost most of his money, and an oil company he had founded went bankrupt. He began to spend less time at home and more with various mistresses. His wife became aware of his many affairs and turned to Frederic for sympathy. At last she agreed to meet him and spend the afternoon in his company.

With high hopes, Frederic rented a room for their rendezvous and filled it with expensive trinkets. He was to meet Mme Arnoux between two and four, and on the appointed day he went to the meeting place at one-thirty. He waited until six-thirty, but she did not appear. In despair he went to see Rosanette, for to him it seemed a just retaliation to make Arnoux's mistress his own.

Mme Arnoux had not kept the appointment because her son was ill. Taking his illness as a sign from heaven, she was ashamed of her interest in Frederic.

During the riots that attended the overthrow of the monarchy and the establishment of the republic, Frederic spent the time agreeably enough in the country with Rosanette. He returned to Paris only after he received word that one of his friends had been wounded. Louise Roque went to Paris with her father, chiefly to see what had happened to Frederic. When she finally met him, she understood that he was no longer interested in her.

While continuing his affair with Rosanette, Frederic took another mistress, Mme Dambreuse. When the banker died, Frederic decided to marry his widow; but in his will, canny Dambreuse had left his money to his niece. Frederic thereupon gave up all thought of marrying the widow.

Frederic had many loves, but none was permanent. When he was nearly fifty years old, Mme Arnoux went to see him. They agreed that they had been right not to love carnally. Deslauriers had been a lawyer for twenty-five years in Nogent. He came to visit Frederic, and they talked over the past. Deslauriers had married Louise Roque, but she had run away with a singer. The old friends concluded that love was fickle, selfish, unhappy—like life itself.

Critical Evaluation:

A Sentimental Education, considered by some critics to be Gustave Flaubert's masterpiece, was without question one of the most influential French novels of the nineteenth century. The novel was a rewriting of a draft by the same title that he wrote two decades earlier. Flaubert drew largely on autobiographical material, and the work was his effort to produce a moral history of the men of his generation. Flaubert's concern is with the organic growth of a personality, and with the unfolding and discovery of the self. Education has, for Flaubert, the almost existential meaning of becoming through action. At the beginning of the book, the protagonist, Frederic Moreau, is little more than a potentiality, an empty page on which experience has yet to leave its mark. It is only as Frederic confronts the world and is forced to make choices and to react among other people that he develops into a complicated and tormented human being. The conflict is always between the man that was and the man that is about to be. To reflect this, the time sequence in the novel is poised between past and future, between the raw youth and the man of experience who is sadder and wiser but not necessarily better.

The question facing Frederic, particularly after he has moved to Paris, is whether he should become a man of the world, successful in love and business, and a man of action who is conventional in his behavior and opinions, or whether he should become a spectator of life, an outsider who remains aloof from the vanity of action and struggles to translate his ideal vision into artistic form. It is the same question that Flaubert himself faced: to be a man of the world, with all of his superficialities and conventions, or a man of art no longer of the real world. At the beginning, by necessity, Frederic stands on the sidelines, watching. He has not been able to enter society, knows few people, and has little money; so he watches the activity of others. This passive quality is emphasized by the repetition of verbs such as "he watched," "he contemplated," "he admired," and "he dreamed." Frederic seems to be a wallflower at a great and glorious ball. Then two events thrust him into the stream of action: love and the inheritance of a fortune from his uncle. With that, his real education begins.

Love is almost a pattern for all the lessons of life, according to the point of view expressed in this novel, and education, in the sense of "education for living," is synonymous with "sentimental education." Thus, the romantic or sentimental education of the hero assumes symbolic proportions. It is love through its many aspects, both sacred and profane, that opens up the world for Frederic Moreau. At first, his vision of love is ideal and pure, but as it becomes more earthbound and physical, he loses both his innocence and his idealism.

"I know nothing more noble," Flaubert once wrote, "than the contemplation of the world," and this novel provides such an opportunity for the reader. *A Sentimental Education* views the world in all of its sordid, beautiful, painful, and pleasurable complexity, and with consummate skill Flaubert presents his vision of the human condition. It was a view that many of his contemporaries considered shocking and disgusting but from which generations have subsequently derived an ironic, profound pleasure.

The heart of the novel is the love affair between Frederic and Mme Arnoux, a fictionalized version of the relationship between the young Flaubert and one Elisa Schlesinger, the wife of a well-known music publisher, who is the prototype for the art dealer Monsieur Arnoux. The real-life relationship continued, off and on, for many years and was one of the central influences in the author's life. There is no doubt that the scene of Frederic's reunion with the white-haired Madame Arnoux had its counterpart in real life. Just as Madame Arnoux is a portrait of Madame Schlesinger, so Frederic is a self-portrait of the author. The principal difference is that Flaubert acted on his dreams and learned to discipline himself in order to realize his ambitions. While Frederic is the ancestor of all the antiheroes of modern literature, Flaubert, himself, transcended the parts of himself that he gave to his hero and found in his literary vocation the strength that Frederic never was able to discover in himself.

It has been claimed that all the characters in the novel—from Frederic's friends and the Marshal, the famous courtesan, to the many minor characters who fill out the spectacular picture of Parisian society—are based on real individuals whom Flaubert knew. Certainly Flaubert based the background events on history, and he did extensive research, particularly on the subject of the 1848 revolution, to ensure historical accuracy. Yet he devoted as much care to describing an operation or a factory as in writing about the historical events. Where a lesser novelist might have let the tumultuous events of his background overpower the human story of his protagonists, however, Flaubert carefully kept a balance between the different parts of the novel. Thus the historical events provide a counterpoint highlighting the personal adventures of his hero.

To later readers, perhaps the most fascinating aspect of *A Sentimental Education* is its detailed portrait of French society at the time that led to the *coup d'état* of 1851. The endless evenings of petty conversation in restaurants and fashionable salons, the bickering and plotting over finances, the quarreling over politics, the scheming of writers and artists to achieve notoriety and attention in periodicals, all is vividly drawn. Frederic wanders among the rich and well-known, as well as among the student class and the less rich, absorbing the lessons that the world around him has to offer. Flaubert's meticulous, graceful style renders the scenes sharply, even when his protagonist is suffering most acutely. The novel gives the illusion of shapelessness, but it is actually carefully constructed. It is both a view of a society in the throes of change and a portrait of a human being discovering his own potentialities.

"Critical Evaluation" by Bruce D. Reeves

Bibliography:

Cortland, Peter. *Sentiment in Flaubert's "Education sentimentale."* Muncie, Ind.: Ball State University, 1966. An excellent starting point. Focuses on analysis of the central character and includes an excellent discussion of the opening scene. English translations and original French provided for quotations cited from the text.

Culler, Jonathan. *Flaubert: The Uses of Uncertainty*. Rev. ed., Ithaca, N.Y.: Cornell University Press, 1985. A classic, still highly relevant study of Flaubert's narrative technique and uses of irony. Structured thematically rather than chronologically. Index is very helpful in locating discussions of specific texts. Translations of French quotations located in Notes section at the end of the volume.

Knight, Diana. *Flaubert's Characters: The Language of Illusion*. Cambridge, England: Cambridge University Press, 1985. A comparative study of Flaubert's fictional characters. Includes a valuable summary of earlier criticism. Chapter 5 offers a provocative interpretation of Frédéric Moreau as an artist creating his life. Quotations from the novels in French.

Paulson, William. *"Sentimental Education": The Complexity of Disenchantment*. New York: Twayne, 1992. A comprehensive book-length study of the novel. Concise background information on literary and historical context. Clear discussion of Flaubert's narrative technique. Excellent annotated bibliography of sources in both English and French.

Porter, Laurence M. *Critical Essays on Gustave Flaubert*. Boston: G. K. Hall, 1986. A collection of essays on Flaubert's canon. See especially "*L'Éducation sentimentale:* Profanation and the Permanence of Dreams," which examines the theme of prostitution.

A SENTIMENTAL JOURNEY

Type of work: Novel
Author: Laurence Sterne (1713-1768)
Type of plot: Sentimental
Time of plot: 1760's
Locale: France
First published: A Sentimental Journey Through France and Italy, 1768

Principal characters:
Mr. Yorick, a sentimental traveler
Madame de L——, a fellow traveler
Madame de R——, Madame de L——'s friend
Count de B——, an admirer of Englishmen
La Fleur, a servant
Maria, a country girl

The Story:

Mr. Yorick felt no kinship with all the different kinds of travelers—the Idle Travelers, the Inquisitive Travelers, the Travelers of Necessity, the Simple Travelers, and the rest. He was a Sentimental Traveler. As such, he collected sentimental adventures as other tourists collected postcards of the points of interest they visited. Mr. Yorick had started his journey because a man had asked him, with a sneer, if he had ever been in France. Yorick had just made some statement on the French and did not like being answered so tartly merely because he did not have firsthand experience. That same evening, he packed some clothes and left by boat for Calais.

While Yorick was having supper at an inn in Calais, a poor monk approached him and begged alms for his monastery. Yorick rebuffed him with caustic and witty remarks. Later, Yorick saw the monk talking with an attractive woman who was also staying at the inn. Afraid the monk might tell her how rudely he had behaved, Yorick approached the couple, apologized to the monk, and offered his shell snuffbox to him as a peace offering. Now that Yorick had made friends with the monk and the lady, he planned to ask the lady to travel with him to Paris. He learned that her name was Madame de L——.

Proposing to make the trip to Paris in a private carriage, Yorick invited the lady to go with him to look over some of the vehicles for sale in a nearby courtyard. Their admiration of each other grew with unusual rapidity. Before Yorick had a chance to ask her to travel with him, however, she was called away by a message that her brother, Count de L——, had arrived. He had come to take her back to Belgium with him. Yorick was brokenhearted. In parting, Madame de L—— asked Yorick to visit her in Belgium if he passed through that country. She also gave him a letter of introduction to a good friend in Paris, Madame de R——.

The next day, Yorick set off in a small carriage for Paris. His baggage fell out of the chaise several times, and he had an uncomfortable trip to Montriul. There an innkeeper suggested he needed a servant, and Yorick saw that the man was quite right. He hired a young boy named La Fleur, whose greatest accomplishments were playing the flute and making love to the girls. La Fleur was delighted at the prospect of traveling around Europe with a generous and unpredictable English milord; he was only sad to have to say good-bye to all of his village sweethearts. Yorick was pleased with the lad's quickness and wit, and he was sure that the young Frenchman would be able to deal with any emergency arising along the way.

The first problem the travelers met on their journey was a dead ass lying in the middle of the road. The horses refused to pass the carcass, and La Fleur's horse threw him and ran away. Proceeding to the next town, they met and talked with the owner of the poor dead beast. He had taken the ass with him from Germany to Italy and was very unhappy at its death, not so much because the beast had been a help to him but because he felt sure that the ass had loved him dearly and had been a good friend to him for many years.

In Paris, Yorick went to the opera. A quotation from Shakespeare popped into his mind, and he suddenly decided to go and buy the works of that writer. He went into a bookstore and found a set on the counter. They were, however, not for sale, having been sent to be rebound for Count de B——, a great lover of English authors and Englishmen. In the shop, Yorick saw an attractive young girl who, he decided, must be a chambermaid. When she left the shop, he followed her and began a conversation about the book she had bought. Yorick was surprised and pleased to discover that the young girl belonged to the household of Madame de R——. He told her to inform her mistress that he would call the next day.

On returning to his rooms, Yorick learned from La Fleur that the police wanted to see him. In his rush out of England, he had forgotten to get a passport, and he had overlooked completely the fact that England and France were at war. Since he did not wish to be put in jail, he decided that he would have to get a passport, but he did not know how these matters were arranged in France. Madame de R—— was the only person in Paris to whom he carried a letter of introduction, and he did not want to bother the lady about the matter. The only other chance of help was from Count de B——, who, as he knew, liked Englishmen.

It took Yorick some time to arrange to see the count; when he did, however, the count was most polite. As an amusing way to introduce himself, Yorick opened one of the volumes of Shakespeare, which had just been sent from the bookseller's. Turning to *Hamlet* and pointing to the passage about the jester Yorick, he said that was his name. The count was overcome with pleasure at meeting so famous a person, and nothing Yorick could say changed the count's mind. The count left the room and did not return for a long while. When he did, he presented Mr. Yorick with a passport that called him the King's Jester. Realizing that he could not correct the mistake without losing his passport, Yorick thanked the count and returned to his room.

The next day, Madame de R——'s chambermaid called to see why Mr. Yorick had not visited her mistress as he had promised. Yorick explained about the passport and asked her to present his apology. Some hours later, after the girl had gone, the manager of the hotel came in and objected to Yorick's having young ladies in his room. In order to keep from being evicted from the hotel, Yorick had to buy some lace from a young woman. He suspected that the manager pocketed most of the profits from such sales.

On Sunday, La Fleur appeared in a fine suit of clothes that he had bought secondhand. He asked if he might be allowed to have the day off, as he had been able to make friends with a young woman he would like to see again that day. Yorick asked him to bring some food before he left for the day. Wrapped about the butter, which La Fleur brought with Yorick's dinner, was a piece of paper that bore on it some old printing. Yorick became interested in the story it told and spent the whole day translating the faded characters to read the story of a luckless notary. Nevertheless, he was never to know the ending of the tale, for La Fleur had used the rest of the paper to wrap up a bouquet for his new friend.

Yorick had a fine time at parties to which he was invited by Count de B—— and the count's friends. Because he agreed with everyone to whom he talked and made no remarks of his own, he was thought the finest wit in Paris. After several minor sentimental adventures, Yorick and La Fleur set out to travel through southern France. At Moulines, Yorick stopped to see

Maria, a poor unhappy girl who wandered about the country grieving for her dead father. He had heard of the girl from his old friend, Mr. Toby Shandy, who had met her several years before. Yorick sat down on a rock with Maria. Moved by her purity and sadness, he shed a few tears with her.

Before ascending Mount Taurira, Yorick stopped and had dinner with a pleasant peasant family. That night, he was forced to stay in a roadside inn. There was only one room in the inn, and Yorick had to share it with a French lady and her maid. In the room there were two large beds standing beside each other and, in a closet connected to the room, a cot. After much deliberation, the lady and Yorick took the big beds and sent the maid into the closet. Yorick had to promise to stay in his bed and to keep silent all night. Unable to sleep, both Yorick and the lady began talking. Afraid that something untoward might occur, the maid came out of the closet and, unseen, stood between the two beds. Yorick stretched out his hand. With this sentimental gesture, Sterne ended abruptly the story of his sentimental journey.

Critical Evaluation:

The full title Lawrence Sterne gave his unconventional mixture of autobiography, travel impressions, and fiction—*A Sentimental Journey Through France and Italy*—is misleading. Sterne told of his travels through France, but he died of tuberculosis before writing the Italian section of his narrative. Sentimental, outrageous, and eccentric in its humorous effects, the novel is replete with delightful accounts and observations of whatever came into the author's mind. Like *The Life and Opinions of Tristram Shandy, Gent.* (1759-1767), the book broadened the scope of prose fiction for later writers by demonstrating that form and unified plot are not necessary for a successful novel.

Both in form and apparent subject, *A Sentimental Journey* follows in the tradition of the grand-tour novel. The depictions of scenes and persons, of escapades on the road, of the cultural adjustments required of an Englishman abroad, and of the things to be learned and the places to be visited were common, enjoyable reading matter for an eighteenth century audience. Sterne's grand tour, however, sports a delightful touch of irreverence. Its hero, Yorick, is not a typical young gentleman matriculating into a peripatetic finishing school but a low-key picaro buffeted by impulse and whimsy. Therefore, his "travelling" seems random. Unplanned, untimed, it accords perfectly with his sole principle, which, it seems, is to have no principle whatever except obedience to natural affections, to his growing sensibility, and his often unseemly passion. He prefers *filles de chambre* to cathedrals and a pretty face to a gallery portrait. Given his free-flowing nature, he does not seek to improve himself in accordance with a travel plan; he prefers to stumble over it in following his heart. The point Sterne makes is that a benevolent nature can be trusted not to err in promoting human goodness.

"Sentiment" and a host of such attendant words as "good nature," "sensibility," and "affections" were all terms with particular significance in Sterne's day. The so-called doctrine of sensibility, popularized by the late seventeenth century Latitudinarian divines, urged an inherent goodness in human beings, a "sense" of moral absolutes that expresses itself in acts of charity and social benevolence. Championed philosophically by the third earl of Shaftesbury (in his *Characteristics of Men, Manners, Opinions, and Times*, 1711) and in fiction by Henry Fielding, this emphasis on good nature ran counter to the often equally influential tradition expounded by Thomas Hobbes in *Leviathan* (1651) and by Bernard de Mandeville in *The Fable of the Bees, or Private Vices, Public Benefits* (1714), a tradition that urged self-interest as the basis of all human action. These two forces collide in *A Sentimental Journey* as Sterne explores what it means to be a good person.

Sterne gave a sidelong glance at Hobbes in several of his characters: the huge oaf who deliberately blocks the view of a dwarf, the postilion who thrashes his horses, and even Yorick himself at the start of the novel when he refuses charity to a monk. Yet this "natural" cruelty—as Hobbes would have defined it—is contrasted with the virtues of a larger number of characters: the old French officer who assists the dwarf, the mourner who laments his dead animal, and the enlightened Yorick who guides the unfortunate Maria. Sterne recognizes only too well human beings' divided nature, in which good and evil are deeply intertwined, yet he wants to insist that the "deeper affections," the "eternal fountain of our feelings," as Yorick says, are also a primary impulse of inordinate strength.

Beneath the surface, *A Sentimental Journey* is something of an allegory, a type of metaphorical journey in which Yorick, and hence also the reader, discovers the primacy of human feeling. It is a travel not just through space and time but into sensibility itself, the common bond of all humanity. Yet on one level, the book is an outrageous comedy, and it is wise not to forget this. The famous ending ("When I stretched out my hand, I caught hold of the *fille de chambre's*—") and the mixed motives of its characters are a reminder that Sterne wrote for delight as much as for instruction. The comedy, however, ought not to obscure a more serious intent in the book. There is a delicate line separating love from lust, Sterne argues, if only because the "web of kindness" has "threads of love and desire . . . entangled with the piece." Too often, the temptation is to rend the whole web (as Yorick says) by drawing out the threads of love and desire. That results merely in people becoming heartless and cold. Instead, they ought to excuse occasional moral lapses in the interest of fostering greater love, for it is love alone that characterizes human beings in their best moments. This is the main point of Sterne's delightful Aristophanic fragment on the town of Abdera: There literature succeeds in making the most profligate town become devoted to Cupid. It is equally the point of Yorick's amorousness and of his belief that, once rekindled at Love's flame, he is all generosity and goodwill again. It underlies his celebration of freedom, La Fleur's Casanovan conquests, the Count de B——'s encomium on the fair sex, and, unforgettably, the French officer's noble lesson that mutual toleration teaches mutual love.

It could also be said that this message underlies Sterne's prose style inasmuch as readers, like Yorick, are sentimental travelers. The associative drift of the narrative precludes expectation; it demands instead that readers allow themselves to be taken wherever their sensibility choose to take them. The novel demands to be read less with the head than with the heart. Many of the scenes, for example, play unabashedly on the emotions, just as Sterne plays on the readers' elementary sense of justice and distinction between what is right and wrong to score his points. In an intriguing way, therefore, *A Sentimental Journey* is not merely about a grand tour but is itself a grand tour. It is an education in the consistency of human nature, not its diversity. It is, like Euripides before Abdera, Sterne before the world.

"Critical Evaluation" by David B. Carroll

Bibliography:

Brissenden, R. F. "The Sentimental Comedy: *A Sentimental Journey*." In *Virtue in Distress*. London: Macmillan, 1974. Argues that the primary purpose of *A Sentimental Journey* is to show the inextricable if ironic link between human beings' capacity for the social virtues of compassion and sympathy and their capacity for sexual responsiveness.

Cash, Arthur Hill. *Sterne's Comedy of Moral Sentiment: The Ethical Dimensions of the "Journey."* Pittsburgh: Duquesne University Press, 1966. Explores ethical rationalism by comparing *A Sentimental Journey* and "the comedy of moral problems" to Sterne's *The Sermons of Mr. Yorick* (1760, 1766) and *The Sermons by the Late Rev. Mr. Sterne* (1769).

Howes, Alan B., ed. *Sterne: The Critical Heritage*. London: Routledge & Kegan Paul, 1974. A thorough and well-organized compilation of criticism, acclaim, and accusations of plagiarism by Sterne's contemporaries in response to the publication of *A Sentimental Journey*. Also discusses other works by Sterne.

Loveridge, Mark. *Laurence Sterne and the Argument About Design*. London: Macmillan, 1982. Explores Sterne's use of pattern, design, and form, and places these concepts within the general cultural and literary context of his day. Chapter 7 deals exclusively with *A Sentimental Journey*.

Moglen, Helene. *The Philosophical Irony of Laurence Sterne*. Gainesville: The University Presses of Florida, 1975. Systematically discusses Sterne's use of stylistic and thematic irony in relation to character, theme development, and thematic unity. Also explores the relevance of his novel to contemporary times.

SET THIS HOUSE ON FIRE

Type of work: Novel
Author: William Styron (1925-   )
Type of plot: Psychological realism
Time of plot: Mid-twentieth century
Locale: Sambuco, Italy
First published: 1960

Principal characters:

CASS KINSOLVING, an expatriate alcoholic painter from the southern United States
PETER LEVERETT, an expatriate American lawyer and friend of Cass
MASON FLAGG, an American millionaire and friend of Cass and Peter
LUIGI MIGLIORE, an Italian policeman and Fascist humanist philosopher
FRANCESCA RICCI, an Italian peasant girl, loved by Cass but raped by Mason Flagg

The Story:

Peter Leverett, the first-person narrator of *Set This House on Fire*, was a lawyer in New York plagued by disturbing memories of and questions about events in Sambuco, Italy, several years earlier, which he partially observed and which culminated in the rape and murder of a young, beautiful Italian, Francesca Ricci, and in the death of Mason Flagg. Mason, a millionaire American temporarily in Sambuco, was found at the base of a cliff a few hours after the brutal attack on Francesca, the Italian police deciding an enraged, lustful Mason attacked Francesca and then killed himself in remorse. Having known Mason Flagg since their high school days some ten years earlier and believing him to be sexually obsessed but not a murderer, Peter had difficulty accepting the official explanation. After seeing a *New York Times* political cartoon drawn by Cass Kinsolving, another American who was in Sambuco when Mason and Francesca died, Peter decided to contact Cass and get his version of what happened, particularly since Cass seemed to have somehow been involved.

Peter left New York for Virginia, where he grew up and where his parents still lived, on his way to visit Cass in Charleston, South Carolina. In Virginia, Peter found his hometown drastically changed and virtually unrecognizable, modernized and urbanized, and street names changed, such as "Bankhead Magruder Avenue" becoming "Buena Vista Terrace," prompting Peter's father to comment that "it's the California influence . . . it's going to get us all in the end."

In Charleston, Peter narrated, via personal flashback and quotation from Cass's comments and notebook, their experiences and observations prior to and after their arrival in Sambuco which, in totality, reconstructed the earlier reality and generated the truth about Francesca's rape and murder and Mason's death. First, Peter related his school-based knowledge of Mason, a Northerner transplanted to Virginia because his unaffectionate movie-mogul father had bought a plantation there, a place of entertainment for his movie-star friends. Peter also explained Mason's unusually close attachment to his alcoholic, virtually deserted mother and related Mason's dismissal from school after his drunken seduction of a thirteen-year-old, imbecilic girl.

Peter then told of his arrival in Sambuco on the afternoon before the murder, interrupting filming of a movie scene; a movie company was in Sambuco partially because of a tie to Mason. Next, Peter described the movie crowd's raucous party and the mysterious scratches around Mason's face. He also observed Mason pursue and threaten to kill a young Italian girl who, with her dress torn, ran from his residence. Later, Peter observed Cass kiss this same girl (Francesca) and observed Mason receive a note which said, "You're in deep trouble. . . . I'm going to turn you into bait for buzzards. C." Peter then watched Mason humiliate a drunken Cass by coercing him to perform a "trained seal" act for the movie crowd (recite bawdy limericks, pantomime the behavior of a French whore, and sing "Old Black Joe," and do the "rebel yell," among other activities). Rescuing Cass from this humiliation, Peter went with him to deliver medicine (stolen from Mason) to Francesca's dying father. Peter then slept, awakening to the news of Francesca's rape and murder, and Mason's death.

Peter next presented Cass's account of his life prior to coming to Sambuco—his lower-class Southern childhood, his determination to become a successful artist, his horrifying World War II experiences, and his subsequent mental problems, including an inability to successfully paint but desperate need to do so and an inability to avoid the alcohol consumption that seemed to dull the pain of his artistic failure but that actually only increased it. A successful painter in Charleston, Cass described himself as guilt-ridden and doubt-filled in Sambuco, haunted by dreams of his prior abuse of an African American family and unable to believe in any divine purpose for or control over the universe. Cass then explained that his love for Francesca and desire to help her impoverished, dying father became his last means of escape from his depression and addiction and that Mason's rape of Francesca and Cass's belief that Mason brutally attacked her a second time, killing her, led Cass to kill Mason, subsequently throwing his body over the cliff. Cass then learned that the second, more brutal attack on Francesca was by Saverio, the idiot of Sambuco, and that Luigi Migliore, Cass's Italian policeman/philosopher friend, concealed the evidence of Cass's attack and attributed Mason's death to suicide, being convinced that "there had been in Sambuco this day entirely too much suffering." Luigi believed that obtaining Cass's freedom would keep him "from the luxury of any more guilt" and force him to face his failings, conquer them, and salvage at least the remainder of his troubled life.

Cass related that he protested violently but eventually acquiesced, returning to the American South and gradually overcoming, at least somewhat, his artistic block, alcohol addiction, and depression. His talk with Peter thus led him to understand the sexual obsessiveness that caused Mason to rape Francesca, and helped Peter to understand the events in Sambuco that ended in Mason's death. Peter then returned to New York, reconciled to Mason's innocence of at least murder and to the tragically confused and violent inevitability of the events in Sambuco.

Critical Evaluation:

Set This House on Fire is William Styron's second novel, published nine years after *Lie Down in Darkness*, the latter generating for Styron the 1950's reputation of America's most promising young novelist. Perhaps partly because of that reputation, *Set This House on Fire* is an ambitious novel—lengthy, complex, graphically emotional, and often profound. However, since Styron's second novel is deceptively different from his first—in length, in location, and in extent of psychological portraiture—many critics found it disappointing, labeling it melodramatic, pretentious, vague, and unconvincing. These criticisms are undeserved, reflecting a failure to comprehend Styron's essential thematic concern and his fundamental technique.

Thematically, *Set This House on Fire* is indeed completely a Southern novel, but often unappreciated as such given its symbolist (even allegorical) technique. This technique accounts for the Italian setting, Sambuco being a place of antiquity where superficialities of cultural accretion do not prevent characters from confrontation with their primeval emotional and philosophical longings. Sambuco represents uncluttered human reality, unlike the modernized and urbanized hometown that Peter Leverett can no longer truly recognize or understand. In Sambuco, though, Peter can realize his true relationship to Mason Flagg (mutual dislike), and Cass Kinsolving can confront his guilt-ridden past and overcome it by purgative actions (serving as Mason's "slave" entertainer; helping the peasant father of Francesca, whom he associates with African Americans he abused in previous years; and killing Mason Flagg).

The killing of Mason has been particularly misunderstood, critics failing to go beyond the symbolism of Mason's last name (Flagg, as in American flag, a symbol of America) to perceive that Styron's symbolism is more pervasive. Mason is also "Mason" of the Mason-Dixon line, specifically the Northern side of that line, the Yankee side. His Northern wealth, his Northern upbringing, and his abrupt transplantation to Virginia via his father's carpetbagger-like assumption of ownership of a Virginia plantation all connote Mason as a symbol of Northern American commercial and industrial power, wealth, and corruption. In contrast, Cass Kinsolving is the "Dixon" part of the Mason-Dixon division. The imagery of the name "Kinsolving" symbolizes the solving of problems created by his kinfolks, his Southern ancestors. Born in North Carolina and most comfortable in Charleston, a center of Old South culture, Cass represents the South's strengths and weaknesses. He is heavily burdened by guilt over his treatment of African Americans but violently opposed to the cultural superficiality, materialism, and sexual callousness of Mason Flagg. Like many Southerners, Cass idolizes women, and his spiritual agonizing and artistic uncertainty are representative of Southern intellectual and cultural nihilism as a result of the Civil War (symbolized by World War II in the novel). Thus, when Cass becomes Mason's "trained seal," he is doing penance for his symbolic enslavement of African Americans, and in helping Francesca's peasant father and killing Mason he is exacting revenge for the Civil War and Northern material and sexual excesses. Thus, Cass regains his self-respect via retribution against the North's oppression of the South as represented, in his mind, by Mason Flagg. He can then return to Charleston emotionally cleansed and able to productively paint and to continue his criticism of Northern America via cartoons in *The New York Times*.

The novel's techniques often reflect the influence of other authors, such as Nathaniel Hawthorne and William Faulkner. Cass's constant psychological self-examination is clearly reminiscent of Robin Molineux in "My Kinsman, Major Molineux," for example, and the frequent use of flashbacks similarly echoes Hawthorne's obsessive self-examination techniques. Also, Styron repeatedly presents Cass's reveries in a state midway between sleeping and waking, in which he may be dreaming or daydreaming, with his repressed feelings of guilt exhibiting themselves in grotesquely altered forms. Styron presents Cass (and implicitly the South) as haunted by its treatment of African Americans. Peter Leverett's father touches on this while looking out at the ocean off Virginia's shore.

> That's where they came in, in the year 1619. Right out there. It was one of the saddest days in the history of man, I mean black *or* white. We're still paying for that day, and we'll be paying for it from right here on out. And there'll be blood shed, and tears.

Although skillfully disguised and symbolized, and distanced via placement of the action in Sambuco, Italy, it is that problem of America which is the focal point of Styron's *Set This House on Fire*. Analogously to Hawthorne's dramatization of the effects of the excesses of American Puritanism, Styron dramatizes the continuing implications of America's racial history, acted out in profound psychological and physical microcosm in the conflict between Mason Flagg and Cass Kinsolving. Clearly, *Set This House on Fire* is a profoundly Southern novel.

John L. Grigsby

Bibliography:

Fossum, Robert H. *William Styron*. Grand Rapids, Mich.: Eerdmans, 1968. Includes a thorough and perceptive chapter on *Set This House on Fire*. Notes the novel's existential bent and purgatorial suffering implications.

Friedman, Melvin J. *William Styron*. Bowling Green, Ohio: Bowling Green State University Popular Press, 1974. Argues that the novel is a caricature of traditional detective fiction and notes the importance of setting but incompletely explains the symbolism.

Pearce, Richard. *William Styron*. Minneapolis: University of Minnesota Press, 1971. Focuses upon the class conflict implications of the economic disparities depicted and the violence underlying the superficial sophistication in American culture as presented by Styron.

Rubin, Louis D. *The Faraway Country: Writers of the Modern South*. Seattle: University of Washington Press, 1963. One of the best analyses of the novel, depicting some of the Southern themes implicit in it and sensitively analyzing the psychological portrait of Cass Kinsolving.

Ruderman, Judith. *William Styron*. New York: Ungar, 1987. A thorough study of the novel that utilizes prior criticism in effectively interpreting some of Styron's symbols and astutely analyzes Mason Flagg's sexual obsessiveness.

SEVEN AGAINST THEBES

Type of work: Drama
Author: Aeschylus (525/524-456/455 B.C.E.)
Type of plot: Tragedy
Time of plot: Antiquity
Locale: Thebes
First performed: Hepta epi Thēbas, 467 B.C.E. (English translation, 1777)

Principal characters:
ETEOCLES, the king of Thebes
POLYNICES, his brother
ANTIGONE and
ISMENE, their sisters
A SPY
THEBAN WOMEN, the chorus

The Story:

After the ruin and exile of Oedipus, the king of Thebes, his sons, Eteocles and Polynices, fell into dispute, each brother claiming supreme authority in the city. The quarrel led to a bloody civil war in which Eteocles was victorious. Banished from Thebes, Polynices went to Argos. There he mustered an army, led by six famous Argive heroes, for the purpose of returning and recapturing the city, which was restless under his brother's rule.

Thebes was besieged with the Argive warriors camped about its walls. Eteocles, consulting a seer, learned that his brother's army was planning to make a surprise night attack and, under cover of darkness, to scale the walls and overwhelm the defenders. Eteocles exhorted all Theban men, young and old, to stand bravely at their posts and to repel the attackers.

While he was speaking, a spy reported to Eteocles that Polynices and his Argives had sworn to raze the city, their vows made with clasps of hands stained by blood dripping from the head of an ox sacrificed in solemn ritual. The spy also brought word that Polynices and the six Argive heroes had drawn lots to determine the city gates against which each of the seven would lead his band of attackers.

Upon hearing the spy's report, the Theban women called upon the gods and goddesses to protect Cadmus' sacred city from the onslaught of the besiegers. Eteocles rebuked the frightened women and declared that they were wasting their time with appeals to the gods at a time of imminent peril. He asserted that the Thebans must depend on their own courage and strength, not upon the unpredictable gods. Angrily he dismissed the women to attend to their children and weaving; they were to leave all other matters to their husbands and fathers.

Eteocles then chose the six outstanding warriors of Thebes who would, with himself, defend the seven gates of the city against the seven Achaean warriors who had sworn each to take a gate of the city by storm. The king chose the defending heroes carefully. Theban Melanippus would oppose Argive Tydeus; Polyphontes, Capaneus; Megareus, Eteocles of Argos; Hyperbius, Hippomedon; Actor, Parthenopaeus; and Lasthenes, Amphiaraus. Polynices was to be the seventh hero leading the attack against the seventh gate, so Eteocles announced that he would stand as his brother's opponent. Their combat, prince against prince, brother against brother, would determine the destiny of their ill-fated house.

Hearing his words, the Theban women again began their wailing lament and warned him against the sin of fratricide. Eteocles, well aware of the blood bath that his family had already suffered because of the curse of Pelops on Laius, his grandfather, ignored the city matrons. Defying the fickle gods, he declared that he was determined to remain the king of Thebes, even if his brother's death must be the price of his crown.

At Eteocles' mention of the curse upon his house, the Theban women deplored the sad story of Laius. Already cursed by Pelops, whose hospitality he had desecrated, Laius had been warned by Apollo that he would prosper only if he sired no child. In spite of the warning, however, he had fathered a son, Oedipus. Later the child was abandoned in the wilderness, where he was saved from death by the intervention of an old household servant and reared to manhood by a good shepherd. Oedipus, in turn, defied prophecies of disaster and doom when he, unaware of his true identity, murdered Laius, his father, and subsequently married Jocasta, his mother. Two of the children of their ill-starred union were Eteocles and Polynices, whose rivalry had caused untold suffering in Thebes. The women wept when they recalled the years of strife and trouble that had been brought upon their city by the doomed line of Cadmus.

Meanwhile the brazen clamor of arms and the shouts of men sounded in the distance; the attack had begun. While the women waited to learn the outcome of the assault, a messenger brought word that the defenders had beaten back the Argive warriors at six of the seven gates. The city had been saved, he announced, but in the fighting at the seventh gate Eteocles and Polynices had both been slain.

At the height of the attack, when the battle was fiercest, the brothers had killed each other, thus fulfilling the prophecy of Oedipus that his sons would share glory by iron, that is to say, by the sword, not by gold. The only land over which they would rule would be the grave, and the soil that had called them masters was now red with their blood.

The bodies of Eteocles and Polynices were carried into the city in preparation for their burial. Antigone and Ismene, sisters of the dead princes, mourned their violent deaths, while the Theban women sang a mournful dirge for the tragic ending of a great family, cursed by the gods but defiant of the doom forecast years before and then unhappily fulfilled.

In the midst of their laments, a herald appeared to announce the decision of the Theban senate. Eteocles, the city fathers had decreed, had been his country's friend; as such, his body was to receive final burial rites and to be interred within the royal tomb. Men would remember him as his city's champion and savior. Polynices, on the other hand, had sowed dissension and civil strife. Demanding fit punishment for his crimes against the state, the senate had proclaimed that his body should be thrown outside the city gates, where dogs and ravens could feast upon his flesh.

Antigone imperiously defied the city fathers. If no one else would give her brother a burial befitting his rank, she declared, she herself would bury him. It was her opinion, since he was the older son and therefore rightful heir to the throne, that he had been no more right and no more wrong than Eteocles had been in his beliefs and deeds.

Her brave defiance brought many sympathizing citizens to her side. Some declared that laws often changed and what is one day right is often wrong tomorrow. The others, surrounding the corpse of Eteocles, maintained that they would obey the decree of the senate. In that division of public opinion more troubles were forecast for the unhappy city.

Critical Evaluation:

In this severely simple drama, in which all the action is described by messengers, Aeschylus presented the third and closing episode in the tragic legend of the royal house of Thebes. The plays dealing with the fate of Laius and of his son Oedipus, have, unfortunately, not survived, but in the surviving drama the deaths of Eteocles and his brother Polynices, sons of Oedipus and grandsons of Laius, culminated three generations of violence, bloodshed, and agony that arose from Laius' ingratitude to Pelops. The delineation of the character of Eteocles in this play marked in Greek tragedy a new departure which was to be perfected by Sophocles and Euripides.

Seven Against Thebes was first produced as part of a Theban trilogy in 467 B.C.E., with which Aeschylus won first place in the Athenian drama competition. By then he had been writing tragedies for more than thirty years. Almost single-handedly he had fashioned an important art form out of the drama with his technical improvements and his gift for stirring dramatic poetry. Aeschylus was a very prominent playwright at that time, and younger men, such as Sophocles, were building on his achievements. Although *Seven Against Thebes* is a mature work, Aeschylus' finest triumphs were still to come.

The two other plays in this Theban series have not survived. Apparently they dealt with the legends of Laius and Oedipus, the grandfather and father of Eteocles and Polynices. *Seven Against Thebes* shows Aeschylus grappling with the theme of the blood curse. Laius was cursed because of his gross ingratitude to Pelops. Oedipus was cursed because he slew his father Laius and married his mother Jocasta; and he in turn cursed his sons Polynices and Eteocles for begrudging him food. This is the background for the fratricidal strife between the two, and for Eteocles' headstrong desire to fight his brother.

With Aeschylus a family curse is something almost palpable, a presence that hovers over a clan and works its doom. Each member of the family has free will, but that will is part of a whole that heads passionately for disaster. The audience sees this in Eteocles, a forerunner of the tragic hero; in Polynices; and in Antigone as she resolutely defies the edict of the Theban council by marching off to bury Polynices. Their fates are chosen, willed by themselves in full knowledge of the consequences, and yet they fit a broad pattern of calamity in the Theban dynasty.

Seven Against Thebes falls into three sections, which diminish progressively in length. The first part handles Eteocles' preparations for battle, the second tells of the war's end and shows the mourning for the sons of Oedipus, while the third deals with Antigone's rebellion against the edict.

In the first section, the audience watches Eteocles in action as an effective leader in defending Thebes. His military address to the troops, his means of getting information about the enemy plans from seer and spy, the way he quells the panicky prayers of the Theban matrons, the type of men he chooses to defend the city gates, and his own willingness to fight, all point to an excellent general. If his right to rule Thebes is questionable, there is no doubt about the quality of his leadership in defending Thebes.

He is manly, disdainful of women who endanger the city through fright and weakness. Eteocles is not impious, for he sees the value of masculine piety in war, but he feels that men should rely chiefly on their own strength. There is, however, a barrier between him and heaven—the curse his father laid on him. He knows that he is doomed, but he takes every precaution to save Thebes. The patriotism of Aeschylus shines through the character of Eteocles. If it were not for his willful sin of fratricide, Eteocles might be an authentic tragic hero.

The second section underscores the idea of the blood curse, announces the Theban victory, and shows the mourning for Eteocles and Polynices. In the final section, with Antigone's defiance of the city elders, the audience realizes that the family curse has not ended. Antigone is making a new crisis in burying her outcast brother. There is an echo of the brothers' feud in the way she leaves with Polynice's body while Ismene, following the edict, exits with the corpse of Eteocles.

It is significant that the audience sees the conflict between the brothers from the Theban point of view—from inside the city. The attackers are depicted as evildoers, as boastful, impious adventurers largely, each intent on sacking and burning the city and carrying off the women as slaves. The audience can understand the panic of the Theban chorus. Aeschylus knew from his experience in the Greek and Persian wars how it felt to be assaulted by foreign troops who wanted to enslave one's homeland. He lived in a heroic era, and his dramas convey the grandeur of Periclean Athens.

Among other things, *Seven Against Thebes* is a rousing martial poem with a wide variety of poetic and rhetorical techniques. There is the military pep talk, the dithyrambic invocation of the gods, invective, choral odes, antithesis in choosing defenders, the dirge, stichomythia in the mourning of Antigone and Ismene, and debate between Antigone and the herald. From a poetic point of view the play is a tour de force.

This drama is usually seen as a prelude to *Oresteia* (458 B.C.E.), Aeschylus' greatest dramas, in which he again takes up the theme of the blood curse. *Seven Against Thebes* is a great work, and if it is not considered of the highest quality, the reason is that readers have the later plays of Aeschylus and the finest plays of Sophocles and Euripides for comparison.

"Critical Evaluation" by James Weigel, Jr.

Bibliography:

Cameron, H. D. *Studies on the "Seven Against Thebes" of Aeschylus*. The Hague: Mouton, 1971. One of the few books to concentrate specifically on this early and often slighted work of Aeschylus. Not a good starting place.

Herington, John. *Aeschylus*. New Haven, Conn.: Yale University Press, 1986. An excellent starting point. Stresses how the play depicts the conflict of two active principles by means of the struggle between Eteocles and Polynices. Notes that the play helped establish tragedy as a form.

Podlecki, Anthony J. *The Political Background of Aeschylean Tragedy*. Ann Arbor: University of Michigan Press, 1966. Relates the action of the play, which concerns conflicts between two would-be leaders of a Greek city-state, to the political disputes occurring in the Athens of Aeschylus' own time. Occasionally dated, crude analysis, but offers insights not readily available in other sources.

Rosenmeyer, Thomas. *The Art of Aeschylus*. Berkeley: University of California Press, 1982. Examines the play from a linguistic, stylistic, and aesthetic standpoint. Does not require any knowledge of ancient Greek to profit from its insight.

Winnington-Ingram, R. P. *Studies in Aeschylus*. New York: Cambridge University Press, 1983. Contains a compelling description of Eteocles as the "first man" of the European stage. Sheds light on Aeschylus' transmutation of his mythological sources and examines the conflict between the playwright's temperamental conservatism and the theme of conflict in the play. Occasionally abstruse and specialized.

SEVEN PILLARS OF WISDOM

Type of work: History
Author: T. E. Lawrence (1888-1935)
Locale: The Middle East
First published: limited edition, 1926; complete edition, 1935

Principal personages:
T. E. LAWRENCE, the author
SHERIF FEISAL IBN HUSSEIN
FIELD MARSHAL EDMUND H. H. ALLENBY
SIR HENRY MCMAHON, High Commissioner in Egypt
JEMAL PASHA, of Syria
SHERIF HUSSEIN, Emir of Mecca

Unless the forces and countercurrents of world history change abruptly or virtually reverse themselves, it is unlikely that an Englishman will ever again have the opportunity to approximate the exploits and terrors, the sense of achievement and frustration, that T. E. Lawrence experienced and described in his *Seven Pillars of Wisdom*. This work is autobiographical history, lived by a most extraordinary and strangely gifted man.

The unusual qualities manifest in the author of *Seven Pillars of Wisdom* developed early. His lifelong interest in archaeology and his field of special study at Oxford brought about his travels as a professional archaeologist in exploratory rambles through Syria, Egypt, and Northern Mesopotamia. When war broke out in 1914, it resulted that Lawrence, who spoke perfect Arabic and who knew the region, served in British Intelligence in Egypt. In 1916, Captain Lawrence sought leave from these duties to try to bring about unity among the Arab chieftains in order to counteract the military and political activities of Turkey. *Seven Pillars of Wisdom* is concerned with these extraordinary years.

Following World War I, Lawrence's life fell into unusual patterns. Granted many military distinctions and special recognition for his achievements during the war years, he refused nearly every honor. For a time, he served as Arab consultant at peace conferences and as a political adviser to the colonial office of his government. By 1921, however, his secretive nature had asserted itself. He enlisted as an aircraftman under the name of Ross; he saw duty as Private T. E. Shaw in the tank corps; and he enlisted again as T. E. Shaw in the air force. Upon completion of this last tour of duty, he returned to England, only to lose his life in a motorcycle crash. His was a strange and unusual life, filled with adventure, heroic achievement, planned self-effacement, and an accidental conclusion.

Just as extraordinary were the events culminating in the final publication of *Seven Pillars of Wisdom*. Working from his own detailed notes, which he destroyed as he completed each major section of the book, Lawrence lost almost the entire first draft. Again he set about his task, this time writing from memory alone. The work appeared first in the limited edition of 1926. In the following year he issued an abridgement, *Revolt in the Desert*, for the general public. Following his death in 1935, the full text of *Seven Pillars of Wisdom* was released. Comparison of the complete work with *Revolt in the Desert* affords no good explanation for the author's insistence upon the delay in releasing the full text.

Strange, even quixotic, as some of the incidents of Lawrence's life and the fortunes of his principal publication may seem, the book itself is far more extraordinary and revealing: a detailed and absorbing recital of two years of striving, of attack and maneuver, of persuasion and rebuff, of privation and intense strain, which culminated in a large measure of success with partial victory of Arab forces over the common enemy, Turkey.

The title of this account is to some extent indicative of the complex mind of the author. Some years before, he had selected the phrase from the first verse of the ninth chapter of the Book of Proverbs: "Wisdom hath builded a house: she hath hewn out her seven pillars." At the time, he planned to use the title for a projected book about seven cities; later he transferred the title to the present work "as a memento" of his early literary enterprise; finally he added the subtitle, *The Seven Pillars of Wisdom: A Triumph*. In essence, the full title suggests the transition from Lawrence the youthful archaeologist to Lawrence the expert in Arab affairs and in military plans and strategy.

This record of a two-year campaign is compact and explicit, although set down from memory. It consists of 122 closely written chapters, comprising an introduction, ten books, and an epilogue, totaling more than six hundred pages.

In the first seven chapters, Lawrence sketched what he termed "The Foundations of Revolt." He described the Arab lands and their troubled peoples, the animosity between Turks and the other loosely knit groups, the lack of trust among various Arab clans, and the absence of fundamental understanding of all of these conflicting circumstances on the part of the British Foreign Office and key military leaders. Lawrence was convinced that the Arab revolt could succeed if the Arab leaders were properly advised.

After securing detachment from his foreign office assignment, he took off to interview Arab chieftains and leaders. He traveled far, on camelback and in Arab dress, to confer with Sherif Feisal Ibn Hussein and other prominent Arab chiefs in an effort to gather first-hand impressions of physical conditions, supplies, and military strength. With this information, Lawrence returned to his superior officers and reported that a tribal war would be feasible if it were adequately supplied logistically. His estimate of the situation was accepted, somewhat surprisingly, and preparations began for an attack on the Turks. A frontal assault soon proved foolhardy, however, because of the preponderant forces of the enemy. Thereafter, the Arabs under Feisal served often as an integral part of the British force and were successful in taking Medina, Akaba; harassing the enemy by cutting railway communications; and aiding in the capture of Damascus. By this time, the Turkish armies were scattered and the Eastern war drew to its end. Lawrence's efforts were expended. He departed as soon as possible, in order not to become involved in the stalemate of establishing authority.

As an account by one intimately acquainted with a successful military endeavor of great significance, *Seven Pillars of Wisdom* merits recognition and thorough study, for it is an excellent treatise of war conducted under extremely difficult conditions. Lawrence's book offers much more than mere history, however; the military story is little more than the framework upon which the author built a deeply absorbing analysis of this part of the Arab world, its people and leaders, its weaknesses, and its hopes for the future. As a professional student of the past history of those areas, Lawrence had chosen to live among the people, to learn their ways, and to share their hardships. With this profoundly sympathetic background, Lawrence was singularly equipped to understand, to reconcile Arab psychology with Allied purposes, and to gain the confidence of justifiably suspicious Arab leaders. In the course of his account, Lawrence constantly describes, explains, and interprets. His style, although at times archaic or difficult, enables him to picture desert scenes, oases, and the teeming Arab cities with consummate skill. His portraits of his associates, his junior colleagues and senior officers among the Allies, and his valued and capable friends among the Arabs, are vivid word pictures.

Lawrence had an eye for human qualities and human character, and he could record them memorably. As few Europeans have ever been able to do, Lawrence undertook to transform himself into an Arab, a member of the people he was working with, and the most understanding and intelligent of them realized this phenomenon and valued his efforts.

Perhaps the most puzzling and stimulating feature of this extraordinary book is almost coincidental: the picture of Lawrence himself that gradually emerges. T. E. Lawrence was an amazing person. He was capable of intense absorption in the task at hand, that of mounting a successful military operation to conquer the Turks. At the same time, he was appreciating the stark beauties of barren lands and ancient cities; he was evaluating human beings and their ways, judging, adapting their strength to the immediate purpose, and enjoying their companionship. He was also subjecting his own way of life and his own people to a very critical appraisal. In the end, he evidently found his own institutions strangely lacking and disappointing. Hence, Lawrence apparently decided to refuse the honors heaped upon him, to cut himself off from the leaders of his own kind, and to submerge himself in obscurity. His was a lofty, powerful mind, honest but stern and implacable. When that mind could not reconcile itself to the English present, he simply chose anonymity. Like the fictional Gulliver, Lawrence's travels among strange peoples and regions left him far from satisfied with the ideals and practices in his homeland.

Bibliography:

Allen, M. D. *The Medievalism of Lawrence of Arabia*. University Park: Pennsylvania State University Press, 1991. Describes *Seven Pillars of Wisdom* as a neomedieval romance; relates elements in it to medieval literary sources and analogues.

Meyers, Jeffrey, ed. *T. E. Lawrence: Soldier, Writer, Legend: New Essays*. New York: St. Martin's Press, 1989. Includes essays by Albert Cook on Lawrence's contrary roles in *Seven Pillars of Wisdom* as observant stranger, military ally, and autobiographical artist; and by Eugene Goodheart on the clash of personal, patriotic, intellectual, and artistic motives in *Seven Pillars of Wisdom.*

____________. *The Wounded Spirit: A Study of Seven Pillars of Wisdom*. London: Martin Brian & O'Keeffe, 1973. Asserts that *Seven Pillars of Wisdom* is beautiful, insightful literature, and views its author as introspective and profound. Defines the book's style as mainly descriptive and narrative, but also comic, dramatic, emotive, epic, lyric, puerile, reflective, and technical.

Tabachnick, Stephen Ely. *T. E. Lawrence*. Boston: Twayne, 1978. Discusses *Seven Pillars of Wisdom* as the autobiography of an aesthete-hero and a dramatized version of the truth. Sees Lawrence as torn by British-Arab cultural and political diversities.

____________, ed. *The T. E. Lawrence Puzzle*. Athens: University of Georgia Press, 1984. Includes essays by Thomas J. O'Donnell on Lawrence's both asserting and denying his will in *Seven Pillars of Wisdom* and by Kenneth N. Hull on *Seven Pillars of Wisdom* as integrating documentary and personal material.

THE SEVEN WHO WERE HANGED

Type of work: Novel
Author: Leonid Andreyev (1871-1919)
Type of plot: Social realism
Time of plot: Early twentieth century
Locale: Russia
First published: *Rasskaz o semi poveshannykh*, 1908 (English translation, 1909)

Principal characters:
SERGEY GOLOVIN,
VASILY KASHIRIN,
TANYA KOVALCHUK,
MUSYA, and
WERNER, five revolutionists
IVAN YANSON and
TSIGANOK GOLUBETS, two condemned men

The Story:

When the police informed a powerful minister that there was a plot to assassinate him, he was terrified. Nevertheless, the police assured him that he would be given ample protection; they knew who the terrorists were, and they would arrest them.

As good as their word, the police seized three men and two women, young people ranging in age from nineteen to twenty-eight years old. A large amount of dynamite was also found. The evidence was so damaging that the prisoners knew they would be sentenced to hang. The trial was swift, and the five revolutionists were imprisoned until the time of their execution, two days hence.

In the same prison were two other condemned men who had been waiting about two weeks for their execution. One was Ivan Yanson, a peasant workman. He was an Estonian who spoke Russian poorly and talked little. His ignorance had made him cruel. Since there were no humans on whom he could vent his rage, he regularly beat the animals under his care. He frequently drank too much, and then his cruelty to animals was worse than usual. Once he had tried to make love to another servant, but he was so repulsive-looking that she had rejected him. One night, Yanson entered the room where his master was and stabbed him to death. He then tried to rape his mistress, but she escaped him. While attempting to flee with some money he had stolen, he was seized, tried, and sentenced to hang.

At first, he wanted the time before his execution to pass quickly. Then, as the time grew shorter, he began to tell his guards that he did not want to die, that he did not understand why he should be hanged. Yanson had no one to love or believe in. Partly stupefied by fear, he was unable to take in much of what had happened to him.

The other condemned man was Tsiganok Golubets, a robber and murderer who took pride in his brutal accomplishments. At times, completely mad, he would get down on all fours and howl like a wolf. Then, for a time, he would be quiet. What little time remained of his life was meaningless to him, for he knew only how to rob and kill, and these pleasures had now been taken away.

The five revolutionists had each determined not to show fear. When Sergey Golovin's father and mother visited him in his cell, however, he could no longer be brave, and he cried. Sergey was young, and life was strong in him; he found it hard to understand that he was soon to die.

Only Vasily Kashirin's mother came to see him, for his father was not interested in seeing his son again. Vasily, who had long ago lost respect for his parents, had no regrets about not seeing his father. Even his mother meant little to him; there was really no one he would hate to leave when he died. While he waited for his execution, he showed no signs of fear.

It was not for herself but for her comrades that Tanya Kovalchuk worried. The fact that she, too, was to die had no meaning for her; she was concerned only for the discomfort and fears of her children, as she called the others. She loved them all.

Musya knew that she would not completely die when she was hanged. She would join the martyrs whom she admired so much, and her name would live forever. She had only one regret; she had done nothing significant enough to justify her martyrdom. She consoled herself with the thought that she had been on the threshold of great deeds. She thought that she had conquered her captors, for the fact that they were going to kill her proved that they feared her. Musya eagerly awaited her execution.

The man called Werner had long been developing a contempt for humanity and was tired of life. There was no one whom he could respect and admire; he was cold and superior even to his comrades. In his cell, however, he suddenly developed a love for humanity in his realization of human progress from an animal state. Loving and pitying other people, Werner felt more freedom in his prison cell than he had ever known outside. It had been a long time since he had felt sympathy for others; the feeling was a good one.

On the day of their execution, the five were allowed to talk together for a short time. They were almost afraid to look at one another, each not wanting to see fear in a comrade's face. Vasily could not control his emotions. The others, particularly Tanya, urged him to be calm and not to allow their guards to see his fear.

When the time came for the execution, Yanson and Golubets joined them. Yanson was still babbling about not wanting to be hanged. Golubets retained his arrogance and made a joke about dying. Transferred to a train, they were allowed to sit together until they reached their destination. Musya was happy to see that Werner had lost his scorn for the others. As they drew nearer their final stop, she smiled; soon she would join those whom she admired so much.

On their arrival, Yanson had to be carried from the coach. Golubets wanted to attack the guards. The night was cold, and often they slipped in the snow as they marched toward the scaffold. All refused the services of a priest who was present. They all kissed one another good-bye and walked in pairs to the ropes. Sergey and Vasily went first, Vasily outwardly calm and in control of himself. At the last minute, Golubets was frightened and asked to go with one of the five brave ones. Musya took his hand, kissed him, and they followed Sergey and Vasily. Musya's hand calmed Golubets; he was arrogant again as he climbed the steps. Werner took Yanson with him, but the peasant had to be carried most of the way. Tanya was the last, and she went alone. Her children had all gone bravely. She was happy.

After Tanya's drop, there was silence for a moment in the wintry night. Then the bodies were taken back over the same road they had traveled a short time before, but only their bodies—their souls were elsewhere.

Critical Evaluation:

In a 1908 letter to Herman Bernstein, his English translator, Leonid Andreyev stated that his task in *The Seven Who Were Hanged* "was to point out the horror and iniquity of capital punishment under any circumstances." That the author was effective in accomplishing this task seems clear, but for many decades criticism has been aware of something called the intentional fallacy, which holds that a work may offer meaning quite apart from what its creator intended. Late twentieth century critical theory has puzzled over the instabilities of language, the tendency of literature to subvert its own apparent goal. Thus Andreyev's novel, while remaining an indictment of the death penalty and its execution, can be viewed as susceptible to a number of interpretations, not necessarily consistent with one another. There may be a bitter irony in linking selfless revolutionaries with common criminals, but then an argument may be made that people who visit death on others to achieve a political aim are themselves no better than common criminals. Feminist criticism might choose to look particularly at the two women among the seven who suffer the death penalty; here again, more than one reading is possible or even desirable. Reducing *The Seven Who Were Hanged* to Andreyev's declared intent or judging it by that intent alone is unwise.

At the same time, there is an advantage to knowing what the author regarded as his task, because it helps the reader to see how Andreyev, reacting to the increased use of the death penalty after the failed revolution of 1905, exercised his exceptional verbal facility to make vivid the brutality of any inflicted death. Andreyev may be seen as a kind of prose Acmeist, Acmeism being a movement in Russian poetry of about the same time that undertook to counter vague symbolism with language, vivid and concrete, that would convey true experience of the natural world. The mental and physical states of the seven who must die are sharply rendered, sometimes in metaphorical terms, as when the slender white arm of one young woman protrudes from the sleeve of a prisoner's coat like "a beautiful flower out of a coarse earthen jug," or when the newly executed prisoners lie "with blue, swollen tongues, looking like some unknown, terrible flowers between the lips." There is little superfluity in this novel, which is not much more than thirty thousand words in length. Of the twelve chapters that make up the book, the capital sentence is pronounced in the second and carried out in the twelfth. Everything in between treats the seven important characters (there are practically no others of consequence) as they prepare to die.

In the chapters in which they are developed, the doomed people have particularity and complexity, but they are not much realized as human beings. This seems to be true for two reasons. First, there is little dialogue. Most of the characters await execution in isolation (two receive brief visits from parents), and what readers know of them is given through the narrative voice. Also, there is a measure of implausibility that may arise from Andreyev's having worked to create sharp impressions. The revolutionaries, where they are not sentimentalized, are idealized, and the common criminals, Yanson especially, are made so brutal as to be incongruent with ordinary experience, even of brutality. The horror of their predicament is clearly understood by the attentive reader, but at the cost of seeing them as people one might encounter in everyday life.

The Seven Who Were Hanged is Andreyev's most successful work, even in its limitations. Andreyev was highly regarded in the first part of his career, but his standing among contemporaries had dwindled even before he died. Early in his literary career, he was befriended by the writer Maxim Gorky, who helped give him a place among his literary peers, and the success of his fiction about capital punishment led some to think that with Anton Chekhov and Leo Tolstoy, Andreyev might be one of the most important of Russian writers of his time. It gradually became apparent that, although he was masterful with language, many of his productions were flawed. Andreyev further compromised his standing by building an opulent house in Finland with money made in Russia by his writing. He lost more sympathy, especially with the rising Soviets, by drifting to the right in politics and supporting Russia's active role in the earlier stages of World War I. His writing might not have been so closely scrutinized had he been more generally approved, but this was not the case, and with no sympathetic indulgence to help him along, the flaws showed through.

Whatever the flaws or limitations of *The Seven Who Were Hanged*, it remains a striking novel in a first encounter. If Andreyev had an avowed purpose in writing this story, he also had the good judgment to avoid leading the reader with direct moralizing, allowing his stark representation of two very different kinds of condemned people—political operatives and common felons—to make his point about the horror they must face. The clean, spare, concrete prose out of which Andreyev created his book gives the reader an impression of distinctly modern fiction. There are moments when Andreyev puts one in mind of writers of the generation that emerged after World War I—the U.S. writer Ernest Hemingway would be an example. His most famous book also strongly resembles the slower, fuller fiction of Russian writers in the nineteenth century.

It is difficult, but not impossible, for a single work by a writer whose reputation has faded to hold its place among books that are sooner or later read. *The Seven Who Were Hanged*, although not an obligatory book, remains one that students of Russian literature should be expected to know well.

"Critical Evaluation" by John Higby

Bibliography:

Connolly, Julian W. "The Russian Short Story 1890-1917." In *The Russian Short Story: A Critical History*, edited by Charles Moser. Boston: Twayne, 1986. Places *The Seven Who Were Hanged* in a historical framework of Andreyev's development. Emphasizes Andreyev's attention to the emotions of the convicted and terms *The Seven Who Were Hanged* his most famous political story.

Hutchings, Stephen. *A Semiotic Analysis of the Short Stories of Leonid Andreev 1900-1909*. London: Modern Humanities Research Association, 1990. A fashionable semiotic study of Andreyev's short stories, placing them within the context of early twentieth century Russian literature and culture.

Kaun, Alexander. *Leonid Andreyev: A Critical Study*. New York: B. W. Huebsch, 1924. Stan-dard critical biography of Andreyev, covering all aspects of his works. Labels *The Seven Who Were Hanged* a masterpiece in both technique and emotional power, because of its simplicity of style, keen psychological analysis, humane sympathy, and lasting effect.

Mihajlov, Mihajlo. *Russian Themes*. Translated by Marija Mihajlov. New York: Farrar, Straus & Giroux, 1968. Far-reaching treatment of Russian writers. Discusses the political aspect of *The Seven Who Were Hanged*, pointing out Andreyev's sympathies for the revolutionaries in their struggle with the czarist regime.

Newcombe, Josephine M. *Leonid Andreyev*. Letchworth, England: Bradda Books, 1972. Brief but pithy introduction to Andreyev, with a pertinent discussion of *The Seven Who Were Hanged* on pages 85-90.

SEVENTEEN

Type of work: Novel
Author: Booth Tarkington (1869-1946)
Type of plot: Comic realism
Time of plot: A summer in the early twentieth century
Locale: A small midwestern town
First published: 1916

Principal characters:
WILLIAM SYLVANUS BAXTER, a seventeen-year-old
MRS. BAXTER, his mother
JANE BAXTER, his sister
MISS PRATT, a summer visitor

The Story:

William Sylvanus Baxter had at last reached the impressive age of seventeen, and as he emerged from the corner drugstore after indulging in two chocolate and strawberry sodas, he tried to impress the town with his lofty air of self-importance. No one noticed him except his friend, Johnny Watson, who destroyed William's hauteur in one breath by calling him "Silly Bill." At that moment, William saw a feminine vision in pink and white. A stranger in town, she carried her parasol and her little white dog with easy grace. William, not daring to speak, managed only an insincere yawn. The vision, taking no apparent notice of William, spoke in charming lisps to her little dog Flopit and disappeared around the corner.

William went home in a daze, hardly bothering to speak to his outrageous little sister, Jane, who greeted him between mouthfuls of applesauce and bread. Scorning her, he went up to his room, his heart full of the mystery of love, and composed a poem to his new and unknown lady. He was interrupted by his mother, who asked William to go with Genesis, the black handyman, to pick up some laundry tubs from the secondhand store. The errand, to William, was worse than being seen in public with a leper, for he looked on Genesis as a ragged, bedraggled, down-at-the-heels pariah, whose presence was an unwholesome reproach to the whole neighborhood.

Genesis was in reality a wise old philosopher, despite his seminudity and the ubiquitous presence of his mongrel dog, Clematis; yet William was in no mood to be tolerant. His worst fears were realized when, on the way home, he heard behind him the silvery voice of the fair stranger referring to Clematis as a nasty old dog. William was hidden by the laundry tub he carried over his head, but his invisibility in no way diminished his growing horror at being taken for a companion of Genesis and the owner of the dreadful Clematis. Clematis, meanwhile, was fascinated by Flopit. When William heard the yips and barks of the two dogs, he ran away, still hidden under his protecting tub.

The young vision in pink and white was the summer visitor of May Parcher. Her name, William learned, was Miss Pratt. Soon the boys in the neighborhood collected on the Parcher porch and swarmed around the adorable girl every evening after supper, much to the disgust of Mr. Parcher, who lay awake for hours in his room over the porch and listened reluctantly to the drivel of conversation below. William had an advantage over the other suitors, for he borrowed his father's dress suit without his parents' knowledge and arrived each night in splendid attire.

During the day, William could not escape his sister Jane, who insisted on appearing in dirty summer sunsuits, her face smeared with her favorite repast of applesauce and bread, just at the moment when William would be walking by the house with Miss Pratt. His angry demands that his sister present a more ladylike appearance irritated Jane to a calm, smouldering intent to get even with William. She knew that William wore his father's dress suit every evening when he visited Miss Pratt. She also knew that Mr. Parcher was nearly crazy over the nightly sessions on his front porch. Putting these facts together, she coldly repeated to her mother some of Mr. Parcher's comments. Mrs. Baxter was horrified that William had worn out his welcome at the Parcher's, and when she discovered Mr. Baxter's dress suit under William's window seat, she took it to a tailor and had it altered to fit only Mr. Baxter. William could not go to see Miss Pratt without the dress suit. He was not among Miss Pratt's evening admirers thereafter.

As a reward to Jane, who had immediately told him of her part in decreasing by one the population of his front porch, Mr. Parcher sent her a five-pound box of candy, much to the amazement of the whole Baxter household. No one suspected Jane's perfidy.

Feeling herself to blame for William's gloomy moods, Mrs. Baxter decided to have a tea for some of her son's friends, with Miss Pratt as guest of honor. The great day arrived, swelteringly hot. Upstairs, William had no sooner broken his only collar button on his fifth and last white shirt than he had the misfortune to tear his white trousers. Another suit was splattered by Jane's paints. By the time he found a heavy winter suit in a trunk in the attic, the guests had gone. Angry and miserable, William sat down on Jane's open, wet paint box.

The time came for Miss Pratt to return home. As a farewell party, the relieved Parchers scheduled a picnic in their guest's honor. To impress Miss Pratt, William bought a package of Cuban cigarettes, but coy Miss Pratt gave all her attention to George, a braggart who stuffed himself with food to impress the beauty with his gustatory prowess. Lunch over, William offered George his cigarettes. Before long, he had the satisfaction of seeing George disappear behind a woodpile. William was blissful once more.

When Miss Pratt unexpectedly granted the weary Parchers the privilege of her company for another week, they gave a final farewell dance in her honor. Mrs. Baxter had her husband's dress suit again altered to fit William. Resplendent, but late as usual, William arrived at the dance to find all Miss Pratt's dances taken, and he was forced to spend the evening with a lonely wallflower. His dignity suffered another blow when Genesis, serving sandwiches, not only greeted William with familiarity but also chided him about the dress suit. His evening was a dismal failure.

The next day, William went down to the train to see Miss Pratt leave. Laden with candy and lush poetry, he found her surrounded by her many admirers. He had the uncomfortable sensation that they were all laughing at him, for they were pointing derisively in his direction. Turning, he saw Jane, who had deliberately come to torment him in company with an equally disreputable female companion. The two pranksters were walking with a vulgar strut that William abhorred. So flustered was he that he merely waved to Miss Pratt and went sadly home, forgetting that he still carried under his arm the box of candy and the poem intended for the pink and white beauty who was going out of his life forever.

Critical Evaluation:

Much of *Seventeen*'s charm for many readers will be found in the novel's quality as a period piece. It provides a solid sense of setting, character, and values as they were in the American Midwest in the first quarter of the twentieth century.

Although the novel's setting is not explicitly identified, Booth Tarkington's midwestern readers of 1916, and particularly his Indiana readers, would assume from the first sentence's reference to Washington Street and Central Avenue that the novel's action takes place in Indianapolis, Tarkington's own hometown. The author's detailed descriptions of costume and customs of white middle-class Americans and his rendering of speech patterns and vocabulary are not only a source of his deliberate humor but also serve to ground the novel in a tangible realism.

Seventeen is, above all, a romantic comedy, a story that focuses mostly on lives that are divorced from any grim concerns of making a living, dealing with illness, or worrying about what evils may lurk in the city or in the hearts of its inhabitants. *Seventeen*'s midwestern setting is a place where there is no crime and little poverty, at least among the white middle-class characters who are the center of the author's attention.

As for the African Americans who appear in the novel, however, they are, socially and historically, only one step removed from slavery. Genesis, for example, is a servant and a worker of odd jobs, thoroughly accustomed to taking orders from his white employers and recognizing his secondary place in this society. Yet Genesis has his own ambitions, as the reader sees when he enthusiastically works part-time as a waiter for catered affairs, a job he considers a definite step upward on the social ladder. Then, too, as an heir to the literary type of the kindly African American father figure, Genesis often looks with amusement and bemusement on the activities of white people, particularly the youngsters. In one notable scene, Genesis embarrasses William at a party, comically suggesting, as a real relative of William might, that the boy has surreptitiously dressed up in his father's evening clothes.

While Tarkington gives no evidence at all of social consciousness, it is also clear that his depictions of African Americans, like his characterizations of white people, is without deliberate malice. There is a naïve innocence in Tarkington's frequent exploitation of African American characters, customs, and speech mannerisms. In his narrator's poking fun at African American tastes in clothing and colors and his accounts of their attitudes toward white people, Tarkington is undoubtedly recalling his own midwestern milieu as he saw it.

Since *Seventeen*'s publication, generations of readers have considered the novel's characters to be familiar or easily imaginable. The Baxter and Parcher families represent a classic American ideal, one of those concepts that has been endorsed by literature and perhaps imitated in reality. William's family, for example, includes a breadwinner father and a mother whose life is defined by motherhood, by rearing her two children—boy and girl—and by maintaining the Baxter household. Both Mr. Baxter and Mr. Parcher are often strict and impatient with their youngsters, while their wives serve as intermediaries between the fathers and the children, softening paternal anger and edicts. In other words, *Seventeen*'s families are those which twentieth century American popular literature, film, and television have perpetuated as "typical."

Critics, even in Tarkington's day, objected to the nature of William's obsession with Lola Pratt, the summer visitor in town who attracts the attention of several young men. William's pursuit of Miss Pratt is essentially that of dreamer after his dream, a pursuit uncomplicated by sexual passion. Indeed, Tarkington's descriptions of Miss Pratt's physical attributes have nothing to do with carnality, and William's behavior never indicates that his admiration of Lola is anything more than aesthetic.

In any case, it is Miss Pratt, the object of William's affections, who becomes the novel's chief comic interest. Miss Pratt is a caricature of femininity, evidently a woman who has been convinced that the best way to get what she wants from male admirers is to emphasize vulnerability and childlike fragility.

Much of *Seventeen*'s success as comedy derives from Tarkington's third-person narrative style, whereby description and advancement of plot are usually expressed in very formal language, even though the events, characters, or motives described are amusing or even trivial. While dialogue is consistently colloquial, the narrator's authoritative, sometimes stilted tone provides a comic contrast that is always amusing.

The novel's final, abbreviated, fairy-tale-like vision, in which it turns out that William is destined to marry Jane's new little friend and not Miss Pratt, is a logical development in a story that largely deals with dreams rather than with reality.

"Critical Evaluation" by Gordon Walters

Bibliography:

Fennimore, Keith J. *Booth Tarkington*. New York: Twayne, 1974. A fine basic study of Tarkington and his work, although it lacks a sustained study of *Seventeen*. The author distinguishes *Seventeen* as a "juvenile" work, different from Tarkington's other novels.

Russo, Dorothy R., et al. "Additions to the Tarkington Bibliography." *Princeton University Library Chronicle* 15 (Winter, 1955): 89-94. An update of the following entry.

Russo, Dorothy R., and Thelma L. Sullivan. *A Bibliography of Booth Tarkington*. Indianapolis: Indianapolis Historical Society, Lakeside Press, 1949. The book remains useful for anyone seriously interested in Tarkington, especially in the receptions his books received in the popular press.

Scott, John D. "Tarkington and the 1920's." *American Scholar* 26 (Spring, 1957): 181-194. Focuses on the social criticism in Tarkington's work.

Woodress, James. *Booth Tarkington: Gentleman from Indiana*. Philadelphia: J. B. Lippincott, 1955. Still one of the most thorough critical biographies of Tarkington, with an emphasis on chronological biography rather than on literary analysis.

SHADOWS ON THE ROCK

Type of work: Novel
Author: Willa Cather (1873-1947)
Type of plot: Historical
Time of plot: Late seventeenth century
Locale: Quebec, Canada
First published: 1931

Principal characters:
EUCLIDE AUCLAIR, the apothecary in Quebec
CÉCILE AUCLAIR, his daughter
COUNT FRONTENAC, the governor of New France and Auclair's patron
PIERRE CHARRON, a Canadian woodsman

The Story:

Late in October of 1697, the last ship left Quebec to return to France, and the colony of New France was isolated from the world until the arrival of the fleet in June or July of the following year. One of the persons who watched as the last vessel passed out of sight down the St. Lawrence River was Euclide Auclair, the apothecary in Quebec.

Auclair lived on the street that wound up the slope and connected the Upper Town on the cliff with the Lower Town, which clustered along the shore of the river at the foot of the mountain. In his home behind his shop, Auclair and his daughter Cécile did their best to re-create the atmosphere they had known in France. So successful were they that many people came to the shop merely to visit and get a breath of the France they had left behind.

Cécile was only twelve years old and her mother had been dead for several years. Although she was content to remain in Canada, her father seemed to live only for the time when he could return to France with his patron, the governor of the colony, Count Frontenac. Auclair, who had served the Count for many years, was a trusted friend of the governor as well as his apothecary.

A few weeks after the last ship had departed, Cécile went to see the Count to ask his aid in obtaining some shoes for a little orphan boy. The governor was glad to see her, for too many of the people who came to him were anxious only to help themselves. He said that when he made his will he would leave the girl a bowl of glass fruit that she had always admired.

The first days of December brought a heavy fall of snow which ushered in a reality of life in Canada, the long, dark winter. The snow also reminded Cécile of the boxes of Christmas presents which had been sent to her by aunts in France the previous summer. On the twenty-fourth of December, the Auclairs brought the boxes out of their storage place. In one was a crèche to be set up in their living room. The crèche was the crowning point of Christmas for many of their friends, for the French colonists were, as a rule, very devout.

One day in March, Father Hector Saint-Cyr put in his appearance. The priest spent several evenings recounting to the Auclairs stories of the missionaries, the Indians, and the hardships of backwoods life. When he left, Euclide Auclair wondered if, after all, the gifts of an educated man like Father Saint-Cyr might not be going to waste in misplaced heroism among the Canadian missions to the Indians.

About the middle of March, the weather changed. There was a continuous downpour of rain which the snow soaked up as if it were a gigantic sponge. The ice in the St. Lawrence broke up and floated downstream in huge gray blocks. It was a season of sickness, and the apothecary was busy from morning until night acting as doctor to many of the inhabitants of the town. Cécile herself caught a cold and was in bed for several days.

One evening while Cécile was ill, Auclair had a strange visit with a misshapen hunchback who secured water and wood for the Auclairs in return for a bowl of soup and a small glass of brandy each evening. Blinker, as the hunchback was called, told Auclair that as a boy he had been an apprentice to his father, one of the king's torturers at Rouen. Blinker had tortured an old woman into admitting that she had murdered her son. Some months after her execution, the son had returned. The shock of what he had done was too great for the apprentice. He ran away, took ship, and went to Quebec to begin a new life. Nevertheless, visions of the old woman haunted him so that he could not sleep. Filled with sympathy, the apothecary gave Blinker some laudanum so that he might have a little untroubled rest.

One day, while Cécile was regaining her strength, her father wrapped her in a blanket and carried her to the door. There, outside the door, Cécile saw the first swallow hunting for its old nest in the wall of the cliff that rose sharply to the chateau above. Delighted at this sign, Cécile had her father inform old Bishop Laval of the bird's appearance. The old man had kept a record of the changing seasons for thirty-eight years, and he had always included the date of the first swallow's arrival.

On the first day of June, the leaves began to bud, and the hunters arrived from the woods with their loads of pelts. Among the first hunters to reach Quebec was Pierre Charron, an old friend of the apothecary and his daughter. Pierre, the son of a rich family in Montreal, had been disappointed in love. His sweetheart decided to build a chapel with her dowry and enter the Church as a recluse. After she had taken her vows, Pierre had become a hunter traveling through the wilderness as far as Michilimackinac and Lake Superior in his quest for furs and forgetfulness. During the spring, Pierre Charron took Cécile with him to visit some friends on the Isle d'Orleans, in the St. Lawrence four miles below Quebec. The squalid and primitive life there disgusted Cécile.

Early in July, the ships from France arrived. The Count had requested the king to recall him from Canada, and he had promised that he would take the Auclairs back to France with him. As each ship arrived through the summer, the Auclairs waited for word of the governor's recall. When late October arrived, the Count called Euclide Auclair to the chateau to warn him that the king's request would never come. When the Count offered to send the Auclairs back to France, Euclide refused, assuring the Count that he could not leave while his patron was forced to remain in Quebec.

The last ship left Quebec in October. Shortly afterward, Count Frontenac became ill. Euclide Auclair knew that his patient could not live through the winter. When the Count died, Euclide carried out his patron's last wish. He sealed the Count's heart in a lead box and sent it with a missionary priest to the English colonies in the south. From there, it was returned to France for burial.

The death of the Count was a great blow to the Auclairs, for security seemed to have gone from their lives. Thinking of returning to France that year, they had not even laid in a proper supply of food to last through the winter. Fortunately for them, Pierre Charron arrived in Quebec with an offer of help. Later he married Cécile. Charron had not the authority of documents and seals that the Count had had to protect them, but he had his knowledge of the woods and the people, which was as good or better in the wilds of Canada. The future was safe.

Critical Evaluation:

To an extent, *Shadows on the Rock* stands apart from other Cather novels because of its setting. Willa Cather is known as a regionalist, one who writes of nineteenth and twentieth century Nebraska and the Southwest. In this novel, she not only does not write about the Midwest; she does not write about the United States. Set in late seventeenth century Quebec, Canada, *Shadows on the Rock* shows the human spirit of a different type of pioneer than those Cather usually writes about. Typically, Cather's immigrants are Swedish, Bohemian, English, and Spanish living on the plains or in the Southwest. In this novel, Cather deals with a French family living in an urban setting about two hundred years before the time of her other novels.

The plot revolves around twelve-year-old Cécile Auclair and her father Euclide, who have settled in New France. Parts of the story are episodic; they are seemingly unrelated events that somehow connect to the lives of the Auclairs. For example, the Auclairs are visited by a hunchback known as Blinker, who tells how he tortured a woman into admitting she had killed her son. The woman was executed for her crime. Then her son returned. This is one of the memorable, haunting stories that appears in Cather's work. As a journalist, Cather often rewrote true stories she knew about into her fiction. She based her short story "Paul's Case," for example, on an incident she had read about in the newspaper.

Cather received her idea for *Shadows on the Rock* from a story she ran across at the Louvre in Paris. She happened upon the diary of an apothecary who had worked for Count Frontenac in Quebec. She began to keep notes on the diary and then formulated a story about it. After the novel was published, a pharmacy company wrote Cather stating that her information was wrong; the drug she had mentioned in *Shadows on the Rock* did not exist at that time. Cather produced her notes from the diary to prove she was right.

Cather also included biographical incidents in her book. For example, on Christmas Day, 1927, Cather was at the family home in Red Cloud, Nebraska. She was arranging her crèche, and her nephew Charles brought a toy cow with him. Cather thought maybe he might not want to give up his toy for the crèche, but Charles said he wanted to give it to Jesus.

Cather went to live in Quebec so she could better research this novel. The novel reflects the relationship between father and daughter, Cécile and Euclide Auclair. Like many of Cather's fictions, *Shadows on the Rock* tends to be autobiographical. She wrote the novel at a time of personal trauma and upheaval. Her father had died, and his death severely affected her. In addition, her mother had recently had a paralytic stroke. Cather's apartment, where she had happily lived for fourteen years, was being demolished, and she had to find somewhere to live. Her research into the history and culture of Quebec and her personal experiences with illness, death, and threats to the home all serve to enrich the novel.

Youth has always been a theme in Cather's works, and *Shadows on the Rock* is no exception. She felt her most important years were between nine and sixteen, and she would often try to recapture the qualities of those youthful years in her fiction. This is probably why Cécile is portrayed as a child and a young woman. Part of Cécile's youth is a sense of the past, of the ancients. Quebec is filled with legends, and the Auclairs are also in contact with France, which also signifies centuries of culture, legend, and history. When Cécile and Pierre travel into the wilderness, they move into ageless, primitive situations. Cécile, the youth, is the past's ambassador to the future; she is the connection between the centuries of French culture and the open wilds of Canada.

Being a novel about youth, the novel is a maturation novel, a *Bildungsroman*. Cécile's varied experiences at home and in the wilderness lead to her maturity. Specifically, after her trip into the wilderness, she is ready to grow up and marry Pierre. The wilderness is symbolic of alienation. In the novel, the wilderness is one of cold and vast areas of nothing. This makes the Harnois family symbolic of alienation; they are isolated on an island surrounded by wilderness.

The isolation and despair contrasts with the domestic life of the Auclairs. Cécile is concerned, much of the time, with cooking and cleaning. The Auclairs lead a simple life, yet their lives are as solid as the Rock of Quebec on which they live. Cather once related that she had, in Cécile's domesticity, caught something new. For Cather, it represented a kind of feeling about human life and fate that she could not accept, wholly, but that she could admire. Cather, personally, could not accept it; she chose a career over domesticity and chose the city over the prairie. She often wrote, however, about those like Cécile. The Auclairs, through their simple lives and hard work, cast their shadows upon the rock of Quebec in this historical fiction.

"Critical Evaluation" by Mary C. Bagley

Bibliography:

Carlin, Deborah. "Tales of Telling Fictions of History: Casting *Shadows on the Rock*." In *Cather, Canon, and the Politics of Reading*. Amherst: University of Massachusetts Press, 1992. Reads the novel as a narrative instead of a history. Says the novel is about the translation of French sensibility into Canadian character.

Greene, George. "A Colloquy with Clio: Willa Cather's *Shadows on the Rock*." *Dalhousie Review* 70 (Summer, 1990): 219-228. Praises *Shadows on the Rock* as one of Cather's best works. Examines the treatment of the northeast wilderness and the Iroquois Indians.

Jacobs, Wilbur R. "Willa Cather and Francis Parkman: Novelistic Portrayals of Colonial New France." In *Willa Cather: Family, Community and History*, edited by John J. Murphy et al. Provo, Utah: Brigham Young University Humanities Publications Center, 1990. Traces the influence of nineteenth century Canadian historian Francis Parkman on Cather.

Nelson, Robert James. *Willa Cather and France*. Champaign: University of Illinois Press, 1988. Discusses the fascination that Willa Cather had in writing about the French on both sides of the Atlantic. Deals with Cather's tour of France and what influenced her to write about the people and their customs.

Stouck, David. "Willa Cather and the Indian Heritage." *Twentieth Century Literature* 22 (December, 1976): 433-443. Claims *Shadows on the Rock* is a historical novel. Sees the Indians as a recurring theme in Cather's novels.

SHE

Type of work: Novel
Author: H. Rider Haggard (1856-1925)
Type of plot: Adventure
Time of plot: Late nineteenth century
Locale: Africa
First published: 1887

Principal characters:
LUDWIG HORACE HOLLY, a teacher
LEO VINCEY, his ward
SHE, a beautiful ageless woman
JOB, Holly's servant
USTANE, a woman of the Amahagger tribe
BILLALI, an old man of the Amahagger tribe

The Story:

Late one night in his room at Cambridge, Ludwig Holly received an urgent visit from Vincey, a fellow student. The man was dying of a lung condition, and because he had no living relatives, he asked Holly to undertake the guardianship of his young son after his death. Vincey explained that the boy would be the last representative of one of the oldest families in the world. He could trace his ancestry back to the ancient Egyptians, to a priest of Isis named Kallikrates, who had broken his vows and fled the country with an Egyptian princess. Kallikrates had been murdered by the queen of a savage tribe, but his wife had escaped and had borne a son, from whom the boy was descended.

Holly agreed to rear the boy. It was understood that he was to be tutored at home, where he would be taught Greek, mathematics, and Arabic. On his twenty-fifth birthday, he was to receive an iron box that Vincey would leave with Holly; at that time, he could decide whether he wanted to act upon its contents. The following morning, Vincey was found dead in his room. Shortly afterward, five-year-old Leo Vincey went to live with his guardian.

Twenty years passed happily for Leo and for the man whom he called his uncle. On the morning of the youth's twenty-fifth birthday, the iron chest was opened. Inside was an ebony box that, in turn, contained a silver chest. Within that chest was a potsherd inscribed by the wife of the ill-fated Kallikrates. A message to her son, it declared that the queen who had murdered Kallikrates had shown them both the Pillar of Life. The message ended by begging that he, or some brave descendant, should try to find the Pillar of Life and slay the evil queen.

In the inmost chest, there was also a letter to Leo from his father, who wrote that he had journeyed to Africa to find the land that his ancestors had visited but had reached no further than the coast. There, suffering a shortage of provisions, he had been forced to turn back. Before he could plan another trip, he had been overcome by his fatal illness.

Leo at once determined that he would carry on from the point where his father had been forced to give up his quest. Three months later, he, Holly, and their servant, Job, were on their way to Africa. Their destination was a rock shaped like a black man's head, a landmark on the eastern coast of Central Africa. As they drew near shore, the little party readied the whaleboat that they planned to use for travel inland. The boat was tied onto the large dhow that carried them down the coast. Suddenly, a squall came up, and huge waves wrecked the dhow. The three white men and an Arab named Mahomed managed to launch the small boat and reach the shore.

Holly and his companions found themselves at the mouth of a river whose teeming marshy banks were crowded with crocodiles. The little party rested for a while and then started inland in the whaleboat. They traveled without much difficulty for five days; then the river grew too shallow to continue farther, and they were forced to branch off into another stream, which proved to be an ancient canal.

During the next four days, the trip became increasingly difficult, and because the canal was full of weeds, the boat had to be towed. The exhausted men were resting on the fourth evening when they were suddenly attacked by a party of about fifty tall, light-colored men who spoke Arabic. They would have been slain on the spot had not the old man who was the leader of the natives ordered that their lives be spared. He explained that word had come from someone whom he called "She-who-must-be-obeyed" that any white men who wandered into the country were to be brought to her. The man, whose name the adventurers later learned was Billali, decreed that Mahomed's life also should be spared. The prisoners were carried in litters to a cave village of the Amahagger tribe. There Billali left them with his people while he went on to report to She-who-must-be-obeyed.

The next four days passed peacefully. The men were well treated, and Ustane, one of the Amahagger women, took Leo for her husband by the simple ceremony of throwing her arms around him and kissing him.

On the fourth night, the three white men and Mahomed were invited to a party. The only refreshment being served was a fermented drink. After the brew had been passed around several times, a woman suddenly slipped a rope around Mahomed's body. At the same time, some of the men reached into the fire around which they were seated, dragged out a white-hot pot, and tried to slip it on the Arab's head. Realizing that the natives were preparing to kill and eat Mahomed, Holly drew his gun and shot the woman. The bullet passed through her body and killed the Arab as well. In the furious struggle that followed, Leo was seriously wounded in the side. The situation was growing desperate when Billali appeared to restore order.

Three days later, when Leo's wound had barely healed, the three white men, accompanied by Billali and Ustane, were taken to meet She in her hidden city of Kôr. The route led through deep swamps that at last gave way to spreading plains. The next day, the travelers reached a tunneled mountain. Their guides led Holly and his friends, blindfolded, through the tunnel to a plain that had once been a lake. There the blindfolds were removed, and the men were taken to apartments cut into the solid rock.

After he had refreshed himself, Holly was taken to the apartments of the heavily veiled queen. She asked about the ancient Greeks and Egyptians and explained that she had been living in the mountain for the past two thousand years. Holly wondered at the strange power that had enabled her to live thus untouched by time or mortality. She declared that she stayed with the Amahagger only to await the return of the man she had once loved, for he was destined to be born again. When Ayesha, as she asked Holly to call her, removed her veil, he saw that she was exceedingly beautiful.

That night, Holly could not sleep from excitement. Wandering in the passages that led off from his room, he saw Ayesha uttering curses over a fire. He discovered that they were directed against an Egyptian woman. Near the fire, on a stone shelf, lay a corpse with a shroud over it. Fearful for his own life if he were discovered, Holly crept back to his room.

The next day, the savages who had plotted Mahomed's death were brought before Ayesha and condemned to death by torture. In the evening, Ayesha went to visit Leo, who was ill with a fever and near death. When she saw his face, the queen staggered back with a scream. Leo had the face of the dead Kallikrates. It was he whose arrival Ayesha had been awaiting. She gave Holly a life-giving fluid, which he forced down Leo's throat. In her jealousy, she would have killed Ustane if Holly had not reminded her of the suffering she had had to bear for killing Kallikrates so long ago. Ustane was sentenced to leave the mountain.

On the following evening, the three white men were invited to attend a dance performed by natives dressed in animal skins. The caves were honeycombed by preserved human bodies, which were used to illuminate the proceedings; when a torch was applied to them they burned brightly. Ustane, who had not been able to bring herself to part from Leo, was one of the dancers. She revealed herself to Leo when he strolled to a dark corner of the room, but she was discovered by Ayesha before she could flee with him. When Ustane refused to leave Leo's side, Ayesha killed her with a fierce look.

Ayesha led Leo and Holly to the place where Holly had seen her uttering her incantations. Drawing back the shroud that covered the corpse, she disclosed the body of Kallikrates. Then over it she poured some acid that destroyed it quickly. With Leo present in the flesh, she explained, she had no more need for the body of the dead man.

Leo quickly fell under Ayesha's spell and forgot Ustane. Several days later, the queen and the white men began their journey to the place where Leo was to bathe in the fire of the Pillar of Life and so be assured of thousands of years of existence. Traveling across the plain through the ruins of the ancient city of Kôr, the party reached a steep mountain. At its foot, they left the litter bearers in the charge of Billali, who had accompanied them, and began the ascent. When, by difficult stages, they reached the top, they were forced to walk a plank across a deep chasm to reach the cave that held the pillar of fire—the Pillar of Life.

When Leo hesitated to immerse himself in the spiraling flame, Ayesha, to show that there was nothing to fear, walked into it. As she stood in its rising flame, a sudden change came over her. Her face and limbs began to shrivel until, before the horrified onlookers, she shrank into a little old monkeylike creature and died. Whether her death was caused by some fatal quality that had crept into the flame or whether her earlier immersion in it had been neutralized, the men did not know. Shaken to their depths, Holly and Leo started back to Billali. They left Job, who had died of shock, in the cave with Ayesha's remains.

Informed of Ayesha's fate, Billali hurried to lead the white men back through the swamps toward the coast before the Amahagger tribe learned that they need no longer fear their queen. Much the worse for wear, Holly and Leo managed to make their way to Delagoa Bay after leaving the old native at the edge of the swamp country. Although they had only spent three weeks in the interior, Leo's hair had turned white.

The two men eventually arrived in England and resumed their old existence. As he sat alone at night, Holly frequently wondered what the next step in the drama he had witnessed would be, and what, some day, would be the role of the Egyptian princess whom Kallikrates had loved.

Critical Evaluation:

England in the 1880's and 1890's saw a great upsurge of interest and popularity in the historical adventure story, especially in the works of three vivid, skillful writers—Robert Louis Stevenson, Rudyard Kipling, and H. Rider Haggard. Although posterity has granted the greater artistic status to Stevenson and Kipling, the prolific Haggard was, in his own time, the most popular and immediately influential of the three. At his very best, as in *King Solomon's Mines* (1885) and *She*, Haggard's work is not unworthy of comparison with his two coromancers. In these two early works, he established plot conventions and character types that became central to the jungle tale from the Victorian age to the present.

Like *King Solomon's Mines* and most adventure tales, *She* centers on a heroic quest. This one, however, is not for anything as mundane as hidden treasure but for something more mysterious and exotic—a white jungle queen who may or may not be a goddess. This shift in emphasis almost turns *She* from an adventure narrative to a dark fantasy. The object of the quest, "She-who-must-be-obeyed," is discovered about halfway through the narrative, and thereafter the question "What will happen to the heroes?" changes to "Who or what is She?" "Where does She come from?" "What does She want?" "What will happen to her?"

Ayesha may never be completely believable, but her vivid, ambiguous presence dominates the book. She is, as American novelist Henry Miller once said, "*the* femme fatale." Haggard succeeds in conveying a sense of her physical perfection and sensuality by judiciously presenting only a few details, leaving her essentially an abstract, idealized vision of feminine beauty. Nevertheless, she is also depicted as very human, as a woman deeply in love who can be something of a coquette, even, for all her two thousand years, somewhat girlish. Ayesha is a determined, ruthless lover and ruler, a contradictory character who combines cynicism and innocence, weariness and eagerness, benign detachment and passionate involvement, generous good and vindictive evil in a single larger-than-life personality.

The scope and ferocity of her character further suggests powers far beyond the merely mortal, although it is difficult to say exactly what she is supposed to stand for. She identifies herself with nature and yet in many ways seems to be supremely unnatural. She finds Kallikrates, the lover she once jealously murdered, reincarnated in Leo Vincey, and she plans a triumphant return to civilization and a use of her supernatural powers to create a magical paradise for humankind with herself and Leo as absolute monarchs. She destroys herself by returning a second time to the Pillar of Fire. In short, Ayesha seems to embody the ultimate paganism, even satanism, which denies the limits set on human beings by a providential divinity—that, at least, is the final interpretation Holly attaches to her disintegration. The ending of the book, however, strongly hints that, despite what readers have seen, she will somehow or other return to "finish" her story.

Such a bizarre, extreme character would be ridiculous if Haggard had not surrounded her with a wealth of images and details that reinforce the mysterious, primordial atmosphere of the novel: the mysterious artifacts and documents that Leo's dying father gives Holly to establish Leo's ancestry; the savage Amahagger cannibals with their "hot-pot" ceremonies; the strange, extinct Kingdom of Kôr, with its peculiar architecture and legends from human prehistory; and, most vivid of all, the incessant images of decay and death. The book abounds with such scenes and details, and they occur increasingly and in more extreme form as the novel develops. They include the killing and torturing of the natives; the tombs of Kôr, where the entombed sleep on burial slabs; the embalmed figures of long-dead Kôr aristocrats, including their greatest king; the great heap of bodies of the less favored; the wild native dance ritual where corpses are burned as torches; and, finally, the image of Ayesha disintegrating before the eyes of her appalled comrades. The novel counterpoints and associates Ayesha's heroic sensuality with death and destruction—"Eros" and "Thanatos"—in a symbiotic relationship that gives the book much of its most disturbing emotional force.

This is not to say that *She* is a great novel. The plot is crude, the prose overblown, falsely ornate, and abstract. The secondary characters are weak; the natives are stereotypes, whereas the whites are bland, stiff, and trite. Although Holly's long rhetorical digressions are intended to expound the book's philosophical and religious themes, these passages are pompous, even somewhat embarrassing. In short, the novel teeters on the edge of absurdity. Nevertheless, it leaves a more lasting and powerful impression than many a more serious book. Perhaps *She* is one of a handful of novels—such as Mary Wollstonecraft Shelley's *Frankenstein* (1818) and Herman Melville's *Pierre* (1852)—that touch such vital centers and provoke such emotional responses in the reader that the flaws in their execution and the implausibility of their ideas become relatively unimportant.

"Critical Evaluation" by Keith Neilson

Bibliography:

Barclay, Glen St. John. *Anatomy of Horror: The Masters of Occult Fiction*. New York: St. Martin's Press, 1979. In the chapter "Love After Death: Henry Rider Haggard," Barclay surveys the writer's supernatural fiction, focusing on *She* and its three sequels. Concludes that Haggard "found an ideal form of expression" in his African adventures, and ranks him above other writers of the supernatural such as Bram Stoker and H. P. Lovecraft.

Haggard, H. Rider. *The Annotated She: A Critical Edition of H. Rider Haggard's Victorian Romance with Introduction and Notes by Norman Etherington*. Bloomington: Indiana University Press, 1991. Etherington's critical introduction is the single best source for the beginner. This edition also includes a brief bibliography.

Higgins, D. S. *Rider Haggard: A Biography*. New York: Stein and Day, 1983. The most accessible and detailed survey of Haggard's life and works. Higgins discusses *She*'s sources and genesis as well as the book's reincarnations on stage and screen. Good bibliography.

Katz, Wendy R. *Rider Haggard and the Fiction of Empire: A Critical Study of British Imperial Fiction*. Cambridge, England: Cambridge University Press, 1987. A study of Haggard's interest in and influence on the British Empire. Important for placing Haggard clearly in the psychological and sociological context of his times. Katz's final chapter, "A Negro Excepted," explores aspects of racism in Haggard's writing.

Moss, John G. "Three Motifs in Haggard's *She*." *English Literature in Transition, 1880-1920* 16, no. 1 (1973): 27-34. Moss summarizes but dismisses most critical interpretations of *She*, concluding that "it escapes definition or explanation." Also faults the sequels for failing to maintain the enigmatic quality of the original.

SHE STOOPS TO CONQUER
Or, The Mistakes of a Night

Type of work: Drama
Author: Oliver Goldsmith (1728 or 1730-1774)
Type of plot: Comedy of manners
Time of plot: Eighteenth century
Locale: England
First performed: 1773; first published, 1773

Principal characters:
MR. HARDCASTLE, an English gentleman
MRS. HARDCASTLE, his wife
TONY LUMPKIN, Mrs. Hardcastle's son
KATE HARDCASTLE, Mr. Hardcastle's daughter
CONSTANCE NEVILLE, Tony's cousin
MARLOW, Kate's reluctant suitor
HASTINGS, in love with Constance
SIR CHARLES, Marlow's father

The Story:

Mrs. Hardcastle, the wife of Mr. Hardcastle by a second marriage, had by her first husband a son, Tony Lumpkin. Tony was a lazy, spoiled boy, but his mother excused his actions by imagining him to be sickly. Mr. Hardcastle vowed that his stepson looked the picture of good health. Kate Hardcastle, Mr. Hardcastle's daughter, was headstrong. To overcome his daughter's wish to be a lady of importance, Mr. Hardcastle had struck a bargain with her whereby she wore ordinary clothes and pretended to be a country girl during part of the day; at other times she was allowed to appear in fine clothes. Knowing it was time for his daughter to marry, Mr. Hardcastle sent for Mr. Marlow, the son of his closest friend, to meet Kate. Kate was pleased by her father's description of the young man in all features except one. She did not like the fact that he was considered shy and retiring.

Mrs. Hardcastle hoped to arrange a match between Tony and Constance Neville, her ward and Kate's best friend. The two young people mutually hated each other but pretended otherwise for Mrs. Hardcastle's sake. On the day of Mr. Marlow's expected arrival, Constance identified the prospective bridegroom as the friend of Hastings, the man whom Constance really loved. Constance described Marlow as being very shy with fashionable young ladies but quite a different character with young women of lower station.

En route to the Hardcastle home, Hastings and Marlow lost their way and arrived at an ale-house, where Tony was carousing with friends. Recognizing the two men, Tony decided to play a trick on his stepfather. When Hastings and Marlow asked the way to the Hardcastle home, Tony told them that they were lost and would be wise to stop at an inn a short distance up the road. Marlow and Hastings arrived at their destination but thought it the inn Tony had described. Hardcastle, knowing nothing of their misconception, treated them as guests, while Hastings and Marlow treated him as an innkeeper, each party thinking the other extremely rude. Hardcastle decided that Marlow's apparent character was in contradiction to the modest person who had been described to him.

When Hastings met Constance, she quickly recognized Tony's hand in the mischief, but

Hastings and Constance kept the secret to themselves. Hastings explained to Marlow that the two young ladies had arrived at the inn after a long journey through the country. When Tony came home, Hastings took him aside and explained his desire to marry Constance, an arrangement quite satisfactory to the rascal Tony. He promised to help the lovers and even to try to secure Constance's jewelry, which was in Mrs. Hardcastle's keeping. The bargain having been made, Tony went to his mother's room and stole the gems. He gave them to Hastings. When Constance asked for the jewels, Tony whispered to his mother that she should tell Constance they had been lost. Thinking it a capital plan, Mrs. Hardcastle complied with Tony's suggestion, only to discover later that the gems actually were gone. Meanwhile, Kate, according to her agreement with her father, had put on a pleasant, simple dress.

Learning of Marlow's mistaken idea that he was at an inn, Kate decided to keep him in error. Marlow, seeing Kate in her simple dress, thought she was a serving-girl and revealed himself as a flirtatious dandy. As he was trying to kiss her, Mr. Hardcastle entered the room, and Marlow fled. Mr. Hardcastle remarked to Kate that obviously she now had proof that Marlow was no modest young man. Kate vowed she would convince her father Marlow had the kind of personality pleasing to them both. However, Marlow's continued impudence aroused Hardcastle to such an uncontrollable state that he ordered him to leave his house. Kate, thinking the time had come to enlighten her deceived suitor, told Marlow about the trick Tony had played. Marlow, still unaware of Kate's real identity, found himself more and more attracted to her, while Kate was discovering him to be a fine and honest person.

Hastings had given Marlow the jewels that Tony had stolen from Mrs. Hardcastle. To protect the valuables, Marlow had sent them to Mrs. Hardcastle, supposing her to be the innkeeper's wife. The servants, under Tony's instructions, then explained to the distraught lady that the jewels had been mislaid because of some confusion in the household. Mrs. Hardcastle discovered that Hastings planned to elope with Constance. Enraged, she decided to punish Constance by sending her to visit her Aunt Pedigree. To add to the confusion, news came that Sir Charles, Marlow's father, was on his way to the Hardcastle home.

Tony offered to drive the coach for Mrs. Hardcastle, but instead of taking the ladies to the house of Aunt Pedigree, he drove them around in a circle for three hours until Mrs. Hardcastle believed they were lost. After hiding his terrified mother in the bushes, Tony took Constance back to Hastings. Constance, however, was determined not to leave without her jewels. When Mrs. Hardcastle at last discovered Tony's trick, she was furious.

Sir Charles, on his arrival, was greatly amused by Hardcastle's account of Marlow's mistake. Hardcastle assured Sir Charles that Marlow loved Kate, but Marlow insisted he was not interested in Miss Hardcastle. Kate promised the two fathers she would prove that Marlow loved her, and she told them to hide while she talked with Marlow. Still under the impression that Kate was a serving-girl, the wretched young man told her he loved her and wanted to marry her. Sir Charles and Hardcastle emerged from their hiding place satisfied that the marriage would be arranged. Marlow was upset to learn that the serving-girl with whom he had behaved so freely was really Miss Hardcastle.

Mrs. Hardcastle reminded her husband that she had full control of Constance's fortune until Tony married her when he became of age. If he should refuse her, Constance would be given control of her inheritance. It was then announced that Tony's real age had been hidden in the hope that the lad would improve his character. Informed that he was already of age, Tony refused to marry Constance. Sir Charles assured Mrs. Hardcastle that Hastings was a fine young man, and Constance obtained her jewels from her guardian. So Kate married Marlow, and Constance married Hastings, and Tony gained his freedom from his mother.

Critical Evaluation:

This charming play has entertained audiences for more than 175 years. Conditions of society on which the comedy is based have long since ceased to exist, but the gaiety of the plot and the racy dialogue are still amusing. Designed to satirize the sentimental comedy of Goldsmith's day, *She Stoops to Conquer* far outshines the exaggerated sentimentality of the author's contemporary stage. Oliver Goldsmith was a poverty-haunted, irritable, and envious man with a great wit and generosity and an essentially lovable nature; all of these contradictory characteristics are reflected in his writings. Hopelessly impractical, especially in money matters, in talk often foolish, he wrote with genius and Irish liveliness in many different forms and left a legacy of at least four masterpieces. Goldsmith was forced, like Samuel Johnson before him, to plod away as a literary hack, trying to survive in London's Grub Street literary world. He did editorial work for booksellers, wrote essays and criticism, and gradually gained a modest reputation. *The Citizen of the World* essays (1762) brought him more recognition; when they were republished, the charm and grace of the satire in these letters, and their humor and good sense, caused a sensation. Although this success eased somewhat the pinch of poverty, Goldsmith continued to find it necessary to write pamphlets and miscellaneous journalism. A philosophic poem, *The Traveler: Or, A Prospect of Society* (1764), brought high praise from Johnson, and *The Deserted Village* (1770) was a wide success. In 1766 *The Vicar of Wakefield*, written to pay his rent, brought Goldsmith fame as a novelist. His collected essays was a further triumph, although his money troubles continued. *She Stoops to Conquer*, Goldsmith's second comedy, received a flattering public response, but the financial returns paid off no more than a fraction of the author's huge debts. The drudgery of his efforts to raise money with his pen caused his health to fail, and he finally died in 1774, only forty-four years old, a victim of his financial failure.

Goldsmith's writings reflect his whimsical, yet serious, nature. As he fluctuated from lighthearted foolishness to depths of depression, so his work demonstrates a somber, earthy thread running through the farce and sentiment. He belonged mainly to the neoclassical tradition; his style and vocabulary are of the eighteenth century, but he avoids the ponderousness of his friend and mentor, Johnson. Even his sentimental streak is lightened with his Irish humor and wistfulness.

Of all of Goldsmith's varied writings, *She Stoops to Conquer* stands supreme, one of the most beloved comedies of all time. The humor and humanity of such characters as Kate Hardcastle and Tony Lumpkin guarantee the play's immortality. The sentimental drama, under the influence of such works as Richard Steele's *Conscious Lovers* (1722), dominated the eighteenth century stage. The middle class craved this kind of drama, and it provided a conventional code of manners for these theatergoers to emulate. In *She Stoops to Conquer*, Goldsmith moves toward real human motivation and escapes the artificiality of the sentimental drama, which was in many respects a flight from reality. He satirizes the posturings of the sentimental plays, but he also does much more than that; his wit and style and shrewd eye for human foibles gives *She Stoops to Conquer* a vitality and sense of real life.

With all of its polish, the eighteenth century was often crude and coarse and cruel; Goldsmith helped to humanize its imagination, to bring it around to his more gentle humor. At the conclusion of *She Stoops to Conquer*, the audience cannot help but be saner and more civilized and to view its fellow mortals with a warmer sympathy. In *She Stoops to Conquer*, the emphasis is not on the outcome (which the audience never doubts) but on how the outcome will arrive. The basis of the plot is the sentimental conflict of the opposed love match and the subordinate trite plot complication (of the mistaken house as an inn, an incident which is said to have happened to Goldsmith in his youth). Goldsmith takes these trifles and breathes life into them, with a pace and humanity seldom approached in the drama. The characters are not cruel to each other; even Tony Lumpkin is essentially a good-hearted rogue. The conclusion is a happy one, without anyone suffering or being left out in the cold. Unlike so many authors of comedies of manners, Goldsmith has no interest in punishing his characters.

Goldsmith was unlearned compared to his friends and compatriots Richard Brinsley Sheridan and Johnson, but he was a natural writer with a loathing for pretense and artificiality. If *She Stoops to Conquer* has any message, it is of the dangers of pretense and pretentiousness. Mr. Hardcastle's rule that Kate and her mother must dress plainly reflects this attitude of Goldsmith. The right of individuals to lead their own lives must be considered the second theme of the play, for both Kate and Marlow at last win their right to love and Tony wins his freedom from his mother.

As a result of the failure of his previous play, *The Good Natur'd Man* (1768), Goldsmith had difficulty getting *She Stoops to Conquer* produced. The great actor David Garrick would have nothing to do with it, and general opinion was that it was too different from the prevailing mode to be a success. It was believed that only plays in the sentimental manner were wanted by audiences. After many difficulties, the comedy finally opened at Covent Garden and Johnson himself led a party to see his friend's play through its hour of judgment. "I know of no comedy for many years," Dr. Johnson said, after, "that has answered so much the great end of comedy—making an audience merry." As usual, Johnson was right, for, while one or two comedies of the time might be considered superior, none of them is merrier. There is, in *She Stoops to Conquer*, something of the quality of the great Elizabethan comedies, a humanity and humor that might have revolutionized the eighteenth century theater. Goldsmith wrote no more plays, however, and he had no followers or imitators, so he produced almost no effect on the drama of the day. Perhaps technically the play is not as perfect as those of Sheridan and lacks the sharp wit of the Restoration comedies, but it reflects the author's own rich and genial personality and will continue to be produced and read and loved as one of the kindliest and funniest of all comedies.

"Critical Evaluation" by Bruce D. Reeves

Bibliography:

Dixon, Peter. *Oliver Goldsmith Revisited*. Boston: Twayne, 1991. Solid introduction to Goldsmith's work in general and *She Stoops to Conquer* in particular. Details the biographical episode that inspired Goldsmith to write the comedy and ties the play to Goldsmith's theories on dramatic writing.

Quintana, Ricardo. *Oliver Goldsmith: A Georgian Study*. New York: Macmillan, 1967. Enthusiastic and graceful study of Goldsmith's work. Places less emphasis on the drama itself and more on the circumstances surrounding the play's production and theatrical success.

Sells, A. Lytton. *Oliver Goldsmith: His Life and Works*. New York: Barnes & Noble Books, 1974. Examines Goldsmith's life and offers a chapter on his writing the play and the problems he faced presenting it on the London stage. Offers two chapters on Goldsmith the dramatist and critically scrutinizes *She Stoops to Conquer*.

Swarbrick, Andrew, ed. *The Art of Oliver Goldsmith*. London: Vision Press, 1984. Ten essays touching on all aspects of Goldsmith's writings. Contains Bernard Harris' engaging "Goldsmith in the Theatre," examining Goldsmith's dramatic career, theater philosophy, and difficulties in staging *She Stoops to Conquer*.

Worth, Katharine. *Sheridan and Goldsmith*. New York: St. Martin's Press, 1992. Intelligent investigation of the playwriting careers of Oliver Goldsmith and Richard Brinsley Sheridan, with special attention given to Goldsmith's intense dislike of the prevailing sentimental comedy. Long chapter on *She Stoops to Conquer* is an excellent discussion of the boisterous play.

THE SHEEP WELL

Type of work: Drama
Author: Lope de Vega Carpio (1562-1635)
Type of plot: Social realism
Time of plot: 1476
Locale: Spain
Written: 1611-1618; first published as *Fuenteovejuna*, c. 1619 (English translation, 1936)

Principal characters:
COMMANDER FERNÁN GÓMEZ DE GUZMÁN, a lustful tyrant
RODRIGO TÉLLEZ GIRÓN, youthful master of the Order of Calatrava
LAURENCIA, a peasant woman desired by the commander
FRONDOSO, a peasant youth in love with Laurencia
ESTEBAN, administrative officer of Fuenteovejuna and Laurencia's father
KING FERDINAND and QUEEN ISABELLA OF SPAIN

The Story:

In the troubled Spain of the 1470's, when King Ferdinand and Queen Isabella were trying to integrate their kingdom and preserve it from the depredations of Portugal, the grand mastership of the military and religious Order of Calatrava fell upon the shoulders of Rodrigo Téllez Girón, a young man scarcely out of boyhood. The new grand master's adviser was the lustful, tyrannical Commander Fernán Gómez de Guzmán, who took women whenever and wherever he saw them and kept his peasants in constant fear of himself and his soldiers. The commander was not loyal to Ferdinand and Isabella, and so he counseled the young grand master to capture the Ciudad Real and hold it for Portugal, which was claiming sections of Spain because the Portuguese queen was Spanish. The grand master took the commander's advice and captured the city.

When the commander returned to his lands, he continued his tyrannous ways with the peasants, especially the women. Among the unmarried peasants was a particularly pretty one named Laurencia, the daughter of Esteban, the administrative officer of the village. The commander had sought her for more than a month, but she had managed to elude his servants by staying in the fields as much as possible. Then the commander had left to capture the city. He returned in triumph, and upon his arrival in the village of Fuenteovejuna he was praised and given two cartloads of foodstuffs as recognition of his military efforts. After receiving the gifts, he requested that the young women, including Laurencia, remain behind to amuse him. The women, however, refused to stay. Ferdinand and Isabella, meanwhile, had received word of the treacherous action of the grand master of the Order of Calatrava and had dispatched a force to retake Ciudad Real.

In Fuenteovejuna, Laurencia was wooed by a good-looking young peasant, Frondoso, but she refused to accept him as her husband. One day, as she was working in the fields, the commander came upon her and attempted to rape her. Frondoso, although a peasant, seized the commander's crossbow and threatened to kill the knight unless he let Laurencia go. The commander, having no choice, let the woman go free but swore vengeance. Frondoso fled with the crossbow.

The commander later went to the village, confronted Laurencia's father, and demanded that he give up his daughter to him. Esteban refused, and he and the other villagers left the commander standing alone in the square. Some of the commander's servants appeared and reported that they thought they had killed Frondoso. Unfortunately, they had cut the throat of the wrong man. As they spoke, a messenger came to inform the commander that the grand master had been besieged by the forces of Ferdinand and Isabella. The commander decided to rush to the grand master's aid.

As they rode away from the village, the commander and his servants tried to force their attentions on several peasant women. The women fled until they reached one of the men of the village. When he tried to protect them, the commander had the man disarmed, bound to a tree, and flogged unmercifully with bridle reins. While that was done, the commander seized one of the women, dragged her into a thicket, and raped her. The soldiers then proceeded on their journey.

During the commander's absence, his subject peasants relaxed a bit. In the quiet interval, arrangements were made for the wedding of Laurencia and Frondoso, the young peasant who had become dear to her after he had saved her from the commander's lust. On the day of the wedding, the commander returned and demanded the woman for his own purposes. When her father again refused, the commander had him beaten, and the wedding was broken up by the soldiers. Frondoso was imprisoned to await hanging; Laurencia was taken to the commander's citadel.

The next day, the town board assembled in the village hall to discuss what might be done to prevent further acts of violence by their wicked master. While they debated, Laurencia, who had escaped from the citadel, ran into the hall, where she roused the men and women of the village to open revolt against the commander who had treated them so brutally and ruthlessly. The people, spurred to action by their anger, stormed the citadel. Once inside, they killed many of the soldiers and finally found the commander. They put him to death and returned to the village with his head held high upon the point of a spear. Their plan was to leave the head in the village square as a symbol of the tyranny they had broken. Not really rebels, the villagers hastened to raise the escutcheon of Ferdinand and Isabella in place of the commander's. Their plan was to place themselves at the mercy of the king and queen.

One of the commander's servants had escaped and carried news of the uprising to the king and queen. The king, anxious to prevent revolt from spreading throughout Spain, dispatched soldiers and a judge to the village of Fuenteovejuna to investigate the happenings. When word came to the village that a judge was coming, the villagers met and decided to stick together, even to hiding the actual murderers of the commander and his men. It was agreed that the entire village had done the deed and that they would hang together, if need be.

The judge had the soldiers bring in villagers for questioning. When the villagers refused to tell who had been the leaders of the revolt or who had actually killed the commander, the judge had them tortured. More than three hundred of the villagers were tortured, including small children, but not one broke his or her vow to claim that the whole town was responsible for their deeds.

At last, the judge and the soldiers returned to the court of Ferdinand and Isabella, where the judge reported that he had made no decision, for in order to punish justly he would have had to wipe out the entire village. He also reported to the king and queen the cruelties of which the commander had been guilty. Villagers he had brought with him to court pleaded with the king and queen, pointing out that they had not rebelled against the crown; they had been forced to rid themselves of a tyrannous lord who threatened their lives and honor. The king, after hearing their stories, pardoned the entire village of Fuenteovejuna and made it a protectorate of the crown.

Critical Evaluation:

Lope de Vega Carpio was the central figure of the great dramatic movement in Spain during the sixteenth and seventeenth centuries. Acclaimed by many scholars as having created the *comedia* that provided the model for the Golden Age of Spanish theater in the seventeenth century, Vega Carpio received the honorary title of doctor of theology before terminating a career that had produced hundreds of plays and extensive volumes of classical epics, lyric verse, one-acts, ballads, epistles, prose stories, and a novelized autobiography.

Vega Carpio was popular with the different levels of society; he was awarded the position of judge by the Spanish Inquisition, becoming an official censor. His popularity reflected his choice to represent the various social strata in his *comedia* instead of limiting his characters to the gentlemen of society. The best of his plays are those, such as *The Sheep Well*, that use peasants as heroes and heroines. Vega Carpio had a sympathy and feeling for those people, because they were of the same class from which he had come. *The Sheep Well*, because of its use of the entire population of a Spanish village as the hero, is sometimes referred to as the first proletarian drama, written some three hundred years before the flood of so-called proletarian literature came out of the Great Depression in the United States.

Vega Carpio formulated concepts regarding the composition of the *comedia* toward the beginning of his career and, in *The New Art of Writing Plays* (1609), read them to the Madrid literary society, who preferred the Aristotelian rules of dramatic composition. Vega Carpio rejected these classical rules in favor of popular dramatic style; his treatise in verse clarified two principal reasons for favoring this style: to give pleasure and to be true to life. In order to impart pleasure to the audience, Vega Carpio decided that comedy could be mixed with tragedy for variety and that the play, observing the unity of action, should be well constructed, with the denouement occurring in the last scene to sustain interest.

In the *comedia*, Vega Carpio portrays realism through natural speech that depicts the social class of the character, as well as through the variety of verse forms that sets the mood of the characters. This treatise establishes Vega Carpio's main theatrical theme as honor, chosen to move people of any age or social class. Soon after Vega Carpio read his formula for composing *comedia*, he wrote *The Sheep Well*, which illustrates his contribution to the development of the Spanish *comedia*: the perspective of the society dedicated to the code of honor. *The Sheep Well* reflects this Spanish code that governs social relationships between king and subject, superior and inferior, friend and friend, and members of the same family.

The significance of the code resides in the correct ordering of social relationships. Since the social group is more important than individual integrity, honor stems from group esteem. The primary theme of *The Sheep Well* revolves around honor; the main plot concerns the village of Fuenteovejuna (Sheep Well) representing the common group, and the commander, the villain, characterizing a superior social class. The two other subplots also involve honor and the commander: Ciudad Real versus the Order of Calatrava and the Spain of Ferdinand and Isabella versus the Portugal of Alfonso. The plot and subplots delineate an assault on the integrity of a societal faction by an exterior power, and this assault is assuaged and avenged. The commander participates in each plot or subplot, spreading his malevolent force to the village, the city, and the nation, until, overcome by his own evil, he is exterminated by the group.

The principal plot involving the commander and the inhabitants of Fuenteovejuna presents different social strata in a realistic manner. The commander reflects his military background through his frequent use of imperatives, hence, speaking with the authority of a conqueror. Upon entering the village in Act I, the soldier shows his excessive authoritarian posture by demanding to be told if the master knows he is in town. The commander then mistreats the girls, women, boys, men, and the town elders; he even asks them if they are his possessions. The commander acts contrary to a typical feudal lord, who protects his vassals and their property. If the feudal lord faithfully renders his service to his vassals, they will perform certain duties; however, the feudal lord's vassals are not unconditionally bound to him. The commander disregards this concept, because he associates the villagers with his stable horses or the wild animals of the forest. For example, he decides that a recalcitrant old man deserves the same castigation as he would give to an unruly horse. Another comparison with animals pertains to the soldier's pursuit of the village women: In addressing Esteban, the soldier shamelessly compares his pursuit of the latter's daughter to that of a greyhound stalking its game. The commander's cruel, obsessive behavior, therefore, severs the normal relationship between a lord and his vassals.

The commander's comparison of the villagers with animals such as horses, hares, and dogs transforms him into an animalistic brute. The peasants, who speak in a rustic dialect with copious homely expressions, recognize the irony and label him as a wild beast, a lynx, a wolf, and a tiger, finally envisioning him as a devil. In order to save themselves from the commander's tyranny, these country people realize that they will have to defend themselves. In Act I, Frondoso intervenes on behalf of Laurencia when he threatens to use the commander's crossbow to defend her from the leader's advances. In Act II, Mengo defies the commander in order to prevent two servants from taking Jacinta to their superior. Mengo's actions are heroic, because his only weapon is his arms. Although Mengo does not succeed in preventing Jacinta's seizure, Vega Carpio is preparing the denouement of the third act by revealing that individual heroic endeavors cannot curb the savage obsessions of the commander. Incited by Laurencia's speech, the villagers agree to end oppression and dishonor because of love. Esteban asserts that they experienced a sort of death when the commander stained their honor, so that their killing the commander is not an act of rebellion, but justice. The villagers prove their adherence to the established social order by going to the court of Ferdinand and Isabella, who acknowledge their bravery, hence establishing the concept of the just monarchs concerned with the honor code of their subjects.

The theme of honor portrayed by a convincing group protagonist composed of courageous individuals provides colorful, animated scenes, which give *The Sheep Well* its success in Vega Carpio's prolific production of *comedias*. It well illustrates Vega Carpio's purpose of creating realistic *comedias* to please the audience.

"Critical Evaluation" by Linda Prewett Davis

Bibliography:

Crow, John A. *Spain: The Root and the Flower*. New York: Harper & Row, 1963. Chapters 6 through 9 contain a readable account of the history of Spain during the epoch of Vega Carpio.

Larson, Donald R. *The Honor Plays of Lope de Vega*. Cambridge, Mass.: Harvard University Press, 1977. Treats the concept of honor in Vega Carpio's *comedias*. Contains an informative section pertaining to *The Sheep Well* in the chapter titled "Plays of the Middle Period."

Parker, A. A. "The Approach to the Spanish Drama of the Golden Age." *Tulane Drama Review* 4 (1959): 42-59. Presents five principles relating to the dramatic construction of the *comedia*. Enhances understanding of the Spanish drama of the seventeenth century.

Pring-Mill, R. D. F. "Sententiousness in *Fuenteovejuna (Sheep Well)*." *Tulane Drama Review* 7 (1962): 5-37. Relates the importance of maxims in *The Sheep Well*. The conclusions concerning the abundance of aphorisms in *The Sheep Well* can be applied to various *comedias* of the epoch.

Reichenberger, Arnold G. "The Uniqueness of the Comedia." *Hispanic Review* 27, no. 3 (July, 1959): 303-316. A critical essay that shows the distinctive characteristics of the *comedia*. Useful in comprehending the Spanish plays of the Golden Age.

THE SHELTERED LIFE

Type of work: Novel
Author: Ellen Glasgow (1873-1945)
Type of plot: Psychological realism
Time of plot: 1906-1914
Locale: Richmond, Virginia
First published: 1932

Principal characters:
GENERAL DAVID ARCHBALD, an aged and aristocratic Southern patriarch
JENNY BLAIR ARCHBALD, his free-spirited granddaughter
AUNT ETTA, the general's neurotic spinster daughter
AUNT ISABELLA, the general's flirtatious daughter
EVA HOWARD BIRDSONG, an aristocratic, formerly celebrated beauty
GEORGE BIRDSONG, Eva's charming, philandering husband

The Story:

"I'm alive, alive, alive, and I'm Jenny Blair Archbald," exclaimed the precocious nine-year-old Jenny, on having thrown aside as tedious Louisa Alcott's *Little Women* (1868-1869). Jenny lived with three somewhat downtrodden females—her widowed mother and two aunts—in the household of her grandfather, General David Archbald. An aged, highly civilized man, the general sought to maintain his aristocratic family amid declining fortunes in a once elegant but rapidly failing Queenborough neighborhood. Jenny, like her mother, grandfather, and aunts, was an ardent admirer of the similarly circumstanced married couple who lived nearby, Eva and George Birdsong, whose marriage was a subject of speculative discussion among the Archbald women.

Eva Birdsong, a queenly belle of the 1890's and still an acknowledged beauty as she approached her forties, had abandoned her social position as well as a planned singing career when she fell in love with George Birdsong. George, a barely successful attorney, was handsome, invariably charming and likable, and a consummate philanderer who recognized Eva's worth but was unable to rise to it. Aware that her beauty and the social attentions that it commanded were waning, Eva refused to acknowledge even the most blatant evidences of George's adulteries.

Increasingly amoral and hedonistic, Jenny Blair Archbald, even as a child, idolized Eva Birdsong for her regal beauty and character, neither of which, she realized, lay within her reach. Jenny was also powerfully drawn to George Birdsong who had cultivated her affections since her childhood. Jenny, moreover, shared a secret with him: Having injured herself falling off roller skates one day in a poorer neighborhood, she was cared for, as it happened, by George and his black mistress. Over the years, Jenny was a frequent and favored visitor in the Birdsong household. Eva, as her fortunes worsened, began to confide in Jenny, explaining how plans for her early career had been jettisoned when, having fallen in love with George, she "stopped wanting anything else," and that a "great love doesn't leave room for anything else in a woman's life." At a grand party attended by all of the Archbalds and Birdsongs, George had an amorous encounter with a pretty young girl in a secluded garden. Eva, distraught, collapsed, and even Jenny and other children present recognized her marital self-delusions.

Eight years later, General Archbald mused over his life and the lives of his family and friends. Eva, whom the general reverenced as the epitome of beautiful and courageous womanhood and thus as a symbol of his dying Southern values, had at the age of forty undergone a maiming operation followed by a nervous collapse. Thereafter she was sickly and lost her striking beauty. Increasingly, she also recognized the price exacted from her for a life of illusions. As old General Archbald devotedly attended her, often in George's company, he pitied Eva for this. Yet while cognizant of the cause of her malaise, he still thought George had the right to philander and that men's adulteries were irrelevant to their love relationships with their wives.

General Archbald also mused about his own youth and the destruction of his poetic talent by his father's callous insistence that he adhere to a traditional Southern male role. The general realized that his conventional marriage had resulted from a mistaken obedience to outworn standards. He had fallen into the right pattern, as he phrased it, but the center of the pattern was missing.

As Eva passively awaited a further operation, it became clear that she was weary of a life of "exacting pretense" and that she wanted to die. The operation stripped her of her remaining beauty, and she succumbed to a post-operative breakdown. Nevertheless, she clung to a faith in her love, excusing George's philandering as a consequence of his kindness. Jenny Blair, then nearly eighteen, hoped to escape home and launch a career. She continued her idolatry of Eva, which Eva reciprocated by confiding her inner thoughts. Eva confessed to Jenny that for forty years she had never really known herself, and she warned Jenny that to surrender everything to love, as she had, was to become a slave to fear.

Despite Eva's soul-baring confidences, Jenny was nevertheless attracted to George. When Eva departed to convalesce, their opportunities for meeting increased. One day after Eva's return, Jenny and George, believing that she was upstairs, were locked in an embrace when Eva inadvertently discovered them. Terrified, Jenny fled into the ruins of Eva's garden. Shortly afterward, Eva fatally shot George amid the blood of his recent kills. Rallying to Eva, General Archbald outfaced the law by describing the murder as an accident, thus continuing to preserve his own and the sheltered lives of his kin from an encounter with reality.

Critical Evaluation:

The Sheltered Life, the last of Ellen Glasgow's Queenborough novels, was appraised critically as one of her finest works and one of the major American novels. Glasgow's tone throughout the work is ironic, at times satiric. The plot is tightly constructed, and the characters, notably General Archbald, Eva, George, and Jenny, are plausible, three-dimensional, and memorable. Glasgow uses deft metaphorical shadings and contrasts. Bright settings become darker and more somber as events proceed, and the encroachments of industrialism become progressively louder and more noxious. The waning of Eva's beauty and marriage are paralleled by her declining fortunes, dress, and gardens, and by the steady erosion of her once elegant neighborhood and her cherished delusions. The characters too are skillfully contrasted. The general and Eva are well-cast evocations of an old and dying order's values. By contrast, George and Jenny are less inhibited and more hedonistic, undisciplined, and vulgar in their vitality; neither is evil, however, and their actions, if not always commendable, are at least understandable. Similarly, General Archbald's daughters reflect a familiar range of feminine repressions: Etta, the homely spinster, neurotic and sexually starved, and Isabella drawn by her flirtations to blend into the commonplace.

Glasgow was one of many who were surprised that *The Sheltered Life* did not garner a Pulitzer Prize. The novel represented Glasgow's most intensive exploitation of themes she had dealt with many times, chief among them her concern with evasive idealism, its subjective and cultural manifestations, and the consequences of its encounters with reality. This thematic exploration was informed by Glasgow's study of Darwinism and its emphasis on the biological imperatives that produced survivors. To satisfy her sexuality, Jenny was, for example, prepared to push others—even Eva, her idol—treacherously aside. Glasgow also drew her thematic material from her keen interest in psychology. Some of her psychological insights she discovered, for example, in the work of Russian novelists and Virginia Woolf, authors who also analyzed the complex connections between people's mental states and emotional decay and the outward appearances they maintained.

In *The Sheltered Life*, Glasgow recounted that she employed two simultaneous yet related points of view that channeled her story like a stream in a narrow valley. One perspective is that of age: General Archbald's view of life as it was and might have been. The other is the perspective of youth as seen in the perceptions of troubled young Jenny Blair. Both perspectives come to bear on the same events and personalities. Yet through the workings of their different thoughts and emotions, each interprets reality differently.

An author whose feminist convictions placed her in advance of her times, Glasgow likewise sought to explore Eva, Jenny, and her other female characters as multidimensional people, not as mere symbols or metaphors for a male perception that predominated in literature, as in Western thought, long after the first decades of the twentieth century. In all of her writing, Glasgow reveals her disdain for sexual love, for homage to males, and for the glorification of a life of feminine sacrifice. Glasgow clearly sympathized with and in many regards admired Eva Birdsong, even to the point of justifying Eva's murder of her husband. As critics have noted, however, Eva destroys herself by shooting George. Glasgow thus remains ambiguous about the desirable role for women's sexuality. This ambiguity is sharpened by her depiction of Jenny, socially and sexually a free spirit, as a shallow, treacherous person. What is not ambiguous is Glasgow's clear message that it is a mistake for women of any kind or at any time to derive their identities from their sexuality.

By choosing to end the story in 1914, the year in which not only the world of the Archbalds and Birdsongs was in conspicuous decline but also Western civilization appeared headed for collapse, Glasgow reflected the questions and interests of her times. Serious philosophical issues were in debate about the hidden springs or motivations of human actions. Human thought and actions were increasingly being described as less the outcome of rationality than of obscure inner drives, primordial passions, and emotions. Human values were being depicted not as traditionally sanctified or divinely ordained but as relative and subject to changing biological and cultural interpretations. Human behavior, therefore, increasingly appeared to be a consequence of self-deception, illusion, or delusion.

Insofar as *The Sheltered Life* signals that not too much should be expected of life or of people—both are full of tricks and deceptions—and yet that love and compassion should not be abandoned, it is a wise book. It is all the wiser because Glasgow identifies courage as "the only virtue that has a lasting quality."

Clifton K. Yearley

Bibliography:

Inge, Thomas M., ed. *Ellen Glasgow*. Charlottesville: University of Virginia Press, 1976. Excellent centennial essays on "Miss Ellen's" work, including pithy critical comments by Louis Rubin, Jr., on *The Sheltered Life*.

McDowell, Frederick P. W. *Ellen Glasgow and the Ironic Art of Fiction*. Madison: University of Wisconsin Press, 1960. Includes lucid analyses of *The Sheltered Life* in chapter 1, which provides fine background, and in chapter 11, which deals exclusively with this novel.

Raper, Julius Rowan. *From the Sunken Garden*. Baton Rouge: Louisiana State University Press, 1980. Fine survey of Glasgow's fiction between 1916 and 1945. Chapter 8 focuses on *The Sheltered Life* and places it in context with other Glasgow writings.

Scura, Dorothy M., ed. *Ellen Glasgow*. Cambridge, England: Cambridge University Press, 1992. An immensely helpful and enlightening collection of contemporary reviews of Glasgow's writings, including an entire section devoted to *The Sheltered Life*.

Thiebaux, Marcelle. *Ellen Glasgow*. New York: Frederick Ungar, 1982. A lucid and informative survey of Glasgow's novels. Includes an analysis of *The Sheltered Life* in chapter 7.

THE SHELTERING SKY

Type of work: Novel
Author: Paul Bowles (1910-   )
Type of plot: Psychological realism
Time of plot: After World War II
Locale: The seaside city of Oran, Algeria; various outposts in the Sahara desert; and a remote Bedouin village
First published: 1949

Principal characters:

PORT MORESBY, an American traveler
KIT MORESBY, his wife
TUNNER, their American companion
MRS. LYLE, an overbearing Englishwoman
ERIC LYLE, her adult son
BELQASSIM, a Bedouin who takes Kit into his harem

The Story:

Port Moresby woke up unable to remember his dream. Later he sat with his wife, Kit Moresby, and their traveling companion, Tunner. They were three New Yorkers who had found that North Africa was one of the few places to which they could get boat passage since the end of the war.

Port explained the difference between tourists and travelers. He was a traveler, a person who belonged to no place, who was not ruled by time, and who questioned his own civilization. His wife, Kit, did not share Port's enthusiasm for maps and remote locations, but was willing to accompany him.

Port then recalled his dream: He was on a speeding train, going ever faster. He was offered the chance to live his life over again, but he refused. Kit left the table crying. Back at the hotel, Kit explained that the dream was too private to tell in front of Tunner, but Port felt that she was being too serious. He left on a walk.

He felt nervous, but he walked until the streetlights were gone, and an Arab man asked what he wanted. Port was offered a prostitute. The man led him to a cliff and pointed to a tent in the valley. Port had sex with a beautiful young girl there, fantasizing that Kit looked on. When the girl attempted to steal his wallet, he pushed her and bolted from the tent. Several men pursued him.

That morning Kit was reflecting on her vanishing relationship with Port. Although she thought Tunner was idiotic, she considered using him as an emotional tool that might force Port back to her. Tunner came to wake her up. Then she noticed that Port's bed was still made. Port arrived and was angry to find Tunner with Kit. She was angry at being accused. Kit and Tunner left. In the hotel bar, Port met Eric Lyle, a revolting character, and Eric's scolding mother. She was a travel writer, and they were touring Africa. Kit returned; she and Port argued briefly.

The argument over Port's whereabouts continued in the morning. Then Eric Lyle invited them to ride in his motorcar to avoid the long train ride to Boussif. Kit refused to travel with the Lyles, or to leave Tunner behind. She and Tunner would take the train. That evening, Tunner wooed Kit over champagne.

Tunner and Kit got drunk in the compartment, riding toward Boussif. Kit left the train momentarily and boarded a fourth-class carriage. She was frightened and soaked by rain when she made it back. She missed having Port to lean on. Tunner took this opportunity to seduce her. By lunchtime the three were reunited at a hotel in Boussif.

Kit and Port, somewhat reconciled, rode rented bikes out toward a cliff. They were finally relaxed and happy together. They climbed and found themselves above the desert. Kit reflected sadly that although alike in feelings, they were hopelessly opposed in their aims. Port, gazing at the sky, said that he had the strange sensation that it was a solid thing protecting them from what lay behind. Kit shuddered and begged him not to talk about it.

Port insisted that they both were barely hanging on to life. Kit said that neither of them had ever gotten into life. Kit felt guilty about Tunner, and she thought that Port knew. After dinner, Port rented a bicycle and rode alone back to the gap. He could never tell Kit that he had gone there again.

Days later, their bus arrived in Ain Krorfa, accompanied by thousands of flies. Tunner, horrified, chose to head to Messad. Afternoon tea left the couple snapping, rather than amused as Port had hoped. To make matters worse, he felt increasingly nervous, and Kit had lost patience with the squalid hotel and the food. She vowed that Port should have to work at getting them back together. Port came to believe that the right time would present itself. Since they both regarded time as nonexistent, they felt eventually everything would happen.

In Bou Noura, Port discovered that he had lost his passport, and he blamed Eric Lyle. Port grew even more distant. The next day Port and Kit left for El Ga'a. On the bus Kit saw that Port was very ill. He was unable to move. The next day at El Ga'a, the hotel proprietor refused to open the door when Kit screamed that her husband was ill. They got a truck out of El Ga'a, a city infected with meningitis.

In Sbâ, a man named Captain Broussard gave Kit something for Port's fever. One could only wait with typhoid. They had a mattress in a small room. Port was unconscious. Once Port said blankly that he did not know whether he would come back. Back from a walk, Kit found Port's fever higher and his speech fantastic. He insisted that he had always lived for her. Kit was revolted by his state; she was moved to violent sobs. He said that she was going away; she shouted that she was not. Kit ran outside into the star-filled landscape just as Port was approaching his death. Captain Broussard attended him and cursed Kit's absence.

Then Kit found herself reunited with Tunner, who had tracked them from Bou Noura. He consoled her, until she felt guilty for leaving Port alone. Tunner scoffed at her concern. Back in the room, Port was alone with one image to accompany his final agony: spots of bright blood on the earth. He also felt the sensation of reaching out to pierce the sheltering sky. Kit told Tunner that they could meet at eight that night; she then hastily returned. When she found Port dead, she was calm. She kissed his forehead and packed her small valise.

Kit locked Port's body inside the room, then she escaped from the fort. She eluded the French soldiers. In the morning, when a caravan approached her, she raised her arms to Belqassim, the younger of the two men in charge. He pulled her onto his camel. Kit traveled with the caravan south into the desert. Each afternoon she submitted to the sexual demands of Belqassim and his older companion. She grew feverishly attached to Belqassim.

At his village, Belqassim dressed her in boys' clothing, then he locked her inside a tiny room within his labyrinthine house. Each afternoon, he visited her for lovemaking.

The household women discovered the deception. When Belqassim was away, the three wives descended on Kit and tore off her clothes. Belqassim arrived shouting. The next day he held a wedding ceremony. As his three humiliated wives looked on, he draped Kit with their gold jewelry. Kit cried and made Belqassim angry. Then she was confined to the room again.

Kit was sentient only during her husband's fiery visits. She lost track of time. When he stopped coming, she became desperate. She escaped the room, and convinced the startled wives (with lipstick bribes and all of her gold jewelry) that they should let her outside. They agreed. In the village, Kit tried to buy food with thousand franc notes and drew a delighted crowd. A man who spoke French took her to send a telegraph that said, "CANNOT GET BACK."

At a convent, Kit was prepared for a trip. She was flown, refusing food, hardly speaking, and with her arms tied down, north to the coast. Her caretakers agreed that she was mad. The hotel people had called Tunner to let him know that she would be there, awaiting passage to the United States. When the cab arrived at the hotel, she seemed frozen into the seat. The proprietress ran for help, but when they returned, Kit had left. A crowded streetcar pulled past up the hill.

Critical Evaluation:

Paul Bowles first won recognition as a composer of modern and theater music. When his first novel, *The Sheltering Sky*, was published in 1949, it was a literary event. Readers of his unique and disturbing stories had eagerly awaited his novel.

Living in Tangier, Morocco, with his wife, the writer Jane Bowles, Paul Bowles was considered a literary outsider. The perception of his work as nihilistic and filled with horror and violence turned many critics away. Others have pointed out Bowles's great capacity for describing the wonder and terror of life.

Many of Bowles's respected contemporaries, such as Tennessee Williams and Gore Vidal, championed the novel. The praise has been echoed by others. Most writers agree that Bowles is a master at depicting the essential separateness of each human psyche.

The Sheltering Sky is about two people who are emotionally estranged from each other. They are in love yet fundamentally separated by emotional impasses, fears, and inabilities. It is also a story about two cultures: the modern intellectual, time-driven American, and the timeless, sensual Saharan. As the story progresses, the American protagonists travel deeper into the desert and inward through many levels of consciousness. The farther south they travel, the less recognizable Kit and Port become to each other. They discard society's trappings and become more strongly impelled to search within themselves for understanding of their problems, desires, and estrangements.

The Sheltering Sky is a novel in three parts. In the first two, Port is the protagonist. His actions propel the novel, and events are filtered through his sensibilities. His melancholy sets the mood, which will grow darker, penetrated only by strained moments of gaiety. Kit's character serves the novel in the same way that she behaves; the reader watches her being propelled by the events Port and Tunner initiate, as if she were on a train she cannot stop. With her superstitions and system of omens, she is at the mercy of other people. She reacts to their signals and takes everything as a sign. Without others, she becomes inert. Tunner, handsome and empty-headed, is the classic foil; because of his attention to her, Kit must examine her loyalty to Port and deal with the consequences of her indecision.

Despite Port's emotional impenetrability, he needs Kit. She is the only person who can connect him to humanity, tenuous as this connection is. The chapters leading up to Port's death give several clues to the couple's mistakes. One fatal error is their fatalism, the belief that events would happen over which they would have no control. They give into this belief and use it as a reason to avoid acting upon their desires to love each other once more. By the time they realize their mistake, it is too late.

The third section of the novel, after Port's death, is Kit's story. As the sexual slave of

Belqassim, she finds freedom from responsibilities. She lives only for the times he comes to her chamber. She slips so far from active consciousness that her sudden return to civilization finds her unable to speak, completely mad. Like Port, Kit has pierced the fabric of the sheltering sky and cannot deal with the emptiness on the other side. Bowles's literary reputation has grown steadily. Once neglected, *The Sheltering Sky* is now recognized as a masterpiece.

JoAnne Balingit

Bibliography:

Bertens, Johannes. *The Fiction of Paul Bowles: The Soul Is the Weariest Part of the Body*. Amsterdam: Rodopi, 1979. Examines the work in light of Bowles's nihilism and attempts to connect the writer to a Calvinist tradition in American literature.

Bowles, Paul. *Conversations with Paul Bowles*. Edited by Gena Dagel Caponi. Jackson: University Press of Mississippi, c. 1993. Bowles discusses the genesis of *The Sheltering Sky*. Interesting background information for study of the novel.

Caponi, Gena Dagel. *Paul Bowles: Romantic Savage*. Carbondale: Southern Illinois University Press, 1994. Interpretive biography that examines the parts of Bowles's life that provide insight into his work. A section on *The Sheltering Sky* examines its influences, its critical reception, and the central characters' relationship. Bibliography and index.

Patteson, Richard F. *A World Outside: The Fiction of Paul Bowles*. Austin: University of Texas Press, 1987. Examines this novel and others through formal and thematic architectural concepts: the story as shelter, both necessary and fragile. Considered the most comprehensive of the full-length studies. Includes bibliography.

Pounds, Wayne. *Paul Bowles: The Inner Geography*. New York: Lang, 1985. Using psychological theories, the author compares *The Sheltering Sky* to Bowles's other works and Edgar Allan Poe's *The Narrative of Arthur Gordon Pym* (1838).

THE SHEPHEARDES CALENDER

Type of work: Poetry
Author: Edmund Spenser (c. 1552-1599)
Type of plot: Pastoral
Time of plot: 1500's
Locale: England
First published: 1579

Principal characters:
COLIN CLOUT, the greatest of the shepherd poets
HOBBINOL, his friend
THENOT, a wise old shepherd
CUDDIE, a young shepherd, an aspiring poet

The Story:

January. Colin, forlorn and rejected by his beloved Rosalind, compared his mood with the wintry landscape:

Thou barrein ground, whome winters wrath hath wasted,
Art made a mirror to behold my plight:
Whilome thy fresh spring flowrd, and after hasted
Thy summer proud with daffadillies dight,
And now is come thy winters stormy state,
Thy mantle marred wherein thou maskedst late.

At the end of this poem, Colin broke his shepherd's pipes and resolved to write no more poetry.

February. An impudent young shepherd, Cuddie, complained of the wintry blasts to the elderly Thenot, and he scorned the old man's philosophical view that one must learn to endure the long succession of misfortunes that this world brings and be concerned only with the safety of the flock. Tired of Cuddie's rudeness, Thenot told the fable of an old oak and a proud briar bush. The briar persuades a farmer to cut down the tree to show off its own beauty. All is well until winter comes; the briar then dies without the protection of the oak against wind and frost. Cuddie was unmoved by this parable of youth and age and broke it off abruptly.

March. Two young shepherds welcomed spring as a time for love. They described Thomalin's encounter with Cupid. Thomalin told a friend how, while he was hunting on one shepherds' holiday, he heard a rustling in the bushes:

With that sprung forth a naked swain
With spotted wings like peacock's train,
And laughing lope to a tree,
His gylden quiver at his back,
And silver bow, which was but slack,
Which lightly he bent at me.

April. Thenot found Hobbinol grieving over the sorrows of his friend Colin Clout and mourning that Colin's unrequited love had deprived all the shepherds of his poems. Thenot asked Hobbinol to recite one of Colin's verses to while away the hours as their flocks grazed, and he complied with an ode on "Fair Elisa, queen of shepherds all." Colin called upon the muses, the graces, the sun, and the moon as he began his praise of the daughter of Pan, the shepherds' god, and Syrinx. Then Colin described Elisa's beauty:

See, where she sits upon the grassie green,
(O seemly sight!)
Yclad in scarlet, like a maiden queen
And ermines white.
Upon her head a cremosin coronet,
With damask leaves and daffadillies set:
Bayleaves between,
And primroses green,
Embellish the sweet violet.

Thenot, convinced of Colin's gifts by this recitation, commented on the folly of giving in to love.

May. Piers and Palinode discussed the corruption of shepherds who neglect their sheep to seek their own profit (indirectly condemning the priests of the time). Palinode, who was discouraged because he could not participate in the spring revels of other shepherds, asked why the good shepherd, the clergyman, should not have a right to the pleasures others enjoy. Piers, who was more serious than his companion, spoke at length about the responsibility of those who care for the flocks. They must, he argued, forsake worldly concerns and trust in God for their living if they are to set a good example for their sheep. He disagreed with Palinode's contention that there is no reason for shepherds to live less pleasantly than anyone else, and, to illustrate the dangers of association with the wicked, he told the familiar fable of the innocent young kid who is duped and carried off by a smooth-talking fox.

June. Colin Clout returned to admire the peaceful life his friend Hobbinol has made for himself in the fields. Hobbinol praised Colin's poetry, but the latter disavowed the possession of any great talents: "But piping low in shade of lowly grove/ I play to please my self, all be it ill."

Colin was content to serve Pan, the god of shepherds; he made no claims to be worthy of the patronage of the Muses. Because his poetic pleas were not powerful enough to pierce the heart of Rosalind, he was forever doomed. He entreated the "gentle shepherds":

Tell the lass, whose flower is woxe a weed,
And faultless faith is turned to faithless fear,
That she the truest shepherds heart made bleed
That lives on earth, and loved her most dear.

July. Thomalin contrasted the simplicity and unpretentiousness of the life of the first shepherd, Christ, and "the brethren twelve that kept yfere the flocks of mighty Pan" with the lavish living of the purple-clad priests of his day. He had recently been shocked to hear of their way of life:

For Palinode (if thou him ken)
Rode late on pilgrimage
To Rome, (if such be Rome) and then
He saw thilke misusage.
For shepherds, said he, there doen lead,
As lords done other where;
Their sheep han crusts, and they the bread;
The chips, and they the cheer.

August. Willy and Perigot contributed alternate lines to a rollicking love lyric, designed to cure Perigot of his melancholy mood, occasioned by an unhappy love affair. When they finished, Cuddie, their judge, recited for them one of Colin Clout's doleful laments to his Rosalind.

September. Diggon Davie returned to the country with news of the miseries he experienced on his travels in the cities, where he found everything filled with greed and corruption. His language was harsh, and his mood was deeply pessimistic. When the shepherds sell their souls to the devil, he argued, their sheep inevitably suffer.

October. Cuddie questioned the value of writing. Even when his work was good, it seemed to bring him little reward. Piers, his older, wiser friend, answered, "The praise is better than the price." He had faith in the didactic effects of poetry:

> O what an honor is it, to restrain
> The lust of lawless youth with good advice,
> Or prick them forth with pleasance of thy vein,
> Whereto thou list their trained wills entice!

He counseled Cuddie to turn to epic, to sing of wars and princes. This kind of poetry, the young man replied, might have been possible in Augustan Rome, where Vergil found willing patrons; in their age, however, there was no climate for poetry. Colin Clout alone might have soared toward the heavens in his verse, but he was the prisoner of love. Piers, a good Platonist, maintained that love had, in fact, freed the poet, given him wings to lift him up out of the "loathsome mire."

November. Colin Clout presented a lament for Dido, a beautiful lady who died young. He spoke first out of deep distress, calling on the muses and all nature to mourn with him. Then the mood changed, and he rejoiced to know that the lady "is installed now in heaven's height," where "lives she with the blessed gods in bliss."

December. Colin reminisced about the carefree days of his youth, the spring of his life, when he climbed trees in search of ravens' eggs and shook nuts from walnut trees and learned the art of song from the good, old shepherd Wrenock. His summer years brought the painful heat of love, which withered his promising poetic talents:

> So now my year draws to his latter term,
> My spring is spent, my summer burnt up quite,
> My harvest hastes to stir up Winter stern,
> And bids him claim with rigorous rage his right.

Colin found himself old and ready to leave the world, and he concluded with a farewell to his art, his flocks, and his friends.

Critical Evaluation:

A new age in English poetry began with the anonymous publication in 1579 of *The Shepheardes Calender*, by Edmund Spenser. The work is a collection of twelve pastoral poems or eclogues, with themes familiar from the time of Vergil: the song contest, the elegy, the lament of the scorned lover, criticism of corruption in church and state. Much of the lasting value of *The Shepheardes Calender* is in its language, the skillfully varied verse forms, the rich imagery of some parts and the direct rustic simplicity of others.

Renaissance Christian humanism generally makes use of the best of classical pagan literature and philosophy, reading it allegorically, or rewriting it as allegory, to teach Christian culture and morality. Spenser engages in this philosophical appropriation more thoroughly, skillfully, and audaciously than any other English poet. *The Shepheardes Calender*, although the work of a young poet just developing his art, startles readers with its political and personal verve and ambition. If Spenser aimed at reforming the state and clergy with his satire, he also aimed at establishing his poetic reputation and gaining court patrons to support and protect him. That he succeeded in these two aims is one of the reasons *The Shepheardes Calender* has remained a landmark in English literature.

Most of Spenser's poetry can be enjoyed for its beauty but exists for the allegory that shapes it. In emulation of Vergil, Spenser begins with youthful pastoral poetry in preparation and anticipation of writing a national epic. *The Shepheardes Calender* contains in embryo many features of *The Faerie Queene* (1590, 1596): fulsome, calculated idealization and praise of Elizabeth; veiled criticism of some of the queen's policies; self-conscious construction of Spenser's own public identity as a poet-prophet; allegorical commentary on contemporary political issues; imitation of classical and continental poetic models; praise of the native English tradition of poetry, and use of archaic language in imitation of Chaucer; love poetry with Petrarchan posturing; didactic purpose of moral reform of church and state; and allegories of poetic identity and inspiration.

Many mysteries haunt the poem, chief among them the identity of the ubiquitous and prolix commentator, "E. K." Knowing E. K.'s identity might enable the reader to know whether E. K.'s frequent obtuseness is unintentional ignorance or a deliberate strategy to obscure some of Spenser's more dangerous criticism of Elizabeth. All that is known about E. K. is that E. K. is a humanist scholar, a bit of a pedant, and eager to promote both Spenser and his friend Gabriel Harvey. Whether E. K. is Spenser or not, his presence is one of Spenser's tactics in an inventive, tireless campaign of self-promotion.

E. K.'s introductory epistle, headnote "arguments" (summaries), and "glosses" (commentary) on each eclogue add another layer in a text already rife with speaking personae. *The Shepheardes Calender* is typically Elizabethan in the complexity of the voices in the text. The allegory and the textual apparatus complicate these matters, but in deliberate and meaningful ways. Most twentieth century critics have read the shepherd speakers as instruments of Spenser's project to create a place for himself in court politics, hyperconscious of how Elizabeth and her powerful counselors and churchmen might react to his words.

The July eclogue provides an example of Spenser's simultaneous caution and audacity. It seems to begin with a debate between the Roman Catholic and Protestant views of holiness and sainthood, but it moves into a more specific and politically charged allegory of Archbishop Edward Grindal's fall from power. Queen Elizabeth had ordered the suppression of Bible study meetings ("prophesyings") among the clergy, fearing they would become hotbeds of Puritan opposition to the official English church. When Grindal defied Elizabeth's orders, she divested him of his power and sequestered him in his home for the remaining seven years of his life. The eclogue's tone and other sources provide strong evidence that Spenser admired Grindal's moral fortitude in standing up to the queen in a matter of conscience. Nevertheless, Spenser shows considerable daring when he has the shepherd speaker Thomalin report that an eagle (symbol of imperial power) dropped a shell on the head of the gentle shepherd "Algrind," an anagram of Grindal's name.

Even more shocking is Spenser's insertion of his opinion into the fiery and perilous debate over Elizabeth's possible marriage to a French Catholic. Many Protestants feared the reestablishment of a Catholic regime, but it was dangerous to castigate the queen too directly for her attentions to her French suitor. A pamphleteer, aptly named Stubbs, had recently lost his right hand as punishment for criticizing the proposed marriage too vehemently, and the pamphlet's printer, Hugh Singleton, had narrowly escaped the same fate. We can only marvel at his and Spenser's courage when, a month after Stubbs's painful public humiliation, Singleton printed *The Shepheardes Calender*, which, in however veiled a way, also criticized the potential marriage. This subtle criticism takes place in the April eclogue, where Hobbinol sings a gushing paean of praise to Eliza, queen of shepherds: Eliza is a goddess of divine descent; she is the fourth Grace; the abashed sun, unable to stand the comparison, retreats from her shining face below; and other Petrarchan conceits. In the midst of this overdone praise, he stresses her virginity and her marriage to England—an implicit denunciation of marriage to a foreign power. Perhaps it is too much to say that such allegorical fables participate in a sustained, underground resistance to Elizabeth's increasing chokehold on public discourse as her reign went on, but these strategies of covert commentary are, in some way, a response to censorship.

The metaphor of the shepherd and his flock points to another key dimension of the poem. In addition to being a commentary on the politics of Spenser's day, the poem may be read as a Christ-centered expression of personal commitment. Yet the image of the Good Shepherd himself, sometimes in the figure of Pan, informs the text. Algrind, for example, in the July eclogue teaches humility, sacrifice, and self-denial, and practices these in imitation of Jesus. If Spenser, in his poetry, acts as political reformer, he also acts as witness to what he sees as God's self-revelation in the person of the Christ.

"Critical Evaluation" by James David Schiavoni

Bibliography:

MacCaffrey, Isabel. "Allegory and Pastoral in *The Shepheardes Calender*." ELH 36, no. 1 (March, 1969): 88-109. Insightful discussion of how Spenser integrates the mode of allegory into the pastoral genre. Offers a sensible working definition of allegory.

Miller, David L. "Authorship, Anonymity, and *The Shepheardes Calender*." *Modern Language Quarterly* 40, no. 3 (September, 1979): 219-236. An early poststructuralist analysis of the poem and its ambitions. Argues that Spenser deliberately created a poem that would stake his claim as a major poet.

Nelson, William. *The Poetry of Edmund Spenser: A Study*. New York: Columbia University Press, 1963. A concise, insightful introduction to the poem and its place in Spenser's career and in English literary history.

Sacks, Peter J. *The English Elegy: Studies in the Genre from Spenser to Yeats*. Baltimore: The Johns Hopkins University Press, 1985. Excellent analysis of Spenser's use of the elegy form in the context of the elegiac tradition in English poetry. Discusses the genre as a literary expression of the psychology of grief and consolation.

THE SHIH CHING

Type of work: Poetry
Compiler: Confucius (K'ung Ch'iu, c. 551-479 B.C.E.)
First transcribed: Twelfth century B.C.E. (English translation, 1875)

The earliest repository of Chinese verse, the *Shih Ching* (or *Book of Poetry* or *Book of Songs* or *Book of Order*) contains 305 poems of both folk and court origins. The court poems are more or less ceremonial in character, designed to be sung at sacrifices, to accompany the dances and feasts in honor of dynastic ancestors, or to adorn such formal occasions as receptions, banquets, chases, and archery contests. The folk songs comprise love lyrics of various kinds, epithalamiums, complaints, satires, elegies, and georgics.

Almost all the poems in the *Shih Ching* were composed in the pre-Confucian period of the Chou dynasty (c. 1122-222 B.C.E.). In the ceremonial odes the wisdom and prowess of its founders—the kings Wen and Wu and the Duke of Chou—are frequently recalled, although a few pieces, hardly of greater antiquity, celebrate the splendid achievements of even earlier dynasties, the Hsia and the Shang. According to a now discredited tradition, Confucius was the compiler of this anthology and rejected nine-tenths of the 3,000 poems then extant; but the canon must have been well fixed by his time, and diplomats and scholars even then knew the poems by heart, quoting them on every conceivable occasion to display their literary attainment or political sagacity. It is easy to see why the court poetry—so vital to the discharge of religious and state functions—should have been saved, but the early preservation of so much folk poetry is a more curious matter. In the absence of better explanation, one must accept the tradition that the Chou kings made a point of collecting the popular ballads of their many vassal states and using them as a political barometer to gauge the happiness or discontent of the populace. All the poems in the *Shih Ching* were meant to be sung, but the tunes were already lost by the time of the Han dynasty (206 B.C.E.-220 C.E.).

The anthology, as it exists today, is divided into four sections: *kuo feng*, the smaller and greater *ya*, and *sung*. While *kuo feng* are the folk songs of the vassal states and both *ya* and *sung* may be indifferently translated as odes, the divisions are hardly clean-cut. Many of the poems in the category of the smaller *ya* are apparently folk songs, and some of the greater *ya* poems are little differentiated from the religious and dynastic odes of the *sung* section. As documents of ancient China, the folk songs and courtly odes are of great historical and anthropological interest. To these, scholars owe the first mention of the sage kings and mythical heroes, the coherent presentation of the animistic beliefs of the early Chinese regarding ancestor worship and the adaptation of human labor to the cyclic changes in nature, the precise details of many a religious and state ritual, and the intimate evocation of the life of a simple people of great emotional integrity: their courtships and marriages, their work on the farm, and their much-detested military service. On the strength of the love poems alone, the French sinologist Marcel Granet reconstructed a fascinating picture of mating customs and fertility rites in the dawn of Chinese history.

Historical considerations aside, the *Shih Ching* is primarily poetry and should be read as such. Confucius once told his disciples, "My children, why do you not study the Poetry? Poetry will stimulate your emotions, help you to be more observant, enlarge your sympathies, and moderate your resentment of injustice. It is useful at home in the service of one's father, abroad in the service of one's prince. Furthermore, it will widen your acquaintance with the names of birds, beasts, plants, and trees." One is hardly surprised that Confucius attached great importance to the *Shih Ching* as a guide to good conduct and a manual of useful information; in ancient Greece, the study of Homer was urged on similar grounds. The poetry, aside from its great social and ceremonial utility, also mentions by name about seventy kinds of plants, thirty kinds each of trees, beasts, and birds, ten kinds of fish, and twenty kinds of insects. The book is a virtual catalog of the more common flora and fauna of the then Middle Kingdom. There are not many other sources for study of ancient China in which such a variety of information is so readily available.

If one reads Confucius correctly, the key message in his little speech above attests his awareness of the humanizing influence of poetry, its power to regulate and refine emotions, to enlarge sympathy. To Confucius, *li* (ritual, etiquette), music, and poetry constitute an inseparable triad. While *li* is designed to bring out the best qualities of people in their everyday social intercourse as well as on the formal occasions of rejoicing and mourning, Confucius is also aware that there is an excess of emotion in people that cannot be rendered in terms of ritual or etiquette. To him, therefore, *li* is the approximation of the ideal and poetry, the expression of the actual, although, as in much of the *Shih Ching*, poetry can be an integral part of a ritualistic occasion. Music is closely allied to ritual and poetry because it serves the dual function of supporting courteous behavior and facilitating the expression of one's true feelings.

To the modern reader, the more vital portion of the *Shih Ching* is surely the folk songs—160 *kuo feng* poems plus many others—because they speak the universal language of one's actual feelings. These songs are quite simple in structure, a series of short rhymed stanzas. The basic unit is the four-word line, and the closing line of each stanza is usually a refrain. Within the simple structure of each poem, however, a little drama unfolds itself. As in all ballad poetry, the poet seldom speaks in person: The speaker may be a woman awaiting her lover by a ford (the wading of a creek or shallow river by a couple may be a symbol of marital engagement), or detaining her lover in bed while the dawn is breaking, or telling her story of woe after her husband has been pressed into military service or has deserted her. The speaker may be the lover who tosses and turns all night in bed thinking of his girl, who takes a walk by the eastern gate and sees women shining like clouds but still prefers his own choice, a modest woman of "plain cloth and gray kerchief." In other poems the speaker is the soldier who climbs a barren hill and acutely misses his kinsfolk; the exile who, seeing the yellow birds pecking in the fields, is seized with the sudden impulse to return home; the farmer who thinks of migrating to another state because the large rats in his fields remind him of the greater rapacity of the officials. This dramatic quality is one reason why the folk songs have a universal appeal and a perennial charm about them.

Another source of poetic appeal is the language. The diction of the *Shih Ching* has an archaic flavor that adds immeasurably to the meaning of the poems. The folk songs, especially, have retained a pristine quality because the simple emotions that they embody are clothed in a language beyond the contamination of modern idiom, beyond the corrosion of time. The language has another strength that is characteristic of Chinese poetry in general: its elliptical density. In a four-word line there is absolutely no room for decoration, for syntactical connectives; each word must have a maximal poetic weight and suggestiveness to merit inclusion.

To a student of English poetry long accustomed to its roses and nightingales, the *Shih Ching*, with its duckweed and dolichos, mulberry and date trees, magpies and orioles, cicadas and locusts, presents a distinctively new landscape. In almost every folk song, nature is an integral part of the human situation: The mulberry tree is shedding its leaves upon the ground and the woman thinks of her state of desertion; ripe plums are dropping from the tree and presently there will be only three left on the boughs, and the woman wonders if she will ever have a lover, because she, too, is ripe for love. The lovers, farmers, and soldiers in the folk songs are so physically close to nature, there is seldom any need to resort to simile or explicit metaphor. The strategy of correspondence, or objective correlative, is characteristic of the *Shih Ching*.

In view of the later development of Chinese poetry, the love songs and complaints appear especially important. Such conventional themes as the separation of husband and wife, the poverty of peasants, the evils of officialdom and war, and the appropriate moods induced by seasonal changes were all first embodied in the *Shih Ching*. The work has remained unsurpassed in its depiction of love. Whereas the later poets, with the exception of an exquisite few, adopt the mask of the forsaken or forlorn woman more or less as a literary convention, the Chinese women in the *Shih Ching* speak out unafraid in the spontaneity of the natural, unashamed womanhood. By contrast, Chinese women of subsequent history, confined in the home and disallowed the privilege of free social intercourse with men, appear sad and dull indeed.

Bibliography:

Dobson, W. A. C. H. *The Language of the Book of Songs*. Toronto: University of Toronto Press, 1968. A grammar of the language of the *Book of Songs* with useful discussions of the linguistic characteristics of each of its four divisions. Argues that the poems derive from different periods.

Legge, James. *The She King*. Volume 4 of *The Chinese Classics*. Reprint. New York: Oxford University Press, 1961. Provides a rich source of materials for the critical reader who can excuse Christian interpretations for Chinese ideas, and who can enjoy stories without needing strictly factual scholarship. Includes translation, notes, and history of the text.

Van Zoeren, Steven. *Poetry and Personality: Reading, Exegesis, and Hermeneutics in Traditional China*. Stanford, Calif.: Stanford University Press, 1991. Principles of interpretation of the text, as they have changed over two thousand years, with a focus on the Mao school and the codes by which the text may have been written and read.

Yeh, Shan. *The Bell and the Drum: Shih Ching As Formulaic Poetry in an Oral Tradition*. Berkeley: University of California Press, 1974. Includes index to references to the 305 poems. Argues composition by oral tradition and formulaic stock phrases, that the work is poetry not because of originality but because of the totality of its cultural associations.

Yu, Pauline. "The Book of Songs." In *Masterworks of Asian Literature in Comparative Perspective*, edited by Barbara Miller. Armonk, N.Y.: M. E. Sharpe, 1994. Best and simplest short discussion of the work. A useful introduction for teaching. Includes topics for discussion and a view of translations of the text.

SHIP OF FOOLS

Type of work: Novel
Author: Katherine Anne Porter (1890-1980)
Type of plot: Allegory
Time of plot: August 22-September 17, 1931
Locale: Aboard the North German Lloyd S.A. *Vera*, at sea
First published: 1962

Principal characters:

JENNY BROWN, a young American painter
DAVID SCOTT, another painter, with whom Jenny lives
MARY TREADWELL, an American divorcée returning to Paris
DR. SCHUMANN, the ship's elderly doctor
LA CONDESA, a middle-aged déclassé noblewoman, formerly resident in Cuba
WILHELM FREYTAG, a young German businessman

The Story:

Many people of various nationalities waited in the heat of Veracruz, Mexico, on August 22, 1931, to board the North German Lloyd S.A. *Vera*, scheduled to arrive at Bremenhaven, Germany, on September 17. Some had urgent errands to perform before embarkation, while others simply killed the time. An elderly professor and his wife, the Huttens, shared their lunch with their fat bulldog; a shrill, obnoxious young woman, Lizzi Spkenkieker, strode about with a little pig-snouted man, Siegfred Rieber; a solitary Swede, Arne Hansen, expressed indignation over the behavior of Mexican revolutionaries; a German couple, the Baumgartners, hushed their young son, dressed in a hot leather riding costume; an American girl in slacks, Jenny Brown, strolled aimlessly with her boyfriend, David Scott; four pretty Spanish girls with their young men, a small *zarzuela* company, prowled through the streets and shops with disobedient six-year-old twins, Ric and Rac; a middle-aged American woman, Mrs. Treadwell, incredulously considered a painful bruise on her arm, inflicted in the street by a beggarwoman.

Aboard the *Vera* Dr. Schumann, the ship's elderly physician, watched passengers mount the gangplank: a hunchbacked dwarf, Herr Glocken, who had sold his newsstand in Mexico City; a dying old man in a wheelchair, Herr Graf, pushed by his young nephew, Johann; a young Mexican woman with her baby and their Indian nurse; two Mexican priests; a Texan youth, William Denny, who continually leered at the Spanish girls; a German Jew, Herr Lőwenthal, lugging a samplecase containing Catholic religious articles; and a beautiful bride and groom on their honeymoon. When the combined freighter-and-passenger ship set sail, the passengers examined the facilities and settled into their cramped cabins. Dinner at the captain's table that evening, presided over by Dr. Schumann, was served to a select German group, which included the Huttens, Lizzi Spkenkieker and Herr Rieber, two elderly widows traveling alone, and Wilhelm Freytag, a presentable young German in the oil business. They ate and drank with pleasure and spoke joyfully of their return to their fatherland.

During the first pleasantly monotonous days of the voyage, both friendly and hostile encounters occurred among the passengers as they became acquainted. Jenny's discreet flirtation with Herr Freytag angered David; Lizzi's loud vulgarity annoyed her cabinmate Mrs. Treadwell; the Huttons and their dog suffered from severe seasickness; Herr Baumgartner embarrassed his family by failing to control or hide his chronic alcoholism; Jenny befriended her cabinmate, an unattractive Swiss teenager returning home with her parents, hoping there to marry. Herr Löwenthal, seated apart in the dining room, cautiously sought amicable conversations with approachable gentiles.

When the *Vera* docked in Havana, many disembarked to amuse themselves on shore while new passengers were taken aboard. Deported from Cuba to their native lands because of a market failure, 876 Spanish sugarfield workers were crowded into steerage, where inadequate accommodations and inhumane conditions awaited them. Six Cuban students made themselves conspicuous by singing "La Cucaracha" endlessly. A mysterious Spanish countess, deported as a dangerous revolutionary by Cuban authorities, aroused considerable curiosity: About fifty, she remained beautiful, dressed elegantly, and adorned herself with jewels; Dr. Schumann treated her nervous disorder with drugs which she habitually used.

As the *Vera* pursued its course toward Germany, the passengers discovered more about each other's personal histories and private lives, and their early affinities and animosities deepened. Many of the Germans voiced anti-Semitic attitudes; Freytag confided to Mrs. Treadwell that his wife was Jewish—a confidence she later betrayed; Ric and Rac threw things overboard, including the Huttens' bulldog (a woodcarver in steerage lost his life saving it); the quarrels of Jenny and David threatened their already unstable relationship; Dr. Schumann and the countess resigned themselves to the futility of the love which had arisen between them; and the young bride and groom floated about the ship blissfully untouched by all these matters.

To celebrate the last night of the voyage, the *zarzuela* troop organized a fiesta designed to affront and insult the fundamental dignity of all the passengers. During this grotesque masquerade, not attended by Dr. Schumann, the dancers usurped the captain's table for themselves; Herr Glocken sported a pink necktie bearing the words "Girls, follow me!"; and the drunken Herr Baumgartner led the children in a Nazi goose-stepping march. The guests dispersed to seek their private pleasures and despairs in fights, amorous encounters, confrontations, or reconciliations. Johann lost his virginity to a Spanish prostitute, for a high price; Mrs. Treadwell, mistaken for a prostitute, hit a passenger in the face with the heel of her shoe. The next morning the passengers, behaving as if nothing unusual had taken place, faced one another with indifferent and incommunicative faces, disembarking at Bremerhaven with their illusions apparently intact, fully expecting to create happiness for themselves by fashioning new lives in other countries.

Critical Evaluation:

For more than three decades, Katherine Anne Porter was renowned for her mastery of short narrative fiction, but only toward the end of her career did she direct her artistry toward the more extended form of the novel. Impressions she retained of a voyage from Veracruz to Bremerhaven in 1931 remained vivid in her mind and, in 1942, began to assume the shape of a complex and intricate work that would reflect her perception of the general spiritual decay of Western civilization during the twentieth century. She formulated an appropriate design for her vision after reading Sebastian Brant's fifteenth century moral allegory *Das Narrenschiff* (1494). The writing progressed slowly, and the book was not completed until 1962. Her *Ship of Fools* enjoyed an immediate popular success and established her reputation firmly as a novelist of vision, of imagination, and of compelling virtuosity.

The theme of the work is stated in a short notice preceding the text, in which Porter explains that the *Vera* (meaning "truth") represents the ship of this world on its voyage to eternity, and the passengers include all humankind on its journey through life. *Ship of Fools* has no conventional plot or unfolding dramatic action; there is no "story" in the traditional sense. Instead, Porter devises nearly forty almost equally vivid and unforgettable characters, of different ages and nationalities, drawn from all walks of life, whose interactions during the voyage reveal truths about the nature of human beings and the human condition and whose behavior reflects common human responses in typical everyday situations.

Porter adopts an omniscient point of view as narrator, which permits her to look directly into her characters, overhear their thoughts, and understand their motivations, urges, and humiliations. Cultivating a classical style of remarkable purity comparable to that of the novelists Henry James and Gustave Flaubert, she employs plain and simple words to formulate sentences of striking rhetorical beauty, which either are concise and direct in their thrust or reveal their meaning gradually as they flow through a series of carefully balanced and modulated dependent clauses. She achieves an extraordinary blend of subtlety and intricacy of thought with simplicity and directness of expression, without ever sacrificing her long-trusted ideal of pristine clarity.

Porter paints a bleak picture of human nature in the book, for rarely does one find instances of kindness or compassion aboard the *Vera*. Base inclinations and mean desires underlie the motivations of most of the characters most of the time. Many people are shown to be merely selfish, greedy, and unconsciously indifferent to their fellows; a few seem to be fundamentally evil at heart, taking pleasure in the suffering of others and occasionally wishing them still greater ill. Animal imagery, often referring to ugly, murderous, or repulsive activities, is appropriately applied to the characters throughout the book as metaphorical judgments upon their indifferent, inhuman, or brutal behavior.

Among the thirty-odd passengers closely observed aboard the *Vera*, a handful are more intrinsically appealing than the others, less mean-spirited, more good-hearted and pleasant. Jenny Brown (a satirical self-portrait of Porter's own youth), entangled in a frustrating relationship with David Scott, seeks her identity as a person and as an artist, expecting new experiences to bring her closer to true spiritual fulfillment. David, arrogant about his talent and maturity, resents her rivalry, twisting their relationship, almost unwillingly, into one of mutual antagonism. Mary Treadwell (another self-caricature) is sensitive and compassionate but harbors an inner reticence that blocks the expression of her feelings for others and causes her to appear cold and aloof. Wilhelm Freytag, ostracized after his marriage to a Jewess is revealed, hides from truth behind a mask of politeness and genteel civility. Dr. Schumann, a deeply religious man threatened by a heart condition, is the most admirable person on the ship. His compassion, illustrated frequently during the voyage, suggests a possibility of hope for humankind's future. His love for La Condesa, expressed tentatively but unmistakably, reflects both tenderness and self-control; she, on the other hand, experiences her love for him as a deeply emotional, unrestrained and nonrational, passion.

Although Porter's sojourn in Germany in the early 1930's provided her with substantial material that she incorporated into the novel to expose the Nazi mentality during its formation, persons of other nationalities are represented as similarly guilty of moral irresponsibility and spiritual decay: Comparable nationalist attitudes, racial biases, and social prejudices are revealed among Americans as well as Germans. Those not actually committed to evil still contribute passively to its augmentation by their silent tolerance or calm indifference. They observe criminal behavior and do nothing, though they may condemn it privately in hushed whispers. The 876 deportees in steerage are looked upon with simple or contemptuous curiosity by those who deign to notice them at all. These representatives of all the suffering lower-classes of the world accept their degradation with patience and stoical endurance, and it is a member of this class, a carver of small wooden figures, who performs the only heroic act during the voyage: He gives his life by leaping into the sea to rescue the Huttons' drowning bulldog. In Porter's view, all the passengers, whether through complacency or turpitude, share responsibility for the moral decadence which the entire book illustrates.

Raymond M. Archer

Bibliography:

Hardy, John Edward. *Katherine Anne Porter*. New York: Frederick Ungar, 1973. Contains interpretations of Porter's major fictional works, with a very good chapter on *Ship of Fools*, though some of the biographical information is inaccurate.

Hendrick, George, and Willene Hendrick. *Katherine Anne Porter*. Rev. ed. Boston: Twayne, 1988. A thorough and well-written overview of Porter's life and fiction, with a chapter on *Ship of Fools*.

Unrue, Darlene Harbour. *Truth and Vision in Katherine Anne Porter's Fiction*. Athens: University of Georgia Press, 1985. A comprehensive and detailed study of Porter's work, written on an advanced level but readable and perceptive.

______________. *Understanding Katherine Anne Porter*. Columbia: University of South Carolina Press, 1988. An excellent beginner's source for analysis of all Porter's major works. Clearly and simply written by an important scholar. Excellent annotated bibliography.

Warren, Robert Penn, ed. *Katherine Anne Porter: A Collection of Critical Essays*. Princeton, N.J.: Prentice-Hall, 1979. Contains an interview (1965) and seventeen essays, many of which deal with *Ship of Fools*.

THE SHOEMAKER'S HOLIDAY
Or, The Gentle Craft

Type of work: Drama
Author: Thomas Dekker (c. 1572-1632)
Type of plot: Comedy
Time of plot: c. 1413-1422
Locale: London and the nearby village of Old Ford
First performed: 1600; first published, 1600

Principal characters:
SIMON EYRE, a London shoemaker
HODGE,
FIRK, and
RAFE, his employees
SIR ROGER OTLEY, Lord Mayor of London
ROSE OTLEY, his daughter
SIR HUGH LACY, the Earl of Lincoln
ROWLAND LACY, his nephew
MARGERY, Simon Eyre's wife
JANE, Rafe's wife

The Story:

Rose Otley, daughter of the Lord Mayor of London, Sir Roger Otley, and Rowland Lacey, nephew to Sir Hugh Lacy, the Earl of Lincoln, were deeply in love. With evident irony, proud Sir Roger declared to Sir Hugh that he could not presume to have his daughter marry above her station. With equal pride, Sir Hugh ironically countered that because of Rowland's dissolute ways it would be far better for Rose to marry a substantial young London businessman. Rowland, who had toured Europe, where he had learned the shoemaker's trade in Germany, was given a command in the army of King Henry the Fifth, who was preparing to invade France. Sir Hugh wanted Rowland off to France as soon as possible, so that the youth might forget Rose Otley.

Rowland had other ideas. Claiming pressing business in London, he turned his command over to his cousin, Askew, after promising that he would join his unit in Normandy, if not in Dover. When the troops assembled to leave London, Simon Eyre, a shoemaker, pleaded to no avail with Rowland to allow Rafe Damport, his drafted journeyman, to stay home with his new bride, Jane. Rafe, resigned to going to the wars, gave Jane as a farewell gift a pair of shoes that he had made for her.

Meanwhile Rose, confined to her father's house at Old Ford, a London suburb, sent her maid Sybil into the city to seek information about Rowland. Rowland, determined to win Rose, disguised himself as a German shoemaker. Singing a German drinking song, he sought work at Simon Eyre's shop. When Simon refused to consider hiring Rowland, Simon's workmen, charmed by Rowland's broken speech, threatened to leave. Rowland, as Hans Meulter, was taken on.

While hunting near Old Ford, Hammon and Warner, two London citizens, pursued a deer into the Lord Mayor's estate. There they encountered Rose and her maid. Hammon fell in love with Rose and Warner lost his heart to Sybil. Sir Roger, welcoming the young hunters, decided that Hammon was just the man to marry Rose.

Rowland, through his friendship with a German sea captain, speculated in a valuable unclaimed ship's cargo, to the enormous profit of Simon, his employer. As a result of this venture Simon was made an alderman, and the genial shoemaker seemed destined for even greater city honors. Sir Hugh, meanwhile, had learned from a servant that Rowland was not in France. Ashamed of his nephew, Sir Hugh sent the servant into the city to discover Rowland's whereabouts.

When Hammon confessed his love, Rose at first dismissed him coyly; finally she declared that she intended to remain single. Even though Sir Roger threatened to force Rose into the match, the offended and impatient Hammon returned to the city. In London, Sir Hugh's servant could learn nothing of Rowland's whereabouts, even though he inquired at the shop of Simon Eyre.

Simon, grown affluent and popular, continued to advance upward in political rank. To the amusement of Simon's journeymen, Firk and Hodge, his wife Margery assumed pretentious manners. Rafe, having been wounded in France, returned to London. Seeking his wife, he wept to learn that Jane had left the Eyre household, where she had been a maid to Margery Eyre, and had not been seen since. The Eyres—Simon was now High Sheriff—visited Sir Roger at Old Ford, where Simon's employees, Rowland among them, performed a morris dance. Rose recognized Rowland in spite of his disguise and drank a toast to him.

Jane, also grown quite independent because of her ability as a seamstress, was courted by Hammon. In his desperate attempt to seduce her, he showed her, to her disbelief, Rafe's name on a casualty list from France. Sorrowfully, she promised Hammon that if she ever remarried she would accept his proposal. Rose, knowing of Rowland's presence in the city, returned to her father's town house and arranged to have Rowland see her on the pretext of fitting a pair of shoes. At the shoe shop, a servant brought in a shoe and ordered that a pair of similar size be made in time for a wedding which was to occur the next day. Rafe recognized the shoe as Jane's; he learned from the servant where the ceremony was to take place.

Roland, as a shoemaker, went to see Rose and talked to her under the eyes of Sir Hugh, who was looking for his nephew, and Sir Roger, who declared to Sir Hugh that he had not seen the young man. When Sybil revealed that Rose meant to marry the German cobbler, Sir Hugh gloated, thinking that Rowland would never be able to marry this middle-class girl. Sir Roger, who secretly had hoped that Rose would marry Sir Hugh's nephew, was furious. At the same time Firk delivered a pair of shoes for Rose and misled the two men into believing that Rose and the German cobbler would marry the next day at the church where Hammon and Jane planned to be married. Sir Hugh, to his alarm, suddenly realized that the cobbler must be his nephew Rowland.

Simon, now Lord Mayor but still his lusty, simple self, declared his gratitude because Rowland had helped him to affluence and promised that he would help the young people to become husband and wife. The next day Dame Eyre accompanied the young couple to the Savoy, while Rafe and his fellow shoemakers, armed with cudgels, encountered Hammon and Jane in front of St. Faith's. Hammon resented the intrusion of the base craftsmen; Jane was filled with misgiving at the sight of Rafe, whom she had believed dead. Hammon patronizingly offered Rafe twenty pounds to relinquish his claims to Jane. Rafe, insulted, would have thrashed Hammon, but he was prevented from doing so by his lameness. Expecting to apprehend Rose and Rowland, Sir Hugh and Sir Roger had waited, too, in front of St. Faith's. Word reached them there that Rose and Rowland had been married at the Savoy.

Lord Mayor Simon Eyre gave a breakfast for all London apprentices; he himself was served by men of his own craft. The king pardoned Rowland and blessed him and Rose. When Sir Hugh and Sir Roger protested the match, the king explained that love was not a respecter of blood. To crown the festivities of Simon's Lord Mayorship, the king granted the shoemakers the privilege of holding two market days a week in the newly-built Leadenhall Market, and accepted Simon's invitation to him to be the guest of honor at a banquet.

Critical Evaluation:

Thomas Dekker, an Englishman of probable Dutch descent, was a true son of London, as his plays, and especially *The Shoemaker's Holiday*, attest. Happy in its blending of quasi-history and ordinary London life, this plot contains young lovers, noblemen, solid merchants, artisans, and even a king. Surely the theme and treatment gave the play wide popularity in Dekker's own day. This drama, with its appeal to patriotic instincts, formed part of the Lord Admiral's Men's answer to the popular history plays being written at the moment by William Shakespeare, who wrote for the Lord Chamberlain's Men. Dekker derived his plot from a prose tale, *The Gentle Craft*, published in 1597 by Thomas Deloney.

The first performance of *The Shoemaker's Holiday* was given for Queen Elizabeth's court. At that time the drama scene in London was experiencing a state of transition; the earlier romantic style of Greene and Lyly now seemed superficial and escapist, but the darkly realistic comedies of Jonson or the later Shakespeare had not yet been written. As comic drama, *The Shoemaker's Holiday* is an excellent example of the transitional period that produced it. Dekker possessed an uncanny talent for mingling realism and romanticism, and this, his first extant play, belongs to two strikingly contradictory literary currents. On the one hand, *The Shoemaker's Holiday* is probably the best illustration of romantic comedy that readers have. Yet, at the same time, subtle, but frequent, realistic touches make the play an effective tool for discussing the transition in English comedy from romance to realism which can be pinpointed as occurring roughly at the beginning of the seventeenth century.

The tone of exuberance—zest for life—that filters through *The Shoemaker's Holiday* may reflect the youthful Dekker who wrote the play. Though he lived for another generation, he never wrote anything better than this early comedy. A poet at heart, Dekker collaborated in writing more than thirty plays and was known as a hack. He was in and out of debtor's prison much of his life.

The play's realistic undercoating—found in the street scenes and whenever the shoemakers are onstage—suggests that even at an early age Dekker was already aware of the dramatic possibilities of realism in comedy. Realism became increasingly evident in his later plays, especially *The Honest Whore* (1604-1605).

The romantic essence of *The Shoemaker's Holiday* may well lie in the absence of a palpable evil, of really dangerous villains in the play. In terms of the genre, it exhibits all the motifs and thematic conventions of romantic comedy. The standard theme of "rival wooers," for example, is carried out through Rowland and Rose and, in the subplot, by Rafe and Jane. Dekker carries the theme through its conventional turns as the true love between these couples is blocked by disapproving and uncomprehending guardians or by circumstances beyond their control, and finally, as they are each in turn separated and then joyfully reunited.

A second major convention is the gentility theme, the idea that true nobility is inborn, not simply inherited. The gentility theme weaves its way through all romantic comedy plots, and it is best displayed in *The Shoemaker's Holiday* by the dignity and pride with which Simon Eyre approaches humble labor. The most succinct statement of the theme also belongs to Eyre:

"Prince am I none, yet nobly born." In Act V, King Henry, whose role is to rectify all the play's complications, makes the gentility theme rule supreme as he chides Lacy's uncle for thinking Rose not noble enough to marry Rowland: "Lincoln, no more. Dost thou not know that love respects no blood, Cares not for difference of birth or state? The maid is young, well born, fair, virtuous, A worthy bride for any gentleman."

Other stock features of romantic comedy in this play are the disguises (Rowland becomes Hans the shoemaker), the song and dance of the morris dancers, and the use of mythic machinery and folklore. Eyre's blazingly quick rise to fortune and fame is perhaps the most romantic touch of all. Dekker's romantic plot is firmly wedded with realistic manners and scenes, a combination reminiscent of Geoffrey Chaucer. During the transition years of 1598 to 1603, comedies began catering to a rising interest in actual city types, and Dekker's choice of Simon Eyre as the central character of his play reflects an innovative turn. Although Eyre is on stage during less than half the scenes, and although the action of his plot involves no conflict, it is his characterization that sets and to a large extent controls the mood of the play. His occupation as shoemaker is definitely a step away from the more aristocratic leanings of Lyly and Greene and reflects a growing bourgeois audience's increasing interest in itself.

More central to the success of Eyre's characterization is its break from the traditional and the stereotyped, for he seems to be a living character. Perhaps the most memorable thing about the play is its brisk, workaday-morning mood of healthy, goodhearted, and not overly sensitive people. Eyre's personality combines with that of his lively shoemakers, his shrewish wife, and Rowland and Rose, to present a copious picture of London life.

The extent of Dekker's realistic touches is indicated by the fact that the play refers specifically to thirty-five landmarks within a radius of three miles of the city. The references reveal that the playwright is mirroring the London of his own time, and not Simon Eyre's time of a hundred and fifty years earlier. Dekker is not careful to avoid anachronisms; but, if comic realism is defined as the frequent interjection of material familiar to the audience—bits of current speech, little natural touches of everyday environment, or references to well-known but ordinary people, Dekker's treatment is clearly realistic.

There is also evidence that the Rose-Rowland story has a parallel to real people and real situations contemporary to Dekker. Sir John Spencer, actual Lord Mayor of London, had forbidden his daughter to marry her chosen lover. He gained notoriety by hiding his daughter so she could not run away and by mistreating her so badly that the law was finally invoked to place her in the custody of an uncle. All of this happened in the months directly preceding the first performance of Dekker's play. Although the stingy Spencer is more an antithesis of the generous Eyre, the comparison offers another intriguing parallel between the play and the time in which it was written.

Dekker's inveterate interest in dialect (Irish, Welsh, French, Spanish, thieves' Latin, and Dutch) may reflect a foreign background, and that may help explain the uncannily perceptive realistic touches imposed on the play. A partly foreign eye can sometimes pick out cultural characteristics that a native observer is blind to. Dekker's best scenes—early morning in Tower Street, Eyre's election to the shrievalty, the party at Old Ford, Jane in the shop, Firk outwitting Otley and Lincoln, the "stir" outside St. Faith's, and the pancake feast at Leadenhall on Shrove Tuesday—demonstrate his ability to see continuity in London life throughout the ages, an ability by which he creates in *The Shoemaker's Holiday* an atmosphere of old and merry England at its jolliest.

"Critical Evaluation" by Jean G. Marlowe

Bibliography:

Dekker, Thomas. *The Shoemaker's Holiday*. Edited by R. L. Smallwood and Stanley Wells. Manchester, England: Manchester University Press, 1979. An edition whose comprehensive introduction places the play in its biographical, historical, and literary context. Also discusses Dekker's use of sources, analyzes the work, and reviews its stage history.

Kaplan, Joel H. "Virtue Holiday: Thomas Dekker and Simon Eyre." *Renaissance Drama* 2 (1969): 103-122. A study of the main character, who rises rapidly from shoemaker to Lord Mayor of London through luck and his expansive good nature. Demonstrates how Eyre's rhetorical skills enhance his pervasive social influence.

Mannheim, Michael. "The Construction of *The Shoemaker's Holiday*." *Studies in English Literature, 1500-1900* 10 (1970): 315-323. An analysis of how Dekker, with apparent ease, unifies his several plots, focusing on the central importance of an attack the playwright has Simon Eyre level at the courtiers in the third act.

Price, George R. *Thomas Dekker*. Boston: Twayne, 1969. One of the few generally available biographical and critical book-length studies of Dekker's plays (including collaborations) and nondramatic works. Especially useful is the discussion of Dekker's social attitudes and the concluding overall assessment of his achievements.

Toliver, Harold E. "*The Shoemaker's Holiday*: Theme and Image." In *Shakespeare's Contemporaries*, edited by Max Bluestone and Norman Rabkin. 2d ed. Englewood Cliffs, N.J.: Prentice-Hall, 1970. An examination of how Dekker presents at once a realistic and romanticized view of London life. Shows how the playwright offers remedies for human faults that cause social deficiencies.

A SHROPSHIRE LAD

Type of work: Poetry
Author: A. E. Housman (1859-1936)
First published: 1896

In 1896, the high point of what has been variously called "the yellow 'nineties" and "the Beardsley period," Victorian poetry was at a low ebb. Alfred, Lord Tennyson and Robert Browning were both dead; Algernon Charles Swinburne had long since retired to Putney. The Pre-Raphaelite movement had subsided. Thomas Hardy was still known only as a novelist. The minor poets seemed stereotyped into two groups: those who, like Oscar Wilde, produced "Swinburne and water" and those who wrote frail imitations of the French of Paul Verlaine. The only new and original talent was that of Rudyard Kipling, who had already published his two most famous volumes. Yet despite Kipling's vigor, the spirit of the age was best represented by *The Yellow Book* and Aubrey Beardsley's illustrations for Alexander Pope's *The Rape of the Lock* (1712). It was in this atmosphere of "purple patches and fine phrases" that there appeared *A Shropshire Lad*, a slender volume containing sixty-three short poems—some only eight lines long—written by the Professor of Latin at University College, London.

Twenty-six years later, in a short preface to his second volume, *Last Poems*, Housman gave some hint of the circumstances attending the composition of *A Shropshire Lad*. He said that most of the poems had been written "in the early months of 1895" and under a "continuous excitement." Exactly what he meant by this last phrase has never been quite clear; indeed, his biography, apparently so uneventful, presents some little mystery. Oddly enough for a man who was to become one of the greatest Latinists in the English-speaking world, he did not take honors in his final examinations at Oxford, and as a result he apparently went through a period of depression. The cause of the "continuous excitement" that resulted in *A Shropshire Lad* remains to be satisfactorily explained.

The reader coming upon the poetry of Housman for the first time will be immediately aware of its extremely narrow range. The poet limited himself to but one theme: the brevity and tragedy of life and the inevitability of death. Spring and youth are beautiful, but they pass quickly, just as the blossoms "stream from the hawthorn on the wind away." People must expect neither happiness nor justice during the brief span allotted to them; life is cruel and filled with injustice. Misfortunes are, however, the common lot of humankind, for, as he wrote in *Last Poems*,

> The troubles of our proud and angry dust,
> Are from eternity, and shall not fail.
> Bear them we can, and if we can we must.
> Shoulder the sky, my lad, and drink your ale.

Humans have no one but themselves to depend on; their own strength must see them through their troubles. They do not have even the hope of immortality, as Horace said in the ode that Housman translated, "pulvis et umbra sumus—we are dust and dreams." Yet the grave, when finally won, brings peace: "Turn safe to rest, no dreams, no waking."

The influence of Housman's classical studies on his own poetry is difficult to measure, and yet it is apparent. Years devoted to the careful editing of texts gave him, if nothing else, a feeling for precise workmanship; the terseness of the Latin language contributed to the characteristic brevity of his poems. Indeed, there is much that might be called "Roman" about his poetry, and it could even be claimed that the following lines of Catullus sum up most of what he had to say:

Soles occidere et redire possunt:
Nobis cum semel occidit brevis lux,
Nox est perpetua una dormienda,
(Suns may rise and set again.
For us, when our short light
Has set, remains no more than sleep
Through one perpetual night.)

That aspect of Roman stoicism that remained in the imagination of subsequent centuries, that "quality of emotional self-restraint," is apparent also in Housman's work and marks it off sharply from the mass of Victorian poetry. There was paganism enough in some of the late nineteenth century poets, but it took the form either of the wild riot of Maenads, Bassarids, and other mythological fauna so dear to Swinburne or of the soft Epicureanism of Edward FitzGerald's 1859 translations of Omar Khayyám verses. A paganism deriving from Roman stoicism and based on restraint, on acceptance of the inevitable tragedy of life, on the idea that "life is never worth preserving at the cost of dishonor," was something quite different. It should, further, be remembered that the patriotism expressed in some of these poems was one of the pagan virtues.

Housman's tragic view of life and his preoccupation with death (particularly with death by hanging) have been criticized by some as artificial. It did not seem plausible that a man whose own existence was so secure could genuinely have viewed life so gloomily, but Housman tried to make his readers aware that the tragedies of which he wrote were "not mine, but man's." He was also criticized for cultivating certain mannerisms of language. It is, for example, true that the lines describing the football game: "The goal stands up, the keeper/ Stands up to keep the goal," sound like an unconscious parody of his own style.

Although Housman declared that "the most poetical of all poets is Blake," he elsewhere stated that the great influences on his own work had been William Shakespeare's songs, the Border ballads, and the poems of Heinrich Heine. Poem 8 in *A Shropshire Lad* shows how he used ballad material; in *Last Poems*, the second stanza of "Sinner's Rue" is a translation of Heine's "Am Kreuzweg wird begraben." Yet the most important effect of the three influences was that of compression. He himself felt that "poetry is not the thing said but a way of saying it," and that "to transfuse emotion . . . is the peculiar function of poetry." His own taste was romantic; he derived his critical judgments from Matthew Arnold, whose dislike for eighteenth century poetry he shared. Nevertheless, the opinions he expressed in his lecture "The Name and Nature of Poetry" (1933) are sometimes curiously at variance with his practice.

As late as 1922 it was still possible for Holbrook Jackson to list Housman among the minor poets of the 1890's. Since then his reputation, which rests chiefly on the 104 short poems in his first two volumes, is as secure as that of any English poet between the Victorians Tennyson and Browning, and the twentieth century masters William Butler Yeats and T. S. Eliot.

Bibliography:

Graves, Richard Perceval. *A. E. Housman: The Scholar-Poet*. New York: Charles Scribner's Sons, 1980. An outstanding critical biography, which connects Housman's work as a Latin scholar and teacher with his poetry, most particularly with *A Shropshire Lad*.

Leggett, B. J. *Housman's Land of Lost Content*. Knoxville: University of Tennessee Press, 1970.

A good overview of *A Shropshire Lad* with close readings of individual poems. Considers carefully the themes of change, loss, and the quest for permanence in Housman's poetry. Includes an excellent bibliography.

_____________. *The Poetic Art of A. E. Housman: Theory and Practice*. Lincoln: University of Nebraska Press, 1978. A reevaluation of Housman's place in the canon of modern poetry. *A Shropshire Lad* is the core work discussed in evaluating Housman's relationship to modern critics such as C. Day Lewis and T. S. Eliot. Housman's own works of criticism are considered in the light of his poetry.

Marlow, Norman. *A. E. Housman, Scholar and Poet*. Minneapolis: University of Minnesota Press, 1958. Considers influences on Housman's poetry and focuses in particular on *A Shropshire Lad*. Examines the influence of Greek and Latin poetry, Shakespeare, the Bible, John Milton, Alfred, Lord Tennyson, Heinrich Heine, Rudyard Kipling, Dante Gabriel Rossetti, and Andrew Lang, as well as folk influences such as border ballads and folk songs.

Page, Norman. *A. E. Housman: A Critical Biography*. New York: Schocken Books, 1983. Discusses Housman's poetry, especially *A Shropshire Lad*, as a special strain divorced from everyday life although influenced by it. Shows that Housman's poetry was written and revised over long periods and therefore difficult to correlate with his life.

THE SICKNESS UNTO DEATH

Type of work: Philosophy
Author: Søren Kierkegaard (1813-1855)
First published: Sygdommen til Døden: En christelig psychologisk Udvikling til Opbyggelse og Opvaekkelse, af Anti-Climacus, 1849 (English translation, 1941)

Søren Kierkegaard gave *The Sickness unto Death* the subtitle "A Christian Psychological Exposition for Edification and Awakening," and he used the pseudonym "Anti-Climacus" when it appeared. Walter Lowrie, in an introduction to his translation of this work, calls *The Sickness unto Death* "one of the most important productions of that most productive period" of Kierkegaard's life. The subtitle and the pseudonym reflect not the wit and eccentricity of a pedant but the conscience and intellect of a modest, though self-assured philosopher in the service of God. The "sickness unto death" that Kierkegaard reveals in his psychological exposition—in so forceful a manner that the work has affected the course of modern philosophic thought—is the sickness of a self that wills to tear itself away from the Power that constituted it.

According to Kierkegaard, human beings are in despair, which they may not recognize, because they are always critically "sick unto death." For a spirit in such a condition, death is no escape; the sickness is "unto death" precisely because it is a despairing longing for death—not for extinction alone but for the experience of not being the self that one is. It is as if human beings were longing for the experience of death—an impossible experience because death, as death, is the end of all experience. Because the self is not content to be itself; because it is not content to relate itself to God; and because it cannot be satisfied with extinction, the result, in Kierkegaard's view, is "the sickness unto death."

Another way of understanding Kierkegaard's account of this dreadful malady of the spirit is through a consideration of what he means by health. Kierkegaard maintains that "to have a self, to be a self, is the greatest concession made to human beings, but at the same time it is eternity's demand upon them." Yet the self is a relation between the infinite and the finite, the temporal and the eternal, freedom and necessity—and as a relation, a synthesis, the self cannot exist before the synthesis is achieved. For that reason, there is some sense in which, as Kierkegaard claims at the outset, "human beings are not yet self": They have not achieved a synthesis with God, with the Power that constituted them. Sickness is this alienation; health is the elimination of despair, achieved when the self, recognizing its dependence on the Power that constituted it, wills itself to be itself.

By using language other than Kierkegaard's in the attempt to understand the book's central thesis, it is possible to say that Kierkegaard is arguing that human beings, considered not as animal but as a spirit, can realize themselves only by admitting that they become something worthy of the name "self" when they accept the whole of their condition. This acceptance of limitations, of opposing powers, even of God's eminence, is not resignation; it is a willingness to live "no matter what" and to be what human beings are in the world as it is.

It is tempting to make Kierkegaard's thesis broader than it is, to argue that the great Danish philosopher has more sense than to suppose that significant acts are possible only by relating the self to God. The term God is, however, not a convenient symbol for power; for Kierkegaard God is the power that relates itself to every spirit and makes possible, through the self's acknowledgment of that relation, the existence of every self.

Atheistic existentialists have found much that is helpful to them in Kierkegaard, but only by eliminating all references to God. Philosophers such as Jean-Paul Sartre are interested in arguing that in humans "existence precedes essence" and that only through action can human beings "make themselves" into some particular self. "Authentic" existence is not given to human beings, but they can create themselves by the life they choose and live. For Kierkegaard also, health of the spirit is possible whenever people choose to be themselves—but only because to be themselves they must relate themselves to God. For Sartre, by contrast, health of the spirit consists not in relating to God, but in recognizing the self's freedom from all such dependent relations. Sartre writes of the nausea and anguish that grip a human being who recognizes creative responsibility, but for Kierkegaard anguish is the condition of a self that is not yet a self, of a self that tries to escape from God and, consequently, from itself.

The despair that is the sickness unto death may take any one of three forms: It may be the despair of not being conscious of having a self; it may be the despair of not willing to be oneself; or it may be the despair of willing to be oneself.

If human beings are in despair, how can they fail to be conscious of it? Kierkegaard asserts that those who are primarily sensuous can be in despair without being conscious of their condition. Those individuals "live in the sensuous categories agreeable/disagreeable, and say goodbye to truth." People who are sensuously happy will resent any attempt to take happiness from them; they refuse to acknowledge the despair that is deep within them. This form of despair—unconscious despair—is the most common. Since the sickness of not being willing to be oneself before God is sinful, it is important that all who are in the anguish of dread come to be conscious of that dread as the first step toward creating a self that is a synthesis. Kierkegaard defines sin as "before God, or with the conception of God, to be in despair at not willing to be oneself, or in despair at willing to be oneself." Both kinds of despair are eliminated by being willing, before God, to be oneself.

The formula that enables someone to escape the sin of dread is, at the same time, a definition of faith: "By relating itself to its own self and by willing to be itself, the self is grounded transparently in the Power that constituted it." The opposite of sin, according to Kierkegaard, is not virtue, but faith.

To emphasize his conviction that the opposition of faith to sin is a Christian concept that is fundamental to all ethical concepts, Kierkegaard stresses the importance of the qualifying phrase "before God." Human beings come to have a reality, a self, "by existing directly in the sight of God," and because of this, their sin—not willing to be themselves before God—concerns God. Kierkegaard admits that the notion of people being invited to exist before God and of God's being concerned for them is unacceptable to many because it is both strange and demanding. Just as it would be puzzling and disturbing if an emperor were to invite a peasant to be his son-in-law, so it is puzzling and disturbing to suppose that God takes enough interest in individual people to wish to have them come to exist before him. Yet this is the Christian idea, Kierkegaard insists, and it is an idea that illuminates the entire area of ethical being and action.

The despair at not being willing to be oneself is called the despair of weakness, and the despair of willing to be oneself is called the despair of defiance. Such forms of despair result from a concern with self as if the self could exist by itself; this delusion is made possible by an absorption in matters that do not properly concern the spirit—matters of business or pleasure.

The sin of despair may give rise to new sins or to a continuation of sin. One may despair over one's sin, so concentrating attention on it as to make impossible the emergence of faith, or one may despair of being forgiven. In the latter case, sinners choose, out of weakness, to be sinners by rejecting the forgiveness that would enable them to be themselves before God. Finally, one may commit the sin of abandoning Christianity, of declaring it to be false. This sin is "offensive warfare," according to Kierkegaard, and it is a sin against the Holy Ghost.

Kierkegaard's conception of God is often difficult to grasp because he explains the relations between God and humanity in a dialectical way, claiming that one understands either God or humanity only by appreciating the subtle effects that the actions and attitudes of the one have on the other. An interesting feature of his account is his conception of God as a being who "can do no other" than make the possibility of human offense a part of the human condition. Dread must be possible for human beings because God is concerned to allow them the possibility of faith.

The influence of Kierkegaard in modern philosophy can be explained, paradoxically, by reference to the widespread loss of religious faith in later times. Dissatisfaction with unexamined creeds quickly leads to the rejection of those creeds. Human beings are then in anguish over the void they find before them, and the writers tell of "wastelands" and "lost generations." At such a time the existentialists are able to arouse interest by declaring that through action a person creates his or her self; the Christian existentialist turns his attention to God as the factor to which a person must be related in order to be a self, while the atheistic existentialist makes virtues out of lucidity, courage, and action. Of the Christian existentialists, none has been more original and persuasive than Kierkegaard.

Bibliography:

Benoit, Raymond. "Fault-lines in Kierkegaard and Hawthorne: *The Sickness unto Death* and *Ethan Brand*." *Thought* 66, no. 261 (June, 1991): 196-206. An insightful interpretation of the two works based on Kierkegaard's concept of despair and literary uses of religion.

Heiss, Robert. *Hegel, Kierkegaard, Marx*. Translated by E. B. Garside. New York: Dell, 1975. Traces the development of dialectical thought and places Kierkegaard's perspective in that context. Provides an insightful discussion of *The Sickness unto Death* in the light of the dialectical philosophy.

Kierkegaard, Søren. *"Fear and Trembling" and "The Sickness unto Death."* Translated by Walter Lowrie. Princeton, N.J.: Princeton University Press, 1954. An excellent starting point for the study of Kierkegaard's work. The introduction provides historical context for the two works, which complement each other.

Malantschuk, Gregor. *Kierkegaard's Thought*. Edited and translated by Howard V. Hong and Edna H. Hong. Princeton, N.J.: Princeton University Press, 1971. Helpful in understanding Kierkegaard's philosophical method, which is represented by *The Sickness unto Death*.

Sontag, Frederick. "Kierkegaard and the Search for a Self." In *Essays on Kierkegaard*, edited by Jerry H. Gill. Minneapolis: Burgess, 1969. Traces the relationship between the self and existence. Sontag's interpretation of Kierkegaard's concept of the self is particularly useful in understanding *The Sickness unto Death*.

SIDDHARTHA

Type of work: Novella
Author: Hermann Hesse (1877-1962)
Type of plot: Bildungsroman
Time of plot: 563?-483? B.C.E.
Locale: India
First published: 1922 (English translation, 1951)

Principal characters:
SIDDHARTHA, the protagonist, son of a Brahmin
GOVINDA, Siddhartha's friend and follower
KAMALA, the courtesan
KAMASWAMI, the merchant
VASUDEVA, the ferryman
GOTAMA, the historical Buddha

The Story:

Siddhartha was a Brahmin's son. He grew up with his friend Govinda. Handsome, intelligent, and graceful, he was loved by everyone—his parents, friends, society, and especially Govinda. At an early age, he listened to the teachings of his learned father, mastered the required Brahminical texts, performed all prescribed religious rites, and practiced the art of meditation. Govinda admired his friend's superior intellect, strong determination, and high vocation. He knew that Siddhartha would be a great man someday, and he wanted to be his friend and follower.

Siddhartha himself was, however, not happy. His soul was restless. Dissatisfied with what the scriptures had told him, he wanted to experience knowledge himself. An inward voice compelled him to leave the idyllic peace and harmony of his father's home and join the Samanas, a sect of ascetics who lived a life of rigorous austerity in the forests. Govinda followed him like his shadow.

While living with the Samanas, Siddhartha learned many ways of losing the Self. He learned how to mortify his flesh, kill his senses, suppress his ego, and dwell at will in the bodies of dead birds and animals. He soon realized that this flight from the self was only a temporary escape, not a permanent release from the life cycle. Still athirst for self-knowledge, he decided to leave the Samanas and went with Govinda in search of Gotama Buddha.

Siddhartha met Gotama Buddha in the Jetavana grove. He immediately recognized that the Buddha had attained the peace of Nirvana, which he was still seeking. He listened to Gotama's sermon on suffering, the cause of suffering, and the release from suffering through the Eightfold Path. He was impressed by Gotama's enlightened presence, but he was not convinced by his teachings. He concluded that, in order to find Nirvana, one must experience what the Buddha had experienced. He therefore resolved to conquer his self, like the Buddha. Govinda became a follower of the Buddha, leaving Siddhartha to wander alone on his solitary path to self-conquest.

Carrying an indelible impression of Buddha's personal example in his mind, Siddhartha turned to himself and said: "I will learn from myself, be my own pupil; I will learn from myself the secret of Siddhartha." With this resolution, he experienced a new awakening and a sense of aloneness, for he had decided to continue his quest alone and never to look back.

With this awakening, the world of appearance became palpable and real; it was no longer the veil of illusion that concealed the truth. Like a newborn child, he looked at the world with great wonder and curiosity. During the night, as he slept in a ferryman's hut beside the river, he had a strange dream in which he embraced and kissed Govinda, but Govinda turned into a woman. For the first time he felt the stirrings of sexual awakening.

He left the river and reached a large town, where he fell in love with a famous courtesan, Kamala. Kamala told him that he could gain her love only after he earned wealth, power, and prestige, and to help him acquire these things she introduced him to a rich merchant, Kamaswami. With Kamaswami as his instructor in acquiring wealth and Kamala as his teacher in the art of love, Siddhartha began to live in excess and surrendered himself to the world of senses, immersing every cell of his being into desire and carnal pleasure.

One night Siddhartha had a dream that Kamala's rare songbird died in its golden cage and that he took it out and threw it away on the road. Suddenly, he felt sad as if he had thrown away the most valuable thing in his life. Next day, he left Kamala and his life of sensual experience and disappeared into the forest.

During his wanderings through the forest, he came back to the river and yearned to be submerged in death. As he was about to commit suicide, suddenly he heard the holy sound "Om" coming from the depths of his inner being and he recognized the folly of his action. The holy sound awakened his slumbering soul, and he remembered all that he had forgotten. Murmuring Om, he sank into a deep sleep.

On awakening from his long sleep, he found Govinda watching over him, and he felt happy once again. It seemed to him that the river had a special message for him. He therefore wanted to listen to the river and learn from it. To understand the river and its secrets, he decided to remain by the river and become the helper of the old ferryman, Vasudeva. Siddhartha learned deep secrets from the river. He learned that there was no such thing as time past or future. There was only the present, just as the water of the river was in a state of continuous flux and yet it was everywhere at the same time, at its source and in the ocean, always the same. The voice of the river was for him "the voice of life, the voice of Being, of perpetual Becoming."

Many years passed. One day Kamala arrived with some followers of the Buddha. She died in Siddhartha's arms and left with him their son, who had been born after his disappearance. Once again, Siddhartha experienced the pangs of love and lost his benign calm. He tried to win the boy's affection and to keep him, but the son ran away, rebelling against him as he himself had rebelled against his father years before. Vasudeva consoled Siddhartha in his suffering, but the river seemed to laugh at his pain. Vasudeva told him to listen to the river and absorb its lesson. Siddhartha tried to listen more intently and discovered the interconnectedness of all life. From Vasudeva, as from the river, he learned about the unity of all things. After Vasudeva's death, he became the ferryman, radiant and benign like his mentor, his face shining with the serenity of the inner awareness of the unity of all things.

Hearing about the old ferryman, Govinda came to the river to see him. When he looked at the face of Siddhartha, he was reminded of the benign and peaceful smile of the Buddha. At Siddhartha's request, when Govinda kissed him on the forehead, he no longer saw the face of his friend Siddhartha. Instead he saw the multiplicity of all life-forms in various stages of development, even the gods, reflected in his unchanging countenance. He recognized then that, like the Buddha, Siddhartha had attained perfect enlightenment and wisdom. In great reverence and humility, Govinda bowed his head before his old friend and tears trickled down his cheeks.

Critical Evaluation:

One of the major twentieth century writers and an important cultural and intellectual force,

Hermann Hesse was awarded the Nobel Prize in Literature in 1946 for his achievement as a novelist, particularly for his masterpiece, *Das Glasperlenspiel: Versuch einer Lebensbeschreibung des Magister Ludi Josef Knecht samt Knechts hinterlassenen Schriften* (1943; *Magister Ludi*, 1949; also *The Glass Bead Game*, 1969). Hesse has stated, "All the prose works of fiction I have written are biographies of souls." *Siddhartha*, his most widely read work of fiction, is a biography of the soul in the essential sense of the term. It evokes the magical realm of the spirit in exploring the protagonist's quest for self-knowledge and the unity of being.

Hesse called *Siddhartha* "an Indic Poem." Of all his fictional works, it is undoubtedly the one most impregnated with Indian religion and philosophy. Hesse himself unequivocally acknowledged his long-standing interest in India and his preoccupation with Hinduism, Buddhism, Vedanta, and Yoga. "More than half of my life," he stated, "I tried to come to an understanding of the Indian view of Life." India had been his family's spiritual homeland for two generations, and he himself had undertaken a voyage to India in 1911 "to go back into that source of life where everything had begun and which signified the Oneness of all phenomenon." *Siddhartha* was an artistic expression of his understanding of the Indian view of life, modified by his own romantic vision.

Using the historical Buddha's life as a framework of his fictional narrative, Hesse appropriated Buddha's given name Siddhartha for his mythical hero and endowed him with many qualities of the Enlightened One. However, he presented them as two separate figures in the novel and used the encounter between them as a catalyst to reinforce his romantic concept of the *Bildungsroman*. Hesse believed that all knowledge must come from personal experience rather than from formal training and doctrinaire teaching. Siddhartha's rejection of the teachings of Buddha served as a turning point in his quest, fortifying his conviction that, to attain the state of perfect enlightenment, he, too, must extinguish his ego and merge with the unity underlying the universe. That he attains his supreme destiny, Nirvana, through pure disinterested love and self-surrender is confirmed by the novel's conclusion.

Because *Siddhartha* deals with themes of initiation and search for the self and focuses on the emotional, intellectual, psychological, and spiritual development of the protagonist, it can be viewed as a *Bildungsroman*, a novel of growth and education. All the major characters, episodes, and symbols in the novel serve as important milestones in Siddhartha's journey toward self-realization.

The most predominant and the all-inclusive symbol in the novel is the river. The river represents the continuum of life and time, the eternal process of being and becoming, and the constant flux in nature. It defines, divides, entwines, and merges the transitions in Siddhartha's journey and ultimately manifests the cosmic vision of totality and timelessness that he attains at the end of his quest. Siddhartha's vision on the riverbank leads to intuitive wisdom.

Though *Siddhartha*, like all great literature, has a timeless dimension, it had a profound impact on the youth culture in the United States from the 1950's to the 1970's. Its gospel of disinterested love appealed to the American flower children, as its emphasis on self-realization, integration, and wholeness attracted many alienated youth to Eastern religions and philosophies. Many Western youth were in rebellion against the institutionalization, growing materialism, and fragmented, scientific worldview of their own society. Written in a lucid, poetic, rhythmical, symbolic, and dignified style, *Siddhartha* presents the spiritual heritage of the East to the West. It came to be recognized as an important landmark in the history of East-West literary relations.

Chaman L. Sahni

Bibliography:

Boulby, Mark. *Hermann Hesse: His Mind and Art*. Ithaca, N.Y.: Cornell University Press, 1967. Scholarly study of the major novels of Hesse. The chapter on *Siddhartha* provides illuminating information on Hesse's Orientalism. Discusses the work "in the context of Hesse's movement away from Buddhism" and views it as the culminating point of his art as a novelist.

Field, G. W. *Hermann Hesse*. Boston: Twayne, 1970. Contains a critical and analytical chapter on *Siddhartha*.

Otten, Anna, ed. *Hesse Companion*. Albuquerque: University of New Mexico Press, 1977. Eight essays on Hesse's work by various scholars. Theodore Ziolkowski's essay, "*Siddhartha*: The Landscape of the Soul," gives an excellent critical analysis of the novel's Eastern background, plot structure, symbolism, and epiphany. Useful glossary and a bibliography of secondary sources in English.

Shaw, Leroy R. "Time and the Structure of Hermann Hesse's *Siddhartha*." *Symposium* 11 (1957): 204-224. A close reading of the text, demonstrating how Hesse communicates his vision of Unity through an intricate blending of form and meaning. A perceptive and illuminating analysis.

Timpe, Eugene E. "Hesse's *Siddhartha* and the *Bhagavad Gita*." *Comparative Literature* 10 (1969): 421-426. Demonstrates that Hesse was deeply influenced by the *Bhagavad Gita* (c. first or second century C.E.) when he wrote his book and that Siddhartha's quest for self-realization follows the path suggested by the *Bhagavad Gita*.

THE SIEGE OF RHODES

Type of work: Drama
Author: Sir William Davenant (1606-1668)
Type of plot: Historical
Time of plot: 1522
Locale: The fortress at Rhodes and the nearby coast of Caria
First performed: part 1, 1656; first published, 1656; part 2, first performed, 1659; first published, 1663

Principal characters:

SOLYMAN II, THE MAGNIFICENT, Sultan of the Ottoman Empire, 1520-1566
PIRRHUS, the general in charge of the Persian army before the arrival of Solyman
VILLERIUS, PHILIP VILLIERS DE L'ISLE ADAM, commander of the fortress at Rhodes
ALPHONSO, a Sicilian duke
IANTHE, Alphonso's wife
ROXOLANA, Solyman's wife

The Story:

In the fortress at Rhodes, seven bastions were maintained by eight Christian nations as united in opposition to the Turks as were the earlier Crusaders. Villerius, a Knight of St. John in supreme command of those forces, was successfully defending the fort from Solyman's assault. Alphonso, the most vigorous among those defending the Cross from the Crescent, considered this battle Christendom's last stand against the infidel. Ianthe, his bride of but a few months, first aided the war effort by sacrificing her jewels to buy arms, and then decided to become one of history's termagants, or Amazons, and fight by the side of her husband. In her attempt to join him, she was captured by the Turks. Two days later she was released by order of the sultan as a mark of respect to her courage and virtue.

In the battle that followed, Alphonso, mad with jealousy because he believed that his wife had been unfaithful to him with the Turkish ruler, fought with the fierceness of many men. Roxolana, Solyman's wife, also became jealous, so highly was Ianthe praised by her husband. The battle was fought so ferociously, especially by the English, that the infidels were repulsed, forcing the sultan to resort to siege tactics. Honor had been preserved in love and battle by participants on the two sides of the fort.

Famine soon became a threat to the beleaguered garrison. While the leaders debated strategy, the populace demanded that Ianthe sue for peace. Alphonso, recovered from his jealousy, refused to allow Ianthe to be used as a hostage, but she, deciding otherwise in order to save her husband and the garrison from slow starvation, stole secretly away to the sultan's camp. Further misunderstanding ensued when Roxolana learned that Ianthe was in the sultan's tent. In her jealousy she sent a note to the aggrieved warrior-husband, word which caused the entire garrison to deplore the sacrifice of virtuous Ianthe to the supposed lust of Solyman. Ianthe's display of virtue, however, won over the sultana, who was fearful only that her son would not succeed to the throne. Solyman declared that his intentions were always honorable, in love as well as war.

As the palace of Villerius was set on fire at the height of the siege, a last abortive attack was made by the Christians in order to rescue Ianthe. The two young lovers were secretly united by Roxolana. Her husband, moved as much by his wife's compassion for the young couple as by their own virtue and devotion, sent both back to Rhodes, leaving the terms of the surrender entirely to Ianthe's discretion. History has it that a general amnesty ensued and that all the Knights of St. John were allowed free egress from Rhodes.

Critical Evaluation:

The Siege of Rhodes was first performed in London in 1656, probably in early September, during the regime of Oliver Cromwell, the great Parliamentarian general who had defeated the forces of King Charles I in the English civil war. Cromwell himself is said to have enjoyed stage plays, but his Puritan supporters most certainly did not. In fact, some years before Cromwell came to power, pressure from conservative religious factions had led Parliament to pass an act closing London theaters and prohibiting the public performance of all "Spectacles of Pleasure." William Davenant was thus forced to present *The Siege of Rhodes* on a cramped, makeshift stage in the rear of Rutland House, the private home where he was living at the time. As a further means of avoiding government sanction, Davenant published his play a month before it was performed, with a title page announcing it as "A Representation by the Art of Prospective in Scenes, and the Story sung in Recitative Music." Thus a drama was passed off as a type of dull recital, a spectacle, perhaps, but without pleasure. Davenant's strategy seems to have worked, for *The Siege of Rhodes* proved a popular success and performances continued without official interference.

Over the next seven years, which saw Cromwell's death and the restoration of monarchy in the person of Charles II, Davenant was an incredibly busy figure in the London theater world. During this period of intense activity, his best-known play underwent a series of complex, confusing, and seldom-discussed transformations, making it difficult even for scholars of the period to know exactly to which play the title *The Siege of Rhodes* refers in any given context.

These transformations began in 1659, when the original was reprinted (with several changes and additions) and was staged at the Cock-Pit Theatre together with a second play, a continuation of the first, titled *The Siege of Rhodes, Part II*. Following the Restoration in 1660, the ban on theatrical entertainments was completely lifted and Davenant became manager of the Duke of York's acting company and owner-manager of the new playhouse in Lincoln's Inn Fields. On opening night in June of 1661, *The Siege of Rhodes, Part I* was revived, and was presented in alternate performances for some eleven days with *Part II*. To add to the confusion, part I and part II were printed together in 1663, with yet more changes. Existing records indicate no performances of either play after 1677.

In spite of its confusing history, however, and in spite of the fact that it is a play that is seldom read and never performed, *The Siege of Rhodes* will always occupy an important place in any account of the Restoration theater. The reasons for this, oddly enough, have virtually nothing to do with the play's literary merits. *The Siege of Rhodes*, rather, will always be known as a play of "firsts": It was the first English play in which movable scenery was employed and the first English play in which an actress appeared on stage playing a female role. It was the first "heroic" play in English as well as England's first opera. The play's music has been lost and the question of which lines were sung in the manner of operatic arias and which recited remains open.

Davenant based the events of his play on the 1522 siege of Rhodes by the forces of Sulieman the Magnificent, sultan of the Ottoman Empire from 1520 to 1566. Davenant's principal source for these events was Richard Knolle's *The Generall Historie of the Turkes* (1603), which gives an inspiring account of the six-month siege in which 5000 Christian defenders (including an international force of 600 Knights of St. John) heroically resisted a combined Turkish force numbering more than 200,000 before finally surrendering. Davenant seems also to have been influenced by several French writers, in particular Madeline de Scudéry. Her work was quite probably a source for both the romantic elements and the general heroic tone given character and action in the play.

Providing the dramatic cornerstone of both parts of *The Siege of Rhodes* is the story of Alphonso, a young Christian nobleman visiting Rhodes who remains to defend the city, and his wife of only a few months, Ianthe, who sails to Rhodes to join her husband. Ianthe's two vessels are captured by the Turkish fleet, and Ianthe is brought to Solyman. Duly impressed by Ianthe's beauty, courage, and virtue, the Turkish sultan orders the release of her ships and commands that she be safely escorted to Rhodes. In the revised version of part 1, the character of Roxolana, Solyman's wife, is introduced, allowing Davenant to develop the theme of jealousy. Part 1 ends somewhat inconclusively, with Alphonso and Ianthe reunited, but with a great battle raging in the background. As a result of the physical restrictions of the original Rutland House stage, the battle was suggested by a painted scene of a "general Assault" and probably—as indicated by stage directions in part 2—by a "Symphony expressing a Battail." In part 2, Davenant continues the essential action, with the siege again serving as background to the Alphonso-Ianthe love story, while bringing into sharper focus the conflict between love and honor that became typical of "heroic" drama. The role of Roxolana is greatly expanded, and she and Ianthe are brought together on stage, with Ianthe emerging even more dramatically as an example of the redemptive power of Christian virtue. Part 2 ends with the final reuniting of Alphonso and Ianthe and with Solyman's gracious and noble treatment of the defeated Christians.

Coming to any final judgment of *The Siege of Rhodes* is made difficult by time and circumstance. On the page, Davenant's language seems hopelessly turgid even by seventeenth century standards, and his characters are at best one-dimensional contrivances. Yet contemporary accounts make clear how thoroughly Restoration audiences enjoyed *The Siege of Rhodes*, and one can readily imagine how a modern audience might enjoy the pomp, spectacle, and music of Davenant's play. The play offers much theatrical entertainment.

"Critical Evaluation" by Michael Stuprich

Bibliography:

Bordinat, Philip, and Sophia B. Blaydes. *Sir William Davenant*. Boston: Twayne, 1981. The best place to begin a study of Davenant and his work. An account of Davenant's life and times is followed by discussions of his major works. Annotated bibliography.

Edmond, Mary. *Rare Sir William Davenant*. New York: St. Martin's Press, 1987. Besides playing a pivotal role in the re-establishment of the London theater following the English civil war, Davenant led a fascinating, multifaceted life. Edmond's biography (the first since the 1930's) provides a solid account of that life as well as a useful discussion of *The Siege of Rhodes*.

Hedback, Ann-Mari, ed. Introduction to *The Siege of Rhodes*, by Sir William Davenant. Uppsala, Sweden: University of Uppsala, 1973. A modern edition of *The Siege of Rhodes*. The textual scholarship is impeccably thorough, and the introduction provides the finest available discussion of the play.

Powell, Jocelyn. *Restoration Theatre Production*. London: Routledge & Kegan Paul, 1984. A delightful study of Restoration drama. Contains a brief but very helpful discussion of *The Siege of Rhodes*.

Summers, Montague. *The Playhouse of Pepys*. London: Kegan Paul, Trench, Trubner, 1935. A chapter on Davenant includes a helpful account of *The Siege of Rhodes*.

THE SIGN OF FOUR

Type of work: Novel
Author: Sir Arthur Conan Doyle (1859-1930)
Type of plot: Detective and mystery
Time of plot: 1888
Locale: London
First published: 1890

Principal characters:
SHERLOCK HOLMES, a crime investigator
DR. JOHN WATSON, his friend
MARY MORSTAN, a client
THADDEUS SHOLTO, an art collector
JONATHAN SMALL, an escaped convict

The Story:

Miss Mary Morstan went to Sherlock Holmes and Dr. Watson with something of a mystery. Her father, formerly an officer in an Indian regiment, had sent her word from London that she was to meet him at a certain hotel. When she kept the appointment, her father failed to appear, and he had not been heard from in the ten years elapsed since that time. His only known friend in England had been Major Sholto, a brother officer, but that gentleman had disclaimed any knowledge of Morstan's presence in London. For the past six years, Mary Morstan had received one large and valuable pearl on a certain date each year. That morning, she had received a note asking her to meet the writer at a certain spot near a theater. She was to bring two friends if she liked, but not the police. Apprehensive and puzzled, she turned to Holmes for help.

Holmes and Dr. Watson eagerly accepted the assignment, Holmes from a need for excitement, and Dr. Watson from a newly kindled love for the young girl. When the three people kept the appointment at the theater, they were met by a coachman who drove them some distance and then deposited them in front of a house in a long row of new, dreary houses of the same design. Inside they were met by Dr. Thaddeus Sholto, the son of Major Sholto, who told them a strange and frightening story that their father had told him and his twin brother shortly before the major died.

In India, Morstan and Major Sholto had come upon a large fortune that Sholto had brought back to England. When Morstan arrived in London, where he had planned to meet his daughter, he had called on Major Sholto. In a disagreement over the division of the treasure, Morstan was stricken by a heart attack, fell, and struck his head a mortal blow. Fearing that he would be accused of murder, Major Sholto had disposed of the body with the help of a servant. On his deathbed, Major Sholto had wanted to make restitution to Morstan's daughter and had called his twin sons to his side to tell them where the treasure was hidden. As he was about to reveal the hiding place, however, he saw a horrible face staring in the window, and he died before he could disclose his secret.

On the following morning, his sons found the room ransacked and on the dead man's chest a piece of paper bearing the words "The Sign of Four." The two brothers differed over their responsibility to Mary Morstan; Thaddeus wanted to help her, and his twin wanted to keep everything for themselves should the treasure be found. It was Thaddeus who had sent her the pearl each year, their father having taken the pearls out of the treasure chest before he died.

The day before his meeting with Mary, Holmes, and Dr. Watson, Thaddeus had learned that his brother had found the treasure chest in a sealed-off portion of the attic in their father's house. Thaddeus declared his intention to take Mary and the two men to his brother and force him to give the girl her share of the wealth. When they arrived at the brother's house, however, they found him murdered and the treasure gone. It was a baffling case, for the door to his room was locked from the inside and the wall to the window impossible to scale. Nevertheless, Holmes found certain clues that led him to believe there had been two accomplices, one of whom had pulled the other up through a trapdoor in the roof. He also ascertained that one of the men had a wooden leg and the other had exceedingly small feet.

During the ten years since Morstan's death, various notes had been found with the names of four men on them, the only English name being that of Jonathan Small. Many of the notes were signed "The Sign of Four," the words that had been written on the paper left on the late Major Sholto's body. Using this clue and the evidence found in the murder room, Holmes went to work. He believed that Jonathan Small was the key to the mystery, and he tracked Small to a steam launch. After a harrowing chase on the river, Holmes caught up with him. Before Holmes could overtake Small, however, he had to kill the little man with the small feet. About to be taken, Small emptied the treasure into the river. After his capture, he told a story that unraveled the mystery.

When he was a young man, Jonathan Small had fled from home because of trouble over a girl. He had joined the army and had gone to India. Soon after his arrival there, he lost a leg to a crocodile. His accident necessitated a wooden leg, and he was invalided out of the army. For a time, he worked on a plantation. When the natives staged an uprising, he accidentally came upon a treasure chest filled with precious jewels. Three natives, his partners in the discovery, swore loyalty to one another and called themselves The Four. After the uprising, the four men were imprisoned. In order to escape, they had entrusted their secret to Morstan and Major Sholto, and Sholto had taken charge of the treasure until the others could reach safety. Major Sholto, however, had tricked his confederates; his treachery had resulted in Morstan's and his own conscience-stricken deaths. Holmes had been right in assuming that Small had left the paper with "The Sign of Four" written on it. Small had escaped from prison and made his way back to England with a native companion, the man with the small feet. After Major Sholto's death, he had waited until the son found the treasure. Small had not intended violence, but his companion had murdered young Sholto with a poison splinter before Small could enter the locked room by means of a rope suspended through the trapdoor.

The rest of the story was known by Holmes. Small, attempting to escape the country with the treasure, had dumped it into the river rather than part with it. To Dr. Watson, the loss was a happy circumstance, for he could now tell Mary Morstan of his love for her. He would not do this while he thought her an heiress. Mary accepted his proposal, and the happy pair received the good wishes of Holmes. As for Holmes, he preferred the stimulation of mystery to the stimulation of love.

Critical Evaluation:

Although considerable dispute exists as to the relative merits of the fifty-six short stories in the Sherlock Holmes series, there is a general agreement among most critics and fans as to the rating of the four Holmes novels. *The Sign of Four* is usually placed second to *The Hound of the Baskervilles* (1902) and solidly ahead of *A Study in Scarlet* (1887) and *The Valley of Fear* (1915). *The Sign of Four* is praised for its picture of Holmes in action and the ingenuity of the initial puzzle for its evocation of the atmosphere of London in the 1880's, for its sharp delineation of character, and for its dramatic effectiveness. It is sometimes faulted, however, for a plot too closely reminiscent of Wilkie Collins' *The Moonstone* (1868), a solution that comes too early in the narrative, and for Jonathan Small's overly long confession. Critic Julian Symons is probably right in his opinion that the main problem in both *A Study in Scarlet* and *The Sign of Four* is that "they could have been condensed into short stories."

Although *The Sign of Four* may seem too long, it still contains some of Sir Arthur Conan Doyle's best writing as well as all the elements that have made the Holmes stories so popular and entertaining. Indeed, the more leisurely structure of the novelette, if unnecessary for the substance of the events described, does allow for a fuller treatment of such "incidentals" as character development, general background, colorful digressions, and atmosphere—"peripheral" elements that are essential to the Holmes stories and that go a long way toward explaining their durability and universality.

One evident reason for this long-standing popularity lies in the characters of the principals and their unique relationship. Perhaps Doyle's most important contribution to the detective story was his "humanizing" of the detective. Edgar Allan Poe's C. Auguste Dupin is little more than a disembodied intellect. Wilkie Collins' Sergeant Cuff is more personable but considerably less skillful. Émile Gaboriau's two early examples, M. Lecoq and Père Tabaret, are ingenious detectives and amiable fellows, but they have almost no distinguishing personal traits. Sherlock Holmes is both an extraordinary investigator and a sharply delineated character, and his relationship with Dr. Watson is the one of the first distinctive partnerships in novelistic crime fighting.

The most obvious characteristics of Holmes are his incredible powers of observation, deduction, and induction (despite what he says, most of Holmes's conclusions are arrived at by induction, not deduction; that is, he draws answers from a mass of small details). This talent is demonstrated again and again in unraveling the most exotic and obscure crimes. Holmes's procedures are always the same: first, his close examination; next, the set of conclusions; and, finally, the minute "elementary" explication. Usually, in the opening passages, Holmes "practices" on the client's superficial characteristics and then, as the substance of the story, he applies his extraordinary talents to the major problem of the narrative. In novels, such as *The Sign of Four*, there is usually a sequence of problems; as Holmes unscrambles one puzzle, the solution points to a new, more sinister one, and this continues until the entire problem is finally solved and the malefactor brought to justice.

Nevertheless, there is more to the Sherlock Holmes stories than ingenious problem solving. If it was Wilkie Collins who originated the practice of "humanizing" his detective by giving him eccentric traits and hobbies (Sergeant Cuff grows roses), it was Doyle who perfected the technique. He supplies Holmes with a wide range of sidelines and interests: beekeeping, violin playing, opera, boxing, toxology, swordplay, food, theater, tobacco ash, and many others. Holmes, however, is no Renaissance man. He prides himself on large areas of total ignorance: art, philosophy, literature, astronomy, and politics, to name a few. The unifying factor is that all of Holmes's diverse knowledge and talent goes into the solving of intricate problems. Holmes is, finally, a monomaniacal rationalist who feels lost without a challenging intellectual puzzle. That is why, he tells Watson near the beginning of *The Sign of Four*, when he is without a case, he must resort to drugs: "Hence the cocaine. I cannot live without brainwork. What else is there to live for? Stand at the window there. Was ever such a dreary, dismal, unprofitable world? . . . What is the use of having powers, Doctor, when one has no field upon which to exert them?"

Thus, although Holmes is infinitely more interesting, he is, like Poe's Dupin, an intellectual freak. "You are an automaton," Watson tells him, "a calculating machine. . . . There is something positively inhuman in you at times." All in all, Holmes is a genius, detached from common society, even a Nietzschean "superman" who has chosen to use his extraordinary powers in the service of humankind, not so much from a sense of justice (although he has a strong one), but out of a need to use those abilities to fight the triviality and meaninglessness of everyday existence. Much of Holmes's long-term popularity comes from the fact that, as an "outsider," Holmes excites the popular imagination, but, as a defender of the status quo, he is ultimately reassuring.

Given the detective's one-sidedness, however, Holmes would be grotesque if he were presented alone. That which really humanizes Holmes is Dr. John Watson. If Holmes is the "superman" and "outsider," Watson is the ordinary professional man, astonished by his friend's capacities but aware of his human imperfections. Watson is neither a slavish worshiper of genius, like Dupin's narrator, nor an amiable drunk, like Father Absinthe, who assists Gaboriau's M. Lecoq. If Watson has little talent for deduction, he is not the blustering fool of many Holmes motion pictures. When Holmes says "a client is to me a mere unit, a factor in a problem," Watson recoils. To Watson, clients are people to be helped, and it is through the good doctor that readers establish their own emotional connection to the characters. Doyle almost always centers his crime on a personal or family situation, and the fate of the people involved is as important as the solving of the puzzle. Because of this, Watson is every bit as important as Holmes.

This relationship is most evident in *The Sign of Four*, which is, in addition to a mystery, a love story in which Watson meets the client, Mary Morstan, falls in love, courts her, and, with the resolution of the problem, wins her. Doyle adroitly weaves this romance in and around the mystery story and deftly shows Watson's emotional reactions without distracting from the main line of detection. The fact that Watson pursues a bride while Holmes chases a criminal adds an extra dimension and flavor to the story as well as sharpening and deepening our picture of Watson as a man. Although his behavior, under the influence of his feelings for Mary, may occasionally be a bit foolish, his actions are admirable and resourceful. He never forgets the main problem, and he assists Holmes in his solution with considerable skill and courage. Readers must admire his resolute determination to rescue the fortune for Mary despite the fact that it will doom their romance. Therefore, when Jonathan Small throws the jewelry into the Thames, readers are glad, since it will enable Watson to realize his romantic ambition.

The Sign of Four has all the ingredients of the best Holmes puzzles: a peculiar situation, a tentative revelation that leads to further enigmas, a vivid London environment that leads to an exotic setting, and, most important, a spectacular and bizarre crime that can be explained only through the most elaborate and imaginative deductions. Mary Morstan's initial problem is strange enough to immediately seize a reader's attention, but it does not become truly threatening until readers are involved with the Sholto family and the sinister events that surround them.

The actual crime, the killing of Bartholomew Sholto, is a variation of the "locked room" murder situation so dear to the hearts of mystery story fans in general and "Sherlockians" in particular. The bizarre quality of the murder is further emphasized by the discovery of "a long dark thorn stuck in the skin just above the ear," the marks of a "wooden stump," and a set of footprints "half the size of an ordinary man."

As soon as these exotic clues are enumerated, however, they lead Holmes directly to Jonathan Small and Tonga, his dwarfish native accomplice. Unfortunately, the novel is at this point little over half-finished. The rest is divided between Holmes's pursuit of the malefactors and a long statement by the villain, Jonathan Small, explaining the events leading up to the crime. The thwarted efforts of Holmes and Watson to track down Small and Tonga with a lumbering mixed-breed dog named Toby are amusing, Holmes's skill in accurately predicting Small's escape route and his strategy in tracing him are impressive, and the final boat chase on the Thames is exciting. Added to all of this is Small's confession, which gives the reader a fascinating villain who is both repulsive and sympathetic. Since the major mystery is already solved, however, all of this is anticlimactic. Once readers have seen Holmes's brilliant mind cut through the tangle of clues and ambiguities that surround Sholto's murder to identify the killers, their methods, and their motives, the other events are superfluous.

"Critical Evaluation" by Keith Neilson

Bibliography:

Carr, John Dickson. *The Life of Sir Arthur Conan Doyle*. New York: Harper, 1949. Because it is based on a thorough perusal of Doyle's private papers by one of the masters of the craft of mystery writing, it is considered the definitive biography.

Doyle, Arthur Conan. *The Annotated Sherlock Holmes*. Edited by William S. Baring-Gould. 2 vols. New York: Clarkson N. Potter, 1967. This work is a veritable cache of information on Victorian England carefully compiled by one of the leading Holmes scholars. It is of particular interest because the bibliography includes references to a number of articles from *The Baker Street Journal*, the official publication of the "Baker Street Irregulars," an organization dedicated to the study of the cases of Mr. Sherlock Holmes.

____________. *Memoirs and Adventures*. Boston: Little, Brown, 1924. While this autobiography leaves many matters untouched and many questions unanswered, it does provide a valuable insight into the life and works of the author at the end of his career.

Farell, Kirby. "Heroism, Culture, and Dread in *The Sign of Four*." *Studies in the Novel* 16, no. 1 (Spring, 1984): 32-51. An interesting study which concentrates on the parallels in the story, especially that between good and evil.

Jaffe, Jacqueline A. *Arthur Conan Doyle*. Boston: Twayne, 1987. An excellent brief introduction to Doyle's life and especially to his works. Two chapters, "The Beginnings of a Modern Hero: Sherlock Holmes" and "The Return of Holmes," deal with Doyle's detective fiction. At the end of the work there is a short but useful bibliography.

THE SIGNIFICANCE OF THE FRONTIER IN AMERICAN HISTORY

Type of work: History
Author: Frederick Jackson Turner (1861-1932)
First published: 1894; revised and enlarged, 1920 as *The Frontier in American History*

On July 12, 1893, an annual meeting of the fledgling American Historical Association was held in Chicago to coincide with the Columbia Exposition. The exposition celebrated the four hundredth anniversary of Christopher Columbus. A man from Wisconsin, Frederick Jackson Turner, got up to deliver a paper before the American Historical Association. "The Significance of the Frontier in American History" permanently altered the study of American history in schools and colleges.

Frederick Jackson Turner's paper was often reprinted, but it was not until 1920 that he put together the first full statement of his theory on the frontier by republishing his original paper with twelve supporting articles in the book *The Frontier in American History*; the second and consequent part of his theory, *The Significance of Sections in American History*, was published in 1932, the year he died. His 1893 paper was preceded by his doctoral dissertation on the fur trade in Wisconsin and two articles on history and American history that show the development of his theory of the frontier. Two events precipitated his paper: first, the work of the Italian economist Achille Loria, with its theories of free land as the key to changes in human society, and of America as the best place in which to test this thesis, came to Turner's notice in the late 1880's. Loria's work influenced Turner's 1892 paper on "Problems in American History." The second event was that the superintendent of the 1890 census had recently announced that insufficient free land existed in the United States for the frontier to feature in the census reports as it had done since the first census in 1790. Turner dramatized this fact in the beginning of his paper. In effect he was directing his fellow historians away from political and diplomatic history, insisting that, no matter what happened in European capitals, American history was made in the hinterland, where the westward movement had been the most important historical phenomenon for Americans. There was, for historians, a vast frontier of local history to investigate in whatever state they might be located. The dramatic setting and occasion for Turner's paper was not immediately appreciated, but it played its part in spreading his ideas rapidly.

The initial paper on "The Significance of the Frontier" was constructed in two parts, with an introduction. The first paragraph asserts that American history is the gradual settlement of the West, and this is followed by four paragraphs defining the frontier as a moving belt between settled and free land; it moved because of the force behind it. As an effect of the environment into which it moved the frontier's chief characteristic is a process of reversion to savagery followed by a slow recovery of civilization which, because its chief influences are indigenous, cannot be an imitation of European life and must therefore be American. If the frontier is the maker of Americans, and they are the makers of their history, then the frontier holds the key to that history.

The first part of the paper presents in rapid survey the different kinds of frontier in American history and the modes of advance from the time when it began as the frontier of Europe on the Atlantic seaboard in the early seventeenth century to its near completion in the 1880's. The changes in the frontier were determined by the different geographical boundaries or barriers to the westward advance—Indians, farm land, salt supplies, and the like. Here Turner draws several vivid sketches of the succession of different types of settlers who followed one another in any one settlement or who could be imaginatively plotted as a series of different kinds of frontier belts such as hunting, trading, nomadic, grazing, farming, and financing. These different types could be traced back eastward from the most advanced settlement at any given point in American history.

The second part of the paper is a provocative summary of changes enforced by the frontier experience on the regions to the east and in Europe, whence the frontier impulse came. First, Turner proposes that the frontier is the real melting pot of immigrant nationalities, and without it the United States would resemble those nations of Europe whence the immigrants came. The next point is the success of the frontier. Although its rate of advance changed, it never faltered, and its increasing distance westward made Americans less dependent on England. Third, the power of the federal government stems from that granted Congress by the Constitution to dispose of the public domain and thus exert federal sway inside the state; without the frontier the federal government would have had little to legislate and less money with which to legislate. Fourth, the products of the frontier determined the development of the national economy, maintaining a rural influence over increasing industrialization in the East. Fifth, the egalitarianism of the frontier kept the states democratic. Last, in struggles with the economic, religious, and educational power of the East, the West came to have a character of its own, which determined that the federalist system would always be a duality of national and sectional interests.

Turner's paper is credited with causing a revolution in American historiography, but it would be truer to say that the paper was so completely in accord with the predilections of American historians in the decades that followed the paper that the paper anticipated and supported what came to be the predominant social and economic interpretation of American history. This version of history came to be preferred to the dynastic, the succession of presidents. It helped to make possible a wholly economic explanation of the causes of the Civil War, for instance, and it had the effect of determining Turner's life work. *The Frontier in American History* coped with his first task: to establish the historical outlines of his moving frontier and then to consider the unique character of postfrontier society, which Turner called the West. Turner's was first of all a new problem in historiography: how to explain that an "uninhabited" area could affect an inhabited area, a problem unknown in European historiography. He used the term "frontier" as the area of overlap between two areas, and since the frontier was always moving westward, however irregularly, Turner conceived it imaginatively as altering the physical shape of the inhabited area behind it by leaving successive belts of post-frontier societies, each of which was a "West" and together formed "the West."

Before analyzing his "West" he outlined the westward or moving frontier from Massachusetts to the "Old West" to the "Middle West," where he expanded his outline to closer study of the Ohio and Mississippi Valleys. "The Significance of the Mississippi Valley in American History" discusses the moving of the frontier and allows Turner to introduce "The Problem of the West," "Dominant Forces in Western Life," "Contributions of the West to American Democracy," "The West and American Ideals," and "Middle Western Democracy." This discussion leads him to the large claim that the West is democratic and that "democracy" is another name for "West." Thus the whole meaning of American history is summed up in "the West." At this point Turner becomes not a narrative historian but a social historian determined to explore "forces," "ideals," and "significances."

In his social history Turner tends to conclude his work with perorations about the virtue of American democracy and that of the West in producing it. "The Significance of the Mississippi

Valley in American History" concludes that the valley realized the American ideal of democracy and constitutes the heartland of America almost an independent nation that has shed its light on the surrounding feebler nations of the South, the East, and the Far West. Turner developed these ideas during his long tenure at Harvard and modified them when he took up residence at the Huntington Library in San Marino, California. In turn, these ideas led him to his pioneer work on sections in American history and life. His methods are summarized in his presidential address to the American Historical Association in 1910, "Social Forces in American History," the twelfth chapter of *The Frontier in American History*, in which he reviews statistics of American growth since 1890, arguing that the statistics provide evidence of the force behind the frontier. Turner summons his fellow historians to continue the work he began nearly two decades before by using statistics available from other disciplines, as he did in using the census bulletin in 1893. His embracing view forecasts the development of American studies, and the discipline he hinted at is given meaning by his insistence that the duty of historians is to engage themselves in the life of their nation by continually reinterpreting the immediate past in terms of the present, as he himself had done in Chicago in 1893.

Turner's concluding chapter, "Middle Western Pioneer Democracy," presents his belief that pioneer life gave Americans a chance for a true democracy, personal freedom, and a free society for the individual.

Bibliography:

Billington, Ray Allen. *The Genesis of the Frontier Thesis: A Study in Historical Creativity*. San Marino, Calif.: Huntington Library, 1971. Traces the process by which Turner developed his frontier thesis through an examination of letters and documents that the historian used in framing his ideas. An important source for investigation of Turner's intellectual evolution, written by Turner's foremost biographer.

Cronon, William. "Revisiting the Vanishing Frontier: The Legacy of Frederick Jackson Turner." *Western Historical Quarterly* 18 (April, 1987): 157-176. An examination of Turner's historical contributions by one of the new scholars of the West. A good overview of how Turner's reputation has progressed over time.

Jacobs, Wilbur R. *The Historical World of Frederick Jackson Turner: With Selections from His Correspondence*. New Haven, Conn.: Yale University Press, 1968. Uses Turner's letters and supplies editorial commentary to outline his emergence as a historian of the West. A fine source for Turner's own words about his historical theories.

Limerick, Patricia Nelson. *The Legacy of Conquest: The Unbroken Past of the American West*. New York: W. W. Norton, 1987. A history of Western settlement by one of the foremost modern exponents of the new Western history, which rejects Turner's thesis about the frontier as only a rationale for Anglo-American conquest of the West.

Nash, Gerald D. *Creating the West: Historical Interpretations, 1890-1990*. Albuquerque: University of New Mexico Press, 1991. An excellent survey of the various historical explanations of Western history that places the Turner thesis into context with other works about the region's development.

SILAS MARNER
The Weaver of Raveloe

Type of work: Novel
Author: George Eliot (Mary Ann Evans, 1819-1880)
Type of plot: Domestic realism
Time of plot: Early nineteenth century
Locale: England
First published: 1861

Principal characters:
SILAS MARNER, a weaver
EPPIE, his adopted daughter
AARON WINTHROP, the man whom Eppie married
GODFREY CASS, Eppie's father
DUNSTAN CASS, his wastrel brother
NANCY LAMMETER, the woman whom Godfrey married

The Story:

Silas Marner, the linen weaver, lived in the small community of Raveloe. Long years at his spinning wheel had left Silas extremely nearsighted so that his vision was limited to only those objects that were very bright or very close to him. Because of an unjust accusation of theft, Silas had left his former home at Lantern Yard and had become a recluse. For fifteen years, the lonely, shriveled man had lived for no purpose but to hoard the money he received in payment for his weaving. Night after night, he took his golden hoard from its hiding place in the floor of his cottage and let the shining pieces run through his fingers.

The leading man in Raveloe was Squire Cass, who had one fine son, Godfrey, and one wastrel son, Dunstan. It was said that Godfrey would marry Nancy Lammeter. Godfrey, however, had become involved in Dunstan's gambling debts. He had lent his spendthrift brother some of the squire's rent money, which Dunstan had lost in gambling. Since neither brother could raise the money, they decided that Dunstan must sell Godfrey's favorite horse, Wildfire, at a nearby fair. Godfrey's one fear was that this affair would harm his reputation in the neighborhood and his chance with Nancy. Another thing that weighed on Godfrey's conscience and prevented his declaration to Nancy was the fact that he was already married. Once he had been drunk in a tavern in a distant hamlet, and in that condition he had married a woman of the lower class. Sober, he had fled back to Raveloe and kept his marriage a secret.

Dunstan rode Wildfire across the fog-dimmed fields and crippled the animal on a high jump. With no means of raising the money, half-drunk and fear-driven, Dunstan came to Silas Marner's cottage. He knew through the neighborhood gossip that the weaver had a hidden hoard of gold. The cottage was empty, and instinct soon led the drunken youth to the hiding place of the gold. Stealing out of the cabin with his prize and stumbling through the night, Dunstan fell into an abandoned quarry pit and was killed.

The robbery of Silas' cottage furnished gossip for the entire community. Another mystery was the disappearance of Dunstan Cass. Godfrey was forced now to tell his father about the rent money he had given Dunstan and about the loss of the valuable horse, which had been found dead. Silas began to receive visitors from the neighborhood. One of his most frequent callers was Dolly Winthrop and her son Aaron, a charming little boy. Nevertheless, Silas could not be persuaded to come out of his hermitage; he secretly mourned the loss of his gold.

On New Year's Eve, a destitute woman died in the snow near Silas' cottage. She had with her a little yellow-haired girl who made her way toward the light shining through the cottage window and entered the house. Returning from an errand, Silas saw a golden gleam in front of his fireplace, a gleam that he mistook for his lost gold. On closer examination, he discovered a sleeping baby. He followed the child's tracks through the snow and discovered the body of the dead woman.

Godfrey was dancing happily with Nancy when Silas appeared to say that he had found a body. Godfrey went with the others to the scene and saw to his horror that the dead woman was his estranged wife. He told no one of her identity, and he did not have the courage to claim the baby for his own. Silas, with a confused association between the golden-haired child and his lost hoard, tenaciously clung to the child. After Dolly Winthrop spoke up in favor of his proper attitude toward children, the villagers decided to leave the baby with the old weaver.

Years passed. Under the spell of the child who, in her baby language, called herself Eppie instead of the biblical Hephzibah that Silas had bestowed upon her, the cottage of the weaver of Raveloe took on a new appearance. Lacy curtains decorated the once drab windows, and Silas outgrew his shell of reticence. Dolly brought her son to play with Eppie. Silas was happy. After many years, he even returned to Lantern Yard, taking Eppie. He searched his old neighborhood hopefully but could find no one who could clear his blighted past.

Godfrey Cass married Nancy, but it was a childless union. For sixteen years, Godfrey secretly carried with him the thought of his child growing up under the care of Silas. At last, the old stone quarry was drained, and workmen found a skeleton identified by Dunstan's watch and seals. Beside the skeleton was Silas' lost bag of gold, stolen on the night of Dunstan's disappearance. With this discovery, Godfrey's past reopened its sealed doors. He felt that the time had come to tell Nancy the truth. When he confessed the story of Eppie's birth, Nancy agreed with him that they should go to Silas and Eppie with their tale. After hearing this strange story of Eppie's parentage, the unselfish weaver opened the way for Eppie to take advantage of her wealthy heritage; but Eppie fled back to the man who had been a father and a mother to her when no one else would claim her. There was one thing remaining to complete the weaver's happiness. Eppie married Aaron Winthrop, her childhood playmate, while Silas beamed happily on the scene of her wedding.

Critical Evaluation:

In four remarkable years, George Eliot published in succession *Scenes from Clerical Life* (1858), *Adam Bede* (1859), *The Mill on the Floss* (1860), and *Silas Marner*. The last, a short novel or novella, is unlike the other works, for its narrative combines elements of myth—some critics have called it a fairy tale—with the otherwise realistic details of English country life centering on the rustic village of Raveloe. Certainly the novel can be understood as a moral tale. Its message, however sentimental to a modern reader, is unambiguous: true wealth is love, not gold. As a myth of loss and redemption, the novel concerns the miser Silas Marner, who loses his material riches only to reclaim a greater treasure of contentment. Silas comes to learn that happiness is possible only for the pure and self-sacrificing. Because of his love for Eppie, he is transformed, as if by magic, from a narrow, selfish, bitter recluse into a truly human, spiritually fulfilled man.

The novel, however, has a dimension other than the moralistic. Eliot skillfully counterpoints the experiences of Silas with those of Godfrey Cass. Whereas Godfrey appears, when the reader first meets him, to be a fortunate man entirely the opposite of the sullen miser, his fortunes fail just as Silas' improve. The wealthy, genial Godfrey has a secret guilt: an unacknowledged marriage to a woman beneath him in social class and refinement. Silas, on the other hand, carries with him the smoldering resentment for a wrong that he had suffered (and suffered innocently) from his friend William Dane. Godfrey's sense of guilt festers, especially after he learns about the terrible circumstances of the woman's death. Nevertheless, he remains silent, fearful of exposing his past. Eppie, the child of his brief union with the woman, becomes the miser's treasure and replaces the sterile gold stolen by Dunstan. Thereafter, the happiness of the old man is Godfrey's doom. His second wife, Nancy, is barren, and when he offers too late to adopt Eppie as his own child, she clings to her foster father. Silas' love has earned what Godfrey's power has failed to command.

By contrasting Silas' good fortune with Godfrey's disappointment, the author expands the mythic scope of her fiction. If some men—the pure and deserving—discover almost by accident the truths of happiness, others, maybe no less deserving, pass by their chances and endure misery. Silas is reformed not only spiritually but also psychologically. Once blasphemous, he returns to the Christian faith of his childhood, but his religious reaffirmation is not so important as the improvement of his psychological health. Freed of his neurotic resentment of past injustices, he becomes a friend to all, beloved of the village. For Godfrey, whose history is realistic rather than marvelous, quite the opposite fate happens. Without an heir, he shrinks within himself. He may endure his disgrace, even eventually make up to Eppie and her husband Aaron some of the material things he owes her; yet he cannot shake his sense of wrongdoing, appease his sorrow for betrayal, nor make restitution for the evils of the past. Eliot, who once described her novel as "rather somber," balances her miraculous fable of rebirth for the favored Silas with another more common human story, that of the defeated Godfrey Cass.

Bibliography:

Draper, R. P., ed. *George Eliot: "The Mill on the Floss" and "Silas Marner."* London: Macmillan, 1977. Useful casebook anthology, containing early reviews and nineteenth century criticism in addition to more modern studies. See especially David Carroll's "Reversing the Oracles of Religion," an authoritative essay on Eliot's humanist religious views.

Ermarth, Elizabeth Deeds. *George Eliot*. Boston: Twayne, 1985. A compact literary biography that addresses various moral and philosophical aspects of Eliot's intellectual development. In the chapter on *Silas Marner*, Ermarth sees a central theme emerging from opposed realms of circumstance and moral order linked by the bonds of human sympathy and trust.

Swinden, Patrick. *"Silas Marner": Memory and Salvation*. New York: Twayne, 1992. Critically sophisticated but readable book-length study that focuses on Eliot's narrative method. Offers a valuable analysis of the historical and societal contexts of the novel's two settings, Lantern Yard and Raveloe.

Thale, Jerome. "George Eliot's Fable for Her Times." *College English* 19 (1958): 141-146. A classic essay; argues that the contrasted realistic and fabular elements of *Silas Marner* are successfully unified by Eliot's moral vision. Also published as chapter 4 of Thale's excellent *The Novels of George Eliot* (New York: Columbia University Press, 1959).

Uglow, Jennifer. *George Eliot*. New York: Pantheon, 1987. Explores the connections between Eliot's life and work, in particular the feminine values her work affirms. In the chapter on *Silas Marner*, sees imagery of rebirth and regeneration at the core of the novel's celebration of nurturing and maternal actions.

SILENCE

Type of work: Novel
Author: Shūsaku Endō (1923-   )
Type of plot: Historical realism
Time of plot: 1632-1644
Locale: Japan
First published: Chimmoku, 1966 (English translation, 1969)

Principal characters:

SEBASTIAN RODRIGUES, a Portuguese Catholic missionary, later renamed Sanemon Okada
FRANCIS GARRPE, Rodrigues' religious associate and companion
CHRISTOVAO FERREIRA, the Jesuit priest who first inspired Rodrigues but who later apostatized and became Sawano Chuan
KICHIGIRO, a weak Japanese convert, who persisted in his faith despite repeated apostatizing
INOUE, Lord of Chikugo, famous for making many Christians apostatize

The Story:

Rumors had it that the respected Portuguese Jesuit missionary, Christovao Ferreira, the leader of the small, underground Christian community in Japan, had apostatized under torture and had cooperated with Japanese officials to expose the faithful. As a result, seven priests (three of them Portuguese and former students of Ferreira) decided to enter Japan secretly in order to exonerate the hero who had inspired them. Juan de Santa Marta, Francis Garrpe, and Sebastian Rodrigues traveled to Goa, India, where they met a timid, hesitant Japanese named Kichigiro; they sought his help in entering Japan. Juan de Santa Marta contracted malaria, however, and he had to be left behind.

After a sea voyage, Garrpe and Rodrigues were left at midnight in the fishing village of Tomogi, near Nagasaki. There Christian Japanese hid them, introduced them to Christians from nearby areas, and received from them church rituals forbidden in Japan. Rodrigues, disturbed at the plight of priestless Japanese Christians, traveled to Goshima to meet more of the faithful; upon his return, however, he learned that Japanese officials had discovered the presence of Christians and that he and Garrpe had to hide. The Tomogi villagers denied their Christianity, but the guards took hostages anyway; Kichigiro was among them. The hostages stamped on the *fumie*, an engraving of the Virgin Mary, as proof that they were not Christians, but the guards noticed their hesitation and made them also spit on a crucifix and call the Blessed Virgin a whore. Kichigiro did so, but two villagers (Mokichi and Ichizo) refused, and, consequently, underwent the water punishment and died as martyrs. The prolonged torture of their deaths, as the tides rose to where they were staked, was not what the two young Portuguese priests had imagined martyrdom would be like.

A further search by guards forced Rodrigues and Garrpe to separate. During this period of hiding, Rodrigues began to fear God's silence meant his nonexistence. Eventually, Kichigiro, claiming to lead him to safety, turned Rodrigues in. In jail, discussions with Japanese prisoners (Juan and Monica) revealed their misunderstanding of church doctrine, but when the Christian prisoners were transferred to Chizukano, Rodrigues had an opportunity to perform some humble religious rituals for them. At Chizukano, he was led before the infamous Japanese Inquisitor, Inoue, whose kindness and mildness defied expectations. Kichigiro was responsible for Rodrigues being in prison, yet Kichigiro begged Rodrigues' forgiveness for his betrayal. Rodrigues, expecting immediate torture and martyrdom, was lulled by the delay, and was, therefore, caught unaware when the guards brought him to a hill near the sea where he and Garrpe were told that three prisoners would be executed unless they apostatized. Rodrigues watched as the three prisoners were rolled up in mats, put on boats, and dumped into the sea to sink like stones. Garrpe ran into the sea screaming, "Lord, hear our prayer," and drowned while trying to rescue the victims.

Inoue continued to use subtle psychological torture to undermine Rodrigues' faith because Inoue believed that Christianity was dangerous for Japan. Inoue believed Christianity could only be stamped out if the European priests could be exposed as unfaithful to their own teachings. He sent Rodrigues to the Saishoji Temple to meet Ferreira, who had adopted the Japanese name "Sawano Chuan," had accepted a Japanese wife, and was writing a book denouncing Christian teachings as erroneous. Ferreira explained that the so-called Japanese Christian converts were simply confused because the Latin word *Deus* sounded to them like the Japanese word *Dainichi*, which referred to the ancient Japanese sun god. The ultimate test of Rodrigues' faith, however, was when he heard sounds like snoring and learned that it was the moaning of Christians, hanging upside down in manure pits, with slits behind their ears to allow blood to drain into their eyes and noses. At this point, Ferreira revealed his secret: His recanting of his faith was not because of personal suffering—he had been in such a pit—but because of the suffering of others for him. He argued that Christ, too, would have apostatized in such a situation. Finally, Rodrigues stepped on the *fumie*, justifying his act by imagining Christ saying, "Trample! Trample! . . . It was to share men's pain that I carried my cross." As he did so, a cock crowed, as it did when Peter betrayed Christ.

An afterword in the form of letters revealed Rodrigues becoming more and more a tool of Inoue, taking a Japanese name and a Japanese wife, and aiding the Japanese in their search for Christians and Christian symbols. Rodrigues' faith persisted despite his repeated betrayals, and, like Kichigiro, he understood that the mystery of faith endured and that God's silence did not negate God's existence or mercy.

Critical Evaluation:

Silence, a short but powerfully realistic fictionalized history, reflects a Japanese interest in the contacts between East and West and in the alien nature of Western religion. Just as James Clavell's *Shōgun* (1975) interprets the Japanese mind for Westerners, so Shūsaku Endō's *Silence*, set some forty years later, interprets the Western Christian mind for the Japanese. Through his Portuguese protagonist, Rodrigues, Endō captures for Japanese the Western image of life and culture in order to help Japanese better understand Western attitudes. In part, Endō's goal is to make Japanese rethink unexamined cultural perspectives and attitudes through a dramatized clash of worldviews. As Japan's most admired and widely read Christian writer, Endō is in a unique position to do so. His exploration of God's silence (the origin of the title) as proof of God's existence, with its paradoxical Zen implications, is meant to puzzle and intrigue Japanese, but his portrait of Japanese cruelties, the historically accurate, hideous tortures used to force captives to recant their faith, is intended to shock and disturb. The description in *The Sea and Poison* (1957) of Japanese doctors vivisecting a captured American pilot during World War II criticized the Japanese for a lack of moral conscience; in *Silence* the criticism continues, as Endō contrasts the image of a compassionate Christ with the bland indifference and sadism of Japanese inquisitors. A Catholic educated in France, and the first Japanese to study abroad after World War II, Endō provides insights into another worldview and another mindset. Endō is similar, in this respect, to Lafcadio Hearn, who introduced the culture and literature of Japan to the West.

The time period of *Silence* is highly significant for Japanese: It is the period following the Shimabara rebellion. The Tokugawa Edicts expelling European Christians from Japan resulted in five thousand to six thousand Christians (both Japanese and Western) being martyred in Japan between 1614 and 1640. Shimabara, a longtime Christian stronghold dominated by Christian *ronin* (lordless samurai), was the center of a spontaneous, Japanese-inspired rebellion against oppression and persecution. This rebellion was a major historical incident. Thirty-five thousand Japanese Christians were killed. Rodrigues and Garrpe arrived shortly after this rebellion was quelled, and this arrival makes clear to Japanese why Inquisitor Inoue fears the effects of Western religious proselytizing on Japan.

Silence, the record of both a physical and a spiritual journey, consists of a series of letters and reports written by Westerners, both Portuguese and Dutch, about the Jesuit mission to Japan, the religious persecutions, and the Japanese enlisting of former priests in the Japanese anti-religious campaign. These documents so closely echo the language and content of seventeenth century church documents that readers might well be convinced that they are reading genuine church records, and, to some degree, they are. Saint Francis Xavier, Alessandro Valignano, Father Christovao Ferreira, and Inouye Mashasige are names from the pages of history, with the library of the Portuguese Institute for the Historical Study of Foreign Lands being Endō's proclaimed source for documentation. Ferreira was, in fact, the historical acting-Vice-Provincial of the Jesuits in Japan, but after six hours of being tightly bound and hung head downward from a gallows into a pit filled with excreta, his forehead and flesh behind the ears slashed in order to vent the blood, Ferreira apostatized. Some time later, he actively helped persecute Christians when he was an assistant to Inouye Masashige, an apostate Japanese and the head of the Christian Inquisition office. Masashige was commissioned to discover and to eliminate hidden Christians. Ferreira also helped Fabian Fukan, author of the virulent anti-Christian book *Ha-Deusu* (God destroyed), orchestrate an anti-Christian campaign.

Endō's descriptions of behavior, cultural interaction, methods of torture, and recanting are detailed and accurate and are in complete accord with the historical record; however, through the first-person narration of Sebastian Rodrigues, in the dominant center of *Silence*, Endō personalizes history and brings to life both religious doubts and the mystery of faith, the compassionate care of the Portuguese missionaries for the peasants who sheltered them and gave their lives for them, and the self-sacrifice, even when the torture proved beyond imagining. Rodrigues was not one of the martyrs of recorded history, though his name echoes the real Jesuit, Joao Rodrigues, but Sebastian Rodrigues' fate is similar to that of a handful of daring missionaries who apostatized in order to save Japanese Christians.

The novel revolves around inexplicable religious mysteries: power in powerlessness; fullness in nothingness; faith in denial; God's silence and the trampling of the *fumie* as evidence of God's existence; the protagonist betraying his faith in order to practice it; and the Japanese attempts to stamp out Christianity assuring its transformation into something more solidly and irrevocably Japanese. The imagery of Japan as a "swamp" into which alien religions sink captures some of the paradox, for in that swamp, religions such as Christianity become diffused and mingle with the local elements until they become an inseparable part of them—another mystery of Christian syncretism. The novel also depends on contrasts in interpretations and in values between Easterners and Westerners. For the Japanese in the novel, the group is most important, and individuals, particularly peasants, are a matter of indifference; however, for Westerners, the individuals are more important than the group, and for this reason, the compassion of the priests for individual sufferers outweighs the priests' consideration of abstract values. Rodrigues' image of God changes because of his Japanese experience, however, and the image of God progresses from a distant, judgmental figure to a worn and care-ridden, humanized figure with whom Rodrigues can personally identify.

The novel also depends on irony, with the ultimate irony being that both Rodrigues and Inoue fail: Rodrigues fails to stand up for and propagate the faith of his fathers—but he does pass on the rituals of the church, and he does teach the Japanese faithful to set up their own religious forms; Inoue fails to stamp out Christianity and, in his persecution of it, lends it a mystical strength that assures its endurance underground.

Gina Macdonald
Yasuko Honda

Bibliography:

Beverly, Elizabeth. "A Silence That Is Not Hollow: The Mindfulness of Shūsaku Endō." *Commonweal* 116 (September 22, 1989): 491-494. Contrasts a Western focus in *Silence* with a Japanese focus and argues that, for Shūsaku Endō, human indifference to the fate of others is a greater sin than being weak or cowardly.

Higgins, Jean. "The Inner Agon of Endō Shūsaku." *Cross Currents* 34 (Winter, 1984-1985): 414-426. Records Endō's shift from Buddhist to Christian perceptions and his resultant identity crisis. Examines *Silence* as Japanese and Western views in confrontation, with the Japanese discovering their spiritual insensitivity and Westerners exchanging a patriarchal for a maternal image of God.

Johnston, William. "Endō and Johnston Talk of Buddhism and Christianity." *America* 171, no. 16 (November 19, 1994): 18-20. A dialogue emphasizing the differences in philosophical perceptions and emphasis between East and West.

Mathy, Francis. "Bookings: Shūsaku Endō: Japanese Catholic Novelist." *America* 167, no. 3 (August 1, 1992): 66-71. Discusses how Endo has made Catholicism more accessible to the Japanese through books such as *Silence*.

Ribeiro, Jorge. "Shūsaku Endō: Japanese Catholic Novelist." *America* 152 (February 2, 1985): 87-89. Discusses the moral issues raised in Endō's canon and the conflicts between the interpretations and assumptions of Japanese and Western critics, with the Japanese missing the spiritual implications in *Silence* and Westerners projecting their own cultural values into the novel.

SIMPLICISSIMUS THE VAGABOND

Type of work: Novel
Author: Hans Jakob Christoffel von Grimmelshausen (1621-1676)
Type of plot: Picaresque
Time of plot: 1600's
Locale: Germany
First published: Der abenteuerliche Simplicissimus, 1669 (English translation, 1912)

Principal characters:
SIMPLICIUS SIMPLICISSIMUS, a vagabond
A PEASANT, his foster father
A HERMIT, his real father
A PASTOR
ULRICH HERZBRUDER, Simplicissimus' friend
OLIVER, a rogue

The Story:

Simplicissimus' beginning was one of a child of pure innocence. Since he lived far removed from any other influences except the small, barely sufficient farm near the Spessart forest, he presented himself as nothing short of a simpleton. His main job was looking after the livestock, and when told to look out for the foxes who came to raid the chickens, Simplicissimus mistook some soldiers for foxes. Since he had never seen either a fox or a knight before, he interpreted them in the only way he knew how. The soldiers were soldiers of the Thirty Years' War and plundered his family's farm as Simplicissimus escaped into the forest.

Deep in the forest, he met a hermit. This hermit asked him many questions that Simplicissimus could only answer in the most naïve manner. He could not even tell the hermit his real name. He stated that his father called him "boy." For two years the boy stayed with the hermit and learned from him. The hermit died and the pastor who gave Simplicissimus supplies was captured by the soldiers. The small town nearby was plundered. Simplicissimus again escaped to the forest but ended up having even his small hut plundered. He was taken as prisoner to the Governor of Hanau. The soldiers questioned Simplicissimus, and again he could not tell his name, nor much of his history. A pastor came to Simplicissimus' rescue by stating that the pastor had seen Simplicissimus in a hermitage with the old man, who happened to be a nobleman disenchanted with the war.

As Simplicissimus' life went on, he began his climb in status. He became a page, but his simpleton ways were not those of the court. He was at a grave disadvantage. He ended up looking and playing a fool. He commented liberally about society, and during a great feast, he saw men acting with such bad manners he thought that they were representing themselves as beasts instead of men. The more he saw the more Simplicissimus realized a fool's ways were better suited for survival than the ways of a courtier.

Again his circumstance changed and he became a prisoner to the Croats. He learned to serve many masters. He escaped dressed as a girl, but he was destined to serve as a lady's maid. He was then discovered to be male and ended up as a horse boy, at which time he met his friend Ulrich Herzbruder. Simplicissimus gave Ulrich money to escape, which Ulrich successfully did, and again Simplicissimus' situation changed.

Simplicissimus was beginning to become educated as to the ways of the world. He had begun to climb the ladder of success. He went through the military ranks, and although he plundered, he never took from the poor, always the rich. He had plenty of wealth and had a reputation as a superior forager, something he was taught by the hermit. Later, Simplicissimus discovered someone had attempted to steal his name and reputation, and had committed crimes in his name, wearing the green garb synonymous with Simplicissimus. Simplicissimus discovered and punished this man. From this time forward, Simplicissimus aspired to become a nobleman, but his fate would not allow it. The Swedes captured him.

During his incarceration with the Swedes, Simplicissimus established himself with the ladies. The Swedes, after hearing of his reputation as a soldier, offered him a position in their armies, but Simplicissimus turned them down. The Swedes allowed him to roam around the city at will. A young daughter of a colonel attracted Simplicissimus and they married. Shortly after, Simplicissimus pledged his alliance to the Swedes.

Then his life changed again. On a trip to Cologne the Swedes convinced him to go to Paris. There he lost his fortune in a robbery, but he gained many adventures in love. Then Simplicissimus used a ruse to return to Germany; he impersonated a doctor. He never made it back to Germany. Instead he was captured and forced to become a soldier in another army. He met Oliver, who had taken advantage of his good friend Ulrich. Soldiers killed Oliver, and Simplicissimus traveled onward.

Following the war, Simplicissimus visited a Swiss spa and stumbled upon an old man who happened to be his peasant father. Simplicissimus discovered that his peasant father was actually his foster father and that the old hermit of noble birth was his real father. From that time on, he had many adventures, including getting married again only to have his wife die after a year. In the end, Simplicissimus returned to the life of his real father, and became a hermit.

Critical Evaluation:

Considered an oasis within a desert of medieval German novels, Hans Jakob Christoffel von Grimmelshausen's *Simplicissimus the Vagabond* was a critical flop but was quite influential and extremely popular. Critics often refer to it as the greatest prose work in German Literature, and it has influenced many others. Grimmelshausen is said to have been influenced by Henry Neville's *Isle of Pines* (1668).

The actual name of the author of *Simplicissimus the Vagabond* was not discovered until 1838. Grimmelshausen's work possesses autobiographical elements, especially in scenes tied to the Thirty Years' War. The novel is a picaresque most of the time, but in addition one could also interpret it as a *Bildungsroman*. In a picaresque novel the protagonist is someone of low birth. This low status gives a worm's-eye view for the narrator to comment, criticize, and assess the different strata of society. The plot is most generally loosely organized. The protagonist never fully develops; he remains a rogue and his experiences do not educate him. On the other hand, the *Bildungsroman* describes the complete development of a character. The protagonist of a *Bildungsroman* slowly achieves moral, spiritual, psychological, and social harmony. The *Bildungsroman* is about a character's struggle toward a better life, whereas the picaresque character merely experiences life. *Simplicissimus the Vagabond* has attributes of both types of novel, but is more picaresque. The protagonist is a rogue, although of noble birth. He tries to fulfill his urge to be noble, but does not yearn for it very strongly. Simplicissimus merely experiences, and comments upon, the various situations happening in his life and never learns much from them.

Grimmelshausen strips his character of familial ties and replaces them with religious ties. All of Simplicissimus' interpretations are religious. The author couples all observances with religious interpretations of action, and in the end the protagonist fulfills the circle as he returns to the life of his father, the hermit. Throughout the work the author has the protagonist complete many circles. Simplicissimus starts out on top of the circle. Then, through his simpleton ways, he falls prey to situations for which he is not prepared.

Janet M. Luehring

Bibliography:

Allen, Ann Taylor. *Satire and Society in Wilhelmine Germany: Kladderadatsch and Simplicissimus, 1890-1914*. Lexington: University Press of Kentucky, 1984. This work has an excellent history and criticism of *Simplicissimus the Vagabond*. Discussion of social problems as related to literature. Bibliography.

Glasberg, Ronald. "The Perversions of Folly in Grimmelshausen's *Simplicius Simplicissimus:* Foreshadowing of Nazism." *CLIO: A Journal of Literature, History, and the Philosophy of History* 16, no. 3 (1987): 253-271. A great discussion of *Simplicissimus the Vagabond* and its characters. Attempts to bring Nazism into the article, but the character analysis is beneficial.

Negus, Kenneth. *Grimmelshausen*. New York: Twayne, 1974. A wonderful book that notes major influences on Grimmelshausen. Includes a chapter on his sources and references. Bibliography.

Richtie, J. M. "Grimmelshausen's *Simplicissimus* and *The Runagate Courage*." In *Knaves and Swindlers: Essays on the Picaresque Novel in Europe*, edited by Christine J. Whitbourn. London: Oxford University Press, 1974. An excellent essay integrating the Thirty Years' War, Grimmelshausen's life, and some of his other works. Bibliography.

Wicks, Ulrich. *Picaresque Narrative, Picaresque Fictions: A Theory and Research Guide*. Westport, Conn.: Greenwood Press, 1989. An excellent beginning source. Describes the various aspects of a picaresque novel. Discusses *Simplicissimus the Vagabond* and its themes.

SINNERS IN THE HANDS OF AN ANGRY GOD

Type of work: Didactic
Author: Jonathan Edwards (1703-1758)
First published: 1741

Jonathan Edwards, a descendant of four generations of Puritan ministers and the most renowned and influential of Puritan leaders, became active when Puritanism was already on the wane. The infamy of the Salem witchcraft trials in 1692, which sent twenty persons to their death and another 150 to prison, festered in the community for a generation as a tragic episode that had exposed the excesses of misguided Puritan zeal. In the early part of the century, New Englanders enjoyed a rising level of affluence which induced a sense of both material and spiritual comfort and eventually led to the introduction of the Half-Way Covenant. Whereas full church membership had been the privilege only of those and the children of those who could testify to a personal experience of conversion, the Half-Way Covenant extended such membership to the third generation of those who had confessed an experiential faith. It was such creeping secularism and spiritual lethargy that Edwards sought to correct in the 1730's through a revival movement called the Great Awakening.

This revival movement stirred many to intensify their religious seriousness, not only in Edwards' own congregation of Northampton but throughout New England. His sermons were intended as a wake-up call for those who underplayed the majesty of a holy God and overemphasized their own worthiness as decent, hard-working, successful citizens. Edwards believed strongly that only a genuine conversion experience should qualify a person for church membership. Revivalist preachers, therefore, sought not only to address the intellect but also to engage the emotions so as to convince the listeners of the seriousness of their sin and activate them to seek salvation from the punishment they could expect from a righteous God. The results were encouraging, but one congregation, that in Enfield, Connecticut, seemed to be immune to the call for radical conversion. Jonathan Edwards was therefore invited to preach there. On July 8, 1741, at the height of the Great Awakening, he delivered a revival sermon in Enfield that was to become the most famous of its kind. He followed the traditional three-part sermon structure: a scripture text, which laid the foundation for the sermon, and an exposition of its implications; discussion of the doctrine that is derived from the text; and the application of the doctrine to the personal situation of the listeners.

Edwards carefully selected the text for this occasion, for it was his single-minded intent to disturb profoundly the comfortable members of his audience. He found the words he wanted in Deuteronomy 32:35: "Their foot shall slide in due time." This short sentence was taken from a long passage, undoubtedly read in its entirety to the congregation, that enunciates God's anger toward the perversity and unfaithfulness of his people Israel. Edwards obviously wished to establish a close connection between those addressed in the biblical passage and those whom he is addressing in his sermon. He begins his sermon by pointing out four features of walking on a slippery slope: The threat of destruction is constant, that destruction is imminent and it is self-generated, and the delay of that destruction is due to God's restraining hand. He is clearly establishing here the foolhardiness of those who choose to walk in such slippery places and that a fatal slide into the yawning abyss is an inescapable certainty. He speaks to both the head and heart in leading his hearers to recognize the nature of such foolishness and to fear the consequences. The warning leads Edwards to his theme: "There is nothing that keeps wicked men, at any moment, out of Hell, but the mere pleasure of God."

In a ten-point elaboration that makes up one-third of the sermon, Edwards pursues his purpose of awakening the spiritually somnolent. Many of his points are interrelated, but cumulatively they persuade the hearers that God's power is terrifying, that his wrath burns hot against the wicked, that the wicked stand condemned by the law and are deserving of hell, and that nothing will save them from such eternal punishment except a saving faith in Christ. Edwards knows, of course, that a cognitive persuasion does not necessarily lead to action. True religion should be a matter of both head and heart, and the emotions too must be engaged and moved to reinforce the will to turn to God for mercy and to a spiritually transformed life.

What distinguishes this most famous example of Puritan revival sermons is its use of imagery so vivid that it left people in the pews trembling and weeping. The imagery in the first part of the sermon graphically underscores the theme of the lot of the unregenerated. They should not deceive themselves about their status or their strength. Their vaunted trust in their own wisdom, prudence, care, and caution is but a self-delusion and will not save them. Before God's almighty power, they are but "heaps of light chaff before the whirlwind" and "dry stubble before devouring flames." They are like worms that crawl on the earth and are easily crushed underfoot; they are hanging as by a slender thread that is easily singed or cut. The glittering sword of justice is whetted and is brandished over their heads. The flames of the fiery pit below them rage and glow, hell's gaping mouth is ready to swallow them, the devils like hungry lions are straining to get at their prey, the arrows of death are poised at them. What Edwards tries to pound into his listeners is the notion of life's uncertainty: Death is always but a breath away. For the unconverted, therefore, and for the unredeemed sinner and those who have not embraced Christ as savior, perdition is but a breath away. They are "walking over the pit of hell on a rotten covering" that cannot be trusted to bear their weight. Only faith in Christ will bear them up. That may not save their life, for they are mortal still, but it will save their soul and awaken the deluded souls in their sinful condition to the wonders of divine grace. That is Edwards' sole concern.

The third part of the sermon, the application, makes up the largest and, to Edwards, the most important part of this sermon. If up to this point he has described the plight of the unsaved in general, he now turns directly to the congregation of Enfield and to the unconverted persons before him. The use of the third person in the sermon's second part changes to the second person in the third part. All of the Bible's warnings about the fate of the unrepentant sinner apply to them, Edwards says: the "lake of burning brimstone, . . . Hell's gaping mouth, . . . the dreadful pit of glowing flames. . . ." He goes on to attack the reasoning of the unconverted, who have tried to persuade themselves that it is not God but their own care and caution that preserves their life. They may point to their religiosity, their ritual of family devotions and church attendance, and the uprightness of their moral life, but Edwards reminds them that unless they have experienced a "great change of heart by the power of the spirit of God" and unless they were made "new creatures" they are still sinners in the hands of an angry God, standing on the slippery slope of disaster, at any moment apt to be "swallowed up in everlasting destruction."

To break down the will's resistance and reinforce the notion of impending doom, Edwards unleashes a powerful arsenal of metaphorical weapons aimed at the emotions. Through metaphors and images, Edwards links the spiritual world to the physical world of the listeners. Images of weight and tension dominate. Sinners "heavy as lead" with their wickedness will "plunge into the bottomless gulf" as surely as a falling rock would plunge through a spider's web. The floods of God's wrath will sweep them off their feet with all the fierce power of a bursting dam. The "bow of God's wrath is bent," the arrow of justice aimed at the heart. The God whose hand is yet staying this ultimate doom is a righteous God of fury to all who reject him. Such are like a loathsome insect in his sight which he holds over the fire of Hell, like a spider hanging by a slender thread above the leaping flames of the "great furnace of wrath."

Edwards wants to ensure that no one take the wrath of this holy and infinite God lightly and he frequently refers to biblical passages that support the point. He stresses that God's wrath is much more terrible than that of the fiercest human warrior and that no one can endure it. Moreover, it will be inflicted without pity upon all who "remain in an unregenerate state." It is, however, Edwards' passion to lead the unregenerate to salvation. All of his dire warnings have led up to what now follows: the announcement of God's grace. Having mercilessly proclaimed the imminence of God's wrath without pity, Edwards now shifts dramatically to the theme that "Now God stands ready to pity you; this is a day of mercy." Woe to those who neglect this opportunity, however. God will show them both how excellent his love is and how terrible his wrath; the God whose hand of wrath will destroy the wicked is the same God whose hand of mercy will save the repentant. In the concluding part of the sermon, Edwards addresses his invitation to receive salvation to everyone in the audience before him—the old, the young, and the children. This, says Edwards, is the time of God's gathering in, the pouring out of his spirit, and now is the time "to fly from the wrath to come" and to "hearken to the loud calls of God's word and providence." This emphasis on immediate response reflects Edwards' conviction that, though emotions can move the will to act, emotions are transient; therefore it is necessary to act before spiritual sloth returns and the door of mercy is forever shut.

This sermon is not typical of the preaching of Jonathan Edwards, but it is typical of revivalist preaching during the Great Awakening. Such sermons were meant to appeal to the head and heart and to destroy vain rationalization and deter delay. According to historical sources, this sermon was not without the desired effect in Enfield. Nevertheless, the Great Awakening movement did not succeed finally in saving Puritanism.

Henry J. Baron

Bibliography:

Cady, Edwin H. "The Artistry of Jonathan Edwards." *Critical Essays on Jonathan Edwards*, edited by William J. Scheick. Boston: G. K. Hall, 1980. Analyzes the sermon as a genuine work of art by looking at its intellectual and literary structure and design.

Pudaloff, Ross J. "'Sinners in the Hands of an Angry God': The Socio-economic and Intellectual Matrices for Edwards' Sermon." *Mosaic: A Journal for the Interdisciplinary Study of Literature* 16 (Summer, 1983): 45-64. A helpful examination of the economic and social history of Enfield, the intellectual and philosophical aspects of Edwards' thought expressed in the sermon, and the rhetoric and metaphors shared by the sermon and the community.

Steele, Thomas J., Jr., and Eugene R. Delay. "Vertigo in History: The Threatening Tactility of 'Sinners in the Hands.'" *Early American Literature* 18 (Winter, 1983-1984): 242-256. A detailed analytical look at the tactile imagery of the sermon as a common method of revivalist preaching and purposeful inducement of a disposition toward repentance and grace.

Stuart, Robert Lee. "Jonathan Edwards at Enfield: 'And Oh the Cheerfulness and Pleasantness . . .'." *American Literature* 48 (March, 1976): 46-59. A sympathetic depiction of Edwards as a loving pastor. Views the sermon as an uncharacteristically forceful approach that was required by the situation. Also examines the sermon's tension between fear and hope.

Yarbrough, Stephen R., and John C. Adams. *Delightful Conviction: Jonathan Edwards and the Rhetoric of Conversion*. Westport, Conn.: Greenwood Press, 1993. Includes an illuminating section that focuses on the experiential imagery of helplessness that points up the need for divine security.

SIR CHARLES GRANDISON

Type of work: Novel
Author: Samuel Richardson (1689-1761)
Type of plot: Fiction of manners
Time of plot: Eighteenth century
Locale: England
First published: 1753-1754

Principal characters:
SIR CHARLES GRANDISON, an English baronet of great virtue
HARRIET BYRON, a virtuous young English woman
LADY CLEMENTINA DELLA PORRETTA, a young Italian woman in love with Sir Charles
SIR HARGRAVE POLLEXFEN, a libertine in love with Harriet Byron
CHARLOTTE GRANDISON, Sir Charles's younger sister
LADY L., Sir Charles's older sister
EMILY JERVOIS, Sir Charles's ward

The Story:

When Harriet Byron, a beautiful and virtuous young English woman of modest expectations, left her aunt's home in rural Northamptonshire to visit in London, she left three men who loved her very much and various relatives who feared that the social life of the city might offer moral pitfalls unknown to a young and unsuspecting woman of virtue such as Harriet. Harriet had spent all of her life in the country; living with an aunt after her parents' deaths, she was excited at the prospect of the London visit. She also went with a happy heart, for she had no one, despite her many admirers, that she was interested in marrying; her suitors had not appealed strongly enough to her sentiments and mind despite their respectable, if ardorous, attentions.

In London, Harriet had connections of a very respectable sort. She was invited to many homes and social events and met many wealthy suitors. One of these was Sir Hargrave Pollexfen, who was determined not to accept a refusal. When told by Harriet that he did not suit her fancy, Sir Hargrave became enraged and vowed he would have both Harriet and revenge. He laid a plot to abduct Harriet from a masquerade ball and force her to marry him.

Sir Hargrave's plot almost succeeded, and the experience was a horrible one for Harriet. Fortunately, however, Sir Charles Grandison heard her screams and rescued her from Sir Hargrave's clutches. Sir Charles took Harriet to his country house, not far from London, where he and his sister invited Harriet to remain as a guest, almost a member of the family. Sir Hargrave sent a challenge to Sir Charles, but the latter refused to fight a duel, insisting that no virtuous man, however brave and skilled, could become a duelist and retain his virtue.

Harriet Byron soon fell in love with Sir Charles Grandison. She realized that he was the very soul of honor and virtue, a man whose time was spent in carefully managing his own affairs and in doing good for others. When his father had died, he had left his entire estate to Sir Charles with no provision for the two daughters of the family. When Sir Charles returned to England from the Continent to take over his estate, he treated his sisters with consideration and devotion. The oldest received his permission for her to marry Lord L., a suitor frowned upon by her father during his lifetime. Sir Charles also began to improve his estates and their revenues so that he could set aside better marriage portions for both his sisters, something more than their father had been willing to do. Sir Charles befriended everyone who would accept his kindnesses, and he always behaved wisely and with decorum. Even those persons who were prepared to dislike him found themselves won over by his sympathetic, friendly, and yet dignified ways. Even to his father's paramour, Mrs. Oldham, he behaved magnanimously, persuading the rest of the family to view her as a fellow human being.

Many women were in love with Sir Charles, including Harriet Byron, but no one could ascertain whether he had any inclinations toward any particular woman. Harriet, however, tried to hide her love for him and to subdue it, although many of Sir Charles's friends and relatives, including his sisters, favored the match. Sir Charles consistently referred to Harriet as a sister and behaved toward her with the same consideration he showed Charlotte Grandison and Lady L. Finally, it became known that two Italian women he had met in his travels had won some favor from him and had some claim to him and his affections. One was Lady Olivia and the other was Lady Clementina della Porretta, whom he had met after saving her brother's life. Lady Clementina's family did not favor a marriage between their daughter and a Protestant Englishman, but the young woman was so enamored of Sir Charles that his departure from Italy unhinged her reason. Feeling a sense of responsibility to the lady and her family as the source of her misfortune, Sir Charles returned to Italy with English medical experts to try to effect a cure. Harriet Byron believed that he would prefer Lady Clementina to her and began to prepare herself for news of his marriage to the Italian woman.

After she had recovered from her malady, however, Lady Clementina refused to marry Sir Charles, despite the fact that her family and he had been able to compromise over religious differences. Lady Clementina, a devout Roman Catholic, feared that she would be tempted by her love for Sir Charles and his virtue to leave her faith to become a Protestant. She asked to be free not to marry at all, since she could not marry him; her family hoped she would marry some other eligible man.

While he was still in Italy, an attempt was made on Sir Charles's life, almost certainly at the instigation of Lady Olivia, who had previously struck at him with a poniard after he had repulsed her addresses. After this incident, Sir Charles felt himself free to pay his court where he desired. He returned to England and immediately began his suit for Harriet Byron's hand, which he quickly won. In the meantime, his sister Charlotte had married Lord G., and Harriet helped the impetuous and willful young woman to learn to bear properly the dignity of matrimony. Harriet's marriage to Sir Charles still faced some small obstacles. She had to learn to accept her suitor in new ways; she was shocked, for example, when he kissed her on the mouth instead of on the cheek. Furthermore, Harriet had to find a place in her heart for Emily Jervois, Sir Charles's young ward. The young girl loved her guardian, and Harriet, aware of the girl's feelings, had to help her accept Harriet's marriage to Sir Charles. Another disturbance was caused by a former suitor of Harriet, Mr. Greville, who tried, while emotionally deranged, to fight a duel with Sir Charles.

Harriet Byron and Sir Charles were finally married. A short time later, they were visited by Lady Clementina, who had run away from her home in Italy because of her parents' insistence that she marry. Through a compromise, Sir Charles managed to arrange a satisfactory agreement between the young woman and her family. Word also came of Sir Hargrave Pollexfen's death. Sir Hargrave, rescued in France by Sir Charles from the outraged relatives of a woman he had attempted to seduce, had discovered the evil of his ways. Wishing to make amends for the abduction and the attempted forced marriage to Harriet, Sir Hargrave left his fortune to her and her husband. Even the mother of Emily Jervois was influenced to become a respectable and virtuous woman. Encouraged by Sir Charles's magnanimity and financial generosity, she interested herself in religion. At one time, the unfortunate woman had looked on Sir Charles as her enemy and she and Mr. O'Hara, her onetime paramour and second husband, had attempted to force Emily into a degrading marriage with a rascal who had promised to share with them the girl's fortune that Sir Charles held in trust; now, however, they mended their dissolute ways and became sober, worthy persons.

Critical Evaluation:

Sir Charles Grandison provides, in a series of 182 familiar letters, the history of a hero who is as different as possible from Lovelace, the villain of Samuel Richardson's earlier novel, *Clarissa: Or, The History of a Young Lady* (1747-1748). Lovelace is many things, all of them bad: a libertine, an atheist, and a rapist, for example. He metamorphoses himself into whatever form of evildoer needed to destroy whatever form of human decency and goodness might be within striking distance. Sir Charles Grandison, on the other hand, is always the same Christian gentleman, whatever he does. The letters in the novel, written by Sir Charles and the other characters in the novel, show him as champion of right social order, compassionate benefactor of the unfortunate, doer of his duty toward his creator, defender of anyone—even a complete stranger—against injustice. He is especially a protector of women in need of protection.

Unlike Lovelace, who engages in no productive activity of any kind, instead spending his fortune and time entirely on furthering his sinister plans for seducing Clarissa, Sir Charles does work and all of it for good. He is seen on his estates caring for his tenants, repairing his buildings, and inspecting his fields. His good husbandry increases the wealth that makes his many charities possible. He makes friends easily. Instead of manipulating people for his own ends, he serves them by solving their problems or helping them to solve their difficulties by themselves.

Another quality of Sir Charles's gentlemanliness is his generosity in his relationships with women. He rescues his father's mistress from certain misery when her keeper dies. He forgives the Lady Olivia, whose unreturned love for him turns into hate, and he forgets the murderous assaults on his person committed by that lady and her accomplices. He assumes the guardianship of little Emily Jervois to preserve her from the bad influence of her immoral mother. He provides dowries for his penniless sisters to enable them to find suitable husbands. His tact helps his younger sister, Charlotte, whose flippancy almost ruins her marriage, to change her behavior so that she becomes a good wife.

His task with Lady Clementina, the delicate, mentally unstable Italian beauty to whom he was affianced, is more difficult. The English physicians he brings with him to Italy to restore her to health cannot deal with her dilemma. Although she loves Sir Charles Grandison, she refuses to marry him unless he abandons his Protestant religion—which he cannot do. So he must extricate himself from a fruitless involvement without causing ill feeling in her family, without precipitating a major breakdown on her part, and without losing her friendship. He carries out this difficult task with quiet discretion, totally unlike the secrecy with which Lovelace conducts his intrigues.

In the case of Harriet Byron, Grandison's generous rescue and subsequent sheltering leads to love—a love that waits a long time for fruition. Harriet, the ideal mate for Sir Charles because she shares his sensitivity, sense of duty, and religion, soon recognizes in him the only man she could marry. Sir Charles must first retain her platonic affection because he cannot declare his love for her and ask her to be his wife until he has freed himself from his obligations and entanglements in Italy.

Just as Sir Charles can be compared with Lovelace, Harriet can be compared with Clarissa.

Harriet is a paragon, beautiful and sought after. She, too, refuses all proposals of marriage in favor of a perfect but still unfound spouse. Unlike the unfortunate Clarissa, who is cast off by her family and subsequently raped by Lovelace, Harriet finds herself rescued by Sir Charles from a rape attempt and then received into his family at Grandison Hall, where, in its warm and sympathetic atmosphere, she falls in love with her rescuer. When Sir Charles goes to Italy on his mission to the Lady Clementina, Harriet becomes ill of a strange malady that resembles the mysterious illness of which Clarissa dies after her rape. Harriet, however, is rescued again by Sir Charles—this time from death—and recovers to marry him and to live as his partner in earthly bliss.

Readers in Richardson's day were accustomed to the epistolary convention in novels. They enjoyed the feeling of intimacy and the thrill of reading other "people's" private correspondence. They reveled in the detail and realism of the letters, which chronicle the slow, circuitous way the union of the lovers becomes possible. They savored the psychological complexity of the action. They welcomed the opportunities to observe manners in good society and the ways these virtuous characters confronted and solved sexual, social, and ethical problems. To many of these readers who wanted to achieve perfect marriages for themselves, Harriet Byron and Sir Charles Grandison provided models. Generations of young writers, among them Fanny Burney, Jane Austen, and Maria Edgeworth, also interested in the theme of good marriage, not only admired Richardson's *Sir Charles Grandison* but also imitated it in their own fiction.

Esteem for *Sir Charles Grandison*, once thought to be a novel far inferior to *Clarissa*, is growing. Several critics now credit the novel with advances in examining the relationship between the sexes, in developing the complexity of narrative, and in broadening the scope of fiction. These critics see *Sir Charles Grandison* as the predecessor not only of the novels by Fanny Burney, Maria Edgeworth, and Jane Austen, but also of the fiction of George Eliot and Henry James.

In many ways Richardson's *Sir Charles Grandison* is a more ambitious work than either *Pamela: Or, Virtue Rewarded* (1740) or *Clarissa*. Its setting is not confined to countryside and town in England; the novel reaches to France and Italy. The range of public and private manners Richardson depicts covers not only those of England but also those of Italy. The sympathetic and tolerant account Richardson gives of Roman Catholic characters and ways is unusual in mid-eighteenth century English fiction. In addition, Richardson provides his letter writers in *Sir Charles Grandison* with a larger and more complicated cast of characters upon whom to exercise their pens. While the novel lacks the single-minded intensity of Richardson's earlier works, which concentrate on the fate of the main character, secondary characters in *Sir Charles Grandison* are granted lives of their own. The way their independent existences are connected one to another and the way their concerns are explored give *Sir Charles Grandison* dimension and realism that Richardson's other novels lack.

"Critical Evaluation" by Margaret Duggan

Bibliography:

Doody, Margaret Anne. *A Natural Passion: A Study of the Novels of Samuel Richardson*. Oxford, England: Clarendon Press, 1964. Sympathetic treatment. Examines *Sir Charles Grandison* as comedy. Discusses the personalities of the women and the imagery in the novel.

Flynn, Carol Houlihan. *Samuel Richardson: A Man of Letters*. Princeton, N.J.: Princeton University Press, 1982. Brief discussions of various aspects of *Sir Charles Grandison*—for example, the use of epistolary method, the figure of the rake, sexual conflict, and the role of romance.

McKillop, Alan Dugald. "On *Sir Charles Grandison*." In *Samuel Richardson*, edited by John Carroll. Englewood Cliffs, N.J.: Prentice-Hall, 1969. Argues that *Sir Charles Grandison* excels in making readers feel "intimacy with a group of characters set in the framework of a familiar society." Suggests that the novel paved the way for later novels of manners.

Marks, Sylvia Kasey. "Man and God in Richardson's *Sir Charles Grandison*." In *Man, God, and Nature in the Enlightenment*. Edited by Donald C. Mell et al. East Lansing, Mich.: Colleagues Press, 1988. Discusses the treatment of Christianity in *Sir Charles Grandison*. Examines Sir Charles's character in light of the Christian religion.

____________. *Sir Charles Grandison: The Compleat Conduct Book*. Cranbury, N.J.: Bucknell University Press, 1986. Examines *Sir Charles Grandison* in its social context. Discusses the novel as "the culmination of the conduct-book tradition."

SIR GAWAIN AND THE GREEN KNIGHT

Type of work: Poetry
Author: Pearl-Poet (fl. late fourteenth century)
Type of plot: Arthurian romance
Time of plot: Sixth century
Locale: England
First transcribed: Fourteenth century

Principal characters:
Sir Gawain, a knight of the Round Table
Sir Bernlak de Hautdesert, the Green Knight

The Story:

On Christmas Eve, many knights and fair ladies gathered in King Arthur's banquet hall, there to feast and enjoy the holiday festivities. Suddenly a stranger entered the room. He was a giant, clad all in green armor, and with a green face, hair, and beard. He advanced, gave his greetings, and then loudly issued his challenge. Was there a knight in the group who would dare to trade blows with the mighty Green Knight? He who accepted was to strike one blow with a battle-ax immediately. Then on New Year's morning, a year hence, the Green Knight was to repay the blow, at his own castle in a distant land. Arrogantly, the Green Knight waited for an answer. From King Arthur's ranks answered the voice of Sir Gawain, who accepted the challenge.

King Arthur and the other knights watched approvingly as Sir Gawain advanced, ax in hand, to confront the Green Knight. The stranger knelt down, bared his neck, and waited for the blow. Sir Gawain struck, sure and true, and the head of the Green Knight was severed from his body. While all gaped in amazement, the Green Knight picked up his head in his hands, leaped upon his charger, and rode toward the gate. As he rode, the lips of the head shouted defiance at Sir Gawain, reminding him of their forthcoming meeting at the Green Chapel on the coming New Year.

The months passed quickly. Noble deeds were legion at the Round Table, and an atmosphere of gaiety pervaded King Arthur's castle. Then, when autumn came, Sir Gawain departed on his promised quest, and with much concern the other knights saw him set forth. Sir Gawain, riding his horse Gringalet, went northward, and at last arrived in Wirral, a wild and uncivilized region. On his way he was often in danger of death, for he faced fire-puffing dragons, fierce animals, and savage wild men in his search for the Knight of the Green Chapel. At last, on Christmas Eve, Sir Gawain saw a great castle in the middle of the wilderness. He entered it and was made welcome.

His host offered Sir Gawain the entire facilities of the castle. In the beautifully furnished chamber which he occupied, Sir Gawain was served the finest dishes and the best wines. The lady of the castle, a lady more beautiful even than Queen Guinevere, sat with him as he ate. The next day was Christmas, and the lord of the castle led in the feasting. Expressing the wish that Sir Gawain would remain at the castle for a long time, the host assured the knight that the Green Chapel was only a short distance away, so that it would not be necessary for him to leave until New Year's Day. The lord of the castle also asked Sir Gawain to keep a covenant with him. During his stay Sir Gawain was to receive all the game that his host caught during the day's hunt. In return, Sir Gawain was to exchange any gifts he received at the castle while the host was away.

On the first morning that the host hunted, Sir Gawain was awakened by the lady of the castle. She entered his chamber, seated herself on his couch, and spoke words of love to him. Sir Gawain resisted temptation and took nothing from the lady. That evening, when the host presented his bounty from the hunt, Sir Gawain answered truthfully that he had received nothing that day. The second morning the same thing happened. Sir Gawain remained chaste in spite of the lady's conduct. On the third morning, however, the day before Sir Gawain was to depart, she gave him an embroidered silk girdle which she said would keep him safe from any mortal blow. Then she kissed him three times and departed. That evening Sir Gawain kissed his host three times, but he did not mention the silken girdle he had received.

On New Year's morning, Sir Gawain set forth from the castle and rode to the Green Chapel. He found it without difficulty; as he approached he heard the Green Knight sharpening his ax. When Sir Gawain announced that he was ready for the blow and bared his head, the Green Knight raised his ax high in the air in preparation for the stroke of death. Sir Gawain first involuntarily jumped aside as the ax descended. The second time, the Green Knight merely struck at Sir Gawain, not touching him at all. With the third blow he wounded Sir Gawain in the neck, drawing a great deal of blood. Then Sir Gawain shouted that he had fulfilled the covenant. The Green Knight laughed loudly at that and began to praise Sir Gawain's courage.

To Sir Gawain's surprise, the Green Knight revealed himself as the host of the castle and explained the blows. On the first two blows Sir Gawain escaped injury, because for two days he had faithfully kept the covenant. The third drew blood, however, because Sir Gawain had failed to reveal the gift to Sir Bernlak de Hautdesert. Together with Morgain le Fay, King Arthur's half sister, the Green Knight had planned this whole affair to test the strength and valor of King Arthur's knights. They had devised the disguise of the Green Knight and persuaded Lady de Hautdesert to try tempting Sir Gawain. Sir Gawain had withstood the test of temptation well, his only fault was the keeping of the girdle. The host forgave him for his act, however, because it was the love of life that had motivated Sir Gawain.

The two knights returned to the castle, and a few days later Sir Gawain journeyed back to King Arthur's court. As he rode he gazed with shame at the girdle. It was to remain with Sir Gawain as a reminder of the moment when he yielded and succumbed to the weakness of the flesh. At King Arthur's castle all the knights and ladies listened to the tale of Sir Gawain and the Green Knight, and then, to show their love for the young knight, they all donned silk girdles. This symbol became a traditional part of the costume of the Knights of the Round Table.

Critical Evaluation:

Sir Gawain and the Green Knight at first glance seems to be a conventional chivalric romance, featuring many of the standard trappings of Arthurian legend: A brave knight of the Round Table is challenged to a seemingly impossible task by a magical creature; on the way to meeting the challenge the knight fights fierce beasts and is charmed by a lovely lady; and he displays almost superhuman courage, skill, and chivalric courtesy to overcome his foe. The poem, however, is concerned with much more than these conventional features of courage and courtesy. In a conventional medieval romance, chivalric courtesy revolves around love, and adulterous love in particular. The "courteous" knight (in the medieval sense, a knight who is "courtly," and who understands and lives by the social rules of the court) is expected to be skilled in love and romantic rhetoric, and devoted to fulfilling the wishes of beautiful ladies. In temptation scenes with the wife of Bernlak, Gawain is forced to choose between this worldly, secular courtesy, which would require giving in to the lady's wishes, and a courtesy of a different sort: spiritual courtesy, which requires fidelity to a host as well as chastity. To refuse the lady without giving offense requires all of Gawain's skill in courteous, roundabout rhetoric.

The wordplay between the seductive lady and the determined but courtly Gawain forms a game of sorts that the poet poses in direct contrast to the exchange-of-winnings game Bernlak has proposed, as well as to Bernlak's own hunting exploits (for wild "game"). The exchange of ax blows between Gawain and the Green Knight is a game too, and Gawain mistakenly believes that it is the game on which his life depends. Ultimately, readers realize that the Green Knight/Bernlak has been enjoying a game of his own at Gawain's expense. Much of the poem's irony rests on the fact that Gawain and readers do not realize on which game Gawain's life depends until the end of the poem. The ironic interplay of these several kinds of games is central to the poem's meaning. By making a series of games into a matter of life and death, the poet offers a subtle criticism of the chivalric ideal of behavior, which places a higher value on honorably obeying the rules of a frivolous game than on saving one's life.

Gawain's failure to give up the girdle forms the central moral question of the poem. It seems clear that, according to chivalric principles, he should surrender the girdle. To do so is part of the game, and Gawain prides himself on his chivalrous qualities, which include keeping his promises. Readers can sympathize, however; after all, the Green Knight, who rode off holding his severed head under his arm, is using some kind of magic; why should Gawain not use what magic he might? The chivalric requirement that he give up the girdle seems ridiculous in the face of death. The reader is not surprised when Gawain conceals the magic girdle in order to save his life. Although Gawain later reproaches himself for covetousness in keeping the girdle, his only fault really is wanting to save his own life. This flaw, however, makes Gawain seem more real, and thus makes it easier to admire his virtues of courage and knightly courtesy.

Much is made of the Green Knight as a symbol of wild nature, contrasted with the civilization of the court and the knightly ideals it admires and represents. This, however, is an incomplete view of the Green Knight. The elaborate description of the Green Knight at Arthur's court details how his green is lavishly embellished by gold embroidery and decoration. The gold can be seen as representing civilization imposed on nature and wildness. With the green-and-gold motif, the Green Knight represents a balance between nature and civilization; he is, after all, the same person as Bernlak, who is a perfect, courteous host. The Green Knight is the real, and is in contrast to Gawain, who represents the ideal. It does, after all, seem rather unnatural that Gawain should be willing to give up his life just to maintain a façade of civilization (that is, if he were to give up the girdle because it is the polite thing to do).

The theme of the poem is the attempt to achieve perfection (spiritual and secular) in the real world. Gawain's ideals for himself are shown to be unrealistic in the face of death. Although Gawain comes about as close to ideal behavior as a real person can expect to, his ideal of perfection is impossible to attain. In the end, he wears the green girdle back to the court of the Round Table as an emblem of his failure and shame. When Arthur's court laughs and congratulates him, paying little attention to his own notions of failure (just as the Green Knight did when he revealed himself as Bernlak), the reader is invited to join in the court's judgment. Gawain is not a two-dimensional embodiment of conventional knightly ideals, but rather is a realistically drawn character facing a dilemma, and demonstrating the compromises involved in putting an ideal standard of conduct into practice in the real world.

Sir Gawain and the Green Knight was first transcribed in the second half of the fourteenth century, the same era in which Geoffrey Chaucer wrote *The Canterbury Tales* (1387-1400) and other works in English. Unlike Geoffrey Chaucer, of whose life many details are known, very little is known about the author of *Sir Gawain and the Green Knight*. Only one original manuscript of the poem is known to exist, which is also the sole manuscript of three other poems. Although in terms of subject matter *Sir Gawain and the Green Knight* has little in common with the other poems of the manuscript, which are religious works, it is generally accepted that all four poems are by the same author. The dialect used in the poem suggests that the author was from the Midlands of England. Although the poet seems to have lived and written far from London and the court, his poem is as sophisticated and urbane as any of Chaucer's works. The author's emphasis on development of character, vivid descriptions, and use of naturalistic dialogue (a quality that, owing to the fact that his dialect has become obsolete, is not immediately recognizable) also mark a common ground with Chaucer. The complexity of the poem's themes, along with the poet's masterful use of irony and skillful artistry in weaving together the temptation game and the exchange-of-blows game, make *Sir Gawain and the Green Knight* one of the most important literary works of medieval England.

"Critical Evaluation" by Catherine Swanson

Bibliography:

Barron, W. R. J. *Trawthe and Treason: The Sin of Gawain Reconsidered.* Manchester, England: Manchester University Press, 1980. Examines Gawain's sin of deception, and the temptation and beheading games, in the context of medieval society and feudal law. Also examines the parallels between the hunting and temptation scenes.

Benson, Larry D. *Art and Tradition in Sir Gawain and the Green Knight.* New Brunswick, N.J.: Rutgers University Press, 1965. Excellent background material and discussion of the sources, literary conventions, style, structure, and meaning of the poem.

Fox, Denton, ed. *Twentieth Century Interpretations of Sir Gawain and the Green Knight.* Englewood Cliffs, N.J.: Prentice-Hall, 1968. A brief but useful collection of critical essays, which also includes brief writings on the poem by such noted critics as C. S. Lewis and A. C. Spearing.

Howard, Donald R., and Christian Zacker, eds. *Critical Studies of Sir Gawain and the Green Knight.* Notre Dame, Ind.: University of Notre Dame Press, 1968. Provides a thorough discussion of all major aspects of *Sir Gawain and the Green Knight.* Essays are grouped by subject and cover such topics as critical issues, style and technique, and characterization and setting.

Waldron, R. A. Introduction to *Sir Gawain and the Green Knight.* London: Edward Arnold, 1970. Offers one of the best and most comprehensive overviews available of the poem's action, themes, and structure. Detailed annotation and an extensive glossary offer insights into the original text that are not found in most critical surveys. An excellent starting point.

THE SIRENS OF TITAN

Type of work: Novel
Author: Kurt Vonnegut, Jr. (1922-   )
Type of plot: Science fiction
Time of plot: The Nightmare Ages, between World War II and the Third Great Depression
Locale: Earth, Mars, Mercury, and the ninth moon of Saturn (Titan)
First published: 1959

Principal characters:

MALACHI CONSTANT, UNK, SPACE WANDERER, the victim of a series of accidents
WINSTON NILES RUMFOORD, a space and time traveler
BEATRICE RUMFOORD, wife of Rumfoord, mate to Constant
CHRONO, son of Constant and Beatrice
BOAZ, a commander in the Martian army
SALO, a Tralfamadorian stranded on Titan

The Story:

Malachi Constant arrived at the Rumfoord estate to witness a materialization. Winston Niles Rumfoord, who was chrono-synclastic infundibula, scattered everywhere between the Sun and Betelgeuse and appeared various places sporadically. He was to materialize and Constant was invited to witness. Constant was a billionaire playboy who had inherited his father Noel's estate.

Rumfoord materialized and told Constant that he, Constant, would eventually go to Mars, Mercury, back to Earth, then to Titan. He and Beatrice Rumfoord, Rumfoord's wife, would have a child named Chrono. Chrono would pick up a good luck piece on Mars and carry it to Titan. Beatrice and Constant were chary of their union. Constant sold the company that owned the only known transportation to Mars, which was a spaceship called *The Whale*, which Beatrice bought. This buying and selling, along with Constant's fifty-six-day party, which ended with him giving away all his oil wells, ruined Constant financially, and Beatrice was likewise ruined financially.

Upon losing all his money, Constant was open for options. Secret agents from Mars recruited him for the Martian army. Beatrice was surreptitiously recruited. On the spaceship to Mars, Constant raped Beatrice. When on Mars, they were separated and their memories were erased from their brains.

Constant began as an officer but after eight years he was made a private and was nicknamed "Unk." His first act after having his memory cleared out for the seventh time was to execute his best friend Stony Stevenson in front of ten thousand Martian soldiers. Before Unk strangled Stevenson, Stevenson managed to tell him "Blue stone . . . Barrack twelve . . . letter." Unk found the stone and the letter. Written on it were things about Stevenson; about the antennas under the soldiers' skulls, which made them do whatever the commanders wanted; about Beatrice and Chrono; and about the Martian army and its plans to make war on Earth. It informed Unk that Boaz, a private first class in the army, did not have an antenna in his head and that he was the one who gave pain to everyone and controlled everyone in Unk's squad. The letter was signed by Unk.

The war on Earth was a complete disaster from the Martian point of view. Before boarding the spaceship, Unk deserted the army and found Beatrice and Chrono. They did not know him or care about him. Unk was returned to his unit, where he and Boaz were put on a spaceship that was designed by Rumfoord to go to Mercury instead of Earth and thus Unk and Boaz missed the war.

Unk and Boaz were stranded deep in a cavern on Mercury where there was no life except for harmoniums, small creatures that lived by eating vibrations. Boaz was especially attached to the harmoniums. He played music from the ship's tape collection, and he allowed his favorite harmoniums to feed from his own pulse. Rumfoord occasionally arranged harmoniums on the walls of the caves to give Unk and Boaz messages. The final message was to turn the ship upside down and it would fly out. Boaz stayed with the harmoniums and Unk traveled on to Earth, where he was greeted as the Space Wanderer, the messiah of the Church of God the Utterly Indifferent. Rumfoord knew of many events that would transpire in future times and had prophesied that Unk would arrive on Earth, exactly as he did, and that when he was asked what happened to him he would reply, "I was a victim of a series of accidents, as are we all." As Unk did exactly what was forecast, the religion Rumfoord had set up became even stronger, as the only one on Earth in which predictions actually came to pass.

Rumfoord staged an elaborate ceremony in which Unk was told by Rumfoord that he had strangled Stevenson. This was Unk's final blow, as he had wished, since reading the message, to find his best friend. Rumfoord explained to Unk that he was Constant before becoming Unk and that Constant was the symbol of evil to the Church of God the Utterly Indifferent. With Beatrice and Chrono, Unk was martyred, sent away in exile to live out his life on Titan.

Upon arrival in Titan, Rumfoord informed Salo, the Tralfamadorian machine who had long been stranded, that the replacement part for his spaceship was now there, in the form of Chrono's good luck piece. Salo did not realize that the entire history of human life on Earth was for his sake. Human life had been made to exist by the Tralfamadorians, who were working to get Salo the replacement part as quickly as they could.

Rumfoord disappeared and Beatrice moved into his home on Titan. Salo self-destructed and Constant lived in Salo's spaceship. Chrono went to live with the giant blue birds of Titan, the most noble creatures on the planet. Chrono's final gesture to Constant and Beatrice was to show appreciation for them having given him life.

Beatrice died and Salo came back to life. Salo gave Constant a ride to Earth, where he died on a street corner. His last thought was a posthypnotic illusion, placed in his mind by Salo, that made him believe that Stevenson came to greet him and took him to paradise.

Critical Evaluation:

The book's disclaimer is a superbly creative and tongue-in-cheek way to begin. It reads: "All persons, places, and events in this book are real. . . . No names have been changed to protect the innocent since God Almighty protects the innocent as a matter of heavenly routine." *The Sirens of Titan*, Kurt Vonnegut's second novel, was originally published as pulp science fiction. There was no respectable hardcover edition. The book's satire and depth was not perceived until many years later, after Vonnegut had achieved fame through *Slaughterhouse-Five* (1969). *The Sirens of Titan* was written in less than two months; the plot line was determined over cocktails at a party. Vonnegut took the job writing it because the magazine market was not as good as the science fiction novel market and he could make more money in two months on a novel. In *The Sirens of Titan*, Vonnegut fashioned several characters and scenes that were employed in his later novels. The invention of the planet Tralfamador is one of these. The Martian recruiters were characters he had used in a story for the *Saturday Evening Post*.

The theme of *The Sirens of Titan* is whether or not human history is meaningful. The answer, and moral, as is often found in Vonnegut's books, is to love whoever is around to be loved, to abandon expectations, and to live fully in the moment at hand. In the caves of Mercury, Boaz states, "I don't know what's going on and I'm probably not smart enough to understand if somebody was to explain it to me. All I know is we're being tested somehow, by somebody or some thing a whole lot smarter than us, and all I can do is be friendly and keep calm and try to have a nice time till it's over."

Rumfoord is the most intricate character in this novel. Vonnegut has said that Rumfoord is based on Franklin Delano Roosevelt. Rumfoord's personal dilemma is that he is used by the Tralfamadorians, just as everyone else is used. He, he thinks, who seems to have so much power and control, should be allowed to determine his own fate and destiny. He is not, and his position is particularly obscure because he arranges the great suicide of the Martian army in order to do what he perceives as a good thing, setting up a religion on Earth in which everyone is equal.

In this religion, people wear handicaps to limit whatever gifts or talents with which they were born. Strong people wear weights, beautiful women wear ugly makeup, people with good eyesight wear glasses to hamper their vision. All the people of Earth participate in this, under Rumfoord's supervision. Rumfoord thinks that, in causing a war and then presenting the world with a new and unified religion, he has accomplished a noble and decent act. He wants to think it was his own idea, that he has been operating of his own free will.

In the end, Rumfoord is found to be no more in control of his destiny than any of the people he controlled. He was made to stage the war and do everything he did by the Tralfamadorians. Vonnegut shows with Rumfoord that even those who appear to have the most power are just as baffled as to the meaning of life as everyone else is. Rumfoord is the only character who seems to be disgruntled with his lack of free will. Everyone else more or less accepts it.

Biblical references abound in the book. Constant adopts the name Jonah and owned a spaceship called *The Whale*. The fortune obtained by Noel Constant was done by breaking the sentences of the book of Genesis into two-letter acronym combinations and finding company names that started with the two letters. The religion Rumfoord founds adopts the same God as is in the Bible, only this religion's God does not care about the plight of humans, or the plight of anything else. Though Vonnegut has claimed he is an atheist, he makes considerable use of the Bible in this and in many of his works.

With *The Sirens of Titan*, Vonnegut not only presents characters that he also uses in later novels, he also uses many themes that will later become Vonnegut hallmarks: middle-class virtues, decency, friendliness, respect, neighborliness, spiritual success through kindness and generosity. He asserts his theory of space and time through Rumfoord. Rumfoord says, "When I ran my spaceship into the chrono-synclastic infundibulum, it came to me in a flash that everything that ever has been always will be, and everything that ever will be always has been." This is as clear an explanation of Vonnegut's sense of fate as can be found.

Beaird Glover

Bibliography:

Giannone, Richard. *Vonnegut: A Preface to His Novels*. Port Washington, N.Y.: Kennikat Press, 1977. Focuses on the method of Vonnegut's novels. The dignified and extensive treatment of *The Sirens of Titan* considers the chapters in small clusters, restating the plot and then discussing the implications from several angles.

Klinkowitz, Jerome. *Kurt Vonnegut*. New York: Methuen, 1982. Discusses *The Sirens of Titan* as a formula novel. Explains it as being like other novels by Vonnegut in adhering to the structures indicative of science fiction, as opposed to later, more experimental and personal novels.

Mayo, Clark. *Kurt Vonnegut: The Gospel from Outer Space (Or, Yes We Have No Nirvanas).* San Bernardino, Calif.: Borgo Press, 1977. A fairly short book adopting Vonnegut's style, voice, and satire while writing about Vonnegut. Discusses *The Sirens of Titan* in detail.

Reed, Peter J. *Kurt Vonnegut, Jr.* New York: Thomas Y. Crowell, 1972. Considers the characteristic themes and fictional techniques of Vonnegut. The subhead to the thirty-page chapter on *The Sirens of Titan* is "Existential Science Fiction." Compares Vonnegut to classic and contemporary writers.

Schatt, Stanley. *Kurt Vonnegut, Jr.* Boston: Twayne, 1976. Extensive quotation and interpretation of *The Sirens of Titan* with attention to plot, structure, style, and technique. Includes a section on Vonnegut as a public figure.

SISTER CARRIE

Type of work: Novel
Author: Theodore Dreiser (1871-1945)
Type of plot: Naturalism
Time of plot: 1889
Locale: Chicago and New York
First published: 1900

Principal characters:
CARRIE MEEBER, a small-town girl
CHARLES DROUET, her first lover
G. W. HURSTWOOD, Drouet's friend and Carrie's second lover

The Story:

When Carrie Meeber left her hometown in Wisconsin, she had nothing but a few dollars and a certain unspoiled beauty and charm. Young and inexperienced, she was going to Chicago to live with her sister and find work. While on the train, she met Charles Drouet, a genial, flashy traveling salesman. Before the train pulled into the station, they had exchanged addresses, and Drouet promised to call on Carrie at her sister's house.

When she arrived at her sister's home, Carrie discovered that her life there would be far from the happy, carefree existence of which she had dreamed. The Hansons were hardworking people, grim and penny-pinching; they allowed themselves no pleasures and lived a dull, conventional life. It was clear to Carrie that Drouet could not possibly call there, not only because of the unattractive atmosphere but also because the Hansons were sure to object to him. She wrote and told him that he was not to call, and that she would get in touch with him later.

Carrie went job-hunting and finally found work in a small shoe factory. Of her first wages, all but fifty cents went to her sister and brother-in-law. When she fell ill, she lost her job and again had to look for work. Day after day, she trudged the streets, without success. It seemed as if she would have to go back to Wisconsin, and the Hansons encouraged her to do so, since they did not want her if she could not bring in money.

One day while looking for work, Carrie met Drouet and told him her troubles. He offered her money which, with reluctance, she finally accepted. The money was for clothes she needed, but she did not know how to explain the source of the money to her sister. Drouet solved the problem by suggesting that he rent a room for her, where she could keep her clothing. A few days later, Carrie went to live with Drouet, who had promised to marry her as soon as he had completed a business deal.

In the meantime, Drouet introduced her to a friend, G. W. Hurstwood. Hurstwood had a good job as the manager of a saloon, a comfortable home, a wife, and two grown children. More than twice Carrie's age, he nevertheless accepted Drouet's suggestion that he look in on her while the salesman was out of town on one of his trips. Before long, Hurstwood was passionately in love with Carrie. When Drouet came back, he discovered from a chambermaid that Carrie and Hurstwood had been going out together frequently. Carrie was furious when Drouet told her that Hurstwood was already married. She blamed Drouet for her folly, saying that he should have told her that Hurstwood was a married man.

Mrs. Hurstwood had meanwhile become suspicious of her husband. Drouet had secured for Carrie a part in a theatrical entertainment that a local lodge was presenting. Hurstwood, hearing that Carrie was to appear, persuaded many of his friends to go with him to the show. Mrs. Hurstwood learned of this and heard, too, that her husband had been seen riding with an unknown woman. She confronted Hurstwood and told him that she intended to sue for divorce. Faced with social and financial ruin, Hurstwood was in despair. One night, he discovered that his employer's safe was open. He robbed it of several thousand dollars and went to Carrie's apartment. Drouet had just deserted her. Pretending that Drouet had been hurt, Hurstwood succeeded in getting Carrie on a train bound for Montreal. In Montreal, he was tracked down by an agent of his former employer, who urged him to return the money and settle the issue quietly. Hurstwood returned all but a relatively small sum and married Carrie under the name of Wheeler. Carrie was under the impression that the ceremony was legal. Then they left for New York, where Hurstwood looked for work but with no success. Finally, he bought a partnership in a small tavern, but when the partnership was dissolved, he lost all his money. Again he started looking for work. Gradually he grew less eager for a job and began staying at home all day. When bills piled up, he and Carrie moved to a new apartment to escape their creditors.

Setting out to find work herself, Carrie managed to get a job as a chorus girl. With a friend, she took an apartment and left Hurstwood to himself. Soon Carrie became a well-known actress. A local hotel invited her to become a guest there, at a nominal expense. Carrie now had many friends and admirers, as well as money and all the comforts and luxuries that appealed to a small-town girl.

Hurstwood had not fared as well. He still had not found work. Once, during a labor strike, he worked as a scab, but he left that job because it was too hazardous. He began to live in Bowery flophouses and to beg on the streets. One day, he went to see Carrie, who gave him money, largely because she had seen Drouet and had learned for the first time of Hurstwood's theft in Chicago. She believed that Hurstwood had kept his disgrace a secret in order to spare her feelings.

Although Carrie was a toast of the town and successful, she was not happy. She was invited to give performances abroad. Hurstwood died and, unbeknownst to Carrie, was buried in the potter's field. As Carrie was sailing for London, Hurstwood's former wife, daughter, and son-in-law arrived in the city, eager for pleasure and social success, which had been made possible by the daughter's marriage and Hurstwood's divorce settlement, in which his family had received all of his property.

Critical Evaluation:

Sister Carrie, like most of Theodore Dreiser's novels, embodies his belief that while humans are controlled and conditioned by heredity, instinct, and chance, a few extraordinary and usually unsophisticated individuals refuse to accept their fate wordlessly and instead strive, albeit unsuccessfully, to find meaning and purpose for their existence. Carrie, the title character, senses that she is merely a cipher in an uncaring world, yet she seeks to grasp the mysteries of life and satisfy her need to matter. In pointing out "how curious are the vagaries of fortune," Dreiser suggests that even when life is cruel, its enigmatic quality makes it all the more fascinating.

Despite its title, the novel is not a study of a family but of Carrie's strangely unemotional relationships with three men and of the resulting and unexpected changes that occur in her outlook and status. A "half-equipped little knight" with small talent, Carrie's instincts nevertheless raise her from a poor girl to a successful actress. The novel traces the rise, through Carrie's increasing reliance on instinct, in three stages of development.

Initially, Carrie is at least partially ruled by reason, but by the end of the first phase of her rise—marked by her accidental second meeting with Drouet and her submission to his promises—she begins to abandon reason, since it has not served her well. During this second portion, her blossoming instinct pulls her to the material advantages offered by Drouet, and her life with him is evidence of her growing commitment to these instincts. Yet it is her almost unconscious and unplanned switch to Hurstwood that reveals how totally she is now following her instincts. Hurstwood offers finer material possessions and more emotional rapport, and Carrie drifts easily into his orbit. Now fully and irrevocably tied to her instincts, Carrie throughout the rest of the novel considers it an obligation to self to let these impulses lead her where they will. When a stage career and her association with Ames replace the relationship with Hurstwood, she is merely proceeding further along that path. As a plant must turn toward the sun, Carrie must feed her unsatisfied urge for happiness.

Closely related to Dreiser's belief that instinct must prevail is his thesis that humans lack responsibility for their fate, a thesis suggested by all three main characters. Drouet leads Carrie to what some consider her moral downfall, but, as Dreiser states, "There was nothing evil in the fellow." His glands are to blame, not he. Neither is there any question of guilt in Hurstwood's case. Since he rarely makes a choice, he cannot be expected to answer for what happens to him. Chance, not conviction, makes him a thief. Hurstwood's wife, not he himself, ends their marriage. Even his attraction to Carrie is a thing of chance, for "He was merely floating those gossamer threads of thought which, like the spider's, he hoped would lay hold somewhere." Although merely a sham without true power or greatness (a fact Dreiser, dazzled by his own creation, seems to forget), Hurstwood, in his decline from semiprominence to degradation, reminds the reader that the forces that send Carrie to stardom can with equal ease reduce a man to nothing.

Dreiser presents his ideas through many symbolic images, most important of which are the urban city, the sea, and the rocking chair. The city, represented in the book by New York and Chicago, is a microcosm of Dreiser's universe. Nature is grim and unfeeling, as is the city. Unless an individual is strong, productive, and fortunate, the world is indifferent, a state magnified in the city where people are perhaps more isolated than elsewhere. When Hurstwood is dying, he is alone, even though Carrie is in a nearby apartment, Drouet is relatively close in a hotel, and his wife is arriving by train. No one knows, or cares, about his tragedy. Dreiser's concept of an uncaring and ever-changing universe is equally conveyed by his use of the sea and the rocking chair. Again and again, Carrie is described as a "lone figure in a tossing, thoughtless sea." Like its counterpart, the city, the sea symbol suggests that only the strong or the lucky survive. The rocking chair hints at the futility of this constant flux, for a rocking chair is in continual motion but goes nowhere. Although Carrie's life would seem to improve, she is sitting miserably in a rocking chair not only at the novel's beginning but also at its end. While this circular development suggests that Carrie has small chance to become truly happy, the fact that she continues to rock provides evidence of her never-ceasing aspiration.

Part of the book reflects events from Dreiser's own turbulent life. In 1886, L. A. Hopkins, a clerk in a Chicago saloon, took thirty-five hundred dollars from his employers, and fled to New York with Emma Dreiser, one of the author's many troubled siblings. Dreiser modeled Carrie on his sister and used Hopkins for aspects of Hurstwood's personality. By the time Dreiser finished the novel in 1900, however, he had gone far beyond the cheap story of adultery and theft to create a work that presented complex questions of innocence and guilt.

The publication of Dreiser's first novel was surrounded by the kind of controversy and confusion that marked the entire career of this man. Apparently, the novel was accepted by

Doubleday during the absence of Frank Doubleday, the senior partner, who upon his return expressed doubt about its content and style. Refusing to release the firm from its unwritten commitment, however, Dreiser demanded that the book be published, and it appeared in 1900. Although it sold poorly (Dreiser earned only $68.40) and was not aggressively promoted by the publishers, stories relating Mrs. Doubleday's violent objections to its moral view and the resulting suppression of the novel are unverified legend. In his own typical confusion of fact and half-fact, Dreiser added to the myths by telling conflicting accounts of what had happened.

Reaction to the book was surprisingly widespread. Many critics attacked its philosophical premises as immoral. Such charges and those that the novel was poorly written, wordy, and melodramatic would later greet each of Dreiser's productions. Yet as Dreiser wrote book after book, exploring the yearning of the young for riches, position, and understanding—a yearning he himself experienced overwhelmingly, coming as he did from a poor and disturbed Indiana family in which he saw reflected much of the irony of the world. Readers were struck, however, by the sincerity, powerful detail, and massive impact of his work. Dreiser became especially known for *Jennie Gerhardt* (1911) and *An American Tragedy* (1925), which placed him securely among the most respected American writers of his time.

"Critical Evaluation" by Judith Bloch

Bibliography:

Gerber, Philip. *Theodore Dreiser Revisited.* New York: Twayne, 1992. A biographical and thematic analysis of Dreiser's major works, which interprets *Sister Carrie* as a naturalistic novel in the tradition of Émile Zola in France and Stephen Crane and Frank Norris in the United States.

Kaplan, Amy. "The Sentimental Revolt of *Sister Carrie*." In *The Social Construction of American Realism.* Chicago: University of Chicago Press, 1988. Excellent discussion of the novel within the framework of American realism. Juxtaposes Dreiser's power as a realist—challenging moral and literary conventions—with his simultaneous reliance on sentimental codes. A second chapter, "Theodore Dreiser's Promotion of Authorship," explores Dreiser's conception of the realist within the literary marketplace.

Pizer, Donald. *The Novels of Theodore Dreiser: A Critical Study.* Minneapolis: University of Minnesota Press, 1976. A classic treatment of Dreiser's novels by one of the most important Dreiser scholars. Discusses the composition history of *Sister Carrie*, its biographical and literary sources, and provides an excellent general introduction to the novel's themes.

_____________, ed. *New Essays on "Sister Carrie."* New York: Cambridge University Press, 1991. Contains, in addition to Pizer's thorough discussion of the novel's historical and biographical background, four essays that explore in depth Dreiser's naturalism, the novel's narrative voice, and the relationship between the author and his heroine.

Sloane, David E. E. *"Sister Carrie": Theodore Dreiser's Sociological Tragedy.* New York: Twayne, 1992. A book-length study of the novel that provides literary and historical context. Interprets the work as a sociological tragedy, focusing on plot, style, metaphor, symbol, and character. Also includes a selected annotated bibliography of criticism.

SISTER PHILOMÈNE

Type of work: Novel
Authors: Edmond de Goncourt (1822-1896) and Jules de Goncourt (1830-1870)
Type of plot: Naturalism
Time of plot: Nineteenth century
Locale: Paris
First published: *Sœur Philomène*, 1861 (English translation, 1890)

Principal characters:
MARIE GAUCHER, later known as Philomène
CÉLINE, her friend
MADAME DE VIRY, the employer of Philomène's aunt
HENRI DE VIRY, Madame de Viry's son
BARNIER, a young doctor
MALIVOIRE, his friend and a doctor
ROMAINE, Barnier's former mistress

The Story:

In a hospital ward, two white-clad Sisters of St. Augustine were making their rounds. One of them, a novice, was Sister Philomène, whose name had originally been Marie Gaucher. She was the daughter of a tailoress and a locksmith and had been orphaned at the age of four, when she was adopted by an aunt who was a servant to the widowed Madame de Viry. In that pleasant household, the child began to thrive, and she soon assumed equal footing with Madame de Viry's son, Henri. Madame de Viry felt this situation to be dangerous and she sent the child, screaming, to a convent orphanage. To avoid confusion with another child there called Marie, the Sisters called her Philomène. Though she was miserable at first, she gradually lost her resentment as she became accustomed to convent routine, although she changed from a vivacious child into a quiet and whining one. She was restless, living only for her aunt's monthly visit. One Sister, the ugly but good and kind Marguerite, paid special attention to Philomène.

At the age of ten, Philomène became the intimate friend of a newcomer, twelve-year-old Céline. Much of Céline's childhood had been spent in reading the *Lives of the Saints* aloud to her infirm grandmother, and she had developed a mystic temperament. She like to deny herself pleasures, to fast, and to invent self-punishments, and she converted Philomène to a course of personal sacrifices. Philomène worked herself up to a state of religious agitation, habitually spending all of Sunday in church and looking forward to that prospect as she once had to her aunt's visits. She became sickly and irritable, and her thoughts were always on death. When her eyes began to give her trouble, the Sisters sent her with her aunt to see an eye doctor. On that occasion, Philomène visited Madame de Viry's house for the first time since she had entered the orphanage.

Back in the convent, Philomène felt miserable and forlorn. She succeeded in maintaining her state of feverish piety for two years, but then her faith became automatic and unfelt. Céline left the orphanage to become a nun; Sister Marguerite left for her health. The convent became unbearable to Philomène; she went into a decline and was so close to death that her aunt was permitted to take her away. Madame de Viry had died, and Philomène now became a servant to Monsieur Henri. Philomène longed to sacrifice herself for him, and she rejected the advances of a coarse groom who hoped eventually, by marrying her, to gain the management of Henri's house.

One night, Philomène overheard Henri telling her aunt that he would have brought a woman home with him had it not been for the presence of an unmarried girl in the house. When he suggested that Philomène marry the groom, she fainted. Later, though assured she would not be sent away, she decided to begin her novitiate to the Sisters of St. Augustine. With seven months of her novitiate to complete before taking her vows, she was sent to a hospital to replace her friend Céline, who had died of typhoid.

The doctors agreed that Philomène was pretty, but Barnier, under whom she worked, said that he preferred the old ones, tried and true. Philomène's original horror of the hospital was relieved by its clean, peaceful atmosphere at first, but later the realization of death and disease tortured her. Mid-morning breakfast was the happiest hour for her, for then, useful and busy feeding and cheering her patients, Philomène gained strength for the rest of the day. By the time she realized that she could do no more than relieve suffering, she was inured to the hospital. She was never hardened, however, and her patients loved her for her tenderness.

Philomène earned the respect of doctors and students alike by her courage and compassion. Soon she was all-powerful, softening hospital rules and lending courage to sufferers.

When one dying patient despaired for her little boy's future, Barnier generously proposed to send him to his mother in the country. Everyone admired his goodness, and he and Philomène became closer. Their chats were her one recreation, for Barnier told her about changes outside the hospital in Paris. She feared that she would be transferred, for the Sisters were not supposed to become attached to a ward, but she was pleased to learn that she was to remain. One day, Barnier, an unbeliever who had often discussed religion with her, was silenced by her announcement that she had just taken her vows. Soon after, Philomène became ill and had to leave the hospital for a month. When she returned, she was very pale but seemed strong and active.

Malivoire told Barnier that he should have a more or less permanent mistress. Because a doctor's profession was so material, maintained Malivoire, the physician needed the illusions of love as well as the brutal fact of sex. Barnier was about to confess a love affair to Malivoire when they were interrupted. Barnier provided Philomène with laudanum to take for her neuralgic headaches. Her laudanum-provoked dream included the illusion of the touch of a kiss.

A new patient arrived. Barnier recognized her as the specter of Romaine, the woman he loved. They had been happy lovers until she left him and began a life of dissipation resulting in a breast injury. When Barnier asked Philomène to prepare Romaine for the operation, Philomène spoke to the woman with unusual harshness. After the operation Romaine, raging in fever, alternately cursed Barnier and begged him not to let her die. As he was leaving, Barnier overheard Philomène say that women like her should not be admitted to the hospital. Romaine died, after a scene in which Philomène's prayers were broken by the woman's curses and singing. Returning, Barnier saw the coffin that was to carry her away.

At a drinking party, Barnier defended the Sisters against a cynic who said that they were tender only toward those who were religious and decent. A suggestion was made that Philomène loved Barnier. Drunk and aroused, he went to the ward and attempted to kiss her, but she slapped him. Sobered, he returned to his friends to say that he would fight anyone who suggested her impurity.

Miserable in his memories of Romaine, Barnier took to drinking absinthe. Intoxication became his real life. When he learned that the house surgeon's coveted medal would not be his, Barnier struggled to resist drink, but when sober he was haunted by thoughts of Romaine. Philomène was ill. After her laudanum dream she searched her heart for symptoms of attachment for Barnier and remembered her jealous reaction to Romaine. Resolving on a course of expiation, she punished herself by remaining in the hospital and suffering the torments of love. One day Barnier asked her forgiveness for the attempted kiss. Her heart too full to speak, she went silently to her closet.

Barnier's student period was soon to end. He told Malivoire that the subject of his thesis was to be Death, that modern existence—a suicide more or less slow—does not use up but breaks life. Having deliberately scratched his hand while dissecting a diseased body, Barnier went to bed to await death.

Philomène went to a priest to have prayers said for Barnier by the Confraternity of Notre-Dame-des-Victoires, who were devoted to those who do not believe. Later, she knelt and prayed beside the dead Barnier. After she had gone, Malivoire was unable to find the lock of Barnier's hair that was to have been sent to his mother.

Critical Evaluation:

The brothers Goncourt are considered to be both theorists and practitioners of the documentary novel in nineteenth century French fiction. They based their plots on newspaper articles, interviews, and personal investigation and, like Émile Zola and Fyodor Dostoevski, they described outrages to contemporary cultural convention. True to their mechanistic and analytical vision of the world, naturalist writers rejected myths of transcendence and brought tragedy into the sphere of everyday existence. Although their novels may have shocked middle-class readership, *Sister Philomène* also inspired sympathy for the poor and for reforms in hospitals and orphanages.

Sister Philomène is based on a firsthand account of a nun's unspoken love for an intern, which was told to the Goncourts by Gustave Flaubert. Initially, the story appealed to the brothers as a romantic tale. Their fictionalized version, however, is decidedly deterministic. The Goncourts believed that character is shaped by milieu, just as animals are formed by their habitat. They rejected realism as a flat imitation of reality and insisted on depicting the physiological causes of psychology. At the same time that they became interested in portraying the impact of the maternal instinct and nervous system on women, they also documented life in city hospitals. The Goncourts' fascination with the pathological and the deviant led them to investigate Paris hospitals, to follow doctors on rounds, and to interview interns. Their account of this social institution, while frequently ironic, seems authentic.

The Goncourts wished to show how a girl could become a nurse on basis of temperament and upbringing. They also trace her search for identity, a search in which she has little choice. Marie Gaucher's life story follows the first chapter in the form of an extended flashback. After being orphaned at an early age, she is sheltered for a time in the household of Madame de Viry, where her aunt, a maid, cares for her. She acquires aristocratic tastes and falls in love with the young master, Henri. Unaware of the social mores that make it impossible to change class, she entertains the illusion that she is a true lady. When the adults realize her illusions, they send her to a Catholic orphanage.

Marie continues her struggle to define her identity at the orphanage, where her name is stripped away—from then on she is called Philomène—and she must rebuild her life. She alternates between acceptance of her new position and an inability to cope. The Church educates orphans on pious legends and miraculous apparitions. When one of her friends, Céline, becomes a mystic, Marie's religious yearnings are expressed by isolation, fasting, and the nervous irritation of constant prayer. The mystical teachings and first communion coincide with her physical maturation. The Goncourts depict the emergence of her senses in detail as she approaches puberty. She really longs for marriage, but when she returns to Madame de Viry's home, Henri barely notices her. The destruction of her fantasy forces her to take up nursing as a substitute for motherhood.

Philomène has naïve and romantic views about her calling. The initial chapter, which shows the nurses making their rounds at night, emphasizes the hospital as a world apart. The moans of patients announce the themes of suffering and pessimism. After presenting this shadowy world of darkness and light, the Goncourts introduce the problem of the perception of reality. The nurses seem to comfort the patients, but they actually prolong the pain of life. The nurses' efforts cannot prevail against the inexorable progress of death. The Goncourts juxtapose the deaths of patients with the joyous cries of the maternity ward—but death always prevails. These scenes also show doctors without idealizing them. Philomène passes through various phases of training that offer more realistic visions of her profession. Trepidation gives way to security, then to overwhelming horror, and, finally, to pragmatism. The hospital must hide the reality of death to give the patients hope.

In the central episode, when Barnier, a young doctor, must operate on a woman who had once been his mistress, all the plot lines are drawn together. Romaine, the mistress, who once symbolized youthful love, had fallen from virtue. Barnier's idealization of love and of his lover dies when he learns that her breast was damaged in an orgy. He thereupon declares that doctors need quick, brutal affairs, like animals. Meanwhile, Philomène has been falling in love with Barnier. At first, he is impatient with her, but then he begins to indulge in shoptalk. Eventually, neither wishes to be transferred from the women's ward, where they meet daily. Each idealizes the other, and their friendship is deepened by Barnier's adoption of an orphaned child.

The strain of unspoken love takes its toll on Philomène's health. When Barnier gives her a drug to help her sleep, her repressed sexuality becomes apparent. The Goncourts portray her dream in an impressionistic style to reveal the psyche beyond the control of the conscious mind. The Goncourts, years ahead of the medicine of their time, recognized that psychological tensions and the will to live complicate physical medicine. Psychological strain affects Philomène's health, and Romaine's condition degenerates as she loses hope. Yet even though Romaine has given up, in her death throes she exhibits the animal desire to live. The constant presence of death leads to more searching religious questions for the characters, and Barnier's doubts regarding an afterlife heighten the horror of his suicide. His death is depicted as a retreat from the atrocities of reality, yet he dies with his illusions about Philomène in place.

The Goncourts try to unify Philomène's character, but the composite nature of her personality as a child, a nurse, and a Sister belies that effort. She is also presented in a vacuum; there are no friends, coworkers, teachers, or family. Although subtleties of plot and character are lacking, the Goncourts skillfully re-create the medical community of their time. In contrast to the Goncourts' usual stories of abject misery and failure, *Sister Philomène* portrays the possibility of independence and some fulfillment.

"Critical Evaluation" by Pamela Pavliscak

Bibliography:

Auerbach, Erich. *Mimesis: The Representation of Reality in Western Literature*. Translated by Willard Trask. New York: Doubleday, 1953. Considers the Goncourts as naturalist writers. Compares their novels with those of Émile Zola and classifies the Goncourts as second-tier writers.

Baldick, Robert. *The Goncourts*. London: Bowes, 1960. A very brief but excellent survey of the Goncourts' novels. Concentrates on biographical background to the novels. Includes some exploration of major themes and aspects of literary style. *Sister Philomène* is cited as their most positive and least sensational novel.

Billy, Andre. *The Goncourt Brothers*. Translated by Margaret Shaw. New York: Horizon Press, 1960. The standard biography of the Goncourts. Shows that their novels emerged from events in their lives. Traces the research efforts that contributed to *Sister Philomène*. Also furnishes contemporary reaction to their novels.

Grant, Richard B. *The Goncourt Brothers*. New York: Twayne, 1972. Surveys the lives and works of Jules and Edmond de Goncourt. Ordered chronologically, the book carefully integrates their lives of the authors with detailed stylistic and thematic analysis of their novels.

Nelson, Brian, ed. *Naturalism in the European Novel: New Critical Perspectives*. New York: Berg, 1992. Essays by prominent scholars of naturalism in England, France, Germany, and Spain. Includes several important discussions of the Goncourts' role in the development of social documentary as a literary genre.

SIX CHARACTERS IN SEARCH OF AN AUTHOR

Type of work: Drama
Author: Luigi Pirandello (1867-1936)
Type of plot: Comedy
Time of plot: Twentieth century
Locale: The stage of a theater
First performed: Sei personaggi in cerca d'autore: Commedia da fare, 1921; first published, 1921 (English translation, 1922)

Principal characters:
THE FATHER
THE MOTHER
THE STEPDAUGHTER
THE SON
THE BOY
THE CHILD
MADAME PACE
THE MANAGER
LEADING LADY
LEADING MAN

The Story:

As a stage manager and a group of actors were preparing to rehearse a Pirandello play, they were interrupted by the appearance of six characters: a man of about fifty, a woman, a young woman, a young man of twenty-two, a boy of fourteen, and a little girl. The man and the young woman were searching for an author who would put all six of them into a drama. They insisted that they were already living characters but that they needed an author to put their drama into suitable form for the stage. The manager, at first annoyed at the interruption of his rehearsal, finally listened with some interest to the rather confused story that the man and the young woman, who, it turned out, was his stepdaughter, tried to tell him.

Years ago the father had gotten rid of his wife, whom he found both boring and pitiable, by providing her with a lover, his ex-secretary, to whom she might go when she was rejected by her husband. Long afterward, the father visited Madame Pace's dress shop, a legitimate business which she operated as a cover for her procuring, and was provided with a pretty young woman whom he did not recognize as his stepdaughter until they were separated by the sudden appearance of his wife. When he learned that his wife was destitute, her lover having died two months before, he permitted her to return to his home with her daughter and two younger children, all illegitimate.

To forestall a refusal by the manager to act as vicar-author for the drama, the father assured him that he need not be bothered about the presence of the two children, for they would quickly disappear from the story. In fact, the daughter would also disappear, leaving only the three original members of the family. The manager dismissed his actors for a few minutes in order to hear more of the plot as it was outlined to him in his office.

Returning a few minutes later from the office conference, the manager set about putting together the play, asking his prompter to take down the most important points in shorthand so that his actors might properly learn their parts later. At this point the father interrupted; the manager, he said, simply did not understand. This was not a play for the manager's professional actors; it belonged to the characters themselves. There was no need for actors when the manager already had six living characters at hand.

After hearing similar objections from the stepdaughter, the manager consented to use the characters, as this was only a rehearsal, but he wondered who would play Madame Pace if they were going to do the dress shop scene. After borrowing hats and other clothes from several actresses to hang on clothes pegs, the father arranged the set. Madame Pace suddenly appeared to play her part, but when she found that she was expected to play it in the presence of the mother, who would be watching the rehearsal from the side of the stage, she was scandalized at such impropriety and left in a rage.

The rehearsal continued, with the mother watching and listening intently, suffering all the while at the reenactment of the scene in which her husband, with honeyed words and actions, planned to purchase the favors of the pretty girl whom he did not recognize as his stepdaughter. The action was suddenly stopped and then repeated, this time with the parts of the father and the stepdaughter being taken by the leading man and the leading lady of the actors' company. The stepdaughter was unable to control her laughter at what seemed to her the ludicrous performance of the leading lady, and the father objected to the way the leading man was portraying him. Again the scene was played with the original characters, this time up to the point where, after the girl had reminded the father that she was wearing mourning, he had suggested that she remove her dress. At that point the action was abruptly stopped by the entrance of the mother, who in horror pulled her daughter away from the father. The manager was well pleased with this action; it would, he decided, make a fine first-act ending for the drama.

Preparations were begun for working up a second act, using a garden scene. The father engaged in a lengthy discussion of the difference between reality and the mere illusion of reality to be found in conventional stage representations, or, for that matter, in life itself. The manager, the father said, must try to perceive what he had so far missed: Ordinary people had illusions about themselves which they later discovered were not the realities they had thought them to be; the only reality the six characters had was that of a permanent, unchanging illusion, more real than any reality the manager himself might have.

The stepdaughter also entered the discussion, which was marked by the manager's increasing irritation and the father's persistence in following his argument through. She, her father, and the other characters had been created by an author who had then decided that he did not want to use them in one of his plays. Having been created, however, they now had existence in drama which must be revealed. But, insisted the manager, drama is action, not slow, dull philosophizing; let the talk stop and the action begin. The manager placed the silent, fourteen-year-old boy behind a tree and some bushes in the garden and the little girl near a fountain. Then he prepared for a conversation between the legitimate son and his mother. But, said the son, there was no such scene in the garden; what happened was that his mother came into his room and he left, refusing to talk to her. The manager asked what happened then. The son replied that nothing happened, that he disliked scenes and simply went away. He seemed very unwilling to discuss the matter or to have anything to do with acting in the drama which his father and his half-sister were trying to have presented.

When his father demanded that he play his part, the son turned violently upon him, asking what madness made him wish to expose the family shame before the world. If the son himself was in the theater, he explained to the confused manager, it was only because his father had dragged him there. However, the manager insisted on knowing what happened after the son left his room. Reluctantly, the son answered that he merely walked in the garden. When the manager urged him to continue, he burst out that it was horrible.

The manager, noting the mother's apprehensive look toward the fountain, partly comprehended, while the father explained that she had been following behind her son. Then the son quickly told what he had found: the body of the little girl in the fountain pool and the brother staring insanely at it. At that moment a revolver shot sounded behind the stage bushes where the boy had been hidden. Amid the resulting confusion the manager asked if the boy was wounded, and the actors disagreed as to whether he was dead or merely pretending to be. The father cried that it was real. The manager, losing his temper, consigned the whole play and the characters to hell. He had lost a whole day over them.

Critical Evaluation:

Six Characters in Search of an Author, Luigi Pirandello's best-known play, contrasts illusion and reality, as do several of the author's other works. It may also be thought of as a dramatic criticism of the popular but artificial "well-made" play of the nineteenth century. Instead of starting with a cleverly constructed drama, Pirandello begins with a group of characters and experiments with letting them—with some professional direction—try to fashion their story into an actable drama. Inexperience, clashes of opinion, interruptions, and above all a lack of poetic understanding defeat their purpose. Yet the attempt itself has produced a drama of a sort, not the characters' but Pirandello's.

One of the greatest Italian playwrights of the twentieth century, Pirandello is now generally recognized as a classic figure of world literature. His stature was recognized when he received the Nobel Prize in 1934, two years before his death. First a poet, then a novelist and writer of short stories, finally a dramatist, Pirandello evolved gradually toward the forms and themes on which his international reputation is based. If his early work is realistic and naturalistic, much of his later, major work may be characterized by his description of *Six Characters in Search of an Author* as "a mixture of tragic and comic, fantastic and realistic." The basic ideas of his major plays are somber, even bitter: the idea that no one can penetrate or understand anyone else's world; the idea that the picture people have of themselves is different from the picture everyone else has of them; that no mental images—about oneself or about others—can encompass the truth about life, which is always changing and always elusive. There is, therefore, no such thing as the Truth: There is simply truth "A" that I believe and truth "B" that you believe. However, you and I are both wrong. To ourselves, however, we are always right. Or, to quote the title of one of Pirandello's plays: *Right You Are (If You Think So).*

It is, of course, no wonder that these ideas should arise in the skeptical twentieth century. Pirandello was not alone among authors in thinking as he did, and a number of his attitudes may be traced to the French philosopher Henri Bergson (1859-1941). Pirandello had a personal reason for his reaction, however, a reason that made the concept that men cannot possibly understand one another become an obsession with him. He was for many years married to an insane wife who gave him no rest. Among other things, her insanity took the form of a violent, raging jealousy. Pirandello did everything he could to reassure his wife; he would not go out, he turned from his friends, he even yielded up his entire salary to her. Nevertheless, his wife's image of him remained the same, so that alongside his own picture of himself as a patient, resigned, pitying family man, there always hovered the image in his wife's mind of a loathsome being who gave her nothing but pain. As far as Pirandello was concerned, such conflicting images underlay even the most normal of human relations, though in insanity the problem is multiplied, or at least seen more clearly.

Six Characters in Search of an Author deals with the problem of conflicting images and with the problem of reality in general, but it also deals with a special aspect of the same set of problems, for the playwright has a particularly difficult task. Not only must he struggle to pin down the very elusive, ever-changing thing he calls reality, but he must also work with the knowledge that he can never deal directly with his audience. Between him and the audience stand the actors and the directors; they give life to the script, but they can never give it quite the sort of life the author had in mind. Thus, we may get Tallulah Bankhead's version of a character, or Vivien Leigh's, or Mary Martin's. Even if Shakespeare were alive today, audiences would not know exactly how he imagined Hamlet. Instead, audiences would know how Laurence Olivier presented him, or John Gielgud, or Maurice Evans: each with his own personality, his own background, his own voice. They can never have quite the personality, background, voice, or mannerisms that Shakespeare had in mind for Hamlet. No wonder, says one of Pirandello's characters, that a playwright may sometimes throw up his hands in despair and decide that the theater cannot present his situations and characters as he wants them presented.

That is what happens in *Six Characters in Search of an Author*. A playwright (Pirandello) gives up. He imagines six very tormented characters and a very sordid situation but has decided not to go on with his play. As one of his characters puts it, "he abandoned us in a fit of depression, of disgust for the ordinary theater as the public knows it and likes it." However, once the characters have been imagined they assume a life of their own. If the playwright refuses to look after them, they will look after themselves. Going to a theater where a play is in rehearsal, they insist that they have a play that must be produced. The story that the characters have to tell emerges in fits and starts. They are much too busy cursing or wrangling with one another to present a very coherent plot. For, as Pirandello insists, each character sees the central situation from his own point of view and each tries to justify himself from that vantage point.

The Father is a great talker and a great explainer. He insists that he put the Mother and his clerk out of his house together because he assumed that they were attached to each other and pitied them; indeed, he asserts that he tried to help them afterward. Still, the Mother, uneducated and nonverbal, insists that the Father threw her and the clerk out of the house and forced her on the clerk. The Stepdaughter refuses to believe that her Mother did not love the clerk initially; after all, the clerk (now dead) was the only father she knew. The Son—the legitimate son of the Father and the Mother—who feels that he has been deserted by both father and mother, attempts to reject both. The Stepdaughter, consumed by a passionate hatred of the Son and the Father, passes up no opportunity to show her contempt and to remind the Father that, at a time when he did not recognize her, he almost had sexual relations with his own stepdaughter. No one is completely right, and no one is completely wrong—but none is able to understand that.

Act II develops the theme of mutual misunderstanding but modulates it into a different key. For now the characters learn, to their consternation, that they will not be able to play their parts themselves (that is, as they were realized by their creator). The actors will do it for them. Of course, the actors cannot possibly play the characters as the characters see themselves. As the Father explains: "It will be difficult to act me as I really am. The effect will be rather—apart from the make-up—according as to how he [the actor] supposes I am, as he senses me—if he does sense me—and not as I inside of myself feel myself to be." Later the act moves to a general attack on the conventions of the theater and the limits of the theater. As the Manager points out, "Acting is our business here. Truth up to a certain point, but no further."

In the last act, the Father gives still another twist to the problem of reality and the artistic presentation of it. In a sense, he insists, the characters are more real than the actors are. For people change from day to day. What a person seems to be one day no longer exists the next day (though his image of himself may persist). The characters, on the other hand, will always remain the same. Or—to turn the statement around—art, since it is static, can never deal with the fluid nature of reality. "All this present reality of yours," says the Father, "is fated to seem a mere illusion to you tomorrow . . . your reality is a mere transitory and fleeting illusion, taking this form today and that tomorrow."

Pirandello is a philosophical dramatist, the maker of a theater of ideas. Inevitably he has been attacked as an author who concerns himself more with concepts than with people and with action. He has also been stoutly defended as one who, immersed in certain basic, tragic facts of human existence, provides them with a hauntingly, overwhelmingly genuine dramatic substance.

"Critical Evaluation" by Max Halperen

Bibliography:

Bentley, Eric. *The Pirandello Commentaries*. Evanston, Ill.: Northwestern University Press, 1986. These essays include an erudite analysis of *Six Characters in Search of an Author*. Bentley explores the abstraction of time and space, the characterizations, and Pirandello's dialectical opposition of reality and illusion in the play.

DiGaetani, John Louis, ed. *A Companion to Pirandello Studies*. Wesport, Conn.: Greenwood Press, 1991. This major source book features four studies on *Six Characters in Search of an Author* and two dozen essays on Pirandello's influence, life, and other works. Appendices include the production history of *Six Characters in Search of an Author* and a bibliography.

Goffman, Erving. *Frame Analysis: An Essay on the Organization of Experience*. Cambridge, Mass.: Harvard University Press, 1974. An extraordinary sociological study, directly influenced by Pirandello, on the epistemological "frames" people use to make sense of the world. Goffman's discussion of the "theatrical frame" is essential for students who wish to understand more about Pirandello's violations of dramatic convention in *Six Characters in Search of an Author*.

Pirandello, Luigi. "*Six Characters in Search of an Author*." In *Playwrights on Play Writing*, edited by Toby Cole. New York: Hill & Wang, 1960. Pirandello's personal account of his motivations for creating characters who, in turn, search for a dramatist to give them life.

Vittorini, Domenico. *The Drama of Luigi Pirandello*. New York: Russell & Russell, 1935. An accessible survey endorsed by Pirandello. Includes a clear, nontechnical exposition of *Six Characters in Search of an Author*.

THE SKIN OF OUR TEETH

Type of work: Drama
Author: Thornton Wilder (1897-1975)
Type of plot: Phantasmagoric
Time of plot: All human history
Locale: Excelsior, New Jersey, and the boardwalk at Atlantic City
First performed: 1942; first published, 1942

Principal characters:
MR. ANTROBUS, a citizen of the world
MRS. ANTROBUS, his wife
GLADYS, their daughter
HENRY, their son
SABINA, their maid

The Story:

A great wall of ice was moving southward over the land, bringing with it an unprecedented cold spell in August. In Hartford they were burning pianos, and it was impossible to reach Boston by telegraph. The people did nothing but talk about the looming catastrophe. So far, only the extreme cold had reached Excelsior, New Jersey, where Mr. and Mrs. George Antrobus lived in an attractive suburban residence. Their rather commonplace lives were to be greatly changed by the extreme form that the weather had taken.

Mr. Antrobus was a fine man, a sterling example for his community. He had invented the wheel, the alphabet, and the multiplication table. Mrs. Antrobus was the picture of the middle-class mother, with the best interests of her children at heart. Their daughter Gladys was much like her mother, but their son was atypical. His name had been Cain until an unfortunate accident occurred in which he hit his brother with a stone and killed him. As the result of that thoughtless action, his name had been changed to Henry, and Mrs. Antrobus went to some pains to keep his past history a secret. Members of the Antrobus household also included Sabina, the maid, a baby dinosaur, and a mammoth.

On this particular day in August, everyone was freezing and the dogs were sticking to the sidewalk because it was so cold. Sabina was in an agitated state because nothing seemed to be going properly. She had milked the mammoth, but she had let the only fire in the house go out. Her plight was doubly humiliating because her career in the Antrobus house had begun when Mr. Antrobus brought her back from the Sabine rape. He had given her a life of luxury until he tired of her; now she was relegated to the kitchen. She, however, was a canny and observant individual, an apex to an age-old triangle.

She was waiting nervously for the return of Mr. Antrobus when a domestic altercation with Mrs. Antrobus prompted her to give a two-week notice. Later a telegram announcing the arrival of Mr. Antrobus and some salvation from the cold caused her to change her mind for the time being. When he arrived, Mr. Antrobus brought news that most of the outside world was freezing and that there was probably nothing they could do to escape the same fate. When some tramps and refugees from the ice came to the house for warmth and food, Mrs. Antrobus was not in favor of admitting them, but Mr. Antrobus insisted. Mrs. Antrobus agreed, but only after the dinosaur and the mammoth had been evicted. The refugees included a judge, named Moses; a blind beggar with a guitar, named Homer; and the Misses E., T., and M. Muse. The Antrobus family attempted to keep up some semblance of hope as they gathered around their small fire. When Henry, in another fit of hate, murdered a neighbor with a stone, Mr. Antrobus stamped out the fire. However, he was cajoled into having faith in humanity again, and all, including the audience, were asked to burn their chairs in order to keep the fire going and save the human race from extinction.

That crisis over, Mr. and Mrs. Antrobus went to the Atlantic City convention of the Ancient and Honorable Order of Mammals, Subdivision Humans. Mr. Antrobus, just elected president of the society for the coming year, made a speech of acceptance, which was followed by a few words from Mrs. Antrobus. During an interview immediately afterward, it was learned that Mr. and Mrs. Antrobus would soon celebrate their five thousandth wedding anniversary. Mr. Antrobus had previously judged a beauty contest in which the winner had been the former maid Sabina, now Miss Lily-Sabina Fairweather from the Boardwalk Bingo Parlor. She had decided, as a result of her victory, to take Mr. Antrobus away from his wife. As soon as she could easily do so, she lured him into her beach cabana. During her father's sojourn in the cabana, Gladys bought herself a pair of red stockings and Henry became involved in an altercation with a boy, whom he hit with a stone. When Mr. Antrobus was finally located, he had decided to leave his wife. Told of his intentions, she handled the situation very calmly and maneuvered him into staying with her. She was aided somewhat by a coming storm, which made it necessary for the family and a large collection of animals to retreat to a boat in order to survive. Under the directions of a mysterious fortune teller, Mr. Antrobus took them all, including Sabina, off to make a new world.

When the great war came, much of the population of the world and most of Excelsior, New Jersey, were wiped out. The Antrobus household, including Sabina, managed to survive, but not without considerable damage. Mrs. Antrobus and Gladys and Gladys' new baby had hidden out in the basement. When the war ended, they came out into the world, which in a very short time began to function very much as it had before the war occurred.

Sabina, dressed now as a Napoleonic camp follower, had enjoyed the war. She felt that everyone was at his or her best in wartime. Henry, following up his stone-throwing activities, had progressed from a corporal's rank to the rank of a general; he had become the picture of hate, the enemy of humankind. Mr. Antrobus ordered that he never come into the house again or he would kill him. When Henry returned, he wanted to kill his father, whom he had hated all these years, and he had brought a gun with which to shoot Mr. Antrobus. When he finally fell asleep from exhaustion, Mrs. Antrobus took the revolver from him. Mr. Antrobus and Henry had an argument during which all the evil in the young man was revealed. Mr. Antrobus, in a fit of self-condemnation, admitted that he would rather fight Henry than try to build a peace with him. His will to survive returned once again, however, and he asked Henry to try to live in peace. Henry agreed, providing he be given a freedom of his own will.

Mr. Antrobus, striving to regain his confidence in humanity, recalled the three things that had always kept him going: the people, his home, and his books. In addition, he remembered the philosophies that he had known and through which he regained his hope for the future.

Critical Evaluation:

To American audiences who saw the original production of *The Skin of Our Teeth*, the play seemed mad and incomprehensible, but highly entertaining. Their reaction was understandable, for few American playwrights have employed such bizarre forms to convey serious content. "Dream plays," German expressionism, the comic strip, musical comedy—Thornton Wilder once listed these as his sources of dramaturgical inspiration. The play is, however, basically a parody of old-fashioned American stock-company productions and vaudeville. European audiences, for whom the play was performed in bomb-scarred churches and beer halls, had less difficulty in grasping Wilder's message. As the dramatist observed, the play "mostly comes alive under conditions of crisis." Since depressions, Ice Ages, and wars have hardly vanished from the scene, *The Skin of Our Teeth* promises to remain a vital part of the world's theater experience.

Despite their range and complexity, Wilder's main ideas can be briefly summarized. In Sabina's first direct address to the audience, Wilder does this. The play is, she says, "all about the troubles the human race has gone through." Such troubles are of two kinds: those caused by nature and those caused by people themselves. The Ice Age and the Flood are examples of the first type, although Wilder makes it plain that the real source of catastrophe in Act II is not the weather but the disordered passions of the individual. Depression and war are clearly human creations. The human race is not, for Wilder, a disconnected assemblage of discrete cultures and generations. Rather, it is a being—a living person who experiences, remembers, and matures. The name "Antrobus" expresses this concept, being derived from the Greek word "for man."

As one learns from the closing philosophic quotations, humanity's best hope for "getting by" lies in the intellect. The first priority for the human race is to establish order in the individual by means of the discipline of reason. In doing so, humanity avails itself of a special energy that Aristotle considered divine. This holy energy is ultimately related to the force that created the heavens and the earth. The greatest threat to human survival is not merely the ego's unruly animal nature, which brings disorder to the soul. The more serious threat is an inclination toward evil, which infects the individual's rational faculties. To counter this threat, people may draw upon their capacity for love as well as upon the accumulated wisdom that history provides.

This set of ideas shapes all aspects of the drama. Mr. and Mrs. Antrobus stand for reason, which has masculine and feminine dimensions. Sabina, the maid, represents the passions, especially those that seek erotic pleasure and social power. Henry, their son, says Wilder, embodies "strong unreconciled evil." Like Sabina, he resists the rule of law in himself and society. His murderous nature reveals a far graver sort of wickedness. Like Cain, he despises God and longs to overthrow his order. Wilder's characters are not merely allegorical types, however. Mr. Antrobus shows himself capable of homicidal intent, and because he loves his theories and machines too much, he is partly to blame for Henry's behavior. Sabina speaks for Wilder when she exclaims, "We're all just as wicked as we can be, and that's God's truth."

No single character symbolizes love in *The Skin of Our Teeth*. Rather this function is fulfilled by the Antrobus family as a whole. In Act I, they share their hearth with the refugees. In Act II, they refuse to enter the ship without Henry. In the final act they readmit Henry to their circle. Since the Antrobuses are a metaphor for humankind, their gestures have wider significance. The refugees are not strangers but relatives. So are members of the audience, a fact that the invitation to "Pass up your chairs, everybody" conveys. Wilder symbolizes this condition by making the father of Gladys' beloved baby an anonymous someone, an Everyman. The final acceptance of Henry is the most powerful moment in the play. Despite Henry's evil, Mr. Antrobus grudgingly must acknowledge that "Oh, you're related, all right." Thus Henry may take his place in a family where all belong.

If the human race is actually one, there is finally only one experience and one memory. Wilder dramatizes this concept in a variety of ingenious ways, all of which involve seeing time as an eternal present. Dinosaurs, Biblical personages, and figures from Greek mythology crowd into the Antrobuses' living room. Each advance in technology requires a remembering of all previous discoveries, so Wilder has the invention of the alphabet "occur" during the era of telegraphic communication. Sabina is, simultaneously, a figure from classical history, a "Napoleonic camp follower," and a contemporary American. The constant interruptions of the action force the audience to dwell in a single time dimension—the present, in which are contained both past and future as well as "real" and "imaginary time."

By these means Wilder also reinforces the notion that the human race is what it is because of the experiences of its forebears. Or, more exactly, human nature has developed in certain ways because humanity has inherited certain principles of interpretation. These principles are found in clearest form in the great books of history. Insofar as such principles shape human thought, the thinkers who expressed them live on. People can forget or ignore the education that history has afforded them and become animals again. Books are instruments of humanization. In this sense, Mr. Antrobus is entirely correct when he says to the book-burning Henry, "You are my deadly enemy." Part of Wilder's optimism about humanity's future stems from the mere existence of books and libraries.

The seriousness and profundity of Wilder's themes tend, unfortunately, to escape most audiences. Indeed, the play's rapid pace and dramaturgical gimmicks draw attention away from its key symbols. Invited to participate on a superficial level, the typical viewer feels puzzled and a bit resentful when, in the third act, the drama suddenly becomes very somber and too heavily philosophical.

"Critical Evaluation" by Leslie E. Gerber

Bibliography:

Burbank, Rex J. *Thornton Wilder*. New York: Twayne, 1961. An excellent introduction to Wilder that emphasizes the humanism of his writings. Asserts *The Skin of Our Teeth* succeeds in communicating its message about human survival, but that "the mixture of comedy and seriousness does not always come off successfully."

Castronovo, David. *Thornton Wilder*. New York: Frederick Ungar, 1986. An effective brief introduction to Wilder and his works. The section on *The Skin of Our Teeth* distills information about the play's writing and staging, interprets the themes, and evaluates the work's strengths and weaknesses.

Goldstone, Richard H., and Gary Anderson. *Thornton Wilder: An Annotated Bibliography of Works, by and About Thornton Wilder*. New York: AMS Press, 1982. An important starting place of finding sources for further reading about Wilder. Numerous bibliography entries concerning *The Skin of Our Teeth.*

Haberman, Donald. *The Plays of Thornton Wilder: A Critical Study*. Middletown, Conn.: Wesleyan University Press, 1967. Explores the philosophical, religious, and mythmaking dimensions of Wilder's dramas. Carefully defends Wilder against the plagiarism issues surrounding *The Skin of Our Teeth.*

Harrison, Gilbert A. *The Enthusiast: A Life of Thornton Wilder*. New York: Ticknor & Fields, 1983. A highly readable source, providing contextual details regarding Wilder's composition of *The Skin of Our Teeth*, as well as information about the play's staging and reception.

SLAUGHTERHOUSE-FIVE
Or, The Children's Crusade, a Duty-Dance with Death

Type of work: Novel
Author: Kurt Vonnegut, Jr. (1922-)
Type of plot: Historical realism
Time of plot: 1922-1976
Locale: Dresden, Germany, and Illium, New York
First published: 1969

Principal characters:
BILLY PILGRIM, foot soldier in World War II
VALENCIA, Pilgrim's wife
BARBARA, their daughter
ROBERT, their son
MONTANA WILDHACK, mate to Pilgrim on Tralfamadore
KURT VONNEGUT, author of *Slaughterhouse-Five*
BERNARD V. O'HARE, Vonnegut's friend

The Story:

Kurt Vonnegut and Bernard V. O'Hare went back to Dresden, Germany, on Guggenheim money in 1967. Before they left, Vonnegut went to O'Hare's house and met his wife, Mary O'Hare. Mary was mad at Vonnegut; she knew he was going to write a book about World War II, and she was sure he was going to make war look glamorous and fun. Vonnegut insisted that he was not going to write a book that made war look glamorous, he would even subtitle the book "The Children's Crusade." This made her like him, and they started being friends.

While in Dresden, Vonnegut and O'Hare met a taxi driver, who showed them around the city and showed them the slaughterhouse where they had been prisoners during World War II.

When Vonnegut returned from the war, he thought writing a book about Dresden would be easy. He expected a masterpiece that would make him a lot of money. The words, however, came very slowly and he became "an old fart with his memories and his Pall Malls," before he actually wrote the book. He liked to call long-lost friends late at night when his wife was asleep and he was drunk, and he liked to listen to talk-radio programs from Boston or New York. He and O'Hare tried to remember things about the war, and they had trouble. Vonnegut suggested the climax of his book would come when Edgar Derby was shot by a firing squad for taking a teapot out of the ruins in Dresden. O'Hare did not know where the climax was supposed to be.

Billy Pilgrim was born in Illium, New York, in 1922. He was tall and weak when he was a child and became tall and weak as an adult. He died in Chicago in 1976 and traveled back and forth through time frequently between his birth and death. Pilgrim was in the infantry in Europe in World War II as a chaplain's assistant. He did not carry a weapon and did not have proper clothing for the climate, which was very cold. He was taken prisoner by the Germans. Before he went to the war, he was on maneuvers in South Carolina, and he was given an emergency furlough home because his father had died. While in the war, Pilgrim was lost behind German lines with three other soldiers; one was Roland Weary. Someone shot at them and Pilgrim heard the bullet go by. Pilgrim let the shooter try to hit him again. Weary hated everyone, including Pilgrim; Weary died in a box car on the way to the concentration camp. He was about to kill or seriously maim Pilgrim when the Germans captured them.

Pilgrim's father had thrown Pilgrim into the deep end of a swimming pool when he was very young. Supposedly he would learn to swim, or he would drown. He would have drowned but someone saved him instead. In the concentration camp, Pilgrim time traveled often. He went to the planet Tralfamadore, where the beings there taught him many things about the irrelevance of time and death. On Tralfamadore he was kept in a zoo. He mated with the beautiful Montana Wildhack, a pornography star who soon came to love Pilgrim. They had a child together on Tralfamadore.

From the concentration camp, Pilgrim and his company were sent to Dresden, Germany, where they worked in a factory that made a vitamin-enriched malt syrup that was for pregnant women. Pilgrim and the other prisoners ate it as much as they could because they were malnourished. While Pilgrim was in Dresden, it was firebombed. One hundred and thirty-five thousand people died in the conflagration. No one had suspected it would be bombed, because it had no armament factories, and almost no soldiers whatsoever. Pilgrim and the Americans with him were some of the only people in the entire city who survived. Vonnegut and O'Hare were with Pilgrim. They helped to clean the wreckage of the city that had been one of the most beautiful in the world and was now like the moon. American fighter planes flew over the city to see if anything was still moving and they saw Pilgrim. They sprayed machine-gun fire at him but missed.

After the war, Pilgrim was back in Illium. He finished the optometry school that he had begun before the war, and he married Valencia Merble, the daughter of an optometrist and a very rich woman. She was also overweight and did not possess an astounding wit or intellect. They had two children, Robert and Barbara. Robert joined the Green Berets to fight in Vietnam. Barbara married an optometrist and came to see Pilgrim frequently after Pilgrim had brain surgery. Valencia died trying to get to the hospital after Pilgrim was in a plane crash.

Pilgrim had the brain surgery shortly following the wreck of an airplane that was meant to carry a group of optometrists to a convention. The plane crashed into a mountain in Vermont, killing everyone except Pilgrim and the copilot. Barbara was very concerned about Pilgrim after the crash and the subsequent brain surgery because Pilgrim was writing letters to a newspaper, telling about Tralfamadore and his time-traveling experiences. He went to New York, to be on a talk-radio program, on which he also told about Tralfamadore.

Critical Evaluation:

Slaughterhouse-Five is Kurt Vonnegut's fifth novel; it was an overwhelming success and established him as one of the best fiction writers of his era. He wrote it while he was a writer-in-residence at the University of Iowa. With money from a Guggenheim fellowship, he went to Dresden, Germany, to complete his research. Kurt Vonnegut appears in the first and last chapters, as a journalist reporting on the work at hand, and he appears three times during the narrative. This device is extremely effective and unique to this novel. It was a great boon to experimental writing and has been thought to be a progressive step in the evolution of literature and narrative stance in particular. Vonnegut makes clear to the reader that he is not Billy Pilgrim. Vonnegut is a character in scenes with Pilgrim; he is watching Pilgrim, like the reader is watching them both. Vonnegut is telling an astounding truth, of the Dresden holocaust, that the allied forces had managed to keep mostly unknown to Americans, while he tells the remarkably funny and moving tale of Pilgrim, who is helpless before the larger powers of the universe.

Vonnegut has the uncanny ability to implant suggestions in the mind of the reader and then work those suggestions into tangible forms in the text. For example, in the first chapter, Vonnegut says that when he has been drinking he listens to talk-radio shows, then, as the novel proceeds, Pilgrim stumbles onto a radio program in which the topic is whether or not the novel, as a literary form, is dead. Also, after the firebombing of Dresden, innkeepers on the outskirts of town offer the soldiers their stable, as a place to sleep. Twenty pages later, Vonnegut reminds the reader of the book's epigraph, "The cattle are lowing,/ The Baby awakes./ But the little Lord Jesus/ No crying He makes." Biblical situations are considered more and more often as the book draws to a close. These include discussion of the following: the friends who took Jesus down from the cross; the possibility that Jesus and his father, as carpenters, made crosses on which other people would be executed; and a time traveler who was the first to check on Jesus at the cross to make sure he was really dead before he was taken down. A new gospel is written in which Jesus is not made the Son of God until the very end, when he is on the cross. Until then he was a nobody. Vonnegut implies that if Jesus was the "wrong" person to kill, then there are necessarily "right" persons to kill, and this is inherently a bad idea.

All these examinations and refigurings are counter to orthodox Christianity, and they are couched in writing that makes extreme pleas for the kindness that people should show to other people. In the first chapter, Vonnegut calls this novel "short and jumbled and jangled . . . because there is nothing intelligent to say about a massacre." His critics have found fault in him and this novel for not taking serious matters more seriously, and for that reason his work was not highly acclaimed or accepted into the academic canon for many years. Vonnegut was categorized in the genre of science fiction, though he believed his work holds more depth than work in that genre usually has. With the eventual acceptance of *Slaughterhouse-Five*, he became classified as a satirist who seeks to make readers laugh, as Mark Twain and Jonathan Swift did before him.

In this book so conscious of time traveling, and postulating that all of one's life can be seen like an expanse of the Rocky Mountains rather than as a one-way train ride, how very fitting for the Pilgrim family car, in the year 1967, to have a bumper sticker on it that said, "Reagan for President." The book was published eleven years before Reagan became president of the United States in 1980. It was not something Pilgrim could have known about, dying as he did in 1976, but still it was an auspicious thing for Vonnegut to have slyly dropped into this book.

Beaird Glover

Bibliography:

Giannone, Richard. *Vonnegut: A Preface to His Novels*. Port Washington, N.Y.: Kennikat Press, 1977. Astute reading of *Slaughterhouse-Five*, marking the biblical references and Vonnegut's personal testimony. Devotes similar attention to other novels by Vonnegut.

Klinkowitz, Jerome. *Kurt Vonnegut*. New York: Methuen, 1982. Explains *Slaughterhouse-Five* as one of Vonnegut's "personal" novels, as opposed to the earlier ones that adhere to the stricter forms of science fiction. Draws correlations among the Vonnegut novels.

____________. *Slaughterhouse-Five: Reforming the Novel and the World*. Boston: Twayne, 1990. A complete study of the novel. Criticism is taken from sources that reviewed *Slaughterhouse-Five* when it was published. Numerous passages of *Slaughterhouse-Five* are explained in depth, as well as Vonnegut's philosophy as it was seen by the reviewers of his time.

Mayo, Clark. *Kurt Vonnegut: The Gospel from Outer Space (or, Yes We Have No Nirvanas)*. San Bernardino, Calif.: Borgo Press, 1977. A short book with considerable insights into *Slaughterhouse-Five* and other novels by Vonnegut. The wit, sarcasm, and style of Vonnegut is prominent in the writing of this text.

Schatt, Stanley. *Kurt Vonnegut, Jr.* Boston: Twayne, 1976. Explores the construction, plot, and structure of *Slaughterhouse-Five* and considers Vonnegut's sense of aesthetic distance from the work. Chapters include the contribution of *Slaughterhouse-Five* to the genre of science fiction and the Tralfamadorian philosophy.

THE SLEEPWALKERS

Type of work: Novel
Author: Hermann Broch (1886-1951)
Type of plot: Philosophical
Time of plot: 1888-1918
Locale: Germany
First published: Die Schlafwandler, 1931-1932 (English translation, 1932): *Pasenow: Oder, Die Romantik-1888*, 1931 (*The Romantic*, 1932); *Esch: Oder, Die Anarchie-1903*, 1931 (*The Anarchist*, 1931); *Hugnenau: Oder, Die Sachlichkeit-1918*, 1932 (*The Realist*, 1932)

Principal characters:
JOACHIM VON PASENOW, a young lieutenant
HERR VON PASENOW, his father
BERTRAND, his friend
ESCH, a bookkeeper
FRAU HENTJEN, his wife
HUGUENAU, a businessman

The Story:

The Romantic. In 1888, Joachim von Pasenow was a lieutenant in the German army. Having worn a uniform for a long time, he looked on it as his natural dress. He believed a uniform hid a man's nakedness; unlike civilian clothes, it made a man amount to something. His friend Bertrand had left the army and now wore mufti all the time; it seemed indecent. Joachim felt a little insecure about his honor, too. His brother Helmuth had been killed in a duel, and his father made much of Helmuth's unsullied honor.

Herr von Pasenow came to Berlin to visit Joachim. He was a funny little man, rotund and intent, and his son was a bit ashamed of him. At a casino they met Ruzena, a Bohemian girl. Von Pasenow stroked her familiarly and gave her money. She accepted the attentions easily, but when the old man joked about marriage she went into the lavatory to cry. Later, perhaps as a kind of penance, Joachim took Ruzena as his mistress.

Bertrand too took a friendly interest in Ruzena, and he helped her get on the stage. Ruzena was happy with Joachim, but she began to distrust Bertrand. He let slip the suggestion that she should leave the chorus and go into a notion shop. Joachim had to leave Ruzena at times to visit his family, for his father was anxious that he should resign from the army and look after the family estate. He was also anxious that he marry Elisabeth.

When Bertrand met Elisabeth, he spoke to her eloquently of a love based on renunciation; the innocent girl was upset. Ruzena, convinced that Bertrand was the evil genius separating her from her lover, shot him in the arm. She then left Joachim and went back to work in a café. Joachim, also believing that Bertrand was a bad influence, settled money on Ruzena and proposed to Elisabeth. With this deed he broke with his past, for he did not ask Bertrand's advice about the marriage.

Before accepting Joachim, Elisabeth visited Bertrand in the hospital. He declared his love for her but was resigned to her marriage with Joachim as inevitable. For a time after their marriage, Joachim thought of Elisabeth as an unapproachable madonna. They did not have their first child for more than one year.

The Anarchist. In 1903, Esch was dismissed from his post as a bookkeeper at a shipping concern in Cologne. Martin, a crippled socialist, somehow learned of Esch's dismissal and told him of a better job in Mannheim. They discussed the matter in Frau Hentjen's restaurant. Esch knew he would have to have a reference. He finally got a good one by threatening to expose the crooked manager under whom he had worked.

In Mannheim, he found employment in a large firm owned by Bertrand. He made friends with Korn, a customs inspector, and with Lohberg, a pallid tobacconist. In a short while, he went to room with Korn and his sister Erna. Erna was unattractive but wanted desperately to marry, and Korn hoped to acquire a brother-in-law in Esch. At last, Esch answered her provocations by going into her bedroom, but Erna reserved her favors until they should be married.

By helping Gernerth, a theatrical manager, with his shipping, Esch received passes to a show and took Korn and Erna with him to the performance. The star attraction was Teltscher, a Hungarian knife thrower, and Ilona, his flashy blonde target. Becoming acquainted with Korn and Esch, the actors visited them at Korn's house. For a while, Esch hoped to win Ilona, but she showed a preference for Korn; at last she slept with him openly.

Arriving in Mannheim during a strike, Martin was arrested at a workers' meeting. Esch was convinced that Bertrand had hired baiters to trap Martin and that Bertrand should have been imprisoned instead. Feeling restless, he accepted Teltscher's offer to join him in the theatrical business. They planned to operate in Cologne. Esch felt an odd responsibility to get Teltscher away from Ilona, because the knife-throwing act endangered Ilona's safety.

Back in Cologne, Esch spent much time with Frau Hentjen, and in time he overcame her scruples against taking him as her lover. She did not like his new job, which was to hire lady wrestlers. Esch wrote an article protesting against Martin's false imprisonment, but the socialist newspaper refused to print it. During his wandering through the town, he stumbled on evidence that Bertrand was a sodomite, but again the paper refused to print his story.

Driven by a vague compulsion, Esch went to see Bertrand. On the way, he stopped off to see the Korns and found Erna engaged to marry Lohberg. Erna had changed; she had no compunction about allowing Esch to sleep with her. Bertrand received Esch kindly but was evasive on the subject of the strike. Bertrand died soon after Esch returned to Cologne. For a while, Esch planned vaguely to go to America. After Frau Hentjen mortgaged her restaurant to provide theatrical capital, she and Esch were married. Eventually they lost their money, and Esch took a good job in Luxembourg.

The Realist. Huguenau, a practical businessman, deserted from the army. By keeping an open countenance and refusing to skulk, he made his way through Belgium to the Ardennes and thence back into the Moselle district. Since he was an Alsatian and knew both French and German, both sides of the Rhine were home to him. In Kur-Trier he spent enough of his carefully hoarded money to set himself up as a hotel keeper.

All about him others were questioning their beliefs during the last months of the war. Hanna, the lawyer's faithful wife, grew more and more virginal during her husband's absence. In Berlin, Marie the Salvation Army girl half-acknowledged her passion for a Talmudic Jew. The wounded in the hospitals had little spirit to live.

Huguenau, however, had no questions, no frustrations; he was intent only on business deals. He bluffed the military commandant, Major Joachim von Pasenow, into supporting him, and on the strength of that backing he persuaded the local dignitaries to put up enough capital for him to buy control of a newspaper owned by Esch. He made the deal easier by circulating rumors that Esch was subversive. Before long, Huguenau was editing the paper and eating Frau Esch's good meals without payment.

Having embraced the Protestant faith, Joachim finally became convinced that Esch was a malcontent and Huguenau a suspicious character. In November, 1918, the workers revolted and took over the town. Joachim was hurt and carried to the basement of Esch's printing house. Observing this, Huguenau took advantage of the confusion and raped Frau Esch. Then he followed Esch, who was returning to guard duty, caught up with him, and slipped a bayonet into his back. After the war, Huguenau tricked Frau Esch by letter into returning the borrowed capital he had invested in the paper. While he continued to amass more money, he prudently married a German girl with a good dowry.

Critical Evaluation:

The Sleepwalkers is considered by many critics to be one of the major literary achievements of the twentieth century, ranking with James Joyce's *Ulysses* (1922), Thomas Mann's *The Magic Mountain* (1924), and Marcel Proust's *Remembrance of Things Past* (1913-1927). Hermann Broch's three-volume novel bears as little resemblance to any of these works as they do to one another; it stands alone, an uncompromising experiment in the art of fiction writing.

The Sleepwalkers consists of three short novels, *The Romantic*, *The Anarchist*, and *The Realist*, held together loosely by the reappearance of some of the characters. In structure, the work is hardly a novel, for the form is incidental. Using this technique, sometimes referred to as essayism, Hermann Broch examines the intellectual, psychological, and moral forces in Germany that culminated in World War I. The book presents an unsparing picture of the character traits and attitudes of the German people that resulted in the glorification of the militaristic personality. These traits are exemplified in the rigid, proud personalities of the Pasenow family.

This carefully constructed novel builds slowly, but with great skill, its power deriving from the cumulative effect of the parts. The narrative relies not on melodrama or romance but on logical development to hold the reader's interest. Each incident serves to make an intellectual point, to symbolize an attitude, or to represent a psychological condition. Like somnambulists, the characters move rigidly and unavoidably to their fates, themselves becoming symbols in a world reduced to dehumanized symbols. Intellectual conversations and the discussion of philosophical and moral attitudes occupy much of the time of these characters, but often they repeat only platitudes and safe assumptions that will not disturb their world. More than anything else, *The Sleepwalkers* is an exploration of moral and ethical principles.

For its characters, correctness of conduct is all-important, regardless of the hypocrisy and deceit lying beneath the proper façade. Safety can be found behind elaborate manners and correct wardrobes and uniforms. Indeed, military uniforms assume symbolic proportions in the novel. When people cast off their uniforms, their true natures and animal instincts are freed—for good and for evil. Joachim's and Bertrand's thoughts about military uniforms become an essay on the nature of uniforms in general. Much space is given to the significance of clothing of all kinds—any human covering becomes, in effect, a uniform, labeling the wearer. Women prefer men in uniform, and men feel more like men when in uniform; above all, men escape responsibility for being themselves when they are in uniform.

The military code has overtaken all aspects of these people's lives, including their ability to love or experience grief. When Joachim was a boy, even the pastor called him a "young warrior" and assumed that the boy would be happy attending the cadet school and devoting his life to military service. Hypocrisy, the narrator explains, is so ingrained in the attitudes of the people that they could not recognize it in any form, but particularly in regard to any aspect of the military code of honor. When Joachim's brother Helmuth is killed in a duel, their father states, "He died for honor." They have deceived themselves so long that they can no longer experience genuine grief. Yet, they still uphold the military code that not only makes duels possible but considers them examples of noble conduct.

The novel moves slowly and, as in an underwater ballet, the characters forever circle around one another, striking dramatic but grotesque poses. The characters are presented in a stylized form; Broch does not attempt to render them as physical human beings, presenting them, instead, as representations of ideas. As such, they clash in an almost dreamlike manner. Most of the characters sooner or later complain of boredom. Most people, Joachim and Bertrand agree, live in a state of vegetative indolence and inertia of feeling. Life, they repeat to each other, consists of compromises. Above all, however, one must protect one's name. Traditions and customs, habits and routines, are the first and last defense of these mediocre individuals. Even murder is permissible, if handled with the proper decorum. Their lives are lived in an aura of unreality, but Bertrand proclaims early in the book that the artificial is always superior to the real, just as play is the true reality of life.

The form of *The Sleepwalkers* is wedded to the content. Particularly in the third volume, readers find a dazzling range of technique, from the total objectivity of the abstract essay to the subjectivity of lyric poetry. The parallel plots of the novel and the interpolated essays serve to broaden the horizon of the narrative, to break out of the mold of the ordinary novel form, and to create new implications of meaning. Broch was striving in this novel to achieve an artistic detachment that would allow the work to stand separate and aloof, its many facets reflecting the reader's interpretation rather than that of the author. Perhaps only André Gide in *The Counterfeiters* (1925) and Hermann Hesse in *The Glass Bead Game* (1943) have attempted any similar experiment.

The progression of the three volumes is philosophic and aesthetic rather than narrative. In the first two books, Broch describes the deterioration of outmoded values in the Prussian Pasenow and the Rhineland proletarian mystic Esch; the final volume, which takes place in 1918, shows the triumph of Huguenau—symbol of the new, valueless society of postwar Germany—over the forces of the past. It is society that is on trial in this book, and Broch is a merciless judge.

Through the first two parts of Broch's trilogy, and well into the third, the reader is kept purposefully under the illusion that one is reading a story written by an objective third-person narrator (to be identified with Hermann Broch). In the middle of part 3, however, it becomes apparent that the narrator of all three parts is in reality the author of the essay "The Disintegration of Values," which has been encapsulated into the fiction. At the close of the book, however, another shift has taken place: The author of the essay turns out to be identical with the first-person narrator of one of the framework stories. The whole novel thus lives in a timeless state of suspension, an aesthetic whole with its own self-contained author and its own laws. Broch has taken a common narrative device, the unreliable narrator, and turned the device back upon itself, rendering the entire novel as a symbol of the chaos of the modern world. In *The Sleepwalkers*, as is often the case with twentieth century literature, the medium is, and must be, the message.

"Critical Evaluation" by Bruce D. Reeves

Bibliography:

Cohn, Dorrit. *"The Sleepwalkers": Elucidations of Hermann Broch's Trilogy*. The Hague: Mouton, 1966. A close reading of Broch's novels. Describes the mechanics of the text's structure and pays special attention to the importance and meaning of narrators in the novels.

Dowden, Stephen D., ed. *Hermann Broch: Literature, Philosophy, Politics: The Yale Broch Symposium 1986*. Columbia, S.C.: Camden House, 1988. *The Sleepwalkers* is specifically discussed in various articles. Each article is paired with a response.

Osterle, Heinz. "Hermann Broch, *Die Schlafwandler:* Revolution and Apocalypse." *Publications of the Modern Language Association of America* 86 (October, 1971): 946-958. Argues that the apocalyptic thrust of the novel carries a paradoxical political message of revolution. Useful for the general reader because it situates the novel in its philosophical and historical contexts. Also refers to other similarly apocalyptic novels of ideas.

Schlant, Ernestine. *Hermann Broch*. Boston: Twayne, 1978. A basic and general introduction to Broch and his works that also provides a sound historical context for the novels. The chapter on the "Mechanics and Metaphysics of Sleepwalking" presents a good introduction to Broch's philosophical and aesthetic project.

Ziolkowski, Theodore. "Hermann Broch: *The Sleepwalkers*." In *Dimensions of the Modern Novel*. Princeton, N.J.: Princeton University Press, 1969. Provides useful background on Broch's philosophical attitudes and how they are transformed into this theoretical and essayistic novel. Argues that Broch's novel, in its rigorous execution, is the logical end point of the modernist consciousness already put forward by Rainer Maria Rilke and Franz Kafka in their modernist novels.

SLOW HOMECOMING

Type of work: Novel
Author: Peter Handke (1942-   )
Type of plot: Philosophical realism
Time of plot: Late 1970's and early 1980's
Locale: The United States, France, and Germany
First published: Langsame Heimkehr, 1979 (*The Long Way Around*); *Die Lehre der Sainte-Victoire*, 1980 (*The Lesson of Mont-Sainte-Victoire*); *Kindergeschichte*, 1981 (*Child Story*) (English translation, 1985 as *Slow Homecoming*); conceived together with the drama *Über die Dörfer* (beyond the villages), 1981

Principal characters:
The Long Way Around:
VALENTIN SORGER, a geologist
LAUFFER, Sorger's friend and fellow scientist
NATIVE AMERICAN WOMAN, Sorger's girlfriend
A FAMILY IN CALIFORNIA, Sorger's neighbors
A STRANGER IN NEW YORK, Sorger's traveling companion

The Lesson of Mont-Sainte-Victoire:
THE NARRATOR

Child Story:
A MAN
A WOMAN
THEIR DAUGHTER

Über die Dörfer:
NOVA, the goddess of Modern Times
GREGOR, a man returning home
HANS, Gregor's brother
SOPHIE, Gregor's sister

The Story:

The Long Way Around. The geologist Sorger was doing research in the vicinity of a small Indian village in Alaska. He knew few people there: his friend and fellow scientist Lauffer, and an Indian woman with whom he had a relationship. At first he and the woman kept their affair secret. However, they gradually allowed their relationship to be apparent to others. The time Sorger had in Alaska was limited. He returned to his house in an unnamed university town in California. Sorger had a close relationship with a neighbor family. On his way eastward, Sorger stopped in Denver to visit an old friend. The discovery that this friend had died made Sorger rethink his relationship with his siblings. In New York, Sorger met a man by chance who, despite all their differences, vaguely reminded Sorger of himself. Sorger's movement, both physically and emotionally, was towards Europe. At the end, Sorger's plane touched down onto European soil.

The Lesson of Mont-Sainte-Victoire. The narrator traveled to the Provence area of France.

Thanks to his appreciation of the paintings by Paul Cézanne, he could view the highway, in all its banality, as pure color. He recalled other journeys, to Yugoslavia and in Upper Austria. He traveled to Mont-Sainte-Victoire, which Cézanne had painted. Near Puyloubier he encountered a large mastiff, and the fear which this animal represented was enough to make him forget all color and form in the landscape. Elsewhere a man threatened his life, then they walked a short way together. In a café on the Cours Mirabeau he saw a scene with card players that was almost exactly like a Cézanne painting. His expedition to the mountain gave him the justification for writing *The Lesson of Mont-Sainte-Victoire*. He became fascinated with the unity of the "thing-image-script" as he learned about it through studying Cézanne. He recalled that his father was German and his mother of Slovenian stock, and that they had lived in southern Austria. Recalling again his writing, he mentioned that he had transformed Sorger, the main character in *The Long Way Around*, into himself. The "lesson" was not to invent, but to realize the world fully. He took a second trip to Provence. He again wanted to go to the mountain. He retraced his steps. The dog was gone. He climbed to the top. In a few months he would return to Austria. He was learning to see, really to see things.

Child Story. A daughter was born to a woman and a man. The family had moved to Paris. While the child was still very young, the family moved to a country where their own language, German, was spoken. There they built a house. The mother decided to resume her career (acting) and drifted away from the man and child. When the child was three, she began to play more with others and go to kindergarten. The father and the daughter moved back to the "beloved foreign city" (Paris). There the girl began school. The school was a Jewish school and this eventually led to problems. Someone even threatened her life (because she represented the people who had persecuted the Jews). She went to another school. Over the next years she would attend several schools, changing because of age or dissatisfaction (hers or his). She preferred German to French, and he decided to send her back to her mother, who lived where German was spoken. He traveled. After a year, he returned. She had her tenth birthday. Father and daughter went through a forest and painted over swastikas others had drawn there.

Über die Dörfer. Gregor was the oldest of three siblings. After the death of their parents, his brother, Hans, wrote to him requesting that he come back home and settle some questions of inheritance. Gregor reflected upon the situation in the presence of the goddess Nova. She advised him to look beyond the villages; that is, he should look beyond the traditional way of thinking about his life and in particular avoid conflict, which seemed inevitable, with his siblings. That conflict arose out of the fact that Hans and their sister Sophie wanted Gregor to relinquish his rights to their parents' house and its lot. Sophie wanted to use the property as collateral. With the borrowed money she planned to set up her own shop. Despite his doubts about Sophie's chances of financial success, Gregor eventually acceded to their wishes. The goddess Nova reappeared at the end and repeated her counsel: go beyond the villages.

Critical Evaluation:

The series in English translation consists of three works of prose that can be considered novels, with the first most closely fitting into that category. The *Slow Homecoming* series, however, is a tetralogy rather than a trilogy. The author, Peter Handke, has designated a play—or dramatic poem as he calls it—-to be the fourth and final work in the series. The play, *Über die Dörfer* (beyond the villages), was not translated into English for the 1985 edition. The series was named for the first book's title, which in German means "slow homecoming."

Handke garnered international attention when he challenged a famous group of postwar German language writers. According to Handke, the Group 47, named for the first year that they met, 1947, had become too much of an institution. Between 1969 and 1972, his daughter was born, he separated from his wife, and his mother committed suicide. From this point on, his writing slowly took on a different character, it became less openly rebellious and showed more self-reflection. It represents Handke's turn to a more subjective, introspective writing, which has been labeled, in reference to Handke and other writers, the New Sensibility.

The *Slow Homecoming* series chronicles Handke's gradual reconciliation with Austria, his home, and its history. In the series, Handke nevertheless maintains a critical attitude toward Austria. The slow trip "home" represents not only a trip back to Austria but also represents a trip back to Handke's poetics, or aesthetic of writing.

The main character in each work of the series may be read as a mask for Handke himself. In the first novel, *The Long Way Around*, the Handke mask is a geologist who decides to return to his home in Europe. Significantly, home is usually expressed as Europe. It is not until the final play, *Beyond the Villages*, that the main character is back in Austria.

The chronology of *Child Story* corresponds to the time in which Handke lived in West Germany (from 1965 to 1969 and from 1971 to 1973) and in Paris (1969-1971). Handke then traveled in the United States, as does Sorger in *The Long Way Around*. The following year Handke traveled around Europe, some of this trip surfaces in *The Lesson of Mont-Sainte-Victoire*. Handke finally returned to Austria and settled in Salzburg, and *Beyond the Villages* takes place entirely in Austria. The homecoming, however, is fraught with family tension. Handke brings back to Austria a concept of home that explodes nationalism. Home is no longer a village; rather, the village (or city, or country) is part of the world. This is the message of *Über die Dörfer*, or "beyond the villages."

The tetralogy does more, however, than investigate the relationship of the personal to the historical. Description of landscape, objects, and the like takes up much of the tetralogy. In the first book, *The Long Way Around*, the world is seen in geographic—not just historical—time. The title of the second book informs the reader that there is a lesson, which seems to be primarily aesthetic, to be learned from viewing Mont-Sainte-Victoire. In *Child Story*, the narrator's daughter teaches him to appreciate color and to recognize form. He learns the "truth about the essence of beauty." From a sense of geologic time in the first work, to the artist Cézanne viewing nature in the second, to a child seeing things for the first time in the third book, the texts present the reader with a world that extends beyond the "village" of human history, activity, and perception.

Although the works are connected in terms of plot, one can speak more easily of theme as the unifying factor. Along with the slow homecoming, a recurrent theme is the art of writing.

Intimately connected to Handke's understanding of writing is his way of looking at the world. In *The Long Way Around*, Handke introduces the reader to his concern for underlying forms. Geologic formations, in their purity (in the sense of being what they are rather than representing something else) and their being what underlies visible, earthly forms, are, in a sense, touchstones for Handke's aesthetic of writing, which he explores in his writing. In his contemplation of the paintings by Cézanne and other artists, Handke seeks to recognize "the form that does not lament transience or the vicissitudes of history, but transmit an existence in peace." What follows from such a recognition is the problem which every artist faces: how to "communicate the essence of things."

Furthermore, the narrator in *Lesson of Mont-Sainte-Victoire* also needs a justification to write. The narrator finds it in his own self-critic. Rather than employing "celestial comparisons" in the face of beauty, he determines to look at and speak of the earth—where ever he might find himself. Throughout *Slow Homecoming*, Handke tries more to narrate nature rather than to tell a story. In his sense of pure narration, the separation of narrated and narration evaporates, and language should be transparent. This means that language should clearly refer to something, and not be a sign dangling outside of meaning. At the same time, Handke tries to create new mythic images that are as relevant and as gripping to the modern reader as the classical myths were to their audience.

Handke is known for experimenting with genres. That experimentation may be in part be a result of Handke's looking for appropriate paradigms for his aesthetics. Handke, who has translated from the ancient Greek, is clearly reflecting, in *Slow Homecoming*, the influence of Plato's theory of forms. Plato's theory of forms, in summary, posits that beyond this, the visible world, a world of ideal, eternal forms exists.

In addition, *Child Story* is clearly influenced the Greek historian Thucydides, and the novel concludes with a motto from the sixth Olympic ode by Pindar. The dramatic poem *Über die Dörfer*, furthermore, is constructed along the lines of Greek drama.

Handke is difficult to read. He eschews story; he mixes and plays with genre; the act of writing is an important theme of his writing. Unlike many modern and postmodern writers, however, Handke strives for (and so, implicitly, believes in) a unity of language with the world it narrates. He looks for beauty and the essence, or form, of things, which many thinker of the twentieth century might consider a waste of time. For them, words have no essence, and the objects of the world do not have ideal correspondences.

Handke's attraction to form may be partly responsible for his interest in classical literature and philosophy. His fascination with classical literature, his concern for aesthetics, as well as his need to re-imagine Austria continue are prominent themes of the *Slow Homecoming* tetralogy. At the end of *Über die Dörfer*, the goddess Nova challenges her listeners (onstage and, implicitly, those in the audience as well) to overcome the past and the crimes of their fathers. However, Handke does not want to heal old wounds by ignoring them. In *Child Story*, the narrator and his daughter make a special effort to paint over swastikas others had drawn in the forest. They protect nature—and by extension their home—from a far-too-present past. It is an ugly past that Austria needs to confront if it is ever to imagine itself into the future.

Scott G. Williams

Bibliography:

Firda, Richard Arthur. *Peter Handke*. New York: Twayne, 1993. Covers Handke's work through the tetralogy (chapter 5) and beyond. Annotated bibliography.

Klinkowitz, Jerome, and James Knowlton. *Peter Handke and the Postmodern Transformation: The Goalie's Journey Home*. Columbia: University of Missouri Press, 1983. Places Handke's work in the context of postmodern literature. Useful for understanding the themes of postmodern literature.

Modern Fiction Studies 36, no. 3 (Autumn, 1990). Provides different perspectives on *Slow Homecoming*. Hugo Caviola's article is especially informative.

Schlueter, June, ed. *The Plays and Novels of Peter Handke*. Pittsburgh: University of Pittsburgh Press, 1981. Provides an overview of Handke's work up to 1981. Includes an interview with Handke.

Wesche, Ulrich. "Peter Handke, Walker Percy, and the End of Modernity." *Essays in Literature* 19, no. 2 (Fall, 1992): 291-297. Establishes a link between the philosophies of Handke and Percy (two of whose books Handke has translated into German). Addresses the postmodernist crisis in language and Handke's desire for the transparency of words.

THE SMALL HOUSE AT ALLINGTON

Type of work: Novel
Author: Anthony Trollope (1815-1882)
Type of plot: Domestic realism
Time of plot: Mid-nineteenth century
Locale: London and the fictional county of "Barsetshire"
First published: serial, 1862-1864; book, 1864

Principal characters:
CHRISTOPHER DALE, the squire of Allington
MRS. DALE, his widowed sister-in-law
LILIAN (LILY), her daughter
ISABELLA (BELL), another daughter
BERNARD DALE, the squire's nephew and heir
ADOLPHUS CROSBIE, Lily's suitor
JOHN EAMES, another suitor
LADY ALEXANDRINA DE COURCY, a young woman of fashion
DR. CROFTS, a man in love with Bell
LORD DE GUEST, Eames's benefactor

The Story:

There were two houses at Allington. The Great House was the residence of Squire Christopher Dale, an unmarried, plain, seemingly dour man whose ancestors had been squires at Allington for generations. In the Small House nearby lived his sister-in-law, Mrs. Dale, and her two daughters, Bell and Lily. Mrs. Dale was the widow of the squire's youngest brother, who had died young and had left his family in modest circumstances. When the squire had offered his brother's widow the Small House rent free, she immediately accepted his offer, not so much for her own sake as for that of her daughters.

The Dales were not the chief family of the neighborhood. Near the town of Guestwick stood Guestwick Manor, the home of Lord de Guest and his sister, Lady Julia. Although not intimate, the families had a tie by marriage. Years before, another of the squire's brothers, Colonel Orlando Dale, had eloped with the earl's sister, Lady Fanny. The colonel had not made a career for himself and now lived with his wife in semiretirement at Torquay. Bernard Dale, their only son and a captain in the Engineers, was the squire's heir.

Mrs. Dale was a woman whose pride was as great as her means were small, and her brother-in-law's gruff manners had done little to retain cordial relations between them during her ten years in the Small House. The uncle had been kind to his nieces in his rather ungracious manner, however, so that they enjoyed the social advantages if not the income of wealth. Bell was her uncle's favorite. It was his secret wish that she would become Bernard's wife and thus mistress of the Great House. At one time, Mrs. Dale had believed that Dr. Crofts, the Guestwick physician, would declare himself; but he had not spoken, and now there seemed little likelihood of that becoming a match.

One summer, Bernard Dale arrived to visit his uncle, bringing with him his friend Adolphus Crosbie, a handsome, agreeable fellow who was a senior clerk in the General Committee Office at Whitehall. At first Crosbie made the deeper impression on Bell, and Lily liked to tease her sister by calling him a swell because he was received in the drawing rooms of countesses and cabinet ministers. Crosbie himself was attracted to Lily. When the squire, more gracious than usual to his nephew's friend, invited him to return in September for the shooting, Crosbie gladly accepted the invitation.

Lily had another suitor in young John Eames of Guestwick, a clerk in the Income Tax office in London. Although he had been hopelessly in love with Lily since boyhood, his meager income of a hundred pounds a year gave him no immediate prospect of marriage. Eames was awkward, callow, and susceptible. While professing adoration for Lily, he had against his better judgment become entangled with Amelia Roper, the scheming daughter of Mrs. Lupex, his London landlady.

Crosbie returned to Allington in September; before long, neighborhood gossip was confirmed—a marriage had been arranged between Lily Dale and Adolphus Crosbie. This was the news that greeted Eames when he arrived in Guestwick to visit his mother in October. He was made even more wretched by the half-languishing, half-threatening letters he received from Amelia during his stay. Lily's engagement made Squire Dale more anxious than ever to see his own plans fulfilled for Bernard and Bell. Encouraged by his uncle, the young officer proposed but in such unconvincing terms that Bell refused him immediately. Not even the settlement of eight hundred pounds a year promised by the squire tempted her to change her mind.

Crosbie had made his choice, and he hoped that the squire would make a financial settlement on Lily, but when he brought up the matter, the squire declared that he felt under no obligation to provide for his niece's future. Crosbie was disappointed, but he consoled himself with the reflection that he was marrying for love and not for worldly advancement. So matters stood when he received from the Countess de Courcy an invitation to join a house party at Courcy Castle before returning to London.

The de Courcys entertained lavishly. One party guest was Lady Julia de Guest, a well-meaning busybody who spread the news of Crosbie's engagement. The countess, who had had some experience in getting daughters engaged and then seeing their engagements broken, said that nothing was likely to come of Crosbie's romance at Allington. She was right, for her campaign to secure the clerk for her own youngest daughter, Lady Alexandrina, was successful. Long before the end of his visit, Crosbie had proposed and was accepted. He had not declared himself to Lady Alexandrina without severe twinges of conscience, it was true; after all, an earl's daughter would offer a better position in fashionable London life than would the penniless niece of a country squire. Hearing what had happened, Lady Julia denounced him as a deceiver and a miserable wretch. Crosbie recognized in her scorn the voice of public opinion; he wished that he could blot out his visit to Courcy Castle.

Meanwhile, Squire Dale, told of Bell's refusal, had gone to his sister-in-law to enlist her aid in furthering the match. He was greatly put out when she insisted that Bell should be free to choose for herself. A short time later, the squire received a letter from Lady Julia telling him of Crosbie's engagement to Lady Alexandrina. Having heard that Crosbie had returned to London, the squire followed him there and tried to see the clerk at his club. Crosbie was conscience-stricken and refused to meet the old gentleman; instead, he sent a disapproving but obliging friend to talk with the squire. The next day, Crosbie wrote to Mrs. Dale and confessed that he had broken his engagement to her daughter.

Shortly before the end of his vacation, Eames saved Lord de Guest from being attacked by a bull on his estate. Gratefully, the earl decided to take an interest in the young man's future, and he invited Eames to spend Christmas with him at Guestwick Manor.

The two months before Christmas passed with heavy slowness at Allington. Mrs. Dale could only hope that time would heal Lily's hurt. The squire felt that there should be some redress for the insult to his niece. Lord de Guest met Eames in London and realized the true state of the young man's feeling for Lily when Eames threatened physical punishment for Crosbie's deed. Meanwhile, Crosbie was preoccupied with financial arrangements for his marriage. Under the fostering hand of Mortimer Gagebee, his future brother-in-law and guardian of the de Courcy interests, he was induced to settle most of his income on Lady Alexandrina.

Crosbie went to Courcy Castle for Christmas. Still involved with Amelia Roper, Eames went to Guestwick Manor. At a dinner, the earl announced his intention of settling some money on Lily and Eames if they married. He asked the squire to do the same, but Lily's uncle refused to commit himself. Returning to London on the same train with Crosbie, Eames was unable to restrain himself when they met on the station platform. He thoroughly trounced Lily's faithless suitor.

Bernard renewed his proposals to Bell and argued their uncle's wishes in the matter; but Bell told him, as kindly as possible, that she could follow no wishes but her own. Stubborn in his desires, the squire became angry with his nephew and niece, and he decided to be angry with his sister-in-law as well if she refused to reason with her daughter. After the exchange of heated words, Mrs. Dale decided that it might be better for all concerned if she and her daughters moved away from the Small House.

A short time later, Lily became ill with scarlatina, and Dr. Crofts was called in. He came daily, ostensibly to see his patient but actually to be near Bell. In the meantime, Mrs. Dale was preparing to move into a small cottage in Guestwick. During Lily's illness, Dr. Crofts declared his love to Bell. Taking her evasive answer for a refusal, he drove away in dejection. Lily, aware of Bell's true feelings, urged him to ask her sister again. Crosbie and Lady Alexandrina were married in London in February.

After Lily's illness, Lady Julia invited Mrs. Dale and her daughters to spend a week at Guestwick Manor. Eames was asked at the same time. Lily, however, saw through the scheme for bringing her and Eames together, especially after she learned that Squire Dale was to make another of the party, and she declined the invitation. The squire was so kind in his concern for Lily that Mrs. Dale began to regret her decision to move into the village. In the midst of her perplexities, Dr. Crofts came to tell her that Bell had accepted him. While the doctor sat with the Dales beside the fire that night as if they were already one family, the anxious mother was almost able to believe that happiness had returned to the Small House.

Eames, manfully escaping from the toils of Amelia Roper, arrived at Guestwick Manor. He had recently been made private secretary to the great Sir Raffle Buffle, largely through the earl's influence, and he was grateful. Since Lily had not come to the manor, it had been decided that the squire and Bell should dine with the de Guests. On the next day, Eames was to call at Allington and declare himself to Lily. To his dismay, however, she would not have him. After his departure, Mrs. Dale added her entreaties to his, but Lily remained firm. She was, she declared, like her mother, widowed; and so matters had to stand.

Mrs. Dale did not leave the Small House after all, for their family troubles had brought her and the squire closer together, and he announced his intention of settling three thousand pounds on each of his nieces. When Bell married Dr. Crofts in June, the squire threw open the Great House for the wedding. Bernard and Eames did not attend.

Crosbie's wedded life lasted only a few months. Lady Alexandrina became bored with the humdrum of a government clerk's life and went off to join her mother at Baden Baden. Crosbie discovered too late that the settlements he had made on his wife left him a poor man, and he went into cheap lodgings—happy at any price, however, to be free both of her nagging and her aristocratic relatives.

Critical Evaluation:

In *The Small House at Allington*, Anthony Trollope continues his investigation of the lives of men and women who inhabit the fictional district of Barsetshire, a country province modeled on those with which the author was familiar. The people of Trollope's imaginary countryside exhibit moral and social values that stand in contrast to those held by the more sophisticated but often more morally bankrupt men and women of London. In this novel, Trollope introduces a number of figures from the city into the lives of his countryfolk, so that the contrast is brought into sharp focus. Although *The Small House at Allington* can be read without reference to the other novels in the Barsetshire series, those familiar with works such as *The Warden* (1855), *Barsetshire Towers* (1857), *Dr. Thorne* (1858), or *Framley Parsonage* (1860-1861) will see how Trollope's vision of society is developed through his exploration of characters from a range of social classes and professions who share a common set of experiences and values. Characters who were featured in major roles in other novels in the series often make cameo appearances in this work, and Trollope introduces additional minor figures whose stories will form the central interest of novels in the author's Palliser series.

Like so many of Trollope's novels, *The Small House at Allington* is concerned with marriage, specifically with the choice to be made between marrying for love and marrying for money or social position. Although the novel contains many elements that resemble those of the romantic novels that achieved great popularity with Victorian audiences, Trollope undercuts the form at key points to highlight the dangers of adhering too closely to the romantic ideal. Instead of meeting his readers' demands for the expected happy ending, which should befall the heroine and hero regardless of how badly they have behaved, Trollope instead uses the familiar structural devices of the traditional romantic novel to explore a theme that intrigued him throughout his career: human perversity. Many of the characters in *The Small House at Allington* seem wilfully intent on making the wrong choices and avoiding the possibility for securing lasting happiness by opting for marriage partners or a single lifestyle that will only bring them unhappiness. To dramatize the universality of his theme, Trollope employs a structural pattern common in Victorian novels, that of multiple plotting. The central story of Lily Dale's unfortunate engagement to Adolphus Crosbie and her subsequent decision to reject Johnnie Eames and to remain a spinster, is complemented by a series of similar love stories in which women and men face choices resembling the one Lily must make between her two lovers.

As he does in so many of his novels, Trollope lavishes a great deal of attention to characterization. Although he himself calls his heroine a "prig," she cannot be dismissed so glibly by serious readers. Lily represents a type of woman common in the Victorian era but not unknown in other times: the strong-willed, independent figure who is determined to make her own decisions but too proud to admit her mistakes, who remains perversely committed to a course of action even when that has been shown to be unwise. Certainly she shares affinities with that other, more famous jilted spinster, Miss Havisham of Charles Dickens' *Great Expectations* (1860-1861). By stubbornly adhering to the notion of constancy in love, she is led to reject the possibility of finding happiness in another romantic relationship. Readers who are disappointed that Trollope does not provide some means to rescue Lily from her self-induced intellectual blindness and have her marry Johnnie Eames have missed the point Trollope is making, that such idyllic resolutions are not plausible in the real world, and that individuals (men as well as women) who refuse to recognize their faults are doomed to a life of unwarranted loneliness. In effect, Lily gets what she deserves.

Johnnie Eames suffers as well from Lily's haughty behavior, but Trollope is careful to show that the hero is not without flaws. His treatment of the unfortunate Amelia Roper demonstrates that he has flaws that may explain why Lily refuses to accept him, both before accepting Crosbie's proposal and later, after her engagement has been severed. In a similar fashion, the author introduces character traits in "villains" such as Crosbie that ameliorate, if they do not exonerate, their actions. A number of characters seem little more than stock figures, however: Lord de Guest and Squire Dale represent the pastoral tradition of the English countryside, whereas the de Courcys embody the false values of London gentry who find amusement in manipulating—and ruining—the lives of others. Trollope does offer readers one traditional "happy ending": that of Lily's sister, Bell, and Dr. Crofts. Like her sister, Bell is torn between two lovers, but she is shrewd enough to reject the dissolute Bernard Dale in favor of the emotionally more stable Crofts.

The vision of society presented in *The Small House at Allington* is noticeably darker than that of earlier novels in the Barsetshire series. Trollope seems less interested in making readers feel comfortable than in exposing human folly. No doubt that is why his contemporaries found the novel less appealing than some of his lighter works. Yet *The Small House at Allington* emerges as one of the finest in the extensive Trollope canon for illustrating the consequences that follow from the willful disregard of common sense and moderation in dealing with others and from the insistence on acting on ill-formed opinion or out of selfish motives.

"Critical Evaluation" by Laurence W. Mazzeno

Bibliography:

Hall, N. John. *Trollope: A Biography*. Oxford, England: Clarendon Press, 1991. Comprehensive scholarly biography of the novelist. Provides information on the composition and publication history of *The Small House at Allington* and a brief analysis of the important characters in the novel who also appear in subsequent works by Trollope.

Kincaid, James R. *The Novels of Anthony Trollope*. Oxford, England: Clarendon Press, 1977. Determines that *The Small House at Allington* is the darkest of the Barsetshire series, which is generally comic in tone; claims that Trollope is intent on undermining the pastoral qualities that characterize earlier novels in the series.

MacDonald, Susan Peck. *Anthony Trollope*. Boston: Twayne, 1987. Discusses *The Small House at Allington* as one of the novels in which Trollope deals with the topic of love. Focuses on the perversity of the heroine, Lily Dale, and explains how Trollope achieves density and verisimilitude through the use of parallel plots.

McMaster, Juliet. "*The Small House at Allington*: The Moth and the Candle." In *Trollope's Palliser Novels: Theme and Pattern*. New York: Oxford University Press, 1978. Excellent analysis of the major themes of the work: the "quest for truth among lies," and the prevalence of human perversity. Links the work to Trollope's Palliser series.

Super, R. H. *The Chronicler of Barsetshire: A Life of Anthony Trollope*. Ann Arbor: University of Michigan Press, 1988. Critical biography of the novelist that provides excellent overview of his major works. Discusses the principal themes of *The Small House at Allington* and points out ways in which Trollope used it as a bridge between the Barsetshire and the Palliser series.

SMOKE

Type of work: Novel
Author: Ivan Turgenev (1818-1883)
Type of plot: Social realism
Time of plot: 1862-1865
Locale: Germany and Russia
First published: Dym, 1867 (English translation, 1868)

Principal characters:
GRIGORY LITVINOFF, a serious young Russian man
TANYA SHESTOFF, his fiancée
KAPITOLINA SHESTOFF, Tanya's aunt
IRINA, a fashionable lady
GENERAL RATMIROFF, her husband
POTUGIN, a retired clerk

The Story:

At Baden, Grigory Litvinoff decided to enjoy a few days of vacation. The fashionable German watering place was full of Russians, and there, in a week or so, Litvinoff was to meet Tanya Shestoff, his fiancée, who was coming to Baden with her Aunt Kapitolina.

Litvinoff was poor, comparatively speaking. His father owned a large farm with forests, meadows, and a lake, but Russian farming was so unproductive that he could barely make ends meet. After his university days, Litvinoff had decided to learn progressive farming, but, because Russia was so far behind in agriculture, he had to go abroad to study. He had been in the Crimea, in France, Switzerland, and England. Everywhere his keen mind had absorbed the latest agricultural methods, and he was particularly impressed by the superiority of the few pieces of American machinery he had seen. Full of ideas, his life was planned; he would make a model farm. First, however, he would marry Tanya.

Quite by chance, he ran into Bambaeff, a former acquaintance. Bambaeff was an ebullient person, filled with windy politics and intimate with the most advanced thinkers in Baden. When Bambaeff took Litvinoff to meet Gubaryoff, the idol of the liberals, Litvinoff was repelled by the company he met in Gubaryoff's rooms. They all talked long and loud in their assertions that Russia produced nothing good, that all virtue resided in Europe proper, that the emancipation of the serfs was a foolish step. He met Bindasoff, a choleric boor who borrowed a hundred rubles from him; he never repaid the debt, although Litvinoff later watched him win four hundred rubles with the money. Only one man in the gathering was quiet; he sat unnoticed in a corner.

After leaving Gubaryoff's room, Litvinoff stopped at a sidewalk café. The quiet man from Gubaryoff's rooms appeared and presented himself at Litvinoff's table; he was Potugin, a former clerk in Moscow. They talked agreeably for a long time. Both men greatly disliked their compatriots who were so sure that nothing good came out of Russia, and they both agreed that by hard work Russia could advance. At last, as Potugin rose to go, he excused himself by saying that he had a girl with him. Seeing Litvinoff's look of polite blankness, he explained that he was looking after a little child who had no parents.

After a short walk, Litvinoff returned to his hotel. He had a letter from Tanya to read; as he read it, he was bothered by a heavy sweet smell. Looking around, he saw a bunch of fresh heliotrope in a glass. Here was a mystery. The servant said that a lady had given him money to get into the room. She must have left the flowers. Suddenly, he remembered Irina.

Ten years before, Litvinoff had been a student in Moscow. He was poor, and he frequently visited another poor family, the Osinins. The family was of the real nobility, but for generations the Osinins had declined, until they existed only on a small pension the father received from some obscure sinecures. Litvinoff was attracted greatly to Irina, the seventeen-year-old daughter of the household, but for a long time Irina paid little heed to the poor student. One day, her haughtiness suddenly changed. Pliant and cheerful, she talked eagerly with Litvinoff of his ambitions. When he declared his love, Irina was pleased and grateful. Without any formal understanding, Litvinoff became her accepted suitor.

By a trick of fate, Prince Osinin, her father, received an invitation to the court ball. Now that Irina was grown, he decided to accept, to show his daughter in fine society. Litvinoff urged Irina to go to the ball. She repeated many times that she was going only at Litvinoff's insistence. On the night of the ball, Litvinoff brought her a bunch of heliotrope to wear. She took the flowers and kissed him passionately. The next day Irina had a headache and refused to see him. Two days after the ball Irina had gone to St. Petersburg with Count Reisenbach, a distant cousin of her mother. The explanation was brief and tragic. The count needed an ornament in his household. Grasping and ambitious as she was, Irina had accepted and had gone to stay with her debauched cousin. Litvinoff put her out of his mind; he had almost forgotten the incident until the heliotrope appeared mysteriously in his room.

Litvinoff wrestled with his conscience and decided not to see Irina again. He held to his resolve until Potugin came to him with a pressing invitation to visit the home of General Ratmiroff. At the party he met Irina again, now the wife of General Ratmiroff, a vain, cruel aristocrat. Litvinoff was as much repelled by the empty smart set as he had been by the empty liberals he had met in Baden.

Irina would not let him ignore her. She begged her former suitor to love her again, and when she came to his rooms he admitted his love had never died.

Tanya and her Aunt Kapitolina appeared. Even naïve Tanya saw at once that something had happened to her fiancé; she was not wholly unprepared when he confessed his affair with Irina. Potugin tried his best to get Litvinoff to abandon Irina. He had good reason to do so. For love of Irina, he had agreed to marry a friend of hers who was soon to bear an illegitimate child. Although the girl fell ill and the marriage never took place, Potugin was burdened with the care of the little girl. He had acted because of his hopeless infatuation for Irina, and he warned Litvinoff that only evil consequences could come of leaving Tanya for the shallow aristocrat.

In his despair, Litvinoff made a deal with Irina. He would not become her secret lover; she must go away with him and be his alone. He named the train on which he would leave. Irina was not at the station, and Litvinoff sadly took his seat. Just then he saw Irina, dressed in her maid's costume, rush to the platform. He motioned her to come aboard; she understood, but she refused by gesture and motioned him to dismount. She stood in a hopeless attitude on the platform as the train pulled out of the station.

Litvinoff recovered almost wholly from his hurt. He was too quiet for his years, but he was fairly happy. He found his father's farm in bad shape, with insufficient income to keep up the house. His father was pathetically glad to see him and abandoned the control of the estate to his son. That end accomplished, he died content. For a long time there was no opportunity to introduce new methods; Litvinoff had all he could do to remain solvent.

After three years, he learned that Tanya was living on a farm a day's journey away. Resolved to mend his life, he decided to go to her and ask her forgiveness. He found Tanya ready to forget as well as forgive, and she was even embarrassed by his penitence. They were soon married. Irina continued to attract admirers in St. Petersburg; despite her thirty years, she retained the freshness of youth. Although many gallants were in attendance upon her, she never singled out a special admirer. The society ladies all agreed that Irina was not generally liked; she had such an ironic turn of mind.

Critical Evaluation:

When *Smoke* appeared in 1867, Ivan Turgenev had been publishing prose fiction for twenty years and was well past the midpoint in his literary career. He had learned most of what he was to know of his craft and had defined his themes, which could be summarized as the Russian question and how it affects, or is affected by, adult love entanglements. The Russian question was simply that of Russia's relation to the community of European nations and what might be done either to change that relation or to preserve it. Turgenev, who lived much in Western Europe and admired its values, saw that in science, industry, social attitudes, political institutions, and general progress, Russia was far behind Germany, France, and England, and he had little sympathy with conservative Slavophiles who felt that their native land was better off for being so. In his complicated relationship with Pauline Garcia Viardot, a highly successful French singer and actress who had both a husband and children, he saw further the impediment to purposeful action in men (or women) who were not secure or even fulfilled in love matters.

Although *Smoke* is set in Baden, a fashionable German spa, virtually all the characters are Russians, falling into three groups. First, there are nonentities such as the liberals Litvinoff meets in Gubaryoff's rooms, brittle and shallow people who pretend to liberalism and intellectuality though they lack the character and purpose to serve their homeland well. Then there are the aristocrats, some of them military men, who have no interest in bringing about change in Russia, which suits them as it is. Finally, there is the novel's hero, Grigory Litvinoff, and a shadowy figure, Sozont Potugin, civilized and thoughtful, with whom Litvinoff becomes acquainted. Both these men seem to embody qualities of character and intelligence by which the condition of Russia and its people might be improved, but both are under the influence of Irina, who is now married to Ratmiroff, a brilliant young general and Russian aristocrat, whose social set Irina detests even as she is unwilling to leave a marriage which gives her power and a comfortable social place. Her brief liaison with Litvinoff seems motivated by genuine passion and true regard, but neither impulse is as strong as the tie that binds her to a world she does not admire but cannot forsake.

Turgenev seems to want his readers to be persuaded that the very people who have gifts that might lead Russia forward are, by virtue of their complete humanity, susceptible to passion, unrequited or impermanent, that would effectively block sustained effort or real accomplishment, thereby guaranteeing that the Russian question will remain unanswered. Such a message would perhaps have been personally gratifying to the author, who believed himself enlightened to true progress as he believed he saw it in the West, but who was nevertheless attached to his own bewitching woman, Pauline Viardot, so that he was content to live in places such as Baden (Turgenev had large hereditary property in Russia) and fill his active life with literary pursuits. That Pauline seems to have been an honorable woman, who remained loyal in friendship to Turgenev even as she must have seen herself as a partial model for characters like Irina, only emphasizes the degree to which Turgenev was captivated by someone stronger than himself. In youth, he had been considerably dominated by an imperious mother, and perhaps domination by a woman was something that he came to need.

It might be well to remember that, when Litvinoff arrives in Baden, he has been engaged in practical study which he hopes to take home to Russia with a view to improving his estate. He is betrothed to a lovely, innocent young woman, Tanya Shestoff, who suffers his adventure with

Irina and accepts him back at the novel's conclusion. Turgenev was to take up the same story again in *Spring Torrents* (1871), but, in that novel, Sanin, the central male character, betrays Gemma, the young innocent, without redemption. After his encounter with Madame Polozova, he fails to return to Gemma, who marries another man and emigrates to America. By 1872, Turgenev was in his middle fifties, old enough to realize clearly that infatuation with an unattainable woman meant the loss of other possibilities in love relations and the conventional happiness (and potential contribution to ordinary Russian life) that might follow from that.

Even if *Smoke* has a happier ending than *Spring Torrents*, there is melancholy near its conclusion. When it becomes clear to Litvinoff that his brief affair with Irina will result in nothing permanent, he leaves Baden alone on a train whose smoke seems to illustrate "his own life, Russian life—everything human, especially everything Russian." He recalls his experiences among the fashionable and pretentious, he recalls the somewhat pessimistic sermonizing of his acquaintance Potugin, and he concludes his reflection with "a gesture of despair."

As happened on more than one occasion when a novel by Turgenev appeared, liberals in Russia were dissatisfied, even bitter, over *Smoke*, which they saw as their betrayal by a landed aristocrat living abroad, of whom they felt they had just cause to be suspicious. However, Turgenev did not feel that liberalism was the same thing as the ideological rigidities he sometimes found in the thinking of progressives among his own countrymen, rigidities that he believed could not result in anything purposeful. Indeed, Turgenev does not seem very hopeful about anything in *Smoke*, as the title implies. About the best thing Litvinoff can expect from life is marriage to Tanya, who has the good grace to take him back as the novel concludes.

"Critical Evaluation" by John Higby

Bibliography:

Magarshack, David. *Turgenev: A Life*. London: Faber and Faber, 1954. An illustrated biography by Turgenev's translator describing Turgenev's life extensively and concentrating on the events shaping it, his relationships with Russian and foreign writers, and the factual circumstances surrounding his works, including *Smoke*.

Matlaw, R. E. "Turgenev's Novels: Civic Responsibility and Literary Predilection." *Harvard Slavic Studies* 4 (1957): 249-262. An interesting view of Turgenev's novels, including *Smoke*. Matlaw concludes that Turgenev was a superlative writer of fiction but was not successful as a novelist, having difficulties integrating social background and the characters appearing against that background.

Seeley, Frank Friedeberg. *Turgenev: A Reading of His Fiction*. New York: Cambridge University Press, 1991. Seeley analyzes *Smoke* both as a novel and as an episode in Turgenev's fight with the critics and readers, seeing it as no less political than *Fathers and Sons* (1862). Through the novel's main characters, Turgenev shows that personal and political life in Russia at that time were reduced to smoke.

Woodward, James B. *Metaphysical Conflict: A Study of the Major Novels of Ivan Turgenev*. Munich: Otto Sagner, 1990. A fine discussion of *Smoke*, especially of the ideas preoccupying Russians in the mid-nineteenth century as they are reflected in the relationships of the characters.

Yarmolinsky, Avrahm. *Turgenev: The Man, His Art, and His Age*. New York: Orion Press, 1959. Yarmolinsky sees *Smoke* primarily as a love story, but he does not neglect the nonliterary components and the impact the novel has had in Russian society, primarily among the intellectuals and social activists.

THE SNAKE PIT

Type of work: Novel
Author: Sigrid Undset (1882-1949)
Type of plot: Historical
Time of plot: Late thirteenth and early fourteenth centuries
Locale: Norway
First published: *Olav Audunssøn i Hestviken* and *Olav Audunssøn og hans børn*, 1925-1927 (*The Master of Hestviken*, 1928-1930, 1934; includes *The Axe*, 1928; *The Snake Pit*, 1929; *In the Wilderness*, 1929; *The Son Avenger*, 1930)

Principal characters:
Olav Audunsson, the master of Hestviken
Ingunn Steinfinnsdatter, his wife
Cecilia, their daughter
Eirik, Ingunn's son by Teit
Olav Half-Priest, Olav's kinsman
Torhild Björnsdatter, the housekeeper at Hestviken

The Story:

After Olav Audunsson received his wife Ingunn from her kin, he returned with her to Hestviken to claim his inheritance. Lime trees were in blossom, and their scent brought back to him childhood memories of the manor which had not been his home since he was seven years old. Hestviken, on a ridge above Oslo fjord, had been a place of chieftains. One of the heirlooms of Viking days was a wood carving showing legendary Gunnar surrounded by vipers in the pit where Atle threw him.

While Olav was growing up as Steinfinn's foster son at Frettastein and during his years of warring and outlawry, an aged kinsman lived at Hestviken. Old Olav, called Half-Priest because he had studied for the Church before an accident crippled him, was more clerk than franklin. Under his stewardship the manor had not prospered, and young Olav had less wealth than he expected. Still, Hestviken was a rich homestead, and so he cheerfully set about repairing the houses, increasing his herds, and outfitting boats to trade by sea. Besides, he liked Olav Half-Priest and spent many evenings listening to stories of his ancestors and their deeds in the old days.

Olav Half-Priest had known four generations of the Hestviken men, and his greatest wish, as he often told Ingunn, was to see her son and Olav's before his death. The child Ingunn bore the summer the old man died lived only a few seconds. In the next four years she had three more children, all stillborn. During part of that time Olav was away on raids against the Danes, but when he was at home there was little cheer between them. Ingunn was fretful and sick, resentful of Signe and Una, Olav's distant cousins, impatient with her maids. Olav knew that she was thinking of the healthy son she had had by Teit, the Icelander he had killed to hide her shame, but there was no mention of the boy between them.

Olav's crime weighed heavily upon his own spirit. If he had proclaimed it at the time, men would have found justice in Teit's slaying; his silence had made his deed secret murder. Unable to confess his guilt without bringing shame to Ingunn, whom he loved, he knew that he must live with the burdens of his sin. Perhaps, he thought, the dead children were part of the chastisement he must suffer. He was always tender toward the useless wife whose misfortune he had taken, by violence, upon himself.

When Ingunn became really ill, Olav hired Torhild Bjönsdatter, whose mother had been a serving woman at Hestviken, to keep his house for him. Afterward the manor was in better order, and for a time Ingunn's health improved, so that one spring she traveled to see Tora, her widowed sister, at Frettastein. While there, she went to see little Eirik, her son, at his foster mother's house. He was half-frightened of the richly dressed woman who gave him gifts and held him so tightly. On her return to Hestviken, Olav asked her if she longed greatly for the boy. She said that Eirik had been afraid of her.

Ingunn's brother Jon died, and Olav rode north to collect her share of his goods. When he returned, he brought Eirik with him. In the neighborhood he let it be known that the boy was his child and Ingunn's, born during his outlaw years and for that reason given to foster parents in the Upplands. Eirik liked Olav and followed him about; Ingunn sometimes grew fretful because the boy preferred her husband's company to her own. Then Olav, for the sake of peace, treated the child coldly. Often it seemed that he was never to have ease because of the Icelander's brat.

After Ingunn gave birth to a son, Audun, Olav realized how foolish his act had been, for in claiming Eirik he had defrauded his lawful son of his birthright. He became sharper in his manner toward Eirik, scolded him for childish lies, and to his own shame beat him for his boasting and loud ways. Sickly Audun died the next winter.

One year Arnvid Finnsson came to Hestviken, Ingunn's cousin and their true friend in the days of Olav's outlawry. Arnvid said that he had given his manor to his oldest son; he himself was to enter the order of the Preaching Friars. Olav told Arnvid the story of the guilt weighing so heavily upon him, saying it was as if God's wrath pursued him and gave him no peace, night or day. Arnvid, kind and good man though he was, could say little to comfort his friend.

Ingunn gave birth to her last child, a fair daughter christened Cecilia. From that time on, the mother seldom left her bed. Years before she had lost the power of her limbs during an illness, and now her old sickness took her again. Sometimes Olav looked at her, pale and wasted, and wondered how the sick woman could have been the beautiful girl he had known years before. He was not completely unhappy, however, in their last years together. He looked after Ingunn with patience and pity for the sad life she had lived. Thinking she might become better if he were to make atonement for the slaying of Teit, he spoke to her one day of the matter, but she begged him to keep silent for her sake. Word came that Arnvid had died at Hamar. Olav felt that the only friend left from his youth was Ingunn, once so fair that he had killed two men for her sake.

The two had lived so much to themselves at Hestviken that they had never been popular with their neighbors. Consequently, there was much gossip when it became known that Olav had fathered a child by his housekeeper. Feeling that his new sin went back to the old one from which he could never be free and anxious to make amends to Torhild for the wrong, he gave her the farm at Auken for her own. Ingunn, who had always been jealous of Torhild's strong, healthy body, said nothing. Eirik showed in every way his dislike for the stern, aloof man he called father.

Torhild's child was a boy, Bjorn. On the day Torhild went to Auken, Ingunn sent to her and asked to see him, a lusty child as fair as her own Cecilia. Afterward Eirik spat after Torhild and cursed her son. Ingunn begged him never to speak so of any woman's child.

Olav was at the Oslo fair when a servant brought word that Ingunn was dying. Memories of the past, remorse, and the conviction that God would be merciful if he would only confess his guilt plagued him as he rode homeward to be at her side. After her death, he was minded to do as he had planned on that night ride, confess and welcome his punishment, whether holy pilgrimage or headsman's ax, but he could not, he realized at last, because of Eirik and Cecilia. Never could he abandon them to a kinsman's care or shame them by letting the world know their mother had been wanton.

Sometimes, in the slow, sleepless nights, he felt that he was Gunnar in the snake pit on the old carving—his hidden sin was the viper that had pierced his heart.

Critical Evaluation:

The Snake Pit is one part of a multivolume novel. The characters in *The Snake Pit* are descendants of the fierce pagan Norsemen whose rough lives and deeds of valor form the substance of medieval sagas throughout the Scandinavian peninsula. The men and women in the novel can barely contain their emotions, and their lives are filled with hatreds and cravings for revenge, and with unendurable remorse. Their family ties are as complicated as they are vital to their mode of existence. The work is filled with portrayals of superstitions, inarticulate fears, and blind religious convictions. Though Sigrid Undset is clearly intent on displaying the superiority of Christianity, especially Catholicism, over the pagan religious practices of her forebears, the people of Hestviken are still caught up in a form of worship which is inextricably tied to ancient terrors and dark legends. The author makes clear that her characters' lives are circumscribed by folk sayings and traditions which are ignored only at great risk, and that their hearts and minds bear a burden of ancient guilt.

The Snake Pit is both a historical picture of a grim age and a human testament of humankind's ability to survive. Undset's story centers on the tragedy of the trapped human lives of the men and women in thirteenth century Norway. While readers may be swept away by the action-filled saga, the novelist has carefully crafted her story so that the moral dimensions are subtly reinforced by a series of symbols and allusions which transform the historically bound tale into one of more universal and timeless significance. The snake pit that gives the work its title is a symbol of considerable flexibility. It seems to Olav Audunsson to illustrate his own predicament, to readers it shows a further aspect of his situation, one which ultimately proves fatal to the protagonist's efforts to achieve salvation. When Olav first comes home to Hestviken, where he has not lived since he was a boy, he sees the ancient doorpost carved with the legendary figure of Gunnar in the snake pit. He applies it in his mind to the Hestvik people's historical propensity to disaster, often brought on by poor alliances or deliberate transgression of God's will. Later, seeing a parallel in his own situation, he congratulates himself for upholding the Hestvik tradition of dogged endurance under misfortune. Throughout his struggles, the heinous crime he has committed—the murder of his wife's lover Teit—seems to him to be a serpent at the heart of his life with Ingunn.

In reality, however, the serpent in his bosom is pride. In that pride, he takes to himself all the guilt and suffering occasioned by Ingunn's fall. His intention in bringing her to Hestviken is to protect and cherish her. At no time does he refer to his wife's liaison with Teit as a sin, or acknowledge her need for expiation, or show concern for the state of her soul. It is almost as though he does not consider her salvation of any importance; of course, he does not understand the nature of salvation, or the price one must pay to achieve it. That self-knowledge will come to him only after considerable struggle, which must include an acknowledgement of his insignificance in the face of God, whose plan transcends any individual's efforts to direct his own life. At this point, however, when Olav is most ready to confess his own sin, he is thrown into confusion by the revelation that Ingunn too has suffered, not for his sin but for her own. He realizes further that were he to confess his own guilt, he would bring shame on his wife and set her suffering at naught. Even her death does not free him from the need to maintain silence about their mutual transgressions, since he cannot bring himself to shame Ingunn before her children. At the close of the novel, Olav finds himself once more contemplating the carvings on the ancient lintel, perceiving himself a lost soul. At the midpoint of his life, and the midpoint of the saga, Undset's hero has reached the moral nadir on his quest for self-knowledge. His salvation is portrayed in the two volumes which follow, *In the Wilderness* and *The Son Avenger*, which reveal his acceptance of Christian principles of dependence on God and acceptance of his sinful nature.

Throughout this novel, Undset shows how blind human beings can be to the inner state of those nearest them, and how selfish their apparent sacrifices are. Although set in the thirteenth century, *The Snake Pit* deals with the darker side of human passions of any age. The greatness of the work lies in the breadth of its vision and the depth of its penetration of human nature.

Bibliography:

Bayerschmidt, Carl. *Sigrid Undset*. New York: Twayne, 1970. For general readers, reviewing Undset's life and major works. A chapter devoted to Undset's novels of the Middle Ages provides commentary on *The Snake Pit*, focusing on the moral development of the hero.

Brunsdale, Mitzi. *Sigrid Undset: Chronicler of Norway*. Oxford, England: Berg, 1988. Summarizes Undset's achievement in the chronicle of which *The Snake Pit* is the second part. Comments on the significance of the symbol of the snake; discusses the hero's relationship with his demanding wife, and his efforts to overcome his pride.

Gustafson, Alrik. *Six Scandinavian Novelists*. Minneapolis: Published for the American-Scandinavian Foundation by the University of Minnesota Press, 1966. Discussion of the four novels that make up *The Master of Hestviken* tetralogy. Describes Undset's concern with the moral development of her hero, and highlights her technique of using historical events to illuminate human concerns.

Whitehouse, J. C. "Sigrid Undset." In *Vertical Man: The Human Being in the Catholic Novels of Graham Greene, Sigrid Undset, and Georges Bernanos*. New York: Garland, 1990. Examines Undset's view of human nature as it emerges in her fiction. Commentary on scenes and characters from *The Snake Pit* are interwoven into a discussion that highlights the novelist's generally optimistic vision of humanity.

Winsnes, A. H. *Sigrid Undset: A Study in Christian Realism*. Translated by P. G. Foote. New York: Sheed & Ward, 1953. A biography of the novelist focusing on the development of Christian themes in her novels.

SNOW-BOUND
A Winter Idyl

Type of work: Poetry
Author: John Greenleaf Whittier (1807-1892)
Type of plot: Idyll
Time of plot: Early nineteenth century
Locale: Haverhill, Massachusetts
First published: 1866

Principal characters:
MEMBERS OF THE WHITTIER FAMILY
THE SCHOOLMASTER
A GUEST

The Story:

One December day a wind from the east and a leaden sky forecast snow. As night came on, the members of the Whittier family brought in firewood, littered the cattle stalls with fresh straw, and fed the stock. All night the storm raged, and in the morning the Whittiers looked upon a world of fleecy snow. The elder Whittier, a man of action, ordered a path dug to the barn, and his sons merrily turned to the work, making a crystal-walled tunnel through the deepest drift. Although the snow no longer fell, all day a north wind drove bits of sleet against the windows of the house. Again, as night fell, wood was brought in for the great fireplace around which the family gathered. While the moon shone on the snow outside and the north wind battered the house, the family stayed snug and warm inside.

As the poet recalled this happy scene of long ago, he paused a moment to think of the many changes that had later taken place. Only he and his brother now remained; death had taken all the others. His memory went back to the old fireside, the stories told there, the puzzles and riddles solved, the poems recited. The elder Whittier told of adventures he had had with the Indians, of fishing trips, and of the witches reputed to have inhabited the land in olden days. The mother told of Indian raids and of the happy times she had had as a girl. To these stories from her own life she added some which she had read in books by famous and revered Quakers. Next the poet called to mind the tales of the world of nature told by his uncle, a man unschooled in a formal way but seemingly filled with a boundless knowledge of moons and tides, of weather signs, of birds and beasts. The memory of the poet's maiden aunt brought her also vividly before him. He remembered how she lived for others instead of bewailing her lonely maidenhood. He saw again his elder sister whose rich, full nature had prompted many deeds of self-sacrifice. Tenderly he recalled his dearly loved younger sister, who had been with him until a year ago, but whose body now lay with the others in the earth.

From the members of his family, the poet turned to the young schoolmaster, a boarder in the Whittier home. The son of a poor man, the schoolmaster had as a boy learned independence. As a student he had helped to pay his way through Dartmouth College by taking varied jobs. Later as a teacher he had, when school was out, joined in schoolboy sports. In the schoolroom he was the earnest shaper of youthful minds. The poet prayed that the cause of freedom might have many young apostles like him.

Another guest of the Whittier household on that night of long ago came to the poet's mind. A strange woman, half-feared, half-welcome, she was as known for her violent temper as she was for her eccentric devotion to religion. Leaving her home, she later went to Europe and the Near East, prophesying everywhere the imminent second coming of Christ. The poet asked for God's mercy upon the poor woman whose mind had seemed so odd to her neighbors.

As the hour grew late the group about the fire retired for the night. The next morning teamsters came to clear the snow-filled roads. The young folks played in the snowbanks. Later, along the cleared road came the neighborhood doctor on his rounds. A week passed before the mailman finally delivered a newspaper to tell of happenings beyond the Whittiers' snowbound world.

The poet shut the covers of his book of memory upon these happy scenes of the past, and he put the book away with the hope that readers in the future might pause with him to view for a little while these Flemish pictures of old days.

Critical Evaluation:

Although John Greenleaf Whittier called *Snow-Bound* an "idyl," the term is not accurate in the sense of what that word means in classical literature. The poem centers on an admiring and pleasant depiction of simple country life, in the tradition of the pastoral, but it does not present that view of rustic life from a detached, aristocratic viewpoint. Rather, the speaker's perspective remains rooted in the values of the community he portrays, even as he acknowledges that the persons and scenes he describes are gone. Similarly, the poem's character as a pastoral elegy is qualified by the speaker's hope. Nostalgia for a former way of life pervades the poem, but the future, in particular the future after abolition of slavery, is imagined as a bright improvement on the past. Two major themes related to this optimistic mood figure in the poem. One of these is the image of an inner light encircled by darkness, and the other is a sense of continuity with the past.

The image of a circle of light within a dark surrounding ground recurs throughout the poem, as the speaker describes the family sitting around the household fire in the midst of winter darkness. The external darkness and the metamorphosis of the landscape under the heavy blanket of snow draw the family closer together. Their sense of fellowship and appreciation for one another grows as they form more intimate relationships through the stories they tell of their lives and experiences. A time of enforced inactivity and restricted movement becomes an opportunity for reflection, insight, and enlightenment.

Whittier's conceptualization of the snowbound home as a place of spiritual and emotional enlightenment and of warmth and light in a dark world is in keeping with his Quaker background and his dedication to Quaker principles of nonaggressiveness, cooperation, and respect for the individual. Quakerism lays great stress on individual enlightenment achieved through a process of meditation and reflection. Each person's inner light of understanding is respected and is sought as an island of light would be in a sea of darkness. The poet's lifelong, impassioned outcry in the cause of the abolition of slavery erupts in the last quarter of the poem: Slavery's degradation of black and white alike will be followed by an almost utopian era of peace, prosperity, education, and communication. The monstrous nature of slavery seems to prompt the poet to lay aside the Quaker principle of nonviolence and admire the schoolmaster's participation in the Civil War that has struck the chains from those in bondage. In keeping with Quaker emphasis on nonrational, intuitive spirituality, an almost mystical bond links the snow-bound New Hampshire farmhouse and the newly freed South in a parallel and intimately felt process of enlightenment.

A major portion of *Snow-Bound* consists of the stories told by the various members of the household community: family, friends, and neighbors. The elders—father, mother, uncle, aunt—impress and entertain their listeners as they rehearse critical turning points in their own lives or retell stories from family and Quaker tradition. The poet dwells on the vividness with which family members, in particular his mother, re-create the scenes of their youth: the father's travels in the deep forests of French Canada, the mother's and her friends' clambakes on the New Hampshire shore, the uncle's hunting and gathering in the rich hills of New England. The poet's spiritual idealism and nostalgia emerge from a rich and almost sensual proliferation of sight, smell, sound, and texture evoked in these memories of far-off days, until they seem almost more tangible than the wintry present.

Storytelling unites the family members and creates their community, through the closeness of intimate and familiar revelation and through the construction of the community's history. The poet places himself and his poem at the end of the Civil War; the snowbound scene he reconstructs occurred many years before. The storytelling that went on in the snowbound farmhouse in turn related the listeners to an even more distant past, so that the historical continuity of the community stretches years back, beyond the memory of individuals long since passed away by the time the poet begins his work. The isolated farmhouse becomes an island in time as well as a beacon of light in space. The continuity of history is forged in the speaker's links with the past and past stories, and time is defeated in the liveliness of the telling, bringing the past more vividly to life almost than the present, where familiar elements of the landscape have been obliterated by featureless drifts of snow. Day and night are rendered nearly indistinguishable by early darkness and the whirling blizzard. The snowbound farmhouse represents a paradox: transcendence of space and time is made possible through imagination and illumination in the most confining of circumstances.

The thematic emphasis on the construction of history emerges particularly in light of the author's prefatory note, prepared for the 1892 edition of the poem, some twenty-six years after first publication. In that note Whittier reaffirms that the characters depicted in the poem were actual members of his family and their neighbors, and offers more information on their lives and personalities. The poem is documentary as well as imaginative. The opening material also emphasizes the poet's central image of a field of light within a darkened ground through the lines quoted from Cornelius Agrippa, linking angelic messengers of spiritual enlightenment with the physical light and warmth of fire. The embracing theme of *Snow-Bound* is that the lives of common, ordinary people—whether inhabitants of a rural New England farm or tormented slaves—are worthy and full of dignity and delight.

"Critical Evaluation" by Helen Jaskoski

Bibliography:

Kribbs, Jayne K., comp. *Critical Essays on John Greenleaf Whittier*. Boston: G. K. Hall, 1980. Includes early reviews and structuralist criticism. Discusses John Greenleaf Whittier's Quaker principles. *Snow-Bound* is addressed in an early review and in an essay on imagistic and structural unity.

Leary, Lewis. *John Greenleaf Whittier*. New York: Twayne, 1961. Summarizes earlier views of *Snow-Bound* and offers lucid paraphrase of each part.

Pickard, John B. *John Greenleaf Whittier: An Introduction and Interpretation*. New York: Barnes & Noble Books, 1961. Focuses on the image of fire. *Snow-Bound* is discussed extensively in the chapter on genre poetry.

______________, ed. *Memorabilia of John Greenleaf Whittier*. Hartford, Conn.: The Emerson Society, 1968. Collects unpublished papers on Whittier and includes an extensive collection of photographs of the poet. Contains one essay on *Snow-Bound*.

Wagenknecht, Edward. *John Greenleaf Whittier: A Portrait in Paradox*. New York: Oxford University Press, 1967. Considers Whittier in light of his philosophy, especially his Quaker principles of pacifism and enlightenment. Considers *Snow-Bound* in relation to these themes.

SO BIG

Type of work: Novel
Author: Edna Ferber (1885-1968)
Type of plot: Social realism
Time of plot: Early twentieth century
Locale: Illinois
First published: 1924

Principal characters:
SELINA PEAKE DEJONG, a woman of strong character and enterprise
PERVUS DEJONG, her husband
DIRK "SOBIG" DEJONG, her son
AUGUST HEMPEL, a Chicago capitalist and, later, Selina's friend
JULIE HEMPEL, August's daughter and Selina's old schoolfriend
SIMON PEAKE, Selina's father
ROELF POOL, Selina's protégé
MATTIE SCHWENGAUER, Dirk's former girlfriend
PAULA ARNOLD STORM, Julie's daughter
DALLAS O'MARA, an artist

The Story:

The first step in Selina's development was her life with her father. He was a man who lived by the whims of fortune; when his gambling went well, he and his daughter lived in the best hotels, and when it went badly, they barely got by in cheap boardinghouses. No matter where they lived, however, they lived every moment, savoring life as a fine meal. This ability to live was, in fact, the true legacy that Simon Peake left his daughter, and it became her most important possession. Her other legacy, after Simon was brought back to the boardinghouse dead from a bullet wound, was two diamonds and almost five hundred dollars in cash. With these, she was able to secure an education for herself and find the means of earning a living.

Simon Peake's death forced Selina to make the step into the next phase of her life, one that was to give shape to her future. She took a teaching position in the Dutch farming country of Illinois. In her new job, she moved into an environment as different from that of her life with Simon Peake as the fine finishing school Selina attended in Chicago was different from the small country schoolhouse where she wemt to teach. When Selina went to live with the Pools, the family with whom she was to stay in Illinois, she saw a life that was not a game but an unending job. There was no time in the Pools' day for magic; every minute had to be spent making a livelihood from the soil: plowing and reaping, repairing farm tools, cooking, and mending clothes. The most striking aspect of life at the Pools', as far as Selina was concerned, was the fact that there was no time for beauty. Up to this point, Selina had only spent her time in the search for beauty; now she found that she had to devote herself to the problems of farming life and to teaching children whose parents were more concerned with their children's ability in the fields than with their ability in the classroom.

Even in the midst of the drudgery of this life, however, Selina was able to find a source of beauty. Among the hardworking Pools there was an artist. Selina gave herself to the task of introducing young Roelf Pool to the magic that life can have. She nurtured his native talents at handiwork and treasured the chest that he built and carved for her. The chest was the reminder that she kept with her after Roelf left and went to find his own life in the world outside Illinois. It was one of Selina's triumphs that Roelf ultimately became a fine and respected sculptor.

Selina's ability to find beauty even in the hard farm life became a guiding principle for her life. She married a beautiful man, capable of beautiful acts. Pervus Dejong was the most unsuccessful farmer in the area, but he was a handsome man who recognized the unusual beauty that marked Selina. When she was subjected to the embarrassment of having the "pretty" basket she prepared for the box supper mocked, Pervus bid a precious ten dollars for her box, turning the laughter to amazement. While Selina's life with Pervus was not marked by beauty, she found it a satisfying life. She became enamored of making things grow; her life became filled with "beautiful cabbages" and asparagus. When Pervus died, she took over the management of the farm and began to build a future for her son.

With the aid of August Hempel, the rich father of Julie Hempel, one of Selina's former classmates at the finishing school, Selina was able to become a successful truck farmer, to send Dirk to good schools, and to give him the opportunity to find the life of magic and beauty of which she had always dreamed. At this point, Selina's story became Dirk's story. The first test of whether Dirk would be able to grasp the chance to pursue beauty occurred when he was at the University of Chicago. There he met Mattie Schwengauer, an Iowa farm girl who represented the innocent goodness of growing things. When Dirk rejected Mattie for the social life of the fraternities, where Mattie would not be accepted, Selina received her first disappointment. Mattie represented the naïve appreciation of life that would be the first step toward discovering the magic that life can offer. Dirk's inability to continue his relationship with her was a foreshadowing of Dirk's future life.

After Dirk became an architect, he met Paula Arnold Storm, Julie's daughter, whom he had known when they were children. She was now a bored, sophisticated woman married to a man old enough to be her father. It was her influence that led Dirk to leave his career as an architect, to leave his dreams of building beautiful buildings, and to go into finance, where he was soon successful. To Selina's continuing disappointment, Dirk lived in a world of position and show. He took a fashionable apartment and acquired an Asian houseboy. He was, according to every conventional description, a success.

Then Dirk met Dallas O'Mara, an artist who reveled in life itself. For a time, it seemed that she would be the force that would pull Dirk back to the course that Selina mapped for him. She fascinated Dirk, and he was as puzzled as he was charmed by her blithe rejection of the social standards that Dirk had come to accept. A battle between the attractions of Paula's world and those of Dallas' world developed. The situation was brought to a crisis when Roelf Pool returned to Chicago in the company of a French celebrity. Suddenly, the Illinois farm boy and his friend were the toast of Chicago society. Paula went to extreme lengths to entertain the celebrated pair, and Dirk was unpleasantly surprised when he discovered that they preferred the company of Dallas. His world was further shattered when he found that the person Roelf most wanted to see was Selina.

When Dirk saw Selina with Dallas and Roelf, all three laughing together, reveling in life itself, he realized the emptiness of the life that Paula represented. He also realized that he had irrevocably committed himself to Paula's world. Ironically, Selina discovered that her own life held the magic she had always sought, for the magic lay in the seeking. Dirk, who earned his nickname by replying once to a question about how big he was that he was only "so big," discovered that there was not necessarily any magic in success.

Critical Evaluation:

Edna Ferber was awarded the Pulitzer Prize for Fiction in 1925 for *So Big*, the first Jewish American woman writer to be so honored. Even though it is one of the earliest of her novels, most critics consider it her best. The decade prior to its appearance in 1924, Ferber had been a newspaper reporter in Wisconsin and a writer of a popular series of magazine stories about businesswoman Emma McChesney. Later she went on to write other regional novels, such as *Cimmaron* (1929) and *Giant* (1952), and to collaborate with George S. Kaufman on stage plays, the most famous being the musical created from her novel *Show Boat* (1926). Working-class America, and particularly its women, provided her lifelong fascination. She was interested in the kind of life provided by the expanding industrial society, the values that controlled America's use of its great wealth, and the meaning of success. Lastly, although it is not an overt theme, but rather an underlying concern, she explored the role women were going to play in shaping America.

Ferber leaves no doubt as to her answers to these questions, opening herself to the frequent criticism of didacticism. Her biographer records that she claimed *So Big* was a book "whose purpose was to show the triumph of materialism over the spirit of America." Nevertheless, the characters she draws as vehicles for her ideas are strong enough, particularly in *So Big*, to carry their weight successfully. When her gambler father tells her that there are only two kinds of people in the world that really count, wheat and emeralds, Selina quickly understands that her two maiden aunts, wizend and fearful because they have shied away from real life, are neither. Physical goods of real value to people, such as farm produce, and nonphysical entities of real value, such as beauty and quality—these are the wheat and the emeralds. Although, on the surface it seems possible to have either a "wheat" life or an "emerald" life, in a deeper psychological reality, Ferber reveals, they are related. If one has one without the other, as did High Prairie's Dutch farmers (wheat, through and through, impervious to the natural beauty of the land around them) or the glittering Chicago social set with their trappings of art and music and leisure (shiny, attractive emeralds), one is only "so big." Selina's hard work saves Dirk the necessity of the grinding physical labor on the farm and of mixing with the lower elements in the Haymarket, freeing him for an artist's life dedicated, in his case, to making the ugly surroundings of Chicago beautiful. Instead, however, it becomes only too easy for him to fall into the trap of the empty rich life. He has emeralds, but, without wheat, they are of no value.

When Selina is emotionally at the lowest ebb after the death of Pervus, on her abortive trip to Haymarket in Chicago to sell his vegetables so that she and Dirk can survive, she seems to deny this philosophy of life. She comments then to August Hempel that she was wrong to think that if one just waited, living one's life as best one could, then beauty would come. She wanted to save Dirk from making that same mistake. Hempel chides her gently that each person must live the life that is natural for him or her. Dirk must make his own mistakes. However, even if she did disavow her passionate belief in beauty (Dirk accuses her of that in the scene in which he informs her that he will never be an architect), her years of living avowed it again and again. The two important artists in the book, Roelf Pool and Dallas O'Mara, both have a natural attraction to the old, mud-spattered farm woman, for they share the grand adventure of a life worth living, doing a work worth doing. Both wheat and emeralds, the three were successful Americans.

Ferber did not preach about the important role of women in shaping the American landscape as much as she preached about success. She did not need to do so. Her women protagonists proved it naturally. Selina herself towers above all the male characters in *So Big*. Her father may have conveyed to her that life is an adventure, but he could not provide consistently for his only child and is even killed by a bullet intended for someone else. Only Selina can see the beauty in the cabbage fields to which the Dutch farmers are blind. Pervus, her husband, does appreciate the beauty she created in her boxed supper and the knowledge of figures she can give him with her teaching, but he cannot implement her excellent ideas to improve the farm, content to continue in his father's ways. Those ways kill him. In contrast, under Selina's control, the farm eventually flourishes with modern technology producing even more beautiful products, ones that were sought after in the best eateries of Chicago. She went into the marketing world, where women were not welcome, to achieve this success. Most important, Dirk, the son Selina loves above all else, though charming, intelligent, and successful by all worldly standards, causes her bitter disappointment when he deserts beauty for the false values of money and leisure with the idle rich.

It may not have been that the female gender was necessarily the stronger or better one for Ferber, although the pattern of a woman succeeding where a man has failed, as with Selina and Pervus, is common in the rest of her fiction. (Indeed, it was the pattern she had observed in her own parents' marriage and business ventures.) After all, Roelf the artist exhibited the very success Selina desired for Dirk (how often she told him so, enough so it must have grated), but even Roelf could not have escaped High Prairie without her help. Then, too, there were the socialite women such as Paula who, like Dirk, refused to live by true values. Nevertheless, the only conclusion to be drawn from *So Big* is that, if all Americans would work hard and think truly like Selina, an uncommon yet representative woman, the country would be truly great.

"Critical Evaluation" by Barbara J. Hampton

Bibliography:

Field, Louise Maunsell. "From Gopher Prairie on to High Prairie: In a Novel Just Published Edna Ferber Invades the Small Town." *The New York Times Book Review*, February 24, 1924, 9. Reviews *So Big* favorably as a novel about values to read and to remember.

Gilbert, Julia Goldsmith. *Edna Ferber*. Garden City, N.Y.: Doubleday, 1978. Ferber's great-niece sets the context for Ferber's novels within her life and is not afraid to ask why the famous Americanist has gone into eclipse.

Gould, Gerald. "New Fiction *So Big*." *The Saturday Review of Literature* 137, no. 3572 (April 12, 1924): 392. A more critical review that suggests that Ferber has created a false dichotomy between art and achievement.

Reed, Paula. "Edna Ferber." In *American Novelists, 1910-1945*. Vol. 9 in *Dictionary of Literary Biography*. Detroit: Gale Research, 1981. Discusses the most important of Ferber's works in the context of her life. Concludes that Ferber's writings are significant for their "recognition of the contributions of women to the growth and development of America."

Shaughnessey, Mary Rose. *Women and Success in American Society in the Works of Edna Ferber*. New York: Gordon Press, 1977. This most thorough examination of Ferber's works claims that women and America are the novelist's two major themes. Ferber believed that "if women ever wake up to their potentialities . . . the world would be a better place."

THE SOCIAL CONTRACT

Type of work: Philosophy
Author: Jean-Jacques Rousseau (1712-1778)
First published: Du contrat social: Ou, Principes du droit politique, 1762 (English translation, 1764)

A Treatise on the Social Contract: Or, The Principles of Political Law (better known as *The Social Contract*) stands as one of the great classics of political philosophy. In three earlier works, Rousseau's basic theme had gradually emerged. Rousseau attacked the basic principles of Enlightenment thought, a philosophy that was dominant in eighteenth century Europe. Enlightenment thinkers sought to free philosophy and religion from the superstitions of the past. They supported the use of reason and science as the foundation for all belief and conduct. In contrast, Rousseau maintained that human understanding is not the sole domain of reason, but is, as he stated, "greatly indebted to passions." Therefore, to understand one's relationship to society, it is necessary to return to a state of nature to search for a better political order.

Political philosophers before Rousseau, most notably the English philosopher Thomas Hobbes (1588-1679), believed that before people formed society, life was a perpetual state of war—"every man against every man." The only way for people to live together in peace, then, was to form a social contract in which the citizens establish a mutually agreed-upon form of social organization.

Rousseau's thinking about the social contract was the exact opposite of what was commonly accepted at the time. He argued that people are not evil and selfish in the state of nature as Hobbes claimed. In Rousseau's view, society breeds inequality and selfishness because society involves the acquisition of power and private property. Thus was born his famous concept of the noble savage, who existed in a time in which all people lived together in peace and harmony, free from the constraints of society.

The Social Contract revolves around the issue of political obligation. The issue is to find a form of association that will defend and protect a person with the united force of society but will allow each person the greatest possible measure of individual freedom. Unlike Rousseau's earlier works, *The Social Contract* recognizes the need for civil society, despite the fact that it deprives citizens of some of their freedoms. In the state of nature, people pursue their self-interest until they discover that the power to preserve themselves against the threats of others is not strong enough. In justifying the transition from the state of nature to civil society, Rousseau argues for a system of government that retains the best instincts that people had in the state of nature while incorporating the added values, such as stability and security, that a political organization can give. This is a radical departure from Rousseau's earlier writings, in which he was extremely suspicious of all forms of central authority. The task of *The Social Contract* is to find the basis for a legitimate compact between people and authority and then describe a legitimate form of government that will represent all people.

To begin, Rousseau first discounts some traditional forms of government that, he argues, can never be the basis of a just political order: the rule of the strongest, any government allowing slavery, and monarchy that claims the sanction of divine right. As for the first, the idea that might makes right has no place in Rousseau's political system. People yield to force out of necessity and fear not because they want to; there is no contract worthy of the name in such a society. Those who rule by force are not bound by any sense of morality, so Rousseau concludes that force does not create right. As for slavery, Rousseau acknowledges that the Greeks and

Romans had slaves, and they believed that slavery was natural for some people, but he argues that for people to surrender their rights to a master is incompatible with human nature, because people do not voluntarily enter into a condition of servitude. As for rule by divine right, Rousseau cannot see how one person could possibly preserve the rights of all of his subjects and at the same time protect his private interests. When the ruler dies, what most often happens is that his empire collapses as a result of the sudden lack of central authority and power. Such a collapse creates disorder and insecurity; the terms of the social contract are not, therefore, honored.

After rejecting each of these illegitimate forms of government, he turns to the idea of the social contract, and he uses it in a very different way than other seventeenth and eighteenth century political thinkers. Thomas Hobbes believed that after the contract is established, the people must surrender all of their authority to a sovereign, who alone would have the power to enforce it. The English philosopher John Locke (1632-1704) rejected Hobbes's conception and argued instead for a limited government in which the contract is formed to establish a market economy, set up a monetary system, and protect property rights. In Locke's government, power is exercised only to ensure safety and settle disputes. Rousseau takes the thinking of Hobbes and Locke a step further. Hobbes argued for a sovereign power, and Locke believed that the people should transfer their collective power to the agencies of government. Rousseau believed that sovereignty must always reside in the people. He states that a government needs executive and judicial functions but argues that their power must be completely subordinated to the power of the people.

The General Will is the key concept in Rousseau's political philosophy. It sets him apart from Hobbes and Locke, who believed that the state was an artificial creation, made necessary by the fear and inequality present in the state of nature. In contrast, in book 2 Rousseau argues that government, established upon the idea of the General Will, is a natural occurrence, and the state of nature teaches that the legitimacy of government must always rest on the consent of the governed. He further defines the General Will by stating that it is determined by two elements: First, it always aims at the general good, and second, it applies to all. In saying this, Rousseau recognizes that unanimous consent in any government is impossible—the vote of the majority also binds the minority, but he does not see majority rule becoming a "tyranny of the majority." Those in the minority, he asserts, do not lose their freedom because they are bound to go along with the majority against their will. Instead, he claims that the minority merely does not recognize the General Will; once the minority sees what their interests are, they will readily assent.

The problem of political representation lies at the heart of Rousseau's political philosophy, because if true sovereignty depends upon the power of the General Will, then no elected legislative body could possibly serve the interests of every individual citizen. Thus, it becomes impossible to achieve a balance of liberty and authority. Rousseau believed that representative democracy is not truly democratic, because unless voters always have a direct voice in the laws enacted by the legislature, democracy is an illusion. However, Rousseau does not adequately solve the practical problem of ruling a large state. His idea of direct democracy may be workable in a small town, but it would not be practical in a country with millions of people. Some states may be too large for Rousseau's ideal government to be possible.

The second problem addressed in book 2 concerns itself with the role of law in a society. For Rousseau, the making of laws is simply another manifestation of the General Will. Laws should be made for the benefit of all and not merely to protect private interests. Laws should never interfere with the individual liberty of citizens, because the laws reflect the citizens' wills.

In book 3, Rousseau gives the reader an idea of what his ideal government might look like. He understands that government is a balance between the General Will of the people and sovereignty or power. In his system, government is merely the agent of the people and possesses no real power. The government administrates and enforces the law, but it always remains accountable to the General Will. This idea is radically different from the writings of previous political theorists. Classical political thinkers such as Plato and Aristotle believed that self-government must surrender itself to good government. Rousseau was the first political writer to attempt to combine good government and self-government through the concept of the General Will. Many critics of Rousseau have argued that he does not clearly show how this is possible. For example, Rousseau would claim that the "separation of powers" found in both the American and British political systems is a denial of democracy and the will of the people. He might, in what for him would be an extreme conciliation to practical reality, place all political power in a supreme legislature that had little or no executive power. In addition, he believed that an ideal state should consist of no more than ten thousand citizens; anything larger would be too difficult to govern.

In surveying the various forms of government that have existed throughout history, Rousseau concludes that no one form of government is best. In looking at each form of government in turn, he sees strengths and weaknesses in each. To the practical question of what constitutes good government, Rousseau answers that the preservation and prosperity of the citizens is the ultimate aim, and any form of government that keeps this goal will, in general, be a good government.

In the fourth and final book, Rousseau talks about how a system of voting and elections should be established. He endorses the principle of majority rule, and argues, oddly enough, that in the small state mentioned earlier as his ideal, most votes would be close to unanimous. Critics have pointed out, however, that Rousseau does not consider the fact that a majority could consist of as little as 51 percent, whose will would then prevail over the other 49 percent. In a time of extreme crisis, Rousseau says, a dictatorship and temporary suspension of civil liberties may even be necessary to ensure the survival of the General Will. Rousseau does not say precisely how the likelihood for the invocation of the General Will to become the basis for a totalitarian state can be avoided.

Rousseau also discusses the role of religion in society. Some religion, he thought, was indispensable to morality. He severely attacks Christianity, believing the Roman Catholic church to be a disruptive force because it claimed to be above the political authority of the state. Thus, in times of war, Christians may find their loyalty divided between defending the state and defending their religious convictions. With this discussion Rousseau concludes *The Social Contract*. He realized that within his discussion about the ideal political system he had omitted many important topics, such as foreign relations, treaties, and laws between nations. He hoped to return to such topics in the future, but did not. The impact of Rousseau's thinking upon the French and American revolutions was enormous.

Raymond Frey

Bibliography:

Cobban, Alfred. *Rousseau and the Modern State*. Hamden, Conn.: Archon Books, 1961. A study of Rousseau's political theory, with particular emphasis on the meaning of the social contract and General Will.

Durant, Will, and Ariel Durant. *Rousseau and Revolution*. New York: Simon & Schuster, 1967.

Rousseau's life provides the setting for this history of England and France from 1715 to 1789. Chapter 7 is an excellent overview of *The Social Contract*.

Ebenstein, William, and Alan O. Ebenstein. *Great Political Thinkers: Plato to the Present*. 5th ed. New York: Harcourt Brace Jovanovich, 1991. Chapter 21 contains an excellent analysis and a good abridged translation of *The Social Contract*.

Miller, James. *Rousseau, Dreamer of Democracy*. New Haven, Conn.: Yale University Press, 1984. A scholarly study of Rousseau's political philosophy. Chapter 3 explores the philosophical arguments underlying *The Social Contract*.

Rousseau, Jean-Jacques. *The Social Contract*. Translated and with an introduction by Maurice Cranston. New York: Penguin Books, 1985. A highly readable and widely available translation.

SOCIETY AND SOLITUDE

Type of work: Essays
Author: Ralph Waldo Emerson (1803-1882)
First published: 1870

Society and Solitude is a group of twelve essays previously delivered as lectures on various occasions and before varied audiences. Each essay is preceded by a few lines of original verse. The volume as a whole lacks the propagandistic fire of Ralph Waldo Emerson's earlier essays, although there is still a tendency to dwell upon humanity's better side, almost as though it had no other. Emerson continues also to see the world as filled with good for those who will receive what is offered. One of Emerson's biographers has called these late writings the cheeriest of Emerson's essays. Several are more discursive than they need be, but on many pages may be found the sparkle, wit, and happy phrasing which mark Emerson at his best.

In the title essay, Emerson makes clear that for humanity both society and solitude are necessary. People differ in their need for these two opposites according to their personalities and their activities. Creative geniuses such as Sir Isaac Newton and Dante Alighieri needed isolation to accomplish their work. Emerson notes, however, that although now and then an ordinary person can and must live alone, "coop up most men and you undo them." A balance is needed. Humanity should not remain proudly alone nor let itself be vulgarized by too much society; one mood should reinforce the other.

"Civilization" may be considered an essay in definition since much of it is devoted to a description of what civilization is not and what it is. Emerson discusses both the civilized society and the civilized or cultured individual. Such a person is marked by the capacity for self-advancement, by the ability to associate and compare things with one another, and by the ability to move from one idea to another. The civilized society, says Emerson, is one that has progressed to agriculture from war, hunting, and pasturage. There are increased means of communication, a division of labor, a raising of the status of women, a diffusion of knowledge, a combining of antagonisms, and even a utilizing of evil so as to produce benefits.

Civilization results from highly complex organization. Climate is often a major force in producing it, but, according to Emerson, any society with a high destiny must be moral. The wise person who would be civilized will use the powers of nature, which exist for the individual. The wise will hitch their wagon to a star and let the heavenly powers pull for them. They will work for the highest ends—justice, love, freedom, knowledge, utility. The test of the civilization in which the wise live will be the kind of people their country creates. In the civilized state all public action will be designed to secure "the greatest good for the greatest number."

"Art" attempts to define both art and the artist. Emerson begins with the simple statement that art is the "conscious utterance of thought, by speech or action, to any end." It is the spirit's voluntary use and combination of things to serve its end; it is the spirit creative. Since this spirit aims at use or at beauty, there are the useful and the fine arts. The universal soul creates all works of art and uses the individual artist to bring them into being. Thus all art complements nature. In the useful arts nature is a tyrant over humanity, forcing humanity to use the tools that nature supplies and to learn which fit best. Turning to the fine arts, such as music, eloquence, poetry, painting, sculpture, and architecture, Emerson points out that each has a material basis that hinders the artist who works with it. Language must be converted into poetry, vibrations in the air into music, and stone into sculpture and architecture. The art resides, observes Emerson, in the model, the plan, and the harmonious arrangement of the material the artist uses. As with the useful arts, nature dominates the artist; the artist is the organ through which the universal mind acts. Believing in a moral universe, Emerson sees all great works of art as attuned to moral nature.

The reader may sense, regarding "Eloquence," that Emerson devoted more space than he needed to this theme. He seeks a distinction between the eloquent person and the mere speaker, and he describes the interrelationships between the speaker and the audience. Much that he says seems rather obvious, the sort of thing a public speaking teacher might use to begin a course. The orator plays on the audience as a master pianist plays the piano. The audience influences the speaker by its reaction. The consummate speaker has, to begin with, a robust and radiant physical health. The speaker, Emerson states, is personally appealing, and the speaker's eloquence illustrates the magic of his or her ascendancy over the audience. The speaker must have the fact and know how to reveal it; reaching higher, however, the speaker must state the law above the fact and must be the means through which the moral law of the universe is revealed.

"Domestic Life" is one of the most pleasing essays in the volume, but one is inclined to wonder what Mrs. Emerson thought of it. It begins with an amusing picture of the infant despot for whom all services are performed. "All day," says Emerson, "between his three or four sleeps, he coos like a pigeon-house, sputters and spurs and puts on his faces of importance; and when he fasts, the little Pharisee fails not to sound his trumpet before him." The home belongs to the adults as well as the child. It must be managed by a wise economy that shall witness that human culture is its end. When visitors come, they shall not be simply fed and put in soft, warm beds; they shall see that here all deeds flow from truth and love, honor and courtesy. Although those who inhabit the home are not themselves divine, they should through their characters reveal that in each nature has laid foundations of a divine structure upon which the soul may build. Finally, the household should cherish the beautiful arts and the sentiment of veneration. It should not, however, attempt to be a museum but only a small work of art itself, nor a church but only an intimate sanctuary for those who dwell there and for their friends who come in.

"Farming" makes some pleasant statements about the occupation, but it is by a man who was better at talking about it than at being a farmer even on a half-acre scale. The farmer, says Emerson, lives by nature's schedule because no person can speed nature up. The farmer is the trustee of health and wealth and is the progenitor of the city dwellers, who, in manufacture and trade, give to the world the products of the farm. The farmer is a continuous benefactor, a minder of nature, who provides not for one generation but for all. The farmer lives in the presence of nature and is ennobled by it.

"Works and Days" opens with a brief survey of the scientific and mechanical tools for labor and leisure newly available to the people of Emerson's day. Emerson observes that humanity, already having much, will have more of these; he even predicts, nearly a half century before World War I, that the next war would be fought in the air.

Emerson is more interested in people than in things, and it means much to him how people spend their days. As he says, "Works and days were offered us, and we took works." Several of the best sentences in the essay are a prose rendering of the famous sonnet "Days," which precedes the essay. Like his younger friend Henry David Thoreau, Emerson laments that humanity wastes its days on trivia when it should write on its heart that every day is the best day in the year and is also doomsday. The measure of humanity, says Emerson, is its apprehension of what a day is.

"Books" was praised by Oliver Wendell Holmes in his biography of Emerson, but its appeal to later readers is limited. Much of it is devoted to recommending particular authors and books to be read, and these are drawn from Emerson's lifetime of reading. Memorable are Emerson's rules for choosing one's reading: "1. Never read any book that is not a year old. 2. Never read any but famed books. 3. Never read any but what you like."

"Clubs" has much about conversation but little about clubs, where conversation abounds, or should in Emerson's estimation. Emerson prizes conversation because it takes one out of oneself and brings one into relation with others. Each talker kindles the mind of another or others. Emerson cares little for those who must be masters of the group, the gladiators who must always win an argument, or the egotists who wish to be heard, not to listen. Emerson sees conversation as "the Olympic games whither every superior gift resorts to assert and approve itself . . . with the rest." He closes with the comment that when discourse rises highest and searches deepest, it is between two only.

In "Courage," Emerson observes that three qualities attract the wonder and reverence of humanity: disinterestedness, practical power, and courage. Courage is thought to be common, he says, but the immense esteem in which it is held proves it to be rare. Fear is based on ignorance, and knowledge is its antidote. The sailor loses fear when he can control sails and spars and steam; the frontiersman when he can aim surely with his rifle. Courage consists in being equal to whatever one faces, in the conviction that the opposition does not excel one in strength of resources or spirit. Each person has his or her own kind of courage, one a fury of onset, another a calm endurance. True courage does not show itself off, and it is a bond of union even between enemies who respect it in each other.

"Success" begins with comments on the multitudinous achievements of Americans and their smug self-satisfaction with what they have done. To show that this is the way of the world, Emerson cites the individual superiority of men in other countries and other times. What rouses his hate is the American passion for quick and effortless success, and his scorn, the boasting when one has succeeded. Drop the brag and advertisement, says Emerson, and following Michelangelo's course in life, confide in yourself and be something of worth and value. Then, as if he were rephrasing a passage from his earlier "Self-Reliance," Emerson remarks: "Self-trust is the first secret of success, the belief that if you are here the authorities of the universe put you here, and for cause, or with some task strictly appointed you in your constitution, and so long as you work at that you are well and successful."

"Old Age," which closes Emerson's book, is one of the best essays in it. "The essence of age," he says, "is intellect," and experience ripens slowly. Elderly men have been honored in many lands and ages because of what they knew. Age has its benefits: It has weathered the capes and shoals of life's sea; it has the felicity of having found expression in living; it sets its house in order and finishes its works, and humanity is ready to be born again in his new and final home.

Bibliography:

Allen, Gay Wilson. *Waldo Emerson: A Biography*. New York: Viking Press, 1981. Notes the reception that various critics have given this work. Provides excerpt from original manuscript not in the published work. Well-indexed, chronology, offers comprehensive notes.

Carpenter, Frederic Ives. *Emerson Handbook*. New York: Hendricks House, 1967. A good research tool, provides background material to the ideas that shape Emerson's texts. Discusses Emerson's writing methods and style. Bibliographies.

Cooke, George Willis. *A Bibliography of Ralph Waldo Emerson*. New York: Kraus Reprint, 1968. Excellent research tool. Gives all publication dates of *Society and Solitude*, including translations.

Emerson, Ralph Waldo. *Journals of Ralph Waldo Emerson: 1820-24*. Vol. 1. Edited by Edward Waldo Emerson and Waldo Emerson Forbes. Boston: Houghton Mifflin, 1990. Rich in comments on key notions present in "Society and Solitude."

Sowder, William J. *Emerson's Reviewers and Commentators*. Hartford, Conn.: Transcendental Books, 1968. A bibliography for criticism in nineteenth century periodicals, including criticism on *Society and Solitude*.

SOHRAB AND RUSTUM

Type of work: Poetry
Author: Matthew Arnold (1822-1888)
Type of plot: Historical
Time of plot: Antiquity
Locale: Western Asia, on the banks of the Oxus River
First published: 1853

Principal characters:
RUSTUM, a Persian chieftain
SOHRAB, a youth in the Tartar army
PERAN-WISA, the leader of the Tartars
FEROOD, the leader of the Persians
GUDURZ, another Persian chieftain

The Story:

The two powerful armies of the Tartars and the Persians were encamped along the banks of the Oxus River. It was night and the soldiers were asleep, but daylight would bring a great conflict between mighty forces. To one Tartar, rest refused to come. In the grayness of the early dawn, he left his bed and made his solitary way through the black tents of the great encampment to the quarters of Peran-Wisa, commander of the Tartar army. He was Sohrab, the youthful champion of the Tartars. Hardly more than a boy, he had developed into the mightiest fighter of the Tartar host. Young in years and famous in arms, he was nevertheless restless and discontented. Above everything else, he wanted to find the father he had never seen, the incomparable Rustum, invincible chieftain of the Persians.

Rustum did not even know that he had a son. He had been told that a woman of Ader-baijan, after his departure from that place, had borne him a child, but that was years earlier. Rustum had given the matter little thought because he believed the child to have been a girl. After Sohrab was born, the fearful mother, hoping to prevent her son from being taken from her and reared for war, had deceived Rustum with that report. Nevertheless, Sohrab had become a warrior, and his mother's ruse had availed nothing except to keep her son from a knowledge of his father.

Peran-Wisa awoke when Sohrab entered and asked an unusual favor of him: Sohrab wished to challenge a leader of the Persians to single combat, the duel to occur as soon as arrangements could be made. He hoped that his fame as a fighter would thereby reach the ears of his father. Peran-Wisa urged patience and questioned his wisdom in thus tempting fate, but at last he unwillingly agreed to Sohrab's request.

Thus challenged by their Tartar foe, the Persians were barely able to conceal their alarm. They had no champion to pit against the redoubtable young Sohrab except Rustum, and Rustum had withdrawn because of slights from the young Persian ruler. When the Persians appealed to him, cleverly implying that Rustum was hoarding his fame and had become reluctant to risk combat with younger men, Rustum was aroused and grudgingly consented to meet the Tartar champion. He stipulated, however, that he would fight unknown to the enemy and in plain armor, for he feared that his great name might otherwise daunt the brash young challenger at the outset. Now that his temper had been aroused, Rustum was in no mood to give up the chance of another single combat.

Halfway between the waiting armies, Sohrab and Rustum came face to face. Before they fought, words passed between them, and a strange disquiet settled over their spirits. The moment passed, however, and the conflict began. Sohrab's misgivings returned; when his nimbleness gave him the initial advantage, he forbore to follow it up. Stung with anger and shame, Rustum gave him no second chance. With a shout of "Rustum" he renewed his attack upon Sohrab, who, thunderstruck at the name, momentarily lowered his shield. Instantly he was transfixed by Rustum's spear and fell to the ground, mortally wounded.

As his life ebbed away, the young man revealed to his adversary the secret of his birth. Rustum, at first incredulous, was convinced when Sohrab bared his arm to reveal the sign of Rustum's own seal, pricked there soon after his birth. The unhappy Rustum, beset by extremes of agony and remorse, could barely be restrained from taking his own life and dying with his son. Broken by grief, he promised to bear the body of Sohrab far away, so that it might be in death where it had never been in life, near the palace of snowheaded Zal, the boy's grandfather. There it would receive burial worthy of a son of Rustum. So ended Sohrab's quest for his father. Life passed from him; the day waned; night came on. The majestic river flowed on into the frosty starlight, and campfires began to twinkle through the fog. Rustum, grieving, remained on the river sands, alone with his son.

Critical Evaluation:

"Sohrab and Rustum" is based on a historical event that took place in Persia about 600 B.C.E. Matthew Arnold acknowledges his source to be Sir John Malcolm's *History of Persia* (1815) and states in his preface to the poem that he intends to "treat a noble action in a somewhat epic fashion." In preparing to compose the consciously Homeric poem, Arnold reread his beloved Homer with the great admiration which he expresses in such poems as "To a Friend" (1849) and such prose works as *On Translating Homer* (1861) and "The Study of Poetry" (1880).

Clearly based on a Homeric model are Arnold's elevated tone, ornate language, and elaborate extended similes, as well as the imposing stature he gives his two main figures, his use of an overriding fate working out their destiny, and his creation of a central dramatic episode of national significance. As an epic poem, "Sohrab and Rustum" is admired for its moving presentation of a dramatic conflict between father and son, its brilliance of language, and its richness of tone. In classical fashion, the poem involves one central action, which takes place in one day, and many critics have commented on the success of the poem's many epic similes and on other parallels.

The main critical interest of the poem lies in its allegorical presentation of the moral and intellectual conflict characterizing the Victorian age and in its dramatization of Arnold's personal dilemmas. The battlefield is Arnold's poetic landscape—the "darkling plain" of the poem "Dover Beach" (1867), "Swept with confused alarms of struggle and flight,/ Where ignorant armies clash by night." The characters Sohrab and Rustum may be seen as the personifications of the warring elements within the hearts and minds of all Victorian writers, who are as two-souled as the narrator of "Dipsychus" (1850) by Arthur Hugh Clough, Arnold's friend and rival for the admiration of his father, who died in 1842.

The single combat between the venerable father Rustum and his son has specifically personal parallels in the conflict between Matthew Arnold, the successful poet, and his father, Dr. Thomas Arnold, the renowned headmaster of Rugby school, who was known for instilling moral earnestness and devotion to duty in his pupils. In many ways, Thomas Arnold resembled the proud and invincible old warrior Rustum. Biographers have suggested that in a sense Arnold, like Sohrab, was engaged in the archetypal search for his father. From early boyhood,

Matthew was both attracted to and repelled by his father's rigorous dedication to educational reform. As Matthew Arnold matures from the youthful poet into the mature prose writer, he takes on the stoic nature and moral vigor of his father. The poet W. H. Auden suggested that the voice of Thomas Arnold kills the poet in the son Matthew just as Rustum kills Sohrab.

Matthew's rebellion against his father began during his school days at Rugby and was manifested for many years in a deliberately flamboyant lifestyle. While Matthew Arnold consciously played the part of the typical dandy, apparently as carefree as his "Strayed Reveller" (1849) wishes to be, his "Romantic" poetry portrayed a lonely and divided soul yearning for peace and unity. It is clear that in part the poet always wanted to embody the virtues he ascribed to his father in his tribute to him in the poem "Rugby Chapel" (1858), in which he described him as one of the "souls temper'd with fire,/ Fervent, heroic, and good,/ Helpers and friends of mankind." In his prose, Matthew deliberately embodies his father's admirable traits and his poetic self dies, as it were, in his father's arms. With the death of Sohrab, the conflict is resolved, but not without Rustum having to endure deep grief and lasting sorrow.

Even more specifically, the battle between Sohrab and Rustum embodies two aspects of Matthew Arnold's internal personal struggle during the 1850's and 1860's, when his poetic self challenged his prosaic self to single combat. That combat ended with the emergence of a sadder and wiser prosaic self. Yet though his youthful poetic self died in the 1860's, Matthew Arnold remains, along with Alfred, Lord Tennyson, and Robert Browning, one of the three great poets of the Victorian period.

Arnold began his transition from rebellious poet to social reformer in April, 1851. That same year, he was appointed to a position as inspector of schools, which he held for thirty-five years; in June he married and settled down to a life devoted to the dissemination of culture with the twenty-two volumes of prose that he wrote during the last thirty years of his life. After 1860, Arnold virtually willed his poetic self to death, and he replaced the writing of poetry with literary and social criticism and various types of religious and educational prose works.

In reading "Sohrab and Rustum" as an allegory of personal internal conflict, it is instructive to consider the very similar story told by William Butler Yeats in his drama "On Baillie's Stand" (1904), in which Cuchulain, the venerable old father character who symbolizes Irish nationalism, kills the young stranger who is his son. Yeats uses the single combat between father and son to define heroic identity in terms of the warring halves of the soul; the heroic self is formed through the dialectical opposition between the self and its opposite or antiself, just as the mature writer that Arnold becomes is formed through the opposition within his consciousness between his poetic self and its antiself.

In one interpretation of a specific image in Arnold's poem, the river Oxus, the chief river of central Asia, has been interpreted as an emblem of human destiny that runs through the desert wasting its energy in frustrations but at last reaching its tranquil goal in the starlit sea. At the beginning of the poem, the river Oxus is obscured by the fog in the gray dawn just as the course of Arnold's life was obscured, even from himself. As the poem ends, the stars emerge to shine on the tranquil waters of the united self of the mature Arnold.

"Critical Evaluation" by Constance M. Fulmer

Bibliography:

Abjadian, Amrollah. "Arnold and the Epic Simile." *Étude anglaises* 42, no. 4 (October-December, 1989): 411-423. A rhetorical study of Arnold's use of epic similies in "Sohrab and Rustum."

Cervo, Nathan. "'Dover Beach,' 'Sohrab and Rustum,' 'Philomela,' and 'Stanzas from the Grande Chartreuse.'" *The Arnoldian* 11, no. 1 (Winter, 1884): 24-31. Cervo discusses Arnold's use of sea and stone imagery as they are related to the Oedipus complex.

Gouws, John. "Matthew Arnold's 'Sohrab and Rustum.'" *Notes and Queries* 30 (August, 1983): 302. This note establishes Goethe as another author whom Matthew Arnold deeply admired. The way Arnold uses his sources demonstrates his practice of measuring his own poetry against "touchstones" from the great literature of the past.

Roper, Alan. *Arnold's Poetic Landscapes*. Baltimore, Md.: The Johns Hopkins University Press, 1969. Examines the degree to which Arnold achieves unity between human significance and literal landscape. In discussing "Sohrab and Rustum," Roper focuses on the tragically fateful dichotomy in Rustum between the individual fulfillment of finding a son of who he can be proud and his public obligation to be a great warrior.

Thorpe, Michael. *Matthew Arnold*. New York: Arco, 1969. Contains a comprehensive treatment of the poem and of the manuscript. Also analyzes specific images and includes a comparison of "Sohrab and Rustum" with Arnold's other poems.

SOLARIS

Type of work: Novel
Author: Stanisław Lem (1921-   )
Type of plot: Science fiction
Time of plot: The future
Locale: A space station suspended above the oceanic surface of the planet Solaris
First published: 1961 (English translation, 1970)

Principal characters:
KRIS KELVIN, a psychologist
DR. SNOW, an expert in cybernetics
DR. SARTORIUS, a physicist
RHEYA, a material apparition of Kelvin's dead wife

The Story:

Kris Kelvin arrived at the Solaris research station to find it in a state of utter confusion. Gibarian, one of the three scientists on staff at the station, had committed suicide. One of the others, Dr. Sartorius, had locked himself away. The third, Dr. Snow, was terrified to the point of madness. While trying to figure out what had happened, Kelvin contemplated the mystery of Solaris: a planet following an impossible orbit around a double sun, seemingly able to do so because the colloidal ocean that covered its entire surface was capable of making continual adjustments to the world's gravity to maintain its path. This living ocean underwent ceaseless metamorphic transformations, producing many kinds of different structures with no discernible pattern; the Solarists studying the world had produced many hypotheses to account for these transformations, but they had been unable to confirm any of them.

After catching a brief glimpse of another person, Kelvin confronted Snow and demanded to know who it was, but Snow refused to tell him anything. Kelvin ascertained, however, that Sartorius, who was equally unhelpful, was not alone in his rooms. Later, Kelvin was visited in his own quarters by his dead wife Rheya, looking exactly as she had when he had last seen her ten years before. Kelvin was horrified by the impossibility of Rheya's manifestation, while she was gradually possessed of an oddly passive anxiety as she realized that she could not understand or explain where she was or how she had come to be at the station. Intent on getting rid of the unnatural visitor, Kelvin tricked her into entering a space capsule; he then blasted her into space.

Knowing that Kelvin might now be ready to believe him, Snow explained that all the station staff had been subject to such visitations. The manifestations invariably solidified guilty secrets of some kind—fetishes, obsessions, or unresolved psychological problems. Snow told Kelvin that as a psychologist, Kelvin should be well aware of the fact that every man has such secrets, and Snow proposed that when men had come to Solaris to confront the alien ocean, the ocean had responded by confronting men with the discomfiting produce of their own inner selves. Snow suggested that if Kelvin wanted explanations he might look at a book called *The Little Apocrypha*, a copy of which Kelvin had already found. Kelvin began to read it, finding it to be a speculative and pseudoscientific counterpart to the disciplined reports issued by the scientists sent to study Solaris.

Kelvin's studies were interrupted by Rheya's remanifestation. Accepting the fact that he was unable to get rid of her for the time being, Kelvin began to study her; slowly they began to reconstitute their loving relationship. Sartorius helped him in the quest, explaining that the simulacra—which Sartorius labeled "phi-beings"—were made of a different kind of matter.

With Snow's help, Sartorius tried to figure out a way to destroy the apparitions; he eventually succeeded in building a device that would break down the matter of which the apparitions were composed. By the time the device was ready for experimental use, however, Kelvin's feelings had become deeply ambivalent. Rheya, aware of her own unhumanness, had to trick Kelvin to be allowed to submit to Sartorius' experiment. It succeeded in destroying her—although the machine promptly broke down—but no sooner was the simulacrum of Rheya banished than Kelvin began wishing for her return.

There was nothing left for Kelvin to do but to try to derive some understanding of Solaris from the strange experience. He suggested to Snow that they might imagine a sick and despairing god with the creative ocean of Solaris as a kind of "hermit of the cosmos" dimly reflecting that god's problematic creative power. Kelvin was able to simulate normality in his outward behavior, but inwardly he remained in turmoil, not knowing whether he could or ought to hope for Rheya's return. Were she to come back again, he felt, it would represent yet another imperfection of creation and of life, which ought not to repeat itself "like a hackneyed tune, or a record a drunkard keeps playing as he feeds coins into the jukebox." At the same time, he stubbornly persisted in the belief that "the time of cruel miracles was not past."

Critical Evaluation:

Stanisław Lem's *Solaris* is science fiction in the purest possible sense, constituting an elaborate thought experiment in which imaginary science is employed to address fundamental questions of epistemology and human psychology in a disciplined fashion. *Solaris* is simultaneously preoccupied with the limits of humans' quest to understand the world in which they find themselves and the limits of their understanding. The ocean of Solaris is a hypothetical test case, bringing both these issues—and the bridge that inevitably connects them—into a dramatic focus that makes up in urgency and ambition what it lacks in clarity and conclusiveness. The English text of *Solaris* is two steps removed from the original, having been translated from the French rather than the original Polish, but it is unlikely that much has been lost, and there is a sense that the serial metamorphoses involved are appropriate to the substance of the plot.

The elaborate technical discourse employed to describe the peculiar behavior of the ocean of Solaris and the makeup of the phi-beings is itself a simulacrum, since most of its terms are imaginary and those borrowed from physics or biology are employed metaphorically. There is much more, however, in the discourse than mere jargon. The form is more important than the content because the issue at stake is how people accumulate knowledge and how they test the accuracy of their conclusions. The physics may be fake but its method is not, and *Solaris* is primarily concerned with the methods people employ in science and in their personal lives, and the problematic relationships between science and personal lives.

Scientific knowledge is supposed to be objective; its truths are supposed to exist independently of people's discovery of them. Physicists do, however, acknowledge the significance of Werner Heisenberg's uncertainty principle, which recognizes that the act of observing phenomena on the smallest scale must of necessity involve a disruptive interference with the phenomena in question. *Solaris* involves both a magnification and an inversion of this kind of interreaction; the vast living ocean responds to observation by disruptively interfering with its observers. The effect of this disruption is to force the observers to look at themselves as well as the ocean—indeed, to look into themselves, to look at awkward but revealing aspects of their own psychoses which have been suppressed or exorcised from the conscious narratives which compose their life histories and representations of themselves.

Kelvin, as a psychologist, is supposed to be able to bring the methods of science to bear on these kinds of phenomena. He is supposed to be able to catalog them and place them within tentative theoretical frameworks, exactly as the Solarists do with the ocean's problematic metamorphoses—but it is impossible to be objective in confronting the phenomena of the psyche, where every act of observation is a disruptive reconstruction. Significantly, neither Kelvin nor the reader is ever allowed to learn exactly what kind of manifestations haunt Snow and Sartorius because they refuse to submit their secrets to public scrutiny, not wanting their guilty secrets analyzed and understood by others. Kelvin can only wonder whether the ocean of Solaris is capable of understanding itself or others—and whether, if so, it has the least desire to be understood.

Andrei Tarkovsky's motion picture version of *Solaris* is better known than the book, but it is very different from it. The print medium is uniquely suited to the kind of technical discourse that forms the core of the project—and, for that matter, to the kind of pseudoscientific discourse that attempts to complicate the method of science and supplement its revelations, a haunting presence represented in the plot by the *The Little Apocrypha*. In isolating and considerably elaborating the personal aspect of Kelvin's predicament, the film denudes his problems of their true context; the whole point of Kelvin's struggle to come to terms with his re-embodied wife is that the struggle is technical and personal at one and the same time—no separation of the two is possible. His painful ambivalence is not the result of mixed feelings about his dead wife—although the fact of the manifestation does, indeed, betray a harmful confusion—but, instead, his ambivalence is an inevitable consequence of a conflict between two very different strategies of understanding.

The dubious resolution of Kelvin's problem raises one of the central issues concerning the role of science in human affairs. Even an incomplete understanding can give rise to technologies that permit people limited but powerful control over the phenomena under consideration. Even in the absence of a sensible understanding of her production, Rheya can still be obliterated. It is far easier to determine what she is made of than the reason for her existence. The same is true of scientific projects in general; it is possible to figure out what things are made of, but people are not sure that it even makes sense to ask why things exist at all.

Even if such questions are set aside in respect to the universe at large—discarding in the process Kelvin's speculations about the sickness and despair of god as empty fantasies—these questions cannot be set aside in regard to people. People have to ask why they have chosen their ways of life, because they could be living some other way if they chose—and they could, like Gibarian, cease to live at all if they could find no reason to live. Kelvin can dispose of the phi-being version of Rheya, but he cannot dispose of the element in his own psyche that provoked her manifestation. That is why, even though he recognizes the folly and futility of endless repetition without transformation, he cannot avoid the hope that the cruel miracle of her return might be reenacted again, and again, and again.

Brian Stableford

Bibliography:

Csisery-Ronay, Istvan. "The Book Is the Alien: On Certain and Uncertain Readings of Stanisław Lem's *Solaris*." *Science-Fiction Studies* 12, no. 1 (March, 1985): 6-21. A consideration of the "hermetic ambiguity" of a situation in which contact with the alien has been achieved and yet remains impossible.

Science-Fiction Studies 13, no. 3 (November, 1986). An entire issue devoted to consideration of Lem's work, including editorial materials and several papers that include consideration of *Solaris*.

Suvin, Darko. "The Open-Ended Parables of Stanisław Lem and *Solaris*." In *Solaris* by Stanisław Lem, translated by Joanna Kilmartin and Steve Cox. New York: Walker, 1970. The afterword provides a general introduction to Lem's work, including an annotated bibliography. Relates *Solaris* to the main traditions of speculative fiction.

Yossef, Abraham. "Understanding Lem: *Solaris* Revisited." *Foundation*, no. 46 (Autumn, 1989): 51-57. Considers the significance of the names given to the characters and the relationship of certain ideas in the text to Judaic theology.

Ziegfeld, Richard E. *Stanisław Lem*. New York: Frederick Ungar, 1985. A general account of the philosophical themes in Lem's work.

THE SOLITUDES

Type of work: Poetry
Author: Luis de Góngora y Argote (1561-1627)
First published: Soledades, 1627 (English translation, 1931)

Few writers have left so decisive a stamp upon the literature of their own and of successive ages as Luis de Góngora y Argote. Góngora is the embodiment of the Spanish baroque. His name also survives as a style, *gongorismo*, or Gongorism. Born in the city of Córdoba into a prosperous and cultivated family, he indifferently studied canon law at the University of Salamanca, although he is said to have led there the life of a dissolute poet rather than that of a student of theology. Returning to Córdoba, he took deacons' orders and in 1577 was made a prebendary of the cathedral. However, he seems to have remained incorrigibly devoted to the pursuit of pleasure, since, in 1589, he is recorded as having received a reprimand from his bishop for a disreputable lifestyle, which included too-frequent attendance at bullfights and consorting with actors and actresses.

By then, he had already attracted the notice and approbation of Miguel de Cervantes for his writing, but with the circulation of his *Romancero general* of 1600, his reputation as a poet was assured. In 1612, he left Córdoba for Madrid, seeking, like other Golden Age writers and artists, the fount of patronage at the royal court. He was appointed chaplain to Philip III, no discriminating judge of literature, and, following the latter's death, served Philip IV in the same capacity. The real source of patronage became the royal favorite, the Count-Duke of Olivares, who seems to have recognized Góngora's merits, but by whom the poet seems to have felt neglected in his last, rather unhappy years in the capital city, where he had failed to acquire the material rewards which he felt were his due.

Góngora's writing is generally opulent and baroque. He adopted the theory of *culteranismo*, first enunciated by the soldier, scholar, and poet Luis de Carrillo y Sotomayor. *Culteranismo*, as conceived by Carrillo, advocates the elevation of literature and especially of poetry. The hallmarks of *culteranismo* are excessive Latinization of the Castilian language, profound erudition, and learned allusion, that, together with deliberate obscurity, restrict comprehension to only the most learned readers. Perhaps no other Spanish poet has been so reviled, so praised, and so imitated. In approaching *The Solitudes*, it is important to be aware of *culteranismo* and *gongorismo*; the reader must work to understand Góngora's intricate, complex, and highly allusive work.

Góngora's years in Madrid, although less rewarding than he had anticipated and leading eventually to decay of his physical and mental capacities, saw the composition of his most notable works. Góngora's writings circulated anonymously and were not published under his name until after his death, although everyone knew they were by him. *Fábula de Polifemo y Galatea* and *The Solitudes* began to circulate in 1613. Perhaps his greatest achievement, the "Fábula de Píramo y Tisbe," began to circulate in 1618. In these works, his pursuit of *culteranismo* was further honed by his adoption of the theory of *conceptismo*. *Conceptismo*, which originated with Alonso de Ledesma, and which at times is difficult to distinguish from *culteranismo*, seeks to achieve in prose, as much if not even more than in poetry, flashes of wit (*concepto*). Such flashes of wit are excessive and often of obscure subtlety. Again, they are aimed primarily for intellectual effect and addressed to a refined readership accustomed to epigram and wordplay. In *conceptismo*, it is the idea that is all-important, while in *culteranismo*, it is the use and play of language: figures of thought, it has been suggested, in contrast to figures of speech. *Conceptismo* appealed to many of the greatest writers of the Spanish Golden Age—for example, Francisco Gómez de Quevedo y Villegas, Baltasar Gracián y Morales, and Pedro Calderón de la Barca. *Conceptismo* also was a pervasive fascination for Góngora, whose many admirers and imitators applied the word *gongorismo* to his uniquely complex melding of *culteranismo* and *conceptismo*. Góngora's famous style is displayed conspicuously in *The Solitudes*. His complexity, obscurity, Latinizations, and neologisms were denounced by some contemporaries such as Quevedo, despite his use of his own version of *conceptismo*, and Lope de Vega Carpio. Lope, it should be acknowledged, sometimes emulates Góngora's style. For centuries, Góngora's writings have been mined by critics and commentators who, perhaps only in the first quarter of the twentieth century, have begun a consistent interpretation of his intentions.

Góngora's great aspiration was to so expand the possibilities of Spanish poetry that the Spanish language could reach the same state of "perfection and sublimity" he believed characteristic of Latin, and he believed that in *The Solitudes* he was accomplishing his goal. Indeed, he is said to be the particular voice that fully and finally changed Spanish literature at a time when the readership was demanding more from poetry. In Spanish poetry, one idiom had until Góngora's time prevailed—the Italianate, in accord with Renaissance poetic dictates. With the publication of *The Solitudes* and *Fábula de Polifemo y Galatea*, a new school of poetry was introduced, and few if any poets of Góngora's language have not since been influenced by his aristocratic, elevated poetic style.

The first modern edition of *The Solitudes* was brought out in 1927, the tercentenary of Góngora's death. In *The Solitudes*, a poem of about 2,000 lines written in the *silva* meter (seven and eleven syllable lines in free pattern), Góngora defies convention and takes as his subject matter the exact opposite of what was expected in Spanish letters in his time. Instead of using the highest level of poetic diction to praise the most heroic and noble of subjects, Góngora employs it to praise the beauties of nature and the virtues of the country and natural life, while deprecating the artificiality and the vices of the court. The characters who speak with wisdom and live with integrity and nobility are the peasants, not the nobility.

It is a paradox of Góngora's art that while his focus is on the rural and the natural as the authentic and desirable, he expresses this vision in poetry of the most complex syntax and of allusively and metaphorically dense qualities accessible only to the intellectually trained reader of poetry, and certainly not accessible to the peasants whom he extols. *The Solitudes* describes rustic life in the most ornate diction.

Many commentators on Góngora, beginning with those in the seventeenth century, have said that *The Solitudes* was to have consisted of four parts, only two of which were written, and only one of which, the first, was completed. Although much has been written on *The Solitudes*, Góngora's critics have failed thus far to determine a thematic, narrative cohesion. It may be suggested, therefore, that the poem works in an associative manner rather than in a linear, narrative manner, and that this quality, along with that of the play of language for its own sake, may have made the poem attractive to the Spanish poets of the Generation of '27.

The Generation of '27 is so named for an important year, 1927, of that group's history. This year marks a high point in the careers of many of that generation, not the year of their birth. The key event in 1927 was the observation of the third centennial of Góngora's death. Góngora's influence may be seen in the work of such members of the Generation of '27 as Vicente Aleixandre and Gerardo Diego.

The first poem of *The Solitudes* begins with a dedication to the Duke of Béjar, replete with images of the hunt. The first thirty-seven lines establish the tone and set the themes of loneliness and of the questionable status of humanity in relation to nature. The poet invokes the muse, acknowledging that some parts of his work, "lonely images," will be as evanescent as the "wandering pilgrim's" footprints on the sand, while others will "live inspired." In typical Renaissance fashion, the poet then dedicates his work to the immortality of his patron, expressing the notion that the arts can make mortals immortal because it is in art that people can live on.

The plot is one thing that is not very intricate. The reader should look to the brilliance of Góngora's prosody for inspiration. There is no cleverly developed plot or characterization in the modern sense of the word. The action opens with reference to spring and to "a pilgrim of love," a nobleman cast out of court life, rejected by a young and false woman, shipwrecked, and washed up on shore thorough the empathy of the "winds and waves." He is able to move a personified nature to sympathize with him and save him from drowning. This young pilgrim serves as the observer of the entire action of both of *The Solitudes*. This is not, however, a psychological narrative, and although readers see the world through his wanderings, he is not the focus of the story. Rather, readers should observe, through the voice of the poet and the vision of the young pilgrim, the life of rural beauty and the state of unspoiled innocence that Góngora sets before the readers to admire. Góngora states that if the poem's difficulties engage the readers, the readers may then find the truth.

The pilgrim's initial action introduces a major motif of the poem: On shore, he wanders until he sees a light in the distance, and he cries out in hope. It is his task to wander until he finds some kind of metaphorical illumination of the primary truth of the universe. He follows the light to a cottage where a band of rustic goatherds welcome him. The "fortunate retreat" of the refrain is a "pastoral temple and a floral bower," a place where "Flattery's voice is banned,/ Siren of royal courts." He stays the night, and in the morning the goatherds show him the beauties of natural vistas. All that he sees, such as vines growing over a castle in ruin, reinforces the notion that nature is enduring while things of this world are fleeting. They observe "mountain maidens" playing "melodious strings" and ornamenting themselves with roses and lilies. A bucolic procession to a wedding feast follows.

An old shepherd, whose son has drowned, invites the young pilgrim (also described as a youth) to the wedding and discourses on the dangers of the sea. Most likely, this is a personal, political interjection by Góngora to show that the sea can be literally as well as figuratively consuming in its providing venues for human greed. When the procession stops by a stream, there follow several lines of praise to the beauties of nature in spring. When finally the procession reaches a village by nightfall, the village is filled with lights. The wedding ensues, and the youth enjoys watching the festivities, the young women dancing and the young men engaging in athletics. A lovely epithalamium is sung, said by many to be the high point of *The Solitudes*. The first of *The Solitudes* ends with the bride and groom going off to their wedding night. The bride is compared to a Phoenix ascending over the static works of humanity, and thus becomes emblematic of the capacity of life to regenerate itself eternally.

The second part of *The Solitudes* begins at daybreak, when many of the wedding guests leave on a boat and the youth joins two fishermen on another boat. Music still plays a large part in creating atmosphere. Overall, the tone changes from one of celebration to one of contemplation. In contrast to the youth's life-affirming attitude of the first part, he sings of the sadness of star-crossed love, of how he has suffered in lonely wandering for five years, and of how he wants to be buried at sea. At the home of the fishermen, they are greeted by their father and six sisters, who garden, and whom the father later characterizes as competent fishers also. Another bucolic scene follows, with the father introducing the youth to the beauties of their island home and with the daughters serving a dinner outdoors among the beauties of nature. They all are relaxed and refreshed by the sounds of birdsong and water. Grace after the meal is followed by the youth's imploring the father to be content with his life. Two of his daughters, Leucipe and Cloris, are beloved of two fishermen, named Lycidas and Micón, who bemoan in song the possibility of dying of love and of being entombed in their own boats.

A personified Night, along with Cupid, the daughters, and others, are moved by the mournful singing of the fishermen. At the youth's pleadings, the father agrees to allow his daughters to marry. Góngora interjects an authorial aside: The poet speaks to Cupid of the effects of his actions.

The next morning, the youth and the two fishermen depart on a boat, from which they hear the trumpet sounds announcing a hunt. There follows a description of the hunt, of a flycatcher who leads a flock of birds away from the hunters, but who is killed by a sparrowhawk. Ravens try to trick an owl into flying during the day by blocking the sunlight to make it think it is night. The ravens envy the owl the color of his eyes. One raven is killed by hawks, and the hunters, their horses, and birds find deserted shelters. The poem stops at this point.

Góngora's great editor and critic Dámaso Alonso has shown him to be the writer in whose works all the great strains of poetry of the Spanish Renaissance reach their artistic culmination. Difficult as *The Solitudes* is to read, it rewards perseverance, especially when the reader can reach that level that reveals Góngora's great "mysterious quality," as Góngora himself described it.

Donna Berliner

Bibliography:

Foster, David William, and Virginia Ramos Foster. *Luis de Góngora*. New York: Twayne, 1973. A chapter on *The Solitudes* and good annotated bibliography, which includes entries for several studies in English.

Gates, Eunice Joiner. "Góngora's *Polifemo* and *Soledades* in Relation to Baroque Art." *Texas Studies in Language and Literature* 2 (1960): 61-77. Situates Góngora's work within the idiom of the visual arts of his time. Examines the ways in which *The Solitudes* is a baroque work.

Green, Otis Howard. *Spain and the Western Tradition: The Castilian Mind in Literature from "El Cid" to Calderón*. 4 vols. Madison: University of Wisconsin Press, 1963-1966. Excellent history of Spanish literature.

Guillén, Jorge. "Poetic Language: Góngora." In *Language and Poetry: Some Poets of Spain*. Cambridge, Mass.: Harvard University Press, 1961. Printed copy of an essay on Góngora delivered at Harvard by one of the great poets of the Generation of '27.

Jones, R. O. Introduction to *Poems*, by Luis de Góngora y Argote. Cambridge, England: Cambridge University Press, 1966. This edition has an introduction by a noted expert on Spanish literature.

Salinas, Pedro. "The Exaltation of Reality: Luis de Góngora." In *Reality and the Poet in Spanish Poetry*. Baltimore: The Johns Hopkins University Press, 1940. Another of the Generation of '27, greatly appreciative of and influenced by Góngora, provides insights of a poet into *The Solitudes*. This short essay, pages 129 to 147, is a good starting place in the appreciation of Góngora's artistry.

A SON OF THE MIDDLE BORDER

Type of work: Autobiography
Author: Hamlin Garland (1860-1940)
First published: 1917

Principal personages:
HAMLIN GARLAND
BELLE GARLAND, his mother
RICHARD "DICK" GARLAND, his father
FRANKLIN "FRANK" GARLAND, his younger brother
HARRIET GARLAND, his older sister
JESSIE GARLAND, his younger sister
DAVID MCCLINTOCK, his uncle
HUGH MCCLINTOCK, his maternal grandfather
PROFESSOR BROWN, principal of the Boston School of Oratory
JOSEPH KIRKLAND, a writer who encouraged Garland in Chicago
B. O. FLOWER, editor of *Arena*
WILLIAM DEAN HOWELLS, the novelist and editor who encouraged Garland in Boston

A Son of the Middle Border begins with the same incident used in "The Return of a Private," probably Hamlin Garland's most popular short story, but more than twenty-six years separates the writing of the two versions. The discrepancies between the two may be caused by Garland's habit of squeezing as much publication out of his materials as possible, or by Garland's tender age when his father returned from the Civil War. There is little doubt, however, about the main lines of his life from 1865 to 1893. The repetition of material chiefly shows that the two series of works for which Garland is best known begin with the earliest remembered dramatic incident in his life and that later reflection showed him some of the depths of meaning contained in that incident. Garland was four or five years old when his father returned from the war; he was thirty when he first published his short story and fifty-seven when he published *A Son of the Middle Border*. This was the first of four volumes of family history which won the Pulitzer Prize in 1921 and reestablished him as a writer. The other three volumes are *A Daughter of the Middle Border* (1921), the story of his marriage and life until 1914; *Trail-Makers of the Middle Border* (1926), the story of his family before 1865; and *Back-Trailers from the Middle Border* (1928), the history of the family after 1914.

Although the Middle Border is Minnesota, Wisconsin, Nebraska, and the Dakotas, the appeal and range of the volumes on this area is national in implication. The story of the Garlands and McClintocks, the two sides of Garland's immediate family, reaches back across the Atlantic to Scotland and forward to the coast of California. It is the American story of nineteenth century immigration and the moving frontier. Garland is a symbol of America at the turn of the century. Born at West Salem, Wisconsin, near the geographical center of the Middle Border, he moved with his parents farther west to Iowa and South Dakota. Then, obeying the attraction of the nation's cultural centers, he moved east to Boston and New York, eventually settling in Chicago in his middle years. In the last chapters of this volume he followed another attraction to California, where he was later to spend his last days. In three other aspects he was also typical: He broke with the land and became a white-collar worker; he left the country for the city; and he was a model son, spending his savings on the unheard-of luxury of taking his parents, pioneer farmers, to visit relations in California, "The End of the Sunset Trail," as Garland calls it. Finally he established "the Garland homestead" in a little house in the old home town of West Salem, Wisconsin.

In the typical Garland way, the story of his first thirty years is an unreconciled mixture of beauty and ugliness, of delight in the success resulting from unremitting hack work and despair at the waste of the human soul in back-breaking labor. The saddest figure in the book is not grandfather Hugh McClintock, who saw his family break up and leave him, nor Belle Garland, the writer's mother, who like many frontier women worked till she dropped. It is his Uncle David McClintock, first seen as a tremendous physical giant, the hero of the boy Garland, and last as an exhausted wreck in California. One of the most moving scenes is that in which Uncle David plays his fiddle for the last time at the family reunion in California, and Garland realizes what a fine musician has been ground down by toil and by chasing the pioneer's rainbow, the promise of ever better land to the west. David McClintock stands for the countless thousands who suffered to make the nation. Garland's own parents could have shared the same fate. His father, at the end of the war a physical wreck, could have perished while trying to revive his neglected holdings. The fact that the story of his parents ends happily is a result of Garland's interference when his father wanted to make one more shift, the fifth, to some new land in the West. The book is thus a monument to the travail of "westering," to the grim reality behind the song that runs through the book, "O'er the hills in legions, boys." Its central ritual is the "send-off," a surprise party for those moving on.

The memoir is in two roughly even halves, the first nineteen chapters being about life on the frontier in Wisconsin, Iowa, and South Dakota. The details are similar to those in local-color work elsewhere: plowing, reaping and threshing, the smell of horses and sweat rising above the smell of fresh biscuits, bare one-room schools, dancing, skating, riding, reading, gatherings at the local store, the ever-present fear of crippling sickness, the tragedies of burnt barns, and death. Garland's sisters die on the frontier, leaving his mother and father alone when the boys depart. The break in the memoir comes near the end of Garland's schooling, when the family spent a year in the town of Osage, Iowa. After that, the family returned to the farm and then made a final move west to South Dakota. In the meantime, Garland was drawn back to the East. After a year spent with his brother Frank exploring Boston, New York, and Washington, D.C., living on odd jobs and a teaching spell in Ohio, he returned to South Dakota to work his quarter-section. After his brother sold his holding and left for Chicago, Garland also sold out and went to Boston. The second part of the book tells an almost incredible story of hardship, self-education, and slow success, first as a "professor" at the Boston School of Oratory under Principal Brown, then as a writer encouraged by those interested in his local-color stories, such writers and editors as William Dean Howells, James Herne, Henry George, and B. O. Flower. Most of this section is Garland's straightforward autobiography and more germane to the study of how to achieve a career by passing through journalism to literature. As is, however, the case with Garland's first piece of writing, "The Western Corn Husking," which is intended to be typical of Middle Border life, so much of the personal detail is seen either by Garland or the reader as illuminating the case history of the Middle Borderer. This effect springs from Garland's sense of duty not only to his parents—his first literary earnings are spent on his mother's first silk dress—but even more to his people, the sons and daughters of the Middle Border.

This realization of himself as a "son of the Middle Border" came only after his first return to the West, when he met Joseph Kirkland in Chicago and was told to write fiction because he was a farmer who could speak the truth about rural life. A second visit in 1889 confirmed this determination and provided material for the stories that make up his first book, *Main-Travelled Roads: Six Mississippi Valley Stories*, published in 1891.

In Garland's story, behind the moves of the family, the daily and seasonal activities on the farm, and the slow successes in the city, stand two figures: Dick Garland, ever westering, and Belle, following faithfully. It was the pathetic image of the latter which troubled Garland during his years in the eastern cities, and it was probably his realization of the cost wives and children paid in pioneering which precipitated his first fiction. Although the vogue for his work did not last, Garland was able to recapture his audience when late in life he began his memoirs of Middle Border life. That his real story was capable of a happy ending was due in part to his own persistence but more to the realization that pioneering was not a glamorous adventure, as many Americans have viewed it. Toward the end of the story, Garland's mother sings an old frontier song, the others joining in the chorus: "We'll stay on the farm and we'll suffer no loss/ For the stone that keeps rolling will gather no moss."

When Garland was thirty-three, he asked his mother what he could bring her from the city; she told him that the thing she wanted most was a daughter—and some grandchildren.

Bibliography:

Browne, Ray B. "'Popular' and Folk Songs: Unifying Force in Garland's Autobiographical Works." In *Critical Essays on Hamlin Garland*, compiled by James Nagel. Boston: G. K. Hall, 1982. All four autobiographical works are discussed to show the importance of music in Garland's life. An unusual approach to understanding Garland's work.

Howells, William D. "*A Son of the Middle Border*, by Hamlin Garland: An Appreciation." In *Critical Essays on Hamlin Garland*, compiled by James Nagel. Boston: G. K. Hall, 1982. Howells discusses Garland's style in his earlier fictional work and then his style in his autobiography. Examines Garland's depiction of prairie life as he lived it.

Nevins, Allan. "Hamlin Garland's Trilogy." In *Critical Essays on Hamlin Garland*, compiled by James Nagel. Boston: G. K. Hall, 1982. Garland's unorthodox autobiographical style is described, along with an analysis of *A Son of the Middle Border*. The trilogy, described as a "disjointed chronicle," was not published chronologically. This unusual approach gave each work more depth.

Pizer, Donald. "Hamlin Garland's *A Son of the Middle Border*: An Appreciation." In *Critical Essays on Hamlin Garland*, compiled by James Nagel. Boston: G. K. Hall, 1982. Theme, style, and plot are discussed. Includes a full plot summary.

____________. "Hamlin Garland's *A Son of the Middle Border:* Autobiography as Art." In *Essays in American Literature Presented to Bruce Robert McElderry, Jr.*, edited by Max F. Schulz with William D. Templeman and Charles R. Metzger. Athens: Ohio University Press, 1967. Shows that Garland's earlier fiction influenced the style and content of *A Son of the Middle Border*.

THE SONG OF HIAWATHA

Type of work: Poetry
Author: Henry Wadsworth Longfellow (1807-1882)
Type of plot: Folklore
Time of plot: Aboriginal period
Locale: Around Lake Superior
First published: 1855

Principal characters:
HIAWATHA, an Indian hero
MINNEHAHA, whom he married
NOKOMIS, his grandmother
MUDJEKEEWIS, the West Wind, Hiawatha's father

The Story:

Weary of the constant fighting of his people, the Great Spirit called together all Indian tribes to reprimand them for their foolish ways. He had given them fertile lands, abundant streams, and forests, but they had continued to hunt each other. He promised to send a prophet who would guide and teach them. Should they fail to follow his counsel, they would perish. Breaking off a piece of a red-stone precipice, he molded a pipe as a symbol of peace among them. He told the warriors to plunge themselves into the stream and wash the war paint from their faces and the bloodstains from their hands.

One evening in twilight the beautiful Nokomis fell to earth from the full moon. There among the ferns and mosses she bore a daughter, Wenonah. As Wenonah grew tall and lovely, Nokomis feared for her daughter and warned her to beware of Mudjekeewis, the West Wind. When Wenonah failed to heed the warning and succumbed to his wooing, she bore a son, Hiawatha. Deserted by the false and faithless Mudjekeewis, Wenonah died grieving for his love.

Hiawatha grew up in the wigwam of Nokomis. From boyhood he was skilled in the craft of hunters, in sports and manly arts and labors. He was a master of speed and accuracy with a bow and arrow. He had magic deerskin mittens that gave him great physical power. Upon his feet he wore magic moccasins that allowed him to stride a mile with each step.

Aroused by the story of his father's treachery, he vowed to visit Mudjekeewis and seek revenge. In the land of the West Wind the two fought for three days. At last Mudjekeewis told Hiawatha that it would be impossible for Hiawatha to kill his immortal father. Pleased with the boy's courage, however, Mudjekeewis sent him back to his people as the prophet who had been promised. On his long journey home Hiawatha stopped in the land of the Dacotahs to purchase arrowheads from an old man. There he saw Minnehaha, the arrow-maker's lovely daughter.

When Hiawatha returned to his people, he built a wigwam in the forest and went there to fast. On the fourth day of his fast, as he lay exhausted on his couch, Hiawatha saw a youth dressed in green and yellow garments with green plumes over his forehead. The stranger informed Hiawatha that his prayers had been heard and that they would be answered should Hiawatha overcome him. In spite of his weakness, Hiawatha struggled bravely until the young stranger yielded himself. He ordered Hiawatha to strip his green and yellow garments and bury him, and then to guard his grave until he leaped again into the sunshine. Hiawatha faithfully guarded the grave until a green shoot appeared, then the yellow silk, and finally the matured ear of corn that was to feed his people.

Hiawatha next shaped a canoe from the birch tree. Then he set out with his strong friend, Kwasind, and cleared the rivers of roots, sandbars, and dead trees, to make the streams safe for the people. At another time he rid the lake of its greatest menace, the sturgeon.

Nokomis then bade Hiawatha to undertake the destruction of Pearl-Feather, the magician, who was responsible for fever, pestilence, and disease. Hiawatha prepared to battle the dozen serpents that guarded the entrance to the wizard's domain. As he approached, he killed them with his arrows. A woodpecker helped Hiawatha to overcome the magician by telling him to aim his arrows at the roots of the wizard's hair. Hiawatha rewarded the woodpecker by dabbing his tuft of feathers with the magician's blood, which the woodpecker wears to this day.

When Hiawatha told Nokomis that he intended to make Minnehaha his wife, Nokomis urged him to marry a woman of his own tribe. Hiawatha refused to listen to her arguments, however, and assured her that the marriage would unite the two tribes. On his return with Minnehaha, they were honored at a huge banquet at which Hiawatha's beloved friend, Chibiabos, sang his famous love songs, and Iagoo related his fanciful tales.

Hiawatha's people prospered in peace and raised abundant crops of corn. In order to keep a record of their tribal history, Hiawatha invented picture writing to tell their story.

One winter, famine struck Hiawatha's people. Snow covered the forests and lakes so deeply that it was impossible for hunters to seek food. Hiawatha's people were starving and dying of fever. When Minnehaha died, Hiawatha mourned her death for seven days.

At last came the warmth and fertility of spring, and life began to return to the earth. There were rumors of the approach of white men in large canoes with sails. Hiawatha confirmed the rumors, for he had seen the white men in a vision. He urged his people to welcome the strangers and be friendly, adding that if they ignored his counsel the tribes would only destroy themselves.

As Hiawatha stood by the wigwam of Nokomis one evening, three white men approached, one of them a priest. Hiawatha welcomed them and invited his people to hear the stories the priest told of the Saviour. That night, as the white men lay sleeping, Hiawatha told Nokomis that the time for him to leave had arrived. Having fulfilled his promises, he left to travel through the portals of the Sunset, to the Land of the Hereafter.

Critical Evaluation:

Longfellow based his story on traditional legend among North American Indians of a warrior hero sent to clear the rivers, forests, and lakes, and to unite the tribes in peace. With this legend the poet combined other Indian traditions. Of particular interest are the folklore stories of the way the woodpecker got a red streak, the introduction of picture writing, the gift of corn to people, and the origin of the peace pipe.

As a renowned and widely respected professor of modern languages, Longfellow traveled and studied the languages and literatures of many European countries. His endeavors in cultural exchange promoted European literature in the United States and American folklore on the Continent. He was a prolific author in a variety of literary forms, including translation, but he is best known for his poetry. Personally, he held high ideals of a conventional sort, but was uninvolved in social issues except for the anti-slavery movement.

In general, Longfellow's literary style was influenced by the German Romantic movement, although Longfellow himself was not an extreme Romantic. His poetry has been described as gentle, sweet, and pure. When it came to writing *The Song of Hiawatha*, Longfellow drew on his knowledge of European literature. He modeled the poem after the Finnish epic the *Kalevala* (1835), written by Elias Lönnrot. The poem uses unrhymed trochaic tetrameter, a memorable departure from the standard verse form in English for serious narrative poetry, iambic pentameter. Longfellow demonstrates great skill at using the unusual trochaic tetrameter. In content, he tells a simple, dispassionate, not-too-imaginative story, sometimes criticized for its preachiness, easy Romanticism, and an overreliance on symbolism. He presents a rather detached and benignly negligent view of the American Indian experience. Hence, Longfellow's *The Song of Hiawatha* has come to be known as a "children's poem," which has little interest for so-called mature audiences. The cadenced meter and the simple content have become victims of frequent parodies.

Hiawatha was a legendary figure with probable historical existence. Longfellow does not recount the legendary traits or exploits of this Indian leader; he used only the name Hiawatha, in typically Romantic carelessness about fact, to lend legitimacy to his narrative. Likewise, after the Romantic predilection, Longfellow incorporates folkloric elements—the woodpecker story, the introduction of pictographs, the gift of corn, and the origin of the peace pipe. Yet there are some qualities that *The Song of Hiawatha* shares with authentic epics, such as supernatural intervention, the long journey of quest, and the heroic sacrifice. Thus, the poem cannot be entirely relegated to the category of children's literature, for it has legitimate claim on serious literary criticism as well.

Bibliography:

Arvin, Newton. *Longfellow: His Life and Work*. Boston: Little, Brown, 1963. Discusses the significance of Longfellow's conscious utilization of American imagery in *The Song of Hiawatha*.

Carr, Helen. "The Myth of Hiawatha." *Literature & History* 12, no. 1 (Spring, 1986): 58-78. Argues that Longfellow made various source materials fit his readers' expectations. Carr discusses Longfellow's use of the Finnish poem *Kalevala* as the source of both certain events in the poem and the poem's rhythm, which is similar to the standard rhythm of the Indian tom-tom.

Gioia, Dana. "Longfellow in the Aftermath of Modernism." In *The Columbia History of American Poetry*, edited by Jay Parini. New York: Columbia University Press, 1993. Argues that Longfellow's poetry has fallen into critical disrepute because of the revision of the American poetry canon by the modernist school of criticism. Places *The Song of Hiawatha* in the foreground of American attempts at producing a national epic.

Millward, Celia and Cecelia Tichi. "Whatever Happened to 'Hiawatha'?" *Genre* 6, no. 3 (September, 1973): 313-332. Discusses the metrics and the poetic devices found in *The Song of Hiawatha* and shows how *The Song of Hiawatha* fits into the traditional epic-poem mold.

Waggoner, Hyatt H. "Beginnings." In *American Poets from the Puritans to the Present*. Baton Rouge: Louisiana State University Press, 1984. Argues that *The Song of Hiawatha* romanticizes the life and culture of the American Indian without resorting to the sentimentality often found in other presentations.

THE SONG OF ROLAND

Type of work: Folklore
Author: Unknown
Type of plot: Chivalric romance
Time of plot: c. 800
Locale: Western Europe
First published: Chanson de Roland, twelfth century

Principal characters:
Roland, a prince in Charlemagne's court
Oliver, his friend
Charlemagne, the Holy Roman Emperor
Ogier the Dane, Roland's friend
Ganelon, a wicked courtier
Bertha, Roland's mother

The Story:

The boy Roland grew up far from his home country and lived with his penniless mother in a cave formerly occupied by a lonely monk. Nevertheless, his mother had taught him that some day he should be a brave hero like his father, Milon, and serve with the great army of Charlemagne. When he asked his mother to tell him the story of his birth, he learned that through his father he was descended from great heroes of old, Trojan Hector on one side and Wotan, king of the Norse gods, on the other. When his father, Milon, incurred the wrath of Charlemagne for taking the king's sister, the Princess Bertha, as his wife, he had come to Italy and had died there fighting pagans in single-handed combat.

One summer, when he was still only a lad, he met his friend Oliver, the son of a local prince, and the two watched the coming of the great Charlemagne into Italy, where the king was to receive the blessing of the pope at Rome. Roland was impressed with the royal pageant but not overawed. That night, he walked into Charlemagne's banquet hall and demanded his own and his mother's rights. Amused by the boy's daring, Charlemagne ordered that Bertha be brought to him. When the emperor recognized his long-lost sister, he rejoiced and gave her and her son a place of honor in his court.

Roland's boyhood years passed quickly and with increasing honors. At first he was merely a page in the court—attending the ladies, carrying messages, and learning court etiquette. He was permitted to accompany the king's knights during war with the Saxons, and he was present when the swan knight, of the race of Lohengrin, appeared at the court of Charlemagne.

When Roland was fourteen years old, he became a squire and made the acquaintance of Ogier the Dane, the son of Duke Godfrey and a hostage prince at Charlemagne's court. The two boys became great friends. When, urged on by a new queen, Ogier's father planned a revolt against Charlemagne. The emperor in retaliation threatened to kill Ogier. Roland intervened and saved his friend's life.

When barbarians attacked Rome, Charlemagne, in an effort to save the pope, ignored the rebellion of the Danes and set off to the south, taking Ogier with him as a prisoner. The great army was assisted on its passage across the Alps by a magnificent white stag that appeared and led the army through the mountain passes.

In the battles that followed, Charlemagne's army was divided. One force, led by the cowardly son of Charlemagne and the false knight Alory, attempted to retreat, thus placing the emperor's life in jeopardy. Roland and Ogier, aided by other squires, donned the garments of the cowards and saved the day. Charlemagne knighted them on the battlefield.

One of the pagan knights proposed a personal combat. In this encounter, Ogier and a son of Charlemagne named Charlot met two barbarians, Prince Sadone and Karaheut. The pagans trapped Ogier and threatened to put him to death, but Charlot escaped. Karaheut, who was to have fought Ogier, rebelled against the unchivalrous action of his pagan prince and surrendered to Charlemagne, to be treated exactly as Ogier would be treated. Reinforcements came to the pagans, among them the giant king of Maiolgre. In a dispute over the marriage of Glorianda, a Danish prisoner, Ogier fought for Glorianda and put his enemy to rout. Charlemagne attacked at the same time, and as a result Ogier and Roland were reunited and the pope was restored to his throne.

Roland was invested with royal arms. His sword was the famous Durandal; his battle horn was the horn of his grandfather, Charles the Hammer. None but Roland could blow that horn. His armor was the best in the kingdom.

A new war began when Count Gerard refused homage to the emperor. Oliver, grandson of the count, was among the knights opposed to Charlemagne. After the French had besieged the fortress of Viana for seven months, it was decided to settle the war by encounter between a champion from each army. Roland was chosen to fight for Charlemagne. Unknown to him, his adversary was to be Oliver, his boyhood friend. When the two discovered each other's identity, they embraced.

A few weeks later on a boar hunt near Viana, Charlemagne was captured by Count Gerard. The two leaders declared a truce, and Count Gerard agreed to be a faithful liege man of the emperor thereafter. Roland met Oliver's sister, Alda, and became betrothed to her.

At Christmastime the princess of Cathay arrived with her brothers at Charlemagne's court. She proposed a contest between a Christian knight and her brother Argalia. If one of Charlemagne's knights were the victor, he should have her hand in marriage. If the knight were defeated, he should become a hostage. Malagis, the wizard, discovered that the princess and her brothers really sought by sorcery to destroy Charlemagne. He visited the apartment of the foreigners but was discovered by them. They complained, and Charlemagne, not understanding the wizard's desire to help him, sentenced Malagis to be imprisoned in a hollow rock beneath the sea forever.

The jousts began. After Argalia had defeated the first knight, the fierce Moor Ferrau began combat. Unhorsed, he fought Argalia on foot and overpowered him. Then the princess became invisible, and Argalia rode away, with Ferrau in pursuit. In the forest of Ardennes he discovered Argalia sleeping, killed him without honor, and seized his wonderful helmet. Roland, having followed them, discovered the murder of Argalia and sought Ferrau to punish him for his unknightly deed.

Reinold of Montalban found the princess of Cathay in the forest after he had drunk from the waters of the fountain of Merlin, and the effect of this water was to make him see the princess as an ugly crone. She thought him handsome, but he felt disgust and hurried away. Roland discovered Ferrau and challenged him to combat, but the Moor suddenly remembered that his liege lord in Spain was in need of his help and he did not remain to fight with Roland. When the princess of Cathay saw Ferrau wearing her brother's helmet, she knew a tragedy had occurred, and she transported herself by magic to her father's kingdom.

Roland went on a quest to the Far East in search of the complete armor of Trojan Hector.

Whether by chance or by evil design, he came to a fountain and there drank the water of forgetfulness. He was rescued by the princess of Cathay and fought many battles for her sake, even though she was a pagan princess.

At last he came to the castle of the fairy queen, Morgan le Fay, where the armor of Trojan Hector was said to be hidden. Overcome for the first time, he failed to gain the armor and was ordered to return to the court of Charlemagne. He arrived home in time to help the Danes resist an invasion of their country. When Ogier's father, Duke Godfrey, summoned help, Ogier and Roland set out for Denmark. The invaders fled. Ogier's father died, but Ogier, on the advice of Morgan the Fay, renounced his rights to his father's holdings in favor of his younger brother.

On his way back to France, Roland heard of a fierce orc said to be the property of Proteus. The orc was devouring one beautiful maiden every day until Roland overcame it and was rewarded by Oberto, the king of Ireland, whose daughter he had saved.

In the meantime Charlemagne's forces were being attacked by Saracens, and Roland set out to help Charlemagne's knights. On the way he was trapped in a wizard's castle. He was released from his captivity by Bradamant, a warrior maiden. She had won a magic ring from the princess of Cathay and was able to overcome the wizard and release all the knights and ladies he was holding prisoner in his castle.

Ferrau, having lost the helmet he had stolen from Argalia, vowed he would never again wear a helmet until he acquired Roland's, which he succeeded in doing by trickery. Roland was set upon by Mandricardo, the fierce knight to whom fortune had awarded the armor of Trojan Hector. They fought for the possession of Durandal, Roland's sword, the only part of Trojan Hector's equipment that Mandricardo did not possess. At last Mandricardo was forced to flee for his life.

Roland visited the forest where the princess of Cathay and Medoro, a Moorish prince, had fallen in love. Some declared it was jealousy for the princess, but others declared it was sheer exhaustion that caused Roland to lose his mind. He cast his armor away from him and wandered helplessly through the forest. Mandricardo seized Durandal and made Roland his prisoner.

Astolpho and Oliver set out from the court of Charlemagne to save Roland. Astolpho journeyed on the back of a flying horse to the fabulous land of Prester John. Having freed Prester John from a flock of harpies, Astolpho journeyed to the rim of the moon and there saw stored up all the things lost on earth. There he found Roland's common sense, which he brought back with him and returned to Roland so that the knight became his former self.

In a battle against the Saracens the wicked Ganelon betrayed the knights of Charlemagne. Greatly outnumbered, they fell one by one to their enemies. Roland, unwilling to call for help, refused to use his famous horn to summon aid, and he died last of all. Charlemagne, discovering the dead hero, declared a great day of mourning. Alda, the betrothed of Roland, fell dead and was buried with many honors. Then Charlemagne died and was buried with great pomp. Only Ogier the Dane remained, and it is said that Morgan le Fay carried him to Avalon where he lives in company with Arthur of the Round Table. It is also said that Charlemagne dwells inside a vast mountain cave with all of his heroes gathered around him. There they wait for the day when they shall march out to avenge the wrongs of the world.

Critical Evaluation:

The Song of Roland is loosely associated with the chivalric romance literature—the adventure narratives—of medieval France. The romance is divided into three types on the basis of content. The first concerns matters of Britain and deals with Arthurian legend and Celtic lore. The second concerns matters of antiquity and takes its cue from the legends of Thebes, the legends of Troy (such as Geoffrey Chaucer's *Troilus and Criseyde*, c. 1382), and the legends about Alexander the Great. The third concerns France and focuses on stories of Charlemagne and his circle, as well as on stories of William of Orange, drawn from the *chansons de geste*. It is in this category that *The Song of Roland* is important, for it is, properly speaking, a "song of great deeds."

Chansons de geste are epic in nature, although the precise origins of the form are unknown. A popular literary form between the eleventh and thirteenth centuries, they are written in French verse, as are the early romances; late romances were written in prose, using first a ten-syllable then a twelve-syllable (Alexandrine) line and assonance. Rhyme was substituted for assonance in the late *chansons*. The lines are grouped in stanzas—called *laisses* or *tirades*—of varying lengths, and series of *chansons* developed into story cycles dealing with a particular person, such as Charlemagne, or a particular theme, such as the conflict between Christians and Saracens. Like the classical epics, the *chansons de geste* concentrate, as the term implies, on battles, heroic feats, and knightly ideals. Little notice is paid to women or the theme of love. These tales furnished the material for the medieval romance, where, however, the emphasis shifts from the heroic to the chivalric, from war to love, and from tragic seriousness to lighthearted adventure. The *Song of Roland* is a narrative of knights in battle, but Lodovico Ariosto's sixteenth century *Orlando furioso* (1516, 1521, 1532) concerns a smitten Roland (Orlando) gone mad over his hopeless infatuation with the faithless Angelica, the princess of Cathay.

Some verification for the events narrated in *The Song of Roland* is provided in the *Annales regni Francorum* of Einhard (or Eginhard), Charlemagne's biographer and chronicler. On this basis, it is possible to pinpoint the essential Roland story as a Basque ambush, in 778, of the rearguard of Charlemagne's army during a retreat through the Pyrenees. One unusual aspect of the story is that it tells of a defeat; although defeat was not a total stranger in the epic world of *chansons de geste*, the heroic ambience that pervaded them precluded an emphasis on defeat. Among the scholars who have suggested explanations for the apparent anomaly, one traces the place names mentioned in the poem to the pilgrimage route to the shrine of St. James of Compostella; according to this theory, clerics on pilgrimage knitted the stories of Roland's defeat into an intrinsically Christian epic, in effect, an adaptation of history to a Christian poem. Another scholar construes the poem as a tribute to courage, loyalty, patriotism, and devotion in the face of overwhelming odds. Yet a third scholar approaches the problem by way of the poem's purpose: If the poem were written to glorify Charlemagne and Christianity, then Roland dies a martyr's death and Charlemagne's vengeance redounds to his credit as a defender of the Faith. Whatever their other merits, these theories suggest two recurring themes in any reading of *The Song of Roland*: the religious and the heroic, both of them major preoccupations of the high Middle Ages.

The religious theme pits Christians against Saracens, imbuing the story with a strong crusading spirit. Charlemagne and his peers display most, if not all, of the seven cardinal virtues. Even the proud Roland dies humble and contrite, and Charlemagne's early indecision is resolved later in the poem when he becomes a courageous leader. The pagans, on the other hand, embody the seven deadly sins. They are treacherous and greedy, and they fight for personal glory or material gain rather than principle or faith. In this world of black-and-white morality, there are no good pagans, and the treasonous, deceitful Ganelon is severely punished for his perfidy. By contrast, the good Charlemagne is rewarded by the direct intervention of the archangel Gabriel, who deals the pagan Saracens a final defeat by slaying their leader, Baligant, while God makes the sun stand still. Divine intervention even affects the trial of Ganelon. The

Christian cause is never questioned, nor is there any doubt about its justice. The forced baptism of the Saracen captives is described without qualm, just as is the battlefield bloodshed. If contradictions appear to later readers, they certainly did not occur to the medieval mind, for religious faith—by no means the least of the cardinal virtues—obliterated any inconsistencies between, for example, the virtue of temperance and the slaughter of pagans.

The heroic theme in *The Song of Roland* is closely linked to the religious, since most heroic deeds are performed in the name of religious principle. The hero's role, however, requires dedication to ideals that have only peripheral, if any, relationship to religious precepts. Loyalty and bravery are held in high esteem, but they are such basic heroic ideals that they are more implicit than explicit in the poem. Decision of major issues, and even major battles by single combat, is another heroic ideal that often manifests itself in the poem. In addition, the motifs of victory and defeat, treason and vengeance, weigh heavily in the balance of heroic ideals. Still another factor, which later readers might call team spirit, is the knightly obligation to subsume individual or personal honor and glory in furtherance of a cause. Thus Roland's early pride, especially his insistence on the use of force to subdue the Saracens and his subsequent refusal to blow his horn to summon Charlemagne's aid until all were dead or dying, is eventually brought low. Finally, Roland regretted his stubborn pride in a vivid demonstration of the need for that heroic ideal, teamwork. Not all is a self-evident exercise in primitive democracy. Charlemagne's word was still law, although the most powerful peers insisted on having a voice in decision making; nor is there much attention paid to morality (as distinct from ethics) or to social courtesies. In fact, a pristine system of social and political justice characterized Charlemagne's court as an essential ingredient in the heroic ideal, quite apart from religious considerations altogether. Thus the unique features of the heroic ideal are distinguishable from religious precepts.

The Song of Roland is a remarkable panorama of medieval life and thought, imaginatively perceived. To those who would say that it is false history, one can answer only with the cliché that fiction is often truer than history, for that is certainly the case in *The Song of Roland*. The poem affords so vivid a picture of medieval reality that its historical accuracy is irrelevant; it presents psychological, emotional, and sociological realities that transcend factual data to reach a new plateau of reality, one reflecting the spirit of the times rather than the substance. In this sense, the *Song of Roland* is, despite its ethical simplicities and its literary primitiveness, remarkably successful as a document of the medieval spirit, a characteristic that may explain its enduring popularity.

"Critical Evaluation" by Joanne G. Kashdan

Bibliography:

Duggan, Joseph J. *A Guide to Studies on the "Chanson de Roland."* London: Grant and Cutler, 1976. A useful bibliographic source.

Haidu, Peter. *The Subject of Violence: The "Song of Roland" and the Birth of the State*. Bloomington: Indiana University Press, 1993. Analyzes *The Song of Roland* as a "beginning moment" in the genealogy of Western culture, a time when Western subjectivity arose alongside a new image of the social body. Haidu combines narrative semiotics and sociocultural history to explain how this change is reflected in the Roland text.

Reed, J. "The Passage of Time in *La Chanson de Roland*." *The Modern Language Review* 87, no. 3 (July, 1992): 555-567. Analyzes the obvious and submerged references to the passage of time in *The Story of Roland* and concludes that the poem spans a period of thirteen days.

Short, Ian. *"La Chanson de Roland."* In *the New Oxford Companion to Literature in French*, edited by Peter France. Oxford, England: Clarendon Press, 1995. A thorough discussion and interpretation of the epic. Discusses the historical context for the work, as well as describing variations among the extant sources.

Vance, Eugene. *Reading the "Song of Roland."* Englewood Cliffs, N.J.: Prentice-Hall, 1970. Analyzes Roland as a legendary character and discusses the work in the context of French epic poetry. Includes bibliography.

SONG OF SOLOMON

Type of work: Novel
Author: Toni Morrison (1931-)
Type of plot: Bildungsroman
Time of plot: 1869-1963
Locale: Detroit, Michigan
First published: 1977

Principal characters:
MILKMAN DEAD, an African American man
MACON DEAD, his father
RUTH FOSTER DEAD, his mother
PILATE DEAD, his aunt
HAGAR, his second cousin
GUITAR BAINS, his closest friend
CORINTHIANS and
LENA, his sisters

The Story:

Milkman Dead, so called because his lonely mother, Ruth Foster Dead, nursed him until he was six years old, grew up hating his family. His mother clung to her faded glory as the only daughter of Detroit's first black doctor. His father, Macon Dead, was a ruthless landlord who built a successful realty business by exploiting his black tenants in Southside (the black section of the city, also called the Blood Bank for its frequent eruptions of violence), and who abused his wife.

At age twelve, Milkman met Guitar Bains. Guitar introduced him to Milkman's father's sister, Pilate, whom Milkman knew his father hated. Pilate supported herself, her illegitimate daughter Reba, and Reba's illegitimate daughter Hagar, by making and selling bootleg wine. Milkman fell instantly in love with the beautiful Hagar, though she was five years older than he, and later maintained with her a sporadic affair that ended in tragedy.

Milkman's first visit to Pilate marked the beginning of his stumbling, almost inadvertent quest for identity. His father forbade him to visit Pilate and tried to explain his decision by telling Milkman what he could remember about his family and his own boyhood. He remembered that Milkman's grandfather, the first Macon Dead, was an illiterate slave freed at the end of the Civil War. He received his unusual name as a teenager in 1869, when a drunken Union army interviewer mistakenly combined his birthplace, Macon, and the status of his father, dead, in the space reserved for his name on his Freedmen's Bureau registration form. This first Macon Dead came north on a wagon filled with former slaves and, sometime before 1887, began building a profitable farm from nothing near the town of Danville, Pennsylvania. His son, the second Macon Dead, was born in 1891, and in 1895, his wife died giving birth to a daughter, Pilate. In 1903, the first Macon Dead was murdered by white landowners, who stole his farm. Milkman's father, then sixteen, and his aunt Pilate, then twelve, were hidden by Circe, a black cook, in her master's mansion until they could escape.

Milkman worked for his father during the years of World War II, and the business prospered. During a dinner-table argument in 1953, Macon hit his wife and Milkman assaulted his father.

His father then explained to Milkman that he hated his wife because she and her father, the late Dr. Foster, had carried on an incestuous affair. Milkman's mother denied the affair and told Milkman that his own father, her husband, had tried to abort him. Milkman's friend Guitar Bains told Milkman that he had joined the Seven Days, a secret society that avenged murdered African Americans.

Disturbed by these revelations, Milkman begged his father to stake him to a new start, inadvertently mentioning a green bag, which Pilate called her inheritance, hanging in Pilate's house. Startled, Macon told Milkman how he and Pilate had hidden in a cave after the murder of their father, how he had fought with and killed a white man also hiding in the cave, and how he and Pilate had found a fortune in gold while hiding the body. Macon had wanted to steal it, but Pilate had stopped him. Macon suspected that the gold was in Pilate's bag, that she had returned and stolen the gold for herself. Milkman and Guitar, who planned to use his share of the gold to bankroll the Seven Days, stole the bag, but it contained nothing but bones, which Pilate said belonged to the white man Macon killed in the cave. Haunted by guilt, she had retrieved them months after the killing. Milkman then went to Pennsylvania to recover the gold.

In Pennsylvania, Milkman found the cave but not the gold, and learned that his grandfather's body, buried in a shallow grave by his murderers, had been washed out by the river and was later thrown into the cave, which meant that the bones in Pilate's bag were actually her father's. Milkman then looked for the gold in the tiny hamlet of Shalimar, Virginia, where Pilate had lived for a time after her father's death. Guitar, thinking Milkman was trying to cheat the Seven Days by keeping all the gold for himself, followed and tried to kill Milkman, but Milkman fought him off. In Shalimar, Milkman heard children singing a song that reminded him of a song he had heard Pilate sing, except the children sang about "Solomon," and Pilate sang about "Sugarman." From local residents Milkman began piecing together his lost family history and discovered that the children's song was that family history. The hero of the song was an African named Solomon who could fly. Solomon tried to carry his twenty-first child, a boy named Jake, home to Africa, but dropped the boy and went on alone. That boy was Milkman's grandfather, Jake Solomon, renamed Macon Dead in 1869.

Milkman went home, returning to Shalimar with Pilate and the bones of his grandfather, which they buried at Solomon's leap, the spot from which legend claimed Solomon had flown. The obsessed Guitar, hiding in the woods, fired a rifle at Milkman, but missed, killing Pilate instead. Milkman charged Guitar, and the story ends with the two locked in mortal combat.

Critical Evaluation:

The first African American to receive the Nobel Prize in Literature (1993), Toni Morrison has achieved a place in the first rank of American writers and is considered by many critics the greatest American novelist of the late twentieth century. Born Chloe Anthony Wofford in 1931, Morrison earned a B.A. degree from Howard University in 1953 and an M.A. from Cornell University in 1955, writing her master's thesis on the theme of suicide in the fiction of William Faulkner and Virginia Woolf, whose influence is apparent in her novels. She later taught at Howard and at the State University of New York at Purchase, and served as a senior editor at Random House. She received a National Book Award nomination in 1975 for her second novel, *Sula*, the National Book Critics Circle Award in 1977 for her fourth novel, *Song of Solomon*, and the Pulitzer Prize in 1988 for her fifth novel, *Beloved*. Perhaps more than any other writer, Morrison is responsible for asserting the influence of African American literature and culture on American culture as a whole. She uses modernistic techniques such as multiple narrators, interior monologues, and discursive, nonchronological narration, so Morrison's fiction is highly complex, but because she possesses a rare skill in breathing life into settings and characters, her prose is also highly readable. *Song of Solomon* combines these qualities in a narrative that frequently employs the grotesque and occasionally the bizarre, yet seldom strains credulity. Telling the story of one man's quest for identity, the novel explores several important African American themes.

The primary theme of the novel is gaining identity through the recovery of a stolen and forgotten past. Multiple narrators in *Song of Solomon* reveal the plot slowly, as Milkman learns his own story piecemeal from his father, his mother, Guitar, Pilate, and the people he meets in Pennsylvania and Virginia on his search for the lost gold. In one sense these characters serve as guides on a journey in the long tradition of the epic quest in Western literature. In another sense, they are red herrings, tempting the reader to a misreading of the novel just as Western materialism tempts Milkman and his family to misread their own history, from which they have been cut off by slavery, by the drunken Union Army officer's accidental renaming of Milkman's grandfather, and by their quest for a materialistic white lifestyle. Milkman's parents and sisters have little knowledge of their history. Like many African Americans, they have derived their identities from absence rather than presence. They are, after all, the Deads, they live on Not Doctor Street, and their values have been borrowed from the dominant white culture. Milkman's mother, Ruth Foster Dead, is known chiefly as Dr. Foster's daughter, and her family history seems to begin with her father. Milkman's father, Macon Dead, can remember very little of his heritage but, like his father, has embraced the American values of rugged individualism and the relentless pursuit of profit. He disowns Pilate, evicts Guitar Bains's family from one of his rental properties because they owe four dollars in back rent, coldly demands that the deranged Porter pay his rent before committing suicide, and develops lakeshore vacation homes in which other middle-class black families isolate themselves from the African-American community. Milkman's middle-aged, unmarried sisters, Corinthians and Lena, are defined chiefly by the absence of husbands. Milkman himself has acquired his own identity from his mother's nursing and from his father's success in business. In seeking Pilate's gold, he seeks his own identity through the materialistic success valued by his father.

The gold, like the quest motif, is a red herring, one of many in the novel. Milkman finds no gold but instead discovers his own identity through a rite of passage in Shalimar, Virginia, where he becomes a warrior (he fights a local man with a broken bottle) and a hunter (the locals take him raccoon hunting, but they kill a fiercer animal, a bobcat). He becomes a part of a community (nearly everyone in Shalimar is surnamed Solomon, the real surname of Milkman's grandfather), and for the first time he learns to give and receive love. He also learns that the real gold in Shalimar is his African heritage, recovered through his rite of passage and through the song of the children. The novel's Old Testament title, *Song of Solomon*, is itself a red herring. It refers not to the Bible of the dominant white culture but to African American folklore. It allows the reader to experience vicariously Milkman's epiphany. Milkman's journey is not an epic quest in the Western tradition, but a rediscovery of African roots.

Craig A. Milliman

Bibliography:

Bloom, Harold, ed. *Toni Morrison: Modern Critical Views*. New York, Chelsea House, 1990. Includes general essays on Morrison, plus Theodore O. Mason, Jr.'s, discussion of Morrison's role as conservator of African American culture and Morrison's own argument for the influence of African American culture on mainstream American culture.

Gates, Henry Louis, Jr., and K. A. Appiah, eds. *Toni Morrison: Critical Perspectives Past and Present*. New York: Amistad Press, 1993. Includes Valerie Smith's argument that *Song of Solomon* invalidates Western concepts of identity and family, replacing those concepts with an African sense of community.

Harris, Trudier. *Fiction and Folklore: The Novels of Toni Morrison*. Knoxville: University of Tennessee Press, 1991. Harris argues that *Song of Solomon* relies on African American folklore rather than Western mythology for its meaning. Solomon's ability to fly, though it seems based on the story of Daedelus and Icarus, actually derives from African American myth.

McKay, Nellie Y., comp. *Critical Essays on Toni Morrison*. Boston: G. K. Hall, 1988. Includes three essays on *Song of Solomon*: Kathleen O'Shaughnessy traces the importance of community, Gary Brenner shows the novel's departures from Western literary traditions and from contemporary feminism, and Genevieve Fabre argues that the novel is a celebration of storytelling.

Samuels, Wilfred D., and Clenora Hudson-Weems. *Toni Morrison*. Boston: Twayne, 1990. Includes a brief biography and discussions of each of her first five novels, stressing *Song of Solomon*'s concern with self-affirmation as the key to identity.

THE SONG OF THE LARK

Type of work: Novel
Author: Willa Cather (1873-1947)
Type of plot: Impressionistic realism
Time of plot: Late nineteenth and early twentieth centuries
Locale: Colorado, Chicago, and New York
First published: 1915

Principal characters:
THEA KRONBORG, a young singer
DR. HOWARD ARCHIE, her friend and adviser
PROFESSOR WUNSCH, a music teacher
ANDOR HARSANYI, a concert pianist
FREDERICK OTTENBURG, a wealthy art patron
TILLY KRONBORG, Thea's aunt

The Story:

Thea Kronborg was the daughter of the Swedish Methodist pastor in the small town of Moonstone, Colorado. A tall, fair girl with grave, candid eyes, her shy awkwardness hid restless depths of thought and feeling. Although she grew up in a lively household of brothers and sisters, she had no real friends among children her own age. Of her family, only her aunt, Tilly Kronborg, seemed to understand her; but Tilly was so ridiculous in her speech and actions that neighbors only laughed when she told them that the day was coming when Thea would make Moonstone sit up and take notice.

One of her few friends was Dr. Howard Archie, the town physician, who, when she was eleven, saved Thea's life during an attack of pneumonia. He was unhappily married to a mean-spirited woman who wanted only three things in life: to have her cigar-smoking husband away from home as much as possible, to keep her house closed against dust, and to live on food from cans. Having no children of his own, Dr. Archie loved Thea in a fatherly way, and he often wondered what would become of a girl so passionate and determined.

Another friend of her childhood was gruff, disreputable old Professor Wunsch, her music teacher. A drunkard, but at one time a talented pianist, he had drifted casually into Moonstone, and Fritz Kohler, the German tailor, had pitied him and given him a home. The two old men, both with memories of their younger years in Europe, became cronies. Fiercely resenting demands of family and school upon her time, he gave Thea her first glimpse of artistic endeavor, just as the Kohler house gave her a knowledge of true Old-World simplicity and friendliness. Wunsch, unable to understand Thea's stubborn reserve, compared her to the yellow prickly pear blossoms of the desert.

Through these friends, she also knew Spanish Johnny from the Mexican settlement on the outskirts of town. He was another wanderer and drunkard, who always came back to Moonstone and his patient wife to recover from his debauches. The neighbors were scandalized when the minister's daughter went with the doctor and Wunsch to hear Spanish Johnny sing Mexican folk songs. Mrs. Kronborg, wiser than her husband, quietly allowed Thea to go her own way. Still another man who took great interest in Thea was Ray Kennedy, a railroad conductor on the Denver run. He was waiting until she grew up; then he intended to marry her. In his own way, he was the most protective of all.

Thea was fifteen years old when old Wunsch, in a drunken frenzy, smashed the furniture in the Kohler house and left town. After his departure, Thea took over his pupils. A year later, Ray Kennedy, injured in a wreck, died, leaving Thea six hundred dollars in insurance. Dr. Archie advised her to take the money and study music for a winter in Chicago. After much discussion, the Kronborgs agreed, if the doctor would take her there and get her settled.

In Chicago, living in cheap rooms and earning extra money by singing in a church choir, Thea was homesick for the sand dunes and deep, silent snows of Moonstone. She hated the city, but she worked hard for Andor Harsanyi, under whom she studied. Like Wunsch, the brilliant young musician was baffled by qualities of Thea's imagination and will. He was almost in despair over her when he discovered that her real talent was in voice. Relieved yet sorry, he told her that she would never make a great pianist. She might, however, become a great singer.

The next summer, Thea went back to Moonstone. There she disturbed her family by refusing to sing at the funeral of Maggie Evans, a neighbor. Persuaded by her mother, she finally consented. Later, she shocked the town and disgusted her brothers and sisters by going to a party in the Mexican village and singing with Spanish Johnny and his friends. Returning to Chicago, she studied under Madison Bowers, a teacher whom she both admired and disliked. At his studio, she met for the first time Fred Ottenburg, son of a rich brewer and an amateur musician. Bowers was cynically amused that the wealthy young man was attracted to the strange girl from the West. Through Ottenburg's influence, Thea was given singing engagements at the parties of his fashionable friends.

That winter, Thea caught a severe cold. Her convalescence was slow, and she felt weak and dispirited. Ottenburg, concerned for her welfare, urged her to go away for a rest at his father's ranch in Arizona. There Thea discovered a West different from the crude, vulgar Moonstone she had known. Prowling among the cliff dwellers' ruins in Panther Canyon, she felt herself part of an older West, a land closer to the everyday simplicities of sun, wind, and water. Thoughts of those primitive people aroused her own half-awakened nature; the desert country, ancient but filled with relics of human endeavor, gave her a realization of art as form given to hope and experience.

Rested, and grateful to Ottenburg, she accepted his proposal of marriage when he arrived at the ranch. On the way to Mexico, however, she learned that he already had a neurotic, invalid wife. Hurt and shocked, she refused his offers of assistance, borrowed money from Dr. Archie, and went to Germany for further study.

Years passed. By that time, Dr. Archie was a widower, his wife having been killed when some cleaning fluid exploded, and he had moved to Denver to take charge of some mining investments that had prospered. From time to time, reports reached him of Thea's progress abroad, and he was pleased when Ottenburg brought word that she had sung Elisabeth at the Dresden Opera. He alone understood why Thea, at a critical point in her career, had been unable to return to Moonstone for her mother's funeral.

He was in New York on that great night when the sudden illness of a famous singer gave Thea her chance to sing Sieglinde in *Die Walküre* (1856) at the Metropolitan Opera House. He and Ottenburg, whom Thea had forgiven, heard the performance together, both pleased and proud because they were the two men who had meant most in her career.

By 1909, Tilly was the last Kronborg in Moonstone. She never tired of boasting to her neighbors about Thea's successes and her marriage to wealthy Frederick Ottenburg after his wife's death. Best of all, she liked to remind the townspeople that Thea had once sung in Moonstone at Maggie Evans' funeral.

Critical Evaluation:

The West, the past—one is the physical background of Willa Cather's writing, the other its spiritual climate. Against her chosen backgrounds, she projected her stories of pioneers and artists, men and women of simple passions and creative energies. The very nature of her material determined her own values as an artist: to find in the people of her creation those realities of the spirit which have been almost overwhelmed in the complexity and confusion of the present. *The Song of the Lark*, which carries Thea Kronborg from an obscure Colorado town to the concert and opera stage, is a novel rich and sustaining in homely realism. The character of Thea was drawn in part from the late Olive Fremstad, but there is much of Cather's own story in the experiences of her heroine. Like Thea, she made common things and disciplined effort the shaping influences of her art. The story of the artist in America is usually sentimentalized or idealized. This novel is a notable exception.

Though it has never shared the success of some of Cather's other works, *The Song of the Lark* is nevertheless a rewarding and significant part of the Cather canon. The novel has been criticized, and perhaps justly so, for its unselective use of detail and episode in developing Thea Kronborg's story; yet such thoroughness is also what has allowed Cather to convey so fully to the reader Thea's passionate spirit for living. Thea's growth as an artist is shown in the context of two themes that run throughout Cather's works: the invigorating, spiritual significance of the Southwest and its history, and the alienation of the artistic temperament from conventional life and values. *The Song of the Lark* is essentially a chronicle of the delicate awakening of the artistic sensibility and its consequent struggle to escape the limitations of a commonplace environment.

This theme is introduced in the novel through Thea's early opposition to the standards and values of Moonstone. The young girl's friends are those who, like Thea herself, display a quality of mind and spirit for life which Moonstone conventionality interprets as either wild and eccentric or blatantly selfish. The lifestyles of Dr. Archie, old Wunsch, Ray Kennedy, and Spanish Johnny are in marked contrast to the provincial conformity and petty materialism embodied in the likes of Mrs. "Livery" Johnson or the community's endorsement of Thea's less talented rival, Lily Fisher. Although Thea's talent and ardent nature set her apart from the rest of her community, she finds happiness and fulfillment in expanding her awareness of things. Visiting the countryside with Dr. Archie, learning German from Wunsch, or singing songs with Spanish Johnny, she is progressively introduced to a broader sense of values and culture than the narrow environment of Moonstone can supply. Her later experience with the ancient pottery at the cliff dwellings in Arizona only makes Thea more conscious of the immense aspirations and possibilities within her own spirit and the human spirit in general.

Seeking to develop her own aspirations to their fullest, Thea becomes more and more dedicated to the disciplines of her art. By the end of the novel, her commitment has left almost no time in her life for other people, but she has fulfilled the artistic impulse that drove her beyond the limitations of a small-town environment and into a world of intense, rapturous feeling for the quality of life. Her disciplined, self-imposed isolation from the conventional world is the price the serious artist must pay for his expansive spirit.

When *The Song of the Lark* was reissued in 1932, Cather revised the novel rather heavily in an attempt to reduce wordage and tighten its style. Most of the changes occurred in the last two books, where the author felt that, because Thea's struggle was now over, the dramatic pull of the story necessarily lagged into the anticlimactic. None of these changes, however, appreciably affected the novel's content or thematic statement.

Bibliography:

Giannone, Richard. "The Lyric Artist." In *Critical Essays on Willa Cather*, edited by John J. Murphy. Boston: G. K. Hall, 1984. Guides the reader through *The Song of the Lark* with short, well-chosen quotations and unifying interpretation. The chapter is preceded by an interesting, anonymous *New Republic* review published in 1915.

Middleton, Jo Ann. *Willa Cather's Modernism: A Study of Style and Technique*. Madison, N.J.: Fairleigh Dickinson University Press, 1990. Middleton's discussion of Cather's deceptively simple style uses *The Song of the Lark* repeatedly as an example. Careful indexing allows the reader to locate these references.

Rosowski, Susan J. *The Voyage Perilous: Willa Cather's Romanticism*. Lincoln: University of Nebraska Press, 1986. Gives a good sense of how *The Song of the Lark* fits into Cather's canon. Rosowski devotes much of one chapter to the novel.

Schwind, Jean. "Fine and Folk Art in *The Song of the Lark*." In *Cather Studies*. Vol. 1, edited by Susan J. Rosowski. Lincoln: University of Nebraska Press, 1990. Investigates the artistic forces at work in the novel. Focuses on the meaning of the title and importance of the epilogue.

Thomas, Susie. *Willa Cather*. New York: Barnes & Noble Books, 1990. Devotes much of chapter 2 to her analysis of *The Song of the Lark* as the most overtly Wagnerian of all of Cather's novels. This excellent reference volume is accessible.

THE SONG OF THE WORLD

Type of work: Novel
Author: Jean Giono (1895-1970)
Type of plot: Impressionistic realism
Time of plot: Early twentieth century
Locale: Basses-Alpes region, France
First published: *Le Chant du monde*, 1934 (English translation, 1937)

Principal characters:
ANTONIO, a man of the river
SAILOR, a woodcutter
JUNIE, his wife
DANIS, their son
MAUDRU, a wealthy ox tamer
GINA, his daughter
CLARA, a blind woman
JÉRÔME or MONSIEUR TOUSSAINT, Junie's brother

The Story:

For years the man called Sailor had lived with his wife Junie and their twin sons in a woodcutter's camp in the forest beyond Christol's Pass. Shortly after one of the twins, who was married and had a child, had been killed by a landslide in a clay pit, the other red-haired twin went north into the Rebeillard country to cut fir trees and raft them down the river. When he failed to return two months later, Junie became alarmed and sent her husband to ask help of Antonio, who lived on the isle of jays.

Antonio was a fisherman, a fierce, hardy, yet strangely compassionate fellow, wise in the ways of streams and the weather. He carried three scars on his body, a knife wound, a man's bite, and the slash of a billhook, for he was as reckless in a fight as he was daring in making love to the maidens and wives of the river villages. Men called him Goldenmouth. He promised to help Sailor search the river and creeks for some sign of Danis, the red-haired twin.

The men started early the next morning, Antonio on one side of the stream, Sailor on the other. Both were armed, for the Rebeillard region was wild country beyond the gorges. There Maudru, the ox tamer, kept his great herds, and his word was the only law. The wind blowing from the north was chill with frost as the two men worked their way up the river. Although they found no sign of Danis or his logs, they saw some of Maudru's drovers and heard their horns, which seemed to signal the coming of strangers into the district. Antonio wondered why Maudru's men were on watch.

At nightfall, he swam across the river to join Sailor. While they sat by a fire that they had built to warm themselves and to cook their food, they heard the moaning of a creature in pain. Investigating, they found a young woman suffering in childbirth. Following the directions of a drover who had been spying on their fire, they carried her and her newborn child to the house of a peasant woman called the mother of the road. The next morning Antonio learned that the woman he had helped, was unmarried, blind, and named Clara. When he saw her for the first time in the daylight, he loved her. That day, over the protests of Maudru's men, he killed a wild boar to provide meat for the house. Four drovers came to the house at twilight. They had been sent to the fields near the river gorges to keep two travelers from leaving the country. Because Antonio and Sailor had come into the district, the watchers were uneasy. While Antonio and

Sailor waited to see whether the drovers would make a fight of the matter, signal beacons flashed on the northern hills. From what was said, Antonio realized that the red-haired twin, for whom the whole country was searching, had been sighted or captured.

Antonio asked the mother of the road to keep the blind woman for him while he and Sailor traveled on toward Villevielle, where they hoped to have some word of Danis' doings from Junie's brother Jérôme, the almanac vendor and healer. On the way, they overtook a cart carrying Mederic, Maudru's wounded nephew. Danis had shot him, Antonio learned from a drover, and the young herder was likely to die. For that reason, beacons had burned on the hills.

Years before, Maudru's sister, Gina, had run away from her brother's farm at Puberclaire with twenty-three of his drovers and had taken the Maladrerie estate as her own. There she ruled her fields and her bed, and bred her sons as she did her bulls. Mederic was the last of her children. Maudru had married and had a daughter, Gina. It had been planned that the cousins should marry, but Danis had shot old Gina's son and carried off her namesake. While Maudru's men were searching for the fugitives, the wounded man was being carried to Puberclaire to die.

Saying they wished to visit the healer of Villevielle, Antonio and Sailor entered the old medieval town and found the house of Jérôme, a hunchback whom the Rebeillard folk called Monsieur Toussaint. Danis and young Gina were hiding in his house. The twin had cut his trees and hidden the raft in Villevielle creek, where it remained. Then he had stolen Gina, but Maudru had sent out an alarm before Danis and Gina could escape down the river. Now his men watched the river and every hamlet and road. The lovers were trapped.

Winter came early in the Rebeillard country. After the first snows, Jérôme sent a messenger to tell Junie that Danis and Sailor still lived. Since they were unknown in the town, Antonio and Sailor visited the wineshops from time to time and heard the news. Gina grew fretful. Sometimes she treated Danis with great tenderness; sometimes she mocked him because he was not stronger and more clever than her father, or complained because they lived like cuckoos in another's house. In spite of Jérôme's efforts, Mederic died. Antonio went to the burial at Maladrerie and met Maudru, a powerful, slow-spoken man. One day, Danis went out on skis to inspect his raft and was almost captured. A short time later, three of Maudru's men, pretending to be sick, came to Jérôme's house. The inmates realized then that the fugitives had been located. When he ventured out thereafter, Antonio came and went through passages connecting the cellars of the old houses.

One day, when there was a touch of spring in the air, Antonio and Sailor went out through the cellars and drank at an inn. Both became drunk. Antonio pursued a woman whom he mistook for Clara and left Sailor alone. Sailor was confused by the brandy; it seemed to him that he was young again and about to embark on a long sea voyage. Forgetting to be cautious, he never heard the two drovers who crept up behind him and stabbed him in the back.

Antonio returned home and discovered that Clara had arrived with Jérôme's messenger. Her child had died, and she no longer wished to be alone. In his joy at seeing her, Antonio completely forgot Sailor, until Jérôme became alarmed by his absence. Then, with Clara's keen sense of hearing to tell them where danger might lurk in the darkened streets, Antonio and the healer searched for the old man. When they found him, they carried his body back to the house and called Danis to look at his dead father. Danis was enraged. That night, he and Antonio went to Puberclaire and set fire to Maudru's barns and house. Many of his prize bulls and tame oxen died in the blaze as the great bull farm was destroyed.

The light of the burning drew off Maudru's watchers; under cover of the confusion, Danis, Gina, Clara, and Antonio started off down the flooded stream on the log raft. Below the gorges they saw green on the trees; spring had arrived. Danis was planning the house he would build for Gina. Antonio thought of his life with Clara on the isle of jays. None of the travelers saw Maudru, alone on horseback, as he watched from a high peak the raft passing below him and out of sight toward the south.

Critical Evaluation:

Jean Giono's novels achieve a quality of timelessness because, in most of his work, he deliberately ignores the discoveries of modern science and mechanical inventions. Instead, he presents in his books pictures of semiprimitive and pastoral life such as survived until the mid-twentieth century in his remote region of France. Giono's feeling for nature is deeply mystical, and he attempts to bridge the worlds of inner and outer reality by the use of poetic images and metaphors. His style is vigorous and sensuous. Nowhere does he show himself a lyric novelist of the soil better than he does in *The Song of the World*, a novel that is both an exciting adventure story and a paean in praise of nature and the simple, rustic life.

Giono successfully combines his interests in the pastoral, simple life of the French peasant with the sociological issue of one's active response to human interaction and strife. Perhaps because of its theme of the maturing of the individual through social growth, *The Song of the World* is the best known of Giono's novels. His first two novels concentrated only on the individual without community; this, his third novel, expresses his love of the peasantry's commitment to preserving the family and its traditional ways, as well as his strong aversion to bloodshed and war. Giono became a pacifist after participating in the Battle of Verdun during World War I.

The Song of the World is an appropriate title for this work, which recounts the myth patterns of the great epics. Giono, in fact, was a great lover of the Latin and Greek epic forms; his favorite was Homer's *Odyssey* (c. 800 B.C.E.), which greatly influenced his writing. The obvious structural correlation is the journey motif. The journey is not only the basic pattern of myth, but also the form of the epic; in this novel, all the elements of the journey theme are employed. First, there is a call to the hero, Antonio, who is widely known as Goldenmouth, to help his friend, Sailor, find a lost son. The hero accepts the call and sets forth on a journey of physical as well as spiritual trials. He is risking his life to preserve life in the sacrificial pattern associated with heroic travels. Symbolically, one of Antonio and Sailor's first encounters is with a woman giving birth to a son. They save the woman and thus the child. She is eventually the hero's prize; her love is his reward for the risk he took to find and save her. Later, great risk is involved in saving his friend's son.

Another familiar element of the epic is the helper motif. This is present in the guise of the barmaid and, more important, in Monsieur Toussaint. As is often the case with the "helper person" in an epic, Toussaint is a hunchback, a philosopher, and a magician doctor of sorts. Although seemingly unchanged by the events in his house, he is the catalyst for change for all those involved with him.

Antonio's goal is to rescue Sailor's red-haired son. The boy has married the daughter of wealthy and powerful Maudru, who controls the whole region. Besides marrying her secretly, in wooing and winning her he has slain her other suitor, the son of Maudru's sister. It is the hero's responsibility to free the boy and his bride from the domination of her father. The goal of the saga is to restore the boy to his homeland so that he may begin living as a man.

The son has experienced the initiation rite essential to his developing manhood. During the course of this process, his father realizes he is dying. Giono employs Sailor's death symbolically as a commentary upon the growth of the son. It is at the death of the father that the son is finally freed to act on his own behalf—freed in will and bursting with power—against the obstacle to his happiness, Maudru. The son boldly risks his life to right the wrong done to his father and thus to himself. He burns all that made Maudru wealthy and leaves the man so much the poorer for his jealousy and vengefulness.

The novel comes full circle when Maudru, on the hill overlooking the river, watches the entourage of his daughter and son-in-law, and Antonio and his new bride drift down the river, just as, when Maudru was powerful, his man watched Antonio and Sailor come into the territory. This river provides life to the foursome and a renewal or rebirth of spirit, as well as a socialization through marriage. The hero, formerly one who lived in a hut in the woods, dreams of creating a home for his bride. The son, now a man, prepares to build a home for his young wife and to care for his newly widowed mother.

The style of *The Song of the World* complements its epic content. The vivid detail and economy of language provide it with a fluidity and rhythmic tempo. Passages describing Antonio and his activities are mainly short, declarative sentences, reflecting the hero's simple, pastoral personality. Antonio's dialogue, however, reflects an eloquence and sensitivity more lofty than is characteristic of a simple peasant. From the first, he is presented as a superior man.

The use of the three-part structural form divides the novel not only by seasons—spring, winter, and spring again—but by location—the setting forth from, absence from, and return to the homeland. Thus, the title is meaningful, not only mythically but also seasonally. One is inextricably tied to the other, as it is the seasons that evoke birth, death, and renewal.

Giono's novel urges the idea that action and risk are the price of freedom. Maudru, clinging to severity and power with an iron hand, loses the people and things he loves because he is unable to accept and respect his daughter's freedom. Giono is searching for those modes of living in which people are free to be themselves and are reunited harmoniously with nature and society.

"Critical Evaluation" by Gayle Steck

Bibliography:

Brée, Germaine, and Margaret Guiton. *An Age of Fiction: The French Novel from Gide to Camus*. New Brunswick, N.J.: Rutgers University Press, 1957. Describes Giono as a novelist who creates private worlds to stand apart from contemporary public issues. Reads *The Song of the World* as a novel concerned chiefly with problems of love and death.

Goodrich, Norma L. *Giono: Master of Fictional Modes*. Princeton, N.J.: Princeton University Press, 1973. Scholarly study aimed at explaining Giono's creative abilities and diversity of expression. Labels Giono as a major figure in twentieth century fiction. Places *The Song of the World* among the significant accomplishments Giono completed during the first phase of his career.

Peyre, Henri. *French Novelists of Today*. New York: Oxford University Press, 1967. One chapter outlines Giono's literary achievements, briefly explicating the plot of *The Song of the World*. Asserts that Giono uses his characters to represent forces of nature.

Redfern, W. D. *The Private World of Jean Giono*. Durham, N.C.: Duke University Press, 1967. Surveys Giono's major works. Includes a section on *The Song of the World*; classifies it as a peasant novel and calls it idealistic in tone and uncluttered in plot and style. Believes Giono intended this work to be a private epic.

Smith, Maxwell. *Jean Giono*. New York: Twayne, 1966. Discusses *The Song of the World* in a chapter devoted to Giono's epic novels. Describes ways in which the novelist achieves unity in a work of great scope and diversity.

SONGS OF INNOCENCE AND OF EXPERIENCE

Type of work: Poetry
Author: William Blake (1757-1827)
First published: Songs of Innocence, 1789; *Songs of Innocence and of Experience*, 1794

Songs of Innocence and of Experience is the foundation of the work of one of the greatest English poets and artists. The two sets of poems reveal what Blake calls "the two contrary states of the human soul." The presentation of these states is deceptively simple, literally childlike in the "Innocence" poems. In both series, clues are offered to deeper meanings and ways out of the apparent trap of selfhood are suggested, so that each reading provides greater insight and understanding, not only to the poems but also to human life.

The first poem in the "Innocence" series, "Introduction," establishes the pastoral background of most of the poems. The speaker in the poem (not Blake) has been playing tunes on a pipe in a pleasant valley when he or she is stopped by a vision of a child on a cloud, perhaps an angel, who functions as an encouraging muse. The child asks the pipe player to pipe a song about a lamb, then asks that the song be repeated and weeps. The child asks the speaker to sing a song, then asks that the songs be written "In a book, that all may read." The child disappears, and the speaker makes a pen from a reed, makes ink by staining water, and writes "happy songs/ Every child may joy to hear."

The last lines establish the apparent audience of *Songs of Innocence*: children. The poems in this series have a simple vocabulary and meter and can be read, and at least partly understood, by small children. This collection is not aimed exclusively at children, however. The child on the cloud tells the speaker to write so that "all may read;" it is the speaker who assumes that "every child may joy to hear" and restricts his or her audience to children. Perhaps "child" does not mean children but everyone, in the sense that all are children of God. Thus, in the first poem, the apparently simple vocabulary leads to complex interpretations.

"Introduction" also describes and wryly comments on Blake's technique. At first, the speaker is playing music, an evanescent expression that only the speaker and the child on the cloud hear. The child asks the speaker to sing songs that can be recorded in a book, specifically a book written and decorated with natural colors. The child, who acts as inspiration, vanishes when the hard work of composing and painting the volumes begins. Also, music strikes the senses directly, but the use of words restricts the audience to those who know and can understand a particular language. *Songs of Innocence*, which appears to be addressed to innocent children, actually requires some sophistication in order to be read, much less understood.

The next two poems, "The Shepherd" and "The Ecchoing Green," continue the pastoral atmosphere established by the first poem, but there is an ominous element at the end of the second poem. An old man has been watching the children at play, and they note that he and the other older people remember that they used to play like that in their youth. In the last line, the area is no longer "ecchoing" but "darkening."

The light apparently returns again in "The Lamb," which returns to the biblical idea of the good shepherd of "The Shepherd." A child asks a lamb if the lamb knows who made it, then informs the lamb that

> He is called by thy name
> For he calls himself a Lamb.
> He is meek, & he is mild.
> He became a little child.

The child is referring to Jesus, but does not explain why Jesus is called a lamb. Adults know that Jesus was the sacrificial lamb of God, who paid for the sins of humanity with death, like those of the animal sacrifices of the Old Testament.

The source of the description becomes clear in the next poem, in which "The Little Black Boy" cries that "White as an angel is the English child:/ But I am black, as if bereav'd of light." Instead of telling the child that he should be proud of who he is, the boy's mother tells him that this physical life is a trial and preparation for the next, spiritual, world. The little boy then imagines a life after death in which the white child will accept him.

A child's acceptance of a cruel fate because society demands it is also present in "The Chimney Sweeper," the first poem with an urban setting. In the late eighteenth and early nineteenth centuries, small boys with heads shaven for streamlining swept chimneys, their lungs filling with soot, doing a job that often led to an early death. In this poem, Tom Dacre, whose head "that curl'd like a lambs back" was shaved like an animal being prepared for slaughter, has a dream in which an angel frees the sweepers from their "coffins of black," another suggestion that only death will bring freedom from life's suffering. The speaker urges the other boys to continue with their work, "So if all do their duty, they need not fear harm."

The idea that God will somehow take care of everyone is reinforced by "The Little Boy Lost" and "The Little Boy Found," in which God miraculously appears to a fatherless boy, lost in a dark swamp, and returns him to his grieving mother. In "A Cradle Song," "Nurse's Song," and "Infant Joy," loving parents or servants watch over helpless babies and playing children. In "Holy Thursday," a description of a religious ceremony in St. Paul's Cathedral, even the orphans of London receive help from "wise guardians of the poor," and the audience of the poem is urged to "cherish pity, lest you drive an angel from your door."

The speaker in "Holy Thursday" is clearly an adult, since he or she has a more sophisticated vocabulary than the speakers in the other poems. The adult viewpoint also appears in "The Divine Image" in which the speaker describes God and the virtues of "Mercy Pity Peace and Love" as dwelling in living human beings, all of whom are entitled to respect and love, no matter what their religion.

Songs of Experience reveals that this acceptance of society as it is and belief in a caring God is naïve. This series does not begin with joy in a pastoral landscape, as does *Songs of Innocence*, but instead the "Introduction" is spoken with "the voice of the Bard . . . Who Present, Past, & Future, sees" and who describes a fallen world with a "lapsed Soul . . . weeping in the evening dew." In the next poem, "Earth's Answer," the earth itself asks to be released from the chains of jealousy and fear. "The Clod and the Pebble" presents two views of love, the clod finding the experience selfless and giving, the pebble stating that love is selfish and restricting.

These poems remind one that there is more than one way to view the same experience, a point further underscored by several other poems in *Songs of Experience* that are answers or companions to poems in *Songs of Innocence*, some even bearing the same name. In the "experience" version of "Holy Thursday," the speaker is appalled by the presence of poverty in such a rich country as England. If people lived in a right relationship with each other and nature, the speaker suggests, hunger and poverty would not exist. In the second "Nurse's Song," the nurse urges the children to come in from their wasteful play, in which she finds no happiness. The "experience" version of "The Chimney Sweeper" makes clear how both a world of misery and the attitude of hopefulness presented in *Songs of Innocence* can exist side by side. A person asks a forlorn chimney sweeper where his parents are, and the child replies that they have gone to church "to praise God & his Priest & King,/ Who make up a heaven of our misery." The society's failings are supported and excused away by the institutions of religion and government, which manage to persuade many that all will somehow be all right, perhaps after death, the same point that is made in "London." The child in this poem has parents, but is more bitter than the orphan of the "innocence" "Chimney Sweeper," because he is intelligent enough to recognize what is being done to him. His response, coupled with that of the accepting adult in the "innocence" "Holy Thursday," show that the sour viewpoint of the "experience" poems is not a result of obtaining wisdom by growing older. Some children are able to see the larger truth; some adults never perceive it. Intelligence and circumstance cause the difference, not age.

The companion poem to "The Divine Image" is "A Divine Image," which points out that cruelty, jealousy, terror, and secrecy are also human properties, and if people are created from God's image, those qualities must belong to God also. In "Infant Sorrow," the baby is unhappy to be born into a dangerous and sorrowful world, unlike the child of "Infant Joy." The companion poem to "The Lamb" is the famous "The Tyger," in which the speaker notes that the same God created the defenseless lamb and the fierce tiger, although he or she seems incredulous: "Did he who made the Lamb make thee?" In the "experience" poems, Blake presents the shock and dismay that arise from the contemplation of the theological problem of evil: If God created everything, God is ultimately responsible for everything, and if God is good, why does evil exist?

There are many answers to this question, including those given in the "innocence" poems, such as the little black boy's mother's contention that this life is a test and those who behave as God or the society directs (as in the "innocence" "Chimney Sweeper") will receive rewards after death, but these answers are emotionally and spiritually unsatisfying for the speakers in the "experience" poems. Nature itself is tainted in such poems as "The Sick Rose," in which the rose is destroyed by a worm—innocence and beauty give way to sin and corruption. In "Ah! Sun-flower" the flower is rooted to its spot and cannot go where repressed youths and virgins go for fulfillment in the next world. In "The Garden of Love," a chapel dedicated to negative commandments, sin, and death has been placed in the midst of what once was a refreshing garden. Now it is clear why the child on the cloud in the "innocence" "Introduction" wept to hear the song piped a second time.

If "innocence" is a naïve viewpoint, Blake shows in the rest of his work that "experience" is also, being fixated on sin and corruption when there is a fuller, genuinely spiritual world at hand. In "The Voice of the Ancient Bard," the speaker urges the audience to "see the opening morn,/ Image of truth new born."

Jim Baird

Bibliography:

Adams, Hazard. *William Blake: A Reading of the Shorter Poems*. Seattle: University of Washington Press, 1963. Interprets *Songs of Innocence and of Experience* from a symbolic and archetypal perspective.

Gleckner, Robert F., and Mark L. Greenberg, eds. *Approaches to Teaching Blake's "Songs of Innocence and of Experience."* New York: The Modern Language Association of America, 1989. A collection of background materials and critical essays by several authors designed to help teachers present *Songs of Innocence and of Experience* in the classroom.

Hirsch, E.D., Jr. *Innocence and Experience: An Introduction to Blake*. New Haven, Conn.: Yale University Press, 1964. Analyzes *Songs of Innocence and of Experience* based on perceived changes in Blake's philosophical and religious ideas while he wrote them.

Leader, Zachary. *Reading Blake's Songs*. London: Routledge & Kegan Paul, 1981. Shows the relation between *Songs of Innocence and of Experience* and Blake's possible models, contemporary children's educational books.

Wicksteed, Joseph. *Blake's Innocence and Experience*. New York: Dutton, 1928. This first book on *Songs of Innocence and of Experience* establishes several foundational critical points, such as the interrelatedness of all the poems. Some of Wicksteed's interpretations of specific poems have been superseded; a good starting place.

THE SONNETS

Type of work: Poetry
Author: Michelangelo (1475-1564)
First published: Rime di Michelagnolo Buonarroti, 1623 (English translation, 1878)

The fame of Michelangelo Buonarroti as a painter and a sculptor has far outdistanced his reputation as a poet. This is unfortunate, for while it is open to question whether Michelangelo could have ever developed into a poet of a stature equivalent to his stature in the plastic arts, his reputation as a poet is less than it should be. Modern critics have discovered that he is an important Renaissance Italian poet, and by many he is considered the best Italian lyric poet of the sixteenth century.

The reasons for the slow growth of Michelangelo's poetic reputation are easy to identify. First, even in his own day, while his poetry was extravagantly praised by a circle of friends, it was Michelangelo's painting and sculpture that drew the eyes of the world at large. Moreover, his poetry was not published until 1623, fifty-nine years after his death, and then only in an incomplete, much edited, and censored edition. By that time the Renaissance style of writing was being replaced by the neoclassical style throughout Europe, and the poems did not attract major attention. It was not until the early nineteenth century, when the Romantics were rediscovering the Middle Ages and the Renaissance, that complete and well-edited editions of the poetry began to appear. Only in the twentieth century were completely authoritative editions published.

Even Michelangelo never took his poetry seriously enough to collect, revise, or preserve the whole of it. While he considered himself a professional painter and sculptor, he, like almost every poet of the Renaissance, thought of himself as an amateur as a poet. Poetry, after all, has never been much of a way to earn a living; in Michelangelo's age poetry was valued as a social pastime and a gentleman's skill. Even if a man did think of himself as a professional poet, it was bad form to act as if he did. This Renaissance attitude has given scholars much trouble, and only after much searching have they managed to locate in various places 343 separate poems and poetic fragments (and many variants) by Michelangelo. Most of these were composed after 1530.

Although the poetry is sometimes written in the traditional Petrarchan manner, and although the conventions of neo-Platonism are also important in the work, the best poems are characterized by Michelangelo's unique style. The structure, syntax, and even the grammar are twisted and full of tension; the poems are often obscure, and the poet sometimes seems to pay scant attention to such relatively simple things as rhyme and metrical regularity. The overall impression of the verse, as critics like to point out, is as if Michelangelo in writing was struggling to shape his complex thoughts into hard, unmalleable language the way a sculptor struggles with marble or granite.

The poems fall into several categories. First in importance are the pieces written to Vittoria Colonna, either proclaiming Michelangelo's Platonic love for her (he met her when he was sixty-three) or lamenting her death, as in this sonnet:

> So that I might at least be less unworthy,
> Lady, of your huge high beneficence,
> To balance it, my poor wits at first
> Took to plying my own wholeheartedly.

But then, seeing in me no potency
To clear the way to grasp that goal exists,
My evil fault for its forgiveness asks,
And the sin makes me wiser constantly.
And well I see how anyone would stray
Who thought my flimsy, transient work could equal
The grace pouring from you, which is divine.
For wit and art and memory give way;
In a thousand attempts none who is mortal
Can pay for Heaven's gift out of his own.

Vittoria was herself a poet of some note and a patron of the arts, and she inspired several notable men of her day to the composition of verse. Generally speaking, there are three levels of love spoken of in Michelangelo's poetry: human, fleshly love, which takes the Petrarchan convention; honest love, a transcendental emotion that takes the neo-Platonic convention; and good love, the spiritual love of God. Good love is the subject of the greater number of Michelangelo's poems, but honest love is the dominant theme in the best of his love poems, most of which are written to Vittoria. Human love is a theme in these poems too, but as an antagonist to honest love. In a typical poem to Vittoria, for example, the poet describes how honest love has come to him forbidding corrupt desire (human love) and raising him to the level of the spirit. This is a conventional, neo-Platonic theme, yet Michelangelo's energetic expression of it reanimates the convention and produces a remarkably unconventional poetry:

I want to want, Lord, what I do not want,
An icy veil hides between heart and fire
And damps the fire, making my page a liar,
Since my pen and my conduct do not fit.
I love you with my tongue, then I lament
Love does not reach the heart, and can't tell where
To open the door to grace so it can enter
And thrust all ruthless pride out of my heart.
Tear the veil thou, O break that wall, my Lord,
Which with its hardness keeps in check the sun
Of your own light; on earth it is put out.
Send that same ray of light to your fair bride
Which we are then to have, so I may burn,
And my heart feel you only with no doubt.

The poems concerning the good love of God are next in importance after the poems to Vittoria. Michelangelo was seriously dedicated to the Christian ideal, and the religious poems are full of his deep, though often agonized love for Christ. Many of them are tortured, self-debasing confessions. Among the most frequent themes in these poems are fear of the judgment day, fear for salvation, the feeling of moral inadequacy, and prayer and supplication:

I live on my own death; if I see right,
My life with an unhappy lot is happy;
If ignorant how to live on death and worry,
Enter this fire, where I'm destroyed and burnt.

Tommaso Cavaliere was a young Roman aristocrat to whom Michelangelo was strongly attracted; a significant group of the poems are dedicated to the poet's admiration and love of that youth. He saw in Tommaso a model of elegance and grace, a man with manners and a social style the opposite of that of Michelangelo himself. The main burden of this group is Michelangelo's statement of admiration of the young man, and the poet's offer of friendship:

I feel how a cold face that fire has lit
Burns me from far, and turns itself to ice;
Two lovely arms submit me to a force
That does not move, but moves all other weight;
Unique, and grasped by me alone, a spirit
That has no death, but others' death can compass,
I see and meet, that binds my heart, being loose;
From one who helps I feel the only spite.
Lord, from a beautiful face how can it be
Effects so far opposed are borne on mine?
It's hard to give to men what you have not.
As for the happy life he's snatched from me,
He may, if you're not kind, act as the sun,
Which heats the world although it is not hot.

Michelangelo's overtures were, apparently, coolly received. All in all, these poems speak of a Platonic kind of love very similar to the kind of affection for a young man readers may be familiar with in William Shakespeare's sonnets. Much different are the forty-eight quatrains to Cecchino Bracci, who died at the age of fifteen in 1544. His uncle, Luigi del Riccio, requested of Michelangelo a tomb design and an epitaph for his nephew. Michelangelo had seen very little of Cecchino, and the moods of the poems represent those of the uncle, not of Michelangelo.

Naturally enough, a group of Michelangelo's poems are concerned with art in general and some of his own works in particular. One interesting piece describes the physical difficulties he endured painting the Sistine Chapel ceiling. Two poems are written as speeches for two of the statues (*Night* and *Day*) that Michelangelo made for the tomb in Florence of the young Duke Giuliano de Medici. A number of the poems use metaphoric structures drawn from aspects of the practice of various arts, painting and sculpture in particular. Among these is Michelangelo's perhaps best-known poem, the sonnet "Non ha l'ottimo artista alcun concetto" ("No conception the greatest artist can have"). Written between 1538 and 1544, the first four lines of this Platonic love poem became famous immediately. Within a few years they were known in Spain and elsewhere, and they were translated into French by Phillipe Desportes, the only verses of Michelangelo translated into French before the nineteenth century. In these four lines is condensed Michelangelo's idea of art. They can be roughly paraphrased as follows: "No conception the greatest artist can have is not imprisoned in the rough marble block; to break away the excess stone to reveal it is all the mind-guided hand can do." This idea of sculpture (and by extension the other arts as well) as the achievement by skill of the artist's intellectual conception was not entirely new, but Michelangelo's unique and authoritative expression of it became, and still is, a touchstone for critics of his art.

Another group of poems is concerned with messages to acquaintances, patrons, and friends, and with the pronouncement of opinion, praise, and condemnations. A friend is lectured on ingratitude; Giorgio Vasari, the great biographer of artists, is praised for his preservation of the reputations of painters; Pope Julius II is angrily denounced; and the deaths of friends and relatives are eloquently regretted. Some of these poems are cautiously political and complain or condemn the actions of powerful contemporaries of the poet. The best-known of this class of poems is Michelangelo's poem in which his statue *Night*, on the Florentine tomb of Duke Giuliano de Medici, speaks. Another poet, Giovanni Strozzi, had praised the statue, carved in the shape of a sleeping young woman. Strozzi suggests that since she is so much alive in art she be awakened. In reply, Michelangelo condemns the excesses of contemporary Medici politics in his native Florence. (Michelangelo, who to some extent identified himself with the exile Dante Alighieri, lived in Rome in self-imposed exile.) He has his statue answer that she would rather sleep than endure the vile corruption which she would witness around her if she were awakened.

The poems that do not fall into any one or more of these major groups cannot be easily classified. Michelangelo wrote in an unsystematic way and, apparently, as the spirit moved him. Many of his poems, for example, have been found jotted down on the back of prints or in the margins of letters or notebooks. It was only in his later years that he wrote consistent groups of poems. Among the unclassified poems are pieces on such various subjects as fire, night, the rustic life, death (he was already writing of his "approaching death" fifty years before he died), cities he had visited, and the manners and morals of his times. Not a few of this last type of poem are satirical burlesques, some full of the earthy language that has always upset censors and self-appointed guardians of public morality.

Bibliography:

Brandes, Georg. *Michelangelo: His Life, His Times, His Era*. Translated with a foreword by Heinz Norden. New York: Frederick Ungar, 1963. Highly readable interpretive biography by great Danish scholar. More than twenty poems cited, with an evaluation of Michelangelo as "in many ways . . . the most compelling poet Italy ever produced." Demonstrates the self-mockery, the satire, even the *buffo* quality of some of the poetry.

Bull, George, ed. *Michelangelo: Life, Letters, and Poetry*. Poems translated by George Bull and Peter Porter. New York: Oxford University Press, 1987. The most accessible collection in English of writings by and about Michelangelo. Includes Condivi's affectionate biography of his teacher, one of the earliest sources for Michelangelo's life, along with selected translations of the master's poems and letters, a fine introduction, and other study aids.

Clements, Robert J. *Michelangelo's Theory of Art*. New York: New York University Press, 1961. An intense and thorough exploration of Michelangelo's formative influences. Attention to relationship between his writing and other forms of artistic expression.

_____________. *The Poetry of Michelangelo*. New York: New York University Press, 1965. Thorough analysis of the poetry in terms of its relation to Italian and broader European literary traditions. Documented discussion of the poetry as a reflection of the life of the artist. Best study in English of Michelangelo's writing.

Ludwig, Emil. *Three Titans*. New York: Putnam, 1930. Comparative biographical study of Michelangelo, Rembrandt, and Ludwig van Beethoven. Dramatic rather than scholarly.

SONNETS FOR HELEN

Type of work: Poetry
Author: Pierre de Ronsard (1524-1585)
First published: Sonnets pour Hélène, 1578 (English translation, 1932)

Hélène de Surgères was the third woman to provide major inspiration for Pierre de Ronsard's poetry. His first poetic love, Cassandre Saviati, whom he met when he was twenty and she only thirteen, married someone else soon after. Marie Dupin, the peasant girl who was the love of his middle years, was separated from him by death. In his late forties, Ronsard took Hélène as his muse. Much younger than the poet, she was a member of the court of Catherine de Medicis (1519-1589). As Hélène's fiancé had been killed at war in 1570, Ronsard addressed his poems to her in order to comfort her as well as to tell her of his love.

A dualism of the personal and the conventional pervades the poetry. Ronsard expresses passionate emotions to Hélène, but he writes in the newly popular sonnet form, which he and his fellow poets of the Pléiade had established as a major French verse form. The Petrarchan sonnet, following the model established by Francesco Petrarca, regularly divides its fourteen lines into an introductory octave and a concluding sestet on distinct but complementary themes. Sonnets were frequently composed in sequences devoted to a single subject. In a sense the entire work may be seen as a sonnet sequence, extremely varied in its details but drawn together by the overriding theme of Ronsard's passion.

The collection is divided into two books that show little progression or distinction between them. There are approximately 130 poems, all sonnets except for an occasional song or elegy (the exact number of poems varies among modern editions). Ronsard varied his subject matter but provides an overall thematic continuity by frequent returns to favored subjects.

The opening sonnet, "Le premier jour de mai, Helene, je vous jure" (The first day of May, Hélène, I swear to you), begins with the appropriate declaration of love on the first of May, a day linked with amorous endeavors. Ronsard swears not only by the vines, the elm tress, and the verdant woods but also by Castor and Pollux, mythological brothers who according to legend became the constellation Gemini. While the June constellation of the zodiac nearly coincides with the springtime setting, Ronsard more likely invoked the brothers because they were also related to the classical Helen of Troy. In appropriate Renaissance tradition, Ronsard invokes the heroes and gods of antiquity, but especially those of Troy because of the analogy of Helen's name. The idea to which Ronsard swears in the octave—his love for Hélène—remains dominated by the images of nature and spring. The sestet turns specifically to his love with another major theme of the work, that of fate. Ronsard calls himself here author of his own fate because he has willingly accepted love's dominion.

The second sonnet, "Quand à longs traits je boy l'amoureuse etincelle" (When I drink deeply of the spark of love), continues the documentation of love's effects on the lover in conventionally physical terms. The first focus is on Hélène's eyes, whose light dazzles Ronsard and troubles his reason so that he staggers as if drunk with love. His hearts beats so hard that he fears the experience will kill him, but Hélène remains aloof, unaware of the pain she causes him. The themes of physical enumeration of love's effects and of the lover's suffering, both common in poetry of the time, recur throughout the work.

The third sonnet, "Ma douce Hélène, non, mais bien ma douce haleine" (My sweet Hélène, no, but rather my sweet breath), combines the poet's suffering with the legend of Troy. Ronsard finds himself fortunate to suffer the pains of love for one with such a name of destiny. She is both his Penelope and his Helen, combining the virtue of Ulysses' faithful wife with the fascination Helen exerted on all the men around her.

Ronsard reinforces the link between classical precedents and his modern love in "Amour, abandonant les vergers de Cytheres" (Cupid, abandoning the orchards of Cythera), in which Cupid comes personally to France to strike him with his light wings so as to implant the feverish need in his heart. The need is that of the poet as much as that of the lover. Ronsard must sing of Hélène's beauty, and when he protests his inability to treat such a heavenly subject, Cupid assures him that he will have exceptional and divine inspiration. The theme of the poet's vocation enters the work, a theme that will recur, especially in the second book, as a gift that love bestows upon the poet but also as a form of immortality with which that poet promises to reward his beloved if she will share his passion.

Just as Cupid's visit drew Ronsard into the classical tradition of poetry, Hélène's beauty links her to classical goddesses. "Deux Venus en avril, puissante Deité" (Two Venuses in April, powerful goddess) compares two figures of Venus, one from Cyprus and the other from the Saintonge region of southwestern France where Hélène was born. Ronsard describes both as born in April but finds the French Venus to be truer than the "Greek lie" that can no longer equal her. He feels fortunate to live at the time of his true Venus, even though she has imprisoned his spirit as one might catch a fish.

Many devices throughout the poems vary the similarities and contrasts that depict the richness of love. Just as the haughty figure of Venus may trap her admirer with an everyday image of fishing, parallel structures bracket opposing feelings. "Tant de fois s'appointer, tant de fois se fascher" (So often drawn to each other, so often angry with each other) lists the stark contrasts of lovers' emotions. They break up only to reconcile, blame love but then praise it, flee each other but then seek each other again. Each of these pairings contained in a single poetic line echoes the frenzied activities leading nowhere from which the lover seems incapable of escape. Thus Ronsard concludes with a wry paradox that inconstancy becomes the sign of constant love.

Toward the end of the first volume, however, Ronsard worries that, even though his love for Hélène persists, she is turning away from him. In "Ma fiéve croist tousjours, la vostre diminue" (My fever still grows, yours diminishes) Ronsard underlines this contrast and continues his use of parallelism when he writes that Hélène "remains cold leaving the heat" to him. Passion is still portrayed in physical terms and the lovers are still linked by parallel language, but the emotions now reflect their separation. Now Cupid takes on the role of fate. Ronsard says that he can never free himself from Hélène's domination because Cupid's arrows have engraved her portrait on his heart.

The final sonnet of the first book, "Si j'ay bien ou mal dit en ces Sonnets, Madame" (If I have spoken well or poorly in these sonnets, my lady), abandons the idea of abstract fate to say that neither it nor Ronsard can be fully responsible for the love his poetry has expressed. Hélène has been his inspiration, and his voice becomes mournful or joyful as she rejects or accepts his love. Ronsard concludes with an image unusual for an author to whom poetic creativity was so important. He is, he says, like a mirror that "always represents what is shown in front of it." This may be true, of course, in the alternations of happy and sad love, without denying the importance of the poet's artistic skill.

The poet's special vocation gains importance in the second book. The opening sonnet, "Soit qu'un sage amoureux ou soit qu'un sot me lise" (Whether a wise lover or a foolish one reads me), links it to Ronsard's preoccupation with his advanced age. The reader, he says, may be astonished by the passion that remains beneath his gray hair as a spark remains under ashes. He notes, however, that dry wood burns more readily than that which is too young and green. Still, Ronsard cautions that he must avoid being like Icarus or Phaeton, two classical figures linked to inappropriate and unsuccessful attempts to rise to heaven.

Images of death multiply as Ronsard expresses fears of his own advancing years and of the possible end of his love. After a sonnet depicting Hélène surrounded by the gaiety of carnival, "N'oubliez, mon Hélène, aujourd'huy qu'il faut prendre" (Don't forget, my Hélène, that today one must take) focuses on Ash Wednesday, a day when she should make atonement for having killed him with her eyes. Amid despair, positive images always offer new hope for happiness. In "Laisse de Pharaon la terre Egyptienne" (Leave the Egyptian land of Pharoah) Ronsard returns to a classical analogy to suggest that they leave Egypt, a land emblematic of the life of the Court, to take refuge in the more bucolic lands on the banks of the Jordan where "I will be your Orpheus, and you my Euridice."

The invocation of Orpheus, whose musical skills offered him the possibility of saving Euridice from hell, leads to what is probably Ronsard's most famous sonnet, "Quand vous serez bien vieille, au soir à la chandelle" (When you are very old, in the evening by candle light). This poem, on which William Butler Yeats (1865-1939) based his adaptation "When You are Old" (1892), combines the ideas of age and death with those of immortality and the power of both love and poetry. Here not only Ronsard but Hélène herself becomes old. Even though he may be long dead, we see Ronsard flourishing in a classical paradise among myrtle bushes while Hélène remains an "old woman stooped" by the fireside. The reversal underlines the importance of their roles, for it is through Ronsard that both will attain immortality. At this future time, both will be remembered because of the beauty of Ronsard's art.

The graceful moral Ronsard attaches to this poem leaves intact Hélène's superiority. In the usual tone of the Renaissance *carpe diem*, he urges her to love him in the present lest she be sad in the future that she has not taken advantage of this possibility. The poet retains the capacity to create immortality but, because of his deference to the woman he loves, he lays his talent at her disposal and allows her to control their actual fate. This appropriately sums up Ronsard's diverse sonnets for Hélène. He has offered her the varied aspects of love, from the physical suffering through the immortality of lovers, and allows her to accept what she will in accepting him.

Dorothy M. Betz

Bibliography:

Bishop, Morris. *Ronsard: Prince of Poets*. Ann Arbor: University of Michigan Press, 1959. A general biography of Ronsard. Chapter 12, "Hélène," gives a detailed description of Hélène de Surgères, the circumstances in which Ronsard met her, and the surrounding atmosphere of court intrigues. Includes limited references to the sonnets.

Cave, Terence, ed. *Ronsard the Poet*. London: Methuen, 1973. Contains eight essays by various authors presenting a largely thematic approach to Ronsard's work. In chapter 2, Grahame Castor discusses Petrarchism and the quest for beauty in the *Sonnets pour Hélène*." Chapter 7, by Odette de Mourgues, on Ronsard's later poetry contains references to Hélène, and an index directs the reader to references in other essays.

Jones, K. R. W. *Pierre de Ronsard*. New York: Twayne, 1970. This standard life-and-work volume discusses Hélène chiefly in chapter 9, "Ronsard's Private World."

Lewis, D. B. Wyndham. *Ronsard*. New York: Sheed and Ward, 1944. Chapter 9, "Hélène," begins with a description of Hélène as Ronsard saw her. A subsequent analysis takes a thematic approach and quotes extensively from the sonnets.

Ronsard, Pierre de. *Sonnets for Helen*. Translated by Humbert Wolfe. London: Allen and Unwin, 1972. This edition provides both English and French texts for a majority of the sonnets. An introductory essay details the circumstances in which the poems were written and their importance to Ronsard's literary reputation.

SONNETS FROM THE PORTUGUESE

Type of work: Poetry
Author: Elizabeth Barrett Browning (1806-1861)
First published: 1850

Whenever English love poetry is discussed, almost invariably the opening of Elizabeth Barrett Browning's penultimate poem of *Sonnets from the Portuguese* is quoted: "How do I love thee? Let me count the ways." The collection represents, variously, depending on the quoter's prejudice, a gem of lyrical eloquence, an oversentimental extravagance, or a tired cliché. Browning's masterpiece, *Sonnets from the Portuguese* went through a complete cycle of literary reception, first being overpraised as "the noblest [sonnets] ever written," then undervalued as overly emotional effusions, and eventually accepted as a major work. Despite minor cavils, Elizabeth Barrett Browning's *Sonnets from the Portuguese* seem assured a permanent reputation as one of the foremost collections of love poetry in the English language.

The recurring criticism of sentimentalism has some validity, but the charge may be met on several grounds. Elizabeth Barrett wrote *Sonnets from the Portuguese* during her passionate courtship with Robert Browning. They record the emotions of that time, and emotions are not always "recollected in tranquility" as William Wordsworth suggested poetry should be. Moreover, the poet never intended them for publication. Then, too, she was writing in a culture whose strictures against poetic display of emotion were less narrow than those of later times; indeed, compared to the other popular love lyrics of her time, *Sonnets from the Portuguese* are less sentimental, as an 1860 review in *The Southern Literary Messenger* attests. Finally, the sonnets were written by a poet to a poet, which makes them unique among love sonnets and allowed for a freedom of emotional language that could be relied upon to be understood.

Browning did not, however, show the poems to her husband until three years after their marriage. When she did, he insisted that she publish the sonnets, which he reportedly deemed the best since William Shakespeare's, in her 1850 volume of collected poems. He suggested the title "Sonnets from the Portuguese" to disguise the work as a translation. Neither of the Brownings believed that it would be in good taste to publicize their private relationship. Robert had admired Elizabeth's early poem "Catarina to Camoëns," which suggested the title, since Luis Vaz de Camoëns was a Portuguese poet.

Although individual sonnets had been written in English since their vogue in the 1590's (except for a 150-year hiatus between the sonnets of John Milton and those of Wordsworth), Browning's *Sonnets from the Portuguese* represented the first true sonnet sequence in English since the Elizabethans. Since Shakespeare's time, sonnets in English had tended to follow the pattern established by Shakespeare's sonnets: three sets of four lines (*quatrains*) concluding with a couplet. The sonnets Elizabeth Barrett wrote before *Sonnets from the Portuguese* followed this Shakespearean or "English" sonnet form. In her sonnet sequence, however, she followed the much more demanding Petrarchan or Italian form, where the first two quatrains share rhyme pairs and form a single unit (the *octave*) that rhymes *abba abba*. The remaining six lines, instead of breaking into quatrain and couplet, are similarly unified; the Italian form allows many variations, but the scheme Elizabeth Barrett settled on was invariably *cdcdcd*. This means that in the entire fourteen lines of each sonnet there are only four rhyme sounds, an unparalleled economy of rhyme.

The opening sonnet of the sequence introduces the biographical element that has always been at least part of the attraction of these love sonnets. In 1845, as she wrote these lines, Elizabeth

Barrett was nearing forty, still living with a domineering father who had forbidden her to marry but encouraged her writing and scholarship. The "antique tongue" represents the ancient Greek in which she was fluent and from which she had translated many classical works. A childhood accident had left her an invalid and doubtful of her prospects for marriage even if her father's ban had been lifted. No wonder, then, that a meditation on her "wished for years" were not just "sweet," like those of the Greek pastoral poet Theocritus (third century B.C.E.) but "sweet, sad" and "melancholy," and "had flung/ A shadow across" the poet.

In the early poems of the sequence, this ambivalence of emotion is traced through the speaker's expectation of Death rather than Love and through skepticism about love. In fact, "Love," the last word of the opening sonnet, comes as a surprise to the speaker just as it surprised Elizabeth Barrett when Robert Browning proposed to her in the summer of 1845. In the second sonnet, the speaker protests that to accept the gentleman's proposal would be to go against God's will. In the third, the objection is to the many differences between them (a letter to Robert Browning, dated March 20, 1845, strikes the same theme), and again the last lines refer to Death as her only expectation: "The chrism is on thine head,—on mine the dew,—/ And Death must dig the level where these agree." Robert Browning was a young poet, six years younger than Elizabeth Barrett, and full of vitality. Miss Barrett saw herself as an aging poet, resigned to death and to the idea of living alone. The earliest sonnets of the sequence reflect this harsh perception of reality; they are far from being idealizations of love.

In sonnet 4, the poet evokes the image of solitude that she saw as her fate. Depicting her suitor as a medieval troubadour, she urges him to sing at a balcony less run-down and deserted, images of the isolation brought on by her injury and consequent opium addiction. She continues to ask the suitor to leave for his own good: If he is staying merely to stamp out the "red wild sparkles" of her grief, she says in sonnet 5, he had better beware that they do not burst into flame. Sonnet 6, one of her most anthologized poems, begins with the same theme, "Go from me," and is no less insistent, yet she is clearly beginning to feel, not a softening of her conviction that the love is wrong, but a resignation to the inevitability of the suitor's presence in her life. "Yet I feel that I shall stand/ Henceforth in thy shadow." The image of solitude in sonnet 4 dissolves into the two-in-one paradox of love: "Nevermore/ Alone," "pulses that beat double," "within my eyes, the tears of two." Sonnet 6 is a major transition in the sequence, the first to acknowledge the change in her life.

That change is the focus of sonnet 7, which opens "The face of all the world is changed." The speaker does not deny the earlier vision of Death but merely presents the suitor's figure as standing between her and death (now lowercased). The suitor has changed her expectations from "obvious death" to life with a vital young man. That poses a problem, however, in the next five sonnets, 8 to 12. In giving her life, the suitor has given her more than she can ever return, "For frequent tears have run/ the colours from my life" (8), leaving her nothing to offer him. She does not quite return to the plea for the lover to go—she has known since sonnet 6 that he is in her heart to stay—but she tells him to "Go farther" than using her life as a pillow for his head; he is to "let it serve to trample on," the total self-giving of love. Yet this image also suggests that lack of self-esteem that is the bane of love. This continues in sonnet 9, where the poet emphasizes the disparity in the exchange of "gifts," but in sonnet 10 the speaker comes to realize that love itself is "beautiful indeed/ And worthy of acceptation" and she can finally say *"I love thee!"* with confidence. "I am not all unworthy" she observes in sonnet 11; "Indeed, this very love," claims the next sonnet, "Doth crown me with a ruby."

Sonnet 14, a justly famous poem, examines the psychology of love, and warns against the danger of focusing love on any one quality of the beloved: "If thou must love me"—even beginning with that "if" reveals how tentative her approach is to this unlooked-for situation—"let it be for nought but love's sake only." Sonnets 13 and 15 respond to the suitor's apparent concern over the fact that she does not put her love into words; sonnet 21 reminds her wordier lover "To love me also in silence, with thy soul."

As the sequence progresses, the speaker grows more confident in her love, yet she is aware of the dangers of idealizing love. In sonnet 22 she imagines her soul "erect and strong" with her lover's and contrasts that with her bed-ridden body; yet she ends the poem preferring earthly love. "The world's sharpness," which before had threatened her, is now more like "a clasping knife" closing harmlessly (sonnet 14). Love is now "as strong as Death" (sonnet 27). There are occasional moments of tears still (sonnet 30); for love does not mean an end to sadness. She is now confident enough to ask him to call her pet names (sonnet 33), and their love is now established enough for her to look back with wonder at its beginning (sonnet 32) and their first kiss (sonnet 38).

The series concludes with three sonnets of hopeful anticipation of life with the beloved: "My future will not copy fair my past" (sonnet 17, originally published separately). The metaphors of a "fair copy" of a manuscript, an impeccable final draft that corrects the false starts and errors of the first, is proper to a poet. Instead of fixing the past, she looks for a new future. Sonnet 48 is the famous "How do I love thee?" As critic William Going first pointed out in 1953, the poem is abstract and enumerative. Its intention is to conclude and summarize the whole sequence, and each of the eight ways of loving echoes a previous sonnet. Though long beloved as an individual sonnet, it gains even more luster as the capstone of the entire series.

John R. Holmes

Bibliography:

Burdett, Osbert. *The Brownings*. New York: Houghton Mifflin, 1936. Though dated, and consequently containing conclusions and facts that have since proven false, this biography contains one of the most readable treatments of the *Sonnets from the Portuguese*, detailing the development of the Brownings' love through a reading of the poems.

Cooper, Helen. *Elizabeth Barrett Browning, Woman and Artist*. Chapel Hill: University of North Carolina Press, 1988. An excellent study of Browning's poetics, relating them to the conflicting roles of women in the Victorian era.

Hayter, Alethea. *Mrs. Browning: A Poet's Work and Its Setting*. London: Faber and Faber, 1962. Though she does not think the *Sonnets from the Portuguese* Browning's best work, Hayter's detailed analyses of them are a good companion to the sequence. Her basic criticism is that the sonnets were written too close to the emotional events of her courtship and lack the objective distance needed for great art.

Lupton, Mary Jane. *Elizabeth Barrett Browning*. Long Island, N.Y.: The Feminist Press, 1972. A general study of Browning combining criticism and biography, this book includes a generous section on the *Sonnets from the Portuguese*, which emphasizes the unusualness in 1850 of Browning's feminine point of view in love sonnets yet notes the irony of that point of view expressing dependence and weakness.

Radley, Virginia L. *Elizabeth Barrett Browning*. New York: Twayne, 1972. A good starting point for the study of Browning, this volume opens with a brief biography and goes on to analyze Browning's works. The chapter on the *Sonnets from the Portuguese* gives background on their composition, analyzes them sequentially, and relates them to the Brownings' love letters.

THE SONNETS OF SHAKESPEARE

Type of work: Poetry
Author: William Shakespeare (1564-1616)
First published: Sonnets, 1609

Although William Shakespeare's sonnets are generally considered to be among the most beautiful and most powerful poems in English literature, the attention of readers and scholars has more often centered on their possible biographical significance than on the literary qualities that give them their greatness. So little is known of the inner life of the poet, so little that helps to explain his genius, that it is not surprising to find critics minutely examining these lyrics that seem to reveal something of Shakespeare the man.

The sonnet sequence was one of the most popular poetic forms in the early 1590's; modeled originally on works by Dante Alighieri and Petrarch, the genre was developed in sixteenth century France and Italy and quickly reached England. Sir Philip Sidney's *Astrophil and Stella* (1591), written a few years before the poet's death in 1586, is a demonstration of how quickly the sonnet cycle achieved excellence in English. Edmund Spenser, Samuel Daniel, Michael Drayton, and many other well-known Elizabethan men of letters followed Sidney's example, paying tribute to the idealized ladies who inspired their almost religious devotion.

Shakespeare's poems, probably composed at intervals during the decade between 1590 and 1600, differ radically from the sonnets of his contemporaries in several ways. They are not based on the traditional Petrarchan theme of a proud, virtuous lady and an abject, scorned lover, and there is in them relatively little of the platonic idealism that fills works like Spenser's *Amoretti* (1595), in which the poet's love for his lady lifts him above human weakness to contemplation of the divine. Shakespeare records a strangely ambiguous, tortured affection for a young nobleman; the emotions he expresses in his sonnets have a depth and complexity, an intensity, that can be encountered elsewhere only in the speeches of some of his greatest dramatic creations.

The narrative of Shakespeare's sequence is exceedingly sketchy. Scholars have, in fact, rearranged the poems many times in an attempt to produce a more coherent "plot" than appeared in the volume published, without the author's supervision, in 1609. It seems likely that the work as it now stands contains at least a few poems that were written as independent pieces, sonnets on popular Renaissance themes which have no real bearing on the subject of the sequence itself.

Three shadowy figures move through the reflections of the poet as he speaks in his sonnets. The most important is the "fair youth," the young nobleman. The fervor of the language with which Shakespeare speaks of his feelings for the youth has led to considerable discussion of the precise nature of the relationship. It must be remembered that the Renaissance regarded the friendship of man and man as the highest form of human affection, for within this relationship there could be complete spiritual and intellectual communication, unmarred by erotic entanglements.

The nobleman is initially idealized in much the same way that most poets envisioned their ladies, as the embodiment of beauty and virtue. Unlike the typical lady of more conventional sonnets, however, he proves to be false and deceptive, shifting his attention to a rival poet, whose identity has been the subject of much speculation. The sequence records the narrator-poet's despair at this betrayal and at the nobleman's affair with the "dark lady," the poet's mistress, who is, in a sense, his evil genius. It is not the loss of the lady he regrets, for he knows her character all too well, but the fact that his friend has yielded to her corruption. Throughout the sonnets the reader feels the poet's agonized sense that there is nothing lastingly beautiful or virtuous.

While it is customary to speak of the "I" of the sonnets as Shakespeare, it is dangerously misleading to overlook the possibility that these poems are dramatic, that "I" is as vividly conceived a creature of Shakespeare's mind as Hamlet, and that the poet is projecting himself into an imagined situation rather than describing a personal experience. Whether the speaker of the sonnets is Shakespeare or not, it does not alter the essential value of the poems themselves.

The greatness of the sonnets lies in their intellectual and emotional power, in Shakespeare's ability to find exactly the right images to convey a particular idea or feeling and in his magnificent gift for shaping the diction and rhythms of ordinary human speech into expressions of the subtlest and deepest human perceptions. He also developed his own sonnet form, the Shakespearian sonnet form, with which Thomas Wyatt and Henry Howard Surrey had experimented earlier in the century. Almost all of Shakespeare's sonnets are divided into three quatrains, each with alternately rhyming lines, followed by a concluding couplet. This form is technically less complex than the Italian pattern, in which the first eight lines are built around two rhymes, rather than four. The technical requirements of the two forms determine to a degree their organization. The Italian sonnet generally breaks down into two sections, with the statement of a problem in the octave and its solution in the sestet, while the form used by Shakespeare lends itself to a tripartite exposition followed by a brief conclusion in the couplet. Shakespeare was, however, capable of varying his development of his subject in many different ways; a thought may run through twelve lines with a surprise conclusion or shift of emphasis in the couplet; it may break into the eight-line, six-line division of the Italian sonnet; or it may follow one of many other patterns.

The organization of the sequence seems somewhat haphazard. Within it are several groups of poems that clearly belong together, but they do not form an entirely satisfying narrative. Shakespeare uses his half-untold story as a basis for poems upon many familiar Renaissance themes: love, time, mutability, the conflict of body and soul, passion and reason. The first eighteen poems, all addressed to the nobleman, are variations on the theme of the transience of youth and beauty and the need for the youth to marry and beget children in order to preserve his virtues of face and mind in them. Shakespeare draws upon nature for images to convey his sense of the destruction that awaits all beauty, referring to "the violet past prime," "winter's ragged hand," "summer's green all girded up in sheaves." Youth becomes more precious and the preservation of beauty more important still when the poet considers that "everything that grows holds in perfection but a little moment."

Shakespeare's sense of the ravages of time leads him to a second important theme: Poetry, as well as heirs, can confer immortality. Sonnet 18 is one of the most beautiful and clearest expressions of this idea:

> Shall I compare thee to a summer's day?
> Thou are more lovely and more temperate:
> Rough winds do shake the darling buds of May,
> And summer's lease hath all too short a date;
> Sometime too hot the eye of heaven shines,
> And often is his gold complexion dimm'd;
> And every fair from fair sometime declines,
> By chance, or nature's changing course, untrimm'd:
> But thy eternal summer shall not fade
> Nor lose possession of that fair thou ow'st;

Nor shall Death brag thou wander'st in his shade,
When in eternal lines to time thou grow'st;
So long as men can breathe or eyes can see,
So long lives this, and this gives life to thee.

The same idea forms the basis for another well-known sonnet, "Not marble nor the gilded monuments of princes," in which Shakespeare affirms the power of his verse to withstand the assaults of war, fire, and death. The sonnets making up the middle of the sequence deal with many aspects of the poet's feeling for the nobleman. Their tone is almost universally melancholy; the haunting language and clear visual images of Sonnet 73 make it perhaps the finest expression of this dominant mood:

That time of year thou mayst in me behold
When yellow leaves, or none, or few, do hang
Upon those boughs which shake against the cold,
Bare [ruin'd] choirs where late the sweet birds sang.
In me thou see'st the twilight of such day
As after sunset fadeth in the west,
Which by and by black night doth take away,
Death's second self, that seals up all in rest.
In me thou see'st the glowing of such fire
That on the ashes of his youth doth lie,
As the death-bed whereon it must expire,
Consum'd with that which it was nourish'd by.
This thou perceiv'st, which makes thy love more strong,
To love that well which thou must leave ere long.

The speaker pictures himself as a man aging, unworthy, despairing. Initially his friendship with the young nobleman provides his one comfort against the frustrations of his worldly state. At those moments, as in Sonnet 29, when he is most wretched:

Haply I think on thee; and then my state,
Like to the lark at break of day arising
From sullen earth, sings hymns at heaven's gate.
For thy sweet love remember'd such wealth brings
That then I scorn to change my state with kings.

A brilliantly conceived image, in Sonnet 33, communicates the impact of the poet's loss of confidence in the youth when the youth turns to the rival poet:

Full many a glorious morning have I seen
Flatter the mountain tops with sovereign eye,
Kissing with golden face the meadows green,
Gilding pale streams with heavenly alchemy;
Anon permit the basest clouds to ride
With ugly rack on his celestial face,
And from the forlorn world his visage hide,
Stealing unseen to west with this disgrace:
Even so my son one early morn did shine
With all triumphant splendour on my brow;

> But out, alack! he was but one hour mine,
> The region cloud hath mask'd him from me now.
> Yet him for this my love no whit disdaineth;
> Suns of the world may stain when heaven's sun staineth.

Many of the poems show the poet's attempts to accept the faithlessness, the fall from virtue, of the youth. While his betrayal cannot destroy the poet's affection ("Love is not love which alters when it alteration finds"), it represents the decay of all good, leaving the speaker filled with despair.

There are, toward the end of the sequence, approximately thirty poems addressed to or speaking of the "dark lady." The lighter of these lyrics are witty commentaries on her brunette beauty—in the sonnet tradition, the lady is fair:

> Thine eyes I love, and they as pitying me,
> Knowing thy heart torment me with disdain,
> Have put on black, and loving mourners be,
> Looking with pretty ruth upon my pain.

The overworked Petrarchan metaphors about the charms of the sonneteer's mistress are parodied in another well-known poem:

> My mistress' eyes are nothing like the sun;
> Coral is far more red than her lips' red;
> If snow be white, why then her breasts are dun;
> If hairs be wires, black wires grow on her head.

Surrounding these relatively happy pieces are verses revealing the pain and conflict in the relationship between the poet and the lady. He knows that his feeling for her is primarily lustful and destructive; yet, as he says in Sonnet 129, he cannot free himself from her: "All this the world well knows; yet none knows well/ To shun the heaven that leads men to this hell."

Irony pervades the sonnets in which Shakespeare declares his full knowledge of her vices and her deceptions both of her husband and of him: "When my love swears that she is made of truth,/ I do believe her, though I know she lies."

The poet's conflict is intensified by the lady's affair with the nobleman, and he tries to explain his reaction in the little morality play of Sonnet 144:

> Two loves I have of comfort and despair,
> Which like two spirits do suggest me still:
> The better angel is a man right fair,
> The worser spirit a woman colour'd ill.
> To win me soon to hell, my female evil
> Tempteth my better angel from my [side],
> And would corrupt my saint to be a devil,
> Wooing his purity with her foul pride.
> And whether that my angel be turn'd fiend,
> Suspect I may, yet not directly tell;
> But being both from me, both to each friend,
> I guess one angel in another's hell.
> Yet this shall I ne'er know, but live in doubt,
> Till my bad angel fire my good one out.

The tremendous appeal of Shakespeare's sonnets through the centuries rests essentially on the same qualities that have made his plays immortal, his phenomenal understanding of the workings of the mind and his incredible ability to distill many aspects of human experience into a few lines. The sonnets are, in many ways, dramatic poetry; the reader is constantly aware of the presence of the poet, the "I" of the sequence, who addresses the nobleman and the dark lady forcefully and directly, not as if he were musing in his study. A brief perusal of the opening lines of the sonnets shows a remarkable number of questions and commands that heighten the reader's sense of a dramatic situation:

> That thou hast her, it is not all my grief,
> And yet it may be said I lov'd her dearly . . .
> Being your slave, what should I do but tend
> Upon the hours and times of your desire?
> Farewell! thou art too dear for my possessing,
> And like enough thou know'st thy estimate.

The compression of language; the vivid images drawn from nature, commerce, the theater, and many other aspects of life; the wordplay; and the flexibility of rhythms of speech that characterize Shakespeare's blank verse—all contribute to the greatness of the sonnets as well. In these poems, as in his plays, he was able to transform traditional forms and raise them to new heights.

Bibliography:

Crossman, Robert. "Making Love out of Nothing at All: The Issue of Story in Shakespeare's Procreation Sonnets." *Shakespeare Quarterly* 41, no. 4 (Winter, 1990): 470-488. Argues that a consistent story line unifies many of the sonnets, focusing especially on Sonnets 1 through 17. In this group, Crossman traces the progress of the sonnet speaker's friendship and warm affection for a fair young man.

Green, Martin. *Wriothesley's Roses: In Shakespeare's Sonnets, Poems, and Plays*. Baltimore: Clevendon Books, 1993. Links historical records with poetic context in various sonnets in an interesting attempt to establish the identities of Shakespeare's fair young man and of the rival poet who seems to compete with Shakespeare's speaker for the affections of the Dark Lady. Provides a good historical background.

Landry, Hilton. *Interpretation in Shakespeare's Sonnets*. Berkeley: University of California Press, 1963. Despite numerous more recent studies, this book remains an excellent introduction to the thematic analysis and interpretation of Shakespeare's sonnets.

Ramsey, Paul. *The Fickle Glass: A Study of Shakespeare's Sonnets*. New York: AMS Press, 1979. A clearly written scholarly examination of critical problems, poetic techniques, and meaning in the sonnets. Explores questions of authorship, order, and date of composition. Excellent discussion of metrical rules and Elizabethan rhetoric in the sonnets.

Smith, Hallet. *The Tension of the Lyre: Poetry in Shakespeare's Sonnets*. San Marino, Calif.: Huntington Library, 1981. General discussion of the sonnets, beginning with an exploration of poetic voice and audience, and including an overview of Shakespeare's world as it is reflected in the sonnets.

Weiser, David K. *Mind in Character: Shakespeare's Speaker in the Sonnets*. Columbia: University of Missouri Press, 1987. Thorough explication of the sonnets. Useful appendix classifies the sonnets by modes of address.

SONNETS TO ORPHEUS

Type of work: Poetry
Author: Rainer Maria Rilke (1875-1926)
First published: Die Sonette an Orpheus, 1923 (English translation, 1936)

Rainer Maria Rilke, one of the great lyric poets of the twentieth century, wrote *Sonnets to Orpheus* in memory of Vera Ouckama Knoop, the nineteen-year-old daughter of a Dutch friend. When she was about seventeen, the girl was stricken with an incurable glandular disease. As her body became heavier and more massive, she stopped dancing and began to play music, and when her body became still heavier, she began to draw. Although Rilke barely knew the girl, he was touched by her story and shaken by the news of her death. At the time *Sonnets to Orpheus* were written, Rilke was staying at a château in Muzot, Switzerland, where he took refuge during several periods in his life after World War I and where he found the solitude he needed to work. It was here that in 1923 Rilke, in a burst of creative genius unlike any that he had ever before experienced, completed *Duino Elegies* and *Sonnets to Orpheus* (a complement to the *Duino Elegies*).

In Greek mythology, Orpheus, the son of Apollo, was the master magician, able to animate nature with his song. When his wife Eurydice died, he obtained her release from the underworld on the condition that he would not look at her until they reached the upper world, but he could not resist glancing back at her at the last moment. Legend had it that he was subsequently dismembered by Thracian women and scattered throughout the universe until all of nature became his song. This introduced a second phase, during which Orpheus became the religious center of a Dionysian sect (Dionysus was the god of uninhibited desire, vegetation, and wine) and presided in his magical divinity over the ancient religious mysteries of Greece. *Sonnets to Orpheus* incorporates this second, magical, aspect of the god.

Rilke's Orpheus symbol is the culmination of a number of themes and motifs dating back to the poet's earliest writing, which coalesce into the figure of the singing god who redeems out of time into space. His function links him with *Duino Elegies* through the principle of transformation. Orpheus is also equated with the poet, and by alluding to his special role as a singer of both realms, Rilke reiterates the need to unite life and death through song and praise. Orpheus has literally sung among the dead. The mortal poet is to do the same.

The two main attributes of the Orpheus symbol are openness toward all experience—a fullness that includes both life and death—to an extent that Rilke refers to as an "overflowing"; and the ordering or forming of this experience through music, that is, art or poetry. The elevation of music as the final court of appeal, after suffering, love, and death have individually failed to reveal their secret, is declared in sonnet 1.

Sonnets to Orpheus speaks of "we," "you," and "I" interchangeably and is thus directed toward no particular person but to humanity in general (the exceptions are the two Vera Knoop sonnets and the one addressed to a friend of Vera). Rilke maintains a certain distance by the sparing use of the first-person pronoun. Although the poems cannot be arranged in any unified metrical scheme, Rilke adheres to a thoroughly symmetrical sonnet composition, with divisions into quatrains and tercets; the individual metrics are flexibly varied. He seems to have set himself the challenge of modifying the sonnet form while at the same time not destroying it altogether.

A kind of metaphorical primitivism may account for the simplicity, grammatical and otherwise, of most of *Sonnets to Orpheus*. In Rilke's later poetry, words are used as signs, and images become "points" or "cosmic configurations." Only in such a pattern, endorsed by Orpheus, can the totality of forms be preserved, a totality no longer viewed in isolation but adapted to the requirements of a universal myth.

Both part 1, which consists of twenty-six sonnets, and part 2, with its twenty-nine sonnets, form a cycle. Rather than forming thematic or chronological groups, the poems may be loosely characterized the Orpheus sonnets, sonnets incorporating poetic memories, and sonnets of a didactic, reflective nature. Twelve poems (all but one in part 1) deal with the Orphic legend. Sonnets, 1, 7, and 26 in part 1 contain the main elements of the Orpheus theme, which opens the series and, as the circle widens to include other motifs, gradually disappears, to resurface finally in part 2, sonnet 26. The initial sonnet of part 1 is pure myth making: At the beginning of the world (or of the poet's art consciousness) stands Orpheus, whose music instills life into trees and stones, breaking down the rigid forms of nature and lending them new rhythms and dimensions. As the archetypal poet, Orpheus does not sing about a tree, he sings a tree, and as he sings the visible ascends into invisibility, while a temple to receive it rises in the ear. Here, as elsewhere, Rilke interchanges acoustic and visual imagery.

The functions of Orpheus in relation to the poet's world are expressed in part 1 in the key sonnet 7. Orpheus is the poet's surrogate, alone able to cross the threshold and, by virtue of his adherence to both the realms of the living and the dead, to praise the things of earth before the dead. In fact, the poet identifies himself with his symbol and they unite. The creative process operates within the paradox of silence and song, perishable and imperishable. It is visualized in the landscape and in the warm vineyards of the south, for whose infinite wine the poet's heart is the perishable wine press.

Praise is only one function of Orpheus' song; the chord of lamentation is its complement. In sonnet 8 in part 1, lamentation is personified and acted out. Sorrow is the youngest sister of Rejoicing, who knows, and Longing, who confesses. Sorrow is still young enough to learn from grief-stricken nights and yet, in abrupt reversal and by virtue of that very experience, is able to represent mortality among the constellations.

Part 1 further defines the Orphic double nature with the aid of nature symbols. In the second quartet of sonnet 6, Rilke draws effectively on folklore and superstitions about the spirits of the dead. To these primitive superstitions, Rilke opposes the gentle knowledge and memory of the dead. Only those who have eaten poppies with the dead (sonnet 9) can register the full scale of Orphic praise. Sonnet 3 contrasts the divine art of the god with human inadequacy resulting from humanity's divided nature. The phrase "Song is being" balances non-Being, humanity's unrelatedness to earth and stars. After the antithesis, the real definition of poetry, its stability and inevitability, provides the final lines. That leads logically to sonnet 4, which introduces the theme of the lovers to whom the Orphic attributes are applied.

Once Rilke has established the basic Orphic myth, about twenty-eight sonnets incorporating poetic memories explore the varied material of the poet's artistic world. Roses, mirrors, dancings, and breathings are transformed into legend. The greatness of Rilke's best poetry lies in the fact that each individual subject or theme, although seeming to possess only aesthetic implications, offers insight. The underlying tensions in Rilke's poetry are between art and life, permanence and change, the formed and the formless. His problem is essentially linguistic rather than metaphysical, and it is to be solved by the transformation of the idea through language. The work's Orphic music is the very element calculated to activate inert space, for it is dynamic. In the "dancer" sonnet in part 2, Rilke fuses the dancer and the dance, the transient motion and the permanent form. The dance actually grows, step by step, out of the functions of language. Rilke perpetuates the movement of the final whirl by projecting the dancer into art forms.

The third type of Rilke's *Sonnets to Orpheus*, the didactic, reflective ones, are among his best. In them, the Orphic lyre conjures up the problems of a machine age and the metaphysical problems of time and eternity, God, and the possibilities of regeneration. Time is present in all of Rilke's poetry, and this is particularly true of these sonnets. Time enters into the unfolding of the machine motif, into the conception of historical and cultural evolution—those "splendid excesses of our own existence"—and into modes of belief. The genetic evolution of human beings, who create their own gods that fate destroys, is a hopeful projection, for eternity still lies before them. This is the timeless Orphic realm of spatial fullness.

Six sonnets deal directly with the role of the machine in the modern age, in the context of aimless motion versus contained repose. In Rilke's view, technology has its function as a means but not as an end. Many sonnets deal negatively with the acoustic unpleasantness of a mechanistic age, the "droning and drumming" of machines. The spiritual impasse invoked by the machine is described in sonnet 24 of part 1, in which humanity has lost the "primeval friends of ours, the unfated,/ ever unsuing gods."

Escape from time, the destroyer, is possible through transformation in Orpheus. Some of Rilke's finest sonnets are concerned with this theme, but none so profoundly as the final ones of part 2, which make up a small cycle of their own. Sonnet 12 urges the readers to be prepared for transformation, like a flame altering all things that slip from their grasp. The theme ends in a mythological figure: Daphne in laurel can only desire that her lover transform himself into the wind that blows through her leaves. Two sonnets describe the inner landscape of transformation, the summer dream world with continuously watered gardens. These gardens of oriental profusion have symbolic reality for those who, with Orpheus, have advanced into another dimension of experience.

Sonnet 13 in part 2 is also concerned with the transformation theme. It is didactic and contains at least six categorical commands to the reader. The full scope of the transformation process is contained in the first verse, its stoic implications in verses 2 and 5: To anticipate departure is to be ever ready for the transformation into new forms. Whatever ultimate moment of experience this may mean, readers are to look forward to it as they look backward at the winter, "almost gone." The poet then moves from the human to the mythical plane in the command to be "ever dead in Eurydice." The poet-god may overcome love that has vanished into the shades by transforming it into art. The conquest of loss restores the individual or the artist to the pure relationship that encloses that more adequate and inviolate world people create in themselves. This world is a declining one, and the realization and full acceptance of this fact is the highest possible accomplishment. Submission to this twofold act of Being and at the same time non-Being, of life and death, raises human beings above themselves, completing the spiral of life. Thus time and destiny can be overcome, and the circle of fullness can be completed.

Beyond exemplifying brilliant structure and innovative use of tradition, *Sonnets to Orpheus* brings the physical and the spiritual together and interchanges their qualities and meanings. The marriage of human being and god, and of concrete and abstract, grief and celebration, changelessness and change, makes reading *Sonnets to Orpheus* a challenging and uplifting experience.

Genevieve Slomski

Bibliography:

Holthusen, Hans Egon. *Rainer Maria Rilke: A Study of His Later Poetry*. New Haven, Conn.: Yale University Press, 1952. Dated but insightful analysis of Rilke's esoteric later poetry, including *Duino Elegies* and *Sonnets to Orpheus*. Contains biographical information.

Mandel, Siegfried. *Rainer Maria Rilke: The Poetic Instinct*. Carbondale: Southern Illinois University Press, 1965. Reflects a thorough knowledge of Rilke's craftsmanship and discusses the deeper reality expressed in his works. Contains a bibliography.

Peters, H. F. *Rainer Maria Rilke: Masks and the Man*. Seattle: University of Washington Press, 1960. Shows Rilke's impact on modern poetry and concludes that the poet consciously tried to express the human predicament of his age by creating new forms, styles, and myths. Contains a chronology of the author's life.

Pollock-Brodsky, Patricia. *Rainer Maria Rilke*. Boston: Twayne, 1988. Excellent introductory analysis to the poet's life and work. Focuses on Rilke's sensitivity to art, his position as a cosmopolitan within the international culture of Europe at the turn of the century, and the contradictory nature of many aspects of his work and life.

Wood, Frank. *Rainer Maria Rilke: The Ring of Forms*. New York: Octagon Books, 1970. Detailed discussion of the growth and structure of Rilke's later poetry. Also discusses the poet's "inverted Christianity."

SONS AND LOVERS

Type of work: Novel
Author: D. H. Lawrence (1885-1930)
Type of plot: Psychological realism
Time of plot: Late nineteenth century
Locale: England
First published: 1913

Principal characters:
GERTRUDE MOREL, a devoted mother
WALTER MOREL, her husband and a coal miner
WILLIAM, her oldest son
ANNIE, her daughter
PAUL, her favorite son
ARTHUR, another son
MIRIAM LEIVERS, Paul's sweetheart
CLARA DAWES, Paul's mistress
BAXTER DAWES, Clara's husband

The Story:

Walter Morel, a coal miner, had been a handsome, dashing young man when Gertrude had married him. After a few years of marriage, however, he proved to be an irresponsible bread-winner and a drunkard, and his wife hated him for what he had once meant to her and for what he was now. Her only solace lay in her children—William, Annie, Paul, and Arthur—for she leaned heavily upon them for companionship and lived in their happiness. She was a good parent, and her children loved her. The oldest son, William, was successful in his work, but he longed to go to London, where he had promise of a better job. After he had gone, Mrs. Morel turned to Paul for the companionship and love she had found in William.

Paul, who liked to paint, was more sensitive than his brothers and sister and was closer to Mrs. Morel than any of the others. William brought a young woman named Lily home to visit, but it was apparent that she was not the right kind of woman for him; she was too shallow and self-centered. Before long, William became aware of that fact, but he resigned himself to keeping the promise he had made to his fiancée.

When William became ill, Mrs. Morel went to London to nurse her son and was with him there when he died. Home once more after having buried her first son, Mrs. Morel could not bring herself out of her sorrow. Not until Paul became sick did she realize that her duty lay with the living rather than with the dead. After this realization, she centered all of her attention upon Paul. The two other children were capable of carrying on their affairs without the constant attention that Paul demanded.

At sixteen years of age, Paul went to visit some friends of Mrs. Morel. The Leivers were a warmhearted family, and Paul easily gained the friendship of the Leivers children. Fifteen-year-old Miriam Leivers was a strange girl, but her inner charm attracted Paul. Mrs. Morel, like many others, did not care for Miriam. Paul went to work at a stocking mill, where he was successful in his social relationships and in his work. He continued to draw. Miriam watched over his work and, with quiet understanding, offered judgment concerning his success or failure. Mrs. Morel sensed that someday her son would become famous for his art.

By the time Miriam and Paul had grown into their twenties, Paul realized that Miriam loved him deeply and that he loved her; for some reason, however, he could not bring himself to touch her. Through Miriam, he met Clara Dawes. For a long while, Mrs. Morel had been urging him to give up Miriam, and now Paul tried to tell Miriam that it was over between them. He did not want to marry her, but he felt that he did belong to her. He could not make up his mind.

Clara Dawes was separated from her husband, Baxter Dawes. Although she was five years Paul's senior, Clara was a beautiful woman whose loveliness charmed him. Although she became his mistress, she refused to divorce her husband and marry Paul. Sometimes Paul wondered whether he could bring himself to marry Clara if she were free. She was not what he wanted. His mother was the only woman to whom he could turn for complete understanding and love, for Miriam had tried to possess him and Clara maintained a barrier against him. Paul continued to devote much of his time and attention to making his mother happy. Annie had married and gone to live with her husband near the Morel home, and Arthur had married a childhood friend who bore him a son six months after the wedding.

Baxter Dawes resented Paul's relationship with his wife. Once he accosted Paul in a tavern and threatened him. Paul knew that he could not fight with Baxter, but he continued to see Clara.

Paul had entered pictures in local exhibits and had won four prizes. With encouragement from Mrs. Morel, he continued to paint. He wanted to go abroad, but he could not leave his mother. He began to see Miriam again. When she yielded herself to him, his passion was ruthless and savage. Their relationship, however, was still unsatisfactory, and he turned again to Clara.

Miriam knew about his love affair with Clara, but Miriam felt that Paul would tire of his mistress and come back to her. Paul stayed with Clara, however, because he found in her an outlet for his unknown desires. His life was in great conflict. Meanwhile, Paul was earning enough money to give his mother the material possessions her husband had failed to provide. Mr. Morel stayed on with his wife and son, but he was no longer accepted as a father or a husband.

One day, it was revealed that Mrs. Morel had cancer and was beyond any help except that of morphine and then death. During the following months, Mrs. Morel declined rapidly. Paul was tortured by his mother's pain. Annie and Paul marveled at her resistance to death and wished that it would come, to end her suffering. Paul dreaded such a catastrophe in his life, although he knew it must come eventually. He turned to Clara for comfort, but she failed to make him forget his misery. While visiting his mother at the hospital, Paul found Baxter Dawes recovering from an attack of typhoid fever. For a long time, Paul had sensed that Clara wanted to return to Dawes, and now, out of pity for Dawes, he brought about a reconciliation between the husband and wife.

When Mrs. Morel's suffering had mounted to a torturing degree, Annie and Paul decided that anything would be better than to let her live in agony. One night, Paul gave her an overdose of morphine, and Mrs. Morel died the next day.

Left alone, Paul was lost. He felt that his own life had ended with the death of his mother. Clara, to whom he had turned before, had returned to Dawes. Because they could not bear to stay in the house without Mrs. Morel, Paul and his father parted and each took different lodgings.

For a while, Paul wandered helplessly, trying to find some purpose in his life. Then he thought of Miriam, to whom he had once belonged. He returned to her, but with the renewed association, he realized more than ever that she was not what he wanted. Once he had thought of going abroad. Now he wanted to join his mother in death. Leaving Miriam for the last time, he felt trapped and lost in his own indecision, but he also felt that he was free from Miriam after many years of passion and regret.

His mother's death was too great a sorrow for Paul to cast off immediately. After a lengthy inner struggle, he was able to see that she would always be with him and that he did not need to die to join her. With his newfound courage, he set out to make his own life anew.

Critical Evaluation:

Although Sigmund Freud was the first to provide a systematic analysis of the Oedipal relationship, this instinct has been a part of the unconscious from man's earliest beginnings as a social animal. The establishment of the taboo against a son's murdering his father and having sexual relationships with his mother was, one may argue, an initial step in the creation of civilization, because, according to Freud, this psychic drive lies deep in every man's subconscious, or id, as a reservoir of anarchistic energy. If man fails to acknowledge this biological compulsion and to incorporate its prohibition into his own ego, he invites annihilation: specifically, in the form of castration by the father; generally, in the loss of freedom and power.

One of the earliest and best-known dramatizations of this drive is Sophocles' play, *Oedipus Tyrannus* (c. 429 B.C.E.). Without foreknowledge and culpable guilt, Oedipus murders his father and marries his mother. Since he has transgressed, however, he must be punished; he blinds himself, a form of castration. William Shakespeare's *Hamlet* (1600-1601) has also been explored and explicated, most notably by Ernest Jones, as a reenactment of the Oedipal myth. *Sons and Lovers*, based directly on D. H. Lawrence's own childhood experiences, is the most significant post-Freudian novel dealing with a young man's murderous feelings toward his father and his erotic attraction to his mother.

Although it would be overly simplistic to explain *Sons and Lovers* as a mere gloss on a psychological concept, Freud's complex does offer a convenient way to begin understanding the character and cultural situation of Lawrence's hero, Paul Morel. He is the youngest and adored son of a mother who has married beneath herself. A member of the failed middle class, she is educated to a degree, refined with pretensions toward the higher matters of life. As a girl, she is attracted to Walter Morel, a miner who possesses a passionate exuberance she missed on the frayed edges of the middle class. Their marriage, however, soon disintegrates under the pressures of poverty and unfulfilled expectations. As the father and mother grow apart and the older children leave home, Mrs. Morel turns toward her youngest child, mapping out his life and intending to free him from the ignominy of the working class. Her ambitions for Paul are not untainted by her own frustrations, and it becomes clear that she wishes to live out her life through him.

Sensitive and frail, Paul finds his father's drunkenness and rough-edged masculinity repellent. Reared by his mother as if he were a fragile hothouse plant, he is further alienated by his father's vulgar habits and degrading job. Without any sympathy or understanding of his father's suffering or his hard and abrupt love for him, Paul withdraws and joins his mother in the domestic battle. Morel becomes enraged and disappointed by the loss of his son and wife and withdraws into self-pity and alcohol.

Bereft of his father's influence, Paul's life becomes dominated by his mother. Smothered by her warm maternity, cut off from the real world, he returns her ardent affection, and they form a relationship designed to hold off the horrors of reality. As he grows up, however, he discovers that he has traded his self for security. His mother's protectiveness has cost him the power and freedom to relate to others. Every relationship he tries to create is inhibited by her jealousy and demands for his entire attention. Indeed, he comes to feel that every relationship he attempts to pursue is in some way a denial of her.

Paul's attraction to Miriam Leivers, which gradually develops into a love affair, is, ironically, both a rejection and a reaffirmation of his mother. Their immature love, which Mrs. Morel rightfully sees as a threat, is in some ways an acting out of the sexual implications of the mother-son relationship. In her passive dominance, Miriam unconsciously assumes for Paul the figure of his mother. If their love manages to remove him temporarily from his mother's sway, it also reinforces it. Both relationships are symbiotic; Paul draws sustenance from the women but loses the power of self-propulsion. That Paul does not completely acquiesce in the symbiosis is evident both in his brutal sexual treatment of Miriam and his sexual ambivalence toward his mother.

Paul's connection with Clara and Baxter Dawes is much more interesting and complex. Clara provides him with an adult sexual experience unlike that which he had with Miriam. She is neither dominating nor submissive, but demands that he meet her as an equal. He therefore must remain emotionally on his own; he is expected to give affection as well as receive it. Unfortunately, Paul cannot maintain such independence, and this fact undermines their love. He cannot exist as a self-sufficient entity, and Clara will not tolerate an invasion of her self. Paul, however, does not understand this about their relationship until after Mrs. Morel's death. His subsequently successful attempt to reunite her with Baxter thus becomes his first sign of health; it is not only an admission that their romance is impossible, but also is a reparation for having alienated her from Baxter.

Paul's act of reparation is also symbolic. Released from his mother's dominance by her death, a death that he hastens, he must continue his growth toward freedom and power by making peace with his father. Unable to confront his father directly, Paul's bringing together Clara and Baxter is an admission of the higher moral demands of marital love, a love he helped to destroy—although in the innocence of childhood—between his father and mother. In this act, moreover, he negates the child in himself and salutes the reality of the father and husband.

"Critical Evaluation" by David L. Kubal

Bibliography:

Balbert, Peter, and Phillip L. Marcus, eds. *D. H. Lawrence: A Centenary Consideration*. Ithaca, N.Y.: Cornell University Press, 1985. Eleven essays on D. H. Lawrence and his novels. Two are effective for research on *Sons and Lovers:* Mark Spilka's "For Mark Schorer with Combative Love: The *Sons and Lovers* Manuscript," and feminist critic Sandra M. Gilbert's masterful "Potent Griselda: 'The Ladybird' and the Great Mother."

Gilbert, Sandra. *D. H. Lawrence's "Sons and Lovers" and Other Works: "The Rainbow," "Women in Love," "The Plumed Serpent."* New York: Simon & Schuster, 1965. Provides introductory biography and information on people behind the fictional characters in this autobiographical novel. Includes Lawrence's plan for the novel, Freudian influences, chapter-by-chapter summary with explication, character descriptions, and critical commentary. A gold mine for researchers.

Kazin, Alfred. Introduction to *Sons and Lovers*, by D. H. Lawrence. New York: Modern Library, 1962. Provides pertinent background information on *Sons and Lovers* as autobiographical fiction; discusses crucial concerns of the content; analyzes style and the Freudian elements in the novel.

Lawrence, D. H. *Phoenix: The Posthumous Papers of D. H. Lawrence*. Edited by Edward D.

McDonald. New York: Viking, 1936. Presents bits and pieces of Lawrence's extant writings; arranged by topic, they range from personal notes to philosophy. Sections 1 and 3, and the concluding autobiographical fragment, are of particular relevance to *Sons and Lovers*. Extensive index, introduction by the editor.

Salgado, Gamini, ed. *D. H. Lawrence, "Sons and Lovers": A Casebook.* Nashville, Tenn.: Aurora, 1970. An excellent collection of materials for researchers of the title novel. Includes the original foreword from the novel, original reviews, criticism, questions, bibliography, and index.

SOPHIE'S CHOICE

Type of work: Novel
Author: William Styron (1925-)
Type of plot: Psychological realism
Time of plot: 1947
Locale: Brooklyn, New York
First published: 1979

Principal characters:
STINGO, the narrator, would-be writer of Great American Novel
SOPHIE ZAWATOWSKA, a displaced concentration camp survivor
NATHAN LANDAU, a brilliant madman, Sophie's lover
STINGO'S FATHER, a Southern, liberal gentleman

The Story:

Stingo, an aspiring Southern novelist in his early twenties, resigned an unrewarding editorship with a major New York publishing firm and moved into economical lodgings in a Brooklyn rooming house to devote all of his energies to his writing. Stingo's father sent him five hundred dollars from a recent discovery of old gold pieces that had been obtained by his great-grandfather for the sale of a slave, Artiste. Although embarrassed by the source of this windfall, Stingo used the money to live on while he created his first literary masterpiece, a novel about Maria Hunt, a high school friend whose suicide Stingo's father related to him as of possible interest. His father wrote him regularly and once came to visit him to try to persuade Stingo to return to his roots in the South. Stingo refused to leave New York, but he often reconsidered that decision.

Soon Stingo was also deeply involved in the lives of Nathan Landau, one of several Jewish boarders, and Nathan's passionate lover, the beautiful Polish, former Catholic refugee, Sophie Zawatowska. Stingo fell in love at first sight with Sophie, but had too much respect for Nathan's prior claim to woo her. He befriended the couple and retold Sophie's story as she gradually unfolded it to him. Sophie was raised in Cracow. Her professor father provided Sophie a strict, oppressive upbringing, while her passive but refined mother taught her a love for classical music that became her only consolation in the madness of Auschwitz and the post-war United States.

At first, Stingo idealized the brilliant, talkative, and volatile Nathan, whose claim to be a cellular biologist Stingo accepted at face value. It soon became clear that Nathan indulged in brutally abusive moods, exacerbated by drug use, ending in gun-waving, threats to kill, physical and verbal abuse, and sexual violence for Sophie. Stingo's perplexity about Sophie's enduring and even clinging to this disastrously destructive relationship was only partially satisfied when he learned Sophie's story. She had inherited guilt for her professor-father's fascist political beliefs, his anti-Semitism, his foreshadowing the Holocaust through a monograph he had written calling for the extermination of Jews, his demand that Sophie distribute the monograph, and his death as the Nazis shot him and Sophie's husband because they were professors and Polish. Sophie's most terrifying burden arose from the few horrifying moments when she had arrived at Auschwitz with her two children, a boy and a girl, and a drunken German physician demanded that she decide which of her two children should be sent to the gas chambers. Such was Sophie's choice.

Her boy lived, and Sophie obtained a clerical position with the camp commandant, Rudolph Hoss. Sophie tried to seduce Hoss, kissed his boots, and begged to see her child—all to no effect. She never saw her son again.

Only her love for Nathan and classical music fueled Sophie's will to live. She constantly filled the neighborhood with strains from Wolfgang Amadeus Mozart, Johann Sebastian Bach, and Ludwig van Beethoven, played on Nathan's gramophone. Stingo learned from Nathan's brother Larry, a wealthy physician, that Nathan suffered chronic mental illness; was not employed as a scientist or anything else; and, between bouts in mental hospitals, occupied the boardinghouse room paid for by his family, on whose patronage he was completely dependent. Now convinced that Nathan might well be homicidal, Stingo offered Sophie an escape, a new life married to him, living on the small Virginia farm his father offered for his use—ironically, inherited from a man of offensively rightist ideology, whom his father tolerated and befriended in traditional liberal American style.

Once again, Sophie became a refugee, on a train bound this time for Virginia, where former slave territory now offered possible liberation, healing, and life accompanied by Stingo, the gallant lover nearly twenty years younger than she. After a stopover in Washington, D.C., so Sophie could have a tourist's introduction to America's political heart, Stingo and Sophie spent a passionate night together. Stingo then awoke to find himself alone. Grieved, Stingo wavered between continuing on toward his life as a Southern gentleman-farmer and writer or returning to New York. At last, his illusions nearly all dispelled, and realizing Sophie's latest choice entailed her death, Stingo frantically returned to the boardinghouse to discover officials removing the bodies of Nathan and Sophie, who had fulfilled their suicide pact.

Critical Evaluation:

Judging by the large body of critical attention given to William Styron, he quickly earned major status among American writers. Many critics consider his fourth novel, *Sophie's Choice*, to be his best achievement.

In *Sophie's Choice*, Styron introduces a theme new to his novels, the Holocaust, and revisits an old theme, the suicide of a woman. *Sophie's Choice* is a memoir narrated by Stingo twenty years after the events it records. As is usual in Styron's fiction, it attempts to connect major themes of recent Western history to a confessional type of story. The parallels between the facts of Stingo's experiences at the rooming house are so consistent with Styron's own life at that age that readers should interpret Stingo as a persona tied extremely closely to Styron himself. Styron did live in such a boardinghouse in order to write and did know such a woman as Sophie, "beautiful but ravaged." He knew her, however, only slightly. This gives an authenticity to the narrative voice, yet allows a freedom to the artist to realize a personal vision. Through Stingo, Styron unifies a complex variety of themes, two of which are central: the difficulty of keep- ing faith with God, religion, and human nature in view of the Nazi atrocities; and the difficulty of becoming a literary artist, in view of those atrocities, as well as in view of the decline of Southern regional writing. As Nathan observes to Stingo, Southern literature is a dying tradition; the difficulty of creating in the wake of such notables as Lillian Hellman, William Faulkner, Robert Penn Warren, and Carson McCullers is Styron's great challenge. A major theme of *Sophie's Choice* is Stryon's focus on this challenge, and he responds by creating a South contextualized in the colorful mixture of many ethnicities and backgrounds. As Stingo notes, the Brooklyn rooming house is a microcosm of American heterogenous types. By placing his South in such a broad context Styron is able to make his point that suffering is universal for human beings, and even the Holocaust may be integrated into a larger picture of human tragedy.

The risk is in proposing such a morally ambiguous world and such a pessimistic vision of life that creativity becomes wholly arbitrary and useless. Styron seems to find a sufficient balance and some rays of convincing hope, but only as Stingo overcomes his youthful naïveté and exercises self-control in his relationships with others. The South of his youth and the European past are as sweet, innocent, and irrecoverable as Sophie's own childhood in Gothic Cracow, resounding with the divine music of the classic composers Mozart, George Frederick Handel, Bach, and Johannes Brahms. The past is not altogether obsolete and archaic, however, nor are the obstacles to happiness the only powers at work. Joy visits at unexpected moments. Whether readers find in these moments sufficient recompense for pain or little more than an interruption of pain will determine the degree to which they find Styron's tragedies absolute. The joy is, in any case, real in Nathan's brilliant conversation, in the progress of Stingo's first novel, in Sophie's friendship, uninhibited sexuality, and beauty. Joy is there even in his father's idealism and old-fashioned manners, his solicitous love for and faith in his son. It is present in Sophie's quasi-mythical youth in prewar Poland; her struggles to help others and make the best of her imprisonment in the concentration camp at Auschwitz; and her efforts to regain her health, to love faithfully, and to rebuild her life in the United States, although she is haunted by memories, especially guilt over her choice.

Structurally, *Sophie's Choice* is a complex achievement. Styron structures the novel on stated and implied parallels—between Poland and the U.S. South, between Nathan's sadistic moods and the Nazi persecution of his race, between Stingo's and Sophie's inability to find permanent happiness through love. Styron's literary output has not been large but has benefited from careful craftsmanship and such deeply considered relationships. Its only serious narrative weakness comes when Stingo gives over his storytelling persona in order to summarize historians' recent scholarship concerning Rudolf Hess's involvement in the Nazi movement, an interruption in the fictional world that jars readers' sensibilities. While critics have rightly observed that Nathan is weak because he is too improbable, Styron's strength rests with his recurring thematic emphasis on tragic women trapped between their need for self-realization and their dependence on unstable and neurotic men. He writes with great sensitivity about traditional women's roles and offers convincing psychological insights into the major dilemmas of feminine existence. While recent history and Styron's autobiography provide a realistic atmosphere, the female character, presented with extraordinary sensitivity and intimacy, is an archetype synthesized in Styron's imagination, the femme fatale become voluntary sacrifice, in a ritual of recompense as old as humanity, a self-assigned offering necessary to balance the scales against man's terrible inhumanity to man.

Men are not immune from pain or victimhood, as the tragicomic adventures during which Stingo tries unsuccessfully to lose his virginity remind us. In Styron's fictional world, no one group, ideology, religion, race, or gender owns exclusive rights to suffering or claims to the superiority of their sufferings. Nor are victims merely passive objects of sadism. Tragedy is defined by the complicity of victims in their suffering, whose commitment to life and goodness ironically traps them as accessories to the evils that befall them. Sophie's so-called choice illustrates the point precisely. One's acceptance of this burden of responsibility restores some dignity to human life, and this theme redeems Styron's literary vision from absolute darkness.

Diane Brotemarkle

Bibliography:

Casciato, Arthur D., and James L. W. West III, eds. *Critical Essays on William Styron*. Boston:

G. K. Hall, 1982. A cross-section of reviews of Styron's fiction, with essays on *Sophie's Choice* and other works.

Coale, Samuel. *William Styron Revisited.* Boston: Twayne, 1991. Chapter seven provides an insightful analysis of characters.

Heath, William. "I, Stingo: The Problem of Egotism in *Sophie's Choice.*" *Southern Review* 20, (Summer, 1984): 528-540. Discusses the novel as competitive storytelling.

Karl, Frederick. *American Fictions, 1940-1980.* New York: Harper and Row, 1983. Broad coverage of the topic, but contains especially high praise for *Sophie's Choice* as Styron's best novel.

Kreyling, Michael. "Speakable and Unspeakable in Styron's *Sophie's Choice.*" *Southern Review* 20 (Summer, 1984): 546-561. Explores thematic relations between language and sexuality.

THE SORROWS OF YOUNG WERTHER

Type of work: Novel
Author: Johann Wolfgang von Goethe (1749-1832)
Type of plot: Bildungsroman
Time of plot: Mid-eighteenth century
Locale: Germany
First published: Die Leiden des jungen Werthers, 1774 (English translation, 1780)

Principal characters:
WERTHER, a young man
CHARLOTTE (LOTTE), a young woman with whom he falls in love
ALBERT, Charlotte's fiancé

The Story:

Young Werther, having left home, wrote to his friend Wilhelm to describe the secluded region where he had gone to forget the unhappiness of his earlier years. He had discovered a pleasant cottage surrounded by a lovely garden, and he felt that in this peaceful retreat he could live in happy solitude forever. A few days later, he reported that his soul had recovered in his rustic surroundings. He did not want books or the companionship of his old friends, for he had been transported into a new world of kinship with nature. He mentioned a nearby hamlet, Walheim, and the village inn where he could drink good coffee, sit in solitude, and read the works of Homer. Several letters to Wilhelm continued describing Werther's simple life among scenes of natural beauty.

Suddenly there was a break in his letters, followed by the announcement that he had met an angel. At a ball, he had been introduced to Charlotte S., the daughter of a judge who had retired to a hunting lodge not far from Walheim. Charlotte was a beautiful and charming girl, and despite the fact that she was betrothed to another young man, who had not been present at the ball, Werther had fallen deeply in love with her at first sight.

Perhaps his passion became all the deeper because he had been warned not to fall in love with her. At the dance, Werther had demanded much of her attention, and he had begun to ask her about Albert, her fiancé, when a storm had suddenly interrupted the dance. The hostess led the guests into a room protected by curtains and shutters. There they played a game called counting. Once Werther kissed Charlotte's hands. When the party broke up at sunrise, he took her to her home through a dazzling world of raindrops and morning sun. From that time on, he called every day on Lotte, as he referred to her in his letters. He grieved over their separation when she went to attend a sick woman. One day, he went with her to visit an old pastor; he noted that her youthful presence seemed to bring new life to the old man.

Because he could not bear to have her out of his sight, Werther began to object to the time Lotte gave to sick friends and other acquaintances. A glimpse of her as she rode away on some errand was enough to set his head spinning and his heart beating wildly. If her finger accidentally touched his, the blood pounded through his veins. He confessed to his friend that he had done little of the painting he had intended; all of his time was consumed with his love for Charlotte.

After he received Wilhelm's advice either to press his suit with Lotte or else relinquish his hopeless passion, Werther decided to see the girl less frequently. His decision was further strengthened by the fact that Albert returned to Walheim. Werther was jealous of Albert but wrote that he nevertheless admired his rival's fine character. In answer to further urging from Wilhelm, Werther replied that he could neither give up Lotte nor hope to win her from Albert. That being so, Werther grew more and more melancholy. Because he could hope to possess Lotte only in his dreams, he succumbed to gloom and despair. At last, deciding that he must leave Walheim, he asked Wilhelm to secure a government post for him. When Wilhelm suggested a post with an ambassador, Werther postponed his acceptance or refusal of the position. Wilhelm, however, obtained the appointment without waiting to hear from his friend, and so Werther's course was decided for him. During the two last hours he spent with Lotte and Albert, he pretended that he was not going away, feeling that their farewells would be more than he could bear.

At first, the official duties of his new position kept Werther from brooding over his sorrows, but as time passed he began to dislike the ambassador for whom he worked. No longer interested in government affairs, he reproached Wilhelm for securing the appointment. He chafed under the responsibilities he had been forced to assume. Finally, he wrote to Lotte. Albert wrote in reply, informing him that the two had been married some time earlier.

Werther resigned his position at court. Failing in his attempt to enter the army, he accepted the offer of a young prince to spend the summer on his estate. When he failed to find in the nobleman's household the peace and calm for which he had hoped, he decided to return to Walheim to be near Lotte. Yet his first encounter with Albert and Lotte threw him into such a state that his letter to Wilhelm was almost incoherent. He could not understand why Albert did not look more distractedly happy. Although Lotte pitied Werther and Albert sympathized with him, they were unable to help him. At the same time, Werther was concerned with the fate of a peasant who had been convicted of murder. Failing to save the man from his fate, Werther was more wretched than ever. At last, following her husband's suggestion, Lotte suggested that Werther visit her house less frequently. In despair, he wrote that when he could bear his sorrows no longer he intended to end his life.

The rest of his story was told by others. One night, while Albert was away from home, Werther went to Lotte's house. Frightened by his speech and appearance, she asked him to read aloud some passages from Ossian. After he had seized her in a wild embrace, she fled and locked herself in her room. He stood outside the door and begged her to speak so that he could hear her voice for the last time.

The next day, he sent a servant to Albert and asked for the loan of a brace of pistols to take with him on an unexpected journey. He shot himself that night, but he was not quite dead when his servant found him the next morning. He died at noon without regaining consciousness. Hearing of his death, Charlotte fell into a swoon so deep that it threatened her life. Workmen of the village carried Werther's body to its resting place under the lime trees at Walheim.

Critical Evaluation:

Johann Wolfgang von Goethe wrote *The Sorrows of Young Werther* in the space of a few weeks in 1774, in a burst of creative energy that charged the whole work with a rare intensity. He drew upon his own experiences, and much of the work is autobiographical. Perhaps because of this, it captured a mood of the times and was greeted with great admiration and enthusiasm by the public. It was the one work that can be said to have made Goethe's reputation; to the end of his life, he was for many readers primarily "the author of *Werther*." At the same time, it was a turning point in his career, for it marked the end of his "storm and stress" period. The outburst of all-consuming emotion was followed by a quieter period, which led to his classical style of the 1780's. Goethe himself later regarded *The Sorrows of Young Werther* as a kind of therapeutic expression of a dangerous side of his own personality, one which he overcame and controlled. He was appalled to find that Werther had become regarded as a model of behavior, influencing men's fashion (blue coat with yellow vest and trousers; long, unpowdered hair) and inspiring a rash of suicides all over Europe.

The immediacy of the work is, in large part, the result of its epistolary form. After a brief foreword by the fictional editor, the reader plunges straight into the world of Werther's mind, and the style of his letters, full of exclamations, broken sentences, and impassioned flights of imagination, expresses his personality better than could any description. Throughout the novel, Werther moves from peak to peak of emotion, and the letters pick out the high points of his life. When he finally becomes too incoherent to write, the editor enters, which creates a chilling effect. The editor observes events from a distance and by observing Werther with a sympathetic but dispassionate eye retards the headlong rush of the story. The novel possessed a further immediacy for its first readers in that it was set in their own contemporary world. The first letter is dated May 4, 1771, and from there Goethe leads the reader through that year's summer, fall, and winter into the next year with its new hope in the spring and the final tragedy at the end of the year in mid-winter. Werther shares the interests of his generation: He reads Homer, Friedrich Gottlieb Klopstock, and Ossian, loves nature and the simple folk in the fashion of Jean-Jacques Rousseau, and chafes against the conventions and fashions of aristocratic eighteenth century society.

Aside from some secondary plot elements that mirror Werther's own predicament, especially the story of the peasant who commits murder out of frustrated love, the work is entirely developed around three characters: Werther, Lotte, and Albert. Lotte is in many ways the pivotal character, since she is placed between the two men, who are almost opposites. She is attracted to both, perhaps more to Werther than to Albert, since Werther appeals to her romantic side and she shares with him a capacity for passionate emotion that Albert lacks. When Goethe first introduces her into the narrative, she is caring for her younger brothers and sisters, the very image of responsibility and self-sacrifice. Her mother is dead, and she has taken over her duties in the family. At the party in the storm, she takes over and organizes games to quiet the fears of her companions. However poetic she may be, she has a calm head and understands that Werther is hopelessly impractical in his emotion-centered life. Albert is a good husband and father, a bit dry perhaps and overly rational, but dependable, devoted, and clearheaded. Lotte, a complex character, would like to have both men in her life. While Werther is certainly the most directly autobiographical of the characters, Lotte is perhaps closer to Goethe's own personality, combining the practical, responsible traits that would find expression in his official activities in Weimar with the poetic imagination that constantly drew him back into the world of literature. This union of opposites is a common feature of Goethe's work, from *Faust, Part I* (1808)—"two souls dwell, alas, within my breast"—to Wilhelm who wants to be an actor but becomes a doctor instead.

From the very beginning, Goethe distinguished his own character from that of Werther. Indeed, *The Sorrows of Young Werther* is more a judgment on the dangers of emotion than an incitement to emulation. The novel is, in fact, a tragedy of character, for the unhappy romance is not the cause of Werther's tragedy. From the very beginning, as Werther exclaims "what a thing is the heart of man," his situation is clear. Werther is important as one of the first modern tragic figures for whom his own personality, not events, is the tragedy. The conflict rests within him, and the world merely provides the occasion for his inner conflict to express itself. He embodies a life-spirit that strives for the absolute and the unconditional, which is carried forward by a stream of emotion that seizes on life and constantly transforms it into an inner experience of great intensity. His life is centered on his own emotions and drawn inward as in a whirlpool. There is no compensating outward flow in the form of activity or other-directedness, no objective pole that can counter the all-transforming subjectivity. It is the spirit of Faust, or of Goethe's tragic poet-figure Torquato Tasso. It is the spirit that he saw as the inevitable consequence of the emotion-centered *Sturm und Drang*, or "storm and stress," writers, not a few of whom ended in madness or suicide. In Werther, Goethe created perhaps the most memorable representative of this tragic type, the embodiment of one extreme of the human personality. In his subsequent work, Goethe continued to keep this aspect of himself alive, to provide the motive force for a series of masterpieces. *The Sorrows of Young Werther* itself became the inspiration for a host of Romantic writers in Germany, England, and France, and thus represents a landmark in European literature.

"Critical Evaluation" by Steven C. Schaber

Bibliography:

Dieckmann, Liselotte. *Johann Wolfgang Goethe*. New York: Twayne, 1974. Discusses the versatility Goethe displayed in his poetry, drama, novels, and tales, and includes a longer discussion of his masterwork, *Faust*. Places the writer's oeuvre within its historical framework, particularly with regard to the impact of the French Revolution and the influence of Goethe's friendship with Friedrich Schiller.

Hatfield, Henry. *Goethe: A Critical Introduction*. New York: New Directions, 1963. Discusses Goethe's influence on later writers. Includes focus on the epistolary novel and the sociological impact of *The Sorrows of Young Werther*.

Reiss, Hans. *Goethe's Novels*. Coral Gables, Fla.: University of Miami Press, 1969. In-depth review of Goethe's earlier novels, with a comprehensive discussion of *The Sorrows of Young Werther* as being representative of Goethe's involvement in the so-called storm-and-stress movement. Compares the novels thematically.

Schweitzer, Albert. *Goethe: Four Studies*. Translated by Charles R. Joy. Boston: Beacon Press, 1949. Of interest because the book reveals parallels between Goethe and Schweitzer, who admired Goethe's simple philosophy of nature and his views on natural science and ethics.

Trevelyan, Humphrey. *Goethe and the Greeks*. New York: Octagon, 1972. Reveals the enormous influence of classical and neoclassical thought and mythology on the work of Goethe. Includes in particular a discussion of the importance of Homer's work for the character of Werther.

THE SOT-WEED FACTOR

Type of work: Novel
Author: John Barth (1930-)
Type of plot: Picaresque
Time of plot: Late seventeenth and early eighteenth centuries
Locale: Maryland
First published: 1960

Principal characters:
EBENEZER or EBEN COOKE, son of Andrew Cooke, owner of a sot-weed (tobacco) plantation in Maryland
ANNA COOKE, his twin sister
HENRY BURLINGAME, their tutor in youth and associate in later life
JOAN TOAST, a prostitute who becomes Ebenezer's ideal love and later his wife
JOHN MCEVOY, her pimp
BERTRAND BURTON, Ebenezer's valet

The Story:

Ebenezer Cooke and his twin sister Anna were born to Andrew Cooke on a tobacco plantation, Malden, at Cooke's Point in the colony of Maryland, in 1666. Their mother died giving birth and their father returned to England, hiring eventually as his children's tutor a young man who had been found floating in Chesapeake Bay with the name "Henry Burlingame III" pinned to his chest. Burlingame hoped to find the secret journal of Captain John Smith. Burlingame had an ancestor who had served with the famous explorer and thought that the secret of his birth might be found in the journal.

Eben went to Cambridge for his formal education. After a period of indecision and carousal with his friends, Eben finally determined that he wanted to be a poet. Henry Burlingame also reappeared to assist Eben during this period. Andrew Cooke asked him to return to Maryland to take over the operation of the family plantation. Two events occurred that were to shape Eben's future. On a dare he met a prostitute named Joan Toast, and Eben was taken by her beauty and personality. Instead of having sex with her, he vowed eternal devotion to her and to preserve his virginity eternally. John McEvoy, Joan's pimp, wanted Eben to pay for the time he spent with her even though there had been no sex. Eben gained an enemy. The second important event was Eben's interview with Charles Calvert, Lord Baltimore and former governor of Maryland, who appointed Eben poet laureate of Maryland and urged the astonished young man to help Calvert regain the governorship of Maryland, which had been wrested from him by a host of villains headed by Jonathan Coode. Calvert had no authority to name Eben to any position because Calvert was no longer governor of Maryland. In fact, Calvert was not Calvert; he was Burlingame, in the first of many disguises.

Eben, Bertrand, and Burlingame headed for a seaport to begin their voyage to Maryland, but brigands set upon Eben, thinking that he would cause trouble for Coode's side of the Maryland conspiracy. Burlingame was separated from the others. Eben and Bertrand exchanged identities to confuse those who were after Eben. Bertrand, pretending to be Eben, got a coquettish daughter of a landowner pregnant and gambled away part of Eben's estate. The ship they were on was attacked by pirates and they were taken prisoner. The pirate ship encountered a ship carrying prostitutes headed for the New World and the passengers were raped. Even Eben was so caught up in the mood that he almost raped a woman who later turned out to be his ideal love, Joan Toast.

The pirates cast Eben and Bertrand overboard. The two made their way to land, which turned out to be Maryland. There they made friends with an Indian chief and eventually made their way to Cambridge, where an open-air court was in session. Eben, thinking that an injustice was about to be done, insisted on making the court's judgment himself, giving some land to the plaintiff. The land turned out to be his own estate. He had given his land to Henry Warren, a blackguard who had turned Malden into an opium farm. Eben was forced to work as a servant on the land that had been his. During this time of servitude he again met Joan Toast, now known as Susan Warren and suffering from smallpox. He was so disillusioned by the course his life had taken that he abandoned his idea of writing an epic about Maryland and instead wrote a bitter satire, "The Sot-Weed Factor."

John McEvoy had reappeared, and he, Bertrand, and Eben were captured by Indians. Eben was able to use his relationship with the Indian chief he had befriended earlier to free himself and his companions. This episode also produced the solution to the mystery of Burlingame's parentage. He was one of three brothers descended from a martyred priest and an Indian maiden. One of his brothers was the consort of Anna Cooke, who had followed her brother to the New World. The governor of Maryland convened a special court to settle the claims to Malden, which were finally resolved in Eben's favor, but in order to reclaim his estate, Eben was forced to marry, and have sex with, the no-longer beautiful, pox-ridden Joan Toast. Burlingame was reunited with Anna. She had loved him when they were in England, and bore him a son, Andrew. At the end of the novel, Ebenezer settled down to run the plantation and take care of his wife, sister, nephew, and servants. Burlingame, who had finally discovered who he really was, disappeared from the novel.

Critical Evaluation:

There was a real Ebenezer Cooke who lived in colonial Maryland and wrote a satirical poem entitled "The Sot-Weed Factor" (1708). Very little is known of the historical Eben Cooke, so John Barth, who was born in Maryland and spent his early life there, set out to write a novel in the style of the time in which Cooke lived. The novel creates the experiences that might have brought Cooke to write such a poem. Barth's novel *The Sot-Weed Factor* is a long, hilarious, complex work, which has echoes not only of eighteenth century novels but also of the other literary models that the eighteenth century novelists used. The ideological viewpoint of the novel, however, reflects its twentieth century origins. Its language and humor are of the eighteenth century; its themes and philosophical implications are of the twentieth.

Barth's most obvious eighteenth century model is Henry Fielding's *Tom Jones* (1749), which Fielding described as a "comic epic in prose." *The Sot-Weed Factor* is comic in the ordinary and dramatic senses; it is filled with jokes of which Eben is usually the butt, yet all is finally resolved in Eben's favor. *The Sot-Weed Factor* also has elements of the epic. An epic is about a heroic figure who fights through difficulties to do good not only for himself but also for his people. Eben finally does help to establish a peaceful and prosperous Maryland after being captured by pirates and savage Indians, reduced to servitude, and physically attacked and threatened with death numerous times. Eben is an ironic, comic hero, and instead of confronting all these dangers and emerging victorious through his own efforts, he frequently escapes through luck or the intervention of others, particularly Burlingame, who reappears in a bewildering number of identities and disguises.

An epic also involves a complex series of events, and Fielding set out in *Tom Jones* to construct a plot so complicated that no one would doubt its epic claims. Barth wanted to write a novel with a plot more convoluted than Fielding's, and he succeeded. There is a plot twist on almost every page of *The Sot-Weed Factor*, and the bare-bones summary given above omits dozens of characters, subplots, and interpolated stories.

Earthy, physical, and sexual humor is also a distinguishing feature of eighteenth century novels such as those of Tobias Smollett, John Cleland, and Daniel Defoe. *The Sot-Weed Factor* is full of such comedy. Eben is often so frightened that he vomits or loses control of his bowels and bladder. The climax of the John Smith subplot is the discovery that, in order to save his life, the captain had to deflower Pocahontas, who had an apparently impenetrable maidenhead, a task that he performed by pasting an eggplant on his sex organ. Barth's Joan Toast, like Moll Flanders, is a prostitute who journeys to the New World. This similarity makes *The Sot-Weed Factor* an imitation of yet another eighteenth century genre, the travel novel. Another of Defoe's novels, *Robinson Crusoe* (1719), and Jonathan Swift's satire *Gulliver's Travels* (1726), are originals in this category. Most people in the eighteenth century had no chance to travel but loved to read of the new lands that the explorers and colonists were visiting. Many of these original travel novels romanticized, idealized, or simply lied about the places they described. In Barth's ironic novel, Eben's naïve view of Maryland as a blissful paradise is shattered when he finds that it is instead a wilderness filled with dangers.

Finally, *The Sot-Weed Factor* is a twentieth century novel that masquerades as an eighteenth century novel. Barth has described his first three novels (*The Floating Opera*, 1956, *The End of the Road*, 1958, and *The Sot-Weed Factor*) as examinations of philosophical nihilism, the theory that there is no ultimate meaning to life or existence. In the first two novels, characters announce their nihilistic attitudes as a result of their philosophical speculations. In *The Sot-Weed Factor*, a nihilistic world is something that happens to the main character, Eben Cooke. He begins life with certain received notions about truth, value, and human relationships. All of his assumptions are left in tatters; he finds that they cannot help him make his way in a world in which nothing is what it appears to be.

Eben thinks that the artificial ideals he has gleaned from his voracious reading will be a guide for behavior in the world. Instead, he finds a society devoted to greed, power, and the satiation of every base appetite. Moreover, the world is so confusing that no one can hope to understand it. For example, Lord Baltimore tells Eben to beware of the evil machinations of Jonathan Coode. Later, Eben discovers that Baltimore is considered by some to be just as evil as Coode, and he is further perplexed when he finds that the "Baltimore" who urged him to watch out for Coode was really his friend Burlingame. Eben's world turns upside down so many times that, in a memorable episode, as he rides along listening to one of Burlingame's typically sophistic discourses, he wonders why he and the horse he is riding on do not tumble off a whirling, topsy-turvy planet.

The Sot-Weed Factor is not merely a hilarious novel offering no values. In the end, Ebenezer abandons his dreams, and he is not bitter. He finds a new sense of value in his commitments to his friends and family. He becomes interested in people, not solely in ideas.

Jim Baird

Bibliography:

Bowen, Zack. *A Reader's Guide to John Barth*. Westport, Conn.: Greenwood Press, 1994. The chapter on *The Sot-Weed Factor* treats the book as both a parody of earlier forms and as a contemporary novel. Extensive bibliography on *The Sot-Weed Factor*.

Miller, Russell H. "*The Sot-Weed Factor*: A Contemporary Mock Epic." *Critique* 8, no. 2 (Winter, 1965-1966): 88-100. Examines the relationships between *The Sot-Weed Factor* and various classical and eighteenth century models, with a point-by-point comparison of Eben's adventures to those of Odysseus.

Morrell, David. *John Barth: An Introduction*. University Park: Pennsylvania State University Press, 1976. An overview of all of Barth's work to 1976, with two chapters analyzing *The Sot-Weed Factor* as a contemporary novel.

Safer, Elaine. "The Allusive Mode and Black Humor in Barth's *The Sot-Weed Factor*." *Studies in the Novel* 13 (1981): 424-438. Discusses the novel in contemporary and postmodern contexts.

Walkiewicz, E. P. *John Barth*. Boston: Twayne, 1986. Excellent short introduction to Barth's work, with numerous comments on *The Sot-Weed Factor*. Bibliography.

THE SOULS OF BLACK FOLK

Type of work: Autobiography
Author: W. E. B. Du Bois (1868-1963)
First published: 1903

The Souls of Black Folk is a passionate and eloquent autobiography. It tells the life story of an individual, W. E. B. Du Bois, and of a group, African Americans. In the process of telling his personal autobiography, Du Bois shows how he is shaped by his community's story. Du Bois inhabits a world in which a color line divides all life into two parts. One part is privileged and white, and it exploits the other part that is constrained and black.

As an author reflecting on his life, Du Bois could not separate himself from "what was then called the Negro problem." Even his consciousness is divided into two parts, becoming a double consciousness. He calls the experience generated by the color line "the Veil." As a man living behind the Veil, part of his being is hidden. One part of his consciousness belongs to the human race, and the other consciousness is shrouded behind the Veil. Du Bois allows his readers to look behind the Veil, to share his pain and humiliation and to celebrate a world populated by heroes and joy. The souls of black folk are the flame of hope and life in a world where hatred diminishes and kills the body and the spirit.

The triumph of African American culture is revealed through the songs of sorrow that introduce each chapter. In the hymns, both suffering from enslavement and surviving through hope are conveyed simultaneously. Although the book is often based on facts, the spirituals connect the information to the heart and soul. The result is a moving story of a race and a man. Spiritual striving shapes the lives of African Americans who search for freedom and fulfillment.

The second chapter begins with one of the most famous lines in this book: "The problem of the twentieth century is the problem of the color line." These prophetic words tell the story of American slaves and their descendants who continue to search for freedom in America and throughout the world. The international dimensions of the color line are rooted in the economy and politics of a worldwide struggle.

One way to address these issues is to work for gradual change. This position was held by Booker T. Washington, the most powerful African American leader in the United States when Du Bois wrote this book. Although Du Bois respected Washington's rise from slavery, Du Bois was opposed to any position that accepted the limitations of African Americans' rights. Washington represented adjustment and submission to an intolerable injustice. The training of the most talented members of the community was central to changing the community, but Washington stressed manual and vocational training at the expense of the most gifted. Du Bois' unflinching criticism of Washington created a public debate about how to fight against discrimination and the reason for engaging in the struggle.

Du Bois tells his personal story of entering Fisk University in Nashville, Tennessee, in 1884. He experiences the Jim Crow world of the South and teaches children who are limited by its cruelty. Their life behind the Veil makes a mockery of the idea of progress and constrains his life as a schoolteacher. Du Bois moves out of the elementary school and on to higher education.

Before leaving the South, he takes the reader on a journey through the black belt. Georgia is the heart of this region where African Americans live behind a color line. Jim Crow railway cars physically and socially segregate black and white passengers. The railroads enforce this segregation throughout the South. Plantations dot the landscape, echoing the slavery that maintained them and continued their legacy years after emancipation was proclaimed but not realized. Churches, however, sustain the souls of black folk, who are isolated behind the Veil.

Du Bois discusses the continuation of the plantation system through tenant farming. The struggle for freedom from economic and political slavery is like the quest for the golden fleece, a journey of epic proportions. Even off the land, segregation is enforced in housing, the economy, politics, and social customs. The vote creates the possibility to fight back, but political corruption subverts this power. Crime and poor public education further weaken the community and sap the strength needed to resist. Sympathy and cooperation, not charity, are necessary to improve the situation.

Faith in God, the community, family, and one another sustains African Americans. Du Bois reveals how the "faith of our fathers" is a communal heritage. The souls of black folk contain a deep religious feeling, a powerful heart nourished by dynamic vigor. The sorrow songs that introduce each chapter are part of the community and its continuing faith. Music, song, and lyrics combine to make a heritage from the past that lives in the present.

The death of Du Bois' first (and only) son, Burghardt, occurred because medical caretakers refused to aid the dying African American infant. Despair and rage at the Veil caused Du Bois to be darkly and perversely glad that his son had escaped its ravages. His baby was beyond the Veil in the valley of death. His keening cry against the evil that murdered his baby is a heart-wrenching paean to lost hope and love.

People are able, nevertheless, to triumph behind the Veil, and the African American leader is the key to ending the despair and suffering behind the color line. Alexander Crummell, a friend and mentor of Du Bois, was such a hero. He survived the temptations to hate, despair, and doubt the goodness of life. After Crummell was denied entry into the ministry because of the color line, he continued to serve others as a witness to the spirit. He fought against the wickedness of the color line and triumphed through his love and generosity until his death after a life of righteousness.

Ordinary people also have the ability to be extraordinary. Their path may be hard to find and filled with stumbling blocks caused by the Veil, but the triumph of the soul is a cause for joy and celebration even in the midst of darkness. This book is a literary masterpiece because it articulates the cost of hatred and celebrates the power to resist it. Although it has never been out of print since its publication in 1903, it assumed an especially important role in the 1960's. It then became a rallying voice and inspiration for the American civil rights struggle. Du Bois' life story is the story of a people: It reaches the soul of all its readers while revealing the soul of black folks. Du Bois forged a new autobiographical form in this book, revealing the contours of his life as rooted in black culture. His essay on Booker T. Washington turned his personal struggle with the man and what he stood for into a national, political statement about the nature of civil rights. Du Bois called for an active demand for social justice that would not compromise with anything less than full equality. Similarly, his grief at his baby son's death became a eulogy for all the African American children slaughtered by white people's hatred.

This technique of telling his life story while he told the story of a people was used by Du Bois during the rest of his long and productive life. Thus, other Du Bois autobiographies tell of friends, struggles, and humiliations over the next sixty years; they do not reach the heights of this first one. *The Souls of Black Folk* is unique in its passion and eloquence. His phrases soar with anguish and anger, reflecting his pain and that of others. His language captures the imagination so dramatically that Du Bois' book reaches out to all people who resist hatred. It offers hope for the triumph of the spirit and the possibility of social justice. Du Bois rose above the Veil.

Mary Jo Deegan

Bibliography:

Andrews, William, ed. *Critical Essays on W. E. B. Du Bois*. Boston: G. K. Hall, 1985. A number of Du Bois' writings are evaluated in terms of their ideas and their impact on the African American community.

Du Bois, W. E. B. *The Autobiography of W. E. B. Du Bois*. New York: International Publishers, 1968. This third socioautobiography is written after World War II and the McCarthy era. Du Bois is living in Africa, realizing some of his pan-African dreams, and reflecting on his long life. This book is filled with the wisdom and peace that Du Bois struggled to achieve.

____________. *Darkwater: Voices from Within the Veil*. Millwood, N.Y.: Kraus-Thomson Organization, 1975. This is Du Bois' second autobiography, containing a critique of the effects of World War I. He also critiques the position of women.

____________. *Dusk of Dawn: An Essay Toward an Autobiography of a Race Concept*. New Brunswick, N.J.: Transaction, 1984. This book continues the autobiography of Du Bois, including the changes brought about after World War II and the Great Depression. This is an angrier book than *The Souls of Black Folk*.

Lewis, David Levering. *W. E. B. Du Bois: Biography of a Race, 1868-1919*. New York: Henry Holt, 1993. The early years of Du Bois' life are examined from another perspective. The author shows the historical context and figures shaping the life of Du Bois.

THE SOUND AND THE FURY

Type of work: Novel
Author: William Faulkner (1897-1962)
Type of plot: Stream of consciousness
Time of plot: 1900-1928
Locale: Mississippi
First published: 1929

Principal characters:
MR. JASON COMPSON, a retired lawyer, the Compson family patriarch
MRS. CAROLINE COMPSON, his wife
CANDACE ("CADDY"),
QUENTIN,
BENJAMIN ("BENJY"), and
JASON, their children
QUENTIN, Candace's daughter
DILSEY, the Compsons' maid
LUSTER, Dilsey's grandson

The Story:

The Compsons, a once-prominent Mississippi family, were in decline. Their sprawling plantation had been sold and turned into a golf course, and their once-splendid mansion was badly dilapidated. At the head of the family were Mr. Jason Compson, a retired lawyer taken to drink, and his wife, Caroline, a hypochondriac who spent most of her day in bed.

Benjamin, the Compsons' youngest child, a mentally retarded man, began to tell the story of his life. On April 7, 1928, his thirty-third birthday, while he walked along the golf course with Luster, his caretaker, Benjy began to reminisce about his childhood years. His mind jumped from event to event, covering more than a dozen events in all.

Several of Benjy's flashbacks concerned his older sister Caddy, to whom Benjy had been quite attached. He described how she cared for him and played with him as a child and how she lay next to him in bed until he fell asleep. Benjy also told of Caddy's wedding and her subsequent departure from the Compson household, which disturbed Benjy profoundly.

Many of Benjy's memories were painful. He related the death of his grandmother, whose wake took place while the Compson children played in a stream, and his brother's death. He recalled the day during his teenage years when he embraced and fondled a local schoolgirl, thinking she was his sister Caddy. Benjy was castrated for that offense.

At the end of his narrative, Benjy returned to the present. He related that he and Luster looked out his bedroom window and watched his niece, Quentin, climb out of the window of her room and run off into the night.

In the second chapter, dated June 2, 1910, Quentin, the Compsons' oldest son, told of the events leading to his suicide. He was a Harvard University student, and he spent the final day of his life getting his affairs in order—delivering suicide notes to his roommate and father and packing his trunk. As he took one more trolley ride around town, his mind flashed back to the troublesome events that led him to suicide. He was particularly upset by his sister Caddy's romantic affairs. The night that she lost her virginity was especially traumatic for Quentin, as was her marriage the following year. (Caddy married because she was pregnant.) Quentin was jealous of his sister's lovers.

Quentin's flashbacks took place while he wandered around Cambridge. He observed some local boys fishing, and he befriended a young immigrant girl whom he met in a bakery. Late in the day, he met some schoolmates and attended a party that ended abruptly when Quentin inexplicably picked a fight with the hostess' son. In his own mind, Quentin had lashed out at one of Caddy's lovers.

At the end of the chapter, Quentin returned to his room, put on a fresh collar, brushed off his clothes, packed a few more articles in his trunk, and departed to take his life. Quentin's brother Jason later revealed that Quentin drowned himself.

In the third chapter, Jason (along with Benjy), related the events of April 6, 1928. He argued with his teenage niece, also named Quentin, before she left for school, accusing her of cutting classes and chastising her for wearing revealing clothing and excessive makeup. He went to work at the local hardware store and argued with his boss. Throughout his narrative Jason made disparaging remarks about Jews, blacks, women, and the members of his own family.

Jason revealed that Caddy, rejected by her husband, had been expelled from the Compson household, though her daughter Quentin remained. Jason explained that he received and cashed Caddy's child-support checks, then delivered phony checks to his mother, which she burned because she would not accept Caddy's money.

On his lunch break, Jason spotted his niece driving around town with a man wearing a red tie. He pursued them but lost their trail after they clandestinely flattened one of his tires.

The events of the final chapter took place on April 8, 1928, Easter Sunday. Dilsey, the Compsons' elderly African American maid, prepared breakfast shortly after daybreak. She fed Luster and Benjy, then waited for Jason, Quentin, and Mrs. Compson to come to breakfast. When Jason emerged, he announced that he had been robbed; the window to his room had been broken and his strongbox pried open. When he found out that his niece Quentin was not in her room, he correctly assumed that she had stolen his savings (which consisted mainly of Caddy's child-support payments). He notified the police and embarked on a long fruitless drive to find Quentin and the man wearing the red tie.

While Jason tried to track Quentin, Dilsey, her family, and Benjy attended Easter services. Dilsey felt the pain that the Compson family had endured over the years and wept, claiming that she had done her best to raise the Compson children properly.

The novel ended with Luster driving Mrs. Compson and Benjy in a surrey to the cemetery. Luster took a wrong turn at town square, and Benjy broke into hysterics. With the help of Jason, who had returned to town following his futile search, Luster regained control and headed the vehicle home.

Critical Evaluation:

The Sound and the Fury is William Faulkner's first masterpiece. His initial two novels, *Soldier's Pay* (1926) and *Mosquitoes* (1927), were apprentice efforts. His third novel, *Sartoris* (1929), was the first set in his fictional Yoknapatawpha County, a territory in northern Mississippi that would serve as the setting for most of his novels and short stories. In telling the Yoknapatawpha County saga, Faulkner was creating a fictional history of the entire South.

What separates *The Sound and the Fury* from his three earlier novels is its technique. Faulkner's first novels are, for the most part, narrated chronologically by an omniscient narrator. *The Sound and the Fury* breaks that pattern. Each of the novel's four chapters is told by a different narrator. The first chapter is told by Benjy, the second by Quentin, the third by

Jason, and the fourth by an omniscient narrator. Faulkner is the first American writer to employ such complex narrative strategies, though they had been used earlier by modernist British novelists such as Joseph Conrad, James Joyce, and Virginia Woolf.

Through the use of multiple narrators, Faulkner is able to relate the Compson family saga from four separate viewpoints. Each of the three Compson sons brings to the story a different set of perspectives and prejudices.

Benjy, whose narrative covers about twenty-five years of Compson family history, is the most honest of the novel's narrators. Mentally incapable of making critical judgments, Benjy simply narrates events as he saw them. Moaning and weeping, Benjy registers the painful episodes in this family's tragic history.

Opening the novel with Benjy's narrative was risky for Faulkner. Benjy's mind is unable to focus on a single event for more than a few pages; he skips arbitrarily from event to event, rendering his tale meaningless unless it is read very carefully. Faulkner's decision to let Benjy speak first was a brilliant one, for it suggests the themes to which the author would return again and again. For Faulkner, a Southerner with a keen sense of his region's tragic past, history was not the linear story of humanity's accomplishments but rather a jumbled tale of pain. *The Sound and the Fury*'s title comes from lines in William Shakespeare's *Macbeth* (c. 1606-1607): "Life . . . is a tale/ Told by an idiot, full of sound and fury,/ Signifying nothing." Benjy's rendering of Compson history is, indeed, the anguished tale of an idiot, full of sound and fury.

Quentin's narrative also features time shifts and stream-of-consciousness narration that Faulkner borrowed from James Joyce and used brilliantly in *The Sound and the Fury* and future novels. Quentin can function better than Benjy in the present, but like his retarded brother, Quentin is unable to keep past events from dominating his present life. He is traumatized and emotionally paralyzed by his sister's sexual promiscuity; he cannot forget these past events and move on with his life. Tormented by the past, and guilty over his own incestuous desire for Caddy, Quentin finds no escape other than suicide. His tragic end suggests Faulkner's view that the past is inescapable; it continues to affect and shape the present and future.

Jason's narrative is, for the most part, chronological, yet he, like his brothers, is unable to escape the traumas of the past. He is an angry man, and his bitterness is rooted in events from the past—his family's willingness to offer Quentin a Harvard education while Jason was not even able to attend the state university and Caddy's failure to arrange a banking career for him through her husband. Though Jason holds a job and functions normally, he is a man on the verge of a nervous breakdown, obsessed with past events. Jason is also a greedy man, and his preoccupation with money reflects the South's drift toward commercialism as the plantation society faded in the post-Civil War period.

The novel's final chapter is told by an omniscient narrator, an attempt by Faulkner to allow an objective speaker to tell the Compsons' story. This chapter focuses on Dilsey, who is depicted sensitively by neither Benjy nor Jason. With Faulkner narrating, Dilsey emerges as something of a heroine, a woman who attempted to hold together the Compson family through decades of tragedy.

Though her three brothers assume the role of narrator, Caddy is never allowed to tell her story in first person. Faulkner once stated that he decided not to use Caddy as a narrator because she was "too beautiful and too moving to reduce her to telling what was going on, that it would be more passionate to see her through somebody else's eyes." As Faulkner suggests, Caddy becomes a symbol of lost innocence. Benjy narrates an episode in which Caddy muddies her drawers in the stream (on the evening of their grandmother's funeral), and Caddy's soiled undergarments foreshadow her fall from innocence. Finding little compassion and love in the

Compson household, she seeks it through sexual encounters, which ultimately leave her pregnant and, later, rejected by husband and family. She becomes a focal point in all her brothers' narratives and the major cause of their anger.

Told chronologically, *The Sound and the Fury* is the saga of a Southern family in decline. Faulkner's portrait of the once-prominent Compson clan shows two dysfunctional parents, a suicidal son, a fallen daughter, a retarded son, and a son racked with bitterness. For Faulkner, the Compsons represent the collapse of the old Southern order in the decades following the Civil War. Faulkner would elaborate on that compelling theme in future works and, in novels such as *As I Lay Dying* (1930) and *Absalom, Absalom!* (1936), perfect the daring narrative such as strategies first employed in *The Sound and the Fury*.

James Tackach

Bibliography:

Bloom, Harold, ed. *Caddy Compson*. New York: Chelsea House, 1990. Contains ten critical essays focusing on Caddy Compson.

Karl, Frederick R. *William Faulkner: American Writer*. New York: Weidenfeld & Nicolson, 1989. A 1,000-page biography of Faulkner that also provides insightful critical analyses of his major works. Karl's discussion of how Faulkner wove together the complex parts of *The Sound and the Fury* is particularly illuminating.

Matthews, John T. *"The Sound and the Fury": Faulkner and the Lost Cause*. Boston: Twayne, 1991. A short but insightful book-length study of the novel, with chapters devoted to its importance in Faulkner's canon and to its composition, critical reception, characterization, setting, and narrative technique.

Vickery, Olga W. *The Novels of William Faulkner*. Baton Rouge: Louisiana State University Press, 1959. One of the first, and most useful, book-length studies of the Faulkner canon. The discussion of *The Sound and the Fury* focuses on the narratives of the Compson brothers.

Volpe, Edmund L. *A Reader's Guide to William Faulkner*. New York: Noonday Press, 1964. The best beginner's guide to Faulkner's work. Appendix contains scene-by-scene rendering of Benjy's and Quentin's sometimes confusing narratives and a useful Compson genealogy.

THE SOUND OF WAVES

Type of work: Novel
Author: Yukio Mishima (Kimitake Hiraoka, 1925-1970)
Type of plot: Idyll
Time of plot: The 1950's
Locale: The Japanese island of Uta-Jima (Song Island)
First published: *Shiosai*, 1954 (English translation, 1956)

Principal characters:

SHINJI KUBO, a young Japanese fisherman
MISTRESS KUBO, his mother
HIROSHI, his younger brother
HATSUE MIYATA, a woman loved by Shinji
TERUKICHI MIYATA, her father and a wealthy boat owner
YASUO KAWAMOTO, a suitor for Hatsue's hand
CHIYOKO, a student at Tokyo University who betrays the lovers
JUKICHI OYAMA, a master fisherman who befriends Shinji

The Story:

Shinji, a young fisherman who was strong beyond his eighteen years, was the provider for his younger schoolboy brother Hiroshi and his widowed mother, formerly the best abalone diver on Uta-Jima. One day, returning from his day's work with Jukichi, a master fisherman and his good friend, Shinji saw an unfamiliar, hauntingly beautiful face among the women helping to beach the fishing boats. The woman was Hatsue, daughter of the owner of two oceangoing freighters, who had been living with adoptive parents on another island. The boy could not get her image out of his mind. The next night, he visited the beautiful Yashiro Shrine, dedicated to the god of the sea and within sound of the never-ceasing waves, and prayed that the god would in time make him a fisherman among fishermen, worthy of a bride such as Hatsue, the beautiful daughter of Terukichi Miyata, the shipowner.

Shinji's prayer was to come true, but not without many trials for the young lovers. On a day when the weather was too stormy for fishing, they arranged to meet in an old ruined tower. Shinji, soaked with the rain, arrived first, built a fire, and fell asleep. He awoke to see Hatsue, unclothed, standing nearby. Innocently, she had decided to dry her wet clothes before the fire while he slept. The tender love scene that followed was as natural, innocent, and idyllic as her act, for Hatsue decided that since they were to be married as soon as her father gave his permission, both had to remain virtuous.

Shinji and Hatsue, however, had been spied on by Chiyoko, daughter of the lighthouse keeper. She, unlike the naïve, wholesome, and unlearned young couple, had spoiled her good nature by too much introspection and by her acquiring a veneer of learning at Tokyo University. Without an inherent sense of honor, she told Yasuo Kawamoto, Hatsue's more acceptable suitor, what she suspected. Yasuo had also been spoiled by the gloss of culture. The whispering campaign that resulted had to be stoically withstood by the lovers, who could no longer be together; even their innocent letters were intercepted.

Terukichi was stern and proud, but not unjust, and he was sufficiently moved by his daughter's devotion to Shinji to try a plan proposed by Jukichi. Shinji and Yasuo were of an age to serve an apprenticeship at sea, so they were signed on one of Terukichi's freighters; the one who showed better character would marry Hatsue. Yasuo, good-natured but lazy, allowed Shinji to do part of his work for him. Neither knew he was being watched. Then, in a heavy storm off Okinawa, when a broken cable threatened to set the ship adrift from its mooring buoy, Shinji swam through the rough seas to secure the vessel from disaster. Young Shinji proved himself, and Terukichi accepted him as his son-in-law.

Critical Evaluation:

Yukio Mishima's artistic accomplishment includes having written in a wide range of genres. For example, he adapted ancient No dramas, wrote science fiction, modern plays, and stories from Japanese history. In addition, *The Sound of Waves* is an idyllic romance, unlike any of the writer's other novels. It is limited in scope and in ambition, showing none of the tedious intellectual debate, emotional strain, or sardonic tone that characterizes much of his other work. Also, evil and perverted love are conspicuous by their absence.

What evil there is in the story remains basically peripheral, for the pure love of Shinji and Hatsue cannot be corrupted. It is the most normal and healthy of his works. *The Sound of Waves* is lyrical, simple, and satisfying, so much so that some have criticized it as being sentimental. While the setting is exotic, it is not exotic in a negative sense. Furthermore, it is the least obscure and reads in English as the least "foreign" of his novels, for it is intentionally unsophisticated and uses simple pastoral elements to tell a story that is concerned with human relationships that are as timeless as the sea that surrounds the island on which the events of the tale occur.

In *The Sound of Waves*, Mishima appears determined to demonstrate to himself that he could create in his writing a world totally different from his own, but even more than that, to show that he could have a place in that world. Several years after the novel was written, Mishima is said to have commented that at about the time of its writing, he had felt a desire to try to turn himself into his own opposite.

Mishima long entertained a hope to visit Greece, and on a voyage around the world in the early 1950's, he found that Greece was even more wonderful than he had imagined. On this voyage, he began to realize that many of the pictures he had painted of human life in the past were highly incomplete; they had dwelled only on the dark side of life. Thus was born the idea of writing an idyllic story that would be based on a classical Greek myth, that of Daphnis and Chloë. It would provide an idyll of a boy and a girl and the sea and would include a fairy-tale-like series of trials that the fisher boy would have to overcome to gain the hand of his "princess." In terms of Mishima's own artistic development, writing this novel based on classical literature demonstrated that, whether that classical background was Japanese or Western, it could serve as an effective substitute for personal experience. Mishima secured some help in locating the kind of island he envisioned for the setting of the story, Kamijima, off the coast of Izu. He spent about ten days on the island, becoming familiar with it. Completed in 1954, the novel became Mishima's best-selling one up to that time, with some 106,000 copies being sold immediately and over 100,000 copies annually thereafter for some years. Soon, major Japanese film companies were in competition with one another for rights. After a film version was released a few months later, Mishima received the first Shinchosha prize for the novel.

The Sound of Waves makes use of a number of important images, not the least of which is the human body, especially the male body. In this respect, it is not unlike some Mishima's other works. In *The Sound of Waves*, the major characters embody the fullness of life through their physical strength. The healthy skin and rosy cheeks of Hatsue and Chiyoko are noted. The sunburned skin of most of the characters is described in detail. It is Shinji's body that is especially important. When he stands against the firelight, he is "like a piece of heroic sculpture," underscoring the classical source of the story. It is the physical strength of that body that is the most important, however, for without superior strength, even Shinji's courage would have been insufficient to win the final test of his fitness during a typhoon at sea, an event that turns the tide for him in gaining the approval of Hatsue's father.

As suggested by the title of the novel, the sea is important in the story. Despite the fact that Japan is an island nation, the sea has not played an especially prominent role in Japanese literature. *The Sound of Waves* is an exception. Early in the novel, the reader is told that "Yashiro Shrine is dedicated to Watatsumu-no-mikoto, god of the sea," making it clear that the fisherman of this island are devout worshipers of this god. Frequently the islanders pray for calm seas, and if one is rescued from some peril at sea, a votive offering at the sea-god's shrine is made immediately. Hatsuo writes Shinji, when he gets a job on the Kamikaze-maru, that she will go daily to Yashiro Shrine to pray for his safety. The sense that the island is favored by the gods foreshadows the happy ending that Shinji and Hatsue enjoy. Very near the end of the novel, Shinji reflects that the blessing of the gods on the little island of Uta Jima had protected their happiness and "brought their love to fulfillment." Mishima uses the sea in characterizing the lovers: Shinji's clear eyes are a gift that the sea makes to those who make their livelihood upon it. Elsewhere, Shinji is said to feel no lack of music in his life because nature itself, the sea, satisfies that need for him. Hatsue's association with the sea as a pearl diver enhances her beauty as it stretches the skin smooth. In the last major scene of the novel, Shinji acts valorously in the sea in Okinawa when he secures the ship to a buoy during a typhoon, putting his own life at great risk, but also enabling him to prove himself to Hatsue's father.

"Critical Evaluation" by Victoria Price

Bibliography:

Napier, Susan J. *Escape from the Wasteland: Romanticism and Realism in the Fiction of Mishima Yukio and Oe Kenzaburo*. Cambridge, Mass.: Council on East Asian Studies, Harvard University, 1991. Declaring *The Sound of Waves* devoid of realism, Napier explores the romantic, idyllic quality of the novel. Emphasizes the story's purity and simplicity.

Nathan, John. *Mishima: A Biography*. Boston: Little, Brown, 1974. In Mishima's biography, the background and context of *The Sound of Waves* are established. Inspiration for the novel is identified as the myth of Daphnis and Chloë.

Petersen, Gwenn Boardman. *The Moon in the Water: Understanding Tanizaki, Kawabata, and Mishima*. Honolulu: University Press of Hawaii, 1979. Sees the classical male body as a dominant figure in all of Mishima's works, including *The Sound of Waves*. Notes associations of fire and desire in the novel.

Scott-Stokes, Henry. *The Life and Death of Yukio Mishima*. New York: Farrar, Straus and Giroux, 1974. A brief section on *The Sound of Waves* discusses Mishima's visit to Greece as an influence on the novel. Explains the widespread popular acclaim given the novel in Japan, unmatched by its critical attention.

Viglielmo, Valdo H. "The Sea as Metaphor: An Aspect of the Modern Japanese Novel." In *The Sea, from Elemental Stirrings to Symbolic Inspiration, Language, and Life-Significance in Literary Interpretation and Theory*. Part 1 in *Poetics of the Elements in the Human Condition:* Boston: D. Reidel, 1985. Argues that unlike Mishima's other novels, *The Sound of Waves* is exceptionally positive and even idyllic. Identifies Shinji and Hatsue as creatures of the sea.

SOUTH WIND

Type of work: Novel
Author: Norman Douglas (1868-1952)
Type of plot: Social satire
Time of plot: Early twentieth century
Locale: Island of Nepenthe
First published: 1917

Principal characters:

BISHOP HEARD OF BAMPOPO, an Anglican clergyman
MRS. MEADOWS, his cousin
DON FRANCESCO, a Catholic priest
MR. VAN KOPPEN, an American millionaire
FREDDY PARKER, the proprietor of a drinking club
MR. KEITH, a hedonist
MR. EAMES, an elderly scholar
COUNT CALOVEGLIA, an antiquarian
DENIS PHIPPS, a student
RETLOW (alias MUHLEN), a blackguard

The Story:

Bishop Heard went to Nepenthe to meet his cousin, Mrs. Meadows. Since her second husband had been unable to leave his post in India, the bishop was to escort Mrs. Meadows and her child to England. The bishop himself was returning from ecclesiastical labors in Bampopo, Africa. The bishop was introduced to Nepenthe society by Don Francesco, a priest he had met on the boat. The social leader was the American-born duchess of San Martino, who was about to join the church through Don Francesco's influence. Other figures were Mr. Keith, a wealthy hedonist; Denis Phipps, a frustrated college student; Mr. Eames, a faithful compiler of material for an annotated edition of a forgotten work on the *Antiquities* of Nepenthe; Count Caloveglia, an antiquarian interested in the Golden Age of Greece; and Freddy Parker, proprietor of a drinking club that served a strange brand of whiskey bottled by his stepsister.

There was also much talk of some religious fanatics, disciples of an unwashed Russian mystic named Bazhakuloff. Because of a virile apostle, Peter, the group was favored by Madame Steynlin and had access to her villa by the sea. One of the few Englishwomen on the island was Miss Wilberforce, who frequently drank to excess and undressed in the streets at odd times of the day and night. Fortunately, the bishop had developed a tolerant point of view while living among African natives, and he was able to accept these strange characters as he found them. Except for a festival in honor of Saint Dodekanus and a visit with his cousin, who did not seem pleased to see him, the first days of the bishop's stay were uneventful. Then one of the old springs on the island suddenly dried up, and the natives reported several unusual births. Next, Mr. Parker's stepsister was bitten by a strange insect. She died swiftly and would have been as swiftly buried if the volcano had not erupted at the same time.

Mr. Parker watched ashes falling over the city and was saddened both by his stepsister's death and by news that a cabinet minister of Nicaragua had been removed from office. Since the minister had made Parker the Nicaraguan finance commissioner for southeastern Europe, the proprietor feared that he was about to lose his pretentious but empty title. Hoping that the

Vatican would intercede for him if he were to become a Catholic, he consulted the parish priest and suggested a procession in honor of the island's patron saint to bring an end to the eruption. The priest was delighted to hear such a pious suggestion from a non-Catholic, and before long, the holy procession was winding through the ashy streets. Miraculously enough, the ashes stopped falling and rain that followed washed away all traces of nature's upheaval.

The eruption ended, and life went on as usual. Several parties were given for Mr. Van Koppen, an American millionaire who visited the island every year. At these parties, the bishop heard more about the life of the colony. He talked with Denis and learned about his problems. He heard with amusement of Van Koppen's promise to contribute liberally toward a clinic for Miss Wilberforce, if Mr. Keith would give a like sum. Van Koppen knew that Keith believed people should be allowed to do what they liked with their lives, and he thus knew that Keith would never part with the amount he had promised.

One day the bishop, visiting Count Caloveglia, found him about to sell the American a small bronze statue of wonderful antique Greek workmanship. To authenticate the statue, which had been unearthed on the count's property, Van Koppen had called in an English art expert. Although the expert declared the piece a real masterpiece and a rare find, Van Koppen knew that the work was a fake. He was willing to pay the price, however, as a compliment to the count's ability to deceive the expert.

The next day, the bishop went for a walk along the cliffs with Denis, who was still perturbed about his problem of where to go and what to do. While they rested, the bishop saw that they were in sight of his cousin's villa. As he watched, he saw Mrs. Meadows come out of her house and walk along the cliff with a man who had called himself Muhlen when the bishop met him on the boat. Later, he had heard that the man was a blackmailer whose real name was Retlow. He wondered what his cousin was doing with such a person. Suddenly, the man disappeared, and Mrs. Meadows walked briskly back to her house. The bishop had just watched a murder.

Suddenly he remembered where he had heard the name Retlow before; it had been the name of his cousin's first husband. Doubtless he had been blackmailing her. So far as the bishop could see, she had been justified in killing him. He remembered that on the boat Retlow had said a particularly annoying child ought to be thrown overboard. The bishop decided that Retlow's own end was consistent with his ideas.

Unfortunately, a gold piece that had belonged to Retlow came to light in the possession of a native boy. When the boy was accused of murder, the case became a battle of rival factions. The boy was a cousin of the village priest, and Signor Malipizzo, the magistrate, was a Freemason who hoped to discredit the church through that relationship. To defend the boy, the priest called in the Commendatore Morena, a lawyer who had risen to fame and power through his membership in the Black Hand. At the trial, the boy was judged innocent, chiefly because of Morena's eloquence. He first called the jurors' attention to the crime they would commit if they removed the boy from his mother, a relationship that had been important to so many famous men. Then, learning that the boy was an orphan, he shifted his argument to show what an injustice they would commit if they convicted an innocent boy. The accused went free. Under the circumstances, the bishop resolved to say nothing of Mrs. Meadows' guilt. With her fears of blackmail removed, she seemed a different woman. Nobody had suffered from the murder but Retlow, who deserved his fate.

Denis finally became angry at Mr. Keith's drunken meddling, and he told the old hedonist to shut up. It was the first time Denis had ever made a decision for himself and carried it through. His visit to Nepenthe had started him on the road to manhood. On the whole, reflected the bishop, most matters affecting the people of Nepenthe turned out well in the end.

Critical Evaluation:

Commentators on Norman Douglas' work have frequently noted that he never wasted material. He not only recycled articles and essays but also viewed his books as opportunities to expound upon the myriad subjects on which he was an expert or at least had strong opinions. *South Wind* is a kind of grab bag of lectures and observations on various, often obscure, aspects of geology, climatology, history, morality, religion, and folklore, among other topics. Douglas' use of articulate characters confined to a restricted setting allows for ample airing of views, and recalls the methods of English novelist Thomas Love Peacock, whose country house novels were once very popular.

South Wind's setting itself is a good example of Douglas' methods. Nepenthe is not to be found on a map, but critics have generally related it to the island of Capri, about which Douglas had written a series of scholarly pamphlets and upon which he was living when he completed *South Wind*. Douglas did not deny his novel's debt to a real location, but insisted that Ischia, Ponza, and the Lipari Islands (all lying off the southwest coast of Italy) were the actual sources for Nepenthe's natural scenery. Douglas even incorporated a version of his observations regarding the pumice stone industry of the Lipari Islands, the subject of one of his first publications. Douglas' creation had deep roots in his own experience—the details of which he drew upon heavily.

The novel's characters are the result of much the same process, which represents a central weakness of *South Wind*. One or two seem to be based on historically obscure acquaintances of Douglas, but others are little more than personifications of facets of their author's own personality. The voluble Mr. Keith is clearly a spokesman for Douglas' hedonistic views, and Mr. Eames and Count Caloveglia represent Douglas' scholarly and antiquarian interests. All are perfectly adequate mouthpieces, but none emerges as rounded or particularly memorable.

As Douglas had difficulty in creating complex characters, so, too, he experienced problems in plotting. When this deficiency was pointed out in reviews, Douglas retorted that *South Wind* was "nothing but plot," and went on to describe that plot as "how to make murder palatable to a bishop." Readers may be forgiven for thinking that Douglas was protesting too much, because few of them turn the pages of *South Wind* to find out what happens next. Instead, readers continue with the book because they are captivated by Douglas' attractive personality and entranced by the sunny mood he captures.

Douglas spent most of his adult life near the shores of the Mediterranean, and he championed the region's values as his own. He prized the Mediterranean's temperate climate (and put his ideas about the relationship between climate and culture into the mouth of Count Caloveglia), its historical associations, and the moderation it seemed to induce in matters of religion, philosophy, and morals. Indeed, *South Wind* might be read as an account of the adjustment of Bishop Heard to the Mediterranean.

South Wind appeared at the height of World War I, and its gaiety contrasts sharply with the bleak, somber mood prevalent throughout Europe and the United States at that time. It also appeared at a time when urbanization and mass production seemed to threaten the individualistic way of life Douglas enjoyed and celebrated. These factors contributed to the book's enormous popularity, and it became the sort of book that anyone with a claim to sophistication read. As British novelist Graham Greene wrote in his introduction to Douglas' last book, "My generation was brought up on *South Wind*."

Indeed, several British writers of Greene's generation were directly influenced by Douglas in general and by *South Wind* in particular. Aldous Huxley's satirical novels *Crome Yellow* (1921, in which Douglas appears as the character Scrogan), *Antic Hay* (1923), and *Point Coun-*

ter Point (1928) bear its stamp. Greene himself generally wrote books of a darker character, but his humorous novel *Travels with My Aunt* (1969) bears similarities to *South Wind*, and was received with some of the criticisms that greeted Douglas' work. Among later British writers, Lawrence Durrell owes a debt to Douglas. Several of Durrell's early novels and Greek travel books exhibit Douglas' hedonistic attitude, his kaleidoscopic interests, and his erudite style.

Among readers, the key to *South Wind*'s enduring popularity may be that it is greater than the sum of its parts. Just as the sirocco, the south wind of Douglas' title, works its magic on Nepenthe's visitors, so Douglas' infectious good humor transforms what might under other circumstances have been indifferent material. *South Wind* is one of the most enjoyable satires in the English language. Douglas' attitudes hardened later in life, but when he wrote his first novel he was content to poke gentle fun at the targets of his satire, and did not hesitate to include himself. For example, Denis asserts his independence by turning on the drunken and garrulous Mr. Keith, Douglas' most obvious alter ego. Concepts of sophistication have changed since *South Wind* appeared, but many of Douglas' concerns remain as important to contemporary readers as they were in 1917. Under these circumstances, Douglas' laughter and his healthy scorn are still important.

"Critical Evaluation" by Grove Koger

Bibliography:

Greenlees, Ian. *Norman Douglas*. Harlow, Essex, England: Longman Group, 1971. A pamphlet-length survey by a man who knew and traveled with Douglas. *South Wind* receives careful attention.

Holloway, Mark. *Norman Douglas: A Biography*. London: Martin Secker & Warburg, 1976. The only comprehensive biography. A warm but judicious consideration by a man who admits to enjoying Douglas' work "almost without reservation." Contains the most thorough investigation available of *South Wind*'s origin, composition, and influence.

Leary, Lewis. *Norman Douglas*. New York: Columbia University Press, 1968. A brief survey that treats *South Wind* prominently. Concludes that the novel remains as fresh as when it first appeared.

Lindeman, Ralph D. *Norman Douglas*. Boston: Twayne, 1965. Easily the best book-length introduction to Douglas and his writings. *South Wind* receives specific treatment. Bibliography.

Matthews, Jack. "Jack Matthews on Norman Douglas's *South Wind*." In *Rediscoveries: Informal Essays in Which Well-Known Novelists Rediscover Neglected Works of Fiction by One of Their Favorite Authors*, edited by David Madden. New York: Crown, 1971. A genial appreciation stressing the novel's intelligence, compassion, and humor. Wonders at the book's neglect. A good starting place for research.

SPAIN, TAKE THIS CUP FROM ME

Type of work: Poetry
Author: César Vallejo (1892-1938)
First published: España, aparta de mí este calíz, 1939 (English translation, 1974)

For the reader who must rely on the English translation of the poetry of César Vallejo, there will always be some sense of distance from the original Spanish. This is all the more the case as Vallejo, like the Irish writer James Joyce, often played with his native language in his poetry, and wordplay is nearly always untranslatable.

César Vallejo, who was born in Santiago de Chuco, a tiny town nestling in the Peruvian Andes, and who died in Paris, is considered by many to be the finest of all Spanish America's poets of the twentieth century. He wrote essays, short stories, a novel, literary criticism, and drama, but he is mainly remembered for his poetry. Vallejo's work falls into five main stages: 1915-1918, *modernismo*; 1919-1926, the avant-garde; 1927-1931, Marxism (Trotskyism gradually transformed into Stalinism); 1932-1935, political disillusionment; and 1936-1938, Christian Marxism. *Spain, Take This Cup from Me* belongs to the culminating phase of Vallejo's work, the Christian-Marxist phase. This collection of poems was written during the first two years of the Spanish Civil War (1936-1938). Vallejo died on Good Friday, 1938, after which the war dragged on for another year. *Spain, Take This Cup from Me* was inspired by the events of the war, about which Vallejo read in newspaper reports. (He used to wait in the railway station in Paris for news from Spain.) Vallejo also drew on his experiences during two visits he made to Spain, one as a reporter in the winter of 1936, the other as the Peruvian delegate at the International Writers' Conference held in Madrid and Valencia in the summer of 1937. Vallejo was not alone in writing poems about the Spanish Civil War. Others, among them the English poet Stephen Spender, the French poet Louis Aragon, the Chilean Pablo Neruda, the Cuban Nicolás Guillén, and the Spanish poets Miguel Hernández and Rafael Alberti, also used the war as a theme of their work. Vallejo's poetry is unique, however, in that it expresses a political faith in the Republican cause through the motif of Christian resurrection, a rather unusual choice given the proletarian and often anticlerical bias of the Republicans and especially the communists who supported the Republican war effort. It was thought for many years that *Spain, Take This Cup from Me* had never been published. The 1939 publication had appeared just before Francisco Franco's troops invaded Barcelona, and to prevent the work's being destroyed, copies were secretly hidden in the monastery at Montserrat, where they were not unearthed until 1981.

Spain, Take This Cup from Me consists of fifteen poems of varying length. The opening poem, "Hymn to the Volunteers for the Republic" (176 lines), which is addressed to the Republican militiamen, imagines a world in which the Republicans have already won the war; it is a utopian world of harmony similar to that envisioned in the prophecies of Isaiah. "Battles" (144 lines) is dedicated to the people of Estremadura, a poor region of Spain on the west near the Portuguese border, which took the brunt of the war effort early on; Franco's troops first landed in southern Spain from the Canary Islands and Morocco and then moved northward. Poem no. 3, "He used to write with his big finger in the air . . ." (45 lines), is based on the death of an imaginary railwayman named Pedro Rojas. Both parts of his name have symbolic connotations, Pedro referring to Peter, the founder of the Christian church, and Rojas to the symbolic color of communism, red. Pedro Rojas therefore stands as a fusion of Christianity and communism. Most striking about the poem is its use of the myth of Prometheus, who was tied to a rock and had his liver eaten by an eagle every day as punishment for having given fire to humankind. In Vallejo's use of the myth, the animal exacting the punishment becomes a vulture to underline the earthiness of the pain of warfare. Vallejo also alludes to the betacism of the Spanish language, the fact that the letters "b" and "v" sound the same in Spanish, in order to emphasize his allegiance with the lower classes, who often misspell words with a "b" instead of a "v." Vallejo reflects the illiteracy of the uneducated classes not in order to ridicule them but to express his political solidarity with them.

Poem no. 4, "The beggars fight for Spain . . ." (25 lines), portrays the struggle for the city of Santander on the northern coast of Spain. Here Vallejo expresses the powerlessness of the have-nots of this world through the image of the beggar. The sinister poem no. 5, "Spanish Image of Death" (45 lines), describes death, here personified and walking around the field of battle. In conclusion, the poet seems to be welcoming the person of death into his own life, as if expressing a suicidal desire. "Cortege after the Capture of Bilbao" (dated September 13, 1937; 28 lines) is based on the final procession of Republicans killed by the assault on the northern Basque town of Bilbao, which fell to the Nationalists on June 18, 1937. Poem no. 7, "For several days the air, companions" (dated November 5, 1937; 26 lines), portrays the movement backward and forward of enemy lines during the struggle for the city of Gijón in the north of Spain; Gijón was finally invaded by Nationalist forces on October 21, 1937. To stress the fact that Franco's troops are the foreign invaders in this war, Vallejo suggests that the land "is Spanish" when it is still loyal to the Republicans. He refutes the legitimacy of Franco's war effort, which was called a "crusade" by the Nationalists, including the Catholic church. Poem no. 8, "Here . . ." (dated September 10, 1937; 38 lines), is devoted to a mythical Republican militiaman, Ramón Collar, who is explicitly compared with Christ. The eleventh poem, "Short Prayer for a Loyalist Hero" (dated September 10, 1937; 22 lines), refers to a militiaman who fell at the battle of Toledo. The opening stanzas of the poem refer to the image at the beginning of the Gospel of St. John, where Christ is referred to as the "Word made flesh." In his poem, Vallejo describes—in surrealist terms—a book as emerging from the dead body of a militiaman. This image also alludes by implication to the poet's verse, which is produced from and transcends death. "Winter During the Battle for Teruel" (33 lines), the tenth poem, is based on the ferocious battle for the city of Teruel in eastern Spain. That battle went on from December 15, 1937, until February 22, 1938, and was interrupted by some of the coldest winter weather ever experienced in that region. In this poem, Vallejo concentrates on the vicarious pain he experiences at witnessing the soldiers' misery. The eleventh poem, "I looked at the corpse, at his visible swift order . . ." (dated September 3, 1937; 14 lines), refers to the way a dead militiaman seemed momentarily to come back to life but was confirmed dead. When the soldiers listened to his heart, they heard nothing but "dates." "Mass" (dated November 10, 1937; 17 lines) is perhaps Vallejo's most famous poem; it depicts the imaginary moment on the battlefield in which a dead Republican militiaman, like Lazarus, rises from his deathbed and begins to walk. Yet it is not Christ who resurrects the dead militiaman but the combined love of all the inhabitants on the globe. This poem is a humanist rewriting of the Lazarus story from the synoptic gospels; in essence it fuses the transcendent Christian belief in eternal life with the human solidarity of socialism.

"Funeral Drumroll for the Ruins of Durango" (30 lines) is based on the bombing of the city of Durango, which was destroyed on April 26, 1937. A rewriting of the Lord's Prayer, this poem in effect sanctifies the dust and destruction that is all that is left of Durango. "Beware, Spain, of your own Spain! . . ." (22 lines) is one of the most confessional of all of the poems in *Spain, Take This Cup from Me.* At the time of the Spanish Civil War, worldwide communism was split between two options: the Stalinist option, which favored "Socialism in One Country," and the

Trotskyist option, which favored revolutionary internationalism, that is, the spreading of the doctrine of communism throughout the world. Vallejo's poem refers to the purges taking place in the Republican zone, which the English writer George Orwell described magnificently in his *Homage to Catalonia* (1938). At this time, the Stalinists were rooting out the Trotskyists and murdering them; in fact, Trotsky would himself be murdered by a Stalinist henchman, though not in Spain but in Mexico. Thus the reference in line 2 to the "sickle without the hammer" should be understood to mean an incomplete communism, a doctrine, such as Stalinism, which is missing an important ingredient. The phrase "Beware of the one hundred percent loyal" (line 15) is a reference to the overzealous Communist doctrinarian who is prepared to sacrifice his friends on behalf of the party.

Finally, "Spain, Take This Cup from Me" (51 lines), the fifteenth poem, from which the title of the collection is taken, describes the possibility that Spain may actually fall to its enemy; this is in fact what did happen, though Vallejo did not live to see the day. Spain, in this poem, becomes a motherlike figure, symbolizing nature (she holds the energy of the earth within her) and culture (she is compared to a schoolteacher who teaches her children how to read and write). As a mother figure, Spain stands not only as a mother for all the citizens of Spain, but also for the citizens of the Spanish-speaking Latin American countries, where Spain is commonly known as "la madre patria," the mother country. The poem concludes by declaring that, should Spain fall, the whole world must go out and search for Spain. This poem, like the fourteen others in *Spain, Take This Cup from Me*, is a gesture of anguished solidarity with Spain and the Republican militiamen who lost their lives fighting for their homeland.

Stephen M. Hart

Bibliography:

Brotherston, Gordon. *Latin American Poetry: Origins and Presence*. Cambridge, England: Cambridge University Press, 1975. The section on Vallejo's posthumous work (pp. 121-131) shows how Vallejo used images taken from the Bible to describe the apocalyptic nature of the Spanish Civil War.

Franco, Jean. *César Vallejo: The Dialectics of Poetry and Silence*. Cambridge, England: Cambridge University Press, 1976. Chapter 9 concentrates on *Spain, Take This Cup from Me* and discusses the use of certain images throughout the poem, such as fire and water, which signify salvation and purification.

Hart, Stephen M. "The World Upside-Down in the Work of César Vallejo." *Bulletin of Hispanic Studies* 62, no. 2 (April, 1985): 163-177. Section on *Spain, Take This Cup from Me* shows how Vallejo uses the image of the prophecy in the book of Isaiah of a world of peace and harmony to portray his vision of a Republican utopia.

Higgins, James. *The Poet in Peru*. Liverpool, England: Francis Cairns, 1982. A good overview, containing a discussion of Vallejo's posthumous work. Analyzes the interplay of the visionary and the socially committed sides of Vallejo's poetic personality.

Vallejo, César. *The Complete Posthumous Poetry*. Translated by Clayton Eshleman and José Rubia Barcia. Berkeley: University of California Press, 1978. Includes a lengthy discussion of *Spain, Take This Cup from Me*. Also provides a helpful introduction to Vallejo.

THE SPANISH FRIAR
Or, The Double Discovery

Type of work: Drama
Author: John Dryden (1631-1700)
Type of plot: Tragicomedy
Time of plot: Fifteenth century
Locale: Aragon, Spain
First performed: 1680; first published, 1681

Principal characters:
Torrismond, son of Sancho the deposed king, defender of Aragon against the Moors
Leonora, queen of Aragon, the daughter of the usurper, engaged to Bertran
Bertran, made a duke by Leonora's father, now in military disgrace
Raymond, foster father of Torrismond
Dominic, a licentious friar
Lorenzo, a young gallant and soldier
Gomez, an elderly usurer
Elvira, his young wife

The Story:

Aragon was in a state of siege because the usurper king, lately dead, had refused to acknowledge and reward the services of the Moors in gaining the kingdom for him. Queen Leonora, promised on her father's deathbed to Duke Bertran, regretted this alliance as well as the fact she held in a dungeon the deposed King Sancho, a righteous and beloved ruler. Bertran's forces had been routed three times by the Moors before Torrismond, supposed son of Raymond, one of the leading nobles, rallied the scattered Christians and saved the kingdom from the infidels.

Young Lorenzo, a valiant colonel in Torrismond's army, brought news of the victory and confided to his friends his desire to celebrate with the first prostitute available. He boasted that he had robbed his Moorish victims of gold and jewels. Elvira, the young wife of a jealous old moneylender named Gomez, made advances to the handsome soldier, but her husband immediately thwarted plans for the assignation that had been put in motion by Friar Dominic.

Upon his triumphal return, Torrismond offended Bertran by openly ridiculing him for ineptness. He also naïvely declared his love for the queen, who, in turn, was smitten with love for the young hero. Bertran vowed vengeance and agreed to her suggestion to kill King Sancho because he thought that would hasten the marriage. Leonora had made the suggestion with the intention of thereby making Torrismond her king-husband. Torrismond, however, remained loyal to the old king and Raymond.

Despite all efforts to the contrary, clandestine love prevailed in the palace, though not in Gomez's mansion. Friar Dominic, ghostly father to Elvira, made a series of arrangements for the young wife and her hopeful gallant to meet, but each meeting was discovered by the near-cuckolded husband. Bertran, too, did his best to keep Leonora and Torrismond apart by testing the reaction of the populace to the supposed murder of King Sancho.

Raymond, incensed by such intrigues, admitted that in the troublesome days of the Moorish invasion King Sancho had entrusted to him his son Torrismond. Raymond urged Torrismond to take over the kingdom and to avenge the old king's death by deposing or killing the usurpers. Torn between his love for Leonora and his filial duty to his foster father and real father, Torrismond was unable to commit so bloody a deed. He declared his belief that Leonora's repentance and his own attempt to thwart the regicide settled that score. After learning Torrismond's decision, Raymond, though he was moved to compassion over his adopted son's predicament, departed to rouse the citizens.

The intrigue involving Elvira and Lorenzo had come to nothing; no amount of bribery, blackmail, or disguise could bring the two together, despite the fact that Friar Dominic was a master of trickery and knavery. The friar was finally exposed when Lorenzo's father revealed that Elvira was his daughter, married to Gomez the usurer in order to prevent her suffering a worse fate in those troubled times. Thus the affection Elvira and Lorenzo had felt for each other was based on the family relationship of brother and sister.

To this double discovery of the true parentage of Torrismond and Elvira came a third: King Sancho was not dead. Bertran, suspicious of the queen's motives and aware of the people's loyalty to the old king, had merely spread the rumor of King Sancho's death. Knowing also that the queen was devoted to Torrismond rather than to himself, Bertran begged forgiveness for his part in the many sad events that had occurred in the kingdom. Leonora, much relieved, wished only for King Sancho's permission for her marriage to his son. Torrismond assured her that the good king, quick to forgive, would grant such a boon.

Critical Evaluation:

The Spanish Friar is a modified form of John Dryden's earlier heroic drama. Features in this play common to the mode are a noble hero of great ability and renown, violently torn between his love for a lady and his honor, which impels him to give her up; an exaggerated, often bombastic style of language; an intricate (and often barely credible) plot, sometimes with a comic, dramatically parallel subplot; and a dramatic movement which threatens, even if it does not actually end in, tragedy. *The Spanish Friar* is a considerably more controlled example of the genre than Dryden's *The Conquest of Granada* (1670-1671), but the family resemblance is clear.

It is easy enough to ridicule the fantastic plot complications of heroic drama, and the often extravagant language in which the heroes and heroines express themselves—as in the line "Despair, Death, Hell, have seized my tortured soul . . ."—but it must be remembered that these plays were designed primarily as entertainment, not as historical dramas or studies of character. "'Tis my interest to please my audience," Dryden noted in his preface. The final revelation that old King Sancho is really alive, saved by Bertran's better nature, tends to render nonsensical Torrismond's earlier anguish over whether or not he must turn against Leonora, and the queen's own painful resolve to renounce her husband and retire to a convent. Yet the earlier dramatic action that leads to this crisis is no less fanciful than the conclusion.

Apart from the unlikely plot twists and the larger-than-life characters, it is apparent how skillfully Dryden, largely through brilliant dialogue, manipulates the intellectual and emotional sympathies of his audiences so that they see the issues of the play from the same points of view as the participants. No one character is either fully unsympathetic or fully sympathetic. Leonora is to be condemned for her crime and her evasion of responsibility but pitied in her plight ("to lose a crown and a lover in a day"); the reader may wish to see justice done but not at the expense of her life or happiness. Similarly, Torrismond is to be admired for his love and devotion, but it is easy enough to see the "womanish" quality in him that makes Raymond despise him for his lethargy in love. The audience—not just the hero—is torn by conflicting sympathies, and Dryden's dramatic prowess in creating and modulating this audience involvement is never more apparent than in the exciting exchange between Torrismond and Raymond at the end of Act IV, in which the conflict between love and honor becomes the focal point.

Dryden, author of the stinging lampoon *Mac Flecknoe* (1682), had a sure hand for comedy, and the comic subplot that gives the play its title is a rollicking one. Friar Dominic is a splendid compendium of all the avaricious, hypocritical, debauched friars that had populated English literature since the Middle Ages. Here again, however, Dryden's dramatic portrait is not purely vitriolic but also sympathetic, even half-admiring; certainly it is difficult to take the part of the near-cuckold Gomez over that of the witty and exuberant "old gouty friar."

In addition to his anti-Catholicism, many other of the playwright's sentiments are apparent in *The Spanish Friar*. Possibly most objectionable is the strain of misogyny (another long-established literary tradition) that characterizes women as the weak, lustful, seductive, and inferior sex: "That toy a woman," says Raymond, "made from the dross and refuse of a man." Finally, Dryden's essential political and religious conservatism, his deeply rooted mistrust of the popular will, and his dread of any kind of rebellion against legitimate power, are everywhere apparent here. Even in a work devoted primarily to thrills and laughter, Dryden's implication is clear: Without the guides of established political and religious authority, morality becomes relative and behavior mechanical, as Leonora realizes when she allows Bertran to perpetrate the murder of the lawful king.

Bibliography:

Eliot, T. S. *John Dryden: The Poet, the Dramatist, the Critic*. 1932. Reprint. New York: Haskell House, 1966. Eliot's discussion helped introduce Dryden to twentieth century audiences and still serves as a starting point for other critiques. Although very generalized, it highlights reasons why Dryden's plays continue to fascinate critics and students.

Hopkins, David. *John Dryden*. Cambridge, England: Cambridge University Press, 1986. Within this updated assessment of Dryden's place among English writers, Hopkins provides an introduction to *The Spanish Friar* for new readers. He includes a plot summary and focuses on Dryden's preface.

Loftis, John. "Chapter Two: Dryden's Comedies." In *Writers and Their Background: John Dryden*, edited by Earl Miner. Athens: Ohio University Press, 1972. Carefully differentiating between the play's comic and serious plots, this discussion calls attention to the English political context, especially the anti-Catholic bias and the Exclusion Controversy.

Ward, Charles E. *The Life of John Dryden*. Chapel Hill: University of North Carolina Press, 1961. This biography puts the play in the context of Dryden's career and details the play's political background, performances, and audience. Ward interprets the main character, Friar Dominic, as a satirization of Catholicism rather than of the clergy.

Wasserman, George R. *John Dryden*. New York: Twayne, 1964. Wasserman gives an overview of Dryden's life and works. He fits *The Spanish Friar* among the tragicomedies and draws heavily on Dryden's interest in Ben Jonson's comedy of humours prototype in discussing style and theatrical context.

THE SPANISH TRAGEDY

Type of work: Drama
Author: Thomas Kyd (1558-1594)
Type of plot: Tragedy
Time of plot: Sixteenth century
Locale: The Spanish and Portuguese courts
First performed: c. 1585-1589; first published, c. 1594

Principal characters:
DON ANDREA, a murdered Spanish nobleman
BALTHAZAR, Prince of Portugal
LORENZO, a Spanish nobleman
BEL-IMPERIA, fiancée of Don Andrea before his death
HIERONIMO, a Spanish general
HORATIO, Don Andrea's friend and Hieronimo's son
ALEXANDRO, and
VILLUPPO, Portuguese noblemen

The Story:

Don Andrea, a Spanish nobleman, was killed in battle with the Portuguese. After his soul went to the underworld, Pluto sent it and the Spirit of Revenge back to learn what had happened after Don Andrea's death. At the Spanish court Don Andrea's ghost heard that the Portuguese had been defeated in war and that Balthazar, Prince of Portugal, had been taken prisoner. Balthazar, Don Andrea learned, was the man who had killed him. A quarrel had developed between Lorenzo and Horatio, each claiming the honor of capturing Balthazar.

Meanwhile, at the Portuguese court, Villuppo told the viceroy that his son Balthazar was dead, having been killed by traitorous Alexandro. Alexandro was then sentenced to death.

Balthazar, while a prisoner, fell in love with Bel-Imperia, as did Horatio. Bel-Imperia, who had been the fiancée of the slain Don Andrea, fell in love with Horatio. Plans were proposed for a treaty of peace between Spain and Portugal. These events were all distasteful to Don Andrea's ghost. He was comforted, however, by the Spirit of Revenge's promise that grim fate would overtake all concerned.

Balthazar, aided by Lorenzo, planned to win the love of Bel-Imperia. Lorenzo sent a servant to spy on Bel-Imperia and to discover whom she loved. When he returned to tell his master that Bel-Imperia was in love with Horatio, Lorenzo and Balthazar plotted Horatio's death.

The King of Spain planned to make diplomatic use of Bel-Imperia by marrying her, his niece, to Portuguese Prince Balthazar, thus cementing the friendship of the two countries. The king warned her that she must do his will. One night, when Bel-Imperia and Horatio met in the garden, Horatio was set upon by Balthazar and Lorenzo and hanged. After his death Bel-Imperia was taken away by Lorenzo and Balthazar. When the body was discovered, Hieronimo, Horatio's father, went mad, as did his wife. Seeing these events, Don Andrea's ghost became even more bitter. The Spirit of Revenge told him to be patient.

The ambassador to Spain, returning to the Portuguese court, arrived in time to prevent the death of Alexandro, because the ambassador brought word that Balthazar still lived. Villuppo, who had plotted Alexandro's death in hopes of preferment, was sentenced to die.

In Spain, Hieronimo, partly recovered from his madness, plotted to avenge his son's murder. Afraid of Hieronimo, Lorenzo and Balthazar planned to murder one of their accomplices, lest he give away their secrets. They had him slain by another of their accomplices. When the murderer was arrested and sentenced to hang, they told him he would be saved with a pardon. The man went to his death in silence, or so Lorenzo and Balthazar believed. Before his execution, however, he had written a confession in which he told the true story of Horatio's death, and he had sent the document to Hieronimo.

Meanwhile Lorenzo and Balthazar had imprisoned Bel-Imperia in hopes of forcing her to marry Balthazar. She, bewildered by all that had happened, finally believed Lorenzo's statement that she would only suffer her father's and the king's anger if she failed to marry Balthazar willingly.

Balthazar and Lorenzo enlisted Hieronimo's aid in presenting an entertainment for the Spanish court and the Portuguese viceroy, who had arrived to swear fealty to the King of Spain. Hieronimo suggested that they do a play that he had written and silenced their protestations with the observation that even Nero had not considered it beneath his dignity to act in a play. The play, he told them, was to be a tragedy befitting royal actors and a royal audience.

In the meantime Hieronimo's mad wife, still lamenting the death of her son, cut down the arbor where he was hanged by his assailants, and stabbed herself. Hers was the fourth death in the action watched by Don Andrea's ghost and the Spirit of Revenge. That evening the royal party gathered for the play that Hieronimo and the others were to present. When the party entered, Hieronimo insisted that they all enter a gallery, lock the door, and throw the key down to him. The king, thinking nothing amiss, agreed to do so. Thus the stage was set for Hieronimo to avenge the murder of his son.

In the play Balthazar played the Emperor Soliman, Lorenzo played a knight, and Bel-Imperia played a Christian woman captured and given to Soliman. While Soliman and the knight argued over the captured woman, a bashaw, acted by Hieronimo, entered and killed the knight, and the captured Christian woman killed the stage emperor. Then, stopping the applause for the fine performance, Hieronimo introduced the body of his dead son and assured the audience that the deaths they had watched were real. Then he ran to hang himself before the royal party could break out of the locked gallery.

Overtaken by courtiers before he could kill himself, he bit out his own tongue to prevent a confession. Told to confess in writing, he gestured for a knife to sharpen the pen. With that weapon he stabbed the king's brother and himself, thus bringing the number of deaths to eight.

At the end, Don Andrea's ghost, who had been watching all the while, announced to the Spirit of Revenge that he was satisfied; all his enemies had received their just deserts. The Spirit of Revenge told him that they would return to the underworld, where Don Andrea could watch his enemies in their torment and consort happily with his friends.

Critical Evaluation:

The Spanish Tragedy, one of the most popular English plays of the sixteenth century, marked a change from the earlier, stilted English drama. Thomas Kyd built his plot on a foundation of three conventional devices found in the Roman tragedies of Seneca. One is a ghost; the second is revenge for a murdered relative, and the third is a liberal use of bombast and soliloquy in the dialogue. To these he added strange characters with perverse psychological twists: madmen, murderers, suicides. He also employed a play within the play, public hangings, and other items new to English drama. As a pioneer playwright, Kyd, in this play, pointed the way to the lurid, bloodthirsty revenge plays of the Jacobean and Caroline stage. The popularity of *The Spanish Tragedy* can be partly seen in the fact that it is known to have gone through at least ten editions by 1634.

The Spanish Tragedy is a nearly perfect example of Elizabethan revenge tragedy. Kyd's spectacular play—with its eight onstage murders and suicides, a public hanging, mad scenes, and the biting out of Hieronimo's tongue—initiated the genre's popularity at the beginning of the seventeenth century. Kyd upstages all his contemporaries in his ability to devise thrilling stage tricks, and the nine extant quarto editions of *The Spanish Tragedy* testify to the play's ability to draw an audience.

The play defines Elizabethan revenge tragedy. The major stock features are all to be found in it, including a revenge, directed either by the father or the son for the sake of the other; a ghost, outside the action of the play, who aids the revenger; hesitation of the hero or revenger (the hero often is contaminated by his passion and becomes, because of the delay, Machiavellian); real or pretended insanity; the presence of suicides, intrigues, scheming villains, and other various horrors.

Comparison between *The Spanish Tragedy* and William Shakespeare's *Hamlet, Prince of Denmark* (1600-1601), written about fifteen years later, is provocative. Both plays have an amiable Horatio, ghosts returning from the dead, father-son vengeance themes, justice retarded by the mental state of the avenger, a dumb show, a play within a play, and profound sensationalism. There is no doubt that Kyd's play in some ways helped shape *Hamlet*. Kyd is in fact attributed as author of the lost play that is probably an earlier version of the Hamlet story.

The Spanish Tragedy withstands the test of critical analysis. Its multiple-subplot construction produces some interesting and sophisticated critical questions. As a result of the liveliness of his play, Kyd is not always regarded as a careful playwright. The revenge motif, for example, plays itself out through three characters, Don Andrea, Bel-Imperia, and Hieronimo. Furthermore, in addition to the audience of the play, there are two other onstage audiences. One is the ghost of Don Andrea and the Spirit of Revenge. The other is the Spanish court, which witnesses the dumb show.

A major critical issue regarding *The Spanish Tragedy* is the question of audience response to Hieronimo. Is he a hero or a villain? Ambiguously, he is both. Judged by Elizabethan ethical and legal standards of behavior, Hieronimo becomes a wholly despicable Machiavellian villain when he decides to effect his revenge by secret—private, rather than public—means. In terms of revenge tragedy, the development in Hieronimo's character from public avenger-hero to private avenger-villain is evidence that Kyd is deliberately turning his audience's sympathy against the revengeful father.

In the play's famous *vindicta mihi* passage, Hieronimo concludes he will act out private vengeance for his son's death:

> And to conclude, I will revenge his death.
> But how? Not as the vulgar wits of men,
> With open, but inevitable ills,
> As by a secret, yet a certain mean,
> Which under kindship will be cloaked best.

Hieronimo chooses his secret plan over the publicly acceptable alternative of open duel, or, better yet, due process of law. Moreover, his final atrocity of killing the innocent Duke of Castile, brother to the king, marks him as total villain. By this deed he departs so far from the English sense of justice that all sympathy is withdrawn. Hieronimo's suicide is then forced by the audience's demand that the villain be properly punished. His death satisfies the stern Elizabethan doctrine that murder by private individuals, no matter what the motive, must not be tolerated.

One may argue that Hieronimo has no choice but to act as he does. His reversal is forced by events in the play. He is the Chief Magistrate of Spain, and his life has been devoted to administering the law. He believes in public justice and wants compensation for wrongs by due process. Hieronimo, in fact, is the only character in the play who attempts to circumvent disaster by appeals to public law. His appeal to the king, however, is blocked. The king is busy when Hieronimo approaches him, and Hieronimo is hit by another fit of distraction at the moment when he most needs to be in complete control of his faculties. Believing that Horatio's murderer must not go unpunished, and believing that no recourse to public vengeance is left open, Hieronimo assumes that he, the next of kin, must be the appointed avenger and he becomes a scourge of God, attempting justice on his own terms. Only if the play is read as a treatise on the nature of divine justice operating on the human level can Hieronimo's character be interpreted as heroic.

Kyd manipulates his audience to feel satisfaction and horror at the catastrophe of the play by using his two onstage audiences to guide the responses of the real audience. The Spirit of Revenge's promise of revenge to Don Andrea sets up a pattern of anticipation for the audience. This response may be described as aesthetic, and Revenge becomes a mouthpiece for the playwright's intent. Revenge says in effect that he is making it all up, that the play is a work of art rather than a piece of reality.

The audience of Hieronimo's dumb show, however, sees not a fiction, but a story with clear ties to reality. Only at the end of his show does Hieronimo reveal that the actors in his play have not been feigning but, instead, have stabbed in earnest. The audience's response is, understandably, horror. The line between art and reality is blurred. Rather than responding to a play, the Spanish court audience finds itself suddenly responding to a real and immediate experience. Kyd's audience is manipulated by this second level of response, so that the general audience sees the play through the eyes of the onstage audience. The general audience, however, is informed, as the onstage audience is not, of the "fiction" that Revenge has created.

The audience members leave the theater with a sense—conscious or not—of having witnessed a play with implications for their everyday lives. Audience response on this level is necessary for any good drama. Kyd seems to have built in a sense of relevancy and meaning on a structural level in *The Spanish Tragedy* that makes the play more than the sensational bloodbath it is often labeled.

Jean G. Marlowe

Bibliography:

Ardolino, Frank R. *Thomas Kyd's Mystery Play: Myth and Ritual in "The Spanish Tragedy."* New York: Peter Lang, 1985. Argues that the play is a combination of murder mystery, allegory, and religious ritual. Heironimo chooses pagan vengeance over Christian forgiveness because the latter does not seem to offer justice.

Barber, C. L. *Creating Elizabethan Tragedy: The Theater of Marlowe and Kyd*. Edited with an introduction by Richard P. Wheeler. Chicago: University of Chicago Press, 1988. Argues that Lorenzo's murder of Horatio violates the social order and disrupts Heironimo's belief in an ordered universe. Heironimo's violence is at first improperly directed but finds a proper focus at the end of the play.

Bowers, Fredson T. *Elizabethan Revenge Tragedy, 1587-1642*. Princeton, N.J.: Princeton University Press, 1940. Still useful, tracing the origins of revenge tragedy to Senecan drama. Shows how *The Spanish Tragedy* follows Senecan patterns closely.

Edwards, Philip. *Thomas Kyd and Early Elizabethan Tragedy*. New York: Longmans, Green, 1966. Analyzes Elizabethan tragedy from the 1560's to the 1580's. Gives a brief biography of Kyd.

Murray, Peter B. *Thomas Kyd*. New York: Twayne, 1969. Puts *The Spanish Tragedy* in its cultural context. Explores the play's influence on later authors. He examines the play sequentially, explaining how its central theme is the corruption of love.

THE SPECTATOR

Type of work: Essays
Author: Joseph Addison (1672-1719) and Richard Steele (1672-1729)
First published: 1711-1712, 1714

Joseph Addison and Richard Steele's *The Spectator* was among the most popular and influential literary periodicals in England in the eighteenth century. Begun on March 1, 1711, this one-page essay sheet was published six days a week, Monday through Saturday, and had reached 555 issues by its last issue on December 6, 1712. Each issue was numbered, the articles were unsigned, and many had mottoes from classical authors. *The Spectator*'s end was brought about by a combination of the other interests of its authors and by a rate increase in the taxes that were levied on paper. In 1714, *The Spectator* was revived from June through December by Addison and two other writers, who had occasionally contributed to the original publication. Reading *The Spectator* yields a vivid portrait of London life in the first decades of the eighteenth century.

The Spectator, like its equally famous predecessor, *The Tatler* (1709 to 1712), was the creation of Sir Richard Steele, who combined a life of politics with a writing career as a poet, playwright, and literary journalist. Steele became a Member of Parliament, was knighted by King George I in 1715, and achieved success as a dramatist with his play *The Conscious Lovers* in 1722. Using the pseudonym of Isaac Bickerstaff, Steele provided lively stories and reports on London society through *The Tatler*, which attracted male and female readers. Joseph Addison, already popular as poet, was also a playwright and a writer on miscellaneous topics who held a series of government appointments. He contributed material to *The Tatler* and then formed a collaborative relationship with Steele to write for *The Spectator*. While *The Tatler* featured both news and short essays on topical matters, *The Spectator*, with the established readers of *The Tatler* as its primary buyers, was composed of one long essay on the social scene or a group of fictive letters to the editor which gave Addison and Steele a forum for moral or intellectual commentary. This was presented in the periodical by the specially created, fictional social observer, "Mr. Spectator."

To give the essays structure, Steele created the Spectator Club and presented the character of Sir Roger De Coverly, a fifty-six-year-old bachelor and country gentleman, as its central spokesman. Other members of this fictional group included a merchant, Sir Andrew Freeport, a lawyer, a soldier, a clergyman, and a socialite, Will Honeycomb, who contributed gossip and interesting examples of social behavior to Mr. Spectator. Although Steele ultimately did not use the Spectator Club as a device as often as he apparently anticipated, the De Coverly essays were the best-recognized and most popular section of *The Spectator*. In later literature of the century, characters similar to those created by Steele for the club appeared in novels and political periodicals. Through De Coverly and Freeport, Addison and Steele are able to contrast the political views of the Tory and Whig parties and, through Honeycomb, to satirize the ill effects of an overly social life on personal morality and good judgment.

The first number of *The Spectator* begins with Addison's general introduction of Mr. Spectator to his readers. As Mr. Spectator explains, readers want to know something about an author, even if the information is general:

> Thus I live in the World, rather as a Spectator of Mankind, than as one of the Species . . . as a Looker-on, which is the Character I intend to preserve in this Paper.

As for keeping some personal details to himself, Mr. Spectator notes that knowing his real name, his age, and his place of residence would spoil his ability to act as a nonpartisan observer. By issue 10 (written by Addison), Mr. Spectator was able to report to his readers that the periodical had a daily circulation of three thousand papers, and, by its height in 1712, nine thousand issues of it were sold daily in London. In addition to essays on a single theme, some issues used letters from readers (written by friends of Addison and Steele) which created the impression of a widespread circulation while offering a means for Mr. Spectator to address specific social problems. Issue 20, for example, written by Steele, is based on a young lady's note about men who stare at women in church. Mr. Spectator gives a detailed and courteous reply which contrasts "male impudence," as he labels it, among the English, the Irish, and the Scots. Several subsequent issues, such as 48 and 53, are composed entirely of these sorts of letters, which become a typical way for the authors to discuss male and female social behavior and, usually, female fashion. The importance of conversation in society is profiled in issue 49, also by Steele, on the role of the coffeehouse as "the Place of Rendezvous to all that live near it, who are thus turned to relish calm and ordinary life." Besides moral and amusing accounts, *The Spectator* featured short pieces of prose fiction with developed characters, plots, dialogue in some cases, and themes specific to the story itself. In issue 50, Addison reworks an idea about cultural encounters that was originally proposed by Jonathan Swift for *The Tatler* in his story of the Indian kings. Earlier, in issue 11, Steele had told the tale of Inkle and Yarico. This story concerned an Indian girl, Yarico, who unwisely, though sincerely, befriends an English merchant, Thomas Inkle, who is more interested in commercial gain than friendship and love.

The Spectator, issues 106 to 131, which cover June and July, 1711, form the De Coverly papers of the periodical to which both Addison and Steele were contributors. Since they were both creating Sir Roger daily, his character evolved into something slightly different from Steele's original portrait in issue 2, as the gentleman's eccentricities and unworldliness made him a comic contribution to literature on the scale of Miguel de Cervantes' Don Quixote. In issue 106, Mr. Spectator accepts Sir Roger's invitation to spend a month with him in the country. Once there, Mr. Spectator is impressed by the freedoms of unstructured country life and the many amusements available to pass each day. Over the course of these letters, Mr. Spectator meets Sir Roger's loyal servants, his chaplain, and an assortment of rural neighbors.

The broad outlines of country life sketched by Mr. Spectator would have been familiar to the London readers as many had country homes of their own, relatives outside London, and opportunities to travel into the cooler northern climates in the summer months. There is more to these lively, pictorial entertainments, however. Through Mr. Spectator, Addison and Steele are able to comment on the positive effects of good household management, the shortcomings of the aristocracy, the benefits of commerce, the landed gentry's role in maintaining social order, the differences between the fear and the shame of poverty, the signs of good breeding—behavior, conversation, and dress—as they are found in the country, and the reach of party politics outside London. The brief accounts of Sir Roger's unrequited love for a "perverse country widow" allow Steele, who wrote issues 113 and 118, to continue his conversation on love and marriage initiated in *The Tatler* and carried on in *The Spectator*. Issue 116, contributed by Eustace Budgell, who later wrote with Addison on the continuation of the paper, offers an amusing and detailed story of Sir Roger's hunt and an opportunity for Mr. Spectator to consider the fickleness of human compassion. At the end of the chase, Sir Roger directs that the hunted rabbit be freed to live its life in its garden as it gave them all good sport. In issue 117, written by Addison, Mr. Spectator relates the story of Moll White, an insensible old woman, believed by many, including Sir Roger, to be a witch. The lack of understanding of the plight of the elderly, abandoned poor is the theme of this more serious essay. Placed back to back as these stories are, the reader quickly sees the contradictions in Sir Roger's attitude toward humans and his attitude toward animals, which sounds a cautionary note to the audience. To complete the cycle, issue 131 announces Mr. Spectator's departure, and issue 132 describes his memorable journey back to London. The entire story of Sir Roger includes four papers on his visit to the sights of London (issues 269, 329, 335, and 383) and one on his death (issue 517) on October 23, 1712. Addison did not want the character to be imitated by other, later periodical writers.

In all, the De Coverly papers are representative of the themes, scope, and treatment of the subjects of *The Spectator* as a whole. These essays also show the balanced style of *The Spectator*, which is maintained through the careful craftsmanship of Addison and Steele. Neither writer concentrated solely on writing either topical or moral essays; they wrote both with equal facility and in complementary styles.

Since the purpose of *The Spectator* was to allow its readers to observe all parts of life, there are a great many topics covered in different degrees in the periodical. One important subject was literary criticism, treated in essays on tragedy (issues 39, 40, 42, and 44), on poetry (issues 70 and 74), on comedy and wit (issues 23, 28, 59-63, 65, 270, and 446), and, interspersed between issues 267 and 463, extended analyses of the writing of John Milton. *The Spectator*'s essays on literature, popular entertainment, and refinement set the standards of taste for the readers, while providing prose composition models and examples of methods of characterization suggestive to other writers. Another series of essays was written in praise of scientific discovery and in response to popular pseudoscientific ideas on animal intelligence and the supernatural. Addison, who composed many of the issues on science, was careful to balance his arguments for the power of science with references to the power of God, as shown in issue 420, in which he discusses the advances in knowledge offered by the microscope and the way that scientific information can be used to heighten faith.

Personal and public morality were also themes of great import in *The Spectator*. For example, Steele wrote on lewd conduct in issues 155, 266, and 274 and on the dangers of plays with situations in which immoral behavior is rewarded in issues 51 and 208. He also used the paper to stress the need for parental responsibility (issues 192, 320, 437, and 479) and marital fidelity. Addison also wrote on religious and philosophical topics with his five hymns, which appeared in issues 441, 453, 465, 489, and 513, reminding readers of his popularity as a poet.

There are, of course, many papers celebrating the diverse characteristics of human nature and numerous portraits of individuals with distinctive traits found throughout *The Spectator*. An interest in and curiosity about people as individuals is one the hallmarks of the eighteenth century, which emphasized, through the philosophy of Enlightenment, the social roles of humans in their societies.

Issue 555, written by Steele and published on December 6, 1712, brought *The Spectator* to a close. In this issue, Mr. Spectator acknowledged the contribution of Addison to the success and variety of the papers in an indirect way and named seven other writers who he claimed had contributed the letters which had enlivened the conversations in its pages. He also announced the impending publication of *The Spectator* in seven volumes, and he clearly blames the higher taxes for driving the paper out of business. In the summer of 1714, Addison, with Eustace Budgell and Thomas Tickell, revived *The Spectator* and published issues through issue 635. These additional essays were collected for volume 8 of the complete *Spectator*, published in September, 1715. Steele, after *The Spectator* had ended, started a political essay periodical, *The Guardian*, in March, 1713, which was succeeded by *The Englishman* in October, 1713. It went into a second series before its end in November, 1715. Donald F. Bond edited the standard edition of *The Spectator* (1965), which has an extensive introduction and identifications of the issues written by Steele, Addison, and the other contributors.

The Spectator was frequently republished throughout the nineteenth century and could be found in many home libraries after 1712. It was an unparalleled accomplishment in eighteenth century periodical journalism and was highly influential on many later English writers. The congenial eye of Mr. Spectator touched on all parts of ordinary life; *The Spectator* compares to Samuel Pepys' *Diary* and James Boswell's *Life of Samuel Johnson* as a work representative of the eighteenth century within cultural history.

Beverly E. Schneller

Bibliography:

Bloom, Edward, and Lillian Bloom. *Educating the Audience: Addison, Steele, and Eighteenth-Century Culture*. Los Angeles: William Clark Andrews Memorial Library, 1984. One of two contemporary studies of *The Spectator* giving a detailed perspective on the readers of the periodical and how the authors appealed to them.

Bond, Richmond P., ed. *Studies in the Early English Periodical*. Chapel Hill: University of North Carolina, 1957. This indispensable history of the eighteenth century periodical provides the terminology currently in use to describe literary essays and magazines.

Dammer, Richard H. *Richard Steele*. Boston: Twayne, 1982. This biography in the Twayne's English Authors series argues Steele used themes from an earlier moral tract, *The Christian Hero* (1701), as a unifying feature in *The Spectator* essays he wrote.

Keatcham, Michael D. *Transparent Designs: Reading, Performance, and Form in "The Spectator" Papers*. Athens: University of Georgia Press, 1985. A significant and careful study of Addison's and Steele's literary styles.

Winton, Calhoun. *Captain Steele: The Early Career of Richard Steele*. Baltimore: The Johns Hopkins University Press, 1964. The first of Winton's two-book biography of Steele covering his early career between 1690 and 1714. Half of this volume is on Steele's periodical journalism and *The Spectator*.

SPECULATIONS ABOUT JAKOB

Type of work: Novel
Author: Uwe Johnson (1934-1984)
Type of plot: Psychological realism
Time of plot: Mid-1950's
Locale: East Germany
First published: Mutmassungen über Jakob, 1959 (English translation, 1963)

Principal characters:

JAKOB ABS, a railroad dispatcher in East Germany
GESINE CRESSPAHL, a worker for NATO in West Germany, lover of Jakob
HERR ROHLFS, an agent of the East German secret service
JONAS BLACH, an assistant in the English department at the university in East Berlin, in love with Gesine
HEINRICH CRESSPAHL, a cabinetmaker in East Germany, Gesine's father and a father figure to Jakob.

The Story:

Jakob Abs was killed when he crossed the railroad tracks as he had done many times in the past. Several people speculated about his death. Rohlfs, the East German secret agent, observed Heinrich Cresspahl in the small Northeastern town of Jerichow because Cresspahl's daughter, Gesine Cresspahl, worked for NATO in West Germany. Gesine met Jakob Abs when he and his mother came to Jerichow as refugees from Pommerania at the end of World War II. She was thirteen and he eighteen at the time. They soon had developed a brother-sister relationship, which they continued during her university years and his time working a railroad job in another town. She finally decided to leave communist East Germany and move to West Germany.

Rohlfs talked to Jakob's mother about the goals of socialism; she asked Heinrich Cresspahl to carry two suitcases for her to the train station, which caused the rumor that Cresspahl had left for West Germany. Jakob, who worked as a dispatcher for the state-owned East German railroad, was contacted by Rohlfs and received a telegram from Cresspahl, saying that his mother had gone to the West.

Jonas Blach left East Berlin, where he taught English at the university; he had met Gesine in the street when she had been walking with American officers to their car. Now in Jerichow, he was introduced to Jakob at Cresspahl's house, where Jakob had gone because his mother had left. As usual, Rohlfs was keeping them all under surveillance. Jakob put his mother's things in order; to him it felt as though she had died. Jonas, involved in a group critical of the communist government, told Jakob and Cresspahl about the group. Sometime before he traveled to Jerichow, Jakob broke up with his girlfriend, Sabine.

Gesine had already heard about it when Cresspahl called her about Jakob's death. She remembered how she, on a surprise visit from West Germany, had run into Rohlfs, whom she did not know at the time. She sat in a restaurant, waiting, and as Jakob walked in, he recognized Rohlfs. Jakob denied Gesine's identity while establishing eye contact with her to meet her later. He then left with Rohlfs to talk about his mother. When Jakob met Gesine outside, they took a cab to another city to catch the train to Jerichow. After an escapelike trip changing trains, long after midnight they ended up at Cresspahl's house, where Jonas still waited. Rohlfs met them all there later, and they discussed the political situation, especially the rebellion in Hungary. Rohlfs allowed Gesine to return to West Germany.

Jonas returned to East Berlin; Gesine sent a telegram from the first post office on the West German side. Coming to his office, Rohlfs discovered that Jakob had disappeared Tuesday evening. Jonas, who had lost his job at the university, visited Jakob that Tuesday, October 30. It was the day when Jakob had to decide for himself whether to delay a troop transport with tanks underway to end the rebellion in Hungary; he let it pass through because he understood that a delay of ten minutes or even a day would not make any difference. In their conversation, Jonas also realized that Gesine had not told Jakob about her love for Jakob.

The next day, Jakob made his trip to the West, officially to see his mother, which Rohlfs had cleared with the authorities. Jakob called Gesine from his hotel, and they spent time together over the next few days. Coming from a visit to the refugee camp, they heard on the radio about the suppression of the Hungarian rebellion by the Soviets and the immanent military action by the West in the Suez Crisis. In their last night together, Gesine asked Jakob to stay in the West, while he asked her to come with him to the East. She took him to the local train station, and he left alone. The next morning, he was very tired, and, on his way to his job, he was struck by a train engine. He died shortly afterward during surgery. Sabine and Jonas, who had in the meantime had been staying with friends and had visited a literature class at another university, notified Cresspahl. Cresspahl arrived in the early afternoon, and Jonas took a train to Jerichow. The next morning, however, Jonas turned himself in to Rohlfs, who arrested him. Gesine met with Rohlfs in West Berlin to talk about what had happened.

Critical Evaluation:

Uwe Johnson is counted among the most important German novelists after World War II. In 1959, three German writers published novels that contributed to reestablishing German literature as world literature. The best known of these is Günter Grass's *The Tin Drum* (1961) with its grotesque allegories. *Billiards at Half-Past Nine* (1962), by the Nobel laureate Heinrich Böll, is the most traditional of these three novels. *Speculations About Jakob* stands out among them as the most experimental novel and the one that focuses on the East-West conflict rather than on the Nazi legacy.

Speculations About Jakob invites its readers to form their own opinions, based on the speculations they encounter. Reader participation is required, which makes the novel challenging and rewarding. The information is presented in three distinct, although at times intertwined, modes: interior monologue, dialogue, and third-person narration. The interior monologues, which are by Rohlfs, Jonas, and Gesine, are scattered throughout the book, but the monologues are easy to recognize because they are in italics. (In contrast to the German original, the English translation identifies the speaker at the beginning of each section of a monologue.) The dialogues, also spread throughout the novel, are marked by dashes, while the contributions by the narrator, which provide the transitions and background information to hold the novel together, are regular text.

It has been pointed out that Johnson's novel is not speculation itself, but rather that it portrays speculation. The technique of flashback dominates the flow of the story, and the story line as it is summarized above unfolds in a fragmented manner within five main divisions, covering a period of about one month. Each character describes Jakob in a different manner because Jakob means something different to each one of them; therefore, readers have to consider the issue of each character's reliability and point of view.

Johnson's narrative technique owes much to the experimental tradition of the twentieth century, especially to the American writer William Faulkner. Faulkner was a master at the abandonment of the omniscient narrator for the sake of multiperspectivism. On the level of vocabulary and syntax, Johnson is also innovative, for instance, when he mixes various kinds of idiom. Some of this, however, is lost in the translation. For example, Gesine tells Jonas about her love for Jakob in biblical language, literally: "It is my soul which loveth Jakob," while the translation reads prosaically: "I happen to love Jakob."

The narrative structure is designed to challenge the reader to piece information together as a detective would. Some of the facts are not quite clear. Jerichow, for example, is Johnson's invention; it bears resemblances, however, to the actual Mecklenburg. Real places, in contrast, are often only alluded to; the name of Dresden is given only toward the end of the novel, with the implication that Jakob works there; however, the description of the city does not match Dresden. Furthermore, the name of the West German town where Gesine works is never given. The true nature of the love relationship between Gesine and Jakob, for example, does not become clear except in later works by Johnson. In another example, the question of whether Jakob's death was an accident or suicide remains unanswered. Readers are challenged to make sense of these and similar uncertainties.

All of this ties in with the novel's overriding issues of identity and reality. Such issues were especially pressing during the Cold War in the divided Germany of the 1950's. Germany provides a focal point for the conflict between these two social systems; the country was divided into capitalist West Germany and communist East Germany. Johnson, who left East Berlin for West Berlin on the day the manuscript of *Speculations About Jakob* was sent to the West German printer's, has been called the writer of the two Germanies.

Characters are represented in terms of what the novel considers most important; there is no simple right or wrong in regard to the social systems. Gesine and Jakob's love is complicated by their mutually exclusive decisions regarding systems. Their decisions are not easy: Just as Jakob struggles to make the Soviet intervention in Hungary fit into his value system, Gesine is disgusted by the military solution to the Suez Crisis by the West. As a consequence, she decides to quit her job with NATO.

The issues of problematic identity and reality also are addressed in the plot, which is in conflict with the demands of Socialist Realism, whose typical elements include an idealistic communist (Rohlfs), a wavering intellectual (Jonas), a citizen who is seduced by the West (Gesine), and another citizen who resists this seduction (Jakob). Jakob, however, dies under mysterious circumstances, and the psychological approach to the novel's issues runs counter to a party-line interpretation of the characters.

Interpretation of the novel, then, lies in understanding that there is no clear-cut truth; what is more, it has been argued that such an objective truth cannot exist in a country in which truth is a commodity and a construct by propaganda machine. Consequently, Jakob's death can be seen as symbolic for the political situation of the Cold War. Caught between the two social systems in West and East Germany, Jakob cannot develop or live by his true identity and is therefore destroyed. It is not possible for an individual to find his or her own place somewhat independently, so to speak—one is either independent or one is not. Jakob is successful at cutting across the tracks of the social systems for only so long. The shocking insight that cutting across the tracks is ultimately impossible, although some people may do it for a short time, is expressed in the first sentence of the novel. Voicing disbelief at the news of Jakob's death, it is one of the famous first sentences in German literature: "But Jakob always cut across the tracks."

Ingo R. Stoehr

Bibliography:

Boulby, Mark. *Uwe Johnson*. New York: Frederick Ungar, 1974. Places Johnson's novel within the context of world literature and German literature. Provides plot summary and character analysis for this intricate novel. All quotes in English translation.

Demetz, Peter. *After the Fires: Recent Writing in the Germanies, Austria and Switzerland*. New York: Harcourt Brace Jovanovich, 1986. Concise discussion of Johnson's complete works. Useful for understanding of *Speculations About Jakob*.

Detweiler, Robert. " 'Speculations About Jakob': The Truth of Ambiguity." *Monatshefte* 63, no. 1 (1966): 25-32. Discusses the main question of what is truth and suggests the terms "juggernaut" and "labyrinth" to describe the novel's structure.

Hirsch, Marianne. *Beyond the Single Vision: Henry James, Michel Butor, Uwe Johnson*. York, S.C.: French Literature Publications, 1981. Interpretation and character analysis, including discussion of each character's function as narrator. All quotes given in the original and in English.

Johnson, Uwe. "'Unacknowledged Humorist': An Interview with Uwe Johnson." Interview by Leslie A. Wilson. *Dimension* 15, no. 3 (1982): 398-413. Contains several questions and answers pertaining to *Speculations About Jakob*; allows immediate access to the way Johnson thinks.

THE SPIRIT OF THE LAWS

Type of work: Politics
Author: Montesquieu (Charles-Louis de Secondat, 1689-1755)
First published: De l'ésprit des loix: Ou, Du rapport que les loix doivent avoir avec la constitution de chaque gouvernement les mouers, le climat, la religion, le comerce . . . , 1748 (English translation, 1750)

In terms of its practical effect, *The Spirit of the Laws* is perhaps the most important political science book ever written. It was one of the primary sources of the United States Constitution and, through that document, one of the major influences on the development of democratic institutions in Europe during and after the French Revolution. All this is out of proportion to Montesquieu's objectives in writing the book, which were to analyze the various types of political institutions known throughout the world throughout history. Montesquieu also aims, in his book, to denounce the abuses of the French monarchical system and encourage a liberal and more equitable monarchical government for France.

In setting out to write his book, Montesquieu's major inspirations were the works of René Descartes, Nicholas de Malebranche, and Niccolò Machiavelli, all of which he viewed with the kind of healthy skepticism typical of Michel Eyquem de Montaigne. This inspiration did not give him his conclusions, but it gave him his method: a rational, descriptive, and analytic approach to the problem of the nature of the good constitution of society. Montesquieu, like most early political thinkers after Machiavelli, was essentially concerned with the problem of the relationship of right and might, of law and power. Many of these thinkers, however, especially those opposed to what they considered the evil in Machiavelli's realistic approach to politics, tried to theorize on a moral base. They sought to find the basis for the right constitution of society in a consideration of right and wrong and a natural law of right and wrong. Such an approach was alien to Montesquieu. Political society, for him, had to be based on civil law. Law should reflect what individuals consider right or wrong, but subjective morals and objective law are two different things. Morals, like law, are relative; what one society might consider both right and legal, another might well consider both wrong and illegal.

In considering the problem of adjusting right and might, law and power, Montesquieu did not attempt to solve the problem. He was convinced the problem could not be solved, but only understood and dealt with in more rational and equitable ways than societies had used in the past. Thus, he was no more a political moralist than he was a political utopian. Montesquieu's political theory rested on the following assumptions: First, there is no universal solution to the problems of politically structuring a society, because there are only kinds of solutions; second, different cultures require different solutions; third, whatever the solution in a given society, it cannot be arbitrary and will not be accidental—it will depend on the cultural tradition and factors of history and geography; fourth, there is no ideal solution for any culture, only better and worse solutions; fifth, no solution is permanent, but is subject to change by conscious or unconscious action and corruption; and sixth, any workable solution must be the result of rational analysis of objective factors.

The book itself is vast in terms of both the ground it covers and the ideas it generates. Nevertheless, it does not, and could not, achieve the objectives set for it. The scope is too large for the author's abilities and resources. The evidence is often incorrect because techniques for gathering information were still undeveloped. Often Montesquieu's interpretation of valid evidence is not logical or warranted by the facts. The excellence of the book, however, far outweighs its relatively minor defects, and it will continue to be read if only for the sake of its most important contribution to political thought: Montesquieu's discovery of the principle of the separation of powers as a method of securing justice and continuing political liberty.

As a result of the great amount of information incorporated into the book, the great number of subjects considered, and the great number of ideas presented in the course of Montesquieu's analysis, *The Spirit of the Laws* has a structure that is random and difficult to perceive. It is not a formless book by any means, but it does not lend itself to a precise analytic outline. The only principle of organization that seems to hold up under examination is one based on the path of the meandering but directed argument. One widely accepted idea of the arrangement is as follows: Books 1 to 13 are concerned with the concept of government as such, and its specific and general functions. Within this larger division are subdivisions. Books 1 through 8 outline the various types of governments, their essential natures, their structures, and the ways their structures are maintained and corrupted. Books 9 through 13 discuss the functions and the purposes of governments; more specifically, books 9 and 10 discuss the army as the protective agency of the state and the problem of war; book 11 discusses ways to protect the citizen and the meaning of political liberty, and considers the accomplishments of Great Britain in this area; book 12 is concerned with problems of individual security, the rights of property, the availability of justice, and the function of legal tribunals. Taxes and taxation are the subjects of book 13.

Books 14 through 19 make up the second large section of *The Spirit of the Laws* and, in general, are concerned with the effect of climate, which is seen as a function of geography on various political considerations: book 14, the relation of law and climate; book 15, civil servitude and climate; book 16, domestic servitude and climate; book 17, the relation of political servitude and despotism to climate. Book 18 is concerned with the effect of geographical situation and the nature of the soil on the development of law and government, and book 19 discusses the relation of law to the national spirit, and the morals and customs of a nation.

Books 20 through 25 are generally concerned with economics and religion. Book 20 presents a general theory of the organic interrelation of commerce, morals, poverty, and system of government. Book 21 examines the relation of law and commerce and historical change, and book 22 comments on law and its relation to the use of money. Book 23 examines the relation of population density and the development of law. Book 24 discusses the effect of religion qua faith, doctrine, and belief on law; book 25 considers the effect of religion qua institution and establishment on law.

Books 26 through 31 are difficult to consider in numerical order. Books 26 and 29, although separated numerically, concern the theory of law and legislative practice; the former discusses kinds of law—positive, natural, canon, and civil; the latter considers the manner of composing laws. Books 27 and 28 are more or less fragmentary considerations of various matters: Book 27 discusses the effect of time on political institutions, and the Roman law of succession; book 28 discusses the origin and evolution of French civil law and the conflict between Germanic and Roman law. Books 30 and 31 examine the development of French feudal laws and institutions: Book 30 is particularly concerned with laws and institutions as they evolved during the period of the establishment of the French monarchy, and book 31 is concerned with feudal law and institutions in relation to the evolution of the monarchy.

One of the most interesting and important sections of *The Spirit of the Laws* is book 2. Here Montesquieu discusses his most famous idea, the separation of powers in the state. Basing his observations on an examination of the English constitution, which he and many other political scientists of the period considered the most advanced and just in history, Montesquieu points out that government has three general functions: the legislative, the judicial, and the executive.

If political liberty is to be preserved for the individual, he says, no one man or body in the state should have control of more than one of these functions. Montesquieu's definition of political liberty is as practical and objective as his method of analysis: It is not a moral or philosophical abstraction, but a simple, relativistic statement. Political liberty—which is not the same thing as independence—is simply the right to do what the law permits. This right, the author demonstrates by reference to history and the contemporary state of affairs in Europe, inevitably is abridged when any person or governmental body falls into control of more than one of the three basic functions of government. Thus, the good constitution should be constructed so as to prevent usurpation of power. The framers of the United States Constitution accepted this observation, as they did many of Montesquieu's other positions, and the result has been manifest in history.

Bibliography:

Cohler, Anne M. *Montesquieu's Comparative Politics and the Spirit of American Constitutionalism.* Lawrence: University Press of Kansas, 1988. Scholarly but accessible work for advanced students. Discusses the narrative content of *The Spirit of the Laws* and explores Montesquieu's conceptualization of liberty, legislation, democracy, and other themes.

Durkheim, Émile. *Montesquieu and Rousseau: Forerunners of Sociology.* Ann Arbor: University of Michigan Press, 1960. Durkheim, a major contributor to the theoretical foundations of sociology, argues that *The Spirit of the Laws* lays down the principles of the then-emerging science of sociology. Outlines and critiques Montesquieu's methodological logic from a classic social scientific standpoint.

Levin, Lawrence Meyer. *The Political Doctrine of Montesquieu's "Esprit des lois": Its Classical Background.* Publications of the Institute of French Studies. New York: Columbia University Press, 1936. A voluminous but straightforward examination of Montesquieu's reliance on Greek, Roman, and other ancient texts as intellectual sources. Includes a large bibliography of studies, predominantly in French, on Montesquieu.

Shackleton, Robert. *Montesquieu: A Critical Biography.* London: Oxford University Press, 1961. Biographical treatment devotes eight lucid chapters to the writing of and concepts in *The Spirit of the Laws.* A useful introductory survey of the work.

Spurlin, Paul Merrill. *Montesquieu in America, 1760-1801.* Baton Rouge: Louisiana State University Press, 1940. Maps the dissemination of Montesquieu's writings in the United States and assesses the influence of *The Spirit of the Laws* on the framers of the U.S. Constitution. Extensive bibliography.

THE SPOILS OF POYNTON

Type of work: Novel
Author: Henry James (1843-1916)
Type of plot: Social realism
Time of plot: Late nineteenth century
Locale: England
First published: 1897

Principal characters:
MRS. GERETH, the mistress of Poynton
FLEDA VETCH, her companion
OWEN GERETH, her son
MONA BRIGSTOCK, Owen's fiancée

The Story:

While visiting one weekend at Waterbath, the country house of the Brigstock family, Mrs. Gereth met and was immediately drawn to a young woman named Fleda Vetch. The basis of the attraction was a mutual sensitiveness to beautiful things; each guessed that the other possessed such a feeling when they met one morning while obviously trying to escape the house and the rest of the party. Their aversion was caused not by the fact that Waterbath was exceptionally ugly, but rather because it was so very ordinary while pretending to be lovely. The house and the garden might have been quite attractive, and should have been so, but the Brigstocks, people without even a hint of feeling or taste, had had everything done over to fit the very latest fashion. It was this air of fashionable conformity to which Fleda and Mrs. Gereth objected. They recognized what the estate would have been naturally, and they could only be repulsed by what it had become.

Mrs. Gereth's horror of Waterbath was particularly acute because of the comparison she inevitably made between it and her own home at Poynton. Everything at Poynton was exquisite. She and her late husband had gradually furnished it after years of scraping and saving so that they might have the best. Every article in the house had been carefully chosen during their travels in various parts of the world, and she rightly considered it the most beautiful place in England. Unfortunately, the estate had been left to her son Owen, and she knew that she would have to give it up, along with her beloved treasures, when he married. Her secret dread was that he would marry a woman with as little a sense of the beautiful as he himself had. She therefore spent much of her time at Waterbath trying to turn his attention from Mona Brigstock, who personified everything she dreaded, to Fleda Vetch, the one person of her acquaintance who would appreciate and preserve Poynton as it was.

When Mrs. Gereth, with somewhat ulterior motives, invited Fleda to come to Poynton as a friend and permanent companion, Fleda, who had no real home of her own, readily accepted. To the chagrin of both women, Owen soon wrote that he was planning to marry Mona and that he was bringing her down within a week to see the estate. Mona, of course, approved. Although she failed to appreciate its beauty and immediately began planning certain changes, she did realize that every article in the house had some value, and she insisted that Mrs. Gereth leave all but her personal belongings as they were. Mrs. Gereth was to be given the smaller, but still charming, estate called Ricks.

At first, Mrs. Gereth refused to be moved, but she finally agreed to make the change when it was decided that she could take a few of her prized objects with her. Owen, who was very much disturbed at being pushed by Mona to the point of having a serious conflict with his mother, had solicited Fleda's aid in getting his mother to make the move quickly. This request only complicated matters, however, for Fleda soon fell in love with Owen and could not really be effective as an agent for both parties in the controversy. She encouraged Mrs. Gereth to move quickly and quietly, leaving Poynton essentially as it was, but, because of her feelings toward both her friend and the estate, she also encouraged Owen to give his mother more time.

During these negotiations, it became necessary for Fleda to go to London to see her father. While she was gone, Mrs. Gereth left Poynton. Her moving was quick and quiet. When Fleda rejoined her at Ricks, she found that the woman had moved virtually all of the furnishings from Poynton. Owen and Mona were less than pleased. In fact, Mona postponed the wedding; she refused to marry Owen until Poynton again held its rightful belongings. Again, Mrs. Gereth was stubborn, and more negotiations ensued, with both sides once more depending on Fleda for aid.

This time it was Owen's turn to fall in love. His strained relations with Mona, which caused a rather close relationship with Fleda, left him emotionally unstable. He had also lately come to realize how much Poynton, as he had always known it, meant to him and to appreciate anyone who understood its beauty and value as Fleda did. He knew that his life would have been much more satisfactory at this time if he were about to marry Fleda instead of Mona. Mrs. Gereth, who had always been willing to give up Poynton to anyone who could love it as she did, would gladly send back everything for Fleda. A realization of this fact finally caused Owen to declare his love for Fleda and to ask her to marry him.

Fleda, although she acknowledged her own feelings, would make no move until Owen had completely broken with Mona Brigstock, and it was to this end that she sent him away. When Mrs. Gereth heard of these developments, she thought that the situation had finally worked out to her liking, and she immediately sent everything back to Poynton. This act proved a mistake, however, for as soon as Mona heard that the furnishings had been returned, she immediately became her former charming self and again captivated Owen. Unfortunately, because of his honor as a gentleman, Owen could not break the engagement unless the lady demonstrated that she wished to do so; Mona Brigstock now made it clear that she did not wish to end the engagement. She quickly married him and moved at once to Poynton in order to acknowledge and secure her possession of the house and its contents. Soon, the couple began an extended tour of the Continent.

Fleda and Mrs. Gereth again took up residence at Ricks and succeeded in making a charming place out of it, in spite of having little to work with and of having to do it with broken hearts. Some time later, Fleda received a letter from Owen asking her to go to Poynton and take whatever object she most prized, and, because of her love both for Owen and for the estate, she resolved to do so. When she arrived at the station, still more than a mile from Poynton, she saw great billows of smoke rising from that direction. It was a porter who told her that everything was lost. Poynton and all of its beautiful furnishings were destroyed in a fire, which was probably caused by a faulty lamp and aided tremendously by a strong wind.

Critical Evaluation:

According to Henry James in his preface to *The Spoils of Poynton*, he perceived the "germ" of the short novel in a friend's casual mention of an acrimonious conflict between a mother and her son over the disposition of the family furniture following the death of the father. "There had been but ten words, yet I recognized in them, as in a flash, all the possibilities of the little drama of my 'Spoils.'" "On the face of it," he went on to say, "the 'things' themselves would form the very center of such a crisis; these grouped objects, all conscious of their eminence and their price, would enjoy, in any picture of a conflict, the heroic importance." The "things" alone, however, must not have been enough to provoke James to immediate creation, since he left the idea unused for almost two years. In 1895, however, needing a story to fulfill an obligation to the *Atlantic Monthly*, James returned to the "spoils" idea and added the necessary missing ingredient, the central character.

Thus, James found the two lines of action that give the story its final shape: the conflict between Mrs. Gereth and her son, goaded on by Mona Brigstock, over the furnishings of Poynton and the romance between Owen Gereth and Fleda Vetch. The problem of who is to get the "spoils" dominates the first third of the book, but by chapter 8, the center of interest has shifted to the question of who will marry Owen. The two issues are completely intertwined since Owen is actually one of the "spoils" himself, and his marital decision also determines the disposition of the "things."

The dispute over the "spoils" is really a trial between two strong-willed, determined women, Mona Brigstock and Mrs. Gereth, who direct their strategies through Owen Gereth and Fleda Vetch. The contest becomes ambiguous and the outcome doubtful because the "agents" prove unreliable: Owen's emotional involvement with Fleda upsets Mona's calculations, and Fleda's ambivalent reactions threaten Mrs. Gereth's design.

It is unlikely that Mona cares much for the "things" of Poynton for themselves. After she finally wins Owen and Poynton, she flaunts her indifference to the house by not even living there. Her tenacity in seeking the "spoils" is a matter of willful pride. "Mona," wrote James, "is all will." She insists on the furniture because it "goes with the house"—and the house goes with Owen. In addition, it is probable that Mona sees the dispute as a "test" of Owen, or, rather, of her ability to control him. If she can force him to act against his mother's deepest wishes, then she can be confident of dominance in their marriage.

Even though Mrs. Gereth is no less strong-willed and ruthless in her passion to keep control of the artifacts of Poynton, she is a considerably more sympathetic figure. If her attitude toward Poynton reveals her to be a thorough materialist, she is at least a materialist with taste; Poynton, the fruit of her labors, is a fine artistic product, and her devotion to it is passionate and complete. If she is a snob, judging people solely in terms of their taste and "cleverness," she seems accurate in her judgments: Mona is vulgar, Owen is stupid, and Fleda is superior. If Mrs. Gereth's actions are arrogant and extreme, they are mitigated by her situation; the English law that grants all inheritance rights directly to the son, regardless of the widow's needs, is an unjust one, and, if she "collected" Fleda to use as part of a scheme to regain Poynton, she does, in the end, show genuine feeling and concern toward the girl as a person, not just a "piece of furniture."

The most sympathetic and interesting person in the story, however, is Fleda Vetch. In his preface, James identifies her as the only real character in the story, that is, the one figure of feeling and intelligence who is capable of development and change. It is through her perception and sensibility that the reader experiences the story and, in James's words, "the progress and march of my tale became and remained that of her understanding."

Not surprisingly, Fleda is the most complex and puzzling character in the book. Although her intelligence and moral superiority are evident throughout, her behavior frequently seems contradictory and self-defeating. Critics have disputed the motivations behind many of her actions and especially those during the crucial scenes that determine the outcome of her romance with Owen. The primary question is this: At the point where Owen says he loves her and wants to marry her, why does she send him straight back to Mona with "conditions" that virtually guarantee losing him? Or, to put it more generally, why does she throw away her one chance for happiness at the very time she seems to have it within her grasp?

In attempting to answer this question, three variables must be kept in mind: Fleda's relationship with Mrs. Gereth, her relationship with Owen, and her own aesthetic and moral values. From the beginning, Fleda is flattered and awed by Mrs. Gereth's attentions and compliments. The older woman sees in Fleda the perfect protégée, a girl gifted with intelligence and intuitive good taste, but with little background experience, who can be influenced, even molded, by an astute mentor. Thus, Mrs. Gereth grooms a replacement for herself who can not only keep Poynton out of Mona's grasp but also minister to its treasures long after she, Mrs. Gereth, is gone. In matters of artistic taste, Mrs. Gereth probably has her way with Fleda, but after Owen becomes a factor her control over the girl becomes doubtful. In addition, as the book progresses, Fleda becomes increasingly aware of being manipulated by Mrs. Gereth, and, while she may not personally object to being a "piece of furniture," she does feel quite guilty about being used as bait in a trap for Owen.

Fleda's relations with Owen are equally problematic. At first, she rejects him on the grounds that he is "too stupid," but even from the beginning, his amiable personality and physical desirability make a strong impression on her. As their relationship grows, Fleda's view of him becomes more and more clouded by self-deception. Her first impressions of him as "stupid" and "weak" are accurate, but, as she falls in love with him, she suppresses these obvious insights or rationalizes them into strengths. She insists that he act with "independence" and "maturity," yet, like Mona, she fully expects to dominate him after marriage, as can be seen when she says, "It's because he's so weak that he needs me."

Fleda feels strongly attracted and obligated to both people, so she gives each of them the impression that she favors their cause. From these contending loyalties come such self-defeating acts as her persistent claim to Owen that she is winning his mother over and her lies to Mrs. Gereth regarding her emotions toward Owen and his toward her.

Thus, conflicting impulses probably determine her final self-defeating act. Because of her innate morality and her Victorian upbringing, Fleda is unable to accept the idea of winning a previously committed man away from his intended; she cannot act the part of the "designing woman"—especially in someone else's design. Given her tendency to self-deception, she probably convinces herself that Owen can, in fact, meet the conditions she imposes; unfortunately, "her Owen" is largely imaginary, and the real Owen cannot resist a captivating Mona Brigstock. Fleda seems to lack the emotional capacity, as Mrs. Gereth puts it, to "let go." These speculations, however, do not answer the central question about Fleda. Does her final act represent a failure of nerve, a running away from life and experience? Or, does it represent the moral victory of a woman too proud to jeopardize her ethics in return for a chance at happiness? Both views, and most positions in between, have been argued by the critics with little consensus.

If Fleda's actions cost her a life with Owen, however, her reaction to that loss demonstrates her strength of character and her mature appreciation of life. It is she who senses the "meaning" of Ricks and brings a measure of solace to the defeated Mrs. Gereth. It is here that readers come really to understand Fleda's aesthetic sensibility; to her, objects have moral qualities and their beauty is a product of the human experience they reflect. If she can succeed in impressing that view on her companion, a mellowed Mrs. Gereth may find a measure of happiness at Ricks—even after the accidental fire which resolves forever the fate of the "spoils" of Poynton.

This novel, written in the middle period of James's career, shows the detailed character analysis, careful development, and acute insight into human affairs for which he has become famous. Here, one has a kind of tragedy, but not one in the classical sense. This novel is tragic first because many beautiful things are unavoidably given up to one who has no appreciation of them and, second, because these same objects are completely destroyed in a freak accident. The human emotions involved are seen to be somewhat mean in spite of the grandeur of the objects with which they are connected, and, throughout the novel, readers have James's astute comments on, and impressions of, the society in which these emotions and events take place.

"Critical Evaluation" by Keith Neilson

Bibliography:

Cargill, Oscar. *The Novels of Henry James*. New York: Macmillan, 1961. Explores the evolution of *The Spoils of Poynton* with careful consideration of James's comments and provides an excellent summary of major contradictory criticisms of the novel.

Clair, J. A. *The Ironic Dimension in the Fiction of Henry James*. Pittsburgh: Duquesne University Press, 1965. An excellent study of the irony in the novel. Sees Fleda Vetch as the center of action and examines her motives and her relationship with other characters in the novel.

Graham, Kenneth. "The Passion of Fleda Vetch." In *Henry James: The Drama of Fulfillment, An Approach to the Novels*. Oxford, England: Clarendon Press, 1975. Views the novel as a story of the conflicting passions of Fleda Vetch, examines James's narrative mode, provides a detailed study of character relationships, and justifies the conclusion of the novel.

Hoffmann, Charles G. *The Short Novels of Henry James*. New York: Bookman Associates, 1957. A good introduction to the novel which argues that the work achieves its dramatic depth from James's decision to emphasize character portrayal and, through that, to focus on possessions. Views Fleda's actions as heroic and based on a code of high conduct but finds the conclusion of the novel unsatisfactory.

Sharp, Corona. *The Confidante in Henry James: Evolution and Moral Value of a Fictive Character*. Notre Dame, Ind.: University of Notre Dame Press, 1963. Explores the unusual role of Fleda Vetch as simultaneously the center of consciousness for the novel and the confidante.

SPOON RIVER ANTHOLOGY

Type of work: Poetry
Author: Edgar Lee Masters (1868-1950)
First published: 1915

Edgar Lee Masters is a rarity among writers: He established his reputation on the basis of one work, *Spoon River Anthology*. Masters was a prolific writer, producing many volumes of verse, several plays, an autobiography, several biographies, essays, novels, and an attempt to recapture his great success in a sequel, *The New Spoon River*. Except for a handful of individual poems from the other volumes, however, he will be remembered as the re-creator of a small Middle Western town which he calls Spoon River. Spoon River is probably Lewiston, Illinois, where he studied law in his father's office and practiced for a year before moving on to Chicago.

In form and style *Spoon River Anthology* is not a work that sprang wholly out of Masters' imagination; it is modeled on *The Greek Anthology* (dating from the seventh century B.C.E.), and the style of the character sketches owes a considerable debt to the English poet Robert Browning. Masters wrote his book with such an effortless brilliance and freshness that years after its first publication it still retains a kind of startling inevitability, as if this were the best and only way to present people in poetry. From their graveyard on the hill Masters lets more than two hundred of the dead citizens of Spoon River tell the truth about themselves, each person writing what might be his or her own epitaph. The secrets they reveal are sometimes shocking—stories of intrigue, corruption, frustration, adultery. On the other hand, the speakers tell their stories with a calmness and simplicity that induce a sense of calmness and simplicity in the reader. As a result of its frankness, *Spoon River Anthology* provoked protest from readers who felt that the book presents too sordid a picture of American small-town life. While many of the poems are interrelated and a certain amount of suspense is created by having one character mention a person or incident to be further developed in a later epitaph, the anthology is not centered around a unifying theme. About the closest approach to such a theme is the tragic failure of the town's bank, chiefly attributed to Thomas Rhodes, its president, and his son Ralph, who confesses from the grave:

> All they said was true:
> I wrecked my father's bank with my loans
> To dabble in wheat; but this was true—
> I was buying wheat for him as well,
> Who couldn't margin the deal in his name
> Because of his church relationship.

Many people suffered from the bank's collapse, including the cashier, who had the blame placed on him and served a term in prison; but a far more corroding effect was the cynicism generated in the citizens when they found that their leaders, the "stalwarts," were weak and culpable.

Masters has pictured many vivid characters in *Spoon River Anthology*. They range from Daisy Fraser, the town harlot, who

> Never was taken before Justice Arnett
> Without contributing ten dollars and costs
> To the school fund of Spoon River!

to Lucinda Matlock, who

Rambled over the fields where sang the larks,
And by Spoon River gathering many a shell,
And many a flower and medicinal weed—
Shouting to the wooded hills, singing to the green valleys.
At ninety-six I had lived enough, that is all,
And passed to a sweet repose.

Others are the town physicians, Doc Hill and Doc Myers, both of whose lives are scarred; Petit, the Poet, whose "faint iambics" rattled on "while Homer and Whitman roared in the pines"; Ann Rutledge, from whose dead bosom the Republic blooms forever; Russian Sonia, a dancer who met old Patrick Hummer, of Spoon River, and went back with him to the town, where the couple lived twenty years in unmarried content; and Chase Henry, the town drunkard, a Catholic who was denied burial in consecrated ground but who won some measure of honor when the Protestants acquired the land where he was buried and interred banker Nicholas and wife beside the old reprobate.

Spoon River Anthology is weighted so heavily on the sordid side—abortions, suicides, adulteries—that the more cheerful and "normal" epitaphs come almost as a relief. Lucinda Matlock and Ann Rutledge fit this category; others are Hare Drummer, who delights in the memory of a happy childhood; Conrad Siever, content in his grave under an apple tree he planted, pruned, and tended; and Fiddler Jones, who never could stick to farming and who ended up with "a broken laugh, and a thousand memories,/ And not a single regret."

One especially effective device that Masters makes use of in his collection is the pairing of poems so that the reader gets a startling jolt of irony. Thus when Elsa Wertman, a peasant woman from Germany, confesses that her employer, Thomas Greene, fathered her child and then raised it as his and Mrs. Greene's, we find in the next poem that Hamilton, the son, attributes his great success as a politician to the "honorable blood" he inherited from Mr. and Mrs. Greene. There is also Roscoe Purkapile, who ran away from his wife for a year, telling her when he came back that he had been captured by pirates while he was rowing a boat on Lake Michigan. After he told her the story, "She cried and kissed me, and said it was cruel,/ Outrageous, inhuman!" When Mrs. Purkapile has her say in the next poem, she makes it known that she was not taken in by his cock-and-bull story, that she knew he was trysting in the city with Mrs. Williams, the milliner, and that she refused to be drawn into a divorce by a husband "who had merely grown tired of his marital vow and duty."

Masters displays an amazing variety of effects in these short poems. His use of free verse undoubtedly helps to achieve this variety, for a stricter form or forms might make the poems seem too pat, too artificial. Sometimes Masters lets his character's only remembrance of life be a simple, vivid description, as when Bert Kessler tells how he met his death. Out hunting one day, Bert killed a quail and when he reached down by a stump to pick it up he felt something sting his hand, like the prick of a brier:

And then, in a second, I spied the rattler—
The shutters wide in his yellow eyes . . .
I stood like a stone as he shrank and uncoiled
And started to crawl beneath the stump,
When I fell limp in the grass.

Bert tells of his death without comment, but when Harry Williams describes how he was deluded into joining the army to fight in the Spanish-American War, in which he was killed, the poem is full of bitterness, horror, and brutal irony.

To say that every poem in this volume is successful would be as foolish as to contend that each entry in William Shakespeare's sonnet sequence is a masterpiece. Masters frequently strains for an effect; for instance, "Sexsmith the Dentist" seems to have been created so that Sexsmith may remark, at the end, that what people consider truth may be a hollow tooth "which must be propped with gold"; and Mrs. Kessler, a washerwoman, was probably included so that she might observe that the face of a dead person always looked to her "like something washed and ironed." There are other poems in which the speakers do not, so to speak, come alive. One suspects that the poet wrote a number of philosophical lyrics, some of them marred by clichés and cloying rhetoric, and then titled them with names selected at random.

In the main, however, Masters has done a remarkable job in *Spoon River Anthology*. Anyone may recognize in these poems the people one sees every day, and, though one may not like to admit it, when these people die they may carry to the grave secrets as startling as those revealed by many of the dead of Spoon River.

Bibliography:

Flanagan, John T. *Edgar Lee Masters: The Spoon River Poet and His Critics*. Metuchen, N.J.: Scarecrow Press, 1974. Examines critical reaction over several decades and discusses attitudes toward *Spoon River Anthology*. Evaluates subject matter and poetic form. Includes descriptions of theatrical presentations.

Hallwas, John E., ed. Introduction and annotations to *Spoon River Anthology*, by Edgar Lee Masters. Champaign: University of Illinois Press, 1992. An excellent starting point. Introduction evaluates style, rhythm, meter, and literary influences. Discusses social attitudes, focusing on the influence of American myths and democratic ideals on characterization. Notes and annotations include textual variations and provide real life counterparts and explanations of period names and information. Annotated bibliography.

Masters, Edgar Lee. *Across Spoon River: An Autobiography*. New York: Farrar & Rinehart, 1936. Autobiography of Edgar Lee Masters, beginning with his early years in Petersburg and Lewiston, Illinois. Reveals incidents that are recreated in *Spoon River Anthology*. Compares and contrasts legal and writing careers and discusses literary influences and Masters' relationships with writers such as Carl Sandburg and Theodore Dreiser.

Primeau, Ronald. *Beyond Spoon River: The Legacy of Edgar Lee Masters*. Austin: University of Texas Press, 1981. Detailed exploration of literary influences, from classical literature to Ralph Waldo Emerson and Walt Whitman. Analyzes style, comparing Masters' poems with those of earlier writers. Discusses unusual blend of regionalism and unsentimental realism.

Wrenn, John H., and Margaret M. Wrenn. *Edgar Lee Masters*. Boston: Twayne, 1983. A good critical source, providing biographical information and tracing literary influences. Discusses organization, style, and language. Explores relationships between characters, stressing realistic portrayals of social repression and sexuality.